NEWBORN METRIC CONVERSION TABLES

Weight (Mass) **Pounds and ounces to grams**

Example: To obtain grams equivalent to 6 lb, 8 oz, read "6" on top scale, "8" on side scale; equivalent is 2948 g.

	Pounds (lb)														
	0	1	2	3	4	5	6	7	8	9	10	11	12	13	14
0	0	454	907	1361	1814	2268	2722	3175	3629	4082	4536	4990	5443	5897	6350
1	28	482	936	1389	1843	2296	2750	3203	3657	4111	4564	5018	5471	5925	6379
2	57	510	964	1417	1871	2325	2778	3232	3685	4139	4593	5046	5500	5953	6407
3	85	539	992	1446	1899	2353	2807	3260	3714	4167	4621	5075	5528	5982	6435
4	113	567	1021	1474	1928	2381	2835	3289	3742	4196	4649	5103	5557	6010	6464
5	142	595	1049	1503	1956	2410	2863	3317	3770	4224	4678	5131	5585	6038	6492
6	170	624	1077	1531	1984	2438	2892	3345	3799	4252	4706	5160	5613	6067	6520
7	198	652	1106	1559	2013	2466	2920	3374	3827	4281	4734	5188	5642	6095	6549
8	227	680	1134	1588	2041	2495	2948	3402	3856	4309	4763	5216	5670	6123	6577
9	255	709	1162	1616	2070	2523	2977	3430	3884	4337	4791	5245	5698	6152	6605
10	283	737	1191	1644	2098	2551	3005	3459	3912	4366	4819	5273	5727	6180	6634
11	312	765	1219	1673	2126	2580	3033	3487	3941	4394	4848	5301	5755	6209	6662
12	340	794	1247	1701	2155	2608	3062	3515	3969	4423	4876	5330	5783	6237	6690
13	369	822	1276	1729	2183	2637	3090	3544	3997	4451	4904	5358	5812	6265	6719
14	397	850	1304	1758	2211	2665	3118	3572	4026	4479	4933	5386	5840	6294	6747
15	425	879	1332	1786	2240	2693	3147	3600	4054	4508	4961	5415	5868	6322	6776

Ounces (oz)

Note: 1 lb = 453.59237 g; 1 oz = 28.349523 g; 1000 g = 1 kg. Gram equivalents have been rounded to whole numbers by adding one when the first decimal place is 5 or greater.

SOURCE: Ross Inservice Nursing Aid No. 1, Ross Laboratories, Division of Abbott Laboratories, Columbus, Ohio.

MATERNITY NURSING TODAY

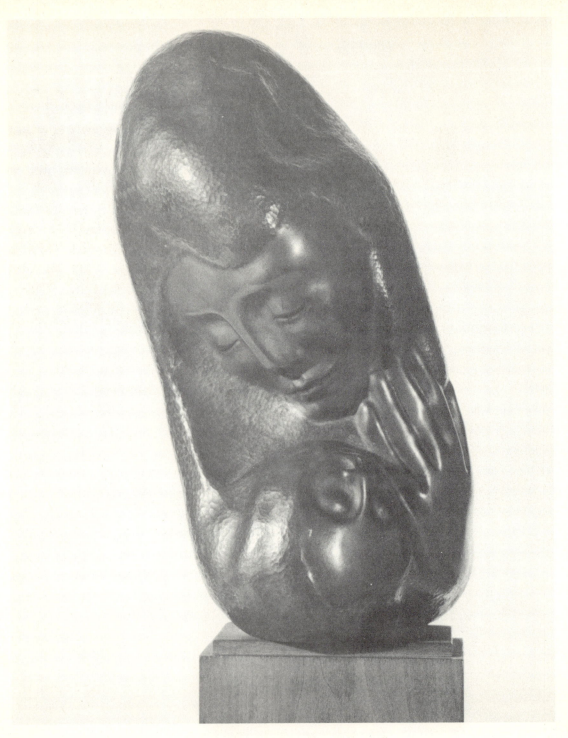

Not Yet. A twentieth-century American sculpture by John Flannagan (1895–1942). *(Reproduced with the permission of the Minneapolis Institute of Arts and the Francesca Winston Fund.)*

SECOND EDITION

MATERNITY NURSING TODAY

JOY PRINCETON CLAUSEN R.N., B.S., M.S., M.A.
Doctoral Candidate, Anthropology
University of Colorado

MARGARET HEMP FLOOK R.N., B.S., M.S.
Assistant Professor
Continuing Education Services
University of Colorado School of Nursing

BOONIE FORD R.N., B.A., B.S., M.A.
Associate Professor, Chairman
Parent–Child Nursing
University of Colorado School of Nursing

McGRAW-HILL BOOK COMPANY
A Blakiston Publication

New York   St. Louis   San Francisco   Auckland   Bogotá   Düsseldorf
Johannesburg   London   Madrid   Mexico   Montreal   New Delhi   Panama
Paris   São Paulo   Singapore   Sydney   Tokyo   Toronto

Library of Congress Cataloging in Publication Data
Main entry under title:

Maternity nursing today.

  "A Blakiston publication."
  Bibliography: p.
  Includes index.
    1. Obstetrical nursing. 2. Infants (Newborn)—
Care and hygiene. I. Clausen, Joy Princeton, date
II. Flook, Margaret Hemp. III. Ford, Boonie.
[DNLM: 1. Obstetrical nursing. 2. Pediatric nurs-
ing.   WY157 C616m]
RG951.M33 1977   610.73'678   76-10233
ISBN 0-07-011284-3

1 2 3 4 5 6 7 8 9 D O D O 7 8 3 2 1 0 9 8 7 6

The book was set in Melior by
Monotype Composition Company, Inc.
The editors were Sally J. Barhydt, Elysbeth H. Wyckoff, and Anne T. Vinnicombe; the designer was
Rafael Hernandez;
the production supervisor was Leroy A. Young.
New drawings were done by J & R Services, Inc.
R. R. Donnelley & Sons Company was
printer and binder.

CONTENTS

LIST OF CONTRIBUTORS

ROSIE L. ACTION, R.N., B.S.N., M.S.
Curriculum Coordinator
Episodic Nursing
Idaho Commission on Nursing and
    Nursing Education
Boise, Idaho

PATRICIA A. BANASIAK, R.N., B.S.,
M.S., C.A.G.S.
Associate Professor
Boston University School of Nursing
Boston, Massachusetts

SANDRA L. BERRY, R.N., B.S., M.S.N.,
M.S.P.H.
Clinical Nurse Specialist Ob-Gyn
North Carolina Memorial Hospital
Associate Professor
University of North Carolina
    School of Nursing
Chapel Hill, North Carolina

R. LA JEUNE BRADFORD, B.S., M.S.
Regional Nutrition Consultant
Region VIII, Public Health Service
Department of Health, Education
    and Welfare
Denver, Colorado

JANE M. BRIGHTMAN, R.N., B.S., M.S.
Master Nurse Clinician,
    Maternal-Infant Care
St. Luke's Hospital
New Bedford, Massachusetts

SYLVIA J. BRUCE, R.N., S.B., M.S.,
C.A.G.S., ED.D.
Assistant Dean,
    Faculty and Academic Affairs
Boston University School of Nursing
Boston, Massachusetts

BARBARA CABELA, R.N., B.S., M.S.
Regional Nursing Consultant, MCH-FP
Region VIII, Public Health Service
Department of Health, Education
    and Welfare
Denver, Colorado

JOAN BARNES CARVELL, B.A., M.U.P.
Consultant
Educational Management Planners
Los Altos, California

FRED CARVELL, B.A., M.A.
Consultant
Educational Management Planners
Los Altos, California

MARILYN A. CHARD, R.N., B.S.,
ED. M., M.S.
Associate Professor
University of Kansas School of Medicine
Department of Human Ecology and
  Community Health
University of Kansas School of Nursing
Department of Community
  Health Nursing
Kansas City, Kansas

STEPHANIE CLATWORTHY, R.N., B.S.,
M.S.
Doctoral Candidate
Counseling Department
Boston University School of Education
Boston, Massachusetts

MARYA M. CORCORAN, R.N., B.S., M.S.
Professor of Nursing
Boston University School of Nursing
Boston, Massachusetts

MILDRED A. DISBROW, R.N., C.N.M.,
B.S.N.ED., M. LITT., PH.D.
Professor, Maternal and Child Nursing
University of Washington
Seattle, Washington

ELIZABETH M. EDMANDS, R.N., B.S.,
M.A.
Associate Professor, Maternal and Child
Health and Public Health Nursing
University of North Carolina School of
  Public Health
Chapel Hill, North Carolina

DAVID M. FULCOMER, PH.D.
Director, School of Family Studies and
  Consumer Sciences
San Diego State University
San Diego, California

BEVERLY M. HORN, R.N., B.S.N., M.N.,
PH.D.
Associate Professor
College of St. Scholastica
Duluth, Minnesota

MARY B. JOHNSON, R.N., B.S.N.
Former Head Nurse
University of Minnesota Hospitals
Obstetrics and Gynecology Outpatient
  Department
Minneapolis, Minnesota

SHARON S. JOSEPH, R.N., B.S., M.S.
Clinical Nurse Specialist
Denver Women's Clinic
Denver, Colorado

KARYN S. KAUFMAN, R.N., B.S.N.,
M.S., C.N.M.
Clinical Nursing Specialist
McMaster University Medical Centre
Hamilton, Ontario, Canada

COLETTE B. KERLIN, R.N., B.S., M.S.
Associate Professor
University of Colorado School of Nursing
Denver, Colorado

VIRGINIA GRAMZOW KINNICK, R.N.,
B.S.N., M.S.N., C.N.M.
Formerly Assistant Professor
University of Northern Colorado School
  of Nursing
Greeley, Colorado

CYNTHIA J. LEPLEY, R.N., B.S., M.S.
Instructor, Continuing Education
  Services
University of Colorado School of Nursing
Denver, Colorado

A. SYLVIA LEWIS, R.N., M.S., PH.D.
Assistant Professor
University of Colorado School of Nursing
Denver, Colorado

VIVIAN MOORE LITTLEFIELD, R.N., B.S., M.S.
Associate Professor
Continuing Education Services
University of Colorado School of Nursing
Denver, Colorado

BARBARA O'NEIL LOWE, R.N., B.S.N., M.A.
Assistant Professor
University of Colorado School of Nursing
Denver, Colorado

MIRIAM T. MANISOFF, R.N., B.A., M.A.
Director, Professional Education
Planned Parenthood–World Population
New York, New York

KATHARINE A. McCARTY, R.N., M.S.
Associate Professor
Maternal and Child Health Nursing
Boston University School of Nursing
Boston, Massachusetts

RANA LIMBO PECK, R.N., B.S.N., M.S.
Former Assistant Professor
University of Nebraska College of
    Nursing
Omaha, Nebraska

MARNA STEINBRONER PRITCHARD, R.N., B.R.E., B.S., M.S.
School Nurse and Teacher and Health
    Educator
Little Valley Central School
Little Valley, New York

ARIANNE SCHRODEL REGESTER, R.N., B.S.N., M.ED.
Assistant Professor of Nursing
Essex Community College
Supervisor of Obstetrics and Gynecology
Women's Clinic
Johns Hopkins Hospital
Baltimore, Maryland

GLADYS MARY SCIPIEN, R.N., B.S., M.S.
Associate Professor
Boston University School of Nursing
Boston, Massachusetts

ANN NOORDENBOS SMITH, R.N., M.S.
Doctoral Candidate, Sociology
University of Colorado
Boulder, Colorado

JANET M. STEWART, M.D.
Assistant Professor
University of Colorado Medical Center
Denver, Colorado

DAVID S. TORBETT, PH.D.
Director
Family Enrichment Foundation
Denver, Colorado

ERNESTINE WIEDENBACH, R.N., B.A., M.A., C.N.M.
Associate Professor Emeritus
Maternal and Newborn Health
Yale University
New Haven, Connecticut

ELIZABETH J. WORTHY, R.N., B.S., M.N.
Assistant Professor
University of Washington School of
    Nursing
Seattle, Washington

PREFACE

The first edition of this textbook was published in 1973, at which time we perceived a need for a nursing textbook which would place family-centered maternity care in a broader, contemporary perspective. Emergent family patterns and social issues challenged the traditionally constrained focus of maternity nursing. In addition, the plethora of research in the behavioral, social, and natural sciences required the publication of a nursing textbook which integrated relevant data from these scientific disciplines for the student and practitioner of maternity nursing.

Family patterns, social issues, and scientific research have continued to change and expand since the first edition of this book was published, thereby necessitating an updated and revised edition. Nurse specialists in maternal and child health, anthropologists, sociologists, ecologists, educators, a nutritionist, and a geneticist have combined their knowledge and expertise throughout this book toward a holistic approach to the care of pregnant women and their families.

The nursing process is the central theme of the book. The process is related to the nursing care of pregnant families through discussion of each of its steps: assessment, development of a plan of action, implementation, and evaluation. Substantive content in some chapters is not intended to be fundamental or exhaustive; in such instances, the reader is encouraged to elicit from the references and bibliographies information which will expand and enhance understanding of the basic concepts upon which the higher-level constructs are founded.

When we undertook the work of editing a maternity nursing textbook, we were well aware, and continue to be aware, of the proliferation of descriptive terms for phenomena in nursing. For example, during work on the second edition, the title "Maternity Nursing Today" was reevaluated. Should a book which encompasses the breadth of information found in this text have a more expansive title? Does the amount of time, energy, and space devoted to the neonate—low-, medium-, and high-risk—justify recognition in the title? "Perinatal Nursing Today" was considered as a possible title, but since perinatal is interpreted differently within the health field, it was decided to retain the original title until a standardized definition of perinatal is accepted.

Nursing today is a profession for both men and women. Therefore, we believe that the word *nurse* should be devoid of gender. There are instances in which the feminine gender has been used, simply because the author intends to individualize concepts about *a* nurse, rather than nurses in general; it could be reasonably argued that the masculine gender could have been used as appropriately.

We generally differentiate between the use of *client* and *patient* when referring to recipients of health care. Client is used when the recipient is cared for on an outpatient basis, and patient is used while the woman is hospitalized in a health care facility.

We would like to call to the readers' attention the fact that, because of our own backgrounds, this book focuses on maternity nursing within the United States. We believe, however, the concepts can be easily transferred to other cultural and geographical locations.

As in the first edition, the book is organized into five parts. Part One, Perspectives in Maternity Nursing, contains a comprehensive discussion of the changing roles and self-concepts of people in general and, more specifically, the changing roles of the maternity nurse. Different family constellations, members' roles, and the *uniqueness* of each family are discussed, as well as the nurse's role as mediated through the nursing process. Part Two, Planning the Family: Childbearing and Childrearing, explores the interplay of many different ecological, psychosocial, cultural, and physiological factors in a human being's life which dictate what family planning means to an individual. Part Three, Childbearing and the Nursing Process, integrates and relates the content from the two previous parts to the normal maternity cycle. Concomitantly, it is essential that the nurse be knowledgeable and competent in the delivery of maternity care. Part Four, Childrearing and the Nursing Process, discusses the needs of the neonate, newly delivered mother, and family. Today's complex, mobile society moves at a rapid pace and little time is allowed for childbearing and childrearing in a relaxed manner. The perceptive nurse recognizes and assists the family in meeting and adjusting to the many demands made upon the members collectively and individually. Part Five, Complications of Childbearing and Childrearing, explores the essential, dynamic, exacting, therapeutic approach used in identifying and caring for pregnant women at risk, fetuses in jeopardy, and high-risk mothers and infants.

This textbook is designed primarily for nursing students. Practicing and nonpracticing nurses will also find the book valuable in improving the nursing care of maternity patients and their families. We have deeply appreciated and benefited from past comments and suggestions in preparing this revision, and additional critique of this edition aimed at improving health care to pregnant families is encouraged.

We wish to acknowledge with gratitude the secretarial assistance of Janet Genow, whose efficiency and patience with our directions, changes, and rewriting simplified our task. We also gratefully acknowledge Sally Barhydt, Betsy Wyckoff, and Anne Vinnicombe whose helpful suggestions are reflected in this revision.

JOY PRINCETON CLAUSEN
MARGARET HEMP FLOOK
BOONIE FORD

PART
ONE

PERSPECTIVES IN
MATERNITY NURSING

UNIT A

MATERNITY NURSING CARE

1

Changing Roles and Self-Concepts of People

MILDRED A. DISBROW

At first consideration the concept *role* might appear to be a clear-cut, unambiguous term which refers to what a person does in a given situation or position. Further consideration, however, begins to raise questions which cast doubt on the clarity of the term. Is role what a person actually does or what he or she should do? Are these two behaviors necessarily different? Who decides what one should do? Do all persons who occupy the same position behave in the same way? Is there consensus even on a particular behavior when it is observed by several persons present at the same time? We might cite as an example an actress's role for a particular part in a play. What she *should* do was first written by the author, then interpreted by the actress and director, and perhaps reinterpreted by both. What she *does* do may be influenced by how she views herself, her past experiences with similar roles in life or in the theater, and what she perceives as cues from her coactors, the director, and the audience. The audience's and critics' *perceptions* of her behavior depend on their own personal experiences, their familiarity with the author's work, and their expectations of the play. If we multiply this one example by all the different actors and actresses, directors, critics, and audiences who have been or will be involved with any one play, we can see that the actress's role for this part is not clear and unambiguous. There are many interpretations of the role of the actress cited here, and we would expect even more equivocation about the roles of persons in less structured positions or situations.

Role, then, is behavior. The term role may refer to the behavior which a person and/or others expect or believe to be appropriate or ideal—the *prescribed role*; it may refer to the behavior actually being emitted—the *enacted role*; or it may refer to how the person thinks he or she behaved or how others view that behavior—the *perceived role*. How one actually does behave, how that person and others perceive the behavior, and what is deemed appropriate all depend on the *self-concept* of the person doing the acting and of the others with whom he or she interacts.

The self-concept is developed through interaction with others, a special kind of interaction called *role taking*. To take the role of another is to put oneself in the place of the other person and, using that person's cues, to look at oneself as the other person would do so. Those others whose roles a person would want to assume in order to evaluate his or her own behavior are significant others, or *reference persons*. When the three categories of behavior—the ideal, the actual, and the perceived—are the same, there should be little or no difficulty.

If, however, there is deviance in any one of these categories, *role conflict* will result. Role conflict may also be experienced when one's different reference persons are not in agreement on the prescribed role. Since each

person may occupy many positions concurrently, such as wife, mother, daughter, student, and editor of the school paper, then role conflict may also be experienced when incongruent sets of behavior are required of one person for the different positions he or she occupies. In the process of resolving role conflict, behaviors are altered and roles change. This chapter will be concerned with the interrelationships of self-concept, reference persons, and role conflict as they pertain to role acquisition and role change.

THE SELF-CONCEPT

The *self*, that conception one has of oneself, is very important. It has been called the self-image, the self-concept, the body image, self-esteem, identity, character, and the "real" person. How one's image of oneself is thought to influence one's behavior can be seen in examples such as the salesperson who tells the customer, "Now that's really you," in an attempt to sell him a suit; the student refusing to become the chairperson of a committee who says, "I could never do that"; or the new mother who tells the nurse, "I can't believe that I'm really a mother." What the salesperson wants the customer to believe is that wearing that particular suit will influence how he acts, and it may do just that. The student refusing to chair a committee may feel that the qualities of a committee chairperson are different from those which he or she possesses; therefore, what the chairperson would have to do cannot be part of his or her repertoire of behavior. The new mother may be thinking that since she does not yet see herself as a mother, she may not be able to behave like one.

Contributions to the literature on self span more than three quarters of a century, starting with the writings of William James in 1892 and continuing to the present. A brief look at some of these contributions might help to clarify just what the self is, how it develops, and how it affects the person's role.

William James dichotomized the self into the "self as known" and the "self as knower."[1] He divided the known or empirical self into the *material self,* the *social self,* and the *spiritual self.* Each of these was viewed in terms of either *self-seeking* or *self-estimating.* Self-seeking had a goal of preservation, and self-esteem was based on a ratio of success to pretentions. For example, manifestations of self-seeking with respect to the social self could include a desire to please, to be noticed, or to be admired, as in the case of the new father who uses cigars as a means of eliciting the attention and congratulations of others. Self-estimation for the material self could be reflected through personal vanity, pride of wealth, or fear of poverty. Both the hoarder and the conspicuous consumer fit this pattern.

Baldwin emphasized the influence of social interaction on the development of the self-concept.[2] He called the "give and take" between a person and a person's associates the "dialectic of personal growth." There were three stages to this: the first, or projective, stage was the one in which the infant adapted to individual variations of others; in the second, or subjective, stage the person became aware of him- or herself, not adapting to others but assimilating them into his or her self; and the third, or ejective, stage was one in which the person saw him- or herself in relation to others who assimilated themselves to him or her. This third stage was the beginning of the social self.

Some of James' formulation was carried further by Cooley who introduced the "looking glass self" through which a person emphasized the importance of the person's interpretations of others' judgments of him or her in the development of self-conception.[3] This was James' "self as known." The three elements of Cooley's construct of self were one's imagination of one's appearance to others, one's imagination of others' judgment of that appearance, and some sort of self-feeling such as pride or mortification. It was the imputed sentiment of the other, that which the person imagined the other thought, that caused the pride or mortification. One might, however, experience both types of feeling with respect to the same act. For example, a youth might brag about his sexual prowess to a friend but be ashamed of it in terms of what his mother might think. Cooley pointed out also the relationship between love and self. One takes on values, attitudes, and attributes of persons whom he loves, and these become part of the self. Thus, love can be seen as necessary for a healthy self. Conversely, since it was felt that one's behavior is consistent with one's self, a substantial self would be necessary if a person were to be capable of loving another person and maintaining the relationship over time. Just as Cooley felt that love was necessary for a healthy self-concept, Coopersmith found that acceptance (a part of loving) was one of the conditions necessary for the development of the "self-esteem" dimension of the self in adolescents.[4]

Mead also followed James' model of dichotomizing the self.[5] Mead's "I" was the portion of the self which reacted to the person's "me," or reflected portion. The me was reflected in that it came into being through the person's *taking the role of the other* and thus defining the situation as the other would define it. In doing this, the person could look at him- or herself as an object just as the other person looked at him or her. *Role taking,* as Mead used it, was evaluating one's own behavior by looking at it through the eyes of another person. This same process was used as part of Rubin's "taking *in* of the maternal role."[6] In Rubin's introjection-projection-rejection operation the mothers tried out bits of the maternal role and used role taking to determine whether or not these bits of behavior "fit" them as reflected in the words and gestures of others.

Mead's main contribution was the introduction of the *generalized other*. The generalized other can be the perceived reactions of many others at one time or in one situation, or it can be the perceived reactions of multitudes of others with whom the person has interacted over time. The latter and more global type of generalized other has been the more acceptable of the two. For example, Brim's "me" in his "I-me" type of relationship is analogous to the generalized other generated from interaction with many others over time.[7]

Schilder extended the body image beyond the body itself to include clothes, the voice, and bodily secretions and excretions.[8] It is this part of Schilder's conceptual framework which could be used as a rationale for today's advertising copy for cosmetics and hygiene products. Schilder suggested that while a change in body image may follow a change in bodily appearance, it was not necessarily a lasting change unless it was congruent with the "psychic attitude" of the person. One's psychic attitude is influenced by the attitudes of others and by the person's projected mirror image. Thus, a physical impairment may change the body image negatively, but it can be rebuilt again. In the same way, a person with a negative body image may have cosmetic surgery to alter a disliked physical appearance, but unless the surgery is accompanied by a positive projected mirror image and by changed attitudes of others, the resulting body image may not be an improved one.

Schilder's work is pertinent when thinking of the alterations of bodily contour which accompany pregnancy. For some women this is a traumatic part of pregnancy, for others it is passively accepted, and for

some it becomes a badge to wear with pride. How each person reacts is largely influenced by previous experience and by the attitudes of peers, parents, and husbands. Treat found that women whom she interviewed in the 6th month of pregnancy were passively accepting of most of the changes accompanying pregnancy but, when given an opportunity to discuss them, concentrated mainly on physical changes, altered body images, and feelings about themselves as feminine.[9] Since most of the body changes due to pregnancy do not persist beyond the puerperium, one would expect any body change to be reversible.

The development of moral judgments about the self was suggested by Cooley and explored further by Sullivan.[10] Sullivan categorized person-other interactions into three types: those which resulted in rewards; those which produced anxiety; and those which inflicted severe anxiety. A different self-concept emerged as a consequence of each type of interaction. The *good-me*, or positive conception, developed out of rewards, such as when a mother rewarded a child for behavior that pleased her. A person would be good-me when he or she did things which he or she perceived would please the rewarder. A *bad-me*, or negative self-concept, is a result of anxiety induced when disapproval of one's actions is manifested or when certain behavior is forbidden. The woman who has been socialized to believe that there is something shameful about the sexual organs and that "nice" women do not enjoy coital relations could see herself as a bad-me when sexually aroused. She might therefore try to avoid stimuli which could produce that feeling or, once aroused, could become frigid. The "too tired" wife or the wife who manages to find emergency ironing to do at bedtime could be protecting herself against the bad-me. The *non-me* does things of which the "me" could have no knowledge. It may be dream behavior, or it may be behavior regarded as dreadful enough to be loathed. The non-me results from experiences which induce anxiety so intense as to obliterate the conscious emitting of such behavior. Examples of the non-me behavior could be the frigidity mentioned above, amnesic behavior when something intolerable is repressed, or the behavior seen in some types of psychoses.

Allport's self was an all-encompassing construct which he called a *proprium*, that which is central to our sense of existence.[11] At first Allport dichotomized the self as James did into the known self and the knowing self. Later he discarded the subjective portion, the knower, which he said he had then consigned to philosophy.[12] Allport's known self was a material self with seven dimensions and functions. These included the bodily self described by Schilder, but without the bodily extensions, and the self-seeking and self-esteem dimensions of James' self. To these Allport added *ego extension* (composed of people, pets, things, ideas, and beliefs which a person could consider his own), a rational facet for problem solving, and a dimension which included one's evaluation of one's abilities today versus what one wanted to become. He also added something which he called *propriate striving* in which the person resisted equilibrium and maintained the tension necessary for accomplishing things. This last dimension was seen as similar to Maslow's "self-actualizing people."[13] Allport offered more cues for detecting manifestations of the self empirically than did others before him.

Turner differentiated between self-images and the self-concept.[14] He viewed the self-image as the picture of oneself that one sees at any given time. It may be one shifting image which is easily changed, or there may be many self-images presenting themselves concurrently. The self-concept, on the other

hand, is more stable and emerges from interaction between the person's goals and values and that person's many self-images. The self-concept is influenced more by what the person would like to be or is trying to be than by self-images. Images may be communicated directly or may be inferred from how one thinks one would appear to someone else. For example, one self-image of a new mother bathing her baby could be inferred from how she thinks she would appear to her absent mother were she present and watching the performance. Other images could be obtained through direct communication with her husband, with a nurse, or with a neighbor, all actually present. These four possible self-images might all be present at the same time and might or might not be congruent. Whether any of these self-images would be a threat to the mother's self-concept would depend on her values, goals, previous experience, and how highly she valued the opinions of these four persons. If she placed a high value on her ability to develop skill in the procedures necessary for caring for her baby, a self-image of herself as inept might be a real threat.

In a study in Los Angeles, breast-feeding primiparas apparently committed themselves to breast-feeding by putting motherhood up as a side bet.[15] This conception of commitment, putting up as a side bet something one does not dare lose, has been suggested by Becker.[16] What this means is that by aligning success in breast-feeding with success in mothering, the woman who failed in the feeding situation would also then have failed in mothering. This kind of failure was intolerable and inadmissible. The mother's image of herself as a failure in this instance would be a threat to her self-concept. A negative self-image may be more of a threat to the self-concept if the person from whose cues the mother detects her self-image is one with whom she will need to continue interaction, such as her husband. This is one of the reasons why the husband's support is so important for the new mother.

In spite of the fact that most of the authors cited so far have pointed out that the social self is both developed and altered through social interaction, there is a tendency to consider the self as an entity or thing. Gordon has reemphasized the point that the self is a process, not a thing.[17] He suggested that each person has a structure of multiple selves of temporal nature: the selves of the past, the selves of the present, and the potential or prospective selves of the future. The comprehensive self must include both social identity and personal attributes. Identity is composed of certain social types, described by nouns. The social types—mother, daughter, wife, church member, and lawyer—may comprise one woman's identity. Her personal attributes, manifested as adjectives, could be pretty, creative, gregarious, and sensitive.

Most of the authors whose contributions have been discussed have at least recognized a dichotomized self, one part knower and one part as known. However, more emphasis in recent years has been on the known or reflected self. Much of the criticism about the James and Mead approaches to self has been aimed at the difficulty or impossibility of testing or measuring something as subjective as the knowing self. There is consensus that the self is primarily social and arises from social interaction. This is of prime importance when working with socially deprived persons, or with social isolates who never learned to take the role of the other. These people are not accustomed to anticipating feedback from others or considering the effect of their behavior on others. If one accepts empathy as a synonym of role taking (and the author does), then one would expect that social isolates would be lacking in empathic capacity.

Empathic persons grow up in an atmo-sphere of acceptance, one which promotes trust and confidence. Most of the action in their lives has been interaction. This has been true at home, in school, and with peers at play. It has been proposed that primary group interaction with peers during the crucial period from the age of five to the early teens is necessary if the individual is to learn to make accurate interpretations of the meanings of the reactions of others.[18] This is because children are frank with one another and criticize freely without worrying about hurting one another or being hurt in the process. Children learn this also at home, but in the home the freedom to reciprocate may be hampered by inequities in power distribution. Adults seldom have opportunity for that easy give-and-take which was part of childhood. With adults, criticism is likely to be offered to other adults not so much with intent to help the other person, but more to let the person know that he or she is interfering with another's goals.

Use of this type of communication, voiced criticism of another's behavior, was found in problem-solving groups only when one member of the group was holding up the group's progress.[19] This can be empirically documented in various daily life situations. Examples of this can be seen when a driver ties up traffic at an intersection, when someone in a supermarket brings his entire weekly grocery order to be checked out between five and six in the evening when commuters are stopping off for one or two items on the way home, or when a patient takes "more than his share" of the nurse's or physician's time. Unless other adults are infringing upon one's rights, it is customary to avoid those whose behavior is not acceptable. Thus, the person who has not learned to correctly interpret others' reactions by the time he or she becomes an adult will most likely continue to have difficulty in interaction with others throughout life.

The tragedy of a lack of empathic capacity

in social isolates is not restricted to how it affects their lives. When these people become parents, the child's life also is affected. Parents who abuse or batter their children have been found to be lacking in empathic capacity.[20,21] (Morris and Gould deny that this is lack of role-taking ability, but unrealistic expectations of children cannot be divorced from a role-taking ability which provides cues for expectations.) Abusive parents are usually socially isolated persons who have themselves been abused and/or reared in a manner to preclude their developing role-taking ability. It follows, then, that the abused children will probably rear their own children as they were reared themselves unless provided with some alternatives to broaden their perspectives.

In maternity nursing, we have an opportunity to work with new parents of all kinds before they have established their own patterns of childrearing through actual practice. How much can be done at this time to promote empathy in a person who has reached adulthood without developing such capacity is questionable, but screening for potential problems and seeking resources for them should be part of the nursing role. Nursing as a profession is not without members who are low in empathic behavior. Ware and Chelgren illustrated this with an incident about nurses who attempted to remove a patient's hands from the bedside rails and in so doing frightened the patient even more.[22] The patient was disoriented and afraid and felt that she was being sent down a slide into a sardine can. One nurse, not knowing of the delusion but recognizing the fear, suggested that the patient hold on to her and assured the patient that she would not let anything hurt her. Similar examples certainly could be drawn from labor and delivery situations.

Since the reactions of other people, obtained either through role taking or through direct communication, are so influential in the development and altering of the self-concept, and since those others whose reactions can have influence are *significant others*, it might be advisable to consider these significant others, or reference persons, in more detail.

REFERENCE PERSONS

Reference persons are significant others—individuals or groups—whose attitudes, values, and opinions have enough salience to influence another person's behavior. Just as one's conception of self develops and changes according to feedback, or perceived feedback, from important others, so also does one's conception of the behavior appropriate for oneself at any given time develop and change as a person makes use of reference persons.

The term reference group was invented by Hyman in 1942 when, in studying socioeconomic status, he found that he could not accurately predict a person's status without taking into consideration the social groups the person used as comparisons for self-appraisal.[23] Prior to that time both Cooley and Mead introduced the idea of referents. Cooley's suggestion that a person takes pride or feels mortification based on how the person thinks he or she appears to others[24] and Mead's "generalized other" or "me" which acts as a conscience to the "I" or acting self[25] imply that such feedback is utilized as a frame of reference.

Many psychologists and sociologists have contributed to reference group literature. Kelly distinguished between two kinds of functions for reference groups: (1) providing values which the person assimilates and (2) serving as a standard of comparison for self-evaluation.[26] Merton and Kitt introduced the concept of "relative deprivation," in which one evaluates one's own condition against that of a reference group which one uses as a standard.[27] Shibutani's definition of a reference group was one whose outlook was used by the actor for a frame of reference for organizing his or her own perceptual field. He also introduced the imaginary reference group as might be used by the artist who was "born ahead of his time."[28] Turner reorganized some of these ideas and renamed the groups as an identification group, which was a source of values; a valuation group, whose influence depended upon the valuation which a person's basic orientations allowed the person to place on the group; and an audience group, which observed and evaluated the person's performance.[29] Eisenstadt made a contribution that was somewhat different from the rest in that he saw the norm itself as the frame of reference to which one oriented oneself and that it was only in specific situations that the norm would be tied to a specific group.[30]

Kemper alone attempted to present this material in the form of a limited theory with reference groups as social mechanisms by which individual achievement was effected.[31] Kemper categorized reference groups into *normative, comparative,* and *audience* groups. Normative referents are persons or groups who establish norms and state values congruent with those norms. These are the individuals or groups to whom one looks to learn what behavior is appropriate for one's given position and situation.

If a person perceives the referent individuals or groups as positive referents, he or she will comply with their norms and internalize their values. However, normative referents may not always be positive. *Negative reference groups,* a term introduced by Newcomb,[32] are individuals or groups whose norms are not only unacceptable to one but which precipitate the setting up of counter norms.

Comparative referents offer a frame of reference by which one can compare oneself with others. The most common of the comparative referents are role models through which one learns how to enact one's role. Comparative referents can also be used to determine the equity of one's fate. When one perceives one's fate as unfair in relation to one's particular reference groups at a particular time and place, such unfairness is called relative deprivation.[33] Homans referred to this same phenomenon as status incongruence.[34]

Another comparative referent group is composed of persons who give legitimacy to one's attitude or behavior. The ubiquitous "they" and "everyone" fit into this category which one uses to give face validity to what one wants to do.[35]

Audience reference groups vary somewhat from the other two types in that they are composed of individuals or groups to whom one has attributed values and norms which one then uses to guide one's behavior. These referents may have espoused the values he or she attributes to them and may have made them known in some way. They could be people with whom the person has interacted, public figures in the news, or authors whose publications he or she has read. On the other hand, they may be persons whose values are not known but only imputed to them by the one who utilizes them as referents. Conformity to the imputed values and norms may in itself be rewarding.

Audience referents may be living persons, heroes from the past, or imaginary characters. This last classification might be illustrated in a study of parents who abused their children.[36] The abusers were social isolates who did not make use of the reference persons normally used by others for help in childrearing such as parents, spouses, neighbors, friends, teachers, or church members. Rather, they imputed to an unknown collectivity of living people their own behavior as the norm. That is, they felt that there were living persons like themselves who, if faced with what the abusers had been faced, would think it appropriate to do what they had done. When questioned about this, they said that they were glad that there were others like themselves. This could be interpreted as support.

Normative reference groups usually make their prescriptions known and impose punishment if there is not compliance. An example of this would be the increasing number of naturalists, earth people, or hippies—there seems to be no agreement on names, only rejection of typecasting by the persons so typed—who want to deliver their babies at home against the advice of some nurses and physicians. When things go wrong, lacerations for example, these persons have hesitated to go to the hospital for assistance because they say they are lectured about the impropriety of their behavior. One couple told of the husband calling the hospital to report that he was bringing his wife in for repair of a perineal laceration. When they arrived at the hospital, they said they were met with statements like, "Oh, you're the one who wanted to have a home delivery." The couple changed their story to one of having planned to come to the hospital but not getting there in time. The attitudes of the hospital personnel changed immediately from punitive to sympathetic.[37] It is often difficult to refrain from making statements like, "I was afraid this would happen" or "I told you so" when the consequences of a person's behavior are serious enough to provoke worry. The deviants themselves may be role models for others. Normative referents seldom reward for compliance except with negative reinforcement, the avoidance of punishing behavior. Rewards come from audience referents.

Physicians have usually been audience referents for their maternity clients as have the women's own mothers, friends, and other women whom they have met in the physician's office or clinic.[38] Nurses are more

often seen as normative or comparative referents than audience referents. In a study on breast-feeding, women were asked what their physicians felt about their choice of breast-feeding. Many responded, "He approves," or "He said 'good.' "[39] It turned out that none of the physicians involved were trying to influence the patients with respect to type of feeding. Usually they were telling them that they were glad they had made a decision regardless of which decision. The patients, however, chose to accept their physicians as audience referents. When these same women were asked what the nurses felt about their choice of feeding their infants, most replied that they did not know or that it did not matter to the nurse. They were not putting the nurses in the role of audience referents.

This does not mean that nurses cannot be audience reference persons. This type of referent depends largely upon image. The image of the physician as one who knows what is best for patients has a long tradition. Even today with criticism of methods of delivery of health services, little criticism is being leveled at the knowledge or capability of the physician per se. Nursing's image in society has not been the same. The image of the nurse has been one of giving comfort, providing emotional support, and following the physician's orders. An example of this can be found in Dalen's study comparing newly delivered maternity patients' and nurses' role expectations for maternity nurses.[40] This image is changing, but to establish the kind of rapport necessary to perceive the nurse as an audience referent takes time. Community health nurses who carry case loads over time, clinic nurses who see the same clients on a regular basis, nurse midwives and maternity nurse practitioners who carry their own case loads of pregnant women, students who follow a pregnant woman and her family throughout pregnancy, labor, and delivery, and into the puerperium and at home, and some office nurses have achieved this kind of rapport and respect.[41,42]

When the maternity patient has a different nurse on each clinic visit, several different nurses during labor and delivery, and different nurses during her two or three postpartum days in the hospital, this kind of rapport does not develop. Usually nurses are seen as normative reference persons who tell patients what they should do and sometimes as comparative referents who show by example how to do something.

The comparative referent, or role model, has an essential quality. He or she "possesses skills and displays techniques which the actor lacks (or thinks he lacks) and from whom, by observation and comparison with his own performance, the actor can learn."[43] Rubin found that maternal grandmothers were not utilized by new mothers as role models. Peers were models. The patients' mothers "seemed too competent, too masochistic, too knowledgeable and too overwhelming to be comfortable models for sustained periods."[44] It would seem unlikely that the new mother would consider the nurse as a role model for the same reasons she rejects her own mother as one. It is familiar to hear the new mother tell the nurse, "You do that so well. I could never handle the baby the way you do."

We might think that exceptions to the rejection of the nurse as a role model would be the nurse who helps the mother manually express milk from her breast after feeding her infant, who demonstrates breathing techniques in an antepartum class or while the patient is in labor, or the nurse who demonstrates how to bathe the baby. These, however, are not role-model behaviors; rather, they are what would be expected of a normative referent, one who tells the patient what he or she should do. When the patient asks

the nurse if she has children, how she handles certain problems with her own children, or what she, the nurse, had as an anesthetic, then the patient is attempting to use the nurse as a role model.

Kemper has proposed that in order to achieve, in this case role enactment, one needs all three types of referents—normative, comparative, and audience. He further suggests what might happen if one or more of the types of referents were missing.[45] When there are both normative and comparative reference persons but no audience groups, there is no inducement to achieve. Many women who plan for psychoprophylactic childbirth find they are unable to carry it through if there is no one present to give support and reward them when they attempt to follow what they have been taught. Obese persons of either sex are more successful in weight loss when there is an appreciative audience to notice the results and commend them. Infants themselves have been used as audience referents through emphasis on infant satisfaction with positioning, type of feeding, or type of holding.

When normative and audience referents are present but comparative types are missing, the person may know *what* to do and may be *motivated* but may not know *how* to do what is appropriate. This is one of the difficulties with the very young mother who does not have peers who are currently involved in behavior like her own. Most aspects of human behavior, unlike that of lower animals, are not guided by instinct.

Whether or not the absence of normative reference persons is serious when both comparative and audience referents are available depends upon the type of behavior involved. Infants face this kind of situation when they first learn imitation for which they are rewarded. However, until norms are set and the infant is mature enough to learn and internalize them, he or she cannot think for him- or herself, use logic, or make decisions about solving complicated problems. Ethical problems concerning some types of behavior control such as brainwashing fall into this category.

We have seen how one's concept of self influences one's perception of one's role, how one actually performs, and how one perceives oneself performing. We have also considered how the presence or absence of significant others influences both the self-concept and one's ability to recognize one's role and to enact it. Now let us consider what happens when various significant others are in disagreement or when one person's many roles are not congruent. These are the two main forms of role conflict.

ROLE CONFLICT

Two other concepts must be included before beginning the discussion of role conflict. One is *role set* and the other is *reference set*. Role set, introduced by Merton, refers to that "complement of role relationships which a person has by virtue of occupying a particular social status."[46] A role set is composed of the *behavioral relationships* of the persons (not the persons themselves) with whom one comes in contact. This is an important point, since a raised eyebrow, an unanswered question, or a hurried response from an otherwise warm and supporting person might change one's self-image and, in turn, one's behavior, or future reflections on this time of one's life.

For example, a few years ago the author was present when a woman returned to her room from the delivery room of a large metropolitan hospital. The husband had been with his wife when she delivered even though she had been heavily anesthetized and was not able to consciously share the birth experience with him. His first words to her were, "You were a perfect lady at all times." I thought this a rather peculiar opening comment, but apparently one of the real worries she had voiced had been whether or not she would lose self-control. Her self-image through his eyes was very important to her and may have influenced whether or not she would have wanted another pregnancy, would have returned to the same hospital, or would have permitted her husband to be present again.

The concept of reference set was coined by Kemper from Merton's role set and the previously mentioned concept, reference group.[47] This set is composed of persons or groups to whom one refers one's behavior for his or her particular role or for his or her role at some particular time. Again, using the labor and delivery situation, part of the woman's role as a natural mother (as contrasted with an adopting mother) is her behavior during the labor and delivery process. Her role set in this situation may be the role relationships with physicians, nurses, anesthesiologists, the father of the baby, other relatives, and student nurses. These named persons with whom she interacts are not necessarily her reference set for her behavior in labor and delivery. Her reference set may be composed of her own mother (present or absent), a member of her club or church group who at some time described in detail her own experiences, a community health nurse or instructor in a parents' class who tried to prepare her for what to expect and do, her husband, someone she overheard on a bus who sounded convincing, or perhaps someone on television or in the movies who was depicted as having a baby or who discussed it on one of the late evening "talk" shows. Intraset conflict in either set—reference or role—could cause ambiguity, frustration, indecision, and trauma for the laboring woman.

Another type of role conflict is that experienced by the person when one or more of the many roles expected of him or her have prescriptions which are not consistent with the others. When one or other of these kinds of role conflict occurs, the person involved can use bargaining or balancing measures. This may involve (1) ranking the referents according to power, legitimacy, sanctioning ability, or intensity of involvement with the individual referents; (2) engaging the referents themselves in bargaining procedures through which they settle their difficulties or at least make them less visible to the person being influenced by them; or (3) insulating the person from stress or strain by physical withdrawal.

The first of the conflict-reducing mechanisms mentioned above, *ranking referents* to determine which to use for a given situation, might use for criteria Merton's suggestion of considering the intensity of the involvement with the referent.[48] Intensity of involvement may be qualitative or quantitative. A graphic description overheard on a bus may have an influence of more intensity than the advice given by the teacher at a parents' class unless the teacher had allowed for discussion of just such encounters.

Gross and associates utilized criteria of the type of a person's orientation—moral, expedient, or moral expediency.[49] The person with a *moral orientation* would give most weight to the referent whom the person feels has the most legitimate claim to his or her opinion. In the case of the laboring woman, she might give more weight to what has been told her by a peer who just had a baby than to what either her male physician or unmarried nurse told her. The person with an *expediency orientation* would place more emphasis on sanctions that could be imposed. If she felt she might be neglected by the nurse or physician by not following their suggestions, she might place high priority on this. There are, of course, positive sanc-

tions also; the desire to have an alert baby rather than one affected by the medication given the mother might be viewed in the category of positive sanction which might influence the laboring woman to insist upon little or no analgesia or anesthesia. The person with a *moral expediency orientation* would weigh the possibility of both positive and negative sanctions and choose the behavior which would show the most profit for her. Since sanctioning in most cases is based on perception which is not necessarily reality, the use of either the expediency or moral expediency orientation is somewhat hard to predict.

The second type of conflict-reducing mechanism, *engaging the referents themselves in settling the difficulties,* has been suggested by Merton.[50] At best, this is a difficult type of solution to use. It is the basis for negotiations when opposing factions strike in the working or business world, and it can be used in patient conferences when the members of the health team get together to discuss and plan care for the patient. For the new mother, however, it is not so easy to get the maternal and paternal grandparents, the nurse, the physician, the neighbors, friends, and newspaper columnists to sit down together and work out the differences of opinion. When the polemics are restricted to conflicting advice given by the physician and nurse, it is simpler to work out, and patients should be instructed to make such differences of opinion known to those involved.

The third type of mechanism used to cope with role conflict, *insulation of the person experiencing the conflict,* is appropriate for use with either intraset conflict in reference or role sets or with intraperson conflict when one's roles require conflicting behavior. Most of these mechanisms have been suggested by Goode,[51] but some of them overlap with suggestions of other people. Unless otherwise stated, the six major coping mechanisms discussed will be Goode's suggestions. He called these mechanisms *role bargains* which are used as a process of selection among alternate behaviors. *Compartmentalism* occurs when one can separate the behavior expected in different roles according to time or situation. For example, a Catholic mother who wants to be a role model for her daughter with respect to the church's teaching about birth control may find this behavior in conflict with her role as a marital partner who is in agreement with her husband that they want no more children. One mother resolved this conflict by keeping her birth control pills at the neighbors, thus compartmentalizing the two roles.[52] This type of solution is similar to Merton's mechanism of insulating role activities from observation by members of the role set.[53] Goode also suggested *delegation* in which obligation for the conflicting role expectation is transferred to someone else. Nurses frequently suggest that a new mother get someone to help her with her housework but keep the care of the baby for herself. If this is a mother who is quite uncomfortable with helpless infants but enjoys caring for older children, she may decide to resolve the conflict between housework and baby care by delegating the baby care to another and doing her own housework. The conflict between the mother's getting enough sleep and also fulfilling her role of providing nourishment for her baby may be settled by bottle-feeding with the father lending a hand, unless of course the mother's most salient referent is one who encourages breast-feeding.

Setting up obstacles against meeting role requirements is another of the insulating coping mechanisms. Pleading the need for additional income might provide a solution for the woman who really doesn't like house-

work or child care. She can't be expected to do all of this if she is working. Commitment to a profession into which was invested much money and time and through which one feels an obligation to make far-reaching contributions to a large population might also be given priority over other role requirements, whether they be childrearing, jury duty, participation in political groups, or working on charity drives. *Setting up barriers* to isolate oneself from others is a frequent method of reducing role strain. Breast-feeding mothers who feel they should give their undivided attention to the young infant in the early weeks of breast-feeding often take their telephones off the hook so others cannot reach them at that time. Goode's last two mechanisms, *eliminating role relationships* and *expanding role relationships*, are self-explanatory. Many a rift between young parents and their in-laws results in elimination, and parents of handicapped children who band together for support and increased involvement reflect expansion.

Regardless of the type of role conflict experienced, some alteration in role usually occurs as a result of the conflict resolution. A method utilized to resolve role conflict or strain in one type of situation at one time may not be the method of choice in the same type of situation at another time. One's role sets and reference sets change over time, and persons who are referents or whose behavior is involved in the role sets are also subject to change within themselves. Social climate is a factor to be considered throughout. Just as the new mother five decades ago would never have considered telling her physician how or where to conduct her delivery, the pregnant woman of today usually feels that it is quite appropriate to make her wishes known and expects to have them considered and, if at all possible, granted. The increasing number of couples wishing to, and succeeding in, delivering their babies at home against the advice of the majority of physicians is a clear example of the changing social climate and its influence on role enactment.

CONCLUSION

It has been the intent of this chapter to show that role is the behavior of a person in a particular position, whether that position is an institutionalized one, requiring patterned behavior, or an informal one as a member of a dyad or larger group. Behavior may be what is expected of a person; it may be the behavior actually emitted, or it may be the behavior as it is perceived by the actor or others.

One's conception of oneself influences one's expectations of how one should behave, how one does behave, and how one thinks one has behaved. The person's self-concept is a social process guided by his or her perception of what he or she thinks others think of him or her and how they perceive him or her from time to time. A person's self-concept has two main dimensions, the subjective one of him- or herself as a knower and the reflected one as the known. Subdivisions of these dimensions may be physical, social, emotional, and temporal. One's self-concept may be stable for periods, such as the self of yesterday, the self of today, or the projected self of tomorrow, or it may be manifested in fleeting images which may or may not have lasting effect on a more permanent self-concept.

The self-concept is influenced by a person's perceptions of how the person appears to others, very important others, sometimes called significant others or reference persons or groups. Reference persons may be living people with whom one interacts, persons once living but now deceased, or they may be imaginary. One's attachment to reference persons may be positive or negative which determines whether there will be compliance with the expectations of the referents or whether there will be overt attempts to be deviant. Reference persons may be utilized as normative referents, role models, or as audiences whose approval one seeks.

Different reference persons may be utilized for different roles or for one role at different times. The collectivity of persons utilized for any given role or role segment is known as a reference set and is to be distinguished from role set, which is made up of relationships, not persons. When there is lack of agreement between persons or behaviors making up a set, role conflict may occur. There may also be role conflict when one person's many different positions place conflicting role expectations upon the person. Role conflict, whether intraset or intraperson, may be resolved through bargaining mechanisms which may rank the referents, eliminate deviant referents, engage conflicting referents in bargaining activities themselves, or provide insulation for the person experiencing the conflict. Interacting with or influencing the choice of conflict-reducing mechanisms is the social climate within which the conflict occurs. Role learning, role enactment, and role change are all social processes. Resolution of role conflict is one of the social processes which frequently is successful in effecting role change.

REFERENCES

1 James, William: *Pyschology: The Briefer Course,* Henry Holt, New York, 1892.

2 Baldwin, James Mark: *Social and Ethical Interpretations in Mental Development,* Macmillan, New York, 1897.

3 Cooley, Charles Horton: *Human Nature and the Social Order,* Scribner, New York, 1902, p. 184.

4   Coopersmith, Stanley: *The Antecedents of Self Esteem,* Freeman, San Francisco, 1967.

5   Mead, George Herbert: *Mind, Self and Society,* University of Chicago Press, Chicago, 1934, pp. 155–156, 173–178, 254–256, and 360–376.

6   Rubin, Reva: "Attainment of the Maternal Role: Part I, Processes," *Nursing Research,* 16:237–245, 1967.

7   Brim, Orville G., Jr., and Stanton Wheeler: *Socialization after Childhood: Two Essays,* Wiley, New York, 1966, pp. 12–15.

8   Schilder, Paul: *The Image and Appearance of the Human Body,* Kegan Paul, Trench, Trubner, London, 1935, pp. 11–16, 188–194, 201–206, 273–282.

9   Treat, Janet Nell: "A Study of the Feminine Gender Identity Crisis of Pregnancy," unpublished master's thesis, University of Washington, Seattle, 1969.

10 Sullivan, Harry Stack: *The Interpersonal Theory of Psychiatry,* Norton, New York, 1953, pp. 158–171.

11 Allport, Gordon W.: *Becoming,* Yale University Press, New Haven, Conn., 1955, pp. 36–56.

12 Allport, Gordon W.: *Pattern and Growth in Personality,* Holt, New York, 1961.

13 Maslow, A. H.: "Self-actualizing People: A Study of Psychological Health," in W. Wolff (ed.), *Personality Symposium No. 1,* Grune & Stratton, New York, 1950, pp. 11–34.

14 Turner, Ralph H.: "The Self-conception in Social Interaction," in Chad Gordon and Kenneth J. Gergen (eds.), *The Self in Social Interaction,* Wiley, New York, 1968, pp. 93–106.

15 Disbrow, Mildred A.: "Any Woman Who Really Wants to Nurse Her Baby Can Do So???" *Nursing Forum,* 2:39–48, 1963.

16 Becker, Howard S.: "Notes on the Concept of Commitment," *American Journal of Sociology,* 66:32–40, 1960.

17 Gordon, Chad: "Self-conceptions: Configurations of Content," in Chad Gordon and Kenneth J. Gergen (eds.), *The Self in Social Interaction,* Wiley, New York, 1968, pp. 115–136.

18 Faris, Robert E. L.: *Social Psychology,* Ronald, New York, 1952, pp. 161–170.

19 Emerson, Richard M.: "A Theory of Communication in Group Problem Solving," paper presented at the American Sociological Association Meetings, Miami, Florida, 1966.

20 Steele, Brandt F.: "Paternal Abuse of Infants and Small Children," in E. James Anthony and Therese Benedek (eds.), *Parenthood,* Little, Brown, Boston, 1970, pp. 449–477.

21 Morris, M. G., and R. W. Gould: "Role Reversal: A Concept in Dealing with the Neglected/Battered Child Syndrome," in *Neglected/Battered Child Syndrome,* Child Welfare League of America, New York, 1963, pp. 29–49.

22 Ware, Alma Miller, and Mary Nofziger Chelgren: "When 'Holding On' Brought Change," *Nursing Clinics of North America,* 6:125–134, March 1971.

23 Hyman, Herbert H.: "The Psychology of Status," *Archives of Psychology,* 269:93, 1942.

24 Cooley: op. cit., p. 104.

25 Mead: op. cit., p. 256.

26 Kelly, Harold H.: "The Two Functions of Reference Groups," in G. E. Swanson, T. M. Newcomb, and Eugene L. Hartley (eds.), *Readings in Social Psychology,* Holt, New York, 1952, pp. 410–414.

27 Merton, Robert K.: "Contributions to the Theory of Reference Group Behavior," in R. K. Merton (ed.), *Social Theory and Social Structure,* Free Press of Glencoe, Glencoe, Ill., 1966, chap. VIII, pp. 225–280.

28 Shibutani, Tamotsu: "Reference Groups as Perspectives," *American Journal of Sociology,* 60:562–569, 1955.

29 Turner, Ralph H.: "Role-taking, Role Standpoint, and Reference-group Behavior," *American Journal of Sociology,* 61:316–328, 1956.

30 Eisenstadt, S. N.: "Studies in Reference

Group Behavior," *Human Relations*, 7:191–216, 1954.

31 Kemper, Theodore D.: "Reference Groups, Socialization and Achievement," *American Sociological Review*, 33:31–45, 1968.

32 Newcomb, Theodore M.: *Social Psychology*, Dryden Press, New York, 1950, pp. 139–155.

33 Kemper: op. cit., p. 33.

34 Homans, George Casper: *Social Behavior: Its Elementary Forms*, Harcourt, Brace, World, New York, 1961, p. 248.

35 Kemper: op. cit., p. 33.

36 Disbrow, Mildred A.: "Deviant Behavior and Putative Reference Persons," in *Fifth Nursing Research Conference Reports*, American Nurses' Association, 1969, pp. 322–346.

37 Healy, Ingrid: "A Descriptive Study of the Social Climate Surrounding Home Deliveries from the Viewpoint of Public Health Nurses and Hippie Type Women," unpublished master's thesis, University of Washington, Seattle, 1972.

38 Rubin, Reva: "Attainment of the Maternal Role: Part II, Models and Referents," *Nursing Research*, 16:342–346, 1967.

39 Disbrow, Mildred A.: "Any Woman Who Really Wants to Nurse Her Baby Can Do So???" *Nursing Forum*, 2:39–48, 1963.

40 Dalen, Audrey: "A Study of the Relationship of Role Conflict to Effective Communication in a Maternity Care Setting," unpublished master's thesis, University of Washington, Seattle, 1970.

41 Lang, Dorothea M.: "Providing Maternity Care through a Nurse Midwifery Service Program," *Nursing Clinics of North America*, 4:509–520, 1969.

42 Runnerstrom, Lillian: "The Effectiveness of

Nurse-Midwifery in a Supervised Hospital Environment," *Bulletin of the American College of Nurse Midwives*, 14:40–52, 1969.

43 Kemper: op. cit., p. 33.

44 Rubin: op. cit., p. 343.

45 Kemper: op. cit., pp. 39–40.

46 Merton, Robert K.: "Instability and Articulation in the Role Set," in Bruce J. Biddle and Edwin J. Thomas (eds.), *Role Theory: Concepts and Research*, Wiley, New York, 1966, pp. 282–287.

47 Kemper, Theodore D.: "The Relationship between Self-concept and the Characteristics and Expectations of Significant Others," unpublished Ph.D. dissertation, New York University, New York, 1963.

48 Merton: "Instability and Articulation in the Role Set," in Bruce J. Biddle and Edwin J. Thomas (eds.), *Role Theory: Concepts and Research*, Wiley, New York, 1966, p. 283.

49 Gross, Neal, W. S. Mason, and A. W. McEachern: *Explorations in Role Analysis*, Wiley, New York, 1957.

50 Merton: "Instability and Articulation in the Role Set," in Bruce J. Biddle and Edwin J. Thomas (eds.), *Role Theory: Concepts and Research*, Wiley, New York, 1966, p. 285.

51 Goode, William J.: "A Theory of Role Strain," *American Sociological Review*, 25:483–496, 1960.

52 Connell, Elizabeth B.: "What Emotional Problems in Family Planning Do You Encounter?" *Medical Aspects of Human Sexuality*, September 1968, pp. 14–15.

53 Merton: "Instability and Articulation in the Role Set," in Bruce J. Biddle and Edwin J. Thomas (eds.), *Role Theory: Concepts and Research*, Wiley, New York, 1966, p. 284.

2

Changing Roles of the Maternity Nurse

SYLVIA J. BRUCE AND
MARILYN A. CHARD

TRENDS AND DIRECTIONS IN PRACTICE

The future of nursing must be determined by nurses. A frightening thought? Indeed it is. There has been a scarcity of outstanding leaders in nursing since the early 1900s, and even today such leaders are rare. Certainly nursing roles are changing, but time and circumstance have done that—*not* nurses. At best, we are keeping up. But with what? Social trends? Institutional demands? Needs of other professions? Patient care?

Nursing has become too isolated. Our behavior is predictable and dependent. As a group we are not risk takers, nor are we socioculturally perceptive. We need nursing leaders who will demand freedom and accept the responsibilities it entails. There is no future in a closed system. And present-day systems of nursing education and nursing practice are indeed closed, female-based institutions. Virginia Cleland has stated,

"My fear is that a desire for protection will win over a bolder plan involving more calculated risks."[1] Female Uncle Toms have charted the direction of nursing all too long. Without boldness, nursing will continue to be consumed by more aggressive groups.

And who are these aggressive groups? At the 1971 convention of the American Medical Association a resolution was passed to take whatever action was necessary "to assure preservation of the physician's authority to use and direct allied health personnel." In a growing number of instances professional nursing has been referred to as one of the allied health groups. During this same convention the chairman of the board of trustees called for programs to expand the role of the nurse in the delivery of basic medical care. "But the American Medical Association wants a moratorium on any licensure laws that would give R.N.'s or P.A.'s (physicians' associates) more specific authority than they now have."[2] The American Nurses' Association supported this moratorium in 1971 and has shown little change since.

Patients are also becoming an aggressive group. The public is no longer willing to accept haphazard care. Yet, the public has not sufficiently defined the multitude of roles assigned to the numerous types, varieties, and levels of health workers providing services. A person will go wherever the service, not necessarily the care, can be found according to his or her medical needs and wants. In all too many instances it is the nonprofessional worker who is there to care. Nursing as an organized group is not visible at block meetings, community-service-center discussions, social-action sessions, legislative hearings, housing-authority meetings, school-committee sessions, or town meetings. Organized nursing does not initiate or lead causes. Parents and lay groups do. So long as we practice isolationism, there

will always be groups who can and will determine the future roles of nursing.

Why have neither nursing as an organized unit nor its leaders been able or even willing to determine and maintain their own direction? There is no valid logic or rationale in discussing trends and directions in maternity nursing roles unless there is first an examination of the larger group—professional nursing practitioners—of which maternity nurses are only one small part. A delineation of the basic issues must be established and discussed before predictions of role potential can be offered.

ACCOUNTABILITY AND INDEPENDENCE

Nurses today are struggling with disjuncture —disjuncture derived from a juxtaposition of vastly different and extremely incongruent beliefs, ideas, and practices. Partial definitions, inefficient proposed models of change, insignificant or unreceptive targets, ineffective attempts at solutions, and inappropriate proposed alternatives all point to the same conclusion. Have we become too preoccupied with the idea of change to examine what to change? If we have, our vision of the future will not halt the diverse, incongruent, and conglomerate programs and systems of care and practice called nursing.

Planned change is grounded in clusters of value commitments. But do we know ours? The crucial question that must be raised and faced squarely at this time by the entire nursing profession is: Do we want to change? Appearances would indicate that we do not. We are at a point where decisions must be made and a direction must be taken. The true test of beliefs is in their implementation. Either we believe in what we say—that change is needed and that change must come now—and act, or we must face the reality that we do not want to change.[3,4]

Model Construction

Role definition and model construction are present-day professional preoccupations. Assuredly, the role of the clinical nursing specialist is not a new one. Discussions about the need for nurses who are prepared clinicians and the potential contribution these specialists could make toward the improvement of nursing practice can be documented in the professional literature as early as 1944.[5] Over a quarter of a century later the role and its potential are still being discussed, not in terms of reporting the results of scientifically controlled research investigations supporting the identified functions of the specialist, and not in terms of rigorously formulated control experiments to measure clinician effectiveness in patient or client care management, but still only in terms of potential model formation and speculative conceptions of effectiveness in practice.

There are a number of reasons why progress in the role development of the clinical specialist has been so slow and confined to such a limited sphere of influence in actual practice. Prevailing inappropriate expectations of nursing roles, underutilization of existing qualified practitioners, lack of physician acceptance of the validity of graduate education for professional nurses, administrative misuse of nursing personnel, rigid systems of organizational structure, and traditional forms of bureaucratic management have all made significant contributions toward stifling the progress of research into the development and testing of models of specialist roles in nursing. Certainly, not the least of these obstacles is the resistance of nurses themselves. No one attributable cause can, or should, be isolated to explain the present dilemma confronting today's activists and innovators in nursing education and practice. However, it would be a propitious move on the part of professional nursing to seriously examine the historical basis of this incongruity of stated role potential that is never transformed into service delivered.

Independent Practice

Although the ANA was founded over 75 years ago, entrepreneurs are still significantly lacking among the national leaders in nursing. This lack is now hopefully being compensated for through the ANA Certification Program. This move has provided the impetus for significant methodological changes to occur in systems of health care delivery. A new philosophy of professional nursing practice is now being formulated—a philosophy of accountable, self-governing independence as opposed to one which promulgates a dependent, for-hire, quasi profession.

Historical Foundations

It is important to examine the evolution of nursing in its close relation to out-group social movements and emancipationist efforts. The ANA can trace its historical development back to an ardent feminist, Lavinia Dock, who developed the bylaws for nursing alumnae groups and later founded the Nurses' Associated Alumnae of the United States and Canada, renamed the American Nurses' Association in 1911.[6] Nursing associations were the "first professional groups to be organized and controlled by women in the United States."[7] The history of nursing has been marked by many firsts, yet the profession seems to benefit least by its own advances. There have been moments of color and humor; yet these events are frequently unknown, misunderstood, or unappreciated by many.

As a dedicated feminist, socialist, and pacifist, Lavinia Dock went to jail three times

in her career as part of her campaign to secure women's right to vote.[8] She, perhaps
more than any other nursing leader, demonstrated how closely the development of
modern nursing was tied to the movements
to secure the emancipation of women. She
once appeared at a nursing convention with
a sign on her chest urging, "vote for women"
and, ignoring the topic assigned to her, pro-
ceeded to make a "fiery suffrage speech to a
somewhat disinterested audience."[9] One of
Miss Dock's most bitter disappointments
came when the ANA voted to *oppose* the
equal rights amendment to the Constitution
—the amendment that gives women equality
with men under the law.

Many believed that the failure of organized
nursing to support the passage of the equal
rights amendment was a great mistake. The
year 1913 also marked another historical defeat. During the first 25 years of existence the
ANA was never able to establish minimum
standards of hours and pay for graduate
nurses. In California in 1913 the legislature
enacted a law to regulate the hours of work
for women. At a mass meeting in San Francisco, before the law was passed, large
groups of nurses met and reluctantly agreed
to the inclusion of student nurses in the provisions of the act but would not agree to the
inclusion of any mention of the graduate
nurse.[10] Their stand was supported by nursing groups across the country, and as a consequence, graduate nurses were not included
in most of the state laws that regulated working hours for women and children.

Over 50 years later the California Nurses
Association and the ANA initiated the present wave of today's dissenting nurses. State
nurses' associations all over the country followed California's lead in demanding equal
employment opportunities and the right to
collective bargaining; the ANA was named
as the official bargaining agent to begin
again the struggle of fair pay and decent

working hours. There is no justifiable reason
for a profession of over 100 years' standing
to have the issue of wages and hours assume
any greater importance than it has for any
other professional group.

Feminist movements in this country have
provided the impetus needed for nursing
development, and the present-day women's
liberation front is once again opening the
doors for nursing. Whether we go through
the door or not is a question only history will
record; however, the time is ripe, the clinical
practitioner's role is established, the need is
great, and the technology for change is available.

Decision and Direction

The idea of self-governance will not be easily
implemented for at least two reasons. *First*,
the tradition of medical and hospital administrative influences on decision making in
professional matters is deeply ingrained. It
will require patience, persistence, and understanding to convince physicians and
administrators of the need for a shift from
their authority to complete independence in
matters of professional nursing practice.
Second, self-governance will require a re-
division of authority within the profession
itself. For example, consider the area of
licensure. Licensure only indicates the meeting of minimum standards of preparation
and knowledge, and it is not in itself sufficient to predict competence levels required
for independent practice—the role demanded of the professional practitioner of
nursing. It will be necessary to evaluate current licensure requirements and the focus of
state board examinations to assess more realistically competence for independent *nursing* practice.

At this writing, 30 of the 50 states have enacted major amendments to or complete re-
visions of the Nurse Practice Act—in the

span of 5 years. Many of these legislative acts call for the monitoring of nursing practice by the state board of medicine, thereby delimiting the practice of nursing. A few states, such as New York (1972), Oregon (1973), and New Jersey (1974), recognize that nursing has the inherent right to define its own standards of practice and to regulate its own standards of practice through a state board of nursing. These three states revised the definition of nursing practice to include the words "diagnose" and "treat" as essential to *nursing care.*

Since the proliferation of the so-called "nurse practitioner" (are not all registered nurses who practice nursing nurse practitioners?), an uneasiness about medical diagnosis and treatment by nurses has prevailed. Yet, have not many nurses only added techniques which provide additional, and necessary, data upon which to base *nursing intervention?*

There is one further issue to consider in the area of professional self-governance. Nurses are reluctant to make peer judgments in the public interest. With operative self-governance this would be a mandatory responsibility. It will be necessary to develop a sophisticated understanding of competence, ethics, due process, and public welfare. To assume that nurses today are primarily responsible for the quality of nursing care provided is absurdly naïve. But nurses should and must be held professionally accountable. It will be incumbent upon the ANA to establish standards for practice, systems of governance and accountability for implementation of practice, and procedures of due process and redress for failure to uphold professional standards of practice.

Although the ANA has had its periods of failure, it has also had brief periods of brilliance. One such period was 1965. The now famous position paper essentially supported two types of nursing preparation: the bac-

calaureate level of preparation for professional nurses, and the associate degree attainment for technical nurses. Unfortunately, this position has not been well received by the majority of current practicing nurses. Since the ANA is more advisory than regulatory in nature, nursing groups have not felt any real pressure to respond actively in setting realistic and urgent targets for implementation. The most serious threat to the viability of nursing as a profession, however, comes from within. Nursing must make of itself, and of its role in the emerging patterns of health services, something much more vital, substantial, and distinctive than it has up to now. Should it neglect this challenge, it may pass quietly from the scene, "a victim of that bad joke of history which, when salvation seems nearest at hand, shuns those who have prayed most fervently and waited most patiently for it, only to bestow the fruits of its promise on them that cared not."[11]

A new dimension in which nurses are becoming involved is quality-assurance programs. Included in these programs are professional standards review organizations and nursing audit committees. Nursing involvement in quality health care through peer review and patient/client care outcomes is essential to accountability and independence. The Maternal Child Health Division of the ANA has been actively writing patient/client outcomes for nursing audits. Educators and practitioners must familiarize themselves with all aspects of quality-assurance programs if they hope to be responsible for defining their parameters of practice.

Emerging Roles

Who will be tomorrow's independent practitioners of nursing? We are rapidly and confusingly developing a myriad of roles, programs, and practices which have achieved little but which have drained off a frightening number of nurses from the mainstream of people available to provide health services. It is inconceivable that such a hodgepodge of programs for specific role practice have actually made a significant impact upon the improvement of current systems of organizing and delivering services to people. Presently we have clinical nursing specialists, often with ill-defined roles; physicians' assistants, with vague programs for role preparation; master clinicians, with rigid and often unscientific curricula underpinning a weak role performance; and a host of other groups, providing fragmented services to families.

Possibly the most tragic circumstance of all is the unnecessary competition between current programs to prepare small groups of nurses for unrealistic or outdated professional practices. Controversy can be a positive and driving force in the creation of improved services only if differences of opinion, preparation, and practice are rigorously evaluated. Controversy for its own sake, however, is a profession's greatest tragedy. Within present educational systems of role preparation philosophical differences of content emphasis and scope of practice delineations exist not only to the detriment of providing significant numbers of qualified practitioners but, more seriously, to the detriment of the welfare of the very fabric of today's family health.

The present-day maternity nursing role both as it is taught and as it is practiced in many areas is definitely obsolete and often ineffective. A maternity nurse whose training, education, and commitment has been confined to the pregnancy cycle alone, minimizing the family's many related needs, cannot be considered within the dimensions of independent nursing practice. All nurses who provide services to families must have both the theory base and the practice experi-

ences encompassing a philosophy of maternal and child health care. A maternity nurse who is not knowledgeable or comfortable in dealing with issues of child development, family-life education, and parent development will provide a professionally deficient service. It is no longer feasible to continue to support programs that cannot provide these experiences.

It would seem logical, therefore, to proceed as rapidly as possible to phase out all specialty preparation programs that are so limited in scope as to develop nurses who cannot provide the care and service that parents need to ensure opportunities for understanding the demands of pregnancy, parenthood, and family development. The place of independent schools of midwifery in such a design is highly questionable. Without a base of maternal–child health knowledge and experience they are mere schools of techniques and procedures of medical practice. With a firm base in maternal–child health theory and practice is there a need to maintain separate schools of mid-wifery or should they be incorporated into existing programs of maternal–child health nursing? Not only must the profession define the parameters of nursing practice, but it must also come to grips with the scope of specialty services and education.

CONFRONTING ISSUES

The trend for health care today is to provide primary care within the community and episodic and exotic care within the hospital setting. With the change in the direction of health care, there is a concomitant change in the direction of nursing. This seems an ideal time to further implement the concept of the independent practitioner in maternity nursing. Before the concept of the independent practitioner in maternity nursing can become a reality, the following issues must be explored by the profession as a whole:

1 Professional concepts for practice
2 Changing parameters in practice
3 Institution roles
4 Sociocultural confrontations

Professional Concepts for Practice

Two sets of concepts need to be examined when contemplating the efficacy of the independent practitioner in nursing. The first set is accountability and self-governance. The second is freedom and authority. Through the utilization of these concepts, the profession of nursing can develop its image.

Accountability and Self-governance

The issue of accountability means that professional nurses are prepared to answer themselves, their colleagues, and their clients in relation to any nursing actions which are based on a *nursing* diagnosis. It presupposes that the nurse can assess nursing needs in a given situation, devise and execute a plan of care based on these needs, and evaluate the effectiveness of nursing actions. No longer would the nurse be under the aegis of the physician or the employing institution. Successes and mistakes become the nurse's own. Because the nurse would be liable for actions based on nursing assessments, malpractice insurance becomes a practical investment.

If professional nurses are to be accountable for their own actions, then it follows that nursing as a profession must be self-governing. Standards of practice concomitant with independent practice must be established. New legislation must continue to be enacted relative to the Nurse Practice Act. Decisions regarding pay scales, area of practice,

and retirement plans would become the responsibility of nursing. Yet, before professional nurses can know those actions for which they are accountable, they must enhance and validate their application of the basic sciences utilized in nursing. In this way nurses can define the parameters of nursing practice. Once this is accomplished, nurses can determine the degree to which they possess the freedom and authority to be self-governing.

Freedom and Authority

Freedom without authority is anarchy. Authority without freedom is tyranny. The professional nurse has authority because of the knowledge of and the ability to apply the basic sciences in the field of nursing. Nurses possess freedom because they can choose a nursing action from several possible plans based on their authority. The degree of authority and freedom they possess depends upon the degree to which they make themselves available to others and the degree to which they allow others to make themselves useful to nurses. In this way trust is built between the nurse and the patients and their families, the nurse and colleagues within nursing and related fields, and the nurse and the community.

If nurses utilize their knowledge and ability to apply the basic sciences as *expert* authority, they may blind themselves to available resources in other people. This presenting image may depict one who is always willing to give information but never to receive, one who is unable to realize that others with whom one is working are also authorities. Thus, nurses decrease their own and others' freedom to choose appropriate action because of lack of information.

In order to become independent practitioners, professional nurses must communicate their authority and freedom to all with whom they are concerned. This has been accomplished to some degree on an individual basis, but it must be done for nursing as a profession. Nurses must document, evaluate, and communicate what they do. Otherwise, they will never be free to determine their roles. The professional nurse may disappear.

Image Development

Regardless of role preparation and setting, professional nurses can communicate their authority and freedom through their actions, both verbally and nonverbally. Once they demonstrate their knowledge and ability to provide meaningful health services, they must document and evaluate their actions. This should then be communicated through publication, not only in nursing journals but also in the mass media. As consumers of health care become aware of the nursing services available to them, they will seek these services more freely. As trust is built between client and nurse, the client can provide the nurse with additional evaluation of nursing actions.

Through documentation and evaluation, the existing body of nursing knowledge will be enhanced and validated. Thus, the basis for defining the parameters of nursing practice is established. Once these parameters are defined, professional nurses can determine those actions for which they are accountable, become self-governing, and establish standards concomitant with independent practice.

Resistance

Resistance to independent practice will come from the profession. Change is threatening. It involves a break with tradition. Documentation and evaluation take time and thought. Some duties traditionally performed by nurses will be taken away, and new ones will be added. In order to prepare nurses for independent practice, the profession must provide continuing and inservice education.

Those who would utilize the services of the independent practitioner (physicians, employing institutions, health care consumers) may also resist this change. Traditionally, the physician and the institution have had authority. The nurse has carried out the physician's orders and abided by institution policy.

Nursing Specialists in Practice

Imagine that Ida Pendent, a clinical specialist in maternal–child health nursing, is working as an independent practitioner with a group of obstetricians. Her parameters of practice include teaching, counseling, history taking, physical assessment, and recording of findings. Her case load consists of women who have uncomplicated pregnancies.

Mary Para, according to Miss Pendent's calculations, is in her 22d week of pregnancy. Mrs. Para has one child, Tip, who is eighteen months of age and mentally retarded. During an office visit, Mrs. Para had complained about the difficulty she was having in toilet training Tip. Miss Pendent had tried, during two office visits and one home visit, to help Mrs. Para view Tip according to his developmental age. These attempts appeared unsuccessful, and Miss Pendent felt frustrated.

Lucy Freedman is a clinical specialist in maternal–child health nursing, working as an independent practitioner with a group of pediatricians. Miss Pendent, realizing that she was in need of nursing consultation, made an appointment with Miss Freedman. The Para family is known by Miss Freedman, who has been involved with Tip and his family since he was three months old. One month ago, Mrs. Para announced to Miss Freedman that she no longer wished her to provide health care for Tip. Miss Freedman has been unsuccessful in her attempts to discover the reason for this.

During the consultation visit, Miss Freedman explained to Miss Pendent that she thought Mrs. Para had been realistic about Tip's potential until 2 months ago. She had not known of Mrs. Para's pregnancy until the meeting with Miss Pendent. As each clinical specialist shared information regarding the Para family, they identified what they thought was the major problem—Mrs. Para's fear of producing another defective child. She was in the dilemma of not having accepted fully the reality of one defective child and being afraid of producing a second defective child. The clinical specialists believed that she was so afraid of the possibility of a second defective child that she was trying to make the first normal. She had refused help from Miss Freedman in regard to Tip. Now, she was also refusing help from Miss Pendent in regard to her pregnancy consultation. The clinical specialists decided that Miss Pendent would continue to work with Mrs. Para around her fears during pregnancy. She would also consult with Miss Freedman periodically in relation to realistic expectations for Tip and try to help Mrs. Para resolve this problem.

Both Miss Pendent and Miss Freedman demonstrated their authority through their application of the basic sciences to their nursing intervention with the Para family— for instance, anatomy, physiology, psychology. They utilized their freedom to consult with one another and to devise a plan of nursing care from several possible alternatives. They displayed their accountability for their own actions through the consultative process and their decision making. By defin-

ing their parameters of practice in working with the Para family, they exhibited their ability to be self-governing.

The authors adjure the readers to attempt to answer these questions. Is this example of independent nursing practice consistent with nurse practice standards? Are there legal implications? Who will stand behind the nurse who sees her commitment to independent practice as a professional right? The ANA? The universities? The public?

Changing Parameters of Practice

Model Obsolescence

Revitalized systems of role-model preparation are mandatory if health services are to be energized and appropriate target programs are to be developed. Tomorrow's independent practitioners of nursing cannot be produced by today's schools of nursing. The 1965 position paper of the ANA was less than a modest beginning. Substantial—but purposeful—change must occur now in the philosophy and value orientation of the faculties of present schools of nursing. Current curricula in nursing education are essentially obsolete and ineffective. Dependent role-model teachers do not produce independent practitioner graduates. Curricula of acquiescence will not develop practitioners of accountability. Teaching medical practices will not produce nursing practitioners.

It is not at all difficult to understand why a profession of 100 years' standing is still attempting to define the art and science of its being. Nursing and nursing care have never really been the central occupation of nursing. Filling vacuums and coordinating a series of independent or isolated services have been nursing's major preoccupation for over a century—and much of that either could or should have been the work of others. It is little wonder that the goals, philosophy, and curricula of nursing are so varied in expectation and production. Designing programs around the unwanted tasks and unmet needs of others does not validate a profession. If nursing is an independent profession, then it should produce persons who can practice the arts of the profession independently. The nurse's service should not be governed, guided, or ordered by another profession; it should be requested or sought just as it is with any other profession.

There seems to be no scientific evidence in the literature to validate continuing the assumption that a doctor and a nurse constitute the core of a health team. Therefore, there is no justifiable reason to assume that the curricula of nursing education or the practices of nursing service should continue to be fashioned after medical models of education and practice. Essentially, medical practice and the preparation of practitioners of medicine focus on illness concepts. Conversely, the art and science of nursing are viewed by many as being broader and more comprehensive but also more general in intent. Consequently, medical models have been inappropriate images and ineffective vehicles to achieve the objectives of nursing practices. Professional nursing should be concerned primarily with wellness and *then* with services for restoration to wellness levels. It is inconceivable that wellness philosophies and wellness models can come from illness constructs and theories.

Not only are the models of medical education inappropriate for nursing preparation, but so are the models of clinical division. Maternity nurses should not consider themselves competent professional practitioners if their preparation has been only in hospital-based obstetrics. Obstetric and gynecologic services are undoubtedly appropriate clinical units to prepare a medical specialist for practice in these areas, but these services do not prepare a nurse for maternity nursing practice. Although model components certainly can vary, any model that is developed to prepare a maternity nursing specialist for the kinds of health care services and practices that will be demanded in the future must concern itself with theories and experiences related to the care of parents and their children.

Maternity nursing will soon become one of the artifacts of American history unless both the role and the preparation to carry out the role are drastically expanded. Maternity nursing has too long confined itself to the physical care of a physiologic condition. Some academic attention has been given to the forces and dynamics of parenthood which dramatically and significantly affect the pregnancy state. However, little or no attention has been given in most academic programs to experiences involving the care of children or the education of developing parents. Health needs and social concerns now and in the immediate future demand professional groups who are competent as well as responsive. Programs preparing maternity nurses will need to be well grounded in the liberal arts and in the basic sciences before any attention can be given to the specific knowledges required for independent maternity nursing practice.

Model Preparation

Programs preparing professional nursing practitioners must be housed in university settings, but these programs—as they now exist—will not be adequate for the kind of educational experiences needed for independent practice. Baccalaureate programs should prepare family health nursing practitioners. The philosophical basis will need to change, as will the teaching methodologies required to implement these programs. Integrated content will not ensure integrated thinking processes. Approaches to learning will require a socioanthropological focus with more attention given to such areas as problem-solving methods, directed and independent study, skill development in the analysis of process and content records of interaction activities, and short-term interventive confrontations. Such skills as the assessment procedures for newborn physical examinations, child development and growth scales, and the physiological progress of pregnancy should be taken out of intermediate or stop-gap programs, such as the current maternity and pediatric practitioner or physician's assistant and associate training experiences, and placed where they are more appropriate and effective—in the first-level professional degree program.

Graduate programs at the master's level would prepare beginning clinical nursing specialists in family health practice. The clinical specialist preparation in maternal–child health care would focus on developing first-level practitioners in both maternity and pediatric nursing; however, future programs in specialty areas will need to consider a philosophical reorganization of the preparation needed and the length of time required to produce the independent professional clinician. There are no valid reasons for lengthening the preparation period for first-level specialty practice. Generally, programs are lengthened not because of knowledge explosions but more likely because of faculty ineffectiveness in developing more advanced teaching methodologies. Problems of faculty development should be faced squarely and handled as such, and not at the expense of students. First-level specialty preparation in maternal–child health nursing can be achieved within the limits of a calendar year and yet include a base of midwifery skills, child development, and family-life experiences for both maternity and pediatric nurses.

Second-level specialization will come from independent nursing practitioners prepared at the doctoral level in nursing science, the basic disciplines, or the functional processes of teaching and administration. Regardless of the focus of preparation, all programs at the doctoral level should have a balanced distribution of nursing and discipline or cognate-based course work. Doctoral education should not continue to foster a spiraling narrowness—frequently referred to as depth. A specialist should be able to develop depth in nursing practice through breadth in educational preparation. Doctoral programs would serve to produce nursing consultants, researchers, scientists, and process implementers. The senseless argument of which degree is best for nurses should cease. The profession needs entrepreneurs of practice, research, and process; routes should be accessible to all approaches.

Somewhere in model preparation, whether on the baccalaureate or master's level, provision should be made for some interdisciplinary educational opportunities. Students of nursing, medicine, dentistry, social work, psychology, physical therapy, occupational therapy, and nutrition have a stake in the provision of health care. If one supports a larger view of health care, students of education, law, anthropology, philosophy, sociology, health care management, and theology must also be included. At the baccalaureate level, at least, joint clinical practice and seminars must be considered.

Model Implementation

Frequent references have been made to a concept of independent practice and the independent practitioner. It would seem, however, that the fullest meaning of the term *independent* must be considered, not only in its vernacular intent but also in its professional implementation. It is well past the time for nursing to assume the same independence that is expected of and afforded to all other professional practitioners. In this respect, then, the idea of nurses having hospital appointments, office hours, and group practices is no longer unbelievable. Maternity nurses in the future will function within just this sort of framework. There is no reason why maternity and pediatric nurses could not open offices for group practice in which the focus of care is on wellness preservation and wellness restoration. Since pregnancy is a wellness concept, it is conceivable that the maternity nurse would make a physical assessment and have a laboratory perform the usual tests to determine the existence of a pregnancy before referring the client to an obstetrician.

During the general course of nursing practice, the maternity nurse might deal with a mother who has a child who is failing to thrive. After consultation with the pediatric family practitioner in group practice, the pediatric nurse might wish to examine the child and possibly admit him or her to the hospital to rule out any physical causes of the child's condition. A resident physician on the staff of the hospital would assume responsibility for this diagnostic admission, but the pediatric nurse practitioner would assume the responsibility for the diagnosis and orders during the period of hospitalization. The maternity family practitioner would continue to see the child's mother, who is pregnant and in need of supportive services as well as pregnancy supervision. For the period of hospitalization of the child the pediatric nurse might work directly with the mother or might serve as a consultant to the maternity nurse.

The idea of hospital appointments is not new for many professional groups, but it certainly is for nursing. No legitimate reason exists to preclude this possibility, but the obsequious nature of hospital nursing would need to change dramatically. Appointments to staff positions in hospital settings would in no way limit or hinder those specialist family health practitioners who will wish the security of working for organizations or institutions. The manner in which they work for the institution would, however, need to be reexamined and reestablished. Any number of possibilities exist for the future independent family health practitioner. The limits will be the visionary limits of nursing.

Institution Roles

With the advent of neighborhood and community health clinics in urban areas, the role of institutions is beginning to change. In the past, hospitals have been primary health care centers. Many planned visits to hospital clinics were never realized. The hospital was quite a distance from the neighborhood. Too much time was spent in traveling to and from the hospital and in waiting to be seen in the clinic. Parents could not be certain that they would be home when their children returned from school. If they had children younger than school age and could not obtain baby-sitters, they would have to bring these children with them to the hospital. This proved to be an exhausting day for both parents and children. For these reasons many parents failed to come to hospital clinics on the appointed day.

Episodic, Exotic, and Primary Health Care

Today neighborhood and community health clinics are centers for primary health care while hospitals provide episodic and exotic care. Thus, the pregnant woman receives antepartum care in a community setting unless complications develop. With complications, such as toxemia of pregnancy, she is followed in a hospital-based clinic which is designed to meet her needs. Admission to the hospital is based on unusual diagnoses, experimental care, and the need for intensive care. The pregnant woman might be hospitalized because of the threat of a spontaneous miscarriage or abortion, preeclampsia or eclampsia, or a multiple pregnancy. She is also hospitalized for the actual delivery of her baby. Postpartum care begins in the hospital and continues in the community setting unless complications are present. If the postpartum course is abnormal, care is provided in the hospital setting. The type of hospital setting, either inpatient or ambulatory services, is dependent upon the nature of the postpartum course.

Americans from all strata of society are making known their belief that good health care is a fundamental right of citizenship. Legislators are responding with various national health insurance plans. Prepaid plans would be underwritten federally and/or privately. Federal monies would come from tax revenues. Private monies would be supplied by payroll levies and by private health insurance plans. One danger of national health insurance is the possible decrease of freedom and authority for the health professions due to federal, industrial, and insurance control. Members of all health professions (medicine, nursing, social work, psychology) must work diligently with legislators and industrial and insurance representatives in order to ensure their rights to freedom and authority and to accountability and self-governance.

One way to accomplish this would be to provide for several private community health centers throughout each state, as formulated by Louis P. Bertonazzi, Massachusetts House of Representatives. These clinics would be designed by members of the health professions. The members of each professional group would collaborate with each other and with community representatives in preparing centers which would meet the health care needs of each individual community. Each center would contract with area hospitals to provide episodic and exotic care. Prepaid insurance plans would furnish the financial needs of the centers and the hospitals. The health centers would be primary care centers for people from all strata of society. This would not preclude private practice for members of the health professions. The members of each health profession would enjoy the right to independent practice, but they would be interdependent in their provision of health care to the community. In order to estimate the efficacy of the community clinics as primary health care centers, periodic evaluation by health professionals and consumers would be necessary. The results of such evaluations would be the basis upon which changes would or would not be made.

The Professional Nurse

Different levels of professional nurses are needed in private community health centers. There is a need for family practitioners and clinical specialists. The type of clinical specialists found in the centers depends upon community health needs. The family practitioner performs health assessments on all family members. As the needs arise, appropriate referrals are made to a clinical specialist in maternal–child health nursing, medical-surgical nursing, adult psychiatric nursing, child psychiatric nursing, rehabilitation nursing, or community health nursing. If family problems are not in the realm of nursing, the family practitioner makes the referral to the appropriate health professional.

In the area of maternity nursing, when a family practitioner discovers that a family member is pregnant, a health assessment is first made. Then a clinical specialist in

maternal-child nursing is consulted. Together, they can design a plan of care and
decide who will implement the care. The
pregnant woman may have many questions
relative to her pregnancy which have physiological and psychological implications. If
she has other children at home, she may
want help in preparing them for the advent of
a new family member. She may have questions relative to toilet training her two-year
old or methods of preventing her four-year
old's masturbation. The father of the expected
infant may have questions in regard to the
pregnant woman's mood swings, sexual
intercourse during pregnancy, and the
growth of the fetus. These are areas in which
the clinical specialist can provide teaching
and counseling, both on a one-to-one basis
and in groups. If parent instruction groups
are being led, the parents can be invited to
join. The parent groups would be a supplement to individual counseling.

As the clinical specialist in maternal–child
health nursing works with the pregnant
woman and her family, nursing problems
may be discovered with which the nurse is
unable to deal. The nurse can then consult
with a clinical specialist in the appropriate
field, and together they can decide who
should work with the family regarding new
nursing problems.

The clinical specialist in maternal–child
health nursing can also be a liaison between
the health center and the hospital. Continuity of care can be ensured by passing the
necessary information to hospital personnel
when the pregnant woman must utilize their
services and by receiving information from
hospital personnel when the patient returns
to the community. In the community setting,
the nurse can provide information to the
pediatric personnel who will be furnishing
health care to the newborn infant.

Different levels of nursing are also needed
within the hospital. Health consumers utilize hospital clinic and inpatient services for
the purposes of establishing unusual diagnoses, follow-up in specialty clinics, and
intensive care. Medical technology is a very
important part of health care in hospitals.
Thus, the bulk of nursing care is technical.
The family nurse practitioner could supervise technical nurses in the various hospital
settings. The clinical specialist is available
for consultation relating to nursing practice
and staff problems.

In maternity nursing there could be family
nurse practitioners in all patient/client care
areas—specialty clinics, labor and delivery
suites, postpartum and rooming-in units,
and high-risk and newborn nurseries—who
could supervise technical nurses and coordinate patient care. The clinical specialist
could be called if any nursing problems
arose which could not be handled by the
staff. Inservice education could be provided
for coaching laboring parents-to-be, care of
high-risk infants, methods of establishing
beginning parent-child relationships, and
the like. The nurse could also be a liaison
between the hospital and the community
health centers.

With the advent of medical technology,
there is a very grave danger. Those providing
health care can become enamored of
machines and their intricate workings. A
client's physiology may assume prime importance. Her feelings and her need to know
what is happening to and within her may
not be recognized or may be ignored. Hopefully, nurses will remember the person and
utilize the machines as extensions of themselves.

Sociocultural Confrontations

The Counterculture

Along with the explosion of knowledge in
this century came great technical advances.
Because of these advances, technical experts
appeared. Many became more interested in
things than people and seemed to perceive

human beings as intellectual beings whose psychic components are nonexistent. The technocracy had arrived. Roszak defines the technocracy as "that society in which those who govern justify themselves by appeal to technical experts who, in turn, justify themselves by appeal to scientific forms of knowledge. And beyond the authority of science there is no appeal."[12] Among a minority of middle-class youths, a counterculture has evolved. It is "a culture so radically disaffiliated from the mainstream assumptions of our society that it scarcely looks to many as a culture at all, but takes on the alarming appearance of a barbaric intrusion."[13] Its members have sought ways to go "beyond the authority of science." Some have chosen communal patterns of family life; some have evolved their own sexual code; and some have turned to psychedelic experiences through drugs, poetry, music, or bastardized versions of Zen. Many alienated youths utilize sensitivity, encounter, and mind-expansion groups as a means of finding themselves. While the technocracy concentrates on the development of the intellective aspects of the personality, the counterculture seeks to develop the psychic aspects of the personality. These groups possess their own authority and freedom, but they do not seem able to exchange this authority and freedom with one another. While they work at cross-purposes, society as a whole must cope with sociological problems, such as alienation, venereal disease, and drug dependence and addiction.

"Hot lines" in many communities are providing counsel for youth with these problems. Help is also available in venereal disease clinics, drug clinics, hospital-based drug units, and mobile health units. Nurses can be found working in the venereal disease and drug clinics, on the drug units, and with mobile health units. A nurse, as a private citizen, may volunteer time to the hot line. Nursing must accept the fact that alienation,

changing sexual codes, and drug dependence and addiction are nursing issues. As independent practitioners, professional nurses will be involved in providing nursing intervention in problems which have arisen as a result of the dichotomy between the technocracy and the counterculture. They *must* be concerned with the broader issues of society in order to define parameters of practice—a practice which will have a more relevant impact on wellness.

Self-concept and the Maternity Nurse

The maternity nurse has the ideal opportunity to begin to equip future generations with the strength to cast aside and conquer alienation. This can be done by fostering parent-child relationships. During the antepartum period, the maternity nurse can encourage parents to discuss their thoughts, feelings, questions, and fantasies regarding their unborn child, their relationship to this future person, sibling relationships, and their own relationships. The nurse can help them to begin to accept the reality of their newborn infant in the delivery room by allowing them to see, touch, hold, and examine the baby. On the postpartum unit, parents can be encouraged to discuss their thoughts, feelings, questions, and fantasies.

An ideal time to observe mother-child relationships is during feeding. How comfortable is the mother? How comfortable is the baby? How does the mother hold, touch, look at her infant? What is her facial expression? The answers to these questions give the nurse the necessary data to begin the assessment of mother-child relationships and to provide nursing intervention.

Although the maternity nurse may have provided parents with excellent information which would aid them in preparing their children for the advent of a new family member, this help should be continued on the postpartum unit. One way to do this would be to provide the opportunity for the siblings to come to the hospital. Seeing their mother and the newborn might dispel many of their own fears and fantasies. Many of their questions could be answered during daily visits to the postpartum unit in the hospital.

Traditionally, the maternity nurse's last contact with the parents would be the 6-week postpartum visit. Continuance of the fostering of parent-child relationships can be ensured by providing pertinent information to the pediatric personnel who will be providing health supervision for the infant. Yet, if the maternity nurse is to be concerned with the broader issues of society, the fostering of parent-child relationships encompasses more than the span of time covered in the antepartum through the postpartum periods. The nurse can become involved with parent groups, church groups, community groups, and teachers who are developing education programs in human sexuality (also known as sex education and family-life education). This education begins in the antepartum period and ends with death. It enhances the self-image in relation to oneself and others, as male and female. It teaches self-respect and respect for others. Thus, a person learns to give as well as receive, and becomes capable of experiencing a loving relationship in all human situations. A person learns that he or she possesses not just intellect but a psyche—that feeling, mystical, mind-expanding part of oneself which is unmeasurable yet so meaningful to personality development and status as an individual.

ACCOUNTABILITY REVISITED

The field of medical technology has come a long way during the last decade and its impact has certainly been felt by nursing. Sweeping away the existing barriers to human achievement through developments in ultratechnology can no longer be tolerated as a desirable or viable goal for the health pro-fessions. Any alteration of the human condition carries with it a concomitant responsibility to measure carefully the ethical impact of the intrusion. Nursing has spent very little time in analyzing the moral-ethical dilemmas created by technology and technological advances.

The New Biology

What do we mean by "the new biology" and what relation does it have, if any, to maternity nursing? Kass identified three categories of biomedical technologies: control of life and death, control of human potentialities, and control of human achievement.[14] Each has its own impact on nursing, and each presents its own dilemma.

Human Potential

Due to advances in medical technology more people with mutant genes are surviving, and surviving longer than at any previous period in our history. Increasing the number of mutant survivors merely serves to perpetuate the potential for greater numbers of genetically defective humans. Modern technology now makes it possible to store spermatozoa and mature oocytes in laboratories thereby allowing one to engage in selective reproduction. It is now possible to mix selectively sperm and ova in test tubes and later transfer the blastomere to a host uterus for eventual delivery of a viable fetus. Cloning, long achieved in frogs and mice, could soon become a step in human evolution. To eliminate cystic fibrosis over the next 35 years for example, 17,000,000 female carriers must be aborted. One can hardly imagine the consequences if each geneticist were allowed "an equal assault on his favorite genetic disorder,"[15] considering each human carries four to eight recessive, lethal genes.

Human Achievement

Neurological and psychological manipulations that alter speech, thought, freedom of choice, emotion, memory, and imagination are now possible through brain surgery, operant conditioning, electric shock, and drugs. Although present techniques are rather primitive, such manipulations do in fact occur and occur in ever-increasing numbers. Any decision to develop or use biomedical technology involves value judgments which cannot be derived from biomedical science. Not only do we overlook this fact, but we also continue to avoid the three serious ethical issues of distributive justice, use of power, abuse of power, and "self-degradation and dehumanization."[16]

Humanhood: Retained or Relinquished?

Medicine's success in extending life is already a major cause of excessive population growth. Death control does indeed point the way to birth control. Modern surgical techniques, advanced biomedical instrumentation, intricate methods of resuscitation, and manipulative chemotherapy may all serve to intrude on the natural human condition until life and living become states of physiological response rather than experiences in being. More and more people are dying in the cold company of pacemakers, defibrillators, respirators, aspirators, oxygenators, and catheters. Few die in the warmth and comfort of human company. Families suffer protracted death watches yet are denied the intimacy of the human experience.

Ethical Issues and Dilemmas

What does it mean to be distinctively human? What does it mean to know, to be knowing? What is knowable? Have human beings become simply raw material for sci-

ence to manipulate and homogenize? Nursing can no longer disengage from the arena of humanhood. The issues of *being* cannot be left to the philosophers, moralists, and students of ethics. What kind of nurses are we to leave the meaning of life to the courts? Human manipulation and human worth have their very genesis in maternity nursing.

Who Shall Live: Situational Ethics

Facing biological realities and but a few of their tragic personal and social implications puts one squarely against the issue of who decides who should live. Within the framework of informed consent* each "defective" newborn infant or child, with and without treatment, must be discussed and evaluated with the family. The most basic issue confronting each of us is the need to come to terms with what is meant by meaningful humanhood.[17] Most individuals would describe meaningful life as the capacity to love and to be loved, to be independent, and to understand, anticipate, and plan for the future. But who among us can prescribe the parameters of how much love or how much independence? Who among us knows what it really means to understand or what should be understood? And when we speak of planning for the future, who among us knows what kind of future is envisioned by the other? Somewhere, however, between the exciting unknown and the dismal now a family must decide if their newborn has the capacity to be.[18]

---

* Informed consent means the voluntary, knowing assent from the individual after he or she has been given a fair explanation of the procedure to be followed, a description of the accompanying discomforts and risks, a description of the benefits to be expected, an explanation concerning appropriate alternatives, an offer to answer any inquiries concerning the procedures, and an instruction that the individual is free to withhold or withdraw his or her consent to the procedure at any time prior to its performance.

Most of the problems we are talking about have no solution at the moment and many will have no solution in the near future. We are tied to biology and the mistakes of nature and natural selection and will continue to be, at least within the foreseeable future for most of us. Biology is not guided by ethics nor does ethics seem to be guided by biology. Many make a sharp distinction between allowing to die and killing. The act itself is emphasized above the result. Modern technology controls so much of our living and dying now that many others consider this distinction to be a moral quibble. Maternity nurses can no longer remain on the sidelines of life while families struggle with the issues of death through informed consent. We have all played God by interfering with natural processes. Each of us has assisted in preventing illness and in postponing death. The issue is not who has the right to play God but how to play God fairly.

Moral Claims of the Fetus: The Unborn Wanted

Current controversy surrounding the question of fetal rights in medical research and abortion has obscured the fact that there is no clear understanding of the nature of our obligations, if any, to the fetus under normal or wanted conditions. What claim does the fetus have on the mother during that period when it is dependent on the integrity of the fetal/maternal relationship? When we can resolve that question we will have clarified some of the issues involved in protecting the fetus against experimentation or in considering abortion after some specified point in gestation.[19]

Generally, in a wanted pregnancy we recognize the needs of the fetus for adequate nutrition and protection and respond in several appropriate ways. Ethical issues arise, however, when these needs conflict with maternal needs. The fetal/maternal relationship is always fraught with conflicts of

a lesser or greater degree. Ethical dilemmas arise when decisions must be made which potentially affect the physical well-being of either the expectant mother or the fetus. Recently, however, there has been a marked change in our understanding of the nature of the interdependency for fetal well-being. We know, for example, that the fetus is in some senses an independent organism. It develops its own circulatory system very early in gestation and soon pumps its own blood through the placental circulation to receive nutrients and to rid itself of wastes. Also, the fetus is not immune to environmental insults. To the contrary, its environment is filled with sensory stimuli—sound, light, tactile stimuli. A loud noise, a high-intensity light, a sudden shift in maternal position— all can elicit a vigorous response from the fetus. We do not know in what way any of these stimuli may be valuable or dangerous to fetal development.

The fetus is also vulnerable to potentially harmful substances, including environmentally derived drugs, chemicals, toxins, and heavy metals, which can produce developmental defects or death. Of course, neither can we ignore maternal risks. Fetal development does not necessarily enhance maternal well-being. It may, in fact, increase the risk of sickness and death through selective weakening of maternal defenses against severe viral infections. Labor and delivery themselves carry a calculable risk of morbidity and death.[20]

Understanding human fetal and maternal vulnerability as well as the concept of maternal responsibility radically increases the range of human choice during pregnancy and moves it well beyond simple avoidance of disease. Advanced technologies have amplified the spectrum of options available for choosing the circumstances and conditions under which conception and successful gestation take place. Lappé defines four special situations where issues related to such decision making are most sharply drawn: (1) where initiation and/or maintenance of pregnancy requires the use of drugs of doubtful safety for the embryo or fetus; (2) where drugs necessary for maternal therapy are potentially injurious to the fetus; (3) where the mother continues to consume potentially harmful substances during pregnancy; and (4) where the mother suffers from an incurable limitation of a genetic, physical, or physiological factor necessary for normal embryonic development.[21] Resolution of these and related problems in the ethics of the fetal/maternal relationship require more knowledge than we now have about maternal and fetal physiology, and about the ethical weights to be given to rights, obligations, and responsibilities owed to *each* participant.

An increasing knowledge of the sources and means of controlling fetal disability will indicate methods by which increased responsibility may be exercised by parents for fetal well-being. It may, in time, even be possible to set precedent for parental legal obligations to the fetus. However, even if we were to justify and to advocate the ethical imperative that society must provide mothers with the conditions for nutritionally adequate, stress-free, and disease-minimized pregnancies, it *may* not follow that the fetus deserves equal protection. However, it does raise a legitimate question we cannot ignore: Does the *fetus* have a legal right to an adequate antepartum environment?[22] If the courts declare that the mother's right to privacy overrides the fetus's right to survive prior to its ability to exist outside the uterus, then it would seem that the courts have seriously reduced their prerogative to regulate other forms of maternal behavior which affect fetal development (experimentation, drug ingestion, and smoking, for example) during that same period.

Nursing has spent very little time weighing the moral-ethical dilemmas created by technology and technological advances. If we are to assume an advocate role, we cannot be reactors to societal forces and change. We must assume a position of centrality in the arena of ethical dialogue and create the forces of social changes. To do less is to have done nothing.

REFERENCES

1 Cleland, Virginia: "Sex Discrimination: Nursing's Most Pervasive Problem," *American Journal of Nursing*, 71:1547, August 1971.
2 Isler, C., S. Rockwell, and B. Shaw: "A Doctor's View of the Nurse: Still a Handmaiden, but . . .," *R.N.*, 34:58, August 1971.
3 Boucher, Rita J.: "Similarities and Differences in Perceptions of the Role of the Clinical Nursing Specialist," vol. I, unpublished doctoral dissertation, Boston University, 1970.
4 Bruce, Sylvia J.: "Valuation of Functions of the Role of the Clinical Nursing Specialist," vol. II, unpublished doctoral dissertation, Boston University, 1970. Materials related to role development and professional independence were drawn from volumes I and II, chapters 1 and 2.
5 Reiter, Frances: "Nurse-Clinician," *American Journal of Nursing*, 66:225, February 1966.
6 Bullough, Vern, and Bonnie Bullough: *The Emergence of Modern Nursing*, Macmillan, New York, 1969, p. 152.
7 Ibid., p. 149.
8 Ibid., p. 154.
9 Ibid., p. 155.
10 Ibid., p. 167.
11 Davis, Fred (ed.): *The Nursing Profession: Five Sociological Essays*, Wiley, New York, 1966, p. 175.
12 Roszak, Theodore: *The Making of a Counter Culture*, Doubleday, Garden City, N.Y.,1969, p. 8.
13 Ibid., p. 42.
14 Kass, Leon R.: "The New Biology: What Price

Relieving Man's Estate?'' *Science*, 174:779, November 19, 1971.

15 Ibid., p. 781.

16 Ibid., p. 782.

17 Kelsey, Beverly: "Which Infants Should Live? Who Should Decide?" *Hastings Center Report*, 5(2):5, April 1975.

18 Ibid., p. 6.

19 Lappé, Marc: "The Moral Claims of the Wanted Fetus," *Hastings Center Report*, 5(2):11, April 1975.

20 Ibid., p. 11.

21 Ibid., p. 12.

22 Ibid., p. 13.

3

The Nursing Process in Maternity Nursing

ERNESTINE WIEDENBACH

Nursing has always been regarded as a helping service, to be rendered with compassion, skill, and understanding to those in need of care, counsel, and confidence in the area of health.* Its practice comprises a wide variety of services, each directed toward the attainment of one of its three components: (1) identification of the patient's need for help, (2) ministration of help needed, and (3) validation that the help provided was indeed helpful to the patient.

Over the years, however, the outward character of nursing has changed. The setting in which the nurse functions is different today. In times gone by, patients were cared for in large open wards, and the nurse's "station" was a table or desk in the center of the ward or at its end. A patient need never

---

* Health is defined by the World Health Organization as a state of complete physical, mental, and social well-being and not merely the absence of disease and infirmity.

feel alone. He or she could readily see the nurse and call for help if necessary, and the nurse could as easily see and call to the patient. Today, on the other hand, in many hospitals, patients are cared for in single-, two-, or four-bed units, with the nursing station centrally located in the corridor outside. Contact between nurse and patient may be established via an intercommunication system (intercom) by pushing a button in the box on the wall. In former days, too, the nurse cared for all of the patient's needs, assisted the doctor with dressings and treatments, and managed the ward. Today the nurse is apt to delegate direct care of patients to other personnel, such as licensed practical nurses and nursing aides, may make rounds with the doctor, and cooperates with unit managers in administrative duties.

Changes comparable to those in hospitals have taken place in the field of community health nursing, too. In earlier days nurses went afield to knock on doors to find and help those in need or to invite them to well-baby clinics or to classes for mothers. Today a patient is more apt to be referred to a nursing agency by a community doctor, hospital, or other agency and then may be visited by the nurse to assess the patient's needs and arrange for follow-up care. Not too often does the community health nurse provide bedside nursing care for patients in their homes. Rather, members of the family are instructed and encouraged to give it, or such care may be delegated to a nonprofessional member of the staff. The nurse is then free to concentrate on measures for disease prevention, to teach classes for expectant parents, and to cooperate with community agencies in developing health and welfare programs. Thus, opportunities for fostering warm, close relationships between nurse and patient are less common today, whether in the hospital or in the field of community health, yet, the

patient's need for care, counsel, and confidence has remained unchanged or, if anything, has increased.

This trend toward impersonalization of nursing care presents problems. Many patients are unhappy about it and frustrated by it. Their experience with nurses—or lack of it—is not in accord with their preconceived image of the nurse as a helping person. Many nurses, too, are dissatisfied and frustrated by this impersonalization. Their desire to give direct care to patients and to meet their needs is as keen as it was when they, as students, entered the nursing world. Pressures, however, due to understaffing, rising patient census, electronics, research, and sophistication of modern hospital management and medical care make it almost impossible for the nurse to develop a close relationship with the patient and derive the satisfactions that result from concerned patient care.

Frustrations exist in the area of maternity nursing, too, particularly in hospitals where most pregnant women are urged to go for care. Except in relatively rare situations in which nursing students have been assigned expectant mothers to follow through their childbearing courses or in which nurse-midwifery programs have been instituted, nurses are unable to give individual mothers the amount of time and attention they know the mothers need. In antepartum and postpartum clinics, on labor and delivery services, and on postpartum units the ratio between number of nurses and number of patients is usually in serious disproportion—especially during the evening and night hours. The lone nurse then is often so overwhelmed by demands made by doctors, telephone calls, students doing research, families of patients, and patient admissions as well as by administrative responsibilities, including tasks such as charting, that it is almost impossible to give uninterrupted attention to patients who are in need of service.

Yet, in maternity nursing, a close and warm relationship between nurse and patient is of special importance. The childbearing process imposes on the woman physical alterations, often accompanied by discomforts and fears, to a greater degree than do other physiological phenomena. Changes, sometimes disfiguring, and frequently not completely understood by the woman, occur in her body; the certainty of labor is anticipated with varying degrees of apprehension. A new life which she must nurture is growing either within her or in the crib beside her, and family relationships and responsibilities can induce strains that are hard to deal with, especially if unaccompanied by love and understanding. Many nurses, in their preparation in both basic and graduate schools of nursing, have become poignantly aware of patients' potential problems and have developed the resources—knowledge, judgment, procedural and interaction skills —so essential to resolve them. But how, amidst the realities of today, does the nurse appropriately apply them? How does the nurse bridge the gap between the desire to meet the needs of patients and the availability to effectively meet them?

Two courses of action are suggested for consideration:

1 Develop understanding of the process that determines nursing actions.
2 Incorporate in practice measures that will enhance the effective functioning of the nursing process.

CONCEPTUALIZATION OF THE NURSING PROCESS

To develop understanding of the process that determines one's nursing actions is a

self-searching and self-revealing undertaking. Difficult though this may be, it is worth doing. The quality of nursing service is measured by the effectiveness of the nurse's individual actions, that is, by the degree to which the nurse succeeds in eliciting behavioral and physiological responses from the patient that are in accordance with the physician's plan of treatment and with the nurse's purpose in nursing. Nursing actions, thus, are significant; they contribute to the patient's ability to realize his or her hopes and needs for health.

Nursing action may be envisaged as an energized phenomenon that occurs within the realities of the existing situation and is carried on with, or in behalf of, an individual involved with restoration or insurance of his or her health. It is the visible portion of nursing practice in which the nurse interacts by word, look, manner, or deed with another person—the patient, another member of the staff, or a member of the patient's family—to bring about results that are desired. Nursing actions, however, do not just happen.

There is a series of operations underlying and powering each one that gives import and direction to each nursing act. This series of operations is regarded as the nursing process, and it is an influencing factor in whatever the nurse may do. It may be activated in many different ways—by bright sunrays striking a sleeping baby's face, an expression of fear in a woman's eyes, or a request for medication to help her go to sleep. Such activating situations are interpreted and made more meaningful to nurses by their personal thoughts and feelings which intensify their awareness of them and give them meaning according to the nurses' knowledge, values, and the realities of the situation.

The meaning the nurse attaches to such awareness, however, represents an interpretation that is based solely upon a subjective view of the situation. Three kinds of subjective interpretations may occur in quick succession within the nurse's mind upon contact with an activating situation: sensation or experienced sensory impressions; perception, or interpretation of a sensory impression; and assumption, or the meaning one attaches to one's perception of a situation. These three interpretations represent levels of awareness that are attained through concentration of attention upon the activating situation.

For example, when the nurse, Miss Black, entered the four-bed maternity unit, she experienced a tightening sensation within her as she sensed that something was wrong. Looking about, she perceived a patient lying on her side with her face buried in her pillow and shoulders heaving; her muffled sobs were faintly audible. In a flash, Miss Black recalled that the patient's baby had a congenital deformity, and she assumed that she was crying because of that distressing fact.

These three levels of awareness—sensation, perception, and assumption—are attained without great mental effort and may be said to represent the involuntary phase of the nursing process. In addition, each could also serve as a staging area for action:

When Miss Black sensed that something was wrong, she might have stopped and spontaneously exclaimed, "Hey, what's going on?"

When she perceived that the patient was crying, she could automatically have gone to her bedside and pulled the curtain around her.

And when she assumed that the reason the patient was crying was because her baby was congenitally deformed, her feelings might have prompted her to whisper, "Oh, don't cry! Your baby will be all right!"

Such acts are spontaneous, automatic, or impulsive in character. They occur on the spur of the moment and are precipitated by unchecked, rampant thoughts and feelings. Occasionally, especially in time of emergency, such spontaneous acts may have useful outcomes. For instance, spontaneous actions have been known to be lifesaving; automatic acts sometimes contribute to preventing the spread of disease; and an impulsive act, indicative of love and understanding, might enable a patient to release pent-up feelings and indulge in a good cry. However, the results of such behavior, as a rule, are open to question and are likely to do more harm than good. The more helpful acts are believed to be those that stem from purposeful deliberation—the voluntary phase of the nursing process. (See Figure 3-1.)

This voluntary phase is brought about when nurses willfully check the random flow of their thoughts and feelings, temper them with reason, and with its aid, bring them under control. In this way, nurses enable themselves to attain a fourth level of awareness, that of realization. It is the crucial level, for it alerts them to the subjective nature of their assumptions and to their need to find out from the patient if their interpretation of the patient's behavior is correct. Such validation or clarification then leads successively to the fifth, sixth, and seventh levels of awareness—namely, insight, design, and decision—from which responsible nursing action then can result.

Had Miss Black, for instance, recognized the subjective nature of her assumption that the patient was crying because her baby was deformed, she might well have realized that the patient's crying could be due to other causes. Then, rather than express an unfounded prediction, she would have tried to find out from the patient the reason for her tears. Knowledge of the cause of distress provides insight into her problem, and then, with clarity about her purpose in nursing, her knowledge, and her skills, she would be

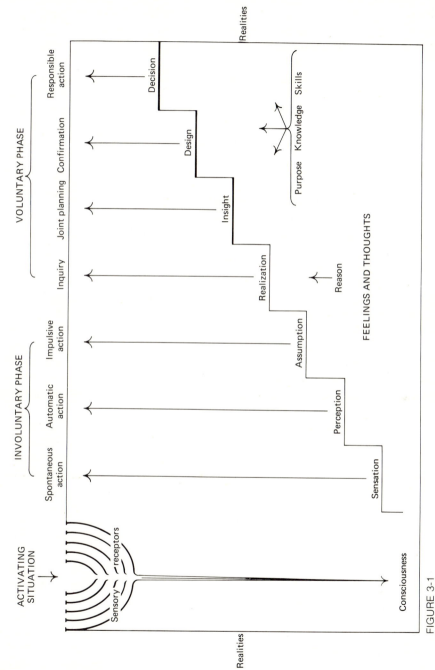

FIGURE 3-1

Conceptualization of the nursing process. Diagrammatic presentation of the influences and forces that raise the consciousness of a situation to higher levels of awareness from each of which a definitive kind of action could result.

able to design a plan of responsible action with the patient, if necessary, and make the decision to act upon it.

The nursing process, thus, is essentially an internal, personalized mechanism. As such, it is influenced by the nurse's culture and subculture, purpose in nursing, knowledge, wisdom, sensitivity, and concern. Furthermore, as an integral part of the nurse, its effectiveness increases as, with experience and resolute intent, the nurse develops clarity about it and its many facets and uses it deliberately to bring about desired results. Regardless of the type of nursing engaged in —community health, medical-surgical, mental health, pediatric, or maternity—the series of operations through which nurses achieve their results follows essentially the same pattern. This means that the mechanism that guides nurses in practice is basically no different in maternity nursing than it is in any other area of nursing. Prevailing circumstances within the realities vary and dictate the kind of knowledge and skills that must be applied, but the process by which the nurse arrives at the decision of what to do and how to do it follows the same general pattern in all types of nursing.

FACTORS THAT ENHANCE FUNCTIONING OF THE NURSING PROCESS

Any mechanism that powers action has parts or areas within it that need special attention to keep it functioning at its best. The nursing process, too, has focal points which, if neglected or ignored, will defeat the effectiveness of the nurse's act. They are identified specifically as:

1 The nurse's beliefs and values
2 The nurse's purpose in nursing
3 The nurse's sensitivity to inconsistencies in the immediate reality situation
4 The nurse's access to reason
5 The nurse's application of knowledge and skills

These five points may be recognized as personal assets that tend to lie latent in the nurse until they are consciously developed and enhanced. This entails special effort: first, clarity about them and their significance to practice must be gained; second, the way in which they may serve best in practice must be ascertained; and third, determination to incorporate them in practice must be sustained.

Beliefs and Values

Beliefs and values supply the energy that motivates the nurse to act, and they determine the attitude displayed in what is done. For example, if the nurse believes the patient has a need, she or he will try to meet it; and if the nurse regards the patient as a worthwhile human being, the nurse will treat the patient with respect and consideration. Together beliefs and values constitute a nurse's *value system*, which is an integral part of the nurse. They develop inconspicuously and may remain unidentified and nebulous unless the nurse takes time to sort them out and make them explicit. Of special importance to a nurse's practice are the beliefs the nurse holds about the significance of life; about the worth, individuality, and aspirations of each human being; and about his or her own responsibilities to both the patient and to him- or herself. By putting these beliefs and values into words, nurses are able to examine them, check their validity, and alter or refine them as their understanding of life, humanity, and themselves is deepened and enlarged. And when the nurse has given expression to them, they enlarge the dimension of his or her nursing process and become a vital part of it.

The Nurse's Purpose

The nurse's purpose in nursing represents a professional commitment. Although the nurse may have been told by others what it is, it will become a useful part of the nursing process only when the nurse has thought it through introspectively and has formulated a personal understanding. Specifically, the purpose in nursing sets forth (1) the qualities that the nurse will strive consistently to sustain, foster, or bring about in the patient with respect to the patient's condition, attitude, or situation and (2) the special responsibilities that the nurse recognizes as belonging to him or her in caring for the patient. The nurse's purpose stems from the nurse's beliefs and values and comes into focus when the nurse clarifies them for him- or herself. As with them, the nurse's purpose in nursing will remain vague and ill-defined unless expressed in a clearly set forth statement. Although the nurse will want to reexamine the statement from time to time and possibly refine it as his or her scope of nursing broadens with experience, the need to have a clearly stated purpose in nursing readily available in explicit terms becomes ever more apparent. It is the guiding force that sets the direction for the voluntary phase of the nursing process and gives stability to the deliberative thinking that it entails. When the nurse makes it a conscious part of the nursing process, it will not only set the course for nursing action, but will also enable the nurse to determine whether the results which he or she obtains are desired. Such understanding by the nurse is the basis not only for responsible action, but also for improvement of the quality of nursing care.

Sensitivity

Sensitivity is an attribute which essentially is part of every individual. It is closely associated with the sensory receptors that are located within the eyes, ears, nose, tongue, and somatic sensory areas and may be considered the principal trigger for setting in motion the operations of the nursing process. Sensitivity alerts the nurse to awareness of inconsistencies in the situation that might signify the presence of a problem or need. Since identification of a patient's need for help is one of the objectives of nursing practice, sensitivity is a key factor in contributing to achievement of this goal. The nurse has responsibility to do all that is possible to enhance personal sensitivity and keep it finely tuned. This is of special importance today when the multiplicity of devices that are laborsaving and efficient militate against the heightening of sensitivity.

For example, a monitoring device had been installed in the labor and delivery suite of a large city hospital, enabling the medical and nursing staffs to keep track not only of the baby's condition during the patient's course of labor but also of the frequency and character of the patient's contractions. The viewing box of the monitoring device was located in the nurse's station, thus allowing the staff, particularly the nurse, to engage in the other activities while "keeping an eye" on the patient's progress. Mrs. Thompson, who had been admitted to the unit earlier in the day, was feeling increasingly apprehensive and uncomfortable as, with wires attached to her abdomen, she labored alone in her room. She wished the nurse would come and talk to her, rub her back, or listen to the baby's heart as the nurse did when she was in the hospital to have her first baby 2 years ago. But she thought the nurse was probably too busy and was reluctant to call for fear of being considered a nuisance or a weakling.

After a while, though, her discomfort overcame her hesitancy, and she mustered enough courage to press the intercom button. A voice from a box on the wall responded, "Yes, Mrs. Thompson, what can I do for you?" The sound of that metallic voice, detached from a visible human being, filled Mrs. Thompson with sudden panic. All she could force herself to say was a whispered, "Could you tell me what time it is, please?" The voice from the box answered, "Surely. Two o'clock." And that was that.

A nurse who was sensitive and clear about purpose in nursing might have recognized the shade of anxiety in Mrs. Thompson's whispered question and responded to it rather than directly to the expressed request. The nurse also might have felt a slight surprise at the question itself and geared a response to the discrepancy sensed, especially if a glance at the monitoring device showed that Mrs. Thompson was having strong contractions with only brief intervals between them.

The finer shades of a person's behavior—the brightness of his eye, posture, gestures, mannerisms, or tone of voice—all tend to reflect the thoughts and feelings that are going on inside the person, and it is to them that sensitivity needs to be directed. Likewise, sensitivity to discrepancies between behavior a patient may present and that which might be expected can alert the nurse to inner conflict or distress.

Susceptibility to such nuances of behavior is increased when they are allowed to reach the nurse's consciousness via several sensory receptors rather than just one. Had the nurse, for instance, actually been in Mrs. Thompson's presence, her facial expression, the sound and rate of her breathing, and possibly the feel of dampness of her forehead or the firmness of her grip would all have been noted. Such behavioral manifestations are telling indicators of a patient's feelings and condition but may go unnoticed by the nurse who relies primarily upon some electronic or other device to reveal a patient's need.

Effort is required to enhance one's sensitivity. It will not happen of its own accord. Not only does it require determined exposure to a multiplicity of sensory stimuli from the patient whenever possible, but it also necessitates continuous search for discrepancies between the patient's behavior and one's expectation of it. Sensitivity that is keen will impel the nurse to higher levels of awareness of the patient and will contribute to establishment of an empathic relationship from which responsible nursing action can result.

Reason

Reason is a tempering agent as well as a stimulator of deliberative thought. It enables one to recognize the blinding quality of one's feelings and to assuage their intensity so that one can view the situation with greater clarity. At the same time, it enables a person to realize the one-sided nature of his or her assumptions and encourages the person to seek their validation. Just as sensitivity alerts awareness to behavioral manifestations in another, so may reason alert the nurse to awareness of inner feelings and assumptions that could cause impulsive actions.

Assumptions are the final level of awareness in the involuntary phase of the nursing process. They result from one's perception of a situation based on one's idea of what it means, and they have potential for evoking strong feelings of anger, joy, or distress that may be totally unjustified by fact. They have an insidious quality, too, for their presence all too often is unrecognized, yet they are responsible for the action that is taken. The nurse, for instance, who responded to Mrs. Thompson by giving her the time of day as she requested, acted on the insidious assumption that time of day was what Mrs. Thompson really wanted to know. Had the nurse, however, resorted to reason and allowed it to bring the assumption into proper focus, its one-sidedness might have been recognized, and the response might have been very different.

The insidious quality of assumptions is also apparent in the following incident. A nurse saw a pregnant woman slowly enter the antepartum clinic area at closing time, just as the doctor was about to leave. The nurse recognized the woman as a registered client and suddenly felt a gush of anger at her late arrival. Consequently the nurse rushed toward her and with a sharp, annoying voice exclaimed, "You know better than to get here at this late hour!" The woman, taken aback, opened her mouth as if to reply, then quickly closed it and dropped despondently onto the clinic bench, tears welling in her eyes.

That nurse let neither sensitivity nor reason preclude the action that brought frustration and unhappiness to a client—a result the nurse surely would not have wanted to bring about. Instead, a full rein was given to the assumption that the woman had intentionally come late to the clinic, and the nurse impulsively chided her for doing so.

Like sensitivity, reason is an attribute with which everyone is to some extent endowed. Furthermore, it complements the awareness to which sensitivity gives rise. Had the nurse in the example noted the nuances in the woman's appearance, manner, or gait, the woman might have been viewed in a clearer light, and reason would probably have helped the nurse realize that the woman was in some sort of distress.

Reason, defined as the ability to think, is a key property of the nursing process. Its introduction elevates awareness to the level of realization which serves as a foundation of deliberative thought. The fact that the nurse has access to reason, however, does not necessarily mean that reason will be utilized. Neither nurse in the two previous examples did. Before effective use can be made of it, the nurse needs to realize the fact that every behavioral manifestation has two aspects: the nurse's view and the view of the other person involved in the situation. When this fact is firmly entrenched in the nurse's mind, then reason can serve as a reminder that assumptions represent a unilateral view of the situation and that to take responsible nursing action the nurse must ascertain the other's view of it. This, too, requires effort to bring about.

Application of a Nurse's Knowledge and Skills

Application of a nurse's knowledge and skills is the substance of the nursing process. The aim of its operations is to enable the nurse to gear nursing action to meet the patient's need. In the field of maternity nursing, most nurses today have acquired the essential knowledge and skills in basic and graduate courses in programs of nursing education. They possess not only theoretic and factual knowledge about parents, their fears and attitudes, and about the childbearing course, but also measures that will contribute to the mother's competence and comfort, promote her health and that of her baby, and safeguard both against illness and distress. Such knowledge and skills represent a tremendous stock of resources for effective functioning, but to have them benefit the patients, nurses must first realize the extent of their knowledge and abilities and then must deliberately apply such skills in their practice.

Timeliness, receptivity, effect, and accountability are four important considerations in the application of a nurse's knowledge and skills.

Timeliness

The childbearing course follows an orderly sequence. The first trimester follows conception; the second trimester follows the first; the third follows the second and culminates in delivery, which brings about the baby's birth. Then, postpartum restoration occurs accompanied by lactation and the newborn's growth and development. Each of these periods is characterized by special happenings, hazards, and responsibilities that give rise to needs of which the nurse is well aware and about which parents also may want to know.

Thus, during the first trimester, when realization of pregnancy first comes with hopes, fears, and apprehensions and the developing baby imposes strains on the expectant mother's entire system, parents may want to know when and how to obtain maternity care for the expectant mother, what to do to keep well, and how to deal with curious feelings and symptoms of which the expectant mother may be aware. They also may welcome information about how the baby grows and the demands it may make of her system as well as suggestions regarding adjustments to make in their daily pattern of living.

During the second trimester, when the expectant mother is apt to feel well and buoyant, parents may want to know when classes in preparation for childbearing are held and how to register for them. The expectant mother may appreciate information about the baby's layette as well as suggestions about eating, bathing, exercising, and just keeping well.

During the third trimester, when weight gain often is a problem for the expectant mother, when her tissues are stretched, her muscles strained and she feels pressure everywhere, and when the day for the baby's birth looms closer, information parents may want includes ways for the expectant mother to maintain her appearance and to be more comfortable, foods to eat and to avoid, and preparations she might make for lactation. They also are usually interested in knowing how to recognize the onset of labor, whom to notify when it has begun, when to go to the hospital, and what to expect there.

During labor, when contractions become progressively stronger, comfort measures and reassurance are what couples usually want.

And during the postpartum period, when the mother has many concerns about herself, her baby, and her family, she usually will appreciate a listening ear and answers to questions she may or may not ask. This is true not only while she is in the hospital but also after she is back at home. In addition, she may also welcome guidance and suggestions for doing exercises that will help her to regain her figure, support for her efforts to nurse her baby (especially if she wants to breast-feed), and counsel for giving the baby the care he or she actually needs.

Voluntarily offering information and suggestions that are relevant to whichever stage the woman is experiencing in her childbearing course is appropriate nursing action, and nurses would do well to incorporate it deliberately in their practice when giving maternity nursing care. Not only may a woman want and need such information and suggestions, but in offering them and, if wanted, giving them, nurses add to their stature as helping persons. This is especially true in antepartum clinics where the nurse, perhaps because of pressures, is often tempted to abrogate nursing responsibility by referring the expectant mother to another worker without first determining her need. Not infrequently, for instance, when the doctor prescribes a low-calorie, salt-free diet for a pregnant woman, the nurse will immediately refer her to the nutritionist in the clinic for information and suggestions. Yet the nurse probably spent hours during student days calculating low-calorie diets and learning about foods that are low in salt! Likewise, when a young high school girl, pregnant and unmarried, registers with the antepartum clinic, the nurse may refer her to the social worker as soon as the doctor has completed his examination of her. These are unfortunate nursing practices, for by passing on to others the responsibilities that are within the province of nursing and that nurses have been prepared to handle, not only do they render useless much knowledge and skill acquired, but they deny their own ability to help.

Receptivity

Receptivity, being ready and willing to accept and make the best use of what is offered or is about to be done, is a state of mind to identify or foster in a patient before initiating definitive nursing action. A patient may indicate receptivity in overt form such as a smiling "Yes," an eager reaching out, or a vigorous drawing away that leaves no doubt in the nurse's mind about the acceptability of what is being offered or is about to be done. Many times, however, the patient does not so obviously reveal her acceptance or rejection. At such times, sensitivity to nuances in patient behavior may give the nurse necessary clues which can be explored verbally to discover if the interpretation is in accord with the meaning to the patient. At still other times, the nurse may have to ask the patient how she feels about intended nursing action and pursue the exploration until a credible response is obtained. When it indicates acceptance, the nurse may feel secure in initiating action. When it indicates rejection, however, the nurse must try to establish the reason for the rejection before initiating definitive action. It may be because the patient has no need, or perhaps she does not

fully understand or could not easily tolerate the nurse's method of offering aid.

For example, in the antepartum clinic, the nurse discovered that Mrs. Brodish, pregnant for the first time, knew practically nothing about the growth and development of the fetus or the mechanisms of labor. The nurse had a *Birth Atlas* in the office and offered to show it. Mrs. Brodish, however, acted reluctant to accept the offer. However, this rejection was unconvincing to the nurse, who also sensed in Mrs. Brodish a curiosity to see the pictures. When the nurse expressed this quandary about Mrs. Brodish's behavior and asked for help in understanding it, Mrs. Brodish then said she would like to see the pictures but not in the nurse's office because she might lose her turn in seeing the doctor. This was an easy adjustment for the nurse to make. The *Atlas* was brought to the clinic area where Mrs. Brodish could give her undivided attention to the pictures and the nurse's explanation of them. Had the nurse not tried to ensure Mrs. Brodish's receptivity but had shown the pictures to her in the office, they would have had little meaning for Mrs. Brodish. Her mind would have been too full of anxiety to be able to comprehend the pictures or the nurse's explanation of them.

Effect

The effect of measures initiated either to identify or meet a patient's need for help is also important to ascertain. The nurse's application of nursing knowledge and skills has no particular value unless it produces desired results. Sometimes the effect of nursing action may be immediately discerned, as in the patient who falls asleep shortly after she has been helped to assume the postpartum relaxation position or in the rapt attention Mrs. Brodish manifested when she was shown the *Birth Atlas* pictures. At other times, the effect may not be known until much later. This is true of dietary information an expectant mother may be given. Its effect may not be known until her next clinic visit when she steps upon the scale or when her blood pressure is taken and her extremities are examined for edema. When results are satisfactory, it is a cause for gratification and for rejoicing with the expectant mother; when results are unsatisfactory, the cause for failure needs to be sought. Rarely does an expectant mother who has placed herself under medical or nursing supervision purposefully disregard suggestions, recommendations, or advice. She usually has a reason for her negative response, such as a lack of understanding, lack of sufficient energy, a serious social problem, a cultural or ethnic bias, or inadequate facilities at home. To scold a patient, as doctors—and nurses, too—have been known to do, serves no useful purpose. It merely alienates the patient. Meaningful application of a nurse's knowledge and skills requires that the cause of unsatisfactory results be sought until uncovered, and then the patient is helped to overcome it. Like Mrs. Brodish, who could not benefit from the *Birth Atlas* pictures until her mind was free of anxiety, so may a patient need help in overcoming whatever may interfere with the patient's ability to respond capably to measures instituted or recommended for her well-being. Therein lies the importance of ascertaining the effect of measures instituted to meet a patient's need for help.

Accountability

Accountability means to accept responsibility not only for the action that one initiates but also for the results. This presents no problem for the nurse when results are satisfactory. In fact, it is a cause for inner gratification when measures are instituted which

provide the beneficial effects that are desired; the nurse is then quite willing to accept responsibility for the consequences of the act. However, when results are disappointing, the nurse may be tempted to blame others or circumstances and thus deny any accountability for what was done. At such times it must be remembered that the action taken represented the nurse's best judgment at the moment; therefore, rather than blame others, the nurse should try to discover how such results were obtained. This can be done by examining the nursing process to determine the level of awareness that was the basis for such judgment. Most likely the nurse will find that it was based on an unvalidated assumption, a level from which effective action seldom results. Such insight is useful. Not only may it suggest what the nurse can do to alter the unsatisfactory results, but it will enable more effective functioning in the future.

CONCLUSION

Maternity nursing is a serious and creative as well as a demanding type of service that all too often is not clearly understood. So much has been said in recent years about the normal physiological aspects of the childbearing process that the fears and apprehensions that parents experience are minimized or overlooked. It is true that most pregnant and postpartum women as well as those who are in labor are essentially well individuals with none of the distressing and debilitating conditions that many patients who are sick in hospitals must endure. However, their needs, though different, are as acute and are apt to be more far-reaching, for they often extend well beyond the period defined by their condition, as in the case of illness. They have implications for the development of the family, the basic structure of our society, which today more than ever needs help to be kept intact. Within the professional nurse are the knowledge and the skills with which to provide that help. The nurse has the ability to enable expectant mothers and fathers to increase their competence in assuming their responsibilities; the nurse can help them have a satisfactory childbearing experience and knows how to support them in their efforts to cope with problems that arise along the way.

When the nurse applies nursing knowledge and skills for the benefit of expectant parents whenever opportunity presents, the nurse contributes to the bond of love between parents and between parents and their children and thus adds strength to the family structure. Maternity nursing care is a vital, significant service which must be appreciated by the nurse who, in turn, should help others to appreciate it as well. To realize full professional potential, nurses must respect their knowledge and abilities, offer them voluntarily (not just in response to the doctor's order or to a patient's specific request), and accept responsibility for their acts. Clarity about the nursing process as the implementing power for nursing practice will enable them to do this. And when this is fully realized and the nurse freely gives of nursing knowledge and skills, when appro-

priate, not only will these services be in demand, but administrative support will be strong for the kind of nursing the nurse both wants and is ready to give. The nurse who is competent and helpful to the patient is a precious asset to any service concerned with patient care.

BIBLIOGRAPHY

Dickoff, James, Patricia James, and Ernestine Wiedenbach: "Theory in a Practice Discipline: Part I, Practice Oriented Theory," *Nursing Research,* 17(5):415, September–October 1968.

—— and ——: "Beliefs and Values: Bases for Curriculum Design," *Nursing Research,* 19(5):415, September–October 1970.

Orlando, Ida J.: *The Dynamic Nurse-Patient Relationship,* Putnam, New York, 1961.

Wiedenbach, Ernestine: *Family-centered Maternity Nursing,* 2d ed., Putnam, New York, 1967.

——: *Clinical Nursing, A Helping Art,* Springer, New York, 1964.

——: *Meeting the Realities in Clinical Teaching,* Springer, New York, 1969.

——: "Nurses' Wisdom in Nursing Theory," *American Journal of Nursing,* 70(5):1057, May 1970.

UNIT B

THE FAMILY OF TODAY

4

The Nuclear Family

DAVID M. FULCOMER

This chapter discusses the nuclear family, the constellation of which is comprised of mother, father, and child or children living within the same household, and the significance of this family type to the maternity nursing process.

Other types of family relationships (alternate family styles) are more common than in former years, but will be discussed in other portions of this book. They are significant to the maternity nurse today, and they should be understood. But the nuclear family remains the most numerous family unit in the United States during pregnancy, childbirth, and early infancy. This is important, even though a growing number of these units change at some point in time to a single-parent type of family, mainly as a result of divorce.

The focus in this chapter is the middle class. Although many children are born to families in other socioeconomic classes, especially low-income families, much of the research data available is on the middle-class family. However, it is very important that the nurse take every opportunity to learn as much as possible about families in different socioeconomic classes. Hopefully, much in this chapter can be applied in the nursing process to families not in the middle class.

Special emphasis will be placed upon the birth of the first child to a married couple and the impact of this birth upon the marital relationship and resulting family relationships. Most "newness" in the husband-wife relationship and the total family constellation comes for the majority of couples during the first birth experience. Although the impact of later children is usually less severe, it is important to remember that there are exceptions.

The nurse is important in any one or a combination of ways to the new parents and the new family. For example, the nurse is often the first member of the health team who meets and has contact with the family. And particularly important is the fact that the nurse is often the most person-oriented member of the team. Often the nurse has an advantageous position as one who is potentially most able to help the family in some significant way.

The analysis the nurse makes of each particular family constellation is very important. A relationship to each family and each family member should be established on the basis of that particular family. The approach must be on a family-to-family basis, recognizing both how each family is different from any other family, and also how each is similar to other families.

What kind of knowledge about nuclear families will be helpful in maternity nursing? How much insight into families can the nurse be expected to know and use? What are the key concepts, perspectives, and insights that will be especially useful to the nurse? This chapter has been written to help

answer these questions. No attempt is made to identify the specific, step-by-step contacts the nurse has with families and family members.

WHAT IS HAPPENING TO FAMILIES?

The professional person who works with families needs to be aware of major changes which are occurring to the family. Our society is complex, and is changing rapidly. Any institution within it must undergo significant changes. The professional person also needs to be aware, however, of the fact that not *everything* about the family is changing. Many of the more traditional concepts, attitudes, values, and feelings are still common.

Families continue to be important and numerous, despite the increase in the number of childless marriages and the stress on the need for population control. Even if reproduction rates continue to decline, all evidence points to the existence of millions of families in the future. Although child care centers will increase rapidly and family-type groupings with alternate life-styles will continue, a more traditional family environment will still be extremely important for a majority of adults and children.

This is not the place to discuss in detail all the specific changes which have occurred and are occurring in American families as they adapt (and families have always adapted) to change. But it is important to call attention to the fact that maternity nurses should be aware of the changes occurring in modern society which affect the behavior of persons involved in family living. Students of the family differ regarding many of the specifics; but most of them agree that the family as an institution is in the process of adapting, rather than disappearing.[1–11]

Some of the significant trends regarding

the American family of which the nurse should be aware are:

1   The rate of marriage is decreasing and the rate of divorce is increasing. There were 970,000 divorces in the United States in 1974, as compared with 913,000 in 1973 and 479,000 in 1965.
2   Single-parent families are increasing rapidly. In 1948 only 1 out of 14 children under six was being reared by one parent. In 1973, 1 out of 7 children under six was being reared by one parent.
3   Fertility among married women in the United States has been declining. The downswing in births that started in the spring of 1971 has continued through the first half of 1975, and every indication is that it will continue.
4   The change in and deemphasis of sex roles is having an important effect upon the family. The male is playing a more active role in many instances. The couple is sharing parenting roles much more often. There is an increasing need for the maternity nurse to know how to relate to and work with both men and women.
5   The increase in the number of married women in the labor force, including mothers, is significant. In fact, the number of working mothers is soaring. Every indication is that the trend will continue, meaning that an increasing number of married couples who have children must give major consideration to their thinking and feelings about how to integrate parenting into their job-oriented life-styles.
6   There is less psychological support for parenting. In some quarters, a couple having children may be considered

suspect or stupid. This influence upon young couples having children is extremely subtle, and little is known about it. But the combination of this negative attitude toward parenting in some parts of society and the extreme difficulties in rearing children in the United States is probably having major effects upon the feelings and coping abilities of many young parents.
7   The role of friends is possibly becoming more important to young parents. At least the need for friends to become involved in rearing one's children is becoming more important. The "good old days" when the extended family was near and played an important part in the day-by-day tasks of rearing children have disappeared. Couples and their children need help, including psychological support and nurturance, from others. The nurse has probably become *more* important to the family constellation than in former years, and it may also be that the nurse should be more alert to the involvement of non-family humans during pregnancy, childbirth, and early infancy.

Yes, the family is undergoing many significant changes. Probably one of the most important things for the maternity nurse to know is that new parents still feel the tremendous pressure of parenthood in our society. This is a definite factor in the reaction of many parents to pregnancy, childbirth, and the coming of children into the marriage relationship. LeMasters speaks of the rate of social change, the conflicting norms, and competing authorities. Big demands are being made upon parents by their children, by professionals, and by themselves. The margin for parental error shrinks as the family system becomes smaller. Each child becomes crucial. Each interaction with the child becomes crucial. All this can lead to fear, frustrations, and even guilt, depending upon the parent's expectations of himself or herself as a parent and of his or her mate as a parent.

Parenthood is terribly important to almost all parents, and yet it is very difficult (although not necessarily undesirable) for most. For many people childrearing and parenthood are more important than marriage as a source of gratification and a sense of self-worth. This is still true for many men and women, and especially for working-class persons. Udry says that marriage is a transition to new roles and responsibilities, but under modern American conditions, the adjustment to marriage is not as difficult as the adjustment to parenthood.[12]

Furthermore, parenthood does not "come naturally" to the average man and woman. It is very demanding. It happens all of a sudden. One has to adjust to it in a much shorter time than either marriage or occupation. And, probably worst of all, less preparation for parenthood is available than for any other major role.[13]

Complicating all this is the romantic approach to marriage and parenthood in our society. For marriage, sufficient preparation is "being in love." For becoming parents, all that is necessary is to want to have one of those wonderful, clean, pretty, smart children! Because having children continues to be highly romanticized in our society, there is a tendency to have a great desire for children but to be unprepared for what they are really like and what it takes to rear them. Many couples are very poorly prepared for the impact of children on marriage.

This is why many parents experience considerable disenchantment with marriage and parenthood, especially during their first months as parents. Parents usually know little about the nature of children. There is evidence to indicate that the over-romanticizing of parenthood and the lack of preparation for it on the part of most couples is a large factor in causing marital difficulties over the years.

Any help the nurse can give parents in coping with pregnancy and childrearing will have positive results that cannot be measured. Therefore, the nurse should remember the following points:

1   Families are still very important and will continue to be.
2   Size of the family is important.
3   Working mothers will increase in number.
4   Divorce will continue to be a significant factor, with many nuclear families having one or both spouses divorced previously.
5   Parents today feel great pressure, often leading to anxiety and even guilt.
6   Parenthood is of great importance to the sense of self-worth of most parents.
7   Parenthood has to be learned, and learned quickly.
8   The over-romanticizing of children and parenthood affects most couples to some degree.
9   In the United States the average adult is unfamiliar with children. Few have any realistic notions of what effects children will have upon the family.
10 All children and all parents can benefit from an effective and well-handled nursing process.

WHAT IS A FAMILY?

What a family *is* is best seen by the way it functions. What are some of the chief characteristics of the family and the way it operates (structure and function) which the nurse takes into account? The following are some important considerations to keep in mind in regard to the couple who are going through pregnancy and childbirth and the early weeks of family life:

1   The myths are out; reality is in. Real people are involved, with all their potentialities for love, hate, and indifference.
2   The family is a special kind of small group. Among other things, it is characterized by:
    a   Deep, continuing emotional involvement among its members.
    b   A combination of sexes.
    c   A combination of ages.
    d   Strong and intense regulation by society, including society's present confusion over what that regulation should be.
3   Individuals make up the family; therefore, individual needs and tasks are directly and intensely involved.

Each member of the family has his or her own combination of needs and tasks at any particular moment. Hess and Handel speak of interaction within the nuclear family of husband, wife, and children as a "bounded universe"—a small world of the family's own making—and within this world, the family members work out a dual pattern in which each person maintains individual separateness, yet remains part of the web of connected relationships. Thus, family life is shaped *within* the participants as well be *between* them.[14]

So, in a very real sense, each person in the family stands at the center of a relationship's context which is peculiar to him or her. At the same time, since there are other persons in the family, personal uniqueness has to be modified and fit into the necessities of living within the family group.

4   A family is a dynamic, living thing, which is constantly changing as the individual members and outside influences change. Yet, it has a continuity because it is a "bounded universe" of relationships among its members.

Interaction is reciprocal action. Roles played by each family member are related directly to roles played by others in the family. A family is a set of interlocking relationships. Each family works out its own specific ways of coping with the combination of persons and societal forces affecting it.

Henry Bowman describes it this way:

The family is a dynamic institution. It changes in slow, evolutionlike fashion as part of overall cultural change. Each family, too, is dynamic. It changes as the number, ages, needs, and behavior of family members change and as the family as a group adapts itself to fluid circumstances. No matter where the family is found, in whatever area, class, or culture, at whatever period in history, certain broad similarities are to be observed in the stages through which it passes, just as there are broad similarities in the stages through which individuals pass in their development from infancy to old age. . . .[15]

Evelyn Duvall puts it this way:

The family is a unity of interacting persons related by ties of marriage, birth, or adoption, whose central purpose is to create and maintain a common culture which promotes the physical, mental, emotional, and social development of each of its members. Modern families fulfill the promise of this definition through at least six emergent, nontraditional functions: (1) affection between husband and wife, parents and children, and among the generations; (2) personal security and acceptance of each family member for the unique individual he is and for the potential he represents; (3) satisfaction and a sense of purpose; (4) continuity of companionship and association; (5)

social placement and socialization; (6) controls and a sense of what is right.[16]

Over two decades ago, Rhoda Bacmeister stated clearly the reciprocity of interaction within a family when she wrote, "This is just human living at close quarters, shifting and frequently illogical, with the love and the flashes of hate, the jolly companionship and the irritations all mixed up. . . ."[17]

In the family, as in all groups, what has gone on before affects what is. Ralph Turner speaks of the sequence of events in the family as a long chain of cause and effect, each link being one episode, and each episode taking some of its unique shape from the sequence of events that preceded it.[18]

This is why the advent of the first child brings a major change in the entire family context. A stranger has been admitted into a close-knit group, and suddenly the balance of the home shifts. Not only has a relationship been added for each older member of the family unit (that member's relationship with the new baby), but the relationships of all former family members to each other are also changed. In addition to the baby being born, a mother is "born" and a father is "born," and usually there are grandparents being "born" as well as aunts, uncles, and cousins.[19]

VARIATIONS AMONG FAMILIES

Each family situation is always somewhat different from any other. It has its own peculiar combination of circumstances and forces. To be aware of and sensitive to the total configuration and combination of factors in each family is a great asset to the assessment phase of the nursing process. To realize that each family has its own particular history influencing it will help the nurse know how to move into that family situation and be more effective in accomplishing nursing goals.

Variation in Form and Structure

Those who criticize our society for being too middle-class, white, and Protestant-centered are correct. Research on families has not escaped this severe limitation. Fortunately, this narrowness is being lessened, but much work remains to be done before we have an accurate overall view and understanding of the many variations among families in our society. The nurse must work within this serious limitation. Yet, the nurse can make use of what knowledge and insight we already have in regard to working with particular types of families.

Minority and ethnic groups have distinct cultural patterns within their families. Different socioeconomic classes have distinctive characteristics which influence their families. Families, taken separately, have their own special combinations of ages, sexes, sheer numbers, rituals, and customs. Families differ in the number of kinfolk who have an influence upon them. They differ, too, in major roles their members play *outside* the home which have to be integrated into the life-style of the family within the home. Work roles outside the family are of tremendous importance. Other outside roles can be equally important.

Variation within Families

There are many ways in which each family differs from any other family, even within its own social class. These differences can influence significantly how the family functions.

Whether or not parenthood is planned can make a big difference in the relationship between a husband and wife during pregnancy and in their reactions to childbirth and becoming a family. Some professional persons believe that involuntary parenthood is far more tragic than involuntary childlessness, for example.[20]

Motivations for parenthood are powerful factors in how humans cope with the actuality of parenthood. Lantz and Snyder discuss immature and mature motivations. Immature motivations include "holding together a poor relationship," "a means of avoiding loneliness," "a means of realizing unfulfilled goals," and "a means of attaining security." They speak of the mature motivation as viewing the child not as a means to a parental end but as an end in itself.[21]

Some parents—many more than we wish existed—reject their children. Bell points out that some mothers severely reject their children either psychologically or physically and that many American women do not love or want their babies.[22]

The problem of the battered child is not new. But the extent to which it exists in our society is alarming to anyone who knows the facts and who is concerned about human relationships. This problem is evidence that not all mothers and fathers are pleased with the arrival and presence of their babies. We need more facts, and they are hard to get. No one who works with couples and young children should be unaware of the evidence available and the studies made of the battered child.[23–25]

Coping with Variations among Families

Nurses need to be aware of the uniqueness of the individual and of the family; yet, it is important to recognize that this uniqueness occurs within a predictable frame of reference. View individuals as unique, but use your knowledge of their age and stage of development to understand better the tasks they may face, the possible reasons for their behavior, and their probable needs. Work with new parents without typing them as just like other members of their group; use your knowledge of the tasks which each person needs to accomplish at this stage of his or her development as a new parent or as a parent again. It does help to know the family life cycle and the developmental sequences experienced by all families, because this aids in making some predictions about a family's behavior and can open the door to anticipating potential problems and needs that are important to a family.[26]

Coping with Personal Feelings about Family Living

Every professional person working with persons and families should be aware of his or her own values and feelings. What if the nurse does not approve of the way people behave in a family? What should be done about one's own values and feelings? Can they be ignored, or do they have to be faced frankly and honestly? To ignore these feelings is to run the danger of letting them interfere with effectiveness in working with families.

The nurse, like any other human being, is influenced by personal experiences as a family member, past and present. Attitudes, feelings, and expectations regarding family behavior are there. The most professional person in the world has them. The important thing is that the nurse learns to recognize, accept, and cope with these feelings so they do not interfere with understanding, acceptance, and effective work with families. It is not necessary to *like* all family members and all the behavior in a family. Feelings of displeasure, anger, and revulsion are just as normal as positive feelings.

Attitudes, feelings, and expectations regarding family behavior can have a sociocultural basis, as well as a personal and familial base. If one has been reared in the middle class, it is almost impossible not to have many middle-class values and biases and the feelings that accompany them. But part of being professional is to know what these are and "allow" for them in the nursing process. In regard to the "naturalness" of biases, one is reminded of the story of the famous Chinese person who, on arriving in the United States, was asked by one of the waiting reporters, "What strikes you as the oddest thing about Americans?" His reply was, "I think it is the peculiar slant of their eyes."

THE NURSE AND THE COUPLE DURING PREGNANCY

Pregnancy involves more than most people realize. What happens *during* pregnancy is very important to the nurse, especially because it has so much to do with what happens *after* pregnancy. It is involved in the whole web of relationships expectant parents have with each other, relatives, friends, customs, rituals, expectations of society, and even laws. Pregnancy is definitely an important part of the parenthood experience.

Each Partner during Pregnancy

Pregnancy, especially the first pregnancy, is quite an experience for both partners. For one thing, each draws upon his or her own experiences, consciously or unconsciously, on how to go about his or her role in pregnancy. It would be very difficult, if not impossible, for anyone to go through pregnancy without some degree of ambivalence. In fact, for most couples pregnancy is filled with many feelings—anxiety, joy, fear, pride, and self-concern, among them. Pregnancy for most couples is a very significant step in further specialization of their relationship. As sex-role differentiation decreases in our society, some of this specialization can be eliminated or lessened. But biology itself dictates certain specialization. Whatever new roles arise for each, it is important that each partner develops feelings of certainty

in the importance of these roles and his or her competence in performing them.

The Expectant Mother during Pregnancy

Much has been said and written about the woman during pregnancy. Both the physical and emotional dimensions have been explained. It takes a keen mind and diligent work to separate the dependable information from the misleading comments and suggestions. This is one area in which the nurse can be both helpful and supportive. The nurse also can help the expectant mother to understand both facts and feelings. The family background and its influence on the pregnant woman at this time can be an important factor. Here is a comment made by a college woman who was making wedding plans:

Maybe motherhood is not foremost in my plans for marriage, because, frankly, I am a little afraid of it. Mother always emphasized that it was very unpleasant. For several years I believed it was next to the worst thing anyone could go through.[27]

These feelings of fear and anxiety were major problems for this young woman during her first pregnancy. Fortunately, she had contact with a nurse who recognized her feelings and helped her understand and accept them.

The Expectant Father during Pregnancy

As females have suffered so long from sexism and role stereotyping, so have males. An aspect of this is the neglect of the expectant father as an important factor in the pregnancy situation after conception takes place.

This carries over into the common tendency to ignore him as a significant parent, except for his financial contribution and "male role image" in parenthood. All members of the family suffer from this.

In many respects, the expectant father's feelings, needs, and problems during pregnancy are not too different from those of his partner, even though this is not usually recognized. Old feelings about pregnancy and childbirth can become important. Mixed feelings, especially shortly after pregnancy is definite, are very common. These feelings are probably reinforced by the popular idea that expectant fathers are lost, afraid, and completely inadequate. One young expectant father wrote:

Something new was on the horizon. New thoughts and ideas started running through my head. The realization that I was going to be a father was too big to swallow all at once. It's a bit hard for the expectant father to realize exactly what his new title implies. I looked at myself and didn't look any different. The word "father" alone made me think of my own father. The comparison made me wonder if I was old enough to handle the job competently. I still wonder. I am determined to be the best father possible. The truth is, doctors don't seem to realize how many questions arise in the husband's mind.[28]

Dr. David Mace comments on the expectant father's mixed emotions during pregnancy (he thinks all men have them) and the fact that it may be easier to be an expectant mother than to be an expectant father:

At a time when he is expected to be pleased and loving, and kind and patient, how can he admit to anyone that his real feelings are often surges of fear and resentment? In many ways, it's harder to be an expectant father than to be an expectant mother. For the woman, all sorts of exciting things are happening. . . .[29]

The socializing of males is significant. They are conditioned not to express their feelings, especially feelings about personal matters. The cultural need for the man to pretend he knows it all and can cope with it all keeps him from letting others, including his mate, know that he, too, needs reassurance and some helpful information. Many males actually feel insecure and inadequate. For many expectant fathers, such feelings may not be a major problem, but the subtle influences of what can be called the "trap syndrome" are probably more far-reaching than is recognized. The nurse who can establish a positive relationship with the expectant father and offer some pertinent information and reassurance is contributing to the pregnancy situation—and the parenthood situation, too. William Genné has written, "The husband who is baffled, bewildered (and, perhaps, belittled) during the nine months of pregnancy will not be able to be a good husband to his wife or a good father to his child."[30]

It is no wonder that in our society many expectant fathers, especially those going through the experience for the first time, become increasingly job or work conscious, feeling that now others must depend upon them. Often they think in terms of whether or not they can provide for the needs of their coming children, especially as they think far into the future. (Insurance salesmen are very much aware of this vulnerability of the expectant father.) In times as uncertain as the 1970s, these concerns of the expectant father are intensified.[31]

Couvade

The existence of an ancient ritual called *couvade* seems to indicate that the need for fathers to have their significance noted during the parenting process is pervasive. Couvade is one of the strangest birth-associated phenomena in the world. Although the details vary from culture to culture, usually in this practice the husband takes to his bed, thrashes around, and groans. When the baby is born, friends pay homage to him; after the child's birth, he may go on a strict diet. Most anthropologists view couvade as a phenomenon most likely to exist in cultural situations in which mothers dominate their sons; where resident patterns are matrilocal, i.e., postmarital residence is with the woman's kin group; where mothers breast-feed their babies for 3 to 4 years; and where mothers sleep in the same room with their children for 6 to 7 years.[32]

Partner Relationships during Pregnancy

Being pregnant is certainly a matter of emotional and social adjustment for both partners. This leads automatically to necessary readjustments in their relationship. A young college man whose wife was pregnant for the first time had this to say:

My wife and I had a lot of important changes and adjustments to make to each other and to things in general . . . things like a changed diet and pills for her to take . . . the doctor didn't want her to work as hard. . . . Those weren't the biggest adjustments, though. Right from the start each one of us had a new part to play—a new role—I found out that expectant fathers have to be more considerate of their wives than before. Then, too, it isn't long before they have to assume a few of the household tasks that their wives did before. My wife and I worked out a lot of these adjustments, talking them over at the dinner table. Some of the others didn't get solved that easily. I hope I haven't painted a dark picture, because waiting for the baby so far has been wonderful.[33]

Sexual relationships may have particular significance during pregnancy. This has probably been less of a problem recently, at least among the well-educated, but it still is a common problem for pregnant couples. Women can easily become apprehensive about sexual relations. It is easy for men to see "sexual withdrawal" as something unpleasant connected with pregnancy. Many men feel this; few verbalize it. Sometimes the nurse can play a significant part in preventing or lessening this kind of a problem. A "word to the women" can help if a word to the men is not possible. Sometimes both are possible.

Another common problem is for the expectant father to feel "left out." As one husband expressed it, "I feel like I'm on the outside looking in." Another expectant father said it this way: "I feel like the doctor and my wife are in cahoots against me." It certainly is easy for many men to feel that their needs are not going to be met (by their mates) in the same way as previously. The facts of the situation tell any man that he will not continue to be the exclusive interest of his mate—probably never again. Women often feel the same way. Here, too, the nurse can be of help. In various ways the nurse may help one or both to become less possessive of the other, help one or both to become more able to give up some of the older dependencies and substitute other things that will make the relationship even more valuable in a personal sense.

Any one or any combination of the following may be important tasks for a couple during the expectancy stage:

1   Acquiring knowledge about and planning for the specifics of pregnancy, childbirth, and parenthood
2   Realigning roles
3   Developing new earning and spending patterns
4   Adapting patterns of sexual relationships to pregnancy

5 Adapting and reorientating relationships with relatives and friends
6 Devising housing rearrangements
7 Adapting and reorientating relationships with friends and the community
at large
8 Learning to communicate even more
effectively and positively

The nurse has many opportunities for
helping the couple. This is truly a teachable
time for both partners, especially during the
first pregnancy.[34-36]

MOVING INTO PARENTHOOD

From "romanticized" parenthood to realistic
parenthood is quite a jump for all too many
couples, especially for those who have no
real opportunity to learn how to be parents.
This is part of the price our society pays for
assuming that persons do not need to be
taught about human relationships and that
even if they did it could not be done.

Most parents have had no "on the job" experience, and it is no wonder that so many
new parents feel overwhelmed and uncertain when they are suddenly faced with the
responsibility for the care and socialization
of the child. Moving slowly into the new situation would be difficult. The sudden step
into this complicated situation is very difficult for many—and very unfair.

Learning to be parents takes time. There is
no automatic inborn instinct of parenthood,
and the skills of parenthood must be
learned.[37]

From a Twosome to a Crowd

Ours is still mainly a paired society. To function "normally," one is supposed to pair up,
especially from adolescence on. Courtship,

the wedding, the honeymoon, and early marriage before pregnancy may all be wonderful. Then comes pregnancy, and all of a sudden the twosome disappears and one has to
operate in a triad—a crowd. Now a third
party becomes an involved member of the relationship. Things will never be the same for
husband and wife! A classic book on the
family states it this way:

No matter how going a concern a marriage may
be, the advent of children causes severe strain between parents. Newborn babies cannot be taken in
their stride; they have none. . . . Any orderly,
smooth, satisfactory relationship carefully
worked out between husband and wife is broken
up the very first night the child is home from the
hospital. The inability of a child to do anything
for itself means that demands are made on parents
which create a new relationship between husband
and wife. . . . Babies are tyrants.[38]

It is clear that with the arrival of the first
child there is a fundamental shift from a
husband-wife relationship to a parental relationship. Since couples are usually not prepared for parenthood (and probably have
highly romanticized or no specific expectations in regard to it), it is often impossible
for them to maintain the centrality of the
husband-wife relationship while they are
rearing a child or children. This is tragic, because a good, healthy marital relationship is
desirable for parents and children.

Each time a baby is born, a new learning
experience begins for everyone in the family.
Being a parent of one child is not like being
the parent of two children, and so on. When
a child is born, every other child in the family has a new position and a new place in the
bounded universe we call the family. Some
behavior and some feelings toward others in
the family change. A crowd is very different
from a twosome! The number of interactions

added with the addition of new members is expressed by the following formula, where x represents the number of interpersonal relations and y represents the number of persons:

$$x = \frac{y^2 - y}{2}$$

The following letter written by a mother needs no explanation:

I suppose we had what is common to all first babies the first month—worry. Shall we call the doctor? Why does she cry so? What is *wrong* with the child? It all amounted to mostly nothing, and a bit of colic. It is still difficult to tell the nothing from the colic, but we are classifying symptoms now, and beginning to learn the difference. . . . I doubt that she was nearly as miserable with it as were we. We'd stand over her bed and commiserate with her difficult breathing. I think I drove the doctor almost out of his mind with telephone calls and idiotic questions. . . . Every time we took her to the hospital she fell into a deep sleep, and remained so during all the doctor's examination. The conclusion was that nothing was wrong with her. We began to feel the doctor thought we were unnecessarily picky about the amount of crying she did. . . . Finally the doctor diagnosed colic. To know that nothing is really wrong with her is such a relief that we have relaxed a bit and perhaps in doing so have actually made her colic less serious. . . .

Our daughter, as you can well imagine from experience, has done a thorough job of reorganizing our home, but for the most part things have settled down and some order has come of the chaos of the first few weeks. . . .[39]

As the new baby brings major changes to the family constellation, including changing needs and changing roles, the nurse can be a help to all family members with whom contact is made. The nurse can assist the persons in the family in understanding and coping with the changes which are occurring.[40–41]

Parenthood: Crisis?

In 1957 LeMasters published an article titled, "Parenthood as Crisis."[42] This was a study of middle-class couples which showed that 83 percent of the 46 couples he studied experienced "extensive" or "severe" crisis after the birth of the first child. Several follow-up studies have raised some questions about his instrument and have added other points. It is fair to conclude, however, from the data at hand that the first child in particular introduces some "crisis" conditions to the marital relationship of many couples.

LeMasters found that the mothers reported such things as loss of sleep, chronic tiredness, exhaustion, extensive confinement to the home and resulting curtailment of their social contacts, giving up the satisfactions and the income of outside employment, additional washing and ironing, guilt at not being a "better" mother, long hours, 7-days-a-week schedules, decline in housekeeping standards, and worry over their appearance. Fathers named many of the same things and added decline in sexual response of wife, economic pressure resulting from the wife's retirement plus additional expenditures necessary for the child, interference with social life, worry about a second pregnancy in the future, and general disenchantment with the parental role.

As Udry says, "Marriage is a twosome; three is a crowd. Studies of many kinds of groups have shown that of all human patterns of association, triads are the least stable."[43]

When the primary reason for having a baby is based on a romantic or unclear conception of parenthood, chances are high that the couple will run into the parenthood-as-crisis situation which LeMasters discusses. The desirability for couples to know what babies are like and what rearing them entails is self-evident if one is concerned about the welfare of the persons involved and the human condition of our society. Parenthood need not be a crisis situation; but, as has been indicated, it can easily be that. Here, again, the nurse can enter the picture and help the couple to cope well with what would otherwise be a very difficult situation.

Shifts in the Partner Relationship

Regardless of how one may rate or measure the changes caused by the coming of the first baby, there is no doubt that they are profound. Radical changes are caused in the interaction between the expectant parents. The following quotation is from a college student reflecting upon herself as a child growing up in the family and her effect upon her parents:

Children are really peculiar possessions. We arrive at a time when they could be very happy together. They could have more money to spend on each other. They are young. They are happy together. They love each other; and then we come along. They find they have to share their love, work twice as hard, spend half as much time and money on themselves. They get away less. Then they have to begin learning all over again. They have to learn how to play jacks, jump rope, skate, and do all kinds of things they once knew but had forgotten.[44]

Something in this statement indicates that having a child is not all bad. It could be tremendously rewarding, even in the 1970s. A great deal depends upon the preparation the couple have had for this big change in their relationship. Have they developed a really healthy relationship as a couple, with good ability in the skills of handling differences and of communicating? The answer to this question would be very important to the nurse, for it would indicate both how and

why the parents cope with a new baby. Also, it would help indicate what information is needed and what would be helpful activity on the part of the nurse.

Specific ways in which the partner relationship can be affected by the birth of the baby are discussed in the following paragraphs.

1   No longer can the man and woman belong *only* to each other. It is possible that one or both may be disturbed that the other has become involved in a new affectional relationship and interpret this as shattering the conception of faithfulness to each other. The romantic approach to marriage in our society makes the closeness and exclusiveness of the couple a symbol of their unity. And this unity is a sacred thing. How romantic and immature are the spouses? This is a very important question.

2   The power relationship and the division of labor can be affected drastically. Blood writes of the revised power structure, division of labor, and personal relationships that are inevitable. He also discusses the loss of mobility, the disruption of routines, the expansion of tasks, and the anxiety about the child's welfare—all of which are common results of the coming of the first child.[45]

3   Each spouse may discover "another" person in his or her marriage partner. Either partner may run into an unexpected syndrome of attitudes, feelings, and behavior that is hard to accept and cope with. The nurse may be able to help them understand what has happened and how to cope with it.

4   A sharp increase in role differentiation and role specialization can occur. (This

has been discussed briefly in this chapter in another context.) Preparental relationships are marked by much sharing of roles and activities. This may or may not continue. Couples vary greatly in how they can cope with this change.

5   Often the sexual relationship has to be adapted to the new family situation. Many partners are not happy about limitations on sexual intercourse; very few are prepared to adjust well to this. It is common to keep sexual activity limited longer than is necessary. Frequently, the sexual relationship of the marriage never recovers after the birth of the baby. This is not necessary, and it has a very negative effect upon the marital relationship. The couple can be helped by the nurse to understand one another's needs and what is healthy and possible for the marriage. Too few couples get this kind of help.

6   Both partners may have difficulty in balancing the needs of the child or children with marital and personal satisfactions. Some sound, effective parent education can be of great help at this stage. A primary problem in this stage is to work toward a balance of developmental experiences which will meet the basic needs of *each* family member and of the family unit as a whole. Lack of achieving this is a very common and a very undesirable characteristic of the early parenthood stage.

7   Opportunity for real husband-wife communication may be cut severely. They often no longer have the free time to be with just each other. This is a point at which many marital couples begin to lose the ability to communicate, and the relationship becomes less and less meaningful to both partners. This is a crucial time for the couple. For many it may be the turning point in

their marriage. Here, too, effective parent education would be highly desirable.

8   This may be the point in their married life when the couple stop enjoying each other—a fatal error. The two may start going off in different directions never to really return to each other and the relationship they once cherished. This is a tragedy because it does not have to happen. A young mother in a sound marriage writes of some of the things she and her husband had to overcome in order to sustain their own relationship:

We can't go out so much. We used to ski and travel a lot; and now we have to decide whether to get away from her or take her places. For me now only about 10 to 20 percent of the time is *mine*. I thought that when the baby was born, I would do all sorts of things around the house. But I am very frustrated to discover that there is little time. Then questions come to my mind like: Should I go back to work? When? My husband has been very good with children, but *now* there isn't much that he can do. He tends to feel that Marsha is my kind of baby. At this stage I guess the baby is the mother's.[46]

9   The mother may resent her confinement and her husband's freedom. That this is a common problem is indicated by the many cartoons on this theme. The young infant and child tremendously complicate the wife's role, very often demanding far more time and emotional energy from her than from her husband. (Middle-class fathers participate much more than lower-class fathers in the rearing of their children.) Women tend to become engulfed in the

motherhood role. They are resenting it more and more.

Here is a letter written by a wife who graduated from college and went into social work until her first child was born. Her husband is a very brilliant young scientist, completely engulfed in his professional roles. This letter was written to a close female friend at 8:00 A.M. [underlining is hers]:

This has been a <u>hectic</u> year for me, to say the least. I am always tired—too tired to write even the family letters I should! I got pregnant six weeks or so after Susan was born. We bought a house and Dad came to be with us for two months, having disposed of his business.

I had my hands full—still have. I went to visit my sister for a few days, but when I got home, my help quit. Such a mess to be in. I managed to get Jake started in kindergarten and two babies fed. It's a gay life. I feel as though I've been <u>sexed</u> and <u>babied</u> out for the rest of my days.

Nothing else to talk about but kids. I don't know what's going on in the outside world. I must close now before the "noisy din" begins. I've been up since 3:00 A.M. and am about ready to retire again! By spring I'll be a mere shadow of my former self.[47]

More and more mothers of young children are in the labor force. There are many ways in which these mothers adapt to the infancy years. The nurse, in working with any family, must be aware of the importance of this type of adaptation.

Kinfolk and friends are important to the young parents. Kinship interaction is different from what it was in the time when extended families were more common, but it is still a vital part of the young family in many cases. One of the frequent difficulties is that roles of nonparent kin—both young and old —are not clear. Confusion and even trouble can result when relatives do not know what is expected of them by the new parents. As said earlier, parenting exacts a big price on parents who do not have a kinship group nearby which can help take care of the infant on a day-by-day basis. Nurses should help modern parents in reaching out for aid in childrearing and should be aware of the type of involvement, if any, of kinfolk and/or friends in the life of the new family.

Although little helpful research is available, the nurse should be alert to the type of situation that exists when there are older siblings in the family. Older children are usually prepared in some manner for the arrival of the infant, but this preparation may be very inadequate. In the family context siblings are very important to each other. Very little help is given parents in regard to the preparation of older children for the coming of a new baby. This, then, is another neglected area in which nurses should become involved.

It would be safe to draw the following conclusions regarding the "moving into parenthood" stage of the family life cycle:

1 No one is ever completely prepared for parenthood, but the right kind of assistance can help.[48]

2 Even if the coming of a baby is a "crisis" in the family, this does not mean it is either good or bad in itself. Properly handled, it is an opportunity. Mishandled, it is a disaster. (It is interesting that the Chinese word for "crisis" is composed of two characters. Respectively, they mean "danger" and "opportunity.")

3 Because the evidence is, in part, conflicting, there is no basis for concluding that the coming of children makes a marriage either happier or less happy.[49]

4　How a particular wife or husband reacts to the arrival and presence of a
baby depends on many factors.

5　Couples who want their marriage to remain vital and satisfying to them will
have to make a deliberate attempt to
achieve this. The husband has a major
role to play in accomplishing this.
(There is no evidence that couples who
keep their husband-wife relationship
of prime importance have children
who are less healthy in any sense.
What evidence there is would point in
the opposite direction; however, there
is little research on this.)

6　The nurse can play a very significant
and helpful role in working with families in which there is a young infant.
There are many points at which the
nurse can move into the relationships
in a desirable way. Most parents are
open to learning how to cope with their
situations.

COMMUNICATION—THE BASIC SKILL

Relating to families and family members
positively and effectively requires good communication. This is not accomplished easily
in a society which gives its members little
help in learning how to communicate well
and, in addition, places many impediments
along the way.

Dorothy Lee, an anthropologist, spoke at
Iowa State University (June 28, 1962) on
"The Human's Potential for Full Existence."
She said that people are protesting against
the alienation *from* life, saying that we are
alienated from ourselves, our own curiosity,
our own wonder. The little child, she said,
has the motivation to grow and learn, but
gradually this feeling is lost. She raised the
question, "How can we get people to the
point of being themselves, being authentic,
being genuine?" She added that we need to
learn to relate fully, that the potential for relatedness is infinite, and that "somewhere
we have lost our feeling of relatedness."

George A. Buttrick once said, "With all the
insistence on intellectual honesty, let us also
be emotionally honest." He is correct. We
tend to be so anxious to be loved that we are
afraid to open ourselves to others for fear of
not being loved, thus making it impossible
for the other person to know us well enough
to truly love us. This basic and tragic fact is
discussed thoroughly in an article by Sidney
M. Jourard and Ardis Whitman.[50] At various
places in his writings, Carl Rogers has
spoken of these necessary elements for effective interpersonal communication:

1　A sensitive ability to hear
2　A deep satisfaction in being heard
3　An ability to be more "real," which in
turn brings forth more "realness" from
the other
4　A willingness to receive warmth and
care from others, and consequently a
greater freedom to give love

He often speaks of the necessity of loving
the *real* person, hearing what he *really* is
saying, and being a *real* person yourself.
This, he indicates, makes any relationship
more meaningful.

Why this comment on communication? It
is the necessary skill for relating. The nursing process is basically the matter of relating
to other humans. Therefore, nothing is more
important than developing the ability to
communicate well. No one can communicate
perfectly. Everyone has his or her limitations. But this skill can be developed and
improved. Without reasonably good success
at it, the nurse can be of little help to young
parents and their babies. With good communicating ability the nursing process can
be of tremendous help to families.

MATERNITY NURSING AND THE NUCLEAR FAMILY

It is fortunate that the nursing profession attracts the kinds of persons who have a deep concern for human development and human relationships. This concern and motivation, plus development of the knowledge and skills necessary, is a combination that will produce a nurse who should relate well to the nuclear family.

As has been indicated, pregnancy, childbirth, and early parenthood are periods in the life of the family when members are open to learning about themselves and how to relate to each other. The maternity nurse is fortunate to be involved with families at a time when they are very "teachable." If the nurse can help the couple move successfully from the relationships developed as a pair, through the process of pregnancy and childbirth, to the realities of parenthood, much will have been accomplished. This is particularly true if the nurse can help the young couple learn to enjoy the rich satisfaction of parenthood and how to practice it for the enhancement of their marriage.

In a society in which feelings are too often unrecognized or belittled, the nurse is in a position to help people understand their feelings and learn how to cope with them. The nurse is not like the census taker in this account:

> *Census taker:* Please give me the number of persons in your household.
> *Lady:* Well, there is Susan, Jackie, Ted. . . .
> *Census taker:* (Interrupting the lady) Thank you, lady, but I don't want their names, I just want their numbers.
> *Lady:* Mister, they ain't got numbers, but they do have names.

If we are to relate effectively with people and teach them, we must regard them as persons, not numbers. This is why it is important that the maternity nurse enjoy encounters with people and families. This is why it is highly desirable that the nurse be aware of and appreciate the ordinary day-by-day joys and sorrows of the young family.

LeMasters and others have warned us against assuming parents to be "guilty" before we even give them a hearing. He reminds us that parents are amateurs, that we should not use professional norms to assess the performance of nonprofessionals. It is indeed important that we learn to relate to people and help people without evaluating them beyond their capabilities.

What is the most important thing a nurse can give to families? It would be very difficult to single out *one* thing. But one is reminded that in her book, *Book of Common Sense Etiquette,* Eleanor Roosevelt wrote that the basis of all good human behavior is kindness. She argued that if you act toward people with genuine kindness, you will never go far wrong.

Pregnancy, childbirth, and early parenthood are indeed short stages in the life of a family, but they are very important "acts" in the play of family living—a drama in which people move in and out frequently. Perhaps Shakespeare described best the dynamic situation the nurse deals with in working with families:

All the world's a stage,
And all the men and women merely players.
They have their exits and their entrances;
And one man in his time plays many parts.[51]

REFERENCES

1 "Newsline," *Psychology Today,* 9:32–34, June 1975.
2 Lerner, Max: "What's Leading the Family Astray?" *San Diego Union,* June 4, 1975, p. B-23.
3 Mace, David R.: "What I Have Learned about

Family Life," *Family Coordinator*, 23:189–195, April 1974.

4 Reiss, Ira L.: *The Family System in America*, Holt, Rinehart, Winston, New York, 1971, pp. 414–415.

5 Scanzoni, John: *Sexual Bargaining: Power Politics in the American Marriage*, Prentice-Hall, Englewood Cliffs, N.J., 1972, pp. 103–164.

6 Vincent, Clark E.: " 'Familia Spongia': The Adaptive Function," *Journal of Marriage and the Family*, 28:29–36, February 1966.

7 "Birth Trends in the United States," *Statistical Bulletin*, Metropolitan Life, October 1974, pp. 3–6.

8 "Trends in Expected Family Size in the United States," *Statistical Bulletin*, Metropolitan Life, January 1975, pp. 8–11.

9 "Married Women in the Labor Force," *Statistical Bulletin*, Metropolitan Life, August 1974, pp. 9–10.

10 Etaugh, C.: "Effects of Maternal Employment on Children: A Review on Recent Research," *Merrill-Palmer Quarterly*, 20:71–93, April 1974.

11 LeMasters, E. E.: *Parents in Modern America*, 2d ed., Dorsey, Homewood, Ill., 1974, pp. 1–17.

12 Udry, J. Richard: *The Social Context of Marriage*, 3d ed., Lippincott, Philadelphia, 1974, p. 381.

13 Rossi, Alice S.: "Transition to Parenthood," *Journal of Marriage and the Family*, 30:26–39, 1968.

14 Hess, Robert D., and Gerald Handel: *Family Worlds: A Psychosocial Approach to Family Life*, University of Chicago Press, Chicago, 1959, p. 19.

15 Bowman, Henry A.: *Marriage for Moderns*, 7th ed., McGraw-Hill, New York, 1974, p. 472.

16 Duvall, Evelyn Millis: *Family Development*, 4th ed., Lippincott, Philadelphia, 1971, p. 5.

17 Bacmeister, Rhoda W.: "Perspective on Parenthood," *Parents' Magazine*, September 1951, p. 29.

18 Turner, Ralph H.: *Family Interaction*, Wiley, New York, 1970, p. 20.

19 Fulcomer, David M.: "Becoming Parents," in Ruth Shonle Cavan, *American Marriage: A Way of Life*, Crowell, New York, 1959, p. 418.

20 Folkman, Jerome D., and Nancy M. K. Clatworthy: *Marriage Has Many Faces*, Merrill, Columbus, Ohio, 1970, p. 188.

21 Lantz, Herman R., and Eloise C. Snyder: *Marriage*, 2d ed., Wiley, New York, 1969, pp. 379–382.

22 Bell, Robert R.: *Marriage and Family Interaction*, 3d ed., Dorsey, Homewood, Ill., 1971, p. 435.

23 Helfer, Ray E., and C. Henry Kempe (eds.): *The Battered Child*, University of Chicago Press, Chicago, 1968.

24 Kempe, C. Henry, and Ray E. Helfer: *Helping the Battered Child and His Family*, Lippincott, Philadelphia, 1972.

25 Kempe, C. Henry: "Pediatric Implications of the Battered Baby Syndrome," *Archives of Disease in Childhood*, 46:28–37, February 1971.

26 Sobol, Evelyn G., and Paulette Robischon: *Family Nursing: A Study Guide*, Mosby, St. Louis, 1970, p. 18.

27 From the personal files of the author.

28 From the personal files of the author.

29 Mace, David R.: "Pregnancy and the Young Husband," *McCall's*, p. 177, April 1963.

30 Genné, William H.: *Husbands and Pregnancy*, Association Press, New York, 1956, p. 15.

31 Powers, Edward A., et al. (eds.): *Process in Relationship*, West Publishing Company, St. Paul, 1974, pp. 47–54.

32 Whiting, John M.: "Effects of Climate on Certain Cultural Practices," in A. P. Vayda (ed.), *Environment and Cultural Behavior: Ecological Studies in Cultural Anthropology*, Natural History Press, New York, 1969, pp. 416–455.

33 From the personal files of the author.

34 Anderson, Wayne J.: *Challenges for Success-*

ful Family Living, T. S. Denison, Minneapolis, 1974, pp. 375–387.

35 Kieren, Dianne, et al.: *Hers and His: A Problem-solving Approach to Marriage,* Dryden Press, Hinesdale, Ill., 1975, pp. 244–254.

36 Kilker, Rosemary, and Betty L. Wilkerson: "Anticipatory Guidance of the Expectant Family," in Debra P. Hymovich and Martha Underwood Barnard (eds.), *Family Health Care,* McGraw-Hill, New York, 1973, pp. 181–187.

37 Fitzpatrick, Elise, Sharon R. Reeder, and Luigi Mastroianni: *Maternity Nursing,* 12th ed., Lippincott, Philadelphia, 1971, pp. 174–176.

38 Levy, John, and Ruth Monroe: *The Happy Family,* Knopf, New York, 1938, p. 243.

39 From the personal files of the author. The last paragraph was written by the new father as a part of the same letter.

40 Maeblus, Nancy K.: "The Nurse and the Expanding Family: A Mother's Viewpoint," in Debra P. Hymovich and Martha Underwood Barnard (eds.), *Family Health Care,* McGraw-Hill, New York, 1973, pp. 198–210.

41 McCabe, Susan Nelson: "Anticipatory Guidance of Families and Infants," in Debra P. Hymovich and Martha Underwood Barnard (eds.), *Family Health Care,* McGraw-Hill, New York, 1973, pp. 211–224.

42 LeMasters, E. E.: "Parenthood as Crisis," *Marriage and Family Living,* 19:354, 1957.

43 Udry: op. cit., p. 365.

44 From the personal files of the author.

45 Blood, Robert O.: *Marriage,* 2d ed., Free Press, New York, 1939, pp. 438–444.

46 From the personal files of the author.

47 From the personal files of the author.

48 Lake, Alice: "Three for the Seesaw: How a First Baby Changes a Marriage," *Redbook,* 144:99, April 1974.

49 Lederer, William J., and Don D. Jackson: *The Mirages of Marriage,* Norton, New York, 1968, pp. 68–74.

50 Jourard, Sidney M., and Ardis Whitman: "The Fear That Cheats Us of Love," *Redbook,* 137:83, October 1971.

51 Shakespeare, William: *As You Like It,* Act II, Scene 7.

BIBLIOGRAPHY

Barman, Alicerose: "Your First Months with Your First Baby," Public Affairs Committee Pamphlet No. 478, New York, 1972.

"Briefs," Official Publication, Maternity Center Association, New York, December 1973.

Coleman, Arthur, and Libby Coleman: *Pregnancy, The Psychological Experience,* Herder and Herder, New York, 1971.

Essex-Cater, Anthony: "The Couvade," *Man,* LIII:144, September 1953.

Farber, Bernard: *Family and Kinship in Modern Society,* Scott, Foresman, Glenview, Ill., 1973.

Feldman, Harold, and Margaret Feldman: "The Family Life Cycle: Some Suggestions for Recycling," *Journal of Marriage and the Family,* 37(2):277, May 1975.

Gelles, Richard J.: "Violence and Pregnancy: A Note on the Extent of the Problem and Needed Services," *The Family Coordinator,* January 1975.

Gordon, Michael (ed.): *The Nuclear Family in Crisis: The Search for an Alternative,* Harper & Row, New York, 1972.

Greenberg, M., and N. Morris: "Engrossment: The Newborn's Impact upon the Father," *American Journal of Orthopsychiatry,* July 1974.

Hymovich, Debra P., and Martha Underwood Barnard (eds.): *Family Health Care,* McGraw-Hill, New York, 1973.

Ruggles-Gates, R.: "An Explanation for the Couvade," *Man,* LIII:89, June 1953.

Russell, Candyce Smith: "Transition to Parenthood: Problems and Gratifications," *Journal of Marriage and the Family,* 36:294–302, May 1974.

Weiss, Robert Russell, and Myron Ray Pexton: *The Expectant Father,* Christopher, North Quincy, Mass., 1970.

5

The Extended Family: Traditional and Communal

MARNA STEINBRONER
PRITCHARD*

One result of mid-twentieth-century social mobility of families in the United States has been a proliferation of research focused on the viability of the traditional extended family as a support system for its members. Some researchers vigorously endorse the premise that the extended family has met its demise. They argue that the extended family is no longer a norm among families in the industrialized United States, with the only possible exceptions being among certain ethnic groups. Other scholars argue that the extended family, as it has been traditionally regarded, is changing, not dying; different forms are arising which basically fulfill the support system responsibilities formerly fulfilled by the extended family constellation.

The Amish family in east-central Ohio, the black family in Watts, the urban commune

* Recognition is given to Ellen J. Mevis who was the original author of the chapter The Extended Family in the first edition of this text.

in San Francisco, the Mexican-American family in Tucson, the Native American family in western New York, and the rural commune in Virginia all have at least one aspect of their existence in common. Their life-style is in the pattern of group living defined by sociologists as "the extended family." Such a family represents interdependent relationships in addition to any biological ties of kinship. This may occur when three or more generations of relatives inhabit a single household, or when totally unrelated individuals elect to form a family relationship based upon concepts of freedom, togetherness, cooperation, and social transformation. The relationships developed here go beyond and are more complex than those of the nuclear family. Therefore, the extended family is often characterized as being closely knit, inner-directed, and often unfamiliar and unfriendly to those outside its bounds.

The relationships among members of an extended family are affected to some degree by their sex, marital status, age, and the generation to which they belong. Each of these factors affects the degree of closeness between any two family members. In addition to these factors, there often occur particular relationships within a specific extended family group which appear for no apparent reason and are simply the result of some special bond established between the members. An example of this would be the grandfather-granddaughter (or grandson) relationship. Occasionally, when such relationships as these occur, their bond is so strong and influential that it ignores the normal authority patterns and preference associations which exist in such families.

Following is a detailed description of an idealized traditional extended family unit and some of the significant events which occur in all families (e.g., courtship, marriage, childbearing, education and instruc-

tion of children, and old age), which demonstrate how such a family unit characteristically reacts to these events.*

THE IDEALIZED TRADITIONAL EXTENDED FAMILY[1]

This extended family unit is composed of a cluster of individual nuclear units who live in their own homes which are usually located near the original household inhabited by the grandparents. Among them is a loosely organized hierarchy of authorities and relationships which are commonly associated with age, actual or potential wealth, and possible utility. This hierarchy often operates as an informal family council through which pressures can be brought to bear on the individual nuclear family units within the larger family structure. Such pressures are utilized to influence members to conform to the family standards and to encourage constant contribution to organized family enterprises and to the welfare and good of all family members.

The integrated extended family circle typically consists of at least three generations. Members included in this unit range from grandparents, through parents and their children, and as far laterally as uncles and aunts, first cousins, and often their children. Although it is more common to find these relatives spread into their own nuclear households, the grandparents' household—and occasionally that of the parents—is often expanded through the inclusion of aging parents, unmarried sisters or brothers, orphaned cousins, and illegitimate children. The structure of this traditional extended family is organized to handle many of the

* *The World of the Family* by Dorothy R. Blitsten has been used as the main reference source for the following discussion of the idealized traditional extended family.

contingent circumstances and individuals which otherwise must be handled by exterior social and welfare agencies.

This extended family maintains between its members established and enforced bonds of responsibility and authority. These bonds may be reinforced by actual affection between these same members. As the result of these responsibilities and authorities, inner tensions occasionally occur and are handled within the family unit itself through pressures and influences. During periods of stress, the family's bonds are drawn even closer to present a united front to outsiders.

The extended family represents a closed circle, and undue communication with strangers and outsiders is usually discouraged. It is not common for strangers to be casually introduced into the family circle. The children usually do not bring their playmates and friends from school into the home. While they might certainly have such associations and friendships at school, their most common playmates and companions away from the school are found within their own kin circle. They associate most commonly with their brothers, sisters, cousins, or the offspring of other families with whom they have been in contact for some time. Neither is it common for the working men of the household to regularly bring their colleagues or friends from work into the home, or for neighbors to casually drop in to introduce themselves or for "idle" chat.

Marriage tends to expand the circle of family associations, and there are occasional introductions of long-term friends from either school or work into the family circle, but such occurrences are rare and significant. Thus, the extended family provides its members with a closed, private world of associations which develop into dependable and lasting relationships. For the women and children, the family provides the majority of their entire range of friendships and associations. Such inner direction adds to the unity and closed nature of the extended family unit. Through inner direction are developed strong feelings of family pride, values, and a sense of obligation to maintain the honor and prestige of the family along with its economic and social advantages. These bonds are further strengthened by the concept of the potential contributions which the members can and do make to each other's feelings of personal satisfaction, careers, and possible benefits to the secondary nuclear subunit in assistance in time of crisis, and finally, in terms of likely inheritance. All of these factors contribute in their own way to maintaining the power and strength of the extended family unit.

The Life Process

Courtship

Since preparation for marriage and later integration into the extended family unit is one of the most implicit aspects of the childrearing process, the children from an early age are oriented toward adult life. They are not encouraged or even, in some cases, allowed to become overly involved in adolescent peer group relations or place their own juvenile or adolescent goals ahead of those goals established for them by their elders. Because of this adult-oriented training and education, by the time adolescents reach the age at which courtship and marriage become primary interests, they are prepared for the demands of married life and the full-time occupation which it will impose.

Generally the young men of the extended family who are of marriageable age postpone their marriage until they have fulfilled their required military training, have entered into an occupation, and have established a means for the support of a family. A variation on this pattern is often manifested in the Native

American and Mexican-American ethnic groups. Within these groups, which are often characterized by impoverished circumstances, the marriage of the members of the family may take place at an earlier age. Occasionally this occurs while they are still in school. Under such circumstances, it is often necessary for the male to drop out of school and go to work to support his new family. The significant factor remains that the male provides capably and immediately for his new wife. This is considered his utmost responsibility to the family and its members.

For the female, marriage alone is assumed to be the fitting and proper career unless the circumstances of her family dictate that she work in order to provide adequately for the family when the head male is incapacitated, deceased, or otherwise absent. It is not uncommon for females to discontinue their formal education after they have finished high school or at about age fifteen or sixteen. They are then expected to perfect their skills in such wifely duties as housekeeping, child care, cooking, and sewing. Their training and education in these duties and skills takes place in their home, along with their siblings, under the supervision of their mother or grandmother. By the age of eighteen or nineteen it is assumed that these skills are perfected, and they are then considered to be ready for marriage. At that time they are encouraged by their parents and other relatives to begin actively seeking a lifetime mate.

Through either direct or indirect means, the parents and family influence the choice of the lifetime mate. One of the more subtle means by which this is accomplished is through the inculcation, over the years, in the child of the family's standards of what is desirable and preferable in a mate. Another means for this is found in the manner in which the extended family limits the range of close associations which its children are allowed to maintain. The associations are restricted to those whom the family would consider to be appropriate mates. A key means by which the parental or grandparental control can be directly asserted is in the fact that they maintain the economic resources and thereby the access to education, career opportunities, and the more desirable living arrangements available to their offspring.

Thus, it is possible for the elders to influence, pressure, or even at times coerce an uncooperative offspring to forgo relationships which they consider to be inappropriate or undesirable to the family.

Actual family approval of the mate in a marriage is particularly important. This is so because of the necessity of the chosen mate's fitting into and adapting well to the circumstances of the extended family situation. There is yet another more significant reason why this approval is deemed so necessary. Without such approval the disobedient offspring could—and very likely would—be deprived of the significant practical economic advantages which emanate from the family, ranging from the prestige of membership to the very real—and sometimes sizable—factors of mutual aid and inheritance.

For all these reasons, when the offspring of a traditional extended family arrive at the point of marriage, they are generally well prepared for new and more responsible circumstances. They realize that the years of childhood and irresponsibility are over, and are armed with the knowledge of a responsible adult which will increase their distinction and authority within the extended family.

Marriage

Once the marriage partner has been approved and the formal and religious aspects of the marriage have been accomplished, the newlyweds generally attempt to establish themselves in a household separate from but adjacent to other members of the husband's family. If this is not practical or possible, they are included quite readily and happily into the household of the parents.

While it is to be expected that some problems will evolve from the newly formed relationships and living arrangement, such strains are effectively reduced because the participants have entered into it with full knowledge and acceptance of its consequences and with highly similar expectations; they have been prepared through their past membership in extended families to deal with such circumstances. With their background and knowledge such a new family relationship has a very high potential for success as compared to the "pioneering" element present in the establishment of completely independent nuclear family life.

Because of the education, training, and orientation of children for adult life present in the extended family, there is a great reduction in importance of the initial period of marriage before parenthood takes place. Since the young couple enter into the marriage with the understanding that the marital relationship is one of interdependence, related closely to their mutual needs, traits, and duties to each other, this usually brief period between marriage and parenthood is a time of preparation for the deeper and more complex marital life which will evolve through parenthood. The emphasis in the extended family is obviously placed on familial continuity, and this concept places a great deal of responsibility and pressure upon the newly wed couple to keep this preparenthood time as short as possible. Because both fatherhood and motherhood have an aura of both authority and sacredness, the young couple, as well as all the associated relatives, hope for the onset of the wife's first pregnancy within a very short time after the marriage takes place.

Childrearing

It is a characteristic of the extended family to perpetuate itself by encouraging large families. Traditionally, it has only been the period of biological fertility which has acted as a limit on the number of the progeny of the extended family. This tradition has resulted in the fact that while the average number of offspring from a fertile couple has been four or five, it is not unusual to discover six to eight or even more children in nuclear units. Through the social significance attendant upon parenthood in the extended family situation, it becomes personally gratifying to each individual member of the couple—especially the woman—to produce as many children as possible. Consequently, nuclear units in the extended family are much larger, and there are smaller age differences between siblings than in the average American nuclear family.

This situation is further helped because within the extended family the burdens of parenthood are significantly reduced through the distribution of the economic costs of childrearing, to those either financially or personally capable of sharing the burden. The relatives are not overly indulgent of the young parents, but they are present and will not shirk any reasonable request for assistance by the young couple if help is needed. The female relatives help the young mother with her household and child care duties, and the male relatives can be counted on in times of emergency to provide labor, produce, or financial assistance. Because they are not isolated from their relatives, their constant presence and willingness to help create one of the strongest bonds between the nuclear family unit and the main extended family.

The strains developing from the childrearing situation result from the general economic conditions under which the entire family lives. Characteristically, the extended family is subject to limited sociocultural and geographic mobility, poor economic conditions, and poor conditions in general, which tend to significantly influence extended family situations. Occasionally wealth and property are spread throughout the members of extended families, but it is more often poverty which is commonly shared. This is possibly the most powerful limiting circumstance of the extended family. As significant and realistic as this factor is, it is generally ignored.

The young mother is expected to keep house well for her husband and children, to live within the financial means which her husband produces, to keep her nuclear family members well fed and clothed, and to teach her children the good manners, respect, and behavior expected of a young member of the family. The father's role is usually somewhat more formally oriented. He is expected to exercise his authority at will over both the wife and children. This does not mean that he normally acts as a dictator and autocrat in the nuclear family situation, but only that the final authority rests in his hands and that he makes those decisions which significantly affect the household. Within this situation, there also lies the powerful, though usually disguised, authority of the mother. Although the authority "officially" rests in the hands of the father, it is often the mother who exerts her influence to direct the course his decision making takes.

Beyond this, the father is affectionate to the children, expecting from them obedience and respect. The child care and household work are considered to be women's tasks, and it is uncommon for the husband to perform them. The father exercises his authority in the lives of his children by deciding how the children should be reared, what they should be taught, and who their friends

should be. Parental approval remains one of the most significant factors in the life of the child and operates as a necessary adjunct to the most significant concern for the extended family: family approval.

Although the birth of children creates new strains and pressures upon the relationship of husband and wife, it does not have a harmful effect upon the marriage. The children are definitely an important aspect of the life of the family, but they are never allowed to dominate either the nuclear or the extended family. The family is adult-oriented and not child-centered, as most American families are. The children are trained early to give full precedence and respect to their elders, and this training is reinforced through the child's observation of his parents' behavior in deference to their elders in the extended family relations. The husband and wife relationship is not threatened in the extended family system because the children, though important, are considered to be an integral part of the marital relationship—not a special development from it. Thus, the children are dealt with as a matter of course—they are not spoiled or given a disproportionate amount of pampering or privilege so that they would seem to be actually competing with their parents. There is an important place for the children of the traditional extended family, but that place is maintained only as long as the children demonstrate that they deserve it by their behavior to their elders. If a child should exceed that place, he or she is immediately brought to the realization and correction of the mistake by both parental and family action.

Education and Instruction of Children

Because in the extended family there are likely to be numerous children and they may be spread over a broad spectrum of ages, there is little distinction made between the initial phases of the childbearing and training process and the later phases of the "launching" of the older children into life. These phases normally are carried on concurrently with several age gradations being present in the family at any one time. It is not uncommon to find the situation in which the last child and the first grandchild are approximately the same age. There can be no sharply drawn line between early training and later launching activities except on a purely individual level. The important element in the training and launching of the children is that of providing an expanded series of associations for the children while training them in the significance and importance *to them* of the extended family association. Training and education does not mean in any way the severance of the child from these functions. The direct opposite is, in fact, its intention.

The parental responsibility operative in the traditional extended family continues over a longer period of time than is characteristic of the American nuclear family. The parental concerns last, in some form or another, throughout the child's entire lifetime. From the training of the child in preparation for adult life and responsibilities, through actual marriage and bearing of children, the training and education of those children, their eventual marriage and entering into their occupations, and the concern of the grandparents for their grandchildren, the parental responsibility is much more extensive than might normally be expected. Beyond these considerations the needs of the older generations for care and housing replace the birth and childrearing cycle in such a way as to further extend the parental responsibility. All in all, there is no period to which the parents can look ahead with the intention of having responsibilities out of the way completely, as is characteristic of the nuclear American family. These responsibilities simply continue throughout life in variable forms.

The children are generally indulged while they are young, but this does not continue throughout their childhood. After the child reaches the age of about five or six, a firmer, more extensive discipline is applied. Parental authority is a constantly exercised and respected force in the life of the child of the extended family. The child is taught to respect the authority of the elders of the household. Through this training, by the time the children reach fifteen or sixteen, they realize the significance and meaning of their position in relation not only to their own nuclear and extended family but also within the society in general. They are thus trained to accept the realities of life and understand their position as subordinate until such time as they have obtained adequate prestige or value to the family—and society—to change this subordinate position to a more dominant one.

Early in life the children are given honest and frank appraisals of their own abilities and potentialities. They are expected to make the best of their natural capabilities. Any behavior seemingly wasteful or less than that of which they are capable is regarded very negatively and is highly disapproved of by both parents and family elders. The child who is doing his or her best and attempting to utilize his or her full capabilities, even though he or she may be doing less than the other children, is rewarded with the admiration and praise of the family.

The punishment of the children of the traditional extended family rarely reaches the point of physical action. It usually takes the verbal form of "tongue-lashing." The withholding of affection and tenderness is another means through which the elders may punish the misbehaving child. The denial of permission for pleasurable activities of the child is another technique which is effectively used. Occasionally the child will actually be held up to the ridicule of others as a means for motivating proper behavior. Actual physical punishment is generally one of the last resorts which may be applied to discipline and enforce the child's proper behavior.

The daily lives of the children of the extended family are organized and planned out well in advance to conform to the needs and requirements of the extended family situation. Beginning with school, the average day of the child progresses in a well-organized and structured manner. After school come first the required household duties which the children have been assigned and for which they are responsible without fail. These tasks are generally sexually separated: The boys usually perform duties assigned by the father which relate to those duties of the male in the household. The girls aid their mothers and older sisters in a relationship which is much like an apprenticeship to prepare them for the time when they will take over those duties in their own nuclear family unit or offer service to other members of the extended family structure. This clear division of labor between males and females continues from the early period of childhood through adulthood and into all aspects of family life.

A primary concern of both the nuclear and extended families with reference to child-rearing is in establishing within the child a firm orientation toward the inner circles of the family structure. The child is not allowed any great extent of social initiative or activity outside the extended family circle. This is often carried to the point at which the entrance of the child into school is regarded by the parents as an incursion into their authority and a threat to regulation by the family. In any case, the child is very deeply inculcated with the idea that the family, and its demands and requirements, has a priority

over any outside demands made upon the child.

The child is taught a strong competitive spirit which is expressed within the family group in a formalized way. Each of the individual nuclear units of the extended family competes with the others to the desired end of obtaining a larger proportion of the overall resources of the family. The gaining of the favor of possible sources of inheritance—from grandparents or unmarried uncles or aunts—is one of the primary objects of this competition. Another area of competitiveness is that of the inner power structure of the family. The power usually rests upon the eldest member of the extended family unit, but there are occasions and incidents in which another member of the family, through wealth, prestige, or special position gained through his own efforts, may be considered as the source of power expressed in the family. Therefore, competition may be a highly effective means for obtaining a base for power within the traditional extended family structure.

As a result of this situation, the child may become adept at the manipulation of the family elders quite early in life. Since the favorite grandchild, niece, or nephew has not only garnered for him- or herself an effective ally against parental authority but has also created a closer link to the source of power and possible wealth within the family, the competition for such relationships is often rather keen. The child who does establish such a relationship has also created some degree of equality with the elders in the family and is treated with more deference and tact than he or she might be otherwise. This applies to treatment both from family members in general and from the child's own parents.

These childrearing and launching activities of the extended family have a goal more extensive than the mere preparation of the children for providing for themselves and their children once they become adults. The desired end result of the childrearing and launching process is the development of a family-centered orientation in the child. The children are to operate always with the family in mind. They are trained to be tools of implementation of the family tradition. They are taught that they must apply their powers and efforts to enhance family resources and prestige. By the time the children have completed this educative and training process, their dependence upon the family is an established behavior pattern, and variation from that pattern is unthinkable.

Old Age

Elderly members do not pose the same problem in the traditional extended family as they do in the average nuclear family. There is little reason for aging members to be anxious over their welfare when they cease to be self-sufficient. Since respect and deference to elders are taught as the primary aspects of behavior and are reinforced through both training and actual practice, aging members are expected to depend upon the family and its individual members more and more as time goes on. The older person is welcomed into the particular nuclear unit which, because of either biological relationship or financial standing, he or she would most reasonably fit. In this way, the family acts as the social welfare agency in providing for its own members.

Persons of advanced age do not face the problem of being disregarded or losing their prestige and family standing because of their age. Family elders are treated with honor and respect. Usually those who are the oldest have the greatest prestige, if not power as well. The aging male usually works at his occupation as long as he is physically able. Upon his retirement, he may help as much as

he can with the normal duties of the male members of the household in which he resides.

For the aging female there are fewer problems in the extended family than may be faced within the nuclear family. They will have gained the confidence and respect of the family members through their past performance as wife and mother. They take great pride in the family which they have engendered and educated into the family tradition. In addition, when the older woman becomes a grandmother she again finds herself in the position of taking a significant role in the childrearing and training process with the children from the new generation.

The care and aid provided for older family members are given as a matter of course and generally without recrimination or resentment. This often entails sacrifice, especially for those families of low income, but it is a duty which must be done—there is little thought of passing the responsibility off onto society in general. The elders do not feel any shame about accepting such aid and care. Since they provided it for their parents, it is expected that their children will do it for them. Any hardship which might derive from this situation is shared by the family on an equitable basis to the extent that it is feasible and possible. Since family unity is the significant factor operative within the extended family unit, this is the only logical means for caring for aging family members.

Present Examples

The traditional extended family pattern exists in many cultural settings in the United States. One which most closely resembles the "ideal" is the Amish family. Of European heritage and strong religious beliefs, these families maintain a life as much apart from the mainstream of American life as possible. Old Germanic tradition describes the philosophy: The blood-related families were the foundation of all private life; the individual member of the house was not a free agent but was a part of an ordered whole with obligations toward the family and from which he or she could not depart without the consent of the head of the household.[2]

The father is the patriarch and head of the household and the farm. Although he has ultimate and unlimited control, he will, without fail, take the ideas and wishes of his children into consideration in any decision relating to farming matters. The woman in an Amish family assumes a subordinate role. This position of subordination is rather common in many extended family living patterns.

The incidence of extended family relationships is also common in the Mexican-American family. Like the Amish culture, this is a highly religion-oriented culture. It would appear that with both the Amish and the Mexican-American family, emphasis on social and religious activities, combined with language barriers, serves to insulate the families from outsiders.

The Mexican-American population of the United States is basically the result of intermarriage. Mexican-Americans are the descendants of the early Spanish colonists who explored North America and the Indians of Mexico. Their physical, social, and religious characteristics result primarily from the extensive intermarriage between these Spanish explorers and the native Indian populations. The two strongest social institutions are the Roman Catholic Church and the family.

Many Mexican-American families reside in small independent agricultural communities. Others inhabit a socially insulated section of large urban centers—el barrio. The term barrio refers to what the Anglo population would call a ghetto. The barrio is a generally economically and physically depressed area which is normally inhabited by extremely poor families, most of which are Spanish-speaking. It is a world which is extremely difficult for an outsider to penetrate.

Within the Mexican-American extended family an additional relationship is established with the godparents of the children in the family. This is identified by the term compadrazgo. The compadrazgo is an old Mexican and Spanish kinship tradition through which each of the children of the family have a set of godparents. The godfather (padrino) and godmother (madrina) act within the family structure as coparents (compadrazgo). They cooperate with the child's real parents to provide additional direction, guidance, and affection for the child. In this sense they actually relate to the family much as the real grandparents of the child might if they were present. The ties of the compadrazgo system are often as strong as blood ties.

It is not an uncommon practice among Mexican-American families to "trade" or "loan out" a child to other members of the family. This trade may last as long as a year. This characteristic of family life is also found in Amish society; Amish families often send a daughter to live and work with another Amish family.

Wives in Mexican-American families are generally subservient to the wishes of their husbands, except in cases in which the husband is absent, negligent, or shirks his duties and responsibilities. Mothers do share the disciplinary tasks of childrearing with the fathers.

There are at least two other groups which provide evidence of the existence of the traditional extended family pattern in the United States: black families and Native American families. Most often these families become "extended" not through a total cultural pattern but due to some external pressure forcing change upon the nuclear family.

These families become extended families when a single-parent family or nuclear family lives with relatives or takes relatives into its own household. The major reason for this kind of arrangement is economic survival, not ideology. The authority structure in such a family shifts, depending upon the combination of family members.

Helping the Traditional Extended Family Meet Health Needs

The Amish family, the Mexican-American family, the black family, and the Native American family all have cultural constraints which inhibit their relationships with the highly structured impersonal health care systems. In each of these instances the ideal health care worker is one who is a member of that particular culture. It is hardly necessary to point out that only a very few health care professionals come from any of these four cultural groups. Until professionals from these extended family groups are abundant, the logical step is for each of us to learn as much as possible about the sociocultural and ideological background of our clients and patients.

Without this understanding health care professionals tend to alienate many of these individuals and their families. Consider for example the following experience in childbirth of a Mexican-American woman. A first-generation immigrant, she delivered her first child in Mexico. She was assisted by a midwife, or *partera* in Spanish. The partera assisted the pregnant mother prior to delivery with hot teas and oil massages. This had the effect of relaxing the mother and engaging her affection for the midwife. The whole experience of childbirth with the partera assisting was a satisfying and success-

ful one. The woman felt highly confident of the midwife's skills and abilities.

After moving to southern California the woman became pregnant again. Little was done until she was about to deliver the second child. At that time her husband set out to find a midwife to assist her, but none could be found. The family had neither relatives nor compadres living nearby to help, and so when the time came the mother gave birth with only the assistance of her husband.

The third child was born in a hospital, where the mother was separated from her family. She was highly disappointed in her experience, feeling that the doctors and nurses were cold and uncaring. She had not been given hot teas or massages. She believes that American obstetric practices are impersonal and totally alien to her experience and her feelings.

Another example occurred in a western New York Amish community. Amish religious beliefs cause them to refuse to comply with New York education requirements for school entrance immunizations. In fact, they run their own school. Suddenly there was a measles epidemic, and the families refused to be immunized. The public health department finally came to understand the situation and provided gammaglobulin. Perhaps prior knowledge and concern on the part of area health care workers could have acted to prevent this emergency, and perhaps not. The fact is, the attempt was not made to provide adequate preventive care to the Amish community.

A highly successful approach to recognizing and meeting the health needs of these cultural groups is through neighborhood health care clinics. Many of the staff are lay persons from the families and neighborhoods served. This staff has the understanding and empathy necessary to identify unique individual needs.

The Essence of the Traditional Extended Family

In their book, *The Family: From Institution to Companionship,* sociologists Burgess and Locke give the following criteria regarding extended families:

1   The feeling on the part of all members that they belong pre-eminently to the family group and that all other persons are outsiders.
2   The complete integration of individual activities for the achievement of family objectives.
3   The assumption that land, money, and other material goods are family property, involving obligations to support individual members and give them assistance when they are in need.
4   The willingness of all other members to rally to the support of another member if attacked by outsiders.
5   Concern for the perpetuation of the family as evidenced by helping an adult child in beginning and continuing an economic activity in line with family expectations and in setting up a new household.[3]

PHILOSOPHICAL COMPARISON OF TRADITIONAL AND COMMUNAL FAMILY

The traditional extended family exists to further the purposes of the family. Each individual member subjugates his or her individual identity and needs to the identity and needs of the whole family. The manner in which this is perpetuated has been the concern of the earlier portions of this chapter.

Within the communal extended family the philosophy is somewhat different. While some communes contend that they exist for the total good of all members, many more emphasize the enhancement of individual identity and growth. Terms like "self-ful-fillment" and "self-awareness" are heard frequently within the communal setting.

With these basic differences in mind, it is important that the reader consider the commune as a kind of extended family life-style, since there are also many similarities.

THE COMMUNE

The Driving Force

There are people driven by the inner conviction that life as they live it cannot be all there is. From comfortable homes in White Plains, the ghetto in Atlanta, an apartment with a view of Lake Michigan or the Charles, they surge forward following the urgent need to find, discover, build "something better." That something is the essence of togetherness: coexistence with other humans and with the earth, the water, and the air. It is clear to such people that a technology which pollutes nature and people in a megalopolis of humans, each competing for some fast-diminishing space, cannot and will not institute any social transformation directed toward slowing our already quickening pace toward extinction.

Communes could not continue to exist without the communard's belief that people who want to change vast social systems must first begin with a change in their own life-style. It is possible that the complex and varied interactions of communal life will enhance individual identity and the potential for interpersonal as well as intrapersonal growth. Communes are the vanguard of an immeasurable social movement addressing itself to the challenge of survival by social transformation. The quest is for that delicate balance between concepts of freedom and togetherness, independence and cooperation, and utopia and realism.

The reader's view of the commune and

those who seek to create a life within its scope will depend on his own vision of the future. Is it the desperate fleeing of revolutionary anti-Establishment youth entrenching themselves in preparation for mass revolt or an outpost of new visions, creative energy, and humanistic values? Is it a threat to be guarded against at all cost or an adventure to be explored and investigated with the hope of discovering some intrinsic worth, some hope for social survival?

Historical Perspective

The communal approach to society is not a new phenomenon. Experiments in utopian living have appeared in America as early as the time of the community of Pilgrims. Idealistic inspiration has been the motivating force as groups of like-minded persons withdrew from the masses in search of a more tolerable life-style. In the 1680s these groups were religious sects which sought shelter for their spiritual visions in the American wilderness. During the nineteenth century more than 130 utopian-style communes were established and disbanded. Among those utopian ventures based on religious belief were the Harmonites in Pennsylvania, the Perfectionists and the Shakers in New York, the Zoarites in Ohio, and the Amana Society in Iowa. Several of these religion-based communes survived only because they became business-minded. Two of the most renowned are the Perfectionists of Oneida, New York, and the Amana Society in Iowa.

Nonreligious communes in the nineteenth century were seeking a change in social order rather than freedom to practice religious beliefs. They identified communal living as the most viable social structure. New Harmony, Indiana, and Brook Farm in West Roxbury, Massachusetts, based themselves on utopian world concepts. Anarchist-social-ist communes or "villages" were founded in Ohio, Louisiana, Georgia, and New York.

At the close of the nineteenth century only a few of these experiments continued to exist. Extinction had come because of pressures, both internal and external. Strict rules and celibacy limited the growth and indoctrination of new generations, and rumors of sexual freedoms and perversions moved neighbors to force the groups to disband.

Commune dwellers today share much with history. Their philosophy insists that the communal pattern for society is *the* life-style which all persons will eventually desire. Their commitment is one of intensity, the magnitude of which established society does not comprehend. Their vision is of a super-culture shaped to fit the way people really are. As with earlier seekers for utopia, they are driven by discontent with the present and a fundamental belief that "surely somewhere somehow there is a better way of living—there has to be."[4]

Haight-Ashbury and the Present

The student of social phenomena can trace the present communal movement to the 1960s and the West Coast of America, to the Haight-Ashbury area of San Francisco. The Haight was an older urban neighborhood experiencing the ritual decomposition common to all large cities. A mutation occurred at some point where it would ordinarily have become a black ghetto. Instead there began a slow gathering of postgraduate "beats," aspiring artists and musicians, and mystics. The lack of housing facilities and money for individual rental and the availability of large Victorian houses stimulated the idea of pooling resources and living communally.

By 1967 the Haight had become the Mecca for dissident youth, an experiment in full sensory awareness and wholeness. A revelation of self led to a heightened perspective of others. The inhabitants were now dubbed "hippies," and the era of acid rock, body painting, and psychedelic stimulation of sight and hearing was under way. The nation was given its first view of the flower children when 20,000 kids turned out in Golden Gate Park in January 1967 for a "love-in," and the mass media recorded the event. With the publicity came thousands of young people groping for some place to belong, to be unique, and yet to conform.

This new movement changed the original settlement into a haven for acid heads, runaways, pushers, and bikers. To them the area offered a little of everything: free food, free clothes, a newspaper, a free clinic, free legal services, head shops, and crash pads. The inevitable followed: tourists, the curious, the narcotic agents, and the commercial-minded seller of "hippie momentos."

With this latest invasion the original settlers began to move, in small communal groups, out of the rapidly degenerating Haight-Ashbury district into houses, shacks, and tent communities on the northern California hillsides. They continued to live in a communal atmosphere and turned their work efforts toward building a community and growing their own food. The era of the modern rural commune had begun.

Between 1965 and 1970, 2,000 communal groups were formed. At the outset it was the visceral reaction of disillusioned youth. Now, it is a movement; the creation of a microculture. They reexamined, tested, reevaluated, and revised. They developed smaller, more self-sufficient communities. They worked for harmony with the environment not only in the cultivation of the land, but in the architecture of their building as well. They tried freer forms of family membership and childbearing and rearing. They established home industries of individual

craftsmanship. They revived old religions, created new ones, and combined the best of both in a rediscovered awareness of divinity.

Today, one or several communes can be found within reach of every major city in America. Travel long enough and far enough, and the seeker will find *that* commune in which his or her own ideals and life-style mesh with those of the members already there. If perchance this is not so, the seeker need only band with other like-minded people; rent or buy a plot of land, a house, or an apartment; and begin developing a communal family of his or her own.

Philosophies of Communal Living

Family

Martha's parents and brothers live in a small town in western New York. Charles's parents were divorced, and he had lived with his mother until now. Isaac's wife and daughter were still in an Eastern city. Each member of the commune has in his past some manner of sociological family unit. Yet the most frequent positive response to the commune is, "For the first time I feel I am part of a family." They refer to each other as "the family." Some even have commune names, such as the "Lynch Family" in California and "The Chosen Family" in New Mexico. Thus, the basic philosophy of communal life-style is the establishment of a new family structure with new roles and developmental processes.

For some communes this means having separate sleeping rooms and family dining, recreation, and work programs. Others establish group marriages with sexual partners changing on a scheduled basis or retain monogamous relationships. Some communes practice celibacy. Childrearing varies from single-parent responsibility through biological family units to a separation of children into a special unit apart from parents.

The most constant family activity observed in comparison of communal practices is the togetherness of sharing certain activities, such as group rituals, singing and chanting, drug experiences, religious services, and the observation of festive holidays. Almost without exception, each communal unit has daily family gatherings for prayers, evening songs, or some other activity in which everyone is a participant.

Group and Personal Awareness

The ever-deepening search for self-awareness and self-fulfillment that is common to human beings is the cornerstone of the intimacy and warmth that the commune members are discovering in their extended families. Therapy-group interaction, mutual criticism, or a policy of honesty and uninhibited expression of feeling and gut reactions provide a proving ground for personal growth. It is a life-style in which all members

FIGURE 5-1
A devotion to religious study is the central focus of this commune, a colony of the Children of God in Burlington, Washington. The sect has colonies across the United States and Europe, sheltering between 2,000 and 3,000 young people. (*By permission from Wide World Photos.*)

of the *family* expect honesty and support from other members and receive it. The potential for social change is heightened even if only a few members can consistently meet this standard of openness.

Robert Houriet experienced the directness of this honest approach when he visited High Ridge Farm in Oregon. His recorded conversations, first with Elaine and then with Jean the following morning, illustrate the atmosphere of concerned helping and caring in which criticism is presented.

Later I lay in my sleeping bag, thinking everyone asleep, furtively taking notes on the day's events by flashlight. Lantern in hand, Elaine entered the A-frame. She saw me and smiled knowingly. Removing her layers of raincoats—so many she looked pregnant—she came and sat down beside me. She is a thin twenty-seven-year-old Jewish girl from New York, who graduated in political science from Swarthmore. She has straight, lustrous brown hair which she brushes over her ears, which protrude slightly. Very thick glasses in oval frames help correct her severe myopia. She always wears the same pair of loose, flowered, pajamalike pants. When she chooses to talk to you, her speech is punctuated with anguished gaps to indicate her extremely careful choice of words. "I've noticed . . . from when you first came here . . . that you've held yourself apart from the family."

I was engulfed by tension. She continued, "You introduced yourself rather formally . . . and you said you wanted to be a member of the family. . . ."

"That's right," I said.

"But there's something about you . . . I guess it was tonight that I first realized what it was . . . the way you broke in with that question about Peter . . . it was a question that *intruded*. I saw that you weren't thinking of yourself as a member of the family . . . you were a detached observer in disguise . . . taking notes in your head . . . and secretly at night." She smiled and looked down at my pad. I felt caught.

"Have you ever tried *not* observing . . . just experiencing . . . or do you always remain detached from whatever you're doing?" Man, this chick was what you call laying a trip! And of course all she said was true.

She concluded, "To catch the essence of communal life, you should put your notebook away, and then you may decide it is more important to live it than to write it." I thanked her for revealing my foibles, and we said good night.

(Next morning)

This morning, I tried to start a conversation with Jean as she ground some flour (she baked a dozen loaves and they were eaten in two days), but she didn't respond to my openers. Instead she said, "I agree with everything Elaine told you last night," and paused to let it sink in, all the time continuing to grind, smiling and jiggling her earrings. "What you said during the meeting was with the tone of not caring about Peter or any of us. It was the tone of a ruthless curiosity, digging for a fact to fill out the story. It was your ego speaking."

There was more. She ground away. "I get the feeling when you talk that you are holding back. An aloofness. And that you don't dig the *feeling* of words, only their logical sense. And, you ask too many questions."

Wowwww! I shook my head dumbly and mumbled about having to think over what she said and went off to dig a hole for a fruit tree.[5]

The meaning of these deeply shared experiences in reaching the depths of other human beings cannot be comprehended without participation. It is the life blood of the commune. It is the philosophical rationale for a life-style. It is seen by the communitarian as the hope for human beings; to the communitarian, social growth is the ultimate result of personal awareness. "We've come together in a commune to channel the Truth to one another. Living alone separates you from the richness of life which is a direct result of creating constantly with a group of kindred spirits."[6]

FIGURE 5-2
A scriptural "rap session" is held at a coffee house operated as an experiment in Christian evangelism in Virginia Beach, Virginia. (*By permission from Wide World Photos.*)

Property and Ownership

The concept of sharing and cooperative venture extends to personal property. Private ownership is, in general, discouraged in most communes. The ideal is for everything to belong to everyone so that everyone treats valuable items, such as tools, with equal care. It is not realistic in view of human nature, past training, and the variation in values placed on material possessions; but

sometimes it works. When it does not, there is inevitably strife.

Some communards own the real property in common and run business affairs as a group. More frequently, two or more members actually own the house or the farm, and others pay rent or just live there in exchange for work and companionship or as family members. With a nuclear family group, it does not matter when one parent owns the house; neither does it matter when this occurs in the extended communal family. When problems do develop, the owner may use legal process to change the membership. The family at Bryn Athym in Vermont experienced this when the owner of the property returned one morning with six others he had met on the West Coast. He announced that they were establishing a work-oriented commune and gave the family 30 days' notice to remove themselves or he would call the state police.[7]

Some owner-members, including Chick at Lorien in New Mexico, are content to live in privacy on the land, allowing life to happen as it will, without intervention. Still others in ownership position become the leaders of the commune, as is the case for Kathy and Constantine at Summit House in Cambridge and the original owners at New Buffalo in New Mexico. In the commune the power usually inherent in ownership is controlled, modified, or rejected by the basic philosophy of communal sharing and by the members themselves. Again, each commune is a unique, distinct entity. There is no stereotype.

There are wide variations among communes in the unwritten rules about personal property, private rooms, automobiles, stereos, and their use. When single persons, couples, or biological families have private sleeping units within the commune, they usually retain rights to the furnishings and personal items in their rooms. All items in the communal rooms and all necessary tools for farming, maintenance, and food preparation are owned and used by everyone. Automobiles and motorcycles seem to be the other item of personal property that may be closely guarded by the owners, much to the dismay of other family members. The farm tractor or truck, however, is communally owned.

The basic philosophy of communal living suggests that all property be given to the commune upon admission to be used by anyone who needs it. However, it is evident that few communal families actually adhere completely to this tenet. One exception is that of Twin Oaks in Virginia, a community based on B. F. Skinner's *Walden Two*.

Autonomy and Self-sufficiency

In the American dream each family unit is able to care for its own needs. This autonomy and self-sufficiency is important to communal philosophy. The remarks are similar across the country: "There are no food stamps here." "We are farmers so we can grow our own food." "Even subsistence farming is better than government funds." Books and pamphlets tell how to build a brick house, grow herbs, preserve foods, and make soap, candles, and clothes. The local library usually has a supply of information on other do-it-yourself ideas. Local farmers have befriended the members in farming communes, particularly in the New England states. Their knowledge is invaluable to the novice farmer.

The distant goal of self-sufficiency is linked to interdependence with the other communes. The urban communes band together in food co-ops to purchase large quantities of food at lower wholesale prices. Sometimes they contract with nearby agrarian communes; they offer planting and harvesting workers from the city in exchange for fruits, vegetables, and grains from the farm. Handicrafts made at both farm and urban communes may be sold at a co-op store.

Several communes are supported, at least in part, by self-contained home industry. Twin Oaks in Virginia makes hammocks. Messiah's World Crusade operates a natural foods restaurant in San Francisco. Bruderhof communities manufacture community playthings.

Some communes are supported by the out-

FIGURE 5-3
Members of The Farm near Summertown, Tennessee, load sorghum for processing
into molasses at a nearby mill. The group of about 400 members came to Tennessee to
establish a communal life-style and have been selling molasses to pay for the
1,014-acre farm. (*By permission from Wide World Photos.*)

side employment of their members. This is particularly valid in urban settings. The members of Summit House in Cambridge are professional persons who pay a monthly fee for the communal finances. There are members with steady incomes from stock dividends, allowances from parents, and their own savings accounts. These are fairly uncommon, however. More likely, the youths receive some kind of welfare assistance, which frequently serves as a constant irritant to the goals of the commune and may be a cause of much discussion.

Male and Female Roles

Women work in the fields beside the men. A male cooks breakfast for everyone. Women care for the children, sew, and cook. Men work at construction of new buildings. What are the expected male and female roles in a commune? That's just the point; the philosophy is respect for each member and his dream. If Bill wants to cook, he is not degraded by the other men because most likely they cook also.

The household chores are done whenever someone feels right about doing something, by a schedule set up through group consensus, or by chosen work credits. In the agrarian communes the traditional role of women seems to be the one most frequently adopted. Women usually assume the responsibility for child care. They cook, sew, and tend to the housekeeping. In the urban areas the power of "women's liberation" seems to be an influencing factor, and the roles in household chores and childrearing are often equally shared.

The idea of equal regard for role identification is basic to the equality of each human being with every other human being. Understanding of self and of one's individual needs and desires leads to a willingness to accept differences in others. The members of the Hog Farm patterned a structure of rotating leadership on a daily basis including both men and women.

The male in both urban and rural communes may be slightly more inhibited about assuming feminine tasks such as sewing, preserving foods, and caring for children. That hesitancy may be due to the early childhood instillation of distinctly male roles. The men tend toward heavy farm and construction labor. Within the commune setting they are freer to express, experiment with, and experience some of the warmer, more "homey" activities traditionally reserved for women. They express a fuller sense of wholeness because they have transcended the strictly masculine role to that of human being.

What is occurring in the change of role identity is not the development of a unisex, as some suggest, but the discovery that male and female roles in American society are arbitrary and passed on by tradition. They belie the human qualities of toughness tempered with gentleness, strength hidden in warmth, and aggressiveness combined with passivity in the same person. The commune dweller is seeking role identity apart from biological sexual identity.

The Children

Childbearing

The most obvious return to the biological, ecological level of living is seen in the almost nationwide communal concept of natural childbirth. Total body-mind awareness, communion with earth and sky, expression of visceral feelings, and the break with technological, plastic, Establishment society negates any desire for the anesthetized, sterile, impersonal nature of hospital-centered labor and delivery. The ultimate goal is not merely natural childbirth but natural childbirth at home.

Childbirth is a spiritual, emotional, physiological experience. There is a whole new movement under way to have babies at home attended by husband, children, and those who mean the most to the mother. Dr. Robert Spitzer investigated this trend and found that his previous value systems were being challenged. He writes of the women with whom he spoke:

They were not kooks, but for the most part were intelligent girls who were not unaware of the medical danger involved. They were willing to take the risk to gain the extreme emotional satisfaction of having their babies at home. To them the advantages of personal growth far outweighed the risk of medical complication. The mothers- and fathers-to-be attended natural childbirth classes and studied the birth process in earnest.[8]

Dr. Spitzer was given the opportunity to participate in a communal birth and found it a joy and spiritual experience not commonly seen in the hospital setting.

It was extremely moving, a unique peak experience for me as well as the others present. The mother delivered rather than was delivered, and I could see that this kind of family home birth was an outgrowth of a new consciousness, an attempt to regain the shared risks and accomplishments of the reality of frontier life. That was a time rich in rituals when the family built its own shelter, grew its own food, and helped its neighbors. Home birth is a rejection of the prevailing abdication to "experts" of those very activities making for individual and family growth.[9]

The rapid increase of home births is evidence of the viability of the communal movement. The basic tenet of total involvement, so much a part of the communal philosophy, is expressed in the complete sharing of father, mother, and friends in the birth process. The height of such an experience is revealed by Mark in the following description of his participation in the delivery of his son.

Sunshine's still handling all well. I no longer worry about her strength, she's on top of it. I decide to move from her head to her feet with Pat and Barb. Pat notices a bulge in the perineum during contractions. We put scissors, syringe, dental floss and navel clamps into boiling water. Pat shows me perineal massage and how to support the perineum with the palm of my hand to prevent tearing. The bulge continues with each contraction. I start to massage. Sunshine handled the contractions so well, I found it hard to tell exactly when some of them began and ended. Soon with each contraction a little of the baby's head was visible. It's got hair. David was holding a mirror for Sunshine, and Claudia sat nearby. The energy mounted. Soon each contraction brings a little more of the baby's head into view, then slowly it disappears. Now it stays visible between each

contraction. I noticed what looked liked a big welt down the baby's head (front to back). To the virgin eye it looked like the umbilical cord. Pat assures me it's only skin forced together, and it's cool. Sunshine starts to push with one foot on Pat's knee, the other on Barb's. I begin to support the perineum which seems very capable of stretching as needed. She pushes. "Far out," "real good," and other such encouragements come from Pat and Barb. It must have been five or six contractions. Each time energy and excitement building, stretching, stretching, pushing, energy, pushing, stretching, then. . . . Like a ball pushed through a bottle neck, the baby's head was in my hand. The head was tightly covered with the caul—remove the caul, my fingernails cut short couldn't dig in, slick as soap on a doorknob. Five hands work fast but gently. Barb gets her finger under the chin and gets ahold of the sac and it tears loose. The face is free.

The face immediately shows expression. Pat sucks a little fluid from the nostrils and throat. It cries. Quickly baby turns sideways as if someone was inside turning it. Another contraction, blam, all red and pink and white-speckled our son was born. Sunshine sits up giggling, and takes him, cord still attached to him and still inside her. I cry.[10]

An experience of that magnitude will not easily be set aside, no matter what the established health workers suggest. Home birth will be a vital part of the communal scene. Most parents are using some variation of the Lamaze method for childbirth preparation. If a physician is utilized by the parents, he must be one who will allow and even encourage natural childbirth. Pamphlets and magazines and newspaper articles direct communal dwellers to books on the Lamaze method.

One result of home births is the lack of identity for the child. (Not in the sense of personal identity; that is most likely enhanced.) For all practical purposes the child is unknown to established authority. As there are no marriage certificates, so there are no birth certificates and no social security numbers. It is the ultimate in liberation of the child from the numbering systems of society. This practice is not adhered to by all or even the majority at present, and the inherent problems are manyfold. In the present society, work, government funds, and scholarships depend upon some identification. To the communard of the future this may be another avenue of social transformation.

Childrearing Practices

Childrearing in most of the communes is an experience shared by the members. Both adults and children seem to thrive in this atmosphere. Each adult has the responsibility and the right to play with, teach, discipline, or just enjoy any of the children at any time. There are many *parents* with many value systems and it seems to be closer to reality.

In contrast, the present American approach is to shape the child's identity and attitudes through the nearly exclusive influence of a single set of adults. It is a very egotistical situation, and the child does not learn to share early in life. Neither do the parents.

Most children live in the same room or unit as their parents. However, each child has a wide variety of adults to interact with during the day. They are shared by many, and an intimacy commonly develops between all of the children and all of the adults. Their primary relationship and loyalty seems to remain with their biological parents.

Some variations are reported. At Olympia, prior to disbanding, each child was free at the beginning of the week to choose an adult to be his official parent that week.[11] The ultimate plans for childrearing at Twin Oaks will be based on the separate units for children suggested by B. F. Skinner in *Walden*

Two. At present there are too few children to warrant assigning a person to child care. The children are reared according to behavioral principles. They are placed as an item on the work credit schedule and divided into shifts. The biological parents take one shift and other members sign up to be with the children during the rest of the 24-hour period.[12]

There have been varied problems with the communal approach to childrearing. Some persons find it extremely difficult to allow others a voice and influence in the lives of their own children. Children are sometimes seen as the most private property. At Sunrise they tried communal child care, but soon found there were so many conflicting theories of childrearing that the children once more were given into the total responsibility of their parents. They did interact with a number of other children and adults, however.[13]

The example of High Ridge Farm in Oregon, reported by Robert Houriet, is one which depicts the common concepts motivating members to rear their children as a shared experience. The following are excerpts from that account:

I spent most of the day playing with the children. They had found some long wooden rods and were engaged in mock swordplay. I watched uneasily, knowing where it would lead. . . . I let them learn the inevitable lesson for themselves: Those who play with sticks get hurt with sticks. Roland got hit hard over the head by Kathy. He retaliated with wild thrusts. At this point, I intervened, jerked the sticks out of their hands, laid down a moralistic trip about the difference between playing and fighting, and diverted their attention to another game. . . . The same situation could have been handled in a number of ways. Claudia, generally authoritarian, probably would have headed off the swordplay at the start. Laura might have allowed it to go further than I did, risking injury. . . . Elaine might have avoided the situation altogether for she avoided the children as much as she avoided everybody; when she did do something with them, it was on her terms, like driving them to the library to see the weekly travelogue film. From time to time, Maureen exploded in violence, usually directed at her own children. . . . Jean was calm and gentle and might have coaxed them into more peaceful play. Altogether, the kids experienced an uneven, inconsistent upbringing by six daddies and five mommies, each of whom could be counted upon to handle the same situation differently. For the kids, the only constant in the

FIGURE 5-4
The sharing of childrearing responsibilities is the accepted practice in many communes. At the Society of Brothers commune in Norfolk, Connecticut, one young woman takes care of children while their families are busy working. (*By permission from Wide World Photos.*)

communal environment was constant inconsistency. . . . Claudia told me, "I think it's a mistake to bring up kids with the notion that there's a single code of what's good, bad, manly or feminine. The fact is, we're living in a world where all the absolutes have been broken. Each man finds his own path. So to prepare the kids for that, it's better to give them a lot of examples of fathers and mothers who are all different personalities and have different values."[14]

The consistent value at High Ridge Farm and in other communes seems to be honesty with the children as with the adults.

Education for the Children

The goal for education within the communal philosophy is the establishment of communal schools completely apart from the public school system. If the present trend in commune schools is followed, the schools of the future will be open classrooms, with all students free to explore and learn as their own interests direct them. It is an effort to retain the natural creativity of childhood and harness it for learning.

The generation of youth now inhabiting communes have found they have much unlearning to do. They spent so many years in the Establishment's educational system that they need a period of *decompression* before they can begin to live communally with satisfaction and success. They want to utilize preventive education with their children. They are determined that each child will be able to find what is most relevant to him or her and learn to share it with others in an intimate, warm relationship.

Most communes do not have enough children to start their own school. Some children now attend the local public schools. Some are tutored at home by one or more of the adults. Generally, school truant officials have not harassed the communes who keep their children home and educate them there. In some of the larger metropolitan areas communes have established cooperative schools. This is true in Cambridge, New York City, Chicago, Los Angeles, and San Francisco. These are the prototype of the future communal schools.

Helping the Commune Meet Health Needs

Variables in Providing Care

The earlier segment in this chapter which presented the trend toward home birth introduced the reader to the wary stance the commune takes in relation to established health care facilities. Their experience with poor care, feelings of contamination, embarrassment, and the hospital's tendency to report everything to the police has placed a distinct barrier of mistrust around much of the commune population. The community, on the other hand, frequently views the commune dweller as filthy, disease ridden, drug addicted, and a threat to the health of the area. In fact, it is frequently the sanitation issue that community officials use to disband a local commune when use of drugs or other infractions of the law cannot be claimed.

Members of the health care professions are becoming leaders in the move to help commune dwellers meet their own needs on their own terms. In many areas the relationships between community and commune have improved to the point of coexistence, if not acceptance. The offer of health care has frequently been followed by involvement of other community volunteers with free legal advice, free farming advice, social service assistance, and offers of part-time employment.

The health needs of the commune member vary to some extent but may include malnutrition, assistance with birth control, hepatitis, venereal disease, and respiratory and psychological problems. They often resist going for care at a hospital or physician's office. Their life-styles and appearance have raised eyebrows and brought lectures and general nonacceptance. If the problem is drug related, they fear being reported to the police. Many cannot afford health care and have no health insurance. Some may be runaways and fear that parents will be contacted. Some have police records and may be fugitives. The usual hospital or clinic admission procedure would bring out most of this judgment-provoking data.

The philosophy and life-style of the commune dweller are the variables which affect any plan for delivery of health care. The objectives of a community health clinic provide for a program designed to offer comprehensive and high-quality medical care in a setting that is convenient and acceptable to the recipient. It encourages the development of an interpersonal relationship between staff and patient, involves the residents in the planning and operation of the facility, and is responsive to the individual needs of the target population.[15] To meet both the philosophy of the commune and the objectives of a community-based health program, new methods of health care delivery were established and still others have yet to be explored and instituted.

Community Health Care Facilities

The urban commune is in the ideal setting for its members to utilize free health clinics which were established in several large cities. The clinic is usually staffed by volunteer doctors, nurses, social workers, and laboratory technicians. Admission procedure requires only name, age, and presenting complaint. If the client decides to use a fictitious name or age, that is accepted. Minimal questions are asked. The atmosphere is non-judgmental. The staff's concern is with the client, not with the client's name, age, or social history except when these have direct bearing on the client's needs. Such free health clinics have received much publicity, particularly those in California (Haight-Ashbury, San Francisco; Los Angeles; Long Beach) and in Cambridge, Massachusetts.

The newest approach to medical care is the mobile unit. This is a clinic which is also staffed by volunteers. The purpose of the mobile clinics is to take free medical care and counseling to the areas where the target population is most likely to be found. Again the atmosphere is nonjudgmental. Frequently a client tests the staff by requesting help with some minor problem. When the client finds that the setting is one in which he or she can be honest and still be accepted and receive care, the client returns to have the more serious problems taken care of.

Many hospital emergency rooms are now staffed by younger doctors and nurses. The red tape has been cut more frequently. Free clinics and some private physicians are referring commune members to the area hospitals where they can find more extensive medical or surgical care without undue hassle.

New Roles for Medical Care

The idea of self-sufficiency is very strong in the commune. When one communal co-op was offered the use of a free medical van their response was, "Leave that for the street kids. Can you teach us about first aid, home delivery, and preventive health maintenance?" The ideal would be a resident health professional—a nurse or doctor who is a member of the commune. In some communes this is a reality.

For the present a more viable plan would be a type of medical-nursing co-op. It could be volunteers from the community who are trusted by the communards. An exchange program could be planned in which health professionals from one urban commune provide services to several other communes in exchange for other services.

There are now birth control and abortion counseling centers in many cities. The future may hold the establishment of centers for home delivery staffed by nurse midwives. The need is to help commune dwellers become self-sufficient in meeting their own health needs, either by utilizing members who are health professionals or by teaching the commune dwellers how to care for these needs themselves.

The Essence of the Commune

If there is any brief description of the commune or the communal movement today, it might be best said in the words of Robert Houriet as he expressed the only commonality in a comparison of communal roles and life-styles.

I was eager to find a commune that *was* working out, a group of people who'd been together a year and were happy. . . . Zablocki cautioned me that there was no such beast as a prototypical commune. Each one is a unique attempt to blend economics, art, agriculture, and the spiritual into the natural round of daily life. . . . Every commune wanted to be—and had to be—unique.[16]

REFERENCES

1 Blitsten, Dorothy R.: *The World of the Family,* Random House, New York, 1963, pp. 145–148, 150–156, 158–159.
2 Schreiber, William I.: *Our Amish Neighbors,* University of Chicago Press, Chicago, 1962, p. 56.
3 Burgess, Ernest W., and Harvey J. Locke: *The Family: From Institution to Companion-*

ship, 2d ed., American, New York, 1953, pp. 71–74.
4 Hedgpeth, William, and Dennis Stock: *The Alternative,* Collier-Macmillan, Toronto, 1970, p. 29.
5 Houriet, Robert: *Getting Back Together,* Coward-McCann, New York, 1971, pp. 60–62.
6 Hedgpeth: op. cit., p. 118.
7 Houriet: op. cit., p. 24.
8 "Home Birth," book review in *Ritual,* Science and Behavior Books, Palo Alto, Calif., 1971, p. 14.
9 Ibid.
10 Ibid., p. 20.
11 Hedgpeth: op. cit., p. 127.
12 Houriet: op. cit., p. 297.
13 Houriet: op. cit., p. 9.
14 Houriet: op. cit., pp. 55–56.
15 Russell, Barbara, and Lynn Lofstrom: "Health Clinic for the Alienated," *American Journal of Nursing,* 71(1):80–83, 1971.
16 Houriet: op. cit., p. 27.

BIBLIOGRAPHY

Beame, Hugh, et al.: *Home Comfort: Stories Scenes of Life on Total Loss Farm,* Saturday Review Press, New York, 1973.
Billingsley, Andrew: *Black Families in White America,* Prentice-Hall, Englewood Cliffs, N.J., 1968.
Brenner, Joseph: "Medical Care without a Hassle," *The New York Times Magazine,* Oct. 11, 1970, p. 30.
Burgess, Ernest W., Harvey J. Locke, and Mary Margaret Thomas: *The Family: From Institution to Companionship,* 3d ed., Crowell, New York, 1966.
Carlson, Lewis H., and George A. Colburn: *In Their Place: White America Defines Her Minorities 1850–1950,* Wiley, New York, 1972.
Cavan, Ruth Shonle: *The American Family,* 3d ed., Crowell, New York, 1965.

Clark, Margaret: *Health in the Mexican-American Culture*, University of California Press, Los Angeles, 1970.

Colorado Commission of Spanish-surnamed Citizens: *The Status of Spanish-surnamed Citizens in Colorado*, Report to the Colorado General Assembly, Denver, 1967.

The Committee on the Family Group for the Advancement of Psychiatry: *Treatment of Families in Conflict*, Science House, New York, 1970.

Daniels, Ada M., and Alaine Krim: "Helping Adolescents Explore Emotional Issues," *American Journal of Nursing*, 69(7):1482–1485, 1969.

Farber, Bernard (ed.): *Kinship and Family Organization*, Wiley, New York, 1966.

Futrell, May D., and Marie J. Kelleher: *The Nurse's Guide to Health Services for Patients*, Little, Brown, Boston, 1973.

Gamio, Manuel: *The Mexican Immigrant*, Arno Press and The New York Times, New York, 1969.

Glazer, Nathan, and Daniel P. Moynihan: *Beyond the Melting Pot*, M.I.T. Press, Cambridge, Mass., 1970.

Goldsborough, Judith: "On Becoming Non-judgmental," *American Journal of Nursing*, 70(1): 2340–2343, 1970.

Gonzalez, Nancie L.: *The Spanish Americans of New Mexico: A Heritage of Pride*, University of New Mexico Press, Albuquerque, 1967.

Goode, William J. (ed.): *Readings on the Family and Society*, Prentice-Hall, Englewood Cliffs, N.J., 1964.

Habenstreit, Barbara: *Fort Greene USA*, Bobbs-Merrill, New York, 1974.

Heller, Celia S.: *Mexican American Youth: Forgotten Youth at the Crossroads*, Random House, New York, 1966.

Helm, June (ed.): *Spanish Speaking People in the United States*, American Ethnological Society, University of Washington Press, Seattle, 1968.

Hommel, Flora: "Natural Childbirth-Nurses in Private Practice as Monitrices," *American Journal of Nursing*, 69(7):1446–1450, 1969.

Hughes, Helen M. (ed.): *Social Organization*, Allyn and Bacon, Boston, 1970.

Josephy, Alvin M., Jr.: *The Indian Heritage of America*, Knopf, New York, 1968.

Kahn, E. J., Jr.: *The American People*, Weybright and Talley, New York, 1973.

Kenkel, William F.: *The Family in Perspective*, 2d ed., Appleton-Century-Crofts, New York, 1966.

Lang, Pat: *Home Birth*, Science and Behavior Books, Palo Alto, Calif., 1973.

Laurel, Alicia B.: *Living on the Earth*, Vintage, New York, 1971.

Lewis, Oscar: *A Death in the Sanchez Family*, Random House, New York, 1970.

———: *The Children of Sanchez*, Random House, New York, 1961.

———: *Five Families: Mexican Case Studies in the Culture of Poverty*, Basic Books, New York, 1959.

———: "Life and Death of a Commune Called Oz," *The New York Times Magazine*, Feb. 16, 1969, p. 30.

Loughlin, Bernice: "Pregnancy in the Navajo Culture," *Nursing Outlook*, 13(3):55–58, 1965.

Melville, Keith: *Communes in the Counter Culture: Origins, Theories, Styles of Life*, Morrow, New York, 1972.

Moore, Joan W., and Alfredo Cuellar: *Mexican Americans*, Prentice-Hall, Englewood Cliffs, N.J., 1970.

"Of Oz and After: Discussion and Letters to the Editor," *The New York Times Magazine*, Mar. 7, 1969, p. 12.

Opler, Morris E.: *Apache Odyssey: A Journey between Two Worlds*, Holt, New York, 1969.

Pelletier, Wilfres, and Ted Poole: *No Foreign Land*, Pantheon, New York, 1973.

Roe, Anne, and Mary Sherwood: *Nursing in the Seventies*, Wiley, New York, 1973.

Samora, Julian, and Richard A. Lamanna: *Mexican-American Study Project: Advance Report 8: Mexican Americans in a Midwest*

Metropolis: A Study of East Chicago, Mexican-American Study Project, Division of Research, Graduate School of Business Administration, University of California, Los Angeles, 1976.

Sankot, Margaret, and David Smith: "Drug Problems in the Haight-Ashbury," *American Journal of Nursing,* 68(8):1686–1688, 1968.

Shanas, Edith, and Gordon F. Streib (eds.): *Social Structure and the Family: Generational Relations,* Prentice-Hall, Englewood Cliffs, N.J., 1965.

Skinner, B. F.: *Walden Two,* Macmillan, New York, 1948.

Skolnick, Arlene S., and Jerome H. Skolnick (eds.): *Family in Transition,* Little, Brown, Boston, 1968.

Smith, David: "Runaways and Their Health Problems in Haight-Ashbury during the Summer of 1967," *American Journal of Public Health,* 59:2046–2050, 1969.

Sprague, W. D.: *Case Histories from the Communes,* Lancer Books, New York, 1972.

Steiner, Stan: *La Raza: The Mexican American,* Harper & Row, New York, 1968.

———: *The New Indians,* Harper & Row, New York, 1968.

Sussman, Marvin B.: *Sourcebook in Marriage and the Family,* 2d ed., Houghton Mifflin, Boston, 1963.

Terrell, John U.: *The Navajos,* Weybright and Talley, New York, 1970.

6

The Single-Parent Family

DAVID S. TORBETT

America today faces a new morality. We live in a society where production and consumption are unlimited and there are few restraints on our use of resources. We are only beginning to be pressed by nature to examine our priorities. Accompanying this trend is a new sexual freedom begging for updated guidelines. Social prohibition against extramarital sexual relationships in the past resulted in unplanned pregnancies being dealt with by quick marriages, by homes for unwed mothers that supplied babies for adoption, or by illegal abortions.

The terms self-actualization and actualization are used throughout this chapter as referents to a form of motivation. The most well-known exponent of a hierarchical organization of motivation is Abraham Maslow, a leader of the humanistic movement in psychology.[1] This hierarchy, from the most basic to the highest level, includes physiological needs, safety needs, love needs, self-esteem needs, and the need for self-actualization. Self-actualization does not necessarily follow even if all prior states have been achieved.[2] Nevertheless, the term is herein used broadly to characterize the essential human quality of self-fulfillment, the fact that people need a purpose in life and a feeling that they are doing things which further this purpose.

THE CURRENT SCENE

While the emphasis of this chapter will be on the single-parent family consisting of an unmarried mother and offspring, there are other single-parent families which result from divorce, separation, and death. In this country about 10 million children under the age of eighteen live in one-parent homes, and 1 out of every 10 families has a female head, reflecting divorce, separation, or widowhood. It is estimated that there are approximately 1,700,000 females who are legally separated from their husbands in this country. Between one-fourth and one-third of all marriages in the United States end in divorce, resulting in about 2,100,000 divorced females at the present time. There are approximately 9 million widows, with an annual increase of about 100,000.[3]

Today women consider keeping their babies as single parents. Abortion is legal and available in every state, and bearing a child for adoption is still a possibility. Marriage for the sake of appearances, hopefully, is no longer valid, and many women seek meaningful, actualizing relationships which contribute to the fulfillment of their lives as individuals. The nursing profession can play a vital role by encouraging individuals to examine their own priorities and by countering society's external pressures working toward unlimited production. The nurse should support families in limiting reproduction within their own minds to the time and family size meaningfully related to their own life plans.

The extended family unit, important during the rural phase of our development when children were economic assets rather than liabilities and survival depended upon cooperation rather than specialization, has given way to a mobile, metropolitanized, and mechanistic unit geared to individualized, industrialized, and immediate gratification. The emergence of a mass-production-oriented society has brought us to a standard of living second to none, while at the same time decreasing the necessity for family interdependence. Today few persons are able to produce the food and fiber necessary for their continued survival. Men and women may, in exchange for money, have their needs met by specialized individuals and groups capable of providing all the necessities of life.

THE FAMILY AND ITS MAJOR SOCIAL FUNCTIONS

The family, sociologically speaking, is a group of two or more persons who are united by blood, marriage, or adoption, inhabiting a common household wherein they create and maintain a common culture. The main functions of the family are production, socialization, and facilitation of meaningful expressions among individuals who care about each other's welfare. If we consider ourselves as having a choice in, and control over, our own lives, it seems most fulfilling for all concerned that adults begin families when they know themselves as individuals, and when they are in a relationship which allows for the continued actualization of all parties involved. When parents feel themselves actualized, they can offer children the enriched environment with realistic limits that fosters the development of individual uniqueness in each of us and thereby the ability to function effectively in groups within society. We need to understand that life itself is a creative process. For individuals to have a meaningful life, they must see themselves as having a creative function within society. Love of self comes from seeing oneself as competent and productive. Such love is basic to sharing love reciprocally, a factor vital to the growth of individuals within families.

Many authors suggest a direct correlation between the rise and fall of civilizations and the stability of the family. Others relegate the family to a rather minor position within the scheme of things and stress the greater importance of political power and economic fluctuations. However the family is viewed, it has appeared in many forms, ranging from the predominantly patrilineal system with evident power held by males, through matrilineages found in early native American tribes such as the Iroquois, Navajo, and Hopi, to the equalitarian and single-parent families of today. Whatever its form or definition, the family has played and will continue to play an important part in the development of individual identity and group and societal functioning.

Women, according to how they are conditioned from early childhood, very often see childbearing as the only possible expression of their creativity in society. The task before us is to develop an awareness in women of their other creative abilities—in areas covering the whole range of human endeavor. Women with such awareness will be capable of making meaningful choices and will begin to change the definition of their own role from mainly reproductive to productive in a variety of ways.

It is necessary to be aware of the cultural norms and patterns for socialization of the sexes which daily influence the adults and children with whom we come in contact.

One of our basic social distinctions is masculinity and femininity. In the United States, we find that sex-role identification is the result of a socialization process wherein males and females are conditioned into their appropriate roles by the way adults react to them on the basis of their sex.

Girls understand their femininity in terms of being unlike boys and by being capable of and interested in different things. At the same time, their identity is based in large part on their ability to be attractive to the opposite sex. The major roles assigned to women have been those of seduction and reproduction, while men have been assigned the power positions in society. Traditional conditioned expectations in society perpetuate women's dependence on men and work against the developing of interdependence between men and women, so vital for survival in today's society characterized by nuclear families and the absence of the support system formerly found in extended families. The powerful male–dependent female relationship also locks the male into prescribed roles, offering him increasingly narrow sectors of success. The male, too, is robbed of optional ways to express his creativity. As he sees his alternatives diminishing, and his future out of his control, he is not in a position to support a woman who is seeking creative channels in her life other than child-rearing.

Demands on the Nursing Profession

The nursing profession itself is an excellent example of how the nurturing role is supported within the American family and is continued outside the home in the hospital, clinic, and health care center. However, present-day nurses, while still rewarded in general for their nurturing care of others, have found themselves confronted with contradictory expectations of them within the profession. The highly specialized, mechanized, and depersonalized hospital or clinic often expects an efficient, highly skilled technician, rather than a nurturing, supportive, and humanistically oriented person. For nurses, being expected to do contradictory kinds of things within the profession often results in confused feelings about themselves, the profession, and those with whom they work.

Obstetric nurses and those dealing with maternity and child care are further confused by the concerns shared with them by pregnant and delivered women. Male and female nurses need to understand how women feel as individuals about their state of expectant parenthood. In the United States pregnancy and childbirth are experiences entered into by women who are often confused by contradictory messages. On the one hand, they are fulfilling their biological role as a woman. On the other, they are becoming aware that independence and personal goals are often difficult to achieve and at times incompatible with motherhood.

Thus we find nurses, themselves the products of contradictory socialization, attempting to deal professionally with a pregnant, birth-oriented woman, who herself is struggling with similar contradictions. The result is often chaos rather than effective professional nurse-client interrelating. It has been well established that the *desire* for a child is of utmost importance in respect to the impact of birth on the delivering mother, the newborn offspring, and the family context within which the mother and child will be involved.

Each of us brings our own values to every situation. The role of the professional is to understand his or her own values, as well as other viewpoints about the question at hand. Our freedom in accepting our own views and relating them to another frees the other person to accept his or her true feelings and relate them as such. Our role as professionals is to help each person get in touch with real feelings as much as possible and to work toward the realistic solution of problems based upon choice.

Therefore, the role of nurses working with pregnant women who are considering single parenthood takes several directions. Nurses need to come to grips with their own feelings about the contradictory socialization they have experienced and their feelings about rearing a child in a one-parent family. In addition, they will need to become competent in reflecting the feelings of the often confused woman who is attempting to decide on the most desirable course of action. The woman's decision often grows out of her own needs at that point in time, making it difficult for her to project into the future the possible implications of rearing a child in a one-parent family with respect to the impact on the child.

A number of implications that expectant mothers should consider prior to accepting the single-parent role as most desirable are:

1 What are the implications for the woman herself? What will keeping the child mean with respect to employment, heterosexual relating, and peer support?
2 What are the implications for the child of being labeled, as is the case in many states, illegitimate and being reared in a single-parent family, which, while increasing numerically, still is outside the framework society considers "normal"? What impact will questions about his or her different status and why he or she has only one parent have on the child's identity formation and personality development?

3 What are the implications in respect to sexual-identity formation for the child? This question is of particular concern if the child is a male being reared by a female and a female being reared without the socializing influence of a male in preparation for educational and community role assimilation. Will the opposite-sex parent modeling result in a tendency, for example, for male offspring to identify with their own sex and become more oriented toward homosexuality or will they become more competent in the areas of emotional expression and non-aggressive relating?

THE UNPLANNED PREGNANCY

Today we are in a state of transition where rapid change is taking place, especially in respect to family forms. While premarital pregnancies have been around as long as human beings have existed, the number of premarital pregnancies that are taking place is increasing as are the number of women who are keeping their children and rearing them as a single parent rather than giving them up for adoption or entering into marriage.

The ability to produce a child and rear that child outside marriage reflects the change in attitude held by society. In the past the stigma of being a parent outside marriage would have been so great that the social pressures would have made it nearly impossible for this to take place in any kind of fashion that would be construed by society as acceptable. However, today, while the stigma is still in evidence, thousands of women are having children, maintaining them outside marriage, and being supported by family and friends to do this without the usual kinds of anxieties.

The responsibility of raising a child or giving life to another human being needs to be understood. Children normally question everything. The more secure an adult can be about his or her own self, the more that adult can accept questioning coming from children. The more adults understand the need for flexibility in living meaningfully, the more flexible they can be in their expectations for their children.

Many unactualized adults do not know or admit to themselves that they are not prepared to take on the responsibility of childrearing. Because of our general social conditioning toward regarding the family structure positively, we rarely question that a two-parent family would produce unwanted children. However, a *single* woman anticipating childbirth confronts an exceptional social situation which causes her to question her commitment to raising a child. This can be looked upon as a positive factor, in that it forces her to make conscious choices regarding her own actualization. When a woman finds herself involved in an unwanted pregnancy, she necessarily must choose a course of action. Abortion or keeping a child are the two most clear-cut options, for once a woman has carried a child to term, it is emotionally tearing for her to give it up. During her pregnancy, she has a symbiotic relationship with the baby and has an acute awareness of parenting.

Abortion

Though the father's emotional involvement cannot be denied, much of the emotional burden for the decision about abortion falls upon the mother, since the fact of bearing or aborting most vitally involves her body and hormones and her emotional responses. This woman needs to be offered the opportunity to look at her immediate and long-range goals in an objective manner. Has she had a chance to understand her own uniqueness? This is a basic prerequisite in working effectively with people who continually question their values as they struggle to fit their own uniqueness into the world.

There are many factors possibly working to influence a person's decision against abortion. These factors include a woman's need to prove her femininity; the need of certain religions and ethnic groups for self-perpetuation; a man's need to prove his virility by showing his capability to impregnate a woman; the need of certain individuals who were deprived of adequate parent figures to right that wrong by being parents themselves; and the need of lonely individuals to fulfill their need for love through a child.

Often inadequate sex education contributes to the woman's lack of understanding of herself and her natural sexual desires which then are not woven meaningfully into her life plan. Such a woman may rationalize her need for intimate relations with a conviction that she indeed intends to bear the child of her mate. For a number of young people, the family and peer response to the unmarried pregnant state or single parent status is one of causative acceptance, primarily because they have proved their femaleness. The adolescent experiencing pregnancy and childbirth outside marriage often becomes a person of great interest to her same-sex peers, whose questions within their own families have been curtailed with respect to sex, pregnancy, and birth.

There are religious and cultural groups within American society who place a high value on children. With individuals from such groups, the conceived fetus most often is not aborted and a place is found for the child within the extended family system.

The nurse needs to be aware of the various possibilities of the cultural expectations of men and how their self-images often cause them to regard childbearing in terms of virility. If the father sees the expected child only as an expression of his need to create life, his feelings must be taken into account, and he advisedly should be offered the option of finding a way to provide for the physical and emotional well-being of the mother and the child.

Finally, many women who have difficulty feeling loved or loving effectively will meet their needs for love through superficial love or sexual relations, and look to the child as a source of continual love which they do not believe themselves capable of achieving in another long-range meaningful way. However, it should be pointed out that babies who fall into this last category of expectations often are victims of child abuse when the realities of the demands of childrearing disappoint and overwhelm the parent seeking mainly to be loved.

THE SINGLE-PARENT FAMILY

Since World War II, the movement of women from the home into industrial positions has increased, rapidly providing the opportunity for them to be self-reliant even though the median salary for women is about one-half of what it is for men, and quality child care is not available for all those in need. In 1970 there were 31,560,000 women, or 43.4 percent of the female population of the United States, holding full-time jobs outside the home, as opposed to 12,845,000 women, or 25.4 percent of the female population, in 1940.[4] The percent of working women continues to increase. Russia has the highest percentage (82 percent) of working women between the ages of fifteen and sixty-four. Percentages in some other countries are: Hungary, 73 percent; Finland, 62 percent; Japan, 56 percent; England, 52 percent; United States, 49 percent; Australia, 45 percent; Norway, 39 percent; Italy, 29 percent; Portugal, 25 percent.[5] This economic self-reliance has made it possible for women to take over financial responsibilities for having and rearing their own children outside the usual context of marriage. Today in America, nearly 7 million families with children under the age of eighteen are headed by women.[6] For a woman who chooses, for whatever reasons, to bear a child as a single parent the following factors need consideration.

Emotional Needs

A woman who feels secure in her ability to raise a child on her own has a range of choice in her life vital to her mental health. She has not based her decision to bear a child on the condition that she will be able to find a father for her family (even though finding a mate to actualize her and join with her in supporting the growth of her child most likely will be one of the options she considers as she considers her own goals in life). A woman needs someone with whom to share her anxieties and concerns about pregnancy, as well as the positive experiences. At the end of her pregnancy she needs someone to help her release emotions about her childrearing responsibilities. Her life with her child may involve feelings of anger, love, irritation, or all three, involving the male, which result from her need for support and help.

Economic Needs

A parent who chooses not to work will need to consider obtaining aid to dependent children (ADC) or some other kind of social welfare assistance. In the one-parent family where the parent is required to work outside the home, the task of meeting the emotional needs of the child will, by necessity, fall to a large extent upon the persons caring for the child while the mother is away. The impor-

tance of early childhood stability, consistency, and security should not be underemphasized. Most people who are able to deal with diversity and are flexible and mature are so largely because of having been raised in an environment which fostered the development of trust as well as a feeling of competence in dealing with the world around them. Most of our status symbols such as job titles, homes, cars, and paychecks are tangible and of great importance in enhancing our self-esteem. For the working mother locked into our kind of specialized, dehumanized work system the tendency may well be to use the same kinds of rewards for her child that are provided for herself. Thus, it is of utmost importance that a person considering a one-parent family give thought to the implication of substituting tangible rewards for emotional ones.

The emotional needs of the mother and the child need to be understood by the mother who will necessarily be making the decisions about and the arrangements for her work and the child's care. According to some childrearing authorities, the implications of women combining work and parenthood has been that these factors frustrate the developmental needs of children. However, a parent who finds her work outside the home actualizing, rather than a job just for money, brings to the situation an element of security about herself and about finding quality care for her child which is vitally instrumental in the child's success. Her actualization sharpens her sensitivity toward what is necessary for the survival and growth of her family. For most parents a balance between mothering at home and working outside for part of each day or week seems most ideal. In our society this points to the need for increasing opportunities for women (and men) to work on part-time, flexible, or free-lance schedules to incorporate parenting more meaningfully into their ways of life. Such flexibility would facilitate the ability of parents, single or not, working cooperatively to provide child care on an alternating basis for each other. In general, the mother who works comes home to the demands of motherhood and unless her job is actualizing she will have a struggle finding adequate time for her own rest and relaxation.

Family Interaction

Unless more than one offspring is produced the parent and child within the family setting will either be in agreement or at odds without anyone to play the role of mediator. When a mother becomes frustrated with the behavior of the child, she needs another adult to listen to her complaints or to relieve her of the demanding role of parenting. It is also valuable for the child to have the option of more than one source of love and nurturing so that if one parent is at odds with the child, the child does not feel abandoned.

Sexual Identification

Evidence supported by Dr. Warren Gadpaille, in an article entitled "Biological Fallacies of Women's Lib," suggests that the brain is "programmed" during early embryonic development for masculine or feminine preferences in behavior. According to Gadpaille, the origin of this normal differentiation is the presence or absence of fetal androgens during very early intrauterine life. After the sex chromosomes determine whether ovaries or testes will develop, fetal hormones take over sexual differentiation. The presence or absence of the male hormone androgen not only determines male or female morphology but also organizes the hypothalamus to release sex-specific and sex-appropriate mating and social behav-

ior.[7] The existence of such early biological differentiation would suggest that males are programmed to be more aggressive and to find satisfaction in aggressive activities while females are more oriented toward passivity. If this is true, what would be the effect of counter-role conditioning by a single parent oriented toward the opposite type of behavior?

The goal of today's family in childrearing is the actualization of the individual and the stabilization of the adult personality. Economic and nurturing roles are interchanged between fathers and mothers. The example of both parents as viable individuals capable of making decisions vital to family survival, which includes making demands upon children in support of such goals, must begin to replace male and female *sex typing*. Often in the two-parent family, the father is absent due to demands of business, his desire to be free of the responsibility of raising children, or for other reasons of personal choice. In contradiction to earlier studies, it has been found that the physical absence of the father seems the least significant of the factors that possibly contribute to juvenile delinquency. However, studies have shown that women who are capable of sexual fulfillment in adult life most likely have shared dependable, caring relationships with their fathers. The ability of women to trust men and allow themselves to be completely free (or at ease) with them is related to their childhood experiences with responsible male figures.

Ideally we will arrive at a point some day where the sexes can be made to feel that they are complementary rather than conflictual, and role assimilation can take place by way of positive examples rather than by negative, opposite-sex examples. In the meantime, it behooves the person considering a one-parent family to give thought to the implications of rearing a member of the opposite sex without the opportunities for the reality of heterosexual involvement. Once she has made the decision to do so, however, a woman need not be uneasy about raising a male child, providing she is aware of the possible implications.

Practical Suggestions

In working with expectant parents and delivered mothers, a nurse plays an important role in the success of the family by relating to the uniqueness of each parent's particular concerns and questions, helping them to identify critical issues, and designing plans of action. As nurses work with prospective parents in considering the implications of single parenthood, they also have the opportunity to create a program for the positive involvement of the male. From starting a dialogue between prospective fathers and boyfriends in the clinic waiting room to working with both parents together, the nurse can build toward the goal of helping all concerned look realistically at the needs of the child. The nurse can stimulate discussion by asking basic, nonthreatening, well-planned questions such as the following: "Can you think of how your parents related to you?" "How would you have changed your parents' approach?" "What do you feel about people?" or "How do you feel about children?"

Nurses' awareness of community resources makes their contribution to the welfare of the new family even greater. Welfare programs, aid to dependent children, housing projects, single-parent dwellings, daycare centers and homes, family planning agencies, academic programs offering financial aid and student placement, and work possibilities conducive to mental health and childrearing are among the possibilities for support the family will need. Nurses' abilities to relate as caring human beings in a community to whom the family can look for realistic emotional support in and out of crisis is their most vital function.

CONCLUSION

It has become increasingly apparent that in spite of the abundant availability of birth control, many women resist avoiding pregnancy. This chapter has attempted to show that increased knowledge of self, including the sexual self, is elementary to fostering the positive choice of parenthood based upon the adult's ability to responsibly rear a child. Family life educators wish for every individual the development of skills which lead to meaningful relating. They know that problems not dealt with directly perpetuate themselves and create an atmosphere of such magnitude that real issues almost completely disappear. Professionals who understand themselves can aid others in airing their true feelings in an atmosphere of understanding. Thus, people who arrive at self-acceptance are better able to employ their energies toward more effective relating, thus setting a new precedent in positive parenting.

REFERENCES

1   Maslow, Abraham H.: "A Dynamic Theory of Human Motivation," *Psychological Review*, 50:370–396, 1943.

2   ———: *Motivation and Personality*, 2d ed., Harper & Row, New York, 1970, pp. 161–180.

3   Schlesinger, Benjamin: *The One-Parent Family*, University of Toronto Press, Toronto, 1969, pp. 113–115.

4   Golenpaul, Dan (ed.): *Information Please Almanac*, U.S. Bureau of Statistics, Simon & Schuster, New York, 1972, p. 126.

5   Schearer, Lloyd: "Intelligence Report," in

Parade section of *The Rocky Mountain News,*
Nov. 23, 1975, p. 6.

6 *U.S. News & World Report,* p. 85, Dec. 2,
1974, from data compiled by U.S. Census
Bureau.

7 Gadpaille, Warren J.: "Biological Fallacies
of Women's Lib," *Hospital Physician,* Medical Economics Inc., subsidiary of Litton,
Oradell, N.J., July 1971, p. 2.

UNIT C

GOALS OF MATERNITY CARE

7

The Impact of Individual Differences on Maternity Care

BEVERLY M. HORN

Individual differences such as age, race, socioeconomic status, cultural background, religion, and education, as well as the geographic areas of residence, have a decided effect on the outcome of maternity care today. The health care delivery system also has a tremendous impact on maternity care. Prior to a discussion of some of these factors, however, it would be advisable to review the current status and trends of maternity care today as reflected in the available statistics.

BIRTH RATES

In the United States, the birth rate has fluctuated over the past three to four decades. The low birth rates of the 1930s plunged to an all-time low of 16.6 per 1,000 population in 1933. This was followed by a gradual increase of births until 1947, when the post-World War II "baby boom" raised the rate to an all-time high of 25.8 per 1,000 population.

A slight decrease in births to approximately 25.0 occurred, and this was maintained at a rather stable level for the next 10 years. In 1958 a trend toward a more marked reduction in births began. By 1963 the rate had decreased to 21.7, and by 1967 the rate was 17.8. Finally, in 1973 and 1974 the rate was 14.9 births per 1,000 population.[1] Racial differences are quite apparent in the birth rate; this can be seen in the data listed in Table 7-1.

TABLE 7-1
Birth Rates by Race 1945–1973*

Year	White	Nonwhite	Total population
1973	13.9	21.9	14.9
1972	14.6	22.9	15.6
1971	16.2	24.7	17.2
1970	17.4	25.1	18.4
1969	16.9	24.4	17.8
1968	16.6	24.2	17.5
1965	18.3	27.6	19.4
1960	22.7	32.1	23.7
1955	23.8	34.7	25.0
1950	23.0	33.3	24.1
1945	19.7	26.5	20.4

* Birth rate per 1,000 population.
SOURCE: U.S. Department of Health, Education, and Welfare, Public Health Service, National Center for Health Statistics, *Vital Statistics 1968*, vol. 1, *Natality*, 1970; and *Monthly Vital Statistics Report, Summary Report Final Natality Statistics, 1973*, Jan. 30, 1975.

When maternity care is under consideration, numbers and rates of births are important. These statistics, which are affected by fertility rates, are computed by the size and the age groups of women who are in the childbearing years, which are considered to be from fifteen to forty-four years of age. The fertility rate remained above the level of the 1930s until 1972. In 1936, the childbearing population constituted 24 percent of the total population, and in 1973 it was 22 percent. As a result of the decline in this population, the fertility of these women cannot maintain the birth rate of the total population at the same level relative to the fertility rate as in the 1930s. In 1973 the fertility rate was 69.2 births per 1,000 women fifteen to forty-four years of age, the lowest ever observed in the United States.[2]

MATERNAL MORTALITY

Although dramatically reduced in recent years, maternal mortality rates are still very important. These rates refer to deaths caused by complications of pregnancy, childbirth, and the puerperium. Because of the drastic reduction in rates that has occurred, the basis for computation of the rates has changed. Prior to 1960, the rate was determined on the basis of 10,000 live births; since 1960 it is based on 100,000 live births. The decline in maternal deaths has been consistent, with the 1973 rate at 15.2.[3] The overall rate in 1973 was 19.1 percent below the rate for 1972, declining 25.2 percent for white women, and only 10.1 percent for nonwhite women. The maternal mortality rate for nonwhite women was 3.2 times that for white women.[4] Table 7-2 shows the decline in maternal mortality for selected years.

Although the maternal death rate is low, it should be remembered that the actual number of maternal deaths in 1973 was 477.[5] This large number of maternal deaths should be of serious consequence for those planning maternity care in the future, as almost all causes of maternal deaths today are preventable. Hemorrhage and sepsis should, theoretically, be completely preventable. Toxemia has been reduced markedly in the past but continues to be the number one cause of maternal deaths.[6]

TABLE 7-2
Maternal Mortality Rates by Race 1950–1973*

Year	White	Nonwhite	Total population
1973	10.7	34.6	15.2
1972	14.3	38.5	18.8
1971	13.0	45.3	18.8
1970	14.4	55.9	21.5
1969	15.5	55.7	22.2
1968	16.6	63.6	24.5
1967	19.5	69.5	28.0
1965	21.0	83.7	31.6
1960	26.0	97.9	37.1
1955	32.8	130.3	47.0
1950	61.1	221.6	83.3

* Per 100,000 live births.
SOURCE: 1950–1968 statistics from U.S. Department of Commerce, Bureau of the Census, *Statistical Abstract of the United States*, 1973. Other statistics from U.S. Department of Health, Education, and Welfare, Public Health Service, National Center for Health Statistics, *Monthly Vital Statistics Report, Final Mortality Statistics, 1973*, Feb. 10, 1975.

The most dramatic reduction in maternal deaths was the decrease in deaths due to toxemia of pregnancy. For the white population, the ages of thirty to forty-five pose a great hazard in relation to toxemia. The nonwhite population is also affected during these years but has a high rate of deaths due to toxemia at all ages. The total rate of maternal deaths due to toxemia for the white population is 2.2 per 100,000 live births, while the total rate of maternal deaths in the nonwhite population due to toxemia is 9.2.[7] In 1973, toxemia was the major specified cause of maternal deaths, followed by sepsis and hemorrhage, respectively. Hemorrhage has been reduced consistently as a cause of death. Frequently, sepsis is indirectly caused from hemorrhage, for the pregnant woman develops infection because of a weakened condition from blood loss.

When the causes of maternal mortality are

examined more closely, it is evident that they are potentially eradicable, especially in the cases of the three major causes of death. They are causes of morbidity that should never occur today. Therefore, the maternal mortality rates should be reduced significantly in the future. Those concerned with maternal care, especially nurses, should continue to focus with vigilance on prevention of maternal mortality and morbidity.

PERINATAL MORTALITY

Perinatal mortality statistics are also important indices of maternity care. Standards of maternity care have improved, and the rate of maternal deaths is no longer considered to be an adequate index of the quality of maternity care that occurs today. The *WHO Chronicle* indicated that this is appropriate inasmuch as care during pregnancy today tends to be aimed at the fetus, and good fetal care implies good maternity care.[8]

Infant mortality, or the number of deaths in the first year of life per 1,000 live births, is the rate most frequently used in comparing the United States with other countries. The United States ranked fifteenth among other developed nations.[9] The reduction in infant mortality rates occurred most dramatically from 1920 through 1950.[10] Since then, the decline has been much slower. The discrepancy that exists between the white and nonwhite population continues. The infant mortality rate in 1973 was 17.7 per 1,000 live births. For nonwhites the rate was 26.2 and for whites it was 15.8.[11]

Neonatal mortality, i.e., deaths per 1,000 live births in the first 4 weeks after birth, has declined from a rate of 32.4 in 1935 to 13.0 in 1973. However, in 1973, the neonatal period accounted for 73.2 percent of infant mortality, just as it did in 1968.[12] Implications for research involving the neonatal period, as well as concerted effort for improvement of health care during this period, should be a high priority for those in the health field.

PERINATAL MORBIDITY

Perinatal morbidity is frequently associated with perinatal mortality as the cause of death. In addition, many infants survive this traumatic period only to be left with serious physiological and neurological deficits. The high incidence of mental retardation, cerebral palsy, and other forms of cerebral dysfunction testify to the grave problems associated with perinatal morbidity. Also, the number of handicapped children born as a result of genetic disturbances or poor intrauterine environment has continued to grow.

Reflection on the preceding array of facts and statements about maternal and infant status today leads to speculation as to what has brought about this situation. Further questions might also be asked, for example: What is maintaining the situation currently? What societal changes are occurring that might direct the way to improved care? What is it about being black, being poor, and living in an urban area, or being Native American, poor, and living in an urban or reservation setting, that precipitates the discrepancy that exists in the quality of care that is delivered? Who is, in fact, the recipient of maternity care today? What is the "high-risk"population in both maternal and infant categories? Probably the most difficult question to answer is: How do the complex variables on all levels—psychosocial, cultural, and physiological—interact? Further, how can health care personnel intervene effectively to promote optimum outcome of pregnancy for the family, based on knowledge of the interaction of these variables?

Much of the research done to determine factors associated with perinatal mortality and morbidity has identified the same factors that are associated with maternal mortality and morbidity. The recurrence in the literature of many of the same factors lends credibility to their importance. Some of the most important are cultural background; ethnicity; socioeconomic status; reproductive history of the mother; geographic location; age of the mother; the course of pregnancy; and antepartum care.[13,14]

PREMATURITY

Prematurity has been identified as a major correlate of perinatal mortality. As a single indicator, it is probably the most sensitive index of the interrelationships of individual differences on reproductive outcome. Prematurity can actually encompass both low-gestational-age infants, under 38 weeks' gestation, and low-birth-weight infants. The differences between premature and low-birth-weight infants must be considered when one is searching for causes of morbidity and mortality. Some ethnic groups, the black population for example, have full-term infants of low birth weight.

Premature onset of labor and infants with low birth weight, resulting more frequently in perinatal deaths, recur among certain groups. Hunt has pointed out that because of the frequent association between mortality and social factors, excessive mortality rates may serve to identify neighborhoods and larger areas in the United States that have a high incidence of social handicaps.[15] Peckham has stated that the relationship of a great deal of fetal and infant morbidity and mortality (reflected in premature onset of labor) relates more closely to psychosocial and economic factors than to specific pathologic conditions of pregnancy.[16] A disproportionate number of perinatal casualties occur in certain segments of the population, such as minority groups and particularly the socially deprived. This relationship of sociocultural variables such as age, race, family, and ecological factors to biological factors was also noted by Nesbitt.[17]

Perhaps the most serious reason for consideration of prematurity as reflecting the complexities of the problem of maternity care is the fact that the incidence of prematurity is actually increasing. Fetal deaths, which are not reflected in either infant or neonatal death rates, often occur with premature onset of labor. If prematurity has been the major cause of perinatal mortality and morbidity in the past, its increase is a fearful sign. Gold, in an introduction to Wallace's article, indicated that even though there has been a 14.2 percent reduction in infant mortality since 1961, the current rate is still high.[18] This statement remains true even though there was a 4.3 percent reduction in infant mortality from 1972 to 1973.[19] Prematurity not only continues to be the major cause of infant death but is increasing in incidence.[20] In studying the problem of prematurity, the previous reproductive history of the mother is of major concern. Tompkins noted three areas that should have priority in obstetric care: adolescent pregnancy, multiparity, and previous history of premature delivery. The mother who has delivered prematurely is very likely to do so again.[21] A previous history of premature delivery, then, signals the presence of a high-risk mother who may deliver a high-risk infant. Shapiro stated that women who have had one or more premature births have from 3 to 4 times the risk of early termination of further pregnancies with low-birth-weight or premature infants than those who have had previous pregnancies ending in mature births.[22]

In addition, Shapiro pointed out that the risk of fetal death in pregnancies preceded by a fetal death is from 2 to 3 times the corresponding rate when only mature live births occurred previously.[22] For maternity care of the future, it is imperative, then, that the past history of the mother in regard to low birth weight, low gestational age, and previous fetal deaths be of major consideration. Wiener, in studying the correlates of low birth weight and low gestational age, used regression analyses with a number of factors and discovered that race and the trimester in which the mother received antepartum care were most significant. Nevertheless, he also stated that these two factors (low birth weight and low gestational age) were not the only causes of maternal and infant difficulties, but that other variables correlated with the mother's race and the trimester in which she received antepartum care.[23]

SOCIOECONOMIC STATUS

A factor in the delivery of maternity care which seems to subsume several other factors is that of the socioeconomic status of the mother. Wallace indicated there was a close relationship between socioeconomic status and infant mortality. She noted that the average infant mortality rates for 1963 for the low-income group (both white and nonwhite) of 17 states was 19 percent higher than the national average.[24] Low birth weight, which in itself can result in morbidity and mortality of the infant, was also associated with low socioeconomic status. The low birth weight of nonwhites, especially blacks, points to the need for further study of the relationship of low socioeconomic status to infant morbidity and mortality. By 1971, 12.5 percent of all families had an annual income under $3,000: 9.9 percent of the white population and 30.9 percent of the nonwhite population had an annual income below $3,000.[25]

Education

A number of studies have shown that education is a variable in the outcome of pregnancy. Rosenwaike viewed educational attainment of the mother as a major indicator of the parents' socioeconomic status. He found that the incidence of low birth weight varied inversely with the educational level of the mother. This relationship of education to low birth weight was maintained even when he controlled for the mother's age, birth order, and source and timing of antepartum care.[26] As previously mentioned, the highest incidence of low birth weight occurs in the black population. In 1973, of those black mothers giving birth, 51.1 percent had completed 12 years or more of formal schooling, whereas white mothers had 73.3 percent completing 12 years or more of formal schooling.[27]

Poverty

Poverty is frequently associated with inferior health, and this is evident in poor maternal and infant health. Bierman, in discussing her experiences in maternity care, noted that very little is known regarding the precise relationship between poverty and health and how the various components of low socioeconomic status affect biological functioning and behavior.[28] The inability of the poor to procure health care is well known. Even when care is available, as in urban areas, it may be inaccessible to a majority of the poor. Various studies have been made to determine precisely why health care is not sought by poor mothers; most frequently, lack of transportation and lack of babysitting services were the ostensible reasons given. The anthropologist Oscar Lewis pointed out that profound feelings of apathy, hopelessness, and despair exist among the poor, as they realize that the values of the dominant middle class cannot be realized.[29]

Nancy Milio, a nurse, proposed and found support for her proposal that the maternity care system, based on values of a middle-class culture, was inaccessible to those who hold an alternate and opposing view of life.[30] Elliot Liebow, an anthropologist, argues that the difference between people in poverty groups and those with higher socioeconomic status is *not* present-time versus future-time orientations, respectively, but rather that the two groups have different future-time orientations—more specifically, different futures.[31] He emphasizes the fact that poverty-group people are acutely aware of the future, contrary to the notions that they are present-time oriented. Poverty-group people visualize their future from observing others around them who have not succeeded and who are in a hopeless state, which leads Liebow to state:

It is a future in which everything is uncertain except the ultimate destruction of . . . hopes and the eventual realization of . . . fears. The most he can reasonably look forward to is that these things do not come too soon.[32]

Valentine, in discussing the behavior of persons who are poor, stresses that they may have values which cannot be realized because opportunities to choose goals are objectively narrowed by the structure of the society in which they live.[33]

Further, Strauss pointed out that the poor are not capable of coping with the complexities of the organization of bureaucracy of the health care delivery system.[34] Large buildings and impersonalization are in direct conflict with their lack of sophistication in an impersonal situation. Accustomed to dealing on a personal basis, they are confounded by the situation of a large organization. Strauss indicated that their sense of discomfort in the middle-class world further alienates them from the system devised to bring them health care. Their reliance on personal relationships to achieve their goals cannot be realized, and they withdraw from the health care system as it exists today. Tompkins noted that in most areas of the United States there has been little change in the character and quality of health services delivered to this most vulnerable group, the poor.[35]

CULTURAL BACKGROUND

Another factor, indicated in the statistics at the beginning of this chapter and closely related to the outcome of maternity care, is that of race. Actually, "race," "culture," and "ethnic group" are terms which do have precise definitions, but in the literature they are used almost interchangeably. There is controversy regarding the definitions of each term, and the area of overlap in the meanings is significant. Even at the risk of obscuring differences, we have chosen to use these terms to refer to differences in *life-style* exhibited by a group. It is believed that in the pluralistic society (a term which is also controversial) of the United States, the primary differences among racial groups, cultural groups, or ethnic groups appear to exist primarily in the life-styles exhibited by them. To the extent that a difference in life-style indicates a difference in value systems and attitudes, behavior will vary. Thus, if a different life-style exists among groups, there will be different approaches to the problems of health and therefore to maternity care.

The dominant group in the United States whose value system has permeated health care delivery is that of the white middle class. Those with a different sociocultural background have the greatest number of problems in attempting to cope with the system of health care delivery. The poor have a particular problem.

The largest number of the poor in the United States is the nonwhite group. For the most part, included within this group is the black population, and the Native American, Mexican-American, and Asian groups. These groups have retained many of the values of their own culture relative to health. The special meanings that childbearing and childrearing have for each group must be considered. The poor results of maternity care in the nonwhite group as witnessed in the statistics cannot be attributed to poverty alone. Each group has special needs that have not yet been met.

Racial and cultural barriers to health care are multiple. The perceptions and belief systems of the nonwhite population regarding the pregnancy area of health care have been shown to vary most from that of the white middle class. Thus, efforts to improve maternity care, based on a value system different from their own, have been significantly unproductive. Maternity care more congruent with the beliefs and life-styles of those for whom it is planned would be more effective.

In 1973, the age-adjusted death rate for the nonwhite population was 1.4 times the corresponding rate for white persons.[36] This fact obscures major differences, for the highest perinatal mortality rates were in the Native American and black groups, respectively; whereas the Japanese-American and Chinese-American rates were actually lower than those for the white population. In 1971, the infant mortality rate of 19.0 consisted of a white rate of 16.6 and a nonwhite rate of 32.5. Of the nonwhite group, 50 percent was Native American and 40 percent was black. Highlighted here, then, is the acute severity of the health problems of both Native Americans and blacks. Gold summed up the problem when he discussed the importance of lack of reduction in our infant mortality rate. He expressed great concern over the disparity in statistics and the differential that existed in pregnancy outcome between the white and nonwhite populations.[37]

The Native American

A group for whom delivery of maternity care has assumed almost crisis proportions, as viewed from the statistical standpoint, is the Native American. While the nonwhite population of the United States is approximately 12 percent of the total population, the Native American population is less than 0.3 of 1 percent of the total population and only 2.3 percent of all nonwhites.[38] A definition of the health problem of this group defies those who have attempted it. Determining exactly who is and who is not a Native American is in itself fraught with difficulty, especially in urban areas.

The poor health of the reservation Native American is well documented. A situation of abject poverty exists for most Native Americans on reservations. Urban Native Americans today are beset by many problems which make them vulnerable to frequent illness and disease and high infant mortality rates, resulting in disastrous outcomes. The urban Native American is lost in the shuffle among all minority groups. The studies of urban poor and of minorities are done predominantly with blacks or whites, and the results have been indiscriminately applied to Native Americans. Few studies have been done to determine factors which have precipitated the poor health status of the Native American both on and off the reservation.

In an unpublished exploratory study carried out recently by the author of this chapter to determine the perceptions of a group of Northwest coast Native American women concerning health care during pregnancy, certain facts emerged, together with their perceptions of the role of the nurse. The importance of other tribal members, especially the extended family, in health care behavior was apparent. All informants expressed constant concern about health matters and a great desire to know what was happening to them during pregnancy. Literature about pregnancy was eagerly accepted by all informants when it was offered to them. A cultural norm expressed by, and adhered to, was that Native American women do not ask questions. Their expectation was that nurses and other health care workers would know what they needed to know.

Although health care was available, albeit fragmented, it was usually used only in crisis situations. Past dehumanizing experiences, associated with prejudice and alienation, kept them from pursuing available health care. Furthermore, the traditional model of antepartum care based on a white middle-class value system, which did not take into consideration daily life crises, was not understood and acceptable to them. Incorporation of the Shaker religion, indigenous to the Northwest, occurred in all aspects of prevention and curing of illness. The Shaker religion combines elements from Native American religion, Catholicism, and fundamentalist Protestantism.

Social scientists are increasingly aware that a dual medical system, the Native American's and the white man's, exists on Native American reservations, and these dual systems are carried over to urban Native American settings. Many Native Americans believe that their "medicine" is complementary to that of the white man. Their medicines, given to them by their Maker, are claimed to cure a vast array of maladies, including gallbladder disease, diabetes, epilepsy, and heart and lung diseases. Indigenous health care and Maker-prescribed medicines are pervasive and are viable cultural components of Native American communities.

Relations between Native American populations and those who deliver health care are often strained due to the fact that two medical systems exist side by side. Each is as dedicated as the other to the end product: prevention of disease and curing illness. However, there is disparity regarding the means to the end. It is the responsibility of the health care worker to understand, appreciate, and incorporate the Native American medical system into the delivery of health care to this population in the United States. This will not be a panacea for the health-related difficulties with which Native Americans are confronted. However, it will be an important step in the attempt to develop more effective systems of health care for the Native American population.

It is encouraging to note that physicians on the Navaho reservation in northeastern Arizona recognize the importance of the indigenous medical system, and that they are engaged in efforts to include Navaho medicine men or shamans as members of the health care team. Monies have been appropriated by the United States government for older shamans to train younger ones so that their healing arts and powers and cultural heritage can be retained.

The birth rate among Native Americans is much higher than in both the white and nonwhite populations. The birth rates for Native Americans in 1971 was 33 per 1,000 live births; for whites, 16.2; and for all other nonwhites, 24.7.[39] Maternal deaths in 1971 had a rate of 38.3 for Native Americans, whereas the overall United States rate was 20.5.[40] These are just a few of the facts that point to the existence of a very complex health problem.

As previously mentioned, infant mortality rates are recognized as important indices of the quality and quantity of maternal health care. The Native American infant mortality rate upholds this assertion; for 1973 it was 18.9 per 1,000 live births.[41] This frightening situation presented a serious challenge to the health care worker, and today most deliveries of Native Americans occur in the

hospital, and the mortality rate for the first week of life has been reduced below that for all United States races. In the postneonatal period, that is from 28 days through 11 months of age, the Native American mortality rate is 11.2, whereas that for all United States races is 4.9.[42] In 1969 the average life expectancy for Native Americans was forty-four years of age, and suicide among teenagers was 5 times the national average.[43] This information should result, it seems, in a mandate for improved maternal and child health care in the future for the Native American population.

The Black American

Problems associated with maternity care and the black population have been well documented, and this group is one of the target populations about which nursing should be especially concerned. Problems of low birth weight and/or prematurity appear to be almost endemic, statistically, to this specific population. In 1973 the proportion of black infants of low birth weight was 13.3 percent, more than twice as high as the proportion of white infants, which was 6.4 percent.[44] There is a much higher incidence of multiple births, frequently accompanied by complications, in the black population. For the total population of the United States, the multiple birth ratio was 18.4 live births in multiple deliveries per 1,000 total live births. For the white population the ratio was 17.7; the ratio for the black population was 22.2.[45]

In 1973, there was a marked discrepancy between white and black pregnant women regarding which month of pregnancy that antepartum care was begun. Almost 75 percent of white mothers began care during the first trimester, while only 51.5 percent of black mothers began care at this trimester.

Only 1.1 percent of white mothers had no care in contrast to 3.4 percent of black mothers.[46]

Among infants born to mothers having no antepartum care, 21.1 percent were in the low-birth-weight category (2,500 g or less), while among those born to mothers with some care, only 7.2 percent were in this category. The proportion of low-birth-weight infants born to white mothers having no antepartum care was 17.5 percent; the proportion born to black mothers having no antepartum care was 27.4 percent. For white mothers having some antepartum care, the proportion of low-birth-weight infants was 6.2 percent; for black mothers having some antepartum care, the proportion was 12.6.[47] Also, in 1973 the infant mortality rate for blacks was 28.1 per 1,000 live births.

In contrast to the Native American, who is scattered throughout urban areas, the black family in the urban area is concentrated primarily in the central city. The problems associated with poor housing, poor education, poor recreational facilities, and overcrowding place a high level of stress on family structure and relationships. A breakdown in health is common, and health care is least accessible to this group.

AGE

Age has been considered a rather crucial variable in the outcome of pregnancy. Basic physiological differences exist at various stages during the childbearing years. The adolescent's physiology differs considerably from that of the young mature adult. Also, the immediately premenopausal woman has problems unique to her age group. Aside from the physiological considerations, crucial psychosocial variables in the different age groups affect the outcome of maternity care. Utilization of birth control methods, parity, infant mortality and morbidity rates,

and maternal complications are just some of the problems that have a direct relationship to the age of the mother.

Adolescence

In women between the ages of fifteen to nineteen a high perinatal mortality rate occurs; this rate declines during the decade of the twenties. During the decades of the thirties and forties there is a rapid increase in the rate of perinatal mortality.[48] As indicated previously, premature labor is one of the most common causes of perinatal mortality, and very young and older mothers are the target groups which have a high incidence of low-gestational-age and/or low-birth-weight infants. Tompkins stated that low-birth-weight and low-gestational-age infants, as determined through reports from maternal and infant care projects, are highest among patients under the age of eighteen and over the age of thirty-five.[49]

The phrase "most vulnerable group" is used repeatedly in the literature to refer to the adolescent who is pregnant. The teenage mother frequently comes from a low-income group. The reproductive outcome for the low-income mother is often poor, and it is even more likely to be poor if she is also a teenager. In a study done with a stable low-income rural population in Florida, Held looked at reproductive trends for the years 1967 through 1969. In this geographic area, the primigravida formed the bulk of the obstetric population, and teenagers comprised 75 percent of all primigravidas.[50] His overwhelming conclusion was that teenagers have to be reached prior to conception. Although births and birth rates have decreased for the general population, there has been an increase for women under fifteen years of age. In 1972, the number of births for women under fifteen years of age increased 6 percent, and in 1973 it increased 8 percent.[51]

Tompkins, in a study aimed at reviewing national efforts to reduce perinatal mortality and morbidity, referred to the school-age pregnant girl who has the stress of pregnancy imposed during a period of maximal growth and development. He noted that society has a punitive attitude toward a school-age pregnant girl, especially if the pregnancy is out of wedlock, and that rarely can such a girl have the quality and standard of care necessary for a healthy pregnancy.[52] This is a rather sad commentary, not only on society, but also on the status of health care delivery to a most important group in the population. Hunscher and Tompkins also noted the relationship between adolescence and maternal and infant mortality and morbidity. They felt it was a mandate for health care workers to make intensive efforts to improve preventive and remedial care of adolescents who are pregnant.[53]

Birth Control

The need to reach the teenager prior to the first pregnancy with birth control information has been set as a priority in many of the maternity care programs. Janus, in a study with low-income groups in the District of Columbia, showed that the consistent use of birth control methods varied, depending on marital status and age. Women under twenty years old and those never married practiced birth control the least.[54] Von der Ahe in Los Angeles asked unwed mothers about the use of contraception, and 87 percent denied using it at all.[55] Thus, clearer understanding of the need for and use of contraceptives by adolescents seems to be a priority for maternity care in the future.

Nutrition

Nutrition is the single factor most responsible for the outcome of pregnancy. Low-income groups may be in a chronic state of malnutrition. The need of the pregnant woman for an adequate diet during pregnancy is accepted by health care workers, but the importance of an adequate state of nutrition prior to the onset of pregnancy is just as crucial. Many cultural patterns pertaining to food affect nutritional status, and ethnic background has a decided influence on nutrition.

Teenagers have always been known for ignoring the rules of good nutrition. Poor eating habits, often associated with food fads such as the macrobiotic diet, have contributed to an increased nutritional deficiency in adolescents today. Since the kinds of food eaten by adolescents are frequently high in calories but of poor quality, obesity may occur. This is especially true if pregnancy imposes an alteration in physical activity.

Poor nutritional status at the beginning of pregnancy imposes a severe hazard. If the vital needs of adolescents for normal growth and development are not met, the needs of the developing fetus are severely endangered. Osofsky, reviewing the data relating antepartum nutrition to subsequent infant and child development, pointed out that malnutrition prior to birth can influence subsequent developmental problems.[56] However, the data relative to the effects of malnutrition on the pregnant woman are not as clear. In the case of the adolescent, the additional demands of the developing fetus upon her state of undernutrition may at least predispose her to irreversible conditions of poor health.

Within the philosophy of maternity care today, it is apparent that focus must be placed on the total family. Nutrition has high priority in this relationship, since habits of good nutrition begin in the family context. Concern about the nutritional status of future pregnancies should begin at the time of the child's birth. Hunscher and Tompkins noted that a considerable amount of scientific literature has accumulated showing the significance of maternal nutrition to the course and outcome of pregnancy. They point out that pregnancy is a unique event, one that reflects the health status of past generations in current reproductive efficiency.[57]

Role Models

Another variable that affects maternity care of adolescents is the imitation of models. For an adolescent, those persons perceived to be most important are considered to be worthy of imitation. This phenomenon is a part of the normal maturation process. Prominent people in sports, politics, and in the entertainment world are frequently used as models.

Many of the models presented to adolescents today deviate considerably from what have been the white middle-class norms of society. This is especially true with regard to sexual practices and modes of family living. The impermanence of marriage, and the questioning of the importance of marriage at all, presents the adolescent with a number of "acceptable" alternatives not openly accepted in other times. The conflicts between what parents propose, and the currently "acceptable" alternatives, impose greater stresses upon the adolescent.

Other Age Groups

Although much of the emphasis in this section has been on health care of the adolescent, other age groups have individual differences which also affect maternity care. Because adolescence has been relatively neglected, the current focus must be on this group. However, the largest number of babies is born to women twenty to twenty-nine years old.

The highest perinatal mortality occurs in mothers fifteen to nineteen years old. The second most rapid climb is in mothers who are over thirty. The major causes of maternal morbidity and mortality are more prevalent in the age groups beyond adolescence. Of the 477 maternal deaths in 1973, distribution was among the following groups: ten to fourteen years, 6 deaths; fifteen to twenty-four years, 174 deaths; twenty-five to thirty-four years, 213 deaths; thirty-five to forty-four years, 81 deaths; and forty-five to fifty-four years, 2 deaths.[58]

In discussing toxemia of pregnancy, Hendricks notes that in certain women over thirty-five years of age there is a much greater tendency to develop toxemia than in those who are twenty to thirty-four years old.[59] This is especially true when there is an impoverished background and five or more previous pregnancies.[60] Toxemia can also be seen in the younger age groups in the presence of the above conditions, but to a lesser degree.

HEALTH CARE DISTRIBUTION

The need for government agencies to become involved in the delivery of adequate maternity care has increased through the years on both the national and local levels. Also, a number of voluntary agencies have become involved in the same endeavor. Tompkins has stated that the present situation concerning perinatal mortality and morbidity is untenable, and medical centers, local health departments, and other health professionals must coordinate their work with government efforts.[61]

Nonprofessionals

Utilization of the indigenous population in an attempt to improve the quality of maternity care has been attempted by many groups. In the District of Columbia, health education aides were used in counseling pregnant women. Success was reflected in a marked reduction in infant mortality and an increase in the number of mothers having antepartum care. Conn's report indicated that the aides moved into the community, and in the area of problems within the inner-city culture, they demonstrated their most valuable asset—familiarity with the life-styles of the women.[62] The aides attempted to deal with whatever stood in the way of the client's getting antepartum care—transportation problems, need for baby-sitting, etc.

In 1968, Denver set up a neighborhood health program with decentralization of services. The neighborhood health centers served a population of approximately 20,000. The reported outcomes were favorable, but the report stressed the fact that community involvement was a prerequisite to an effective program.[63]

Morton discussed experiences with a maternity and infant care project in the Los Angeles County Health Department. A multidisciplinary team was used, including the extended role of the nurse in antepartum care. One of the measures to determine success was the rate of broken appointments at the clinic. Prior to the project there were from 30 to 50 percent broken appointments, but after the project was begun these were reduced to 9 to 24 percent. Morton attributed the success of the project to the interdisciplinary teamwork that was involved plus close follow-up of the patients.[64]

In a study conducted by Planned Parenthood, New York City,[65] the use of paraprofessionals to motivate women to return for postpartum checkups was attempted. The paraprofessionals were recruited from the same neighborhood as the patients and had the same sociocultural background. Two comparative studies were done with patients from two hospitals: (1) persons who accepted family planning versus those who did not and (2) women who had failed to keep their postpartum appointments. It was felt that the use of paraprofessionals was very effective, both in getting the mothers back for their postpartum checkups and in helping them to decide on some form of family planning.

In the above mentioned studies, the message that successful delivery of maternity care appears to be dependent on self-involvement of those for whom it is planned comes through loudly and clearly. Although not specifically noted in these examples, the fact that programs planned and executed by outsiders exclusively seem doomed to failure is clearly demonstrated in the literature.

The Free Clinic

A phenomenon of recent years that has had a decisive impact on health care, including maternity care, is the free clinic. In the "First National Survey of Free Medical Clinics 1967–1969," Jerome Schwartz noted that the first free clinic was opened in the Haight-Ashbury district in San Francisco in 1967, followed in the same year by clinics in Cincinnati, Detroit, Seattle, and Vancouver, Canada. By the beginning of 1971, the total number of clinics was at least 135, and they have continued to multiply. A "free clinic" does not necessarily mean that there is no charge but that it is free of eligibility requirements, questions, and "bureaucratic hassle."[66] However, it was noted that free clinic patients have one thing in common: the are without resources to pay for medical care.[67]

This study identified four types of free clinics: neighborhood clinics, street clinics, youth clinics, and sponsored clinics. Not all clinics offered all types of services. Of 59 clinics studied, antepartum and postpartum care was provided by 24 clinics. Street clinics, of which there were 20, included 6 which offered these services, and neighborhood clinics, of which there were 23, included 14 which offered these services. Only 2 of the 9 youth clinics offered antepartum and postpartum care. Lastly, 2 of the 4 sponsored clinics offered these services.

The age groups served by each of the clinics were as follows: *Neighborhood clinics* served families with persons over thirty-five years old and children under twelve. Adolescents represented the smallest proportion of clients, but there was a moderate number of women clients nineteen to twenty-four years of age. The *youth clinics* have mostly sixteen- to eighteen-year olds, but also a sizable number of twelve- to fifteen-year olds. When one considers the previous information regarding age levels, with emphasis on the needs of the teenager during pregnancy, the information relative to free clinics poses a problem. Those clinics with the smallest number of adolescents, i.e., neighborhood clinics, offered both antepartum and postpartum care, whereas those which handled the largest number of teenagers, the street clinics, offered the least. In the *street clinic* group, only 6 offered these services, with the remaining 14 offering neither antepartum nor postpartum care. One would feel more comfortable about this fact if there was an adequate referral system with follow-up. However, the article on free clinics noted that although many centers made referrals for obstetric care, only four made direct arrangements for delivery and hospitalization.[68]

Home Delivery

An increasingly frequent phenomenon is the desire for home delivery. Dissatisfaction with previous antepartum and hospital care has led many disenchanted mothers to request home delivery with subsequent pregnancies. Some members of the so-called "youth subculture" also desire delivery at home, attended or unattended. The "do it yourself" way of thinking has entered into

maternity care. This trend seems to many to be totally out of line with what has been considered ideal maternity care in our society. Maternity care supervised by professionals, culminating in delivery in a hospital and followed by at least 6 weeks of care, has been the model. Many facets of this kind of care have been rejected by what is considered to be a significant segment of the population. In the Seattle–King County area the number of home deliveries in 1966 was 32 out of 18,676 or 1.5 per 1,000 births. In 1969, the rate had risen to 2.0 home deliveries per 1,000 births. In 1971, the rate of reported home deliveries was 5.8 per 1,000; in 1972, the rate was 8.2; and in 1973 it was 12.4. The number of home deliveries reported in 1973 was 167, and the number reported for the first half of 1974 was 122.[69] How accurate a picture this is of the total number delivered at home is not known, because there is evidence that some who have delivered at home without medical supervision did not register the births.

Some women planning home delivery attend classes held by nurses and physicians, but there may be many more who do not seek professional advice. Certainly there are many women who do not care to have professional persons in attendance at the delivery itself.

The implications of the trend toward home deliveries will have to be explored. Rejection of the traditional method of delivery of maternity care has been complete by this group. It would seem that new and unique approaches to maternity care will have to be instituted if this group is to be considered in planning for maternity care of the future.

ANTEPARTUM CARE

In this discussion of how individual differences affect maternity care, the concept of antepartum care has only been alluded to. This was not meant to negate its importance. Antepartum care has been shown to have a direct effect upon the outcome of pregnancy, and helps to ensure a healthy mother and baby. In looking at correlates of low birth weight, Wiener has noted that the trimester in which the mother obtains antepartum care has been significant.[70]

Which factors within the complex of what is called antepartum care are important is not really known. A number of relationships are established, and services are rendered by professionals to the pregnant woman and her mate. Which of these are crucial and which are not remains to be determined by further study. According to Milio, the structure of the antepartum care system is based on assumptions of middle-class culture,[71] and the system is effective for that particular group. The disparity in maternity outcome that exists between middle-income and low-income persons, however, has demonstrated that the traditional antepartum care model is ineffective for some segments of the population. Thus, a challenge for health care workers exists; they must be able to meet the needs of all groups in our society, not just the middle class.

CONCLUSION

A great deal can be learned about individual differences that affect maternity care by looking at the statistics of birth rates and of maternal and infant mortality and morbidity rates. The groups having successful maternal and infant outcomes as well as those with less satisfactory consequences can be readily seen. The discrepancies in levels of socioeconomic status, in age, in ethnic background, and in care sought or obtained are evident.

Prematurity, as an example of poor obstetric outcome, is intimately related to all the factors of individual differences. Inasmuch as prematurity is the major cause of infant mortality, it can be studied in some detail.

Further, because in most cases of prematurity there is no demonstrable physiological basis, answers are sought by looking at variations in cultural and social factors.

It is important to recognize that no single factor determines the outcome of pregnancy. Poverty is associated with a poor educational background, and both are associated with a poor nutritional background. Minority groups are more likely to be at low-income or poverty level than are middle-class whites. Poor people and those in minority groups frequently live in areas where health care is inaccessible or culturally alienating.

Whatever the relative importance of the various differences among groups, a health care system not responsive to these differences can result in the discrepancies we see in maternity care. Many women obtain very fine care, with excellent outcomes, while others either receive inadequate care or turn away from the system entirely and inaugurate their own system of maternity care. If health care workers in the area of maternal and infant health can meet the challenge presented by the special needs of different groups, the entire picture of maternal and child care in the future could be altered.

REFERENCES

1 U.S. Department of Health, Education, and Welfare, Public Health Service, National Center for Health Statistics: *Monthly Vital Statistics Report, Summary Report Final Natality Statistics, 1973,* Jan. 30, 1975, p. 1.
2 Ibid.
3 ———: *Vital Statistics Report, Summary Report Final Mortality Statistics, 1973,* Feb. 10, 1975, p. 2.
4 Ibid.
5 Ibid.
6 Ibid., p. 18.
7 Ibid.
8 *WHO Chronicle,* Geneva, Switzerland, June 1971, pp. 268–269.

9 U.S. Department of Commerce, Bureau of the Census: *Statistical Abstracts of the United States*, 94th ed., 1973, p. 806.

10 Wallace, Helen M.: "Factors in Mortality and Morbidity," *Clinical Obstetrics and Gynecology*, 13:16, 1970.

11 U.S. Department of Health, Education, and Welfare: *Monthly Vital Statistics Report*, Feb. 10, 1975, p. 2.

12 Ibid.

13 Wallace: op. cit., p. 14.

14 Hunt, Eleanor: "Infant Mortality Trends and Maternal and Infant Care," *Children*, 17:88, 1969.

15 Ibid., p. 89.

16 Peckham, Ben M.: "Optimal Maternal Care," (editorial) *Obstetrics and Gynecology*, 33:864, 1969.

17 Nesbitt, R. E., Jr., and R. H. Aubry: "High-risk Obstetrics. Value of Semiobjective Grading System in Identifying the Vulnerable Group," *American Journal of Obstetrics and Gynecology*, 103:974, 1969.

18 Gold, Edwin M.: in Wallace, op. cit., p. 11.

19 U.S. Department of Health, Education, and Welfare: *Monthly Vital Statistics Report*, Feb. 10, 1975, p. 3.

20 Gold: loc. cit.

21 Tompkins, Winslow T.: "National Efforts to Reduce Perinatal Mortality and Morbidity," *Clinical Obstetrics and Gynecology*, 13:53, 1970.

22 Shapiro, Sam, and Mark Abramowicz: "Pregnancy Outcome Correlates Identified through Medical Record-based Information," *The American Journal of Public Health*, 59:1638, 1969.

23 Wiener, G., and T. Milton: "Demographic Correlates of Low Birth Weight," *American Journal of Epidemiology*, 91:262, 1970.

24 Wallace: op. cit., p. 25.

25 U.S. Department of Commerce: op. cit., table 548, p. 335.

26 Rosenwaike, Ira: "The Influence of Socioeconomic Status on Incidence of Low Birth Weight," *HSMHA Health Reports*, 86:641, 1971.

27 U.S. Department of Health, Education, and Welfare: *Vital Statistics Report*, Jan. 30, 1975, p. 4.

28 Bierman, J.: "Some Things Learned," *The American Journal of Public Health*, 59:931, 1969.

29 Lewis, Oscar: "The Culture of Poverty," *Scientific American*, 215:21, 1966.

30 Milio, Nancy: "Values, Social Class and Community Health Services," *Nursing Research*, 16:29, 1967.

31 Liebow, Elliot: *Tally's Corner*, Little, Brown, Boston, 1967, pp. 64–66.

32 Ibid.

33 Valentine, Charles A.: *Culture and Poverty*, University of Chicago Press, Chicago, 1968.

34 Strauss, Anselm: "Medical Ghettos," in Anselm Strauss (ed.), *Where Medicine Fails*, Aldine, Chicago, 1970.

35 Tompkins: op. cit., p. 23.

36 U.S. Department of Health, Education, and Welfare: *Vital Statistics Report*, Feb. 10, 1975, p. 1.

37 Gold, Edwin M.: "Identification of the High-Risk Fetus," *Clinical Obstetrics and Gynecology*, 11:1070, 1968.

38 Hill, Charles A., Jr., and Mozart I. Spector: "Natality and Mortality of American Indians Compared with U.S. Whites and Non-whites," *HSMHA Health Reports*, 86:233, 1971.

39 U.S. Department of Health, Education, and Welfare, Public Health Service, Health Services Administration, Indian Health Service, Office of Program Statistics: *Indian Health Trends and Services*, 1974, table 2-2, p. 13; and *Vital Statistics Report*, table 1, Jan. 30, 1975, p. 6.

40 U.S. Department of Health, Education, and Welfare: *Indian Health Trends, 1974*, table 3.7, p. 30.

41 Ibid., table 3.1, p. 22.

42 Ibid., table 3.3, p. 25.

43   Schusky, Ernest L.: "An Indian Dilemma," *International Journal of Comparative Sociology,* 11:58–66, March 1970.

44   U.S. Department of Health, Education, and Welfare: *Vital Statistics Report,* Jan. 30, 1975, p. 3.

45   Ibid.

46   Ibid., p. 5.

47   Ibid.

48   Wallace: op. cit., p. 31.

49   Tompkins: op. cit., p. 53.

50   Held, B., and H. Prystowsky: "Research in the Delivery of Health Care-changing Reproductive Trends," *American Journal of Obstetrics and Gynecology,* 109:32, 1971.

51   U.S. Department of Health, Education, and Welfare: *Vital Statistics Report,* Jan. 30, 1975, p. 2.

52   Tompkins: op. cit., p. 48.

53   Hunscher, Helen A., and Winslow T. Tompkins: "The Influence of Maternal Nutrition on the Immediate and Long-Term Outcome of Pregnancy," *Clinical Obstetrics and Gynecology,* 13:132, 1970.

54   Janus, Z., and R. Fuentes: "Participation of Low-Income Urban Women in a Public Health Birth Control Program," *Public Health Reports,* 85:862, 1970.

55   Von der Ahe, C. B.: "The Unwed Teen-age Mother," *American Journal of Obstetrics and Gynecology,* 15:279, 1969.

56   Osofsky, H. J.: "Antenatal Malnutrition—Its Relationship to Subsequent Infant and Child Development," *American Journal of Obstetrics and Gynecology,* 105:1150, 1969.

57   Hunscher and Tompkins: op. cit., p. 130.

58   U.S. Department of Health, Education, and Welfare: *Vital Statistics Report,* Feb. 10, 1975, table 6, pp. 10–11.

59   Hendricks, C. H., and W. Brenner: "Toxemia of Pregnancy—Relationship between Fetal Weight, Fetal Survival, and the Maternal State," *American Journal of Obstetrics and Gynecology,* 109:323, 1971.

60   Ibid.

61   Tompkins: op. cit., p. 56.

62   Conn, R. H.: "Using Health Education Aides in Counseling Pregnant Women," *Public Health Reports,* 84:981, 1968.

63   Cowen, D.: "Denver Neighborhood Health Program," *Public Health Reports,* 84:1030, 1969.

64   Morton, J.: "Experiences with a Maternity and Infant Care (MIC) Project," *American Journal of Obstetrics and Gynecology,* 107:362–368, 1970.

65   Westheimer, R. K., S. H. Cattell, E. Connell, et al.: "Use of Paraprofessionals to Motivate Women to Return for Post Partum Checkup," *Public Health Reports,* 85:625, 1970.

66   Schwartz, Jerome L.: "First National Survey of Free Medical Clinics, 1967–69," *HSMHA Health Reports,* 86:788, 1971.

67   Ibid., p. 786.

68   Ibid., p. 780.

69   Personal communication with Mr. Harry Dunning, Director of Vital Statistics Section of the Seattle–King County Health Department, 1975.

70   Wiener and Milton: op. cit., p. 266.

71   Milio: op. cit.

8

Methods of Teaching and Counseling

SYLVIA J. BRUCE AND
MARILYN A. CHARD

FREEDOM TO CHOOSE

What is there about parenthood and prospective parenthood that has created a need for educational programs? Why has this particular period in our history generated such a need to become more knowledgeable? Why did the myth "mother (or father) knows best" break down so completely? This increasing push for education and preparation is by no means confined to affluent and suburban families. Serving the educational interests and needs of parents is fast becoming a professional business. To be sure, it is still one of the weaker aspects of the health care package, and the quality of the educational commitment is frequently secondary to the business enterprise. Nevertheless, the business of educating parents and preparing prospective parents is here to stay, and it must be examined and evaluated carefully and completely.

The effects of the midcentury knowledge

explosion and the resulting development of today's technocracy have left no group untouched, including the fabric of family-life tradition, belief, and practice. Many forces in today's modern world have influenced family stability, sex roles, kinship relationships, and childbearing practices. The characteristics of our time have cut off many young people from family influences and traditions. There has been a growing awareness of the need to reexamine customs and practices in order to determine purposes and values. Only children used to ask the "why" of things. Fortunately, adults are now beginning to question the purposes of what they do, what they allow done to themselves, and what they have done for themselves.

A flood of unsorted, poorly presented, and ill-digested information has confused both parents and educators. Knowledge will always be used and misused. Helping parents to sort out knowledge and facts will be one of nursing's most critical contributions of the future. The essence of validation of independent practice for nursing will be in the development and advancement of concepts of wellness, prevention, and restoration. Nursing has a choice, and a decision must be made. Our uniqueness, if such it must be, may be in a commitment to concepts of wellness and programs of restoration.

Many prospective parents either are a part of the current movement that is attempting to change the quality and tradition of family life or are already participating in newer forms of social living and child care practices. What was once considered the appropriate domain for maternity nursing practice and expectant parent preparation is now woefully inadequate. Prospective parents are no longer willing to limit their preparation for parenthood only to those needs and understandings which prepare them for the briefest of all their lifetime commitments—

pregnancy. Expectant mothers and couples are grappling with such ecological issues as overpopulation and their fear of rearing children in what they view as a substantially polluted world. Knowledge of the so-called freedom experiences manifest in such practices as yoga, hallucinogenic drugs, organic diets, fasts related to social issues, communal living, and transitory coupling is a critical part of the substantive content of today's programs for expectant parents. To continue to limit the scope of programs offered to expectant parents is to ignore the urgency of parental concern and the relevancy of social change and childrearing practices.

One serious caution must be noted, however. Parents and expectant parents should have the freedom to choose the educational program they feel is best suited to them. Making such a choice can be the most difficult and frustrating aspect of the entire pregnancy experience. Generally, educational offerings for parents are not presented or advertised in the most clear and open way. An amazing variety of programs which are offered as preparation for parenthood are actually programs of preparation dealing only with specific aspects of a pregnancy. Education for expectant parents should be broadly based in scope and should include issues beyond the pregnancy cycle itself. If a program is to do less, it should be so advertised. There is no reason why programs for specific pregnancy cycle preparations should not be offered. They are critical to the process, essential to the experience, and needed by many. They should, however, make no direct or vague claims to being more than they are.

Just what is offered to pregnant women or couples? Some programs are designed specifically to help women cope with the labor process only. Generally, these programs focus on a particular method of self-preparation which may or may not include care-taking and support tasks for the prospective father. Issues related to labor and concerns or questions relevant to pregnancy physiology are also raised but are, for the most part, didactically or prescriptively handled, since they are secondary to the basic purpose of the program. Not only are these programs limited to a specific aspect of a pregnancy experience, but many are also limited to just one major approach. Consequently, many expectant women or couples enroll in the course not realizing that only one method will be analyzed and taught. There is nothing wrong in approaching preparation programs in this way *provided* that those who choose to attend are fully apprised of the purposes, goals, and scope of the offering. Perhaps these programs would serve expectant parents more effectively if they were made available to those who have just participated in broader experiences, have had the opportunity to make their preparatory selection from a variety of methods, and are more settled in just how they wish to cope with one specific task—labor.

Another major source of educational offerings for expectant parents could legitimately be referred to as the promotional giveaway programs. The fundamental premise of these programs is that they must sell something—good relations, a specific institution, products, or businesses. The education of prospective parents is blatantly secondary. The qualifications of the nurses conducting these programs may not be a matter of great concern to the sponsors, but they are of critical importance to parents. Given the opportunity, parents or prospective parents will challenge leadership qualifications. Generally, leaders of the promotional giveaway programs are in a safer position if the offerings are geared to imparting facts and dazzling participants. Again, there is nothing fundamentally inappropriate with these

offerings *if* the participants know what is being offered as well as what will not be provided.

Promotional giveaways do, however, lay the groundwork for an almost unconscious proclivity to sift out material unrelated to the sponsor and to dwell on facets of content or experience that is of a decided advantage to the supporting business or institution. An example of such a program may be found in the layette section of a large department store. A careful analysis of the content of these offerings would demonstrate an uneven distribution of subject emphasis; more time is expended on bathing supplies, layette items, nursery equipment, and feeding methods than on parental concerns of first trimester issues or preparations and methods of encouraging labor and delivery. Upon completion of a series of lectures or classes the parents are usually given a certificate and a sample case of creams and lotions for the baby. Institutions also provide promotional programs under the guise of preparation for parenthood. The programs are generally shorter, consisting of only two or three sessions during which couples are introduced to the chief of staff and the maternity supervisor, attend lectures given by the hospital's nutritionist and chief of pediatrics, and are taken on a tour of the facilities. The main focus of the program is "this is what this hospital can do and has done for you." It is probably only by the sheerest coincidence that these tours usually end just outside the cashier's office. As Sylvia Bruce put it:

Theoretically there is a need for as many kinds of programs as there are expectant parents to attend them. If the purpose of the program is clear and the goals well defined, expectant parents can make intelligent choices regarding the kinds of experiences they feel will be most appropriate for them.[1]

FREEDOM TO LEARN

The traditional expectations of the adult learner involve a situation in which the teacher is the authoritarian communicator of knowledge and the student is a passive receiver of information. Because of past experiences, the student anticipates the ingestion of "pearls of wisdom" which will be regurgitated at a later date as proof to the teacher and to the student that learning has taken place. Thus, the teacher is seen as the expert authority, the guardian of all available knowledge on a particular subject, and the learner is denied the educational resources within him- or herself and within his or her fellow learners. Yet every adult has a repository of knowledge culled from his or her experiences. If adults can be freed to share their knowledge with their teachers and their fellow learners, then discovery of knowledge will involve a mutual exchange of ideas, beliefs, and experiences. Learning will be side by side rather than face to face. Both teacher and learner will utilize their authority in the educational process.

The independent practitioner in maternity nursing possesses authority because of knowledge of anatomy, physiology, and the social sciences in relation to the antepartum, intrapartum, and postpartum stages of pregnancy and in relation to menopause. In addition the nurse has sufficient knowledge of human development to provide teaching and counseling experiences for parents regarding offspring of all ages. The parents and prospective parents whom the nurse is teaching and counseling possess authority because of their experiences concerning the physical and psychological changes during the antepartum, intrapartum, and postpartum periods of pregnancy and their experiences as parents of children in various stages of human development. The ability of the independent practitioner in maternity nursing and parents or prospective parents to exercise their freedom to learn will depend upon their exchange of authority. If authority is shared, all participants will be able to assimilate that information which has the most meaning for them.

Malcolm Knowles compares assumptions and design elements of pedagogy (traditional teaching-learning model) and andragogy (adult education model). His assumptions concern self-concept, experience, readiness, time perspective, and orientation to learning, while his design elements cover climate, planning, diagnosis of needs, formulation of objectives, design, activities, and evaluation. He postulates that adult learners are a rich resource for learning; they are increasingly self-directed, involved in developmental tasks of social roles, interested in immediate application of their learning, and problem-centered in their orientation to learning. The climate for learning has the elements of mutuality, respectfulness, collaboration, and informality. Planning, diagnosis of needs, and formulation of objectives are done mutually by teacher (facilitator) and learner. The design of the learning experience is sequenced according to the learner's needs and in problem units. Learning activities encourage inquiry. Evaluation involves mutual rediagnosis of needs and mutual measurement of the program.[2] His model is one that can be adapted to either group or individual teaching and counseling situations and ensures the freedom to learn.

Principles of Teaching-Learning

Aline Auerbach, a recognized leader in the parent education movement, has identified nine basic assumptions which underlie parent group education and which are based on her experiences over a number of years.[3] The assumptions are as follows:

1 Parents can learn.
2 Parents want to learn.

3   Parents learn best what they are interested in learning.

4   Learning is most significant when the subject matter is closely related to the parents' own immediate experiences.

5   Parents can learn best when they are free to create their own response to a situation.

6   Parent group education is as much an emotional experience as it is an intellectual one.

7   Parents can learn from one another.

8   Parent group education provides the basis for a remaking of experience.

9   Each parent learns in his or her own way.

The authors have identified five main steps in the teaching process based on their experiences as group leaders. They are as follows:

1   Recruit the group.
2   Develop the agenda.
3   Develop the content.
4   Examine the process.
5   Evaluate the group experience.

Table 8-1 shows the intimate relationship between Auerbach's nine learning principles and the authors' five steps in the teaching process. The fundamental teaching-learning processes can be broadened further and subsequently viewed as methodologies of recruitment, procedure, and process.

Recruitment

The independent practitioner's first step in recruiting a parent group involves identification of philosophy and goals relative to parent education. Nurses should also be aware of their own strengths and limitations as group leaders and as authorities. The nurse then must investigate the various parent education programs which are available in the community. Once this is accomplished either of two things can be done. The nurse can develop a separate program or can serve as a consultant to or a coordinator of existing programs. The latter choice may necessitate suggesting the termination of some programs, the merger of others, or the development of a new program. As a group leader, the independent practitioner must make the choice which is personally as well as professionally acceptable.

Parent education groups are discussion groups based on expectant or actual parent needs. The order and range of topics depend upon group needs. Yet, if it is believed that pertinent material has not been covered, the leader has a responsibility to remind the group of this oversight and to stimulate discussion in the neglected, but important, areas. The group experience "should provide for acquisition of new information as a means of broadening the point of view and enlarging perspectives"[4] based on information culled from the group members.

Because parents can and want to learn, parent group education should be an integral part of antepartum and postpartum nursing care. Independent practitioners in maternity nursing should be familiar with all parent group educational experiences which are available. This information should be discussed with the parents and potential parents with whom the nurse works, thereby affording them the opportunity to choose that group which best meets their needs. Parents can also be recruited into groups through referral. For example, a clinical specialist in maternity nursing may be conducting a prospective parent group in which the topics discussed include the physiology and psychology of pregnancy. Toward the end of the series of eight meetings, a set of

TABLE 8-1
The Teaching-Learning Process

Steps in teaching	Learning principles
1 Recruit the group	1 Parents can learn
	2 Parents want to learn
2 Develop the agenda	3 Parents learn best when interested
	4 Learning is most significant when based on personal experiences
3 Develop the content	5 Parents can learn best when they are free to respond in their own way
	6 Parent group education is both an emotional and an intellectual experience
	7 Parents can learn from one another
4 Examine the process	8 Parent group education provides the basis for a remaking of experience
5 Evaluate the experience	9 Each parent learns in his or her own way

prospective parents express their wish to be together during the intrapartum period. The clinical specialist can refer them to an available group experience which will meet their needs. There may be other parents who desire more information regarding their two-year old. The clinical specialist in maternity nursing can refer them to the clinical specialist in pediatric nursing who will be conducting a series of parent group meetings which will meet this parental need.

Regardless of the work setting (hospital, community clinic, obstetrician's office), the independent practitioner should provide for parent education. The time for conducting meetings and the composition of these groups will be dependent on parents' schedules. For example, prospective fathers may not be free to meet at the same time as prospective mothers. Therefore, there could be two separate groups—one for the men and one for the women. When prospective parents are scheduled for pregnancy assessment appointments and are also attending prospective parent groups, the day for the appointment should coincide with the day of the group meeting and the time for the appointment should be set for one-half hour before or right after the group meeting. The

major purpose of parent education is to provide services that are actually needed, at times that are practical, and in combinations that are really helpful (sets of parents, mothers only, fathers only). Regardless of the type of group, the time, and the place, the crucial point is that parents and prospective parents know what the group leader truly plans to provide and in what areas help can be provided for them.

Procedure

Although it has been implied, the authors' premise must be made unmistakably clear: *The teaching-learning interaction or process lends itself best to those situations in which the participants can discuss the topics or issues which are of the most immediate interest or concern to them.* Undoubtedly, there are some leaders who can provide this type of learning situation through methods other than discussion. However, since the more traditional forms of teaching methodologies, such as lectures, panels, symposia, and conferences, are familiar experiences for most, only the discussion process and procedure will be developed in detail.

The discussion procedure involves agenda

and content development. At the initial group meeting, the leader first hands out cards to be filled out with certain information, such as name and telephone number. At the same time each group member is given a card with the leader's name and telephone number. The purpose of this exchange is to enable the group members and the group leader to fulfill their obligations to one another. Thus, if the group leader has to change a meeting date, each group member can be telephoned and given the information. By the same token, if a group member is unable to attend a given meeting, he or she can inform the group leader. Missing members do affect group process and procedure. With the mechanism of mutual responsibility established, the leader can inform other group members if a member or members will be absent from individual meetings. If a group leader wishes any additional information, it should be made quite clear why such information is requested and what is to be done with it.

"A first meeting in any group experience is unquestionably a vital one. At this time, the leadership role is explained, and the purpose and function of the group, as well as its limitations, are described."[5] Thus, following the written exchange of information and an explanation of its purpose, the following information is shared with the group members: who the group leader is, why the group leader is there, and the philosophy and goals of parent group education. The participants are then asked to explain who they are and what they hope will be discussed and covered in this discussion series. If their expressed areas of interest and concern are stated broadly, the leader should request more specificity by such questions as: "Can you give me an example?" "Do you have something particular in mind?" Following this "go-around" the leader summarizes the

topics raised, grouping the related items under appropriate headings. The leader explains that, as meetings progress, both the leader and the members may add to the agenda. There is no particular sequence in which these topics must be discussed and developed. Thus is the agenda developed and two learning principles are fulfilled: Parents can learn best when they are interested. Learning is most significant when based on personal experiences.

At a recent first meeting of an expectant parent group series, the initial agenda was very superficial, as indicated by the expectant couples who stated the following: "I'm interested in seeing the hospital and delivery room." "I'm interested in care of the baby at home." Since the leader was inexperienced and there were 25 participants in this particular group, the shallowness of the agenda could probably be attributed to the leader's ineptness in working with large discussion groups. However, a more experienced leader would have collected a more meaningful agenda. For example, one expectant father said he was interested in "just what caused it all." The group laughed at this, but the leader never responded to his comment. Yet, had the group leader said, "I'm not so sure I really understand what you're saying. Can you tell me more?" many pertinent items could have been uncovered, such as, "Why did we become pregnant? It wasn't the right time." "We were practicing the rhythm method of contraception. Why didn't it work?" "I know my wife would know when she is in labor, but what starts labor anyway? The doctor gives you a vague idea of when the baby is expected, but is there anything we can do to start labor? Or does it just happen? Why does it happen?"

By being more sensitive to what seems to be an offhand remark, many issues can be opened, such as the following:

1 Family planning and contraception—techniques, methods, physiology
2 Changing roles from husband and wife to father and mother
3 Unwanted pregnancy—psychological adjustments
4 Becoming parents—responsibilities, fears, worries
5 Harming a pregnancy, i.e., what a couple or mother might do that could start premature labor and result in a deformed infant
6 Physiology of labor—what is true labor, what is false labor?

Not only will the group identify what they want to explore and discuss, but also the leader must assume professional commitment and responsibility to the group in order to help them see the relationship of their general questions and concerns to topics that are specific and pertinent to prospective parents.

Content development involves the identification of a body of knowledge related to the area covered by the group's experience. Content includes a balance between emotional and intellectual material. Its development presupposes the leader's encouragement of open exchange among group members. The first step involves establishing a focus for group discussion; this demands a concentration of attention and the pinpointing of the emotional involvement in the group around a given topic. Therefore, not only is the group better informed, but it is also less fearful and better able to cope with the physical and psychological aspects of the subject matter. The focus helps the members to discuss the same topic and provides a structure which teaches by examples supplied by the members. The group may begin

to sense and understand why its members may be concerned about a particular subject.

The group arrives at a focus through a process of clarification—separation of the superficial from the meaningful. The leader picks up the question or request from the group for the purpose of helping the group to become clear about their concerns, feelings, and thoughts around a chosen subject. The leader now carries the responsibility for enabling the group to discuss the topic as productively as possible. The leader must be aware of and sensitive to purposes and readiness for discussion. Input is provided as needed, either to supply information or to correct misinformation, when this is not forthcoming from the group. Underscoring and restatement of what individual group members have said and periodic summarization of what has happened up to a given point in the discussion are leadership techniques which help to maintain a productive meeting.

The ultimate goal of any educational parent group discussion is the enhanced ability of the members to cope with present and future demands of parenthood. In the later phases of the group discussion, the members can be enabled to evolve ways of coping which are suitable to them. They can be helped to see the implications of their choices and to face realistically those issues which may not offer a choice. This is content development and in it three learning principles are fulfilled: Parents can learn best when they are free to respond in their own way. Parent group education is both an emotional and an intellectual experience. Parents can learn from one another.

At a fourth meeting of a recent expectant parent group series, the leader collected a small agenda and a topic was selected. The group was told that the leader would prefer to be more specific. Thus, the topic went from "What causes abnormal babies?" to "What can I do to prevent having an abnormal baby?" The original question was academic and general. The second question was more personal and meaningful to the members. This is a step the leader took for the group rather than letting them do it. Had the topic remained "What causes abnormal babies?" the leader could have turned to the mother who originally raised the question and asked, "What do you have in mind?" The group might have discussed specific diseases and conditions for awhile. The leader then could move in with a restatement of the original question, such as, "Are you perhaps asking if there is anything you can do to prevent or to be sure you won't have an abnormal baby?" The group will usually nod in the affirmative. The leader's next question can be, "What are you doing now that is helping to ensure a good baby?" If there is silence, the leader can say, "Well, let's look at what we've discussed already." The leader will then summarize and have the group select a place to begin. Many issues could have been opened, such as the following:

1   What the parents give to the baby to ensure a healthy start in life
2   What the parents cannot control to any predictable degree
3   What the parents, especially the expectant mothers, can do to ensure the best possible outcome

Thus, the focus could have been reached and maintained, and the group could have had a productive discussion through meaningful content development.

As can be seen in the above example, the potential for a productive discussion was there. However, the quality of the learning experience is dependent upon professional competence and sociocultural relevancy. The procedures utilized by the leader in discussion groups are merely facilitating devices. They do not take the place of maternity nursing expertise. These same procedures of agenda and content development provide the participants with a more systematic approach to problem solving.

Process

Process involves the utilization of individual behavior as a method of moving the group forward. Therefore, in order to be effective, the group leader should observe and understand individual behavior—words, gestures, silence, facial and bodily expressions, and tone of voice. Individuals possess certain attitudes and predispositions based on previous experience which tend to influence the way in which they interact with each other and with the group leader. Although it may not be possible to fully understand all the meanings of behavior of an individual within the group, the leader must try to see beyond the overt behavior because it has personal significance for the individual who is utilizing it. The leader's key to response to individual behavior is acceptance of the person. Nevertheless, the leader does have a responsibility to intervene when individual behavior is inappropriate and disruptive to the group. The leader seeks to understand through careful listening and maintains focus on the content rather than on the personality.

Once the group has been recruited, its members have expressed their interests and concerns, and a focus has been found, the leader should utilize process to enhance the group experience. In order to pave the way, it might be helpful to set aside time either at the beginning or at the end of the first two or three sessions to discuss the process of forming a group. Thus, members can be prepared for initial feelings of disappointment. They may have expected to take notes while the leader talked. Once in the group they discover that they are expected to be active participants. This is difficult to do with a group of strangers. People (participants and leader) have to get to know one another before they can take risks. Before the group is really formed, some people may elect to leave and new members may arrive. It usually takes three meetings before the group becomes "permanent" and cohesive.

The group leader should identify process very subtly to the group; this can be done when the group process is *not* working because members are directing all their questions to the leader and not using each other, or when they are "doing their own thing" and not listening to each other. At such times the leader might say, "We don't seem to be working as a group. Let's slow down." Or "What's the matter with everyone tonight? No matter what we agree to discuss, it just falls apart." A summary of what has occurred up to that point may then help the group to refocus.

Remember the father who wondered "just what caused it all"? The response of the group to this was just laughter. The leader could have seen this group laughter as a cue. Was it anxious laughter? Was it hilarious laughter? Did it mean that other group members also had questions or concerns about how such things happen? The leader must be sensitive to group as well as individual behavior in order to provide a productive meeting. The leader's use of behavior and content will determine the participants' freedom to share their authority with one another and to try new behaviors. Not only should group members feel free to explore

and analyze a situation presented within a group, but they also should be able to apply this learning in their daily lives.

Evaluation of the group experience is provided when both leader and parents discover for themselves what they have learned and ascertain how they could have learned more. It is important that the leader realize that each person learns in his or her own way and at his or her own rate. Members should be encouraged to do this and to come to their own decisions. Because this experience is one which is freely chosen by the participants, the leader should not demand a verbal or written evaluation. Rather, this should be anticipated, on a behavioral level. Toward the end of the series, group members may exhibit their unwillingness to leave by congregating at the end of a session "just to talk." An expectant mother may deliver before the last session but attend this last session with her newborn. Some members may just say, "Thank you. This really helped."

The leader can enhance personal learning by keeping records of each session in a series. Through careful examination of these records, the leader can ascertain what has been done that was helpful to the group or that hindered the group process. The leader can also realize the clues that were missed and the quality of content which was discussed, analyzed, and utilized by the participants.

In parent group education, the leader teaches procedure to the parents through agenda and content development. Process is used to facilitate the group's learning. Through process, the last two learning principles are realized: Parent group education provides the basis for a remaking of experience. Each parent learns in his or her own way.

Through the exploration of recruitment, procedure, and process, the relationship between the nine learning principles and the steps in teaching have been established. Yet this chapter is concerned not only with teaching but also with counseling. Is counseling different from teaching? Is it inherent in teaching? Are the terms counseling and teaching synonymous? Herein lies a dilemma.

The Dilemma of Teaching-Counseling

Some may see teaching as mechanical fact-giving and counseling more personal and feeling-oriented. This does not mean that they cannot be offered simultaneously in a teaching situation. Others believe that counseling is something which is beyond the scope of teaching. The authors use the terms interchangeably. Teaching is not effective unless it deals with feelings. Emotions such as fear, hate, and anxiety can inhibit learning, while love, openness, and trust can enhance learning. The feelings dealt with during the teaching-counseling process are based on the present. Delving into the unconscious would be therapy. The independent practitioner in maternity nursing, when working with parents and prospective parents, is interested in how parents perceive facts and how they deal with them as applied to the present. This practitioner is not equipped to handle psychological problems, which are the realm of the clinical specialist in psychiatric nursing.

Much of this chapter has been directed toward parent group education. This does not preclude the efficacy of teaching-counseling on an individual basis. There may be times when problems cannot be handled appropriately in the group. Although feelings have relevancy to the individual and to group members, one participant's feelings are not always relevant to the entire group.

They may be too personal and thus embarrassing to other group members. The leader should be sensitive to this group feeling, intervene, and arrange to see the participant personally.

Individual teaching-counseling can also be provided by the independent practitioner in maternity nursing in practice settings (hospital, community health center, obstetrician's office). Problems which are of immediate concern to the parents and prospective parents should be handled as they arise rather than being deferred to the parent group meeting time. *The same teaching-learning principles of group settings apply in these situations.* The great difference lies in the fact that the nurse and the parent must give more of themselves because they are the only two involved as opposed to a group of six to eight couples.

In a counseling, as in a teaching, situation, the maternity nurse helps the client to realize worthwhile objectives and to produce desired, valued outcomes. That is, counseling involves a helping relationship. It is *not* advice-giving. Both counselor and counselee enter the relationship as unique human beings, each having something to offer the other. *Both* enter the relationship intentionally, *both* determine the goals of the relationship, and *both* possess the means to attain these goals. The maternity nurse has information necessary to the client in the attainment of desired outcomes. At the same time, the client holds information about him- or herself, *unknown to the nurse*, which is important to the realization of worthwhile objectives. Both nurse and client must recognize what each has to offer if counseling is to be effective.

Once the counseling need is established, all available information known about the specific need is given to the client. The client also supplies information about him- or herself—beliefs, feelings, culture, and so forth—which may be important to any ultimate decision making. *Together,* the nurse and client explore alternative actions. The client then chooses that action, or those actions, which will best help the client attain his or her goals.

Parents will have freedom to learn when they are aware of the educational opportunities which are available to them as parents and prospective parents. This knowledge presupposes their right to choose from a variety of parent group education experiences when the philosophies and goals of each program have been interpreted to them. Then they can choose that program which will meet their educational needs. Their freedom to learn will be enhanced when group leaders acknowledge parents' authority and supplement it with their own.

FREEDOM TO TEACH

Parents who are free to learn need nurses who are free to teach. As simplistic as this statement appears to be, it in no way ensures an easy implementation. Classes, courses, tours, and demonstrations traditionally offered to expectant parents by maternity nurses have not been widely known as free experiences for either the nurse or the participants. The content or focus of a majority of these classes and courses generally has been instructive in approach and physio-medical in scope. Nursing theories, science, and practice have been abysmally absent. Nursing knowledge and skills are certainly not unknown to maternity nurses. The freedom to use these knowledges, unfortunately, is a little used freedom. Just why this is so is a point of historical interest but is not ger-

mane to the decision to change. If change is wanted, change can occur. Why it has not occurred can become a preoccupying exercise of little academic merit.

Professionalism Revisited

The maternity *nursing* role as it is practiced today can best be described as static and passive. Maternity nursing practice is a mere reflection of the larger issue—professional obsolescence. Whether nursing ever *was* or now *is* a profession is a moot question. What it *will* become is an issue of urgent concern. Other professions have defined their parameters of practice, stated their goals, and developed the content of their role while simultaneously implementing their service. But nurses have practiced their role as defined by others and are only now beginning to evolve their own definition of what nursing care should be.

Today's practitioners must have the integrity required to allow changes to occur that will ensure the rebirth of their profession as a legitimate form of practice and service. Nursing, however, and maternity nurses are no exception, must earn the right to professionalism and independent practice. This can only occur when present-day practitioners can recognize and value the strength and integrity that is realized through standards, knowledge, research, and scholarship. When nursing *practices* are carefully examined they leave much to be desired, for the art and science of nursing is remarkably absent. When nursing *thought* is evaluated the tragedy rests in the omission of implementation. Although obviously overdue, it is not too late to legitimize thoughts, ideas, and intuitions.

Parents have a right to learn, and nurses have a right to teach, but only if they first accept the responsibility to learn. The freedom to teach assumes there is a willingness to learn.

Self Reexamined

Self-development is a professional responsibility of the independent practitioner in maternity nursing. In order to develop, one must have something on which to build. Hopefully, the independent practitioner has a broad background in the liberal arts, including anthropology, psychology, sociology, history, literature, and human development. Today, a historical sense of nursing seems to be sadly lacking. How many independent practitioners can determine whether history has changed nursing or nursing has changed history? How has history affected nursing? Upon what must independent practitioners build in order to change their self-image and earn the freedom to teach parents and prospective parents?

When anthropology, psychology, sociology, literature, and theories of human development are taught from a historical perspective, the learner begins to acquire a sense of history. In teaching parents, the nurse who has experienced this approach will be able to identify practices and values held by some parents who seem to belong to a different era. The nurse can begin to understand why these values and practices are important to colleagues.

In order to understand and deal with the social issues of today the independent practitioner must have an understanding of our technocracy and how it developed historically, with the impact of two world wars, the philosophy of pragmatism, and the explosion of knowledge in the fields of technology, medicine, and psychology. How many independent practitioners can understand the reasons why the counterculture has emerged and delved into the area of psychedelic experiences? Where have members of this culture seen value placed? They have seen value placed on the authority of scientific knowledge which espouses the development of the intellect and ignores the psyche. Thus, they perceive human relationships as lacking in love and understanding.

Suppose an expectant mother who had taken LSD came to a community health center. She had read that fetal chromosomal abnormalities can be determined through analysis of amniotic fluid. Upon her request an amniocentesis was performed. Examination of the amniotic fluid showed no abnormalities. Although the expectant mother has been assured that the fetus has no known chromosomal defects, she is still fearful and expresses her anxiety to the clinical specialist in maternity nursing who works out of the community health center. If the clinical specialist places nursing values on the authority of scientific knowledge alone, the expectant mother will be referred to the test results. If the clinical specialist believes in the authority of the psyche as well as the intellect, not only will the test results be used as assurance, but the expectant mother also will be helped to explore her feelings. Until the reasons for her feelings are understood, the expectant mother may be unable to believe that the fetus is doing well. Thus *care* has been demonstrated by the clinical specialist.

Professional nurses have a responsibility to themselves and to their clients to come to grips with today's sociocultural issues. The quality of parent teaching and freedom to teach will be limited if they do not face these issues. The parents' freedom to learn will be inhibited through their lack of knowledge. Without a firm background in the liberal arts and in *nursing*, how can nurses help parents to find relationships between knowledge and feelings in order to reshape their own learning? How can they teach legislators what nursing is? And how can parameters of practice be defined so that a nurse practice act congruent with the professional concepts for nursing practice can be legislated and enacted? These nurses must reexamine themselves as professionals, enhance their strengths, and acknowledge their limitations by building upon what is already known, identifying what needs to be known, and accepting the responsibility to learn it. Only then will the nurse have the background to merit the freedom to teach.

FREEDOM TO DEVELOP

Education for parent development and expectant parent preparation should be viewed as a parental right. The quality of programs offered to parents and prospective parents should be no less than the quality of educational experiences provided for children and young adults. In this respect the development of new programs and the consultation provided to existing ones should be the responsibility of institutions involved in the teaching-learning interaction. To do less would be to undermine the fundamental assumption that a democratic system of government works best when its members are informed, are free of unrealistic concerns, and are operating in a state of wellness.

The University and the Community

Colleges and universities have long been under attack for what has been perceived as an insensitivity to the sociocultural and educational needs of the communities in which they are located. All too few communities view institutions of higher education as in-

tegral and necessary components of an efficient and productive human condition. One is more likely to hear them described, and this is particularly true of highly congested urban areas, as institutional forms that take the services, facilities, and resources of the community but remain uncommitted to the realities, issues, and ills of human need. Without question, there are variations of both forms of practice. There is no valid reason, however, why universities should continue to remain patently unresponsive to the country's largest and most neglected group—parents. Parenthood is the only occupation for which there is no systematic mode of preparation and few continuing education programs for parental development. Is there any reason why universities and colleges should not develop these programs and courses for parents?

Certainly it is a justifiable expectation to look to and depend upon the universities for the development of a wide variety of learning resources and materials. If the premise that schools of nursing should produce general family health practitioners at the baccalaureate level and specialist practitioners through programs at the graduate level is accepted and operative, then the need for providing practitioner experiences commensurate with societal needs will be of critical concern to the faculties of nursing. There is no doubt of the benefits of mutuality when schools of nursing provide educational programs for parents and these same programs provide teaching-learning sources for students and faculty. Services for parents and expectant parents should be ongoing and continuous even though there will be times when these experiences are needed more by parents than by students and faculties. Such services should not be provided just for those periods when students need particular learning experiences.

Parents and the Video World

A variety of teaching-learning devices and approaches can be developed and utilized to enrich and vitalize programs and services offered to parents. Video tapes can be developed around particular developmental tasks of children, can focus on certain common but troublesome family interactions, or could follow a parent discussion series. These tapes could be used by nurses from outside the university who are leading discussion groups either for their own continuing education or to facilitate the process and development of their groups. Parents who wish to direct their own learnings also should have access to these video tapes. There is no reason why parents and expectant parents should not be able to use university facilities to meet their own needs in learning how to cope with or manage their children or their pregnancy.

The Right to Develop

Parents have a right to learn the roles they must assume in helping their families to grow and develop, and universities have an obligation and sociocultural commitment to be sensitive and responsive to meeting the fundamental purpose of their being. Maternal–child health services must begin to accept the continuing education of parents as a service of equal importance to the education of nurses and physicians in the field of maternal–child health care.

REFERENCES

1   Bruce, Sylvia J.: "Do Prenatal Educational Programs Really Prepare for Parenthood?" *Hospital Topics,* November 1965, p. 104.
2   Knowles, Malcolm: *The Adult Learner: A Neglected Species,* Gulf Publishing Company, Houston, 1973, p. 104.
3   Auerbach, Aline B.: *Parents Learn through Discussion,* Wiley, New York, 1968, pp. 23–28.
4   Bruce: op. cit., p. 105.
5   Bruce, Sylvia J.: "What Mothers of 6- to 10-Year-Olds Want To Know," *Nursing Outlook,* 12:40, September 1964.

PART TWO

PLANNING THE
FAMILY:
CHILDBEARING AND
CHILDREARING

9

Ecological Factors in Family Planning

JOAN CARVELL AND
FRED CARVELL

Ecology refers to the study of the relationships between organisms and between organisms and their environment. Until recently most people concentrated on the biological aspects of ecology without giving much consideration to the human and sociocultural considerations that deal with the spacing of people and institutions and their interdependency. The discussion in this chapter will emphasize these aspects of ecology rather than the biological.

The concept of ecology involves a complex network of dependency among living things. Many of the interrelationships go unnoticed by human beings until the delicate balance of nature is disturbed. Some ecologists have attempted to explain the network of natural interdependency through the use of a multilayered pyramid. At the base of this pyramid lies the earth and the sea, which support all life. The next layer consists of all forms of plant life which support insects and smaller forms of animal life. The remaining layers of the pyramid are composed of various members of the animal kingdom. Ultimately, humans see themselves at the apex of the pyramid. (See Figure 9-1.) It may be argued that this topmost position of homo sapiens is more correctly attributable to ego than to animal superiority; however, it is difficult to find another living thing that has done more to exploit the environment or endanger the existence of living things in each layer of the pyramid.

Although the pyramid is a simple representation of a very complex network of relationships, it serves to illustrate several important points. First, each layer of the pyramid supplies the food and resources for the layers above it. In turn, each layer is dependent upon the layers below it for survival. Second, ecological balance is maintained as

long as each layer reproduces in sufficient numbers to ensure its continuance while supplying the needs of the layers above it, resulting in a system of complex interdependencies.

The critical question for the survival of all living things, including humans, is how to maintain a level of population through reproduction that will not overtax the supportive environment. Nothing is more germane to our survival than the birth and death rates; yet these two factors alone are not the primary determinants of our standard of living. A sound and healthy environment for people implies much more than maintenance of ecological equilibrium, the conservation of natural resources, and the control of the biological layers that occupy the pyramid beneath us.

FIGURE 9-1
Ecological pyramid.

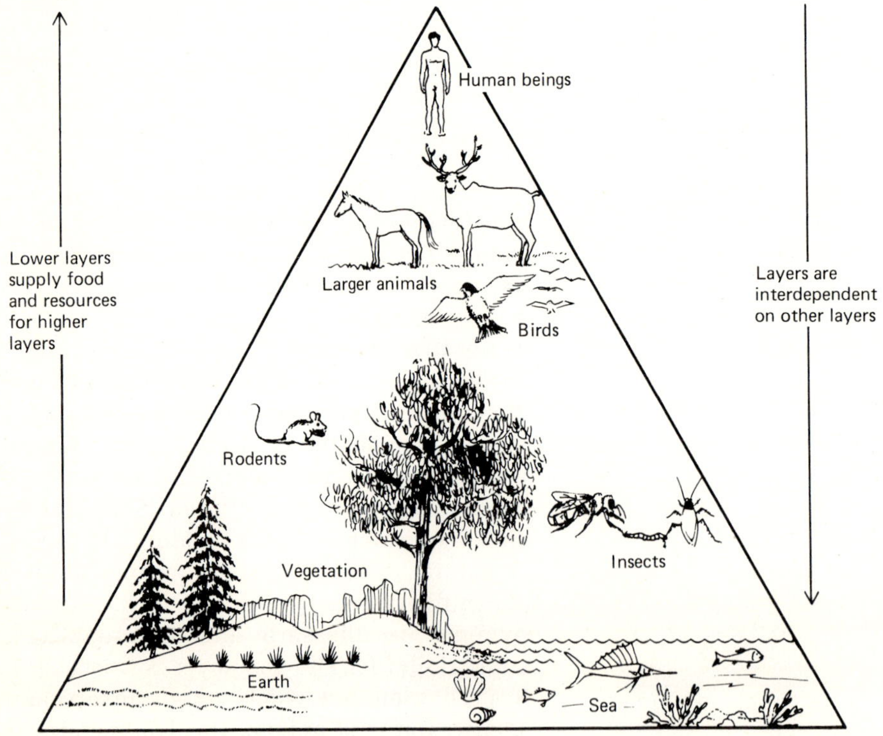

Lower layers supply food and resources for higher layers

Layers are interdependent on other layers

Human beings

Larger animals

Birds

Rodents

Vegetation

Insects

Earth

Sea

We not only survive and function in our environment, we are shaped by it—psychologically, physically, and socially. To be healthy, the environment and standard of living sought by us must therefore provide conditions that favor the development of desirable human characteristics. Each set of parents *should* consider this factor before making the decision to add another human life to the existing stock. However, it may be unrealistic to expect human beings to become suddenly concerned about such a broad topic as ecology when we have so little understanding of the factors that affect the social and psychological environment in our own families.

We can take three philosophical approaches when considering our impact on the environment.

First, we can believe that the ultimate control of the earth lies outside the realm of human action. Therefore, we are justified in neither worrying about its problems nor taking action to prevent catastrophe.

Second, we can believe that our destiny, and the earth's, lies in our own hands. Thus, we should plan our evolutionary process so that the best kind (and number) of human beings in the best kind of world results.

Third, we can believe that we cannot and perhaps should not control our entire destiny, and yet by virtue of our rational nature, we will always act to control significant portions of our future.[1]

If we are to act in accordance with the third philosophical approach and make the attempt to control our own population growth, we should begin by understanding the importance of our relationship to other elements in the ecological system. To do this requires new insights and knowledge. This chapter begins with a general explanation of what environmental education is about and why it is important in helping to attain such insights. Other topics relate to various aspects of population growth and the impact such growth has on resource utilization, urbanization, pollution, and living standards.

Each potential set of parents should consciously make the decision whether or not to have children. Those who make no decision may end up reproducing by default. Obviously, not all potential parents will attempt to engage in the thought-provoking mental process that leads to making either a positive or negative decision. However, those who do decide to curb their own reproductive process will also have to make the decision on the appropriate means to be used for taking such action. The means should be appropriate for them and in accordance with their own values and beliefs.

Other chapters in this book deal more specifically with methods of birth control. This chapter, hopefully, provides information that can be used as the framework within which the decision to control population can be made by individuals more intelligently and with greater understanding.

WHY ENVIRONMENTAL EDUCATION?

For more than a decade human beings have shown an increasing awareness of the changing ecological balance and the role we have played in it. Ecology has become a *cause célèbre* for crusades and conferences both at local and international levels. State and federal legislation has been affected, advertising campaigns launched, and ecology-related fads in organic foods, natural cosmetics, clothing, and posters have become prevalent. Life-styles based on *a return to nature* have had widespread appeal among those who have joined rural communes.

There are variations in the levels of concern and understanding among those who are advocates of conservation and other environmental programs. The viewpoints of scientists, industrialists, land developers, physicians, students, farmers, or politicians are colored by their spectrum of experience. In short, people's perspectives of ecology are influenced by their own understanding and ideals and their vested interests in either protecting or exploiting natural resources.

Despite the increased publicity on ecology, understanding of the interdependence and interrelationships among living things and their environment is more apparent than real among the majority of people. Yet the future course of human history depends on our comprehension of the consequences of our exploitation of nature. The allocation of natural resources and the resulting changes in the environment will vary according to our priority of demands from the earth. Until priorities change, we seem destined to continue to pollute the environment, overpopulate, and create environmental problems that endanger our life-style and health.

The urban dweller is confronted by environmental problems resulting from overcrowding, rats, roaches, poor solid waste and sewage disposal, air pollution, and environmental blight. The rural dweller faces the consequences of ruinous strip-mining practices and timber harvesting, excessive or inappropriate use of agricultural chemicals, and the encroachment of the overflow of urban population. It is little wonder that the urban dweller trapped in the squalid living conditions of the ghetto does not share the same degree of concern over the purity of mountain streams that the rural dweller or Sierra Club conservationist may voice. Yet, inhabitants of both environments ultimately must face the consequence of air, water, and surface pollution.

Not only do the urban and rural environmental problems impose visual and aesthetic distractions, they pose genuine health hazards and have long-range consequences for the survival of both animal and plant life. An important implication of the widespread and growing concern humans are showing toward the environment is our increasing awareness that should an ecological disaster occur, it will not differentiate between nations as political units, races, ideologies, ages, or geographic locations. Thus, the importance of ecological awareness affords a point of view not limited to the narrow approach that often accompanies temporary solutions framed by economics, politics, or singular nationalistic interests.

The ecological balance has never been static, but with the recognition of the threat to the human environment, concern and steps toward action are emerging. The individual in this complex world who wants only to understand the problems of his or her immediate locale or whose perspective is limited to his or her own technical field (and this would include nursing) is, at the least, a hindrance to society and more likely a threat to the environment.

Today we possess much of the scientific and technological knowledge necessary to solve many environmental problems. However, decisions regarding human use of the environment are seldom based solely on scientific knowledge. Human decisions are affected by emotion, custom, oversight, economic feasibility, political expediency, social desirability, or religious belief. Certainly individual human decisions regarding planned parenthood are influenced by the same factors.

It is difficult to make wise decisions about the environment without an understanding of economics, history, political science, sociology, psychology, the humanities, and the physical and natural sciences. This calls for a new approach to education which will provide an ecological perspective for all aspects of learning. The need for such an approach was the force behind the passage of the Environmental Education Act of 1970. This act was an outgrowth of a national commitment to a search for enlightened life-styles and provides a working definition of environmental education.

Environmental education is an integrated process which deals with man's interrelationship with his natural and man-made surroundings, including the relationship of population growth, pollution, resource allocation and depletion, conservation technology, and urban and rural planning to the total human environment. Environmental education is a study of the factors influencing ecosystems, mental and physical growth, living and working conditions, decaying cities, and population pressures. Environmental education is intended to promote among citizens the awareness and understanding of the environment, our relationship to it, and the concern and responsible action necessary to assure our survival and to improve the quality of life.[2]

Under the broad, general definition adopted by Congress in the Environmental Education Act of 1970, population growth becomes a key element in understanding the interrelationship of human beings, our environment, and the quality of life we enjoy. This relationship is germane to the health care sciences of which nursing is a part and, more specifically, to the role of planned parenthood which is discussed in this part of the book. The following sections of this chapter deal with the magnitude of population growth and the factors that contribute to continued growth.

POPULATION GROWTH

The term *population explosion* has been used by demographers to describe the rate of increase in the world's population during the past several decades. The use of the term implies that a problem exists—overpopulation. This perception is reinforced by the news media and reports from such agencies as the United Nations indicating that nearly two-thirds of the existing population live at the edge of survival with malnutrition or starvation. These reports indicate that in certain parts of the world there are more people than can be supported by existing food supplies and necessary health services. According to reports from the Food and Agriculture Organization of the United Nations, food production is failing to keep pace with rising population growth in many sectors of the world. This means there will be little relief unless a better balance can be struck between people and food production.[3]

The United Nations *Demographic Yearbook* reports that the world population, which exceeded 3.6 billion in 1970, is expected to reach 4.5 billion by 1980 and 6.5 billion by the year 2000. Some demographers project even higher world population levels by 2000. Although there is no statistical evidence to indicate precisely how many people the earth can support, it can be assumed that earth, having finite and exhaustible resources, cannot indefinitely support such increases in population.

Concern about implications of the population explosion might best be understood by reviewing the past record of population growth. The world's population did not reach 1 billion until 1850. In 1925, 75 years later, it reached 2 billion; it only took 37 years (until 1962) to reach 3 billion. World population is expected to expand by another billion, reaching 4 billion by 1977. This latest 1 billion increment is expected to take just 15 years.

The accelerated population growth is the result of a sequence of industrial, medical, and agricultural revolutions that began nearly 200 years ago in England. Until then, the doubling time for the world's population took about 1,500 years. The first doubling time after that was 75 years; to double the second time (from 2 to 4 billion) it will take about 52 years. Thus, it is easy to see that the term population explosion is no misnomer.

An average person has approximately 38 million pulses per year. Nearly two infants will be born for each of these pulses. At present the world population expands by 80 million persons each year. This means that, in theory, every 6 to 7 weeks the world population increases sufficiently to populate the world's largest city, Tokyo—that is, roughly 9 million persons.

In addition to the problems posed by the absolute increase in population, further complications accrue as a result of the extraordinarily uneven growth rates around the world. In the industrialized and technologically advanced nations, those mainly of Europe, the Soviet Union, North America, Oceania, and Japan, the annual rate of increase is relatively low—about 2 percent. However, in other locations where nations are still in the early stages of technological development—namely, Asia, Africa, and Latin America—the yearly rate of increase is rapid, often twice the rate of the more developed nations. At the current rate of increase, by the year 2000 the developing nations will add more than five times as many people to the world as the more advanced nations.

Factors of Population Growth

Thus far, the discussion has centered on population growth. Two factors have contributed to this growth: natality (birth) rates and mortality rates. Although birth rates have played a role in population growth during the past 25 years, there is little question that the reduction of mortality rates has become the dominant factor for increasing populations.

Approximately half the population in the world today has been born since 1945. Improved medical care has resulted in a substantial reduction in infant mortality rates,

allowing a greater number of infants to survive than ever before. At the same time that a higher portion of infants live to the age of procreation, improved health services and technology have helped to extend the life expectancy of persons born prior to 1945. The extension of life expectancy for adults is the reason people under the age of twenty-five do not constitute an even higher portion of the total population. For example, in the United States the life expectancy of a person advanced from thirty-three to seventy years (more than doubled) between the time the Pilgrims first settled New England and 1970.

Although the recent emphasis on youth in the United States has given the illusion that the average age of the population is getting younger, actually the opposite is true. In 1970 the median age in the United States was 25.9 years. In 1910 it was only 24.1 years. The net result of more people living longer has been that the average age of the population has risen, even though more youths under the age of twenty-five are alive today than ever before.

The large portion of youths approaching or at childbearing age has major implications for world population. In the underdeveloped and emerging nations roughly 40 percent of the population is under fifteen years old compared with 25 to 32 percent in the more advanced nations of Europe and North America.[4]

Because birth rates are related generally to the number of women of childbearing age (ages fifteen to forty-four) in a given locale, the avalanche of youth in emerging countries is an ominous sign for future population growth in such areas as Latin America, South Asia, and Africa. In these areas the birth rate is often 40 per 1,000 persons, nearly double that of the more developed nations. Until the 1950s the majority of demographers believed that the maximum birth rate that was physiologically possible in a given country was 45 births per 1,000 persons. During the 1960s and early 1970s this belief proved to be unwarranted, and nearly a dozen developing countries exceeded 45 births per 1,000. For example, Costa Rica had a birth rate of 44.9 in 1940; in 1950 it was 49.2; and in the mid-1960s it was 50.2.[5] Such high birth rates are occurring in the countries with the largest *potential* child-bearing populations.

When high birth rates are combined with lowered mortality rates, it is not difficult to understand that even if birth rates were reduced to the replacement level (i.e., limited to two children) population would continue to expand. It is estimated that it would take nearly 60 years, or almost a lifetime, before the world's population would stop growing.[6]

POPULATION GROWTH AND USE OF NATURAL RESOURCES

The quality of life is irrevocably tied to the quantity of people and the level of their material demands for goods and services. As the population increases, assuming that a given standard of living is to be maintained, increases in resource utilization must also occur. In simple terms, production must keep up with the requirements of the population. In the United States most citizens have high levels of expectation regarding these requirements. Although, as a nation, we are the world's greatest producer, we are also one of the world's most avid consumers. Robert and Leona Rienow illustrate this point:

Every 8 seconds a new American is born. He is a disarming little thing, but he begins to scream loudly in a voice that can be heard for 70 years. He is screaming for 56,000,000 gallons of water, 21,000 gallons of gasoline, 10,150 pounds of meat, 28,000 pounds of milk and cream, 9,000 pounds of wheat. . . .[7]

American children will also scream for school buildings, clothes, housing, automobiles, paper, plastic, steel, electric power, and other materials and services that they consider their share. Their total share, when combined with the shares of adult Americans, constitutes about half the total material production of the world.

The expectations of Americans continue to grow. It is estimated that in 1880 each American used roughly 50 tons of raw materials per year to sustain his or her standard of living. By the mid-1960s the amount of raw materials had grown to 300 tons per year. Based on an average life span of seventy years, each American is supported by 21,000 tons of raw materials which are not replaceable within many lifetimes.

Aside from the depletion of natural resources—i.e., iron, oil, coal, wood—to provide material goods for our expanding population, these raw materials are the basis for supplying the energy we require to supply electricity and heat for our homes, run our factories, and provide our transportation. It is estimated that the standard of living we currently enjoy in the United States uses 150,000 calories per person each day. Three thousand or less of these calories are required for physical nourishment; the remaining calories are used for production, transportation, and running laborsaving appliances.

Modern life-styles in industrialized nations are supported by raw materials used at a rate never before known to human beings. The rapid utilization of materials and energy has been brought about because our material needs and wants have accelerated. The technology of production has kept pace with the demand to convert increasing quantities of raw materials into more usable or desirable forms—automobiles, washing machines, housing, highways, television sets. Technology has helped people apply scientific knowledge in such fields as medicine, aerospace, communications, and production. At the same time that technology has extended our power over nature, it has contributed to the pollution of our air, water, and landscape which detracts from the habitability of our environment. Often other living things that are part of the ecological system pay the price of our unbridled application of technology. Insects and plant life die because of indiscriminate use of chemicals. Living things in rivers, lakes, and even the oceans are unwittingly diminished or altered because of industrial and human wastes that are deliberately or unthinkingly pumped into waterways.

URBANIZATION

Mass production has provided the material goods for the populations who live in technologically backward countries as well as those who live in industrialized nations. Both beneficial and nonbeneficial effects have resulted from the mass production processes man has developed. Industrialization creates jobs, and thus the people can work to earn the means to acquire the material goods that are produced. Industrialization also has accelerated the increasing concentration of populations in urban centers around the world. Not only have nations grown in population, but cities with their suburban areas are getting larger. Less than 15 years ago the world had only 29 cities which had 1 million residents. Now there are 133 such cities. Not only are big cities getting larger and more numerous, but middle-sized cities are increasing in number. According to the United Nations *Demographic Yearbook*, in 1970 the world had 1,784 cities with more than 100,000 people residing in each one. This was a 20 percent increase in the number of such cities over the previous decade. In 1973, over half of the population in North America and almost half of the population of Oceania live in cities of 100,000 or more. In South America and Europe, about one-third of the population live in cities of this size. About 10 percent of the population in Africa and Asia reside in such urban centers. Now more than one-third of the world's population lives in urban areas—quite a transition from the days when the farm was the primary living and production unit of society.

Throughout the world people have been moving from rural areas to more densely populated urban areas. In the United States alone, two-thirds of the population live on one-fiftieth of the land area in and around urban centers. With the current population trends indicating that we will number nearly 300 million by the year 2000, accommodations for the increase of 100 million people will mean crowding them into existing cities or building the equivalent of a new city with a population of 250,000 every 40 days for the next 30 years—35 more Los Angeleses, or 250 Newark, New Jerseys.

POLLUTION

The impact of an urbanized concentration of people in all areas of the world has resulted in a concentration of waste—solid, liquid, and gaseous—that has increased per capita along with the growing per capita use of materials and energy, intensifying pollution problems. The types, sources, and amounts of wastes increase with population growth, industry, and use of technology and natural resources. Many types of wastes are expected to increase even more rapidly than population.[8] Unless dramatic changes are made in our existing production processes and energy utilization patterns, increases in consumption will continue to mean compounded increases in pollution.

Since people have conceptualized the planet earth as a self-contained spaceship, they have been faced with the reality that they can no longer dispose of garbage merely by dumping it over the backyard fence. This is true whether they are seeking to dispose of aluminum cans or radioactive waste materials.

LIVING SPACE

In addition to rising pollution problems resulting from the interaction of population growth, industrialization, urbanization, and increased consumption patterns, other factors have become significant in assessing the quality of life we enjoy—population density and the living space each person has at his or her disposal. Although these two space factors are interrelated, they are not the same thing.

Population Density

Population density refers to the number of people per designated area and is most frequently calculated on the basis of a square mile. This gross index is an indication of the amount of land that is available in a given country to support each individual living in it. It indicates how much land is available to grow food, provide recreational space, erect homes, and accommodate other human uses.

The figures in Table 9-1 indicate the approximate populations, density, and land area for selected countries. It will become apparent that population density varies among nations without regard to their global location or stage of technological development. For example, in the most populous nation in the world, Mainland China, the density is less than in some highly industrialized nations in Europe (West Germany, United Kingdom, France). Yet China's density is considerably higher than any country in North America (United States, Mexico, Canada). Comparison of population densities

TABLE 9-1
Population Size and Density for Selected Countries

Country	Approximate population, millions	Density per square mile, millions	Area in square miles, thousands
Mainland China	800.7	216.9	3,690.5
India	563.5	446.5	1,261.5
Soviet Union	247.5	28.6	8,647.2
United States	208.8	57.8	3,614.3
Japan	107.0	748.0	142.8
West Germany	59.6	620.8	95.7
United Kingdom	55.8	593.5	94.2
Mexico	52.6	69.2	761.4
France	51.7	245.1	211.2
Argentina	23.9	22.3	1,071.9
Canada	21.6	5.6	3,850.8

SOURCE: Adapted from the *United Nations Demographic Yearbook*, 1972, and the *United Nations Monthly Bulletin of Statistics*, July 1973.

provides a gross basis for determining how much land is available for population expansion, but it does not provide any indication of how rich in mineral deposits the land is, nor does it tell about the topography which might make the land uninhabitable. These factors are important in determining the usability of the land.

Since 1970, a number of states in America have initiated planning efforts aimed at determining better land use for the future. Such plans reflect the need to take into account population growth, as well as the need for strict control over future land development to ensure that industrial use and urbanization will be balanced with appropriate open space so that a healthy living environment will result. In California, one proposed environmental plan states that a new kind of comprehensive planning is called for, one which is highly responsive to human needs as well as sensitive to the needs of that portion of the planet occupied by human beings.[9]

Concern about the use of available land and the distribution of population is a new and growing factor in industrialized nations where large segments of the population are clustered in or around large urban centers. However, concern about the number of human beings the land in a given region can support is becoming an unavoidable environmental consideration in developing as well as developed countries.

When all things are considered, it can be said that countries with the most fertile soil, abundant water, moderate climates, and bountiful natural resources attract and support the highest number of people. This may be reflected in population density; however, population density alone does not indicate the standard of living of the population. Other factors, such as the status of technology and access to material resources, affect living standards more than the land-people ratio.

Crowding

Social scientists have turned increasing attention toward other factors of people-space relationships. In the face of burgeoning cities with crowded living conditions, a number of studies have been conducted to determine the effects of limited space on behavior. Citing evidence gained from observing the behavior of rats placed in overcrowded conditions, the anthropologist Edward T. Hall has attempted to project the effects of crowding on human behavior. Hall's analysis leads to the conclusion that the stress produced from overcrowdedness contributes to a sense of disorganization and ultimate breakdown of normal social relations among people. The term "behavioral sink" was used to designate the gross distortions of behavior among the rat population that was subjected to excessive crowding. Delinquency, sexual deviations, violence, and crimes along with

other symptoms of behavioral breakdowns such as drug addiction, mental illness, nervous tension, and other physical and psychological disorders are often attributed to the overcrowded and squalid conditions found in inner cities and ghettos, where as many as a quarter of a million human beings are crowded into a few square miles, as they are in Harlem.

Hall sums up his conclusion regarding overcrowding in cities with this statement:

The implosion of the world population into cities everywhere is creating a series of destructive behavioral sinks more lethal than the hydrogen bomb. Man is faced with a chain reaction and practically no knowledge of the structure of the cultural atoms producing it. If what is known about animals when they are crowded or moved to an unfamiliar biotope is at all relevant to mankind, we are now facing some terrible consequences in our urban sinks. Studies of ethology and comparative proxemics should alert us to the dangers ahead as our rural populations pour into urban centers. The adjustment of these people is not just economic but involves an *entire way of life*.[10]

Not all social scientists agree that overcrowding has the effects of which Hall warns. Opponents of Hall's theory say that crowding seems to have little effect on juvenile delinquency or mental illness. As evidence, they refer to the fact that New York City, which is the most densely populated city in the United States, has a lower crime rate than many other cities. More important, within New York City, areas with the highest densities do not necessarily have the highest crime rates. However, even those who do not agree that population density is a causative factor in social breakdown do find that lack of sufficient space in the home is associated with more crime, mental illness, and probably other forms of social disorientation.

Living space is related to status and economics not only in amount but also in quality. The high-status and upper-income individual has better space and more of it. Most attempts to equalize the situation on a limited scale seem to fail because persons with higher incomes also have greater mobility and will move to places where more space is available and where their prerogatives will be recognized.[11] It is not surprising that people will avoid juvenile delinquency, congestion, and air and noise pollution if they can. Thus, the last two decades have seen a mass migration of families from the city to the suburbs. This move has been largely among the middle-income and higher-income population who have abandoned the core city and left behind concentrated populations of the elderly, nonwhite, and low-income families. Although the blighted living conditions of the inner city may have been reason enough to escape, the suburb, in many cases, was no utopia. Lack of architectural imagination, conformity, poor construction, and social isolation were often the price for families who sought to own their homes on a 20×40 m treeless lot. The move of many families to suburban developments only postponed rather than eliminated the declining social and living conditions.

POPULATION AND LIVING STANDARDS

Before discussing the implications of family planning as it affects the individuals involved, it might be useful to summarize a few generalizations about population and its impact on standards of living.

1   With the present status of technology and social organization among nations, there is little possibility of raising the material standard of living for the vast majority of people living in underdeveloped nations to the level enjoyed by those living in developed nations. As the population in the underdeveloped countries multiplies, the likelihood of raising their standards of living to Western levels becomes even more remote.

2   There is a strong probability that the standard of living enjoyed by the developed nations will have to be modified, if not lowered, as more people in underdeveloped nations acquire and demand more material goods and as pollution becomes an increasing barrier to existing production methods.

3   The production processes and consumption patterns of modern society are creating pollution problems at a faster rate than human beings have been able or willing to solve. Therefore, even if population growth ceases to be a factor, people will have to improve their efforts to clean up the environment if they wish to improve the living conditions of the millions of people who reside in urban centers.

4   The population base of the world is accelerating at an increasing pace with each generation. Although there is no known optimal long-range population level, given a finite set of resources to support and feed the population, growth cannot continue indefinitely. Therefore, human beings individually and collectively will ultimately have to face population control or a substantially reduced standard of living.

It has already been established that the efforts of the medical and health fields have resulted in lower mortality rates among all age groups. Therefore, reducing the birth rate will not, by itself, solve the population-related environmental problems faced by human beings. However, one cannot forgo or eliminate the long-range consequences if birth rates are not reduced. The question is: How should the reduction be brought about?

REDUCTION OF BIRTH RATES

Many demographers have observed that certain conditions tend to reduce birth rates. Rapid economic development and rising manufacturing and industrial production accompanied by increasing urbanization and limited living space have resulted in a relative disadvantage for large families. The downward trend in birth rates in the United States strongly indicates that there has been a voluntary reduction in birth rates. This self-imposed reduction was noted five or more years before contraceptive pills became widely available or the intrauterine device (IUD) widely used. During the past decade birth rates in seven European countries have dropped below the replacement level. A half dozen other European countries are rapidly reaching the zero population growth (ZPG) level. Although the migration of workers between countries may distort the growth rate of some countries, taken as a whole, birth rates in both Eastern and Western Europe have shown an absolute decline. In a number of other countries, most notably Sweden and Japan, declines in birth rates are attributed to legalized abortion rather than contraception. But the picture of human fertility does not approach ZPG in the majority of developing countries. Mainland China, India, Brazil, and Mexico made inroads on curbing birth rates, but the gains are not great, and even these limited examples are exceptions rather than the rule. Growing populations in most developing countries bear testimony that significant reduction of fertility is not occurring in countries where illiteracy and poverty are endemic. Perhaps economic and technological development would reduce

birth rates in such countries, but development seems to elude them because their limited resources are habitually spent to feed their ever-increasing numbers.

The race between population and famine in two-thirds of the world is a major concern not only to countries whose people are starving but to the major food-producing nations whose food reserves are being eliminated. In 1974 a United Nations International Children's Emergency Fund (UNICEF) report noted that 400 million children in underdeveloped countries face severe malnutrition and starvation. In November 1974, a World Food Conference was held in Rome. During this conference discussions centered on the problems associated with the growing number of starving persons living in underdeveloped nations and how the food-producing countries might better distribute their surplus food supplies. Unfortunately, no long-range solutions for meeting the needs of the undernourished peoples of the world were forthcoming from the conference.

One means of reducing starvation is to increase food supplies and to develop more efficient distribution systems. Another approach calls for reducing birth rates in the world so that existing food supplies can be used to sustain human health and existence. Both solutions require time to implement, and offer little comfort to those already suffering from hunger and malnutrition.

To achieve lower birth rates, sterilization of males by vasectomy and sterilization of females by tubal ligation has been used and promoted in a number of developing nations. India, for example, reported that 4 million males have undergone vasectomies during the past few years. However, it is also reported that sterilization among males in India has shown a decline in popularity despite measures to promote it. The Indian government has found it difficult to administer family planning services over its vast territory. Furthermore, it is the contention of the Indian government that couples must be motivated not only to practice contraception but also to plan smaller families. Many who presently practice contraception in India have four or more children and many of those that do not engage in family planning also already have large families.[12]

At the same time that sterilization procedures have shown lagging interest in such nations as India, they have gained popularity in the United States. Although sterilization is not as popular as oral contraceptives, which were used by an estimated 8 million persons in 1970, or the condom, employed by another 5 million, it was obtained by an estimated 1 million Americans in 1974.

In the mid-1960s, more women than men requested sterilization, but by the early 1970s, 75 percent of the requests were from males. Even though there has been increasing concern over the possible side effects or long-range consequences of sterilization of males, the Association for Voluntary Sterilization reports that the most frequent requests came from middle-aged fathers of three or more children. Another trend appears to be the rising number of calls for sterilization from younger people with no children.[13]

Reduced birth rates have also been attributed to a number of changes in social patterns and institutions. It is claimed that postponement of marriage until a later age, along with a growing acceptance of oral contraceptives, has helped reduce birth rates in Mainland China. This reflects a major cultural change on both counts for the Chinese people.

It is noteworthy that the number of marriages in the United States has stabilized at 10.9 per 1,000 persons. In 1963, a decade earlier, the marriage rate was 8.8 per 1,000. What the long-range effects of postponed marriages or reduction in the rate of marriages will be on birth rates is yet to be measured; however, if the pattern of the past decade continues, the developed nations will see a substantial reduction in average family size by 1980. At present the average completed family in the United States includes about 2.7 children; by 1980 it is expected to drop to 2.4 children.

Barriers to Population Control

Proponents of ZPG have launched a strong campaign against reproduction. Neutral observers could easily conclude that if anti-population groups have their way human beings would soon become an endangered species. Although there are signs, most notably in more developed nations, that reduced birth rates can and will be attained, there are many widespread factors that militate against sustained reduction in birth rates. Paul R. Ehrlich discussed one of the deep-rooted barriers to birth control in his book on population growth:

Billions of years of evolution have given us all a powerful will to live. Intervening in the birth rate goes against our evolutionary values. During all those centuries of our evolutionary past, the individuals who had the most children passed on their genetic endowment in greater quantities than those who reproduced less. Their genes dominate our heredity today. All our biological urges are for more reproduction, and they are all too often reinforced by our culture. In brief, death control goes with the grain, birth control against it.[14]

In addition to cultural habits, other social and political forces oppose the practice of birth control or abortion. For example, some nations promote the theory that a larger population will contribute to their own political, economic, or military power. Some nations have and do reward marriage and childbirth with acclaim or actual financial benefits.

Although many nations do not overtly reward childbirth or large families, there is still a strong cultural belief that growth is good. It may make little difference as to the type of growth—gross national product, number of cars produced, tons of steel, sales volume, or population—as long as the current figures show increases over previous ones. Cities take pride in their population increases between censuses. Nations look to their increased numbers for military strength and a larger labor supply. As long as a culture treats quantitative increases as having intrinsic value, there will be little substantial action to make anything smaller. This will be true whether one is dealing with population or the number of automobiles produced. Thus, population will tend to increase in such a culture because of the implicit sanction given to growth.

For some people a major barrier to birth control is direct religious opposition, most notably the Roman Catholic Church. On numerous occasions Pope Paul VI has expressed the attitude of the church toward artificial birth control.

Instead of increasing the supply of bread on the dining table of the hunger-ridden world, as modern techniques of production can do today, some are thinking in terms of diminishing, by illicit means, the number of those who eat with them. This is unworthy of civilization.[15]

Opposition to "illicit means" of birth control will undoubtedly delay the reduction of birth rates in underdeveloped nations where a large portion of the population is Roman Catholic. Time will tell whether the Roman Catholic Church will change its position about birth control or whether developing nations in the sphere of its influence can gain a foothold on economic progress so that reduced birth rates will occur as they did

prior to widespread use of contraceptive technology in the advanced nations.

If all cultural, political, and religious sources of resistance to contraception were eliminated, the long-range effectiveness of birth control methods in many underdeveloped nations would still depend upon the development and implementation of inexpensive, less burdensome methods than presently exist. In many countries the level of illiteracy is a hindrance to widespread distribution of information and medical advice on family planning and birth control. Pills that must be taken daily will no doubt have to be replaced by methods that may last for longer periods of time if contraception is to become truly workable for many women who are confused about present methods. Perhaps the future lies with the development of a safe temporary male sterilization technique.

THE DECISION TO PLAN A FAMILY

Although proponents of ZPG often give the doctrinaire impression that *no* family should have more than two children (i.e., replacement of the parents), most groups encouraging family planning emphasize that it is a means for *spacing* children as well as regulating their number. Most parents when considering family planning are not concerned with futuristic abstractions or global population forecasts.

Another simple and unscientific factor acting as a force in family planning is the fact that many people love children. This is not often discussed by proponents of ZPG, but many men and women of all races and national origins share this human emotion. Such a factor is germane to family planning in all countries, whether or not they are wealthy or technologically advanced. Love of children is not an abstraction, and persons contemplating raising a family should be directly concerned with their own physical ability and psychological willingness to incur the added responsibility for rearing a child.

This poses questions that each family must be prepared to answer. After careful consideration some couples may decide that despite cultural pressures they will remain childless. Others may find that despite the publicity of ZPG they want to have more than two children. In either case family planning has stressed the right of parents to have the number of children they want, not the right of society (church, government, and so on) to have the number of children it needs. When the majority of parents want children, population will continue to increase. Thus, many population and environmental experts agree that the effectiveness of a self-limiting population is dubious when the decision to procreate remains with the discretion of the parents. Yet the idea that anyone else should share in the decision is regarded by many as an extreme danger to personal freedom.

Although the self-limiting population concept may prove inadequate over the long run, there is little chance that it can succeed if people remain unaware of the human and environmental consequences of overpopulation and the role each individual plays in creating such a condition.

REFERENCES

1 Carvell, Fred, and Max Tadlock: *It's Not Too Late*, Glencoe, Beverly Hills, 1971, pp. xix–xx.
2 U.S. Department of Health, Education, and Welfare, Office of Education, Environmental Education Studies Staff: *Environmental Education Act*, 1970.
3 Brody, Samuel: "Facts, Fables, and Fallacies on Feeding the World Population," in Paul Shepard and Daniel McKinley (eds.), *The Subversive Science*, Houghton Mifflin, Boston, 1969, p. 74.
4 Kormondy, Edward J.: *Concepts of Ecology*, Prentice-Hall, Englewood Cliffs, N.J., 1969, p. 83.
5 Paddock, William, and Paul Paddock: *Famine 1975!*, Little, Brown, Boston, 1967, p. 22.
6 For further discussion on the impact of limited birth rates on the population of specific countries in the world see *The Two-Child Family and Population Growth: An International View*, compiled by the U.S. Bureau of the Census, 1970.
7 Rienow, Robert, and Leona Train Rienow: *Moment in the Sun*, Ballantine, New York, 1967, p. 3.
8 Lamson, Robert W.: "The Future of Man's Environment," *The Science Teacher*, 36(1), January 1969.
9 Heller, Alfred: *The California Tomorrow Plan*, William Kaufmann, Los Altos, Calif., 1972.
10 Hall, Edward T.: *The Hidden Dimension*, Doubleday, Garden City, N.Y., 1966, p. 155.
11 Sommer, Robert: "Planning *Not Place* for Nobody," *Saturday Review*, Apr. 5, 1969, p. 69.
12 Gaud, William S.: "AID Policy on Family Planning and Population Growth," policy paper distributed by the Agency for International Development, U.S. Department of State, February 1968, p. 9.
13 Tuthill, Sue: "Today's Health News," *Today's Health*, October 1971, p. 8.
14 Ehrlich, Paul R.: *The Population Bomb*, Ballantine, New York, 1969, p. 34.
15 Excerpts from Pope Paul VI, *Christmas Message to the World*, 1963.

BIBLIOGRAPHY

Clarke, John: *Population Geography and the Developing Countries*, Pergamon, Oxford, 1971.
Coale, Ansley: "The History of the Human Popu-

lation," *Scientific American*, 231:41–51, 1974.

Demeny, Paul: "The Populations of the Underdeveloped Countries," *Scientific American*, 231:149–159, 1974.

Dreitzel, Hans Peter (ed.): *Family, Marriage, and the Struggle of the Sexes*, Macmillan, New York, 1972.

Ehrlich, Paul R., and Anne H. Ehrlich: *The End of Affluence*, Ballantine, New York, 1974.

Feldman, Saul D., and Gerald W. Thielbar: *Life Styles: Diversity in American Society*, Little, Brown, Boston, 1972.

Freedman, Ronald, and Bernard Serelson: "The Human Population," *Scientific American*, 231:31–36, 1974.

Heer, David: "Economic Development and the Fertility Transition," in D. V. Glass and Roger Revelle (eds.), *Population and Social Change*, Edward Arnold, London, 1972.

Huber, Joan (ed.): *Changing Women in a Changing Society*, University of Chicago Press, Chicago, 1973.

Mamdani, Mahmood: *The Myth of Population Control: Family, Caste, and Class in an Indian Village*, Monthly Review, New York, 1972.

Nag, Moni: "Anthropology and Population: Problems and Perspectives," *Population Studies*, 27:49–68, 1973.

Polgar, Steven (ed.): *Culture and Population: A Collection of Current Studies*, Schenkman, Cambridge, 1971.

Revelle, Roger: "Food and Population," *Scientific American*, 231:161–170, 1974.

10

Infertility

ELIZABETH M. EDMANDS

Family planning in its broadest sense encompasses the desire on the part of a couple to determine whether or not they will have children, how many, and at what intervals they will conceive. Currently the emphasis is on curbing a rapidly expanding population in the United States and abroad. However, this situation has little meaning for most couples who are having difficulty in producing at least one child of their own. *Infertility* is a relative term implying inability to have children as readily as most couples do. The terms sterility and infertility are commonly used interchangeably, but *sterility* actually represents the incapacity to conceive.

Nurses have been involved for many years in the education, counseling, and care of persons who seek assistance for the problem of infertility. New knowledge and techniques of diagnostic and therapeutic procedures have had a profound effect on the nature and extent of nursing responsibilities in this area.

They call for all the sensitivity, compassion, and understanding the nurse can give, for they involve not only intimate relationships between the couple, but also a need for confidence and trust in the professional staff.

HISTORICAL PERSPECTIVE

Human beings may not have realized the relationship between coitus and pregnancy until they were well along in their cultural and intellectual development. However, we do have evidence that barrenness was recognized over 4,000 years ago (Egyptian medical papyri), and there are numerous references to it in the Old Testament. In the fifth century B.C. Hippocrates developed theories about woman's inability to conceive and wrote of his prescribed remedies. Soranus, a Greek physician in the second century, wrote a number of books on gynecology. His writings indicate that he recognized the relation of emotional factors and good physical health to conception.

It was not until the year 1677 that Leeuwenhoek and his German medical student, Ham, while examining human semen, saw what they called *animalcules* through a simple microscope. They were spermatozoa. It was also in the seventeenth century that de Graaf described the ovarian follicle, but not until 1827 did von Baer see the first ovum.[1]

Numerous were the contributions of many medical scientists to the development of knowledge both before and after these critical discoveries. Names such as Rubin (tubal insufflation), Knaus-Ogino (fertile-infertile period), and Klinefelter (chromosomal abnormalities) are prominent today. These men and others did their work in the twentieth century. Less than 100 years ago, experts were writing that the best time to achieve pregnancy was just before and after the menstrual period. They even hypothesized that male children were conceived premenstru-

ally and females postmenstrually. Therefore, it is evident that scientific diagnostic procedures and treatment of infertility are modern accomplishments, based on concepts that had their origin in antiquity but their critical refinements only in this century.

There have been few religious prohibitions to the procedures involved in the study of infertility. A notable exception is the objection of the Roman Catholic Church and strict Orthodox Jews to masturbation, withdrawal, or use of the condom to obtain semen samples for the study of the male factor.

INCIDENCE AND CAUSES

Fifteen percent of all couples will experience difficulty in producing a child. They are either infertile or sterile. The drive to reproduce is nearly universal, and failure to do so is regarded as a major tragedy in some cultures and some families. Fortunately for the infertile couple, the same search for an effective way to limit reproduction has provided insight into ways to stimulate it.

Infertility is found cross-culturally. It occurs in all economic groups and social classes. However, there is a difference in its etiology depending on some of these factors. For example, in the United States within the lower-income groups, pelvic inflammatory disease and postabortal sepsis contribute to a high incidence of tubal closure. Behrman and Kistner state, "An overall review of recent literature dealing with the major causes of infertility reveals a gradient of this order: cervical factor, 20 percent; tubal factor, 30 to 35 percent; male factor, 30 to 35 percent; hormonal factor, 15 percent. Among private patients the cervical factor is much lower and the hormonal factor much higher."[2]

Four factors that contribute generally to a couple's ability to conceive are (1) the age of the female partner, (2) the age of the male partner, (3) the frequency of intercourse, and

(4) the length of exposure. The peak of fertility in the female is reached at about twenty-four years of age. There is a gradual decline until about age thirty, then the decline becomes more rapid. It is a rare exception for pregnancy to occur after the female is fifty years of age. The male peak is also reached at twenty-four to twenty-five years. The decline is also gradual, but there are reported cases of male fertility remaining as late as eighty to ninety years of age.

It is estimated that a frequency of sexual intercourse averaging 4 times per week is most likely to produce conception in a 6-month period. Depending on all other factors, average couples not using contraception will conceive at the rate of 25 percent the first month, 65 percent in 6 months, 80 percent in a year, and 90 percent in 18 months.[3]

Infertility often has multiple causes. There are male and female factors and those that relate to the couple as a unit. For each partner these factors can be grouped as general, developmental, endocrine, and genital disease. For the couple as a unit, there are the factors of sexual knowledge and adjustment, immunologic incompatibility, and minor factors which might not be significant in one partner, but in combination produce a subfertile threshold.[4]

In spite of the fact that infertility management has made considerable progress, there probably will remain from 5 to 10 percent of all couples for whom no medical reason for their barrenness can be determined.[5]

DIAGNOSTIC APPROACH AND THERAPY

The Couple

Although it is usually the female partner who first seeks medical assistance for infertility, it is considered unwise to subject her to more than the most simple diagnostic procedures unless the male partner also agrees to an evaluation. The couple is entitled to a full explanation of the tests and procedures involved and the reasons why they are done. An overall plan is made in progressive steps, and testing usually continues until critical defects are found, pregnancy occurs, or the plan is completed. The length of time required is usually estimated from 6 to 18 months. The couple should fully understand what is expected of them, for their consistent cooperation is essential to the study. They will also want to know something about costs. These estimates will obviously vary according to the findings, but they should know that complex diagnostic evaluation or corrective surgical procedures requiring hospitalization will increase the costs of the investigation.

The decision of a couple with an infertility problem to seek help is frequently therapeutic in itself. Some physicians and infertility clinics report conception occurring before tests have been made or soon after—sometimes before any treatment is possible. It may be that there is improvement in psychological outlook, followed by release of tension when the couple realizes that their problem is not unique or that they have transferred their burden to someone who is skilled in helping them.[6]

The basic premise of fertility has been described in a booklet published by the American Infertility Society.[7] The following clear, concise statements describe quite simply what processes must take place in order for pregnancy to occur:

1 *Male:* The husband must produce a sufficient number of normal, motile spermatozoa which have access through patent pathways to be discharged on ejaculation from the urethra.

2 *Male and female:* These spermatozoa must be deposited in the female in

such a way that they reach and penetrate the cervical secretion and ascend through the uterus to the tube at the time in the cycle appropriate for fertilization of the ovum.

3 *Female:* The wife must produce a normal fertilizable ovum which must enter the fallopian tube within a period of a few hours and become fertilized. The resulting conceptus must move into the uterus and implant in an adequately developed endometrium, and there undergo normal development.

In some women who have no other demonstrable cause for infertility, sperm-immobilizing or sperm-agglutinating antibodies have been found in their blood plasma. When the male partner uses a condom only and the woman does not use any vaginal lubricants, her titer of circulating antibodies tends to fall in time. These findings suggest that some women make antibodies to their male partner's sperm, and some become pregnant after the antibody titer falls.[8]

Couples need to realize that infertility problems may be complex, often involving psychosocial and cultural factors as well as physical impairments. Some couples will be extremely embarrassed because of the necessity to reveal aspects of their personal life which they have considered private. Infertility diagnosis and treatment can be a threatening experience for any couple. It can also be a time when wise counseling and skillful interpretation of findings can promote understanding and empathy between the couple regardless of the outcome of the investigation.

The Male Partner

Usually the male partner is referred to a urologist for diagnosis and evaluation. Only recently have some gynecologists included the actual examination and treatment of the male. In either case, close cooperation and coordination of testing and reporting are essential.

History

A complete history is of primary importance. This will include medical, social, sexual, and occupational factors. Medical factors of vital importance are past and present illnesses, especially mumps, orchitis, venereal diseases, and surgical procedures. Social habits to be noted include excessive smoking, alcoholism, and fatigue. Sexual aspects such as use of precoital lubricants, premature ejaculation, impotence, and coital positioning may all have significance. Occupational exposure to radioactive substances, gasoline and carbon monoxide fumes, excessive heat, or certain metals may be etiological factors. Prolonged excessive heat to the genital area may affect spermatogenesis.

Examination

Physical examination includes special emphasis on observation of secondary male characteristics, endocrinopathy, presence of congenital abnormalities such as undescended or atrophic testicles, hypospadias, cryptorchism, and absence of vas deferens.

Laboratory Studies

Laboratory studies include those of basic routine evaluation appropriate for age or any presenting symptoms of pain or dysfunction. Nearly all clinicians include tests for thyroid function and, if indicated, may add other endocrine studies. A complete semen analysis is usually done. Authorities differ on the number of specimens required, but if the first is abnormal, usually a minimum of three, collected at intervals of 2 to 4 weeks, are sufficient. A period of continence corresponding to the usual frequency of intercourse is recommended prior to obtaining the specimen. The specimen is obtained by masturbation or coitus interruptus and collected in a clean, dry, glass jar. It should be transported to the doctor's office as soon as possible and no later than 2 hours after collection.[9]

Factors and standards (not absolute) for examination of the seminal fluid are as follows:

1 Liquefaction: complete within 10 to 30 minutes
2 Volume: 2.5 to 5 ml
3 Motility: proportion of forward-moving sperm related to time of ejaculation
4 Count: minimum normal 40 million sperm per ml or a total count of 125 million per ejaculate
5 Morphology: normal sperm heads in 80 percent of count[10]

Treatment

In general, treatment of male infertility has been discouraging. Correction of underlying conditions affecting general health can be instigated. Elimination of external factors such as heat, radiation, or exposure to certain fumes and metals may be beneficial. Habits of excessive smoking, drinking, and fatigue can be curtailed. Surgical treatment of congenital abnormalities and obstructions may be possible. Coitus at regular intervals of approximately every 2 or 3 days will encourage sperm motility without appreciably decreasing sperm count. All these measures increase the probability of conception and certainly are in no way harmful. Frequently reassurance, instruction in coital techniques, and emphasis on timing of intercourse in relation to ovulation are helpful to the male partner who is subfertile but not sterile.

The Female Partner

Often the female partner who is having difficulty in achieving a pregnancy prefers to consult her own source of medical care first. This procedure is advisable for if there is any chronic medical condition or known abnormality, this information can be communicated on referral to the physician or infertility clinic. However, few general practitioners are equipped to do a complex study, and unless there is an obvious minor correctable condition, most generalists will not delay referral to a specialist. Infertility studies are ideally conducted by a team of specialists, such as gynecologists, endocrinologists, psychiatrists, and marriage counselors with consultation from others, depending on the nature of preliminary findings.

History

The history required of the female is even more detailed than that of the male partner. In addition to medical, surgical, and sociocultural factors, a complete menstrual history including onset, frequency, duration, pain, and amount of flow should be recorded. It is important to know about use of contraceptives—kind, duration and cessation of use, and side effects, if any. Coital frequency and timing in relation to ovulation must be explored. Other factors include vaginal and pelvic infections, abdominal and pelvic surgery, and use of intravaginal lubricants and douches.[11] If a previous pregnancy has been achieved, full details on the course and outcome are essential. During history taking it is possible to obtain some estimate of the woman's attitudes toward coitus, relationships with her mate, and the degree of anxiety in relation to her failure to conceive.

If no previous evaluation of the time of ovulation has been made, the patient is instructed to keep a basal body temperature

(BBT) chart. During the monthly cycle, women who ovulate have biphasic curves. The term *biphasic* means that there are two levels of temperature occurring during the menstrual cycle. For example, following menstruation temperatures generally remain at a low level for approximately 14 to 16 days. Then just before or during ovulation the temperature shifts to a higher level due to the rupture of the ovarian follicle. (See Figure 10-1.) It is estimated that ovulation takes place within a 24- to 72-hour period of the temperature shift.[12] There are other tests for ovulation, notably the cervical mucus test described below under the Sims-Hühner test. The important factor to determine for purposes of infertility evaluation is whether ovulation occurs at all. Menstruation alone does not ensure that prior ovulation has occurred.

Examination

A complete physical examination is performed, during which time observation is made of the general body contour, the relation of weight to height, breast development, and evidence of a female pattern of hair distribution. A thorough pelvic examination includes evaluation of any abnormality or infection. Specifically in relation to the woman's ability to conceive, the examiner evaluates the hymen, clitoris, cervical os, and the size and position of the uterus and also looks for evidence of tumors, malformations, or endometriosis.

Laboratory Studies

Laboratory procedures begin with basic routine urinalysis, serological examination for syphilis, blood count, sedimentation rate, and chest x ray. Tests for thyroid function and a Papanicolaou smear are always done. If any purulent secretion is noted on vaginal

examination, it should be stained and cultured for gonococci.[13] Some examiners also do a hanging drop slide for *Candida* (*Monilia*) and *Trichomonas*, especially when there is a complaint of dyspareunia. If there is a history of irregular menses, amenorrhea, hirsutism, acne, or excessive weight gain, basic endocrine studies are also done.

Three important diagnostic tests that can be done in the physician's office or on an outpatient basis are discussed in the following paragraphs.

The Sims-Hühner test is a postcoital examination of cervical mucus. It is done at the time of ovulation and from 1 to 12 hours after coitus. The purpose of the test is to determine sperm survival and motility. Also, the characteristics of the cervical mucus can be determined. Normally at ovulation it forms a thin, continuous thread when pulled apart (spinnbarkeit) and when dried on a slide takes on a fernlike pattern called arborization. Both of these phenomena disappear during the progesterone phase following ovulation.

The endometrial biopsy is performed to test for ovulation. The optimal time is the sixth to eighth day after the shift in BBT, or if this is obscure, at the first day of menstruation. It is then possible to determine whether uterine bleeding is anovulatory. If the biopsy shows abnormal tissue, it should be followed by curettage to be sure there is no malignancy.

Tubal insufflation is also known as the Rubin test. It is diagnostic but may also be therapeutic. The best time to perform the test is 3 to 4 days after menstruation. It is preceded by a pelvic examination to rule out any evidence of infection, which would be a contraindication. With the woman in the lithotomy position, carbon dioxide is introduced into the fallopian tubes, through the cervix and uterus. Pressure readings under normal conditions show a rise and fall. Also

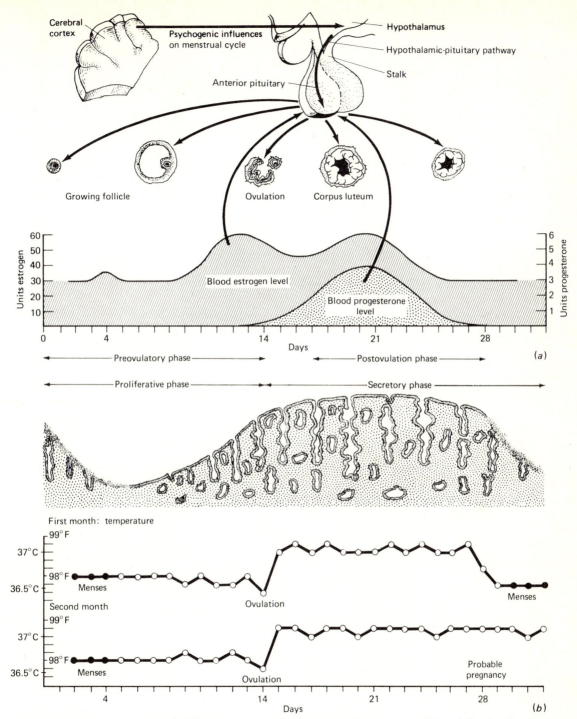

FIGURE 10-1 Hormonal control of the menstrual cycle. (a) Hormonal changes paralleling follicular changes;
(b) endometrial changes correlated with body temperature. (*Reproduced with permission from R. C. Benson,
Handbook of Obstetrics and Gynecology, 5th ed., Lange Medical Publications, Los Altos, Calif., 1974.*)

significant is the pain in the shoulder experienced by the woman with tubal patency. Tests should be repeated if pregnancy does not occur after a normal test or if there is evidence of obstruction.

As a result of these tests, other examinations may be indicated. *Hysterosalpingography* enables the examiner to investigate tubal patency by visualizing the tubes through fluoroscopic or x-ray examination. *Culdoscopy* is done as an inpatient procedure, usually under spinal anesthesia. By injecting methylene blue into the cervix with the culdoscope in place, further visualization of the tubes is feasible. *Laparoscopy* is being done more frequently as instruments have been perfected. Some examiners believe this is preferable to culdoscopy because, if indicated, corrective procedures can be carried out immediately after the examination.[14]

Treatment

The defects found on examination of the female are more likely to be amenable to treatment than those of the male. However, the degree of severity, the type of defect found, and the relationship of multiple defects are critical factors in the probability that their correction will enable pregnancy to occur.

Estrogen deficiency may be treated with small doses of this hormone over a period of several months. Other endocrine defects may be more difficult to assess and treat in relation to infertility because of their complexity and interrelatedness. Anovulation is often successfully treated with drugs like clomiphene or human menopausal gonadotrophin. Removal of any vaginal or uterine obstruction to the flow of seminal fluid may require only a simple surgical procedure. Gradual dilation of a closed cervix and treatment of cervical inflammation with antibiotics have been used, but it is questionable

how specific such measures are in improving the woman's fertility. Pelvic endometriosis may be treated both by surgery and by suppression with progestagens. Disease and obstruction of the oviducts are the most common organic causes of infertility in women, and the treatment is usually plastic surgical repair.

The purpose of the complete diagnostic study is to uncover all contributing causes for infertility. Return of fertility is usually the result of a change of threshold, rather than the discovery and correction of a single blocking factor. Successful outcome in the study of infertility can be measured by the discovery of a cause or by an exhaustive study which determines no known medical impediment. Psychosomatic factors may impinge on the ultimate achievement of pregnancy in either of these groups. However, the supportive measures provided by skilled counseling have been known to be effective to the couple's resolution of their problem. This may be their ability to produce a child, successful adaptation to childlessness, or adoption.

ALTERNATIVES

Adoption

For the couple found to be permanently sterile or even for the couple for whom no medical cause for infertility can be found, adoption may fulfill their desire to become parents. The physician usually is not equipped to make judgments or provide the complex guidance that prospective adopting parents need to determine if this course of action is advisable for them. It is the physician's responsibility to see that those who desire to pursue adoption are referred to a responsible counselor or agency.

Not all couples who are unable to have children of their own can provide the care and nurturing needed by adopted children. Some couples who seek diagnostic help are motivated by a desire to know whether they are fertile or infertile so they can decide about continued use of contraceptives. Still others consider their infertility as evidence of something abnormal. They do not desire a child, but only reassurance of their normalcy.[15]

It is not as easy today to adopt a baby of the desired sex as it was a few years ago. Availability of contraception and abortion are decreasing the number of women who carry an unwanted pregnancy to term. However, older children, those of mixed race, and those with physical and mental deficiencies are still available and just as much in need of love and support. Wise counseling can often make such an adoption a satisfactory and fulfilling experience for the parents and the child.

There are few, if any, well-documented studies on the incidence of conception after adoption. Two studies, one of which was reported by Hanson and Rock[16] in 1950, and the other by Tyler, Bonapart, and Grant[17] in 1960, and two surveys by Banks in 1960 and 1961[18,19] found very small percentages of adopting couples who later achieved pregnancy. Evaluation of couples who did conceive suggests that they may not have received an exhaustive infertility work-up or may have been among the 10 percent who spontaneously achieve pregnancy with or without adoption when no medical cause can be found. The reason that it is such a common belief that pregnancy follows adoption may be due to the drama involved or the optimistic expectations generated by this achievement when all the facts are not known.

Artificial Insemination

There are two types of artificial insemination possible today. They are known as AIH (artificial insemination by husband) and AID (artificial insemination by donor).

For those couples in whom no medical pathology can be found and yet pregnancy does not occur, the physician may suggest that a semen specimen from the husband (AIH) be introduced by syringe into the vagina at the mouth of the cervix. This is a simple procedure which is timed to coincide with the ovulation period. Usually three inseminations are carried out during each cycle over a period of 3 months or until pregnancy is achieved.[20]

When it has been proved by exhaustive study that the male is azoospermic but the female is capable of producing a child, the couple may want to consider artificial insemination by a donor (AID). Although this is a medically sound procedure, it may have legal complications in some states. Further discussion of technique, medical and legal aspects, and social implications may be found in specialized texts dealing more extensively with this subject.

NURSING INVOLVEMENT

Case-finding, Counseling, and Referral

A nurse living or working in a community needs to be sensitive to local attitudes toward women's roles, motherhood, parenthood, and the meaning of children. Although many couples desire at least one or two children of their own, there is growing evidence that this factor may be changing. Particularly in industrialized countries, there is concern about rapid population growth, the increasing cost of rearing children, and the critical shortage of natural resources, and there seem to be ever-widening opportunities for the employment of women. However, for those couples who do want children, they usually expect to produce their first child within 3 or 4 years.

In many situations, whether at work or as a neighbor in the community, a friendly, approachable nurse may be the first person to learn that a woman or a couple are doubtful about their ability to conceive. Others, however, will be reluctant to initiate a query because of embarrassment or lack of knowledge that anything can be done. Perhaps the first manifestations may be marital stress or physical and emotional symptoms.

How can these couples who need help be approached? There is a time for subtle suggestion, and there is a time for the direct approach. When nurses must talk about any delicate or serious problem, they try to find a time when privacy can be assured, when the subject can be introduced naturally into a conversation, and when the recipients of their messages are most likely to understand. When the subject is infertility, they may expect that this emotionally charged topic can bring forth denial, resentment, blame toward anyone but self, and frequently profound grief. One woman described her reaction: "I've been frantic to talk about this to someone. I'm glad you brought it up, but now I feel exposed."[21] Mixed reactions are common, but when handled by a skillful, compassionate interviewer, there is usually relief and gratitude.

Perhaps one of the most important things for the nurse to know is that any couple who desires a child and have cohabited normally for a year without using contraceptives are entitled to a full infertility evaluation. If either partner is over thirty-five years of age, they should be referred for medical help after 6 unsuccessful months.[22]

Community health nurses working in their districts are frequently approached by a mother-in-law, a relative, or a neighbor to ask what can be done. This situation can involve sensitive and complex relationships. Two actions are possible. Preferably, nurses can suggest that the woman or couple be referred to them for discussion and information. If this seems unlikely to happen, then necessary knowledge and means of referral to competent resources should be given.

It is not always the couple who has never reproduced that needs counsel; it may be the couple with one child who is experiencing problems with a second conception. Age and the interval since last delivery are critical factors. Those couples who have been using contraceptives and stop because they desire a pregnancy should be counseled regarding expectations and medical intervention if they are not successful. The interval will depend on age and the type of contraceptive used.

Counseling in infertility requires that the nurse be knowledgeable about human reproductive anatomy and physiology, sexual practices such as frequency and timing of intercourse, likelihood of conception for age and length of coital exposure, procedures involved in male and female fertility investigations, and available resources for referral. The nurse also must be able to gauge the amount of information that can be absorbed by the particular individual or couple at a given time. The first objective may be simply to establish a comfortable relationship that will invite discussion.

Procedures in counseling will vary with the situation. A formal or informal history is often the opening wedge to ascertain the direction for further exploration. If the counseling is in response to a query, a base line of the couple's knowledge needs to be established before the counselor can proceed.

Even today there are married couples with an abysmal lack of knowledge of how conception takes place. Many do not understand when ovulation occurs or that it is of short duration. Old wives' tales and superstitions abound, not only in the poorly educated, but in some who give an outward appearance of sophistication. Perhaps it is in this basic teaching that nurses can make a unique contribution. Women who have doubts or apprehension about intimate, personal female problems are far more likely to seek out another woman, and particularly a nurse, whom they believe has the answers. The male nurse also has a unique contribution to make in relation to the male sex partner. Answers to some of these questions may be all that is needed by some couples in order to achieve a pregnancy.

Referral procedures will vary with the circumstances within which the case-finding and counseling take place. It is obvious that those who have a private physician should be referred to this source first. If there is an infertility clinic within the community, medical referral may be required. If so, a medical clinic or private physician may be the actual referring agent. However, the nurse should be knowledgeable about resources within the community, state, or region and about costs, eligibility, and the number of visits usually required for a basic evaluation. This information can be helpful to the couple seeking advice and may enable the nurse to work in partnership with the physician to provide a supporting referral team.

Care and Support

After the couple has been referred to a diagnostic resource, they may still need the interest and encouragement that can be provided by the referring nurse. Inquiry regarding progress and further clarification of the reasons for procedures may provide the stimulus to continue the diagnostic process. The community health nurse is often in a position to give such continuity of care.

The nurse working in an infertility clinic or with the physician who is carrying out the procedures has a critical role to perform. The female nurse can relate closely to the woman, and the male nurse can be helpful to the man. A dignified yet friendly approach, an unhurried manner, patience, and understanding are qualities that can make the nurse an invaluable member of the examining team.

Although procedures may have been explained innumerable times, clients in their anxiety often have questions about these procedures or want reassurance that a test is really needed. Nurses learned long ago that people frequently wish to appear self-confident, knowledgeable, and unafraid when interacting with their physician but will express their concerns and ask for interpretation of information from the nurse. This pattern should not be discouraged, nor the fact belittled, for each profession has its own role in relation to the delivery of health service.

Some of the procedures may be painful, unpleasant, tedious, and require repetition. A nurse who can explain the procedure and inform the clients what is expected of them will not only make the procedure more endurable, but may actually encourage the relaxation that is essential for the test or treatment to be properly done. During the gynecological examinations, women appreciate a kind, sympathetic nurse by their side who can anticipate their needs or ease their discomforts.

Nurses must be aware that both partners are under stress and that it will increase as procedures become more complex. For the client and staff, each test holds the expectation that it will reveal what is wrong. While waiting for the results of these tests, hopes may soar that a remediable defect will be found. It is one of the few situations in which the determination of medical normalcy is not always a welcome diagnosis.

Coordination with Other Disciplines

Throughout the nurse's contact with the client or couple, more information will be received. Some of it will have little pertinence to the evaluation, but some may be highly significant. A nurse who is alert and sensitive to subtle clues and has the judgment to decide their relevance is a great asset.

Opportunities for communication and co-ordination of activities with other disciplines occur under a variety of circumstances. Prior to referral nurses may need to discuss their plans with the local physician or a social worker. At the time of referral, their knowledge of the situation relayed by telephone or written report may give focus to an immediate problem or to a complex, involved background. The nurse in the infertility clinic or specialist's office works closely with other members of the team. Communication with others, such as the physician, the marriage counselor, the social worker, or the psychologist, takes place during routine procedures as well as at case conferences.

Nurses engaged in multiphasic screening may be the first to detect unrecognized or subconscious infertility among apparently normal persons. In counseling people receiving contraceptives, or women seeking abortion, a nurse must be aware of their interrelatedness to infertility. When appropriate, such information should be given to the couple. In areas of the country where health personnel are scarce, physicians may not be able to give as high a priority to infertility as to lifesaving measures. It may be that a well-informed nurse can provide the counseling, referral, and guidance that is needed in many of these circumstances.

REFERENCES

1   Guttmacher, A. F.: "Past Attitudes Especially toward Female Infertility," in C. A. Joel (ed.), *Fertility Disturbances in Men and Women,* S. Karger, Basel, Switzerland, 1971, pp. 317–326.
2   Behrman, S. J., and R. W. Kistner: "A Rational Approach to the Evaluation of Infertility," in *Progress in Infertility,* Little, Brown, Boston, 1968, p. 1.
3   Ibid., p. 3.
4   Ibid., p. 6.
5   Ibid., p. 3.
6   Ward, Mildred W.: "One Thousand Pregnancies in Infertility Cases," *International Journal of Fertility,* 10:7, 1965.
7   *How to Organize a Basic Study of the Infertile Couple,* The American Infertility Society, Birmingham, 1970.
8   Personal communication from Dr. Robert W. Noyes.
9   *How to Organize a Basic Study of the Infertile Couple,* p. 11.
10 Ibid., pp. 11–12.
11 Behrman and Kistner: op. cit., p. 10.
12 Iorio, Josephine: "Infertility and Sterility," in Josephine Iorio (ed.), *Principles of Obstetrics and Gynecology for Nurses,* 2d ed., Mosby, St. Louis, 1971, p. 360.
13 Behrman and Kistner: op. cit., p. 12.
14 Ibid., pp. 13–17.
15 Iorio: op. cit., p. 355.
16 Hanson, F. N., and J. Rock: "The Effect of Adoption on Fertility and Other Reproductive Functions," *American Journal of Obstetrics and Gynecology,* 59:311, 1950.
17 Tyler, E. T., J. Bonapart, and J. Grant: "Occurrence of Pregnancy Following Adoption," *Fertility and Sterility,* 11:581, 1960.
18 Banks, A. L., R. N. Rutherford, and U. A. Coburn: "Fertility Following Adoption," *Fertility and Sterility,* 12:438–442, 1961.
19 Banks, A. L.: "Does Adoption Affect Infertility?" *International Journal of Fertility,* 7:23–28, 1962.
20 Guttmacher, A. F.: *Birth Control and Love,* Macmillan, Bantam edition, New York, p. 233.
21 Personal communication.
22 Guttmacher: *Birth Control and Love,* op. cit., p. 203.

BIBLIOGRAPHY

Beacham, D. W., and U. D. Beacham: *Synopsis of Gynecology,* 8th ed., Mosby, St. Louis, 1972.
Behrman, S. J.: "Management of Infertility,"

American Journal of Nursing, 66:552–555, 1966.

———: "The Complete Fertility Work-up," *Hospital Practice,* October 1966, p. 50.

Benson, R. C.: *Handbook of Obstetrics and Gynecology,* 5th ed., Lange Medical Publications, Los Altos, Calif., 1974.

Cavanaugh, John A.: "Rhythm of Sexual Desire in Women," *Medical Aspects of Human Sexuality,* 3:29, 34, 35, 39, 1969.

Danforth, D. N. (ed.): *Textbook of Obstetrics and Gynecology,* 2d ed., Harper and Row, New York, 1971.

Dillon, Harriet B.: "The Woman Patient," *Nursing Clinics of North America,* 3:195–203, 1968.

Hafez, E. S. E., and T. N. Evans (eds.): *Human Reproduction: Conception and Contraception,* Harper and Row, New York, 1973.

Kaufman, Sherwin A.: *A New Hope for the Childless Couple,* Simon and Schuster, New York, 1970.

———: "Impact of Infertility on the Marital Sexual Relationship," *Fertility and Sterility,* 20:380, 1969.

———: "Male and Female Infertility: In an Age of Population Explosion, Why a Child Isn't Born," *Medical Insights,* 3:14–21, 1971.

———: "Physical Clues to Sexual Maladjustment in Women," *Medical Aspects of Human Sexuality,* 4:38, 1970.

Kleegan, Sophia J., and Sherwin A. Kaufman: *Infertility in Women,* Davis, New York, 1966.

Mai, F. M.: "Conception After Adoption: An Open Question," *Psychosomatic Medicine,* 33(6), November–December 1971.

McCulley, Lee B.: "Health Counseling of Women," *Nursing Clinics of North America,* 3:263–273, 1968.

Novak, E., and Seegar G. Jones: *Novak's Textbook of Gynecology,* 7th ed., Williams and Wilkins, Baltimore, 1965.

Westin, Bjorn, and Nils Wisvist (eds.): *Fertility and Sterility: Proceedings of the Fifth World Congress,* Excerpta Medica Foundation, New York, 1967.

11

Abortion

SANDRA L. BERRY

Nurses have been caring for women having therapeutic abortions for years. Today, many nurses are caring for women having legally induced abortions. Historically, the term therapeutic abortion has referred to those abortions which were done on the basis of poor health of the mother and which were usually recommended by several physicians. Women, or women and their sexual partners, now have the opportunity to decide if they want to continue a pregnancy, and after consulting a physician, they may be eligible for an abortion. The two terms, therapeutic abortion and legally induced abortion, have become synonymous in medical usage. Abortion, as used throughout this chapter, refers to legally induced abortions performed under the auspices of the new legislation.

As the law is instituted and abortion becomes socially acceptable, nurses throughout the United States will be caring for women who elect to undergo these procedures. Therefore, it is the nurses' responsibility to be aware of the facts regarding abortions, the effects on women having abortions, and the effects on the nurses who are giving care.

HISTORICAL PERSPECTIVE

Even the earliest written records give evidence that physicians and scholars have had something to say about abortion. Some were concerned about the ability of a family or a state to care for a large number of children. Others sought a means to select for survival only those who were physically and mentally sound. Still others were interested in finding a safe way for a woman to rid herself of a pregnancy that was poorly timed or sired by the wrong male.

Apparently, in these ancient times abortion brought forth few feelings of condemnation, for the custom was universally practiced. Often the failure to dislodge a fetus or the birth of an unwanted child resulted in the practice of infanticide, the exposure of an infant to harsh elements and lack of care or feeding.

In the royal archives of China about 3000 B.C., the first description of an abortive technique was recorded. In 1550 B.C. the Egyptian papyri also recorded abortion methods. The Greek philosopher Aristotle recommended that abortion take place "before life and sense have begun," especially for those who have "an aversion to exposure of offspring."[1]

Early Greek, Roman, and Egyptian writings contained many descriptions of methods, ranging from herbs to foreign objects inserted in the vagina to produce irritation of the uterus. Few advocated surgery, although some gynecological instruments had already been developed. Although Hippocrates is credited with stating opposition to abortion in his famous oath, recent scholars have questioned whether the antiabortion section may not have been written by his disciples, the Pythagoreans, who believed that the soul was present from the moment of conception.[2]

It is over the issue of *when life begins* that most legal, moral, and religious controversies have taken place throughout the centuries. Some writers express the view that even now "we seem no nearer agreement than the Greeks."[3] Aristotle claimed that the soul entered the body 40 days after conception for the male and 80 days for the female. Plato, at about the same time, was arguing that life begins at birth. At the other extreme, the Stoics maintained that the soul was infused at puberty.[4] It is evident that individual philosophers and scientists had many different opinions, and also that these opinions influenced how society dealt with this issue in relation to abortion at different periods of time.

The early Judean and Christian teaching about the value of an individual life had the strongest influence on the moral issue. "In actuality, previous to 1803, abortion appears to have been largely regarded as a church offense and was punishable only by religious penalties. The first English Abortion Statute, the law of 1830, made abortion a crime."[5] No one knows for certain what combination of circumstances motivated the passage of this law at this time. Possibly widespread disease, poverty, and high death rates were providing little enticement for couples to attempt to raise large numbers of children, and the government decided to intercede.

In 1821, Connecticut became the first state to pass an abortion law. Throughout the remainder of the nineteenth century various states gradually developed their own laws. A number of factors influenced the adoption of these laws. Prior to these statutes, abortion was done chiefly by barbers, who also did minor surgery and bloodletting to cure various ailments. Gold was discovered in 1849, and the Civil War lasted from 1861 to 1865. The need to settle the West was hindered by the loss of life from war casualties and by the increased demand for abortion due to wartime pregnancies. This demand brought unskilled, unscrupulous amateurs into the abortion business, and as a result, the maternal mortality rate soared. Legislators sought some way to stem the practice and to increase the birth rate so they made abortion a criminal offense. It is pertinent to note that in the impetus for enactment in most states, neither ethics nor religion played a major part.[6] However, the latter part of the century was also the Victorian era, noted for adherence to Puritanical concepts of sin. The pregnant unmarried girl had to be punished and was not allowed to conceal evidence of her wrongdoing. Abortion would have removed this evidence.[7] So the laws on the books were made more stringent by revision and by stronger attempts at enforcement.

In spite of the fact that there was no national law and each state had enacted its own legislation, there were few changes during the first half of the twentieth century. By midcentury, evidence accumulated that demand for abortion had reached a figure equal to a substantial proportion of live births. In the face of this demand only a small percentage were done by physicians in hospital settings, and illegal abortion has flourished.[8] Only in the last two decades has there been an attempt to inform the public of the horrors that take place in the clandestine, degrading, unclean places of most illegal abortionists. Lader states, "Untrained and often thoroughly incompetent abortionists are surely the most terrifying product of the underworld which feeds on the abortion system."[9]

ABORTION REFORM

"The first decisive move for reform in either Britain or the United States originated in 1938 in the solitary courage of an eminent London surgeon, Aleck Bourne."[10] A fourteen-year-old girl had been raped by soldiers, and Bourne decided to perform an abortion and then notify the police. This test case made medical history and his acquittal provided the first liberalized guidelines for practicing physicians.

Four European countries—Sweden, Denmark, Norway, and Iceland—pioneered in abortion reform to produce laws that allowed for liberalization for "humanitarian" needs. However, none of these countries has approached the marked permissiveness found in Japan or other Eastern European countries. In spite of this movement for reform, abortion is still prohibited except for medical emergencies in nearly two-thirds of the world.[11]

As of 1971, one of the countries in which abortion was still restricted was the United States. The American Law Institute in 1962 developed a model code which was used as a basis for most of the reform legislation. In 1967, Colorado was the first state to adopt new legislation, and within the next 4 years, 16 other states passed modifications of their original laws.[12] Four of these states—Alaska, Hawaii, New York, and Washington—were the most liberal. Their reform called for no restrictions for the nonviable fetus and provided for "abortion on demand" or arrangements made between the patient and her physician.

On January 22, 1973, two landmark decisions were handed down by the Supreme Court of the United States (*Doe v. Bolton* and *Roe v. Wade*), invalidating the abortion laws of most states. The court ruled that during the first trimester, "the abortion decision and its effectuation must be left to the medical judgment of the pregnant woman's attending physician." After the first trimester, "the State, in promoting its interest in the health of the mother, may, if it chooses, regulate the abortion procedure in ways that are reasonably related to maternal health." After the fetus has reached viability "the State . . . may, if it chooses, regulate, and even proscribe, abortion except where necessary, in appropriate medical judgment, for the preservation of the life or health of the mother."[13]

By mid-1973, the decision of the Supreme Court had not been fully implemented throughout the United States. In some states, the legislature, or law enforcement officers, as well as hospital boards and administrators, have taken a variety of actions designed to delay implementation, some of which have been challenged in the courts and will doubtless be declared unconstitutional in due course. Efforts are being made in the Congress of the United States to initiate a constitutional amendment which would nullify the decision of the Supreme Court.

ATTITUDES OF MAJOR RELIGIONS

In the United States, attitudes toward abortion and consequently abortion reform are influenced by the positions of its three major religions: Roman Catholicism, Judaism, and Protestantism. In other parts of the world where one religion predominates in a country, the position closely adheres to the accepted attitude of that specific faith. Neither Buddhist nor Hindu theology contains any scriptural prohibitions against early abortion. Islam holds to the belief that life begins 150 days after conception, and the Shinto religion holds that life begins at birth. There-

fore, the debate over abortion as a moral or ethical issue rarely occurs for them.

The Roman Catholic Church has taken a firm position on abortion. Since 1869 when the church abolished the 40- and 80-day theories of animation, it has strictly prohibited abortion when termination of pregnancy is the prime motive for the operation. Only when there is underlying pathology for which an operative procedure is required and the termination is a natural by-product is it tolerated.[14] The church has been strong in its opposition to abortion reform, calling it an outrage against humanity. It deals harshly (by immediate excommunication) with those Catholics who deliberately procure an abortion or help someone to do so.

The Jewish theologians have been more flexible in their interpretation of when life begins. Although there is some disagreement among them, generally they consider the moment of ensoulment as belonging to those "secrets of God." They usually consider the fetus as part of the mother until it is born.[15] In this interpretation there is no conflict with their legal and ethical standards in relation to aborting a pregnancy. The Jewish position has been handed down by great rabbis and teachers through the centuries.[16] There may be some rejection of modern interpretation by Orthodox Jews, but in general, the emphasis has been on protecting the life of the mother.

The Protestant position can hardly be said to be uniform. There is wide range of belief of many religious tenets, which hold to positions of extreme conservatism and equally unrestricted liberalism. However, the National Council of Churches of Christ in 1961 issued a statement stressing the sanctity of potential life and condemning abortion as a method of birth control *but* approving hospital abortion "when the life or health of the mother is at stake." The General Assembly of the United Presbyterian Church issued a similar statement on policy in 1962. Prior to this in 1958, the Lambeth Conference which included representatives of the American Protestant Episcopal Church, as well as those of the Anglican Communion, also declared that abortion is allowed "at the dictate of strict and undeniable medical necessity."[17] Other denominations during the decade of 1960 through 1970 have brought the issue to their assemblies with the result that a number of them have issued statements equally free in their interpretation.

In many communities Protestant clergy and Jewish rabbis have formed Abortion Counseling Services. Their primary purpose is to provide guidance to qualified medical care as a deterrent to the use of the illegal abortionists. Some of these services also include provision for guidance to the woman or couple who wish to continue with the pregnancy but need medical or financial assistance.

HEALTH AND SOCIAL ASPECTS

Medical Contraindications

The issue of abortion is surrounded by multiple aspects of health and social concern. The legal change in the United States has not necessarily altered attitudes, and there is considerable polarization in the positions on abortion taken by individuals.

Medical indications for abortion as a life-saving measure have decreased, and the focus has changed to concern for the health of the pregnant woman and the risk of a defective child. However, conditions such as hypertension, cardiac disorders, cancer of the breast or cervix, kidney disease, and psychiatric illness are still indications for medical intervention, depending on their severity. In some of the psychiatric indications such as severe psychoneurosis, previous postpartum psychosis, schizophrenia or neurological disease, mental deficiency and situational reactions, the decision to perform an abortion must be considered in relation to its effect on the woman's future mental health.[18]

The major studies involving the degree of psychological sequelae in women having legally induced abortions have been done in Sweden. These few studies show that the stronger the indication for abortion the greater the risk of unfavorable psychological sequelae. Approximately 25 percent of the women expressed mild to serious self-reproaches on follow-up 22 to 30 months later.[19]

The Osofskys studied psychological reactions to abortion in New York City in 1970.[20] They interviewed approximately 400 patients immediately after the procedure with the following results:

60 percent happy
66 percent no guilt
78 percent relieved
15 percent unhappy
 6 percent guilt
 9 percent angry

There were no significant negative sequelae. Positive attitudes of staff made for significant acceptance of the procedure.

According to Woods, "It is generally believed that the psychologic sequelae of abortion are usually short-lived and tend to reflect the circumstances surrounding the abortion and the attitudes conveyed by significant others in the peer group, the family, and the health care setting."[21]

Threat of Deformity of the Child

Each year in the United States between 80,000 and 160,000 defective children are born.[22] In states in which reasons for abortion are reported, less than 1 percent have been performed on the indication of potential fetal abnormality.[23] Rubella during the first trimester, massive exposure to x rays, history of previous genetic defects, and the consumption of teratogenic drugs, prescribed or self-administered, are a threat of deformity to a fetus.

Two procedures are used to detect fetal deformities. A small percentage are detected by amniocentesis, a microscopic examination of fetal cells. Amniocentesis is limited in use because of possible complications, such as infection or initiation of labor. When there is probable exposure to German measles, a second method, positive rubella blood titer, indicates the disease did occur. Most abnormalities will not be detected until birth or years after.

Age of the Mother

The age of the mother is an important consideration in determining the degree of pregnancy risk. Pregnancy before the age of sixteen and after forty is generally considered to involve increased risks of complications.

Rape or Incest

It has been calculated that there are approximately 800 rape-induced pregnancies in the United States per year.[24] It was often difficult for the woman who had been the victim of rape or incest to obtain an abortion. There were complicated legal requirements of proof as well as state restrictions.

Some women had abortions done under the guise of a psychiatric condition due to the emotional trauma of forcible rape.

Social or Family Problems

Social issues such as poverty, marital stress, unwanted pregnancy, and excess number of children do not elicit the same acute emotional impact as do issues such as rape or incest. However, these issues are the major reasons women seek abortion, both legal or illegal. Reports from the few studies, surveys, and lay literature concerning attitudes of nurses, physicians, and laymen reflect prevailing opposition to abortion for social reasons.[25-31] The controversy over legislation for abortion on request is another clue to the interest of society in the protection of the embryo.

INCIDENCE OF LEGAL AND ILLEGAL ABORTION

Nurses should be aware of the extent of society's demand for abortion. The demands for abortion are coming from several sources: (1) women seeking therapeutic abortions, (2) women having criminal abortions, and (3) women with unwanted pregnancies who are now seeking legal abortions.[32] The demand for abortion increased dramatically following the new legislation.

Before the new legislation, the estimated number of therapeutic abortions performed annually in the United States was about 8,000. Estimates on the number of illegal abortions per year in the United States were between 200,000 and 1,200,000.[33] The total number of abortions reported to the Center for Disease Control in 1973 from 50 states, the District of Columbia, and New York City was 615,831.[34]

Variables

In 1958 Mary Calderone reported on a former Baltimore abortionist, Dr. Timanus, who told of having performed 5,210 abortions in a 20-year period. Of these abortions, the majority of women (84 percent) were between twenty-one and forty years old; 53 percent were married, and 35 percent were single. Of these patients, 3,149 had no children while 2,061 had one to five children; more than one-third of the women (35 percent) were between twenty-one and twenty-five years old, 24 percent were between twenty-six and thirty years old, and 25 percent were between thirty-one and forty years of age.[35]

The late Dr. Kinsey published a study of a sample of 8,000 white females with a pregnancy total of 6,300. Among all women in the sample ever married, 22 percent had abortions in marriage by the age of forty-five. Among all the single white females who had coitus, 20 percent had abortions.[36]

The foregoing statistics were collected before liberalization of the abortion laws. Unfortunately, reporting systems are not in effect in each state. Based on the information that is available from selected states, it is possible to describe demographic characteristics of the population of women who have received legal abortions.

Age

The age distribution of women who have had legal abortions (Table 11-1) shows that the largest number of abortions (62.3 percent) were obtained by women between the ages of fifteen and twenty-four years. Unmarried women under the age of eighteen still have the disadvantage of required parental permission in most states.

TABLE 11-1
Induced Abortion by Age in Selected States, 1973*

Age groups	Number of abortions	% of total
Under 15	7,329	1.5
15–19	147,112	30.0
20–24	151,060	30.8
25–29	83,618	17.1
30–34	46,925	9.6
35–39	25,930	5.3
Over 40	10,414	2.1
Unknown	17,347	3.5
Total	489,735	100.0†

* Alaska, Arkansas, California, Colorado, District of Columbia, Georgia, Hawaii, Illinois, Indiana, Kansas, Maryland, Mississippi, Missouri, Nebraska, Nevada, New York, North Carolina, Oregon, South Carolina, South Dakota, Tennessee, Vermont, Virginia, and Washington.
† Note that the total is actually 99.9 because of rounding off of percentages.
SOURCE: *Center for Disease Control: Abortion Surveillance: 1973*, U.S. Department of Health, Education, and Welfare, Public Health Service, May 1975, p. 15.

Race

The majority of women seeking induced abortion are white (67.7 percent); 25.7 percent are black or of other races. In a study among black women of both poverty-level and lower-middle income groups, it was shown that 80 to 87 percent opposed abortion. Revealed also was a positive and consistent association between education and favorable attitude about abortion. (See Table 11-2.)

Marital Status

Table 11-3 shows that over two-thirds of the women who received abortions were not married at the time of their abortions. Married women have decreased since 1971, from 33.1 then to 27.9 percent in 1973.

The classification of unmarried women includes those who have never married and those who are separated, widowed, or divorced.

Parity

Approximately one-half of the women (47.3 percent) who had abortions in the reporting states had no living children. (See Table 11-4.)

TABLE 11-2
Induced Abortion by Race in Selected States, 1973*

Race	Number of abortions	% of total
White	314,843	67.7†
Black and other	119,620	25.7‡
Unknown	30,506	6.6
Total	464,969	100.0

* Alaska, Arkansas, California, Colorado, District of Columbia, Georgia, Hawaii, Illinois, Indiana, Kansas, Maryland, Mississippi, Missouri, Nebraska, Nevada, New York, North Carolina, South Carolina, South Dakota, Tennessee, Vermont, and Virginia.
† White category includes Caucasian, Mexican, Puerto Rican, and Cuban.
‡ Black category includes Negro, American Indian, Chinese, and Japanese.
SOURCE: *Center for Disease Control: Abortion Surveillance: 1973*, U.S. Department of Health, Education, and Welfare, Public Health Service, May 1975, p. 17.

TABLE 11-4
Induced Abortion by Parity in Selected States, 1973*

Number of living children	Number of abortions	% of total
0	196,250	47.3
1	76,054	18.3
2	57,313	13.8
3	35,010	8.4
4	19,302	4.7
5 and over	19,878	4.8
Unknown	11,246	2.7
Total	415,053	100.0

* Alaska, California, Colorado, Georgia, Illinois, Indiana, Kansas, Maryland, Mississippi, Nebraska, Nevada, New York, North Carolina, South Carolina, South Dakota, Tennessee, Vermont, and Virginia.
SOURCE: *Center for Disease Control: Abortion Surveillance: 1973*, U.S. Department of Health, Education, and Welfare, Public Health Service, May 1975, p. 22.

TABLE 11-3
Induced Abortion by Marital Status in Selected States, 1973*

Marital status	Number of abortions	% of total
Married	87,056	25.6
Unmarried	230,717	67.9
Unknown	22,207	6.5
Total	339,980	100.0

* All states with data available: Alaska, Arkansas, California, Colorado, District of Columbia, Georgia, Hawaii, Illinois, Indiana, Kansas, Maryland, Mississippi, Missouri, Nebraska, Nevada, New York upstate, North Carolina, Oregon, South Carolina, South Dakota, Tennessee, Vermont, Virginia, and Washington.
SOURCE: *Center for Disease Control: Abortion Surveillance: 1973*, U.S. Department of Health, Education, and Welfare, Public Health Service, May 1975, p. 19.

Gestation

Most women have abortions performed by the 11th week of gestation; 77 percent were performed before the end of the 12th week of gestation and 91.2 percent by the end of the 20th week. (See Table 11-5.)

Methods

Since most abortions were performed by the 12th week of gestation, the majority of women had a dilatation and curettage (D&C)

TABLE 11-5
Induced Abortion by Menstrual Week of Gestation in Selected States, 1973*

Weeks of gestation at time of abortion	Number of abortions	% of total
Less than 9	163,988	33.5
9–10	133,883	27.3
11–12	31,350	16.6
13–15	31,457	6.4
16–20	36,322	7.4
More than 21	7,701	1.6
Unknown	35,034	7.2
Total	489,735	100.0

* Alaska, Arkansas, California, Colorado, District of Columbia, Georgia, Hawaii, Illinois, Indiana, Kansas, Maryland, Mississippi, Missouri, Nebraska, Nevada, New York, North Carolina, Oregon, South Carolina, South Dakota, Tennessee, Vermont, Virginia, and Washington.
SOURCE: *Center for Disease Control: Abortion Surveillance: 1973*, U.S. Department of Health, Education, and Welfare, Public Health Service, May 1975, p. 25.

or evacuation (D&E) procedure. (See Table 11-6.) It appears that women are becoming educated concerning the safety of having abortions early in their pregnancies.

PROCEDURES

Abortion Resources

A woman who is faced with the possibility of an unwanted, unplanned pregnancy usually needs counseling and referral services. In large metropolitan areas there are agencies which provide pregnancy testing as a part of their counseling services. In smaller cities and rural areas it is more difficult to obtain this kind of help. However, in some areas, pregnancy testing is now being offered through the resources of health departments, outpatient facilities, neighborhood clinics, and doctors' offices. Frequently in these settings, nurses are called upon to counsel and refer.

When the test is positive for pregnancy, a woman must make her next decision—what to do about it. She needs basic information about medical, legal, and financial aspects of abortion and about the alternatives that are open to her. If she is considering abortion, she needs to know that her decision cannot be postponed indefinitely because of the developing fetus.

Today, regardless of where a woman is in the United States, she does have access to an abortion referral group or agency.[37] Local resources will vary according to availability and the legal status of abortion in a particular state. Such resources might be a private physician, a hospital, a Planned Parenthood affiliate, a clergy consultation service, or a health or social service department. If assistance cannot be found locally or in the state, national groups such as the Abortion Reform Association, the Association for the Study of Abortion, the National Association for Repeal of Abortion Laws, the National Clergy Consultation Services, and the headquarters

TABLE 11-6
Procedures Used for Induced Abortion in Selected States, 1973*

Procedure	Number of abortions	% of total
D&C	61,642	13.2
D&E	342,510	73.6
Amniotic fluid replacement	47,402	10.2
Hysterotomy and hysterectomy	3,056	0.7
Other	2,569	0.6
Unknown	8,367	1.8
Total	466,546	100.0†

* Alaska, California, Colorado, District of Columbia, Hawaii, Illinois, Indiana, Kansas, Maryland, Mississippi, Nebraska, Nevada, New York, North Carolina, Oregon, South Carolina, South Dakota, Tennessee, Vermont, and Washington.
† Note that the total is actually 100.1 because of rounding off of percentages.
SOURCE: *Center for Disease Control: Abortion Surveillance: 1973*, U.S. Department of Health, Education, and Welfare, May 1975, p. 24.

of Planned Parenthood—World Population may be of assistance.

If a woman wishes to explore the services available to her if she should decide against abortion, local agencies such as social service, health departments, or private physicians may be equipped to help her carry the pregnancy to term. Several new national organizations such as Birthright, Birthchoice, and others with similar titles have recently been developed. They state that their chief purpose is to provide a pregnant woman with the opportunity to make a choice.

Medical, Psychological, and Social History

In any abortion, the need for a complete history consisting of social, psychological, and medical aspects cannot be overstressed. Various professionals may be involved, including nurses, social workers, and physicians. In some instances, different aspects of the history may be taken by several persons, thus breaking the continuity of care. If it is possible, within the system, for a counselor or nurse to follow the client throughout her entire abortion experience, this will assist in the client's self-acceptance and a more positive approach toward the entire procedure.

In many instances, there is a general format (record system) which can be used as a guide. If nurses take the initial history, they should individualize their questions to the client and be attuned to important cues given by the client which need further investigation. During this time, rapport can be established with the client which may reveal important details that should be passed on to the physician to be utilized when a medical history is taken or the physical examination is performed. Many histories can

bring forth information which will assist nurses in caring for the client throughout her abortion experience, including follow-up in the community.

Methods by Length of Gestation

The commonly used methods of legally inducing abortion are (1) menstrual extraction; (2) D&C; (3) D&E (suction method); (4) saline or prostaglandin induction; and (5) hysterotomy. (See Figure 11-1.)

Menstrual Extraction

Menstrual extraction or regulation is a promising method of fertility control which may reduce the demand for late first or second trimester abortion. The technique is simple and safe, and effects are minor or nonexistent; the procedure can be provided on an outpatient basis, and requires only a few minutes. The procedure is done within 14 days of a missed menstrual period (42 days from last menstrual period, LMP).

The procedure is as follows. With the patient in a dorsal lithotomy position the cervix is exposed with a speculum. Some physicians cleanse the cervix and vagina with an antiseptic solution. The cervix is then stabilized with a tenaculum or forceps. At this point, a sound is used to determine the depth of the uterine cavity. Without cervical dilatation (except in selected patients) a flexible cannula is inserted into the uterus. This cannula is connected to a vacuum source (syringe, hand- or foot-operated pump, or an electrical vacuum). When the pressure is secured, the cannula is rotated 180 degrees and at the same time moved back and forth in short strokes within the uterus until all the interior has been reached. The operator notices a characteristic grating sensation when the uterus is completely empty.

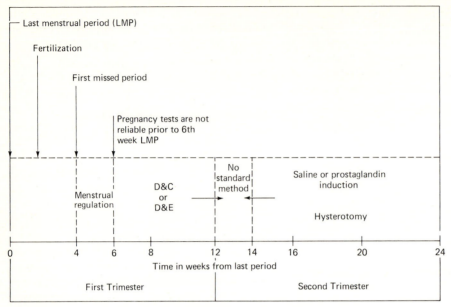

FIGURE 11-1
Methods of pregnancy termination by week of pregnancy. (*Adapted from Theresa Van Der Vlugt, "History, Present Status, and Applications of Menstrual Regulation,"* Journal of Obstetric, Gynecologic and Neonatal Nursing, *June 1974, p. 36.*

Dilatation and Curettage; Dilatation and Evacuation

Up to the 12th or 14th week of gestation, abortion is usually performed by either D&C or D&E. Either of these procedures may be done in a hospital, a clinic, or an abortorium. Wherever the procedure takes place, the room is set up similar to an operating room. The patient is given a preoperative medication and either a regional or inhalation anesthetic. The cervix is gradually dilated until a curette or suction tube can be inserted. If curettage is used, the uterus is scraped clean with the curette. If suction is used, a rubber, glass, or plastic tube is inserted into the dilated cervix, and the uterine contents are evacuated.

Prostaglandin or Saline Induction

If the pregnancy is past 14 weeks of gestation, prostaglandin $F_{2\alpha}$ or saline induction can be done. This procedure is usually carried out in a hospital examining or treatment room, and the patient will remain hospitalized until the abortive process is complete and her vital signs have stabilized. Local anesthesia of the abdominal wall is used. A 4- to 6-inch 18 or 20 gauge needle is inserted through the abdominal wall until the amniotic sac is entered. If saline is used, amniotic fluid is withdrawn in an amount approximating the volume of saline to be used. If prostaglandin is used, a smaller volume is inserted, and thus in most instances amniotic fluid is not withdrawn.

Following the injection, the patient must await the onset of "labor." Within 48 hours most patients abort.[38]

With prostaglandin $F_{2\alpha}$ it has been shown that sedation with meperidine does not inhibit the abortion process or uterine activity.[39] Although analgesia will sedate the woman having a saline abortion, there is no proof that this will prolong the abortion time.

Hysterotomy

Hysterotomy is a surgical procedure performed after the 15th week of gestation. A small incision is made transabdominally, through the uterine wall. The contents of the uterus are then removed. This method is sometimes referred to as a mini cesarean section. Usually the procedure is accompanied by tubal ligation.

Complications

Complications due to abortion vary according to the method used and the age, health status, and psychological well-being of the client. In general, the longer the gestation, the more likely are the chances for complications. (See Table 11-7.) According to Dr. C. Hendricks' report on pregnancy termination,[40] the following range of percentages have been reported:

D&C	0– 8.2
D&E	0.5– 1.2
Saline induction	4.0–12.6
Hysterotomy	9.3–24.8

Since abortion has been legalized, maternal mortality has lessened, the number of admissions to hospitals because of incomplete abortions has decreased, the premature and infant death rates have dropped, and the rate of illegitimate births has decreased.

Those complications arising from prostaglandin $F_{2\alpha}$ inductions which differ from saline are vomiting and diarrhea. The other complications for midtrimester abortions are given in Table 11-7.

Contraception

One of the effects of liberalized abortion laws in general has been the availability of information about methods, or more effective methods, of contraception and sexuality. Women now seeking abortions are from all socioeconomic levels; thus, for the first time women have a more equal opportunity to decide the number of children they want.

TABLE 11-7
Reported Complications of Induced Abortion, by Method

Complications	D&C	D&E	Saline induction	Hysterotomy
Incomplete abortion	+*	+	+	–
Postabortal bleeding	+	+	+	+
Postabortal infection	+	+	+	+
Perforation	+	+	–	–
Cervical lacerations	+	+	–	–
Hypernatremia	–	–	+	–
Hypofibrinogenemia	–	–	+	–

* A plus (+) indicates complications which apply to method; a minus (–) indicates complications which do not apply to method.
SOURCE: Charles H. Hendricks, "Pregnancy Termination: The Impact of New Laws," *The Journal of Reproductive Medicine,* 6:60–70, 1971.

Recidivism

The number of women seeking repeat abortions and the proportion of repeats to total abortions are small, but both have increased with time. From 1970 to 1972, 2.5 percent were repeats in a study from New York City by Daily and Pakter. However, during the last 6-month period there was an increase of repeats to 6 percent. The proportion of all abortions which were repeats were similar for each ethnic group over the 2-year period. Repeat abortions of women in their twenties was the highest. Teenagers seventeen or under exhibited the smallest proportion of repeats followed by women thirty-five and older. The difference by age may be explained by differences in fecundity and intercourse frequency. When pregnancy order was known, over 40 percent of abortions were of women experiencing their first pregnancy; 38 percent of repeat abortions were of women who had only two pregnancies. Women having repeat abortions were more likely to have them performed early in pregnancy by the suction method.[41]

The respondents in the study were interviewed concerning contraceptive practices and their reasons for another pregnancy leading to a repeat abortion. Although nothing can be deduced from the data concerning contraceptive practices the dominant reasons for repeat abortion are similar to those heard in other health care facilities.

Reasons for repeat abortion:[42]

Not using method	47.3%
Failure to use according to instructions	28.7%
Method failure	19.2%
No reason	4.2%
Planned pregnancy	0.6%

Major reasons for nonuse:[43]

Experienced bad things with method	31.0%
Heard bad things about some methods, afraid	17.3%
Ran out of supplies, did not return to clinic for checkup and/or supplies or supplies were too expensive	8.3%
Did not want a method	6.0%
Thought she would not, could not get pregnant, or did not know pregnancy could be prevented	5.4%
Does not believe in birth control	3.6%
No plans to have sexual relations	1.2%
"Stopped for medical reasons"	1.2%

The chief of obstetrics at Elmhurst Hospital in New York City has been looking at the problem of recidivism both psychologically and socially. From his experience, the young teenager does not appear to be a repeater. Women that are repeating seem to have poor ego development in that they do not use or are inconsistent users of contraceptives, thus exposing themselves to the risk of repeated abortion. Dr. Zigmond Lebensohn, a District of Columbia psychiatrist, believes that these women are in need of psychiatric care but do not recognize their problems and are not interested in treatment.[44]

PSYCHOLOGICAL AND EMOTIONAL IMPLICATIONS FOR THE CLIENT AND FAMILY

In spite of the fact that the issue of abortion is more freely discussed today than in the past, there is no universal justification or acceptance of abortion. Proabortion groups are strong in advocating that it should be a decision between a woman and her doctor. Antiabortion groups proclaim loudly that it is murder and cannot be sanctioned under any circumstances. Opinion polls indicate that most people have their own concepts of when it is right and when it is wrong. Yet, many say they are confused and don't know what they believe.

Against this background, it is understandable that persons who are confronted with an unwanted pregnancy are ambivalent in making their own decision. Professional people and all those in counseling roles need to be aware of the potential factors that may impinge on the decision-making process. Generally, the husband or the sexual partner is not directly involved in the counseling sessions. Yet, he may be the one upon whom the ultimate decision rests.

The woman carrying an unwanted fetus has some very personal concerns, both physical and psychological. For example, she may question whether she is really destroying a life, or whether the procedure will be more painful or distressing than a full-term delivery. She may wonder what other people will think of her, particularly her family and nursing staff. She may have concerns about expense or the people in whom she has put her trust. Fear of the unknown cannot be completely eliminated by the best of counselors, but it can be diminished by skillful interviewing and emotional support.

Institutionalization

During the client's institutionalization, whether it be an outpatient or inpatient procedure, she should be treated as a person who has many feelings that need continuous attention. Everything that the woman having an abortion encounters should be carefully explained. Many clients expect to be rejected and disapproved of by nursing personnel and physicians.

After undergoing the abortion procedure, the woman does not expect a visible reward.

She has experienced a procedure which, when finished, brings her a feeling of relief; it is over.

Psychological Sequelae

What about a few hours or a few days after the abortion when the client is at home and a feeling of depression suddenly appears? How accountable does she feel now for the decision that she made? Is this guilt she now feels? To whom can she go? What if she does not feel any guilt or contempt for what she has done? Dr. Margolis has reported on a follow-up study and corroborated his data with four other studies in the United States. He concluded that abortion is "often helpful to the life situation adjustment of these women. The legal, social, and medical sanction for interruption of pregnancy results in minimizing untoward guilt and depressive reactions, leaving the majority of women a sense of rightness of their pregnancy terminations, now culturally approved."[45]

NURSING CARE

Counseling and Interviewing

The woman wanting an abortion comes to the hospital or abortorium either with no previous counseling or with counseling by someone who has prepared her for the procedure she is about to experience. It is very important for the nurse who initially interviews the woman to find out what she has already been told and to restate anything that has been misunderstood or not synthesized. A follow-through with the same information by the nurse can help the client to feel more relaxed and able to concentrate on the deluge of information that accompanies legal abortion, regardless of the method. The woman may appear to have no knowledge of what will occur even when she has been counseled by someone before admission. This client may be experiencing some ambivalence in her decision, or a low frustration level, and needs reassurance and support to be able to follow through with her decision.

The nurse is in a unique position as the one person to whom the client may communicate with the most freedom, if she is given the opportunity. Communication by the client may be an expression of positive or negative feelings. Regardless of what the client's expression may be (hostile, fearful, angry, flippant), the nurse can assist her by being aware of why she is reacting in such a manner and encouraging her to express her feelings. Every woman will not verbalize her feelings to the same extent. Those who hesitate to express their feelings may respond to nonverbal cues such as touch or the frequent presence of a caring, accepting nurse.

Interviewing should include a medical and obstetrical history, social history, and discussion of the procedure and contraception. In some hospitals forms are being used to assist the nurse in accomplishing all aspects of interviewing and counseling. (See Figures 11-2 to 11-4.) These forms are not all-inclusive but do give the nurse direction regarding what should be included when talking with any client seeking an abortion regardless of the type of procedure to be done.

In many settings where abortions are done there is a team approach to care. Questionnaires can be used to ensure that all nurses, social workers, doctors, and ancillary health care workers are aware of where a client is in working through her feelings concerning abortion.

Care during Procedures

The setting the client enters is dependent upon gestation and procedure and will be a major factor in the amount of nursing time

she receives. If the client comes into a hospital, clinic, or abortorium for a D&C or D&E, the procedure is completed, the woman is observed for several hours, and then she is released if there are no complications. If the client is hospitalized for a prostaglandin or saline induction or hysterotomy, she will be in contact with nurses from 2 to 6 days. These procedural differences thus create variations in nursing care.

Depending upon the situation, the client may or may not have been in the clinic for her counseling and laboratory work-up. The work-up should include a pregnancy test, urinalysis, complete blood count, serology, gonococcus smear, Rh type (Rh-negative women should be given RhoGam after abortion), and a Pap test. The clients will see a nurse for an interview and, if indicated, a social worker. The doctor will examine the client and schedule her for the procedure. In some instances, the woman returns at another time, and in other cases, the procedure is done that day.

Regardless of the particular routine of the clinic, there are reported experiences from nurses and clients which can serve as a basis for nursing care. One very important aspect of abortion is the nurse's ability to exhibit a relaxed and comfortable atmosphere. The more frank and direct the nurse can be, the more the client will feel free to interact, whether on an individual or group basis. In many instances, the woman is accompanied by her male friend or husband. He should be encouraged to sit in on the counseling sessions (individual or group) if the woman concurs. If the woman is to be hospitalized for a prostaglandin or saline abortion, then the sexual partner should feel free to be with her whenever he is able. In the case of some adolescents, a parent or both parents may accompany the girl. After the nurse has interviewed the girl alone, together they should decide on the amount of time her parents will spend with her during the procedure.

NURSE (date and signature)	PROCEDURE	DATE OF PROCEDURE Return appointment (where)

Procedure explained including complications and risks:

Contraception (instructions and appropriate literature):   Type chosen:

If IUD, request form signed by patient (or parent if under 18):

If pills, referral to Health Dept. (parent's consent if under 18):   Rx

If sterilization, request signed by patient   husband   witness

Operative permit and therapeutic abortion request signed by patient (or parent if under 18):   witness

Phone number during day: Location:

Permission to give microscopic and pathologic reports to:

Allergies: Do you faint easily?   Transportation:

For infusion: Admit today   Admit   To Social Service for scheduling

For day of operation: Instructions   Urine to Lab   X Ray   EKG

N.P.O. after midnight   No URI or sore throat   Time voided   Baseline B.P.

Record on schedule*   Chart to therapeutic abortion clerk[†]

Pre-op B.P.:   Post-op B.P.:

Pre-op medications: IV Fluids

Procedure notes:

Post-op medications:

Recovery notes: Adm. B.P.   Discharge B.P.

Hematocrit   Group and type

Urine

RhoGam given   Explanation of Rh   "After D&E" given[‡]   Discussed

Can read thermometer: Has or will get thermometer: Thermometer given:

Fluids tolerated: Ambulatory: Voided:

Bleeding at discharge: minimum   moderate   heavy

Discharged: Time: R.N.:

Return appointment date _____

FIGURE 11-2

Therapeutic abortion checklist. At * the nurse adds client's name to schedule with the procedure to be done. At [†] the therapeutic abortion clerk checks the chart for completeness. At [‡] the nurse would anticipate questions and answers such as those in Figure 11-4. (*By permission from North Carolina Memorial Hospital, Chapel Hill, North Carolina.*)

THIS INFORMATION WILL BE CONSIDERED CONFIDENTIAL

We ask that you complete the following questions so we may know how to best serve you during your visit to North Carolina Memorial Hospital.

Are you (circle one):   single   married   separated   divorced   widowed

Do you work now? ___ yes   ___ no   Occupation _____
Do you go to school? ___ yes   ___ no   Grade _____

		Yes	No
1	I have mixed feelings about whether to get an abortion.	___	___
2	It is hard for me to talk about this pregnancy and abortion.	___	___
3	I would like to talk with someone today about being pregnant and getting an abortion.	___	___
4	I am undecided about whether to get an abortion.	___	___
5	The decision to get an abortion was a very difficult decision for me to make.	___	___
6	I feel that I had a part in making the decision to get an abortion.	___	___
7	The pregnancy has caused problems between my family and me.	___	___
8	The pregnancy has caused problems between my sexual partner and me.	___	___
9	Getting an abortion may cause problems between my family and me.	___	___
10	Getting an abortion may cause problems between my sexual partner and me.	___	___
11	I was using a method of birth control when I got pregnant.	___	___
12	I have heard bad things about birth control.	___	___

I have talked about the decision to seek an abortion with (you may check more than one):

Husband ___   Doctor ___   Guidance counselor ___
Parents ___   Family planning worker ___   Psychiatrist ___
Clergyman ___   Boyfriend ___   Psychologist ___
Nurse ___   Social worker ___   Friend ___

FIGURE 11-3
Client information form. (*Courtesy of Janet Runquist, A.C., S.W., North Carolina Memorial Hospital, Chapel Hill, North Carolina.*)

Dilatation and Curettage or Dilatation and Evacuation

A woman having a D&C or D&E should be told what she can expect throughout the entire procedure. There are two ways the procedures are done. The woman may go to the operating room and be given a local or general anesthetic or she can have the procedure done in a clinic setting under local anesthesia. When she is awake she will probably be given an intravenous short-acting narcotic or a tranquilizer intramuscularly. If she is to be awake during the procedure, she needs to know this in advance and have a nurse with her during the abortion for support. The blood pressure should be taken before and immediately following the procedure. The procedure itself generally takes 7 to 10 minutes. After the abortion she will be taken to a recovery area where the nurse will check for excessive bleeding and frequently monitor vital signs. In most cases, the woman can be given something to drink and ambulated with assistance to the bathroom to void within an hour. If the client complains of feeling weak or tired, she should be assured that this is not unusual and may persist for a day or two. The client may be given an oxytocic which could cause

How do each of the following feel about the abortion decision?

Sexual partner:
   He suggested the abortion _____
   I have not told him of the pregnancy _____
   We made the decision together _____
   He let me make my own decision _____
   He does not approve of abortion _____

Parents:
   They do not know of the pregnancy _____
   They suggested the abortion _____
   We made the decision together _____
   They let me make my own decision _____
   They do not approve of abortion _____
   Nonapplicable _____

We feel that an important part of our clinic program is the discussion of future contraception. We encourage each woman to make a decision for herself regarding a method of future contraception.
Have you decided on a method of future birth control? _____ Yes   _____ No
   If yes, what method? _____
Will you be coming back to NCMH for your followup medical examination? _____ Yes   _____ No
   If no, where will you be having the checkup? _____
Name _____   Age _____

FIGURE 11-4
Abortion decision questionnaire. (*Courtesy of Janet Runquist, A.C., S.W., North Carolina Memorial Hospital, Chapel Hill, North Carolina.*)

her to have more severe cramping than usual. Local heat application over the area of the symphysis pubis and an analgesic may be given every 4 hours to make the client more comfortable.

Most abortion settings have either a group meeting to go over postoperative instructions and answer questions, or individual consultation with a nurse before discharge. Most women are still feeling too many effects of medication to retain this information. A printed sheet for future use is of great value. (See Figure 11-5.)

Saline or Prostaglandin Induction

After the client has been interviewed and adequately counseled concerning saline or prostaglandin induction, she may be ad-

mitted immediately or go home to return at a later time. Depending on the hospital, the procedure may be done on an inpatient or outpatient basis. In some places, an enema is given to lessen the pressure at the time of the abortion. The abdomen may be shaved and the woman is asked to void just prior to the injection to make the level of the bladder as low as possible. The nurse may find that the client asks some very disturbing questions while the doctor is injecting the solution. These questions need to be faced by both client and nurse as honestly as possible.

The women are not given any medication or anesthetic (except local anesthetic at the injection site) so that they will be able to report any sensations related to possible side effects of the procedure. Intravascular injection of saline would produce heat sensation, dry mouth, tinnitus, tachycardia, or severe

How much bleeding will I have?

Each woman is an individual, and so it is difficult to predict her bleeding pattern. A woman who usually has heavy periods may have more bleeding than a woman who normally has light periods.

What is considered an average amount of bleeding?

Bleeding no heavier than a normal period for 5 to 7 days after the abortion. Some women will have some spotting for 2 to 4 weeks following the abortion. Those who have had an IUD inserted are more likely to notice some spotting. You may pass a small amount of clots, and bleeding may seem to increase when you get up suddenly or if you are on the toilet.

How will I know whether I am bleeding too much?

Bleeding heavy enough to soak through one pad in 1 hour or bleeding as much as a heavy period which persists for 4 to 5 days should be considered too much bleeding.

What should I do if I feel I am bleeding too much?

Call the Ob-Gyn Clinic at (give telephone number). At night call the Emergency Room at (give number). It may also help to lie down and massage the lower abdomen.

What if I have little or no bleeding after the abortion?

It probably is perfectly normal for you.

What if the bleeding stops completely and then begins again several days later?

This seems to happen to a number of women. It should not be considered cause for alarm unless it is heavy, excessive bleeding.

Take your temperature twice a day. Why?

Fever is almost always the first indication that an infection has developed after the abortion. Therefore, it is very important that you take your temperature twice a day when you first get up in the morning and again in the early evening, for the first 5 days. A fever is most likely to occur on the second or third day following the abortion. The fever is often accompanied by tenderness of the lower abdomen. There may be a vaginal discharge with an unpleasant odor. If these symptoms occur, notify your physician.

What should I do if I have a fever?

If your fever is 38.9°C or more, immediately call the Clinic or Emergency Room. If your temperature is 38.6°C two times in a row, you should call for advice.

How much pain and cramping will I have?

You may experience some mild cramping for the first day or two. Antifever pain medications usually control the discomfort. Women with an IUD may have cramping for several days.

When will I begin to feel normal again?

You should begin to feel normal within 24 to 48 hours following the abortion. Your body will be undergoing some changes in that time due to a dramatic drop in the hormones of pregnancy. The nausea you may have experienced will disappear. You may feel a mild depression for a few days.

May I resume my normal activities?

Yes, but it is probably best to avoid very strenuous activities during the first week after the abortion.

How about horseback riding, swimming, or bicycling?

These activities should be avoided for a few days. Common sense tells you to perform less vigorously than usual until the bleeding has almost stopped.

When will I be able to go back to work?
Some women plan and feel able to return to work on the day after the abortion is done. You may return to work whenever you feel up to your job.

When may I take a tub bath?
Tub baths may be allowed right away, depending upon your physician's preference. The tub should be cleaned thoroughly first.

Will it be permissible to douche?
Many doctors feel that douching is undesirable at any time. However, if you feel you must douche, wait 6 weeks.

When may I wash my hair?
Whenever you so desire.

When is it safe to have sexual relations?
It is recommended that you have no sexual relations until after you have had your 2 week check-up.

Is it all right to eat whatever I want?
There are no restrictions. However, if you have been experiencing nausea and vomiting, it is wise to eat soup and soft foods until it ends.

I have experienced breast soreness. Will it disappear soon? Will there be milk produced?
You may experience a slight increase in soreness, in the first few days. Occasionally, a woman will have breast fullness about the third day after the abortion. She may even have some milk which requires breast pads to be placed inside her bra to protect her clothing. A tight fitting bra should be worn. The milk usually subsides within a day or two.

When may I use tampax?
You may use sanitary pads. However, you must wait 2 weeks before using tampax.

Is it okay to drive a car?
The day after the abortion is fine.

After everything has returned to normal, will a doctor be able to tell that I have had an abortion?
No.

When will I have a period?
If you are taking birth control pills, you will start your period 2 or 3 days after you have taken the last pill. If you are using another method of contraception (IUD, diaphragm, foam, condom), you should have a period 4 to 6 weeks following the abortion.

When should I have my check-up?
You should have a check-up 2 weeks after the abortion. You should make an appointment in the Gyn Clinic or return to your family doctor.

FIGURE 11-5
After an abortion: questions commonly asked by women and answers. (*By permission from North Carolina Memorial Hospital, Chapel Hill, North Carolina.*)

headache. A small amount of the saline solution is injected; if none of these symptoms occur within 1 minute after injection, the remaining saline is infused. Generally women do not experience pain during the procedure except at the beginning when the needle penetrates the peritoneum. Vital signs are checked every 15 minutes until stable, and they usually stabilize rapidly. The woman is then allowed activities and food as desired.

Fetal movement generally decreases soon after saline injection, and fetal death has been documented within 1 hour. With the infusion of such a hypertonic solution into the amniotic sac, all surrounding tissue is dehydrated. However, the exact reason for fetal death or the induction of uterine contractions is unknown.[46]

There is a latency period from the time the woman receives the injection until she experiences labor. She may complain of an intense thirst for a few hours after injection, and she should be encouraged to drink as much as she desires. During the time, she may become quite talkative or she may be totally uncommunicative. Of all times during the whole abortive process, this appears to be the time that is most stressful. If there are several women undergoing the same procedure, they may group together and support each other to the exclusion, at times, of the nursing staff and family or friends. If the clients are talkative with the nurse, they should be encouraged to ventilate their feelings. Often while these women are awaiting labor, members of the hospital staff will walk into their rooms several times during each shift to ask, "Is anything happening?" A client may begin to wonder if there is something wrong because nothing is occurring.

Once the woman begins experiencing contractions, the "crisis" situation seems to come to an end. Such a labor period is one of negative expectation due to the end result. Regardless of the result, however, the woman needs physical and psychological support throughout the laboring process. Medication for pain should be given if needed to provide relief and rest. A clear liquid diet should be provided to supply some caloric intake. Once the woman has partially dilated, she is kept in bed until she aborts.

The client should be instructed to call the nurse when she feels rectal pressure. During the abortive process, the nurse may deliver the fetus and placenta. If the placenta is not expelled immediately, the cord should be clamped and cut and the fetus removed. The placenta generally separates on its own or with the Credé expression (gentle traction on the cord along with fundal massage). After 2 hours, if the placenta still remains attached, surgical removal may be necessary. The placenta must be checked to ascertain whether or not fragments have been retained.

Following complete abortion, the patient may be given lactation inhibitors to prevent breast engorgement. The woman usually expresses feelings of relief. After she is bathed and offered something to drink, she will probably feel exhausted and fall asleep. If there are no complications, she will usually be discharged within 4 to 6 hours.

The client who is having a prostaglandin $F_{2\alpha}$ induction is injected the same way as the woman receiving saline induction but she does not experience the same side effects. Also, the latency period with prostaglandin $F_{2\alpha}$ is much shorter in duration (15 to 30 minutes); thus she may be in need of parenteral analgesics sooner and throughout the procedure. Management of the other side effects such as vomiting and diarrhea can be attenuated by use of antiemetics and antidiarrheal agents. This client has the same needs for a supportive and caring nurse.

Hysterotomy

The client experiencing a hysterotomy usually has two areas of concern; one is the abortion, the other the loss of capability to re-

produce. Abortion combined with sterilization indicates that the woman has come to a
decision concerning family size. When this
client enters the hospital, she is usually
treated by the staff very much like any client
having abdominal surgery, often with complete disregard for the pregnancy or approaching abortion. This is reflected in the
fact that this client, generally, is not given
the emotional support she needs as an abortion patient. Just being given a chance to express her feelings might assist in her recovery. What she does receive is routine
postoperative physical care such as instructions on turning, coughing, and deep breathing which do not meet her psychological or
emotional needs. She usually remains in the
hospital for about 5 days.

Referral

Referral following an abortion can be very
detrimental to the client if she has not been
consulted in this decision. Many women are
fearful of the knowledge of the abortion getting back to their homes. Many have had the
abortion done away from home and do not
want community health, mental health, or
private physicians knowing about their decision. In other instances, the client was initially referred for abortion by these same
agencies or physicians, and the follow-
through assists the client in obtaining continuing care back in her own community.

Follow-up Care

It is of great importance that all women going home after having an abortion be aware
of possible complications. Vaginal bleeding
will continue for 1 to 3 weeks, but if it becomes heavier than a menstrual period, or if
she passes large clots or tissue with the
bleeding, she should consult her physician.
She should also see her physician for fever
over 38.1°C, severe persistent pain, or burn-

ing on urination. The first menses usually
occurs 2 to 8 weeks after the abortion and
may differ from that which the woman has
previously experienced. The menses may be
heavier or less in quantity and may be either
of a longer or shorter duration.

If lactation begins, it is usually mild and
lasts less than 48 hours if the breasts are not
stimulated. Using a tight brassiere, or binding the breasts and using an ice bag, will
ease the discomfort until the engorgement
decreases.

Normal physical activity can be resumed
as rapidly as desired. Increased fatigue is
often noted for a few days. Showers and
washing hair can be done immediately, but
tub baths or swimming will depend upon
physician preference and common practice
in different geographical locations. Figure
11-5 cites questions commonly asked by
women postabortion.

Return appointments are made for 2 to 4
weeks after the abortion. It is of utmost importance for the woman to have this examination to ensure that the reproductive
organs have returned to the prepregnancy
state. Although most physicians suggest that
women abstain from sexual intercourse until
after their return appointment, most women
resume sexual activity when they so desire.

Contraception

At some time during the abortion experience, the nurse should introduce the subject
of contraception if the woman has not already requested information. In some instances in which the women are having
D&C's or D&E's, they have given permission
for an IUD (intrauterine device) to be inserted at the end of the procedure. If this
service is available, it is of importance to include family planning in the preabortion
counseling.

During the time the woman is making her
decision for abortion is not when she would

be motivated toward thinking about a method of birth control. Once the decision is reached, then she is ready to pursue the outcome—abortion. After the abortion, the woman is discharged within a few hours, and at this time she is emotionally drained. The next possible contact with her is 2 to 4 weeks later, if she returns for her postabortion examination, and this may be too late. Probably the optimum time to approach the subject of contraception is when the woman has been settled into her hospital room after admission to the hospital or during the precounseling period.

Counseling on contraception is of importance to these women who are or have been faced with the reality of an unwanted pregnancy. The nurse may find several opportunities which will be psychologically right for discussion of contraception with these patients.

PSYCHOLOGICAL AND EMOTIONAL IMPLICATIONS FOR THE NURSE

Since 1967, when Colorado and North Carolina liberalized their abortion laws, nurses have been expected to be part of the health team providing care to women having abortions. However, there were no considerations made with regard to the psychological reactions that might occur in the nursing personnel working with abortion cases.

In 1970 *RN* polled 500 subscribers concerning the attitudes of nurses toward abortion and clients who have abortions.[47] The majority of nurses were opposed to abortion on demand, but 93 percent could accept having abortions for some reasons. The reasons given for abortion were rape, fetal defect, and physical impairment of the mother. Abortion for psychological reasons was not an acceptable indication. The greatest opposition toward abortion for out-of-wedlock pregnancies came from the younger nurses.

Medical personnel in Colorado reported having problems in accepting the care of patients having abortions under the new laws.[48] Some personnel refused to take part in abortions, particularly those done for psychiatric reasons when the need for the procedure was not completely obvious. Inservice training and reeducation helped to alleviate some of the difficulties which occurred.

Dr. John McDermott, Jr., presented a paper on the unexpected crisis in patient care in Hawaii when their abortion law was repealed.[49] Within 1 month after the change, hospitals began to ask for mental health consultation because of psychological reactions of the nursing staff. The reactions were of varying intensities among the staff, depending on the procedure involved. The description was of a kind of "combat fatigue" which resulted from an increased work load and emotional stress. Part of the problem here, as with other medical institutions performing abortions, was that the nurses were not well prepared for the new procedures or for the new kinds of clients they were to encounter. Most nurses who select maternity nursing as their occupational role think in terms of bringing life into the world, not taking it away. Consequently, it was quite evident from the negative reaction which was encountered that nurses were unprepared for this shift in role.

The nurses' persistent identification with the fetus seemed based on their inability to identify with the abortion client themselves. Nurses were horrified at women who talked about the fetus as though it had no human characteristics, while they, the nurses, placed very definite humanizing characteristics on the fetus. The young girls receiving abortions aroused anger in the nurses, who felt that they were playing games with sex.

Ambivalent feelings were expressed over women becoming pregnant in spite of excellent contraceptive methods being available.

Small group sessions were utilized with these nurses, first allowing for ventilation of feelings and then looking at general client dynamics.

Because of continuing problems evolving from attitudes of health personnel toward abortion, the Center for Disease Control interviewed health care providers in 16 states in an effort to find out how they felt about abortion in late 1970 and in 1971. They found that religion was an obvious, but not the most important, personal factor. The most important factor was the person's general feeling about social change: "Those who identify on some level with the forces of change are quite likely to view legal abortion as an improvement in society's way of handling unwanted pregnancy, while those who see societal change as the cause of problems fear legalized abortion as one more in a series of steps down the road to moral decay."[50]

They found that the attitudes of the nursing staff directly affected the morale of the clients. When the nurses expected their clients to feel some remorse over the abortion, the women did feel guilty and sad. On the other hand, if the nurses communicated to clients that they were not sick, but had a solvable problem, they seemed to feel much better after the procedure, and the nurses felt better also.

The abortion situation is a complicated one with many variables to be considered as we prepare student nurses to care for patients having abortions. Working with such patients and having understanding staff members and instructors who are available for verbalization of feelings will assist the student in caring for the client seeking or having an abortion.

REFERENCES

1 Lader, Lawrence: *Abortion*, Bobbs-Merrill, Indianapolis, 1966, p. 75.
2 Ibid., p. 76.
3 Knutson, Andie L.: "When Does a Human Life Begin? Viewpoints of Public Health Professionals," *American Journal of Public Health*, 57:2163–2177, 1967.
4 Ibid., p. 2163.
5 Guttmacher, Alan: "Abortion Yesterday, Today, and Tomorrow," in A. Guttmacher (ed.), *The Case for Legalized Abortion Now*, Diablo Press, Berkeley, 1967, p. 4.
6 Personal communication from Arthur Jones and Elizabeth M. Edmands.
7 Lader: op. cit., p. 89.
8 Lebensohn, Zigmond: The Right to Abortion, in "Abortion and the Law," *Res Ipsa Loquitar*, 23:15, 1970.
9 Lader: op. cit., p. 64.
10 Lader: op. cit., p. 103
11 Westoff, Leslie A., and Charles Westoff: *From Now to Zero*, Little, Brown, Boston, 1971, p. 137.
12 Ibid., p. 138.
13 Tietze, Christopher, and Deborah Dawson: *Reports on Population/Family Planning, Induced Abortion: A Factbook*, No. 14, The Population Council, Inc., New York, December 1973, pp. 8–9.
14 Guttmacher, Alan: *Birth Control and Love*, Bantam, published by arrangement with Macmillan, New York, 1970.
15 Westoff and Westoff: op. cit., p. 129.
16 Lader: op. cit., p. 98.
17 Lader: op. cit., p. 99.
18 Ryan, Joseph A.: "Liberalized Abortion Laws—Immoral and Dangerous," *Medical Opinion and Review*, February 1966, pp. 104–105.
19 Ekblad, Martin: "Induced Abortion on Psychiatric Grounds: A Follow-up of 479 Women," *Acta Psychiatrica et Neurologica*

Scandinavica, supplementum 99, 1955, p. 170.

20 Osofsky, J. D., and J. H. Osofsky: "The Psychological Reactions of Patients to Legalized Abortion," paper presented at American Orthopsychiatric Association Meeting, March 1971.

21 Woods, Nancy Fugate: *Human Sexuality in Health and Illness,* Mosby, St. Louis, 1975, p. 83.

22 Hardin, Garrett: "Abortion—or Compulsory Pregnancy?" in Garrett Hardin (ed.), *Population, Evolution, and Birth Control,* Freeman, San Francisco, 1969, p. 295.

23 Kahn, James B., Judith P. Bourne, John D. Asher, and Carl W. Tyler, Jr.: "Surveillance of Abortions in Hospitals in the United States, 1970," *HSMHA Health Reports,* 86:426, 1971.

24 Hardin: op. cit., p. 294.

25 Westoff, Charles F., Emily C. Mors, and Norman B. Ryders: "The Structure of Attitudes toward Abortion," *Milbank Memorial Fund Quarterly,* 47:33, 1969.

26 Rossi, Alice S.: "Abortion Laws and Their Victims," *Trans-Action,* 3:8, 1966.

27 Vincent, Clark E., C. Allen Haney, and Carl M. Cochrane: "Abortion Attitudes of Poverty-Level Blacks," *Seminars in Psychiatry,* 2:311, 1970.

28 Frye, Bobbie S.: "Attitudes toward Abortion of a Selected Group of Nurses," unpublished master's thesis, University of North Carolina, Chapel Hill, 1971, pp. 17–21.

29 "What Nurses Think about Abortion," *RN,* 33:40–43, 1970.

30 Sherwin, Lawrence, and Edmund W. Overstreet: "Therapeutic Abortion," *California Medicine,* 105:337–339, 1966.

31 Peck, Arthur: "Therapeutic Abortion: Patients, Doctors, and Society," *American Journal of Psychiatry,* 125:105–115, 1968.

32 Tyler, Carl W., Jr., and Jan Schneider: "The Logistics of Abortion Services in the Absence of Restrictive Criminal Legislation in the United States," *American Journal of Public Health,* 61:490, 1971.

33 "Abortion Surveillance Report—Legal Abortions, United States Annual Summary, 1970," *Center for Disease Control: Family Planning Evaluation,* U.S. Department of Health, Education, and Welfare, Public Health Service, pp. 3–5.

34 *Center for Disease Control: Abortion Surveillance: 1973,* U.S. Department of Health, Education, and Welfare, Public Health Service, May 1975, p. 1.

35 Calderone, Mary S.: *Abortion in the United States,* Harper, New York, 1958, pp. 60–61.

36 Ibid., pp. 50–55.

37 Ebon, Martin (ed.): *Every Woman's Guide to Abortion,* Pocket Books, New York, 1971, pp. 119–147.

38 Staurovsky, Linda G., William Brenner, James Dingfelder, and Thamysu Kumarasamy: "Induction of Therapeutic Abortion with Intraamniotically Administered Prostaglandin $F_{2\alpha}$: A Comparative Study of Two Single Dose Schedules," speech presented at VIIIth World Congress of Fertility and Sterility, Buenos Aires, November 1974.

39 Staurovsky, Linda G., et al.: "The Effect of Meperidine Analgesia in $PGF_{2\alpha}$ Induced Midtrimester Abortions," accepted for publication in *American Journal of Obstetrics and Gynecology.*

40 Hendricks, Charles H.: "Pregnancy Termination: The Impact of New Laws," *Journal of Reproductive Medicine,* 6:60–70, 1971.

41 Daily, Edwin F., Nick Nicholas, Frieda Nelson, and Jean Pakter: "Repeat Abortions in New York City: 1970–1972," *Family Planning Perspectives,* 5:89–92, Spring 1973.

42 Ibid., p. 92.

43 Ibid.

44 Harting, Donald, and Helen J. Hunter: "Abortion Techniques and Services: A Review and Critique," *American Journal of Public Health,* 61:2101–2102, 1971.

45 Margolis, Alan J., et al.: "Therapeutic Abor-

tion Follow-up Study," *American Journal of Obstetrics and Gynecology*, 110:246, 1971.

46 Cronenwett, Linda R., and Janice M. Choyce: "Saline Abortion," *American Journal of Nursing*, 71:1754–1757, 1971.

47 "What Nurses Think about Abortion," *RN*, 33:40–43, 1970.

48 Thompson, Horace, David L. Cowen, and Betty Berris: "Therapeutic Abortion: A Two-Year Experience in One Hospital," *Journal of the American Medical Association*, 213:995, 1970.

49 McDermott, John F., Jr., and Walter F. Char: "Abortion Repeal in Hawaii: An Unexpected Crisis in Patient Care," paper presented at the 48th annual meeting of the American Orthopsychiatric Association, Washington, D.C., Mar. 23, 1971.

50 Bourne, Judith: Report presented at the Conference on Abortion Techniques and Services, New York, June 3–5, 1971.

BIBLIOGRAPHY

Bauer, H.: "Abortion Counseling: Before, After and Again," *Medical Insight*, 6:6–11, January 1974.

Bennett, Elizabeth: "Abortion," *Nursing Clinics of North America*, 3:243–251, 1968.

Branson, Helen: "Nurses Talk about Abortion," *American Journal of Nursing*, 72:106–109, 1972.

Burchell, R. Clay: "Professional Perspectives on Abortion," *Journal of Obstetric, Gynecologic and Neonatal Nursing*, 3:25–27, November–December 1974.

Burnhill, Michael S.: *Physician's Manual, Standard Medical Procedures*, 3d ed., Preterm Institute, Newton, Mass., 1975.

Donovan, Cornelia M., Rhoda Greenspan, and Faye Mittleman: "Postabortion Psychiatric Illness," *Nursing Digest*, 3:12–16, September–October 1975.

Felton, Geraldine, and Roy Smith: "Administrative Guidelines for an Abortion Service," *American Journal of Nursing*, 72:108–109, 1972.

Fronseca, Jeanne D.: "Induced Abortion: Nursing Attitudes and Action," *American Journal of Nursing*, 68:1022–1027, 1968.

Gedan, S.: "Abortion Counseling with Adolescents," *American Journal of Nursing*, 74:1856–1858, 1974.

Goldman, Alice: "Learning Abortion Care," *Nursing Outlook*, 19:350–352, 1971.

Keller, Christa, and Pamela Copeland: "Counseling the Abortion Patient Is More Than Talk," *American Journal of Nursing*, 72:102–106, 1972.

Malo-Juvera, Dolores: "Preparing Students for Abortion Care," *Nursing Outlook*, 19:347–349, 1971.

"Personal Experience at a Legal Abortion Center," *American Journal of Nursing*, 72:110–112, 1972.

University of Colorado School of Nursing, Workshop on Family Planning: "Abortion," *American Journal of Nursing*, 70:1919–1925, 1970.

Williams, Jean Morton, and Keith Hindell: *Abortion and Contraceptions: A Study of Patients' Attitudes*, Berridge, London, 1973.

Wilson, Robert R.: *Problem Pregnancy and Abortion Counseling*, Family Life Publications, Saluda, N.C., 1973.

12

Genetic Counseling

JANET M. STEWART

The ultimate goal of every pregnancy is to produce an individual who is anatomically perfect, intellectually normal, and functionally capable of an independent and productive life. Most pregnancies culminate in such an individual, but in a certain percentage—small, but significant—something goes wrong. A child is born with a congenital anomaly which may be immediately obvious or which may not become apparent until later on in childhood or even in adult life. The child may be mentally retarded, or his or her behavior or emotional stability may be such that the child is not capable of functioning independently in society. In some instances the cause for such a problem is known; in others, it cannot be determined. In the minds of the parents, however, many questions are raised: "Will this happen again? Can it be prevented? What are my chances of having a normal baby next time?" Genetic counseling is an attempt to answer these questions. Genetic factors are of major importance in some abnormalities, in others they are a contributing factor, and in a third group their role is negligible. We as medical personnel may know into which group a certain abnormality falls; but parents rarely do, and they usually imagine the worst.

The incidence of congenital abnormalities is estimated to be 3 to 5 percent of all births with an even higher occurrence if an individual is followed into adult life. This incidence is fairly constant, but the significance of these defects is increasing. Perinatal mortality due to prematurity and infection is decreasing. Improved nursery and surgical techniques are allowing children to survive who previously would have died. These children are now living reminders of the pain, expense, and frustration of rearing a handicapped child. Parents, in their increasing sophistication, are seeking to learn the genetic implications of the defect in their particular family.

CHROMOSOMES AND CHROMOSOMAL DEFECTS

All hereditary material, in the form of deoxyribonucleic acid (DNA), is carried as genes on the chromosomes. All somatic cells in the human body contain 46 chromosomes (diploid number), or 23 pairs of chromosomes; one member of each pair is maternal in origin, the other paternal. Twenty-two of these pairs are known as autosomes; the remaining two chromosomes are called the sex chromosomes, two X chromosomes constituting a female (46, XX) and one X and one Y a male (46, XY). These somatic cells divide by a process called mitosis. (See Figure 12-1.)

Each chromosome becomes shortened and thickened and splits longitudinally into two chromatids joined at a point called the centromere. This is the form in which most chromosomes are pictured. They are then aligned on a central spindle and split longitudinally through the centromere, thus separating the two chromatids which then migrate to opposite ends of the cell. Cleavage occurs to produce two genetically similar cells.

In the germ cells of the body, a unique process known as meiosis occurs. (See Figure 12-2.) The chromosomes again shorten and thicken and split into two chromatids joined at the centromere. Homologous pairs are arranged together, and at this time material may be exchanged between the paired chromosomes (crossing-over). The paired chromosomes then separate (disjunction) and move to opposite poles, forming two cells with 23 chromosomes each (haploid number). Each cell contains either an X or a Y. This is then followed by a mitotic division in which there is a longitudinal split at the centromere and migration of the chromatids to opposite poles. In this manner ova and sperm are formed, each with 23 chromosomes. At the time of fertilization, one ovum and one sperm unite to form a cell with the full diploid chromosomal constitution, and from this cell the fetus develops.

Chromosomes are most commonly studied in lymphocytes. Phytohemagglutinin is added to peripheral blood to stimulate mitosis and agglutinate erythrocytes. After 3 days, the cells are arrested in mitosis by the addition of colchicine to the culture medium. At this stage the chromosomes have split into chromatids and are readily visible under high magnification. The photographic record of the chromosomal constitution of a cell is called a karyotype. (See Figure 12-3.)

In 1970, Caspersson described a fluorescent stain which enables each individual chromosome to be identified by its characteristic alternate bright and dark bands. Several such staining techniques are now available (quinacrine-induced fluorescence, Giemsa

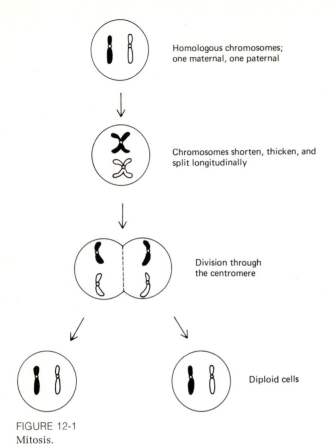

Homologous chromosomes;
one maternal, one paternal

Chromosomes shorten, thicken, and
split longitudinally

Division through
the centromere

Diploid cells

FIGURE 12-1
Mitosis.

stain, reverse Giemsa, etc.) and are routine in many major cytogenetic laboratories. Minor deletions and translocations and more subtle chromosomal abnormalities can thus be detected and studied. If an unusual chromosome abnormality is suspected, at least one of the new banding techniques is essential before the karyotype can be called normal.

Abnormalities may occur during meiotic or mitotic division, producing an individual with a chromosomal defect. These abnormalities may involve one of the autosomes or the sex chromosomes and consist of too much or too little chromosomal material. Approximately 1 in every 150 live-born in-

fants will have a chromosomal defect; half of these will involve the autosomes and half the sex chromosomes. As high as 25 to 50 percent of spontaneous abortions will also have a chromosomal aberration. In addition recent studies have shown that 5 to 10 percent of perinatal deaths are associated with chromosomal abnormalities, many clinically unsuspected.

Autosomal Defects

The most common autosomal defect is known as Down's syndrome, or mongolism. The affected individual has an extra number

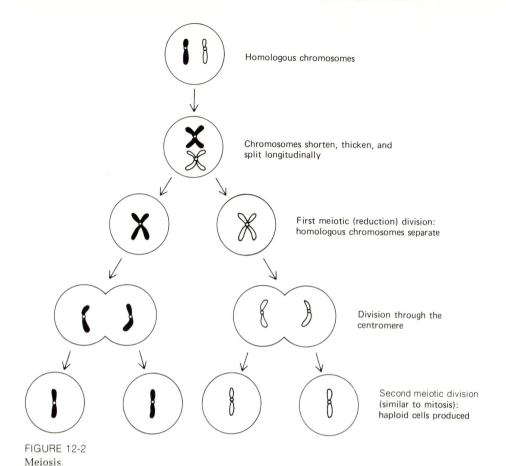

Homologous chromosomes

Chromosomes shorten, thicken, and split longitudinally

First meiotic (reduction) division: homologous chromosomes separate

Division through the centromere

Second meiotic division (similar to mitosis): haploid cells produced

FIGURE 12-2
Meiosis.

21 chromosome for a total of 47, trisomy 21. (See Figure 12-4.) During meiosis, the two paired 21 chromosomes fail to separate (nondisjunction), and two dissimilar cells are formed, one with 24 chromosomes and one with 22. The latter cell is nonviable and dies. The former cell then unites with a haploid gamete, and the result is an individual with 47, XX (or XY), 21+ karyotype. The clinical features of Down's syndrome are well known and are listed in Table 12-1. Most children with Down's syndrome are born to mothers over thirty-five years of age. At the time of the birth of a female child all ova are in the

early stages of meiosis. They remain dormant until the time of ovulation, as long as 35 years later. It is believed that these older ova are more prone to nondisjunction.

Down's syndrome can occur in two other cytogenetic forms. An occasional child with Down's syndrome will have only 46 chromosomes. This includes one large abnormal chromosome which consists of the translocation of the extra 21 to another chromosome, usually a number 14. (See Figure 12-5.) One of the parents, usually the mother, may have a balanced translocation, that is, 45 chromosomes including the translocation. (See

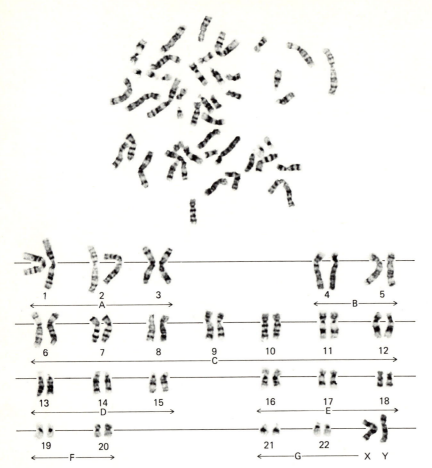

FIGURE 12-3
Normal female karyotype using trypsin-Giema staining.

TABLE 12-1
Clinical Features of Down's Syndrome

Small head	Short, broad neck
Slanting palpebral fissures	Congenital heart disease
Epicanthic folds	
Speckling of the iris	Short, broad hands
Low-set, simply formed ears	Transverse palmar creases
Protrusion of the tongue	
High palate	Curved fifth finger
	Hypotonia
	Mental retardation

Figure 12-6.) Although the number of chromosomes is deficient, the amount of chromosomal or genetic material is essentially normal and the translocation carrier is clinically a normal individual. She is, however, at an increased risk for having subsequent children with Down's syndrome. Translocation Down's syndrome is more common in younger mothers, but the most common type of Down's syndrome born to a young mother is still the standard trisomy

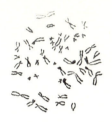

FIGURE 12-4
Karyotype of a male with trisomy 21, or Down's syndrome.

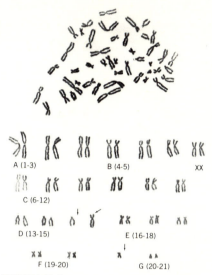

FIGURE 12-6
Balanced translocation carrier for Down's syndrome. Vertical arrows indicate missing D and G chromosomes; oblique arrow points to D/G translocation chromosome.

FIGURE 12-5
Translocation Down's syndrome with abnormal chromosome shown by arrow.

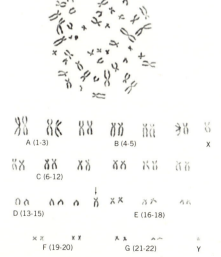

21. Clinically, the child with a translocation type of Down's syndrome is indistinguishable from the child with the more common form.

Occasionally an individual will have a mixed population of cells, some normal and some with an extra 21. This is known as mosaicism and is due to nondisjunction at a later stage of cell division. The clinical features and intellectual potential of these individuals vary with the proportion of abnormal cells.

Infants have also been born with trisomy 13 and trisomy 18 but have many severe abnormalities and rarely live beyond a few months of age. (See Table 12-2.) Translocations are fairly common in trisomy 13.

The total absence of an autosome is felt to be incompatible with life, although a few exceptions have been reported. Partial deletions of the short arm (p−) or the long arm (q−) of various chromosomes have been de-

TABLE 12-2
Clinical Features of Trisomy 13 and Trisomy 18

Trisomy 13	Trisomy 18
Arhinencephaly	Low birth weight
Microphthalmia/	Low-set, malformed ears
anophthalmia	Prominent occiput
Facial clefts	Micrognathia
Polydactyly	Short sternum
Scalp defects/	Overlapping fingers
hemangiomata	Flexion contractures
Congenital heart	Spasticity
disease	Congenital heart disease
Severe retardation	Genitourinary anomalies
	Severe retardation

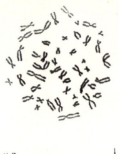

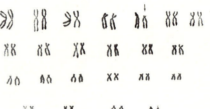

FIGURE 12-7
The cri du chat syndrome. Arrow shows deletion of short arms of chromosome number 5.

scribed and, in a few instances, seem to comprise specific syndromes. A deletion of the short arm of chromosome 5 results in severe mental retardation and a catlike cry in infancy, the cri du chat syndrome. (See Figure 12-7.)

A deletion of the long arm of chromosome 18 may be associated with maxillary hypoplasia, stenotic ear canals, and a conductive hearing loss. Material may be lost from both the long and the short arms of a certain chromosome, and during cell division, these two arms may become adherent, forming a ring. (See Figure 12-8.) These individuals clinically resemble the picture seen with a single deletion.

Sex Chromosome Defects

Unlike the loss of autosomal material, an individual may lose one of the sex chromosomes with surprisingly little effect. The 45, Y zygote is not viable, but the 45, X individual (Turner's syndrome, see Figure 12-9) has a female appearance or phenotype with the abnormalities listed in Table 12-3. She also has streak ovaries, develops few secondary sex characteristics, and is usually in-

fertile. She is most often of normal intelligence but may have perceptual difficulties. It is usually not known if the lost chromosome is of maternal or paternal origin, and, indeed, this probably varies.

FIGURE 12-8
Karyotype of a male with a ring 18 chromosome indicated by arrow.

FIGURE 12-9
Turner's syndrome (45, X).

The presence of the Y chromosome is essential for the early development of a male phenotype, but it actually carries few, if any, known genes. At first glance it would appear that the normal female has a double dose of the genetic material carried on the X chromosome. The work of Barr and others, however, has shown that females have a darkly staining body found adjacent to the nuclear membrane in nondividing cells, a body not found in the normal male. It has been postulated that this Barr body represents one of the X chromosomes which is randomly inactivated early in fetal development. Thus, the genetically active material on the X chromosome

TABLE 12-3
Clinical Features of Turner's Syndrome

Short stature	Hyperconvex and/or deep-set
Lymphedema	nails
Low hairline	Excessive nevi
Webbed neck	Renal anomalies
Cubitus valgus	Broad chest
	Wide-spaced, hypoplastic
	nipples

is equal in males and in females. (See Figure 12-10.) This is known as the Lyon hypothesis.

A female may have a 47, XXX constitution and have two Barr bodies, representing two of the three X chromosomes that have been inactivated. While it has been felt in the past that these individuals are retarded and infertile, more recent evidence indicates that many may be normal. A male with a 47, XXY

FIGURE 12-10
(a) Normal male cell, no Barr body; (b) normal female cell, single Barr body indicated by arrow.

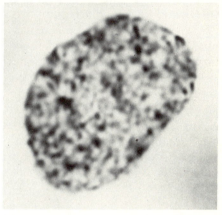

(a)

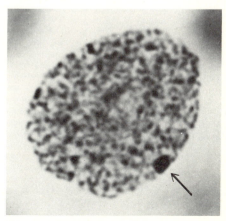

(b)

chromosomal picture may have testicular atrophy and sterility. This is known as Klinefelter's syndrome. (See Figure 12-11.)

Recent attention has been focused on the 47, XYY karyotype and its possible association with tall stature and aggressive or criminal behavior. This association has not been proven. Individuals with more X chromosomes (48, XXXX or 48, XXXY) usually have more severe physical abnormalities and mental retardation.

For many years, a simple technique has been available to screen for abnormalities of the X chromosome. Cells from the buccal mucosa or from the amnion can be stained and the Barr body identified. The number of X chromosomes in the karyotype is equal to the number of Barr bodies counted (inactivated X's) *plus* 1 (active X). In our laboratory a normal female will have 20 to 40 percent chromatin-positive cells (one Barr body) in a buccal smear. Variations in the size of the Barr body or in the percentage of positive cells may indicate a structural abnormality of the X chromosome or mosaicism, and a

full karyotype should be done. The interpretation of a buccal smear in the newborn infant can be extremely difficult and mistakes have caused much parental anxiety and confusion. The cells of the amniotic membrane are more reliable if available, and a full karyotype should certainly be done if there is any question of the sex chromosome constitution of the infant.

With the introduction of the new fluorescent stains described above, it has become possible to screen for Y chromosome abnormalities as well. The Y chromosome can be identified as a brightly staining body even in the interphase or nondividing cell of the buccal mucosa, amnion, or umbilical cord. (See Figure 12-12.) The number of Y chromosomes in the karyotype is *equal* to the number of fluorescent Y bodies seen in the resting cell. The distal part of the long arm of the chromosome provides the fluorescent portion which is visible on screening. Certain males have short long arms, and the fluorescent body may not be evident. Certainly the identification of both Barr and fluorescent Y bodies should be considered a screening procedure only. If an abnormality is suspected, a full karyotype is mandatory.

PATTERNS OF INHERITANCE

The chromosomal defects that have been discussed are grossly obvious in a standard karyotype. Defects involving single genes, however, are much more discrete and invisible by any currently used technique. The determination of the hereditary nature of an abnormality is done in two ways: (1) by the careful study of an individual family, and (2) by a study of the inheritance pattern of that particular defect as previously reported in the literature.

Genes occur in pairs and are located on homologous chromosomes. One is maternal in origin and the other paternal. If the two

FIGURE 12-11
Klinefelter's syndrome (47, XXY).

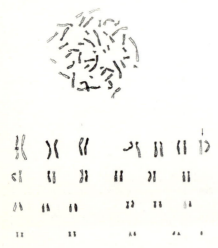

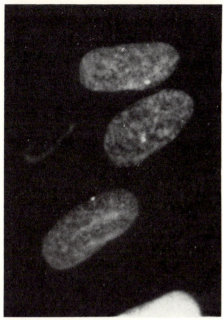

FIGURE 12-12
Fluorescent Y body in interphase or resting cell;
this indicates the presence of a single Y chromosome.
(*Reproduced by permission of* Journal of Pediatrics,
79:305, 1971.)

genes have the same effect, the individual is said to be homozygous; if the effect is different, the individual is said to be heterozygous. The expression of each gene depends upon its interaction with other genes and with the environment.

Genetic defects can be inherited in three well-known ways and in a fourth less well understood but commonly occurring manner.

Autosomal Dominant Traits

A condition or trait is said to be dominantly inherited if it is manifest in the heterozygous state. This is a vertical type of inheritance with an affected individual having a 50 percent chance of passing the gene on to each of the individual's offspring. An unaffected individual, in most cases, does not carry the abnormal gene, and all of that individual's offspring will be normal.

Case 1. A. G. (see Figure 12-13, III-1) is a five-year-old boy with bilateral cataracts and a left club foot noted at birth. The club foot has been corrected by casting, and his development has been normal. The cataracts are small and do not interfere with vision. His mother (Figure 12-13, II-1) has bilateral cataracts and colobomata, as does a maternal aunt (II-2). A maternal uncle also has cataracts (II-3) and has one son with cataracts and aniridia (III-2), a daughter with cataracts and colobomata (III-3), and a second daughter with cataracts and aniridia (III-4). The maternal grandmother (I-1) also has cataracts and colobomata. All other family members are normal. The affected family members carry a dominantly inherited gene for eye abnormalities, variously expressed as cataracts, colobomata, and aniridia.

Dominantly inherited traits have several distinguishing characteristics. They are usually milder, since the gene is passed on by the affected individual who is able to reproduce. Occasionally, the onset of symptoms does not occur until after the reproductive years, e.g., Huntington's chorea. There is much variation in the clinical manifestations of a dominant gene, as shown in Case 1. This is known as variation in expressivity. A few individuals are severely affected, while those at the other end of the spectrum may be so mildly affected that they have no obvious clinical manifestations of the gene. If this occurs, a gene is said to have decreased penetrance. Often, however, if sought, some mild and clinically insignificant finding is present which identifies the abnormal gene.

Key to symbols

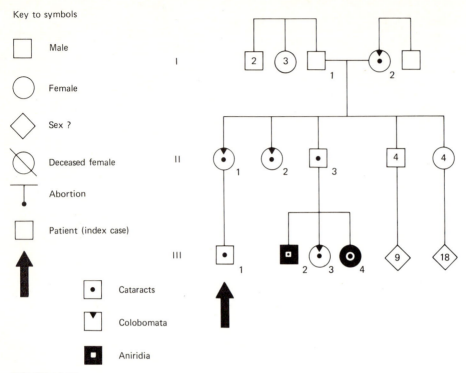

FIGURE 12-13
Case 1: Pedigree illustrating autosomal dominant inheritance.

On occasion a dominant trait will seem to appear *de novo*. An affected child will be born to normal parents with a negative family history. In this case, a spontaneous gene mutation has occurred. The parents of such a child are not at an increased risk for future pregnancies, although the affected individual would have a 50 percent chance of passing the trait on to his or her offspring. Many dominantly inherited traits have a high mutation rate, and, indeed, some of the more severe conditions seem most often to be new mutations. Increased paternal age has been implicated as a factor in the spontaneous mutation of certain dominant abnormalities, e.g., achondroplasia, Apert's syndrome (acrocephalosyndactyly), fibrodysplasia ossificans progressiva, and Marfan's syndrome.

Autosomal Recessive Traits

A condition is said to be recessively inherited if it is manifest only when the individual is homozygous for the defective gene. This is a horizontal type of inheritance with the carrier parents often being asymptomatic and having a 25 percent chance with each pregnancy of producing an affected child. There is a 50 percent chance that a child will be a carrier like the parents and a 25 percent chance that the child will be genetically normal. In many cases, recessive conditions are more severe as the abnormality is passed on by the asymptomatic carrier and the affected person need not reproduce. If a particular recessive condition is rare, there is an increased incidence of consanguinity in the parents. Conversely, if parents are related, there is an increased chance that an abnormality in a child is recessive in nature.

Case 2. M. W. (see Figure 12-14, II-10) is a 14½-year old girl with a profound bilateral sensorineural hearing loss first suspected at one year of age. She wears a hearing aid and has attended schools for the hearing handicapped. M. has two older sisters, ages thirty-one and thirty-two (Figure 12-14, II-4 and 5), who also have profound hearing losses and goiters. They have been diagnosed as having Pendred's syndrome, an autosomal recessive condition characterized by hearing loss and a goiter which appears in adolescence. Both sisters have children with normal hearing. M. has no thyroid enlargement to date. Both parents have normal hearing, and there is no other family history of deafness.

The distinction between dominant and recessive inheritance is not strictly true. If our tools are sophisticated enough, an abnormality can be detected in the "normal" carrier parents. Galactosemia is a defect due to the deficiency of the enzyme galactose 1-P uridyl transferase. The homozygous individual has little or no detectable enzyme. The carrier has an enzyme level that is roughly 50 percent of normal. Although clinically asymptomatic, the carrier is not biochemically normal, and the gene does manifest itself in the heterozygous state.

Sickle-cell anemia is another example of what some have called "intermediate" inheritance. The individual with sickle-cell disease is *homozygous (S-S)* for hemoglobin S. The carrier, or the person with sickle-cell trait, is *heterozygous (A-S)* and therefore has an abnormality which can be detected on hemoglobin electrophoresis. The sickle-cell carrier is clinically normal except in unusual circumstances such as high altitude where the carrier may become symptomatic.

Sex-linked Traits

If the gene for a particular trait or abnormality is located on the X chromosome, the condition is said to be inherited in an X-linked, or sex-linked, manner. The condition is X-linked recessive if it is manifest only in the

FIGURE 12-14
Case 2: Pedigree showing autosomal recessive inheritance.

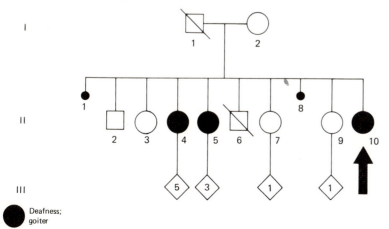

male who is hemizygous, that is, the abnormal gene on the single X chromosome is genetically unopposed. The female who has a normal gene on one X chromosome and an abnormal gene on the other is a carrier and usually asymptomatic. In reality, because of the random inactivation of the X chromosome, the female carrier may have varying degrees of symptomatology. This is an oblique kind of inheritance. The carrier female passes the gene on to 50 percent of her sons, who then manifest the abnormality, and 50 percent of her daughters, who are also carriers. An affected male has all normal sons and all carrier daughters. The cardinal feature of an X-linked trait is the lack of male-to-male transmission, since the male may only pass on his Y chromosome to his sons.

Case 3. T. N. (see Figure 12-15, IV-2) is a twelve-month-old boy with an athetoid form of cerebral palsy diagnosed at ten months of age. Laboratory studies including serum uric acid and ceruloplasmin are normal. He has an older normal brother. A maternal first cousin (Figure 12-15, IV-4), an uncle (III-3), a second cousin (IV-6), and two first cousins of the mother (III-5, 6) are all males who have a similar type of cerebral palsy and associated mental retardation. This is a rare X-linked form of cerebral palsy. The carriers (I-1; II-1, 2, 3; III-1, 2, 9) are clinically normal.

More rarely, an X-linked trait may be dominantly inherited, e.g., vitamin D resistant rickets. In this case, heterozygous females are also affected but less severely than the hemizygous male. Again, there is no male-to-male transmission.

Polygenic Abnormalities

Many of the more common congenital abnormalities, such as cleft lip, cleft palate, spina bifida, and pyloric stenosis, are not inherited in one of the manners described above, and yet these defects often cluster in families. It has been postulated that multiple genes contribute to these defects and that each individual has a threshold above which the abnormality will be manifest. This is known as polygenic inheritance. The more severe the defect, the more predisposing genes present. The less commonly affected sex requires more predisposing genes to demonstrate the abnormality. Unlike single gene defects, the recurrence risk varies with the number of affected persons in the family. Practically, the principles of polygenic inheritance are often applied in genetic counseling situations. Normal parents who have one child with a cleft lip and cleft palate have a 4 percent recurrence risk figure for future pregnancies. If one of the parents is also affected, the risk increases to 17 percent. With normal parents and two affected children the risk is about 9 percent.

INBORN ERRORS OF METABOLISM

Metabolic errors are disorders of protein, often characterized by abnormal or deficient enzymes which interfere with the metabolism of certain endogenous or exogenous substances. A few of these abnormalities are dominantly inherited (type II hyperlipoproteinemia), some are X-linked (Hunter's syndrome), but most are autosomal recessive disorders. Most metabolic errors are rare, but they assume an importance out of proportion to their frequency. There are several reasons for this. First, they are often associated with mental retardation; second, if detected early, many of the metabolic errors can be treated and the retardation thus prevented; and

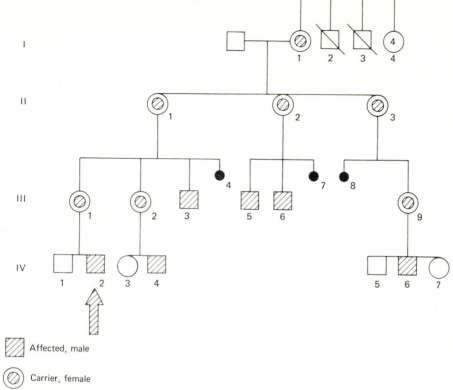

☒ (hatched square) Affected, male

⊘ (slashed circle) Carrier, female

FIGURE 12-15
Case 3: Pedigree demonstrating X-linked recessive inheritance.

third, an increasing number of these conditions can be diagnosed early in pregnancy (see following paragraphs). Three inborn errors of metabolism will be considered here briefly.

Phenylketonuria (PKU)

PKU is one of the best known of the metabolic errors. It was first described in 1934 by Følling, and in 1953 Jervis identified the missing enzyme as phenylalanine hydroxylase. Affected persons are unable to convert phenylalanine to tyrosine, resulting in an accumulation of phenylalanine and certain

metabolic by-products. Infants with PKU are usually normal at birth but within the first few months of life they show progressive developmental delay, often with eczema and seizures. Untreated, most phenylketonurics are severely retarded. Dietary treatment was first attempted in the mid-1950s and, with some modifications, is the therapy used today. After the diagnosis has been confirmed, the infant is put on a diet restricted in phenylalanine. Since this is one of the essential amino acids, certain amounts are necessary to ensure normal growth. In essence, this is a diet with little protein which is supplemented by a commercial milk substitute containing low levels of phenylalanine. Results of early dietary treatment have been encouraging; mental retardation is either prevented or markedly ameliorated. It is apparent, however, that for dietary restriction to be effective, it must be started within the first few months of life. For this reason, several screening methods have been developed, and in many states PKU screening of the newborn has been made compulsory by law.

The incidence of PKU ranges from 1:15,000 to 1:20,000, and it comprises 1 percent of the population in an institution for the mentally retarded. It is an autosomal recessive condition and carriers are identified by a phenylalanine loading test with measurement of phenylalanine levels and the phenylalanine:tyrosine ratio. Although this test is helpful, there may be overlap with normal, and carriers cannot always be identified with certainty. Unfortunately, the missing enzyme, phenylalanine hydroxylase, has only been found in the liver, making the measurement of exact enzyme levels an impractical method for the diagnosis of the disease or the identification of carriers. At this time, PKU cannot be diagnosed in utero.

Many questions remain unanswered about this abnormality. The exact cause of the mental retardation is not understood. There are some individuals with the disease who have a normal or near normal IQ. No consistent metabolic differences have been identified in these individuals. The exact level at which the serum phenylalanine should be maintained during treatment has not been determined, nor has the age at which the diet can be discontinued. It would seem that most brain growth has been completed by the age of five or six years and that the diet can be safely discontinued at this time. It is also known that mothers with PKU give birth to a very high percentage of children with mental retardation and microcephaly. Since most of the treated individuals will now marry and reproduce, some type of maternal treatment during pregnancy must be devised which will ensure enough phenylalanine to allow normal fetal growth but not so much as to cause retardation.

Maple Syrup Urine Disease (MSUD)

MSUD is a much less common metabolic error in which there is an accumulation of the branched-chain amino acids leucine, isoleucine, and valine. This is believed to be secondary to the absence or depression of the decarboxylase enzyme or enzymes. Clinically, these infants are also normal at birth but by one week of age, they develop poor feeding, vomiting, lethargy, hypertonicity, and seizures along with a characteristic odor to the urine suggestive of maple syrup. Untreated, most infants die shortly after birth; survival is associated with severe retardation. Treatment is similar to PKU. An artificial diet is used which contains restricted amounts of leucine, isoleucine, and valine. Again, early treatment seems to be effective in preventing mental retardation, but the diet is more difficult to maintain with frequent fluctuations associated with infection. Dietary treatment may be necessary throughout life. This, too, is an autosomal recessive condition. Carriers can be identified and an intrauterine diagnosis can be made in the first trimester of pregnancy.

Galactosemia

A third metabolic error, galactosemia, is due to a deficiency of the enzyme galactose 1-phosphate uridyl transferase, resulting in an inability to convert galactose 1-phosphate to glucose 1-phosphate. These infants develop failure to thrive, vomiting, diarrhea, and signs of liver disease shortly after milk is introduced into the diet. Untreated, many go on to develop cataracts and mental retardation. Therapy consists of the elimination of galactose from the diet by using commercial milk substitutes which are galactose-free. Dietary treatment has been quite effective. A second, less common form of galactosemia is due to a deficiency of the enzyme galactokinase. Affected persons may have cataracts but seem to be spared the liver disease and the mental retardation. Both forms of galactosemia are autosomal recessive. Enzyme levels can be determined in fibroblasts and leukocytes, and heterozygotes have 50 percent of the expected normal enzyme value. An intrauterine diagnosis can be made by measuring the enzyme level in fetal fibroblasts.

Undiagnosable and Untreatable Errors

The three conditions discussed above represent three broad categories: (1) PKU—a disorder not diagnosable in utero but with a relatively simple and effective therapy; (2) MSUD—a disorder detectable in utero with a very difficult dietary therapy and less predictable effectiveness; and (3) galactosemia —a disorder diagnosable in utero with a good therapeutic regimen available. There are many other inborn errors of metabolism, and most fall into a fourth category—not diagnosable and not treatable, at least at this time. Although rare, these conditions must be considered in children with early deterioration or mental retardation, particularly if the family history indicates other similarly affected persons or if there is consanguinity.

GENETIC COUNSELING

Most frequently, genetic counseling is given to parents who have had one abnormal child. It should also be offered to siblings of such an individual and to the affected person when he or she approaches marriage and parenthood. Less commonly, more distant relatives may seek genetic counseling, or related individuals who are contemplating marriage may want genetic advice.

The genetic evaluation and counseling may be done effectively in many places by a variety of persons, and there are advantages to having the counseling done by a person familiar with the family. It is absolutely imperative, however, that the diagnosis be correct. The less common dominantly inherited form of cleft lip and cleft palate must be differentiated from the usual polygenic type. The child with multiple abnormalities who fits into a previously described recessively inherited syndrome must be identified. For this reason, referral to a genetic center is often advisable.

The actual steps involved in genetic counseling vary with the complexity of the problem, but often the process is simpler and less expensive than expected. A careful history is always taken, and it should include any environmental factors in the pregnancy which might explain the abnormality. The family history is taken in pedigree form and is as extensive as possible. It is often necessary to obtain medical records or photographs of relatives who may have a similar abnormality. A careful physical examination is made of not only the affected individual (the propositus or proband) but often of other family members as well. The detailed history, including a pedigree, and the careful physical examination are the hallmarks of a good genetic evaluation. The amount of laboratory work required prior to genetic counseling varies considerably. Some of the tests which may be done on the proband and other family members are listed in Table 12-4. It is not necessary to do a karyotype prior to genetic counseling unless a chromosomal defect is suspected.

When the evaluation has been completed and the diagnosis made, the parents then return for the actual counseling session. Both parents are encouraged to attend, and the counseling is done in an unhurried and relaxed atmosphere. They are given the final diagnosis and the risk figures for future pregnancies. In most centers, actual advice about future children is not given, but rather an attempt is made to give parents the factual knowledge necessary to make a wise decision. This not only includes the recurrence risk figures but also the significance of the diagnosis and the prognosis for the child. Parents who have not yet lived with a child with cystic fibrosis will not comprehend the severity of the disease. When possible, an attempt is made to minimize guilt; however, in situations in which one parent is obviously the carrier of the gene causing the defect, it is often better to acknowledge the guilt and help the parent deal with it. In many instances one counseling session is not enough. Parents may hear nothing beyond the term "Down's syndrome." Additional sessions may be necessary to review the information, answer questions, and clear up misconceptions. A nurse or social worker may be the key figure in these follow-up meetings.

If a malformation is environmental in origin or if both the risk and the burden of the disorder are low, parents will usually elect to proceed with a pregnancy if they desire future children. On the other hand if the risk is high or the burden great, there may be concern and reluctance to plan future pregnancies. In this case, various alternatives should be discussed with the family. Because the adoption of a normal, healthy infant is becoming increasingly difficult, other courses must be explored.

Artificial Insemination

If the father has an autosomal dominant trait which he does not want to pass on to his offspring (neurofibromatosis, some types of blindness, type II hyperlipidemia, etc.), or if he is the potential carrier of a condition such as Huntington's chorea, artificial insemination is a medically and genetically acceptable alternative. A father who himself has an X-linked trait such as hemophilia or anhydrotic ectodermal dysplasia may elect artificial insemination over the reappearance of the disorder in the male offspring of his carrier daughters. Artificial insemination is also feasible in certain autosomal recessive disorders where the carrier state can be detected (thus assuring a normal donor) or where the gene is rare enough that the procedure would markedly lower the recurrence risk figure. Artificial insemination has not been generally discussed in many genetic counseling clinics, in part because of the discomfort of the counselor and in part because of poor acceptance by the families. In certain cases, however, it may be the best and even the only way of lowering an unacceptably high recurrence risk figure.

TABLE 12-4
Some Laboratory Tests Done on Proband and Family

Viral titers	Carrier tests
Viral cultures	X rays
Dermatoglyphics	Other blood tests appropriate
Buccal smear	for suspected disorder
Karyotype	

Intrauterine Diagnosis

With recent advancements in cytogenetic, biochemical, and obstetrical techniques, it has now become possible to diagnose an increasing number of disorders in the second trimester of pregnancy. The liberalization of abortion laws and newer obstetrical techniques have made the interruption of pregnancy at this point both legal and increasingly safe. At the 14th to 16th week of pregnancy, a needle can be inserted into the uterus and amniotic fluid removed. This fluid contains cells of fetal origin which are grown and may then be analyzed chromosomally or biochemically. The indications for amniocentesis are listed in Table 12-5. This procedure is most often done where there is an increased risk of producing a child with a chromosomal aberration because of (1) advanced maternal age, (2) a previous child with such an abnormality, or (3) either parent a translocation carrier. It can also be done to determine sex in X-linked disorders when the parents desire to abort any male with a 50 percent risk and carry to term any female who would be asymptomatic although a possible carrier. Certain autosomal recessive disorders are diagnosable in utero by assaying specific enzyme levels in the growing fetal cells. A partial

TABLE 12-5
Indications for Amniocentesis

1 Previous child with a chromosomal defect
2 Either parent a balanced translocation carrier
3 Both parents carriers for a diagnosable metabolic defect
4 Mother a carrier for an X-linked disorder. A potentially affected male could be aborted and a female carried to term
5 Mother over thirty-five years of age
6 Previous child with a neural tube defect

TABLE 12-6
Metabolic Disorders Diagnosable in Utero

Tay-Sachs disease	MSUD
Niemann-Pick disease	Glycogen storage disease
Hurler's syndrome	Galactosemia
Hunter's syndrome	Lesch-Nyhan syndrome

list of such conditions is found in Table 12-6. This is by no means complete, and a genetics center should be consulted when any question arises.

In 1972, Brock and Sutcliffe reported that the alpha-fetoprotein level (AFP) was increased in the amniotic fluid of pregnancies leading to infants with anencephaly and myelomeningocele. AFP is a fetal-specific α_1-globulin made by normal embryonal liver cells, the yolk sac, and the gastrointestinal tract. The level increases from 6 weeks of gestation, peaks at 12 to 14 weeks, and then decreases to term. The major source of AFP in amniotic fluid seems to be urine from the fetus. Subsequent studies have shown that AFP levels are elevated in the second trimester of pregnancy in the case of anencephaly, some myelomeningoceles, Turner's syndrome (45, X), congenital nephrosis, and fetal death. The reason for this elevation is not completely understood. In neural tube defects, it has been postulated that this is due to leakage of AFP from the fetal cerebrospinal fluid (CSF); in Turner's syndrome, it may be secondary to the AFP escaping from a cervical cystic hygroma. Today the combination of ultrasound and the measurement of the AFP level in amniotic fluid at 14 to 16 weeks is believed to be 90 to 95 percent accurate in predicting an infant with a neural tube defect. Most likely to be missed are skin-covered lesions where there has been no CSF leakage.

Macri et al. have described a protein substance in amniotic fluid (beta-trace protein, specific to the CSF) which they believe may be more specific in predicting neural tube defects. In addition, maternal serum-AFP levels have been screened in an attempt to identify women who may be at an increased risk for a child with a neural tube defect. Results are varied but work is continuing in this area.

While intrauterine diagnosis is essentially equated with amniocentesis, other techniques are possible. Some are still considered research procedures (see below), but at least two are generally available and practical today. An oblique film of the abdomen at 20 to 22 weeks will outline the fetal skeleton. Bony abnormalities such as severe osteogenesis imperfecta, certain types of dwarfism, tetraphocomelia, etc., can thus be diagnosed early enough to interrupt pregnancy if the parents so desire. Ultrasound has been used in conjunction with AFP to diagnose anencephaly. It has also been used in detecting intrauterine hydrocephalus and infantile polycystic kidneys.

THE ROLE OF THE NURSE

When an imperfect child is born, the parents often see many physicians, and the child may be immediately transferred to a medical center many miles away. Their most frequent and consistent early contact may be with the maternity nurse. It is important, therefore, that this nurse recognize the need and indications for genetic counseling. After the initial shock, the parents will have many questions and will need to talk with someone who is comfortable discussing their child. They need to be encouraged to voice their many questions. "What is the significance of my child's defect? What caused it? Is it hereditary?" Although the nurse may be unable to answer many of these questions,

the parents can be guided to appropriate resources, such as genetic counseling clinics, after discussion with the pediatrician, obstetrician, or family practitioner.

Prior to discharge, the nurse, with the approval of the attending physician, should make the arrangements either to follow the family personally or to refer them to a community health nurse. The importance of this long-term, continuing contact with the family cannot be overemphasized, and through it the nurse can play an important role in the genetic counseling process.

Before Counseling

The nurse can help the family contact a genetic counseling clinic and should arrange transportation if necessary. The family can be prepared for their appointment by discussing what will be done and by collecting information on family members who have similar medical problems. The family can also be helped to formulate their questions and their apprehension can be eased.

During Counseling

It is most desirable that the nurse attend the counseling session with the family. The role of liaison between the family and the genetic counseling clinic will be much more effectively filled if the nurse has talked with the counselor and has heard directly the information given to the family.

After Counseling

It is at this point that the nurse becomes one of the most important figures in the counseling process. By virtue of educational background and close contact with the family, the nurse is the ideal person to follow through on genetic counseling. To do this there must be a good understanding of the basic principles of genetics as described above. The nurse can answer questions and elaborate upon information given to the family. If the questions are too complex or if the family's basic understanding of the information is poor, a return appointment to the clinic can be arranged. As parents make decisions about future pregnancies, the nurse can discuss contraceptives and make referrals to family planning clinics or adoption agencies.

In the majority of cases, after the genetic counseling has been completed, the parents must learn to live with their handicapped child. The nurse now becomes a major source of support for the family by answering questions about prognosis; by helping with daily problems of feeding, development, etc.; and by referrals to appropriate places for medical care and educational planning. Intimate knowledge of community resources makes the nurse one of the most important contacts for the family.

The "luxury" of genetic counseling has traditionally been confined to the middle and upper classes. These people have been verbal enough to ask their questions, and their physician, often an old friend, has been able either to answer them or to find the answers. The same questions exist in the minds of parents of all classes, but those of a lower socioeconomic group or those with a language barrier may have difficulty expressing them. Traditions inherent in their culture may discourage such questioning or may supply erroneous answers. Medical care is often fragmented and sporadic, and families may never see the same physician frequently enough to raise more than the very urgent questions about immediate problems. The community health nurse is in a unique position and knows people of all classes and all ethnic backgrounds. Such a person is often the only consistent contact many people

have with the professional community. It is important, therefore, that the nurse recognize those families who need, but who are unlikely to get, genetic counseling and discuss the issue with them, arranging for referral. It is important that the family wants this information, as this motivation is essential for the genetic counseling to be effective. If there is a language barrier, the nurse should either function as or provide an interpreter for the counseling session.

The establishment of regional or satellite genetic counseling clinics has made genetic counseling more available to people of all socioeconomic levels, regardless of where they live. In Colorado, there are currently eight regional clinics which serve the Rocky Mountain area. Consultants from the medical center work with local physicians, nurses, and health departments. Many of these nurses have come to the medical center for training in basic genetics, pedigree taking, etc., and work with families before, during, and after the counseling sessions. Similar programs are available in other states.

It is obvious that the nurse, both in the hospital and in the community, is of vital importance in genetic counseling. A nurse makes the referrals and answers the questions which arise after the counseling and is the single most important person in the expansion of genetic counseling to people of all classes. A sound background in genetics is essential to fill this role effectively. Such a background will be increasingly important in the future.

ADVANCES IN GENETICS AND GENETIC COUNSELING

The field of genetics is old, antedating even the work of Gregor Mendel in the 1860s; yet, in another sense, it is very new. Not until 1956 were human chromosomes accurately counted, and it was in 1959 that LeJeune described the first chromosomal abnormality—the trisomy 21 associated with Down's syndrome.

Many of the "new advances" described in the previous edition have moved from the area of research to the area of service and are now generally available. While the long-term implications of amniocentesis are not yet known, there is increasing evidence that this is a safe as well as an extremely valuable procedure. Most major cytogenetic laboratories are now routinely using at least one of the new banding techniques on all karyotypes.

Investigation continues and much of it centers on new and improved methods of making a diagnosis of an abnormality in utero. There is continued research in the intrauterine diagnosis of hemophilia, muscular dystrophy, cystic fibrosis, and other autosomal and X-linked recessive disorders. Since many autosomal dominant conditions do not have a known biochemical basis, intrauterine diagnosis has been difficult. On the other hand, the risk is high (50 percent). In certain instances it has been possible to link the mutant gene with a marker which can be detected in utero. Myotonic dystrophy has been linked to the secretor locus, the nail-patella syndrome to the ABO blood group, and a form of congenital cataracts to the Duffy blood group. Even where linkage has been established, only certain matings will produce the combination necessary to provide the information needed. Linkage studies are being done to increase the number of dominant traits linked to biochemical markers potentially detectable in utero.

At this time it is theoretically possible to diagnose sickle-cell anemia during pregnancy, since the beta chain of hemoglobin S is synthesized by the 11th to 15th week of gestation. The major problem has been obtaining fetal blood. Placental aspiration and direct-vision endoamnioscopy have been used. In the latter method, a fiber-optic instrument is inserted through the abdominal wall into the uterus. Blood can be aspirated from cord vessels and biopsies taken. In addition, a fiber-optic endoscope can be used to directly visualize the fetus, looking for specific structural abnormalities. This procedure is known as fetuscopy. Fetography or the introduction of contrast material into the amniotic fluid may be useful in the detection of certain abnormalities of the fetal kidney, gastrointestinal tract, etc.

All of these procedures are new and still experimental. If the field of genetics continues to progress at the rapid rate seen in the past, these and other techniques yet to be described may become part of a service genetic counseling program.

This progress in the development of new genetic techniques must be accompanied by similar progress in the expansion of genetic counseling, increasing its availability to all those in need. The role of the community nurse in genetic counseling has been described. The nurse can also fill an expanded role in a genetic counseling center and can be taught to take the pedigree, print and interpret dermatoglyphics, examine family members for certain specific abnormalities, and do much of the initial evaluation under the supervision of a physician who would assist in making the diagnosis. The nurse could then participate in or even do the genetic counseling and follow through with the family as has been described.

The nurse may also play an expanded role in the community itself. By spending a period of time in preparation at a genetic center, a nurse can be taught the techniques of a genetic evaluation and can then return to a job in the community, the schools, the state health department, etc. In appropriate situations, the nurse could begin an evaluation, discuss the findings with a physician from the genetic center, and go with the family for an abbreviated counseling session during which the diagnosis would be confirmed and the specific risk figures discussed. Further interpretation and discussion could be done by the specially instructed nurse after the family has returned home. The expanded role of the nurse in genetic counseling is new, but it is feasible today and potentially very rewarding.

Some of the most exciting medical advances today are being made in the field of genetics. A maternity nurse or a community health nurse with basic genetic knowledge or with expanded skills can be in the center of this new and exciting activity.

BIBLIOGRAPHY

Bauld, R., G. R. Sutherland, and D. Bain: "Chromosomal Studies in Investigation of Stillbirths and Neonatal Deaths," *Archives of Disease in Childhood*, 49:782–788, 1974.

Bearn, A. G.: "Cell Culture in Inherited Disease—With Some Notes on Genetic Heterogeneity," *New England Journal of Medicine*, 286:764–767, 1972.

Bergsma, D. (ed.): "Intrauterine Diagnosis," *Birth Defects: Original Article Series*, 7(5), April 1971.

Brock, D. J. H., and R. G. Sutcliffe: "Alpha-Fetoprotein in the Antenatal Diagnosis of Anencephaly and Spina Bifida," *Lancet*, 2:197–199, 1972.

Carr, D. H.: "Chromosomal Abnormalities in Clinical Medicine," in A. G. Steinberg and A. G. Bearn (eds.), *Progress in Medical Genetics*, vol. 6, Grune & Stratton, New York, 1969, pp. 1–61.

Carter, C. O.: *An ABC of Medical Genetics*, Little, Brown, Boston, 1969.

———, J. A. F. Roberts, K. A. Evans, and A. R. Buck: "Genetic Clinic: A Follow-up," *Lancet*, 1:281–285, 1971.

Caspersson, T., L. Zech, C. Johansson, and E. J. Modest: "Identification of Human Chromosomes by DNA-binding Fluorescent Agents," *Chromosoma* (Berlin), 30:215–227, 1970.

Eller, E., W. Frankenburg, M. Puck, and A. Robinson: "Prognosis in Newborn Infants with X-Chromosomal Abnormalities," *Pediatrics*, 47:681–688, 1971.

Gordon, H.: "Genetic Counseling," *Journal of the American Medical Association*, 217:1215–1225, 1971.

Greensher, A., R. Gersh, D. Peakman, and A. Robinson: "Screening of Newborn Infants for Abnormalities of the Y Chromosome," *Journal of Pediatrics*, 79:305–306, 1971.

Hecht, F., H. E. Wyandt, and R. W. Erbe: "Revolutionary Cytogenetics," *New England Journal of Medicine*, 285:1482–1484, 1971.

Lubs, H. A., and M. L. Lubs: "Genetic Diseases," in G. N. Burrow and T. F. Ferris (eds.), *Medical Complications of Pregnancy*, Saunders, Philadelphia (in press).

Lynch, H. T., G. M. Mulcahy, and A. J. Krush: "Genetic Counseling and the Physician," *Journal of the American Medical Association*, 211:647–651, 1970.

Macri, J. N., R. R. Weiss, M. S. Joshi, and M. I. Evans: "Antenatal Diagnosis of Neural-Tube Defects Using Cerebrospinal Fluid Proteins," *Lancet*, 1:14–15, 1974.

McKusick, V. A.: *Human Genetics*, 2d ed., Prentice-Hall, Englewood Cliffs, N.J., 1969.

Milunsky, A.: *The Prenatal Diagnosis of Hereditary Disorders*, Charles C Thomas, Springfield, Ill., 1973.

Milunsky, A., J. W. Littlefield, J. N. Kanfer, E. H. Kolodny, V. E. Shih, and L. Atkins: "Prenatal Genetic Diagnosis," *New England Journal of Medicine*, 283:1370–1381, 1441–1447, 1498–1504, 1970.

Nadler, H. L., and A. B. Gerbie: "Role of Amniocentesis in the Intrauterine Detection of Genetic Disorders," *New England Journal of Medicine*, 282:596–599, 1970.

Reisman, L. E., and A. P. Matheny: *Genetics and*

Counseling in Medical Practice, Mosby, St. Louis, 1969.

Robinson, A.: "Clinical Genetics," in E. S. Taylor, *Beck's Obstetrical Practice,* 9th ed., Williams & Wilkins, Baltimore, 1971, pp. 626–646.

Seller, M. J.: "Alpha-Fetoprotein and the Prenatal Diagnosis of Neural Tube Defects," *Developmental Medicine and Child Neurology,* 16:369–371, 1974.

Smith, D. W.: *Recognizable Patterns of Human Malformation,* Saunders, Philadelphia, 1970.

Stanbury, J. B., J. B. Wyngaarden, and D. S. Fredrickson: *The Metabolic Basis of Inherited Disease,* 3d ed., McGraw-Hill, New York, 1972.

Stevenson, A. C., B. C. C. Davison, and M. W. Oakes: *Genetic Counseling,* Lippincott, Philadelphia, 1970.

13

Psychosocial and Cultural Factors in Family Planning

MIRIAM T. MANISOFF

The decision by any individual couple to delay or limit childbearing is based on a most complex interaction of social and economic conditions and pressures, cultural norms, conscious and unconscious motivational factors, and emotional attitudes toward childbearing. With the introduction of highly effective, coitus-independent methods of conception control, many of the former barriers to effective contraception were removed. Indeed, many of the so-called motivational problems were eliminated, as is attested to by the studies on the increasing use of contraception.

According to a 1974 report of the U.S. Bureau of the Census, "It appears that the two-child family will be the wave of the future." More than 58 percent of all married women eighteen to thirty-nine years of age expect to have two or fewer children during their lifetime. Fewer than 10 percent of wives eighteen to twenty-four years of age expect to have four or more children, and 17 percent of wives eighteen to nineteen years old expect to have no or one child.[1] The trend toward smaller families continues as more couples are using more effective methods of contraception than a decade earlier.

INCREASING ACCEPTANCE OF FAMILY PLANNING

Many factors are now operating to bring about greater parental choice in conception. Newer, more effective, more acceptable methods have been developed. There is greater professional and scientific acceptance and commitment as well as public interest in contraception, and a number of social trends now favor individual choice. These trends in family life include a shift from the "institutional" to the "companionship" family in which children may be a liability, even though they are desired; the change from having children as a duty to having "wanted" children; the altered parental roles with the woman working and the male helping to rear children; and a willingness to plan and interfere with "nature."

The United States is moving toward a universally favorable attitude of acceptance of family planning among the majority of American women, whether urban or rural, white or nonwhite, rich or poor, Catholic or non-Catholic. Among the factors which may be contributing to this norm of acceptance are the increasing number of working women and the greater number of two-income families required by our high standard of living. Increased urbanization makes the large family an economic liability rather than an asset and imposes additional penalties for large families in that obtaining adequate housing is difficult. The effect of the women's liberation movement is also a factor.

CAUSES OF UNWANTED FERTILITY

Despite this norm of acceptance, and improvements in availability and use of birth control measures, births considered unwanted at the time of conception are still unacceptably high, averaging 15 percent of all births to married women. The rate of unwanted births is higher when the family is poor (27 percent) than when the family is not poor (12 percent). When the family is both poor and black, the rate of unwanted births is higher (40 percent) than when the family is poor and white (23 percent), but black-white differences disappear as income levels rise above poverty.

Although most couples in the United States have used or plan to use contraception, there appears to be a divergence in the methods typically used by various socioeconomic groups. Couples in the higher socioeconomic levels who can afford private medical care tend to use more reliable, medically supervised methods of birth control, while white low-income couples who have less access to such care depend more on the less reliable, nonmedical methods available from drugstores.

Only 34 percent of all poverty-status couples in the United States use the most effective or moderately effective methods, compared with 41 percent of couples above poverty level. An additional 34 percent of poor couples use no method or less effective methods, compared with 29 percent of couples above poverty level.[2]

Some of this unwanted fertility can also be accounted for by the fallibility and difficulty of current methodology. Only the oral contraceptives are almost 100 percent effective, but they require constant and repeated use and have side effects. To reduce unwanted fertility there must be more research to develop better methods of birth control. Extension of organized family planning programs to provide access to the most effective methods for all segments of the population, regardless of income or age, and provision of elective abortion for contraceptive failure are vitally important in further reducing unwanted births.

Although the poor have higher fertility rates, this does not alone account for the growth in American population, since this group makes up only one-fourth of our population. The significance of unwanted high fertility among the poor lies in the additional burdens it imposes on the poor themselves.

The disparity between poor and nonpoor use of effective contraception is related to accessibility—financial and otherwise—of services. Wherever free or low-cost family planning services have been offered at convenient locations under conditions of respect, dignity, and free choice, unusually high patient acceptance has been found. However, while the network of government and private services is expanding, there is still a gap between need and availability. In 1974 organized programs were providing medically supervised family planning services to 3.5 to 4 million poor and near-poor in two-thirds of the nation's 3,070 counties. There are an estimated 6 million poor, fertile, sexually active women. Out of this number, two-thirds of them are being served through organized programs as well as private physicians.[3] But each year brings another group of women into the childbearing years. With improved education and services, they need not add to the statistics of unwanted fertility.

One particular group for whom services are still most inadequate is the sexually active teenager. The American Medical Association, American Academy of Pediatrics, the American Academy of Family Physicians, and the American College of Obstetricians and Gynecologists have endorsed the recommendation that teenage girls who are likely to conceive should have access to medical consultation, contraceptive advice, and methods consistent with their needs.

Teenage pregnancy carries high risks medically, as well as social, economic, and psychological complications. Out-of-wedlock birth rates have dropped in all age groups except among teenagers. The high ratio of abortions to live births in this age group indicates a high rate of unwanted fertility. Less than 20 percent of sexually active teenagers consistently use contraception of any kind.[4] An estimated 1.3 to 2.2 million never-married teenage girls need family planning services, but only 460,000 were served in organized programs in 1972.[5]

Legal barriers to obtaining contraceptive services by teenagers have been increasingly removed. Unmarried girls of eighteen can now consent for their own care in 45 states and the District of Columbia.[6] There is, however, a serious lack of information and services for younger girls under eighteen.

More effective and more sensitive programs of sex and family planning education, starting at an early age in schools, churches, and other agencies, are essential. The special needs of teenagers for nonjudgmental counseling and for the opportunity to participate in making decisions affecting their lives must be considered.

VOLUNTARY NATURE OF FAMILY PLANNING

In the United States today there is no official national policy of population control. Couples who practice family planning do so to achieve personal objectives, based on their own goals and not as part of a government population policy. Our governmental family planning program is designed to help people achieve their own desires as to family size and spacing, based on individual voluntary decisions.

All the major religions now agree that family planning is an obligation of responsible parenthood. Pope Paul's encyclical of 1968 continued the approval of the rhythm method only.

Through the Department of Health, Education, and Welfare, the government defined its policy with regard to population and family planning in 1966 in terms of improving the health of the people, strengthening the integrity of the family, and providing freedom of choice to parents to determine the spacing of children and the size of their families. The Commission on Population Growth and the American Future was established by Congress in 1970. Its final report in 1972 was a milestone in the development of a national policy. Population growth was identified as an intensifier or aggravator of problems affecting the quality of life in this country, and the report concluded that the United States should "welcome and plan for a stabilized population" as one factor contributing to the nation's ability to solve its problems. The commission's specific recommendations were aimed at increasing opportunities to exercise freedom of choice and concomitantly to contribute to slowing population growth. These included expanded family planning services for all Americans, together with improved antepartum and pediatric care, voluntary sterilization, and increased research funds to find better contraceptives. Rights for children and women were to be improved through adequate daycare services, elimination of discrimination against children born out of wedlock, reform of adoption laws, adoption of the Equal Rights Amendment, and alternative roles to childbearing for women. While cautioning that abortion *not* be considered a primary means of birth control, the commission rec-

ommended wide liberalization of restrictive abortion statutes and inclusion of abortion services in programs of health insurance. Population education and family-life education in schools through community organizations and the media were to be fostered by a Population Education Act, and guidelines for population distribution and migration were to be developed.[7]

PSYCHOSOCIAL AND CULTURAL FACTORS IN FAMILY PLANNING

The reasons couples use or fail to use contraception, in addition to the factor of availability, stem from many psychological, cultural, and social needs. In contemporary society, many consider parenthood the norm. Social pressure is often felt by those remaining deliberately childless. Among the poor, even more than among the nonpoor, social scientists believe parenthood brings a sense of status and a sense of personal adequacy. And, of course, among rich and poor, the birth of wanted children is a joyful event.

Many cultural values and concepts emphasize the importance of childbearing. Parenthood may be used to "prove" an individual's femininity or masculinity, virility, or potency. Some parents may continue to conceive in the attempt to have a child of each sex; others in the belief that children will hold a fragile marriage together. Some religious beliefs hold that children are an expression of God's will or punishment, not to be changed by human decision. Conception and pregnancy are interpreted by psychologists as a possible way to show independence from parents, or as payment or punishment for having sex. Couples may feel that good parents should have as many children as they can afford. Bearing children may be used to compensate for the male partner's neglect; to express his conscious or unconscious hostility by repeatedly making his mate pregnant; to obtain increased attention from a spouse; to relieve boredom; to provide a creative outlet in an otherwise uncreative life; or to prove male dominance or female importance. Parents may believe that large families are better for children or may want to give their child a sibling. The child may be viewed as an extension of oneself or a way for reliving one's life vicariously.

Motivations for the use of contraception are often expressed in terms of economics. The financial costs of rearing children are high. It may cost more than $40,000 to rear and educate a child through college. Psychosocial and cultural reasons often operate on the subconscious level and are less likely to be acknowledged because they may appear selfish. Childbearing and rearing can interfere with a mother's social life, career, and physical appearance. It subtracts time from enjoyment and self-development. It may represent a sacrifice of male-female relationships and impair intimacy, romance, and sexual relations. The shift in attention from mate to child may evoke jealousy in the opposite mate. However, these psychological "costs" of children may, by some parents, be seen as rewards rather than penalties. Ignorance and fear of contraceptive methods may also be factors in their nonuse, but such barriers are usually most amenable to correction through education.

Motivation and Contraception

The stronger the desire to avoid conception, the more effective contraceptive practice is likely to become. Parents approaching or achieving desired family size tend to use more effective methods and to use them more skillfully and consistently. They take fewer chances and achieve a lower rate of unwanted conceptions.

The acceptability of specific methods also affects contraceptive use. In the days when the diaphragm was almost the only female method available, patient motivation was considered to be a great problem, and much attention was focused on improving it. With the introduction of methods which did not involve vaginal manipulation—repugnant to many women because of its possible association with masturbation—patient motivation was found to be much less of a barrier. Since the most effective methods—the pills and the IUD—have troublesome and possibly frightening side effects, it is most important to prepare patients in advance for possible difficulties, so as to reduce anxiety and to enable them to cope.

According to Dr. Hans Lehfeldt unwanted pregnancy may be due to conflicting motivation.[8] Some couples fail to use contraception consistently and regularly because they are ambivalent about pregnancy and willfully expose themselves to possible failure by misuse of the method or "forgetting" to take their pills. They alternate between contraception and exposure and may need psychological help to elicit and clarify their ambivalence so that they can either practice effective contraception or become happy parents.

Couples may also harbor fears related to the use of contraception that they will lose their capacity for sexual enjoyment or ability to give sexual pleasure. A male may feel that it will lead to extramarital activity by his partner or that inability to impregnate her will lessen his status in the eyes of his socio-cultural group. Among minority groups, there may be beliefs that the motivation for offering contraception is racist in origin and that family planning programs are designed to keep them a minority, rather than to help them. Women who, because of poor sexual adjustment, have used fear of pregnancy to avoid coitus may be unable to use a method which would eliminate that excuse.

Dr. Robert E. Gould has identified reasons

people often give for having children—reasons which are not uniformly valid for child or parents:[9]

1 Our parents want grandchildren.
2 We can afford it.
3 I want to be somebody.
4 I need to be needed.
5 A baby will give me something to do.
6 It will help our marriage.
7 It's the only way to prove you're a man.
8 We don't want to be different.
9 I want him to have the things I never had.
10 A child is my only claim to immortality.
11 A baby will keep a woman in her place.
12 Children are a blessing.
13 Children are a gift of destiny or chance.
14 Children ensure security for parents in their old age.
15 Many sons are needed to ensure continuation of the family name.
16 Children are useful and can help parents in the home and at work.
17 Additional children are no problem.

Since family planning encompasses assistance in achieving desired family size through spacing and limiting pregnancies as well as through help in cases of infertility, we need to consider some of the psychosocial factors which may exist among those denied a child.

Psychosocial Factors in Infertility

The desire for children, stemming from basic human desires and reinforced by societal pressures for parenthood, can produce in those who are involuntarily childless feelings of guilt, frustration, and inadequacy as males or females.

The effects and role of psychological and emotional factors in infertility are most complex. Although a number of writers agree that such factors exist, they also indicate that it is difficult to identify them or to document them scientifically.[10,11] For example, indirect clinical evidence exists, based on repeated findings, that a small percentage of women with sterility problems become pregnant soon after registering for infertility therapy and before any medical treatment has been instituted, or after adopting a child. The occurrence of pseudocyesis in a woman anxious to become pregnant is also cited as an example that psychological factors are operating in infertile women. The reciprocal nature of psychological factors and infertility is pointed out by Drs. Buxton and Southam.[12] Psychological conflicts about pregnancy and marriage also affect fertility.

Inability to conceive affects the psychological condition and state of mind of both males and females. Social pressures on couples to reproduce can produce tension within the individual who finds him- or herself infertile and may put that person on the defensive. This in turn produces feelings of guilt and inadequacy which can further affect fertility. Very often tension arises between partners; each blames the other for the infertility.

Many theories have been advanced to account for the effect of emotional factors in achieving pregnancy. Dr. James A. Peterson indicates that inadequate emotional integrations operate (1) by directly affecting endocrine or tubal functions, (2) by inhibiting sexual adjustment essential to conception, or (3) by interfering with the development of sympathetic understanding between marital partners needed for cooperation in achieving parenthood and in child nurture.[11]

The relationship of sexual response and

sexual adjustment to fertility is implicated in Dr. Peterson's findings of a "low order of sexual adjustment" in many cases of infertility. The emotional disturbances which influence success or failure of infertility programs, he explains, must be dealt with through exploration of:

1   The *meaning* of sterility for the patient in her social setting, along with attempts to ventilate and minimize guilt or self-demeaning reactions
2   The degree of adjustment of the couple's marriage and ways of dealing with possible marital conflicts
3   The degree of sexual adjustment and any frigidity or impotence which may interfere with impregnation
4   The degree of emotional disturbance in the husband and wife to determine to what extent neurotic conflict may be interfering with medical therapy

SERVICE-RELATED FACTORS IN FAMILY PLANNING

Nurses working in community health family planning programs among the medically indigent should be concerned with clinic-related factors. While many studies have surveyed factors of family planning knowledge, attitudes, and practice among patients, few have addressed themselves to relating the purveyor's knowledge, attitudes, and practices to patient needs. It is possible that the most difficult obstacles may exist not in the patient, but in the professionals responsible for making services available.

Nurses in family planning clinics should keep in mind that family planning is an elective service; the patient is not propelled by acute pain or disease. Patients can easily be deterred from attendance if they find demeaning, unsympathetic attitudes among staff, lack of privacy, or long waiting periods. Other practical issues which may affect acceptance are cost, inconvenient clinic hours, distance which the patient must travel to reach the clinic, availability of public transportation and baby-sitters, and the variety of methods from which patients may choose, together with full information as to their use.

NEGATIVE STAFF ATTITUDES

Concepts of the Goals of Family Planning

Other problem areas may involve staff. The basic beliefs held by the doctor or nurse as to the goals of family planning may be negative. Some consider family planning as a means to control population (with the frequent implication that particular groups should be singled out). It is important to distinguish between family planning, as a voluntary individual decision, and population control, a societal issue. If the nurse's approach to patients is based on the concept of population control, it is likely to have repercussions and the service may be rejected by the patient. The statement, "Nobody should have more than two children" as an introduction of family planning to a couple has proved a disaster. The nurse who critically says, "*How many* children did you say you have?" is conveying to the patient personal family planning goals—not necessarily the patient's. The primary goal of family planning is to reduce the gap between desired and achieved family size. There are also important secondary objectives, including (1) improving the physical, emotional, and economic health of the family; (2) fostering happier, more fulfilling sex relationships for parents; (3) giving parents the freedom to decide the number and spacing of children; and (4) reducing abortion and illegitimacy.

Attitudes toward the Poor

Some nurses hold negative, punitive, or demeaning concepts about the poor. These may be expressed in such phrases as "They're too dumb, too lazy, too uninterested to use family planning." "People who have had fun should pay for it." "If they don't accept family planning, they're just stupid." "They can't support what they have now, why should they be allowed to have more." "Why should we use tax money to support promiscuity?" "They don't care how many they have." Most of the time these statements are not true. More important, these attitudes can be serious obstacles to patient education and acceptance. While the phrases may vary, contempt or disrespect in word, tone, or facial expression of nurses or other staff members will predictably evoke unfavorable patient reaction. The family planning staff should be selected for positive attitudes to family planning because basic attitudinal changes take time, training, and effort, and for some, change may not be desirable or possible. Those without acceptance should be reassigned to other, less sensitive services. To underline the importance of these attitudes, a study by William Darity showed that almost 90 percent of patients interviewed cited "kind treatment" as the characteristic they most liked about a health department family planning program.[13]

Concepts of Self

Into our functioning as professionals we bring our concepts of self, both positive and negative. The negative may easily interfere with adequate functioning in family planning. For example, nurses may feel they do not know enough to discuss family planning properly with patients. Young unmarried nurses may feel they cannot discuss family planning at all. Outmoded beliefs that this teaching invades patient privacy still persist.

Nurses may harbor fears that patients will be offended; they may feel that "It's none of my business." "Why should I force my attitude on someone else?" "I feel too uncomfortable talking about this." These attitudes can prevent the nurse from offering information which the patient has a right to know. Identifying this sense of inadequacy in staff can lead to its early resolution. Role playing has been found an effective antidote, as well as assigning a neophyte to work with an experienced family planning educator.

Attitudes toward Sexuality

Negative concepts of sexuality may exist in both patients and staff and may make effective education more difficult. Such attitudes may be conscious or unconscious, and essentially they consist of the idea that sex is sinful and pregnancy is an appropriate punishment for it. Reflections of this are the attitudes that unmarried girls should not be told about birth control, that family planning promotes promiscuity, or that people with many children are oversexed.

It is difficult, if not impossible, to divorce sex and one's attitude toward it from family planning. Because of our cultural and family conditioning, sex is for many an anxiety-laden area. Yet acceptance of one's own sexuality influences the ability to help effectively with problems of sexuality and fertility control in others. Nurses who consider sex as a positive, good, even joyful part of life, who see their own sexual being as an intrinsic and wholesome part of their total personality, can accept a wide range of sexual behavior in others. Masturbation, homosexuality, bisexuality, oral/anal/genital sex, group and extramarital sex are variations which nurses as well as others in the helping professions are expected to understand. If one is working with young people, such understanding is not merely helpful, it is essential. Nonjudgmental, nonpunitive attitudes can be achieved or at least aimed for. Seminars, books, films, and discussion groups are more and more available to nurses interested in achieving self-understanding. The professional goal is better health care, but the bonus can be better sexual health and interpersonal relationships for the nurse.

Service Providers and Service Consumers

Another source of difficulty may lie in the whole relationship of service providers vis-à-vis service consumers. Often reflected in the styles used with patients is the underlying assumption that the providers know—ipso facto—what is best for the patient. Professional education and experience do prepare nurses to assess a problem from an objective viewpoint. But nurses can learn much about the "hard knocks" and existential know-how upon which patients base their views.

CONSUMER ATTITUDES

Effects of Previous Experience

Patients' views of family planning services are influenced by their previous experience with community medical care facilities. Since family planning is so intricately connected with such emotional areas as sex and reproduction, staff in these services must use particular tact in dealing with patients who may already be hostile to care provided from such "charity" agencies. Every staff member, professional or nonprofessional, will need to be trained to be respectful of patient feelings and sensitivities. Regulations set by the administration will need to be flexible enough to take into account the life circumstances and attitudes of patients.

Attitudes among the Poor

Consider for a moment the implications of the fact that community health programs of family planning are directed at low-income groups. Among these groups there are a number of incentives for the use of family planning. These include the fact that no one wants pregnancy at all times, the desire for sex without danger of conception, the influence of peer attitudes, and economic and health reasons. Realistically, there also exist among low-income groups some explicit barriers to the use of family planning. What has been called the "powerlessness syndrome" can be a very real thing. This may be expressed as "the odds are against you anyway, so live for today, take a chance, and what will be, will be." To be offered power against births without power in any other sphere may not be enough for some. The dominance of the male in sex relations among this group, with the woman dependent on the man for companionship, sex attention, and groceries, may also be a problem, particularly if the man equates his virility with impregnating a woman. Among low-income groups there may also exist a dislike and mistrust of health personnel and facilities, since the obvious power of doctors and nurses may serve to emphasize the patient's own lack of power.

Lack of Consumer Participation

Among the poor, and among poor minority groups in particular, family planning programs have come under criticism for the lack of involvement of the consumer in planning, policy making, and decision making. It is increasingly important that consumer participation be considered in an area such as family planning so that services will be responsive to and representative of those for whom they are intended.

CONSIDERATIONS FOR THE NURSE

In the development of a personal working philosophy and role, nurses are reaching for a better understanding of some of the obstacles which may exist within the patient, in the services, and within themselves. We can perhaps emphasize the need for nurses to see and place the patient's needs above their own and to respond to those needs, even if talking about sex or birth control makes the nurse uncomfortable at first. If this is an area of patient need, the professional responds with help for that need. Linked to this is the ability to observe and understand the scene from the patient's point of view, for nurses must be able to put themselves in the patient's position as a recipient of service. For example, students or staff nurses in clinics can "shadow" a patient through a clinic, wait with the patient, hear the instructions and questions he or she gets, note the time spent waiting, observe where and how he or she is directed and the times he or she gets lost, and find out how the patient feels about the experience.

In trying to help patients who forget or misinterpret their instructions or who say they want to use family planning but never get around to attending the clinic, nurses can try to analyze and understand their own feelings. By considering the effects of the patient's environment and experiences, nurses can gain a better understanding of why patients act or react as they do, and minimize their own feelings of anger and impatience. The nurse can attempt a more open approach to methods of patient education and to search for more realistic teaching which involves the patient in the process. Nurses can encourage greater patient participation in clinic administration, possibly through use of neighborhood advisory committees.

Nurses must have faith in patients' ability to grow, improve, and learn. They should try to be nonjudgmental, to refrain from imposing their values, attitudes, standards, and ways of life on families with different cultural or economic orientation. If possible, they should learn to understand and operate within the patient's cultural framework—to meet patients at their own level and proceed from there. Above all, in their relationships they should try to create an atmosphere of mutual respect and understanding by encouraging patients to feel a sense of freedom in choosing—or refusing—a family planning method.

Nurses need to consider both initial and continuing inservice education, through cooperative efforts for all staff members in contact with patients—clerks, receptionists, aides, etc. Attempts should be made to provide continuity of service, such as bringing together hospital and clinic nurses. There are hospital family planning programs in which a patient is begun on a method with no provision or follow-through to see that she or he continues that method at a community facility when the hospital clinic is not convenient. Improved interagency communication is another goal for achieving better service. Nurses, nurse educators, and students need opportunities—in small groups —to discuss and evaluate their feelings about sex and sexuality so that they can develop ability and comfort in talking with patients about matters related to family planning and sexuality.

HEALTH CONCERNS IN FAMILY PLANNING

A concern for maternal and infant health is integral to the interest in and provision of family planning services. Perhaps of greatest concern are those who are socially and economically deprived and with whom high-risk conditions are most commonly associated. Among the factors which are implicated in increased risk to mother or child are parental age (under eighteen and over forty), birth interval (less than 18 months between pregnancies), and a history of premature births, infant deaths, abortion, obstetrical complications, diabetes, cardiovascular disease, or venereal disease.[14]

Studies have repeatedly shown the relationship of infant mortality and other adverse pregnancy results to high parity and short intervals between births. Such relationships are intensified among poor women with repeated pregnancies in rapid succession whose health is already impaired by inadequate nutrition and living conditions and poor medical care. Nowhere in the health field is poverty as directly implicated in the cost of human well-being and life.

Maternal and infant mortality and morbidity rates increase when the interval between children is less than two years. Among births which occur at less than 18-month intervals, the infant mortality rate is 4 times the natural rate. The premature birth rates among babies born less than 12 months apart occur at double the rate for those born at 24-month intervals. After the fourth child the risk of fetal and neonatal death increases. Studies have also substantiated the fact that perinatal mortality increases with the age and parity of the mother. The unmarried mother and her infant are at significantly greater risk from mortality, premature births, and pregnancy complications. A definite correlation has been found between multiparity and obstetric and gynecological complications. Multiparity also has an aggravating effect on many other diseases, such as cardiovascular disease, cancer, epilepsy, hypertension, and rheumatic heart disease. Women who have had five children have about 3 times the chance of developing diabetes as nulliparous women. Since low-income women are more likely to suffer from

malnutrition, anemia, chronic vascular disease, tuberculosis, and toxemia, it is important that pregnancy be postponed in women with such conditions until they can be treated, for the protection of both mother and child.

In assessing the need for family planning guidance, nurses can utilize their knowledge of the patient's and the family's medical and sociocultural history. While all women in the childbearing years can be considered as potential family planning candidates, the following are particular indicators for offering information:

1   The woman has just had a pregnancy.
2   The last two pregnancies were less than 18 months apart.
3   The woman appears physically or emotionally depleted.
4   The parents or other family members have a history of physical or emotional disability.
5   The woman is under eighteen or over forty years old.
6   The family already has four children.
7   There is a history of premature births, obstetric complications, tuberculosis, or heart disease.
8   The woman is unable to cope with her existing children.
9   There is marital conflict related to the birth of unwanted children.
10 There is a seriously handicapped child requiring much care.
11 There are one or more out-of-wedlock children.
12 The woman is working or plans to work.
13 A sexually active teenager is present in the home.
14 The family is having difficulty in maintaining economic independence

or is already receiving public assistance.

15 There is evidence that any of the children in the family are abused or battered.

Although nurses, as health educators, are rightly concerned with the knowledge, attitudes, and values of their patients regarding family planning, it is interesting that one professional health educator considers such factors often not sufficient as causal factors in the adoption of preventive health behavior, such as family planning. Lawrence Green has found that individuals often have the appropriate beliefs and attitudes and adequate knowledge to produce a recommended behavior, and yet it does not materialize.[15] Conversely, the expected preventive health practice is seen in those without such knowledge and attitudes, or they may be acquired following the behavior. Green suggests that social pressure and social support may be more important than knowledge and that influence in matters of health tends to come from informal social sources close to the individual. The use of indigenous paraprofessional workers with whom patients can identify can be a valuable way to increase patient utilization of family planning services. The "satisfied patient" is, of course, an excellent source of such influence and in many family planning clinics, the primary source of new patients.

Psychosocial factors in family planning are only recently being given the attention of psychiatrists and social scientists. Yet, as early as 1898 Sigmund Freud wrote:[16]

Theoretically it would be one of the greatest triumphs of mankind, one of the most tangible liberations upon the bondage of nature to which we are subject, were it possible to raise the responsible act of procreation to the level of a vol-untary and intentional act, and to free it from the entanglement with an indispensable satisfaction of natural desire.

REFERENCES

1 "Birth Expectations among U.S. Wives," *Family Planning Perspectives*, 7(1):5–6, January–February 1975.

2 "1970 National Fertility Study," *Family Planning Digest*, 1(6):9–12, 1972.

3 Jaffe, Frederick S.: "Fertility Control Policy, Social Policy and Population Policy in an Industrialized Country," *Family Planning Perspectives*, 6(3):164–169, Summer 1974.

4 Zelnik, Melvin, and John F. Kantner: "The Resolution of Teenage First Pregnancies," *Family Planning Perspectives*, 6(2):74–80, Spring 1974.

5 Morris, Leo: "Estimating the Need for Family Planning Services among Unwed Teenagers," *Family Planning Perspectives*, 6(2):90–97, Spring 1974.

6 Paul, Eve W., Harriet F. Pilpel, and Nancy F. Wechsler: "Pregnancy, Teenagers and the Law, 1974," *Family Planning Perspectives*, 6(3):142–147, Summer 1974.

7 *Population and the American Future: The Report of the Commission on Population Growth and the American Future*, New American Library, New York, 1972.

8 Lehfeldt, Hans: "Psychology of Contraceptive Failure," *Medical Aspects of Human Sexuality*, May 1971.

9 Gould, Robert E.: "The Wrong Reasons to Have Children," *New York Times Magazine*, June 1970.

10 Van de Velde, T. H.: *Fertility and Sterility in Marriage*, Heinemann, London, 1931, p. 167.

11 Peterson, James A.: "Emotional Factors in Infertility," in Edward T. Tyler (ed.), *Sterility*, McGraw-Hill, New York, 1961, pp. 282–299.

12 Buxton, C. Lee, and Anna L. Southam: *Human Infertility*, Harper, New York, 1958, pp. 203–216.

13 Darity, William: "Continuing/Discontinuing Users of Oral Contraceptives," in A. Sobrero and S. Lewit (eds.), *Advances in Planned Parenthood*, Schenkman, Cambridge, Mass., 1965.

14 Manisoff, Miriam: *Family Planning: A Teaching Guide for Nurses*, 4th ed., Planned Parenthood—World Population, New York, 1973, pp. 13–23.

15 Green, Lawrence N.: "Status Identity and Preventive Health Behavior," *Pacific Health Education Report*, School of Public Health, University of California, Berkeley, 1970.

16 Freud, Sigmund: "Sexuality in the Aetiology of the Neuroses," collected papers, vol. I, Hogarth, London, 1949 (quoted in Lee Rainwater, *And the Poor Get Children*, Quadrangle, Chicago, 1960).

BIBLIOGRAPHY

Berelson, Bernard: "Beyond Family Planning," *Studies in Family Planning*, Population Council, February 1969.

Bumpass, Larry, and Charles F. Westoff: "The Perfect Contraceptive Population," *Science*, September 1970.

International Planned Parenthood Federation: *Relations between Family Size and Maternal and Child Health*, London, July 1970.

Kessler, A., and S. Kessler: "Health Aspects of Family Planning," in E. Diczfalusy and U. Borell (eds.), *Control of Human Fertility*, Wiley, New York, 1971.

Lidz, Ruth W.: "Emotional Factors in the Success of Contraception," *Fertility and Sterility*, 20(5), September–October 1969.

Manisoff, Miriam: *Family Planning: A Teaching Guide for Nurses*, 4th ed., Planned Parenthood—World Population, New York, 1973.

———: *Family Planning Training for Social Service*, Planned Parenthood—World Population, New York, 1972.

Pohlman, E. J.: *The Psychology of Birth Planning*, Schenkman, Cambridge, Mass., 1969.

Rainwater, Lee: *And the Poor Get Children*, Quadrangle, Chicago, 1960.

Tourkow, L. P., R. W. Lidz, and L. Marder: "Psychiatric Considerations in Fertility Inhibition," in Hafez and Evans (eds.), *Human Reproduction*, Harper & Row, New York, 1973.

14

Methods of Conception Control

MIRIAM T. MANISOFF

All current as well as experimental methods of family planning are based on the principle of "intervention," that is, the interposing of barriers to or the interruption of the complicated series of physiological events in humans which constitute the process of conception. The ideal method would be completely safe, reversible, inexpensive, free of all side effects, simple to obtain and use, 100 percent effective, and not related to the time of coitus. Although we have approached some of these ideal standards, no single method meets all these criteria. Research to develop new and improved methods is a vital need if we are to achieve the ideal. Methods now in use can be categorized as those which require medical services (pelvic examination, prescription, or surgery) and those which an individual can obtain and use without medical supervision.

HELPING COUPLES TO CHOOSE

In guiding couples to a choice of a method, it is important to ascertain which one will be most acceptable to them, since consistency of use is a critical factor in effectiveness. A method may be considered highly effective theoretically, but if the couple finds it unpleasant, distasteful, or difficult to use, it is unlikely they will use it consistently, if at all. This, of course, implies that they be given enough detail about each method so that they may make an informed initial choice and so that they be made aware of the availability of alternative methods; in this way they may choose another method if the first choice is found to be unsatisfactory. The availability of legal elective abortion for contraceptive failure has made it possible to use less effective older methods with a high degree of safety.

Consideration should always be given to the acceptability of the method to the male partner, since his opposition can be a serious barrier to effective use. Therefore, both factors of acceptability and effectiveness need to be considered, the aim being to select the most effective method which will be used consistently.

ORAL CONTRACEPTIVES

Oral contraceptives contain synthetic forms of the hormones progesterone and estrogen, either in combined form or in sequence. The dosages and types of hormones in the pills vary among the many formulations now on the market, and the schedules for taking them also vary. With 20-day pill regimens the woman starts taking the pill on the fifth day of her menstrual cycle, counting the day that menses begin as day one and taking one pill a day for 20 days. She then stops taking the pills, waits for her next menstrual cycle, and repeats the procedure. The woman

should be cautioned not to skip any days. She should be instructed to take the pill at approximately the same time each day and never to wait more than 7 days for the next menstrual period. If her period has not started by the seventh day, she should begin the next cycle of pills that day. If menses do not appear by the seventh day following the second pill cycle, she should report this to the physician. If the woman forgets to take her daily pill, she is to take it as soon as she remembers, even if this means taking two the next day. If she neglects her pill for 2 days in a row, she should be advised to continue the daily schedule, but to use an additional contraceptive (such as foam or the condom) for the remainder of the cycle. Women should also understand that they are protected from pregnancy at all times, even on those days when they are waiting for their next menstrual period. The protection starts with the first series of pills if they are begun within the first 7 days of the menstrual cycle. Women who decide to discontinue the pills in favor of another method should be informed that their next menstrual period may be delayed for up to 3 weeks and in some cases longer. Cessation of pill taking at any point prior to completion of the full cycle of pills will result in withdrawal bleeding. Guidance to women, therefore, should include mention that it is advisable to complete a pill series in its entirety before discontinuing oral contraception unless there are medical indications for immediate withdrawal.

Oral contraceptives are also available in the more convenient 21-day regimens in which the woman takes a pill each day for 3 weeks continuously, then suspends for 1 week and resumes for the next 3 weeks—the so-called "3 weeks on, 1 week off" method. The menstrual period usually occurs during the 7 days off the pill, but women must restart the pill after 7 days whether or not menses have occurred. In another variation, the pills are in a 28-day package and the woman takes the pills continuously and in sequence. The final seven pills are placebos, or they may contain iron. All varieties described above consist of hormonal combinations.

Sequential pills are packaged so that 15 or 16 consecutive pills containing only estrogen are taken, followed by five pills containing both estrogen and progestin. The sequential pills were designed to simulate the natural hormone events more closely than the combination pills, but they have a somewhat lower effectiveness rate.*

Minipills differ from other oral contraceptives in that they contain no estrogen and only a small dose of synthetic progesterone. They are taken every day without stopping, beginning with the first day of the cycle. They are not as effective as combination pills in preventing pregnancy and irregular bleeding or spotting is frequently experienced in their use.

Morning-after pills have been approved by the Food and Drug Administration for emergency use only, following midcycle unprotected coitus. They contain a synthetic estrogen, diethylstilbestrol (DES) and must be taken no later than 72 hours after unprotected coitus. The 25-mg pills are taken twice a day for 5 consecutive days. Nausea and vomiting are common side effects and may interfere with the full course of treatment required for effectiveness. If a pregnancy does occur, termination must be considered because of the possibility of carcinogenic or teratogenic effects of DES on the woman or fetus.

* As this book goes to press, there is much controversy over sequential pills, and the Food and Drug Administration has proposed restrictions on the prescription and use of these pills.

Mode of Action

The primary action of the oral contraceptives is the suppression of ovulation through the inhibition of the hypothalamic hormones; it is similar to the mechanism in pregnancy. The progestin contributes to the contraceptive effect by causing the cervical mucus to become thick and less penetrable to sperm, and by suppressing the midcycle surge of luteinizing hormone (LH) and follicle-stimulating hormone (FSH) required for ovulation. The pill also alters endometrial development so that it is out of phase for implantation. It may interfere with tubal transport of the ovum.

The effectiveness of combination oral contraceptives is considered virtually 100 percent in preventing pregnancy *provided* that they are taken as prescribed. This proviso emphasizes the importance of careful instruction and checking for understanding. The nurse, using language appropriate to the level of the woman's comprehension and education, plays an important role in ensuring proper use.

Side Effects

Side effects similar to those of early pregnancy are experienced by some women due to the pregnancylike hormonal status produced by the pills. Most of these side effects are slight. They include nausea, dizziness, bloating, breast tenderness, headache, weight gain, and breakthrough bleeding. The symptoms usually disappear within the next two to four cycles, but if they persist, a shift to another preparation may be necessary. If side effects persist with various preparations, discontinuance of the medication and provision of a different method may be necessary.

Since the pills can suppress lactation, it is usually advised that they not be used for newly delivered mothers who plan to nurse their babies.

Other side effects, which are considered desirable, are a decrease in the menstrual flow; reduction of dysmenorrhea and premenstrual tension; improvement in acne conditions; and regulation of the menstrual cycle. In rare instances women report increases in libido and feelings of euphoria, perhaps induced by the release from worry about unwanted pregnancy. A few women have also reported depression and reduction of libido.

Less common side effects also include an increase in skin pigmentation (chloasma), which takes a long time to clear when the medication is discontinued, and an increase in acne or hirsutism. Vaginal infections may be more common. In women who have menstrual irregularities before starting the pills, amenorrhea may persist after discontinuing them. Pre-existing uterine fibroid tumors may enlarge when the oral contraceptives are used.

The most severe side effect which has been noted is thrombophlebitis. There is an increased risk of morbidity and mortality from pulmonary embolism or cerebral thrombosis among women using the pill, and the risk is higher in those over thirty-five years old than in younger women. A history of thromboembolic disease is a contraindication to use of oral contraception. Pregnancy carries a 6 to 10 times higher risk of thrombophlebitis and embolism than does the use of pills. Therefore, use of the pill by women without such history is considered justified by most physicians.

Other contraindications to the use of oral contraceptives are a history of breast or uterine cancer, serious liver disease, or undiagnosed vaginal bleeding. Use with medical caution is indicated in patients with migraine, uterine fibroids, heart or kidney disease, asthma, high blood pressure, diabetes,

and epilepsy. No causal relationship has been found between the oral contraceptives and any type of malignancy. Recent studies show that there is an increased risk of myocardial infarction in women using the pill, especially if they are 40 years or over, if they are obese, or if they are smokers.

It is apparent that careful and continuing medical supervision is required for the use of this method. A careful history, pelvic and breast examination, blood pressure determination, urinalysis for glucose and protein, and a Pap smear should be completed before the initiation of pill therapy. Women should be educated as to the necessity for periodic medical examinations and reporting of untoward symptoms.

The Food and Drug Administration now stipulates that all pill manufacturers include with their product a standard information flyer cautioning women about possible side effects and suggesting that they ask their doctor for a booklet with further information. Physicians prescribing the pills must be able to provide patients with this pamphlet, which has been prepared by the American Medical Association.

Acceptability

The oral contraceptives appear to be the most acceptable of all methods for American women, with 10 million using the pills. It is estimated that 50 million women are using these pills throughout the world. However, in the United States, about 32 percent have discontinued use of the pills by the end of 1 year, and 47 percent by 2 years because of the side effects encountered.

INTRAUTERINE DEVICES

Intrauterine devices, often referred to as IUDs, are small plastic or metal forms to which a "tail" of nylon threads is usually attached. Some popular types of IUDs are shown in Figure 14-1. Many others are under study. The device is inserted through the vagina and the cervical canal into the uterine cavity. IUDs are usually inserted via a straw-shaped, plunger-type inserter. The device is pulled into a straight line as it is loaded into the inserter, and can be easily introduced without dilating the cervix. The inserter is then disengaged and withdrawn from the vagina. The nylon threads extend into the vagina and are used to check on the presence of the device in the uterus. The device can be removed by pulling the threads. The IUDs regain their original shape after placement in the uterus and can be left in place for an in-

definite time except for those which are bioactive.

Devices can be inserted by a physician, nurse midwife, or a nurse trained to do the procedure. The practitioner uses sterile gloves, and the device and inserter are sterilized before use. Cold sterilization is used for the plastic devices and inserters, and pre-sterilized packs of them are now available. A complete history, pelvic examination, and Pap smear are done prior to insertion to rule out contraindicating conditions or pelvic disease. A tenaculum to stabilize the cervix is used, and a uterine sound is passed to ascertain the direction and tightness of the uterine canal. The preferred time for inser-

FIGURE 14-1
Types of IUDs. (a) SAF-T coil; (b) Lippes loop; (c) copper 7 device; (d) copper T device.

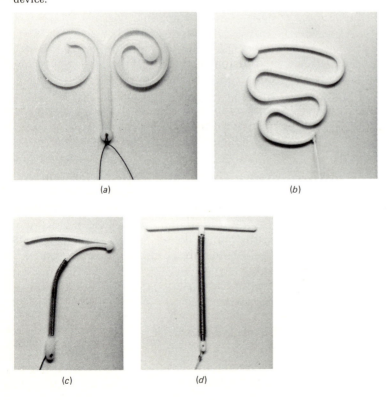

(a)   (b)

(c)   (d)

tion is during the last few days of the menstrual period, since this usually rules out an existing pregnancy. The device is also somewhat easier to insert at this time, and the slight bleeding which usually follows insertion is less alarming to the woman, since she can consider it as part of her menses.

Mode of Action

The exact way in which the IUD works to prevent pregnancy in humans has not as yet been determined. It was originally thought to increase tubal motility and speed ovum transport. Thus, the egg, if fertilized, would be too immature for nidation on reaching the uterus. However, this theory has not been substantiated. It is now believed that the IUD, like the pill, may have more than one effect on the reproductive chain of events. One possibility is that the presence of a foreign body in the uterus produces a spermicidal or blastocidal substance. Another theory is that the IUD's presence causes an increase in macrophages in the uterine cavity and that their increased numbers are hostile and destructive to a fertilized ovum. Another mechanism which may be operating is an alteration in the normal endometrial phase needed for the reception of a fertilized ovum. Copper-bearing devices release copper ions which appear to be spermicidal or antinidative.

Effectiveness

The IUDs, while less effective than the oral contraceptives in preventing pregnancy, are still among the most effective methods available. Approximately 20 to 30 percent of women either expel the device involuntarily or have it removed because of side effects. Among those who retain the device, there is a failure rate of about 2 to 4 percent of women per year during the first year of use,

but this rate declines in later years. Older multiparous women retain the device better than nulliparous women. If pregnancy occurs with the device in place, the IUD is usually removed if the cervical threads are visible, since there is a higher rate of spontaneous abortion among women who become pregnant with the device in place. Since IUDs are more effective in preventing intrauterine pregnancies than ectopic pregnancies, there is a higher rate of ectopic pregnancy among women who become pregnant while wearing the IUD than among those without the IUD.

Side Effects

The most common side effects are bleeding following insertion and heavier menstrual periods for some months after insertion. If the bleeding is severe and continues, the device may need to be removed. Cramping or pelvic pain is also common and may be severe enough to warrant removal. Involuntary expulsion of the device, particularly at the time of menstruation, may occur. It may be reinserted and will usually be retained in about half of such cases. Women should be instructed to check with their finger for the presence of the nylon threads in the vagina about once a week and always after their period. If they cannot feel the threads, they may have expelled the device without noticing it and should be instructed to return to the doctor and to use an alternative method until they have been reexamined. Although the threads are discernible to the woman's examining finger, it is rare for her partner to be aware of them during intercourse. Women should be told that they may experience the side effects noted above and that if the side effects are severe, to report them to the doctor.

Among the more serious side effects of IUD insertion are possible occurrence or exacerbation of pelvic inflammatory disease, and uterine perforation during insertion. Pelvic inflammatory disease can usually be treated without removal of the device. Perforations may occur, but they are rare; these are often symptomless but may require removal of the device if it contains copper. There is no evidence that the IUD causes cancer of the uterus or endometrium.

The contraindications to the insertion of an IUD are pregnancy or suspected pregnancy, the presence of acute or chronic pelvic inflammatory disease, and a history of infected abortion or postpartum endometritis during the previous 6 weeks. Severe dysmenorrhea, abnormal genital bleeding, and abnormally low hemoglobin may also contraindicate IUD use.

The Dalkon shield has been found to be associated with a disproportionate number of pregnancy-related infections and spontaneous septic abortions, with some maternal deaths possibly related to its multifilament tail. It has been taken off the market. Patients already wearing a Dalkon shield who become pregnant or miss a period should be advised of the need to remove the device immediately or may be offered an abortion.

Acceptability

IUDs have been found highly acceptable to clinic patients, judging by the rates of continuation observed. About 80 percent were found to be still using this method after 1 year and 70 percent after the second year. Continuation rates for private patients are not available. Among the possible reasons advanced for this high acceptability are the facts that the IUD, once inserted, requires little, if any, further action or decision by the woman; it is coitus-independent and therefore aesthetically preferable; its cost or upkeep is low; and it is easily removed and completely reversible.

The nurse is often expected to explain this method and to answer the questions of women who will have or have had an IUD inserted. It is reassuring for the client to be shown the device and to be instructed as to how and where it will be inserted, using a model or diagram. She can see that the device is not likely to be lost inside her, and she should be informed as to what the possible side effects are so that she will not be unduly alarmed if they occur. She can also be told that the IUD will not interfere with sex relations, the use of tampons, or the douche. Most women will also want to know how reliable the IUD is in preventing pregnancy, and it is important that they be aware that the IUD is not 100 percent effective.

DIAPHRAGM WITH JELLY OR CREAM

The diaphragm is a shallow cup of soft rubber with a flexible metal rubber-covered rim. It is designed to fit snugly in the upper vagina between the symphysis pubis and the posterior fornix, covering the cervix. There are also some special diaphragms in other shapes for women with very relaxed vaginal tissues or other anatomical difficulties who cannot be fitted with a standard diaphragm. Diaphragms come in various sizes, measured in millimeters (50 to 105 mm), and each woman must be individually measured and fitted by a physician or trained nurse to ensure proper cervical coverage. The thimble-shaped cervical cap, made of rubber or plastic, is designed to fit snugly over the cervix. This device, however, is not used very frequently in the United States.

The diaphragm is always used with contraceptive jelly or cream spread on it. In addition to careful fitting, this method requires that women understand female anatomy, how the diaphragm works, and how to insert the diaphragm properly. They also need to be given the opportunity to practice insertion and checking for correct diaphragm placement. Women should be instructed that the size may need to be changed after the birth of a child or pelvic surgery or if there is a considerable loss or gain of weight (4.5 kg or more).

Mode of Action

The diaphragm acts as a mechanical barrier to the entry of sperm into the cervix, as shown in Figure 14-2. The primary function of the diaphragm, however, is to hold the spermicidal jelly or cream in contact with the cervix. This fact should always be emphasized in instructing patients.

Effectiveness

The theoretical effectiveness of the properly fitted, correctly used diaphragm with jelly or cream is high, with a failure rate as low as 3 pregnancies per 100 women per year. However, it is a fairly complicated method and

FIGURE 14-2
Entry of sperm into the cervix is prevented by use of the diaphragm. (*Drawing by Mary McGovern.*)

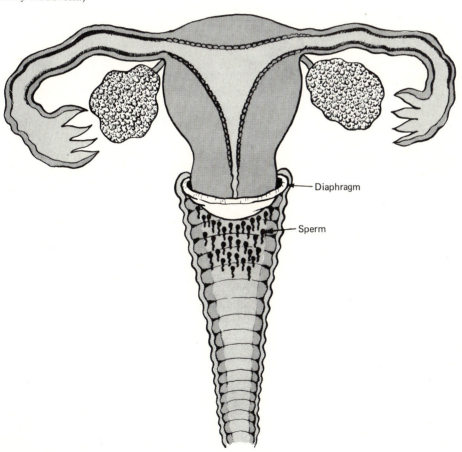

— Diaphragm

— Sperm

requires consistent and repeated use, involving some degree of vaginal self-manipulation—distasteful to many women—and preplanning in relation to coitus; therefore, its actual use and effectiveness is much lower than in theory, with 10 to 15 pregnancies per 100 women per year. It also requires the availability of privacy and sustained motivation on the part of the woman, which may be in short supply for many women in the lower socioeconomic groups. It has no medical side effects. About 5 percent of patients in Planned Parenthood clinics now choose this method. Prior to the advent of the pills and the IUD, it was probably the most prescribed method for women in the United States.

Instructions for Use

Probably no other method requires as much careful and often time-consuming instruction for the woman. Two visits are usually needed before the woman may use the diaphragm for protection. On the first visit she is examined, a Pap smear is taken, and the proper size diaphragm is ascertained. She is then asked to insert the diaphragm herself, first compressing the rim between the thumb and forefinger and passing it into the vagina, aiming it in the direction of her coccyx, as shown in Figure 14-3. She then pushes the rim nearest the front of her body up behind the symphysis pubis. Alternatively, she may attach the diaphragm to an inserter and push this as deeply as possible into the vagina, give it a half turn to release the diaphragm, and remove the inserter. The woman then checks to see if the cervix is covered by the rubber dome of the diaphragm by inserting her longest finger into her vagina and feeling for the rounded knob of the cervix. This procedure is demonstrated in Figure 14-4. It is advisable to have the woman feel her cervix before and after

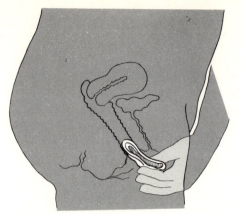

FIGURE 14-3
Insertion of a diaphragm. (*Drawing by Mary McGovern.*)

insertion so that she can distinguish the proper covering of the cervix by the diaphragm. She can be told that the cervix will feel like the tip of her nose.

It is most helpful to show a model of the pelvic organs, into which a diaphragm can be inserted, so that the woman will better visualize what she is doing. She is usually given a "practice" diaphragm to take home with her before actually relying on the method for protection. She is instructed to

FIGURE 14-4
The woman uses her longest finger to check for proper positioning of the diaphragm. (*Drawing by Mary McGovern.*)

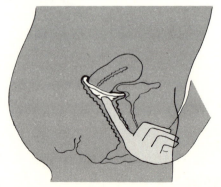

return in a week, having inserted the diaphragm at home, so that her positioning of the diaphragm can be checked again after she has had the opportunity to practice insertion and removal. She may insert the diaphragm in a squatting or lying-down position, or standing up with one foot raised and resting on a chair or toilet seat. Removal of the diaphragm is done by hooking a finger around the rim nearest the front of her body and pulling. The woman should also understand that when using the diaphragm for contraception, it *must always* be coated thinly with about a teaspoonful of contraceptive jelly or cream. The diaphragm may be inserted with the dome up or down, if both sides have jelly or cream on them. After removal, the diaphragm is to be washed with mild soap and water, patted dry with a towel, lightly powdered with unmedicated talcum or cornstarch, and replaced in a container or safe place.

At the return visit, when the woman is again examined, it can be ascertained if she has properly placed the diaphragm. It may be at this time that the size of the original diaphragm given her will be changed; some women are tense on the first visit and more relaxed on the return visit, when a larger size is a better fit.

Women should also be encouraged to adopt the habit of inserting the diaphragm before retiring every night as part of their usual routine, whether they expect to have sexual intercourse or not. This reduces the likelihood—and bother—of having to get up and insert it during the night. If intercourse does not take place, the diaphragm is simply removed in the morning. In any case, the woman should be told to be sure to insert the diaphragm before intercourse, regardless of when it takes place. If intercourse occurs more than 2 hours after the diaphragm has been inserted, additional jelly or cream should be inserted with an applicator before

sex relations. Following intercourse, the diaphragm must not be removed for *at least 6 hours,* although it can remain in place longer. The 6-hour interval is necessary to ensure that the sperm deposited in the vagina will all be inactive or dead. If sex relations occur again during the 6 hours, the woman should insert more cream or jelly and leave the diaphragm in place for 6 hours following the last coitus.

Women should understand that they may urinate or defecate while they wear the diaphragm. If menses should start, the diaphragm will not interfere with flow. They should also examine the diaphragm from time to time to check for holes or tears, particularly around the rim, by holding it up to a strong light. Women often need reassurance that the diaphragm cannot get lost inside them. They can readily see this if the nurse can show them the pelvic model and point out the absence of any passageway large enough for the diaphragm to go through from the vagina into the interior of the body.

Patients should be told to return once a year or sooner if any problems arise with the method. Young women who are just beginning regular intercourse should return in about 3 months to have the size rechecked. Women should also know where they can obtain additional supplies of the cream or jelly as they need them and should be cautioned against using any other lubricant, such as petroleum jelly, as a substitute, since these may cause the rubber to deteriorate and are not spermicidal.

STERILIZATION

Voluntary elective sterilization of either male or female is a medically accepted means of conception control which is legal in all states. It differs from other methods of contraception in that it involves a surgical, usually irreversible procedure. It is the most reliable way to avoid unwanted pregnancy.

Voluntary sterilization should be actively considered for those couples who have achieved a family of desired size, particularly in cases in which there are serious medical contraindications to another pregnancy or in which other temporary contraceptive methods have been found to be unacceptable. Couples interested in this method should be fully informed as to its nature and consequence, since male sterilization is considered reversible in only 20 to 40 percent of cases. There is no way of predetermining this for specific individuals. Although newer techniques are improving the chances of reversibility, couples who expect possible reversal should be advised to use other methods.

Both partners should be emotionally mature and sure of their determination not to have any more children. They should also have a clear understanding of the permanence of the procedure. Doctors may expect both husband and wife to give written consent. Since these procedures do not involve removal of any glands or organs, normal potency and functioning of the hormonal system are not affected.

In women, there are a number of procedures, involving tubal ligation or partial or total salpingectomy, which may be used. These usually involve an abdominal incision so that the tubes may be ligated, and a portion excised or the two cut ends cauterized. Female sterilization can also be done vaginally (culdoscopy) or through a very small abdominal incision using a laparoscope. Sterilization in women is preferably done in the immediate postpartum period, since at this time the tubes are more readily accessible. Hysterectomy is also sometimes used as a sterilizing procedure, but unless there is uterine pathology, it is hard to justify its use in place of the more conservative steriliza-

tion procedures which have lower mortality rates.

For the male, vasectomy involves merely the closing of the vas deferens which carries the sperm. An incision of 12.5 to 18.5 mm is made in each side of the scrotum so that the tubes can be lifted out, cut, and tied off, thus blocking the passage of sperm. The testicles continue to form sperm which are then absorbed in the body. Usually, this minor operation is performed in the doctor's office under local anesthesia.

After sterilization, the male will still have orgasm and ejaculate, although the semen contains no sperm. The quantity of the ejaculate does not diminish noticeably after a vasectomy, since the secretion of the testes which contains the sperm constitutes only about one-tenth of the amount of ejaculated semen.

Vasectomy does not produce sterility immediately, since mature sperm remain in the vas deferens beyond the area of ligation. Men who have been sterilized should be cautioned to continue contraceptive use until their semen can be reexamined by the physician about 8 weeks or following 10 ejaculations after the operation to ensure that it is sperm-free.

Although voluntary male sterilization has been widely used in India, its acceptance in this country appeared relatively low until recently (an estimated 100,000 Americans yearly). Through education and understanding of the fact that vasectomy does not castrate a man or "change his nature" but simply removes his ability to impregnate a woman, it is becoming an increasingly popular method of permanent contraception. Public acceptance, combined with greater availability of the procedure from physicians and clinics, has resulted in a startling increase. In 1974 the Association for Voluntary Sterilization estimated that over 800,000 sterilizations on men and almost 400,000 on women were performed. Among couples over thirty who want no more children, sterilization is the first method of choice; among couples of all ages wanting no more children, it is second only to the pill in popularity.

THE RHYTHM METHOD

The rhythm method is the only birth control method (besides total abstinence) which is officially approved by the Roman Catholic Church. It is also referred to as "safe period," "periodic continence," or "temporary abstinence."

This method is based on the fact that a woman is fertile only around the time of ovulation and that if she abstains from sexual intercourse during that time, she is unlikely to conceive. Usually a woman ovulates once during each menstrual cycle. The ovum has an active life of 12 to 24 hours during which it can be fertilized. Sperm cells, once within the uterus, are viable for about 72 hours during which they can fertilize the ovum. Thus, there is a minimum total of 96 hours (4 days) during each menstrual cycle when conception is possible. To these 4 days an additional margin of several days is added to allow for variation in the exact day of ovulation.

To calculate the safe period by the calendar method, the woman should have a written record of the date of onset of her last 12 menstrual periods. From this record, the number of days in each of these menstrual cycles is listed, counting from the first day bleeding began to the day before the onset of bleeding of the next menstrual period. From this list, the longest cycle and the shortest cycle are selected. The number 18 is subtracted from the number of days in the shortest cycle to give the first day of the fertile or unsafe period, and the number 11 is subtracted from the number of days in the longest cycle to give the last day of the fertile pe-

riod. Thus, if a woman had cycles ranging from 25 to 31 days, she would abstain from intercourse from the seventh day of her current menstrual cycle ($25 - 18 = 7$) until the twentieth day of her cycle ($31 - 11 = 20$). The woman will need to continue her written record of menstrual periods so that the calculation is always based on the 12 most recent menstrual cycles.

The accuracy of the safe period method can be improved by charting the woman's basal body temperature. This is based on the fact that the basal temperature (taken immediately on awakening and before any activity whatsoever) of a woman is more or less constant during the first part of the menstrual cycle until the day of ovulation. At that time it drops slightly and then rises to a level somewhat higher (usually five-tenths to seven-tenths of a degree) than it has been and remains at the higher level for the balance of the cycle. If there is no cold or infection to account for this elevation, the woman can consider herself beyond the fertile period when the elevation has persisted for 3 days. Special basal temperature charts are available from Planned Parenthood—World Population for recording the temperature curves, and special basal thermometers may be used.

Recognition by the woman through observation of changes in her cervical mucus is an additional guide in estimating her safe period. The appearance of peak m cus symptoms, typically clear, abundant and stretchy—like egg white, coincides with ovulation and the temperature rise, usually 14 days before menstruation. It subsides in a few days and the unfertile period follows.

The effectiveness of this method can be considered satisfactory for highly motivated, carefully selected women with fairly regular cycles, who have the motivation and self-discipline, as well as a cooperative partner, to understand and practice it correctly and rigorously. It also costs nothing. However, many couples find it impossible to have "sex by the calendar" instead of by inclination. The use of the rhythm method has also been implicated in studies that indicate it may predispose to fetal abnormalities or abnormal gestation because when accidental pregnancies occurred the ovum or sperm involved were more likely to be "past their prime."

Most couples who, because of religious convictions, prefer to use this method will need assistance and considerable support from the doctor and nurse. It is contraindicated in women for whom a pregnancy poses a serious medical danger.

CONDOMS

The condom, a latex rubber or animal cecum sheath, is the most widely used device for contraception in this country and in many other parts of the world. It is also the oldest device and one of the few under male control. It is highly effective, particularly when used in conjunction with the insertion of contraceptive vaginal jelly or cream by the woman. The spermicide provides protection in case the condom should break or slip during intercourse.

The condom ranks almost with the diaphragm in effectiveness, having an accidental pregnancy rate of about 3 percent. The popularity of the condom is no doubt due to the fact that it is relatively inexpensive, simple to use, and readily available without a doctor's prescription. It carries the additional advantage of protecting against venereal disease and is also used clinically in the treatment of vaginal moniliasis and trichomoniasis to prevent reinfestation by the male. Condoms are particularly appropriate for use when intercourse is not taking place frequently and regularly, as among unmarried young couples, and when there are con-

traindications or difficulties in using other methods.

Its disadvantages include the fact that the sexual act must be interrupted to apply the condom to the erect penis, and many couples find that it dulls sensation. The latter fact, however, may be an advantage in cases of premature ejaculation.

Condoms are made with plain ends or with teat tip, prelubricated or dry. They are now available in a variety of colors. To use the condom correctly, care should be taken in unrolling it over the erect penis to see that no air is left in the condom's tip or, if it has a plain end, that it is not drawn too tightly over the end of the penis, since the air may cause it to burst or may cause an overflow of semen from the open end. After orgasm, the penis must be withdrawn before the erection disappears. The upper rim of the condom must be held firmly during withdrawal so that it does not slip off into the vagina.

VAGINAL FOAMS, JELLIES, AND CREAMS

These preparations contain spermicidal chemicals and materials which immobilize sperm and form a film over the cervix to deter sperm from entering. They are inserted deep into the vagina with a plastic applicator which has been filled from a container. Insertion must take place within an hour before each coitus. If intercourse is repeated, or if more than an hour has elapsed since insertion, another full applicator of the preparation should be inserted. Douching is not necessary, but if used, it *must be delayed until 6 hours* after the last intercourse, since the protection of these materials may be washed away before the sperm are dead or inactive.

Foams are considered somewhat more effective than jellies or creams and are also less likely to be messy or drippy. These methods are rated less effective than the diaphragm or condom. Like the condom, they are readily available without prescription, relatively inexpensive and simple to use, and are especially useful as an alternative or temporary method (e.g., when a woman has forgotten to take her pills for 2 days) or for women who are having infrequent intercourse.

VAGINAL FOAMING TABLETS, SUPPOSITORIES, AND SPONGES

These methods are not as widely used in the United States as other vaginal methods and are ranked among the least reliable. Their main advantage is their simplicity, availability, and low cost. The foaming tablets are moistened with water or saliva to start their foaming action and are inserted no more than 1 hour before intercourse.

The woman must wait at least 5 minutes after insertion to allow the foam to be generated. Vaginal suppositories do not need moistening, but require a brief time—about 10 minutes—after insertion to allow them to melt and disperse in the vagina. The vaginal sponge is used by moistening with a spermicidal liquid and squeezing it to produce a foam. The sponge is inserted deep into the vagina and left in place until 6 hours after intercourse. No douching should be used with these methods until 6 hours after coitus.

WITHDRAWAL (COITUS INTERRUPTUS)

This is an ancient technique which requires the male to interrupt coitus by removing his penis from the woman's vagina prior to orgasm so that the ejaculate is deposited well away from the vagina or external genitals. It requires no devices or chemicals and is available under all circumstances at no cost.

Estimates as to its effectiveness vary, since

this depends on the ability of the individual male to judge and control his time of orgasm. Studies indicate that it may rank with the diaphragm and condom for effectiveness, but many men lack the control necessary for its successful use. Many couples consider the interruption psychologically disturbing, and anxiety about whether withdrawal will take place in time can also be a deterrent to satisfactory sexual intercourse. For couples who have found this method acceptable and reliable, there is no need to urge a change to another method. It can also be useful as an emergency method when other means are unavailable.

UNRELIABLE METHODS

The postcoital douche is a very ineffective method of contraception, despite its fairly wide use, since the sperm enter the cervical canal within seconds after ejaculation, from where they cannot be flushed by douching. Its main value, since it reduces the number of sperm still within the vagina, is in an emergency, such as after the breaking or slipping of the condom.

Prolonged lactation is widely used in developing countries since it delays the return of ovulation for varying periods of time. It is not considered a reliable method in the United States since the return of fertility is unpredictable and supplementary infant feeding reduces its reliability even further.

RESEARCH METHODS

Possible sites and means of intervention in the reproductive chain of events are being studied in the effort to develop new and more effective means of contraception. Such experimental methods are, of course, not available for general use.

Continuous administration of progestins to women by means of injections, subdermal implants, and long-acting once-a-month pills are being tested. Bioactive IUDs and vaginal rings containing progesterone are under research. Combination steroids for men to suppress sperm production are being sought. They could be administered via pills, injections, or subdermal implants. Reversible male sterilization, using valves or removable clamps, have been tested. The use of prostaglandins to terminate pregnancy or prevent fertilization, and other compounds which suppress corpus luteum activity required for pregnancy maintenance, are other interesting possibilities.

BIBLIOGRAPHY

Davis, Hugh J., and John Lesinski: "Mechanism of Action of Intrauterine Contraceptives in Women," *Obstetrics and Gynecology*, 36(3), September 1970.

Guttmacher, Alan F., W. Best, and F. S. Jaffe: *Birth Control and Love*, Macmillan, New York, 1969.

Harkavy, Oscar, and John Maier: "Research in Reproductive Biology and Contraceptive Technology: Present Status and Needs for the Future," *Family Planning Perspectives*, 2(3), June 1970.

Hartman, C. G.: *Science and the Safe Period*, Williams & Wilkins, Baltimore, 1962.

Karim, S. M. M., and G. M. Filshie: "Use of Prostaglandin E2 for Therapeutic Abortion," *British Medical Journal*, no. 5716, July 25, 1970.

Manisoff, Miriam: *Family Planning, A Teaching Guide for Nurses*, 4th ed., Planned Parenthood—World Population, New York, 1973.

———: "Intrauterine Devices," *American Journal of Nursing*, 73(7), July 1973.

Neubardt, Selig: *A Concept of Contraception*, Trident, New York, 1967.

Peel, J., and M. Potts: *Contraceptive Practice*, Cambridge, New York, 1969.

Segal, Sheldon J.: "New Approaches to Contraception," *Clinical Obstetrics and Gynecology*, 17(1), March 1974.

Wood, H. Curtis, Jr.: *Sex without Babies*, Whitmore, Philadelphia, 1967.

PART
THREE

CHILDBEARING AND
THE NURSING
PROCESS

UNIT A

MANAGEMENT AND SUPPORTIVE CARE DURING PREGNANCY

15

Initiating the Nursing Process

ROSIE L. ACTON

Antepartum care, or management and supportive care given during pregnancy, has maternal and fetal safety and health as its goals. In recent years these goals have expanded to encompass supporting an informed, rewarding life experience for a family. Emphasis is on the *informed, participating* family. With this has come increased counseling and teaching in antepartum settings plus more written material on parenthood which focuses on expectant parents. The management and supportive care given during pregnancy differs in relation to many social, cultural, ethnic, and financial circumstances. The differences are also reflected in the nature of the professional delivering the service.

Economic circumstances limit the number of families who seek antepartum care. Efforts are being made to make services readily available to the economically deprived. With the emphasis on health as a *right*, perhaps more women will seek antepartum care, and the risks of childbearing for the poor may be reduced. Maternal-child, high-risk programs have brought antepartum care to many women. Whims of federal funding have made these programs precarious in some areas, however, and long-term continuous support is necessary if positive results are to be realized.

PROFESSIONAL ROLES WITHIN THE HEALTH SYSTEM

The nurse, physician, midwife, and other specialized personnel collaborate in providing services for the family. The nurse acts as the consumer advocate, teacher, and counselor concerned with the client's total health care experience. The midwife or physician is the diagnostician and technical specialist. The physician differs from the midwife in his or her ability to *both* diagnose and treat medical complications of pregnancy. These roles are not clearly defined and much duplication results. Nurses, doctors, and midwives have many similar skills; all are process facilitators.

The following factors may influence who provides what services to clients.

1   The strength or weakness of a particular skill makes a difference in how the professional performs. Nurses have technical and interpersonal skills. If interested in technical performance, the nurse may act mainly as a technician to other health team members. When the nurse values interpersonal and teaching skills, more time is spent counseling, listening to, and teaching clients.
2   Circumstances may often dictate the practice of a nurse. If the nurse works in an antepartum facility that serves 100 women a day, individual teaching and counseling may be difficult. In this

setting group sessions and perhaps collaboration with skilled volunteers from the community would be beneficial.
3   Women's prior conceptions of nurses influence the early nurse-client interactions. If women have not had previous experience with nurses as counselors and teachers, the nurse will need to be articulate in interpreting and establishing this role. The role is often overtly supported by physicians when they refer clients to the nurse for information. In return the nurse keeps the physician informed of the woman's response, which nurtures a collective, informed response to clients' needs.
4   The availability of other professionals influences how the nurse works with families. Small rural communities have limited numbers of allied health personnel, such as dietitians and social workers. In large, urban clinic-type organizations, there are often social workers and dietitians available to meet the needs of women in such areas as placement of babies of unwed mothers or to handle specific dietary problems. Some facilities, when able, use allied health personnel in teaching sessions with pregnant women and their families. Usually they have a minimum of time available, and they see only those clients with the greatest need. This emphasizes the need for nurses to make accurate client assessments and to refer those who require other professional services.
5   If there is a physician shortage in the community, nurses may practice differently. The minimal number of physicians providing care to clients emphasizes the need for collaborative effort and the use of the services of the most appropriate person for meeting the clients' needs. This points toward the

probable use of nurses and midwives to provide more antepartum care to women with apparently normal pregnancies. We may see nurses working with families to facilitate self-monitoring and also as the primary health worker for the family. This would support a trend toward family care, not merely maternity care.

6   The nurse's sound educational preparation in interpersonal skills influences the health services available to clients. This preparation enables the nurse to work effectively with pregnant women and their families.

A pregnant woman seeks the person she believes will meet her present perceived needs and proceeds on a trial-and-error basis. This is especially true regarding information seeking. Often the woman may not know where to find the most appropriate source of information. The nurse needs to be skilled in watching for cues. Establishing relationships with reception personnel so that they will refer patients who seem hesitant or uncertain is one step. Emphasizing this part of nursing practice when talking with physicians will increase the opportunity for nurses and physicians to collaborate toward meeting client needs. Nurses must keep physicians informed so that they know how to work with them, and nurses follow through by keeping accurate, concise, clear records to facilitate the work of other health care professionals in the delivery of service to clients.

Clients come to health facilities with various perceptions or stereotypes of physicians and nurses. We can determine what these are and perform that way; we can ignore them; or we can try to understand their expectations and attempt to interpret what services we can offer. Studies have shown that clients are willing to use nurses as coun-

selors rather than physicians if nurses can meet their needs.[1] Edith Anderson speaks of programs in which the maternity nurse manages the normal pregnancy of a mother after the initial medical assessment.[2] These trends indicate more and more responsibility for nurses and emphasize the need for skill in establishing long-term relationships with clients. The nurse needs interpersonal communication skills to interpret the nursing role to clients, and knowledge and judgment to perform it.

THE NURSING PROCESS

The nursing process is problem solving applied in an interpersonal relationship between a client and a nurse. The phases of this process are:

1   The assessment
2   Development of a plan of action
3   Implementation of the plan
4   Evaluation of the assessment, plan, and implementation

The *assessment* is an outline of important data about a client. Data from the client profile, the physical examination, and the laboratory are analyzed. This data, the analysis, and setting of priorities make up the client assessment. The establishment of a client profile may be accomplished with the assistance of questionnaires the client completes, but due to the personal information involved in maternity nursing the addition of an interview is essential. From the time of the initial client contact the nurse makes observations and seeks information to formulate a plan of care.

After the data is gathered an analysis is made to decide problems, potential problems, and the needs of the client. These are then validated with the client. She may not be aware of either problems or potential problems but she will usually be aware of some of her needs especially in the knowledge area. Priorities are set based on her total physical and emotional needs, and her knowledge and ability to cope with them.

Using the assessment and the priorities a *plan of action* is developed by the nurse, client, and perhaps other health care personnel who will be involved with care. The plan will vary with individual needs and the stage of pregnancy. Information is one of the key components of antepartum care. Through knowledge of the process of a normal pregnancy and the anticipated physiological changes, a woman can do much to ensure the health of herself and her baby.

The client's plan of action is *implemented* through educational programs, specified therapy, monitoring, and reassessment as she makes each visit to the office or clinic during her pregnancy. At each of these appointments the nurse *evaluates* the woman's physical and emotional status plus her knowledge level to determine if the plan has been effective. The nurse alters and/or proceeds with the plan based on the individual's health status.

The initial assessment of the client's situation is the base-line tool of the nursing process. The nurse validates the information obtained with the client and develops a plan of action which is subsequently implemented and evaluated. The assessment will be altered as the client situation changes. This is a nonstatic matrix which changes with the living process.

THE CLIENT SEEKS ENTRY INTO THE HEALTH CARE SYSTEM

A woman who thinks she is pregnant may have a family physician or gynecologist; if not, she will need to decide where and from whom she will seek antepartum care. Re-

ferral by a trusted friend who is pleased with her own care, or convenience and availability may be the deciding factors. Parents classes are also more and more cited by women as the reason for going to a particular physician and/or facility.

The woman telephones an office or clinic to make an appointment; she is asked some identity questions by a receptionist, and an appointment is made for a pregnancy test. When the results of the pregnancy test are positive, an appointment is set for the woman to see the nurse and the physician.

When the woman arrives, an admission clerk or a secretary gathers initial data and begins a record. This gives the nurse and physician some basic information prior to seeing the client.

In a clinic that uses nurses as assessors of client needs, the nurse and client meet; the nurse puts the client at ease by exhibiting a relaxed, caring, knowledgeable attitude, and conducts an initial interview. From this an assessment of the woman is written, and a plan of care is entered in the chart. This antepartum record with its nursing assessment and plan of care facilitates the client's pregnancy experience and coordinates the work of the various people the client will contact during her pregnancy. An example of an antepartum record is shown in Figure 15-1. The record is updated at each antepartum visit. It is sent to the hospital labor and delivery areas when the woman is admitted to deliver her baby. Her experience will be recorded as she goes through labor and delivery and is admitted to the postpartum unit. It will also be used by physicians and nurses to provide care while she is in the hospital and to plan for her care when she goes home. The information may generate a referral to a community health nurse. The community health nurse uses it for the home visit and returns it to the clinic where it is used for the first postpartum visit. By this

DATE
_____

PATIENT'S NAME: LAST   FIRST   INITIAL   AGE
_____

MAIDEN NAME   BIRTH DATE   RACE   RELIGION   OCCUPATION
_____

ADDRESS   PHONE   MARITAL STATUS M-S-W-D-SEP   EDUCATION
_____

HUSBAND   AGE   OCCUPATION   HEIGHT   WEIGHT

MEDICAL HISTORY
_____

FAMILY MEDICAL HISTORY: (Tuberculosis, Hypertension, Heart, Diabetes, Neurology, Epilepsy, Allergies, Multiple Births, Congenital Anomalies)

MEDICAL HISTORY	POS		POS
Nephritis	_____	Psychological disorders	_____
Heart disease	_____	Epilepsy	_____
Hypertension	_____	Drug sensitivity	_____
Rheumatic fever	_____	Allergies	_____
Tuberculosis	_____	Blood dyscrasias	_____
Venereal disease	_____	Blood transfusions	_____
Gynecologic disease	_____	Operations, accidents	_____
Iso-immunization	_____	German measles	_____
Diabetes	_____	Virus infections	_____
Thyroid disfunction	_____	X rays	_____
Phlebitis varicosities	_____	Smoking	_____

COMMENTS:

MENSTRUAL HISTORY
_____

Onset Age	Interval	Duration	Amount
LMP	PMP	Normal?	EDC

PREVIOUS PREGNANCIES

No.	Date	Place of confine-ment	Duration of gestation	Duration of labor	Type of delivery	Born A/D	Sex	Weight	Complications Maternal Child
1									
2									
3									
4									
5									
6									
7									

Summary, number of pregnancies

	Full term	Premature	Abortions Stillborn	Children now alive	Multiple births

FIGURE 15-1

Example of an antepartum or obstetric record.

PRESENT PREGNANCY

Nausea	_____	Edema	_____
Vomiting	_____	Abdominal pain	_____
Indigestion	_____	Urinary complaints	_____
Constipation	_____	Bleeding	_____
Headache	_____	Breast changes	_____
Dizziness	_____	Fatigue	_____
Visual disturbance	_____	Weight gain	_____

COMMENTS:

PHYSICAL EXAM: T   P   R   BP   WT   WT before LMP

EENT	Abdomen
Fundi	Height of fundus
Teeth	Breasts
Thyroid	Nipples
Heart	Tumors
Lungs	Fetal heart
Extremities	Presentation or
Varicosities	position
Edema	Pelvic exam
Skin	
Nodes	

COMMENTS:

Bony pelvis _____
Diag.: Conj.   cm   Trans. diam. outlet   cm   Shape sacrum

Arch   Coccyx   SS. notch

Ischial spines   P. sag

Inlet	Midpelvis	Outlet	Prognosis for delivery
___Adequate	___Adequate	___Adequate	
___Borderline	___Borderline	___Borderline	
___Contracted	___Contracted	___Contracted	

LABORATORY EXAMINATIONS: Blood Type and Rh_____Hgb _____

Urinalysis: Albumin_____ Sugar_____ Microscopic _____

Pap smear: Date _____ Results _____

G. C. culture: Date _____ Results _____

FIGURE 15-1 (Continued)

PRENATAL RECORD

EDC	Parity	Nonpregnant weight	

Date of visit

Week of gestation

Blood pressure

Weight

Headache

Dizziness

Nausea

       Vomiting

Edema

Urine tr. sym.

Bleeding

Height of fundus (cm)

Presentation and position

Station

Fetal motion

Fetal heart rate

Est. fetal weight

      Urine protein

L   Urine sugar

A   Antibody titer

B   Hemoglobin

Next visit

M.D. initials

SPECIAL INFORMATION

Type of delivery planned   Sensitivities

Anesthesia planned   Nutritional status

Hospital   Breast-feeding planned?

                            Physician's Signature _____

FIGURE 15-1 (Continued)

PROGRESS NOTES AND/OR CONSULTATIONS

Date:

Postpartum exam

Time: post delivery _____ Complications _____
T _____ P _____ BP _____ WT _____
Breasts and nipples _____
Abdomen _____
Perineum _____ Vagina _____
Uterus: Position _____ Size _____
Cervix _____ Adnexa _____
Rectal _____
Cytology _____
Infant's condition _____
Remarks _____
Recommendations _____
Referrals _____
Date _____

Physician's Signature _____

FIGURE 15-1 (Continued)

time it tells the entire story of the woman's pregnancy, labor and delivery, postpartum recovery, and home adjustment. At the first postpartum appointment, 5 or 6 weeks after delivery, an evaluation is made of the woman's childbirth experience, and family planning services are offered.

In some institutions the antepartum record is a combined medical and nursing record. In others, the records are separate, with some overlapping of information, and are used by both types of professionals. A separate nursing record form may be sent to the community health nurse to use when making a home visit. (See Figure 15-2.)

INTERVIEWING SKILLS: THE KEY TO THE NURSING PROCESS

There are three basic purposes of the interview:

1　To establish a relationship
2　To gather information
3　To disseminate information

All three goals are sought in an interview, but all require different emphasis at different times, both during the initial interview and during subsequent visits.

Interviewing is a basic skill involved in the problem-solving phases of the nursing process. We will discuss it as a nursing skill in itself and later relate it more fully to the problem-solving process.

Perspectives of Interviewing

In a new interpersonal situation, people have the need to maintain self-esteem. This is intensified in situations that will extend over a given time. When expectant parents come to a health facility, they are interested in what the health care workers are like and how they will be treated. If the nurse is able to demonstrate caring, respect, and value of people, this will enhance the service rendered. This sets the atmosphere of the interview situation. If the nurse is concerned with what clients think of nursing knowledge and tries to impress them, difficulty may arise. Trying to impress clients may be perceived as patronizing. The probable result is that the client only tolerates the nurse, when indeed the goal is a relationship of honest caring and give-and-take.

An interview may be a personal or an impersonal experience. Assuming that a personal experience is desirable for maternity clients, the nurse needs to understand what is happening in the interview situation and why.

The following assumptions about the nurse-client interactions may be helpful.

First, assume the client wants this to be a meaningful interview.

Second, the interview will be more successful if the nurse first tells the client why she is being interviewed. Parents of first babies especially desire and need information, since they know little of what to expect from this kind of encounter with a health worker.

Third, it is the responsibility of the nurse to put the woman at ease. The nurse must be warm, open, and accepting if the client is to feel comfortable and reciprocate. The focus should be on looking forward to meeting a new person and anticipating the advantages for both participants. The nurse is encountering a person undergoing one of nature's most fascinating processes—reproduction—and will have the opportunity to be an involved participant and observer. The client requires a knowledgeable ad-

NURSING INFORMATION RECORD

E.D.C._____

Date of 1st Clinic Visit:_____

Phone:_____

Patient:_____ Age:_____

Occupation:_____

Future Plans:_____

Husband:_____ Age:_____

Occupation:_____

Family:_____

_____

_____

_____

_____

_____

Concerns of the Patient:_____

_____

_____

_____

_____

_____

_____

Problems|Observed by Staff:_____

_____

_____

_____

_____

Knowledge and Attitudes Concerning Labor and Delivery:_____

_____

_____

_____

Infant Care:_____

_____

_____

_____

_____

_____

_____

_____

FIGURE 15-2

The nursing information record. This record is used at the University of Minnesota
Hospitals to record the nursing assessment and plan of care. It travels from the clinic

Date of Interview and Tour of Obstetrical Area:_____

General Observations:

   1. Appearance:

   2. Behavior During Interview:

   3. How Patient Communicates:

Previous Hospitalizations:_____

Reason(s) for Hospitalization:_____
_____
_____
_____

Comments:_____
_____
_____
_____
_____
_____
_____
_____
_____
_____

Hospital Discharge Notes:_____
_____
_____
_____
_____
_____
_____
_____
_____
_____

Family Planning:_____
_____
_____
_____
_____
_____
_____
_____

to the labor rooms, to the postpartum unit, to the community health nurse, and back to the clinic. This circle movement provides continuity throughout the childbearing experience.

vocate in this experience. Both have the opportunity for personal growth and understanding.

Fourth, nurses should realize that most women have some ambivalent feelings about being pregnant. Few events in our lives have all positive ramifications and no negative ones. If the nurse remarks about how happy the woman must be, she may not feel that she can say anything about being unhappy. Unhappiness may be very real, even when it is a planned pregnancy. The new baby means having someone completely dependent who takes, takes, takes, and gives very little in return. Many American people today, in a culture which values independence and freedom, find this a difficult adjustment.

Fifth, the responsibility for clarity of information offered rests with the nurse. To fulfill this obligation one must use all of the senses to detect signs of misunderstanding. This means watching eye and facial expressions as well as body movements. It means telling the woman to please ask questions if statements are not clear.

The categories of information sought in an interview are flexible. Some beginning queries are as follows:

1   Who is the client and what is she like? This would include age, marital status, occupation, ethnic group, size, appearance, and personality.
2   What are her resources? Relationships with family and friends, energy level, and apparent ability to cope with change or stress might be included in this area.
3   What are her goals and values? This might include body image, whether this is a planned pregnancy, if the woman is working and if her job is important to her, and her life-style.
4   How much knowledge or experience does she have? This would include whether this is the first baby, the existence of younger brothers and sisters, if she has cared for small babies, and whether she has read any books for expectant parents or attended expectant parent classes.
5   What are her expectations and concerns? A difficult and uncomfortable pregnancy, the change of life patterns with this addition to the family, economic concerns, and worry about labor and delivery should be noted.
6   Does she have any problems which may influence the course of the pregnancy? Examples might be existing diabetes or heart disease. She may be having financial problems, or she may be overweight. This might be an unwanted pregnancy, or she might be unmarried.

From this information a plan of nursing care and a patient record is established which facilitates work with the family. This record is used to plan for teaching and the use of community resources, and as a base to anticipate problems the family might encounter during the course of the pregnancy.

The Initial Interview

The goals of the initial interview are identical to the three basic purposes of the interview stated previously: to establish a relationship; to gather information; to disseminate information.

If a reciprocal relationship is not established, the interviewer will not have an accurate perception of the client and the woman will not be able to assimilate the information given at this time. With this in mind, the steps in the initial interview are:

1　Meet the client and introduce yourself.
2　Explain the purpose of the interview.
3　Ask the woman to tell you how her pregnancy is progressing. Let her tell all she wants.
4　Listen to the woman. Be attentive; ask questions based on the information or cues she has given.
5　Follow through on information she has given. Clarify points of misunderstanding.
6　Find out how the woman feels, physically and emotionally, and how she has been coping until now.
7　Offer information pertinent to the trimester of pregnancy she is in. Ask if she understands the changes and if they are affecting her activities. (Refer to Figure 15-3 for areas pertinent to that stage of the pregnancy.)
8　Ask if you may explain the services of the clinic. If she answers "no," offer to explain during her next visit.
9　Explain the purpose of seeing the doctor, the physical examination, the regular checks she will have each time she comes to the clinic, the regular discussion of her progress, and the offering of information.
10　Close by asking for more questions and by making sure she does not leave without having her questions answered.

During the initial interview, the nurse attempts to put the client at ease and establish a relationship which reflects trust and confidence. Understanding of nonverbal cues which might be displayed during an interview can be facilitated by role playing an initial interview and discussing the interaction.

The nurse assesses the client's comfort level and observes posture, expression, and signs of possible anxiety. Further nurse-client interaction is aimed at establishing a relationship and beginning data gathering.

The nurse checks the record after the client has been examined by the physician to study the client's history and physical examination and laboratory results. Nursing findings are recorded describing the client's knowledge and information level, family status, attitude toward the pregnancy, general emotional and physical health, and voiced personal values. The nurse looks for cues to current and potential problems and individual needs. There is usually a basic or standard plan of care for the normal pregnant woman, but the nurse analyzes an individual client's data for cues that *that client* has unique needs or problems which require altering the standard plan. As the record is reviewed, the nurse notes areas in which it will be necessary to gather more data at the next appointment.

The Nurse in the Interview

If all goes well, the nursing interview meets the needs of the nurse and the client. It may sound strangely self-centered at first, but the nurse must be introspective and think about why the interview is taking place before it begins. The following paragraphs discuss areas of thought the nurse might like to pursue before interviewing.

The nurse must first meet the client. If the nurse really does not enjoy meeting new people and discussing their concerns, this will be communicated in some way to the client. Women and men become nurses predominantly because they care for people.

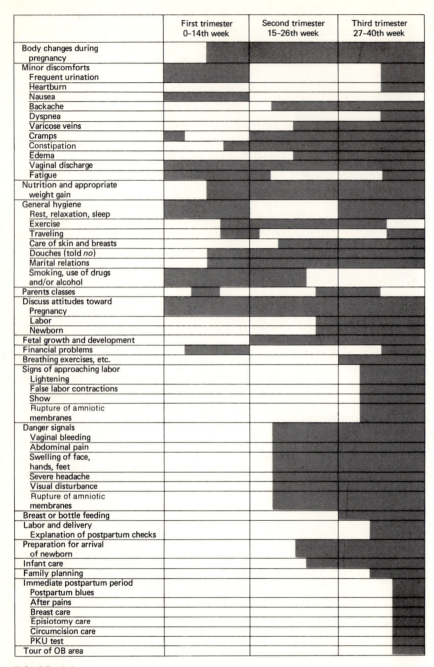

FIGURE 15-3

This bar graph demonstrates the approximate times during pregnancy a woman
will experience concerns or needs information in each category. From this data,
a plan for teaching is made to present the information prior to her need, enabling
the woman to better understand and be prepared for her experience.

They should allow themselves to relax and enjoy meetings with particular persons. Nurses should not think of other clients or how many are yet to be seen. They should concentrate on the person they are talking with and listen to what the client is saying and asking.

The ability to communicate both verbally and nonverbally is necessary for a successful interview. The understanding must be conveyed to the client that the nurse wants to be with her, that not only is she important but the nurse has no one who is more important than she is at this time. That the nurse will maintain privacy is an assumed prerequisite.

The nurse should "listen" with eyes, ears, feelings, even intuition. If a nurse has a hunch, it should be checked out. If there is something that makes a nurse think a client is not comfortable, he or she should try to find out why. Nurses may even need to have someone else follow a particular client if there is some barrier to communication. Consulting another colleague may provide valuable answers in some situations. If a nurse sees a woman with tightly clenched hands, the nurse might assume she is tense or nervous. The situation should not be ignored— the "message" conveyed by those clenched hands may be important. The nurse should tell the client what he or she has seen, and ask if the interpretation is correct. This may free the woman to ask an embarrassing or worrisome question.

It is helpful if nurses understand themselves and the mechanisms of nurse-client relationships. Bermosk speaks of those attitudes of warmth, acceptance, objectivity, and compassion as necessary for effective interviewing.[3] In the personal area of maternity nursing, these are especially important. How can nurses demonstrate these attitudes to clients? Perhaps by smiling, introducing themselves, making sure they hear and understand the client's name, and explaining why the interview is taking place. The nurse and client should mutually set the goals. Nurses should be relaxed and tolerant, remembering not to be annoyed when required to explain something in more than one way to a person. If a nurse admits having difficulty clarifying certain information, it may make the client feel more relaxed and able to ask questions in return.

The Client in the Interview

Many factors about the client influence the interview, one of which is the stage of pregnancy. Most of the concerns or questions a woman has during the first trimester have changed by the third trimester. Figure 15-3 indicates many of the areas commonly discussed with clients in various trimesters. (These time spans are not definite, but give a general picture of which questions, at what times, are of concern to many women.) The nurse in turn tries to give the information prior to the time the client needs it. Many of the times are influenced by physiological changes in the body. For example, body image may be more significant in the third trimester, when the body form is dramatically changed. Often body image is so important and so threatened by pregnancy that this is what concerns the woman most on her first visit to a health care facility.

The following situation occurred when a model sought antepartum care. She and her mate had planned to work for 2 more years before starting a family, and she was concerned about her career. They were dependent on both their incomes to maintain their present life-style. She had many questions on her first visit to the clinic. For example, would dieting hurt her baby? How soon after the baby was born would she be able to regain her figure, or would there be permanent figure changes? Helping her find alternatives and allowing her to make choices freely and participate in planning her own care were very important. This exemplifies some of the individuality necessary in planning care.

The client's values about babies and families and about pregnancy itself all influence what information is needed and how it is best presented. A general guideline to follow is to allow the woman to question and lead the interview as much as possible. This will often disclose the woman's value system, and indicate how information may most effectively be introduced.

Where the family obtains health information is another factor directly affecting the client's perception of pregnancy. What kind of experiences do the woman's parents talk about when babies are discussed? Everyone develops ideas, perceptions, and values related to pregnancy, labor, and delivery. When families were larger and communities smaller, much of this was gained from family members, especially mothers, sisters, and grandmothers. Today there is still much influence from parents, but it is tempered by educational and cultural influences and peer contact. No matter where values and perceptions originate, they will influence the pregnancy experience. With this in mind it is often wise to ask the family what their mothers said about having babies. A variety of replies will be offered from "pure hell" to a "joyous, fulfilling experience." Allow the clients to elaborate on what their parents told them and, more important, ask what they thought of what their parents said. If the woman's mother had a bad labor and delivery, does she expect the same experience? How does she think it would be best to handle her fear? What is she afraid of? Being alone? Pain? Death? Something being wrong with the baby? It is wise not to dwell on apprehension but to leave the subject open for discussion. Be sure to allow enough time and opportunity for the client to express herself.

Family resources and how the woman is accustomed to using them are influential factors. If she and her mate regularly use written resources when they want to know something, she may wish to read some of the books written for expectant parents. As a consequence, she may have fewer questions than someone who is used to getting information by word of mouth. The latter may need special sessions with more time for questions and more generous use of pictures and demonstrations.

Our society often assumes everyone knows how to be a parent, but "mothering" and "fathering" behavior is learned. Many men and women unconsciously perform these roles the way their parents performed them. Many women are astounded by the fact that when the baby arrives they do not have an overwhelming feeling of being a mother. When new mothers are with someone they trust, they often admit, "It doesn't seem real," or "I don't feel like a mother." Because motherly and fatherly feelings are assumed to be so natural, it is usually up to the professional to introduce learning behaviors in anticipation of the new role to help prepare the parents. Often they need to know that they will learn, that the baby will not break, and that it is normal not to "feel like a parent" right away.

The Father in the Interview

The nurse's first contact is usually with the woman client, but including the man in the relationship and plan of care is very helpful. Ideally the plan of care is developed by the family, the nurse, the physician, and possibly social workers and dietitians.

Nurses often state that when they ask the man if he wants to come into the interview he refuses, so they seldom include him. This may be because he does not know what is going to happen and nonverbally gets the message that his presence is not necessary.

Nurses might find men more eager and willing to join interviews if they really make an effort to include them. This could be a significant step toward the reality of family planned health care. A word of caution: There may be reasons why the man does not want to be included, such as his cultural values. He may regard childbearing as feminine and feel threatened if he must be included. Perhaps he is not the father of this child. Maybe he really does not want to be there because of other interests. Choice should be maintained, but the opportunity to participate should be encouraged. He may want to be included later and should be offered the opportunity to join the conversation each time he accompanies the pregnant woman.

One of the primary reasons a man often does not accompany the woman to a clinic is the time of day antepartum appointments are made. Most men work and do not want to relinquish a day's pay to accompany their mates. If we believe seeing both parents is important, we should make efforts to have evening maternity clinics or clinics at times congruent with *both* parents' personal schedules.

If there appears from talking with the woman to be some difficulty regarding the man's understanding and support of her during pregnancy, the nurse should suggest that the woman bring him along on one of her visits to allow the three of them to talk. This may provide the opportunity to clarify the psychological and physiological changes pregnancy brings which are best dealt with by both parents. When both parents are more knowledgeable, they are likely to be more patient with each other.

Follow-up Interviews

The pattern of nurse-client interview subsequent to the initial encounter and establishment of the relationship may be as follows:

1 Greet the client.
2 Ask how she is getting along. If she gives the polite social answer of "being fine," ask about specific concerns. An example might be, "Are you still so tired?"
3 Allow her to explain what she is doing, what she is coping with. For example, a nurse might ask what the client has done about the early morning nausea she was previously experiencing.
4 Ask about problem areas involving weight, diet, discomfort, etc., pertinent to the particular time of pregnancy.
5 After answering her questions, again offer information and resources she may not have asked about in areas related to that time in her pregnancy or the near future.
6 At each visit (at the end if it has not been brought up) offer information on her physiological changes, personal care, and fetal growth and development.

As one can see, the key is to put the woman at ease, answer her questions, and then introduce new information so she will know what to expect as she goes through each phase of her pregnancy.

During antepartum care, assessment, plan of action, implementation, and evaluation often flow together. If an emotional problem is noted, the nurse plans an interaction to bring the emotions out in such a way that the people involved can discuss them. Afterwards, the success of the interaction in solving the emotional problem is evaluated; if it was unsuccessful, another plan is devised for meeting these client needs. At times a nurse will find it necessary to consult with the physician and a mental health professional regarding a client's plan of care.

Women who develop symptoms, who are

worried, or who have a question which is bothering them are encouraged to call the office or clinic. These telephone calls are usually handled by the nurse. If the relationship already established is a sound one, the nurse can do much to clarify information, allay groundless fears, or assess the need for the client to be seen sooner than her next appointment. A good telephone manner is of course a valuable asset to the nurse. The nurse's interviewing skills are strongly tested when making a telephone assessment since the client is not present to provide cues to appropriate questions. The nurse will need to quickly review the client's record while taking the call. Clear concise recording is an invaluable asset in this, as well as in other, situations.

Within an interaction setting the problem-solving process is a vital force. It can be used by the nurse in a very effective way. The first goal in an interaction is to ensure that the problem is clearly understood by all participants. The second goal is to bring out several alternative solutions and explore what the various results might be. The third goal is to allow the participants to select an alternative. The fourth goal is to clarify and support the decision. This process again is problem solving with the nurse acting as a facilitator.

Nursing in antepartum care is largely counseling and teaching. Physically doing something for the client is a small part of the services rendered. A clear understanding of the nursing process and the role of interviewing and interaction is vital.

Plan for Offering Information

In counseling and teaching during pregnancy some subjects fall automatically into trimesters. Other items of information for discussion may be important to the client at different times, depending on the client. General times when certain topics are usu-

ally important to the woman are listed in Figure 15-3. If a woman asks about something it is discussed at the time she asks. An example might be sexual intercourse. Many young couples think they may hurt the baby and have questions regarding abstaining. If the nurse has established a trust relationship and put the family at ease, often this will be brought up by the client. This is a very personal area and one which concerns many clients. The nurse should be well versed in information on this subject and should not be embarrassed by the question. If the nurse shows embarrassment, the woman will probably not want to be the cause of more embarrassment and will refrain from asking personal questions in the future. The interviewer should assess how comfortable the woman or couple is, and if they do not ask about intercourse, this information should be offered. (See Chapter 18.)

It is believed that the best learning occurs when the client indicates a readiness for it, but there must be some consideration for the woman who does not know what to ask the nurse. The following areas of discussion can be introduced by the nurse even if the client does not request the information.

Subjects introduced during the first trimester
Nutrition and basic diet information
Minor discomforts with comfort measures
    Frequent urination
    Nausea
    Vaginal discharge
    Fatigue
    Constipation
General hygiene
    Rest, relaxation, and sleep
    Douches
    Exercise
Employment
Travel

Marital relations

Smoking, drugs, or alcohol

Parents classes (attendance is usually recommended during the third trimester; many classes have strong emphasis regarding preparation for labor and delivery which may mean poor recall and application if taken too early)

Attitudes toward pregnancy

Fetal growth and development (often introduced during either the first or second trimester)

Subjects introduced before or during the second trimester

Minor discomforts with comfort measures
  Backache
  Varicose veins
  Cramps
  Edema
General hygiene
  Care of skin and breasts
Parents classes
Attitudes toward expected child
Fetal growth and development
Danger signals (caution of what to look for and do)
Preparation for arrival of newborn
Infant care

Subjects introduced before or during the third trimester

Minor discomforts
  Frequent urination (different cause at this time)
  Heartburn
  Backache
  Dyspnea
  Fatigue
General hygiene
  Rest, relaxation, sleep (different reasons)
Travel
Parents classes
Attitudes toward labor and delivery
Financial problems

Breathing exercises

Signs of approaching labor

Breast- or bottle-feeding

Labor and delivery itself, what to expect

Family planning (contraception after baby is born)

Explanation of immediate postpartum period

Tour of the labor rooms, delivery rooms, postpartum unit, the nursery, and rooming-in facilities

Although the above plan attempts to ensure readiness, information is often introduced long before it is needed because of the keen interest of clients. An increasing number of books are written for expectant parents, and many women come to the interviews quite early in their pregnancy armed with questions.

Through the interviews an assessment of the client is made, and the care plan is varied to meet the individual needs of clients. The aim of a plan for giving information is for it to be a supplementary tool in the nursing process. As the nurse assesses the client on each visit, data is gathered, the plan is validated with the client, and the plan is implemented by giving the client information appropriate to her needs at that time. The success of each interaction is evaluated by the nurse as application of the nursing process is evaluated. This process of explore, act, and explore again is a continuous cycle, existing over several months, which involves the relationships among the nurse, the pregnant woman, and her family. Through this process the nurse helps the family find the information and services they need and want. When properly executed this process also results in growth and increased understanding by both the nurse and clients about how to deal with life problems. The emphasis is on maintenance of health, early detection of complications, and preventive measures.

The nurse plays a key role as the advocate, counselor, and teacher of families in maternity settings.

THE MEDICAL ASSESSMENT

The first time a woman sees the physician a thorough work-up of the client is usually, but not always, done. Some women spontaneously abort during the first trimester, and if this is a possibility, the physician might wish to delay the thorough history and physical examination. As the pregnancy progresses, the pelvic floor is more relaxed, making it easier for a total examination with a minimum of discomfort to the woman. The physician does want to establish that the woman is pregnant and get enough information to anticipate any problem. This means the total work-up is often done about the 12th week, after which a spontaneous abortion is not likely to occur.[4]

During the *total* medical assessment, a medical history is taken and a general physical examination is performed, including examination of eyes, ears, nose, and throat as well as breasts and pelvis. With a first pregnancy, the woman may not know what to expect and will feel more comfortable if the content of this initial visit is clarified. The physician wants an assessment of the expectant woman's general health. If she has an undetected problem, it is better to know and deal with it now than to have it appear later in her pregnancy when it might be difficult for her and the unborn child.

Heart disease, kidney disease, and diabetes are problems which may exist undetected and would be dangerous during pregnancy. When these underlying diseases are known, steps can be taken to make the pregnancy as safe and nontraumatic as possible for the mother and the unborn child. A basic knowledge of her condition early in pregnancy also gives the physician a more accurate perspective from which to view any complica-

tions. The medical history section of the sample antepartum record (Figure 15-1) gives a list of the many disease phenomena and conditions the physician needs to know about.

General Antepartum Care

General care for most women during the antepartum period follows a regular pattern after the initial history, physical examination, and establishment of a plan of care. This pattern is demonstrated in Figure 15-1. This type of record is established to show any physiological changes that may occur during the progression of the pregnancy. Fluctuations of any degree often signal some type of complication. The signs and symptoms are interrelated and must be evaluated in the context of the total client situation. The goal is to identify problems early enough to prevent serious complications.

The client usually sees a physician once a month until the 8th month, then every 2 weeks until the 9th month, and then once per week until she delivers. This, of course, is altered if there are complications, or if the client is considered high-risk.

Cardinal checks done on each antepartum visit include blood pressure, weight, edema, and urine protein and sugar. The hemoglobin is checked 3 to 4 times during the pregnancy.

Fetal circulation puts an added burden on the woman. Because of the extra body tissue requiring perfusion, there is an increase in circulating fluid volume with some dilution of hemoglobin; this is more slowly remedied during pregnancy by the increased production of cells. A high concentration of hemoglobin is needed to provide necessary oxygen for both mother and fetus. Most women are advised to take iron supplements throughout their pregnancy, since the increased iron required is difficult to get by diet alone.

Antibody titers are done on Rh-negative women. The antibodies that build up in the mother's blood against the Rh-positive baby usually do not rise appreciably until after the 4th month, although this varies from person to person. This is especially true if the woman has experienced more than one pregnancy. These titers are usually started about the 4th month, but the schedule varies with each physician's mode of practice.

Usually the only physical examination done on these visits is to palpate the abdomen, check the height of the uterus, and listen to the fetal heart rate. This brief physical plus the above checks will usually indicate need for further exploration.

Weight gain, increased blood pressure, proteinuria, dizziness, persistent frontal headaches, epigastric pain, and blurred vision may signal toxemia, one of the more complex complications of pregnancy. Bleeding, cramps, or abdominal pain early in the pregnancy might indicate a threatened abortion. If there are signs that the pregnancy is not proceeding normally, a pelvic examination may be performed. Indications might be bleeding, pain, or failure of the uterus to enlarge. Another reason for an early pelvic exam is a history of an incompetent cervix which might require a Shirodkar procedure or other corrective measures.

Pelvic Examination

At one time a woman always had a nurse or other female in the room when a pelvic examination was performed. This is no longer required unless the physician anticipates some difficulty or assistance is needed in performing a procedure. In making an assessment of a woman and deciding whether the nurse's presence is necessary, several factors may be considered. These would include the client's need for support and information, the age and marital status of the woman, whether it is the first pelvic examination, whether pain is anticipated or pathology is suspected, and the woman's apparent level of understanding and apprehension. Language barriers, learning difficulties, and mental retardation also pose dilemmas in deciding how best to help a client.

The nurse's role is to explain to the woman what to expect and why the pelvic examination is done; ask her to disrobe; provide her with appropriate drapes which ensure as much privacy as possible; and assist the woman in understanding how she may participate most effectively through relaxation. When the pelvic muscles are tight and tense, the physician cannot accurately assess the condition of the pelvic organs and the woman will experience more discomfort. Nurses try various means to help clients to relax. A nurse might ask a woman to place her hands on the middle of her chest and relax them; to breathe through her mouth and not hold her breath; and to allow her knees to fall to the sides when her feet are in the stirrups. Nurses may suggest that the examination will be easier if the client concentrates on moving her toes, relaxing her ankles, and making her stomach soft. There are ways to go about relaxing, and nurses will find which suggestions help which clients by careful observation.

The nurse should always ask the woman to empty her bladder before the pelvic examination. Clients are asked to provide a urine specimen to be tested for albumin and sugar when they arrive at the clinic. Therefore, unless the woman has been waiting a long time, a full bladder usually should not be the problem.

Pelvic Measurements

Pelvic measurements are assessment tools which provide one scientific basis for the physician's decision about the mode of delivery: vaginal or cesarean section. Measurement of the diameters of the pelvis is termed *pelvimetry*.

The safe delivery of a fetus depends upon the adequacy of the maternal pelvis. A small, contracted pelvis makes delivery very difficult or even impossible. Efforts are made by the physician during a woman's antepartum phase of pregnancy to anticipate and diagnose disproportion between the maternal pelvis and the fetal size.

The Pelvis

The pelvis is a basin-shaped bony ring by which the weight of the body is transmitted to the lower extremities. The female pelvis is of particular form specially adapted to childbearing functions. The sacrum, the coccyx, and the two hipbones (innominate bones) comprise the pelvis. The innominate bones are composed of the ilium, ischium, and symphysis pubis. They articulate with the sacrum at the sacroiliac joint.

There are two main divisions of a pelvis, the *false* and the *true*. The false pelvis is the upper, flaring portion; the true pelvis comprises the area through which the fetus actually passes during birth. The *linea terminales* is a bony ridge which separates the upper, false portion from the lower, true portion. Figures 15-4 and 15-5 illustrate a pelvis and its landmarks.

The true pelvis is divided into three parts: the *inlet*, the *outlet*, and the *cavity*. The linea terminales forms the uppermost boundary of the true pelvis and designates the beginning of the inlet. This inlet cannot be directly measured in a living woman for it is entirely surrounded by bone. However, its measurement can be estimated from the dimensions of the diagonal conjugate (discussed below) and from the anteroposterior diameter measurements.

The symphysis pubis and pubic arch form the front boundary of the pelvic outlet, while

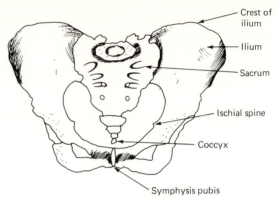

FIGURE 15-4
The pelvis and important bony landmarks.

the ischial tuberosities form the side boundaries, and the coccyx and greater sacrosciatic ligaments form the posterior boundary. The outlet can be visualized as a triangle with the distance between the ischial tuberosities forming the base of the triangle and the pubic arch forming the apex. Obstetrically, this triangle is of paramount importance, for the

FIGURE 15-5
Lateral section of the pelvis illustrating bony landmarks, and false and true portions.

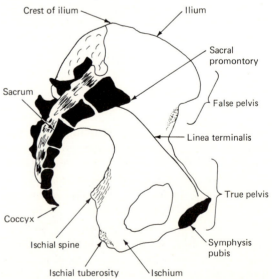

fetal head must pass through this area in order to be born. Anatomically, this triangle is wider in women than in men.

The pelvic cavity is the area between the inlet, the outlet, and the anterior, posterior, and lateral pelvic walls. The upper canal of the pelvic cavity is nearly cylindrical, and only the lower portion is curved. This curvature complicates the birth process, for it necessitates the baby's accommodation to it.

The *Caldwell-Moloy classification* delineates four basic pelvic shapes. The *android pelvis* is basically triangular in shape at the inlet, narrow at the outlet, and is found in about 32 percent of white women and about 15 percent of nonwhite women The *anthropoid pelvis* is oval in shape with the longest portion in the anteroposterior plane. It is found in about 23 percent of white women and about 40 percent of nonwhite women. The *gynecoid pelvis* is a rounded, oval, rather heart-shaped pelvis with only a slightly larger transverse measurement than anteroposterior diameter. It is known as the "normal" female pelvis, and is found in about 42 percent of women. The *platypelloid pelvis* is most like the gynecoid but is more flat with a much narrower measurement from the sacrum to the symphysis pubis. It is found in about 3 percent of white women and about 2 percent of nonwhite women. Figure 15-6 illustrates these four types of pelvises.

Measurements

There are two types of pelvic measurements taken, external and internal. External measurements are approximations, and may be taken any time during pregnancy; a Thom's pelvimeter is used for these measurements, as shown in Figure 15-7. External measurements are considered by many obstetric authorities to be of dubious value, although they are still recorded by many physicians.

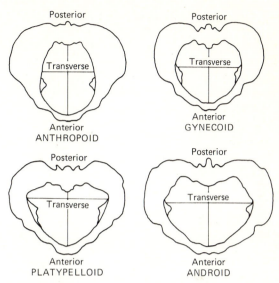

FIGURE 15-6

The four pelvic types. Note the transverse and anteroposterior dimensions.

For all the external pelvic measurements, the woman lies on her back or side, depending on the measurement being taken. She is draped to ensure privacy, with only the area from the xiphoid process to the top of the mons pubis exposed. Table 15-1 summarizes the external pelvic measurements.

Internal pelvic measurements are more accurate than external, but the degree of accuracy is dependent upon the method. Internal measurements can be done by manual vaginal examination, x ray, or sonic waves. The most common method is manual vaginal examination. Some physicians prefer to postpone the manual examination until the early third trimester, at which time the maternal tissues are soft and hence there is less discomfort to the woman. The most accurate methods of internal pelvic measurement are x ray and sonic waves.

One internal pelvic measurement of primary importance is the *diagonal conjugate*. The woman is placed in lithotomy position and through a pelvic examination the dis-

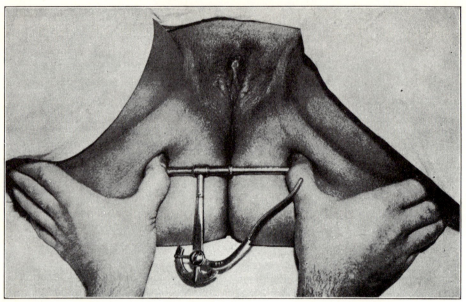

FIGURE 15-7
Measurement of biischial (transverse) diameter of outlet with Thom's pelvimeter.
(*By permission from Louis Hellman and Jack A. Pritchard,* Williams Obstetrics,
14th ed., Appleton-Century-Crofts, New York, 1971.)

TABLE 15-1
External Pelvic Measurements

Measurement	Description	Average, cm
Interspinous	Distance between the outermost edges of the anterosuperior iliac spines	26
Intercristal	Distance between the most prominent outer edges of the iliac crests	29
Intertrochanteric	Distance between the most prominent parts of the femoral trochanters	31
External conjugate (Baudeloque's diameter)	Distance from the depressed area above the first sacral vertebra spine to the mid-upper border of the symphysis pubis	20
Right and left oblique (right and left diagonal)	Distance from one posterosuperior iliac spine to the opposite anterosuperior iliac spine; right oblique usually slightly greater than left oblique	22
Biischial (transverse diameter, tuberischii diameter, intertuberous diameter)	Distance between the ischial tuberosities	8

SOURCES: Adapted from Arthur Osol (ed.), *Blakiston's Gould Medical Dictionary*, McGraw-Hill, New York, 1972; Clarence W. Taber, *Taber's Cyclopedic Medical Dictionary*, Davis, Philadelphia, 1965; Louis M. Hellman and Jack A. Pritchard, *Williams Obstetrics*, 14th ed., Appleton-Century-Crofts, New York, 1971.

tance is palpated and estimated between the undersurface of the symphysis pubis and the sacral promontory. The length of the diagonal conjugate is measured by passing the index and middle fingers of one hand into the vagina. They are pressed inward and upward until the middle finger reaches the sacral promontory. The index finger of the other hand is used to mark the place on the examining hand which touches the undersurface of the symphysis pubis. The examining hand is then withdrawn, keeping the other index finger in place. The diagonal conjugate constitutes the measurement from the tip of the middle finger of the examining hand to the mark measured by the other index finger. A stationary measuring device attached to a wall is the preferred standard to use in calculating this measurement.

Another very important internal pelvic measurement is the *conjugata vera,* or *true conjugate.* This represents the distance between the middle of the sacral promontory and the upper edge of the symphysis pubis. However, this measurement must be estimated from the diagonal conjugate due to the fact that it cannot be directly taken on a living woman except by x ray. In order to arrive at a measurement for the conjugata vera, 1.5 to 2 cm is deducted from the total length of the diagonal conjugate, the deduction amount based on the height and inclination of the symphysis pubis. The measurement of the conjugata vera is of paramount importance, for it is the smallest area of the inlet through which the fetal head must pass.

A term which often brings confusion to students *and* practicing registered nurses is *obstetric conjugate.* This measurement, in order to be fully accurate, must be taken by x ray; it begins at the sacral promontory and ends just below the conjugata vera on the inner surface of the symphysis pubis. This represents the shortest measurement of the

maternal pelvis through which the fetal head must pass.

Figure 15-8 illustrates the hand maneuvers for measuring the diagonal conjugate and indicates the angles of the internal pelvic measurements. Table 15-2 summarizes for the reader the major internal pelvic measurements, their description, and average findings.

X-ray pelvimetry is usually done very late in pregnancy during the advanced third trimester when an exact measurement of the pelvis is needed. It may be done when the fetal head is not engaged and disproportion

FIGURE 15-8
Hand maneuvers for measuring the diagonal conjugate. Positions of the conjugata vera, the obstetric conjugate, and the diagonal conjugate are indicated.

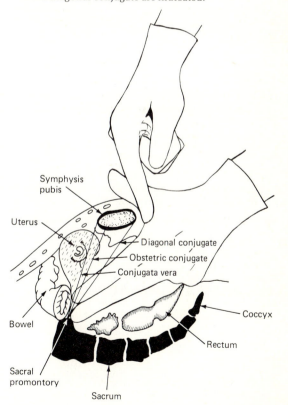

TABLE 15-2
Internal Pelvic Measurements

Measurement	Description	Average, cm
Diagonal conjugate	Distance between the sacral promontory and the undersurface of the symphysis pubis	12.5
Conjugata vera (true conjugate; the term conjugata diagonalis also is used when diameter estimated from diagonal conjugate rather than verified by x ray)	Anteroposterior diameter of the pelvic inlet measured from the middle of the sacral promontory to the upper edge of the symphysis pubis	11
Obstetric conjugate	Distance from the sacral promontory to just below the conjugata vera on the inner surface of the symphysis pubis	10.6

SOURCES: Adapted from Arthur Osol (ed.), *Blakiston's Gould Medical Dictionary*, McGraw-Hill, New York, 1972; Clarence W. Taber, *Taber's Cyclopedic Medical Dictionary*, Davis, Philadelphia, 1965; Louis M. Hellman and Jack A. Pritchard, *Williams Obstetrics*, 14th ed., Appleton-Century-Crofts, New York, 1971.

with the maternal pelvis is suspected. The physician may have already measured the diagonal conjugate and other diameters, and found them to be within normal limits, but may suspect a large baby in relation to the maternal pelvis. The physician considers the woman's obstetrical history, her pelvic measurements, her progress in labor, and the size and presentation of the baby.

X ray does present a risk to the infant and is, therefore, postponed until very late in pregnancy. It is used then only if there are clinical symptoms which indicate its necessity, because such procedures early in pregnancy may harm the fetus. If chest or other x rays are required for some medical problem, care should be taken to shield the fetus with a lead apron.

THE ANTEPARTUM RECORD

Antepartum records vary in format. Some have very detailed information as demonstrated in Figure 15-1. Others will have more generalized categories of information. Some of this variation is dictated by the setting in which the client seeks care. Medical center clinics and obstetricians who see clients with more pregnancy complications tend to have more detailed records. General practitioners who care for mostly normal pregnancies may find less need for complex records. Regardless of the setting, Weed's idea of the problem-oriented record is beginning to affect the way many maternity client records are kept. Pregnancy, a normal predictable process, is quite amenable to the problem-oriented format.

The Traditional Record

Traditional records are referred to as *narrative* records, in that they tell a story of the client in narrative fashion or order. Basic information is gathered about a client, after which different practitioners each have a section of the record in which to enter information. A progress note is written on each visit by health professionals seeing the client. The person recording might write in symptoms, or tests done, or make a comment on condition. When only one practitioner sees a client each visit, as in many office settings, this form of record is often adequate. In group practices and medical center clinics where many professionals see the client and the record is used for educational purposes, the narrative record does not function well as an effective communication tool between professionals.

The Problem-oriented Record

Problem-oriented records are organized according to problems and the problem-solving process. Basically there are four sections to the record.

1   The data base
2   Problem list
3   Plans
4   Progress notes

The *data base* consists of all the basic information about the client, including history and physical, client profile, and laboratory reports and tests. In maternity nursing one assumes pregnancy is a normal process rather than a problem but problems or complications of pregnancy can occur. The *problem list* would name pregnancy as the diagnosis, and list other problems if they develop. *Plans* consist of anticipated nursing actions dictated by the client's condition, therapy prescribed, and the education planned. *Progress notes* in the problem-oriented recording system are organized in a specific manner. The format is referred to as SOAP with each initial standing for a component of the note: S, subjective; O, objective; A, assessment; and P, plan.

SOAP names the types of information one records when recording nursing process or problem solving. S and O represent the two types of information which are gathered in looking at the client's situation. *Subjective* refers to the client's verbal and/or non-

verbal behavior; *objective* refers to what the nurse observes or measures. *Assessment* refers to the nurse's interpretation of the situation based on scientific knowledge and analysis of the subjective and objective information. The *plan* is a recording of intended direct nursing intervention which results from the assessment. An example of this type of recording on a maternity client is as follows:

Problem: Possible preeclampsia
Subjective: Complains of dizziness and seeing spots; blinks eyes long, with some fluttering of lids
Objective: Blood pressure, 150/110; 8 months pregnant; ankles swollen; urine protein positive; 4-kg weight gain in past 3 weeks
Assessment: Preeclamptic
Plan: Physician notified. Placed on rest regimen at home. Placed on 1,000-ml fluid restriction per 24 hours. To return for blood pressure check in 3 days

In actual recordings, the initials S, O, A, P are used for brevity.

Flow sheets are recording devices which enable the practitioner to follow the recordings of data over time; they facilitate comparisons. They are ideal for monitoring conditions and recording client teachin or behavior. Figure 15-1 is an example of ε low sheet used to monitor those items necessary to the physical progression of pregnancy.

Flow sheets can also be designed to monitor other parameters. They are often used to monitor client learning. (See Figure 15-9.) Those items that only need be recorded once or twice may have boxes to be checked, whereas those frequently monitored require a grid.

The problem-oriented record is more time-

Instructions: Check when instructed. Date when demonstrates or verbalizes understanding.

Expected delivery date _____

Instructed	Demonstrates or verbalizes	Instructed	Demonstrates or verbalizes
____Nutrition—weight gain	____	____How to participate during labor and delivery	____
____Hygiene	____	____Postpartum checks	____
____Activity, exercise, rest, sleep	____	____Postpartum period	____
____Parents classes (date when attended)	____	1 Postpartum blues	____
____Signs of approaching labor	____	2 Afterpains	____
____Danger signals	____	3 Breast care	____
____Breast-feeding (breast preparation)	____	4 Episiotomy care	____
____Bottle-feeding	____	5 Circumcision	____
____Tour of OB area	____	6 PKU test	____
		____Sibling preparation	____
		____Infant care	____
		____Family planning	____

Date								
Weight								
Blood pressure								
Headaches/dizziness								
Nausea/vomiting								
Urine protein								
Sugar								
Edema								
Bleeding								
Fetal heart rate								
Fetal movement								

Date	Problem	Assessment and plan

FIGURE 15-9
Maternal care flow sheet. This flow sheet contains items the nurse monitors for a
client. Additional progress notes may be required if the client develops complications
or problems.

consuming to write initially. Once established, however, a problem-oriented record with its flow sheets actually takes less time and will contain more concise, complete information. It offers the professional the opportunity to demonstrate the nursing process in writing in a way difficult to implement in the narrative record.

Ethics

Ethics in health care is often taken for granted. However, certain problems in ethics, for example, those involving confidentiality, come up in our practice every day. Confidentiality does not mean that everything said by a client is top secret. It does mean that all information should be used with discretion. We can share with clients the fact that the reason we gather information is so that we can provide appropriate care.

Referring to the earlier section in this chapter covering the categories of information included in client assessment, one can see that many areas of very personal information are involved. If this information is not respected and kept private and safe by the personnel gathering and using it, such personnel should not be involved in health care.

In some group situations in which parents share their experiences, very personal information is revealed. However, this information is offered voluntarily, and the nurse should not divulge group-shared information without the permission of the client involved.

Establishing a relationship means setting the ground rules and expectations of the relationship so that those involved will know how to behave. Health personnel who disclose very personal client information may not be breaking the law, but they are "breaking the rules." There are certain ethi-

cal guidelines for interpersonal relationships, and good judgment must always be used. Nurses learn about ethics in nursing ethics and philosophy classes, but the direct client interactions in which these ethics are practiced provide the opportunities to develop trust relationships supported by genuine concern and respect for human dignity.

REFERENCES

1   Nunnally, Dianne: "A Nurse Establishes Prenatal Program at Med-School Clinic," *Journal of Obstetric, Gynecologic and Neonatal Nursing*, 3(1):41–47, January–February 1974.
2   Anderson, Edith: "Today's Parents and Maternity Nursing," in Betty Bergerson et al. (eds.), *Current Concepts in Clinical Nursing*, Mosby, St. Louis, 1967, p. 362.
3   Bermosk, Loretta Sue: "Interviewing: A Key to Therapeutic Communication in Nursing Practice," *Nursing Clinics of North America*, 1(2):208, June 1966.
4   Hellman, Louis M., and Jack A. Pritchard: *Williams Obstetrics*, 14th ed., Appleton-Century-Crofts, New York, 1971, p. 494.

BIBLIOGRAPHY

Apgar, Virginia: "Drugs in Pregnancy," *American Journal of Nursing*, 65(3):104–105, March 1965.
Bates, Barbara: "Doctor and Nurse: Changing Roles and Relations," *The New England Journal of Medicine*, 283(3):129–134, July 16, 1970.
Beebe, Joyce E., et al.: "Bench Conferences in a Large Obstetric Clinic," *American Journal of Nursing*, 68(1):85–87, January 1968.
Berggren, Helen J., and Dawn A. Zagornik: "Teaching Nursing Progress to Beginning Students," *Nursing Outlook*, 16(7):32–35, July 1968.

Bishop, Barbara E.: "First OB Nurse Visit—A Tool of Assessment," unpublished paper, 1971.

Cahil, Imogene D.: "Mutual Withdrawal: The Nurse and the Low Scoioeconomic Mother," in Betty Bergerson et al. (eds.), *Current Concepts in Clinical Nursing*, Mosby, St. Louis, 1967, pp. 365–371.

Carrieri, Virginia K., and Judith Sitzman: "Components of the Nursing Process," *Nursing Clinics of North America*, 6(1):115–124, March 1971.

Clark, Al: "The Generation Gap and Childbearing Practice," *Nursing Forum*, 11:177–184, 1972.

Clark, Ann L.: "The Unwed Mother: Design for Nursing Intervention," in Betty Bergerson et al. (eds.), *Current Concepts in Clinical Nursing*, Mosby, St. Louis, 1967, pp. 400–406.

Clausen, Joy P.: "Nursing Leadership of Expectant Parent Discussion Groups," *Journal of Obstetric, Gynecologic and Neonatal Nursing*, 2(3):46–49, May–June 1973.

Fitzpatrick, Elise, et al.: *Maternity Nursing*, 12th ed., Lippincott, Philadelphia, 1971.

Fodor, John T., and Gust Dalis: *Health Instruction: Theory and Application*, Lea & Febiger, Philadelphia, 1968.

Haswell, J. N.: "Clear the Clutter—Problem Oriented Records for OB-GYN," *Medical Record News*, 44(1):64–65, February 1973.

Hennel, Magdalena: "Family-centered Maternity Nursing in Practice," *Nursing Clinics of North America*, 3(2):289–298, June 1968.

Horowitz, Mardit Nancy: "Psychologic Effects of Education for Childbirth," *Psychosomatics*, 8:196–202, July–August 1967.

Iffrig, M. C.: "Body Image in Pregnancy. Its Relation to Nursing Function," *Nursing Clinics of North America*, 7(2), December 1972.

Langner, S. R.: "The Nursing Process and the Interview," *Occupational Health Nurse*, 21: 19–23, December 1973.

Lesser, Marion S., and Vera R. Keane: *Nurse-Patient Relationships in a Hospital Maternity Service*, Mosby, St. Louis, 1956.

McCoffery, Margo Smith: "An Approach to Parent Education," *Nursing Forum*, 6(1):77–93, 1967.

McCulley, Lee B.: "Health Counseling of Women," *Nursing Clinics of North America*, 3(2):263–273, June 1968.

Peplau, Hildegarde E.: "Professional Closeness . . . ," *Nursing Forum*, 8(4):342–360, 1969.

Preparation for Labor: Breathing and Relaxation Techniques, Minnesota Department of Health, Division of Special Services, Section of Maternal and Child Health, Minneapolis, March 1969.

Rubin, Reva: "Maternity Care in Our Society," *Nursing Outlook*, July 1963, pp. 519–521.

———: "Cognitive Style in Pregnancy," *American Journal of Nursing*, 70(3):502–508, March 1970.

Smith, Dorothy M.: "A Clinical Nursing Tool," *American Journal of Nursing*, 68(11):2384, 2388, November 1968.

Standeven, Muriel: "What the Poor Dislike about Community Health Nurses," *Nursing Outlook*, 17(9):72–75, September 1969.

Stroh, Natalie G.: "A Maternity Nurse Practitioner in Public Health Clinics," *Journal of Obstetric, Gynecologic and Neonatal Nursing*, 3:40–42, March–April 1974.

Walker, Lorraine: "Providing More Relevant Maternity Services," *Journal of Obstetric, Gynecologic and Neonatal Nursing*, 3:34–36, March–April 1974.

Weed, L. L.: *Medical Records, Medical Education and Patient Care*, Press of Case Western University, Cleveland, 1971.

Wiedenbach, Ernestine: "Family Nurse Practitioner for Maternal Child Care," *Nursing Outlook*, 13(12):50–52, December 1965.

———: "The Nurse's Role in Family Planning," *Nursing Clinics of North America*, 3(2):355–365, June 1968.

Wonnel, E. B.: "The Expectant Father," *Nursing Clinics of North America*, 6(1):501–603, December 1971.

16

Physiological Changes during Pregnancy and Antepartum Management

COLETTE B. KERLIN AND
A. SYLVIA LEWIS

Pregnancy produces normal physiological adaptive processes in most body systems in order to maintain homeostasis between mother and fetus. The expectant woman's physiology is changed during pregnancy in several ways. First, changes occur in the reproductive organs and breasts to provide for development of the fetus and nutrition for the newborn infant. Second, all metabolic functions are increased to supply sufficient nutrition to the growing fetus. Finally, production of certain placental hormones causes many changes which are related to the maintenance of homeostasis between the woman and developing fetus. An understanding of these altered physiological processes is required for optimal care and management of the pregnant woman.

HUMAN REPRODUCTION AND FETAL DEVELOPMENT

Menstrual Cycle

There are three interacting cycles that control the menstrual cycle: the pituitary, the ovarian, and the endometrial. From day 1 to day 12 of the cycle, the pituitary gland excretes the follicle-stimulating hormone (FSH). This stimulates the secretion of estrogen from the ovary and the development of the graafian follicle. The estrogen from the ovary produces changes in the uterus, and the endometrium thickens. Enzymes, proteins, and water content increase. This is called the proliferative phase. At about day 13 to 14, the pituitary secretes luteinizing hormone (LH), which initiates ovulation and causes FSH to decrease with the formation of the corpus luteum. It also stimulates the theca cells to produce estrogen. At this time, the ovary expels the egg and the endometrium continues to remain about the same. From day 14 to 24, the pituitary excretes the luteotropic or lactogenic hormone (LTH), which stimulates the corpus luteum to produce progesterone. It maintains the corpus luteum until it reaches maturity in about 10 days. The ovary is then in the corpus luteum phase and the endometrium begins the secretory phase. There is further increase in the thickness of the endometrium with deposits of glycogen due to action of progesterone and estrogen. If conception does not take place, estrogen and progesterone levels begin to decrease and the corpus luteum changes to the corpus albicans about days 25 to 28. The endometrial lining desquamates. If conception does take place, chorionic gonadotrophin from the pituitary stimulates the corpus luteum to continue to secrete progesterone and estrogen which keep the myometrium quiescent. In the meantime, in the uterus, the cellular layer of chorion secretes chorionic gonadotrophins. The placenta and decidua are developed and the placenta becomes a source of progesterone, estrogen, and chorionic gonadotrophin. (Refer to Figure 16-1.)

General Structural Characteristics of the Sex Cells

All the genetic material a human being inherits from his or her parents is contained in two sex cells, the egg and the sperm. The human egg is a spherical cell about $\frac{1}{7}$ mm in diameter. Such small measurements are usually given in microns (μ), and 1 micron is 1/1,000th of a millimeter. The diameter of the human egg is about 140 μ. In spite of its relatively minute size, the egg is one of the largest cells in the human body. This exceedingly small unit of material contains the genetic contribution of the woman to her child. The egg cells, or *primary oocytes*, are produced in two ovaries, organs about the size of walnuts, which are attached to the dorsolateral wall of the female abdominal cavity. In the female fetus, as early as the 3d month of gestation, some germ cells have already developed and are in the first stage of meiosis. (See Chapter 12 for further description of the meiotic process.) By the 7th month, almost all the germinal cells have been transformed to these primary oocytes. They remain in this stage until puberty, and only then, under the influence of hormones, does the meiotic process continue with the formation of the spindle and the first reduction division. The above phenomenon has significance in that it has been implicated or associated with the increased incidence of trisomy 21, a variety of Down's syndrome, with increased maternal age. That is, in the female fetus, eggs have already moved into the first stage of meiosis and then remain dormant, some up to the age of menopause. Since proper placement and separation of chromosomes during cell division depends on their attachment to the spindle, increased age may progressively impair this attachment and nondisjunction may occur more frequently.

In the ovaries, then, at the time of puberty, each egg cell (or primary oocyte) is surrounded by a wall or layer of cells called follicular or pregranulosa cells. Concurrent with the growth of an egg cell, the follicle cells multiply and secrete an amorphous or hyalin substance which forms a coating directly around the egg cells. This noncellular area composed of the hyalin substance is called the *zona pellucida*. As the follicular cells continue to multiply, fluid-filled gaps appear between their cells. These spaces increase and coalesce to form a single fluid-filled space which in turn splits the follicu-

lar cells into external and internal layers. Thus a mature ovarian follicle originates. It consists of an outer layer of follicular cells which later will be referred to as the *membrane granulosa*, and a fluid-filled center containing the egg cell, which, in turn, is located within the inner layer of follicular cells (this inner layer of cells is later termed the *corona radiata*). The egg cell and the inner layer of follicular cells remain connected on one side with the outer layer of follicle cells. (See Figure 16-1.)

The ovarian follicle continues to develop, and approaches the surface of the ovary. The increased pressure of the follicular fluid (liquor folliculi) stretches the thin sheets of tissue until the wall of the ovary bursts and

FIGURE 16-1
Section through the ovary showing primary and maturing follicles (×88). (*By permission from L. Langley, I. Telford, and J. Christensen*, Dynamic Anatomy and Physiology, *4th ed., McGraw-Hill, New York, 1974.*)

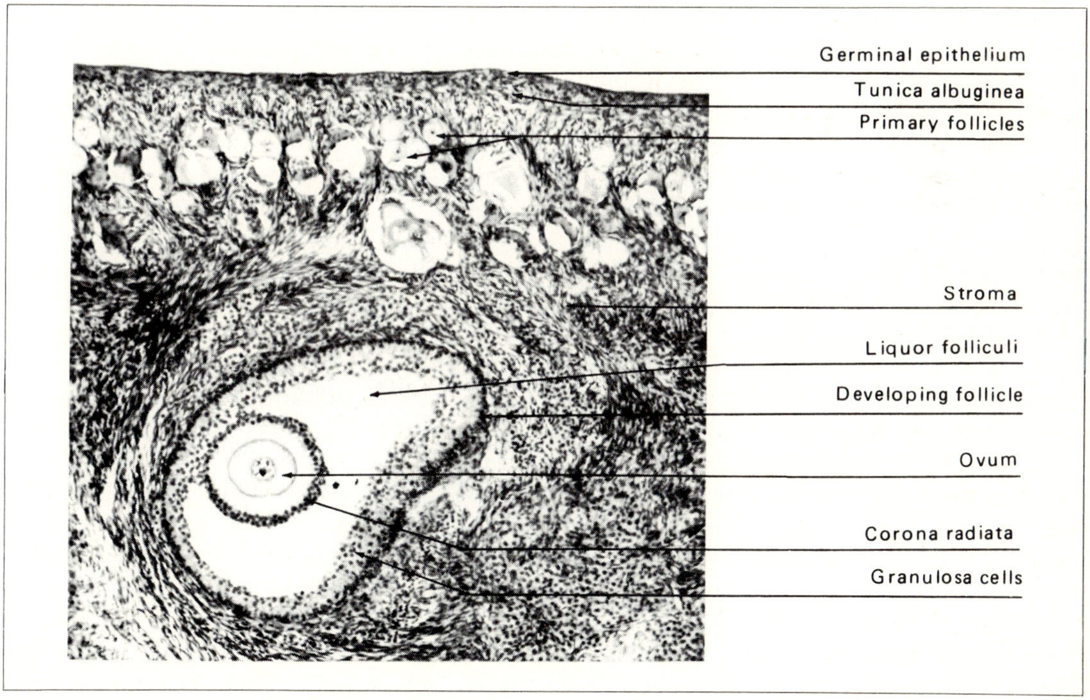

ovulation occurs, releasing the egg cell (*oocyte*) into the abdominal cavity. Here, it enters a funnellike opening of the oviduct or fallopian tube and starts its journey down into the uterus. If the oviduct is free of sperm, the egg cell disintegrates inside the uterus. If, as a result of recent coitus, live sperm are present, the egg may be fertilized in the oviduct and preembryonic development is initiated. While undergoing the first steps of this process, the fertilized egg, now called a *zygote*, moves into the uterus where it becomes embedded in the uterine wall and remains there during the 9 months of antepartum development. Normally, only one mature follicle develops during each monthly cycle. Occasionally, however, more than one follicle matures at the same time, either in the same ovary or both ovaries. Consequently, more than one ripe egg may be present for fertilization at the same time and a multiple pregnancy may occur.

The male genetic contribution to a child is contained in the spermatozoon or sperm cell. Sperm cells are produced in the testes, the primary male sex organs which are located within the scrotum of the external male genitalia. The testes are enclosed by a membrane, the *tunica vaginalis*, under which lies a tough fibrous capsule, the *tunica albuginea*. The latter covering sends septa into the organ, dividing it into lobules. Each lobule contains several coiled seminiferous tubules, each of which empty into a network of channels called the *rete testes*, located on the posterior thickened portion of the tunica albuginea. These channels converge to form the efferent ductules which pass into the long, torturous duct of the epididymis. Near the lower portion of the epididymis (tail), the convolutions cease and the duct forms the *ascending ductus deferens*, which joins the urethra as the latter travels through the prostate gland. (See Figure 16-2.) The epithelium of the seminiferous tubules has a basement

membrane on which lie germinal cells called *spermatogonia* and supporting cells called the cells of *sertoli*. The development of spermatogonia into mature spermatozoa is cyclical; that is, there are four cycles, each lasting 16 days; during this time the germinal cells are transformed into mature sperm cells. Between the seminiferous tubules are clusters of epitheloid cells, called interstitial cells, which secrete testosterone. (See Figure 16-3.)

The cellular structure of the mature sperm cell is less obvious than that of the egg; it consists of several parts, head, middlepiece, and tail. The sperm's overall length is 35 to 60 μ, and the width of the head is 1.4 to 4 μ. Thus it is considerably smaller than the egg. Prior to the maturation process, spermatogonia or the germinal cells present themselves as typical cells, consisting of a mass of cytoplasm and a nucleus. In the course of maturation, striking changes take place. The nucleus becomes smaller and more compact and forms the head of the mature sperm. A minute body in cytoplasm, called the *centriole*, sends out a bundle of fibers which are embedded in a cylinder of cytoplasm and this forms the middlepiece and the tail. Most of the original cytoplasm of the immature spermatogonial cells is cast off and disintegrates in the testes. Another unique feature in the cellular transformation to a mature sperm cell is the formation of the *acrosome*, a structure that contains several enzymes which play an important part in fertilization.

In summary, the major portion of the testes consists of fine tubules, lined with germinal cells, which are constantly being transformed into mature sperm. These are transported and stored in ducts that lead to the outside via the penile urethra. A discharge of human semen consists of more than 200 million sperm suspended in the fluid secretions from glands in the male genital system. The average ejaculate is 3.5 ml, and the average density of sperm is 100 million per ml.

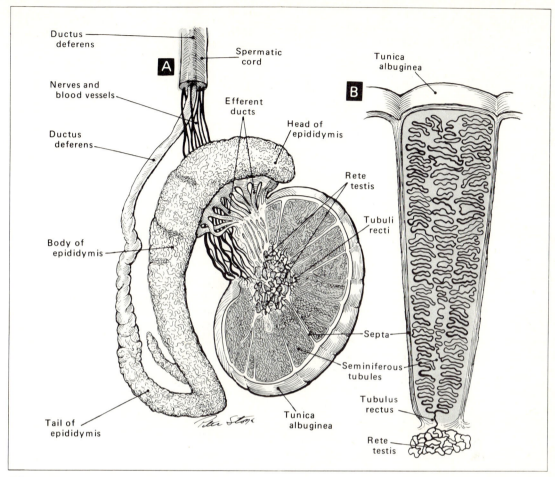

FIGURE 16-2
(A) Epididymis and testis. Testis is shown in sagittal section. (B) A single lobule of
the testis. (*By permission from L. Langley, I. Telford, and J. Christensen,* Dynamic
Anatomy and Physiology, *4th ed., McGraw-Hill, New York, 1974.*)

Studies have indicated that, on the average,
20 to 25 percent of these sperm are in abnormal form (e.g., double or small heads or
tails); and over 75 percent are mobile.[1,2]
Sperm cells are capable of moving 2 to 3 mm
per minute, but their actual speed varies
with the pH of their environment. They are
nonmobile during storage but become highly
mobile in the ejaculate. Their velocity is
probably quite slow in the acid environment

of the vagina but increases after reaching the
alkaline environment of the uterine cavity.
Semen is rich in hyaluronidase, an enzyme
important as a spreading factor which causes
lysis of intercellular mucopolysaccharides.
This facilitates the passage of sperm through
the cervical mucus and penetration of the
cover of follicular cells which surrounds the
egg cell. Approximately 10 to 15 percent of
marriages are childless, and it is estimated

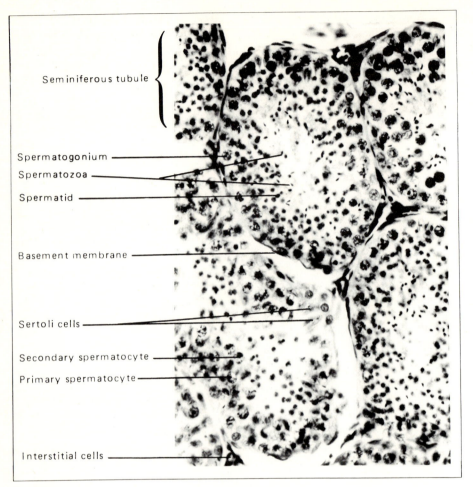

Seminiferous tubule

Spermatogonium

Spermatozoa

Spermatid

Basement membrane

Sertoli cells

Secondary spermatocyte

Primary spermatocyte

Interstitial cells

FIGURE 16-3
Cross section through seminiferous tubules. Mature sperm are at the center of a
tubule. Interstitial cells can be seen between tubules (×265). (*By permission from
L. Langley, I. Telford, and J. Christensen, Dynamic Anatomy and Physiology, 4th ed.,
McGraw-Hill, New York, 1974.*)

that the cause in one-third to one-half is due
to male infertility.[3,4] This may be due to endocrine disorders, defective spermatogenesis, or obstruction of the genital ducts.
Semen analysis may reveal a low seminal
volume (less than 2 ml) or a low sperm count
(less than 20 million per ml). For potential
fertility, at least 40 percent of the sperm

should remain mobile 2 hours after ejaculation, and some should remain mobile for 24
hours. Additionally, the abnormal forms of
sperm should be less than 40 percent. A deficiency of hyaluronidase in the semen as
well as unfavorable conditions of the cervix
may contribute to infertility. These conditions may be revealed by Hubner's test,

which is an examination of the cervical mucus after coitus. The general topic of infertility is discussed in more depth in Chapter 10.

In addition to the changes occurring during the maturation of the sex cells, important alterations take place simultaneously at the chromosomal level. Essentially, the diploid number of chromosomes (46) is reduced to a haploid number (23) by the process of meiosis. As mentioned earlier, the meiotic process in the female has already been initiated during fetal growth. During ovulation, meiosis proceeds to the formation of the *secondary* oocyte stage. In the male, maturation of sperm is complete.

Time Periods of Pregnancy

It is the usual practice to calculate the duration of pregnancy on the basis of menstrual or gestational age. Menstrual or gestational age begins on the first day of the last menstrual period or about 2 weeks before ovulation/fertilization. On the average, 280 days or 40 weeks elapse between the last menstrual period and delivery of a full-term infant; 280 days corresponds to $9\frac{1}{3}$ calendar months or 10 units of 28 days. A unit of 28 days has been commonly referred to as a *lunar month* of pregnancy. In order to evaluate the expected date of confinement or delivery (EDC), one counts back 3 months from the first day of the last menstrual period and then adds 7 days. This method of calculation is referred to as Naegele's rule and is illustrated by the following example: If a woman's last menstrual period began on October 6, 1976 (10/6/76), the EDC would be July 13, 1977 (7/13/77). This method yields only an approximate expected date of delivery; 40 percent of women go into labor within 5 days of the calculated date and nearly 66 percent within 10 days.

The period of gestation or length of pregnancy is usually divided into three units of calendar months, and each unit is referred to as a trimester. These time units have significance, since certain important obstetric events may be categorized by trimesters. In obstetrics, the length of pregnancy is based on the first day of the last menstrual period (gestational age). Embryologists are more exact and cite events of development from the time of ovulation/fertilization (conceptual age). This means there is a difference of 2 weeks between gestational and conceptual age. In the following section, a brief description will be presented on fertilization, cleavage, implantation, and the development of the embryo and fetus. The development of the placenta will be presented in a separate section.

Developmental Stages of the Fetus

The length of time for fetal development is divided into three stages: (1) the preembryonic stage, which covers the first 2 weeks after ovulation/fertilization (conceptual age), or 4 weeks since the first day of the last menstrual period (gestational age); (2) the embryo stage, which covers the 3d to approximately the 8th week after ovulation (conceptual age), or the 5th to 10th week since the first day of the last menstrual period (gestational age); and (3) the fetal stage, which begins at about the 8th week after ovulation/fertilization, or the 10th week from the first day of the last menstrual period.

Preembryonic Stage

This stage covers the developmental events occurring from the time of ovulation/fertilization to the implantation of the blastocyst, approximately 2 weeks. Substages include fertilization, cleavage, and implantation.

FERTILIZATION At the time of ovulation, the fimbriated end of the fallopian tube becomes closely applied to and partially covers the ovary, so that the egg (or secondary oocyte) is swept into the tube. Sperm deposited during coitus travel up through the uterine cavity and enter the tubes within a few hours. Fertilization normally occurs in the outer third portion of the tube. As the sperm approaches the egg, the acrosomal cap of the sperm head dissolves and releases hyaluronidase. This enzyme causes a separation and falling away of the cells forming the corona radiola and facilitates the sperm's penetration through the zona pellucida. When the sperm reaches the oocyte, it adheres to the cell membrane. At this point of contact, the cytoplasm of the oocyte is extruded and engulfs the sperm. This contact also activates the oocyte, which results in complex changes on the oocyte's cellular surface and prevents or reduces the possibility of other sperm entering the oocyte. This activation process also causes the oocyte to complete the second meiotic division of the chromosomes in the cell nucleus or *pronucleus*. The head of the sperm which contains the nucleus (containing the haploid set of chromosomes) increases in size and is now referred to as the male pronucleus; the rest of the sperm (middlepiece and tail) disappears. The male and female pronuclei migrate toward the center of the oocyte's cytoplasm; the pronuclear membranes disappear and the chromosomes become arranged on an equatorial plane. Fertilization results in the restoration of the diploid number of chromosomes, and this results in a cell which is now called a *zygote* (i.e., fertilized egg). Sex of the future individual is determined at this point, depending on whether the oocyte was fertilized by an X- or Y-carrying sperm. It has been estimated that as many as 25 to 40 percent of all fertilized zygotes fail to develop to a point at which there is

either a normal or premature birth. Causes for such loss are manifold, but it is now known that a large fraction (approximately 20 to 50 percent) of abortions expelled spontaneously are chromosomally abnormal. The most common chromosomal aberrations encountered are somatic trisomies and the XO (Turner's syndrome) constitution, which affects the sex chromosome. In addition, in approximately 15 percent of spontaneously aborted fetuses, *polyploidy* (a complete extra set or sets of chromosomes) is also present.[5]

CLEAVAGE AND IMPLANTATION Very soon after the formation of the zygote, cell divisions occur; these initial divisions are referred to as cleavage divisions. These series of divisions result in a mulberry-shaped cellular mass called the *morula*. The morula remains surrounded by the zona pellucida. The cleavage divisions involve a series of rapid mitotic divisions with the synthesis of chromosomal DNA, but without synthesis of additional cytoplasm. The oocyte at the time of ovulation is an atypical cell; that is, it has an enormous amount of cytoplasm compared to the size of its nucleus. Consequently, these cleavage divisions reduce the amount of cytoplasm and return the resulting cells to the usual cytoplasmic-nuclear ratio. These smaller cells are called *blastomeres*; they are highly active and undergo changes of shape and position relative to each other. The morula stage is completed in 3 to 4 days and by then consists of 16 to 32 cells or blastomeres. The time required to reach the completed morula stage is also the same amount of time required for passage through the fallopian tube. During the next 3 to 4 days, while free in the uterine cavity, the morula changes. That is, fluid-filled spaces appear between the centrally placed cells, and soon coalesce to form a cavity. At this point, the morula is transformed into the *blastocyst*.

The blastocyst has an external wall of cells called *trophoblasts;* within the cavity, there is an eccentrically placed inner cell mass. Certain formative cells of the inner cell mass will form the embryo, while all remaining trophoblast cells will form the extraembryonic membranes. On about the 7th day after fertilization, the zona pellucida disappears and exposes the trophoblastic layer of cells. These cells possess active invasive properties which erode the maternal epithelial lining of the uterus and blood vessels. As this erosion takes place, it forms a cavity in the uterine lining into which the blastocyst is embedded. Thus, at approximately $7\frac{1}{2}$ days after fertilization, the blastocyst has initiated implantation (nidation) into the uterine epithelium. The wall of the blastocyst which faces the uterine cavity consists of a single layer of cells; the thicker opposite wall comprises two zones, the trophoblast and the embryo-forming inner cell mass. The walls of the implantation cavity and the attaching trophoblast cells are concerned with the future development of the placenta, and are discussed in a separate section. By this time, the inner cell mass has differentiated so that the cells destined to form the embryo are clearly defined to form a two-layered or bilaminar disc-shaped mass, called the *embryonic disc.* The two layers of cells consist of the *primary endoderm* and the *embryonic ectoderm.*

As the products of conception continue to grow, more maternal uterine epithelium is eroded. As a result, maternal blood forms small lacunae or pools surrounding the blastocyst. At the same time, strands branching off the outer surface of the trophoblastic layer form *primitive villi* which enter into the blood-filled lacunae. These villi, which cover the entire outer surface of the vesicle, eventually disappear except over the most deeply implanted portion which is the future placental site. The inside of the vesicle becomes lined with a membrane, the *chorion.* The cells which form the chorion are derived from the trophoblastic cell layer. At the same time, the amniotic cavity also is apparent and is lined with a membrane, the *amnion.* At this point of development, the product of conception is called the *chorionic vesicle.* By the 12th day after fertilization, cells within the cavity of the vesicle condense to form the body stalk, which will eventually join the embryo to the nutrient chorionic membrane and later develop into the umbilical cord. (See Figure 16-4.) A third layer of cells also becomes apparent, lying between the ectodermal and endodermal layers of the embryonic disc. This intervening layer of cells is called the mesoderm. These three cellular layers give rise to the various organs in the body. The ectoderm forms the entire nervous system, the epidermis, the crystalline lens of the eye, the hair, and the nails. The endoderm gives rise to the lining of the gastrointestinal tract from the pharynx to the rectum; it also forms the liver, pancreas, and thyroid. The mesoderm develops into the dermis, skeletal tissue, connective tissue, the vascular and urogenital system, and most of the smooth and skeletal muscle tissue. Around the 12th day after fertilization, a thickening of the ectodermal layers arising in the middle of the preembryonic disc can be recognized. This area is called the *primitive streak.*

The Embryo Stage

This stage covers approximately 5 weeks, from the 3d to 8th week after fertilization or from the 5th to 10th week after the first day of the last menstrual period. During this time the major organs and structures are formed. By the 3d week of development, the primitive streak becomes a prominent feature which leads to the recognition of the cephalic and caudal ends of the embryo. A

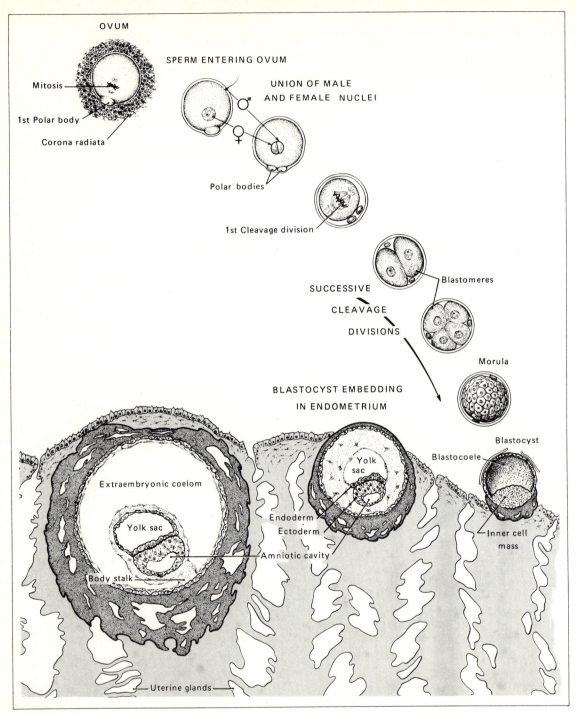

FIGURE 16-4

Early stages of embryogenesis. Schematic illustration showing fertilization, cleavage, blastocyst formation, implantation, and formation of germ-cell layers. The endometrium is shaded. (*By permission from L. Langley, I. Telford, and J. Christensen, Dynamic Anatomy and Physiology, 4th ed., McGraw-Hill, New York, 1974.*)

thickened portion of the ectodermal layer forms the *neural plate* which soon develops into the *neural groove* and, eventually, the *neural tube*. At the same time, the mesodermal layer is divided into segmented blocks called *somites*. These give rise to skeletal and connective tissues, muscle, and the dermis. The cephalic end of the embryo remains relatively large during the embryonic period, and development of structures follows a cephalocaudal sequence. By the 4th week, the formative heart is quite prominent and pulsations have begun; arm and leg buds are present, and the amniotic membrane is beginning to ensheathe the body stalk. During the 6th week of development, the fingers and

toes are beginning to appear. In addition, beginnings of the external ear, oral and nasal structures, and the eyes are becoming apparent. The external genitals are apparent, and the sex glands have become differentiated into either female or male gonads. Centers of ossification also begin to appear. (See Figure 16-5.)

The enlarging uterus can be felt bimanually by the end of the 4th week after fertilization or 6 weeks after the beginning of the last menstrual period. Morning nausea and vomiting may begin at this time as well as an increase in urination due to the enlarging and anteflexed uterus. Breast tingling may also be reported. By the end of the 6th week

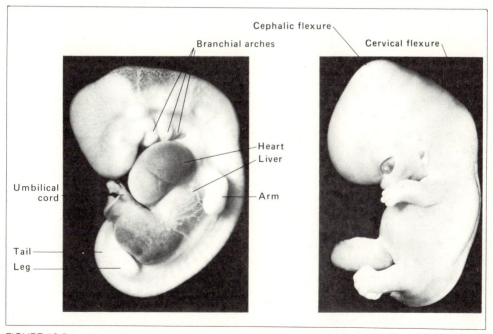

FIGURE 16-5
Photographs of a thirty-one-day old embryo on the left and a forty-day old embryo on the right. The limb buds on the right show beginning finger and toe differentiation. Note the more advanced development of the upper limb. (*By permission from L. Langley, I. Telford, and J. Christensen, Dynamic Anatomy and Physiology, 4th ed., McGraw-Hill, New York, 1974; Chester F. Reather, Photographer, Carnegie Institution of Washington.*)

of growth, the product of conception measures 3 by 5 cm and the embryo is 2.5 cm. The uterus is 6 by 10 cm; Hegar's, Goodell's, and Chadwick's signs are also present. At the end of the embryonic stage, the embryo has assumed a characteristically human form, and the length is approximately 4 cm.

Fetal Stage

The fetal stage arbitrarily begins during the 8th week after fertilization and continues until the birth of the infant. Few if any new structures develop, and the fetal stage is characterized by cellular growth, maturation, and changes in proportions of the structure. By the end of the 10th week after fertilization, the fetus is 7 to 9 cm in length. Centers of ossification have appeared in most bones; fingers and toes are differentiated and have nails. The external genitalia are beginning to show sexual differentiation, and the fetus may make spontaneous movements. By the end of the 14th week (16 weeks postmenstrual), the external genitalia are sufficiently differentiated to be able to definitely distinguish the sex of the fetus. Between 14 and 18 weeks (or 16 and 20 weeks postmenstrual), fetal movement (quickening) may be felt by the mother and fetal heart tones may be auscultated with a fetoscope. By the end of the 18th week (20 weeks postmenstrual), the fetus weighs approximately 300 g and the maternal fundus has grown to the level of the umbilicus. The fetus shows the presence of downy hair, or *lanugo,* and *vernix caseosa,* a white cheesy substance on parts of the body. The fetus has attained the weight of 600 g, and deposits of fat occur by the end of the 22d week (24th week postmenstrual). At the completion of the 26th week (28th week postmenstrual), the fetus weighs approximately 1,000 g. The thin skin is red and covered with vernix caseosa. If the fetus is born at this time, the survival rate is approxi-

mately 32 percent.[6] With an additional 4 weeks in utero, the fetus attains a weight of 1,700 g and chances of survival are greatly improved. By the end of the 34th week (36 weeks postmenstrual), the fetus weighs 2,500 g and deposits of subcutaneous fat give a more rotund appearance to the body. Infants born at this time have an excellent chance of survival if given proper care. Term pregnancy is reached at 38 weeks after fertilization, or 40 weeks after the last menstrual period, and the fetus is fully developed.

Development of the Placenta

The placenta is an organ derived from fetal and maternal tissues. Its main functions are nutrition of the fetus and the maintenance of physiological exchanges between the mother and the fetus. The placenta consists of the chorion, amnion, and umbilical cord (all derived from fetal tissue), and decidua basalis of maternal endometrium. As mentioned earlier, the fertilized ovum is covered with the chorionic trophoblastic layer of tissue during the first few weeks after implantation. During this stage, nutrition is provided to the growing ovum by trophoblastic digestion of the uterine endometrium. This trophoblastic period of nutrition lasts through approximately the 12th week of pregnancy (postmenstrual age). It may be recalled that by the 3d week after fertilization, the embryonic heart begins to function; in addition, the forming blood vessels in the trophoblastic villi coalesce with those in the chorionic membrane and body stalk to produce an early functioning circulatory system. By the 12th week, this system has developed to a point where nutrition of the growing embryo is adequately sustained by the developing placenta. Since the fertilized ovum is abundantly nourished by the chorionic trophoblastic villi, it grows rapidly, exerting pressure in all directions on the surrounding uterine endometrial tissue (also called *decidua*). The thinner covering of decidua which faces the uterine cavity is called the *decidua capsularis;* the deeper layer which lies between the ovum and uterine musculature is called the *decidua basalis.* The remaining endometrial lining of the uterus is called the *decidua vera* or *parietalis.* These various portions of the decidua are identified in Figure 16-6. The chorionic villi in contact with the decidua basalis proliferate to form the *chorionic frondosum;* this structure, by the end of the 12th week of pregnancy (postmenstrual), in combination with the decidua basalis, forms the placenta. It may be noted that the chorionic villi in contact with the decidua capsularis eventually cease to grow, and degenerate.

Certain villi of the chorionic frondosum extend into the decidua and act as anchoring villi; most villi, however, end freely in the intervillous spaces where they are bathed in the circulating maternal blood. As the placenta develops, these early or initial villi (called *stem villi*) branch repeatedly, forming progressively finer subdivisions and greater numbers of small villi which contain fetal blood capillaries. Fetal blood flows into the capillaries of the placental villi, and nutrients diffuse from the maternal blood circulating in the intervillous spaces across the placental villi into the fetal blood supply. Each main stem villi and its ramifications constitute a placental or fetal cotyledon. These cotyledons are separated by fibrous tissue walls called *septa;* the number of main cotyledons is fairly constant, approximately 10 in number. The gross anatomic structure and blood circulation of the placenta are depicted in Figure 16-7.

At term, the placenta is discoid in shape, weighs approximately 500 g, and is approximately 15 to 20 cm in diameter and 2 to 3 cm in thickness. It is generally located in the an-

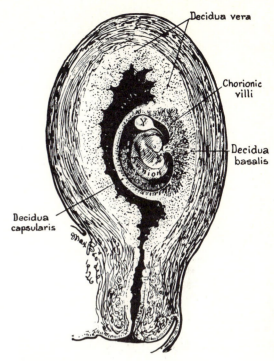

FIGURE 16-6
Diagram of more advanced stage of pregnancy. The label Y stands for yolk sac. (*By permission from Louis M. Hellman and Jack A. Pritchard,* Williams Obstetrics, *14th ed., Appleton-Century-Crofts, New York, 1971.*)

terior or posterior portion of the uterus near the fundus. The fetal side is covered by the transparent amnion, beneath which chorionic vessels course; on the maternal side, the irregular lobes or cotyledons can be distinguished.

Uterine Changes

The increased size of the uterus during pregnancy is due to hypertrophy of the muscle cells and stretching. The uterine walls are thicker during early pregnancy than in the nonpregnant state. With continuing gestation, however, the walls thin. During early

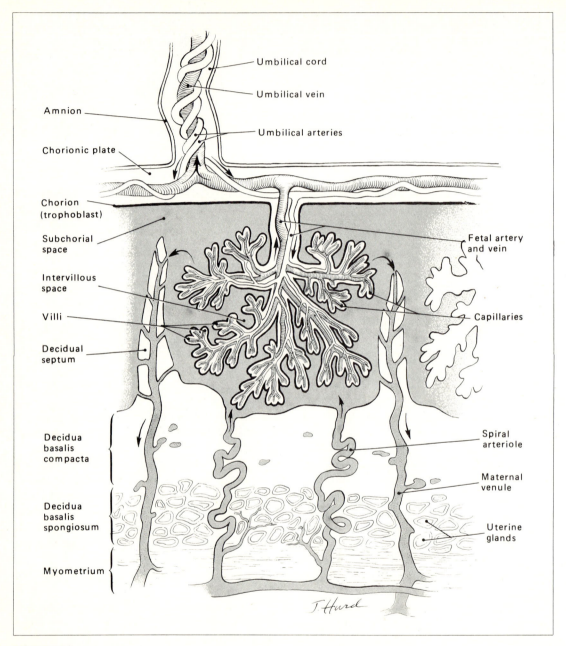

FIGURE 16-7
Section through the placenta. Nutrients, gases, and wastes are exchanged across intervillous space. Arrows indicate the direction of flow. Blood from the embryo moves from the placenta through umbilical veins and returns by way of umbilical arteries. (*By permission from L. Langley, I. Telford, and J. Christensen, Dynamic Anatomy and Physiology, 4th ed., McGraw-Hill, New York, 1974.*)

pregnancy, the uterine walls lose resistance and firmness, and later in pregnancy, the uterus becomes a muscular sac with easily indented thin soft walls. This is why one can palpate the fetus by palpating the abdomen and why the uterus yields to fetal movement.

Uterine enlargement is mostly in the fundal portion. The part of the uterus around the placental site enlarges more quickly than other areas. The middle layer of the uterus is the portion in which most of the blood vessels are found. They lie between an interlacing network of muscle fibers, which provide a protective mechanism after delivery because as the muscles contract, they constrict the blood vessels. During the first few weeks of pregnancy, the uterus maintains its pear shape; then it changes to a more globular form in the corpus and fundus, until by the 3d month, it is spherical. Later it becomes ovoid as the length increases more than the width.

The upper border of the fundus will be found midway between the umbilicus and the symphysis pubis by the 4th month. The fundus can be measured with a tape measure and will be found to be about 1 cm above the symphysis pubis for every week of pregnancy up to about 32 weeks. The pregnant uterus is quite mobile.

PHYSIOLOGICAL CHANGES IN BODY SYSTEMS

Hair, Skin, Eyes, and Nose

Hair

There can be depression, stimulation, or no change in rate of hair growth during pregnancy. There are two phases to hair growth, the growing phase and the resting phase. The latter phase ends with depilation. During pregnancy there is a decrease in hair loss as there is a decrease in the percent of hair follicles that are in the resting phase. During the postpartum period there might consequently be a loss of hair as the hair readjusts to the usual cycle of growing and resting. The sebaceous glands might provide more or less sebum. If more oil is produced, the hair might become dull and hard to handle.

Skin

The pituitary gland secretes a melanocyte stimulating hormone which controls melanin pigmentation. There is an increase in this hormone from the 2d month of pregnancy to term. This leads to pregnancy-related development of chloasma, darkened nipples and vulva, the linea nigra, and increased growth and darkening of existing nevi. This pigmentation will decrease after pregnancy but will not completely disappear.

There is an increased sensitivity to ultraviolet light from the 2d to the 7th month. Some pregnant women might have to refrain from overexposure to sunlight and use protective substances. The white or red line created by dermography stays for a longer period of time in 75 percent of pregnant women.

There is an increase in sweating during the last trimester of pregnancy due to an increase in the thyroid hormone, which leads to feelings of heat and erythema of the skin. There also can be a prickly heat rash which can be relieved by cooling the environment and decreasing the humidity.

Heavy women might get maceration in areas where skin surfaces are in contact such as the breasts, groin, axilla, and abdomen, if these areas are not kept dry. If the skin should break down, it needs to be treated by thorough cleansing, drying by exposure to air, and dusting with powder as there is danger of secondary infection by *Candida albicans*. Twenty percent of pregnant women harbor *Candida albicans* during pregnancy.

If this should happen, the macerated area would be overgrown with pustules.

There is controversy as to whether there is an increase or decrease in sebum from the sebaceous glands. Higher levels of progesterone lead to an increase in sebum, and circulating estrogens inhibit the sebaceous glands. Some women have a "glow" to their complexion while others develop skin eruptions. An increase in corticosteroid hormones weakens the elasticity of the muscles, contributing to the possible development of abdominal striae.

Eyes

There is an increase in pigmentation of the lids. Some women develop slight myopia. Many opthalmologists believe, however, that pregnancy is not the time to do routine refractions, but prefer to wait until the eyes revert to the prepregnant state. There can also be temporary changes in the curvature of the cornea, and contact lenses should not be fitted at this time. In examining visual fields, concentric field contractions may be found. This could be from fatigue and is considered functional.

Nose

Pressure from increased blood flow to the nasal mucous membrane leads to an increased incidence of epistaxis. There is also an increased incidence of noninfectious rhinitis and sinusitis. There might be nasal stuffiness, watery discharge, or postnasal drip. On examination of the nose, swollen, moist, red, mucous membrane and turbinates may be seen. It is thought that this is a vasomotor response to a local disturbance of the autonomic nervous system. Drugs must be used conservatively in pregnancy; however,

a nasal spray containing a corticosteroid and vasoconstrictor (except Privine) can be used if the symptoms become very disturbing.

Cardiovascular System

Certain physiological changes occur in the cardiovascular system during pregnancy, and one of the most striking alterations is the volume of circulating blood. Recent investigations report an average increase of 48 percent in plasma volume over the prepregnant state; red blood cell volume (a component of total blood volume) also increases by an average of 32 percent. Pritchard reports the average nonpregnant blood volume to be 3,200 ml and the red blood cell mass to be 1,355 ml.[7] At term of a normal single fetus gestation, the values increase to 4,820 and 1,790 ml, respectively. The amount of increase varies with individuals; some show only a modest increase while others nearly double the volume existing in the prepregnant state. In addition, twin gestations average an increase of 67 percent in blood volume over the prepregnant state.

The change in total blood volume during pregnancy is typically characterized by the following pattern: There is a moderate increase in volume by the end of the first trimester; a more marked increase is noted during the second trimester; and during the last trimester, the volume continues to rise slightly, then plateaus during the last few weeks. Initially, plasma and water volume are relatively greater than the production of red blood cells. In late pregnancy, the reverse situation occurs. Overall, however, the increase in plasma volume is disproportionate to that of red blood cells. Consequently, the average hematocrit value is lower during pregnancy. This phenomenon is commonly referred to as physiological anemia of pregnancy. That is, without iron supplements, the average hematocrit may be as low as 35.8 percent (the normal prepregnant value is 41.7 percent). If iron is readily available, the *average* hematocrit can be raised to 37 percent. Hemoglobin concentration also decreases as a result of hemodilution. When the plasma volume is at its maximum, the mean hemoglobin concentration is at its lowest value, i.e., 11 to 12 g per 100 ml; usually if the hemoglobin is 10.6 g or below, this is regarded as a pathological anemia. The increase in circulating red blood cells is due to an acceleration of production rather than a prolongation of the life-span of the red blood cell. The stimulus for the increased production is not clearly defined, although it is thought to be related to the increased production of erythropoietin due to the influence of certain placental hormones. Since there is an increase in red blood cell production, there is a need for increased iron intake particularly during the second and third trimester.

Hypervolemia associated with pregnancy serves to meet the demands of the enlarging gravid uterus and to safeguard the woman and her fetus from adverse effects associated with supine and erect posture of the woman. In addition, this increased blood volume extends the safety limits for the woman and her fetus at the time of parturition, since the average total blood loss at this time is estimated to be approximately 500 ml.

Other components of the blood also change during pregnancy. The leukocyte blood count varies considerably; the usual range is from 5,000 to 12,000 per ml. Certain clotting factors are increased, and this is viewed again as a safeguard against hemorrhage. The most significant increase is seen in the plasma fibrinogen concentration, which increases by approximately 50 percent. (The mean nonpregnant value is 300

mg per ml; the pregnancy mean is 450 mg per ml.) Maternal plasminogen (profibrinolysin) also increases; however, fibrinolysis or clotlysis is distinctly prolonged compared to the normal nonpregnant state. Symptomatic thrombosis is uncommon during pregnancy despite an increase in several blood procoagulants, reduced fibrinolytic activity, and stasis of blood in the lower half of the body imposed by pregnancy.

During pregnancy, the diaphragm is progressively elevated, and consequently the heart is displaced to the left and upward as well as being rotated slightly on its axis. The heart increases in size by approximately 10 percent over the prepregnant state due to myocardial hyperplasia. Certain systolic heart murmurs are heard during pregnancy and are believed to be due to the displacement of the heart and the associated great vessels. The work of the heart during pregnancy is increased. Cardiac output (the amount of blood flow per minute) is increased by approximately 30 to 40 percent (that is, 1.2 to 3.1 liters per minute). Most of the increase is established by the end of the first trimester and is maintained at this level until term. The increase in cardiac output is related largely to an increase in stroke volume (amount of blood pumped by the heart per beat). The heart rate also increases slightly; the maximum increase is approximately 10 beats per minute. Arterial blood pressure changes are minimal during pregnancy. Systolic pressure remains essentially the same or slightly lower during pregnancy, while the diastolic pressure is significantly lower during early and midpregnancy. Return to normal prepregnant volumes occurs during the last trimester.

Venous blood pressure in the lower extremities during the latter part of pregnancy is position-dependent. That is, in an erect or supine position, femoral venous pressure steadily rises from 8 to 24 cm of water pressure. This retardation of blood flow in the lower extremities is due entirely to the pressure of the enlarging uterus on the pelvic veins and the inferior vena cava. Venous pressure returns to normal when position is changed from supine to a lateral recumbent position. Mechanical obstruction to venous flow due to the increasing weight of the uterus contributes to the development or aggravation of leg and vulva varicosities. In addition, it contributes to dependent edema of the lower extremities which occurs in approximately 40 percent of normotensive pregnant women.

Peripheral resistance is decreased during pregnancy. It may be recalled that arterial blood pressure remains essentially the same during pregnancy, and cardiac output increases. It follows then that peripheral resistance must decrease. During the second trimester, vasodilation occurs, particularly in the hands. Microscopic studies reveal the dilation of the capillary vascular bed as well as an increase in the number of capillaries. Dilation of the small cutaneous vessels causes the formation of so-called "spiders," a common feature of the pregnant state. The increased peripheral flow also has been associated with the increase in fingernail growth. This increased peripheral flow apparently acts to maintain a thermal balance in the pregnant woman. The developing fetus produces heat which is dissipated by the woman by increasing skin blood flow. The causative mechanism involved for the increased peripheral blood flow is not definitely known, although a release in vasoconstrictor tone has been implicated.

A final important point needs to be presented relative to the effects of posture during pregnancy on the dynamics of the cardiovascular system. As mentioned earlier, a supine position has an associated increase in venous pressure in the lower extremities due to the enlarging gravid uterus. This is due to the *partial* or *complete* occlusion of the inferior vena cava by the uterus. Studies dealing with the effect of the pregnant uterus on compression at the vena cava indicate that, in addition to the increase in venous pressure, there is also an associated drop in cardiac output; at the same time arterial blood pressure remains unchanged.[8] Blood pressure is maintained by an increase in systemic vascular resistance, and return venous blood flow is maintained by collateral venous systems (the azygous and vertebral veins). However, a small number of pregnant women (approximately 5 percent) experience hypotension when reclining in a supine position. Associated with this supine hypotension syndrome is bradycardia, pallor, hypoxia, sweating, and syncope. There is also an associated drop in fetal heart rate and fetal hypoxia. Relief is obtained immediately when the woman turns to a lateral recumbent position. In cases where the supine hypotension syndrome occurs, the alternate routes of collateral venous channels mentioned above are inadequate. Recent studies also indicate that a supine position has an associated decrease in uterine arterial pressure, and in cases of hypotension, this is even more markedly decreased. These changes in hemodynamics certainly have implications for positioning pregnant patients who are placed on bed rest as part of their medical/nursing regimen.[9]

Respiratory System

Pulmonary function changes to some extent during pregnancy. The primary respiratory function is to maintain optimal partial pressures of oxygen and carbon dioxide throughout the tissues. Due to the enlarging uterus, the diaphragm is elevated and impinges upon the base of the lungs, which results in a decrease in the air volume in the lungs at the end of a normal expiration (called functional residual capacity). In addition to the elevation of the diaphragm, the rib cage expands; this is related to a hormonal influence which increases the mobility of the rib attachments, and the phenomenon is similar to the changes taking place in other skeletal joints. The expansion of the thoracic cage leads to an increase in circumference of about 6 cm and in transverse diameter of 2 cm.

Pulmonary tests show the respiratory rate and the total volume (the amount of air breathed with an ordinary respiration) to be increased. Consequently, the minute volume (amount of air ordinarily breathed per minute) is also increased by 40 percent. This increase is more than adequate to meet the 10 to 15 percent increase in oxygen consumption needed during pregnancy. This physiological hyperventilation is believed to be related to the change in progesterone level.

The mucous membrane of the nasopharynx and larynx is frequently hyperemic. This condition in the latter trimester affects the vocal cords, and as a result, voice changes may be noticed during pregnancy.

Gastrointestinal System

The changes which occur in the gastrointestinal tract are the result of hormonal as well as mechanical factors. The gums often become hyperemic, spongy, and swollen, and the incidence of gingivitis increases. Bleeding of the gums often ensues after brushing the teeth. Occasionally, a focal vascular swelling of the gums may occur, a condition called *epulis of pregnancy,* which usually regresses after delivery. This change in the condition of the gums is believed to be due to the influence of increased estrogen levels, which affect the ground substance of the gum tissue. It has been observed that the activity of the salivary glands is also increased.

Teeth that have been well cared for show no tendency for increased caries during pregnancy.

Elective surgery or reconstructive procedures requiring a lot of drilling should be postponed. Preventive dental care should include daily flossing and thorough brushing with a soft toothbrush.

The common complaint of heartburn during pregnancy is due to the reflux of acidic secretions passed from the cardiac sphincter into the lower portion of the esophagus. This is due in part to the altered position of the stomach due to the enlarging uterus. In addition, the musculature of the stomach is generally now relaxed and motility is decreased; this situation is apparently the result of the effects of high levels of progesterone and contributes to the reflux of acidic secretions. With some women the amount of gastric secretion is reduced, while with others there seems to be no change in secretory activity during pregnancy. Since the motility of the stomach is decreased, the emptying time is also prolonged. The general lack of tone and decreased motility may be related to the common tendency of nausea and vomiting. However, hormonal changes affecting the metabolism of carbohydrates are also implicated in contributing to this phenomenon. Decreased motility and general reduction of muscle tone also occur in the small and large intestine. In the small intestine, increased time for passage of food allows a longer time for digestion and absorption, and gut function here has been reported to be improved. For example, the absorption of iron increases by nearly threefold. As stated above, the large intestine also has a general relaxation of smooth muscle structure. There is also an increased absorption of water; consequently, constipation is another common complaint during pregnancy. The reduction in muscle tone also occurs in the gallbladder, and emptying time is prolonged. This coupled with the fact that the bile becomes more concentrated and viscous during pregnancy favors the formation of cholelithiasis.

Renal System

The ureters dilate as early as the 10th week of pregnancy. This was formerly attributed to general smooth muscle atony caused by progesterone. Recent research indicates that the right ureter dilates more than the left with involvement of the renal pelvis. These changes are more often found in primigravidas and often decrease after 6 months of pregnancy, especially on the left side. This has led to other theories of causality. The lesser dilation of the left side may be the consequence of cushioning by the sigmoid colon. The right-side dilation may be due to compression of the ureter by the dilatation of the ovarian venous plexus, the iliac artery, or dextrorotation of the uterus. There is also angulation of the ureters.

The renal plasma flow is higher in pregnancy, with a decrease at the end of pregnancy. It is believed that the decrease at the end of pregnancy might be postural. The gravid uterus places increased weight on the renal veins when the woman lies on her back. Consequently, renal function tests, in order to be accurate, should be done in the lateral recumbent rather than the supine position.

Renal blood flow is also increased during pregnancy. However, it falls slightly throughout pregnancy because of decreasing hematocrit levels. The average level in the second trimester is 1,200 ml per minute, falling to 1,100 at 34 weeks; the average nonpregnant level is 800 ml per minute. The glomerular filtration rate is also raised during pregnancy. This accounts for glucosuria, urinary excretion of a number of vitamins, and aminoaciduria. Some studies indicate

the rate is increased throughout pregnancy, while others show there is a fall as term gestation is approached.[10] The glomerular filtration rate increases as much as 50 percent by the second trimester. The concentrations of creatinine and urea decrease during pregnancy due to the increased glomerular filtration rate. At times urea levels might be so low as to suggest liver disease. Urea and creatinine clearance are higher in pregnancy and their plasma levels are lower. Davison and Hytten found 24-hour creatinine clearances of 150 ml per minute the first half of pregnancy, and 130 ml per minute in the third trimester.[11] Plasma urea-nitrogen levels found by Sims and Krantz were 8.7 ± 1.5 mg from the 15th week of pregnancy to term, compared to 13.1 ± 3.0 mg in nonpregnant women.[12] Uric acid clearance is also elevated. The serum levels of uric acid in nonpregnant women are 3.86 mg per 100 ml compared to 2.72 mg before 16 weeks, 2.60 mg between 17 and 28 weeks, and 3.61 mg after 28 weeks in pregnant women.

In pregnancy, the total amount of sodium in the body is higher than in the nonpregnant state and is mostly found in the expanded maternal extracellular water space. However, the sodium concentration and osmolality are lower than in the nonpregnant state. This would usually cause the kidney to take corrective measures, but since this does not happen, it can be assumed that this is important in preserving a new homeostasis. The mechanism that controls excretion of sodium exhibits some changes. About 60 percent more sodium is filtered and most recovered, probably at the proximal tubule. The release of renin through angiotensin and aldosterone might be triggered by the high sodium levels in urine when it reaches the terminal nephron. The greatest amount of sodium and water is excreted at night, especially if the woman has edema. This is because of changes in gravity, with the vascular compartment receiving what is like an isotonic saline infusion.

Little is understood about the function of the renin-angiotensin system in the body. In pregnancy, the enzyme renin increases 5 to 10 times. Angiotensin is formed by the action of renin on plasma x2 globulin substrate. This protein, along with others, has a higher concentration when estrogen is administered. A study by Gordon, Parson, and Symonds found that women who later developed preeclampsia had higher renin activity. This led to the hypothesis that angiotensin might play a role in abnormal rises of blood pressure.[13] Another possible effect of the system might be stimulation of aldosterone production, which is high in pregnancy as the result of the body's need to respond to the sodium-depleting effects of progesterone.

Glucose excretion is common in pregnancy. There are many individual excretion differences among pregnant women in amount, time of day, and regularity. This is probably because with the increased glomerular filtration rate, the tubules can not reabsorb all that is presented to them. Lactose and fructose secretion is also increased, along with ribose, xylose, and fucose. Lactosuria increases from 12 percent in the first trimester to 50 percent during the third trimester. Amino acid excretion is up in pregnancy, perhaps because of increased circulating cortisol. Also, water-soluble vitamins are excreted in higher amounts during pregnancy. Early in pregnancy there is a diuretic response to ingested water. Later in pregnancy there is a tendency to retain water. Hytten et al. found an increase in pregnancy of 6.8 to 7.2 liters of body water with edema in the legs.[14] If the water content of the placenta, amniotic fluid, and fetus is summed, it accounts for 3.5 liters. Increase in size of breasts and uterus and the increased blood volume accounts for the other 3 liters.

According to Hellman and Pritchard, water retention is due to many factors, many of which are not known, but the following factors can be identified as playing a role:

1. Effective intracapillary hydrostatic pressure favors filtration from vascular bed.
2. The effective colloidal osmotic pressure of the plasma limits filtration and effects reabsorption of filtered water.
3. Increased capillary permeability.
4. Sodium retention.[15]

There is little change in the bladder until the 4th month of pregnancy after which there is an increase in size. There is hyperemia and hyperplasia of muscle and connective tissue which raise the *trigone* and cause a thickening of the posterior or interureteric margin. The deepening and widening of the trigone continue. After the fetal head is engaged, the base of the bladder is pushed forward and upward, which makes diagnostic and therapeutic procedures difficult. In addition, the pressure of the presenting part on the bladder and surrounding tissue hinders the drainage of blood and lymph and can lead to edema and possible trauma to the bladder. These conditions predispose the woman to urinary tract infections.

Another predisposing factor to urinary tract infections is the high nutrient content of the urine. If stasis in the urinary tract exists, an ideal culture media in which bacteria can colonize is created.

Endocrine System and Metabolism

Placental Hormones

The hormone chorionic gonadotrophin is used in most pregnancy tests. It maintains the corpus luteum during early pregnancy until the steroids needed for development can be sufficiently produced by the fetal-placental unit. It can be found in the urine as early as the 26th day, and peaks between the 60th and 70th day. This early occurrence of chorionic gonadotrophin makes it possible to run relatively accurate pregnancy tests early enough so that an unwanted pregnancy might be aborted if this is the choice of the client. The levels then drop between the 100th and 130th day. Serum levels run 10 units per ml at the first missed menses to 100 units per ml between the 60th and 80th day after the last menstrual period.

The physiological effects of this hormone on the placenta, fetus, and the pregnant woman are not known. Relationships such as human chorionic gonadotrophin acting as a stimulus for the fetal adrenal cortex and maternal adrenal gland in estrogen synthesis have been studied, but no conclusive evidence has arisen.

Chorionic somatomammotropin (CSM) can be detected as early as the 3d week after ovulation/fertilization. Its role is mediated by the woman, not the fetus, as it is found primarily in the woman's circulation. It plays a preparatory role for lactation and has a role in various metabolic activities. It is a source of energy for maternal metabolism in that it induces lipolysis and elevates free-floating acids. Because of this, glucose and protein are spared by inhibiting gluconeogenesis and glucose metabolism. Protein synthesis is favored, and a source of amino acids is mobilized for transport to the fetus, which is the result of CSM's insulinogenic action leading to high levels of maternal insulin. It is assumed that CSM aids fetal growth by maintaining a steady flow of chemical energy from the mother to the fetus. Maternal serum levels differ between some complicated pregnancies and normal pregnancies, leading some to believe that a distressed fetus may be detected by measuring serum levels.

Investigations are now being done to determine if the levels might be indicative of placental functions.

Estriols are produced by the placenta. There is a rise in urinary and blood levels throughout pregnancy. The average blood levels are about 14 mg at 32 weeks, rising to 26 mg at term. However, there is considerable variation found among clients and among the times of day the samples are drawn. Samples taken at 4:30 P.M. are lower by an average of 25 percent than those taken at 8:00 A.M., indicating a diurnal variation. Estriol levels are used to indicate placental function and fetal condition. Upon fetal death, there is a marked reduction in urinary and serum estriols. Due to variations from times of day the samples are taken and normal variations among clients, it is essential that serum-level results be used which are taken at the same time of day. "Except in the anencephalic fetus, levels of three to four milligrams a day in the third trimester indicate fetal death or difficulty."[16]

A woman carrying an anencephalic fetus has about one-tenth the amount of estrogen in her urine as a woman carrying a normal fetus. It is believed that the adrenal cortex of the fetus is the site of origin for substances which serve as precursors for placental estrogens. The major role is to control the function and growth of the uterus.

The polymerization of acid mucopolysaccharides may be altered by estrogens. This leads to water retention in the skin during pregnancy as the hygroscopic qualities of mucopolysaccharides is increased. It also may have an effect on the ability of the cervix to stretch in late pregnancy. This results from altered polymerization, which affects the chemical-physical properties of substances which act as adhesives between fibers in collagenous tissues; the cervix is high in collagen.

It was formerly believed that estrogen and progesterone had an effect on breast development—estrogen for duct growth and both for lobule alveolar development. In lower animals only prolactin is needed, so the question remains whether they play a role in human breast development.

Estrogen may cause leukocytosis during pregnancy. It probably is in part responsible for serum protein alteration, including clotting factors and increased avidity of binding proteins. The increased sensitivity of the respiratory centers may also be due to estrogen.

The placenta produces more progesterone than estrogen. There is an increasing amount of pregnanediol excreted in urine which reaches a plateau at about 32 weeks. The placenta utilizes precursors supplied by the mother. The main purpose is to protect the fetus by reducing uterine muscle tone because hollow organs have a tendency to expel their contents.

It has long been thought that progesterone reduces the muscle tone of smooth muscle like the stomach and colon. However, labor starts when progesterone levels are at their highest. It is thought that progesterone might act centrally by influencing the hypothalamic centers or by suppressing oxytocin at the source.[17] It has been suggested that progesterone might render the uterine membrane inexcitable by preventing the movement of calcium and promoting the firm binding of calcium in the myometrial cells.[18]

The secretion and vascularity of the cervix, the growth of the uterus, and the extensive storage of depot fat in pregnancy might be governed by progesterone. There is also evidence that it induces overbreathing, which reduces arterial and alveolar P_{CO_2}.[19]

There is an indication that the fetus uses progesterone to build molecules such as hydrocortisones. Fetal tissues conjugate neutral steroids; pregnenolone is formed in the placenta and is a precursor of neutral steroids used in the formation of estrogens. The functional significance of this is not known.[20]

Maternal Hormones

The thyroid gland enlarges during pregnancy and can be manually palpated. There is increased vascularity and hyperplasia of the glandular tissue. The metabolic activities of the products of conception and the increased body surface of mother and fetus increase the body's need for oxygen, and the basal metabolic rate increases. The thyroid hormone increases in the plasma in the 2d month of pregnancy. The level then plateaus until the time of delivery. The level at plateau is 7 to 12 μg per 100 ml protein-bound iodine compared to 4 to 8 μg in the nonpregnant state. This incorrectly suggests a hyperthyroid state. The thyroxin-binding proteins are increased due to the increase in circulating estrogens.

The pituitary gland increases some in size. Pituitary somatomammotropin (PSM) decreases during pregnancy, while CSM is abundant in the pregnant woman's blood. After delivery the CSM disappears rapidly and the PSM levels remain low for some time. The lack of these anti-insulin hormones might account for reduced insulin requirements of diabetic women early in pregnancy.

There is little known about the function of the parathyroid during pregnancy. Pregnant women who have a low calcium intake make a physiological adjustment by secondary hyperparathyroidism in order to maintain homeostasis for mother and fetus.

There is little change in the adrenal gland, although there is an increase in cortisol, both unbound and that bound to the protein transcortin. Cortisol is metabolized at a slower rate due to the effect of estrogen. It secretes more aldosterone so that by the third trimester, 1 mg per day is secreted. More aldosterone is secreted if sodium intake is decreased. Increased aldosterone is created by increased levels of renin, angiotensin, and renin substrate. It has been suggested that the protection against the sodium-depleting effect of progesterone is from the elevated levels of aldosterone.[21]

In addition to the physiological changes presented earlier, alterations in protein, fat, and carbohydrate metabolism also occur in response to the growing fetal-placental unit. However, the effects of placental, maternal, and fetal hormones on these processes and the interrelationship among them in regulating energy metabolism in the mother and fetus are poorly defined at this time.

An extensive storage of fat takes place during early and midpregnancy. It has been postulated that this mechanism serves to protect the mother and fetus at times of prolonged starvation or hard physical exertion. During the second half of pregnancy, the previously stored lipids are released to free fatty acids and serve as a source of fuel in the maternal peripheral tissues and diminish maternal glucose utilization. There is substantial evidence which indicates that human placental lactogen (alternatively called human CSM) is closely implicated in the adaptation of carbohydrate-lipid metabolism in late pregnancy. This mechanism is currently viewed as an adaptation for the rapidly growing energy requirements of the fetus nearing the end of gestation. Since an alternative source of fuel (free fatty acids) is supplied to the mother, glucose, which is the principal energy source for fetal protein synthesis, is more available for the maternal brain and for transfer to the fetus.

Fasting blood sugar and mean daily blood sugar are found to be decreased during pregnancy. The daily averages for pregnant and nonpregnant individuals are 80 mg per 100 ml and 99 mg per 100 ml, respectively. In addition to the reduced amount of circulating blood sugar, there is an increase in circulating insulin during pregnancy. However, there is a more rapid enzymatic destruction of insulin by the placental insulinase. The increased secretion of insulin and its rapid destruction consequently can tax the maternal economy of insulin to the extent that diabetes mellitus may first become manifest during pregnancy.

SIGNS AND SYMPTOMS OF PREGNANCY

Signs and symptoms of pregnancy are divided according to presumptive signs of pregnancy, probable signs of pregnancy, and positive signs of pregnancy.

Presumptive Signs of Pregnancy

Presumptive signs of pregnancy include conditions which may indicate the possibility of pregnancy but which also could be caused by other factors.

Cessation of Menses

When conception takes place, the pituitary secretes chorionic gonadotrophin. This stimulates the corpus luteum to continue producing estrogen and progesterone so that the endometrial lining does not desquamate; hence cessation of menses occurs.

Breast Changes

The breasts become tingly and tense due to hormonal changes. Hypertrophy of the alveoli causes the breasts to become nodular.

The veins of the breast can often be seen. Increased pigmentation causes nipples and the areola to darken.

Nausea and Vomiting

Some women experience morning sickness (nausea and vomiting). Physiologically this is probably due to changes in carbohydrate metabolism. This may begin at the time of the first missed menstrual period and usually ceases by the end of the first trimester.

Discoloration of Mucosa and Skin of the Vulva and Vagina

Chadwick's sign, or the bluish appearance of the vagina and cervix, is found upon examination. This is due to the increased vascularization of the area.

Urinary Disturbances

As the uterus increases in size, but has not yet risen out of the pelvis, there is a frequency of urination. This is due to the pressure on the bladder from the enlarging uterus.

Fatigue

Another symptom causing clients some discomfort in the first trimester is fatigue. This is due to the decreased basic metabolic rate and decreased blood sugar.

Probable Signs of Pregnancy

Elevated Chorionic Gonadotrophin

A urine sample is taken and a variety of immunoassays or bioassays may be run to detect pregnancy. The basis for these tests is that chorionic gonadotrophin is present in the woman's plasma and is thus excreted in the urine.

Enlargement of the Abdomen

This is more pronounced in multiparas who have lost much of their muscle tone. Sometimes the uterus sags forward and downward so as to produce a pendulous abdomen as the result of flaccid muscles. There is less abdominal prominence in the supine position.

Cervical Changes

Increased congestion due to increased vascularization causes a softening of the cervix called Goodell's sign. The softening of the isthmus is called Hegar's sign.

Ballottement

A sudden light fingertap on the abdomen during the 4th and 5th months of pregnancy causes the fetus to sink in the amniotic fluid and then rebound to the finger. This is due to the fact that the fetus is small in relation to the amount of amniotic fluid.

Braxton Hicks Contractions

These are painless contractions of the uterus and start early in gestation.

Positive Signs of Pregnancy

Outlining the Fetus

One can palpate and at times visually detect fetal parts in the second half of pregnancy. The gestational sac, illustrated by a white ring in the fundus of the uterus, can be detected by ultrasound (which is harmless to the fetus) around the 6th week of pregnancy. It is usually after the 5th month that the fetal skeleton can be detected by x ray.

Fetal Heart Tones and Fetal Movement

About the 20th to the 22d week of pregnancy, fetal heart tones can be heard with a fetoscope. The fetal heart tones range from 120 to 160 beats per minute. By placing the hand on the abdomen, fetal movements can be felt after the 5th month of pregnancy.

Other Associated Signs and Symptoms

Other signs and symptoms that are not included under presumptive, probable, or positive signs of pregnancy may cause clients some concern.

An increase in acidity in the mouth stimulates the salivary glands to secrete more saliva so women might complain of increased salivation. During the second trimester, the woman may become physiologically anemic. This is due to increasing circulating blood volume without an increase in red blood cells. This is not a problem if the woman takes in adequate iron, maintaining hemoglobin levels above 12 g or hematocrit above 35 percent. The joints of the pelvis become more movable due to the hormone relaxin. This causes a characteristic waddling gait. Stretching of the round ligaments and consequent muscle spasm can cause sharp pains that radiate to the groin. The basic metabolic rate increases, giving the pregnant woman more energy and generally a feeling of well-being.

The pH of the vagina varies from 3.5 to 6 due to increased lactic acid from increases in vaginal glycogen. The high acidity of increased vaginal secretion protects against bacteria prone to live in a high alkaline environment. However, candidiasis and trichomoniasis are common during pregnancy due to increased glycogen content and are difficult to control during pregnancy. Itching and burning create much discomfort. Other nonspecific vaginal infections are also common. A mucus plug is also formed in the cervix to prevent bacteria from entering the uterus. These conditions increase the amount of vaginal discharge.

Chloasma, or the mask of pregnancy, can occur along the nose, cheeks, and forehead. Vascular spiders due to large amounts of estrogen may appear on the breasts, face, neck, chest, and arms. Striae gravidarum, or stretch marks, may appear on the abdomen, upper arms, and thighs. The linea nigra, a dark line, appears from the umbilicus to the symphysis pubis. All of these disappear or diminish in intensity after pregnancy, but they may create body image anxieties during pregnancy.

MANAGEMENT OF PREGNANCY

Pregnancy produces normal physiological adaptive processes in most body systems in order to maintain homeostasis between mother and fetus. An understanding of these adaptive physiological processes is certainly required for optimal care and management of the pregnant woman. This section of the present chapter augments Chapters 15, 17, 18, and 19, which deal with nursing management during the antepartum period. It is suggested that the reader relate the physiological changes presented here to the detailed information on nursing management given elsewhere.

The knowledge of the physiology of pregnancy is necessary to assess and diagnose the progress of pregnancy and to detect high-risk pregnancy. It is important in explaining signs and symptoms to the client, and in offering advice on measures that can be used to decrease the discomfort of some signs and symptoms and minor complications.

Data are assessed at each visit to ensure the normal progress of pregnancy. Pregnant women are seen on a routine basis. The progressive routine moves from every 4 weeks to every week as the pregnancy advances. It can be advantageous to see the client weekly from 18 weeks gestation until fetal heart tones are heard. Determining when fetal heart tones are heard is an important piece of data, as is eliciting information as to quickening, menstrual history, and height of the fundus, in establishing the accuracy of the EDC.

At each visit urine should be tested for protein and sugar to detect signs of preeclampsia and diabetes. Weight should be taken to be sure weight gain or loss is not excessive. Vital signs are monitored including fetal heart tones.

A study by Gant et al. might change procedures in blood pressure taking between 28 and 32 weeks. In the study, 15 of 16 patients who had a positive supine pressor response developed pregnancy-induced hypertension. A positive supine pressor response is indicated when there is a 20-mm rise in diastolic pressure between the lateral position and the supine. Of the 22 patients with a negative supine pressor response, 20 of 22 remained normotensive. They found a positive correlation between increased sensitivity to infused angiotensin II and a positive supine pressor response.[22]

Hematocrits are repeated at 28 and 34 weeks; a vaginal beta streptococci culture is run at 34 weeks.

At every visit the increase in size of the uterus should be noted by measuring the distance from the symphysis pubis to the top of the fundus. This is called McDonald's measurement. The fundus will be about 1 cm above the symphysis pubis for every week during gestation until about 34 weeks. After this point the measure is not very accurate. The fundus is at the umbilicus at 24 weeks. If the fetus is large enough to palpate, fetal weight and size, presentation, and position can be estimated by abdominal palpation. These assessments should be made at every visit to keep a running data base of pregnancy. Leopold's maneuver can be used to assess these data. (See Figure 16-8.) If the fetal size is inadequate for gestational age, an ultrasound examination might be ordered by the physician.

First Trimester

The first need is to gather base-line data from a history, physical examination, and laboratory data. A history form is presented in Chapter 15. It is the most essential component of management. It provides a focus for the physical examination and additional laboratory work to be done as well as areas of counseling and teaching needed. The physical examination should be complete so as to detect any possible diseases that the client might have and of which she may not be aware.

Determining the last menstrual period is important. After the client relates the date of her last period, a description of the previous period is then requested. Many women will have slight vaginal bleeding at the time their period would have been due. It is not uncommon for some women to have some bleeding during the first trimester. If a woman has been taking birth control pills, it takes 40 to 60 days to establish a normal menstrual period, so it is important to find out if she has been taking the pill, how long she has been off the pill, and the nature of her periods since coming off the pill.

It is also important to elicit information regarding the signs of pregnancy. This can be used as substantiating data. The woman's

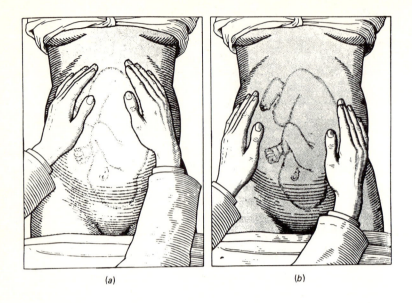

(a)   (b)

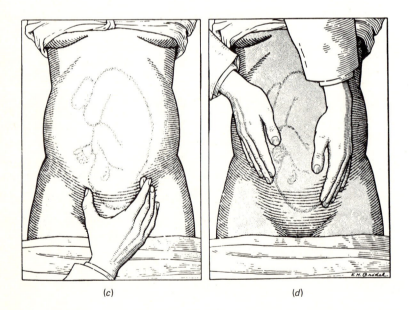

(c)   (d)

FIGURE 16-8
Palpation of left occiput anterior position (maneuvers of Leopold). (*By permission from Louis M. Hellman and Jack A. Pritchard, Williams Obstetrics, 14th ed., Appleton-Century-Crofts, New York, 1971.*)

height and weight should be ascertained and information collected about the average weight before pregnancy and at the beginning of pregnancy. This is to determine if there has been excessive weight gain. Even though there is not as much emphasis on weight gain as in the past, excessive weight gain can cause the same kind of problems obesity causes. It places an extra burden on systems of the body, especially the cardiovascular system, which must perform additional work because of the products of conception. Excessive weight is not easy to remove and can create problems relating to body image. (See Chapter 17.)

On physical examination some normal physical differences will be found in pregnant women as compared with nonpregnant women. (See section above, Physiological Changes in Body Systems.)

The thyroid might be slightly enlarged. The heart rate increases steadily until about 30 weeks to an average increase of 10 to 15 beats a minute over normal. The systolic and diastolic blood pressure will be a little below the nonpregnant state. Pulmonic and apical systolic murmurs might be heard. If diastolic murmurs are heard, they are always pathological. There will be a strong supraclavicular pulse.

A pelvic examination should be done. The cervix is examined for its condition and for Chadwick's sign of pregnancy. The size of the uterus is ascertained and evaluated in relation to the last menses. The cervix and uterus are examined for softening. Internal pelvimetry is ascertained. (See Chapter 15.) The vagina is examined for color changes, vaginal discharges, and herpes. The vulva is examined for discoloration or lesions.

Laboratory data are collected. A complete blood count, hemoglobin, hematocrit, serologic test for syphilis, rubella titer, and blood sugar are determined. A urine specimen is tested for protein and sugar. A Pap smear is performed, as is a culture for gonorrhea. Laboratory normals for blood are as follows:

Component	Amount
RBC	4.2–5.4 ml/mm^3
WBC	5,000–10,000 mm^3
Reticulocytes	0.5–1.5%
Platelets	150,000–250,000
Hematocrit	37–47%
Hemoglobin	12.3–16.7 g/100 ml

A rubella titer less than 1/20 indicates there is not adequate immunity to rubella.

Clients should be informed that if they have any signs such as swelling of the hands and feet, vaginal bleeding, continuous or severe headaches, dimness or blurring of vision, abdominal pain, chills and fever, persistent vomiting, dysuria, or loss of fluid from the vagina, they should seek medical help.

If a client complains of nausea and vomiting, the nurse might suggest trying more frequent small feedings, eating crackers before arising, staying in bed for a while in the morning, not brushing her teeth right away, or eating a dry breakfast. Assure the client that these symptoms usually disappear by the 4th month.

Fatigue may last up to the end of the first trimester. In the meantime, naps may be suggested to ameliorate fatigue.

Breast tingling and urinary frequency will pass by the end of the first trimester. Alert the client to watch her dietary intake because there will be an increase in appetite. (See Chapter 17.)

Vaginitis is not uncommon. *Candida albicans* causes severe itching and a cottage-cheese-like discharge. The vulva becomes red and edematous and the cervix is reddened. *Trichomonas* yields an odorous greenish gray discharge which is foamy and bubbling. The cervix is a speckled red color.

Both male and female should be treated. Gonorrhea yields a copious discharge. The vagina and cervix are red. If the cervix is manipulated, it is tender to the touch. The culture incubates on chocolate and blood media in a carbon dioxide environment. It takes 1 to 2 days to receive the laboratory report. Penicillin is the drug of choice for treatment if not contraindicated by client allergy.

Second Trimester

The second trimester tends to be the most labile of all trimesters. Expectant mothers generally feel good. Increased blood flow to the periphery causes the loss of heat to the extremities. This can cause some discomfort and one should reassure the client that this symptom is normal. The most uncomfortable problem of this trimester is heartburn and gas, due to relaxation and compression of the stomach and a decrease in gastric motility. Antacids that do not contain sodium can be suggested. It might also help to put the head of the bed on blocks to relieve the pressure of the fetus on the stomach. If certain foods cause heartburn, the client should not include them in her diet.

The client might also complain of sharp pain in the lower lateral region of the abdomen as the result of round ligament stretching. The only aid is reassurance and explanation of causality.

If measurements of the size of the uterus are small for dates or large for dates, an ultrasound may be ordered to rule out intrauterine growth retardation, multiple birth, or polyhydramnios. Possible placenta previa is an indication for ultrasound.

Third Trimester

There are many discomforts that might cause concern to clients in this trimester. Anemia caused by disproportionate increase in plasma volume and red blood cells may be present. Consequently, hematocrits should be checked at 28 and 34 weeks. An iron supplement may be prescribed by the physician.

If the client complains of leg cramps, information should be elicited which reveals the calcium intake from food and pills. Calcium needed daily during pregnancy is $1\frac{1}{2}$ g. From studies carried out with animals, it has been shown that muscle contractions are stronger with increased amounts of calcium.[23] If the calcium intake is found to be very high, the nurse can suggest a decrease in calcium intake. A lack of calcium can create a tetany response. If this occurs, instruct the client to place her hand on the ball of the foot and bring the foot forward. In addition, the client may also need to rub the muscle spasm. The client should also be counseled to increase her intake of foods rich in calcium. Her physician may prescribe supplementary calcium.

During pregnancy, the center of gravity might be out of line because poor abdominal muscle tone allows the uterus to fall forward. The lumbar curve is exaggerated, putting a strain on that area. Poor body mechanics in lifting, stooping, working, etc., can cause a strain on the lumbar area. The relaxation of the pelvic ligaments can cause backache. Evaluation and teaching about posture and use of a firm mattress should be done. Pelvic rocking is a very good exercise for relief of backache, as is adequate rest with good alignment. The expectant mother might need a supportive girdle. Teach the client proper means of lifting, utilizing the proper body mechanics, and the use of firm supportive shoes.

Another possible complaint is varicosities of the legs, vulva, or anus caused by problems in venous return created by the pressure of the enlarging uterus. To help prevent leg varicosities, the client should be encouraged to rest with her legs elevated periodically throughout the day; support hose will be of help. Exercise, adequate diet, stool softeners, and adequate fluid intake should help to prevent hemorrhoids. Witch-hazel compresses as well as topical anesthetics and warm soaks can be used to relieve the discomfort of hemorrhoids. If varicosities of the vulva develop, a foam rubber pad held by a sanitary belt can be used for support. Advise the client to sleep on her side if possible, for lying on the back increases venous pressure.

To relieve dyspnea caused by pressure on the diaphragm from the enlarged uterus, the nurse can suggest placing blocks under the head of the bed. Sleeping with more than one pillow often relieves this symptom.

Urinary tract infections are fairly common in the last trimester. If the client complains of burning, pain, urgency, or frequency, a urinalysis for culture and sensitivity to antibiotics should be run. Treatment is initiated depending upon the number of gram-negative bacteria found in the urine.

Another problem in late pregnancy is edema. Edema needs to be assessed in feet and legs and hands and face. Amount of edema present can be evaluated by depressing the skin and observing how fast it rebounds. There are conflicting ideas as to the indication for restricting sodium. If hypervolemia which is present in pregnancy sensitizes the vascular receptors to the effects of endogenous amines or peptides, excessive salt could be harmful. If the vasoconstriction of preeclampsia is due to an overcompensation to intravascular volume contraction, then salt restriction could be harmful. Most research seems to suggest a middle-of-the-road approach: salt to taste, but keep from excessive indulgence. There are many risks associated with diuretics and there is no proof that they are beneficial; therefore, they are not used for edema unless associated heart disease is present. The best treatment for asymptomatic edema is bed rest, with the woman lying on her side to enhance diuresis.[24]

Heartburn can continue to be a problem. Urinary frequency returns as the fetus descends into the pelvis.

As term approaches, a vaginal examination should be done to evaluate the condition of the pelvis and its readiness for labor. When a client goes past term, an amnioscope might be used to be sure the amniotic fluid is clear. To evaluate the maturity of the fetus, an amniocentesis might be done or serial serum estriols might be drawn.

REFERENCES

1 Williams, P. L., and C. P. Wendell-Smith: *Basic Human Embryology*, 2d ed., Lippincott, Philadelphia, 1969, p. 26.

2 Stern, Kurt: *Principles of Human Genetics*, Freeman, San Francisco, 1972, pp. 13–15.

3 Williams and Wendell-Smith: op. cit., p. 26.

4 Assali, N. S. (ed.): *Biology of Gestation*, vol. I, Academic, New York, 1968, pp. 67–76.

5 Stern: op. cit., pp. 131–133.

6 Kempe, C. Henry, Henry K. Silver, and Donough O'Brien: *Current Pediatric Diagnosis and Treatment*, 3d ed., Lange, Palo Alto, Calif., 1973, p. 16.

7 Pritchard, J. A.: "Changes in Blood Volume during Pregnancy and Delivery," *Anesthesiology*, 26:393–399, 1965.

8 Hellman, Louis M., and Jack A. Pritchard: *Williams Obstetrics*, 14th ed., Appleton-Century-Crofts, New York, 1971, p. 258.

9 Ibid., p. 259.

10 Davison, J. M., and F. E. Hytten: "Glomerular Filtration during and after Pregnancy," *Journal of Obstetrics and Gynecology of the British Commonwealth*, 81:588–595; cited in F. E. Hytten (ed.), *Clinics in Obstetrics and Gynecology*, Saunders, Philadelphia, August 1975, p. 350.

11 Ibid., p. 347.

12 Sims, Earl, and K. E. Krantz: "Serial Studies of Renal Function during Pregnancy and the Puerperium in Normal Women," *Journal of Clinical Investigation*, 37(1):64, 1958; cited

in Frank Hytten and Isabella Leitch, *The Physiology of Human Pregnancy*, Blackwell, Oxford, 1971, p. 156.

13 Gordon, R. D., S. Parsons, and E. M. Symonds: "A Prospective Study of Plasma-Renin Activity in Normal and Toxemic Pregnancy," *Lancet*, 1:347, 1969; cited in Frank Hytten and Isabella Leitch, *The Physiology of Human Pregnancy*, Blackwell, Oxford, 1971, p. 156.

14 Hytten, F. E., A. M. Thomson, and N. Taggart: "Total Body Water in Normal Pregnancy," *Journal of Obstetrics and Gynecology of the British Commonwealth*, 73:553, 1966; cited in Louis M. Hellman and Jack A. Pritchard, *Williams Obstetrics*, 14th ed., Appleton-Century-Crofts, New York, 1971, p. 248.

15 Hellman and Pritchard: op. cit., p. 249.

16 Hellman and Pritchard: op. cit., p. 183.

17 Hytten, Frank E., and Isabella Leitch: *The Physiology of Human Pregnancy*, Blackwell, Oxford, 1971, p. 191.

18 Ibid., p. 190.

19 Ibid., p. 192.

20 Fuchs, Fritz: *Endocrinology of Pregnancy*, Harper & Row, New York, 1971, p. 92.

21 Hytten and Leitch: op. cit., p. 228.

22 Gant, N. F., S. Chand, R. J. Worley, J. Whally, U. D. Crosby, and F. C. MacDonald: "A Clinical Test Useful for Predicting the Development of Acute Hypertension in Pregnancy," *American Journal of Obstetrics and Gynecology*, September 1974, pp. 1–8.

23 Williams, Sue R.: *Nutrition and Diet Therapy*, Mosby, St. Louis, 1973, p. 1288.

24 Lindheimer, M. D., et al.: "Sodium and Diuretics in Pregnancy," *New England Journal of Medicine*, 288:891–894, April 1973.

BIBLIOGRAPHY

Adams, D., J. Carney, and D. Dicks: "Pregnancy Gingivitis: A Survey of 100 Antepartal Patients," *Journal of Dentistry*, 2:106–110, 1974.

Aladjem, Silvio, and Audrey K. Brown: *Clinical Perinatology*, Mosby, St. Louis, 1974.

Barnes, Allen C.: *Intra-uterine Development*, Lea & Febiger, Philadelphia, 1968.

Beazley, J. M., and K. Bingham: "Changes in Hair and Skin Condition during Pregnancy," *British Journal of Clinical Practice*, 27:425–428, 1973.

Bonica, John J.: "Maternal Respiratory Changes during Pregnancy and Parturition," *Clinical Anesthesia*, 10:1–19, 1974.

Boots, Larry, J. B. Younger, J. W. Mullis, and L. R. Beck: "Endocrinology of the Maternal-Feto-placental Unit—Use of Serum Estrogens as a Practical Index of Fetal Well Being," *American Journal of Obstetrics and Gynecology*, 120:515–524, September 1974.

Bowes, Watson A., Yvonne Brachbill, Esther Conway, and Alfred Steinschneider: *Monographs of the Society for Research in Child Development*, University of Chicago Press, (137)35 (4), June 1970.

Brewer, D., and R. Aubry: "The Physiology of Pregnancy, Clinical Pathologic Correlations," *Post-graduate Medicine*, 52:110–114, 1973.

Gaspard, U., H. Sandpunt, and A. Lyckx: "Glucose-Insulin Interaction and the Modulation of Human Placental Lactogen (HPL) Secretion during Pregnancy," *Journal of Obstetrics and Gynecology of the British Commonwealth*, 81:201–209, 1974.

Kerr, M.: "The Mechanical Effects of the Gravid Uterus in Late Pregnancy," *Journal of Obstetrics and Gynecology of the British Commonwealth*, 72:513–529, 1965.

Lynfield, Y. L.: "Effect of Pregnancy on the Human Hair Cycle," *Journal of Investigative Dermatology*, 35:323–326, 1960.

Reed, Duncan E., and C. D. Christian (eds.): *Controversy in Obstetrics and Gynecology*, Saunders, Philadelphia, 1974.

Rovinsky, Joseph J., and Alan F. Guttmacher (eds.): *Medical, Surgical, and Gynecologic Complications of Pregnancy*, 2d ed., Williams & Wilkins, Baltimore, 1965.

Rovinsky, J., and R. Jaffin: "Cardiovascular Hemodynamics in Pregnancy," *American Journal
of Obstetrics and Gynecology,* 93:1–15, 1965.
Victor, J. J.: "Normal Blood Sugar Variations during Pregnancy," *Obstetrica et Gynecologica
Scandinavica,* 53:37–40, 1974.

Walters, W., and L. Yean: "Changes in the Maternal Cardiovascular System during Human
Pregnancy," *Survey of Gynecology and Obstetrics,* 131:765–784, 1970.

17

Nutrition during Pregnancy and the Postpartum Period

R. LA JEUNE BRADFORD

The nurse's nutrition role during pregnancy may be as simple as instructing a pregnant woman who has been eating a nearly adequate diet to drink a little more milk, or it may be as complicated as understanding the scientific basis of the role of nutrition in the development of the fetus. Between these two extremes there is knowledge and understanding that can help women with simple or complex nutrition problems. This chapter presents some scientific evidence which describes the importance of nutrition in pregnancy, but it focuses primarily upon the role of the nurse in the nutrition care of pregnant women.

This is a revision of the chapter written by Joan E. Carter for the first edition of *Maternity Nursing Today* (1973). The chapter was revised by R. La Jeune Bradford in her private capacity. No official support or endorsement by the Public Health Service, U.S. Department of Health, Education, and Welfare, is intended or should be inferred.

IMPORTANCE OF NUTRITION DURING PREGNANCY

It is well known that an infant starts as a single fertilized cell that is not even visible to the eye. If all goes well, about 9 months later a baby is born, consisting of billions of cells, complete with flesh, bones, blood, and other tissues. Between conception and birth, the fetus obtains materials for body-building from food the expectant mother eats and nutrients stored in her body. It was once thought that the fetus was a perfect parasite, able to obtain all needed nutrients from the mother regardless of her food intake. There is now considerable evidence that the fetus may be damaged when the woman's nutrient stores are poor and when her calorie and nutrient intake during pregnancy is inadequate. Similarly there is convincing evidence that well-nourished pregnant women have fewer complications and healthier babies than poorly nourished women.

There are two kinds of research related to nutrition during pregnancy. First, there are studies of nutrient and food intakes of groups of pregnant women which are compared with the course and outcome of pregnancies. Second, there is basic nutrition research which shows the functions of nutrients during pregnancy.

Nutrient Intake Related to Pregnancy Outcome

Strong evidence of the relationship of maternal nutrition to the outcome of pregnancy is reported in the following studies. Frequently cited studies during World War II point to a definite relationship between the adequacy of the woman's diet and the outcome of pregnancy. In a report by Antonov[1] on children born during the siege of Leningrad in 1942 during which time both the quantity and quality of food were poor, he reports an inci-

dence of 41.2 percent premature births during the period of food shortage compared with 6.5 percent when food was not so scarce. Newborn mortality for prematures was 30.8 percent, whereas for full-term babies it was 9 percent. Stillbirths more than doubled during this period. Antonov concluded that severe quantitative and qualitative nutritional deprivation of the woman decidedly affects the development of the fetus and the vitality of the newborn. During the wartime food shortage in Holland, Smith reports widespread amenorrhea among the women and a markedly reduced birth rate.[2,3] Infants conceived before the months when food was short but born during the hunger period were significantly below expected heights and weights; Smith suggests that this can be correlated with maternal nutrition during the last trimester of pregnancy. He reported a slight increase in prematurity.

Burke and her coworkers[4,5] found in a study at Boston Lying-In Hospital that every stillborn, every infant who died within a few days of birth (except one), all prematures, all functionally immature infants, and the majority of infants with congenital malformations were born to women with very inadequate diets. In this study the diets of the women and the condition of the infants were evaluated. The woman's diet was rated as "excellent," "good," "fair," or "poor." The infants at birth and during the first 2 weeks of life were rated by pediatricians who had no knowledge of the mothers' dietary ratings. The ratings of the infants were then correlated with the ratings of the mothers' antepartum diets. They found that when the maternal diet had been excellent or good that 95 percent of the infants were in excellent or good condition, and only 5 percent were in fair or poor condition. On the other hand, when the maternal diet had been poor only 8 percent of the infants were in excellent or good condition, but 65 percent were in poor condition, and 27 percent were in fair condition.

In a later study by Jeans et al. of 404 pregnant women in a Midwestern state, it was reported that all the stillbirths, all the neonatal deaths, and all the infants with congenital anomalies were born to women whose diets were poor or very poor.[6] Also, the incidence of prematurity rose sharply with the decrease in nutritional status of the women, and the premature infants born to poorly nourished women were smaller and weaker than premature infants born to better nourished women.

Evidence is accumulating from both animal experiments and observations of human pregnancies that serious malnutrition during pregnancy may result in impaired mental functioning of the offspring.[7]

Kilocalorie and Nutrient Needs

Since pregnancy is normal, a pregnant woman's nutritional status and her diet should be thought of as contributions to normal processes leading to the birth of a healthy, full-term baby; they should not be thought of as means of forestalling or treating possible complications.[8]

The earlier interest in diet in pregnancy was stimulated by a desire to have smaller babies—at that time many women's pelvises were contracted as a result of rickets and deliveries were difficult. Today, interest is focused on reducing the incidence of births of underweight babies.[9] Such babies are more likely to die, to become mentally retarded, or have other handicapping conditions.

During pregnancy there is an increased need for kilocalories and nearly all nutrients. The recommended dietary allowances of the Food and Nutrition Board of the National Academy of Sciences for nonpregnant and pregnant women of childbearing ages are found in Table 17-1.[10] These allowances

have been designed to maintain good nutrition in practically all healthy people in the United States. These allowances include only about one-third of the nutrients known to be essential for humans. More research must be done before allowances can be established for other essential nutrients, and it is even possible that some essential nutrients have not yet been discovered.

Kilocalories

Fetal growth, which means tissue growth, requires energy, and the increase in maternal tissues during pregnancy also requires energy. The energy in foods is expressed as *kilocalories* (kcal), the scientific term for calories. An additional 300 kcal is recommended during pregnancy for building fetal and placental tissue, for storing fat as an energy reserve for lactation, for supporting the increase in the woman's basic metabolic rate, and for providing energy to move the woman's greater body weight. In addition, adequate kilocalories are needed to guarantee that protein will be used for building tissue and will be stored in the pregnant woman's body; when kilocalories are inadequate, protein is used for energy.

Adequate weight gain is considered very important to the successful outcome of pregnancy.[11–13] Three important factors are: (1) the total amount of weight gain, (2) the pattern of the gain, and (3) the quality of the diet responsible for the weight gain.

An average weight gain during pregnancy of 24 lb [11 kg] (range 20–25 lb [9 to 12 kg]) is commensurate with a better than average course and outcome of pregnancy. This would be a gain of 1.5 to 3.0 lb [625 to 1,250 g] during the first trimester and a gain of 0.8 lb [370 g] per week during the remainder of pregnancy. There is no scientific justification for routine limitations of weight gain to lesser amounts.[14]

TABLE 17-1
Recommended Daily Dietary Allowances[a]

	Age, years	Weight, kg	Weight, lb	Height, cm	Height, in.	Energy, kcal	Protein, g	Fat-soluble vitamins Vitamin A activity, RE[b]	Vitamin A activity, IU	Vitamin D, IU	Vitamin E activity,[c] IU
Females	11–14	44	97	155	62	2400	44	800	4,000	400	12
	15–18	54	119	162	65	2100	48	800	4,000	400	12
	19–22	58	128	162	65	2100	46	800	4,000	400	12
	23–50	58	128	162	65	2000	46	800	4,000	...	12
Pregnant						+300	+30	1,000	5,000	400	15
Lactating						+500	+20	1,200	6,000	400	15

Water-soluble vitamins

Ascorbic acid, mg	Folacin,[d] μg	Niacin,[e] mg	Riboflavin (B₂), mg	Thiamine (B₁), mg	Vitamin B₆, mg	Vitamin B₁₂, μg
45	400	16	1.3	1.2	1.6	3.0
45	400	14	1.4	1.1	2.0	3.0
45	400	14	1.4	1.1	2.0	3.0
45	400	13	1.2	1.0	2.0	3.0
60	800	+2	+0.3	+0.3	2.5	4.0
80	600	+4	+0.5	+0.3	2.5	4.0

Minerals

Calcium, mg	Phosphorus, mg	Iodine, μg	Iron, mg	Magnesium, mg	Zinc, mg
1,200	1,200	115	18	300	15
1,200	1,200	115	18	300	15
800	800	100	18	300	15
800	800	100	18	300	15
1,200	1,200	125	18+[f]	450	20
1,200	1,200	150	18	450	25

[a] The allowances given are designed for the maintenance of good nutrition of practically all healthy people in the United States. They are intended to provide for individual variations among most normal persons as they live in the United States under usual environmental stresses. Diets should be based on a variety of common foods in order to provide other nutrients for which human requirements have been less well defined.

[b] Retinol equivalents.

[c] Total vitamin E activity, estimated to be 80 percent as α-tocopherol and 20 percent other tocopherols.

[d] The folacin allowances refer to dietary sources as determined by *Lactobacillus casei* assay. Pure forms of folacin may be effective in doses less than one-fourth of the recommended dietary allowance.

[e] Although allowances are expressed as niacin, it is recognized that on the average 1 mg of niacin is derived from each 60 mg of dietary tryptophan.

[f] This increased requirement cannot be met by ordinary diets; therefore, the use of supplemental iron is recommended.

SOURCE: Food and Nutrition Board, National Research Council, National Academy of Sciences (revised 1974).

The pattern of weight gain is more important than the total number of pounds gained, and Figure 17-1 illustrates the ideal pattern. The curve was derived from the weight gain of women whose outcome of pregnancy was desirable. Figure 17-2 illustrates a woman of standard weight at the beginning of her pregnancy whose weight gain followed the ideal pattern. Figure 17-3 shows a woman who was obese when she became pregnant and in spite of her obesity was counseled to follow the ideal weight gain pattern. This resulted in a desirable course and outcome of pregnancy.

FIGURE 17-1

Ideal pattern of weight gain during pregnancy. (Clinical Obstetrics, *Lippincott, Philadelphia, 1953. Reproduced by permission.*)

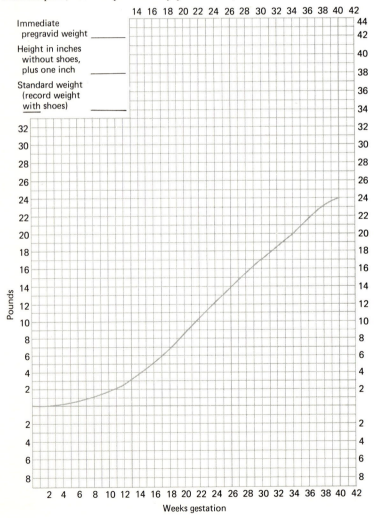

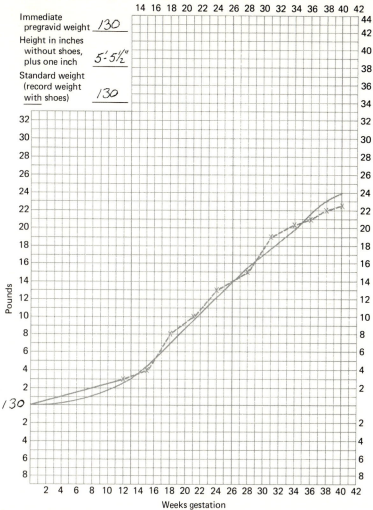

FIGURE 17-2

Ideal pattern of weight gain during pregnancy for woman of standard pregravid weight. (Clinical Obstetrics, *Lippincott, Philadelphia, 1953. Reproduced by permission.*)

It has been common practice in the past to restrict the weight gain of overweight and obese pregnant women. Included in the policy statement of the American College of Obstetricians and Gynecologists is the following: "Weight gain during pregnancy should not be restricted unduly, nor should weight reduction be normally attempted."[15] There is little supporting evidence that excessive weight gain during pregnancy predisposes women to toxemia and other complications of pregnancy such as abortion, dystocia, postpartum hemorrhage, or mechanical difficulties during childbirth.[16]

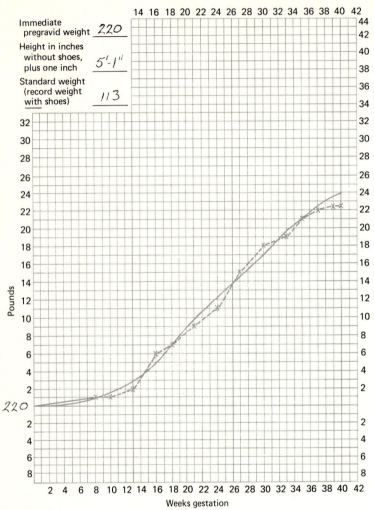

FIGURE 17-3
Ideal pattern of weight gain during pregnancy for woman of excessive pregravid
weight. (Clinical Obstetrics, *Lippincott, Philadelphia, 1953. Reproduced by
permission.*)

The idea that limitation of weight gain by caloric restriction protects against toxemia goes back to the observed reduction in the incidence of eclampsia in Germany and Austria-Hungary during World War I. Because of a war-imposed scarcity of meat and fats, pregnant women gained less, and it was concluded without further study that a restricted diet was protective. Caloric restriction

to limit gain in weight during pregnancy became widely advocated as a means for preventing toxemia and many other complications. The idea found its way into textbooks of obstetrics and was widely adopted by the medical profession. Seldom has a medical idea with such a basis (hearsay evidence) been applied so widely and subjected to so little scientific study.[17]

The underweight woman, rather than the overweight woman, is the one who runs a greater risk of developing toxemia. Tompkins reported that the incidence of toxemia in women who are markedly underweight was nearly twice that found in those who are overweight.[18] He reported that failure to gain an average amount of weight during the second trimester is associated with a relatively high possibility of developing toxemia.[19] Low weight gain during pregnancy is associated with infants who are either smaller than average at birth or who are premature.[20-22] Tompkins also reports that an excessive weight gain of 4.2 to 4.5 kg during the last weeks of pregnancy for extremely underweight women is compatible with a minimum risk of developing toxic symptoms.[23]

One final objection to restricting kilocalories during pregnancy is the possibility that protein will be used for energy. This reduces the availability of protein for essential functions.[24] In addition, many foods high in nutrients are also high in kilocalories, e.g., meat, milk, and certain fruits and vegetables. Therefore, a restriction in kilocalories usually results in a restriction of nutritious foods.

The ideal weight gain pattern should reflect the accretion of actual tissue resulting from a nutritionally adequate diet. It is possible for a woman to eat a nutritionally inadequate diet and retain fluid. Such a woman could show an increase in weight in accordance with the ideal weight gain curve, but this increased weight would be due to fluid retention and not tissue growth. The latter case is likely to result in a poor rather than desirable course of pregnancy.

Protein

During pregnancy an increase of 30 g of food protein per day is recommended in order to provide amino acids and nitrogen for syn-thesis of fetal and placental tissues; for increases in the woman's total amount of blood, breast, and uterine tissues; and for amniotic fluid. Some authorities believe that high quality (animal) protein can prevent toxemia and some believe it is even helpful in the treatment of toxemia, but more evidence is needed.[25]

Calcium, Magnesium, and Iron

The pregnant woman needs additional calcium for deposition into fetal bones and teeth, for her ongoing needs, and for the extra storage observed in pregnant women. If the calcium intake is inadequate, fetal needs will be met by demineralizing the woman's skeleton.[26] Some authorities believe that their observance of subnormal bone density in females, which they have found to be associated with high fracture risk, may be associated with "calcium losses incurred during pregnancies and previously existing calcium deficits which have not been adequately repleted by diet or prescribed prenatal supplements."[27]

Magnesium is an important constituent of bones and is found within all living cells. This mineral is important for the activity of many enzymes including those involved in cellular oxidation, protein and lipid metabolism, and the synthesis of DNA and RNA. Magnesium deficiency is not generally found in the American population.

Increased iron is recommended for the pregnant woman to provide hemoglobin for the increased number of maternal red blood cells; for the placenta; for the formation of fetal hemoglobin, myoglobin, and a number of enzymes; for enough fetal storage to last for the first 3 months of the infant's life; and for blood losses during childbirth.

The woman's iron stores and dietary iron are sources which meet these needs. However, a significant number of women enter pregnancy with inadequate or no iron stores.

The recommended dietary allowance is 18 mg per day for the nonpregnant woman of childbearing age[28]; this amount provides for her daily needs and for storing iron in preparation for pregnancy. However, 18 mg of iron per day is not easily or usually obtained in the normal diet. Since dietary iron and maternal iron stores are usually inadequate to meet iron needs during pregnancy, a daily supplement of 30 to 60 mg per day is recommended.[29]

Sodium

Sodium is an essential body mineral. Its primary function is to control body fluid volume. The need for sodium is greater during pregnancy to permit the expansion of maternal tissues and for fetal needs.[30] The typical American diet provides a generous amount of salt (sodium chloride), and the pregnant woman's needs will be adequately covered unless her sodium intake is restricted.

In the past it has been common obstetric practice to routinely restrict sodium in the diets of pregnant women. This practice was based on the belief that sodium restriction would prevent toxemia. An accumulation of research has now brought about a change in thinking. The Food and Nutrition Board makes the following statement: "It is difficult to justify sodium limitation in healthy women during pregnancy on the basis of either animal or clinical evidence."[31] The *Policy Statement on Nutrition and Pregnancy* by the American College of Obstetricians and Gynecologists states: "Essential nutritional elements (such as sodium) should not be restricted during normal pregnancy."[32]

The amount of sodium in the body is regulated by aldosterone. This is a hormone secreted by the adrenal glands which promotes the reabsorption of sodium from the kidneys.

Pike and Smiciklas[33] cite studies of pregnant animals showing that when sodium intake is restricted, the adrenal glands secrete additional aldosterone to conserve body sodium. When restriction is severe this compensatory mechanism is increased and leads to hyperplasia and hypertrophy of the secretory cells in the adrenal glands; the inability to expand blood volume and tissue fluids; a reduction in the renal blood flow and glomerular filtration rates; and the development of hyponatremia in fluids and tissues. It is possible that pregnant humans may suffer similar undesirable consequences when sodium intake is restricted.

Sodium restriction in pregnancy has also been used to prevent edema. Pike and Smiciklas present an historical review of this practice and note that it was first advocated by Cramer in 1906 and later supported by Zangmeister. Cramer and Zangmeister emphasized the relationship between weight gain and edema and suggested that impairment in sodium restriction in pregnant women was responsible for toxemia. Some edema appears to be natural in pregnancy when it is confined to the lower limbs, is not generalized, and is not accompanied by hypertension and proteinuria. Studies show that women with edema, uncomplicated by other symptoms, have larger babies and reduced rates of prematurity. Evidence indicates that simple edema in pregnancy is not associated with increased perinatal mortality.[34] Pike and Smiciklas cite studies in which the condition of pregnant women with toxemia was improved when given additional salt.

In practice, when pregnant women attempt to reduce their sodium intake, the nutritive quality of their diets suffers because many foods high in nutritive value (and relatively low in cost) are also high in sodium, e.g., milk, canned meats and fish, canned vegetables, peanut butter, and cheese. In addition, women find low sodium meals unpalatable and simply eat less. One last disadvantage of sodium-restricted diets during pregnancy is that iodized table salt is the main source of iodine for most Americans. When salt intake is restricted, the iodine intake is also restricted.

Zinc and Iodine

Zinc is a constituent of enzymes involved in most major metabolic pathways. Stored zinc is not readily available to the body; therefore, a constant food source is important to keep the body in good health. Zinc deficiency results in growth retardation and lack of appetite in children.[35]

Iodine, which is present in all body tissues, is an essential constituent of thyroxine and other related compounds secreted by the thyroid gland. Thyroxine is essential for normal metabolism and growth.

In adults, an iodine deficiency results in simple goiter which is an enlarged thyroid gland. In infants and children a deficiency causes hypothyroidism, also known as cretinism and juvenile myxedema, with symptoms of retarded physical growth and mental development. Iodine deficiency in the pregnant woman can predispose the infant to iodine-deficiency disease.

Vitamin A and Vitamin D

Vitamin A is essential for the health and functioning of the epithelial cells of the body found in the eyes, skin, and the mucous membranes lining the gastrointestinal, genitourinary, and respiratory tracts. In addition, vitamin A is necessary for growth and for normal cartilage cell development and is essential for normal bone and tooth formation. The most well-known function of vitamin A is its role in making it possible for the eye to see in dim light, especially after exposure to bright light. This is called *dark adaptation*. During pregnancy an additional 1,000 IU per day are recommended for fetal use and storage.[36]

Pure (preformed) vitamin A is colorless and is found in animal products such as milk, butter, liver, cod liver oil, and most multivitamin supplements. Vitamin A is fat-soluble and can be stored in the body. Ingesting too much vitamin A can lead to toxic symptoms characterized by loss of appetite, dry skin, abnormal skin pigmentation, pain in the long bones, and general fragility of all bones. The Food and Nutrition Board recommends that "The regular ingestion of 6,700 I.U. of pre-formed Vitamin A, above that already in the diet, should be carefully monitored by a physician."[37]

Carotene is a yellow compound found in dark green and deep yellow vegetables. It is a precursor of vitamin A and is converted into vitamin A in the body. People who consume excessive amounts of carotene by drinking large amounts of carrot juice, for example, get a yellow-colored skin which disappears when the carotene intake is decreased.

Vitamin D promotes intestinal absorption of calcium and probably directs the incorporation of calcium and other minerals into bones and teeth. Since bones are calcified in the fetus, this vitamin is important during pregnancy. For all growing persons and pregnant women 400 IU of vitamin D are recommended. Nonpregnant adults can synthesize sufficient vitamin D in the skin when exposed to ultraviolet light.

Excessive amounts of vitamin D (above 2,000 IU per day, or 5 times the recommended allowance) for prolonged periods have produced hypercalcemia in infants and nephrocalcinosis (deposition of calcium in the kidneys) in infants and adults. According to the Food and Nutrition Board, "It should be emphasized that the ingestion of Vitamin D in excess of the recommended amounts provides no benefits and that large excesses are potentially harmful."[38]

Folacin

Folacin, also known as folic acid or pteroyl-glutamic acid, is a water-soluble vitamin essential for the formation of DNA and RNA which are required for cell division and protein synthesis. Folacin plays a role in the formation of white and red blood cells and the metabolism of certain amino acids. Since folacin is essential for cell division it is essential for fetal growth and therefore very important during pregnancy.

Studies indicate that the megaloblastic anemia of late pregnancy due to folacin deficiency and low blood folic acid levels during pregnancy are not uncommon. Some studies suggested that folacin deficiency may be implicated in fetal damage, late pregnancy bleeding, and fetal malformation and abortion, but additional research has not confirmed these results.[39]

The recommended dietary allowance for folacin is set at 800 μg per day (twice the allowance for the nonpregnant woman) because of studies indicating a marked increased need during pregnancy. Dietary levels of folacin may or may not be adequate to meet this recommended intake, so authorities advocate a routine supplementation of 400 μg for all pregnant women.[40]

Water

Water is the largest constituent of the body, and fluid intake is necessary for life. Water continues to be important during pregnancy, but the fluid intake should be neither greatly reduced nor increased.

Interrelatedness of Nutrients

Nutrients have multiple interrelated functions in the body. For example, although calcium is an important constituent of bones and teeth it is also necessary for blood coagulation, myocardial function, and muscle contractility; for the integrity of intracellular cement substances and various membranes; and for controlling the excitability of peripheral nerves and muscle. In addition, all body organs and systems need a multiplicity of nutrients for their proper functioning. For example, protein, iron, folacin, vitamin B_{12}, vitamin C, and other nutrients are necessary for proper blood cell formation.

This summary has not attempted to provide all the current knowledge about the functions of the known essential nutrients. The nutrients discussed were selected because there is a substantial increase in the need for them during pregnancy. The nurse should consult a nutrition text for more complete information about the essential nutrients and their functions.

FOODS TO PROVIDE NUTRIENT NEEDS DURING PREGNANCY

Since people eat foods and not nutrients, various food plans are devised by nutritionists and dietitians to assist clients to understand the need for and eat the foods that provide nutrients in the amounts stated in the *Recommended Dietary Allowances* for pregnancy. Many different combinations of foods supply the recommended nutrients. Food plans are prepared to suit the food habits and economic standards of populations to be served. As more knowledge about nutrient needs of humans is accumulated, food plans are revised to accommodate this information. The nurse should use the most appropriate food plan available for teaching clients.

A sample food plan, entitled "Daily Food

Plan for the Expectant Mother," is illustrated in Figure 17-4. This plan uses the format of the four food groups from the U.S. Department of Agriculture's *National Food Guide*,[41] which lists foods of similar nutrient content together. Table 17-2 shows the nutrient content of one day's meals and of individual foods chosen according to the plan. An examination of the table illustrates the following points:

1   The basic foods, chosen in accordance with the plan, provide about 1,800 kcal.

2   Additional foods are needed to provide sufficient kilocalories and to complete the day's meals. These may include additional basic foods and/or candy, cake, and other high-calorie foods. Most of these foods also contribute some essential nutrients. There is no need to prohibit the pregnant woman from eating desserts and snack foods unless she is gaining weight in excess of the ideal weight curve.

3   It is recommended that women consume three glasses of milk a day, preferably fortified with vitamin D. The milk provides 300 IU of vitamin D and almost all of the recommended amount of calcium. Enough calcium is obtained from the rest of the foods in the diet to meet the allowance. Additional vitamin D is available from the action of sunlight on the skin.

4   Most of the vitamin C in the diet comes from orange juice. Other foods contribute some vitamin C, but if orange juice is omitted, the amount of vitamin C in the day's meals is not adequate.

5   Most of the vitamin A in the diet is provided by carrots. The amount of this vitamin in the daily diet is 10,000 IU, while the allowance is 6,000 IU. However, several other foods listed as vitamin A foods do not contain as much vitamin A as carrots.

6   Foods selected according to the plan do not provide vitamin D, vitamin B_6, zinc, or magnesium in the recommended amounts. Although the foods do not provide enough niacin, the tryptophan in protein foods is converted to niacin in the body. This will supply enough to provide the recommended amount. The plan provides a generous amount of high-protein foods and stresses the use of whole-grain breads and cereals in an effort to provide as much zinc and magnesium as possible without requiring a drastic change in eating habits.

Experience has proved that most pregnant women will not follow dietary recommendations if they require radical changes in eating habits and if the cost is prohibitive. There are two ways to provide the recommended amounts of vitamin D, vitamin B_6, zinc, and magnesium. The first is to include them in vitamin-mineral supplements. If the supplement is free to the client, this could be a solution for low-income women who cannot afford the amount of high-protein foods recommended in the plan. The second way of providing these nutrients is to devise a daily food plan that is a departure from the four food groups. Such a plan is found in the California Department of Health booklet *Nutrition during Pregnancy and Lactation*.[42] Either solution is appropriate if it is practical.

7   An examination of the nutrient content of individual foods reveals that most foods contain a variety of nutrients. For example, orange juice provides not only vitamin C, but some of all the other nutrients listed except vitamin D.

Foods	Daily Amounts

MILK GROUP

   Over eighteen years of age   3 cups ($\frac{3}{4}$ quart)
   Under eighteen years of age   5 cups ($1\frac{1}{4}$ quart)

A serving is:
   1 cup whole milk, buttermilk, low-fat milk, nonfat milk, cocoa, chocolate milk
    drink, malted milk, milk shake, ice cream, yogurt, custard
   $\frac{1}{2}$ cup evaporated milk
   $\frac{1}{3}$ cup nonfat *dry* milk
   1 ounce hard cheese

MEAT GROUP   2 servings

A serving is:
   120 g cooked meat, fish, or fowl
    (as 150 g hamburger after it is cooked)
$\frac{1}{2}$ serving is:

4 slices luncheon meat	$\frac{1}{2}$ cup cottage cheese
2 frankfurters	4 tablespoons peanut butter
2 eggs	1 cup cooked dry beans
$\frac{1}{2}$ cup canned fish	$\frac{1}{2}$ cup nuts

VEGETABLE AND FRUIT GROUP

Dark Green and Deep Yellow Vegetables and Fruits $\frac{1}{2}$ cup

Acorn squash	Cantaloupe	Mustard greens
Apricots, dried	Chard	Pumpkin
Banana squash	Collard greens	Spinach
Broccoli	Dandelion greens	Sweet potatoes
Beet greens	Hubbard squash	Turnip greens
Carrots	Kale	Yams

Citrus Fruits and Other High-Vitamin C Foods $\frac{1}{2}$ cup

Broccoli	Grapefruit or juice	Orange or juice
Brussel sprouts	Guava	Papaya
Cantaloupe	Green pepper	Strawberries
Cauliflower	Mango	Turnip greens
Collard greens	Mustard greens	Tomato (raw)

Other Fruits and Vegetables   2 servings (1 cup)

Apple	Green beans	Raisins
Banana	Green peas	White potato
Cabbage	Lettuce	Additional servings of
Corn	Prunes	high-vitamin A or C food

BREAD AND CEREAL GROUP (Whole Grain or Enriched)   5 servings

A serving is:

1 slice bread	$\frac{1}{2}$ cup macaroni
1 tortilla	$\frac{1}{2}$ cup spaghetti
$\frac{1}{2}$ cup cooked cereal	$\frac{1}{2}$ cup rice
$\frac{1}{2}$ cup grits	$\frac{3}{4}$ cup ready-to-eat cereal

IODIZED SALT   Use moderately

ADDITIONAL FOODS TO COMPLETE YOUR MEALS

Margarine, butter, salad dressing, desserts, additional servings of bread,   As you wish if
   fruit, vegetables, meat, etc.   weight gain is
                                              all right

Coffee, tea, other beverages   As you wish

FIGURE 17-4
Daily food plan for the expectant mother. (*Adapted from "What to Eat before the
Baby Comes," Nutrition Program, Community Health Services, Department of
Health Services, County of Los Angeles, 1974. Reproduced by permission.*)

It is also apparent that it takes more than one food to provide the recommended amounts of any nutrient. For example, most of the suggested amount of calcium is provided by milk, but other foods contain some calcium. It is for these reasons that nutritionists recommend that people eat a variety of foods.

8 Calculations for iodine are not given. Iodine is found in seafoods, vegetables grown in soil containing iodine, and in milk and eggs from animals who eat iodine-rich foods. These foods are undependable sources of iodine for most Americans, because seafoods are not generally eaten daily and most American soil does not contain iodine. Consequently, the daily use of iodized salt is recommended and will take care of the needs of the pregnant woman.

Some type of vitamin-mineral supplement is recommended for the pregnant woman. However, certain precautions must be noted.

1 Vitamin-mineral supplements can give a false sense of security to the physician, nurse, and client who might assume that the supplement ensures a satisfactory nutrient intake even if a nutritionally inadequate diet is consumed. However, supplements contain neither protein nor calories, which are essential for pregnancy. The amount of calcium found in most supplements is usually not more than that found in one glass of milk. It is also possible that a poor diet may be lacking in one or more of the essential nutrients for which no allowance has been established and which are not found in vitamin-mineral supplements.

2 The reason for prescribing the supplement must be carefully explained to clients. Studies show that pregnant adolescents do not like to take medications, especially if they are not told the reasons. One-fifth to one-third of such clients failed to take supplements that were given without charge.[43] Many mature women feel and behave the same way.

3 If sound reasons for taking supplements are not given to clients, they may assume that foods are not adequate sources of nutrients. This lends authority to the widespread but false notion that the quality of foods in the United States is inferior. The pregnant woman may think that it does not matter what she eats as long as she takes the supplement. She may also think

TABLE 17-2
Nutrient Content of One Day's Meals Chosen in Accordance with the "Daily Food Plan for the Expectant Mother"

	Amount	Kilocalories	Protein, g	Vitamin A activity, IU	Vitamin C, mg	Folacin, μg	Niacin, mg
Basic foods							
Whole milk	3 glasses	477	26	1026	6	66	0.6
Beef patty	4 oz	329	28	45	....	460	5.2
Dried beans, cooked	1 cup	212	14	....	....	14	1.3
Eggs	2	163	13	1180	....	30	0.1
Carrots	½ cup	23	1	7615	5	2	0.4
Orange juice	½ cup	54	1	240	54	5	0.4
White potato	1 medium	93	3	....	20	12	1.7
Apple	1 medium	87	....	135	6	3	0.1
Shredded wheat	1 biscuit	90	3	....	....	5	1.1
Whole wheat bread	4 slices	244	10	....	....	40	2.4
Total		1772	99	10241	91	637	13.3
Additional foods							
Banana	1 medium	100	1	230	12	32	0.8
Head lettuce	¼ head	15	1	345	6	210	0.3
Mayonnaise	1 T	101	....	40	....	....	....
Margarine	2 T	204	....	940	....	....	....
Coffee	3 cups	....	....	....	....	....	....
Sugar	1 T	46	....	....	....	....	....
Cupcake with icing	1 small	129	2	60	....	2	0.1
Chocolate candy	1 small bar	72	1	40	....	....	0.1
Total		667	5	1655	18	244	1.3
Total basic & additional foods		2439	104	11896	109	881	14.6
RDA, pregnant women 19–22 years		2400	76	5,000	60	800	16.0
RDA, lactating women 19–22 years		2600	66	6,000	80	600	18.0

that the physician or nurse are not serious about her eating, or do not trust her to eat the recommended foods.

THE NURSE'S ROLE IN NUTRITION CARE

Recognition of nutrition as a component of nursing care has been accepted since the days of Florence Nightingale. In her many writings it was evident that she recognized that food played an important part in a person's health and well-being. She encouraged nurses to accept their responsibility in this area of nursing.[44]

Nurses function in several important ways in the nutrition care of pregnant women. They assist in seeing that women who need counseling from a nutritionist or dietitian get this care; they reinforce this counseling; they participate as members of interdisciplinary

Riboflavin, mg	Thiamine, mg	Vitamin B$_6$, mg	Vitamin D, IU	Calcium, mg	Iron, mg	Magnesium, mg	Zinc, mg
1.23	0.21	0.294	300	864	0.3	96	3.0
0.24	0.10	0.529	....	13	3.7	24	4.9
0.13	0.25	0.252	....	90	4.9	67	2.7
0.28	0.09	0.090	50	54	2.3	12	1.4
0.04	0.04	0.022	....	24	0.5	5	0.2
0.01	0.11	0.036	....	11	0.1	14	0.1
0.04	0.10	0.200	....	9	0.7	22	0.2
0.03	0.04	0.045	....	15	0.5	8	....
0.03	0.06	0.081	....	11	0.9	27	0.8
0.12	0.24	0.180	16	100	2.4	44	2.8
2.15	1.24	1.729	366	1191	16.3	319	16.1
0.07	0.06	0.373	....	10	0.8	54	0.2
0.06	0.06	0.063	....	21	0.6	12	....
0.01	....	....	....	3	0.1	....	0.1
....	....	....	....	6	....	....	....
....	....	....	....	....	....	....	....
....	....	....	....	....	....	....	....
0.04	0.01	0.005	....	47	0.3	3	0.2
0.05	....	....	....	32	0.2	....	....
0.23	0.13	0.441	....	119	2.0	69	0.5
2.38	1.37	2.17	366	1310	18.3	388	16.6
1.7	1.4	2.5	400	1,200	18	450	20
1.9	1.4	2.5	400	1,200	18	450	25

health teams working with individuals who have nutrition problems; and they directly counsel women about nutrition.

The following section discusses conditions and problems of clients (1) who should be referred to a nutritionist or dietitian, (2) who should preferably be referred to a nutritionist or dietitian, (3) who may need the services of several disciplines or an interdisciplinary team, and (4) who can be counseled by the nurse. To some readers, this may seem like an artificial breakdown of counselors and clients. It should be remembered, however, that it is often necessary to categorize and break down concepts in idealized terms. More often than not depending upon geographical location and resources, the nurse may very well be the only health professional available to offer any type of nutrition counseling.

Women Who Should Be Referred to a Nutritionist or Dietitian

Pre-existing Medical Conditions Requiring Therapeutic Diets

Pre-existing medical conditions requiring a therapeutic diet include diabetes; renal disease; active tuberculosis; hepatic diseases such as hepatitis and cirrhosis of the liver; food allergies or intolerances such as allergy to wheat and milk intolerance; cardiovascular disease; phenylketonuria and other inborn errors of metabolism; cystic fibrosis; and diseases of the gastrointestinal tract such as ulcers. In conditions such as these, the therapeutic diet must be modified to provide for the nutrition needs of pregnancy. The clients may need frequent and lengthy counseling to ensure their food intake is in accordance with the prescribed diet.

Conditions Developed during Pregnancy Requiring Therapeutic Diets

These conditions include transient diabetes, toxemia, cardiovascular disease, diseases of the gastrointestinal tract, and renal diseases. These women will need a therapeutic pregnancy diet and will also need frequent and lengthy counseling to ensure their food intake is in accordance with the prescribed diet.

Unusual Eating Patterns

Groups with unusual eating patterns that can cause problems during pregnancy include *vegans* (pure vegetarians who eat no animal products), particularly if they also refuse to eat canned foods or take a vitamin-mineral supplement; some health food enthusiasts; persons eating fad diets which are grossly inadequate in nutrient content; and members of certain religious groups whose beliefs pro-

scribe eating foods commonly used in American diets.

Women with strong beliefs about food who also have unusual eating habits are often difficult to counsel and are sometimes resistant to change. These women will need diet recommendations tailored to fit their eating habits. In some cases they can be persuaded to make some minor changes in their practices so that they consume a nutritionally adequate diet. Counseling sessions for such women may be more lengthy and frequent than for the average woman.

Women Preferably Referred to a Nutritionist or Dietitian

Individuals who are preferably referred are those with problems during a past or current pregnancy which are nutrition-related. These women usually require frequent and lengthy counseling sessions involving the following: determination of fairly precise information about the amount, frequency, and types of foods eaten; information about the nutritive value of many foods; and recommendations that are practical in terms of costs, attitudes, and beliefs about foods. Such clients may also have social, cultural, emotional, and physical problems which make it difficult for them to carry out nutrition recommendations. When these women are referred for counseling, the nurse continues to play a helpful role in their nutrition care during regular counseling sessions with them. At that time the nurse determines any problems clients may have with their diets, offers them information, and shares these factors with the nutritionist or dietitian.

When nutrition personnel are inadequate in number to counsel these women, nurses can and do assume this responsibility. Nutritionists and dietitians assist nurses by providing practical information as part of inservice education or by consultation. The disadvantage of this situation is that it may be very time-consuming, detracting from the time the nurse has for counseling about other important matters. Alternatively, the nurse may not spend enough time providing nutrition counseling to these clients to make it effective. Some information the nurse can use in counseling these women is found in the section Suggestions for Nutrition Counseling.

Poor Past Obstetric and Health History

Women preferably referred to a nutritionist or dietitian include those with the following obstetric histories: neonatal deaths; stillbirths; low-birth-weight babies (premature or small for gestational age or both); a handicapped child; an excessively large baby (4.2 kg or more); repeated spontaneous abortion; therapeutic abortion; abruptio placenta or placenta previa; cesarean section; and infertility problems. Poor nutrient stores and poor pregnancy diet may have contributed to past outcomes, and a nutritionally adequate diet during this pregnancy could be important in bringing about a good outcome.

Women with high parity, five children or more, are at greater than average risk for a poor pregnancy outcome and are preferably referred to a nutritionist. Women with a multiple pregnancy have greater nutrient needs than women with a single fetus, and careful attention must be paid to the diet of such women.

Primigravidas may have poor nutrient stores, particularly when they have recently attempted to lose weight. In addition, these women may be nauseated, may vomit often, and may have morning sickness, heartburn, muscle cramps, food intolerances, and constipation. Some of these women may lack information about nutrition and food needs during pregnancy. All of these factors may be compounded by the adjustment problems of a new marriage and by financial problems.

A detailed assessment about eating habits during prior pregnancies and during this pregnancy is needed. Clients should be counseled often enough to ensure they are eating a good diet during this pregnancy.

Women who have had the following conditions in their health history are included in the ones preferably referred: tuberculosis; hepatic diseases; rheumatic heart disease; ulcer; and other diseases of the gastrointestinal tract. Pregnancy imposes a burden upon the client whose health has been impaired in the past, and there is a risk of recurrence. Careful monitoring, therefore, during pregnancy is important, and an adequate diet is an important part of health care at this time.

Weight Factors

Clients whose prepregnancy weight is 10 percent or more under expected weight for height or whose weight gain during this pregnancy is less than the ideal weight gain curve are at higher than average risk for complications of pregnancy and poor outcome. They may have poor appetites, previous poor dietary habits, and poor nutrient stores, and they may be hyperactive.

Prepregnancy weight 20 percent or more above expected weight for height is an indication of overweight or obesity. Clients may have poor past dietary habits and poor nutrient stores. In-depth information about past and present eating habits is needed.

Too rapid weight gain may be a result of the woman retaining an excessive amount of fluid and may be the result of eating a nutritionally inadequate diet. Excessive caloric intake may also be the cause. It is necessary to take a careful dietary history, including the kinds and amounts of foods being eaten, to determine the areas counseling should focus on.

In all these situations the client is preferably referred to a nutritionist or dietitian. Careful assessment and in-depth interviewing regarding past and present dietary and activity patterns are required. These women may need frequent counseling sessions in order to find acceptable solutions.

Anemia

Clients with folic acid deficiency, or sickle-cell and other anemias, are preferably referred to a nutritionist or dietitian. Iron-deficiency anemia is the most common anemia found in pregnant women. These clients are usually eating poorly, and may resist taking iron supplements because such supplements upset their stomachs. They will need frequent counseling to improve their diets and make sure they are taking the iron supplement.

Very Inadequate Diet

When a diet is lacking in foods from two or more of the groups in the four food groups, for example, no milk or fruits, it can be classified as *very inadequate*. Clients may have poor nutrient stores and their current diet may not be providing sufficient nutrients. Careful, in-depth interviewing is needed to determine the reasons for the problems, which may be culturally, socially, economically, or individually based.

Priorities for dietary changes must be established. Numerous suggestions for ways of improving the diet must be offered until clients find an acceptable one. They will need frequent and possibly lengthy counsel-

ing sessions and may need the help of workers in other disciplines, such as a social worker or home economist.

Economic Factors

The impact of economics upon pregnancy is manifest most profoundly in those clients whose income is at or below the poverty level; in clients whose income is adequate but who have unusually high expenses or debts; and in clients whose income is adequate but who have money management problems. These women frequently have difficulty purchasing a nutritionally adequate diet. The nutrition counselor must know both the nutritive value and cost of a wide variety of foods in order to make appropriate suggestions for dietary improvement. Clients may need food buying suggestions, menu ideas, and recipes. They may need referral to additional sources of money, such as the U.S. Department of Agriculture (USDA) Food Stamp Program, the Commodity Food Program, or the Supplemental Food Program for Women, Infants, and Children (WIC).

Cultural Factors

Women from Mexican-American, other Latin American, Southern United States, Oriental, Native American, and European cultures may eat foods and have cultural beliefs about foods that are unfamiliar to the nurse. Thus, evaluating the nutritional adequacy of eating patterns and making appropriate recommendations for change will be difficult. Many such clients are also low income, which complicates the problem of making appropriate suggestions for changes in eating patterns.

When nurses work with different cultural groups in nutrition counseling, it is necessary to gain knowledge about the culture and cultural eating habits. In many instances, adequate intake of the four basic food groups can be accomplished using foods which are already being eaten or which are culturally acceptable as desirable foods.

Women Needing Interdisciplinary Health Services

This group includes women with complex problems that require the services of many disciplines or an interdisciplinary team. Women with complex problems have difficulty carrying out suggestions for health care, including nutrition suggestions. The nurse assists by suggesting and/or making referrals to members of various disciplines. The nurse may convene the interdisciplinary team and/or contribute to the team's deliberations about the problems and the development of the client care plan. The nurse also participates in the implementation of the care plan.

Adolescent Pregnancy

There are approximately 200,000 births a year among girls aged twelve to nineteen. Medical and nutrition problems are increased for these teenagers, and they are at greater risk for complications of pregnancy. Their infants are at greater risk of low birth weight and handicapping conditions. Nutrient stores are likely to be poor, especially in older teenagers who may have led a busy life with irregular meals and poor food choices. Younger teenagers are usually under parental influence regarding eating. Teenager rebellion against parents is frequently expressed through rebellion against family eating patterns.

Girls aged twelve to seventeen years are still growing, and 8 percent of their total growth is attained during these years. The nutrient needs of the fetus are superimposed upon the girl's own growth needs. Pregnant teenagers frequently have problems of anemia, and too little or too much weight gain.

Studies indicate that diets of pregnant teenagers are likely to be deficient in milk, fruits, and vegetables.[45] Of this group, 20 to 30 percent do not take the vitamin-mineral supplements given them, and most teenagers do not like to take medication, especially if they do not know the reason.[46] One study indicated pica in 28 percent of teenaged clients.[47]

The food and nutrition needs of the older teenager, aged seventeen to nineteen, are the same as those of the adult woman, but the twelve- to seventeen-year old needs more calories, protein, and other nutrients. (Refer to Table 17-1 and Figure 17-4.)

There are several barriers preventing pregnant teenagers from following an adequate diet:

1   Income: Studies indicate that married teenagers have low incomes and unmarried teenagers are often on welfare.[48]
2   Food habits: Past poor food habits persist during pregnancy.
3   Lack of information: Teenagers usually do not know their own nutrient needs or those of the fetus. Married teenagers often do not have cooking, meal planning, money management, or other homemaking skills.[49]
4   Lack of control of the food supply: Many teenagers live with parents, other relatives, friends, or in an institution. These caretakers as well as the teenager must be counseled to provide the necessary foods for the young client.

5   *Lack of motivation:* When pregnancy is unwanted, clients are not motivated to eat well in order to bear a healthy baby. Adolescents may be concerned about losing their figures and getting fat. Emotional maladjustment and upset[50] may be the cause of unwanted pregnancies, as well as the cause of rebellion against adult food habits. Poor relationships with adults may cause resistance to suggestions made by other authority figures such as the physician, nurse, and nutritionist.

Pregnant adolescents appear to do better when they have comprehensive services provided by an interdisciplinary team. This includes provisions for them to continue school, plus medical, nursing, nutrition, social work, and home economics services.[51,52]

Social or Emotional Disturbances

Examples of this group include clients with out-of-wedlock pregnancies; clients not receiving support (financial or psychological) from spouse or other family members; cases involving alcohol or other drug addiction in client or spouse; emotionally immature clients; and clients or their families who are socially or emotionally distressed for complex reasons that require in-depth analysis to determine. Clients may be unable to carry out medical or nutrition suggestions and may be unable to purchase or eat a nutritionally adequate diet. Emotional disturbance interferes with nitrogen and calcium utilization and possibly the utilization of other nutrients.

Clients may need psychological counseling and emotional support. Some may need help in changing or arranging for a different living situation. Help from social services is often necessary, while some women may require the services of a psychiatrist or psychologist.

Homemaking, Family, and Physical Factors

Some clients may need help in all areas of homemaking—shopping, use of credit, use of household equipment, childrearing, cooking, budgeting, etc. Women with large families may need help with time, energy, and money management. The client who is unwed, widowed, or divorced may need help with homemaking skills, as well as advice regarding time- and energy-saving methods associated with housekeeping. When the expectant mother is deaf, blind, or crippled, she may need special devices and methods for homemaking.

For some clients, home economics classes can be a helpful adjunct to nursing and nutrition education endeavors. For others, a home economist or home economics aide can teach the necessary skills and facilitate learning, and for still others, a combination of these services may be needed.

Individual Factors

Women who are illiterate will need special teaching devices to augment and reinforce their learning, such as pictures or other teaching aids, and they may need more frequent counseling sessions. Women whose mental abilities are below normal may need simpler diet instructions, more frequent counseling, and more detailed information about food buying, cooking, and serving.

When the client does not speak English and health workers do not speak the client's language and have no written materials in the client's language, problems of communications are profound. An interpreter is needed as well as teaching materials in the client's language.

In these situations, once again, home economics classes, home economists, and home economics aides may be helpful in problem solving in particular instances.

Women Who Can Be Counseled by the Nurse

This group includes women whose physical, social, and emotional conditions are essentially normal. There is an uncomplicated pregnancy, adequate income, no previous disease requiring a therapeutic diet, no previous disease that could recur during this pregnancy, high school education or more, adequate homemaking skills, no severe emotional problems, ordinary or familiar eating habits, and reasonable acceptance of dietary counseling. Such women do not need lengthy, frequent, or intensive nutrition counseling. Nutrition counseling is easily incorporated into the nurse's overall counseling.

Some of the problems clients may complain of are nausea, morning sickness, heartburn, gas, vomiting, leg cramps, food intolerances, or constipation. Clients may need minor modifications in eating patterns, while some may need information about food and nutrition needs during pregnancy.

The nurse has many opportunities to provide nutrition guidance to these women. They are seen at regular intervals—in the office, in the clinic, and in the home. The nurse is in a good position to know and understand the individual in the family situation. The nurse develops rapport with clients and is able to discuss nutrition as a part of the overall counseling at times that are appropriate in terms of the woman's interests and needs.

THE NURSE AS NUTRITION COUNSELOR

When counseling women about nutrition, the nurse uses the same skills employed when counseling about other subjects. The most important factor in successful nutrition counseling is the nurse's nonjudgmental attitude of caring and respect.

Counseling, as used in this chapter, does not mean simply giving the woman a leaflet or telling her what she should eat and why. Experience shows that women do not usually change their eating habits when instructed in this way. Nutrition counseling should include the *maximum involvement* of the client. The objectives are to find out the woman's current problems about food, make suggestions for solving these problems, determine how she feels and what she thinks about nutrition and food needs during pregnancy, determine her current eating pattern, evaluate the nutritional adequacy of her diet, provide information about the functions of nutrients and the nutritive value of foods when appropriate, offer suggestions for changes in her dietary pattern when needed, and assist the client in making a decision to change. The client should do most of the talking during the counseling session.

Prerequisites for Counseling

1   A teaching leaflet stating how many servings of which foods should be eaten daily is useful. (An example is the Daily Food Plan for the Expectant Mother given in Figure 17-4.)
2   Knowledge about the nutritive value of ordinary foods is necessary. This information may be included in the teaching leaflet.
3   The ability to evaluate the nutritional adequacy of one day's food intake is

important. It is sufficient for most women to simply count the servings of the various foods they eat. This is a simple qualitative evaluation. When necessary, nutritionists and dietitians can get more quantitative information about exact portion sizes, methods of food preparation, and the number of times various foods are eaten during the week. The nurse needs more information about which specific foods belong in each of the four food groups than is practical to include in a teaching leaflet. A more complete list is given in the section A Guide for Evaluating Food Intake at the end of this chapter.

4 Knowledge about the function of nutrients and the ability to explain this to clients in an understandable way is necessary.

5 Teaching aids, such as charts showing the nutritive content of foods or the increased nutrition needs during pregnancy, are useful. These aids may be obtained from a nutritionist or dietitian; from commercial companies; from city, county, or state health departments; and from agencies of the federal government.

6 Practical suggestions given to expectant mothers to help them make dietary changes are important. (See the section Suggestions for Nutrition Counseling.) The nurse can obtain additional ideas from the nutritionist or dietitian. The nurse may also ask women how they solved certain problems or how they avoided them. The women themselves are the best source of practical suggestions.

7 The nurse may need specialized knowledge about the foods eaten and the beliefs of people belonging to specific cultural groups. This is true when a nurse's clientele consists of a substantial number of women belonging to different cultural groups, and when nutrition personnel are limited and the nurse must counsel these individuals.

8 The nurse may need consultation from a nutritionist or dietitian when giving nutrition guidance to a client whose needs require specialized nutrition information.

Steps in Nutrition Counseling

1 Establish rapport with the client. Explain that the purpose of the meeting is to talk about nutrition, and that what a woman eats is important for her health and for the baby. The prospective father should be included in the sessions when possible, for frequently he has a strong influence on what the family eats. He may need help in understanding the importance of an adequate diet for his mate, or conversely he may be very interested in knowing what foods are appropriate so that he can support his mate's good eating habits. Effective nutrition education during this time could well improve food habits and start the family on the road to better nutrition.

2 Determine what the client knows and how she feels about eating during pregnancy and what problems she might have. It is not unusual for expectant mothers to complain about nausea, morning sickness, gas, leg cramps, new food intolerances, and cravings. Women often have knowledge about the functions of nutrients and the nutritive value of foods, and the nurse should answer questions and give suggestions for solving problems be-

fore proceeding to gather information about eating habits. If more information is needed about what the client is eating before questions can be answered, explain this to the woman.

3 Use the diet record method or the dietary interview method for determining what the client is eating. When the food record is used, ask her to take the form home and write down all the foods she eats on a typical day. Ask her to return the form on her next visit. A sample dietary intake record form is found in Figure 17-5. Alternatively, the client may be asked to fill out the food record while she is sitting in the waiting room. Either method has the advantage of saving the nurse's time because clients do not quickly recall what they typically eat in a day. In addition, when the counseling session begins, the client's thoughts will be focused on food and she will respond more quickly to a discussion about nutrition. The disadvantage of this method is that clients may forget to bring the food record from home or their recording of foods eaten may be incomplete. In either case, the nurse may then use the dietary interview method.

The dietary interview method involves simply asking the client what she ate yesterday or what she eats on a typical day. Avoid getting information about foods eaten on weekends or holidays, since these are not usually typical days. The client should be seated at the nurse's side as the information is recorded, so she can see what is being written and can participate more closely in the process. Open-ended questions should be used. For example, "When was the first time you ate yesterday?" and "Did you drink anything?" are better than "Did you eat breakfast?" or "Did you drink milk?" The latter questions may evoke unreliable answers because the client may not want to reveal that she did not eat breakfast, and she may assume that she should tell you she drank milk. The disadvantage of the dietary interview method is that it takes considerable time to obtain the information.

4 Evaluate the nutritional adequacy of the diet with the client. With the client seated beside the nurse, both can count the number of servings of basic foods (milk, meat, fruits, vegetables, bread, and cereals) the client consumed. Next, both can compare the number of servings the client ate with those recommended. (See Figure 17-4.) The client can then identify where changes in her diet are needed. These changes are written on the client's leaflet, or appropriate sections can be underlined. This individualizes the leaflet and makes it more meaningful to her. At this point, the nurse can ask her if she knows why it is important for her to make changes. It is not unusual for pregnant women to know both the nutritive value of foods (e.g., milk is a good source of calcium) and the function of nutrients (e.g., calcium is important for strong bones and teeth). If the client needs information, provide it. See the section Suggestions for Nutrition Counseling for ideas. The client should indicate that she understands and accepts the need for making dietary changes before the nurse proceeds to the next step.

5 Ask the pregnant woman which changes she is willing to make and how she will go about making them.

DIETARY INTAKE RECORD

INSTRUCTIONS:

Write down everything you ate yesterday.
Include foods eaten at meals and between meals.
Give specific foods and amounts of foods, for example:

$\frac{1}{2}$ cup of orange juice, *not just fruit juice*
2 slices roast beef, *not just meat*
2 slices of white bread with bologna, *not just a sandwich*

NAME OF FOOD	AMOUNT	TIME OF DAY

Is this the way you usually eat?   Yes _____   No _____

Date _____   Day _____

Patient's Name _____

Patient's Record Number _____

PLEASE NOTE   Physician _____   Other _____

Dietitian _____   Social Worker _____

NURSE'S RECORD

Food Groups	Amounts Eaten
Milk	
Meat	
Vegetable-Fruit	
Vitamin A . . .	
Vitamin C . . .	
Other	
Cereal-Bread . . .	

Modified Diet

Problems

Recommendations

Nurse's Signature _____

_____ (Date)

FIGURE 17-5
Dietary intake record. (*Adapted from Nutrition Program, Community Health Services, Department of Health Services, County of Los Angeles. Reproduced by permission.*)

Allow her enough time to consider these questions and to answer them. Clients will frequently solve the whole problem and make a decision for change. If a client has difficulties finding solutions, the nurse can make suggestions. Give her enough time to decide which suggestions are acceptable. When she has decided, write this information on the teaching leaflet. Ask her to keep the leaflet in a conspicuous place in the kitchen where she can refer to it.

6   The nurse informs the client that she will see her again to find out if she has been able to carry out her plan, or if new problems develop. It is desirable to discuss nutrition with clients at more than one session. Some women who were eating an adequate diet at the time of the first conversation may subsequently experience problems. When problems such as anemia, constipation, diabetes, or others develop, additional counseling is required. If the client has not made the anticipated changes, then the nurse will need to determine why and to make additional suggestions. It is important to remember that it is difficult for people to make changes in eating habits, and more than one counseling session is usually necessary.

Suggestions for Nutrition Counseling

This section provides some suggestions for counseling pregnant women with nutrition problems using words and expressions the author has found successful. Over time, the nurse will gain additional ideas from clients, nutritionists, dietitians, other nurses, and physicians. None of the following expressions, approaches, or suggestions will be successful for all clients. However, they do serve as a basis for each nurse to develop a *smorgasbord* of ideas to present to the client for her selection.

Gastrointestinal Complaints

GAS   Advise the client who complains of gas not to eat rapidly, for this can result in swallowing air. Also suggest that the client not eat foods that cause *her* to form gas; this is a highly individual matter. Foods that cause gas for some people include onions, cabbage, cauliflower, brussel sprouts, collard greens, dried beans, and sweet potatoes eaten with buttermilk at the same meal.

HEARTBURN AND REGURGITATION   Symptoms of heartburn and regurgitation of foods may be relieved if the client eats smaller meals, that is, does not overload her stomach. It may also be helpful to avoid fried foods and other foods that are high in fat. These foods remain in the stomach longer than other foods. During pregnancy the stomach is less efficient in digesting food and emptying the stomach. Food may stay in the stomach too long and come back up through the esophagus because of reverse peristalsis. The acid content of the stomach burns the esophagus and causes heartburn. The physician may prescribe medicines which may temporarily relieve the problem.

NAUSEA AND VOMITING   Physicians vary in their dietary suggestions for nausea and vomiting, and clients vary in their responses. The following ideas work with some women: avoid foods that are fatty, highly spiced, or tend to be gassy. Eat several small dry meals a day. Drink liquids only between meals. When nauseated, eat a small amount of the following: carbonated beverage, sugar-coated cereal without milk, caramel corn, grapefruit juice, orange juice, or grape juice.

MORNING SICKNESS Physician recommendations and client responses to *morning sickness* (nausea and vomiting only in the morning) vary. The following may be helpful: Before getting out of bed, eat dry bread, toast, or crackers. Get out of bed *very* slowly. Sleep with enough fresh air to avoid smelling household odors or soiled clothing. When cooking, have enough ventilation to get rid of cooking odors.

CONSTIPATION Adequate liquid intake can relieve constipation. Suggest drinking 6 to 8 glasses of fluids a day, including water, milk, tea, coffee, and fruit juices. Foods, such as whole-grain breads and cereals and raw vegetables and fruits, especially prunes and apples, may be helpful. Advise the client to establish regular elimination habits.

Leg Cramps

This condition may be caused by fatigue. Frequent changing of the position of the legs may help. In some pregnant women there is a disturbance in calcium metabolism which results in leg cramps. If calcium intake is inadequate, advise the client to increase intake from the milk group. Some physicians prescribe calcium tablets to relieve the condition.

Lack of Knowledge about the Four Food Groups

MILK GROUP These foods are the main source of calcium and riboflavin in our diets. They also contain a considerable amount of protein and all the nutrients a baby needs for growth except iron and vitamin C.

MEAT GROUP This group includes meats and other high-protein foods such as fish, poultry, eggs, dried beans, dried peas, nuts, and cheese. These foods are the major source of protein in our diet. They also contain iron,

thiamine, niacin, vitamin B_6, and zinc. Some of them also contain vitamin B_{12}, vitamin E, iodine, and magnesium.

Some people may be *lacto-ovo vegetarians;* that is, they do not eat meat but do drink milk and eat cheese and eggs. An adequate diet can be built around this eating preference by suggesting that the client drink recommended amounts of milk and eat recommended amounts of high-protein nonmeat foods such as cheese, peanut butter, nuts, cooked dry beans, and imitation meat products made from soybeans.

VEGETABLE-FRUIT GROUP Certain vegetables and fruits have more nutritive value than others. It is important to distinguish the following:

> *Dark green and deep yellow vegetables* contain large amounts of carotene, which our bodies convert to vitamin A. (See Figure 17-6.) They also contain other vitamins and minerals. Dark green vegetables like spinach contain much more vitamin A than green beans. Dark yellow vegetables like carrots contain much more vitamin A than corn.
> *Citrus fruits and certain other fruits and vegetables* are high in vitamin C. (See Figure 17-7.) Compare the vitamin C in orange juice with that in apples.
> *Other fruits and vegetables* contain vitamins and minerals but are not as rich in specific vitamins as the dark green and deep yellow vegetables or citrus fruits.

BREAD-CEREAL GROUP This group contains worthwhile amounts of thiamine, iron, niacin, and riboflavin, and smaller amounts of other vitamins, minerals, and protein. Whole-grain breads and cereals are important sources of magnesium and zinc.

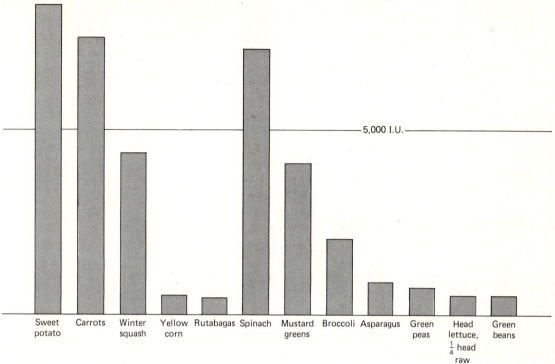

FIGURE 17-6

Vitamin A in foods (½ cup cooked). (*Adapted from Nutrition Program, Community Health Services, Department of Health Services, County of Los Angeles. Reproduced by permission.*)

Lack of Knowledge of the Function of Nutrients

It is better to talk about nutrients in terms of *promoting health* rather than preventing disease since most overt clinical deficiency diseases are rare in this country and unknown to clients. The following paragraphs give simple ways to explain the functions of nutrients.

CALORIES Calories are what we need for energy. We need energy to live and babies need energy to grow. We obtain energy from foods and this source of energy is called calories. Life is not possible without calories.

PROTEIN Protein is the substance of which life is made. It is in every cell of our bodies. The body throws away a certain amount of protein every day, and we have to replace this with protein from foods. The unborn child needs protein to build its body.

VITAMINS AND MINERALS

Vitamin A is important for proper vision and healthy eyes, for growth, and for the functioning of mucous membranes. Run your tongue around the inside of your mouth. Feel how slick and moist it is. This kind of tissue lines your stomach, intestines, lungs, and other organs. Vitamin A is necessary to keep these tissues moist, firm, and healthy.

Vitamin C is necessary for the cementing material that glues the body cells together. Our bodies are made of cells.

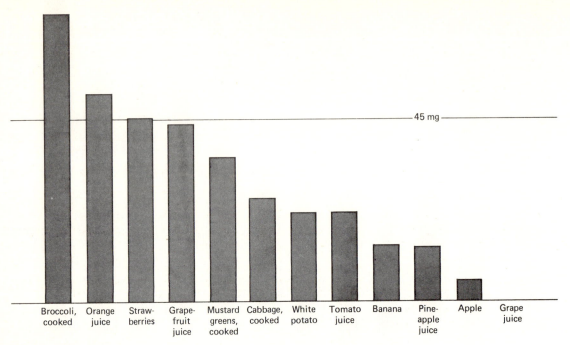

45 mg

Broccoli, cooked — Orange juice — Straw-berries — Grape-fruit juice — Mustard greens, cooked — Cabbage, cooked — White potato — Tomato juice — Banana — Pine-apple juice — Apple — Grape juice

FIGURE 17-7

Vitamin C in foods (½ cup). (*Adapted from Nutrition Program, Community Health Services, Department of Health Services, County of Los Angeles. Reproduced by permission.*)

Imagine a brick wall without mortar to hold the bricks together; it would be a weak wall. When we do not eat enough vitamin C, we feel weak and tired and we may bleed easily. Vitamin C helps bind the cells together in the baby growing in your body.

The B vitamins include thiamine, riboflavin, niacin, and vitamin B_6. They have many functions; one important one is to help us get energy from foods. Our body uses foods by a very complicated process that requires B vitamins. If we do not eat enough of these vitamins we do not have enough energy, which may result in a poor appetite, nervousness, and poor digestion. Folacin and vitamin B_{12} are also called B vitamins and are important for making blood as well as for other functions in the body.

Vitamin D is necessary for hard bones. Bones are hard, and the substances that make them hard are calcium, phosphorus, and other minerals. We get calcium from food, but we need *vitamin D* in order to get the calcium from the food into our bodies and then into our bones and teeth.

Calcium is one of the substances that makes our bones and teeth hard. For some reason we lose a little calcium from our bodies each day, and we must replace it. The unborn baby also needs calcium to make bones hard.

Iron is one of the substances we need to make hemoglobin. Hemoglobin is what makes our blood red. Hemoglobin carries oxygen to body cells where the oxygen is used to burn food for energy. If we do not eat enough foods containing iron, we do not have enough hemoglobin and we become anemic. Symptoms of anemia include loss of energy and tiredness. The unborn baby needs to store enough iron in the liver to last from 3 to 5 months after birth. After birth, the baby must obtain iron from foods.

Insufficient Milk Intake

The client may like milk and/or buttermilk, and only need encouragement to drink it, or the client may dislike regular milk but be willing to drink buttermilk or skim milk. When clients drink coffee, tea, and soft drinks, suggest replacing these with milk, or suggest that clients drink milk plus these beverages at the same meal. Clients can be instructed to take in some of the milk in the form of hard cheeses, foods cooked with milk (e.g., puddings), and milk served with food (e.g., milk on cereal). It is not practical for women to try to eat three glasses of milk a day in cooked foods.

Some clients do not like the taste of milk. It can be suggested that they flavor milk with coffee, vanilla, cocoa, or molasses. They can drink double-strength milk made by adding one-third cup nonfat dry milk to one glass of milk, and flavorings can be added to this mixture.

Some clients cannot or will not drink milk. These women will need to eat an additional 90 g per day of meat, fish, poultry, or meat alternative, plus calcium tablets and a supplement containing riboflavin.

Insufficient Intake of Foods High in Vitamin A or Vitamin C

Clients may not know which foods are high in vitamin A, and Figure 17-6 can be used in teaching. They may be willing to eat raw vegetables rich in vitamin A such as carrots, or raw spinach in a salad. Sweet potatoes and winter squash are often acceptable and palatable.

Clients may not be acquainted with foods high in vitamin C, and Figure 17-7 can be used for teaching. Most women like citrus fruits. If they are allergic to foods high in vitamin C, or dislike them, a vitamin C supplement is recommended.

Poor Meal and Snack Habits

When clients do not eat at least three meals a day, they are unlikely to consume all the recommended foods. Breakfast is frequently missed or skipped.

Suggest a minimal breakfast, such as milk and toast, and suggest that the client plan a midmorning snack, such as eggs and fruit. Alternately, it can be suggested that a woman skip an early breakfast and eat a late one instead of a midmorning snack. Nontraditional breakfast foods such as sandwiches, dinner leftovers, and other foods usually eaten for lunch or dinner can be eaten for breakfast.

Some clients may simply not plan for lunch, or may be unaccustomed to eating at this time. It can be suggested to the woman that she write menu plans for lunch, and that she have simple-to-prepare foods available for lunch such as cheese, peanut butter, luncheon meat, and fresh or canned fruit.

Some women eat many snack foods which are high in calories and poor in nutritive value. Instead of suggesting that they stop eating snacks, suggest a menu pattern like the one below.

Breakfast: citrus fruit, cereal and milk, toast, margarine
Snack: egg sandwich and milk
Lunch: cottage cheese or peanut butter sandwich, vegetable or fruit, milk
Snack: milk and fruit

Dinner: meat, fish, or fowl, dark green or deep yellow vegetable, potato, coffee or tea, dessert

Snack: milk and cookies

Suggest that the client eat a good source of protein for each snack to provide satiety and maintain a constant blood sugar level. Clients may not follow the exact plan suggested, but they will get ideas for planning meals and snacks themselves.

Underweight and Failure to Gain Adequate Weight

Women who were underweight before becoming pregnant and those who fail to gain adequate weight during pregnancy are frequently hyperactive with poor appetites. Recommendations that are acceptable to them will be done on a trial-and-error basis. The following measures may be suggested to such clients.

Schedule rest periods to slow the pace of activities and to reduce total physical activity. A short nap or rest before mealtimes may enhance the appetite. Plan regular meals and plan to sit down and eat. Eat six or seven small meals a day rather than three large ones. The menu given above might help. Try eating extra portions of high-fat foods such as butter, margarine, mayonnaise, and cream. Add cream to milk and coffee, and use cream over cereals. Use extra butter on bread and use both jelly and butter on bread. Eat more desserts and sweets in addition to the basic foods. Include high-calorie foods in snacks, such as dried fruits, eggnog, nuts, and hard cheese.

The client may be nervous or emotionally upset and may need counseling to help with such problems.

Overweight and Gaining Too Much Weight

If overweight is recent, find out if the client has had recent emotional or social problems. If so, counsel her about these problems or refer her to a social worker or psychologist for counseling. Review the diet with the client to see if she is eating adequate amounts of basic foods. If she is not, counsel her accordingly. Next, review the quantities of basic foods eaten to see if servings are too large or too many, e.g., too much bread or milk. Suggest a reduction in quantity if necessary. Last, determine which foods the client is eating in addition to the basic foods by asking her to check the foods on the following list. Let the patient decide which foods she can eliminate or reduce.

Foods high in fat

Avocado	Fried beans
Bacon	Gravy
Chocolate candy	Half-and-half
Cream cheese	Ice cream
Coconut cream	Mayonnaise
Cream	Nuts
Corn chips	Pie crust
Doughnuts	Potato chips
Fatback	Salad dressing
Fat on meat	Sausage
Fried meat, fish, fowl	Vegetables and beans cooked with fat meat
Fried potatoes	

Foods high in carbohydrates or alcohol

Beer	Jelly
Cake	Liquor
Candy	Molasses
Corn chips	Sherbert
Cookies	Soft drinks
Fruit canned in heavy syrup	Sugar
Honey	Sweet rolls
Jam	Syrup
	Wine

If the client has a large appetite and is frequently hungry, suggest the menu and snack pattern outlined in the section Poor Meal and Snack Habits.

Fear of Overweight

Some women deliberately limit their food intake for fear of gaining too much weight and losing their figures. Explain that average weight loss from childbirth and within the first week postpartum is 8 to 9 kg. Most women continue to lose some weight during the first 3 months after delivery and return to normal weight by that time. Explain to the client that she can hasten the return to her normal figure by eating a nutritionally adequate diet and by doing special postpartum exercises.

Anemia

Women who are anemic often eat irregular meals and eat very few vegetables and fruits, and their diets are often inadequate. The nurse can counsel the patient to help her eat a nutritionally adequate diet and encourage her to eat some of the following high-iron foods as often as possible: cereals highly fortified with iron, liver and liver sausage, dark green leafy vegetables, dried beans, dried fruits. Suggest adding dry infant cereal to regular cereal because the infant cereal is fortified with iron, does not detract from the flavor or texture of the regular cereal, and is inexpensive and easy to use.

When discussing anemia with clients, remember they often do not understand the terms hemoglobin and hematocrit and these terms should be explained to them.

Iron supplements may cause upset stomachs; hence, clients may refuse to take them.

Suggest that iron supplements be taken with meals, which reduces the frequency and intensity of the nausea.

Antepartum Classes

Many nurses teach one or two sessions about nutrition during pregnancy as part of a series of antepartum classes. The most effective method for a class is a modification of the principles suggested for individual client counseling. The following steps have been found to be helpful.

1 Start out by asking the women to bring a record of what they ate on a typical day to the class.
2 Have each person score her own diet, i.e., count the number of servings of foods she ate and compare this with those recommended in an antepartum diet plan.
3 Make a composite count of how many members in the class ate the recommended number of servings of each of the basic foods (milk, meat, fruits, vegetables, cereals, breads). Record this information on a blackboard.
4 Have the group discuss why they are not eating the recommended amounts of the basic foods. This can include information about why these foods are important, the nutritive value of the foods, the function of nutrients they contain, and the importance of nutrition during pregnancy.
5 Have the group exchange ideas about how they can improve their diet. The nurse can participate and offer ideas.
6 Have each member of the group write down the changes she intends to make before the next class session.
7 At the next session, have the group dis-

cuss which changes they have made and not made. Discuss additional suggestions for making the desired changes.

8 Visual aids can be helpful to the nurse in teaching.

NUTRITION AND FOOD NEEDS DURING THE POSTPARTUM PERIOD

The postpartum woman benefits from nutrition counseling which ensures that she continues to eat an adequate diet. She will need to maintain a good state of nutrition to prepare for a subsequent pregnancy, and/or to help her continue to be a healthy, productive person. The postpartum woman should be encouraged to continue to take antepartum vitamin-mineral supplements until the supply is exhausted, for the supplements can help replenish nutrient stores. The postpartum period is also an appropriate time to counsel women about nutrition when they need to gain or lose weight, as the case may be.

There are differences in the calorie and nutrient needs of the postpartum woman depending on whether she is lactating, taking oral contraceptives, using intrauterine devices, or none of these. These differences are important for the nurse to understand.

Lactating Women

The recommended dietary allowances for the woman who is breast-feeding are shown in Table 17-1. The increased needs of the lactating woman above those of the nonpregnant woman include the following.

Calories and Protein

The breast-feeding woman needs an additional 500 kcal above the nonpregnant woman during the first 3 months of lacta-

tion.[53] Milk production requires energy, and breast milk contains kilocalories. The Food and Nutrition Board estimates that the fat stored during pregnancy plus 500 kcal per day will be sufficient for milk production for the first 3 months of the infant's life. Subsequently, the fat stored for this purpose is depleted, and the kilocalorie intake must be increased to a level that will maintain the woman's desired weight.[54] It is unlikely that a lactating mother will eat enough calories to gain excess fat. Most lactating women need help in consuming enough calories to maintain their desired weight.

An additional 20 g of protein per day is recommended for the lactating woman. This provides for the protein content of breast milk.

Calcium and Iron

Additional calcium is needed to provide for the calcium found in breast milk. This increase can readily be attained by diet. The lactating woman needs no increase in iron over the nonpregnant woman, since breast milk contains a very small amount of iron.

Vitamins D, A, and C

During lactation an intake of 400 IU of vitamin D is recommended to make it possible to use and metabolize calcium and deposit it into breast milk. An additional 1,000 IU of vitamin A above the level recommended for the nonpregnant woman is needed to provide for the vitamin A secreted in breast milk.[55] The amount of vitamin C recommended for the lactating woman is almost twice the amount for the nonpregnant woman. That double amount of vitamin C ensures that the infant will be able to obtain enough of this vitamin to meet his or her needs.

Other Vitamins and Minerals

There is an increased allowance above that for the nonpregnant woman for all the recommended vitamins and minerals except iron. The increases reflect either needs for nutrients in producing breast milk and/or the provision for the nutrient in breast milk.

A dietary plan that meets the recommended dietary allowances for pregnancy will also meet the allowances for lactation, with the exception of kilocalories. The lactating woman can simply continue to eat her antepartum diet plus additional calories. (See the calculations in Table 17-2.)

Women Taking Oral Contraceptives

There is some biochemical evidence that suggests an increased need in this group of women for vitamin B_6, vitamin B_{12}, vitamin C, and vitamin A and a decreased need for iron and copper. However, no recommended daily allowances have been established. The clinical significance of the biochemical evidence is not clear at this time.[56]

Some clinicians have observed a number of generalized symptoms in women taking oral contraceptives. The symptoms are subtle in their onset and appear to represent nutritional deficiency symptoms. These symptoms are most likely to occur in postpartum women who were in a poor state of nutrition when they became pregnant and who were not in a good state during pregnancy. They may also occur in women who were in a mild deficiency state when they started taking the contraceptives. These symptoms have not been validated by scientific study and are not reported in the literature. However, the nurse may wish to be alert for them and refer patients exhibiting such symptoms to the physician for clinical evaluation and treatment. They are as follows: hypotonia of the gastroin-

testinal tract, exhibited by gas, indigestion, and constipation; headaches; hyperirritability; depression; loss of appetite; poor sleep; mild anemia; weakness; changes in weight, up or down; menstrual disorders; splitting nails; hair falling out; cracked lips; and sore tongue.[57] Most women do not experience these symptoms and should be counseled to eat a normal, nutritionally adequate diet.

Women Using Intrauterine Devices

Some women who use an intrauterine device (IUD) experience a greater than normal menstrual blood loss which can result in anemia. It is important to monitor the hemoglobin levels in women using an IUD and to take appropriate action if anemia develops. For some of these women, counseling about a nutritionally adequate diet and recommendation of an iron supplement are advisable. Most women do not experience this problem and should be counseled to eat a normal nutritionally adequate diet.

Nutrition during the Interconceptional and Preconceptional Period

Women who have been well nourished during infancy, and through childhood, adolescence, and adulthood, are most likely to have an uneventful pregnancy and a good outcome. Counseling clients about a normal, nutritionally adequate diet during these periods can have beneficial effects in increasing the number of healthy babies born to healthy women.

CONCLUSION

There is considerable evidence that nutrition is an important factor during pregnancy and has an influence on the health of the woman and her baby. The following points should be considered:

An average weight gain of 11 kg during pregnancy is recommended. The suggested rate of weight gain is 625 to 1,250 g during the first trimester, and 370 g per week during the remainder of pregnancy.

Special attention should be given to the nutritional needs of adolescents.

The underweight woman who becomes pregnant needs special attention.

Weight reduction regimens should not be undertaken until after pregnancy.

Routine restriction of salt during pregnancy is not recommended.

The nurse has an important contribution to make in the nutrition care of the pregnant and postpartum woman.

GUIDE FOR EVALUATING FOOD INTAKE*

Milk Group

Milk to drink	*Count as 1 serving*
Whole milk	240 g, 1 cup, 1 glass, $\frac{1}{4}$ liter
Buttermilk	
Low-fat milk	
Nonfat milk, reconstituted	
Evaporated milk, reconstituted	
Cocoa made with milk	
Malted milk	
Milk shake	

Milk to eat	
Cream soups (1 can plus 1 can of milk)	1 cup

* Adapted from information put out by Nutrition Program, Community Health Services, Department of Health Services, County of Los Angeles. Used by permission.

Hard cheeses, (cheddar, swiss, processed)	1 slice or 30 g
Macaroni and cheese	1 cup
Yogurt	1 cup
	Count as $\frac{1}{2}$ serving
Ice milk	$\frac{1}{2}$ cup
Ice cream	$\frac{1}{2}$ cup
Milk on cereal	1 serving—count $\frac{1}{2}$ cup of milk on cereal
Puddings and custards	$\frac{1}{2}$ cup

Do not count
Cream
Cream cheese
Cottage cheese ($\frac{1}{2}$ cup is a serving; count this in the meat group)
Blue cheese
Butter or margarine

Meat Group

A serving of meat is the amount of meat you would have if you cooked 150 g of raw hamburger. The meat would shrink to 120 g. This is a small serving of meat, and many pregnant women can easily eat two servings at a meal, e.g., two meat balls, two chops, a large slice of roast meat, etc. Lower-income women may eat smaller servings of meat, fish, and poultry.

Foods in the meat group	*Count as*
Meat, fish, or poultry	1 serving, 90–120 g of meat
Canned fish, chicken, or meat	$\frac{1}{2}$ serving, 60 g of meat

Frankfurters	$\frac{1}{2}$ serving, 60 g of meat	Carrots	Mustard greens
Luncheon meat	4 slices, 60 g of meat	Cantaloupe	Pumpkin
Chili con carne with beans	$\frac{1}{2}$ serving, 60 g of meat	Chard	Spinach
		Collard greens	Sweet potatoes
Canned meat, fish, or poultry in sandwiches made at home	$\frac{1}{2}$ serving, 60 g of meat	Dandelion greens	Turnip greens
		Hubbard squash	Winter squash
		Kale	Yams
Meat, fish, or poultry sandwich made at restaurant	1 serving, 120 g of meat		

Citrus and other high-vitamin C foods (a serving is $\frac{1}{2}$ cup or 1 medium piece of fruit)

Broccoli	Mangoes
Brussel sprouts	Mustard greens
Cantaloupe	Orange or juice
Cauliflower	Papayas
Collard greens	Strawberries
Grapefruit or juice	Turnip greens
Green pepper	Tomato, 1 raw medium
Guava	

Meat alternates	*Count as*
Eggs, 2	$\frac{1}{2}$ serving or 60 g of meat
Cottage cheese, $\frac{1}{2}$ cup	
Cooked dried beans, 1 cup	
Peanut butter, 4 tablespoons	
Nuts, 1 cup	

Other fruits and vegetables (a serving is $\frac{1}{2}$ cup or 1 medium piece of fruit)

Two servings of the fruits below will provide about as much vitamin C as $\frac{1}{2}$ cup of orange juice; when clients regularly eat two servings of these foods a day, they do not need to eat a citrus fruit or other food high in vitamin C.

Meat extenders	*Count as*
Chicken and noodles, homemade, 1 cup	$\frac{1}{2}$ serving or 60 g of meat
Fish chowder, homemade, 1 cup	
Hash, 1 cup	
Stews, homemade, 1 cup	
Pizza	
Vegetable soup, homemade, 1 cup	

Asparagus	Honeydew melon
Bean sprouts	Lemonade
Cabbage	Tangerine or juice
Chili pepper (a serving is 1 to 2 tablespoons)	Tomatoes, canned
	Tomato juice
	Watermelon

Vegetable and Fruit Group

Dark green and deep yellow vegetables (a serving is $\frac{1}{2}$ cup)

Acorn squash	Banana squash
Apricots, dried (4 apricots)	Broccoli
	Beet greens

Foods which are good iron sources

Peas (green), $\frac{1}{2}$ cup serving	Raisins, 1 tablespoon serving
Prunes, 4	
Prune juice, $\frac{1}{2}$ cup serving	

Foods containing small amounts of a variety of vitamins and minerals (a serving is $\frac{1}{2}$ cup or 1 medium piece of fruit)

Apples

Bananas

Bamboo shoots

Berries (except
strawberries)

Beets

Celery

Corn

Cucumber

Eggplant

Figs

Fruit cocktail

Fruit in gelatin
desserts

Fruit in pies

Grapes

Green beans

Lettuce

Mushrooms

Onions

Parsnips

Peaches

Pears

Plums

Plantains

Radishes

Rutabagas

Summer squash

Turnips

Vegetable soup

Vegetable soup
with beef or
chicken

Zucchini

Bread and Cereal Group

Whole-grain breads and cereals are preferred to enriched products because they contain zinc, magnesium, vitamin B_6, and other nutrients in addition to the thiamine, riboflavin, niacin, and iron found in enriched and fortified products. Some cereals are labeled as a food supplement and contain over one-half of the recommended amounts of all the nutrients listed in the *Recommended Dietary Allowances.*

Thirty g of meat, or its equivalent from the meat group, can substitute for one serving of bread or cereal. Meat and its equivalents from the meat group contain all the vitamins and minerals found in grains plus more protein than bread and cereals.

Bread (a serving is 1 slice)

White bread

Whole-grain
bread (wheat,

rye, oatmeal,
etc.)

Biscuits

Crackers

Corn bread

Muffins

Pancakes

Rolls

Tortillas

Waffles

Cooked cereals (a serving is $\frac{1}{2}$ cup)

Buckwheat

Oatmeal

Whole wheat

Farina

Grits

Macaroni

Spaghetti and
other pastas

Rice—brown,
converted,
enriched

Ready-to-eat cereals (a serving is $\frac{3}{4}$ cup)

Shredded wheat

Wheat flakes

Corn flakes

Puffed rice

Puffed wheat

Other

Canned chicken
noodle soup

Canned beef
noodle soup

Doughnuts

Oatmeal cookies

Peanut butter
cookies

Foods to Be Counted Only if Overweight Is a Problem

Foods high in fat

Avocado

Bacon

Butter

Chocolate candy

Cream (sweet
or sour)

Cream cheese

Coconut cream

Corn chips

Doughnuts

Fatback

Fat on meat

Fried meat,
fish, fowl,
potatoes, etc.

Fried beans

Fried foods

Gravy

Half-and-half

Ice cream

Margarine

Mayonnaise

Nuts

Pie crust

Potato chips

Salad dressing

Salt pork

Sausage

Vegetables and
beans cooked
with fat meat

Foods high in carbohydrates or alcohol

Beer	Liquor
Cake	Molasses
Candy	Sherbert
Cookies	Soft drinks (pop)
Fruit (canned in	Sugar
heavy syrup)	Sweet rolls
Honey	Syrup
Jam	Wine
Jelly	

Foods Not to Be Counted

Artificially	Mustard
sweetened	Other condiments
beverages	Pickles
Catsup	Tea
Coffee	

REFERENCES

1   Antonov, A. N.: "Children Born during the Siege of Leningrad in 1942," *Journal of Pediatrics*, 30:250–259, 1947.

2   Smith, C. A.: "Effects of Maternal Undernutrition upon the Newborn Infant in Holland (1944–1945)," *Journal of Pediatrics*, 30:229–243, 1947.

3   Smith, C. A.: "The Effect of Wartime Starvation in Holland upon Pregnancy and Its Product," *American Journal of Obstetrics and Gynecology*, 53:599–608, 1947.

4   Burke, B. S., V. A. Beal, A. B. Kirkwood, and H. C. Stuart: "Nutrition Studies during Pregnancy," *American Journal of Obstetrics and Gynecology*, 46:38–52, 1943.

5   Burke, B. S., S. S. Stevenson, J. Worcester, and H. C. Stuart: "Nutrition Studies during Pregnancy, V, Relation of Maternal Nutrition to Condition of Infant at Birth: Study of Siblings," *The Journal of Nutrition*, 38:453–467, 1949.

6   Jeans, P. C., M. B. Smith, and G. Stearns: "Incidence of Prematurity in Relation to Maternal Nutrition," *Journal of the American Dietetic Association*, 31:576–581, 1955.

7   Martin, H. P.: "Nutrition and Its Relationship to a Child's Physical, Mental and Emotional Development," *American Journal of Clinical Nutrition*, 26:766–775, 1973.

8   *Maternal Nutrition and the Course of Pregnancy*, Committee on Maternal Nutrition, Food and Nutrition Board, National Research Council, National Academy of Sciences, Washington, D.C., 1970, p. 3.

9   Ibid., p. 182.

10   *Recommended Dietary Allowances*, 8th ed., Food and Nutrition Board, National Research Council, National Academy of Sciences, Washington, D.C., 1974, p. 129.

11   Pitkin, R. M., et al.: "Maternal Nutrition: A Selective Review of Clinical Topics," *American Journal of Obstetrics and Gynecology*, 40:773–785, 1972.

12   *Nutrition in Maternal Health Care*, American College of Obstetricians and Gynecologists, Chicago, 1974.

13   *Maternal Nutrition and the Course of Pregnancy*, op. cit., p. 190.

14   *Maternal Nutrition and the Course of Pregnancy, Summary Report*, Committee on Maternal Nutrition, Food and Nutrition Board, National Research Council, National Academy of Sciences, Washington, D.C., 1970, p. 13.

15   *Policy Statement on Nutrition and Pregnancy*, Executive Board of the American College of Obstetricians and Gynecologists, Chicago, Dec. 1, 1972.

16   Pitkin: op. cit., p. 779.

17   *Maternal Nutrition and the Course of Pregnancy*, op. cit., p. 176.

18   Tompkins, W. T., and D. G. Wiehl: "Nutritional Deficiencies as a Causal Factor in Toxemia and Premature Labor," *American Journal of Obstetrics and Gynecology*, 62:898–919, 1951.

19   Tompkins, W. T., D. G. Wiehl, and R. M. Mitchell: "The Underweight Patient as an In-

creased Obstetric Hazard," *American Journal of Obstetrics and Gynecology*, 69:114–123, 1955.

20 Pitkin: op. cit., p. 779.

21 Bergner, L., and W. Susser: "Low Birth Weight and Prenatal Nutrition," *Pediatrics*, 46:946–966, 1970.

22 Tompkins, W. T., R. M. Mitchell, and D. G. Wiehl: "Maternal and Newborn Nutrition Studies at Philadelphia Lying-In Hospital," *The Promotion of Maternal and Newborn Health*, Milbank Memorial Fund, New York, 1955, p. 48.

23 Tompkins, W.T., et al.: "The Underweight Patient as an Increased Obstetric Hazard," op. cit., p. 117.

24 *Recommended Dietary Allowances*, op. cit., p. 47.

25 *Maternal Nutrition and the Course of Pregnancy, Summary Report*, op. cit., p. 12.

26 Pitkin: op. cit., p. 776.

27 Albanese, Anthony A.: "Nutritional Aspects of Bone Loss," *Food and Nutrition News*, December–January 1975–76, p. 1.

28 *Recommended Dietary Allowances*, op. cit., p. 94.

29 Recommended Dietary Allowances, op. cit., p. 54.

30 *Nutrition in Maternal Health Care*, op. cit., p. 3.

31 *Recommended Dietary Allowances*, op. cit., p. 90.

32 *Policy Statement on Nutrition and Pregnancy*, op. cit., p. 1.

33 Pike, R. L., and H. A. Smiciklas: "A Reappraisal of Sodium Restriction during Pregnancy," *International Journal of Gynecology and Obstetrics*, 10:1–8, 1972.

34 Hytten, F. E., and L. Leitsch: *The Physiology of Human Pregnancy*, 2d ed., Blackwell, Oxford, 1971, p. 348.

35 *Recommended Dietary Allowances*, op. cit., p. 100.

36 *Recommended Dietary Allowances*, op. cit., p. 54.

37 *Recommended Dietary Allowances*, op. cit., p. 54.

38 *Recommended Dietary Allowances*, op. cit., p. 56.

39 *Maternal Nutrition and the Course of Pregnancy*, op. cit., pp. 91–92.

40 *Recommended Dietary Allowances*, op. cit., p. 74.

41 *National Food Guide*, U.S. Department of Agriculture Leaflet 288, March 1957.

42 *Nutrition during Pregnancy and Lactation . . . for Professional Use*, California Department of Health, Berkeley, March 1975, pp. 34–41.

43 Weigley, E. S.: "The Pregnant Adolescent," *Journal of the American Dietetic Association*, 66:588–591, 1975.

44 Cooper, L. F.: "Florence Nightingale's Contribution to Dietetics," *Journal of the American Dietetic Association*, 30:121–127, 1954.

45 Weigley: op. cit.

46 King, J. E., S. H. Cohenour, D. H. Calloway, and H. N. Jacobson: "Assessment of Nutrition Status of Teenage Pregnant Girls, 1, Nutrient Intake and Pregnancy," *American Journal of Clinical Nutrition*, 25:916–925, 1972.

47 Weigley: op. cit., p. 588.

48 King: op. cit., p. 918.

49 Meyer, R. J., et al.: "Who Cares for the Pregnant Adolescent?" Community Pediatric Society and other organizations, no date.

50 Egan, Mary: "Nutrition Services for Adolescent Girls," in R. J. Meyer et al., "Who Cares for the Pregnant Adolescent?" Community Pediatric Society and other organizations, pp. 26–30.

51 Weigley: op. cit., p. 591.

52 Meyer et al.: "Who Cares for the Pregnant Adolescent?" Community Pediatric Society and other organizations, p. 47.

53 *Recommended Dietary Allowances*, op. cit., p. 32.

54 *Recommended Dietary Allowances*, op. cit., p. 55.

55 *Recommended Dietary Allowances*, op. cit., p. 54.

56 *Oral Contraceptives and Nutrition*, statement by the Committee on Nutrition of the Mother and the Preschool Child, Food and Nutrition Board, National Research Council, National Academy of Sciences, Washington, D.C., 1975.

57 Tompkins, W. T.: personal communication, October 1974.

18

Safety and Activities during Pregnancy

MARY B. JOHNSON

Most of the advice given to women about activities and safety during pregnancy focuses upon the physical aspects, but the emotionality inherent in each aspect cannot be denied. Pregnancy is both a physiological state and an emotional experience. Maintenance of the best possible physical condition is one of the prime goals of antepartum care. However, the health team's efforts cannot be directed to the physiological needs alone. Emotional care and understanding by professional health personnel are necessary in order to treat the client within the totality of her pregnancy. Good antepartum care considers the woman as an individual within her specific medical and sociocultural situation.

The nurse usually works within one of three settings—a private doctor's office, a clinic, or in the community. Wherever the work setting is, nurses must identify the population of clients with whom they are working before they can begin to advise women about their activities and safety during pregnancy. Age, marital status, habits, motivation, levels of knowledge, culture, socioeconomic level, and many more factors will influence the nurse's approach to clients.

The initial contact between the nurse and client is important because it may set the tone of their relationship for the duration of that woman's pregnancy. The nurse should be a sympathetic listener, a friend, and a resource person. Not only a thorough knowledge of the physiological and psychological aspects of pregnancy are needed, but also a recognition on the part of nurses as to their own feelings in relation to pregnancy, motherhood, sex, and femininity. Insight, not intimidation, is the key to establishing a role as a caring, resourceful person.

The nurse's role is to augment the obstetrician, not to displace his or her philosophy and advice. There is considerable difference of opinion concerning the details of management of pregnancy. The directions given here are basically generalities. Within a health care setting, the physician and nurse consider the client as an individual with a unique pregnancy.

EMPLOYMENT

Today women of childbearing age are a major factor in the labor force, and it is difficult to say "yes" or "no" when a client asks if she should continue working. Realistic adjustments in her mode of life must be made if employment is physically or mentally jeopardizing her health or pregnancy. Some of the most important factors involved are economic, psychological, and physical. The order of importance of these factors will vary with each client and even with each subsequent pregnancy.

Many women are not content to stay home, and others are simply unable to stop because of their financial situations. Whether she is unmarried or has a husband who is in school or is unemployed, her job and salary become very important. Also, many women today intend to pursue their careers after pregnancy and view the baby's birth as a temporary stopping point in that career. Today many companies have lifted severe restrictions on pregnant workers, but the woman should check to see if she needs a work approval letter from her physician or if it will be necessary to resign after a certain period. Working up to and including the 7th month of pregnancy is a very common practice. Many hospitals do not have work-termination limits, and nurses often work up to their date of delivery. One obstetric nurse worked in the delivery area while having contractions, gave report, went home and picked up her suitcase, and returned to check herself into the labor area.

Women work not only for the money but also as a "mental health break," as one woman with small children described it. Conversely, some women who stay at home feel this is their last chance to be themselves and capture time alone with their husbands. Both points are valid, and the individual feelings of each woman are to be carefully considered. A woman who works must realize that the physical and mental strains of pregnancy should not be imposed upon her coworkers. Also, different grooming and a larger wardrobe are often expected of women who work outside the home.

Whether a woman works at home or outside, she must be aware of her physical activities and how they affect her and her fetus. Ideally she should:

1   Avoid physical strain and not work to the point of fatigue.
2   Know the correct ways to lift and carry objects.

3 Avoid occupations involving toxic substances.
4 Take adequate rest periods either at home or at work.
5 Consider restrictions made by her physician to decrease her amount of physical work or strain. These recommendations might be made with the knowledge of a previous history of obstetric complications.

In general, long hours of physical work should be avoided. This includes standing or sitting for hours at a time, rotating night shifts, heavy lifting, and jobs requiring a delicate sense of body balance. Pregnant women do not have a ready reserve of energy upon which to draw. Instead they become fatigued easily and are unable to regain their usual energy level as quickly.

Correct methods of lifting or carrying will decrease possible physical strain. By squatting or kneeling, bringing objects as close to the body as possible, and lifting from the legs, strong thigh muscles are used and back strain can be avoided. Instead of lifting children, the pregnant woman should encourage them to climb onto a footstool and then onto her lap. Activity at home may be just as strenuous as at any outside position or job. A fall is basically the same whether it is from a stepladder while painting the nursery or from a chair at the office.

Occupations which involve toxic substances are to be avoided. Women working in industry especially should be urged to contact their company physician or nurse about possible hazards in connection with their work. The following is a partial list of toxic substances considered to be dangerous during pregnancy. It was compiled by the Maternal Child Health Service of the United States and stated in their *Standards for Maternity Care and Employment of Mothers in Industry.*

Aniline
Benzene and toluene
Carbon disulfide
Carbon monoxide
Chlorinated hydrocarbons
Lead and its compounds
Mercury and its compounds
Nitrobenzene and other nitro compounds of benzene and its homologues
Phosphorus
Radioactive substances and x rays
Turpentine

Rest during work, either at home or in the office, is important for every pregnant woman, even if it is only a chance to elevate her feet for 10 minutes and regain some of her lost energy.

For women who have a previous history of not carrying a baby to term or who show a tendency to abort, the physician may advise rest as a necessity, and she may be encouraged to work only part time or to stop work altogether.

EXERCISE

As with employment, exercise should never be carried to the point of fatigue. Women who are pregnant do not have their normal resilience and do not recover as easily from physical exercise. Women who previously felt rested an hour after a game of tennis may need half a day to recover during pregnancy. Walking outdoors at a good brisk pace seems to be the most universally recommended exercise. Exercise of any kind is beneficial and ideally should be combined with fresh air and sunlight. Clients should be asked about their usual amount of activity, and it must be decided which activities should be increased or decreased. This also will change between the early and later periods of pregnancy.

The strenuous sports such as tennis, golf, skiing, horseback riding, backpacking, or canoeing should not be condemned immediately but should be individually considered for each woman. Pregnancy is not a reason to drastically change a way of life, but women should be warned that their sense of balance and timing may be altered by their increasing size. Many physicians do advise against taking part in active sports in which there is a greater likelihood of a direct blow to the abdomen. Exceptions are, of course, made. One woman went skiing during her 7th and 8th months with the blessing of her obstetrician, himself an avid and expert skier. Another woman, with no obstetric complications, continued to raise and train horses until late into her pregnancy.

Body-slimming exercises need not be stopped because of pregnancy and a disappearing waistline. Modified knee bends, sit-ups, or stretches as well as shoulder-relaxing exercises are usually allowed but must again be considered in relation to the individual client and her pregnancy. Women who have never been active or exercise-minded should be cautioned against starting strenuous exercise regimens or taking up new sports at this time, not only because of a certain inherent clumsiness, but also to avoid pushing themselves to the point of fatigue.

SLEEP, REST, AND RELAXATION

During pregnancy it is not just extra sleep at night that is needed, as so many women believe, but an entirely new pattern of rest and relaxation. Besides an adequate amount of sleep each night, she should try to nap or rest for a half hour every morning and afternoon. Obviously not everyone can follow this schedule, especially the woman who works outside the home during her entire pregnancy or who is the mother of other small children.

"Rest and relaxation" is an individual concept, and what it means to each woman must be carefully defined before any attempts are made to modify her schedule of activities. Age, nervous disposition, marital status, culture, and normal activities must all be considered with each client.

Flexibility is perhaps the key word in counseling pregnant women about resting; it can be explained that relaxation not only means sleep but the ability to sit down alone, elevate her feet or relax tense muscles, and simply do nothing for a while. This method of relaxation can help overcome some of the discomforts of pregnancy. Elevating the legs on a chair or even up against a wall or headboard may be recommended to help overcome edema or varicosities. Sims's position may be advised for vulvar or rectal varicosities.

Emotional rest is just as important as physical rest. The woman's physical activity is changed, but she also senses and reacts emotionally to many more things. Sounds seem louder, smells seem stronger and are sometimes nauseating, taste sensations change, and small annoyances may produce unwarranted irritation or anger.

Physically, sleep may be a problem, especially in the last trimester. Digestive discomforts and frequency of urination contribute to sleeplessness, as do nightmares and fears. The protruding abdomen itself is usually a major cause of discomfort. Some women find waterbeds extremely comfortable, offering the only way they can sleep on their abdomens while pregnant. There is virtually no sleep position that is harmful, but the most comfortable is usually on the side with a pillow under the top knee which has been brought forward. This pillow can also be used to support the abdomen if this is comfortable.

TRAVEL

Discretion is encouraged for women when traveling or vacationing. Some of the most commonly asked questions are, "How long can I stay?" "What precautions should I take along the way?" "Does it matter how I get there?"

The old myth about pregnant women not traveling far from home was disproved soon after World War II when it was shown that no significant increase in abortions occurred in wives of military personnel who followed their husbands all over the world.[1]

With a client who has no apparent or anticipated obstetric complications, the time spent away from home is not as important as the fact that there will be a physician nearby in case of complications. For prolonged stays, arrangements should be made for the woman to see another physician on a regular basis until she returns home. If possible, no long trips should be planned during the last trimester in order to avoid delivering in a strange hospital where her obstetric history is unknown.

Each client's individual pregnancy must be considered when advising her about traveling. Often women delay "asking" permission from their obstetrician until just before they leave, and nurses and physicians should urge pregnant women to have their vacation plans approved earlier. They should also be advised to take along only those medications prescribed specifically for them by their obstetrician. If travel ordinarily makes the pregnant woman nauseated, her physician should be informed of this fact.

Since indigestion and heartburn do not enhance a vacation, special care should be taken with what and how much are eaten and drunk. The amount, of course, also depends on how weight-conscious both the woman and her physician are.

Means of Transportation

For women who are prone to travel sickness, the train or airplane is probably the best choice. Railroads have no restrictions on carrying pregnant passengers and provide comfortable travel in either the day coach or the sleeper. Air travel, especially during the first trimester, has caused controversy on the basis of questionable fetal hypoxia during this formative period. Well-pressurized commerical airlines, as opposed to small private planes, are to be recommended. Some airlines have restrictions on carrying pregnant women; restrictions for domestic and foreign flights may also differ. Some airlines require letters with differing amounts of information from the physician before they will allow the woman to fly with them.

Air travel may be faster, but bus and car travel offers the advantage of frequent rest and bathroom stops. Clients should be advised not to try to finish their trip all in one day. Rest stops every 150 to 250 km will help to eliminate stiffness, cramping, and poor circulation. A rest stop should include stopping the car, getting out and walking around, going to the bathroom, and elevating the feet periodically.

Driving

As long as the pregnant woman can comfortably sit behind the wheel there is no reason for her to stop driving. During the last trimester for obvious reasons she should be advised not to drive alone at night or in uninhabited areas. It might be suggested that pregnancy is a very poor time to learn to drive, not only because of the inherent clumsiness of some pregnant women but also because beginning drivers are more prone to accidents.

Seat belts are another controversial matter among obstetricians. Although the rare case of uterine rupture has been reported due to a seat belt, seat belts definitely decrease the possibility of maternal mortality in severe car accidents.[2] Seat belts should be recommended and should be worn low, comfortably under the abdomen and in conjunction with a shoulder strap if possible. Both belts must be properly adjusted—not too tight and not pressing high against the neck or abdomen. The shoulder strap is rapidly replacing the seat belt.

Vaccinations

The question of vaccinations is important in view of the widespread travels undertaken by many pregnant women. The diseases a woman may be exposed to must be considered when making travel plans and when considering the possibilities of pregnancy.

Vaccinations are a precaution but are questionable at the same time. Many live viruses are able to cross the placental barrier and infect the fetus. Therefore, all routine immunizations with live vaccines are to be avoided during pregnancy. The following list of vaccinations is based upon reports of the Advisory Committee on Immunization of Infectious Diseases of the American Academy of Pediatrics as reviewed by *The Medical Letter on Drugs and Therapeutics*.[3]

Smallpox: Vaccinia virus given during pregnancy can occasionally infect the fetus. Fetal vaccinia has almost always been associated with primary vaccination. Thus, primary vaccination should only be used in essential cases because of exposure in an endemic area.

Mumps and measles: These live viruses should never be given to pregnant women.

Rubella: This virus vaccine has been shown on occasion to infect both the placenta and the fetus, the significance of which is uncertain. Pregnancy is a contraindication for administration of the live rubella vaccine.

Yellow fever: This is a live virus that should be given to pregnant women only if there is a very great risk of exposure.

Poliomyelitis: Since polio has almost been eradicated in this country, immunization during pregnancy is rarely indicated.

Cholera: This killed bacterial vaccine should be given only if there is a danger of infection. There has been no convincing documentation of an abortogenic effect.

Other vaccines and tests: No recommendations were made by the Advisory Committee about vaccination against influenza, epidemic typhus, and typhoid. Tetanus and diphtheria toxoids are considered safe. The tuberculin and histoplasmin tests are also permissible.

The fact that the occasional fetal abnormality due to vaccinations cannot be ruled out leaves one definite course open to physicians and nurses; clients should be urged to have necessary immunizations before pregnancy and to then allow the correct amount of time following immunization before conceiving. This precaution as well as avoiding exposure to the diseases will help reduce problems with infections and possible risks to fetal health and development. General good health is also a major factor in reducing threats to fetal development in that it reduces chances for infection or disease. Pregnant women should be urged to report every illness to their physician no matter how minor it may seem to them.

DENTAL CARE

It is a common misconception that the baby absorbs calcium from the mother's teeth or jawbone. It should be explained to the client that a proper diet will supply the baby with all the calcium and other necessities for healthy teeth and bones.

The baby's teeth are already developing during the 2d month of pregnancy and by about the 6th month the permanent tooth buds have started to form. Heredity is the major determinant of tooth size and shape, but the diet, health, and activities of the pregnant woman can affect their quality. It goes without saying that good dental health should be maintained at all times, but especially during pregnancy. Gums may have a tendency to bleed more readily and may appear somewhat red or swollen at times. Nausea, acid regurgitation (heartburn), omission of brushing the teeth (maybe because of gagging), excessive salivation (ptyalism), and changing day-to-day eating habits are all conducive to dental problems during pregnancy. Usually conditions that have gone unattended give the impression that pregnancy in itself aggravates dental problems.

The dentist should be informed early in pregnancy of either the possibility or the actuality of pregnancy. Dental visits, and especially any extensive work, should be discussed with the dentist and obstetrician so that they can decide together the best time for dental work and the safety and choice of drugs and anesthetics. Very seldom is dental work contraindicated, but extensive elective work may have to be postponed. The most favorable time for dental work is from the 4th to the 7th month.[4] The fetus is well along in development and, just as important, the client is usually feeling much better, less nauseated, and yet is not so large that she cannot sit for a period of time.

Dental x rays, a diagnostic procedure,

should be postponed until the latter half of pregnancy.[5] When used properly in connection with a lead apron over the abdomen, the dental x-ray machine should have no adverse effects with its small 3-cm beam aimed only at the face.

X RAYS FOR DIAGNOSTIC PURPOSES

Occasionally obstetric clients rebel at the idea of x rays taken during their pregnancies. These women have heard many of the misconceptions regarding all forms of irradiation, including such examinations as the routine antepartum chest x ray.

In a recent guide to good practice of x-ray examinations prepared by the American College of Radiology, it was stated that the optimal period of examinations of the abdomen and pelvis of women of childbearing age is the first 14 days after the onset of the menstrual cycle. At this time the woman is definitely not pregnant. Routine antepartum chest x rays may be taken at any time with a lead apron over the abdomen, but the procedure is usually delayed until after the 6th month.

Obviously when the woman is definitely pregnant the physician must make a choice as to the urgency of the procedure. For example, if she has active gastrointestinal bleeding, there would be very little need to question a barium enema and upper gastrointestinal series, even in the first trimester when the fetus is the most susceptible. The radiologist should be informed of the pregnancy so as to shield the abdomen with a lead apron if possible and also to minimize the level of radiation. If the pregnancy is undetermined and the x-ray procedure has been performed, usually there is little to worry about, since the radiation dose for most procedures is relatively small. Some studies of the evidence relating to the harmful effects of diagnostic x-ray exposure suggest that such exposure may be less harmful than has been previously claimed.[6] However, in the case of extremely large dosages from a particular procedure or combination of procedures, experts should be consulted about the amount of radiation the fetus has been exposed to and the possible hazard to fetal development.

Ultrasound is a diagnostic procedure using high-frequency sound for the evaluation of the gestational age of the fetus, placental localization, fetal presentation, and multiple pregnancies. Studies so far have shown no known deleterious effects upon either mother or fetus.[7,8]

SMOKING AND DRINKING

Alcohol is usually not prohibited during pregnancy, although cocktails and beer are very high in calories. Taste is a sensation that changes with pregnancy, and many women find themselves unable to drink alcohol in any form. The quantity of alcohol in one or two drinks is eliminated rapidly from the bloodstream, and therefore only small quantities reach the fetus. The secondary effects of alcoholism, however, may lead to fetal underdevelopment because of maternal malnutrition. Research is increasingly pointing to the fact that women who are alcoholics give birth to infants who have a significantly higher proportion of anomalies than those born to nonalcoholic mothers.

Smoking, unlike drinking, may affect the child more directly.[9,10] Studies have confirmed that cigarette smoking during pregnancy is associated with low-birth-weight babies in general and with, specifically, an average weight reduction of 200 g. Nicotine and carbon monoxide are the main components of tobacco smoke that have been studied. They are probably absorbed in the blood-

stream and passed to the fetus by means of the placenta. The amount absorbed, of course, depends on the amount inhaled. Some experts believe that this causes no more than a harmless increase in fetal heart rate, whereas others believe that it may somehow lead to fetal underdevelopment. Size of infants at birth is probably affected by the number of cigarettes smoked per day. Very heavy smokers—those who smoke more than one pack a day—seem to have smaller infants than nonsmoking mothers. There is still a great deal of controversy in recent literature regarding the possibility of stillborns, fetal abnormalities, prematurity, or maternal complications caused by smoking.

For general health reasons, perhaps pregnancy is a good time to urge women to try to stop smoking; many are nauseated in the first trimester and cannot tolerate the smell or taste of cigarettes anyway.

MATERNITY CLOTHING

Maternity fashions have changed greatly over the past few years. Clothing today is practical, attractive, and nonrestricting. To avoid constriction around the waist, dresses or tops should be hung from the shoulders and should not have tight elastic around the waistline. The importance of properly fitting girdles, brassieres, and shoes should be discussed with clients.

Usually a girdle is a deterrent to complete comfort, since many pregnant women feel as though they are encased in an elastic strait jacket. The properly fitted maternity girdle may be a necessity, however, for the woman who has always worn a girdle or who needs extra support for stretched muscles due to multiparity. The woman should lie on her back to put on the girdle and hook or adjust it starting from the bottom. It should not be so tight that when she sits up it constricts or is uncomfortable. After the 4th or 5th month, backache may be relieved for some women by proper abdominal support, but it must be pointed out to women that girdles do not prevent striae or stretched muscles.

Pregnant women should buy properly fitted and supportive brassieres in one cup size larger than usual. This is especially true for those women who have large pendulous breasts. These women may even find that it is necessary to wear a breast support to bed at night.

Tight bands or garters tend to accentuate any varicosities or edema of the lower extremities. Maternity garter belts or the more commonly worn panty hose are much safer and easier to wear.

The postural changes of pregnancy may be aggravated by either very high-heeled or very flat shoes. Both accentuate poor posture and may contribute to backache and fatigue. Low-heeled, comfortable shoes are advised, but higher heels can be worn on occasion if the woman is aware that she may be inclined to tip forward due to the increasing size of her abdomen.

GENERAL HYGIENE

At one time tub baths and intercourse were prohibited during pregnancy because it was thought that water or semen which entered the vagina could cause infections harmful to the fetus. This concept has been negated.

Bathing

There are now no restrictions on bathing during pregnancy unless the membranes have ruptured, and then tub baths are strictly prohibited. Women should be cautioned that they are not as agile during the later months and are more prone to fall. Rubber mats on the floor of the bath or shower, and even handrails, can be recommended. The tem-

perature of the bath or shower is not a matter for concern, as long as it is comfortable to the expectant mother.

Douching

Douching is very rarely needed and should be done during pregnancy only when recommended by the physician. Vaginal discharge or irritations should be reported to the physician, who may advise more frequent change of underwear, suppositories, or a douche. Nylon underwear and panty hose, which so many women wear today, have the irritating effect of retaining heat in the perineal area and preventing the evaporation of normal perspiration, thus providing an incubator effect for organisms in the discharge. Sometimes changing to cotton underwear, bathing daily, and keeping the vaginal or perineal area as dry as possible helps to clear the irritation. Douche bags, when prescribed and with the correct solutions, should be held low to decrease the force of gravity and should be inserted no more than 4½ to 6½ cm into the vagina. The woman may be seated on the toilet instead of in the bathtub, a very awkward position under any conditions. Hand bulb syringes should never be allowed as they can theoretically introduce air into the vagina, resulting in air emboli.

SEXUAL INTERCOURSE

Many couples and physicians in the past believed that intercourse during pregnancy would harm the baby or the woman. Misconceptions such as this, and ignorance about sex in general and sex during pregnancy in particular, still exist even in this sexually open and permissive culture. At one time intercourse was prohibited during the entire 9 months of pregnancy or on the date of the expected period, but these beliefs have been shown to be without any factual foundations.

Today the main restrictions that most physicians adhere to are no intercourse if the membranes are ruptured or if the woman is bleeding or threatening to abort. Clients with a history of repeated abortions may be advised to restrict intercourse during certain times of the pregnancy.

The openness of the physician and the nurse counseling the woman or couple about sexual matters is clearly of the utmost importance. Clients may be reluctant to ask these personal questions unless there is a trusting doctor- or nurse-patient relationship. If the nurse is a woman, she may be consulted for information because she may have had similar experiences. If she is going to be utilized as such a resource person, she must take steps to prepare herself thoroughly for this role. Besides knowing the physiological and psychological aspects of sexuality, the nurse, if a woman, must also examine herself in regard to her own feelings in relation to pregnancy, sex, and her own femininity before she can successfully function as a resource person to others. If a man, the nurse must be able to empathize and establish a rapport with the pregnant woman and/or couple he is counseling. Just as important is a thorough understanding of the physician's philosophy about intercourse and his or her client population. Some doctors are restrictive during the last month and this of course is entirely based on the individuality of the woman and her pregnancy. Some clients also have a greater inherent risk of venereal disease and infection, and the sexual activity of this group may be limited during the last month in contrast to those less vulnerable and better informed.

The nurse should be also aware of clients who are unable to communicate their questions, whether from embarrassment, ignorance, or cultural factors. Misinformation may promote silence or misunderstanding within the counseling situation. At some point it may become simply a volunteering of information in an interested, matter-of-fact, open-ended manner. The nurse's ability to listen and reflect during the conversation becomes essential. The nurse should encourage couples to communicate with each other about their feelings regarding their changing sexual relations. Then, hopefully, they will feel free to ask professional health personnel those questions they themselves cannot answer; this in turn will clarify misconceptions and misunderstandings regarding sexual intercourse.

Misunderstandings which have led to restriction of sexual activity during pregnancy include the following: pregnant women are uncomfortable and do not enjoy intercourse at this time; the membranes may rupture because of penile thrusts; an orgasm, which causes uterine contractions, might bring on early labor.

Some women have a decreased desire for intercourse during pregnancy. It may be uncomfortable, or it may be seen as unnecessary, since she is already pregnant. An unexplained aversion to her mate may occur and must be explained as a temporary idiosyncrasy accompanying the new condition of pregnancy. Many women for whom contraception was a hindrance find sex more enjoyable now, and their desires and responses may be heightened. This is especially true after the third month.

The membranes are so well protected by the cervix and mucus that they would be very difficult to rupture. Fear of infection caused by rupture of the membranes during intercourse is an old misconception. This concept dates back to the preantibiotic period in medicine and is largely negated today. Depending on the dilation of the cervix and the immediacy of delivery, the couple may be advised to restrict intercourse altogether or to restrict the depth of penetration.

Orgasm has not been definitively shown to

bring on premature labor. Uterine contractions occur regardless of what causes the orgasm—masturbation or natural or artificial intercourse. Cases have been reported of labor onset immediately after orgasmic experience, however.

With conservative, traditional medical counseling, sexual intercourse might formerly have been completely restricted for 4 to 6 weeks before birth and for 6 weeks postpartum; the couple would eventually resume sexual relations after a period of 3 months. Understandably, many couples did not adhere to this advice. Guilt feelings about this might lead to a subsequent lack of communications or problems with the marriage during pregnancy. Men often do not understand the prolonged period of restrictions and are not willing to endure this period of abstention; subsequently, some men look elsewhere for their sexual gratification.[11]

The couple's perception of their sexual relations plays a major part in the determination of their familial roles and subsequent sexual enjoyment. Men, as well as women, may experience lessening sexual drives during the third trimester. Pregnancy and childbirth also create emotional problems for the expectant father; some even experience symptoms of pregnancy along with their mate. Some men see pregnancy as a verification of their virility, and others see it as a test of their masculinity. Also, when a first pregnancy precedes or follows marriage, or occurs during an open living arrangement, many couples' sexual adjustment to each other must immediately include the further adjustment to the psychological and physiological changes that occur during pregnancy.[12]

Women may equate the act of intercourse with an act of love, and during pregnancy intercourse may become a symbol of protection or of reaffirmation of femininity or basic sexuality. This, of course, varies with every union and is dependent on such factors as age, marital status, culture, and basic feelings about this particular pregnancy. A woman may begin to look at her mate not only as a lover and provider, but also as the father of her child. Thus, new familial roles begin to be defined. The fact that the woman carries and nurses the child casts her into an essentially nurturing role and the man into a protective or supportive role. These roles, however, are changing and overlap within current sociocultural patterns in the United States.

Frequency of intercourse and positions are the decision of the couple, within the restrictions set by the physician. Frequency will change with the alteration in desire, and positions will have to be modified during the later part of pregnancy. In the last trimester, many women find it more comfortable astride the man or in a side-by-side position. Gentleness, use of lubricants if necessary, and avoidance of uncomfortable positions are to be endorsed. Mutual petting can be substituted during periods of medically forced abstinence. Couples should be cautioned, however, about unusual sexual activities that might be dangerous during the last weeks of pregnancy. There have been a few accidental deaths reported as a result of air emboli caused from precoital oral-genital contact.[13] Substitute sexual acts, if actual intercourse is prohibited, should be clearly specified.

CONCLUSION

A thorough knowledge of the physiological, psychological, and sociocultural aspects of pregnancy is needed to counsel pregnant women about safety and activities during pregnancy. It is also essential for nurses to recognize their own feelings about pregnancy, motherhood, sex, and femininity.

Their role within the clinical setting is to augment the physician in treatment and advice to individual clients through operationalizing the nursing process.

REFERENCES

1   Guilbeau, J. A., and J. L. Turner: "Effect of Travel upon the Interruption of Pregnancy," *American Journal of Obstetrics and Gynecology,* 66:1224, 1953.
2   Crosby, W. M., and J. P. Costiloe: "Safety of Lap-belt Restraint for Pregnant Victims of Automobile Collisions," *New England Journal of Medicine,* 284:632–636, March 1971.
3   Drugs and Therapeutic Information, Inc.: "Safety of Immunizing Agents in Pregnancy," *The Medical Letter on Drugs and Therapeutics,* issue 291, 12(5), Mar. 6, 1970.
4   Alk, Madelin (ed.): *Expectant Mother,* prepared in cooperation with the American College of Obstetricians and Gynecologists, Trident Press, New York, 1967.
5   United States Department of Health, Education, and Welfare: *X-ray Examinations . . . A Guide to Good Practice,* prepared in connection with the American College of Radiology, Maryland, 1971.
6   Oppenheim, B. E., M. L. Griem, and P. Meier: "The Effects of X-ray Exposure in the Human Fetus: an Examination of the Evidence," *Radiology,* 114:529–534, March 1975.
7   Woodward, B., J. B. Pond, and R. Warwick: "How Safe is Diagnostic Sonar?" *British Journal of Radiology,* 43:719–725, 1970.
8   Hellman, L. M., G. M. Duffus, and I. Donald: "Safety of Diagnostic Ultrasound in Obstetrics," *Lancet,* 1:1133, 1970.
9   O'Lane, J. M.: "Some Fetal Effects of Maternal Cigarette Smoking," *Obstetrics and Gynecology,* 22:181–184, August 1963.
10 Haworth, J. C.: "Cigarette Smoking during Pregnancy and the Effect upon the Fetus," *Canadian Journal of Public Health,* 64:20–24, March–April 1973.
11 Masters, W. H., and V. E. Johnson: *Human Sexual Response,* Little, Brown, Boston, 1966, chap. 10.
12 Clark, A. L., and R. W. Hale: "Sex during and after Pregnancy," *American Journal of Nursing,* 74:1430–1431, August 1974.
13 Aronson, M. E., and P. K. Newson: "Fatal Air Embolisms in Pregnancy Resulting from an Unusual Sex Act," *Obstetrics and Gynecology,* 31:127, July 1967.

BIBLIOGRAPHY

Bancroft, V.: "Pregnancy and the Counter Culture," *Nursing Clinics of North America,* 8:67–76, March 1973.
Best, M. C., and C. K. Warrick: "The 10-Day Rule," *Nursing Times,* 70:1474, Sept. 19, 1974.
Fitzpatrick, E., et al.: *Maternity Nursing,* 12th ed., Lippincott, Philadelphia, 1971.
Guttmacher, A. F.: *Pregnancy and Birth,* Viking, New York, 1962.
Hall, Robert E.: *Nine Months Reading: A Medical Guide for Pregnant Women,* rev. ed., Doubleday, New York, 1963.
Hellman, L. M., J. A. Pritchard, and R. M. Wynn: *Williams Obstetrics,* 14th ed., Appleton-Century-Crofts, New York, 1971.
Israel, S. L., and Isadore Rubin: *Sexual Relations during Pregnancy and Postdelivery Period,* Sex Information and Education Council of the United States, study guide no. 6, 1967.
Liley, H. M. I., with Beth Day: *Modern Motherhood: Pregnancy, Childbirth and the Newborn Baby,* Random House, New York, 1961.
Maternity Center Association: *Preparation for Childbearing,* 3d ed., Maternity Center Association, New York, 1971.
Montgomery, W. P., et al.: "The Tuberculin Test in Pregnancy," *American Journal of Obstetrics and Gynecology,* 100:829–831, Mar. 15, 1968.
Peterson, W. F., et al.: "Smoking and Prematurity," *Obstetrics and Gynecology,* 26:775–779, December 1965.

Pugh, W. E., and F. L. Fernandez: "Coitus in Late Pregnancy," *Obstetrics and Gynecology*, 2:636, 1953.

Quirk, B., et al.: "The Nurse's Role in Advising Patients on Coitus during Pregnancy," *Nursing Clinics of North America*, 8:501–507, September 1973.

Rubovits, F. E.: "Traumatic Rupture of the Pregnant Uterus from 'Seat Belt' Injury," *American Journal of Obstetrics and Gynecology*, 90:828–829, 1964.

Seacat, M., and L. Schlachter: "Expanded Nursing Role in Prenatal and Infant Care," *American Journal of Nursing*, 68:822–824, April 1968.

Solberg, D. A., et al.: "Sexual Behavior in Pregnancy," *New England Journal of Medicine*, 288:1098–1103, May 24, 1973.

Zabriskie, J. R.: "Effect of Cigarette Smoking during Pregnancy," *Obstetrics and Gynecology*, 21:405, 1963.

19

Preparation for Childbirth*

PATRICIA A. BANASIAK AND
MARYA M. CORCORAN

EVOLUTION OF CHILDBIRTH PROGRAMS

Historical Perspective

Everyone who comes to the experience of childbirth is prepared. The crux of the matter is whether the preparation is positive and realistic or negative and inaccurate. Preparation occurs throughout all life experiences and is influenced by family, church, school, and peer relationships. Without the word "childbirth" ever being used, a definite impression can be given to the young child whose mother says, "What I went through to have you, and look at what you're doing to me!" The nature of the preparation, then, becomes a primary concern for nurses, since it affects the entire maternity cycle. In order to assist clients in this endeavor, it is important

* The authors gratefully acknowledge the contribution of Rose LeRoux whose work on the Lamaze method in the first edition served as background for this writing.

to assess where we have been, determine where we are now, and map the course for future developments in the practice of childbirth education.

Prior to the 1900s, childbirth usually occurred at home. One need only recall an old movie or novel in which childbirth took place. The scene depicted was that of the laboring woman at home with the old family physician or midwife in attendance. If other children were present it was the husband's responsibility to keep them occupied. The father's paramount task, however, was to boil water in preparation for the birth. It should be noted that the quantity of water boiled far exceeded that which probably could be used. In any event, the entire family tended to be involved, in some way, with the arrival of the new baby.

Preparation for the new arrival, though probably not formally discussed in the family, took place nonetheless. The agrarian society, prior to this century, provided much of the sex education in its most natural settings. Since it was common to raise animals, even in the city, children learned about reproduction and birth as a normal, natural part of life. The knowledge acquired about animals was transferred to humans. Pain was experienced, but it was not the singular focal point during pregnancy, labor, and delivery.

The turn of the century brought many changes in childbirth practices. Concern over maternal and infant mortality rates grew, and hospitalization for childbirth became the trend. The advantages which were offered in the hospital were countered with several disadvantages. On one hand, a woman could expect to have her baby in an aseptic environment. In the efficient, sterile hospital, however, the father was recognized solely for his ability to provide transportation and to finance the event. He managed to bring his wife to the hospital at the onset of labor and returned 10 to 14 days later to pay the bill and take his family home. The

woman shared her labor room with several other laboring women under the strict supervision of hospital personnel. From the moment of birth, the baby was whisked to the nursery to be cared for by efficient experts. The mother was completely removed from any involvement with her new baby, and only the more progressive hospitals allowed even a visiting period for the mother and her infant. The baby was cared for on a rigid schedule; and upon discharge from the hospital, the mother had little or no idea of who her baby was and what was involved in caring for the baby.

Hospitalization also offered the mother more analgesia and anesthesia than were practical at home. She was assured a comfortable, and most probably an unconscious, labor. Regardless of her needs or wishes, she was medicated. In an attempt to make the experience a comfortable one for the patient, and a manageable one for the nurses, medications were given singly or in combination. The desired effects became complete unawareness of the discomfort and total amnesia about the event. With the woman completely medicated and safely attended by the nurses, the doctor could continue practicing, to be summoned only at the time of delivery. And woe be to the nurse who did not get the doctor there in time!

The homecoming was another noteworthy event. The mother, father, and new baby were united after approximately 2 weeks of hospitalization. The mother and father had to reestablish their relationship, and the baby was a stranger to both of them.

Since the parturient woman was kept on complete bed rest for the duration of her hospitalization, she was naturally weak upon her return home. Any children who were at home, as well as other young women in the family, learned through conversation and through their own observations that childbirth was at least incapacitating, if not painful.

Formalized preparation for childbirth was virtually nonexistent. Since the entire experience was managed *for* the woman, there was no need for her to have knowledge of anything aside from how to recognize the onset of labor. That preparation was frequently limited to the simple, but unsettling, statement, "You'll know."

A shortening of the hospital stay and an increase in the mother's involvement, at least in the feeding of the infant, occurred in the 1940s. It might be noted, however, that this trend evolved more from the hospital's need than from concern for family relationships. The increased birth rate and the decreased number of hospital personnel due to World War II made previous practices impractical.

During the 1950s the father was once again recognized as a member of the family. The demands of fathers returning from the war, as well as changes in medical and nursing education, fostered their inclusion during the hospital stay. The father became a more familiar sight at the bedside of the laboring woman. Unprepared as he might be, the frightened father stood there bravely.

Today's practices are influenced by historical developments. Although 90 percent of all births presently take place in the hospital, several factors may create a return to planned childbirth at home. Among these factors are the skyrocketing cost of hospitalization, the desire of couples to avoid the mechanized, unnatural hospital setting, and the evolution of different family structures with a greater emphasis upon shared experiences. In addition, the couple who plans for childbirth at home retains some measure of control over this significant event.

SELECTED CHILDBIRTH PRACTICES

It is impossible to deal with the subject of preparation for labor and delivery without some mention of pain, since this is the general expectation of the childbirth experience.

Anthropologists have demonstrated that in all cultures in all parts of the world, women may experience pain during childbirth. Reduction or elimination of the discomforts has been a vital component of obstetrical management, particularly in the Western world, and, thus, the focus of programs of preparation. A thorough understanding of the variability of pain response is necessary for cogent guidance and support of those involved in childbearing. The subject of pain can consume an entire book and more, but the important point to emphasize is the complexity and the individuality of response to pain. Numerous studies over the years have only served to underline the complexity of pain. It is clear that there is a physical stimulus and a psychic modification and that multiple factors influence both aspects in any given person. Since there are no universal characteristics which define pain, there can be no set prescription for a means of pain relief. In its complex nature, one finds the reason for the wide variety of means employed to alleviate the pain of childbirth. Due to the complexity of pain phenomena and to the abundance of pharmacological agents available for the relief of childbirth pain in the United States, it was thought unnecessary to condition women for childbirth.

The strong resistance to childbirth preparation methods and the people who tried to proselytize them in the United States may have been partially a product of cultural orientation. Some members of the health professions viewed women who chose to employ one of the "natural childbirth" methods suspiciously because often they refused analgesics or anesthetics. They were suspected of being martyrs, so committed to a method that they would suffer needlessly, unknowingly jeopardizing safe obstetric care. The concept of preparing for childbirth may have been foreign to the thinking of an American "drug-oriented" society in which pain or emotional discomfort could be readily relieved by medication. Little attention was given to other possible ways of relieving discomfort and enhancing awareness experiences.

Pharmacological Intervention

As hospitalization for childbirth became the rule rather than the exception, women began to rely heavily on analgesia. The concern of practitioners to combat the discomforts of childbirth went hand in hand with the rapid development of pharmacological agents. Hospitalization, with its concomitant equipment and trained personnel, provided the environment conducive to a pharmacological approach. Large doses of depressant and amnestic drugs were administered to the patient, and unconscious labor became the trend. The most popular physician was one who would guarantee that his or her patients would not experience any pain in labor.

In addition to medication for labor, a general inhalation anesthetic was frequently administered for delivery. It was discovered, however, that the chemical agents utilized passed into fetal circulation with deleterious effects to the infant. Both the type of agent and the large amounts used contributed to the high perinatal morbidity and mortality rates. As concern for maternal and infant well-being grew, techniques were developed aimed at the reduction of pharmacological intervention which might be harmful. As so often is the case, the pendulum swung, the trend took a complete reversal, and one fear replaced another. Rather than a fear that drugs might be withheld, women now feared that drugs would be administered which would endanger their babies. For some women, all energies were directed toward achieving that state of physical and/or psychological preparation which would eliminate any need for medicinal relief.

The Read Method

Dr. Grantly Dick-Read was responsible for the original natural childbirth movement in England. The basis of this program was that childbirth was a normal physiological occurrence and as such should not be painful. Dr. Dick-Read believed that the experienced pain of labor and delivery was mental in origin. He attributed the cause of pain to culturally induced fear and anxiety. His writings, and the writings of both those who supported him and those who denigrated him, demonstrate that he had a persuasive personality. Dr. Dick-Read, who was described as an evangelistic crusader for his program, utilized every conceivable means of publicizing his beliefs. He widely incorporated emotional and sentimental phraseology which added to the impact of his pronouncements. The basic premise of the Read method, introduced to the United States by Dr. Thoms of Yale, centered around the triad of fear-tension-pain. The belief was that fear of labor and delivery was a learned response. This fear created tension and was responsible for the pain which occurred. Dr. Dick-Read's program, and the publicity which it received, coincided with other circumstances. The concern of physicians for the welfare of women and their unborn babies and the genuine desire of women to be more involved in the birth process contributed to the spread of this program. Utilizing the premise of fear-tension-pain, the Read method attempted to interrupt this syndrome through education, psychological training, and physical conditioning.

The physical exercise component of the Read method was largely due to the work of Helen Heardman, a physiotherapist in England, who strongly supported Dr. Dick-Read's contentions. She believed, as he did, in the necessity of a healthy, positive mental attitude in the prospective mother. In addition, she advocated a vigorous program of physical education in preparation for parturition. Thus, through the combined efforts of Dr. Dick-Read and Mrs. Heardman, education, psychological training, and physical exercise to enhance relaxation comprised the original natural childbirth program.

Education was aimed at preparing prospective parents thoroughly in the anatomy, physiology, and process of pregnancy, labor, and delivery. Along with presentation and discussion of factual material, the Read approach included demonstration and practice of exercises to foster relaxation and to condition muscles involved in the birth process. Another component part of the Read method was the group process. Emphasis was placed upon deriving support from other group members as an inherent part of the program.

Read technique exercises were intended to prepare a woman physically for the muscular work of labor. They were designed to increase the elasticity of perineal muscles, to exercise the pelvis and back, and to foster the general improvement of circulation in the pelvic region. Among the exercises included to fulfill these objectives were tailor-sitting, squatting, kneeling, and pelvic rocking. Some authorities believed, however, that exercises which involved the pelvic girdle might damage the symphysis and lumbosacral joints.

Breathing exercises in the Read methodology included slow abdominal breathing, diaphragmatic breathing, and panting. Slow abdominal breathing was used primarily for the first stage of labor. This technique was aimed at raising the abdominal wall off the contracting uterus. Its purposes were to reduce the discomfort created by opposing forces and to promote general relaxation. Diaphragmatic breathing, to expand the ribs sideways, was said to enhance comfort in late active labor prior to pushing. Panting was included in the breathing techniques to

avoid a forceful, rapid expulsion of the infant. Read proponents cautioned against excessive use of panting, since it might lead to hyperventilation and its resultant problems.

The nurse's role with Read preparation was one of teacher, demonstrator, and coach. With medical guidance and approval, the general format and guidelines for the program were established, and the nurse generally was responsible for implementing the program. Classes were geared to the presentation and discussion of factual components, and a period was allotted for demonstration and practice of the exercises. The nurse became vital as a coach—encouraging, explaining, and restating goals throughout the program. Attempts were made to carry through this same role once labor began, either by the same nurse or by other nurses equally grounded in the theoretical and technical aspects. Obvious areas of difficulty arose. An uninformed practitioner, or one who did not share an attitude of value in the approach, might fail to continue the support and guidance in the manner familiar to the patient. An overly enthusiastic nurse might become so involved in the goal of successful achievement that she might fail to correctly assess the patient's status. The nurse might also fail to utilize any measures other than that of cheering the patient on. Another problem lay in the consistency of the support. It was generally agreed that consistent sustainment in labor enhanced the patient's ability to progress more positively. With hospital personnel traditionally working a scheduled shift and the unpredictability of either the onset or the termination of labor, many contacts with multiple approaches might occur throughout the course of one labor.

However, aspects of the Read approach could be readily instituted with patients in labor who had never been instructed in the techniques and who did not need to have the techniques labeled as such. Relaxation positions and slow abdominal breathing assisted patients in reducing tension. This created a quieting approach which generally enhanced patient comfort.

Dr. Dick-Read's philosophy and approach were both stoutly defended and soundly denounced. In general, the strongest resistance arose from the all-or-none attitude engendered by the proponents of natural childbirth. For women who viewed training for childbirth as the panacea, disappointments stemmed from several sources. Women might need medication for parts of their labor, but since they were not prepared for this, they considered either the program or themselves failures because neither had achieved their aims. Many a skeptical doctor allowed his patient to prepare for natural childbirth, only to follow his own practiced regimen of medication once the patient was hospitalized. Practitioners who were the strongest proponents of the Read method often withheld medication when it was not only necessary but crucial for the patient.

Although Dr. Dick-Read never proposed that analgesics or anesthetics be withheld, an attitude prevailed that to utilize such assistance was the ultimate failure of a woman in her most supreme achievement. Dr. Dick-Read repeatedly stated that medicinal support could be utilized, but the focus of his approach and the words which he used gave quite another message. Repeatedly in his own writings appear such phrases as "ability to endure" and "artificial aids." This terminology suggested that such assistance should not be needed, and thus many would not dare to request medication.

Another facet of the all-or-none approach was the belief that any patient was suited to this technique, regardless of her physical or psychological constitution. Some women selected this means because it was the thing to do rather than because they believed it to be either necessary or rewarding. Little empha-

sis was given to the disadvantages or the need for alternatives, and as a result, many physical and psychological traumas were attributed to natural childbirth.

A report by Dr. Paul A. Bowers revealed that the women who availed themselves of the Read technique could generally be categorized into four groups. A large group appeared to be medically allied in some way. A second group perceived natural childbirth as a superior intellectual activity. The other two groups included women whose friends wholeheartedly recommended the approach and those with borderline or actual mental illness who viewed natural childbirth as a form of therapy.[1]

In the first group (those with some health orientation), many understood the program thoroughly, accepted it for themselves, and demonstrated a high rate of success. There were also, however, those with this orientation who suffered through it silently with what appeared to be success but only because they believed this behavior was expected of them. Another aspect is illustrated in the following example:

At a time when the Read method was highly favored in a given hospital, a clinical psychologist encouraged his wife to utilize this method. They arrived at the hospital to share the labor experience. What truly was shared, however, was in doubt. He was extremely enthusiastic about the classes, the exercises, and the labor. She said little, but when she experienced a mild contraction, she appeared tense and clenched her fists. For a while she attempted to smile and to show enthusiasm. Before labor progressed very far, however, she dissolved into tears with complete loss of control. She begged not to have "to go through with it." Her husband apologized to the hospital staff for his wife's failure. He was utterly dejected when his wife was heavily medicated and he was asked to leave the labor room. His wife was greatly relieved to receive medication for labor and general anesthetics for delivery. Later, she was extremely upset, because she knew she had disappointed her husband.

In the group of those who chose natural childbirth, because they felt it was a sign of superior intelligence, there were those who actively engaged in preparation and who achieved their goals successfully. There were also those who believed that it was easy to perform in the prescribed manner with little or no preparation. Unfortunately, this group did not always meet their goal, which resulted in feelings of failure and/or guilt.

Of the women who selected this method by endorsement, success was more likely if they grew to accept the method for themselves. Many who began the program because of another's endorsement failed to complete the program of preparation.

Women with borderline or actual mental illness were those with perhaps the greatest liability in accepting this approach. Their reasons for selection were complex or negative, and for many, irreparable scars occurred. One example was the type of woman who utilized this approach to punish herself or to punish her mate. His *expected* presence precluded any relief from witnessing his mate's "suffering."

In general, it might be said that the highest predictor of successful achievement lay in the woman's motivation for selection of this technique. The woman who chose the Read method and who believed in its appropriateness for *herself* was far more likely to achieve its goals.

Regardless of which aspects of the Read method remain valid, acceptable, or usable, Dr. Dick-Read must be recognized as a pioneer in the movement for preparation for childbirth. Conscious, cooperative labor and family involvement have many of their roots

in the Read method, and Dick-Read established the mental component of childbirth. This awakened many practitioners to the need for incorporation of psychological aspects into a responsible, safe, therapeutic practice of obstetrics.

The Lamaze Method

The Lamaze method, also referred to as psychoprophylaxis, is a means of childbirth preparation based on Pavlov's principle of conditioned reflex training. Lamaze, an easier word to pronounce, is used most frequently; psychoprophylaxis, which literally means mind prevention, is, however, the more precise term.

Psychoprophylaxis was developed by Russian scientists who postulated that through stimulus-response conditioning during pregnancy, women could learn specific behaviors which they would automatically use during labor and delivery to eliminate the pain associated with childbirth. This method, practiced with great success in Russia, became equally popular in France through the efforts of Dr. Fernand Lamaze. Dr. Lamaze became acquainted with the method while attending an obstetric conference in Russia. The Lamaze method spread quickly throughout many European countries and was introduced to the United States in the early 1950s. The outstanding pioneer of psychoprophylaxis in the United States was Elisabeth Bing, a physical therapist trained in England. Her initial efforts in this country were in association with Dr. Alan Guttmacher in the Childbirth Education Program at Mt. Sinai Hospital in New York City. Psychoprophylaxis gathered a following through the appeal of Marjorie Karmel's book, *Thank You, Dr. Lamaze*, which was published in 1959.

The Lamaze method, as described by Bing, differentiates between Dr. Dick-Read's natural childbirth and psychoprophylaxis.

This method [Lamaze] is *not* a technique of so called "natural childbirth." On the contrary, it is a technique which is not at all natural, but acquired through concentrated effort and hard work on the part of the expectant mother and her husband. It is a method which provides an analgesic (or lessening of pain) achieved by physical means instead of by drugs or chemical means.[2]

In 1960, interested physicians, nurses, physical therapists, and parents formed a nonprofit organization to further the goals of the psychoprophylactic method of preparation for childbirth during the antepartum, labor, and delivery periods. The organization was called the American Society for Psychoprophylaxis in Obstetrics (ASPO) and presently has member chapters throughout the United States.

Psychoprophylaxis has been modified throughout the years. However, the basic concepts of the method remain the same: *education* and *training*. The educational component includes content on the anatomy and physiology of the reproductive system and extensive study of the labor and delivery process. Effort is made to replace misinformation and superstition with valid scientific information. The training part of the program consists of learning controlled breathing, exercises, and effleurage.

The exercise component of the Lamaze method includes: (1) neuromuscular control (concentration-relaxation) and (2) body-building exercises. Neuromuscular exercises are intended to develop muscle control, giving the woman the ability to isolate muscle groups. Through concerted effort and conscious control one learns to promote action of one set of muscles while relaxing others. This type of exercise is intended to prepare the woman to control her entire body during labor while the uterine muscle contracts and

relaxes. The body-building exercises are essentially the same as those in the Read technique. They are intended to strengthen back and abdominal muscles, improve the tone of the pelvic floor muscles, and promote general physical well-being. Body-building exercises are incorporated into all programs of childbirth preparation. The goal is to bring the body to its optimum level of functioning in order to reduce muscle strain during pregnancy and to prepare for the work of labor and delivery.

Three basic types of breathing, to be employed during labor, are learned.[3] Each type begins and ends with a deep cleansing breath to promote complete relaxation. The first type of breathing is utilized during the preliminary phase of labor (30- to 60-second contractions with a 5- to 20-minute interval). Deliberate chest breathing is done, inhaling through the nose and exhaling through the mouth. During the accelerated phase (45- to 60-second contractions with a 2- to 4-minute interval) the breathing pattern changes to one of rapid, shallow panting. Until the transition phase occurs, this pattern is increased as the intensity of contractions increases. Breathing during the transition phase (60- to 90-second contractions with a 30- to 90-second interval) is composed of a pant-blow combination. It is a pattern of 4 to 6 pants followed by a short blowing out, and the pant-blow pattern is repeated until the contraction is ended. The rapid, shallow type of breathing has received strong criticism because it often results in hyperventilation which can cause problems for both mother and baby. However, clients are taught methods which counteract the symptoms of hyperventilation should they occur.

Abdominal massage, *effleurage*, provides an additional focus for concentration and affords comfort by helping to relieve abdominal tension during contractions. A gentle fingertip massage in a circular motion begins at the bottom of the abdomen and works upward during inhalation, and the circle is completed with downward massage during exhalation. Effleurage is performed in time to the breathing, thus increasing in rapidity as labor increases in intensity and breathing accelerates.

Lamaze emphasizes the crucial nature of the mate's role both in the educational and training phase and as a collaborative partner during childbirth itself. If the mate is not available, a trained monitor may be present to provide supportive physical care and encouragement throughout the labor process. With increased utilization of the Lamaze method, labor-room nurses have begun to overcome their initial resistance to the presence of a mate or monitor and are now functioning as the third member of the labor-room team. In addition to monitoring vital signs and progress of labor and collaborating with the physician, nurses function in a supportive role to both partners. The mate or monitor is allowed to function in areas of competence and comfort, with the nurse providing supplementary physical and/or emotional support where indicated.

The success or failure of this method for any patient is dependent again upon the individual's motivation for selecting this approach to childbirth preparation and to the support provided by health team members. Since the Lamaze-prepared patient is well educated as to what to expect in labor and delivery and insists on the type of care she wants, this often has an unsettling effect upon professional practitioners.

In the United States, the concept of "painless childbirth" has gradually given way to the concept of "education for childbirth." Empirical evidence has demonstrated that some women have easy labors and some women do not. Women learn that having a baby is not like entering a contest in which one succeeds or fails. They are taught that analgesics and anesthetics are administered when necessary according to their individual needs and the discretion of their obstetrician. Although some studies indicate that women trained by the Lamaze method require less medication during childbirth, there is much controversy concerning the physiological mechanism by which the method reduces the perception of pain. Apparently the element of distraction plays an important part. It has long been observed that people intensely absorbed in activity are less sensitive to painful stimuli. It has been postulated that when many stimuli are sent to the cerebral cortex, the cortex will respond only to the strongest stimuli. Therefore, if during a uterine contraction a series of activities are carried out which require the woman's complete attention, the perception of the contraction as a "pain" will be diminished. Adherents of the Lamaze method seem to refer more to the satisfaction they have experienced during childbirth than to the presence or absence of pain.

Hypnosis

Hypnosis is one of the oldest techniques known to the medical world. Its origins were in the spiritual realm where it was the province of the temple priests and mystics to employ hypnotic techniques. Within the health care system, it has been considered both beneficial and inappropriate, sometimes simultaneously.

Authoritative sources clearly demonstrate that hypnosis is a powerful and effective anesthetic agent. There have been repeated demonstrations of its use in obstetrics.

Certain obvious advantages exist with hypnosis. For any patient with a pathological condition which contraindicates the use of pharmacological agents, hypnosis can be utilized to provide a comfortable, controlled labor and delivery with amnesia as a possible option. It can also be a useful tool for the upset or disturbed patient. When hypnosis is not completely effective, only minimal analgesia or anesthesia is generally required.

Hypnosis requires skilled application and judicious use. In some settings where hypnosis is utilized, no interaction or noise of any kind is permitted. Many authorities agree, however, that the approach to the hypnotized patient in labor is one of quiet, unstartling commands and reassurance. This approach will enhance, not disrupt, the hypnotic state.

All patients are not suited to the technique of hypnosis, and there are obvious dangers if it is used indiscriminantly. One such danger, mentioned repeatedly, is that by removing the ability to perceive pain one removes a first-line defense mechanism of the body. The description of pain perceived by the patient can be a valuable diagnostic aid. Pain is often the signal of impending danger, such as in the instance of uterine rupture. Another frequently voiced objection to the use of hypnosis is the time requirement. Hypnosis requires training for the practitioner and is time-consuming for both the practitioner and the client in the conditioning phase. Another challenge to its obstetric use is that although the patient is not under pharmacological influence, she may remain unaware of and be a nonparticipant in her labor and delivery. Proponents of the use of hypnosis point to the possibility of producing a state of waking hypnosis in which the patient is able to converse, interact, follow instructions, and participate with awareness in her own labor and delivery.

Hypnosis and the Read technique are intertwined in almost all of the literature. Dr. Dick-Read repeatedly denied that his method

was hypnosis because a friend of his who was a hypnotist said it was not. Most authorities, however, maintain that the Read method is a form of hypnosis in that it utilizes the same basic approach and techniques. Dr. Dick-Read himself referred to some of his patients as being in a "trance from the beginning of their labor until the end." Other observers maintain that any of the psychophysical methods for relief of childbirth pain are in fact hypnosis. They cite the quiet, repetitive pronouncements to patients that their labor is not painful and that they are doing well as examples. According to them, this approach has a hypnotic effect upon the patient. Buxton carefully distinguishes between hypnosis, which artificially produces sleep, and "hypnotic effect" whereby a person may be profoundly affected although he is not asleep.[4] Some have always considered hypnosis quackery and therefore unsound for use in medicine. It is, however, regaining its popularity and is worthy of consideration.

PREPARATION FOR CHILDBIRTH TODAY

Factors Influencing Preparation

There has been a steady increase in the number of formal programs to prepare parents for the childbirth experience. It is noteworthy that the growth of programs has been largely due to their acceptance by the public. Although many professionals currently attest to the necessity and value of such preparation programs, resistance to this movement remains observable. Many who interact with prospective parents demonstrate their disapproval of the involved, knowledgeable parent who intends to participate in the childbearing experience. There are many reasons for such attitudes among doctors and nurses alike. Often, professional practitioners believe that by virtue of their education and experience, they are more qualified to select what is best for the client, including how she should bear her babies. It would appear that client involvement represents a threat to some egos, and many who resist the movement feel that they are being asked to surrender their professional control. For some practitioners, it is more convenient for parents not to be concerned with details of process and care. The "I'll handle everything for you" approach often demonstrates that it is easier for the practitioner not to be bothered by questions and explanations. A third attitude is reflected by professionals whose experiences and education engender other beliefs. Their statements, such as "Why should a woman suffer to bear her child?" and "Why should any man want to witness his partner's pain and suffering?" are the antithesis of the philosophy held by parents who desire understanding of and participation in their childbirth experience.

Advances in professional education have fostered inclusion of parents in more of the activities surrounding childbirth. Prospective parents frequently attend the physician's office together, and in the clinic setting it is more usual to see parents together for regular antepartum visits. Parents are being referred to existent childbirth education classes offered in the community, and it is increasingly common for hospitals to offer programs of antepartum education. Many private physicians provide programs of preparation for childbirth, usually under the guidance of the office nurse or nurse practitioner.

The influence of the mass media has been instrumental in stimulating the public's demand for increased preparation. Lay publications, movies, and television have often presented their own, one-sided and biased, views. An avalanche of popularly consumed articles proffer simplified and glorified approaches to childbirth. Through communication media, false interpretations and misconceptions may arise. The overzealous endorsement of some professional practitioners also contributes to misnomers and misconceptions. These misunderstandings in many instances only serve to do more harm than good to the general premise of prepared childbirth.

Peer influence cannot be minimized. It is often observed that a close friend's or a neighbor's experience is given more credence than the explanations offered by professionals. Even a very positive recital of the wonders of the childbirth experience can be very detrimental. When the listener only hears the end result, with no assessment of the reality of such an approach for her, her experience frequently bears no resemblance to what she had expected.

Two of the familiar methods, namely Read and Lamaze, acquired the titles of natural childbirth and painless childbirth, respectively. Inherent in the terminology "natural childbirth" is the idea that any medicinal or mechanical assistance defeats the naturalness of the event. If the goal of unassisted labor and delivery is not met, extreme frustration is likely. Resistance to appropriate medical intervention jeopardizes maternal and fetal welfare. "Childbirth without pain," on the other hand, conveys the impression that a certain practiced regimen abolishes the discomforts associated with childbirth. This descriptive, simplified terminology, applied to each program, often defeats preparedness for the realities of labor and delivery.

Whether programs had their origin in professional practice or in popular demand, all programs directed toward preparation for childbirth share similar goals or ideals. Essentially, these programs are aimed at reducing the amount of drugs needed and increasing the satisfaction of participants.

Contemporary Practices

Purists in a given method still exist within professional ranks. Many preparation programs are practiced as they were originally developed. Today, however, many practitioners in the field of childbirth education are moving away from rigid adherence to a given technique. Programs sponsored by educational institutions, hospitals, and other community health agencies are more likely to be representative of a combination of techniques tailored for the needs of those enrolled.

The objective of increasing satisfaction is being met by judicious combinations of techniques and pharmacological agents, rather than by the ability to tolerate labor and delivery by technique alone. Adherence to the belief that ultimate femininity lies in an unmedicated labor and delivery has given way to goal achievement through more realistic and appropriate means. The administration of analgesics and anesthetics need not negate the achievement of conscious, cooperative childbirth. Regardless of the technique utilized, all authorities agree on the value of education to reduce anxiety and to enhance involvement in the childbirth experience.

Education to eradicate needless or unfounded fears is certainly valid. Programs of preparation attempt to provide knowledge and understanding in a realistic, factual way. Most preparation programs also include exercises to achieve physical or psychological conditioning. No single rationale or purpose exists for the exercise component in childbirth education. All psychophysical programs include these techniques, and claims have been made that exercises shorten labor, reduce pain, and avoid complications. Although no such obstetric effectiveness has been proven, authorities do agree that exercise contributes to general physical and mental health. Some women state, however, that the sole value of the exercises for them was one of distraction.

Relaxation techniques are frequently utilized as supportive measures with the patient in labor. Posture and positioning are vital to both comfort and relaxation, since they reduce the stress and strain on muscles. The ability to control breathing can enhance relaxation or may simply provide distraction.

Anticipation of pain heightens anxiety. Anxiety intensifies pain perception. The terminology which is utilized when a person is under stress can contribute to heightening or lessening this stress. An expectation can be created through word selection. Thus, avoidance of repeated reference to pain and the utilization of less charged words is likely to evoke a positive, relaxed response. Terminology selection is also vital in the collection of accurate data. Asking the patient to describe what she feels is more likely to elicit her perception of sensations than asking her, "How often are your pains?" or "Are you in pain?" The number of women who deny that contractions are painful is noteworthy. Many speak of accompanying sensations such as backache, tingling, pressure in the groin and vagina, and radiating sensations along the thigh, but rather than describing these sensations as "pain," they characterize them as giving rise to "discomfort" in labor.

Each individual or couple comes to the experience of childbirth with a unique and complex background. All have differing expectations and fears and have been differently prepared. Regardless of the approach or method of preparation, the primary goal remains one of a safe outcome for the parents and the baby. Achievement of this goal is enhanced by a knowledgeable nurse who is sensitive to the needs of others. Sensitivity necessitates self-awareness and an honest recognition of the impact of attitudes and values upon others. The ultimate goal is to accomplish satisfaction with dignity.

The following examples illustrate divergent patient and personnel expectations:

A young husband was with his wife during her labor with their second child. No visible expressions of discomfort were observed in the wife, and by all measurements she was well established in active labor with frequent moderate to firm contractions. The husband did not fit the expected pattern of a supporting, back-rubbing, coaching helpmate, but rather appeared to agitate consistently and "pick an argument" with his wife. A continuous bantering, bickering interaction was noted. A nurse who was well schooled in the Read technique was concerned about what she perceived to be lack of husbandly support. She encouraged the husband to leave his wife and go to supper. The nurse failed to note that there had been no hostility or anger observed in the couple's interaction. The wife was quite active in joining, and at times initiating, the interchange. Within minutes of the husband's departure, the wife became restless, grimaced, and stated, "Oh, the contractions are much stronger now!" The labor pattern was unchanged, but her perception was different. Apparently, a familiar pattern of behavior had been utilized successfully for those involved. It was disallowed because of the nurse's perceptions and expectations.

A nurse related the story of how change in approach affected her own labor awareness and behavior. Admitted in labor to a busy unit at a time when most of the patients were heavily medicated, she met a great deal of resistance and intolerance to her "natural childbirth" ideas. She was highly motivated to participate in the birth of her baby and well educated in the theory and techniques. She described her first hours of labor as time spent busily defending her right to her own means. These were hours of continuous battle with an unkind, rough resident who considered her to be quite "nuts." She has little recall of this part of her labor. She stated that she was too busy fighting and being angry to be physically uncomfortable. At the time a different resident came on duty, she was amazed and thrilled to find a compassionate, supportive person. He demonstrated the approach which she believed to be important

for success. Almost immediately, she became conscious of discomfort and perceived her labor as quite painful. In this instance, apparently the distraction of the battle and the sudden change in approach had unpredicted effects.

An appropriate and meaningful childbirth experience is one which considers the needs, desires, and capabilities of a given family unit. The family-centered approach has been developed in an attempt to meet these needs. "Family centered" is often interpreted to mean a shared labor and delivery experience, rooming-in, and breast-feeding as a natural follow-up. While it is true that these experiences are very often related and extremely rewarding for some parents, it is appalling to see that frequently this is the only interpretation of a family-centered experience. Too often, under the guise of a family-centered program, a hospital really provides a staff-centered program, one based upon their beliefs and facilities, permitting little or no deviation from the stated program. Focus on familial needs recognizes that each family unit may "share" in different ways. When agreed upon mutually, selected experiences can be more rewarding than the total package. Insistence upon a prescribed set of activities denies the family's right to determine what is meaningful to them.

Much emphasis is given to preparing a family unit for the birth experience of their first child. However, more intensive preparation may be necessary for the multiparous family, since the strongest influence on attitudes and beliefs is the previous childbirth experience. If this experience was difficult or frightening, positive attitudes will be more difficult to achieve than in a family in which no such sensitization has occurred.

Assessment of the individual or group to be prepared is vital in planning and implementing any program or technique. Perusal of a program frequently demonstrates that it is based upon practitioner beliefs with little or no regard for the needs of the participant. It is true, of course, that the learner does not always know what he or she needs to know. It is also true that he or she cannot and will not learn until initial needs are met. "The primary purpose of education is not reassurance, but honest recognition of anxiety and examination of the realities on which it is based."[5]

An increasingly larger segment of the childbearing public demands education. The age of ignorance and alienation is being replaced by the era of enlightenment, personalization, and involvement. Mass means of care for patients in labor are giving way to more personalized and individualized approaches. Large labor rooms are being modified to hold one or two laboring women. Provision for fathers as an integral part of the team of attendants is a more common practice. The hospital is coming to realize its responsibility to provide safe, humane, personalized care.

What the hospital has yet to do is to assume responsibility for more far-reaching, inclusive parent education. This is demonstrated in the adherence to programs of preparation for childbearing. Little attention is focused on assisting parents to cope with childrearing. Preparation for parenthood is not totally the hospital's province; however, there are those aspects which are appropriately the hospital's responsibility.

Programs aimed at preparation have grown over the years. Programs of education which encompass all aspects of family life are beginning to evolve.

Implications for Other Preparation Programs

The sensible approach to preparation for childbirth is that which concerns itself with the attitudes, values, and beliefs of the participants. It attempts to allay unrealistic fears, to provide means of coping with unavoidable fears and stress, and to promote selection of techniques which best meet the needs of each individual and family group.

Obviously, preparation is most effective if it occurs throughout one's life. Our ultimate aim is to increase its consistency and accuracy which would foster its occurrence as a normal part of life. This type of preparation would bring any participant to the actual reality of pregnancy with basic, factual knowledge and healthier, more positive attitudes. Even with improved preparation, fear and misconceptions may continue to create problems. With this background, however, the realities and the specifics relative to the problem could be handled more easily and quickly. If all who are now involved in childbirth were adequately prepared, there would be fewer fantasies and misconceptions in the succeeding generation. The point here is not to devalue programs of preparation, but rather to emphasize the need for utilizing knowledge and techniques toward the most satisfying experience possible within the therapeutic milieu of each client.

We are, however, a long way from that point. Many people have not benefited from explanations and education which could have enhanced their childbirth experience, regardless of the approach. When we begin to appraise the needs of clients and their families more honestly, we will begin to identify what constitutes minimally adequate, if not totally satisfying, preparation. In order to satisfy the needs of clients primarily and professional practitioners secondarily, we must begin to look at who is involved in programs of preparation.

Programs for prepared childbirth have historically been structured for the typical married couple. Repeated references to "husband" and "wife" cement this impression.

Although partners were involved in creating the child, for a variety of reasons there may be no future involvement of the male. Yet absence of the male because of death, separation, or disinterest frequently provides the reason for a woman's exclusion from some programs. The usual rationalization is that it would be uncomfortable for *her*. Must the presence of a husband be a ticket of entry into these programs? Whose comfort are we *really* considering? Since single parenthood may give rise to problems, is this not all the more reason for professional assistance? Emphasis needs to be placed on the fact that absence of marriage or of a partner need not exclude clients from such programs.

We have begun to include husbands in the activities related to childbirth. We are much slower to include *fathers*, as opposed to husbands, and are particularly resistant to the inclusion of significant others who fit neither the husband nor the father category. It may be a male friend, father, mother, aunt, or other close friend whose role interaction with the pregnant woman is most significant. If this relationship is one which provides support in times of stress and crisis, does it not follow that presence or involvement at the time of labor and delivery might be not only permissible but beneficial? If so, then to increase the value of this interaction, the significant other(s) may need to be part of the preparation. All client contacts need not move into the hospital setting with the parturient woman, but again, assessment of a given situation provides the basis for evaluating what is shared by whom.

If preparation is to be meaningful, it appears logical that professional practitioners and clients need to work together in formulating and implementing a practical, rewarding experience. Establishing an appropriate approach includes the citation of possible alternatives which may be indicated by either client or practitioner requirements. Thus, the

elements of defeat inherent in the failure to meet a prescribed regimen are less likely to occur. In this way, ultimate professional responsibility for the safety and welfare of those concerned is in no way jeopardized. Most patients are relieved to have realistic, safe decisions made for them. Difficulties arise when no rationale is given for decisions and all rights in the decision-making process are denied them.

Prior to the fact of a given experience, it is irrational and dangerous to espouse an approach that will require *no* adaptation. Each individual who arrives at the time of childbirth is unique. So, too, is each program or technique of prepared childbirth a unique entity with its own strengths and weaknesses. Thus, it is impossible to dictate *one* means of preparing for childbirth.

The very nature of pregnancy can be a predictor of readiness to learn. Thus, the timing and sequence of content will influence the effectiveness of learning. Thorough understanding of the physical and psychological aspects can increase awareness of when critical issues are likely to emerge. According to Reva Rubin,

There is indeed a cognitive style in pregnancy, one of inconclusive questioning and uncertainty. Two sets of questions and an underlying sense of uncertainty alternate during the course of the pregnancy to effect, in harmony with the biological changes, progressive developmental stages of pregnancy.

One set of questions is concerned with time within the life space, the other with a personal sense of identity. Both sets of questions are salient to a sense of feminine identity.[6]

Early in pregnancy, the physiological changes which create gastrointestinal problems and fatigue, accompanied by the disquieting thought of pregnancy as a fact, hardly provide the impetus to become pre-pared for labor and delivery. At this time, ef-forts are most appropriately geared toward assisting resolution of the *reality* of the preg-nancy.

In the second trimester, when physical symptoms are usually not problematic, there is a general sense of well-being. This period affords an opportunity to begin to deal with the realities of pregnancy. Now the focus is upon impending role change for the parents, and plans for the event of childbirth begin. If diapering or bathing an infant is a learning activity, it serves as a vehicle for trying on this impending role. This is a valuable tool in assisting role transition, but it should not be confused with the belief that learning to handle, bathe, and diaper an infant has been achieved. This learning can only occur when their infant is a reality. Thus, it belongs prop-erly with activities aimed at establishing parent-infant relationships in the postpar-tum period.

The third trimester of pregnancy generally brings a return of discomforts, a sense of physical and emotional burden, and a more introspective manner. Educational and sup-portive techniques now can be directed to-ward expression of the impatience and fears. These can assist the identification of appro-priate coping means. The aim, late in preg-nancy, is to assist the family in garnering reserves which will enable them to tolerate the threats of labor and delivery.

Preparation for childbirth can foster inter-nalization of the impending occurrence with acceptance of its realities. Through a learn-ing experience which increases problem-solving skill, participants can come to trust in their own ability and cope with both the predictable and unpredictable aspects of childbirth. Trust in oneself fosters trust in others involved and in the interventions which may become necessary in a particular situation.

The selection of appropriate resources by each person is to be applauded in the quest for prepared childbirth. Clients and practi-tioners respect each other's rights and re-sponsibilities through prior awareness and knowledge of what those rights and respon-sibilities entail. An adequately prepared woman arrives at the time of labor and de-livery with a sense of dignity and control which can be maintained regardless of un-foreseeable events.

FUTURE PROGRAMS IN CHILDBIRTH PREPARATION

One of the best opportunities for health pro-motion is in the field of obstetrics. Antepar-tum care has long demonstrated its effective-ness in reducing perinatal mortality. Thus, it is conceivable that through a program of *pre-vention* rather than intervention, the crisis of childbirth might be reduced or perhaps eliminated.

Within the childbirth experience there lies an excellent opportunity to demonstrate con-tinuity of care and comprehensive services. There can be no doubt that assisting families, of whatever composition, ultimately affects society at large. It is long overdue that we of the profession assume more leadership in the preventive aspects which we know are pos-sible. Too often we discharge our responsi-bilities to parents with a miniature course in labor and delivery and the traditional baby bath. Our larger responsibility is the assis-tance of each parent in the assumption of his or her parental role.

Various programs which have been de-veloped have attracted given segments of so-ciety but have failed to contact all strata. Those who avail themselves of these pro-grams are generally the more economically advantaged or more informed. To reach those who are uninformed, untouched, and alienated becomes our goal. In order to accomplish this goal, health care professionals must abandon their restrictive approach to care. Community resources can help us learn what approaches and methods will be accepted. We can look for guidance from colleagues who continue to experience success in the community. Honest evaluation of success and failure can assist in the identification of health care services to be provided.

The nurse who engages in parent education must be well prepared in all aspects of childbearing and childrearing. A background in the physical, behavioral, and social sciences which encompasses growth and development is vital. It is mandatory to have knowledge and experience in various teaching methods as well as an understanding of the cultural variations in particular communities. These are the qualifications necessary to help parents clarify issues through a problem-solving approach, rather than making decisions *for* them.

It is predicted that the next decade will see the continued development of out-of-hospital services with more concentration on health and less preoccupation with illness. This trend demands the development of new roles for nurses and greater efficiency in their utilization.

There is a new role for tomorrow's nurse. She could in the next decade or two be responsible for the health of families in the community and for their nursing care in the hospital if a member of the family required this specialized nursing service. . . . This new nurse would move freely from the home to the hospital and back. She would become the family's nurse and her main concern would be *health*.[7]

Traditional means of operating must be abandoned—the old must give way to the new, more rational, more efficient. The nurse

is envisioned as an independent practitioner accountable to the physician for a specific medical regimen, and responsible for prescriptions to meet the nursing needs of the client and her family. As an independent practitioner the nurse will utilize the nursing knowledge, experience, and expertise of all colleagues and will provide consultation when it is sought. These nurses will give direct patient care and will act as liaisons between the hospital and the community. Above all, they will be responsible to and for their clients and accountable to the profession.

REFERENCES

1 Bowers, Paul A.: "Natural Childbirth," *Medical Clinics of North America*, 39:1789–1799, November 1955.
2 Bing, Elisabeth: *Six Practical Lessons for an Easier Childbirth*, Grosset & Dunlap, New York, 1967, p. 15.
3 Ibid., p. 65.
4 Buxton, C. Lee: *A Study of Psychophysical Methods for Relief of Childbirth Pain*, Saunders, Philadelphia, 1962, p. 53.
5 Bruce, Sylvia J.: "Do Prenatal Education Programs Really Prepare for Parenthood?" *Hospital Topics*, November 1965, p. 106.
6 Rubin, Reva: "Cognitive Style in Pregnancy," *American Journal of Nursing*, 70(3):502, March 1970.
7 Mussallem, Helen K.: "The Changing Role of the Nurse," *American Journal of Nursing*, 69(3):515, March 1969.

BIBLIOGRAPHY

Auerbach, A. B.: *Parents Learn through Discussion: Principles and Practices of Parent Group Education*, Wiley, New York, 1968.
Bean, Constance A.: *Methods of Childbirth*, Doubleday, Garden City, N.Y., 1972.
——— (ed.): *The Adventure of Birth Experiences*

in the Lamaze Method of Prepared Child-birth, Grosset & Dunlap, New York, 1970.

Chabon, Irwin: *Awake and Aware*, Delacorte Press, New York, 1966.

Chertok, L.: "Psychosomatic Methods of Preparation for Childbirth," *American Journal of Obstetrics and Gynecology*, 98:698–707, July 1967.

Dick-Read, G.: *Childbirth without Fear*, 2d ed., Harper, New York, 1959.

Eastman, Nicholson: *Expectant Mother*, Little, Brown, Boston, 1963.

Fielding, W., and L. Benjamin: *The Childbirth Challenge: Common Sense versus "Natural" Methods*, Viking, New York, 1962.

Fitzpatrick, E., S. Reeder, and L. Mastroianni: *Maternity Nursing*, 12th ed., Lippincott, Philadelphia, 1971.

Hoff, Florence E.: "How Any Nurse Can Help," *American Journal of Nursing*, 69(7):1451–1453, July 1969.

Hommel, Flora: "Natural Childbirth—Nurses in Private Practice as Monotrices," *American Journal of Nursing*, 69(7):1446–1450, July 1969.

Howard, Robert E., and Sister Jan Marie: Initial Experience with a Prepared Childbirth Program," *Journal of Obstetric, Gynecologic and Neonatal Nursing*, 1(3):30–34, September–October 1972.

Karmel, M.: *Thank You, Doctor Lamaze*, Lippincott, Philadelphia, 1959.

Leonard, Roger F.: "Evaulation of Selection Tendencies of Patients Preferring Prepared Childbirth," *Obstetrics and Gynecology*, 42(3): 371–377, September 1973.

Maternity Center Association: *Seminar on Childbearing and Family Life: Prelude to Action*, New York, 1969.

Mead, Margaret: *Cultural Patterns and Technical Change*, The New American Library of World Literature, New York, 1955.

Mulcahy, Rae A.: "Effectiveness of Raising Pain Perception Threshold in Males and Females Using a Psychoprophylactic Childbirth Technique during Induced Pain," *Nursing Research*, 22(5):423–427, September–October 1973.

Pomerance, Jeffrey, Louis Gluck, and Vincent A. Lynch: "Physical Fitness in Pregnancy: Its Effect on Pregnancy Outcome," *American Journal of Obstetrics and Gynecology*, 119(7): 867–876, August 1974.

Sasmor, Jeannette L.: "Stress Adaptation. A Theory for Childbirth Education," *Journal of Obstetric, Gynecologic and Neonatal Nursing*, 2(6):48–50, November–December 1973.

Sasmor, Jeannette L., Constance R. Castor, and Patricia Hassid: "The Childbirth Team during Labor," *American Journal of Nursing*, 73(3): 444–447, March 1973.

Sclare, A. B.: "Psychoprophylaxis in Obstetrics," *Nursing Times*, 61:1373–1374, October 1968.

Shapiro, Howard I., and Leonore G. Schmitt: "Evaulation of the Psychoprophylactic Method of Childbirth in the Primigravida," *Connecticut Medicine*, 37(7):341–343, July 1973.

Smith, Barbara, Robert M. Priore, and Mona K. Stern: "The Transition Phase of Labor," *American Journal of Nursing*, 73(3):448–450, March 1973.

Tanzer, Deborah: "Natural Childbirth: Pain or Peak Experience," *Psychology Today*, October 1968.

Vellay, P., and A. Vellay: *Térmoinages sur l'Accouchement sans Couleur*, Éditions du Senil, Paris, 1956.

Wright, Erna: *The New Childbirth*, Hart, New York, 1968.

Yahia, C., and P. Ulin: "Preliminary Experience with a Psycho-physical Program of Preparation for Childbirth," *American Journal of Obstetrics and Gynecology*, 93(7), 1965.

20

Emotional Considerations for the Pregnant Family

VIVIAN MOORE LITTLEFIELD

It is essential to treat the entire family when one member is ill and to consider the family as a whole when attempting to promote emotional health.[1] Maternity nursing also emphasizes family-centered care. Therefore, considering the entire family "pregnant" when one is concerned with emotional needs is appropriate. Family members expect a change in the family makeup as well as changes in their roles within the family. The preparation period during pregnancy is important for each family member in different ways and will have an important influence on the emotional environment of the "new" family after the birth of the baby. The type of support and guidance a family receives during the preparation period of pregnancy influences the family's ability to cope with the stresses of pregnancy and to be prepared emotionally to provide a healthy environment for its newest member. (See Figure 20-1.)

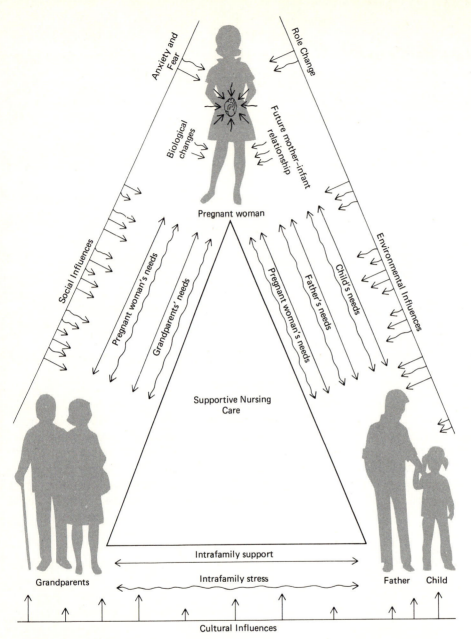

FIGURE 20-1

This diagram indicates the influence of each family member's needs on the needs
of other members during pregnancy. The straight lines indicate positive support and
the wavy lines indicate negative influences. The supportive role of the nurse in
assisting each family member (primary and extended) in coping with stressful
situations is indicated by the triangle in the center.

The goal of health care is one of promoting optimum health since childbearing is relatively safe for most families. A review of current theories of psychopathology and psychophysiological disorders indicates that child battering, mental illness, and many psychophysiological illnesses result from unhealthy mother-infant-family relationships. There is some evidence, too, that many of the complications of pregnancy such as habitual abortion, hyperemesis gravidarum, pseudocyesis, toxemia, prematurity, and prolonged labor are emotional in origin, or are at least enhanced by stressful emotional situations in the pregnant woman's biologic, psychosocial, and cultural environment.[2-4] There is also evidence that suggests that the emotional stress of the pregnant woman may have some influence on the fetus in utero and on the baby's behavior at birth, and may even cause congenital abnormalities.[5] Therefore, it becomes essential to promote optimum psychological health in the pregnant woman and her family unit.

There are various socioeconomic, cultural, and environmental situations that influence the amount of stress present during pregnancy. These situations include poverty, marital difficulties, inadequate living conditions, and difficult work situations. These situations also influence the family's ability to handle the stress that the biological and psychological changes bring about in the family members, individually and as a whole. In evaluating the emotional needs of a family, all of these factors must be considered so that the family can be helped to cope more effectively with the various stresses present. This can be done by helping the family use its strengths in creative ways to eliminate or decrease various stressful situations and to enhance its ability to cope with the stressful situations that cannot be avoided.

Professional nurses are in extremely important positions by virtue of their educational background and job situation to provide emotional support to pregnant families. But more important is the fact that of all the professional workers who assist the pregnant family, it is the nurse who has a sociological closeness that other health professionals sometimes lack. Caplan believes that this closeness is a unique function of nursing. He sees this as an extremely valuable tool in relating to the pregnant woman and her family. He suggests that nurses' "wise sister role" allows clients to be more free in their relationships with nurses and to more readily trust them with their problems and concerns.[6]

In order to provide "emotional support" for the pregnant family the nurse needs knowledge of the biological and physical changes that pregnancy initiates in the expectant woman. In addition to this knowledge, the nurse must understand, within a cultural context, the needs of other family members who face these changes with the pregnant woman and what is involved in assuming a new role within the family. The nurse cannot overlook how *all* of these factors interact to influence the emotional tone of the family.

This chapter attempts to provide a basis of knowledge about the emotional changes of pregnancy and how they influence the pregnant woman and her family. How these needs are interdependent and how the family handles the stresses will be discussed. Throughout this discussion some suggestions will be made concerning intervention by the nurse which assists the family to cope. Some attention is given to emotional situations that are pathological.

THE PREGNANT WOMAN— CHANGED AND CHANGING

Biological and Physical Changes That Influence Emotional Needs

Pregnancy is a biological state that changes the woman's chemical and physical makeup. These changes in hormones and physical appearance greatly influence the woman's emotional needs and state. Among the physiological changes initiated by conception are changes in protein metabolism, carbohydrate metabolism, level of electrolytes, blood volume, and amount of body water as well as numerous endocrine changes in the thyroid gland, pituitary gland, and ovaries. There is an increased production of estrogen and progesterone.[7] According to Benedek, Caplan, and Richardson, all these changes are important in producing the "pregnant personality," or what is termed "the mood of pregnancy." Some of the most common psychological changes during pregnancy are the woman's general introversion, passivity, and primary narcissism (the increase in the energy which a woman turns in on herself during pregnancy). It is believed that these traits of pregnancy are due to the increased production of progesterone.[8] The reader is referred to a text on physiology and Chapter 16 of this text for a more complete description of the physiological changes taking place.

Depending on the pregnant woman's psychological and sociocultural background, these physiological changes may or may not cause stress. Whether or not she chose to be pregnant influences her emotional acceptance or rejection of her condition and all the changes that are taking place within her body. Her methods of resolving previous psychological developmental stages also influence the way she views pregnancy and her changed emotional state.

Psychological Mood of Pregnancy

Introversion and Passivity

One of the most common changes in the emotional response of many pregnant women is their introversion and passivity. The need to rest, to do quiet things, and a lessened interest in previous activities may be frustrating to the woman and/or her family. One client described this feeling as being "detached" from others and from the situation. If the pregnant woman knows this introversion is a possibility, she is less likely to be frustrated by it. However, if she is not aware of this "turning-in," she could become concerned about her lack of interest in things about which she was previously enthusiastic. Passivity and introversion are less acceptable to some women, and often husbands, mothers, and relatives are somewhat confused and concerned by the change.

Some women become more physically active, outgoing, or extroverted during pregnancy. These women state they feel better than at other times. This appears to occur less frequently than introversion, but since it is a possibility, one should think of the consequences or confusion of both client and family as well as friends or an employer when the pregnant women's personality is "different" from what it was previously.

Primary Narcissism

Primary narcissism is a trait of pregnancy that may be frustrating to family and friends. This trait, however, is viewed as an important protective mechanism. It causes the woman to consider her own needs during pregnancy and to begin to attach feelings to the fetus as an extension of her own body. The woman who is busy caring and doing for others at her own expense is assisted in caring for herself more appropriately in order to maintain pregnancy at an optimal state. The self-centeredness that is often evident may be upsetting to the pregnant woman or to various family members, relative to their degree of dependence on her before pregnancy. At any rate, this is an extremely important change for the nurse to consider, since it might be frustrating to the family, the pregnant woman, or to other health workers who ask the woman to follow certain regulations regarding rest, activity, or nutrition for the baby. The pregnant woman is concerned about *her* needs and the restrictions that pregnancy may place on *her*. It is highly possible that the nurse who understands this need might be more effective in getting the pregnant mother to follow necessary medical, nutritional, and physical regimens since it is the nurse who understands how the pregnant woman may view these requirements. The nurse can help put restrictions in the context of being beneficial for the pregnant woman herself, rather than *always* placing emphasis on doing everything "for the baby." If the nurse feels guilty about giving extra attention to the pregnant woman, who seems to be healthy and well and appears somewhat self-centered, it should be considered that this giving to the pregnant woman is helping her prepare psychologically for giving to her child.

Changes in Sexual Desire

If one spends time talking with the pregnant woman about her concerns, it becomes clear that there are changes in sexual desire. Some women indicate their best sexual experiences are during pregnancy; others indicate little interest in sex during pregnancy. Masters and Johnson, in a study of 107 gravidas, found that there was an increase in frequency of intercourse and sexual interest during the first trimester, a marked increase in the second trimester, and diminished interest in sexual relations during the third trimester.[9] A study by Landis, reported by Falicov, found a decrease in sexual desire on the part of husbands and wives as pregnancy progressed in 212 first-time pregnant couples.[10]

Falicov in a small study involving 19 primigravidas found decreased frequency of sexual intercourse, decreased sexual desire, and decreased eroticism that carried over to the postpartum period. Ten of the women in the study expressed a fear of harming the infant. Figure 20-2 demonstrates Falicov's findings.[11]

Changes in sexual desire are likely to cause emotional stress on the part of the pregnant woman and her mate. Anticipatory guidance concerning possible changes in sexual desire is needed early in pregnancy with assurance to both parents that this is quite common. A combination of introversion, passivity, and narcissism coupled with decreased sexual desire might increase fam-

FIGURE 20-2

Direction of changes in sexual adjustment. n = the number of women in the study population. (*By permission from Celia J. Falicov, "Sexual Adjustment during First Pregnancy and Post Partum,"* American Journal of Obstetrics-Gynecology, *Dec. 1, 1973, p. 994.*)

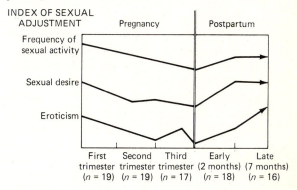

ily stress. One can visualize the various problems encountered by each family member when varying degrees of these changes occur.

Emotional Lability

Mood swings, emotional lability, irritability, and increased sensitivity have been said to be a part of the mood of pregnancy. The degree to which a client is irritable and overly sensitive depends on the individual and is influenced by the woman's basic personality, her level of emotional and physical maturity, and her desire to be pregnant.

One author indicates that women who were, prior to conception, demanding, complaining, unstable, and unable to adapt to changes or stress were found to be moody, uncooperative, self-indulgent, self-pitying, and full of somatic distress during pregnancy. Likewise, those rated stable during pregnancy were generally rated stable during everyday life.[12] There were exceptions to the rule, however, and so we must realize that a relatively stable and mature woman may experience a fair amount of emotional stress during pregnancy.

The fact that such changes are possible is probably difficult for the family to handle. In Dr. Robert Bradley's book *Husband-coached Childbirth*, he writes to husbands, "Let us . . . explore in detail the problem of living with pregnant women. Let's face it, they're nuttier than a fruitcake! . . . A pregnant woman is a changed and ever-changing woman. She gradually not only looks different but she feels different and acts different."[13] This colorful way of getting the idea across to the husband dramatizes the difficulty the husband may have adjusting to mood swings and the fact that a woman during pregnancy is "different" and at times unpredictable.

Such a statement also indicates the need to discuss these changes with the expectant father.

Ambivalence toward Pregnancy

Gerald Caplan's research on the emotions of pregnancy indicates that 80 percent of the women who become pregnant admit they are disappointed and anxious when they find that they are pregnant.[14] Dunbar indicates that even those women who wanted to become pregnant have doubts when they actually accomplish their goal.[15] This ambivalence results from many complex factors and may be expressed in some of the mood swings, nausea and vomiting, increased anxiety, or various somatic symptoms such as constipation, diarrhea, disturbed sleep, or overeating.

Although there is disagreement in the literature concerning the origin of somatic symptoms during pregnancy, psychophysiological theory indicates that emotional stress can be expressed by physical symptoms. Emotional influence seems highly possible in the most common physical symptoms of early pregnancy—nausea and vomiting. Although most authors agree that there is a physiological basis for this symptom, there is evidence that there are psychological factors involved. An example of a cultural variable illustrates this point. Some Native American cultures have not had a term for morning sickness, and few of the women in these cultures have experienced morning sickness in early pregnancy. However, when a particular group of Native Americans moved to California, the women developed nausea and vomiting during early pregnancy.[16]

When nausea and vomiting is excessive, as in hyperemesis gravidarum, it is interpreted by many as a symptom of emotional distress. Deutsch's description of the vomiting of pregnancy is perhaps the most psychologically oriented. She says that vomiting tries to rid the mother-to-be of the child, but a triumphant feeling (that the fetus is still intact) after emesis represents the conflicting wish to keep the child.[17] Other authors indicate that the psychological origin of vomiting in pregnancy is due to undesired sexual relations or to an undesirable relationship between the pregnant woman and her mother.[18,19] Regardless of the origin of the physical symptoms of nausea and vomiting, most authors agree that emotional stress can increase the symptoms or prohibit effective treatment of such symptoms. Emotional influences are important for nurses to remember when nausea and vomiting are problems for pregnant women.

Oral Tone of Pregnancy

Another important trait of the pregnant personality is the oral tone, or, as Chertok indicates, the emphasis on "hypersomnia, interest in food, greed, dependence, and susceptibility in relation to the environment."[20] This need may cause conflict when restrictions are placed on food intake. Caplan indicates that pregnant women often disagree with the dietitian over diet because of their emphasis on oral needs. These needs, coupled with the revival of childhood conflicts between the woman and her mother, sometimes make it difficult for the pregnant woman to follow the dietitian's advice. Better results have been obtained when the diet for the pregnant woman was given to her by the obstetrician as a medical prescription.[21] This information has important implications for nursing, especially if the nurse finds difficulty in persuading a client to follow dietary advice.

Disequilibrium between Ego and Id

Bradley's remark that the pregnant woman is "nuttier than a fruitcake" is descriptive of a psychological condition that some authors feel is the result of changes between the equilibrium of the ego and id. Caplan, Montagu, and Guttmacher indicate that psychological development is relived during pregnancy, and the pregnant woman works through developmental tasks she was unable to solve appropriately in the past. Caplan describes this as allowing a "great deal of id material to come to the surface."[22] During this time fantasies, needs, and repressed wishes become conscious. In any other situation, this would only happen when a person was psychotic. However, the difference between the pregnant woman and the psychotic is that the pregnant woman is aware of reality. This reworking of old conflicts is thought to help the woman become a more mature individual. What a good preparation for motherhood if this is in fact the case! However, problems may arise if the pregnant woman verbally shares these ideas with family members or health workers who fail to realize this aspect of pregnancy.

Caplan also believes that many of the pregnant woman's fears are linked to old conflicts becoming conscious. Some of the fears he mentions that are a result of this reworking of old conflicts are dying during childbirth, giving birth to a monster, or fear that the baby may die.[23] Depending on the support given during pregnancy, the environmental stress present, and the maturity of the pregnant woman, this reworking of earlier developmental stages may or may not be positive. Nevertheless, it brings with it anxiety and emotional needs that are not clearly evident on a conscious level. Therefore, even though the pregnant woman and her family seem to be in a fairly stable life situation during pregnancy, there may be unconscious conflicts that cause anxiety. This could cause the nurse to miss many of the client's signals of need for support and help if the nurse does not consider that there may be anxiety present in the pregnant woman without obvious cause.

The nurse's responsibility in handling this ego-id disequilibrium is to be aware that many types of comments may be made by the pregnant woman that might not be said or tolerated at other times. In this respect one could help the woman discuss how she will handle psychosexual development in her own children. Also, by not being shocked by the ideas the woman brings up, such as "hating" her mother or various sexual difficulties, the nurse allows the woman to "work through" these feelings without unnecessary anxiety. Caplan believes this is the reason that many obstetricians and nurses avoid talking with and working with pregnant women on a closer level.[24] He believes that nurses and obstetricians are upset by the kind of things that pregnant women talk about openly. If the nurse indicates anxiety about the topics the pregnant woman wants to discuss, it might be difficult for the client and the nurse. The nurse who teaches pregnant women in groups should have knowledge and appreciation of these psychological factors of pregnancy. The pregnant woman, as a result of the changes taking place, can usually handle the ideas that are now hers. The registered nurse, social worker, or nursing student may be somewhat unprepared and unable to handle these ideas comfortably.

Body-Image Change

Physical changes occurring during pregnancy affect the pregnant woman's concept of self and influence her response to preg-nancy. Many authors indicate that there is always some change in body-image concept during pregnancy. The degree of difficulty perceived by the pregnant woman will depend on many things: the degree of threat that change in body image presents to her; the views of her family, friends, neighbors, and others of her sociocultural background; and her acceptance of pregnancy. If the pregnant woman's mate continually reminds her of her size or awkwardness, this is likely to have a negative influence on her. If, on the other hand, the mate views her pregnant state as a manifestation of his manliness and reminds her of her beauty, the threat of body-image change may be less stressful. A survey of current dress and the resultant advertising for such dress for pregnant women will give the reader an idea of contemporary acceptance of pregnancy.

Anxiety over Labor and Delivery

Pregnancy can be viewed as a period of crisis, a period of increased vulnerability, or as "a normal biological state, yet it tests the physiological and psychological reserves of [the] woman."[25]

The fears associated with the labor and delivery process—fear of pain, disability, and/or death—may cause stress.[26] The idea that a woman must go to a hospital to have a baby may indicate that birth is a difficult and painful procedure to some families. Many women hear of friends' and neighbors' labors and deliveries which are not always positive experiences. The practice of anesthetizing patients just before delivery also may have some influence on women as they believe they missed "so many of the terrible things of childbirth." Cultural background heavily influences interpretations of the labor and delivery experience. Many tales of bad experiences are often reinforced because occasionally mothers are "cut, torn, and injured, [and] babies are born with congenital defects."[27]

Dr. Grantly Dick-Read's description of the fear-tension-pain syndrome in labor indicates some of the problems that have arisen because of lack of knowledge and fear of the labor and delivery process. Dick-Read reported that if fear is reduced, the tension and resultant pain will be decreased. Since he has had success in providing a less painful labor and a better outlook for many patients, one could assume that helping the woman deal effectively with this aspect of reproduction would indeed benefit her greatly. Other psychoprophylactic methods of childbirth preparation have also had beneficial results in improving the patient's experience during labor and delivery. A number of studies have been done that indicate that prepared women, or women who have known what to expect during labor and delivery, have had a better experience during delivery and have felt more satisfaction in their achievement. Other studies have shown that if certain comfort methods are utilized, the pregnant woman is better able to handle the stress of labor.[28] Buxton's study of the various methods of preparation for labor and types of self-help during labor points out that information and certain techniques do improve the situation for the pregnant woman.[29] Other studies indicate that if the woman is helped to handle the stress of labor and delivery, she can more quickly and readily relate to her infant and assume the mothering role with less difficulty.

Role Change and Its Influence

In addition to mood changes, changes in personality, weakening of defenses, and change in body image, there is an overriding factor of change in role that pregnancy is preparing

the woman to assume. Regardless of whether the woman desires a role change—from wife to mother, or from first-time mother to second-, third-, or fourth-time mother—the pregnant woman must at the close of pregnancy assume a new role. This may bring countless psychological problems and conflicts or emotional growth.

Taking on the Maternal Role

Reva Rubin has described role change during pregnancy and how the woman experiences this change psychologically. She has taken Mead's "taking-in the role of other" and Sarbin's "adopting-the-ways-of-others" and has studied how the specific role of mother is assumed.[30,31]

The various methods used by the woman during pregnancy in order to take on the mother role are identified by Mead and Sarbin as (1) play, (2) fantasy, (3) empathy, and (4) copying.[32] Rubin indicates that this process is "a quiet, continuous process, but not a passive one." She also relates that the underlying motivation for taking-in is the "intent to become," and is characterized by five categories: *mimicking* and *role play,* which are forms of the *taking-on* process; *fantasy* and *introjection-projection-rejection,* which are forms of the *taking-in* process, and *grief-work,* which is a form of the *letting-go* of a former role process.

Observing actions of a group of pregnant women in a doctor's office, in an antepartum clinic, or at a neighborhood gathering for coffee reveals a number of taking-on processes. The pregnant woman may wear maternity clothes before they are necessary to accommodate her new shape. She establishes friendships with pregnant women in various stages of pregnancy and mimics their behavior. She offers to baby-sit for friends, relatives, or acquaintances so that, as Rubin puts it, she can "try-on" the role of mother (role play). She may decide to adopt a pet to practice her mothering activities. One pregnant woman attempted to adopt a pet during late pregnancy and was told by a pet adoption agency to come back after her baby was born. They had had too many pregnant women who wanted a pet to "practice mothering," and who, after the baby arrived, returned or neglected the pet.

Another way the pregnant woman prepares for mothering is to *fantasize* how it will be. This talking about and exploring how they will behave when the baby does certain things gives the nurse an excellent opportunity for anticipatory guidance concerning infant care, what babies need psychologically in the form of mothering, and what kinds of problems arise for the new mother. As the pregnant woman suggests positive acts of mothering which would assist the infant in gaining a sense of trust, the nurse can reinforce those behaviors. As the pregnant woman mentions behaviors that do not necessarily create a healthful environment for the baby, the nurse can suggest more appropriate behaviors. By helping the pregnant woman explore what she will do in areas of infant care, including problem areas such as crying, illness, or feeding, the nurse can help the woman prepare a variety of approaches to mothering which she adopts or rejects (introjection-projection-rejection). This process is beneficial to the pregnant woman and provides her with opportunities to maximize her coping ability to assume a new role.

Another important process of the mothering role as seen by Rubin is the "letting-go" of the former role (grief-work) that is "incompatible with the aspiration of the maternal role."[33] Again, the choice of the client to be in this situation (pregnant) will make a great deal of difference in the difficulty with which she lets go of former roles. Previously,

it was mentioned that the pregnant woman's desire to be pregnant influences her response to the changes taking place. This is also true of the difficulty or ease with which she lets go of former roles. Regardless of her desire to be pregnant, the pregnant woman will most likely have ambivalent feelings about giving up former roles. Rubin indicates that most women have difficulty in this respect. The pregnant woman actually grieves over her loss of role. This grieving is a "review in memory of the attachments and associated events of a former self. This memory of details of former self helps to loosen the ties with that self."[34]

Perhaps an example will be helpful. A pregnant woman recently indicated how she and her husband packed away the various articles of his school days and her work days in a trunk in preparation for becoming parents. Parenthood in this situation necessitated his becoming the financial support of the family. This was described as a ritual during which there were tears as they remembered experiences in this past life together. After this experience, this couple seemed to move very rapidly and more easily into doing the things necessary to prepare for parenthood. It should be noted that this pregnancy was planned for many years to be at this point in time. This process of letting-go is not pathological but therapeutic and necessary for the mother, and perhaps the father, if the parent role is to be assumed. This grieving is often seen on the postpartum unit, and the new mother is not able to move into mothering activities until this psychological step is well advanced.

One might speculate as to the most appropriate time to work through this letting-go process. Should the pregnant woman begin this during pregnancy? Should she be encouraged by the nurse to begin this process? It is highly possible that many women should be encouraged to begin thinking about their new role so that it is not difficult to move into it after the birth of the baby. Other women indicate little readiness for this process during pregnancy. It is also possible that naturally, or as a course of pregnancy, the woman herself will begin this process, and some assistance and encouragement will be all that is needed. The number of women on the postpartum unit who have not begun this grieving process seems to indicate that some research is needed into the most conducive way to support and encourage this process so that the client has the least amount of stress and does work through this in an acceptable way that does not impede her assuming the mothering role.

This process of letting-go was demonstrated very vividly by a young, attractive, immaculately groomed mother who had given birth to a little girl 2 days previously. She was in a rooming-in unit, and various efforts had been made to assist this mother in learning how to care for her infant. However, her fingernails were of such length that she could not handle the baby, pin the diaper, or bathe the baby because the staff feared she would injure her baby. There were quite a few nurses who were critical of this new mother. "Why doesn't she cut those fingernails?" The nursing student who had been working with the young mother had an understanding of the letting-go process and of the patient's difficulty in giving up her former role and accepting her new role, and she listened with understanding and assisted with baby care the mother could not do. On the last hospital day, the new mother asked for scissors and cried while she was cutting her beautifully manicured nails. The student accepted this and provided opportunities for the new mother to care for the baby that morning. She performed the tasks well and when the student later made a home visit, the student reported that the client was "mothering well."

It should be noted that this letting-go process is not limited to the prepregnant state—that is, grieving over loss of one's status as a bride, professional woman, or single girl—but that the mother who has previous children is affected by the loss of a relationship with her youngest child as the baby. Women pregnant for a second time do grief-work over the prepregnancy state *as well as* over the relationship with their first baby. Third- and fourth-time mothers grieve over loss of financial income and independence that a job might have offered them.[35]

Reva Rubin indicates that the ability to perform the tasks of mothering is facilitated if the grieving process as well as the taking-in process is complete. In light of this idea, it seems important to help the mother work through this process quickly so that she can care for her new baby as soon as possible because our system of maternal care requires the mother to function as a mother very soon after the baby's birth. Since grandparents are often far away, there is less help for the new mother and she has less time to take in and let go before taking on the mothering role. We need to look at how our mobile families, stripped of grandparents, and the short hospital stay cause stress as well as how the stress can be lessened.

Maternal Role Achievement

Certain specific behavior by the pregnant woman indicates she has assumed the identity of mother. Knowing these behaviors is most important to the nurse if the nurse is to ascertain if the woman is prepared psychologically for her new role. Role achievement can be said to be accomplished when:

1   The pregnant woman refers to mothering activities as *I* without reference to models.

2 The tense used in describing her actions as a mother is *present* rather than *future*.

If childbirth is imminent and there are *no* signs that role identity is progressing in the pregnant woman, this should alert the nurse to watch for problems as the new mother assumes this role after the birth of her baby.

The role of the nurse in helping the client take on the mothering role during the antepartum period is summarized in the following list:

1 Provide opportunities for the pregnant woman to express her concerns about mothering and to discuss what she will do as a mother.
2 Provide opportunities for the process of mimicry, role play, fantasy, and introjection-projection-rejection by offering group classes, and encouraging interchange among pregnant women in clinics, doctor's offices, or in neighborhood groups.
3 Provide appropriate reading material concerning mothering activities and opportunities to discuss same, and use anticipatory guidance concerning appropriate activities necessary in the care of newborns.
4 Encourage the pregnant woman to express anticipated difficulties in giving up former roles.
5 Encourage the family to be supportive and to understand that the grieving process involved in giving up former roles is normal and important to the pregnant woman psychologically.
6 Be open and nonjudgmental when the woman expresses ambivalent feelings or if she has difficulty assuming the mothering role.

7 Assess the woman's progress in taking on the mothering role and relay this evaluation to the postpartum nursing staff so that they can be supportive and provide opportunity for this process to take place after the baby arrives.

Establishment of Mother-Infant Relationships

SELF-LOVE AND ITS INFLUENCE Pregnancy is a time for the pregnant woman to begin to establish a relationship with her child. Previously it was mentioned that the pregnant woman was narcissistic. This turning-in of energy on herself is a process that allows her to love the fetus as an extension of her own body. Each woman develops a feeling for the fetus in an individual manner. Caplan indicates that the more narcissistic a woman is, the quicker she develops love for the newborn.[36] If the pregnant woman develops such a feeling for the fetus, she comes to feel the fetus has a personality and a relationship with her. She may name the fetus, ascribe various traits to it, and talk about the fetus as if the fetus had feelings, needs, and wishes. Usually the fetus is not seen as a person until after quickening.

INFLUENCE ON RELATIONSHIP WITH THE FETUS Observation of pregnant women reveals that they have varying degrees of feeling for their fetuses. Some women have no feeling or a negative feeling for their fetuses. Caplan indicates that negative feelings usually carry over to the newborn. After the baby is born, women who have developed a feeling for the fetus in utero seem to move into positive mother-infant relationships more readily. One exception to this sometimes occurs when the baby does not match the expectations the mother had of her future baby. In other words, if the baby is of the opposite sex than that which she wanted, is of a different personality, is quiet and passive rather than active and aggressive, or has a defect that is disturbing to the mother, she may not develop a feeling for the baby as quickly as she might have if the baby "fit" her imagination.

Since there is usually a *time lag* between the birth of the baby and true maternal feeling for that baby, the pregnant woman needs to be aware of this during pregnancy so that she does not feel there is something wrong with her when she does not love her baby immediately. This maternal love can develop a few hours to several weeks after the baby's birth and usually comes on suddenly. A number of factors influence the onset of maternal love. Some of these factors are:

1   The relationship the mother had with the infant as a fetus
2   The type of labor and delivery experience, including fatigue, response to large amounts of medication, or postpartum complications
3   The fit of the child to her needs and desires

4   The pregnant woman's personality
5   Cultural expectations of the family unit
6   Hospital routines that keep mother and baby apart

Since women have fantasies about this baby during pregnancy, Caplan contends that nurses can pick up clues and predict problems in the future mother-infant relationship by listening to their fantasies. Table 20-1 indicates the various clues and the possible predictions that the nurse might make.

CIRCULAR REVERBERATING PROCESS   Another area that helps the nurse assess the future mother-infant relationship is the amount of impersonal references she makes to the fetus. If the pregnant woman does not think of the fetus as human, speaks of the fetus as "it," and has not given any thought to a name for the infant even in late pregnancy, this may be a clue to problems in the early postpartum period. It should be stressed, however, that any prediction of a relationship during the

TABLE 20-1
Fantasies of Pregnant Women about the Fetus

Fantasy	Predictive value
Regarding age of the baby, the pregnant woman sees the baby as an infant 4 to 5 months old.	If she *always* talks of the infant as older than a newborn baby, there may be problems during early infancy.
The pregnant woman's daydreams about the fetus revolve around what the child will be when grown.	The pregnant woman may not see the child as an individual but may attempt to meet her own ambitions through the child.
The pregnant woman talks of the baby as *always* a boy or *always* a girl.	Problems may arise if the child is of the opposite sex. Better if the mother is ambivalent about the sex in her fantasies.
The pregnant woman knows *exactly* what the baby is like.	She may not be able to see the baby as he or she is, with individual needs and personality.
After the baby is born, the new mother pictures a "marvelous baby" beyond all estimates of people around her.	The new mother may be unable to see the baby's real needs.

SOURCE: Developed from Gerald Caplan, *Concepts of Mental Health Consultations, Their Application in Public Health Social Work*, Children's Bureau, Washington, D.C., 1959.

antepartum period will need to be verified; the opposite conclusion may be drawn once the baby arrives because the relationship then becomes a circular, reverberating process between two individuals. Whether a positive or negative relationship develops depends on each individual—mother and baby—meeting or not meeting the needs of the other.

For example, the woman's attitude toward the fetus may be judged as negative because of her talk about the fetus, lack of naming the baby, or not making any preparations for the baby as well as complaints about "it" kicking her and disturbing her sleep. When the baby arrives, the baby is a boy. Her culture indicates the importance of having a boy. Her mate is pleased with this and becomes very supportive, and the baby responds extremely well to feeding and the mother's caretaking activities. This negative feeling portrayed during pregnancy will probably develop into a positive one. Therefore, any indication on the part of the nurse that there may be a negative mother-infant relationship should be resolved after the baby has arrived. It is also possible that the future relationship between mother and baby is predicted as being positive, but because the baby does not fit the mother's expectations, as well as various other situations, the relationship does not develop. The nurse must be alert for negative relationships during pregnancy and after the baby is born.

The student of nursing may ask, "Why is it important to predict problems?" The importance of knowing if all will be well with a particular mother, infant, and family is emphasized because of the problems that may result if this mother-infant relationship is negative. The mother is all-important to the infant. She is essential not only to the baby's physical health but also to emotional health and development. Exploration of Bowlby's studies of the failure of infants to grow and

mature normally without mothering even when all aspects of their physical needs were met emphasizes the need to detect faulty mother-infant relationships early so that steps can be taken to correct the situation *before* there is severe damage to the infant.[37] Even if the situation is not as drastic as in what is called *the battered child syndrome*, it may deprive the infant of adequate love to meet the baby's needs so the baby can establish a sense of basic trust; this in turn causes a less than healthy emotional personality.

Table 20-2, which summarizes some of the disordered mother-infant-family relationships, should aid in carrying out the assessment process successfully.

THE ROLE OF NURSING IN PROMOTING POSITIVE MOTHER-INFANT-FAMILY RELATIONSHIPS The supportive aspect of nursing related to preparation for childbearing is demonstrated symbolically in Figure 20-3. As the pregnant woman receives support during the childbearing period, this "spills" over into her ability to care for her infant. Nursing care during this time involves encouraging the mother to talk about her relationship with

FIGURE 20-3
Symbolic representation of the support and care that a pregnant woman receives "spilling over" into her ability to care for her infant.

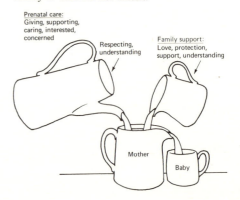

Table 20-2
Disordered Mother-Infant Relationships

Type of disorder	Behaviors indicative of disorder	Comments	Behavior predictive of disorder
Open hostility and neglect.	Battered child syndrome (50,000–70,000/yr). Failure to thrive (can result in death or permanent brain damage).	Passed on from generation to generation: cycle of dehumanization and pain that must be broken.	Finds no pleasure in infant behavior of dependency. Finds no pleasure in mothering. All negative descriptions of baby and baby's needs. Lack of interest in learning tasks of mothering in last trimester. Evidence of severe emotional deprivation or discipline as a child. Constant worry about defects or death of the child.
Perfectionism.	Rigid expectation that infant will follow set pattern. Negative feelings toward child expressed in overdoing mothering role.	Negative feelings toward child justified in making child perfect, therefore, acceptable; overdoes mothering tasks to make child perfect.	Overdoes learning and takes advice literally. Adheres to diet schedules, and early bowel training. Insists on specific, detailed advice in child care.
Overprotection.	Resents child because of own disrupted goals.	Problem becomes more acute when child grows up and attempts independence.	Indicates strong resentment toward pregnancy. Feels she has to sacrifice everything for baby. Extreme concern over every action of baby.

SOURCE: This table was developed from John Bowlby, *Maternal Care and Mental Health*, World Health Organization, Geneva, 1952; Raye Helfer and C. Henry Kempe, *The Battered Child*, University of Chicago Press, Chicago, 1968; and Elise Fitzpatrick, Sharon Reeder, and Luigi Mastroianni, Jr., *Maternity Nursing*, 12th ed., Lippincott, Philadelphia, 1971.

her baby and facilitating the pregnant woman's mimicry, role play, fantasy, and establishment of identity. The nurse also helps the pregnant woman to understand the infant's need for love, attention, and dependent care. All steps that help decrease stress associated with pregnancy and childbirth as well as increase respect for the individual's uniqueness are positive steps in fostering positive mother-infant relationships. If the pregnant woman has accepted her new role, understands her changed needs, receives respect and support during antepartum care, and has a positive birth experience, it will be easier for her to give love and attention to her infant.

Sociocultural Factors That Influence the Pregnant Family

Cultural Variability and the Pregnant Family

In order for the nurse to be helpful to the family in reducing emotional stress, the nurse must understand how the cultural background of the family influences the response to childbearing. Some perusal of cross-cultural studies of how reproduction is handled in a variety of ways will call attention to the differences in beliefs and attitudes and the effects on the behavior of the family as well as its individual members. Because culture also influences the nurse and the medical profession's beliefs and behaviors concerning reproduction, there is always the possibility of conflict between the client and the caretaking professional that often causes emotional stress for all concerned. Research and general observations have led to the recognition that cultural understanding often makes the difference between helping and turning away certain families.

Niles Newton writes, "All known human societies pattern the behavior of human beings involved in the process of reproduction. Beliefs concerning appropriate behavior in pregnancy, during labor, and in the puerperium appear to be characteristic of all cultures."(38)

Culture influences such things as nutrition, spacing of children, what clothes should be worn, and what kind of help the pregnant woman should have during pregnancy, labor, and delivery. All of this patterning influences attitudes, thought processes, medical help sought, and restrictions adhered to during pregnancy.

In the chapter on cultural patterns of prenatal behavior in the book *Childbearing—Its Sociocultural and Psychological Aspects*, Niles Newton and Margaret Mead indicate different cultural attitudes toward pregnancy in various areas. (See Table 20-3.) All these aspects of the influence of culture may be seen in this country. They vary with the subculture, the area, and the individual family. If cultural beliefs differ between the medical and nursing staff and the client, conflicts occur. If, for example, a woman views pregnancy as a shameful situation, the emotional overtones will be different from those of a woman who sees pregnancy as proof of her mate's virility. If the nurse's view of pregnancy is different from that of the pregnant woman and the nurse fails to see the client's point of view, the nurse may misread clues to problems or assume there are problems when, in fact, there are none.

Two other important aspects of the influence of culture on emotional needs are the family's view of reproduction in terms of privacy, and cultural beliefs concerning the couple's responsibility for the outcome of pregnancy. For example, some cultures stress that reproduction is a very private affair and seek to provide the pregnant woman with extreme privacy even from her mate, especially during birth. In other cultures, childbearing is a very open occasion and may be shared with many people. In our society attitudes toward pregnancy and birth run the gamut from one of these extremes to the other, with all the varying in-between positions represented. It may be very stressful to some women to have many medical personnel available and watching, while to other women this procedure is perfectly acceptable. It is important to be aware of how various individuals view roles of male and female during pregnancy and delivery. If a couple prefers privacy for the woman, and the baby's father would be uncomfortable being part of the delivery team or participating publicly in any other aspect of pregnancy, it is important that they not be forced into "family-centered care," especially that of expecting the baby's father to be present during birth.

On the other hand, if the family sees pregnancy and birth as a family affair, it would be unfortunate to exclude the father from classes, discussions, and participation in the birth process. The consideration of the individual's beliefs about privacy is important because it can cause unnecessary stress to the couple. When the man's and woman's views of pregnancy differ, it is important to listen and help the couple to come to some form of compromise that is comfortable and not stressful for either.

Our culture believes that "the outcome of pregnancy and childbirth is of considerable public concern. It emphasizes the special value of each human infant and mother and

TABLE 20-3
Cultural Attitudes toward Pregnancy

Cultural attitudes	Possible areas of conflict
Responsibility for fetal growth.	This attitude results in restrictions in dietary habits, sexual practices during childbearing, and guilt if all is not well when the baby is born.
Feelings of solicitude toward the pregnant woman.	This may influence the amount of attention and help the woman receives with her daily tasks. Conflicts may arise when cultural beliefs are vastly different from medical philosophy. Newton indicates that American culture seems to view pregnancy in light of pathology, since American obstetricians are so "obsessed with pathology" and can't see a woman who needs their services as not sick.[39]
Pregnancy as proof of sexual adequacy.	People of some cultures feel it is important to marry only *after* pregnancy occurs. Conflict may occur between cultures who hold this belief and middle-class health workers.
Pregnancy as a time of vulnerability and debilitation.	The pregnant woman is isolated and kept away from others. A certain degree of this is evident in some cultures in which the pregnant woman is kept from various activities and functions such as maintaining certain jobs and performing certain tasks.
Pregnancy as a time of shame and reticence.	Various cultures and subcultures do not tell that the woman is pregnant until she is "showing." Also, this view of pregnancy may have some influence on seeking medical help late in pregnancy or taking necessary precautions concerning certain aspects of care. This also may influence the person's attitude toward pregnancy. If this condition is something that is not talked about, then perhaps it is considered shameful. Such attitudes may cause some anxiety in the pregnant woman.[40]

SOURCE: Adapted from N. Newton and M. Mead, "Cultural Patterns of Prenatal Behavior," in S. A. Richardson and A. F. Guttmacher, *Childbearing—Its Sociocultural and Psychological Aspects,* Williams & Wilkins, Baltimore, 1967, pp. 164–171.

their right to live and be cared for regardless of personal qualities and defects."[41] Such an idea brings with it various emotional problems because when the outcome of pregnancy is abnormal, the couple often feels guilty. Some stress may occur when the pregnant woman and her family recognize the responsibility they have for caring for the child, regardless of such an outcome. Such a cultural belief may also result in increased stress if abortion is recommended or when genetic counseling has indicated that the

couple should not have children because of some genetic problem. Those who do not hold this belief may not have as great a problem accepting abortion or intervention to terminate pregnancy.

In addition, culture influences the length of the transition period after birth. The transition period is the time of close relationship between mother and child before she takes on other tasks of primary importance. This total commitment to the newborn may last a few minutes or 4 to 5 years. It determines when the woman gets pregnant again and what type of activities she assumes while caring for her young child. Varying views in this respect may influence the family's choice of spacing children and may be in conflict with what is physically healthy for the woman. Emotional stress results when views differ between partners as well as between the couple and the medical recommendations.

Our society, which emphasizes hospital deliveries, conveys the idea that pregnancy is an illness. The medical treatment of many of the discomforts of pregnancy also indicates to pregnant women that pregnancy is an illness. Various groups tend to promote "natural childbirth," or physiological childbirth, and encourage the woman not to take any kind of medication during pregnancy. This conflict between practices may cause unnecessary stress as the pregnant woman and her family listen to various ideas about antepartum care. On the one hand, she is encouraged to seek all types of medical aid for her discomforts; on the other, she is told that having a baby is natural and not complicated. She may be made to feel guilty no matter which method she chooses, especially if the outcome of pregnancy is not normal.

The influences of culture, subculture, and geographic area are very complex, and the student of nursing should always be aware that each individual views reproduction in a different light. This view may in fact be the key to unlocking problems or to helping the family solve problems that are emotionally disturbing because of cultural beliefs about pregnancy which are different from the view of the health workers or institution. The nurse must help clients come to some acceptable compromise when conflicts arise which jeopardize emotional health or physical safety. However, care should be taken to be absolutely certain that any advice or restrictions placed on pregnant women and their families are absolutely important to health rather than the nurse's personal and cultural beliefs about childbearing.

A nurse encouraged a couple with four children to marry. This couple was effectively caring for the children and was satisfied with their common-law marriage. They could see no advantage to spending the money for a license or taking the time or effort to marry and were comfortable in the present situation. Stress seemed apparent when the nurse insisted they were wrong by not marrying. It would most likely be quite upsetting to know how much unnecessary stress has been caused by forcing cultural values on those who are not part of that culture. It is hoped that as nurses more fully comprehend the influence of one's beliefs and background on one's behavior that they will question traditional requirements for pregnant families and consider only health needs when making suggestions to the family about their care.

SIGNIFICANT OTHERS—THEIR NEEDS AND CONFLICTS

The Father

The role of the father during the reproductive period is culturally determined. Newton indicates that primarily our culture emphasizes mandatory financial support and excludes the father from the childbearing process.[42] A survey of the visiting practices in some maternity hospital units as well as opportunities for the fathers to attend "mother's" classes indicates that having a baby is a woman's business. However, many of the methods of preparation for childbearing now include fathers, and many maternity units have instituted family-centered maternity care. Fathers are becoming more involved and are helpful during labor and delivery. Some obstetricians and nurses have sessions for both the man and woman so that their questions can be answered.

Figure 20-4 shows an entire family coming to the antepartum clinic. What an opportunity to help the entire family with their individual needs and concerns!

Emotional Problems Facing a Father-to-Be

ADJUSTMENT TO PREGNANT STATE IN HIS MATE As pregnancy progresses and becomes more obvious, the father has certain adjustments to make. The pregnancy experience can allow the male an opportunity to assume the fathering role in the same way pregnancy allows the woman to take on the maternal role. Table 20-4 demonstrates the steps in the process of assuming the fathering role and the potential problems this process may produce.

ADJUSTMENT TO A NEW ROLE The role of father in the United States is not always well defined; therefore, it may be necessary to help the father assume the fathering role.

A. D. Colman and L. L. Colman, in *Pregnancy: The Psychological Experience*, indicate that it is rare for a man to admit pregnancy is a "profound emotional experience" although research studies have indicated a "higher incidence of physical symptoms among men whose wives were pregnant." One man in ten is affected by physical symptoms; common examples are "weight gain, nausea, stomach distress, loss of appetite, toothache and even abdominal bloating."[43]

In addition to the research findings, Colman and Colman indicate there may be a high incidence of anxiety, depression, and alienation during pregnancy which causes marriage instability.[44]

Nurses should study the needs of the father and find appropriate ways that are helpful and supportive to the expectant

FIGURE 20-4
The entire "pregnant family" is visiting the clinic. This is a good opportunity for the nurse to identify needs of the significant others, as well as the pregnant woman's, and enhance the family's coping ability and support of each other in preparation for a new family member. (*By permission of the University of Colorado Medical Center, Denver, Colo.*)

father. It should be remembered in helping the expectant father to assume his role that it must be done in light of his cultural and socioeconomic background. The nurse must not insist that an expectant father perform a role that is acceptable to the nurse or the medical staff but must help the couple understand that they have to work out something that is comfortable for each of them.

What is needed for the pregnant woman and her mate is "an emotional alliance, an agreement to be sensitive to one another's needs, to communicate what is needed more now from one another, to share experiences, to help the other cope with the unfamiliar and frightening."[45]

The nurse assists the pregnant woman in

TABLE 20-4
Taking on the Paternal Role

Trimester	Emotional issues confronting father	Possible emotional responses	Nurse's role
First trimester	Discovery of pregnancy.	1 Acceptance or rejection. 2 Sense of pride in making woman pregnant. 3 Increased sense of masculinity. 4 Sense of link with immortality. 5 Concern over his paternity.	Collect data from the expectant father to determine his individual response. Allow him to express his concerns and encourage acceptance of the pregnant state.
	Increased responsibility.	1 Reevaluation of his job and income.	Explore anxiety around increased responsibility; help know these are common concerns. Refer to social services if unable to cope.
		2 Worry concerning competence and security.	
		3 Represses his feelings and response because of wife's more obvious changes physically and emotionally.	Help father express his concerns to appropriate person(s).
		4 Response to wife's enlarging breasts and size.	Identify amount of stress this poses. Assist him to understand physical changes.
Second trimester	Confirmation of pregnancy through feeling fetal movement.	1 Increased need for physical relationship and touch of fetus. 2 Relationship with fetus as an individual.	Educate as to the development of the fetus. Discuss factors concerning safety so excessive fears are decreased.
	Sexual issues are focused.	1 Usually increased during this trimester and can be demanding or satisfying.	Assess potential for sexual problems, educate about sexual functioning, and changed needs.
	Woman's increased passivity and dependency.	1 Woman's increased dependency may be difficult. 2 Father may respond to pregnancy by trying to be creative.	Educate the father as to psychological changes that commonly occur in pregnant women. Encourage his creative activities, acknowledge his needs are important for his adjustment.

Phase				
Third trimester	If previous trimesters coped with, this trimester can bring insights and rewards.	1	Positive or negative adjustment.	Allow father to explore problems; encourage positive adjustment.
	More active involvement through preparation for childbirth and the baby.	1	Becomes involved in preparation and classes that assist the process of becoming a father; tension, however, is present.	Inform couples of a variety of opportunities and resources for involvement.
	Both pregnant woman and father-to-be move from separate worlds.	1	Relationship can be enhanced unless there has been a negative response to pregnancy.	Help couple reassess their emotional response through individual counseling or group sessions.
	Loss of previous family role and size.	1	Recognition that the couple will no longer be only two or that they will relate to only one child, etc.	Assist with the process of loss.
	Relationship with older child than newborn.	1	Fathers generally fantasize about a child older than newborn. May have trouble relating to newborn.	Begin to use anticipatory guidance concerning the newborn.
	Fears of labor and delivery and resultant loss of wife and/or infant.	1	Fantasies and fears concerning labor and delivery and his role are common.	Educate the couple as to the process of labor and delivery and acknowledge fears, dispelling them when they are inappropriate.
Labor and delivery	Reality of the situation.	1	Noninvolvement may be difficult and increase insecurity and fear and feelings of isolation.	Allow involvement if desired. Educate as the process continues.
		2	May prefer noninvolvement. Other family members may assume supportive role.	Accept choice.

SOURCE: Process of taking on paternal role developed from Colman and Colman, *Pregnancy: The Psychological Experience,* Herder and Herder, New York, 1971, pp. 96–144.

405

understanding her partner's needs. Many women instinctively recognize the rivalry situation that is possible between father and the new baby and have ideas on how to handle this. Obviously, new babies do take a great deal of time, and usually the obstetrician discourages sexual activities for 2 to 6 weeks after birth. Therefore, the father relinquishes some of his needs in order to establish his new family. If he has become sole provider of the family, this may place additional strain on him. The nurse who reminds the pregnant woman of these needs of the expectant father may help her avoid some of the stress that might otherwise prevent the partner from being understanding and supportive.

The Grandparents

One must consider the needs and influence that the extended family members have on the pregnant woman. In some subcultures the grandparents and other relatives play a significant role during the childbearing period. If the nurse fails to recognize this, it may cause stress to her or him personally as well as to the family unit.

In our mobile society, many young parents are separated from grandparents and lack the help and support these family members provide. At such times the nurse may be needed to help the pregnant woman do more planning than would be done otherwise. Reva Rubin's study, mentioned previously, indicated that the mother of the pregnant woman was seen more as help and support than a role model by the pregnant woman. Absence of this support in our society for many women may be frustrating. Grandparents can often be helped to be very supportive of prospective parents and should be included in the family's plan of care when they are available.

Inclusion of the grandparents in antepartum instruction and in the current practices of the day may be important, since these practices are likely to be very different from those at the time they were raising children. Grandmothers who attend nonstructured classes for pregnant women can share ideas and experiences of infant care. Inclusion of grandparents in these classes or discussions gives the nurse opportunities to clarify misconceptions that these expectant grandparents may have that could contribute to the pregnant woman's anxiety. Some new ideas as to how these expectant grandparents may be educated and helped to be more supportive to the pregnant couple should be explored.

The Unborn Baby

Any discussion regarding the emotional considerations for the family during pregnancy would be incomplete without some discussion of the influence of the emotional response of the pregnant woman on her unborn baby. Previously, such ideas might have been considered folklore or myth and not scientific. However, studies with animals and retrospective studies with humans have pointed to the possibility of the influences of emotions on the unborn baby. Some authors believe that clinical evidence indicates that emotional stress in the mother *does* have some influence on the unborn baby. Ferreina, in his book *Prenatal Environment,* says that "so much positive evidence has now been accumulated that the question is no longer about whether the pregnant woman's emotions have an impact upon the fetus but about the pathways, the nature, and the consequences of such an impact."[46] Ferreina reports in his book a number of studies that point to the fact that increased emotional stress can result in such congenital abnormalities as cleft palate, antepartal complications such as toxemia, habitual abortion, and hyperirritability of the infant at birth. These studies, as well as some of the conclusions of M. F. Ashley Montagu in his book *Prenatal Influences,* point out the need for further study of the effects of the emotional stress on the fetus. However, it is not conclusive that such stress in the pregnant woman will cause problems that result in reproductive malfunction (toxemia, prematurity, difficult labor), congenital malformations, or disordered personality in the newborn infant. Certainly enough evidence has been gathered for one to consider this as a possibility and to recognize that the emotional environment may be extremely important not only in terms of family stability but in terms of the infant's start in life.

Direct Influence on Fetal Development

It should be noted that many of the studies that point to the influence of maternal emotions on fetal development and conditions at birth are retrospective in nature, indicating that memory of the mother may be influenced by the outcome of her pregnancy. Such studies should be considered in this light and additional studies be undertaken. Montagu attempted a study with better controls. This latter study determined stress levels before the baby was delivered. He found increased fetal activity when there was increased maternal stress and when this increased, stress remained high over a period of weeks after birth. Of the 61.5 percent babies who were hyperactive after birth, 38.5 percent had mothers with emotional disturbance during pregnancy.[47] What of the other babies who were hyperactive? What of severely disturbed mental patients who deliver perfectly normal babies? These and other questions arise when considering this subject. Ferreina found that pregnant women

who had a great fear of having a baby, and who had extreme attitudes, as rated on a scale, had babies who behaved in deviant ways. This was a double-blind study with 163 mothers and infants and was statistically significant.[48]

Perhaps an explanation of the effects of stress and how these might be relayed to the fetus through the placental barrier, as described by Ferreina, will be helpful in indicating the possibility of emotional influence on the fetus. During stress in prolonged emotional states there are high levels of corticosteroids as well as disturbances in plasma proteins. Also, there is often hyperventilation associated with anxiety. This changes the levels of oxygen and carbon dioxide present in maternal blood. It is possible that high levels of corticosteroids and changes in plasma proteins as well as lack of oxygen at various stages of pregnancy may in fact be beyond a level of tolerance for the fetus at that particular stage of development. The idea of individual differences for stress tolerance in the pregnant woman, as well as in the individual fetus, must be researched. Ability to tolerate such changes depends on individual susceptibility and the period of gestation during which the stress occurs.

Montagu suggests that chromosomal anomalies fail to be expressed in fetal development if pregnancy proceeds in a favorable environment.[49] A favorable antepartum environment is, then, important in fetal development. Montagu also suggests that emotional disturbances in the male or female are capable of disordering spermatogenesis and ovulation. If this is true, then there is a possibility that the processes of cell division may also be affected. Montagu argues that if pseudocyesis is possible, why not psychologically induced abortion? The fact that psychotherapy alone is sometimes successful in habitual abortion also indicates the influence of the emotions on reproduction.

Indirect Influence on Fetal Development

Numerous studies can be quoted which state that there is indeed the possibility of some emotional influence on the unborn baby. Some authors indicate that maternal activity and the response to stress in the form of over-eating, smoking, and not following medical advice are also ways in which emotional stress can influence the newborn infant. These activities may be more accepted as ways in which maternal stress influences the baby. This indicates the need for the nurse to help the pregnant woman cope with stressful situations appropriately, so that dietary requirements and limitations of activity, when necessary, are not as difficult for her. Also, the nurse should help the pregnant woman to cope with minor discomforts of pregnancy such as nausea, diarrhea, leg aches, and constipation by suggesting proper diet, exercises, and activity so that she does not seek medication to ease her anxiety and/or discomfort. The probability of causing defects in the unborn by taking drugs early in pregnancy is now an accepted fact. Since little is known about specific results of many drugs and individual response on the part of the mother and fetus, it is important to help the pregnant woman avoid the use of medication when at all possible.

When the possible pathways of conveying maternal stress to the fetus are considered, the possibilities of the resulting influence on fetal development can be logically considered. This influence will, however, depend on the developmental stage of the fetus as well as the individual fetus's susceptibility to various stresses.

Awareness of the possibilities of how stress might influence the fetus directly through high levels of corticosteroids and maternal activity and indirectly through such behaviors and activities in the pregnant woman as overeating or not following medical advice, should make the nurse more determined to assist the family in reducing the number of stressful situations, and in dealing with stress constructively.

Emotional Needs and Conflicts of Children

Other family members to consider in the pregnant family are the children. Their needs for emotional support and education during pregnancy are great. Pregnancy can be a difficult time, or it can be a time for learning and growing, depending on how it is handled by the parents. An important variable to consider in determining the effect that a new brother or sister will have on these children is their age when the additional family member arrives. The type of explanation given to the expectant child, the timing of the explanation, and the type and amount of emotional preparation will again depend on the age of the child. The very young child will not be as aware of the change in the mother's body as the older child but may be somewhat upset by the emotional changes in the mother and in turn may respond by behavior that is regressive or frustrating to the pregnant woman. When the child recognizes the change in the mother's body and the activity within her lap area (fetal movement), he or she should be given an explanation of what is occurring and how the baby is growing in the mother's womb.

The young child may be upset by changes in the household, such as preparation for the new baby, and will need to be prepared for this well in advance, especially if the child is to change rooms or beds when the baby arrives. Depending upon the child's age, and the questions asked by the child, he or she should be given an explanation of what is happening as clearly and openly as possible. The advent of a new baby provides an extremely good opportunity to help the child with sex education. The nurse may need to help the mother and father recognize the child's (or children's) needs and help them handle situations that may cause problems. The recognition that a child may have ambivalent feelings toward the new baby is important because the child may respond with aggression toward the baby or regressive behavior, and this in turn may be frustrating to the parents.

The possibility of sibling rivalry should be mentioned during the course of pregnancy, since the parents should be prepared for it and armed with ideas as to how to cope with it. Also, some planning and proper timing are necessary so that the parents can prepare the child before the new baby arrives.

Previously, it was mentioned that the woman who is pregnant for the second or third time must work through her grief at giving up the "baby" relationship with the last child. This may be difficult for the mother and for the child, depending on the child's age. Efforts by the nurse to assist the parents in making plans and begin working through this stage are helpful.

THE FAMILY—EACH INDIVIDUAL'S INFLUENCE ON THE WHOLE

Consideration for the wholeness of the family should be made. The family is influenced by each individual's needs and conflicts. If one member is under stress, this is likely to influence the other members' amount of stress. Pregnancy places different kinds of emotional stress on different members. The complexity of how this might influence other family members and in turn influence the individual should be considered when a plan of care is proposed by the nurse. Figure 20-1 demonstrates this idea of the effects of each member on the other members. Each family

member's individual strengths must be considered as well as how each member may be supportive to the other. The nurse should not provide all the support, but rather should guide and encourage the family to use their own coping mechanisms to support and help each other. After all, having a baby is a family affair.

New theories and research are needed to help determine how the nurse, through psychological closeness, can best intervene and assist families during the childbearing process.

NURSING INTERVENTION IN MEETING EMOTIONAL NEEDS

A summary of needs follows, indicating what is involved in providing emotional support to the pregnant family. The nurse should:

1 Assess the emotional needs of the pregnant woman and her family. Consideration should be given to assessing the pregnant woman's:
   a Response to the physical and chemical changes of pregnancy
   b Readiness for the mothering role
   c Need for supportive relationships with mate, parents, and family
   d Influence of the woman's cultural background on her response to childbearing
   e Level of anxiety concerning pregnancy, childbearing, and child-rearing
   f Future mother-infant-family relationships
   g Amount of family support and help
   h Environmental situation and its resultant stress on the pregnant family

TABLE 20-5
Characteristics of High-Risk Families

Behaviors indicating possible severe emotional stress	Possible problem	Nursing role
	Pregnant woman	
Nausea and vomiting continue beyond the first trimester.	Possible rejection of pregnancy. Depending on severity, can become hyperemesis gravidarum.	Observation and assessment of severity of symptoms. Awareness of any indications of rejection of pregnancy or other emotional stress. Inform physician. Assist client with decreasing vomiting and stress. When advanced, help maintain food and fluid needs.
Reporting of a number of abortions prior to current pregnancy.	Habitual abortion which may have some basis in severe rejection of pregnancy.	Explore woman's feelings toward this pregnancy and previous pregnancies when appropriate. Convey this information to the physician. Assume supportive role indicated by psychiatric assessment.
Physical signs of toxemia, increased blood pressure, increased weight, edema, dizziness, albuminuria, etc.	Combination of physical and mental stress resulting in toxemia (etiology unclear). Can be enhanced by emotional stress.	Explore family situation to detect possible areas of emotional stress such as marital problems, financial stress, overwork, poverty, etc. Assist family in lessening stress and provide emotional "rest" as well as physical rest.
Extreme anxiety over pregnant state, childbirth, etc.	Misconception, unconscious conflicts, and lack of information.	Offer explanation of pregnancy and childbirth processes and assistance in helping woman and family cope with anxiety. Provide opportunity to attend classes, obtain literature, and explore feelings openly.
Verbal indication of inability to relate to new baby or expression of severe emotional deprivation and harsh discipline as a child.	Possibility of child battering or neglect or at least less than optimum relationship with new child.	Observations of the family situation and relating information to physician and child battering team if available. Make arrangements to explore further on postpartum unit and in early home situation.
Expression of difficulty in accepting maternal role and/or no evidence of taking in or taking on of this role.	Difficulty in mothering.	Explore client's view of pregnancy. Help client find opportunity to work through her negative feelings. Relate problems to obstetrician and a psychiatrist if indicated. Follow up observations on the postpartum unit to determine status.

Evidence of attempted abortion.	Rejection of pregnancy and mothering.	Maintain a nonjudgmental attitude, listen to client, assist in eliminating guilt. Refer client to obstetrician and psychiatrist for evaluation and possible therapy or therapeutic abortion.
Sleeplessness, excess irritability, anxiety, excessive depression or excitement, suspiciousness, preoccupation with trivia, and tense agitation.	Psychoses of pregnancy. Usually occurs postpartially and is estimated to occur 1 in 400 to 1,000 pregnancies.	Relate symptoms to obstetrician and encourage pregnant woman to seek psychiatric help.
Fetus		
Signs of fetal distress such as extreme hyperactivity, failure to grow, increase in heartbeat.	Possible response to severe emotional stress in mother or family situation.	Relay observations to obstetrician. Explore with pregnant woman possible areas of stress. Help reduce stress.
Father (expectant)		
Extreme nonacceptance of mate's changes during pregnancy. Lack of support to mate and her increased stress because of this attitude.	Misunderstanding, lack of maturity or inability to be a father figure.	Explore problems and misconceptions and provide anticipatory guidance and support so father can support mate. Encourage seeking help from obstetrician, psychiatrist, or family counselor as indicated.
Indications of nonacceptance of role of father or background indicating possible child battering.	Nonacceptance of father role and possibly faulty relationship to child, resulting in battering or neglect.	Explore problems, support and help in minor situations; if possibility of severe situation, refer to child battering team or psychiatrist.
Children (expectant)		
Fear of replacement or change in environment as a result of change in room or bed and/or parent's stress.	Regressive behavior, change in behavior, emotional anxiety (assessed in regard to age and normal areas of stress).	Anticipatory guidance before occurrence. Plan with parents considering age and individuality of child so as to decrease the amount of stress the child experiences.

  i Behavior that is indicative of pathological emotional situation (see Table 20-2)

2 Make plans for nursing intervention that include enhancement of the family's coping mechanisms and assist the family in preparing emotionally for the new family situation. The ultimate goal should be a positive emotional climate for the new baby. The nursing tasks involved will include:

  a Anticipatory guidance as to the course of pregnancy, the occurrences during birth, and the tasks of mothering and fathering

  b Listening to fears and anxieties and taking some steps to eliminate stress that causes emotional overtones

  c Supportive measures that assist the family in dealing with stress of an emotional nature or assistance in finding ways to eliminate stress that causes emotional overtones

3 Periodically evaluate how the family is coping with its pregnant state and reassess needs as they change as well as make plans for different intervention when planned nursing intervention is not decreasing stress.

Throughout the assessment process the nurse must be aware of predicting the high-risk family emotionally as well as physically. Some indications of pathological situations have been discussed, but because of the complexity of the emotional situations that could become pathological, Table 20-5 has been prepared to facilitate identification of pathological emotional stress.

Nursing intervention for a family who is pregnant can truly be a creative process, for there are many factors, variables, and individual needs to consider when planning and implementing care. Hopefully, such intervention will assist the family in maintaining a more favorable emotional environment during the childbearing years so that the task of generativity is fully met. It is when such intervention is helpful that good maternity nursing care becomes preventive child care.

A word of concern and caution should perhaps be presented in a discussion of such lofty goals of preventive care. The fact is not that we should not aspire to such heights, but that at the present time, research has not indicated those aspects of care that *actually* promote mental health or those factors that cause mental illness. Much needs to be done in this respect, and nursing should be involved in discovering what can be done to promote emotional health. Caplan, in an introduction to *Prevention of Mental Disorders in Children,* perhaps says it most effectively:

We cannot afford to sit back and wait for our lack of knowledge of the etiology of mental disorders in children to be remedied by many long years of patient research. Intensive research must be carried on, but it also seems important to survey relevant systems of etiologic theory and clinical experience and to attempt to arrive at a judgment regarding etiologic factors operating at a community level and also to plan for amelioration of the factors decided upon.[50]

Hopefully, nursing intervention will proceed along this course as it relates to emotional support for pregnant families. It is necessary to make every effort to detect emotional stress, to help the family cope in the most knowledgeable way, and to evaluate the intervention and revise it when necessary. The challenge can be great to the student of nursing to find new ways to assist families to have a positive experience with childbearing in preparation for childrearing.

REFERENCES

1 Ackerman, Nathan, Frances L. Beatman, and Sanford N. Sherman: *Expanding Theory and Practice in Family Therapy*, Family Service Association of America, New York, 1967.

2 Richardson, Stephen A., and Alan F. Guttmacher: *Childbearing—Its Sociocultural and Psychological Aspects*, Williams & Wilkins, Baltimore, 1967.

3 Ferreina, Antonio J.: *Prenatal Environment*, Charles C Thomas, Springfield, Ill., 1969, p. 125.

4 Montagu, M. F. Ashley: *Prenatal Influences*, Charles C Thomas, Springfield, Ill., 1962, p. 169.

5 Ferreina: op. cit., pp. 125–138.

6 Caplan, Gerald: *Concepts of Mental Health Consultations, Their Application in Public Health Social Work*, Children's Bureau, Washington, D.C., 1959, pp. 264–265.

7 Ferreina: op. cit., pp. 23–31.

8 Caplan: op. cit., p. 46.

9 Masters, W. H., and V. E. Johnson: *Human Sexual Response*, Little, Brown, Boston, 1966.

10 Falicov, Celia J.: "Sexual Adjustment during First Pregnancy and Post Partum," *American Journal of Obstetrics and Gynecology*, Dec. 1, 1973, p. 991.

11 Ibid., p. 994.

12 Mason, Edward A.: "Emotional Reactions in Pregnancy—Are They Predictable?" *The Bulletin of Maternal Welfare*, March–April 1958, pp. 18–22.

13 Bradley, Robert A.: *Husband-coached Childbirth*, Harper & Row, 1965, p. 108.

14 Caplan, Gerald: "Normal Emotions in Pregnancy—Are They Predictable?" *Briefs*, 21(3): 35–39, March 1957.

15 Dunbar, Flondus: *Emotional and Bodily Changes*, 4th ed., Columbia University Press, New York, 1954.

16 Ferreina: op. cit., p. 127.

17 Deutsch, Helene: *The Psychology of Women*, Grune & Stratton, New York, 1944.

18 Newton, Niles: *Maternal Emotions*, Hoeber-Harper, New York, 1955.

19 Deutsch: op. cit., p. 405.

20 Chertok, Leon: *Motherhood and Personality*, Lippincott, Philadelphia, 1969, p. 32.

21 Caplan, Gerald: *Concepts of Mental Health Consultations; Their Application in Public Health Social Work*, op. cit., pp. 70–71.

22 Caplan, Gerald: *Concepts of Mental Health Consultations, Their Application in Public Health Social Work*, op. cit., p. 53.

23 Caplan, Gerald: *Concepts of Mental Health Consultations, Their Application in Public Health Social Work*, op. cit., p. 54.

24 Caplan, Gerald: *Concepts of Mental Health Consultations, Their Application in Public Health Social Work*, op. cit., p. 53.

25 Lewis, Couper: "Emotional Stress in Pregnant Woman," *Nursing Times*, 57:79, Jan. 20, 1961.

26 Kroger, William S.: *Psychosomatic Obstetrics, Gynecology and Endocrinology*, Charles C Thomas, Springfield, Ill., 1962, pp. 34–35.

27 Morris, Marion C.: "Psychological Miscarriage: An End to Mother Love," *Trans-Action*, 3(2):8, January–February 1966.

28 Littlefield, Vivian: *An Experimental Investigation into the Effects of Supportive Nursing Care on Primiparous Patients during Labor*, unpublished study presented to the graduate faculty of the University of Colorado, 1964.

29 Buxton, C. Lee: *A Study of Psychophysical Methods for Relief of Childbirth Pain*, Saunders, Philadelphia, 1962, p. 102.

30 Rubin, Reva: "Attainment of the Maternal Role, 1, Processes," *Nursing Research*, 16(3):237–245, Summer 1967.

31 Rubin, Reva: "Attainment of the Maternal Role, 2, Models and Referents," *Nursing Research*, 16(4):342–346, Fall 1967.

32 Ibid., pp. 342–346.

33 Ibid., p. 242.

34 Ibid., p. 243.

35 Ibid., pp. 243–244.

36 Caplan, Gerald: *Concepts of Mental Health Consultations, Their Application in Public Health Social Work,* op. cit., p. 63.

37 Bowlby, John: *Maternal Care and Mental Health,* World Health Organization, Geneva, 1952.

38 Richardson and Guttmacher: op. cit., p. 147.

39 Richardson and Guttmacher: op. cit., p. 171.

40 Richardson and Guttmacher: op. cit., pp. 164–169.

41 Richardson and Guttmacher: op. cit., p. 163.

42 Richardson and Guttmacher: op. cit., pp. 190–191.

43 Colman, Arthur D., and Libby Lee Colman: *Pregnancy: The Psychological Experience,* Herder and Herder, New York, 1971, p. 116.

44 Ibid., p. 116

45 Ibid., p. 116.

46 Ferreina: op. cit., p. 133.

47 Montagu: op. cit., p. 176.

48 Ferreina: op. cit., p. 133.

49 Montagu: op. cit., p. 187.

50 Caplan, Gerald: *Prevention of Mental Disorders in Children,* Basic Books, New York, 1961, p. 7.

BIBLIOGRAPHY

Aladjem, Silvio: *Clinical Perinatology,* Mosby, St. Louis, 1974.

———: *Risks in the Practice of Modern Obstetrics,* Mosby, St. Louis, 1972.

Assali, Nicholas: *Pathophysiology of Gestation,* Academic, New York, 1972.

Auerbach, Aline B.: *Parents Learn through Discussion: Principles and Practices of Parent Group Education,* Wiley, New York, 1968.

Bancroft, A. V.: "Pregnancy and the Counter Culture," *Nursing Clinics of North America,* 8:67–76, March 1973.

Caplan, Gerald: "Psychological Aspects of Maternity Care," *American Journal of Public Health,* 47:25–31, January 1957.

Carty, Elaine A.: "My You're Getting Big," *Canadian Nurse,* 66:40, August 1970.

Cassidy, J. E.: "A Nurse Looks at Childbirth Anxiety," *Journal of Obstetric and Gynecological Nursing,* 3:52–54, January–February 1974.

Clark A.: "The Adaption Problems and Patterns of an Expanding Family: The Prenatal Period," *Nursing Forum,* 5:93–108, 1966.

——— et al.: "Sex during and after Pregnancy," *American Journal of Nursing,* 74(8):1430–1431, August 1974.

D'Angelo, A. C.: "Psychological Effects of Pregnancy and Contraception," *Journal of American Pharmaceutical Association,* 14:667–670, December 1974.

Fitzpatrick, Elise, Sharon Reeder, and Luigi Mastroianni, Jr.: *Maternity Nursing,* 12th ed., Lippincott, Philadelphia, 1971.

Fuchs, Fritz: *Endocrinology of Pregnancy,* Harper & Row, New York, 1971.

Gunn, A. D.: "The Normal Pregnancy," *Nursing Times,* 66:69, January 1970.

Heicks, G. M.: "What Makes a Good Parent?" *Children,* 7:207–212, November–December 1960.

Helfer, Ray E., and C. Henry Kempe: *The Battered Child,* The University of Chicago Press, Chicago, Ill., 1968.

Horney, Karen: *Feminine Psychology,* Norton, New York, 1967.

"How Mother Affects Unborn Baby," *Woman's Day,* 33:12, July 1970.

Howells, John A.: *Modern Perspective in Psycho-Obstetrics,* Oliver and Boyd, Edinburgh, 1972.

Iffrig, M. C.: "Body Image in Pregnancy: Its Relation to Nursing Functions," *Nursing Clinics of North America,* 7:631–639, December 1972.

Jefferies, Derek: "The Sequelae of Childbirth," *Nursing Mirror,* June, 1963, pp. 283–284.

Kempe, C. Henry, Federick Silverman, Brendt F.

Steel, William Droegemueller, and Henry K. Silver: "The Battered-Child Syndrome," *Journal of the American Medical Association,* 181:17–24, July 7, 1962.

Lilley, M. J.: "Emotional Needs of Parents," *Nursing Mirror,* 139:61–63, July 19, 1974.

Littlefield, Vivian: *Maternal Satisfaction with the Birth Experience and Maternal-Child Adjustment,* unpublished study presented to the graduate faculty of the University of Colorado School of Nursing, 1964.

Mann, David, Luther E. Woodward, and Nathan Joseph: *Educating Expectant Parents,* Wolff, New York, 1961.

Maternity Center Association: *Meeting the Childbearing Needs of Families in a Changing World,* Maternity Center Association, New York, 1962.

McKinlay, J. B.: "The Sick Role, Illness and Pregnancy," in P. J. M. McEwan (ed.), *Problems in Medical Care,* Tavistock, London, 1971.

Meek, L.: "Maternal Emotions and Their Implications in Nursing," *Registered Nurse,* 32:38, April 1969.

Miller, W. B.: "Relationships between the Intendedness of Conception and the Wantedness of Pregnancy," *Journal of Nervous Disorders,* 159:396–406, December 1974.

Painter, Charlotte: *Who Made the Lamb,* New American Library, New York, 1966.

Parsons, T.: "Sick Role, Illness and Pregnancy," in Elise Fitzpatrick, Sharon Reeder, and Luigi Mastroianni, Jr., *Maternity Nursing,* 12th ed., Lippincott, Philadelphia, 1971.

Peplau, Hildegard: "Anxiety in the Mother-Infant Relationship," *Nursing World,* May 1960, p. 134.

Quirk, Barbara L., and Ruth Hassanra: "The Nurse's Role in Advising Patients on Coitus during Pregnancy," *Nursing Clinics of North America,* 8:3, September 1973.

Reeder, Leo: "Social and Cultural Meaning of Pregnancy," in Elise Fitzpatrick, Sharon Reeder, and Luigi Mastroianni, Jr., *Maternity Nursing,* 12th ed., Lippincott, Philadelphia, 1971, p. 174.

Rich, Olive J.: "Hospital Routines as Rites of Passage in Developing Maternal Identity," *Nursing Clinics of North America,* 4(1):101–109, March 1969.

Rubin, Reva: "Basic Maternal Behavior," *Nursing Outlook,* 9(11):683–686, November 1961.

———: "Cognitive Style in Pregnancy," *American Journal of Nursing,* 70:502, March 1970.

———: "Maternity Care in Our Society," *Nursing Outlook,* 11:512–521, July 1963.

Selye, Hans: *The Stress of Life,* McGraw-Hill, New York, 1956.

Shereshefsky, Pauline M.: *Psychological Aspects of a First Pregnancy and Early Postnatal Adaptation,* Raven, New York, 1973.

Solberg, D. A., et al.: "Sexual Behavior in Pregnancy," *New England Journal of Medicine,* 288:1098–1103, May 24, 1973.

Waleko, K. F.: "Manifestations of a Multigravida's Feeling of Vulnerability," *Maternal-Child Nursing Journal,* 3:103–131, Summer 1974.

Warrick, Louise H.: "Feminity, Sexuality and Mothering," *Nursing Forum,* 8(2):212–224, 1969.

Wiedenbach, Ernestine: *Family-centered Maternity Nursing,* Putnam, New York, 1967.

UNIT B

21

The First Stage of Labor

KARYN S. KAUFMAN

The entire process of labor is subdivided into four stages:

First stage: from labor onset through complete dilatation of the cervix

Second stage: from complete dilatation of the cervix through delivery of the infant

Third stage: from the delivery of the infant through delivery of the placenta and membranes

Fourth stage: from delivery of the placenta and membranes through the first hour or two of the puerperium during which the vital signs should stabilize and any tendency for immediate hemorrhage should be controlled

This chapter discusses the first stage of labor.

The process of expelling the products of conception is aptly called labor, since this implies expenditure of energy to accomplish work. The work of labor effects the necessary changes in maternal reproductive organs and generates the intrauterine pressures necessary to accomplish birth itself.

Uterine contractions are the forces of labor. These involuntary, powerful muscle contractions overcome the resistance of the soft tissues to achieve dilatation of the cervix. The contractions are characterized by their rhythmic and increasing frequency as labor progresses. The first stage of labor is therefore a function of contractions recurring in time to accomplish cervical dilatation and other changes in both the pregnant woman and her fetus.

PRELABOR CONTRACTIONS

The uterus does not lie dormant until labor begins. Apparently, contractions are present throughout pregnancy (and in the nonpregnant state) and become increasingly more apparent to the pregnant woman and to an examiner as term approaches, although considerable individual variation is clinically evident. The distinguishing characteristic between prelabor contractions (often termed Braxton-Hicks contractions) and true labor contractions is their ability to accomplish cervical dilatation, i.e., their ability to be effective in the work of labor. That prelabor contractions can be converted to labor contractions at any time during pregnancy is also apparent, since spontaneous abortion or premature labor is documented throughout gestation. Labor does occur, though, most frequently at term, or around 40 weeks after the last regular menstrual period.

LABOR ONSET

What mechanism is responsible for triggering the change from prelabor contractions to the "real thing"? The precise answer is not known. It is probable that a combination of factors, perhaps both maternal and fetal, is responsible for labor initiation.[1–4]

Uterine muscle (*myometrium*) is responsive to oxytocin, a hormone produced by the hypothalamus and stored in the posterior pituitary. It is possible that a rise in oxytocin levels plays a role in labor onset. Certainly the widespread use of commercially available oxytocinlike drugs for induction of labor suggests a role for oxytocin in initiating spontaneous labor.

Progesterone is produced by the placenta and may exert a blockade effect on myometrial activity. Falling levels of progesterone may produce an increase in uterine activity or may make the myometrium more sensitive to oxytocin.

Premature labor occurs more often in women with a multiple pregnancy or with *polyhydramnios* (excess amniotic fluid). This suggests that distension of the uterus is implicated in triggering labor onset. Somewhat related is the purposeful stretching of the cervix by medical personnel as a method of inducing labor contractions. Cervical stretch also appears to be implicated in the premature labor associated with an incompetent cervix.

A group of compounds called *prostaglandins* have been found in amniotic fluid and in maternal blood during labor. The mechanism of action of these compounds is unknown, but prostaglandins are being increasingly used to induce labor.

Finally, there may be involvement of fetal factors, perhaps fetal steroids, in initiating labor. It is interesting to speculate that the fetus plays some role in timing its own delivery.

Whatever the precipitating factor or factors, prelabor contractions do convert to effective labor contractions. The change may not be very evident subjectively to the pregnant woman; i.e., the felt effects may be the same or little changed from prelabor activity. The change may only be evident to the objective examiner whose criteria are cervical effacement and dilatation, the true distinguishing difference between "false" and "true" labor. On a symptomatic or experiential level, it may be difficult to define differences.

PHYSIOLOGICAL UTERINE CHANGES

Cervical Effacement

Prior to labor the cervix usually undergoes a softening process (also referred to as *ripening*) and is often described as pliable, patulous, soft, or ripe. In addition, the position of the cervix within the vagina changes so the external os is aligned with the vaginal canal rather than lying toward the posterior vaginal wall as it does prior to labor. Prelabor contractions may accomplish these preparatory changes, and in fact may cause *effacement* to begin.

Effacement is defined as the shortening of the cervix. Normally, the cervix is 1 to 2 cm in length. When effacement is complete, the cervix is a circular opening with paper-thin edges. (See Figure 21-1.) To accomplish this change the cervical muscle fibers are "pulled," during contractions, up and into

FIGURE 21-1
Effacement and dilatation in the primigravida. Effacement may occur before dilatation begins. (*Used with permission from Ross Clinical Education Aid No. 13, Ross Laboratories, Columbus, Ohio.*)

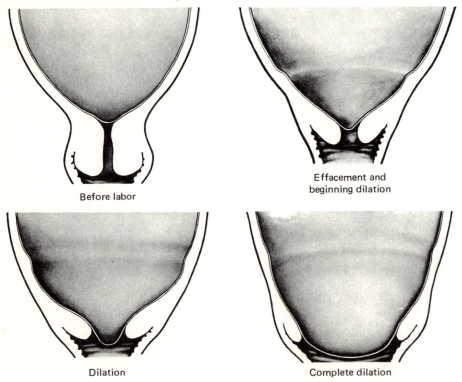

Before labor

Effacement and
beginning dilation

Dilation

Complete dilation

the lower uterine segment (the portion of the uterus located just above the cervix). Effacement is somewhat facilitated by the expulsion of the mucus plug which is formed during pregnancy by the secretory mucus glands lining the cervical canal.

Clinically, effacement is measured during a sterile vaginal examination. The cervix is palpated by the examiner's gloved fingers, and an estimation is made of the amount of shortening which has occurred. A cervix about half its normal length is 50 percent effaced; a paper-thin cervix is 100 percent effaced. The measurement is subjective and is dependent on the experience and judg-

ment of the examiner. Noting that change is progressing is more important than the precise measurement at each examination.

Clinically, it is apparent that effacement may precede actual dilatation or may occur concomitantly. Frequently in primigravidas, effacement is complete before dilatation begins. This is usually not the case with multigravidas, as shown in Figure 21-2.

Cervical Dilatation

Cervical dilatation is the enlargement of the cervical os. During pregnancy, the internal os is usually closed but may dilate suffi-

FIGURE 21-2
Effacement and dilatation in the multigravida. Effacement may occur concomitantly with dilatation. (*Used with permission from Ross Clinical Education Aid No. 13, Ross Laboratories, Columbus, Ohio.*)

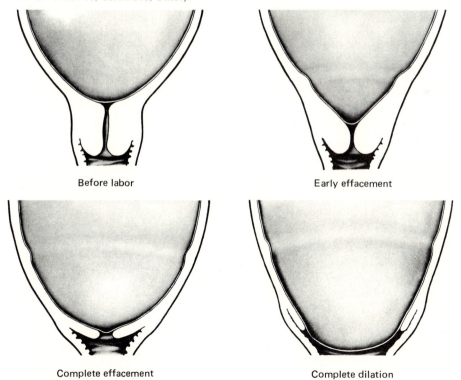

Before labor

Early effacement

Complete effacement

Complete dilation

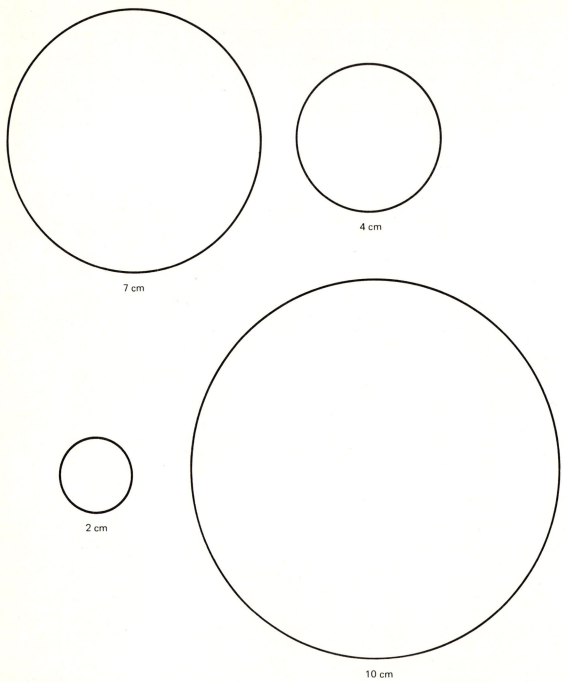

7 cm

4 cm

2 cm

10 cm

FIGURE 21-3
Centimeters of dilatation. Progressive dilatation is depicted by the dimensions of the circles.

ciently to pass a fingertip during the latter weeks of gestation.

Under the influence of rhythmic coordinated contractions, the uterine contents are subjected to increased pressure which is transmitted through the amniotic fluid in all directions. The cervical opening is the point of least resistance. Hydrostatic forces cause the amniotic sac and/or fetal head to act as a wedge in accomplishing dilatation. The cervix is fully dilated when it is a circular opening approximately 10 cm in diameter. This amount of dilatation permits the full-term fetus to be expelled from the uterine cavity.

Clinically, dilatation is assessed by an examiner during a sterile vaginal examination. As with effacement, this is a subjective assessment, dependent on judgment and experience. Figure 21-3 shows circles with actual diameters in centimeters to give the reader a visual description of changes in cervical os size.

Earlier in this chapter it was stated that the first stage of labor is a function of contractions over time accomplishing cervical dilatation. The rate of dilatation, however, is not uniform throughout labor. This may be a reflection of the changing strength of uterine contractions, or related to overcoming the resistance of the cervix to dilatation, or both. Dilatation of the cervix is conceptualized as an S-shaped curve. Translated into the clinical situation, the first few centimeters of dilatation takes a much longer time than the later phase of dilatation. (See Figures 21-4 and 21-5.)

The labor curve of the multigravid woman is compressed when compared to the primi-

FIGURE 21-4

Labor progress curve—primigravida. The various phases of dilatation are identified. The latent phase was 8¼ hours during which 2½ cm of dilatation occurred. The total active phase was 5 hours during which 7½ cm of dilatation occurred.

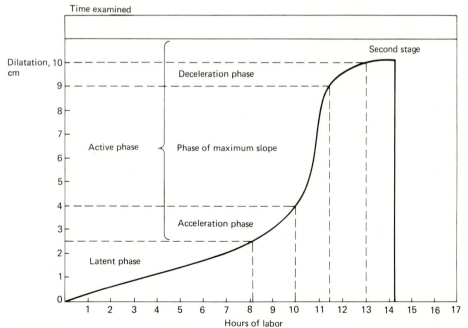

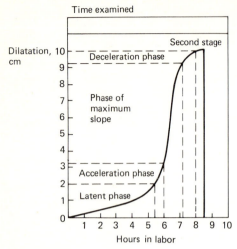

FIGURE 21-5

Labor progress curve—multigravida. The curve is compressed compared to primigravid labor. The latent phase was 5½ hours, resulting in 2 cm of dilatation. The active phase was 2½ hours, resulting in 8 cm of dilatation.

gravid curve, but retains the same curvilinear shape. Variations in labor progress produce abnormally shaped curves. Plotting cervical changes as labor progresses is an effective way of assessing normal progress and identifying complications. (See Figure 21-6, a sample chart form.)

Uterine Fundus and Lower Segment

The force of uterine contractions during the first stage of labor creates changes in the uterine body as well as the cervix. Contractions may originate from *pacemakers* located in the upper portion of the uterine body (*fundus*). During each contraction the muscle fibers in the fundus thicken and become shorter, and tension rises, as with any muscle when it contracts. Unlike other muscles, however, when the contraction ends the muscle fibers in the fundus do not return to their original dimensions, even though the tension returns to resting levels.[5] This unique property of the fundal myometrium is termed *muscle retraction*. Functionally, this gradual accumulative thickening of the fundus creates less room in the upper portion of the uterus for the fetus and gradually propels the fetus downward. Uterine contractions are therefore characterized by fundal dominance and are palpated most easily by the examiner's hand when it is placed lightly on the pregnant woman's abdomen immediately over the fundus.

In order for the fundus to gradually thicken and diminish its volume, the lower uterine segment must stretch to accommodate an increased volume. Muscle retraction is a phenomenon only of the upper segment, and relaxation is characteristic of the lower segment. As the cervix effaces and dilates, it becomes continuous with the lower uterine segment. This thinned-out portion of the uterus allows the fetus to be accommodated as it is pushed out of the upper portion by the actively contracting fundus.

The changes in the cervix and uterus are apparently responsible for the discomfort or pain experienced in the first stage of labor. The impulses arising from the cervix and lower segment are transmitted via afferent (sensory) nerves to the spinal cord at about the level of the 10th, 11th, and 12th thoracic nerves. These spinal cord segments supply skin *dermatomes* of the lower abdomen, lower lumbar spine, and upper sacral spine. These are the areas in which most pregnant women experience their labor discomfort. The skin sensation, then, is referred pain arising from stimuli in the lower uterine segment and cervix.[6,7]

The efferent (motor) component of uterine contractions arises from thoracic segments. These pathways are important in maintaining adequate contractions. This information

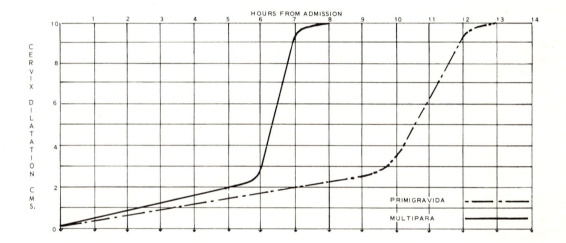

McMASTER UNIVERSITY MEDICAL CENTRE

LABOUR SUMMARY

EDC		LABOUR ONSET DATE TIME		WEEKS AMENORRHEA
BLOOD GROUP	RH TYPE	GTPAL		
ANTIBODIES: NIL_____ .1/____		ADMISSION TO LABOUR FLOOR DATE TIME		
MEMBRANES I ☐ DATE AND TIME R ☐		SPECIAL INFORMATION (ALLERGIES, ETC.)		
TIME OF LAST ORAL IN-TAKE				DOCTOR

HOURS FROM ADMISSION

PRIMIGRAVIDA — — — — —

MULTIPARA ————

TIME (EACH DIVISION = ONE HOUR)

COMPLETE RELEVANT DATA FROM
ADMISSION PHYSICAL HERE AND
EXPAND IN PROGRESS NOTES

EXAMINATION DURING LABOUR

DATE	HOUR	B.P.	FHR	CERVIX ASSESSMENT			CONTR.	MEMB.	POS. & PRES.	R/V	EX.	COMMENT (ANALGESICS, ETC.)
				ST'N.	DIL'N.	DESCRIPTION						

FIGURE 21-6
Sample labor progress chart form. The actual dilatation found with successive
vaginal exams is plotted on the graph and compared to the normal curves printed
on the form. (*Courtesy of McMaster University Medical Centre, Hamilton, Ontario,
Canada.*)

is clearly valuable when considering the effects of various regional analgesics. (See Figures 21-7 and 21-8.)

FETAL-PLACENTAL UNIT CHANGES

Fetal Position Changes and Descent

Accompanying the changes in the maternal reproductive organs during the first stage of labor is some amount of descent of the fetus in the birth passageway. The anatomic structure of the pelvis and reproductive organs produces a curved line of descent. (See Figure 21-9.) This curve is the pelvic axis, defined by the various planes of the pelvis. A study of Figure 21-10 will illustrate these planes and the pathway through the pelvis.

During descent, the fetus also changes *position* to accommodate to differing pelvic dimensions. Since in the majority of births the fetal head is the presenting part in the passageway, the changes in fetal position described below are in reference to the head.

Classically the fetal head enters the pelvic inlet with the sagittal suture in a transverse or oblique relationship to the inlet. Therefore, the position of the baby may be LOA or ROA; LOT or ROT; LOP or ROP. (See Figures 21-11 to 21-13 for these positions.) In the majority of pregnant women, the fetus is in the LOT or ROT position at the pelvic inlet because the diameters of the fetal head are most easily accommodated in this position. All the possible positions mentioned presume that the fetal head is well flexed, i.e., the chin is tucked onto the chest. This allows the head to present its smallest diameter as it descends; the process is analogous to tucking in the chin when pulling on a turtleneck sweater.

As the head continues to descend, the resistance of maternal soft tissue and the dif-

FIGURE 21-7
Diagrammatic representation of nerve pathways. The motor component arises above the level of sensory input. An epidural block attempts to place local anesthetic near the sensory nerves.

FIGURE 21-8
Skin sensation from uterine contractions. The darker areas indicate skin areas where the sensation of uterine contractions is most perceived in the first stage of labor.

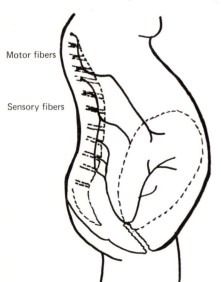

Motor fibers

Sensory fibers

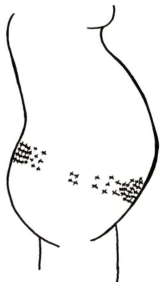

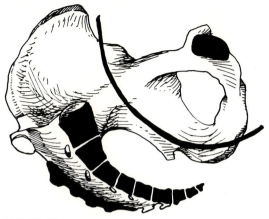

FIGURE 21-9
Curve of the maternal pelvis. The curved line indicates
the direction of passage through the maternal pelvis.
(*Drawn by Knud Skov, Audiovisual Department,
McMaster University Medical Centre, Hamilton,
Ontario, Canada.*)

fering pelvic dimensions of the midpelvis rotate the head to a direct anterior position
(termed *internal rotation*). This position is
the usual one at delivery and is discussed in
Chapter 22.

Clinically, during the first stage of labor, it
is important to estimate the descent of the
fetus as another measure of labor progress.
Like effacement and dilatation, this estimate
is made during a sterile vaginal examination.
The examiner is usually able to define the
sagittal suture and the posterior fontanel as
the head is palpated and can, therefore, determine fetal position. The examiner then
palpates the ischial spines of the maternal
pelvis to estimate the level of the fetal head
in relation to those spines. This is the measure of descent of the fetal head and is
termed *station* of the presenting part. If the
presenting part is above the spines, the station is a minus number; if below the spines,
a plus number. (See Figure 21-14.)

The ischial spines are a landmark of the
midplane of the pelvis. (Refer to Figure

21-10*b*.) When the fetal head is level with
the spines (0 station), the head is in the midpelvis, or is said to be *engaged* in the pelvis.
Engagement technically means that the largest diameter of the fetal head has passed the
pelvic inlet, but clinically that fact cannot be
assessed. When the presenting part reaches 0
station, the assumption is that the inlet has
been cleared, and this is the significance of 0
station.

Although the rate of descent of the fetus is
slower in the first stage of labor than in the
second stage, there should be some measurable descent occurring to meet the criteria of
normal labor progress.[8] In primigravidas,
the fetal head may be at 0 station at labor
onset or descend to that station during the
early hours of the first stage. In many primigravidas, the fetal head may be at +1, +2
station when the cervix has fully dilated.

In multigravidas, the fetus descends more
rapidly later in labor, nominally because of
lower resistance in the birth passageway.
Therefore, it is not uncommon to find minus
stations at labor onset, with engagement
achieved only during the active phase of dilatation.

In summary, the rate of fetal movements
varies from patient to patient, but the pattern
is similar:

Flexion of the head
Descent
Engagement
Internal rotation

This pattern of fetal movements is called
*cardinal movements in the mechanism of
labor.* The entire list includes three more
movements which occur in the second stage
of labor:

Extension
External rotation
Expulsion

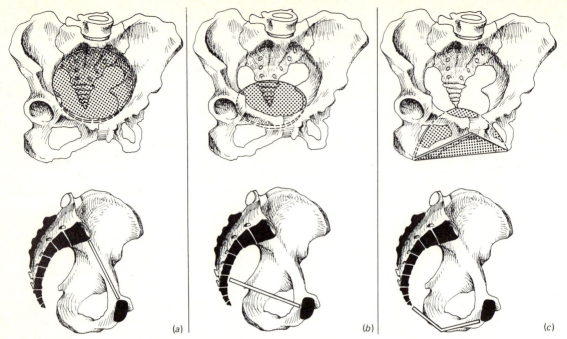

FIGURE 21-10
(a) Plane of the pelvic inlet. The inlet is represented by the dotted area in the upper sketch and the bar in the lower sketch. (b) Plane of the midpelvis. The midplane is represented by the dotted area in the upper sketch and the bar in the lower sketch. (c) Plane of the pelvic outlet. The outlet is represented by the dotted area in the upper sketch and the bar in the lower sketch. (*Drawn by Knud Skov, Audiovisual Department, McMaster University Medical Centre, Hamilton, Ontario, Canada.*)

FIGURE 21-11
Fetus in occiput anterior positions. (*Used with permission from Ross Clinical Education Aids No. 18, Ross Laboratories, Columbus, Ohio.*)

FIGURE 21-12
Fetus in occiput transverse positions. (*Used with permission from Ross Clinical Education Aids No. 18, Ross Laboratories, Columbus, Ohio.*)

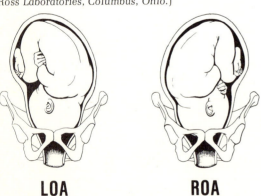

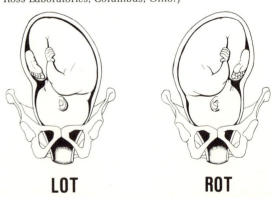

LOA   ROA   LOT   ROT

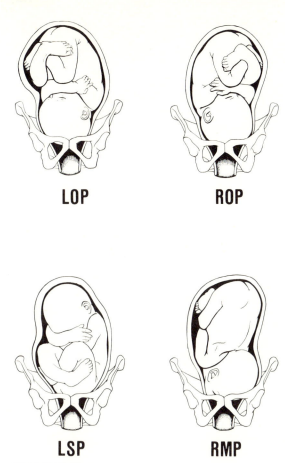

LOP   ROP

LSP   RMP

FIGURE 21-13
Fetus in occiput posterior positions. (*Used with
permission from Ross Clinical Education Aids No. 18,
Ross Laboratories, Columbus, Ohio.*)

As a whole, the list denotes the positional
changes required for completion of childbirth.

Fetal Physiological Changes

In addition to accomplishing positional
changes in the fetus, the contractions of the
first stage of labor may also evoke changes in
fetal physiology.[9,10] Labor is a stressful period for the fetus. During each contraction

the myometrium contracts and in effect
squeezes the fetus and interrupts the circulatory supply of the uterus and placenta.

Under normal circumstances, the fetus is
able to tolerate the stress of labor, and in fact
profits from the stress. Neonatal adaptation
is known to proceed more slowly in infants
delivered by cesarean section (when performed for reasons other than asphyxia) than
in those who experience a normal vaginal
delivery.

Assessment of the fetus by continuously or
periodically monitoring its heart rate is the
method of evaluating the response to labor
contractions. The normal range of the fetal
heart rate is 120 to 160 beats per minute. The
optimal response of the fetus is little change
in heart rate during a contraction. Many
times, though, the fetus responds with an accelerated heart rate for the duration of the
contraction and then resumes the previous
rate as the contraction ends. This is interpreted as a healthy response, indicating a
normally functioning myocardium.

There is different equipment which can be
used to monitor and evaluate fetal heart rate.
A conventional stethoscope or the fetoscope
applied to the abdominal wall at periodic intervals permits sampling of the fetal heart
rate. Various types of ultrasound sensors applied to the abdomen also detect the fetal
heart and produce an audible signal for the
observer to count.

Electronic devices are also available and
are becoming used more frequently. These
devices continuously monitor the fetal heart
rate and produce a graphic recording so that
changes may be easily seen. (See Figure
21-15.)

The electronic monitor has an external
sensor, which is applied to the pregnant
woman's abdomen, or an internal sensor to
detect the fetal heart. The internal sensor is a
small clip or wire electrode applied directly
to the fetal scalp (or other presenting part) to

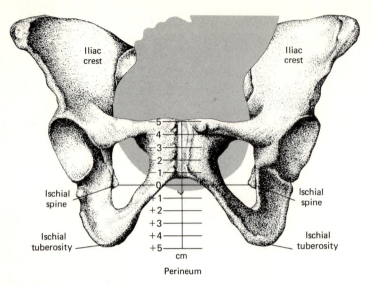

FIGURE 21-14
Stations of the fetal head. The scale depicts the location of the fetal head with
reference to the ischial spines; minus numbers are for locations above the spines
and plus numbers for locations below the spines. (*Used with permission from Ross
Clinical Education Aid No. 13, Ross Laboratories, Columbus, Ohio.*)

detect the ECG pattern. The heart rate is calculated from the pattern and the ECG complex can be directly observed.

The fetal heart rate pattern is evaluated for
changes as the labor progresses, particularly
changes in relation to the recurring uterine
contractions. Specific patterns have been
identified which are symptomatic of fetal
distress. These are discussed in Chapter 31,
"Complications during Labor and Delivery."

Another direct effect of contractions and
the resultant intrauterine pressures are the
changes in shape of the fetal head throughout labor. These changes are most evident
when membranes rupture early in labor.
They are apparent at delivery when often the
head appears elongated in the anteroposterior dimension. This elongation is achieved
by the ability of the skull bones to override
at their margins since they are not firmly

united. This molding of the fetal head allows
the fetus to maximally accommodate to the
maternal pelvis. In addition, an edematous
area, called a *caput succedaneum*, may form
in the most dependent area of the head.

**Changes in Placenta, Cord,
and Membranes**

Uterine contractions during labor exert an
effect on the placenta, membranes, and
amniotic fluid. The uterus is supplied with
blood vessels which are subjected to compression during a contraction. During strong
contractions, the pressure may be sufficient
to occlude the vessels totally or at least diminish blood flow. Since exchange of blood
gases and nutrients at the placental site is dependent on intact maternal circulation, it is
evident that contractions represent a poten-

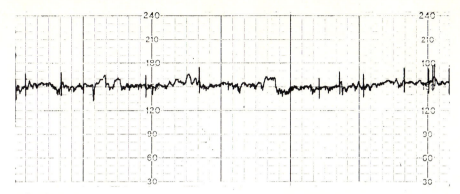

FIGURE 21-15
Fetal heart rate obtained with electronic monitor. The pattern exhibits a stable heart
rate of 150 beats per minute with a normal amount of oscillation.

tial threat to oxygenation and nutrition of the
fetus. Under normal circumstances, the fetus
is able to compensate for any momentary interruptions in blood exchange, and the uterine contractions are followed by sufficient
rest periods to restore adequate circulation in
the intervillous space.

The umbilical cord is also subjected to the
increased intrauterine pressures generated
by labor contractions, and the pressure may
be sufficient to impede blood flow in the
cord vessels. The position of the cord
changes throughout labor as the fetal position changes. If there is cord compression resulting in diminished blood flow to the fetus,
the resultant hypoxia is reflected in a typical
fetal heart rate pattern.

An event that accompanies almost every
first stage of labor is rupture of the membranes. This refers to the breaking of the amniotic and chorionic sac with the subsequent
loss of amniotic fluid. Spontaneous rupture
of membranes can occur at any point in the
first stage of labor, and, in fact, can occur
prior to labor onset. If spontaneous rupture is
awaited, it appears that most often this does
not occur until late in the first stage. This is

likely beneficial to the fetus since an intact
sac protects the fetal head from direct compression during each contraction.[11]

Membranes are often ruptured artificially
(*amniotomy*) as a method of inducing or accelerating labor. If the cervix is soft and partially dilated, rupture of membranes is usually followed by spontaneous contractions.
During spontaneous labor, if the membranes
have not ruptured before the active phase of
dilatation, they are often artificially broken
during a vaginal exam by using an instrument with a hook or sharp point. This is a
painless procedure for the patient. There
may be a sudden gush of a large quantity of
fluid or only a small trickle. This depends to
some extent on the station of the head and
the amount of fluid in the sac immediately in
front of the head (forewaters). It is recommended that membranes not be artificially
ruptured until the head is at 0 station to prevent the possibility of a prolapsed cord.
There are conflicting points of view in the
literature about the value of accelerating
labor by this method.[12-14]

Amniotic fluid is continually produced by
the amnion. Consequently, there will be

fluid around the fetus and a trickling from the vagina from the time of membrane rupture to delivery.

CHANGES IN UTERINE CONTRACTIONS

Since labor contractions are responsible for causing the described changes in the uterus itself, in the cervix, and in the fetoplacental unit, it is necessary to evaluate and describe the characteristics of those contractions as labor progresses. *Wavelike* is a term often used in the description of contractions. This conveys their ebb and flow from a subjective perspective and also suggests an objective picture of their appearance. In fact, when electronic devices are used to monitor contractions, the resulting graph depicts wavelike contractions. (See Figure 21-16.)

This wavelike or bell-shaped curve demonstrates the increasing of the pressure, the hold at the peak pressure, and the decline in pressure. These three phases are labeled *increment, acme,* and *decrement* of the contraction. Clinically, there are three parameters of importance:

Frequency: how often the contractions are occurring, expressed (for example) as 3 contractions in 8 minutes or as 2 to 3 minutes apart. When measuring frequency, it is important to report the numbers of total contractions in an elapsed time, or, in another method, to count the interval from the beginning of a contraction to the beginning of the next contraction, and so on.

Duration: how long the contraction lasts from its beginning to its end.

Strength or amplitude: how much pressure is generated by the contraction compared to the intrauterine pressure at rest.

Contractions are evaluated by placing the fingertips *lightly* over the contracting fundus. Uterine tensing will be felt as progressive hardening under the abdominal wall. During a contraction, the uterus tips forward a bit, and so if the pregnant woman is lying on her back, this can be observed as a rise in the abdominal wall over the fundus. With fingertips in place, it is possible to determine the frequency and duration of contractions quite accurately. The determination of strength is subjective and depends somewhat on experience. The subjectivity is further handicapped by an obese abdomen and changes in the maternal position.

When an electronic sensor is used, it may be internal or external. An external sensor is secured to the pregnant woman's abdomen over the fundus and is sensitive to the ab-

FIGURE 21-16
Uterine contraction pattern obtained with electronic monitor. Note the fairly consistent frequency and intensity with relaxation between contractions.

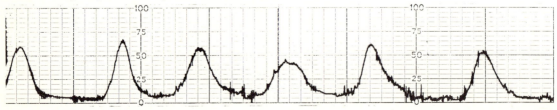

dominal displacement that occurs with a contraction. The signal is transmitted to the machine, and a graph is produced. Frequency and duration of contractions can be measured very accurately by the external route, but amplitude is still subjective and varies with placement of the sensor and thickness of the abdominal wall. (See Figure 21-17.)

The internal sensor is a thin plastic tube, filled with sterile water and introduced into the uterine cavity during a vaginal examination after membranes have been ruptured. The catheter is attached to a pressure-sensitive transducer on the monitor. When intra-

uterine pressure rises during a contraction, the pressure in the catheter also rises, is sensed by the transducer, and transmitted to the machine for graphic recording. This method results in a tracing which accurately displays frequency and duration as well as intrauterine pressure measured in millimeters of mercury. Whenever it is desirable to have highly specific information (as with some high-risk patients), the internal method may be selected.

In general, the frequency, duration, and strength of contractions gradually increases as labor progresses. While minute-to-minute comparisons may not reflect that pattern,

FIGURE 21-17
External sensors of the electronic monitor. These sensors are secured with straps and must be adjusted for patient comfort and accurate recordings. (*Courtesy of Elizabeth Sturrock and Sally Ann Yeomans, nurse midwives.*)

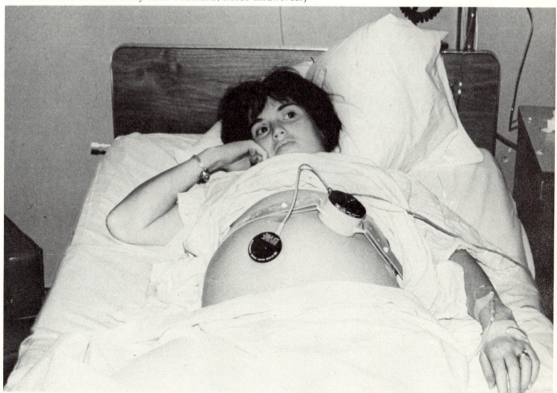

the tendency is in the direction of increasing uterine activity. Detecting regressive changes in the contraction pattern may provide early clues to abnormal labor progress.

PHASES OF LABOR

It is apparent from the preceding description that labor is a dynamic process, that changes are constantly occurring. But those changes do not occur uniformly throughout the duration of labor. For ease in describing this lack of uniformity, various phases of the first stage are described.[15,16]

1   *Early phase or latent phase:* These terms are often used synonymously to describe the period from labor onset to 3 or 4 cm of cervical dilatation. This phase usually lasts longer than the rest of labor, but there is less progress. This phase may last many hours, but averages 5 to 9 hours depending on parity.

2   *Active phase:* This is a general term applied to the remaining first stage and is marked by more rapid progress of the labor. This phase is shorter and averages from 2 to 6 hours depending on parity. This phase can be subdivided in different ways.

  Figures 21-4 and 21-5 illustrate the following subphases:

  a   Acceleration phase: 3 to 4 cm of dilatation

  b   Phase of maximum slope: 4 to 9 cm of dilatation

  c   Deceleration phase: 9 to 10 cm of dilatation

It is apparent from the graphs that the labels for these subphases are derived from the rate of cervical dilatation occurring at those times.

  The active phase can also be subdivided into the:

a   Midactive phase: 4 to 7 cm of dilatation

b   Transition phase: 7 to 10 cm of dilatation

This subdivision is based on clinical observations of the behavior of pregnant women in labor.

Nursing care of the laboring woman is based on an understanding of the process of labor and on the responses and needs of the woman as she experiences the process. Nursing care is discussed in relation to the early, midactive, and transition phases since the behavioral cues that signal change from one phase to the next should be familiar to labor-room nurses.

EARLY PHASE

Signs of Labor Onset

During the latter weeks of pregnancy many pregnant women experience Braxton-Hicks contractions. These are felt by some women as an intermittent backache, or a cramping sensation in the groin or above the symphysis pubis, or as painless tightenings of the abdomen. These irregular sensations may occur at rest and often cease with activity. The variation in type and amount of sensation is marked. The woman usually regards these episodes with some anticipation: Will this be the "real thing" or will the sensations go away only to return another time? Some women can become quite frustrated with repeated episodes of "false labor" and may also become fatigued if these episodes interfere with sleep. It is not uncommon to find women who have made trips to the doctor's office or the hospital with high hopes that the awaited day has arrived only to be disappointed by a disappearance of the symptoms. These women need understanding, support, and reassurance that their experience is not unusual. They may need help exploring ways to acquire more rest and encouragement to return when symptoms reoccur. Since some softening or even effacement of the cervix may result from these prelabor contractions, the woman can be reassured about the value of this period in preparing for actual labor.

Eventually rhythmic contractions begin and actual labor gets under way. Classically, these early contractions may be as much as 10 or 15 minutes apart, but this is variable. Some women begin labor with contractions recurring every 4 to 5 minutes. Others experience contractions which recur in a *regular pattern* rather than recurring regularly. The contraction pattern, for example, may be several contractions close together and several further apart, and then several close together again. This is a regular pattern but *not* regular contractions. It is important to explain this difference to expectant parents who may sit waiting for contractions to occur with specific regularity. Subjectively, these early contractions may be perceived as low pelvic cramps and/or as a backache.

With beginning cervical dilatation, the protective mucus plug is expelled and blood-tinged vaginal mucus appears. This discharge is termed *show* or bloody show, and pregnant women should be instructed to watch for its appearance as another sign of labor onset.

Occasionally, the membranes rupture as another sign of labor onset. If this occurs, it is best for the woman or her supportive companion to notify the appropriate health professional and go to the hospital for admission.

With the appearance of any or all of these signs, most women experience relief and anticipation: "Finally something is happening." But there is also an edge of apprehension and anxiety: "Will I be able to cope?" "Will I be okay?" "How long will it last?" These are feelings shared by almost all women in early labor.

Patient Activities

Since the early phase of labor may last several hours, it is usually unnecessary to have the woman in hospital during the entire phase. Premature rupture of membranes, vaginal bleeding (as opposed to blood-tinged mucus), and multigravidas with previous rapid labors are some obvious exceptions. Most women can be encouraged to stay at home for much of the early phase. In general, they will be more relaxed and comfortable in familiar surroundings. Time may pass more quickly at home than in a small labor room.

What can the pregnant woman do at home? She may continue light housework, watch television, have a nap, take a shower or bath, or take a walk. Multigravidas can begin making final arrangements for the care of other children as well as continuing with activities such as listed above. The woman or her companion can make notes about the frequency of contractions, and their progress can be reported to the appropriate health professional by telephone or upon admission.

Women or couples who have prepared for this experience by learning about labor and delivery, and practicing a method of prepared childbirth, will often begin utilizing breathing techniques during the latter part of the early phase. Contractions at labor onset are usually mild and do not interfere with walking and talking. As the contractions increase in strength and frequency, the woman pauses in her activity, allowing the contraction to pass. At this time, breathing techniques become helpful by offering a controlled purposeful activity for the period of the contraction. Often the suggested breathing pattern is a slow regular one accompanied by body relaxation.

There is controversy regarding whether pregnant women should eat once labor is under way. Physiologically, the body requires a source of energy to accomplish the necessary work of labor, yet there is an element of risk involved if sudden general anesthesia is necessary and food is present in the stomach. If foods are recommended for early labor, they should be fluids and sources of energy. A helpful list includes gelatin, tea with sugar, and broth with crackers.

At some time during the early phase most women begin to be sufficiently aware of the contractions, and frequency and intensity increases, to the point at which hospital admission may be warranted. With some exceptions, this does not need to be a hectic, frantic race. Distance from the hospital, time of day, and the character of the labor will influence the timing of the decision to leave home.

Hospital Admission

The nurse is frequently the first person the woman and her companion meet at the hospital. The nurse has an opportunity to swiftly assess the woman's response to contractions during the first moments of contact. The nurse proceeds with the admission, balancing the need to acquire information with the need to maintain a comfortable pace for the woman that is consistent with her labor status. Admission during the early phase generally allows time for adequate history taking, assessment of labor status, assessment of the woman's responses to contractions, and teaching or reinforcement of coping skills (such as relaxation and slow breathing) if the woman appears quite tense and anxious. The nursing history should include a review of the appearance of early signs of labor, the woman's responses to these signs, the preparation of the woman and her companion for this experience, and their goals for the labor and delivery. The nurse should also review a summary of the antepartum period, including past history, estimated date of confinement, blood type and Rh, and any problems of the current pregnancy. Table 21-1 outlines the kind of information most frequently secured at admission.

Base-line measures of physiological parameters and the labor status need to be established upon admission. These include maternal vital signs (temperature, pulse, respirations, blood pressure); urinalysis; hemoglobin/hematocrit; characteristics of uterine contractions; status of the cervix; presentation, position, and station of the fetus; and fetal response to contractions. The prepared, experienced nurse can perform all of these assessments, and the student nurse, during the early phases of his or her education, can assist the experienced nurse during the admission procedure. While carrying out assessment and history-taking activities, the nurse continues to evaluate the woman's responses to her labor and the relationship between the woman and her companion, and provides support and explanations to both of them as appropriate. Comfort measures are also provided, e.g., helping the woman find a comfortable position, altering the room temperature, helping her into comfortable clothing, and checking body relaxation during contractions.

Nursing Care in the Early Phase

When the data base has been compiled, the care is jointly planned by the nurse, the labor patient, her companion, and perhaps others in her family who may be present.

TABLE 21-1
Information to Obtain upon Admission

1 Review prenatal record for:
  Parity
  Estimated date of confinement
  Significant problems of previous pregnancies, e.g.,
    Hemorrhage
    Fetal distress
    Prolonged labor
  Medical problems of present pregnancy, e.g.,
    Hypertension
    Infection
    Anemia, etc.
  Allergies—food and drug
  Weight gain during pregnancy
  Rh, blood type—other laboratory work
2 History of labor onset:
  When last slept
  When last ate, what
  Contractions
    When they began, frequency
    Where they are felt
    What helps to relieve discomfort
    Preference for being up and about or lying down
    Progression of frequency—pattern up to ad-
     mission
  Membranes—intact/ruptured, when, describe fluid
  Show—absent/present, when appeared, describe
  Fetal movements
3 Goals of patient:
  Preparation for childbirth, type of classes
  Desire for use or nonuse of medication(s)
  Desire for companion during labor and delivery,
   preparation for this
  Desire regarding infant contact following delivery,
   breast-feed, etc.
4 Base-line parameters:
  Contraction pattern
  Fetal heart rate pattern
  Blood pressure
  Pulse
  Respirations
  Temperature
  Weight
  Pelvic assessment

Activity

If labor seems to be in the very early phase and membranes are intact, the woman may be more comfortable moving around, sitting in an informal lounge, watching television, etc. If membranes are ruptured but the fetal head is well engaged, these same activities are appropriate. If the woman prefers to be in bed or her labor status indicates she should be in bed (ruptured membranes with high presenting part, elevated blood pressure, anticipated complications), she can be helped to find a comfortable position. Optimally, the pregnant woman should not lie flat on her back in bed. This can lead to impairment of venous return with a drop in blood pressure and syncope, as the heavy uterus lies on the inferior vena cava (*supine hypotensive syndrome*). Elevating the head of the bed counteracts this tendency, and a Sims's position prevents it altogether.

Fluids

Fluids may or may not be permitted. The use of intravenous fluids may depend in part on the policy regarding oral fluids. Ice chips for moistening the mouth and hard candy for a sugar supply are helpful if other foods are not permitted. Meticulous mouth care is essential for patient comfort.

Contractions

The nurse continues to evaluate the labor status by noting the frequency, duration, and strength of uterine contractions. Either the nurse or the woman's companion can determine changes in the contraction pattern by gently palpating the abdomen. The fundal area should not be poked or massaged in an attempt to feel the contraction. This is most uncomfortable for the patient. The fingertips are kept in place through several contractions. The uterine relaxation between contractions and fetal activity can be assessed as well as the contractions themselves. If available and indicated, the external uterine contraction sensor of the fetal monitor can be applied. This sensor is usually attached to an elastic belt, and it is important to adjust this for the patient's comfort and for a clear tracing.

Fetal Heart Response

By using a fetoscope, an ultrasound sensor (e.g., Doptone), or the external fetal monitor, the fetal heart rate can be evaluated in relation to contractions. The fetal heart monitor supplies continuous data whereas the other instruments are used to obtain intermittent data. Interpreting the various fetal heart rate patterns and using the fetoscope in a manner to detect some of these patterns is discussed in Chapter 31.

When the nurse applies the external fetal monitoring sensor, it is important to adjust the belt and to place the sensor over the area of the abdomen where heart tones are most clearly audible. This location varies with fetal position and thickness of the abdominal wall. Often, the heart sounds can be heard at the umbilicus since there is less maternal tissue to mask the sounds. The rate should be 120 to 160 beats per minute between contractions. Palpating the maternal pulse simultaneously ensures that the fetal rate and not the maternal rate is being heard. As the fetal position changes during labor, the location of the sensor also needs changing.

External sensors provide continuous data about contractions and fetal heart responses, but they do restrict patient movement. If the monitoring sensors are used, the belts should be removed at intervals so the patient can change position or get out of bed.

If the patient is unfamiliar with the apparatus, it is very important to explain its purpose and function before attaching the monitor. Electronic equipment appears very threatening to many people, and some patients may feel its use indicates that a problem exists.

Physiological Parameters

The nurse is also responsible for continual evaluation of the parameters assessed at admission. The vital signs are measured and recorded at intervals appropriate to the patient situation, but usually not less than hourly. The temperature can be measured less frequently unless there are circumstances like premature ruptured membranes or urinary tract infection. Intake and output records and urinary assessments of protein and acetone at each voiding give information about fluid status and possible metabolic problems. The bladder should be kept emptied, since even a small amount of urine can create discomfort if the fetus is at a low station. Conversely, a full bladder can interfere with normal fetal descent. When able, the woman may use the bathroom. If this is contraindicated, the woman can be assisted to sit on the bedpan in bed rather than lie on it.

Hygiene

There is little rationale for the formerly routine practices of shaving the entire vulva and perineum, and giving an enema to every patient when admitted. Partial shaves ("mini preps"), or no shave at all, are becoming more common. An enema is given if the bowel is full. However, since many women have frequent bowel movements in the early hours of labor, they are usually unnecessary. Individual assessment rather than routine is a more rational and patient-centered approach.

Attention to perineal hygiene—with or without a shave—is important nursing care for the laboring woman. Fastidious women are often concerned about the "mess" they make as bloody show appears. Keeping the woman and bedding clean is important in preventing infection and in maintaining the self-image of many women. Perineal pads are

contraindicated in labor since they hold secretions at the vaginal introitus. The downward flow of mucus and amniotic fluid after
membranes have ruptured probably helps
prevent ascending infection. Soft wipes and
washcloths can be used to cleanse the perineum. Strong soaps and abrasive materials
are avoided. The direction of cleansing is
from front to back to prevent contamination
of the vaginal area.

Supportive Care

Even for prepared couples who look to each
other for reinforcement of positive feelings
about labor, hospital personnel become very
important people during the experience.
Positive responses of personnel can help the
couple cope and achieve their goals. Appropriate responses of personnel can also help
reduce the feelings of failure often expressed
when, for instance, a cesarean section is
needed, the labor lasts a long time, or the
woman becomes very distressed. Couples
and health professionals should see labor as
an experience with many options, and they
should be encouraged not to view labor as a
success-failure polarity. That view is unrealistic and unnecessary. Every woman in every
labor will have a different experience, and
there is no one right way to cope. Success
can be defined differently for each situation.

For the nurse this means acknowledging
with the woman that each labor is a new and
therefore anxious time, that she is doing
well, that she will not be left alone unable to
summon help, that her companion is important and helpful. These are examples of supportive messages to incorporate into nursing
care.[17]

Pain Relief

In the latter part of the early phase when
stronger contractions are present, light stroking of the abdomen, especially in the supra-

pubic region, while relaxing and controlling
breathing is helpful. Back pressure can be
applied if the sensation of contractions is primarily in the sacral region. Changing position from time to time also seems to ease discomfort.

Very often these measures, provided by
supportive personnel and reinforced by a
supportive companion, will see the woman
through the early phase. In general, she remains talkative between contractions, paus-
ing during them. She may be able to nap for
brief periods. The contractions tend to recur
about every 4 to 5 minutes and last about 45
to 60 seconds. There is generally noticeable
excitement and happiness, although some
women experience discomfort, are tense and
anxious, and may receive some type of medication during the early phase. Timing of
medication administration is important
since there is a desire to relieve pain, but not
prolong the labor. In very tense patients,
medication may be given to relax the
woman. This may actually quicken the pace
of labor because circulating epinephrine apparently can inhibit uterine contractions. If
medication is administered during this
phase, it is most commonly one of the bar-
biturates or tranquilizers (see Table 21-2).

Induction of Labor

A discussion of labor induction is included
at this point, since induction usually
shortens and alters the character of the early
phase of labor. As labor progresses there is
little difference from the labor of spontaneous onset.

Induction of labor is the initiation of labor
by a medical attendant who uses one or more
of the following methods:

1 Rupturing membranes
2 Administering oxytociclike drugs

TABLE 21-2
Drugs Administered in Early Phase

Type of drug	Maternal effects	Fetal and neonatal effects

Sedatives:
  Seconal
  Nembutal
  Phenobarbital
  Amytal
  Phanodorn
	Sleep, sedation, mild tranquilizer, mild antiemetic; may slow labor depending on dose and timing	Can cause respiratory depression and, possibly, depressed muscle tone

Atarax Vistaril	Sedation, relaxation, potentiate narcotics, antiemetic	Not known
Valium	Reduce anxiety, muscle relaxant	Some loss of normal heart rate variability, hypotonicity, possible effect on thermal regulation, respiratory depressant

Tranquilizers:
  Phenothiazines
  Thorazine
  Phenergan
  Sparine
  Compazine
  Trilafon
	Reduce apprehension
	Sedation, relaxation, mild antiemetic, potentiate narcotics, respiratory depression
		May cause poorer muscle tone

SOURCES: Adapted from David Fisher and John B. Paton, "The Effect of Maternal Anesthetic Analgesic Drugs on the Fetus and Newborn," *Clinical Obstetrics and Gynecology*, 17(2):275–286, 1974; and J. J. Bonica, *Principles and Practice of Obstetric Analgesia and Anesthesia*, vol. 1, Davis, Philadelphia, 1967.

3   Stretching the cervix
4   Administering one of the prostaglandinlike drugs

The method most commonly used is administering an oxytociclike drug via intravenous infusion with or without concomitant artificial amniotomy.

Induction may be indicated by maternal or fetal conditions. Maternal conditions such as severe preeclampsia, vaginal bleeding, kidney disease, and severe hypertension are sometimes better controlled after delivery. Other maternal conditions may be a history of previous rapid labors or problems in the socioeconomic environment sufficient to hasten labor in a term gestation. Fetal indications include intrauterine growth retardation, Rh incompatibility, or clear threat of infection from prematurely ruptured membranes. Unless there is some compelling reason, induction is not carried out until deter-

minations of fetal maturity are made. Every attempt should be made to avoid delivering an immature infant unless the intrauterine environment is life-threatening.

Oxytocin Induction

Medical induction methods vary from hospital to hospital and among physicians. Professional groups recommend using diluted intravenous solutions of oxytocin. Generally an initial infusion is begun with a standard solution, and the oxytocin dilution in a second infusion is "piggybacked" to the original. The rate of infusion is titrated against the uterine response to the oxytocin. In this way, the infusion can be easily controlled. The piggyback line can run by gravity drip, but is better controlled if fed through some type of mechanical infusion pump. These pumps control to a high degree of accuracy extremely small doses of the oxytocin infusion. The rate can be very gradually increased according to some established protocol until rhythmic contractions are established.

It is impossible to predict individual sensitivities to oxytocin. Nursing care must include very close observation of uterine activity. Oxytocin induction is known to increase the uterine tone at rest; therefore *uterine relaxation between contractions is a critical observation.* For this reason fetal monitors are often used when labor is induced. They permit continuous observation of uterine activity and fetal response. When this technique is utilized, the patient may feel overwhelmed at the technical apparatus involved in this labor (see Figure 21-18), and it is very important that explanations to the woman and her companion precede the

initiation of the induction. The woman should be reassured that although nurses and other medical attendants must look after the functioning of the equipment, she remains the focus of concern.

The object of the induction is to establish contractions like those of normal labor, for example, contractions recurring every 2 to 3 minutes lasting 60 to 75 seconds, with good relaxation between the contractions. Very long or very frequent contractions diminish uterine blood flow and may cause fetal hypoxia. Nursing care includes documenting the frequent observations of the contraction pattern, the changes in rate of the intravenous infusion, and the fetal and maternal responses to the induced contractions. Vital signs are often measured more frequently, particularly while the infusion rate is in-

FIGURE 21-18

Supporting equipment in a labor room. At left is the Harvard infusion pump used for administering oxytocin and at right a fetal electronic monitor for displaying uterine contractions and fetal heart rate. (*Courtesy of Elizabeth Sturrock and Sally Ann Yeomans, nurse midwives.*)

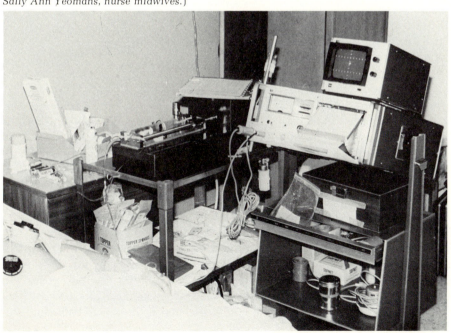

creasing. The patient may need increased assistance to cope with the contractions of an induced labor because she may experience frequent, strong contractions from the onset, as opposed to spontaneous labor, when the frequency, duration, and intensity of contractions increase gradually.

Oxytociclike drugs have been administered by buccal, intramuscular, and subcutaneous routes. The problem with nonintravenous routes is that the dose cannot be turned off if uterine activity is excessive. The hazards of induction are real, and standards and policies that encourage safe use are a protection for everyone. Many hospitals and professional groups have recommended standards to be observed when oxytocin inductions are occurring.[18-20]

Rupture of Membranes

Amniotomy, i.e., artificial rupturing of the membranes, may be performed to induce labor. Amniotomy alone may stimulate spontaneous contractions. If contractions do not occur, an oxytocic infusion is usually begun. At other times, an infusion is initiated and amniotomy is deferred until the active phase when there is certainty that the labor will proceed.

If amniotomy is performed or if membranes rupture spontaneously during the early phase, the nurse's first action is to listen for the fetal heart rate (or watch the monitor closely) and evaluate the fetal response to this change in the environment. The sudden loss of amniotic fluid can "wash" the cord into a new position where it may be compressed during contractions. With a high presenting part it is possible for the cord to prolapse into the vagina ahead of the presenting part. This is a grave threat to the fetus since prolapse may occlude the cord vessels. With the loss of amniotic fluid the fetal head is subjected to the direct force of contractions and heart rate changes may develop.

The leaking fluid is observed for color, consistency, odor, and amount. Normally the fluid is clear and watery with no specific odor. Fluid which is brown or greenish brown is colored by meconium and indicates recent fetal hypoxia. Greenish yellow fluid usually indicates older meconium that was passed during an earlier hypoxic episode. Blood-tinged fluid is abnormal and should be reported immediately. Fluid of term infants often contains numerous particles of vernix caseosa.

The volume of fluid may vary from a large gush to only a small trickle with spontaneous or artificial rupture of membranes. If there is a question that a small trickle may not be amniotic fluid it can be tested with a pH-sensitive paper that changes color in the presence of alkaline amniotic fluid.

If spontaneous membrane rupture occurs while the woman is up and about, she should be quickly helped into bed so the fetal response can be evaluated.

MIDACTIVE PHASE

Patient Response

At about 4 to 5 cm the laboring woman exhibits some changes in her response to contractions. Characteristically the contractions become more frequent and stronger. The woman now concentrates on getting through each contraction. Emotionally she may experience feelings of helplessness and fear. She may feel as if her body is controlling her, that she is subject to forces over which she has no control. The observant nurse often detects flushing of the woman's face at this time. Muscle tension may appear now in women who were able to relax easily during the early phase. Most women will seek positions of comfort in bed if they have been ambulatory up until the active phase. Most women continue to perceive the discomfort of contractions in the suprapubic and/or sacral regions.

The woman's companion and the nurse are important attendants during this phase. Both may be involved in timing contractions and in coaching the use of breathing techniques. If the couple has practiced before labor, the woman will respond to the familiar voice and cues of her companion. With these brisk contractions the breathing pattern accelerates while the contraction increases in strength, and decelerates while the contraction wanes. Stroking the abdomen and applying pressure to the sacral area continue to be effective ways of coping with the discomfort. In addition this touching can convey nonverbal messages of relaxation. The woman can be encouraged to relax and let go when tense areas are massaged. The nurse can support and reinforce the prepared couple who work well together. For the couple unfamiliar with these methods, the nurse can provide direct care and teach the companion these supportive care measures.

Most women begin to doubt that they can cope with these contractions. Verbal and nonverbal messages of support and reassurance that this phase is expected and that she is doing well can reduce fear and encourage the woman to trust her body and the people around her to help her through the experience. It is important not to leave the woman alone. This increases her fear and interferes with coping skills.

Hospital Admission

If the woman is admitted to hospital during this phase of labor, the nurse must be sensitive to the emotions of the midactive phase. It may be necessary to quickly have the patient examined and obtain a few cursory details about labor onset to determine the labor status. Once this is accomplished, the nurse can spend some time getting the patient comfortable, and by working between contractions, obtain the necessary history and vital signs. If the patient is quite tense the nurse may need to use touch and massage to encourage relaxation. During contractions she can *focus on the patient's eyes,* count out the breathing pattern, and breathe with the woman as a way of establishing some control. With this technique the nurse can usually settle the fear and tension to levels which permit the admission to proceed. These measures are useful when any patient seems unable to remain in control. If the nurse works through each contraction with the frightened patient, the patient receives a message that she is important enough to merit this time and attention, and that she will be able to cope.

Vaginal Examinations

When the behavioral changes of the midactive phase are noticed, a vaginal examination is usually performed to confirm progress in cervical effacement and dilatation. During the examination the station and position of the fetal head as well as cervical changes are noted. The educated and technically trained nurse performs this examination in many settings or assists with it in other settings. Coaching the patient to relax and continue the breathing pattern will alleviate the increased tension commonly seen with examinations during active labor. The nurse can be helpful to the woman by appropriately draping the perineal area during a pelvic examination and providing perineal care before and after the examination.

As mentioned earlier, amniotomy may be performed during this phase or membranes may rupture spontaneously. The nursing actions are those described previously under Early Phase.

Physiological Parameters

The nurse has a continuing responsibility to assess the contractions and fetal heart rate whether monitors or conventional methods are utilized. The frequency of the assessment is increased as labor becomes more active.

Internal monitors can be applied after membranes rupture. When the cervix is about 4 cm dilated and the head has descended into the pelvis, these sensors are more easily applied. The nursing role is usually to assist with this procedure. Explanations, coupled with encouraging the woman to keep her pelvic floor relaxed, facilitate the placement of the internal sensors. Once they are placed, the patient is free to move about in bed. Her movement will not significantly interfere with the recording being obtained. The nurse is responsible for observing the record and reporting alterations in the contraction or fetal heart pattern. The specific techniques of maintaining a properly functioning monitor vary from one type of instrument to another and are best learned in the clinical setting.

Periodic evaluation of fetal heart rate and contractions should be frequent enough to detect changes in the pattern of either parameter. It is difficult to specify the frequency of fetal heart auscultation since changes can occur abruptly. The nurse must use judgment and evaluate the frequency of contractions, maternal condition, size and maturity of the fetus, and medications administered in deciding how frequently to assess fetal heart tones.

Other maternal signs are also evaluated at less frequent intervals since they are less subject to change. Throughout the midactive phase there is little change in blood pressure and pulse that is attributable to the labor itself if these parameters are measured between contractions. The effect of contrac-tions will produce a rise in blood pressure at peak intrauterine pressures. Strong emotional reactions and/or medications will affect these parameters, and the frequency of measurement is a judgment based on the patient's situation.

The nurse continues to monitor intake and output and encourage frequent voiding. Every attempt should be made to avoid catheterizing a woman in labor. The procedure is difficult when the head has descended into the pelvis, it is uncomfortable for the woman, and there is always the possibility of introducing bacteria into the bladder. As the pace of contractions increases most women spontaneously refuse oral fluids. Ice chips may be welcome to keep the mouth and lips moist. Intravenous solutions may be used to provide glucose, water, and electrolytes, particularly if the early phase has been extended and oral intake limited.

Physical Comfort

Mouth care becomes very important during the active phase when the breathing pace accelerates. Unprepared patients often respond to contractions with rapid mouth breathing and may need extra attention to oral hygiene in addition to specific teaching and coaching of more controlled breathing patterns. Keeping the lips well lubricated and the mouth moist contributes to patient comfort.

Women who are in labor many hours can benefit from a bed bath and a change of bedding and clothing. Frequent perineal care is a vital nursing function. These activities can be provided at the patient's pace, ceasing during contractions and resuming between them. The nurse provides support by continual presence, by respecting the patient's need to be undisturbed during contractions, and by providing physical care that says nonverbally, "You are an important person."

The nurse can assist the woman into different positions (such as sitting and leaning across an overbed table, propping her with extra pillows to a semisitting or side-lying position, standing for brief periods) to see which is most helpful. The nurse can check muscle tension and encourage relaxation, or can provide encouragement and support to a companion who is participating in these labor care activities. The nurse can employ a variety of comfort measures for the woman who experiences intense back pressure with each contraction. Counterpressure or massage over the sacrum, a heating pad or moist warm compress, a firm pillow or rolled towel may be tried. Similarly, for suprapubic discomfort, warm compresses and/or light massage using talcum powder to avoid skin irritation may be helpful. Women vary in their response, and no one measure will be successful all the time.

Analgesia

If or when these measures are no longer effective in coping with the discomfort of contractions, some form of analgesia may be indicated. Analgesia for the active phase can be systemic or regional. If the labor has moved into the acceleration or maximum-slope phase of the labor-progress curve (refer to Figures 21-4 and 21-5), there should be minimal interference with labor progress. The decision about type of analgesia should be a shared one between the patient and the health care professionals responsible for labor management. The choice is based on patient condition, labor status, knowledge of risks, accessibility of skilled personnel, and to some extent local practice.

Narcotic Analgesics

Systemic analgesia was first introduced in the early 1900s as a boon to maternal suffering during labor. "Twilight sleep" induced by morphine and scopolamine provided pain relief and partial amnesia to laboring women but also produced longer labors and an increase in asphyxiated newborns. Morphine is now seldom used, but other types of narcotic analgesics play a large role in labor management in many settings.[21] Typically these drugs may be meperidine hydrochloride, alphaprodine hydrochloride, dihydromorphine hydrochloride, oxymorphone hydrochloride, and anileridine hydrochloride. When systemic narcotics are used, the objective is to give adequate maternal analgesia and avoid neonatal depression and prolonged labor. Side effects include a lowering of blood pressure, nausea and/or vomiting, and a tendency to urinary retention.

Intramuscular (IM) or intravenous (IV) routes can be used to administer analgesics. The IM route produces longer action, but the peak activity of the drug on the fetus is delayed several hours. This contributes to—or produces—the neonatal respiratory depression often seen at delivery after narcotic analgesia. The IV route produces a faster action for the laboring woman, peak effects in mother and fetus within an hour, and more rapid decline in drug action. Small repeated doses may be necessary to maintain analgesia.

Nurses are often responsible for administering analgesics and for making the decision about when to give them if using p.r.n. orders. The nurse must have *specific* information about the drug(s) administered; the foregoing is only a general description of a broad class of drugs. The timing of analgesics is a complex judgment involving subjective and objective data. The rate of labor progress, parity, patient response to labor, size of mother and fetus, gestational age, characteristics of the drug itself, and presence of complications are some of the important considerations.

Regional Blocks

Regional analgesia for labor is a more recent development and appears to have a wider margin of safety for the fetus. These methods seem to offer the advantage of providing complete (or nearly complete) pain relief in regions of the body without affecting the level of consciousness. The pregnant woman remains awake to participate in the labor experience. However, these methods can slow labor progress and produce hypotension and other side effects, and skilled personnel must administer them. The epidural block and caudal block are forms of regional analgesia. The continuous epidural block is becoming more popular in many settings. (See Figure 21-19.)

When an epidural block is used to provide labor analgesia, a local anesthetic is injected into the epidural space (the space outside the spinal cord and layers of dura) in the lumbar region. A skilled physician performs this technique by placing a needle between the appropriate vertebrae into the epidural

FIGURE 21-19
(a) Placement of needle and catheter for epidural block, below, and for saddle block, above, which is a true spinal injection; (b) placement of needle for caudal block. (*Used with permission from Ross Nursing Education Aids, No. 17, Ross Laboratories, Columbus, Ohio.*)

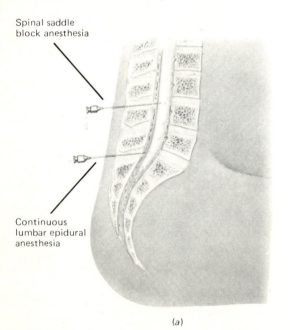

Spinal saddle block anesthesia

Continuous lumbar epidural anesthesia

(a)

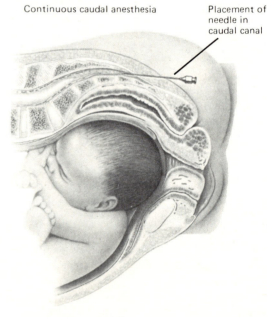

Continuous caudal anesthesia

Placement of needle in caudal canal

(b)

space. When the correct location is identified, a small catheter is advanced through the needle to remain in the space until after delivery. Initial and subsequent doses are administered through the catheter. Since sensory stimuli from contractions in the first stage are mediated at the upper lumbar–lower thoracic region, the epidural block can be limited to those areas and theoretically not interfere with the motor pathways to the uterus. A large epidural block in first stage will slow labor progress and interfere with internal rotation of the fetal head. During second stage the block can be enlarged to the perineal area.

Nursing responsibilities include assisting the patient to assume a side-lying position with her lumbar region slightly arched during the procedure. Once a dose is administered vital signs are measured very frequently for 20 minutes or so. Careful evaluation of the fetal heart and contractions is carried out frequently. Most obstetricians and anesthesiologists recommend an IV in site and a fetal monitor in place as preventive measures when continuous epidurals are used. Subsequent doses are in some cases administered through the catheter by nurses with special preparation for that function. With each dose the vital signs and fetal heart must be carefully observed.

For a complete discussion of the advantages, disadvantages, and techniques of epidural block and a description of other blocks, e.g., caudal and spinal, see specific anesthesiology references.[22–24]

Another type of regional block used during labor in many settings is the paracervical block.[25] This block is performed more simply than those mentioned above and involves interrupting sensory pathways at the site of origin. With the patient in lithotomy position, a local anesthetic is injected into the lateral vaginal fornices with a guarded needle at what corresponds to the 3 and 9 o'clock locations of the cervix. The duration of the dose is approximately 1 to 2 hours and can be repeated as labor progresses, although it is difficult to administer the block when the cervix is dilated 7 cm or more. There is usually prompt relief of pain for the woman, and few maternal side effects are noted. Many authorities believe that dilatation is accelerated by the block, and with many patients this seems to be the case.

However, fetal bradycardia is common and can be prolonged. This problem has reduced the use of this technique. Continuous fetal monitoring is advisable when paracervical blocks are given, and subsequent doses are contraindicated if a sustained bradycardia develops. (See Figure 21-20.)

When assisting with any of these procedures the nurse must be very aware of the properties of specific medications being used. The nursing responsibility is to provide support and comfort measures to minimize the patient's need for analgesia, since all of them carry some degree of risk, and to provide assessment of the responses when analgesia is given. The pharmacologic effects of various drugs on the fetus are under increasing study. There is little doubt that every medication given to the laboring woman is transmitted to her fetus. The precise effects are not well known, however. Nurses with continuing responsibilities in the care of laboring women should keep informed of current findings about fetal pharmacology.

Other methods of analgesia are also available but are not as widely used. Of interest are hypnosis and acupuncture as well as newer types of systemic analgesics.[26,27]

Simultaneously there seems to be increased awareness of the value of prepared childbirth.[28–31] Parent education classes are in demand in many locales. Consumer

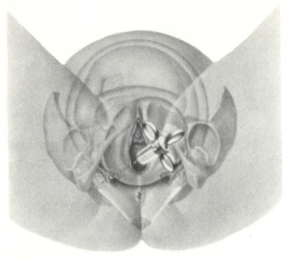

FIGURE 21-20
Placement of needle for paracervical block. (*Used with permission from Ross Nursing Education Aids No. 17, Ross Laboratories, Columbus, Ohio.*)

awareness of the risk of many medications, and continued research directed toward providing safer drugs, should result in increasing improvement in the management of labor discomfort.

The Oxytocin-induced Labor

The foregoing discussion of the midphase describes the typical picture of a spontaneous labor. An induced labor may not be very different, but the nurse must provide more careful monitoring of the contraction pattern and the fetal heart response. Once an effective contraction pattern begins there is usually no need to continue increasing the oxytocic dose; however, a maintenance dose continues. The nurse must carefully supervise the intravenous drip to prevent excessive uterine activity. During an induction uterine resting tone is frequently elevated. This, if combined with too strong or too frequent contractions, can interfere with placental perfusion and produce fetal hypoxia.

Women who have experienced spontaneous and induced labors report some subjective differences between them. Many feel that the contractions of an induced labor accelerate more swiftly and they get "caught" at the peak before they are prepared. Women who intend to utilize prepared childbirth breathing techniques report more difficulty staying in control. Whether these subjective impressions are a reflection of different uterine behavior during induction is not known. Because of the labor's more rapid pace and the subjective difference of contractions, pain relief measures may be needed at an earlier time. Epidural blocks are often used for analgesia during inductions since they appear to be safest for the fetus.

Because induction is more commonly associated with high-risk situations there may be multiple factors jeopardizing maternal and/or fetal health. The nurse must be aware of these factors, realize that an induced labor may not resemble the "normal" or typical situation, and provide care appropriately.

TRANSITION PHASE

Patient Responses and Comfort Measures

This last phase of the first stage of labor is characterized by *hard work*. This is the shortest phase, but the most intense. The laboring woman needs to concentrate intensely during each contraction. She may be frightened by these powerful overwhelming contractions. They are felt in the sacrum, deep in the pelvis, in the upper thighs, and the lower abdomen. As each contraction subsides she appears exhausted and slumps into the pillows, unresponsive to people in the room. During the peak of contractions her legs may involuntarily shake. She may hiccough or belch. Nausea and vomiting may occur. She perspires freely, complains of being too warm, and throws off the covers, and yet she may have cold feet. Profuse medium dark red bloody show is usually present as the cervix dilates to its maximum diameter.

During this intense phase the woman may feel as though labor will never end and that she is helpless to make it end. She is irritable, has no wish to respond to questions or conversation, does not want to be touched, but does *not want to be left alone*. Staying in control (which to most North Americans means staying quiet) may be very difficult. Grunts and moans are involuntary responses. Many women feel guilty about making noise, and hospital personnel are usually intolerant of loud verbal behaviors. Most women wish to remain stoically quiet, and are often surprised to hear themselves making noise. Nurses can demonstrate acceptance of this, and, in effect, give "permission" for verbal expressions.

Other comfort measures the nurse can employ are loose, light bed clothing, a cool room, a damp, cool cloth for wiping the patient's face, lip moisteners, clean perineal underpads, and a quiet environment. Mini-mizing distractions and activity helps the patient to remain in control.

The supportive presence of a nurse during transition is helpful to every laboring woman. For the patient who desires to remain unmedicated, the nurse can be, or assist the woman's companion to be, an effective guide who reinforces that this is hard work, that the end is in sight, that soon (in second stage) she will feel better. These messages help confirm the reality that labor will end, despite the woman's feeling that labor is interminable. Encouragement and short specific directions regarding the more rapid and precise breathing pattern will help the patient manage one contraction at a time.

Because transition is stressful for the laboring woman, it can also be more stressful for those providing care and support. A couple who has worked together effectively until now may experience difficulty. The woman may feel unable to carry on and express her frustration and irritation toward people she had appreciated until this phase. The prepared couple will expect different behavior, but may need confirmation when it appears. The unprepared couple or woman may be quite distressed during this phase of labor. Supportive reassurance ("Labor is like this," "I'll help you through each contraction") and directives ("Breathe with me," "Watch me count the pattern") should help to reduce loss of control.

Analgesia

Transition may be experienced somewhat differently if analgesia was administered during the midphase. Narcotic analgesics given during the midphase may continue to give pain relief during the greater discomfort of transition. Because narcotics cloud the sensorium, it may be difficult for the woman to practice breathing patterns that augment the drug effect. The narcotic analgesics tend to obscure a contraction until it is reaching its peak, making it difficult for the woman to anticipate and begin using breathing techniques. She has difficulty concentrating and remembering the breathing pattern. The analgesia contributes to amnesic behavior between contractions. If repeat doses of narcotics are administered during this late phase, their effect must be carefully considered in relation to labor progress because peak effects that coincide with delivery can produce a depressed baby.

When a paracervical or epidural block is initiated during the midphase, repeat doses can be given for transition. Both types of block will usually markedly increase patient comfort. The woman should be encouraged to continue rhythmic breathing with contractions, change her position frequently, and rest between contractions. If the woman continues to participate, augmenting the effect of blocks, lower doses will be required for her to remain in good control. Low doses of local anesthetic are encouraged to prevent fetal bradycardia in the case of paracervical blocks and to prevent interference with the woman's ability to push during second stage with an epidural block.

Physiologic Parameters

Measuring vital signs and providing personal hygiene are continuing nursing care tasks. These activities should be performed efficiently between contractions to minimize their disturbing effect during brief rest periods. The frequency of measurement of vital signs is dependent on total length of labor to this phase, previous patient condition, and presence of any medication and its potential side effects. There appears to be little effect of the labor itself on the maternal parameters. The blood pressure and pulse may be somewhat elevated during this phase, but significant differences are not the norm and should be carefully monitored and investigated.

The fetal response to this intense phase also needs careful evaluation. The more frequent contractions provide only brief rest periods of uninterrupted placental blood flow, and the increased intensity of contractions may sufficiently compress the fetal head and/or umbilical cord to produce fetal heart rate changes. External sensors for fetal heart rate and uterine contractions are usually uncomfortable for women in transition. If they are being used the nurse can periodically loosen or remove them, which does interrupt the data recording but enhances patient comfort. Periodic auscultation of the fetal heart rate is also uncomfortable, but can be used to sample the intervals between contractions. If an internal sensor is being used, continuous data about fetal response is available. During continuous monitoring it is not uncommon to see fetal heart rate decelerations during contractions, particularly when membranes have ruptured.

Uterine contractions are more frequent, more intense, and of longer duration in transition. It is not uncommon to see contractions recurring every 2 minutes, each one lasting over 1 minute.

By watching the monitor or feeling the fundus the nurse can cue the patient to begin her breathing pattern before she is overwhelmed by an intense contraction and unable to get into the rhythmic breathing. The nurse should gently palpate the fundal areas since many women find constant palpation uncomfortable and a source of irritation.

Measuring Labor Progress

Vaginal examination(s) are performed to confirm labor progress. There is normally more rapid descent of the fetal head and more rapid cervical dilatation during the transition phase. The examiner determines the dilatation and the station and position of the fetal head. Internal rotation begins when the head reaches the midpelvis (0 station). The examiner, therefore, is interested in assessing the amount and kind of internal rotation that is occurring.

If the fetal head is in an anterior position (LOA or ROA) in the midpelvis, the fetus will usually descend more quickly, resulting in a shorter labor, than when a transverse or posterior position is found.

The frequency of examination will depend on the parity, the anticipated progress if a labor curve is being charted, the patient's behavior, the frequency and strength of contractions, and the presence of medications or blocks which mask behavioral cues.

When progress is confirmed by vaginal examination, the patient and her companion should be informed. This reinforces the reality that labor is moving to an end point and offers encouragement that is so helpful during transition.

The membranes may spontaneously rupture during this phase if they have remained intact, or an amniotomy may be performed. The nursing actions are those described in earlier phases.

As the fetus moves through the positional changes of internal rotation, the experienced nurse may detect these changes when performing abdominal palpation. Often the cue is the change in location of heart sounds. Classically as the fetus descends and rotates anteriorly, the heart sounds are found in the lower abdominal midline.

When the fetal head reaches the perineal floor the woman feels an irresistible urge to push. Very often this amount of descent coincides with complete cervical dilatation, and voluntary pushing with each contraction is appropriate and needed. An examination can confirm or negate full dilatation. If the cervix is incompletely dilated pushing is inappropriate. The woman is coached to resist the urge by utilizing a pant or blowing technique of breathing during contractions. This renders her unable to hold her breath, lock the diaphragm, and exert downward pressure.

If a regional block has been used for analgesia the sensation of having to push is blocked by the anesthetic. This cue of probable complete dilatation is, therefore, absent, and vaginal examination is necessary to determine this end point.

With complete dilatation this difficult transition period ends. The second stage of labor involves new work and the woman feels better able to participate and accomplish that work.

Difficult Situations

The transition phase is commonly the time when patients are most uncomfortable and frightened and lose control of their own responses. Labor attendants can then become frustrated and angry. It is important not to get so caught in that frustration that punitive responses are directed at the patient. Such responses ("You're old enough to know better") are inappropriate and make a hurting patient feel more hurt. A frustrated nurse needs the opportunity to express personal feelings and needs support to reassess the situation and formulate positive approaches while someone else assumes care of the patient for a brief period. Restoring the objectivity and self-confidence of the nurse may enable the nurse to do that for the patient.

A patient may lose control more easily if the environment is noisy and confusing, if there are conflicting directions given to her, or if there is tension among health professionals caring for her. The nurse can often help clarify who will provide primary support so the patient listens and responds to one person, and the nurse can keep the environment as calm and controlled as possible.

Admitting a patient to hospital when she is in advanced labor can be a situation with the above problems. The nurse must be very clear about the priorities of this situation and proceed accordingly. This is a difficult time for the woman. Meeting a controlled, organized environment will help to maintain her control.

Nurses who provide care to specific cultural groups need to learn the values and cultural meanings of labor and delivery in order to provide sensitive supportive care to laboring women. The behaviors discussed in this chapter are representative of large segments of the population, but may not be typical of specific groups.

CONCLUSION

Providing nursing care for the woman in labor is one of the most challenging and satisfying experiences of maternity nursing. The unique character of each labor means the nurse must continually integrate new observations with previous experience and must exercise continual clinical judgment in interpreting those observations. For the laboring woman, her feelings about the labor and delivery are part of the whole process of attachment that determines how she will participate in the mothering experience.[32] The quality of a labor and delivery experience is difficult to define, but it has to do with a woman's perceptions of her own adequacy and capabilities to participate in this unique life experience. Nurses who actively support and enhance this experience have a rare opportunity to influence a vital moment of family life.

REFERENCES

1 Quilligan, Edward J.: "Maternal Factors Influencing the Onset of Labor," *Clinical Obstetrics and Gynecology,* 16(4):150–158, 1973.

2 Fuchs, Fritz: "Endocrinology of Labor," in F. Fuchs and A. Klopper (eds.), *Endocrinology of Pregnancy,* Harper & Row, New York, 1971, chap. 13, pp. 306–327.

3 Turnbull, A. C., and Anne Anderson: "Uterine Function in Human Pregnancy and Labour," in R. R. Macdonald (ed.), *Scientific Basis of Obstetrics and Gynaecology,* J. & A. Churchill, London, 1971, chap. 3, pp. 59–86.

4 Thorburn, Geoffrey: "The Initiation of Labor," in *The Endocrine Milieu of Pregnancy, Puerperium and Childhood,* Report of the Third Ross Conference on Obstetric Research, Ross Laboratories, Columbus, Ohio, 1974, pp. 89–100.

5 Hellman, Louis M., and Jack A. Pritchard: *Williams Obstetrics,* 14th ed., Appleton-Century-Crofts, New York, 1971, pp. 351–357.

6 Akamatsu, Toshio J., and John J. Bonica: "Spinal and Extradural Analgesia—Anesthesia for Parturition," *Clinical Obstetrics and Gynecology,* 17(2):187–192, 1974.

7 Bonica, J. J.: *Principles and Practice of Obstetric Analgesia and Anesthesia,* vol. 1, Davis, Philadelphia, 1967, pp. 98–114.

8 Friedman, Emanuel A.: *Labor, Clinical Evaluation and Management,* Appleton-Century-Crofts, New York, 1967, pp. 201–209.

9 Hon, Edward: *An Atlas of Fetal Heart Rate Patterns,* Harty, New Haven, Conn., 1968, pp. 39–54.

10 Klaven, Marshall, and Mary Ann Boscola: *A Guide to Fetal Monitoring,* distributed by Hewlett-Packard, 1973.

11 Schwartz, R. L., J. M. Belizan, and R. Caldeyro-Barcia: "Conservative Management of Labor," in L. S. Persianinov, et al. (eds.),

Recent Progress in Obstetrics and Gynae-cology, Proceedings of the VIIth World Congress of Obstetrics and Gynaecology in Moscow, 1973, Amsterdam and Prague, 1974, pp. 106–115.

12 Caldeyro-Barcia, R., et al.: "Effects of Rupture of Membrane on Fetal Heart Rate Pattern," *International Journal of Gynaecology and Obstetrics,* 10:169–172, 1972.

13 Friedman: op. cit., pp. 245–260.

14 Schwartz, et al.: op. cit., pp. 106–115.

15 Friedman: op. cit., pp. 34–41.

16 Wiedenbach, Ernestine: *Family-centered Maternity Nursing,* 2d ed., Putnam, New York, 1967, pp. 256–259; 300–302.

17 Edwards, Margot: "Ego States and Stroking in Labor," from *Communications: Dimensions in Childbirth Education,* Lange, Palo Alto, Calif., 1973, pp. 19–22.

18 Hellman and Pritchard: op. cit., pp. 845–846.

19 American College of Obstetricians and Gynecologists: *Standards for Obstetric-Gynecologic Hospital Services,* Chicago, 1969, pp. 34, 41.

20 *Statements re Policy on Special Procedures for Registered Nurses, Nursing and Technical Personnel,* Consolidated by College of Nurses of Ontario, Toronto, May 1975.

21 Ricciarelli, Eveline A. M., et al.: "Opioids and Obstetrics," *Clinical Obstetrics and Gynecology,* 17(2):259–274, 1974.

22 Akamatsu and Bonica: op. cit., pp. 193–198.

23 Cohen, Harry: "Complications of Regional Anesthesia in Obstetrics," *Clinical Obstetrics and Gynecology,* 17(2):211–225, 1974.

24 Bonica: op. cit., pp. 473–650.

25 Hamilton, Lewis A., and William Gottschalk: "Paracervical Block: Advantages and Disadvantages," *Clinical Obstetrics and Gynecology,* 17(2):199–210, 1974.

26 Kennedy, Roland L.: "General Analgesia and Anesthesia in Obstetrics," *Clinical Obstetrics and Gynecology,* 17(2):227–239, 1974.

27 Scott, David L.: *Modern Hospital Hypnosis,* Loyde-Duke, London, 1974, pp. 93–98.

28 Arms, Suzanne: "How Hospitals Complicate Childbirth," *Ms.,* May 1975, pp. 108–115.

29 Bing, Elisabeth: *Six Practical Lessons for an Easier Childbirth,* Bantam, New York, 1967.

30 Haire, Doris: *The Cultural Warping of Childbirth,* International Childbirth Education Association News, Spring 1972.

31 Kitzinger, Sheila: *The Experience of Childbirth,* 3d ed., C. Nicholls, London, 1972.

32 Klaus, Marshall, and John H. Kennell: "Mothers Separated from Their Newborn Infants," *Pediatric Clinics of North America,* 17(4):1015–1035, 1970.

22

The Second Stage
of Labor

ARIANNE SCHRODEL REGESTER

THE LABOR PROCESS

Description

The second stage of labor begins when the cervix is fully dilated and ends with the delivery of the baby. During this stage, the fetus descends from the uterus through the birth canal; therefore it is often described as the expulsive stage. In the multiparous patient the expulsion process may require only a few contractions, whereas other patients, especially nulliparous ones, may need an hour or longer of expulsive effort.

The accelerated descent of the second stage requires accommodation of the fetal head to the maternal pelvis and a simultaneous distention of the maternal muscles and connective tissue. Upon engagement, the fetal head enters the pelvis in a transverse position (LOT or ROT) or in an oblique position (ROA, ROP, LOA, or LOP). (See Chapter 21.) The position is largely, but not entirely, determined by the shape of the maternal pelvis. To be delivered, the head must rotate internally so that the anteroposterior direction of the head corresponds to the anteroposterior direction of the pelvis. Only with this alignment can the head pass under the symphysis pubis.

Descent and rotation are controlled by the size and shape of the maternal pelvis, the size and flexion of the fetal head, the quality of labor, and contractions of voluntary muscles. Flexion, descent, and internal rotation occur simultaneously, begin during the first stage of labor, and continue throughout the second stage. During delivery, the head extends under the symphysis pubis and restitutes to align with the shoulders; the shoulders rotate to an anteroposterior plane and are then expelled. Figure 22-1 illustrates the mechanisms of labor.

As the head descends, it stretches the muscles and fascia of the pelvis. Resistance of the maternal tissue to distention is greatest in the nulliparous patient. After delivery some

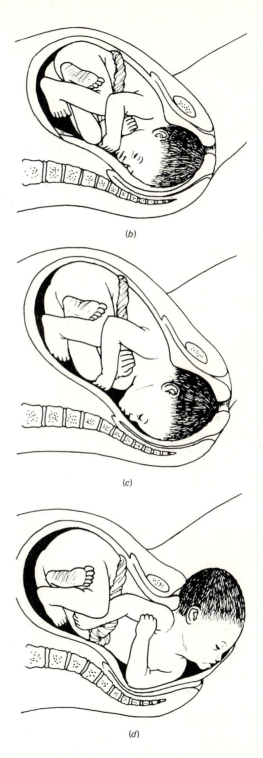

(b)

(c)

(d)

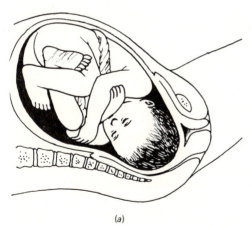

(a)

FIGURE 22-1
Mechanisms of labor. (a) Engagement, descent, flexion; (b) internal rotation; (c) extension beginning; (d) extension complete; (e) external rotation (restitution); (f) external rotation; (g) expulsion. (From Ross Clinical Education Aid No. 13, Ross Laboratories, Columbus, Ohio.)

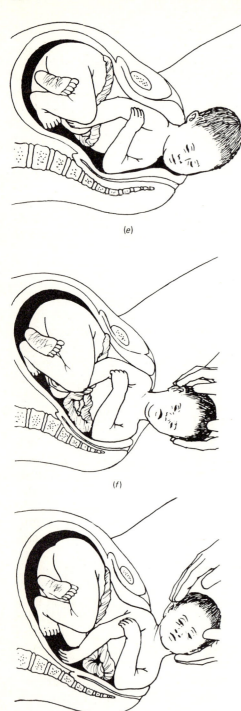

(e)

(f)

(g)

degree of relaxation persists, which is somewhat increased with every subsequent delivery. Consequently, one can expect the second stage to become progressively shorter with each labor.

Nursing Assessment and Intervention

The Transitional Phase

As the first stage of labor ends and the second begins, the patient experiences her longest, strongest, and most frequent contractions. (See Chapter 21, Transition Phase.) Even the best-prepared patient will have difficulty maintaining control over feelings of panic and frustration. Often she expresses hostility toward her partner and those caring for her. It is imperative that she not be left alone at this time when she most needs encouragement. The nurse must be present not only to reassure the patient and her partner that such reactions are to be expected but also to identify clinical signs of the second stage. A vaginal examination may be indicated to confirm that the cervix has completely receded around the fetal head. A nursing diagnosis, however, can usually be made by astute observations of symptoms manifest by the patient.

Manifestations of the Second Stage

Observable indications that the second stage has been reached are numerous, but the nurse should not expect any one patient to demonstrate all of them.

The uterus changes in shape during the contractions. It becomes longer as a result of stretching of the lower uterine segment, and also because the fetus is lying in a more vertical position. While the uterus is lengthening, it diminishes in the transverse and anteroposterior diameters.[1] If there has been no bloody show previously, it now appears as the cervix recedes; but if there has been bloody show throughout labor, it now increases in amount and becomes brighter red. This is caused by the rupture of capillaries and possibly from the fetal membranes separating from the decidua in the lower uterine segment.

The patient frequently becomes nauseated, with emesis occurring at the time of complete dilation.[2] If the fetal membranes have not ruptured previously, this may now occur. The patient indicates she has a desire to bear down. She may verbalize this to the nurse, or she may begin to hold her breath and strain involuntarily. She usually has the sensation or desire to urinate or defecate. A late sign of complete cervical dilatation is the characteristic grunt during straining or pushing, usually followed by flattening of the perineum and rectal bulging. Regardless of her past progress, when the patient says "The baby is coming," she is almost always right.

With the onset of the second stage, the contractions occur at regular intervals with a predictable acme and decline. As the unremitting discomfort of transition from the first to the second stage of labor ends, and as contraction patterns return, the patient's reactions become organized, her concentration is intense, and her behavior is deliberate.

NURSING CARE DURING THE SECOND STAGE OF LABOR

The decision to transfer the patient to the delivery room must be made on an individual basis, because moving the patient prematurely causes her unnecessary discomfort and anxiety, and too long a delay in transfer leads to a last-minute frenzy, which causes tension in the patient, her partner, and the hospital staff. Moreover, preparations for delivery are compromised. A multiparous patient who is having strong, regular contrac-

tions is usually transferred during the transition phase when the cervix is dilated 7 to 9 cm. The nulliparous patient usually remains in the labor room until the bearing-down effort advances the fetal head sufficiently to cause a bulging of the perineum. However, should evidence of fetal distress be observed, the patient is transferred immediately.[3] Unless delivery is imminent, the nurse confers with the physician or nurse midwife before moving the patient. Before, during, and after the patient is transferred, the nurse continues to respond to the patient's needs, makes observations, coaches, and comforts.

Coaching

Patients are encouraged not to bear down until the cervix is completely dilated due to the fact that premature bearing down simply causes the cervix to become edematous and prolongs labor. When a period of bearing down is necessary, the nurse ensures that the patient fully understands the importance, technique, and value of this hard work. Patients who have had no childbirth preparation will need explicit explanations. Prepared patients will need some reinforcement of past instruction during the stress of labor. The expulsive force of an involuntary uterine contraction is approximately 50 mmHg. If this force is coupled with effective, simultaneous use of voluntary abdominal muscles, pressure may exceed 100 mmHg.[4] Consequently, the descent and rotation of the fetal head can be accomplished more effectively with proper bearing-down techniques. Prior to the second stage conscious relaxation techniques ease labor discomfort. But during the second stage, the harder the patient pushes, the better she feels. Despite the tremendous physical effort exerted, most patients experience relief, even exhilaration, during the second stage. Concentration is shifted from the stimulus of the contraction to the response to the contraction. For the first time, the patient can make a positive effort, hastening delivery. In most labors, the interval between contractions increases during the second stage. The patient should be encouraged to use those moments for complete relaxation since pushing is done *only with a contraction.*

Bearing down is a reflex response, and maximum achievement is attained when the patient is properly positioned and coached. The woman's partner may be prepared to be an excellent labor coach, but this is no substitute for the nurse's vitally needed presence.

The trunk of the patient's body is elevated 45 to 75°. The sensation of perineal pressure causes the patient to move toward the head of the bed or table; the elevation prevents this. In addition, sitting up facilitates breathing and the downward direction of the push. Next, the patient flexes her knees on the abdomen and grasps her legs below the knees. Some patients may prefer holding their thighs but care must be taken that pressure is never applied to the popliteal area. Flexing of the legs serves two purposes: the patient has something to pull against; and the gluteal and perineal muscles are prevented from tensing.[5]

Fixation of the diaphragm is necessary for increased intraabdominal pressure.[6] The patient is instructed to take one or two quick, cleansing breaths and then a deep breath which she holds. She grasps the handgrips and bends her elbows to a 90° angle. She strains downward as if to pass a stool, and pulls her head forward toward her chest. (See Figure 22-2.) This position greatly resembles the primitive and effective squatting position which is used by many non-Western women throughout the world.

Short, grunty pushes accomplish little. Obviously the patient can sustain a push no longer than she can hold her breath. If the

FIGURE 22-2
Patient positioned for bearing down.

coach matches his or her own breathing to that of the patient, the coach is better able to judge timing directions. One technique is to request the patient to hold her breath while the coach counts to 20. When exchange of air is needed during a contraction, the woman is asked to quickly exhale, and follow this by a very rapid inhalation. The patient soon adapts to a rhythm of breathing and pushing.

If the patient has been given caudal or epidural anesthesia, her sensations and muscular control are diminished. It is necessary for the nurse to palpate the fundus for contractions and inform the patient when to begin and when to stop pushing. If the patient is unable to position or flex her legs, the nurse assists her. The patient pulls against the sides of the bed or the handgrips of the delivery table.

On some occasions the bearing-down response is contraindicated. This may occur in the latter part of the first stage, during transfer to the delivery room when delivery is imminent, or during the actual delivery of the baby. Telling the patient not to push is useless. Instead, the patient is coached to pant until the contraction subsides. It is helpful if the nurse demonstrates how to pant by actually panting with the patient. Prolonged panting can lead to hyperventilation; therefore, it should be done only during the contraction. When it is possible to turn the patient, the Sims's position is a useful adjunct to panting.

Observation of the Patient and Fetus

During the second stage, the nurse observes the effect of each contraction on the fetal heart. As the head descends deeper and deeper into the pelvis, head compression occurs. This compression may cause a fetal vagal response, which in turn causes a significant bradycardia. The nurse should be alert for these variations. (See Chapter 21, the section on Fetal Physiological Changes.) If constant fetal heart monitoring devices are not available, auscultation with the fetoscope should immediately follow each contraction. As labor progresses, the fetal heart tones are located lower in the maternal abdomen and more centrally.

Inspection of the perineum with each contraction enables the nurse to report progress to the patient. The patient should always be informed when the fetal scalp appears. Furthermore, uncontrolled, precipitate deliveries are usually prevented when the perineum is watched closely.

As the fetal scalp becomes visible, the nurse notes whether it recedes between contractions and whether there are concurrent perineal changes. Perineal bulging is caused by beginning extension of the head which never occurs until internal rotation is complete. Perineal bulging, illustrated in Figure 22-3, is first apparent by dilatation of the

rectal sphincter. Further extension of the head causes spreading of the labia, and gradually an oval, vertical patch of scalp becomes visible. The frequency and quality of the contractions are assessed regularly. Strong, sequential, patterned contractions are essential for progress.

Sending the partner from the room during internal or perineal examinations heightens anxiety in both the partner and the patient.[7] Careful draping and appreciation of the *patient's* needs should help eliminate feelings of embarrassment that the nurse might have.

Comfort Measures

Physical care during the second stage of labor is directed at providing patient safety, conserving energy, and relieving incidental discomfort. Many patients interpret rectal

FIGURE 22-3
Bulging of the perineum of a multigravida. A primigravida would be prepared for delivery at this time. (*Courtesy Childbirth Education Association, Baltimore, Md.*)

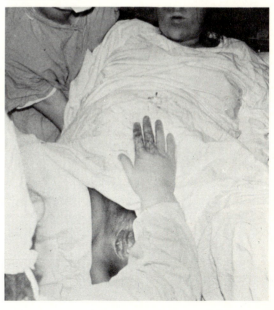

pressure as the need to defecate. After explaining to the patient that the reason for her sensation is descent of the fetal presenting part, the nurse should assure the patient that protective bedpads are in place. Following her own inclination, the patient may exhaust herself getting on and off the bedpan. With each expulsive effort, some involuntary voiding or even defecation may occur. The patient needs frequent cleansing and pad changes both for her comfort and her sense of dignity. The nurse is also better able to identify an increase or change of vaginal discharges: blood, perhaps meconium, or amniotic fluid.

Most patients appreciate cold cloths to the forehead or nape of the neck. This often gives the woman's partner or supporting person a feeling of contributing to her care. Sometimes a backrub or application of sacral pressure with the hands gives relief. Small pillows strategically placed under the lower back or sacrum, and change of position, promote comfort.

Nurse-Patient-Family Relationships

Labor and delivery create stress; stress increases dependency and lessens behavioral restraints. Assessments of the needs of the patient and her family require keen insight, knowledge, and perceptual skills, particularly since the average patient stays in the labor and delivery suite less than 12 hours.

Because the nurse-patient relationship lasts for a relatively short period of time, consistency can be extremely beneficial. Postpartum analyses of care at one family-centered obstetrical service concluded that both parents found the one-nurse concept very valuable.[8]

Unfortunately, conventional assignments of schedules and work are not always congruent with continuous care. Recognition of the importance of the nurse-patient relationship has led to implementation of pilot on-call systems. In essence, an on-call system is one in which nurses are assigned to predesignated *patients* rather than predesignated *working hours*.[9] Not every agency, or every nurse, could incorporate this approach. What is crucial is that nurses establish a philosophy of improving patient care, and that they continue with experimentation and research to meet the improved standards they set.

Nurses who wish to overcome the limitations of rendering short-term, acute care may plan methods to extend their relationships with patients. Some nurses, primarily those assigned to labor and delivery areas, have expanded their role to include rotation to antepartum clinics. Patients appreciate a familiar face when they are admitted in labor, and nurses can anticipate and identify which patients will have special needs in labor. These nurses use their specialized knowledge of labor and delivery to augment teaching by community health and clinic nurses.

Nurse-patient interaction can also be expanded and improved by visits to patients in the postpartum unit. Patients appreciate being remembered and often have questions about their delivery experience. Patients' perceptions can be useful in evaluating the care given and planning alternative courses of action for the future.

Although maternity nursing should continue with innovative plans for meeting patients' needs, most systems will succeed with knowledgeable, caring nurses. To establish a helping relationship with the patient and her family, the nurse applies knowledge gained about the patient's sociocultural background. A person's social milieu and culture influence childbearing behavior, and an understanding of these factors aids the nurse in assessing family needs and developing a plan of action to meet the needs.[10]

For example, many inner-city adolescents characteristically are supported by their mothers during labor, despite an ongoing relationship with their "boyfriend." Rarely have these mothers of pregnant adolescents attended childbirth preparation classes. Most of them work and/or have responsibilities or households which prevent them attending classes. Therefore, their knowledge is based on their own deliveries, which were probably handled very differently from that of their daughter. Past life experiences have very often failed to give the mothers trust or understanding of the health care system. The nurse is an effective ambassador for all health professionals. The nurse makes sure the mother of a pregnant adolescent knows that her concern is appreciated and helps her understand the value of the care that is being given to her daughter. Mothers, as labor-support persons, seldom wish to be in the delivery room, but they should know that they are welcome if so desired. The nurse's concern can be demonstrated by frequently reporting developments. Since the grandmother of the baby assumes varying amounts of the child's care, from partial, intermittent care to total, continuous care, it is vitally important that she develops positive feelings toward health services.

The nurse should never assume that the patient's control, or lack of it, is directly related to nursing support. One pregnant adolescent screamed and fought throughout her entire labor and delivery. Nothing seemed to help until she finally delivered. Later, the patient told the nurse that she really had not minded the pain, but she thought if she "carried on a lot" the nurse would be afraid to leave her. Perhaps past emotional deprivation led the girl to conclude that no one would pay attention to her unless she was "bad." The patient's seemingly inexplicable behavior was apparently caused by her great dependency and limited ability to communicate. Even uncontrolled behavior may be goal-directed.

Conversely, other patients direct excessive energy at maintaining control. As a result of childbirth education, many women have replaced the fear of dying at delivery with the fear of not performing well.[11] Fear creates tension regardless of the source. As the nurse offers frequent praise and reinforcement, it should also be conveyed to the patient that she is not being evaluated on her performance.

NURSING CARE IN THE ADMINISTRATION OF ANESTHESIA

Normal deliveries *can* be completed with no anesthesia. Evaluation of anesthesia methods available, however, requires weighing potential disadvantages against the patient's discomfort. The primary consideration must always be safety for both the mother and infant.[12]

All pain-relieving agents eventually cross the placental barrier. The agent's effect upon the fetus is influenced by amount of drug and time of administration to the mother. For the fetus who is in stress, anesthesia compounds the situation. With infants who are known to be high-risk, minimal or no anesthesia is indicated. Unfortunately, many of the patients who have high-risk infants are not prepared to deliver without medication, and in addition the mothers of high-risk infants seem to have an increased need for operative deliveries.[13]

Anesthetics which cause central nervous system depression in the mother may lead to narcosis and respiratory depression in the neonate. Whenever complications of any anesthetic occur in the mother, the fetus is in jeopardy. Both immediate and long-term effects of anesthesia on the fetus and neonate are being studied.

Many anesthetics administered decrease uterine contractibility which in turn slows the progress of labor. Prolonged atony may lead to hemorrhage in the postpartum period.

Systemic Anesthesia

Systemic anesthetic agents are capable of producing loss of consciousness. There are many theories as to the pharmacologic action, but all anesthetic agents have an effect on all excitable tissue. The response to the agents is, first, loss of muscle tone and analgesia, then stupor.[14] Systemic anesthetics discussed below are all inhaled through a mask.

General anesthesia poses potential danger to both the mother and fetus. Aspiration of stomach contents is always a serious risk with loss of consciousness. For this reason, foods and fluids are withheld from labor patients when it is anticipated that general anesthesia will be used for delivery. During labor the stomach does not continue normal digestive process. Labor patients may vomit food eaten 12 hours or more before. Anesthesia is a major cause of maternal death, and aspiration is the most common cause of anesthesia-associated deaths.[15] General anesthesia increases the probability of newborn depression; the long-term significance of this depression has not been determined. Another disadvantage of general anesthesia is that it causes loss of maternal muscle contractibility.

Despite recognized risks, general anesthetics are widely used on an elective basis.[16] General anesthesia is indicated when emergencies necessitate maneuvers that require a relaxed uterus. Also, general anesthesia might be necessary when the welfare of the patient or fetus requires operative

intervention and there is a specific contraindication to regional anesthesia. When general anesthetics are used for cesarean section, the usual practice is to administer low doses of several agents.

Nursing Implications

Prior to delivery of a woman by general anesthesia, the nurse is responsible for having the patient remove dentures and removable bridges. In many institutions it is the nurse who is responsible for notifying the nurse anesthetist or anesthesiologist that delivery is imminent. Some authorities claim that registered nurses working in delivery rooms may be requested by the anesthetist to apply pressure to the cricoid cartilage in the event the patient vomits, thus freeing the anesthetist for other life-saving actions.[17] Delivery-room nurses may also be asked by the anesthetist to assist in some aspect of patient suctioning.

If a delivery-room crisis situation arises from the administration of general anesthesia, it is the nurse anesthetist or anesthesiologist who is in charge of resuscitative measures, and it is they who direct the actions of other health personnel present.

Depression of the newborn is anticipated, especially if narcotics and barbiturates are given during the first stage of labor. It should be emphasized that there is a direct correlation between the amount of agent used and the length of time it was administered to the mother before delivery, and the degree of depression which results in the newborn.

It is helpful for the nurse to be aware of some characteristics of common systemic anesthetic agents. *Cyclopropane* is highly explosive. It is contraindicated on that basis alone when the necessary safety precautions cannot be carried out. When ergonovine is administered to a patient receiving cyclopropane, the drug combination may cause an appreciable rise in blood pressure postpartum. In addition, cardiac arrhythmias arise when oxytocics and vasopressors are administered simultaneously with cyclopropane. Low concentrations may give relief of pain during delivery with no depressant effect on the neonate.[18]

Halothane causes marked uterine atony. For the management of some obstetrical emergencies, this may be beneficial. *Ether* is one of the oldest and safest inhalation agents. It is unpopular because it is irritating to skin and mucous membranes, causes vomiting in the recovery period, and has an unpleasant smell.

Methoxyflurane can produce anesthesia. In obstetrical practice it is used mostly for inhalation analgesia. *Nitrous oxide* is a valuable analgesic agent. When it is used for anesthetic purposes, it is used with other agents, such as methoxyflurane, halothane, or analgesics in conjunction with muscle relaxants. Nitrous oxide may also be used with cyclopropane under *highly controlled* situations where safety precautions associated with administration can be met.

Inhalation Analgesia

Nitrous oxide, cyclopropane, methoxyflurane, and trichloroethylene are all volatile analgesics which are given to relieve discomforts associated with late first stage labor and delivery. Very low concentrations are administered; therefore the patient does not lose consciousness and can continue to be coached. The low concentrations do not lead to fetal depression. Local perineal anesthesia must be used in conjunction with these agents if an episiotomy is performed.[19]

Nursing Implications

Methoxyflurane and trichloroethylene may both be self-administered by the patient. The liquid is poured into a special inhalation device which is strapped to the patient's wrist. The patient holds the mask over her nose and inhales when she has a contraction. In theory, the patient releases the mask as she becomes drowsy. An overdose is more likely to occur if someone other than the patient holds the mask. Sometimes, however, the patient does not spontaneously release the mask. The nurse, therefore, must observe her for excessive drowsiness. The patient may very well be anxious about the responsibility for self-administration of anesthesia, and the nurse's supervision is essential both for her safety and for her acceptance of the technique.[20]

If trichloroethylene is used during labor, anesthetic agents administered by a closed-system anesthesia apparatus cannot be utilized for delivery. The trichloroethylene reacts with the soda lime in the machine to form a toxic substance in the patient's lungs. The nurse should be very certain that the anesthesiologist or nurse anesthetist is informed of prior use of trichloroethylene.

Low concentrations of nitrous oxide (also called laughing gas) are often given with contractions at delivery. Nitrous oxide is an effective analgesic; the patient receives increased oxygen, and is awake to see her baby immediately. However, it can have an adverse effect in that the patient is often distressed by her uncontrollable emotions. She should be reassured that her behavior is caused by the gas and that this effect will pass quickly. The nurse should remember that the patient has distorted perceptions while she inhales the gas. Conversation should be kept to a minimum, since the patient can easily misinterpret what is said. Many patients become talkative and are less inhibited. With tact, the nurse can usually prevent the patient from saying things that might later cause embarrassment.

Nurses *do not* administer anesthesia unless they have had special education in an accredited school of anesthesia. There is direct correlation between the safety of anesthesia and the knowledge and capability of the person administering it. In their standards of care, the Nurses' Association of The American College of Obstetricians and Gynecologists states that the administration of anesthesia is *not* an acceptable practice for the obstetric nurse.

Regional Anesthesia

Regional anesthesia is achieved by the injection of an agent that blocks the transmission of nerve impulses. It is administered either by an anesthesiologist or the attending physician. Pain is alleviated without loss of consciousness. Agents used include procaine, lidocaine, tetracaine, mepivacaine, and dibucaine. Choice of the agent is determined by the desired onset and duration of action. The technique of administration limits the extent of blockage. All blocking agents are capable of causing circulatory collapse. Care must be taken that they are not accidentally administered intravascularly. Regional anesthesia does not cause narcosis of the newborn. However, transmission of the agent across the placenta may, in some cases, cause fetal bradycardia. Figure 22-4 illustrates the injection site for pudendal anesthesia. Figure 21-19 illustrates injection sites for other types of regional anesthesia.

Subarachnoid Anesthesia

Subarachnoid or spinal anesthesia is performed by inserting a needle through the lumbar intervertebral space into the subarachnoid space, injecting the blocking agent directly into the cerebrospinal fluid. Generally the extent of blockage is regulated by the position of the patient during and immediately following injection. The hyperbaric blocking agent is weighted with dex-

trose, which controls drug concentration in the lower spinal cord.

The *saddle block* is a very low spinal block. Patients respond much better to the term "saddle" than to "spinal," which often leads to imprecise interchange of terms. A true saddle block relieves the pain of distention of the vagina and totally anesthetizes the perineum; it does not block pain sensations from the cervix or uterus. Consequently, the saddle block is appropriate only for delivery. A higher spinal blocks uterine pain sensations, but at the same time it arrests labor; therefore, it too can be used only at the time of delivery, or for cesarean section.

Contraindications to the use of subarachnoid anesthesia include the patient's objections, excessive restlessness, marked obesity, a known allergy to blocking agents, deformities of the spine, and precipitous labor.

Complications include postspinal headache, hypotension, and respiratory arrest. Spinal headaches are relatively uncommon,

FIGURE 22-4
Site for injection of pudendal anesthetic. (*From Ross Clinical Education Aid No. 17, Ross Laboratories, Columbus, Ohio.*)

Pudendal block

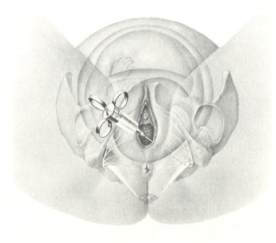

but they may incapacitate the patient for weeks; she is relieved only by lying flat. It is believed that headaches result from leakage of cerebrospinal fluid. Keeping the patient flat for 6 to 12 hours, use of a fine-gauge spinal needle, and good hydration may help prevent the occurrence of headache. Hypotension may occur from the coincidental loss of sympathetic innervation of the vascular system. Respiratory arrest is very rare and results from spinal anesthesia reaching an excessively high level. Injection of the blocking agent during a contraction is the most likely cause. The nurse is responsible for informing the physician when a contraction begins, thereby hopefully preventing this complication.

Epidural Anesthesia

The epidural space is a potential space between the ligaments connecting the vertebrae and the dura mater. The needle is introduced between the lumbar vertebrae using a needle with a rounded end to help prevent accidental perforation of the dura.

Continuous epidural anesthesia is begun during the first stage of labor. A catheter is passed through the lumen of the needle, the needle is withdrawn, and the catheter is taped into place. Intermittent doses of a blocking agent can then be administered. Epidural anesthesia should not affect uterine contractions, but many clinicians believe that labor is sometimes slowed. It may be necessary to allow the effects of the epidural to subside during the second stage, enabling the patient to bear down more effectively. At delivery, anesthesia can be achieved by a single-dose epidural, or by injecting the blocking agent into the in-place catheter. The single-dose technique does not include the placement of a catheter; the physician must be able to anticipate the time of delivery about 30 minutes in advance. To modify the continuous epidural for delivery anesthesia, a larger dose of the blocking agent is given and the patient is placed in a more vertical position.

Contraindications to epidural anesthesia are similar to those for subarachnoid anesthesia. The most serious potential complication is hypotension. Headaches may occur if the dura mater is accidentally perforated. Continuous epidural anesthesia can be used for cesarean section and sterilization procedures immediately following delivery.

Caudal Anesthesia

The chief difference between caudal and epidural anesthesia is the insertion site of the needle. The caudal space is entered through a foramen of the sacrum. Like epidural anesthesia, caudal anesthesia may be given on a continuous or single-dose basis. The action, contraindications, and complications of epidural and caudal anesthesia are similar; the danger of infection is somewhat greater with the caudal route. Accidents have occurred when the fetal head was perforated by the caudal needle. Both the caudal and epidural techniques require specialized skill to be administered safely and effectively. The experience of the anesthesiologist or the attending physician determines his or her preference of the two. The use of caudal and epidural anesthesia is restricted to those obstetric services that have qualified personnel who can perform the technique and then provide ongoing supervision of the patient.

Nursing Responsibilities in Regional Anesthesia

Prior to assisting with the administration of caudal, epidural, or spinal anesthesia, the nurse ascertains whether the patient should be left in the labor room or transferred to the delivery room. The nurse determines from the physician whether the patient should be placed in a sitting or lateral position. When a sitting position is utilized, the patient sits with her buttocks at the edge of the table or bed. She bends forward slightly and places her head on the nurse's shoulder. The patient may sit tailor-fashion, or her feet may be supported by a chair or stool. When the lateral position is used, the patient's back is aligned with the edge of the bed. The nurse helps the patient maintain her neck and knees in a flexed position. With both positions the physician instructs the patient to arch her back, which increases the intervertebral space.

When caudal anesthesia is initiated, the patient is assisted into a Sims's or knee-chest position. All the above positions are tiring and uncomfortable for the patient. Lumbar punctures are much more technically difficult when the patient tenses her muscles. Encouragement and explanations are necessary to promote relaxation. The patient is repeatedly assured that soon her discomfort will be gone.

Since the patient's position largely determines the level of anesthesia, the nurse must know exactly what position the physician desires and for what period of time. The nurse then makes the patient as comfortable as possible in the prescribed position.

The patient must be watched very closely for a fall in blood pressure, for the fetus suffers from even moderate degrees of maternal hypotension. Should a drop occur, immediate intervention is necessary. Either the patient is turned on her left side, or the uterus is manually displaced from midline. Both actions remove the weight of the uterus from the vena cava, with subsequent improved cardiac return and increased cardiac output.

Oxygen is given to the patient for the welfare of the fetus. Whenever epidural, caudal, or spinal anesthesia is initiated, an intravenous infusion is mandatory. Should hypotension occur, the intravenous rate is increased. The nurse must remember, however, that although 250 ml in 15 minutes may be therapeutic, 1,000 ml in an hour is potentially dangerous. If the intravenous drip rate is increased, the nurse determines with the physician when the rate is to be reduced.

Vasopressors are contraindicated in pregnant women. Vasoconstriction causes reduced placental blood flow, which further insults the fetus. With a fall in blood pressure, many patients experience nausea and feelings of apprehension. Anxiety compounds the existing problem, so that every effort should be made to promote patient relaxation.

When caudal and epidural anesthesia are used, an anesthesiologist or the attending physician should be immediately available. The nurse should seek physician consultation if any changes in the patient's vital signs are observed. The nurse reports the onset of tremors, or complaints of dizziness or dyspnea. Whenever regional anesthesia is used, the patient is fully conscious of her surroundings. This fact must be remembered when her condition is discussed by health personnel.

The patient may be disappointed when she realizes that regional anesthesia does not block sensations of touch and pressure. The nurse reassures her that she will remain comparatively free from discomfort even though she continues to experience these sensations.

Nursing care of the patient receiving regional anesthesia necessitates follow-up. Patients who have received spinal or saddle blocks should be instructed to force fluids and remain flat for a designated time. The possibility of a headache should not be suggested to the patient. After delivery, if the epidural or caudal anesthesia was continuous, the catheter must be removed; the nurse may need to remind the physician to do so.

Pudendal Nerve Block

Pudendal nerve block anesthesia is injected by the physician or nurse midwife after the patient is draped for delivery. A successful block relieves discomfort caused by distention of the perineal tissue and provides anesthesia for incising and suturing the episiotomy. Pudendal block anesthesia does not affect uterine contractions, discomfort produced by the contractions, or the patient's ability to bear down.

To execute the technique, the operator inserts a 10-cm-long needle directly through the perineal tissue; or the needle may be covered with a guide and inserted through the vagina. In either case the ischial spines are palpated and used as landmarks for the injection of the blocking agent. Frequently, inhalation analgesia is used as an adjunct to pudendal block. Pudendal block anesthesia is relatively safe for both the mother and baby.[21]

Local Infiltration

Local infiltration is one of the simplest and safest methods of anesthesia used at delivery. A nerve blocking agent is injected directly into the tissue posterior to the introitus. Its only function is to prevent discomfort associated with performing and repairing the episiotomy. Following delivery, the blocking agent may be manually infiltrated into the surrounding tissue to permit pain-free suturing.

The nurse ensures that the patient receiving any form of regional anesthesia is prepared for each step. Verbal explanations are offered to the patient prior to, during, and after procedures, taking care to explain the details. The unknown causes apprehension, and simple explanations are vital.

Available methods of anesthesia are generally discussed with the patient during pregnancy. However, unforeseen developments of labor and delivery may necessitate change of plans. Some patients discover that labor is more uncomfortable than they had anticipated; others have complications that influence the choice of anesthesia. Nursing explanations that reinforce and augment the physician's explanations are valuable in helping the patient accept the method used.

PREPARATION FOR DELIVERY

Transferring the Patient

The patient is transferred *unhurriedly* to the delivery room; last-minute rushed trips should be avoided. The patient is already apprehensive, and frantic activity adds greatly to her general uneasiness. The anxiety of her partner will also increase at this time, particularly if he will not be present in the delivery room. The parents-to-be need a brief moment to share words of encouragement, perhaps an embrace. The nurse should, if possible, offer the couple this privacy.

During this period an atmosphere is created in which the patient develops confidence and trust in those caring for her, an atmosphere in which she feels her behavior is accepted and realizes she is a very special woman.

The nurse can demonstrate caring and enhance this feeling by simply explaining occurring events. Delivery rooms are designed for asepsis and efficiency. To the uninitiated they appear stark and foreboding. The nurse anticipates this reaction and encourages the couple to ask questions about the environment and predelivery activities.

The move to the delivery room requires that the nurse plan for some problems of logistics. Contemporary obstetrical care requires considerable equipment. The couple themselves may have been instructed to bring their own supplies for the process of "natural" childbirth. The nurse must know which medical equipment needs to be transferred, as well as how to disconnect and/or transport it quickly. Patients are very sensitive to skill in those upon whom they are so totally dependent. The nurse is also responsible for safe storage of the couples' personal belongings.

Oxygen may have been given to the patient for the benefit of the fetus. The nurse should plan for immediate continuation in the delivery room. The patient may need help in moving from the bed to the delivery table. The bed is held securely against the delivery table as the patient transfers so that it will not roll away as weight is shifted. Movement is planned for the interval between contractions. The nurse should remember that to the patient, who usually slides and wiggles to the delivery table on her back, the short distance she actually moves may seem enormous. A hand extended to the patient from the opposite side of the table is both symbolically and physically helpful. This may necessitate the presence of a second person in the delivery room. Teamwork is needed for the movement from the labor room to the delivery room, and from the labor bed to the delivery table.

The Delivery Room

Setting Priorities

The delivery-room nurse sets priorities. It is necessary to keep the patient as comfortable as possible, monitor fetal heart tones by watching the electronic monitor or by listening with a fetoscope, take the blood pressure and pulse, prepare the sterile supplies at the appropriate time, call the anesthesiologist, or have equipment available for the attending physician to insert a regional or local

anesthetic. The nurse prepares oxytocic drugs, may monitor an intravenous infusion, scrubs the patient's perineal area, prepares identification for the newborn, charts necessary information, assists the physician, monitors contractions by observing the electronic monitor and/or by palpation, and at the same time reassures and supplies information to the patient and her partner.

The nurse reassures the patient best by talking slowly into her ear, letting her know that she is progressing well and that her baby will soon be born. The nurse realizes that the patient is very introverted at this time, and it is necessary to gain her attention in order for her to understand what is going on about her.[22] This usually requires much repetition in helping her to know what is occurring during this stage of labor. The nurse may have the father, if present, relay information to the patient.

It is believed by some health care personnel that if the father is permitted in the delivery room, the staff find themselves with two patients. Instead, experience has shown that an informed father is of great benefit, not only to the parturient but to the health care team. Few nurses who work with prepared couples have had to assist the father from the delivery room. It has been found, primarily through trial and error, that the father is most effective and can best share in the birth process if he is positioned on a chair or stool close to the patient's head. In this position he can continue supporting and coaching her. Mirrors are positioned so that both parents can observe the progress being made and the actual delivery. If the prospective parents so desire, the father can be guided by the nurse to the end of the delivery table for the actual birth of the infant.

The technical skills of the delivery-room nurse are not complex. But the nurse must be capable of performing them precisely and quickly while she or he continues to observe and encourage the patient. Setting priorities is of utmost importance.

Nursing Tasks in the Delivery Room

Final positioning and cleansing of the patient is delayed until *immediately* prior to delivery. During the actual delivery, the nurse plans to stand at the patient's head so that she can be observed closely and given the needed encouragement and instruction. Immediately following delivery, the neonate requires the attention of the nurse. Nurses learn with experience to organize nursing tasks. Optimally, a second nursing staff member assists. When this is impossible, the nurse assesses which tasks to perform first, and which might be postponed until the new mother and baby no longer require immediate attention. Organization is based on applying knowledge of the sequence of events. For example, the baby must be placed in a warm receptacle before he or she is identified. Therefore, if the nurse is hurried and must choose whether to prepare the warmer or the identification bands, obviously the warmer would be prepared first. In like manner, the doctor will need gloves before the forceps.

The prompt administration of oxytocic drugs is crucially important in the prevention of hemorrhage. The nurse must know the drug, the dosage, and the administration route that the physician prefers in order to readily prepare and administer it. Injectable lactation-suppressant drugs are usually given with delivery of the fetal shoulders; these too must be prepared in advance.

Accurate charting is essential for both legal reasons and optimal patient care. Information recorded in the delivery room is used later for planning care both for the new mother and the neonate.

Nursing tasks are dictated by the direct or indirect needs of the patient. Hospital procedures define the method used in performing tasks. Task performance is only one portion of nursing care, but task mastery frees the nurse to *care* for the patient.

Aseptic Technique

At the time of delivery, the patient's normal defenses against infection are disrupted. Organisms can enter the body through breaks in the mucous membrane of the birth canal. The endometrium of the uterus is also exposed to invading organisms. Delivery-room care incorporates many aseptic principles of the operating room. While the nurse is responsible for the provision of sterile equipment, ancillary departments and personnel may actually prepare and package the equipment and supplies. Nursing knowledge, however, is necessary for use, planning, and evaluation.

The instrument table is prepared when the patient is transferred into the delivery room, or it may be prepared a short time in advance and uncovered at the time of delivery. Basically, instruments are provided that enable the physician or nurse midwife to cut the cord, perform and repair the episiotomy, and inspect the cervix and vagina. The instrument table also includes sterile drapes which cover the patient's legs, thighs, and abdomen at the time of delivery. Other items are added according to the attendant's preference and needs and hospital routine.

Nurses may or may not scrub and gown to assist with a vaginal delivery. The nurse assists the physician or nurse midwife with gowning and gloving, and continuously observes for breaks in aseptic technique. Nurses who care for patients in the delivery room should refer to a manual of operating-room aseptic technique because infections

constitute one of the three most fatal complications of pregnancy. Every effort is made to
prevent those infections which are acquired
at the time of delivery. Because the neonate
and parturient are so vulnerable, personnel
caring for them must comply with stringent
regulations regarding possible and diagnosed infections.

Scrub suits and dresses are generally worn
in the delivery room. Personnel change
clothing upon entering the labor and delivery suite to reduce the possibility of carrying in organisms from other parts of the hospital and the outside. Furthermore, some
soiling of the clothing is inevitable in the
care of the delivery patient. For both aesthetic and aseptic reasons, frequent changes
of clothing are necessary. Masks are worn to
protect the patient from pathogenic organisms that may be present in the respiratory
tract. The parturient is especially vulnerable
to streptococcal infections.

Positioning the Patient

The position of choice for delivery in hospitals in the United States and the Western
world is the lithotomy. This position is favored by physicians who claim better control
during expulsion of the head and shoulders;
suturing is facilitated, and improved application of aseptic technique is permitted.

These arguments supporting the lithotomy
position are debatable in that they may very
well be more physician-oriented than patient-oriented. Physiologically as well as
anthropologically speaking, this position
may not be optimum for facilitation of the
childbearing process. Primates, of which
humans are just one division, have for time
immemorial delivered their newborn in a
squatting position. Peoples of the non-Western world continue to use this squat position
for delivery. It is only in the modernized,
technically and scientifically advanced
Western world and like areas of the non-
Western world that the lithotomy position,
or in some countries the Sims's position, is
thought to be the optimum. But is it really?
Are not the body muscles involved in the
birth process so constructed to function most
efficiently in a squat position? Do health
care personnel not attempt to simulate the
squat position, albeit rather ineffectively, by
utilizing the lithotomy position for delivery?
Are not the physiological forces of gravity
functioning optimally when the patient is in
the squat position? Has adaptation to the
squat position not proved for other primates
to be the most efficient birth position for
millennia? Answers to these questions can
only be found through research in this area.
Currently, there is a dearth of such research
relative to this issue; the field is wide open
for *nursing research.*

The patient's legs are not placed in stirrups until the obstetrician or nurse midwife
scrubs for the delivery. The nurse positions
and adjusts the stirrups, however, and explains their function and purpose to the
patient.

She is asked to move her buttocks (or
whatever term she will understand) to the
section where the table separates. The stirrups are then adjusted properly. Pressure on
the popliteal region can cause nerve damage
or predispose to thrombophlebitis. The
weight of the leg should be supported so that
the foot is approximately the same height as
the knee. Exaggerated spreading of the
thighs can also cause injury to the patient.
(See Figure 22-5.)

To adjust the stirrups, the patient draws
her legs up in a bent position at the knees.
The nurse places the stirrups at the same
height as the patient's knees. The length is
adjusted according to the patient's leg. The
stirrups must be turned slightly outward,
away from the site of delivery. The patient's
legs are then placed *simultaneously* in the

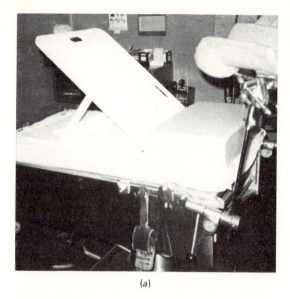
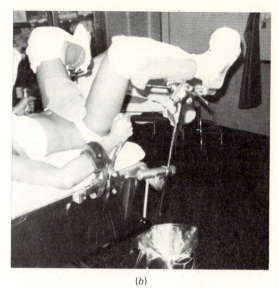

(a)   (b)

FIGURE 22-5
Suggestions for positioning a patient. (a) A backrest can be added to the table for
elevation. Stirrups may be omitted, in which case the table remains extended.
(b) The leg is extended straight from the knee to prevent popliteal pressure. Further
protection is provided by padding the stirrups with foam rubber and then covering
them with heavy plastic. The wrist straps permit the arm to slide but not reach out. A
handgrip has been grasped.

stirrups after the adjustments are made to determine if they are properly fitted; again they
may need to be altered. If the stirrups are adjusted correctly in height and length, the patient will be more comfortable, and cramps
in the legs may be prevented. In the event
that leg cramps do occur, the nurse
straightens the patient's leg, slips one hand
under the patient's knee, and then applies
pressure against the patient's toes with the
other hand causing the foot to bend toward
the body. Leg cramps generally disappear
with this prompt action.

Handgrips are adjusted, but the wrist cuffs
are not fastened until the patient is cleansed
for delivery. Wrist cuffs are one of the most
disliked parts of the delivery process. Patients state they do not like being strapped
down, or object to "wearing handcuffs."

There is probably a feeling of being deprived
of independence and human dignity. At the
time the cuffs are fastened, reasons for their
use are explained.

Many delivery rooms have overhead mirrors which the patient may use for viewing.
She should be given the opportunity to decide if she wants to use the mirrors or not.
The nurse makes sure that the patient who
wants to watch her delivery has the mirror
adjusted properly. Eyeglasses which may
have been removed during labor are returned
to the patient at this time.

Cleansing the Patient

Immediately after she is placed in lithotomy
position, the patient is cleansed for delivery.
Cleansing procedures vary considerably

from one hospital to another, but the nurse should be aware of certain basic points: the equipment and technique are designed to remove tenacious contaminants from the skin; soaps are irritating and need to be rinsed off; iodophors are the most efficacious antiseptic agents, and tinctures are not recommended for perineal cleansing unless the area is anesthetized. Solutions are cold, and the patient is prepared for this before the nurse begins the procedure.

The nurse prepares the patient for delivery by scrubbing the vulva and lower thighs. The general principle is to scrub from the labia outward, without retracing the movements. (See Figure 22-6.) The nurse *never* removes the gloves and does not leave the end of the delivery table until replaced by the physician. The nurse is responsible for observing the perineum and protecting the baby should birth occur. In the meantime, the attendant has scrubbed, gowned, and gloved for the delivery.

THE DELIVERY

After the patient is draped, the physician or nurse midwife makes a final check of the position and station of the fetal head or presenting part. If the head has rotated, or is rotating well, and if the patient is able to bear down when instructed, a spontaneous delivery may be anticipated. At this time, the patient again needs the nurse's reassuring presence and will also need an interpretation of the actions expected of her.

As the attendant directs the patient, the nurse nonverbally supports the patient in her efforts by perhaps placing a hand on her shoulder or wiping her forehead. It is very difficult for the patient to respond when more than one person directs her. She may have to be informed when a uterine contraction is occurring, depending on the type of anesthetic being administered, and she may need continuous help in bearing down or panting, or a whispered "It won't be long now."

As the fetal head bulges the perineum, the attendant prepares to slowly and guardedly deliver the head. After the occiput passes under the symphysis pubis, the Ritgen's maneuver is employed. (See Figure 22-7.) The attendant places a towel over the rectum and gently presses the baby's chin, at the same time holding the other hand over the occiput. Extension is completed with the Ritgen's maneuver. The attendant attempts to deliver the head slowly between contractions to prevent trauma to the fetal head and maternal tissue. Upon delivery of the head, the infant's neck is examined to ascertain if the umbilical cord is encircling it and, if so, it is slipped over the head. If the cord is too short and tight, it must be clamped and cut immediately to prevent fetal asphyxiation.

As soon as the head emerges from the vagina, it restitutes to the position in which it entered the maternal pelvis. The oropharynx is then suctioned with a Davidson bulb, catheter, or mucus trap to prevent aspiration of amniotic fluid, mucus, or meconium in case the infant should gasp or inhale prior to complete expulsion. The shoulders, which entered the pelvis in the same position as the head, must now rotate to an anteroposterior position. The physician or nurse midwife

FIGURE 22-6
Perineal scrub before delivery.

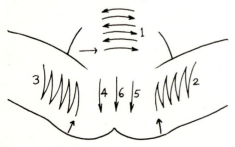

FIGURE 22-7
Ritgen's maneuver. (From Elise Fitzpatrick, Sharon R. Reeder, and Luigi Mastroianni, Jr., Maternity Nursing, 12th ed., Lippincott, Philadelphia, 1971, p. 265.)

guides the delivery of the shoulders by grasping the head with both hands and directing the head, first downward to deliver the anterior shoulder, and then upward for the posterior shoulder. (See Figure 22-8.) If the mother is watching in the mirror, she may be distressed by this maneuver. The nurse can redirect her attention by telling her to "listen for the baby." With delivery of the shoulders, the chest emerges immediately, the infant gasps, and the lungs promptly expand. Once the shoulders are delivered, there is no further delay in expulsion. The nurse may be asked to apply suprapubic pressure to help bring the anterior shoulder under the symphysis pubis.

The mother is informed of the baby's sex and is given opportunity to see and touch the infant as soon as possible. This is a time when the nurse can share with the mother in her achievement and joy. It is a climactic moment for the mother and father when the doctor holds the baby within their view. Often the infant is placed on the mother's abdomen for initial care. If the nurse or father helps the mother lift her shoulders, the mother can

watch this activity. (See Figure 22-9.) The nurse notes the exact time of birth for charting and for legal certification of the birth.

The length of time between the delivery of the newborn and the clamping of the cord varies among physicians. Hellman and Pritchard state that it is still unclear what the ideal time for the cord to be clamped is. They also state that an advantage from placental transfusion is the addition of approximately 50 mg of iron which helps to prevent later iron deficiency anemia.[23] Babson and Benson believe that the umbilical cord should be clamped and cut 15 to 20 seconds

FIGURE 22-8
The infant's head is held to assist the delivery of the shoulders. (By permission from Louis M. Hellman and Jack A. Pritchard, Williams Obstetrics, Appleton-Century-Crofts, New York, 1971, p. 413.)

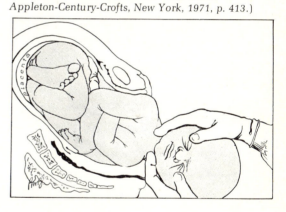

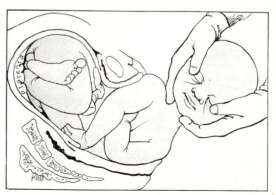

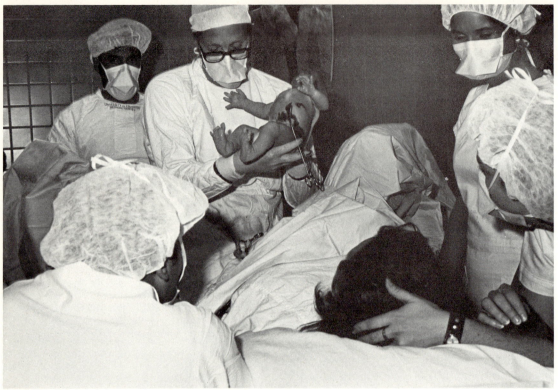

FIGURE 22-9
A successful delivery is promoted by the cooperative interaction of all members of
the health team and the family. (*Courtesy of The University of Colorado Medical
Center, Denver, Colo.*)

following delivery and that the attendant should wait, holding the baby at the placental level, until the infant takes a breath or two. However, they do not believe the time period should be extended if a breath has not been taken.[24] Preliminary findings by Moss, Duffie, and Fagan recommend delaying clamping of the cord. Their evidence reveals that clamping of the cord before the beginning of respirations could be a factor in pathogenesis of respiratory distress syndrome.[25] Taylor, Bright, and Birchard suggest late clamping of the cord may cause overinfusion with placental blood and believe the addition of blood from the placenta

does not benefit the premature infant.[26] The cord is cut immediately if the mother is receiving general anesthesia or if she is Rh-negative. In the former case, it is done to reduce narcosis in the neonate; in the latter, to reduce maternal sensitization. The physician places two hemostats on the baby's cord and cuts the cord between the clamps. After the cord is cut, either an umbilical clamp or a tie is securely placed approximately 2 cm from the baby's abdomen.

Many hospitals use the Apgar score for the evaluation of the newborn. This is done at 1 and again at 5 minutes following birth and includes evaluation of the infant's heart rate, respiratory effort, muscle tone, reflex irritability, and color. An example of an Apgar score chart can be found in Chapter 25. The physician and/or the nurse determines the Apgar score and the infant's condition. It has been found that Apgar scores determined by the attending physician are often higher than the values estimated by a more objective attendant, such as a nurse or anesthetist. The evaluation results are noted on the chart. The infant is then placed on his or her side in a heated crib, since this position facilitates drainage of mucus secretions. The infant is dried to reduce loss of body heat through evaporation and covered.

Most mothers have a strong need to touch the baby immediately. The actual touching of the infant affirms the infant's reality. As soon as the nurse is satisfied that the infant is breathing well, one of the mother's hands should be freed, and the infant carried to her so that she can hold her infant for a few minutes if so desired. The nurse should arrange the position of the heated crib in a way that the mother can watch the care of her baby.

Episiotomy

An episiotomy is an incision which enlarges the vaginal outlet. It may be made medially or mediolaterally when 3 to 4 cm of the fetal head become visible. (See Figure 22-10.) By making an incision, the attendant decreases chances of lacerations of the vulva, vagina, and rectum occurring with delivery of the head and shoulders. Incisions heal more readily than lacerations. Excessive stretching of the fascia and muscle of the pelvic floor may lead to later bladder and bowel control problems; the episiotomy reduces the amount of stretching necessary for expulsion. Injury to the fetal head may result from the propulsive force of labor and the counterresistance of the perineum; premature infants are especially vulnerable. Conse-

quently, the episiotomy may be done to protect the infant.[27] Except for patients of high parity and patients with severe varicosities of the vulva, the episiotomy is a regular procedure at delivery.

A midline incision has advantages in that it repairs more easily, heals better, and causes less postpartum pain than the mediolateral episiotomy. The latter may also cause later dyspareunia. Justification for the use of the mediolateral approach is based on the possibility that the midline incision may be insufficient for delivery, and consequently extend and tear the rectum. Many authorities believe that a well-repaired rectal (fourth-degree) extension is preferable to a mediolateral episiotomy.

The patient is forewarned when the episiotomy is done, because it is possible she may feel pressure or, perhaps, some discomfort. In an emergency situation, an episiotomy may be done with no anesthesia. The pressure of the emerging head causes ischemia and reduces sensitivity of the perineum. During closure of the episiotomy, the patient

FIGURE 22-10

Episiotomy. Incision site (A) is for the median episiotomy and (B) is for the mediolateral.

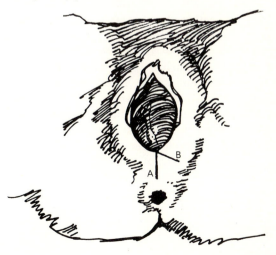

is informed that the sutures will be absorbed by the body. Many patients worry needlessly about having their episiotomy stitches removed.

The Forceps Delivery

When the fetal head is visible and has rotated completely to an occiput anterior position, the physician may elect to do an outlet forcep delivery. Control of the head, gained by the use of outlet forceps, may reduce trauma to the fetal head and maternal tissue. The tired patient is spared another 15 to 30 minutes of pushing. Forceps are used only if the patient has received some type of anesthesia. In the event of maternal or fetal complications, forceps may be indicated. However, the cervix must be fully dilated and the head fully engaged.[28]

Patients often have negative feelings about use of forceps. The nurse can reassure the patient that the baby will be benefited by their use.

The Leboyer Method

The Leboyer method is based on the premise that the infant suffers psychological shock at the time of delivery.[29] Effort is made to reduce the contrast between the intrauterine environment and the outside world. Lights and voices are kept low in the delivery room. Cutting of the cord is delayed until pulsation stops; the infant is then immersed in a tub of warm water. Skin-to-skin contact with the mother is provided, and the infant is fondled and stroked. In his book *Birth without Violence,* Dr. Leboyer gives a detailed explanation of this method of delivery.

THE BABY

Assessment and care of the newborn at the time of delivery initiates an ongoing process. Delivery-room care always includes measures that ensure safety, ventilation, maintenance of body temperature, and identification. The Apgar score, by definition, must be determined immediately after birth. Prophylactic eye care may be done in the delivery room or at the time of admission to the nursery. Chapter 25 describes the nursing process for the neonate.

CONCLUSION

Each woman in labor is unique in that she reacts to discomfort, expresses fear, and responds to the nurse differently. With the nursing process, these differences are determined, and patients and their families are evaluated as individuals and as family units. The nurse, patient, and family form a plan to meet their needs, although unexpected needs may necessitate revision of the original plan.

The nurse's actions are focused on the patient's and the baby's welfare. After the baby is born is an appropriate time to review the nursing care that the patient received and evaluate what was effective, what the nurse would change if the experience could be repeated, and what was gained by this family through the role the nurse played. Did the type of nursing help to make the delivery a truly meaningful experience for this family? By this type of evaluation, maternity nurses are born.

REFERENCES

1 Hellman, Louis M., and Jack A. Pritchard: *Williams Obstetrics,* 14th ed., Appleton-Century-Crofts, New York, 1971, p. 362.
2 Fitzpatrick, Elise, Sharon R. Reeder, and Luigi Mastroianni: *Maternity Nursing,* 12th ed., Lippincott, Philadelphia, 1971, p. 258.
3 Danforth, David N.: *Textbook of Obstetrics and Gynecology,* 2d ed., Harper & Row, New York, 1971, p. 567.

4   Ziegel, Erna, and Carolyn Conant Van Blar-
    com: *Obstetric Nursing*, 6th ed., Macmillan,
    New York, 1971, p. 299.
5   Fitzpatrick, et al.: op. cit., p. 259.
6   Oxorn, Harry: *Human Labor and Birth*, 3d
    ed., Appleton-Century-Crofts, New York,
    1975, p. 112.
7   Jordan, Doreen A.: "Evaluation of a Family-
    centered Maternity Care Hospital Program—
    Part III," *Journal of Obstetric, Gynecologic
    and Neonatal Nursing*, 2:17, 1973.
8   Ibid., p. 18.
9   Kowalski, Karren E.: " 'On-Call' Staffing,"
    American Journal of Nursing, 73(10):1725–
    1727, October 1973.
10 Lubic, Ruth Watson: "What the Lay Person
    Expects of Maternity Care," *Journal of Ob-
    stetric, Gynecologic and Neonatal Nursing*,
    1:30, 1972.
11 Cassidy, Jean E.: "A Nurse Looks at Child-
    birth Anxiety," *Journal of Obstetric, Gyneco-
    logic and Neonatal Nursing*, 3:53, 1974.
12 Hellman and Pritchard: op. cit., p. 430.
13 Wallace, Helen M., Edwin M. Gold, and Ed-
    ward F. Lis: *Maternal and Child Health Prac-
    tices*, Thomas, Springfield, Ill., 1973, p. 407.
14 Bergersen, Betty S., and Andres Goth: *Phar-
    macology in Nursing*, 12th ed., Mosby, St.
    Louis, 1973, pp. 294–296.
15 Shnider, Sol M.: *Obstetrical Anesthesia, Cur-
    rent Concepts and Practice*, Williams & Wil-
    kins, Baltimore, 1970, p. 151.
16 Shnider, Sol M., and Frank Mayo: *The Anes-
    thesiologist, Mother and Newborn*, Williams
    & Wilkins, Baltimore, 1974, p. 69.
17 Ibid., p. 124.
18 Ibid., p. 61.
19 Shnider: op. cit., p. 82.
20 Ziegel and Van Blarcom: op. cit., p. 316–318.
21 Hellman and Pritchard: op. cit., pp. 439–442.
22 Rubin, Reva: "Puerperal Change," *Nursing
    Outlook*, 9:754, 1961.
23 Hellman and Pritchard: op. cit., p. 415.
24 Babson, S. G., and Ralph C. Benson: *Primer
    on Prematurity and High-Risk Pregnancy*,
    Mosby, St. Louis, 1966, p. 81.
25 Moss, A. J., E. Duffie, and L. M. Fagan: "Res-
    piratory Distress in the Newborn: Study on
    the Association of Cord Clamping and the
    Pathogenesis of Disease," *Journal of the
    American Medical Association*, 184:50,
    1963.
26 Taylor, P. M., N. H. Bright, and E. L. Bir-
    chard: "Effect of Early versus Delayed
    Clamping of the Umbilical Cord on the Clini-
    cal Condition of the Newborn Infant," *Ameri-
    can Journal of Diseases of Children*, 98:650,
    1959.
27 Oxorn: op. cit., p. 407.
28 Danforth: op. cit., pp. 577, 630.
29 Leboyer, Frederick: *Birth without Violence*,
    Knopf, New York, 1975.

BIBLIOGRAPHY

Bryan, William: "Care and Repair of the Peri-
    neum," *Nursing Times*, 7(9):301–302, Feb.
    28, 1974.
———: "Careful Maternity Nursing," *Nursing 73*,
    3(3):36–43, March 1973.
Eyres, Patricia J.: "The Role of the Nurse in
    Family-centered Nursing Care," *Nursing
    Clinics of North America*, 7(1):27–40, March
    1972.
Fleming, Georgianna: "Delivering a Happy
    Father," *American Journal of Nursing*, 72(5):
    949–950, May 1972.
Grim, Linda M.: "Maternity Continuity Care
    Clinic," *American Journal of Nursing*,
    73(10):1723–1725, October 1973.
Sasmor, Jeannette L.: "Stress Adaptation: A Theory
    for Childbirth Education," *Journal of Ob-
    stetric, Gynecologic and Neonatal Nursing*,
    2(6):48–50, November–December 1973.

23

The Third Stage of Labor

VIVIAN MOORE LITTLEFIELD

To be effective, complete, and patient-centered, nursing care should be goal-directed. This is particularly important in the third stage of labor, the placental stage, since the baby has just arrived and requires skilled nursing care that will establish the infant in his or her new environment physically, psychologically, and socially. The mother's care is extremely important, too, for it is during this stage that there is high incidence of postpartum hemorrhage. In addition to the physical care of the mother and newborn, the nurse should encourage the mother to feel she has successfully accomplished a great task in giving birth to her new baby.

Most hospital routines require the completion of various charts and forms by the nurse. If the nurse does not have specific nursing goals in mind, nursing care may become disorganized and therefore incomplete. The rush and excitement often present in delivery rooms has lessened during the third stage, and if no complications arise, the nurse could relax and become busy with the numerous forms and reports required at this time unless there are specific goals in mind. Therefore, this chapter will identify specific goals, based on the needs of the mother, newborn, and family following childbirth, through the placental stage, and until the patient leaves the delivery room. Following the identification of these goals, the basic knowledge necessary to accomplish them will be presented as well as identification of various tasks that accomplish each.

The overall goal in patient care during the third stage of labor should be *to provide as physically healthy a mother and infant as possible and encourage the establishment of the family unit.*

The third stage of labor, or the placental stage, begins with the birth of the baby and is completed with the expulsion of the placenta. During this stage the placenta separates and is expelled. This involves the forces of uterine contraction and intraabdominal pressure.

The first hour immediately following the expulsion of the placenta has been termed the *fourth stage of labor.* This critical time *after* the expulsion of the placenta is the time postpartum hemorrhage due to uterine atony is most likely to occur. The nursing care of the patient after leaving the delivery room will be discussed in the following chapters.

In order to provide adequate care and to set proper nursing goals, the nurse must know the changes taking place in the new mother and the newborn during this stage of labor. Since the needs and the immediate care of the newborn were covered in the previous chapter and will be further discussed in following chapters, goals for the newborn's care will only be summarized. The nurse should remember that as care is given to the mother in the third stage, care for the newborn is going on concurrently. Often the nurse must set priorities for care between the mother and

the newborn because of the problems that each might develop which require reordering of care. The nurse may need to call for assistance from other nurses or specialists, such as a pediatrician or obstetrician, when the situation indicates.

There are also several goals of nursing care that were begun prior to the third stage of labor which the nurse must keep in mind as goals specific to the third stage are carried out. Since the tasks involved in meeting these goals have been covered in previous chapters concerning labor and delivery, they will only be identified here for completeness. Goals that were begun previously and should continually be met are:

1 Prevention of infection in the mother and infant by strict aseptic technique
2 Provision of safety for the mother and infant by maintenance of equipment, control of personnel in and out of the delivery room, proper administration of medications, proper positioning of the new mother, and proper care in handling the newborn
3 Assistance to the attendant so that there is adequate equipment or information essential to providing adequate obstetric care
4 Assurance of the maintenance of dignity and self-respect for the new mother, her husband (or significant other), and baby

ESTABLISHING TWO SEPARATE INDIVIDUALS—MOTHER AND BABY

Nursing Knowledge Needed

The knowledge needed by the nurse to meet the goal of establishing two individuals, mother and baby, concerns the physiology involved in the placental separation and delivery. The nurse must know methods used

478

to assist in the separation and expulsion of the placenta when this occurs naturally, and the problems that can result from inadequate placental separation and expulsion. By knowing the signs of inadequate placental separation, the nurse can detect any problems present and assist the attendant in solving them. The nurse also must know which drugs can be used to prevent hemorrhage, as well as the side effects of these drugs. The nurse needs to know why it is important for the entire placenta to be delivered and the appropriate procedures when it is not entirely delivered. By knowing these purposes and procedures, an explanation

can be offered to the patient in the event the placenta is delivered incompletely. The nurse also needs knowledge of the technique by which the cord is cut and the physiology involved in this process.

After the baby is born, the uterus contracts at regular intervals. There is less content without the baby, and consequently, the area of placental attachment is greatly reduced. This disproportion between the uterus and the placenta brings about a folding of the maternal surface of the placenta and causes separation to take place. Bleeding occurs in the placental folds and expedites placental separation. The placenta then moves into the

FIGURE 23-1
The climax for a family that has actively participated in the birth process. The nurse can do much to facilitate this participation. (*By permission of The University of Colorado Medical Center, Denver, Colo.*)

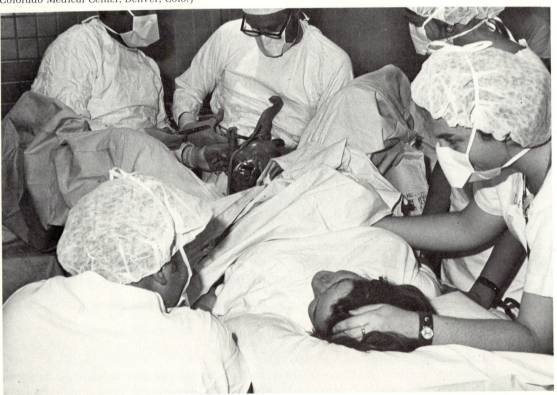

lower uterine segment or upper vagina as an unattached body. The nurse should be familiar with the signs which suggest the placenta has separated. These are:

1   The uterus rises upward in the abdomen because the placenta has moved down into the lower uterine segment. Figure 23-2 indicates the shape of the uterus when this occurs.

2   The umbilical cord protrudes 7 or more centimeters from the vagina which indicates that the placenta has descended.

3   The uterus assumes a globular shape and becomes more firm. (See Figure 23-2.)

4   A sudden gush of blood often occurs and is the result of the separation of the placenta.

5   The cord fails to recede when the uterus is elevated.[1]

These signs of placental detachment usually appear from 1 to 5 minutes after the delivery of the infant. As long as the uterus remains firm and there is no excessive bleeding, the attendant waits until the placenta is separated. No massage is practiced before placental detachment since massage is usually futile and possibly dangerous.[2] The major goal in managing the separation and explusion of the placenta is to prevent unnecessary blood loss. This is accomplished by making sure that the uterus is firmly contracted and that the placenta is expelled as soon as possible.

Awareness that there are many open areas from which the uterus might bleed helps the nurse understand the importance of the uterus contracting and becoming globular immediately after the placenta has separated. If the uterus relaxes after the placenta separates, the chance of hemorrhage is great.

Once the placenta has separated, it must be expelled. This usually can be accomplished by the patient's bearing down in the same way as when she assisted with the birth of the baby. The mother at this point may be dozing, distracted from the birth process, or engaged in watching her newborn. The nurse should coach her in bearing down so

FIGURE 23-2

Shape of the uterus before (left) and after (right) separation of the placenta. (*From E. Stewart Taylor, Beck's Obstetrical Practice, 9th ed., Williams & Wilkins, Baltimore, 1971, p. 199, by permission of the publisher.*)

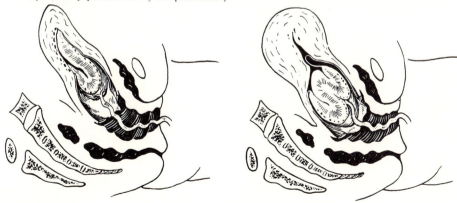

that the placenta is expelled with the least amount of effort and trauma. It has been stated that when the mother is involved and uses her own efforts, it prevents some of the fetal blood present in the placenta from entering the maternal blood. This crossing of fetal blood into the maternal blood often occurs with manual assistance and causes sensitization of the maternal blood when the mother is Rh-negative.

When the patient is anesthetized she cannot fully assist with expelling the placenta. Therefore, she must be assisted by the attendant or, in some situations, by the nurse under the attendant's guidance. This procedure is as follows: (1) palpate the fundus to be *certain* that the uterus is firm; (2) exert downward pressure with one hand on the fundus of the uterus; and (3) employ the placenta as a piston, and push the placenta out of the vagina.[3] This placental expression should be done with gentleness and without squeezing. If it is attempted when the uterus is boggy, *inversion of the uterus,* an extremely dangerous complication, may occur. After separation of the placenta, expulsion should occur quickly in order to prevent unnecessary blood loss. The uterus cannot contract properly until the placenta has been removed. In order to prevent blood loss, constant application of the hand to the uterine fundus *after* birth of the infant to detect first signs of placental detachment, vigorous massage after separation, and immediate delivery of the placenta will decrease the amount of blood loss.[4] Some attendants may follow this procedure and may ask the nurse's assistance in detecting the detachment of the placenta, in massage of the fundus, and expression of the placenta after delivery. This is especially true when anesthesia prevents the patient from bearing down to assist in this procedure. Figure 23-3 demonstrates the expression of the placenta. It is also the nurse's responsibility to note the time of expulsion of the placenta.

The placenta is delivered by two methods which can be differentiated in Figure 23-4.[5] The first method, Schultz's mechanism, is said to occur in about 80 percent of deliveries. The placenta is turned inside out and is expelled with the fetal side presenting. The second method is called Duncan's mechanism and occurs in about 20 percent of the deliveries. In this method, the maternal side presents on delivery of the placenta.

It is estimated that even with efficient management of the third stage of labor, approximately 250 to 300 ml of blood are lost from the average patient. It is extremely important to estimate the amount of blood that is lost so that, if necessary, blood or intravenous fluids can be administered to the mother. It is important for the nurse who is caring for patients in the delivery room to be accurate in the estimation of blood loss. Knowing that the mother has lost an extra amount of blood will alert the nurse to assess the effect of the blood loss on the new mother. The patient's blood pressure and pulse should be taken frequently. The nurse must watch for other specific signs of hypovolemic shock, such as pale color, increase in respirations, euphoria, vertigo, restlessness, and air hunger. The nurse must also be prepared to administer blood or intravenous fluids immediately when ordered.

If the placenta does not separate promptly or if there is bleeding from the uterus, the obstetrician will proceed to remove the placenta manually. Figure 23-5 demonstrates this procedure.

A study of Figure 23-5 indicates that one disadvantage of manual removal of the placenta is introduction of infection into the uterine cavity. The nurse may need to assist the attendant in changing gloves, drapes, etc., if the delivery field becomes contaminated.

Taylor indicates that if manual removal is necessary, the more time between the birth of the baby and the manual removal of the placenta, the greater the chances are of infection in the uterus.[6]

The attendant inspects the placenta immediately after delivery to determine if any cotyledons have been retained. If placental fragments or entire cotyledons are retained, the chance of hemorrhage is increased because the uterus cannot contract completely. Retention of placental fragments is also conducive to infection. When the uterus attempts to contract but is unable to do so because of the retained fragments, these contractions cause the mother pain. If the fragments must be removed later, the procedure may cause additional bleeding and discomfort to the mother.

If the mother is experiencing pain during the placental expulsion, the nurse should provide support by assisting her to relax and providing an explanation of the events taking place. Coaching the mother by speaking into her ear is helpful in reinforcing the attendant's requests. The nurse can also support the mother by placing the hands gently but firmly on the mother's shoulders.

Retained placental fragments are a cause of late postpartum hemorrhage and often necessitate the mother returning to the hospital for dilatation and curettage after she has been dismissed.

Nursing Tasks

Care of the Mother

The nursing tasks involved in caring for the mother immediately after delivery are as follows:

FIGURE 23-3

Expression of the placenta. The fundus should be firm before this procedure is carried out. (*From Louis M. Hellman and Jack A. Pritchard,* Williams Obstetrics, *14th ed., Appleton-Century-Crofts, New York, 1971, p. 416, by permission of the publisher.*)

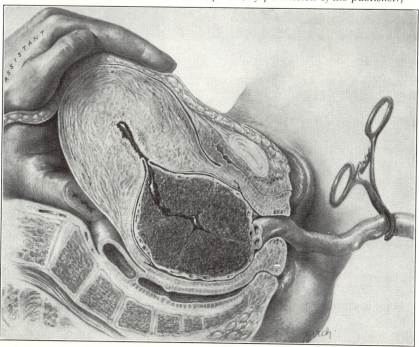

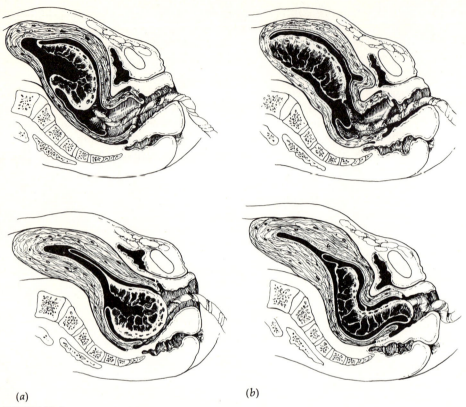

(a) *(b)*

FIGURE 23-4
Two methods of placental delivery. (a) Schultz method; (b) Duncan method. (*From Ralph C. Benson, Handbook of Obstetrics and Gynecology, 4th ed., Lange Medical Publications, Los Altos, Calif., 1971, pp. 134–135, by permission of the publisher.*)

1 Support and assist the mother in expelling the placenta.
2 Assist with the delivery of the placenta if indicated.
3 Observe blood loss and estimate the amount as accurately as possible.
4 Detect signs of uterine relaxation and hemorrhage by:
    a Taking the blood pressure and comparing it with previous readings.
    b Palpating the pulse and detecting a weak beat, increased rate, or other irregularity.
    c Measuring the height and degree of firmness of the fundus.

    d Apprising the attendant of any change in the mother's condition and, if none, informing him or her that all vital signs are stable and the fundus is firm.

Care of the Infant

The nursing goals and tasks involved in caring for the infant are as follows:

1 Assess the status of the newborn in relation to adaption to the extrauterine environment.

2 Assess the gross normality of the new-born infant.
3 Establish a patent airway.
4 Maintain adequate oxygenation.
5 Maintain body warmth.
6 Provide proper identification of the baby.
7 Prevent infection.

The reader is referred to Chapters 25 and 26 for detailed information regarding the tasks outlined for the newborn.

It should be emphasized that the nurse will have to set priorities, depending on the amount of assistance available and the problems that arise with either the mother or the baby. For example, let us say the nurse is checking the mother's vital signs to detect any sign of hemorrhage, and it is observed that the newborn's color is somewhat dusky. The nurse must immediately return to the newborn, identify the problem, and institute appropriate measures. After the baby's condition is stable the nurse must return to the assessment of the mother's situation.

FIGURE 23-5

Manual removal of the placenta. (a) Method of introducing the internal hand and creating pressure on the fundus with the external hand. (b) Technique of separating the placenta before it is removed. (From E. Stewart Taylor, Beck's Obstetrical Practice, 9th ed., Williams & Wilkins, Baltimore, 1971, p. 201, by permission of the publisher.)

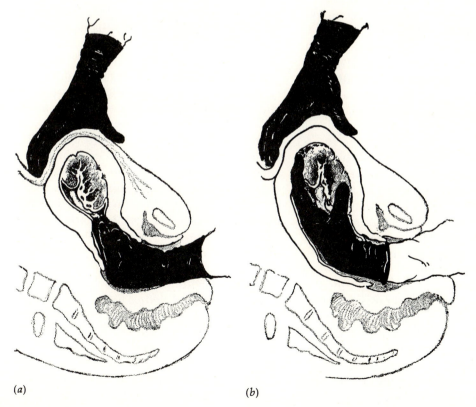

(a)   (b)

At the same time if there is *any* indication that the mother is bleeding excessively, then the nurse must ask for assistance from another nurse or from the attendant. Setting priorities, especially when complications arise, is a complex situation and requires knowledge, judgment, and action on the part of the nurse.

PREVENTION AND DETECTION OF HEMORRHAGE AND OTHER MATERNAL COMPLICATIONS

Nursing Knowledge Needed

The third stage of labor is dangerous for the mother because of the possibility of postpartum hemorrhage and resultant hypovolemic shock. Hemorrhage is said to occur if there is more than 500 ml of blood loss.[7] This amount of blood loss is fairly common even with the most skilled obstetric care. Every effort should be taken to avoid such an occurrence and to detect signs that might lead to hemorrhage before the hemorrhage occurs. Bleeding of 500 ml is encountered once in every 20 to 30 deliveries. Hemorrhages of 1,000 ml and over are encountered once in about every 75 cases, whereas a blood loss of 1,500 to 2,000 ml is only occasionally encountered. Based on this information, the nurse must constantly be aware of the status of bleeding in the new mother. Hemorrhage can be a result of *uterine atony, lacerations,* or *retained placental fragments.*

Hemorrhage in the delivery room and in the first hour postpartum is usually due to uterine atony, as this is the most common cause of hemorrhage at this time. If there is a blood loss of 1,000 ml, a blood transfusion may be given to prevent the possibility of infection, shock, acute kidney tubular necrosis, and pituitary and/or adrenal necrosis.[8]

The large blood vessels within the muscle fibers of the uterus and especially those in the placental site are open and gaping. Therefore, the nurse should recognize the necessity for the uterus to contract and stay contracted. If there is only a slight degree of relaxation, the uterus may fill with blood, which will further prevent the uterus from contracting. More bleeding may occur. The nurse should ascertain the level of the fundus in relation to the umbilicus. If it is closer to the umbilicus during the next check, the attendant should be apprised of this finding. The nurse and attendant would then collaborate as to the plan of action in order to prevent hemorrhage. Care must be taken that massage of the fundus is not done during repair of the episiotomy without consulting with the attendant. On the attendant's request, the nurse then proceeds to massage the fundus and expel the blood. *Care should be taken to avoid exerting pressure on the fundus when it is not contracted.* The proper method of palpating the fundus is described in the following chapter, "The Fourth Stage of Labor."

It is important for the nurse to anticipate complications so that care can be planned and implemented. Considering the many tasks and priorities in the delivery room with a new baby, a new mother, and the necessity to help the family feel they have achieved success in their efforts, the nurse must be able to identify patients who are more likely to have postpartum bleeding. However, the nurse should never forget there are patients who hemorrhage for the first time. If the nurse knows those patients who may more likely hemorrhage for whatever reason, extra care and watchfulness for such a complication can be provided. This might require checking the fundus, pulse, and blood pressure more frequently than hospital routine requires. The nurse should be prepared to administer intravenous aqueous infusion with oxytocin during the third stage of labor, since this treatment may be ordered by the obstetrician if hemorrhage is suspected. Hellman indicates the usual dosage of oxytocin is 20 to 40 units per liter of infusion administered at 30 to 60 drops per minute.[9] Some of the predisposing factors to hemorrhage during and/or following the third stage of labor due to uterine atony in the new mother are as follows:

1 Any condition that distends the uterus beyond what is "normal" (large babies, hydramnious, multiple pregnancy)
2 Premature separation of the placenta and placenta previa
3 Operative delivery, such as forceps extraction
4 Large amounts of medication late in labor or general anesthesia
5 Uterine atony after the third stage of labor in previous pregnancies
6 Prolonged first and second stages of labor
7 Very rapid labor
8 Labor induced and maintained with oxytocin
9 Older women of high parity
10 Preeclampsia and eclampsia[10]

To help prevent postpartum hemorrhage due to uterine atony, the nurse should be familiar with the various drugs used to assist the uterus to contract. It is often the nurse who administers these drugs in the delivery room, and, therefore, the nurse must be alert for signs and symptoms of side effects. Table 23-1 lists the most commonly used drugs, their action, advantages, disadvantages, and side effects. This information should be familiar to the nurse.

The use, especially the timing of administration, of these drugs varies from physician to physician and from hospital to hospital. At times, various combinations of these drugs are used, at other times no drugs are used.

It should be noted that oxytocin acts quickly, but does not last as long as ergonovine and methylergonovine.[11] However, oxytocin avoids the problem of blood pressure elevation more common with ergonovine and methylergonovine.[12]

One of these oxytocic drugs is usually given after the placenta is delivered or in some cases with the delivery of the anterior shoulder of the baby. The latter procedure requires skilled obstetric care as it may cause the placenta to be retained. However, excessive bleeding may be avoided when this procedure is carefully executed. The nurse must be aware of the different use of these drugs and should anticipate their use so that they are administered when the attendant requests them. The attendant's plan of care depends on the proper timing of these drugs, and the nurse should recognize that such timing is important in order to prevent unnecessary bleeding in the new mother. If the drugs are given too soon, it is possible that the placenta cannot escape from the uterus, thereby causing unnecessary difficulty. If they are given too late, the mother may lose unnecessary amounts of blood. Precautions must be taken so that patients who have elevated blood pressure are not given ergonovine or methylergonovine. Any of the side effects of these drugs should be watched for and reported to the attendant immediately.

The second most frequent cause of hemorrhage is lacerations of the perineum, vagina, and cervix. Inspection of the cervix and vagina is done by the attendant to determine if there are any lacerations. If an episiotomy has been performed, this will usually prevent the possibility of tears in the pelvic floor. Since the nurse is often responsible for "cleaning up the patient" and placing a perineal pad on the patient before leaving the delivery room, it is necessary to be aware of

TABLE 23-1
Drugs Commonly Administered during the Third Stage of Labor

Name	Effects	Route	Disadvantages
Ergonovine (ergotrate)	Produces uterine contractions of 3 or more hours, acts rapidly and sustains uterus in contracted state	Orally, IM, IV	Given IV, blood pressure increase of 20 mmHg or more in 22% of patients. Given IV, headache and vertigo in 30–50% of patients. Given IV, temporary chest pain, palpitation, dyspnea, 5–10%. Cannot be given prior to placental expulsion
Methylergonovine (methergine)	Produces stronger and longer contractions than ergonovine	Orally, IM, IV	Given IV, blood pressure increase of 20 mmHg or more in 10% of patients. Given IV, headache and vertigo in 30–50% of patients. Given IV, temporary chest pain, palpitation, dyspnea, 5–10%. Should not be given prior to placental expulsion
Oxytocin (Pitocin and Syntocinon, the latter a synthetic drug that has replaced posterior pituitary extract, Pituitrin, because of vasopressor effect)	Produces contraction of uterus like ergonovine for first 5–10 minutes, then normal rhythmic contraction of amplified degree and intermittent periods of relaxation. Avoids elevation of blood pressure	IV	Few, except antidiuresis

SOURCE: Adapted from E. Stewart Taylor, *Beck's Obstetrical Practice*, 8th ed., Williams & Wilkins, Baltimore, 1971; Louis M. Hellman and Jack A. Pritchard, *Williams Obstetrics*, 14th ed., Appleton-Century-Crofts, New York, 1971; *Physicians' Desk Reference*,

Available dosage	Rate of action	Precautions	Side effects
1 ml, 0.2 mg	Rapid	Sensitivity with prolonged use. Store below 15°C room temperature acceptable if kept *no* more than 60 days	Nausea and vomiting rarely, increase with IV route; transient hypertension when associated with regional and general anesthesia, IV route of administration
0.2 mg/ml (1/320 g)	30–60 seconds after IV, 2–5 minutes after IM injection, 5–10 minutes after oral administration	Administer 1 ml slowly over 60 seconds. Check blood pressure frequently and at intervals of 1 hour after	Nausea and vomiting, transient hypertension, dizziness, tachycardia. When administered as dilute IV infusion, has little effect on blood pressure or electrocardiogram
10 units/ml	Acts quicker than ergonovine, but effect is not as lasting	Not used by more than one route of administration because of inherent problem of controlling dosage. May exchange buccal Pitocin and IV route. Has antidiuretic effect. Watch if patient receiving IV fluids	

Medical Economic Company, Oradell, N.J., 1975; and Betty S. Bergerson and Andres Goth, *Pharmacology in Nursing*, Mosby, St. Louis, 1973.

bleeding from lacerations and/or sutures. At this time, the lacerations will have been sutured and inspection of these sutures for bleeding and/or a hematoma should be done before allowing the patient to leave the delivery room. Lacerations are fairly common in primigravidas and precipitous births.

An episiotomy is often done to avoid lacerations in the perineum and rectal sphincter. An episiotomy heals more readily than a laceration. The nurse should be aware of why lacerations occur, as these cause additional trauma and pain to the mother in the postpartum period.

The causes for lacerations of the perineum include:

1   Rapid and sudden expulsion of the presenting part during delivery
2   Large size of the infant
3   Difficult forceps deliveries and breech extractions
4   Contraction of the pelvic outlet
5   Exaggerated lithotomy position
6   Friable maternal tissues

Since the nurse is responsible for positioning the patient on the delivery table, he or she should be aware of the problems that may occur if the patient is improperly positioned in the lithotomy position. Refer to Chapter 22 for the proper positioning of a patient.

The third cause of hemorrhage is retained placental fragments. The nurse must recognize the importance of inspecting the placenta to be sure that it has been completely removed. Retained placental fragments cause late postpartum hemorrhage and increase the chance of infection in the new mother. This type of hemorrhage causes a complication that interferes with mothering activities and often causes a return to the hospital or the operating table.

Nursing Tasks Involved in Prevention of Hemorrhage

In summary, the nursing tasks involved in obtaining this goal are:

1   Identify previous predisposing factors from the patient's history which might indicate the possibility of hemorrhage.
2   Check the fundus frequently. This may entail constant check by maintaining the hand on the fundus to detect the slightest fundal change, or it may entail checking the fundus every few minutes.
3   Massage the uterus and expel clots of blood as necessary.
4   Check vital signs frequently, basing the time interval on previous assessment of the possibility of hemorrhage and other factors that indicate need for frequent check of vital signs, such as spinal anesthesia, maternal cardiac complications, and amount of medication and anesthetics received.
5   Administration of the oxytocic drug or drugs in the prescribed amount and at the appropriate time.
6   Complete reevaluation of the patient's signs of bleeding *before* leaving the delivery room, with an assessment of the type of care needed in the recovery room. If the patient indicates various predisposing signs of hemorrhage, arrangements for constant surveillance in the recovery room may be essential. If the patient is doing well, then frequent sequential checks must be arranged. These postpartum checks are described in detail in Chapter 24. Assessment of the state of the episiotomy should be done prior to leaving the delivery room.

NURSING GOAL: ESTABLISHING MOTHER-INFANT-FAMILY RELATIONSHIPS

Nursing Knowledge Needed

During the third stage of labor, the attendant is busy facilitating the delivery of the placenta, determining if there is hemorrhage present, and establishing the respirations of the newborn infant. The nurse also is involved in tasks that assist this process, which have been described in the previous section. However, once the baby is born, the new mother may be intensively engaged in seeing her new baby and ascertaining what he or she is like. New mothers' behaviors, once their babies arrive, are as varied as are the women themselves. Some laugh, some cry, some are quite verbal and share their feelings, others are extremely quiet in their response to their babies. It is important for the nurse to recognize this individualism and not to insist that a mother behave in a manner different from her pattern or her ability to behave at this point in time. Many factors seem to influence the way the new mother behaves toward her baby.

1   The mother's own personality and her way of responding to situations of excitement, stress, or joy
2   The mother's cultural background and the way she feels she should respond in this situation
3   The type of labor and delivery and the degree of fatigue, pain, or fear she has experienced during this process and whether or not she wanted to have a baby
4   Her marital status and whether she is keeping the baby
5   The baby and his or her responses; whether the baby "fits" the baby the

mother wanted as to sex, size, and condition; whether she is aware of how newborn babies look, regarding color, size, vernix caseosa, blood
6   The tone and atmosphere of the delivery-room staff and whether she feels comfortable, important, and accepted, regardless of her response
7   The presence or absence of the baby's father; if he is present, his response may in turn influence the mother's response
8   The amount of medication or type of anesthesia she has received

Discussion of whether the father should be present in the delivery room is widespread, and there are differing opinions about the value of this procedure. If the father is present, his needs should be considered so that he can participate in holding the baby and supporting his mate. If he is not, consideration should be given as to how he might be included in the birth of the baby from afar. Often women who have just delivered a baby prefer to let the father know of the baby's birth in a specific way. Some women will want the nurse to inform him immediately that all is well when the baby is born. Other women will want to wait until they can tell the father themselves. The nurse should have explored this with the couple *before* delivery so that the mother can inform the father in the desired manner.

Many psychologists indicate the importance of the mother establishing a relationship with the newborn baby immediately after birth. Dr. Bradley, who advocates *husband-coached childbirth*, and many of the physicians who propose psychoprophylactic methods of preparation for childbirth, indicate the importance for the new parents of immediately seeing and holding the baby.[13] Caplan indicates that if this initial reaction is delayed, often the establishment of a positive relationship between the mother and her baby is delayed. Maternal feelings are said to develop more readily when the mother is confronted with her baby immediately and is able to touch and hold her baby. Response to the newborn initiates the *release* of oxytocin that stimulates the mother's uterus to contract. Indeed, then, nature intended for the mother to hold her baby immediately and the procedure, still seen too frequently, of not allowing the mother to touch and handle her baby is an unnecessary restriction in most situations.

Every effort should be made to allow the mother to see and hold her baby. The mother will need to establish the baby's identity very soon and respond to the baby's needs and desires. The sooner she can see the baby as an individual with a specific sex and personality, the better she can care for the child. Touching and holding the baby is extremely important, and the mother should not be denied this opportunity. (See Figure 23-6.)

If the condition of the mother does not warrant immediate contact with her baby, arrangements should be made as soon as the mother's condition allows. Many times ob-

FIGURE 23-6
Interaction of the mother, father, and child immediately after delivery. Positive interaction will encourage a satisfying relationship between the mother and her infant. (*By permission from The University of Colorado Medical Center, Denver, Colo.*)

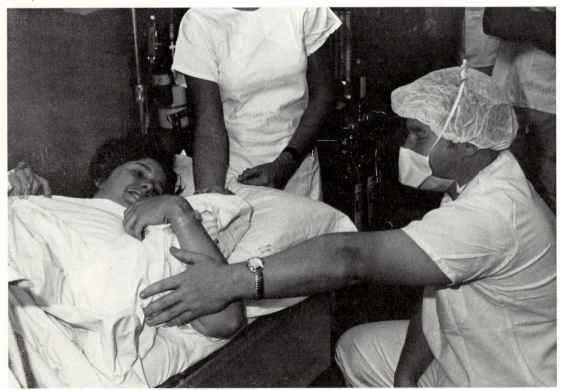

stetric staff has the idea that if the mother missed this experience, she will have to wait until "babies are brought out" according to hospital procedure and schedule. If the nurse believes that maternal-infant relationships are fostered and enhanced by early encounter between mother and baby, every effort will be made for the mother to see and hold her infant as soon as possible.

In making judgments about whether a mother should be allowed to hold her baby after delivery, the baby's condition should be evaluated and the judgment made on the basis of this condition. Normal newborn infants who are of adequate size, in good condition, and not depressed by too much maternal medication are not traumatized if the parents hold them or look to see if the baby is "all there."

However, babies who are small for gestational age, who are born prematurely, who have problems breathing, or who are listless because of medication may not be able to tolerate this procedure. When this is the case, certainly the safety of the newborn must take precedence. The baby may need to be transferred immediately to an intensive nursing unit. If the baby's condition prevents the mother from holding the baby, the nurse must see to it that the mother is brought to the baby or the baby is within seeing distance of the mother at the earliest time possible.

A frequent argument for not allowing fathers to be present in the delivery room or for not allowing the parents to be able to see and hold their baby immediately after delivery is that the baby has a defect. Parents must adjust and accept this situation. If parents wish to hold their baby who has a defect, they certainly should not be denied this privilege. A mother who saw her baby, with a cleft lip, for the first time several days after delivery explained with a sigh of relief on seeing her baby, "Oh it is not nearly as bad as

I imagined!" How disconcerting to allow this mother to imagine a defect many times worse than the one present by delaying showing her the baby!

When there is a complication present in the newborn that threatens life, the parents should know what is happening to their child and should be able to see their infant and the efforts being made to assist the baby. Often the parents are shielded from knowing about the baby's condition and prevented from seeing the care the baby is receiving. This may be detrimental to the parents. If the parents see the concentrated care given their baby, they are often less upset; they feel everything possible is being done. If the staff is truthful and open about the condition of the baby, the parents learn to trust the staff.

Helping the mother feel she is close to her baby still needs to be accomplished. This can be accomplished in different ways. Some of the ways that closeness when apart may be accomplished include letting the mother know where the baby is going, and reporting the baby's condition and what is happening to the baby as frequently as possible.

The birth of the baby gives the nurse an excellent opportunity to enhance the mother's and the father's level of achievement in the birth process. This need for achievement is great and can often forestall guilt feelings that come later when the mother feels that she was unable to cooperate to the degree she wanted to during labor and/or the birth of her baby. Positive accomplishments by the patient need to be reinforced by the nurse. The mother needs to feel successful. After all, having had a baby *is* an achievement! The following example, which emphasizes the patient's need to feel she has successfully given birth to her baby, might demonstrate this point more completely.

A nurse was talking with a newly delivered mother who had a severe cardiac complication. The purpose of the discussion was to help the new mother plan her postpartum activities to compensate for her cardiac condition in the care of her new baby and her other young child. Not much progress was being made, and the patient appeared very sad and finally started crying. The nurse asked the patient what was wrong. The patient replied, "I was a failure, I *couldn't* help but push when the baby was born! That doctor was so angry at me! I tried, really I did . . . !" The patient was feeling some guilt, and possibly her mothering activities would be hindered. The patient had done well, with her cardiac condition, to deliver the baby safely, and yet she was deeply concerned about being an uncooperative patient. The physician was tense because of the patient's condition and relayed his tension to the patient by strongly insisting that the patient not push, a necessity to this situation. Time was spent in exploring how difficult it would be not to push, that she was not to blame, that the doctor was expressing his concern for her, and that she had done well. Her labor nurse was asked to reinforce this. Patients seem to be very sensitive to their performance and need reassurance that they did well in light of their particular situation.

The procedure of allowing the mother to carry the baby from the delivery room walking or in her bed is an important one in establishing mother-infant relationships and in allowing the new mother to feel important, for she has indeed achieved a great task. This should be done when the condition of the mother and her infant allow such a procedure. Also, the desire of the patient should be considered. If the new mother does not desire to hold her baby at this time, this procedure should certainly not be forced upon her, but she should not be denied this privilege because of "hospital routine."

Some hospitals allow the mother and baby to occupy the same room during the first hour postpartum and allow the infant to remain with the mother at all times in a rooming-in situation. Skilled nursing care is done concurrently rather than separately in this situation.

Women who have already decided not to keep their babies often are not allowed to see and hold them. This should be an individual decision and should not be dictated by hospital policy. If the mother desires to see and hold her baby, she should not be denied this opportunity. After all, it is her baby and it may be important for her to see that the baby is normal and healthy. She must make her decision to relinquish the baby in light of all the facts and in light of her response to the baby. If the mother does not wish to see her baby, it should not be forced upon her. This subject is complex and highly individual and should be planned with each person involved as well as some knowledge of how the patient is handling the situation of relinquishing her baby.

Nursing Tasks Involved

1   Assess the condition of the mother and the infant to determine if the mother can see and hold her baby.
2   Facilitate the mother's touching of her baby, the exploration of all parts, and encourage her to fondle the baby as desired in relation to the condition of the baby.
3   Dry the infant to prevent overexposure, provide warmed blankets and a warmed crib.
4   Create an atmosphere that encourages the mother to feel comfortable in handling the baby.
5   Include the father in the birth of the baby if he is present. If the father is absent from the delivery room, inform

him in the manner he and the mother wish.

6 Compliment the mother on the task she has just completed, encourage the attendant to do so if he or she has not done so already, point out things the mother did well in order to enhance the patient's sense of self-esteem and well-being.

7 Foster continuity of the mother-infant relationship by allowing the infant to remain with the mother when possible, or inform the mother of the baby's condition, and what is being done for the baby.

PROMOTION OF SAFETY, COMFORT, AND RELAXATION IN THE NEW MOTHER

Nursing Knowledge Needed

The term labor is an appropriate one, since the pregnant woman has indeed labored. There has been a great expenditure of energy, physically and psychologically. She may have had a long labor that interfered with her normal sleep; she may have had times of discouragement, anxiety, pain, and fear. All of this as well as having had her food and possibly her fluids restricted may have decreased her energy stores, and she may be tense and fatigued, even though she is excited and happy. She may or may not become aware of uterine contractions and feel discomfort as the placenta is delivered. Her response to the entire birth process may be one of relief, or it may be one of excitement. Regardless of her reaction, the nurse needs to help the mother relax and become comfortable.

The type of anesthesia the patient had will influence the patient's needs and the nursing actions to meet the goal of promotion of comfort, relaxation, and safety. For example, if the patient has had a general anesthetic, the nurse's activities immediately after the baby is born would center around tasks that detect the patient's response to this anesthetic and help provide safety and adequate recovery. If on the other hand, the patient has had a regional anesthetic, such as a caudal or saddle block, the patient may not experience physical pain but will have emotional responses that will need nursing support or intervention. If the patient has had a local anesthetic, she may be aware of uterine pain which may interfere with establishing a relationship with her newborn.

At times, the physician may order a tranquilizer when the patient is extremely tense or a pain medication when pain is a problem. The nurse should make every effort to help the patient relax because it is essential that the mother is relaxed, rested, and fully restored from fatigue or anxiety as soon as possible so she can take on the mothering role. The nursing care which facilitates patient rest and relaxation is described in Chapter 24.

Various other needs of the new mother may have been interfered with because of the labor process. The new mother may be experiencing some degree of discomfort because of any or all of the following:

1 Lack of adequate food and fluids
2 Inadequate elimination as labor progressed
3 An uncomfortable position in stirrups, wet linens because of the obstetric preparation
4 Coolness because of the delivery-room temperature
5 Interference with her need to be with her mate and family
6 Anxiety due to stress of labor and delivery

The nurse should take steps as soon as possible to relieve situations that cause discomfort. The nurse might provide ice chips or a drink that provides some calories, check the position of the stirrups and reposition them if there is any pressure on the popliteal space, and remove the patient from the stirrups as soon as possible. The nurse should provide dry linens, a clean gown, and a warm blanket when the patient is transferred from the delivery table.

To allay emotional discomfort that may be interfering with the patient's ability to relax, the nurse should assess the patient's reason for anxiety and take steps to help the mother relax. Perhaps an opportunity to communicate with her family will help her relax.

Special care should be taken to avoid trauma as the patient is removed from the stirrups and placed on a bed or stretcher. The type of care in taking the patient down from the delivery table depends on the type of anesthetic administered. If the patient has had none or only a local anesthetic, the nurse can help her move her legs. She may experience some difficulty if she has been in stirrups for a long time or if she has been improperly positioned. If the patient has had a regional anesthetic, such as a saddle or caudal block, she will not be able to move her legs. Her legs must be moved by the nurse. Care should be taken to move both legs at the same time, in the same way, and with adequate support. If one leg at a time is moved, then there will be stress on the ligaments that may cause pain and trauma in the future. If the patient has had a spinal anesthetic, special care should be taken to avoid an elevation of the patient from the vertical position. She should be carefully lifted or log-rolled from the delivery table and her head should not be elevated for 6 to 8 hours, or as ordered by the physician.

If the mother received general anesthesia during delivery, she may need reassurance that she has given birth and that all is well. Her need for relaxation and sleep may be demonstrated by intermittent dozing. This should be allowed as much as possible, since this is her taking-in time. She will need extra food, sleep, rest, and attention so as to move into taking-on activities of mothering. The goal of providing comfort and rest is extremely important and should be begun as soon as possible.

Nursing Tasks Involved in Providing Rest, Relaxation, Comfort, and Safety

1 Assess the individual mother's needs. Is she excited, tense, anxious, fatigued?
2 Create an atmosphere conducive to rest.
3 Provide physical comfort by appropriate position, clean linens, blanket, or medication, if indicated.
4 Use caution in removing the patient from the stirrups of the delivery table to avoid discomfort or future trauma.
5 Provide fluids, as needed by the patient.
6 Provide an opportunity for the patient and her family to visit with each other as soon as possible.

PROVIDING CONTINUITY OF CARE THROUGH ADEQUATE REPORTING AND RECORDING

Since nursing care for the newly delivered mother at this time is usually divided between delivery room, recovery room, nursery, and postpartum areas, extra care must be taken to provide continuity of care. It is hoped that innovations in nursing across the country will bring changes which will provide nurses for patients rather than "area" nurses in the maternity units. The frequent change of nurses necessitated by days off and change of shifts heightens discontinuity of care during the patient's short hospital stay.

Since the patient's care is likely to be ministered by a number of nurses within the same day or even within an 8-hour period, it is extremely important for the delivery-area nurse to communicate appropriate and accurate data in writing and by an oral report which will be informative to the nurse who will be caring for the patient after leaving the delivery room. The nurse who receives the new mother needs information concerning the patient's needs and previous problems, as well as the patient's preference in care.

Regardless of the various reports and charts that are unique to a particular delivery-room setting, the delivery-area nurse should recognize various areas of information that are important to the nurse who will be caring for the mother and the baby so that care can proceed without interruption. The knowledge the delivery-area nurse should pass on to the nurse who cares for the patient immediately postpartum, regardless of *where* the patient is cared for, should include:

1 The patient's gravida and para, an assessment of fundal height and consistency of the uterus, as well as the amount of blood loss during delivery. The estimate of blood loss should include the amount in the delivery room and a specific description of the amount lost on perineal pads, e.g., the number and the amount of saturation of the pads during a specific period of time.
2 The amount and type of drugs received by the patient that might affect her care, such as narcotics, tranquilizers, anesthetics (local, regional, or general), and oxytocics; unusual response or allergies to medication.
3 The type of episiotomy and if there were lacerations or unusual trauma.
4 The physician's or nurse midwife's orders for the patient.
5 The last time the patient voided.
6 The predisposing factors that indicate the possibility of postpartum hemorrhage.
7 The parents' response to the newborn and their desires regarding seeing and holding their baby.
8 Intravenous feedings and/or blood transfusions during labor and delivery or which may be currently running, amount remaining, orders to discontinue or continue.
9 Factors that indicate the possibility of infection, dehydration, or extreme fatigue or exhaustion in the patient.
10 Previous vital signs, especially when problems are anticipated.
11 The condition and sex of the baby.

The knowledge the delivery-area nurse should pass on to the nursery nurse should include:

1 Condition of the infant at birth, Apgar score at 1 minute and at 5 minutes
2 Amount and type of anesthetic or analgesic the mother received
3 Type of resuscitation used for the infant
4 Sex of the baby, time of birth, and considerations such as spontaneous or forceps delivery, prolonged labor, meconium in the amniotic fluid, tachycardia, bradycardia, or arrhythmia during labor and delivery
5 Response of the mother and father to the newborn and plans made with

them in regard to establishing a relationship with the baby

6 Condition of the mother
7 Method of feeding the infant
8 Type and amount of medication given
to the infant
9 Bracelet information that identified
the infant with his or her parents
10 Baby's pediatrician or general practitioner

Whether these are written or verbally reported depends on several factors. Most hospitals require all of the above information to
be written. In addition, the nurse should
mention many of these factors verbally when
they influence the care the nurse will give
the patient. Discussion of a plan of care is
valuable, since the nurse who has cared for
the patient in labor and delivery may have
identified various patient needs that only the
nurse who cares for the patient later in her
postpartum period can provide. Some of
these needs would include the new mother's
need for teaching and support in mothering
activities.

This chapter deals with a very brief time in
the patient's birth experience. However,
nursing care during this time is very important to the new family, as it may help prevent
a postpartum hemorrhage, which can result
in death. More frequently, this is the time in
which the mother may experience a delay in
recovering from the birth experience and/or
a delay in taking on the mothering role. The
nurse who cares for the patient in this stage
also can do much to enhance the patient's
sense of achievement for her efforts in the
birth process. In addition to assisting the
newborn in adjusting to the extrauterine environment, the nurse can also help establish
a positive family experience by providing
opportunities for the mother and father to relate to their baby and begin building a rela-

tionship. Rather than being distracted by
menial tasks, nursing care during the third
stage of labor can become one of magnitude
and importance and may be extremely satisfying to the nurse and helpful to the mother
and father as they *begin* the all-important
task of becoming parents.

REFERENCES

1 Taylor, E. Stewart: *Beck's Obstetrical Practice*, 9th ed., Williams & Wilkins, Baltimore,
1971, p. 199.
2 Hellman, Louis M., and Jack A. Pritchard:
Williams Obstetrics, 14th ed., Appleton-
Century-Crofts, New York, 1971, p. 415.
3 Ibid., p. 416.
4 Calkins, L. A.: "Management of the Third
Stage of Labor," *Journal of the American
Medical Association*, 101:1128, 1933.
5 Fitzpatrick, Elise, Sharon Reeder, and Luigi
Mastroianni: *Maternity Nursing*, 12th ed.,
Lippincott, Philadelphia, 1971, p. 223.
6 Taylor: op. cit., pp. 201–202.
7 Fitzpatrick, et al.: op. cit., p. 493.
8 Taylor: op. cit., p. 202.
9 Hellman, et al.: op. cit., p. 42.
10 Ibid., p. 421.
11 *Physicians' Desk Reference*, Medical Economics Company, Oradell, N.J., 1975, pp.
927, 1301, 1140–1141.
12 Bergerson, Betty S., and Andres Goth: *Pharmacology in Nursing*, Mosby, St. Louis, 1973,
p. 527.
13 Bradley, Robert A.: *Husband-coached Childbirth*, Harper & Row, New York, 1965.

BIBLIOGRAPHY

Alexander, L.: "Fathers in the Delivery Room,"
American Baby, 34:24–25, January 1972.
Biard, R. W.: "Active Management of Labour,"
Midwives Chronicle, 86:374–376, December
1972.

Bordon, D.: "The Setting of Childbirth and Its Effect on Mother-Neonate Interactions," *Midwives Chronicle,* 87:343–346, October 1974.

Bradley, Robert A.: "Father's Presence in Delivery Rooms," *Psychosomatics,* 3(6), November–December 1962.

Caplan, Gerald: *Concepts of Mental Health Consultations, Their Application in Public Health Social Work,* 2d ed., Children's Bureau, New York, 1966.

Fleming, G.: "Delivering a Happy Father," *American Journal of Nursing,* 72:949, May 1972.

Kennedy, J. C.: "The High-Risk Maternal-Infant Acquaintance Process," *Nursing Clinics of North America,* 8:549–556, September 1973.

Littlefield, Vivian: "An Investigation into the Effects of Supportive Nursing Care on Primiparous Patients during Labor and Delivery," an unpublished study presented to the graduate faculty of the University of Colorado School of Nursing, 1964.

———: "Maternal Satisfaction with the Birth Experience and Maternal Child Adjustment," an unpublished study presented to the graduate faculty of the University of Colorado School of Nursing, 1964.

Moore, M. L.: "The Importance of Culture in Childbearing," *Journal of Obstetric, Gynecologic and Neonatal Nursing,* 1:29–32, July–August 1972.

Phillips, C.: "Neonatal Heat Loss in Heated Cribs vs. Mothers' Arms . . . Watsonville Community Hospital," *Journal of Obstetric, Gynecologic and Neonatal Nursing,* 3:11–15, November–December 1974.

Rising, S. S.: "The Fourth Stage of Labor: Family Integration," *American Journal of Nursing,* 74:870–874, May 1974.

Rubin, Reva: "Attainment of the Maternal Role. 1. Processes," *Nursing Research,* 16(3):237–245, Summer 1967.

———: "Attainment of the Maternal Role. 2. Models and Referents," *Nursing Research,* 16(4):342–346, Fall 1967.

Wiedenbach, Ernestine: *Family-centered Maternity Nursing,* Putnam, New York, 1967.

24

The Fourth Stage of Labor

JOY CLAUSEN

As illustrated in the preceding chapters, the first three stages of labor are sequential delineated events. Similarly, the fourth stage of labor is a distinct phase of the birth process, beginning with the expulsion of the placenta and terminating at the end of the following hour.

In 1946 Emanuel M. Greenberg, a physician, reviewed the literature and found that Manfred Leff was the first medical doctor to recognize the fourth stage of labor.[1] Greenberg refined Leff's definition, and is the man primarily responsible for delimiting this critically important stage of labor:

I propose that the first hour following the delivery of the placenta be considered as the normal duration of the fourth stage of labor, until further exhaustive studies will either add or detract a few minutes from the already rather arbitrarily accepted "postpartum hour."[2]

The 1-hour duration for the fourth stage of labor should not be thought of in rigid terms. If the maternal condition has not stabilized within the first hour postpartum, the time span of this stage should be extended to the period during which the mother's condition does become stable. Like the other three stages of labor, the time interval for the fourth stage is contingent upon the individual woman's recuperative powers and the quality of care she receives.

This chapter will focus on normal events during the first hour postpartum. It will illustrate how nurses utilize the nursing process at this time to: (1) promote stabilization of the mother's condition; and (2) deliver quality care which augments the mother's inherent recuperative powers. Recognition by nurses that this stage of labor is physiologically unique and that it has its own normalities and its own aberrations should enable knowledgeable, purposeful care to be delivered with confidence and with some degree of uniformity, albeit the individuality of each mother is never forgotten.

THE NURSING PROCESS DURING THE FOURTH STAGE OF LABOR

In Chapter 3, Ernestine Wiedenbach cited two interrelated courses of action nurses can take in their attempts to meet the needs of maternity patients:

1 Develop understanding of the process that determines nursing actions.
2 Incorporate in practice measures that will enhance the effective functioning of the nursing process.

Theoretically, the nursing process is a problem-solving approach, but unfortunately, some R.N.'s have never learned the theory; some who have learned the theory are unable to apply it in health care situations. Many nurses have been educated by the case-study method which emphasizes the medical rather than the nursing process.[3] The result of this teaching-learning process is that the nurse learns to deliver health care intuitively, and consequently nursing actions are frequently "an automatic response to the situation or the result of a hunch, rather than one that is based on a rational replicable judgment."[4]

For those readers who are students, the following discussion of the nursing process may be a reiteration; for those who are practicing R.N.'s it may be either new material or a reorganization of previously known material; for some, regardless of status, it may be somewhat awesome. Hopefully, for all readers, the discussion about the utilization of the nursing process will be thought-provoking and applicable to the care of maternity patients and their families. It is beneficial as well as pleasing to think of nurses as persons who are flexible in the practice of their profession. From the very nature of this thought it follows that some readers will find it fitting and appropriate to reassess and reevaluate their nursing actions to incorporate the utilization of the nursing process therein. It must be remembered that the nursing process applied to maternity nursing is essentially no different in purpose, structure, or function than the nursing process applied to other types of nursing situations such as pediatrics or orthopedics; the content may vary but not the process.

As briefly discussed in Chapter 15, the operations which comprise the nursing process include assessment of the patient situation; development of a plan of action; implementation of the plan of action; and evaluation of the assessment, plan of action, and implementation phases.

Assessment of the Patient Situation

Assessment of the maternity patient's situation and condition is based on three reference points: *the chart,* particularly the prenatal record, laboratory reports, nurses' and physicians' notes, and physicians' orders; (2) *the report,* written and oral, as received from labor- and delivery-room nurses, which includes pertinent facts and information about mother, father, and baby (see Chapter 23, "The Third Stage of Labor"); and (3) *observation* of and *interaction* with the mother, father, and baby. In carrying out a patient assessment nurses use their sight, hearing, smell, and touch senses.

It is important during the assessment phase to collect as much pertinent data about the patient and her family as possible. The recovery room or postpartum nurse usually finds that much of the initial assessment data has been collected during the antepartum and intrapartum periods and documented in the chart by the labor- and delivery-room nurses. Operationally, then, the chart and report serve not only as an assessment of the patient's past situation but also as a base line against which the patient's present and future condition can be evaluated.

It is important that the following factors are assessed during interaction with and observation of the parents and the new baby:

Sociocultural
Emotional
Mothering and fathering behaviors initiated
Intrafamilial relationships
Energy stores
Reaction to and ability to cope with environment
General comfort and safety

In addition to assessment of these factors, it is necessary to assess physical factors relevant only to the mother:

Tone and size of the fundus of the uterus
Degree of distention of the bladder
Character and amount of lochia
Condition of the perineum
Deviations in blood pressure and pulse
Body hygiene
Absence or presence of nausea/vomiting
Absence or presence of varicosities in legs and/or vulva
Site and type of pain if experienced

The factors listed above are not placed in order of importance; only the nurse caring for the mother and her family during the postpartum period has the knowledge to set assessment priorities. However, it can be realistically stated that the factors of assessment which usually carry the highest priority are those associated with the tone and size of the fundus of the uterus and the character and amount of the lochia. These factors ultimately affect life-sustaining abilities of the mother; therefore, it is understandable why they carry high priority. If these factors are assessed first and are found to be within normal limits, the assessment of the other factors subsequently develops in a logical, patient-individualized order. Both the order and the factors will be expanded upon in the following sections.

From the above discussion, it should be clear that the first phase of the nursing process in the fourth stage of labor is a thorough assessment of the patient situation which includes intrafamilial characteristics as well as the physical condition of the newly delivered mother. Without an initial, comprehensive assessment, the subsequent fulfillment of the remaining three operations of the nursing process is not attainable.

Development of a Plan of Action

Nurses base their plans of action for patient care upon their nursing knowledge and upon their assessment of the patient situation. An inherent process in the development of a plan of action is interpretation of the assessment, or in other words, the attachment of significance to that which has been observed.

The development of a plan of action begins as a mental process which can be likened to a screening technique. Assessment factors are delimited, individually and/or in clusters, in order of importance for patient safety and welfare. These delimited factors are then utilized in conjunction with nursing knowledge and patient input to formulate plans for patient-oriented nursing care.

The mental process becomes operationalized as the nurse verbally articulates the plan of patient care with the patient, and with nursing peers. The ultimate expression of the plan of action occurs when the nurse concretely conceptualizes it to the extent that it is written in the form of a nursing care plan. This plan, in turn, can be elaborated, restructured, refocused, or even discarded depending on continuing assessment and reassessment of the patient situation.

An example of the interconnectedness of the assessment and plan of action phases of the nursing process is as follows:

Assessment: The nurse observes that the mother has saturated two perineal pads within the past 10 minutes. The possibility of overdistention of the uterus antepartum is explored, as is the length of labor, drugs administered during the labor and delivery, and the mother's parity. The fundus of the uterus is palpated to ascertain its tone. Bleeding as the result of cervical laceration is ruled out. The bladder area is visually checked and palpated for distention. The blood pressure and pulse are taken and compared with previous readings, and all data is recorded. The mother is asked if she has cramping in the uterine area. Her skin and behavior are observed for symptoms of circulatory shock.

The patient's antepartum, labor, and delivery records are checked and found to contain no information which suggests predisposition to hemorrhage. Cervical bleeding is ruled out by validating that the lochia is dark rather than bright red; there is no bright red continuous "trickle" of blood from the vagina. The following plan of action is formulated:

Plan of action:
Check the tone of the fundus at least every 5 minutes, being cautious not to overmassage, hence, overstimulate it which may cause uterine atony.
Change the perineal pads as necessary and save them in a covered container for purposes of comparison of bleeding, and for inspection by the physician.
Facilitate voiding by use of nursing measures; follow doctor's orders if unable to void and if bladder is full.
Monitor the pulse every 5 minutes, the blood pressure every 10 minutes until condition stabilizes.
Have in close proximity, not necessarily in the patient's room but accessible, intravenous solution, tubing, vials of oxytocics anticipated as those which might be used; and an intravenous tray which includes syringes, needles, tourniquet, sponges, and antiseptic.
If bleeding not controlled by nursing actions, notify the physician immediately.
Record observations concisely and precisely in patient's chart.

In this example, as the reader can readily determine, it may not be possible to write out the plan of action by virtue of the fact that the patient demands practically constant surveillance. However, this does not preclude the fact that the nurse completes a thorough assessment of the potential hemorrhage situation and develops a concomitant plan of action in his or her mind.

Implementation of the Plan of Action

It can be difficult to behaviorally differentiate between this phase of the nursing process and the development of the plan of action phase, for both often occur seemingly simultaneously, particularly in emergency situations. In nonemergencies, however, the parameters are much clearer, and conceptually, it is important to identify this phase. By doing so, further order and meaning can be brought to the nursing process.

Simplistically stated, the implementation phase of the nursing process is the nursing action phase, the point in time when the nurse behaviorally carries out the assessment and plan of action phases. The implementation phase is the acting out of the plans for patient care. In the example cited above, implementation occurs when the nurse behaviorally executes the steps listed in the plan of action.

The implementation phase is characterized by the purposeful use of self as a maternity nurse in combination with the use of knowledge and skills general to the practice of nursing, and use of knowledge and skills specific to maternity nursing. Implementation of the plan of action necessitates that the nurse set priorities on which action is first, which is second, which can be done in combination with another, which can wait, and so forth.

Nursing actions during the implementation phase are heavily dependent upon the assessment and plan of action phases; if the latter two have been neglected, nursing actions will be incomplete, inconsistent, and generally haphazard, resulting in reduced quality of patient care. Nursing action in the implementation phase must be scientifically based, purposeful, orderly, and meaningful, and nursing action can take on these characteristics only when patient assessment and plans for care have been fully developed.

Evaluation

The process of evaluation is often misunderstood as the *fourth* phase of the nursing process. Evaluation should, rather, be conceptualized as an ongoing or continuous process, one which is integrally connected to all parts of the other three phases.

Evaluation enables nurses to appraise the effectiveness and value of their patient assessment, the plan of action developed with and for the patient, and the nursing actions taken. It is a critique of the nursing process utilized by the nurse. It permits a continuous study of the results of the nursing process in terms of patient response, thereby allowing for specific alterations, substitutions, deletions, and general rethinking of all phases. Evaluation is a recycling process.

Evaluation enables nurses to predict with confidence the results of nursing care and consequently forms one scientific base for the practice of nursing. It enhances patient care in that through the evaluation process, nursing care becomes dynamic and enthusiastic rather than static and lifeless.

"The nursing process is one of the few things we can measure. . . . [it] allows nurses to organize nursing practice, communicate with other members of the health team about nursing care needs and helps to assure continuity of care."[5]

TRANSFER TO THE POSTPARTUM AREA

Not all hospitals have postpartum recovery-room facilities. However, nursing care is facilitated and patient care enhanced when a well-planned, well-equipped, and proficiently staffed recovery room is available for newly delivered mothers and their families.

If the mother has had general anesthesia during delivery, she should be under the constant surveillance in the delivery room of the anesthesiologist or nurse anesthetist until she is fully awake. Nurses should not transfer the mother to the postpartum area until deemed advisable by the person who administered the general anesthesia.

The mother is transferred via a litter or bed to the postpartum area. The nurse attends to the utmost safety precautions while the mother is being placed on the transfer vehicle as well as before the vehicle begins to move. These precautions include a comfortable position and proper body alignment; nonstatic blankets which provide privacy and warmth; safety straps secured; and side rails raised. An emesis basin and paper handkerchiefs should be placed on the transfer vehicle in the event they are needed. If the mother is receiving an IV infusion, the nurse must check for patency and possible infiltration. The wheels of the vehicle, locked as the mother moved from the delivery table, are unlocked during the transfer. They are locked as soon as the movement ceases.

If the baby is transferred with the mother, it works well if the mother lies on her side with the baby nestled in her arms. Maintenance of body heat is critically important for the newborn and is a body function which is not fully activated at this time. The baby should be wrapped securely in dry, warm blankets which will not create static electricity. Patency of the baby's airway must be ascertained and maintained before and during the transfer. An aspiration bulb syringe can be placed near the baby to be used if necessary. The baby's umbilical cord is checked immediately before movement of the vehicle in order to rule out bleeding.

These safety precautions will ensure that the mother and baby are physically safe in an environment which protects their well-being. The nurse will then find it appropriate to step aside and allow mother, father,

and baby a few moments of privacy before the actual transfer to the postpartum area begins.

In some institutions, the nursery nurse is called after this initial visit to transfer the baby from delivery room to nursery. In others the delivery-room nurse wheels the mother and baby, accompanied by the father, to the nursery and transfers the baby to the nursery nurses. In other institutions, the baby is transferred to the nursery before the mother is out of the delivery room, and in still others the father carries the baby to the nursery. These procedures are dictated to a large degree by hospital policies, and differ widely. Whatever the procedure, the nurse who is responsible for the care of the mother during the fourth stage of labor is responsible for providing mother, father, and baby the opportunity to be together if they so desire as soon after delivery as possible.

The nurse can use ingenuity during the mother's transfer to make sure the father is included, thus initiating interaction between family members. The father can help with and facilitate the transfer. He can help steer the cumbersome cart or bed, help arrange furniture in the postpartum room to allow for the transfer vehicle to enter, and he can help lift the mother or help her roll from the transfer cart to the bed. He is an integral part of the childbearing process and should be helped to realize that he is needed and important at this time.

DYNAMICS ASSOCIATED WITH THE FOURTH STAGE OF LABOR

Physiological and Anatomical Considerations

The fourth stage of labor should be understood as the tapering off of the labor process; the height of the process has been previously attained with the birth of the baby and delivery of the placenta.

Profound physiological and anatomical changes begin during this stage of labor. Although these changes, as discussed below, are considered within the limits of normality, they closely approximate a pathological state, for by their very nature, they are catabolic. In conditions other than the postpartum condition, such catabolic processes result in the patient's departure from a healthy state.

Uterus

The uterus continues to contract and relax during the fourth stage of labor, thereby controlling postpartum hemorrhage by compressing the patent blood vessels at the placental implantation site located in the spongy decidual basalis lining of the uterine cavity.

Following delivery, what was once the placental implantation site now becomes an irregular, nodular, somewhat elevated region approximately the size of the palm of the hand in which there are numerous thrombosed vascular sinuses.[6] The lumens of the vessels become smaller and transgress through various stages which results in the recanalization of some and the formation of endometrial (lining of the uterus) scar tissue. This process, if not rectified by nature, could act as an inhibitory mechanism to future pregnancies. However, nature corrects this process by undermining the scar tissue area with endometrial tissue; hence exfoliation of the area occurs with each menses. The exfoliation process, then, prevents the buildup of endometrial scar tissue.

The uterus at this time resembles a solid, firm mass, weighs approximately 1,000 g, and lies about 12 cm above the symphysis pubis.[7] The posterior and anterior uterine walls lie in close proximity to one another and each is about 5 cm thick. Within a few weeks, by the process of *atrophic involution*, the uterus will be reduced to between one-twentieth and one-twenty-fifth of its full-term pregnancy size. Involution is the result of the removal of excess cytoplasm from the uterine muscle cells by the breakdown of uterine wall protein into less complex substances; these substances in turn are eliminated through the urine.

Occurring simultaneously with uterine atrophic involution is regeneration of the lining of the uterus. The decidual lining differentiates into two layers: a necrotic one adjoining the uterine cavity; and a well-preserved layer adjoining the muscularis, or muscle wall. The necrotic layer is discharged gradually in the form of lochia, a postpartum vaginal discharge. The muscularis layer remains intact and functions as the basis for regeneration of new endometrium.

Cervix and Vagina

The cervix is soft and collapsed after birth of the baby, and the cervical os slowly contracts. During the fourth stage of labor the os is opened about 2 cm, but by the end of 1 week, it is usually so tightly contracted that it is difficult to insert a fingertip. The entire cervix begins to retract and shorten from its elongated shape immediately post delivery. The minute lacerations resulting from childbirth begin to heal.

The vagina has been greatly overdistended as the result of childbirth, and it takes some time to return to its predelivery state though rarely does it return to its nulliparous size. During the fourth stage of labor, the walls of the vagina are smooth, and not until about the third week postpartum do the vaginal rugae reappear.[8] The hymen is no longer present but has been replaced by small tissue tags at the vaginal opening.

The broad and round ligaments which

support the uterus intraabdominally are relaxed due to the release of tension on them after evacuation of the gravid uterus. It takes some time for these ligaments to recuperate from the stretching and loosening which they have experienced.

Urinary System

The bladder during the fourth stage of labor is characterized by edema, hyperemia, sometimes extravasation of blood, and increased capacity.

Bladder edema is caused by trauma, and may be so marked that the urethra is obstructed. This, coupled with its insensitivity to filling as the result of anesthesia and disturbed innervation, may result in overdistention and/or incomplete emptying of the bladder.

Diuresis may begin as early as the fourth stage of labor, during which time the body excretes large amounts of fluids accumulated during pregnancy.

Abdomen

In some women the abdominal skin is marked by reddish colored striae; other women have none. It is estimated that about 50 percent of women who have been pregnant have striae. They are caused by hyperactivity of the adrenal cortex.

Although the muscle fibers in the abdominal wall are undergoing hyperplasia and hypertrophy, the abdominal wall, as well as the skin, appear soft and flabby due to the profound overdistention of pregnancy.

Diastasis, or separation of the longitudinal abdominal rectus muscle, is particularly pronounced during this stage of labor as the result of uterine distention during pregnancy. As a consequence the abdominal viscera in that region is covered only by the peritoneum, a thin layer of fascia, and the skin.

Sociocultural Considerations

The terms *culture* and *society* are not synonymous. Societies may exist, as among non-human animals, in the absence of culture. Society and culture are interdependent phenomena among human beings; one exists only in the presence of the other. When the focus is on *ideas* shared by a group, the frame of reference is cultural. When the emphasis is on the *group* that shares ideas, the frame of reference is social.

The terms cultural and social are often used interchangeably, thus giving rise to the term sociocultural. In the United States, anthropologists prefer the terms culture or cultural when explaining observed phenomena, while sociologists prefer the terms society or social.

Culture is defined as "the totality of all the learned and transmitted behaviors of a particular group of people."[9] It functions subtly and systematically as a device for perceiving the world. Perceptions of the world vary because cultures vary. The culture incorporated by an individual through the process of socialization begins to be inculcated at birth. A person's culture prescribes for that person how his or her world will be classified, divided, distinguished, and named.

The delivery of health service by nurses and other health professionals is complicated by disparities between cultural groups and how they classify, divide, and name the world around them. People vary widely in the manner by which they segment the health-illness, pregnancy-nonpregnancy, maternal-paternal gradients. The thin lines which divide these gradients change from one cultural group to another; hence we witness cultural variation.

Nurses continually attempt to understand different systems of perceptions, aims, and interests. Recognition of differences is the first step toward understanding, and although this does not explain the differences or automatically clear up misconceptions, it does lay the groundwork for understanding and effectively responding to sociocultural differences.

If maternity nurses are to understand the total delivery of health care to women and their families and render effective family-centered maternity care to this population, they must become knowledgeable about cultural groups, their concepts of health and illness, and their health practices. By doing so, the nursing care offered will be in concert, rather than in conflict, with the client's health needs. Madeleine Leininger, a nurse anthropologist, makes this poignantly clear:

The patient's cultural background alerts the nurse to a range of possible health problems and the ways a patient's health problems may be culturally expressed.... The culture aspect of behavior is as crucial in the treatment of a patient as the physical and psychological aspects of his illness. The culture concept can help nurses to understand broad patterns of human behavior as well as highly specialized behavior modalities, and it can help them understand why behavior which is culturally learned and transmitted from one generation to the next is often difficult to change. With today's concern about fair treatment of minority group members, it is imperative that nurses be aware of the culture concept and adjust their nursing care accordingly.[10]

People who are members of different cultural groups have their own sets of health norms and practices, and several things can occur as the result of this. The person may find that the health beliefs and practices of the dominant culture are incongruous with his or her beliefs; hence they build resistance to the health care offered by the dominant group, thereby neglecting care except in crisis situations. Or, as with many Native Americans in the United States, two systems of health care exist side by side: the scientifically based system of the dominant culture, and the indigenous, spiritual system, with its "medicine bundle." At times one system may conflict with the other, causing the client to become confused and distrustful.

Nurses should certainly question whether or not they have the right to impose their standards of health and health practices upon members of distinct cultural groups. They should also question if past imposition of these standards is not partially responsible for alienation of clients.

Without dispute, America is a pluralistic society, one in which cultural diversity permeates the American way of life. Emphasis until very recently has been upon assimilation of all groups into the melting pot, which tended to obscure the multicultural nature of our society. It must be remembered, however, that concepts of health, illness, disease, pregnancy, childbirth, sexual relations, self-exposure, pain, happiness, and body functioning have different meanings for different cultural groups.

How can nurses learn about the various cultural groups to which they deliver health service? Some are fortunate to have a broad background in the social sciences, which enables them to call upon past learning and to be cognizant of where to look for information. Other nurses have backgrounds which have brought them into contact with different cultural groups. Still others need direction and help in seeking such information.

Schools of nursing should accept the responsibility for educating students systematically and comprehensively about different cultural groups, and their health beliefs, habits, and needs. Some schools of nursing are offering this type of education but until this becomes a national norm, it becomes a matter of independent responsibility and knowledge seeking on the part of the nurse.

The scope of this book precludes a detailed analysis of cultural groups in the United States. However, independent study by the nurse can be a very exciting and rewarding adventure. We often become quite parochial in our self-directed, educative endeavors; this is one opportunity to reach out of the realm of nursing into other related disciplines, such as anthropology, sociology, and social psychology, for the purpose of learning about cultural groups within the United States and elsewhere.

At the end of this chapter is a bibliography which is a beginning for the interested person to learn about how other groups understand and cope with health, illness, and maternity-cycle phenomena.

The theme which runs throughout this textbook is that few if any health-related concerns during the maternity cycle can be defined and solved within the confines of a narrow analysis. Deepening our insight into the concepts of culture and society broadens analysis.

A social concern to many people in the United States and elsewhere today is the variety of ways the family unit is defined. In contrast with the traditional definition, the family unit of today may consist of the mother of the baby; the father of the baby, who may not be the mother's husband according to the legal definition, or a man who is not the father of the baby; and the baby. It is sometimes difficult for nurses to assume the role of initiator of mother-father-baby interaction because of these new and different family configurations. Often it is necessary for nurses to spend time working through personal feelings in order to arrive at a place in their careers at which they can deliver objective care to populations holding different moral and ethical values.

Family Relationships

During the second and third stages of labor the woman is concentrating on herself, working diligently on childbearing. The nurse may find that during the fourth stage of labor the mother is not really anxious to see or hold the baby. This may indicate several things, one of which may be that she has not yet transcended the turned-in phase of the previous stages of labor. Then too she may be truly fatigued from the childbearing process. The fatigue, either by itself or in combination with the residual turned-in phase, affects the degree to which the mother can extend herself to her new baby. The father may choose to adhere to the mother's wishes regarding seeing and holding the baby.

In some instances it may be the nurse's assessment that it is wise *not* to urge the parents to interact with the baby immediately, but instead wait until such time that fatigue and the turned-in phase subside. When the parents indicate readiness, the baby should be taken to them, allowing sufficient time for them to examine and cuddle the baby, and to become acquainted.

If the mother had general anesthesia during delivery and/or if the father was not allowed in the delivery room, there is a possibility that they have not had an opportunity to hold and caress, cuddle and inspect, the baby together. The needs of the mother and father relative to seeing and holding the baby can be assessed if the nurse will *listen* to what they say, and ask a few questions of them.

The fetus has now become a living, breathing baby. However, the human mother and father, unlike other mammals, are not parents by instinct. Humans must learn to be parents. They must learn to cultivate an affective relationship with the baby. There is often a time lag of a few hours to a few days or weeks before the mother and father experience feelings of motherliness or fatherliness toward the baby. Mothers in particular, if questioned about when they first experienced a maternal feeling, can often identify almost the exact instance the feeling occurred. They usually say the feeling came upon them suddenly, and describe it as a warm, protective, nurturant kind of feeling.[11] If the conditions of mother and infant permit, in order to foster maternal attachment, every effort possible should be made to unite them during the infant's alert stage which usually occurs during the first 30 to 60 minutes after birth.

Figure 24-1 illustrates a form developed by Sharon Schindler Rising and tested by students and staff nurses at Yale University School of Nursing. This form facilitates nursing observations of mothers and infants during the fourth stage of labor.

It can be a frightening experience for a mother to experience lack of feeling for her baby, particularly when she believes that she should, in fact, have immediate motherly feelings when the baby is first placed in her arms. The same is true for the father. If a nurse assesses from the parents' behavior that this is a concern, it can be explained to them that there is sometimes a period of time before maternal and paternal feelings toward the baby are experienced. The optimum time for such anticipatory guidance, however, is before delivery. If parents know about the possibility of a time lag, they will be more cognizant of their lack of feelings toward the baby, should this occur, and some of their concern might be allayed. The maternity nurse plays an integral role in helping the mother and father anticipate and understand present and future parent-child relationships.

Parents who are not familiar with so small

FIGURE 24-1

Observations of responses of the mother during the fourth stage of labor. (*Courtesy of Sharon Schindler Rising, University of Minnesota School of Nursing.*)

Patient's name:_____

Please circle appropriate responses:

Verbal responses
1   Calls baby by name
2   Calls baby affectionate terms
3   Comments on beauty of baby and on realistic defects
4   Voices unhappiness over sex of baby
5   Calls baby "it"
6   Uses unhappy or scolding inflections
7   Asks husband or nurse if baby is all right
8   Talks about baby
9   Answers in monosyllables
10 Complains of difficult labor and delivery
11 Does not talk about baby
12 Requests that baby be taken to nursery
13 Seeks considerable support for own discomfort

Nonverbal responses
1   Looks, reaches out to baby
2   Hugs, touches baby
3   Smiles at baby
4   Kisses baby
5   Undresses baby
6   Does not touch baby

a human being as a newborn baby may feel intimidated, and hence reluctant to interact with their new family member. They display their insecurity in the manner by which they hold the baby, usually awkwardly and tensely. Their facial expressions and tone of voice indicate tension, and they are seemingly unable to find a comfortable position. These feelings and behaviors affect the smooth and comfortable patterns of family-infant interaction which nurses strive for and which new parents set forth as their ideal. The nurse can offer to show the parents methods by which they can comfortably and safely hold their baby, thereby acting as a role model whose behavior can be emulated by the parents.

Emotional Factors

There is a wide range of emotions displayed by mothers and fathers during the first hour postpartum. The manifestation of emotions to a great extent is dictated by the fatigue level of the parents. Many exhibit profound fatigue similar to that experienced after strenuous physical exercise. However, even when fatigue is present, elation and excitation can also be present, and it is not unusual for parents to share with the nurse that they feel utterly tired out, but excited and wide awake at the same time.

It is not uncommon for the parents to cry, laugh, shout, embrace, talk constantly, and kiss lavishly, and these emotions may be

  7   Does not look at baby
  8   Pushes baby away
  9   Tenses face, arms
 10   Sleepy, not drug induced
 11   Turns away from baby
 12   Turns away from husband, nurse, visitor
 13   Positive eye contact, emotional feeling with husband
 14   Unresponsive to husband, nurse, visitor
 15   Cries unhappily
 16   Holds husband's hand
 17   Breast-feeds baby

First comments made in delivery room by mother about baby:

_____

Visitor with mother during fourth stage:_____

Involvement of husband or visitor: _____

Problems with baby: _____

Subjective opinion of response of mother: _____

Analgesia within last 4 hours:_____   Parity: _____

Anesthesia: _____   Age: _____

Complications: _____   Marital status: _____

Significant social history:_____   Feeding method: _____

_____   Service: _____

_____   Race: _____

Behavior of baby:

    Crying: None_____periodic_____almost continuous_____

    Affect: Difficult to arouse_____dozes_____eyes open_____very alert_____ heightened when the baby is being cuddled between them. It is important for the nurse to observe and record these behaviors, for not only do they aid in tension reduction for the parents, but they can serve as indicators of intrafamilial relationships.

It is important to remember that this is a period of time for the parents during which important role transitions are taking place. These transitions demand different parental behaviors, and the parents often respond on an emotional level to such demands. It takes time, fortitude, patience, and knowledge to become a parent, and none of these is without its unique emotional implication.

A common complaint of mothers during the fourth stage of labor is a feeling of chill. This chill often occurs while the mother is being prepared for transfer to the recovery room, while she is being transferred, or immediately after the transfer. The mother may actually tremble or shake as a manifestation of the chill. The chill usually does not last over 10 to 15 minutes.

There are numerous hypotheses regarding cause of the chill, some of which include the following.[12–15]

1   The mother's nervous reaction and exhaustion related to childbearing are manifest in chilling.
2   Muscular exertion during labor and delivery causes disequilibrium between the internal and external body temperature.
3   There is a sudden release of intra-abdominal pressure after the uterus is emptied, which in turn affects the central nervous system.
4   Lack of aseptic technique during labor predisposes to infection in the mother, giving rise to chills as one manifestation of the infection.
5   Postpartum chills probably represent minute, circulatory amniotic fluid emboli and are associated with scanty amniotic fluid volume.
6   Previous maternal sensitization to elements of fetal blood, as well as fetal/maternal transfusions at the time of delivery, cause a reaction in the mother manifested by chills.

The chills are annoying and are sometimes frightening and embarrassing to the mother and father. Whether this reaction is emotional, physiological, or an interaction of the two, the nurse can be helpful by truthfully reassuring the mother and father that chills are not uncommon after delivery and that they may have a multifactor etiology. Comfort measures should be offered by the nurse; these might include a warm, dry blanket and gown, an increase in room temperature, and, if not contraindicated, warm fluids by mouth.

Mothers often ask the same questions over and over again about their delivery and about the baby. The nurse should recognize this as a normal emotional reaction, a necessary process allowing the mother to move out of the symbiotic relationship she has had with the fetus during pregnancy.[16] The baby must be a separate person before the mother can become acquainted with him or her. This psychological separation of baby from mother is an important phase in the development of the maternal role and for the future of the mother-child relationship. Disengagement of the symbiotic mother-fetus relationship of pregnancy is sometimes referred to as "cutting the psychological cord."

CONTINUITY OF CARE DURING THE FIRST HOUR POSTPARTUM

Organization of Patient Assessment

The nurse is responsible for assessing the mother's physical condition as soon as she has been settled in her postpartum bed. The technique of the assessment should be organized in order that important observations are not deleted. The assessment includes:

1 Palpation of the fundus of the uterus
2 Massage of the fundus if it is boggy and observation for bladder distention
3 Expression of clots and free blood from the uterus
4 Measurement of the fundus in relation to the umbilicus
5 Inspection of the perineum for discoloration and swelling; inspection of lochia and change of perineal pads
6 Recording of blood pressure and pulse
7 Assessment of pain
8 Offering food and fluids if allowed
9 Promotion of comfort and safety

It is important for the assessment to be done at specific time intervals so that the nurse is able to compare the mother's condition on a sequential basis. The American College of Obstetricians and Gynecologists recommends that the postpartum patient be under constant observation by the nurse and that the mother is checked at least every 15 minutes for 1 hour postpartum for uterine atony, hemorrhage, deviations in blood pressure and pulse, and other indicators of complications.[17] The mother must be checked more often than every 15 minutes if her condition is not stable.

Each step of the assessment is explained to the patient. This should be, indeed, a basic nursing skill, but it must be reinforced once again that the nurse must take time, especially before the initial check, to explain to the mother and father what is involved in the nursing care about to be administered. The care involved in palpation, massage, and expression of the uterus may be uncomfortable for the mother, and she should be prepared for this possibility. Relaxation by the patient

of her abdominal muscles will expedite the check, and this should be shared with her.

A basic nursing skill which is often neglected on maternity wards is provision of privacy for the mother. Too often there is unnecessary exposure of the mother's body during the postpartum check because of lack of adequate screening devices or draping techniques.

It is usually not necessary for the father to leave the room while the nurse works through the assessment. Certainly there are times when this is appropriate, but most of the time it is not. The father and mother should be consulted regarding their desires in this situation, and if they decide for him to remain in the room, the nurse can be creative in providing privacy for the mother. For example, the nurse can have the mother elevate and flex her legs so that the bed linens form a tentlike structure, as shown in Figure 24-2. The mother is asked to hold the bed linen taut by pulling the linen to her upper chest and neck. The nurse then approaches from the side, and exposes the mother's abdominal and perineal areas by lifting the loose linen flap formed by the mother's thigh and

FIGURE 24-2
Providing the mother with privacy during the postpartum check by fashioning a tentlike structure from the bed linens. (*Courtesy of Abbott-Northwestern Hospital, Minneapolis, Minnesota, Calista Arneson, and A. M. Haukebo.*)

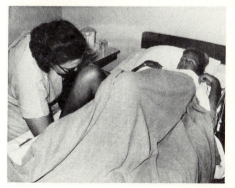

lower leg. The linens on the side facing the father are left intact, thus providing the mother with privacy.

If the mother is unable to flex her legs because of effects of anesthesia, another means of providing privacy can be employed. The nurse approaches the mother from the side on which the father is sitting, thus using the body to shield her from undue exposure during the assessment.

More often than not, if the father remains in the room he will look out the window, read, or become otherwise engaged during this time. He most often senses the mother's need for privacy and behaves accordingly.

The postpartum assessments should not be lengthy procedures. As the nurse acquires competence in checking the mother, it will be found that these checks can be completed thoroughly and efficiently in just a few minutes without conveying haste to the mother and father. Sufficient time is spent to ensure that the needs of the parents are met, and for the nurse to be assured that the mother's physical condition is fully supportive of life processes.

Palpation, Massage, Expression, and Measurement of the Uterus

Oxytocic medications are administered to the mother intravenously or intramuscularly during the delivery of the baby's anterior shoulder, during delivery of the placenta, or immediately after the placenta is delivered. These medications stimulate uterine contractions, the effect of which may last several hours.

Oxytocics work well in prevention of uterine atony, the most common cause of postpartum hemorrhage. Nonetheless, the action of these drugs is contingent upon the overall physical condition of the patient. It must *not* be assumed because sufficient doses of oxytocics were administered to the mother that

assessment of uterine tone is not necessary. The tone of the uterus is dependent on many factors other than whether or not the mother has had oxytocics, some of which include antepartum hydramnios, size of the baby, parity, multiple births, uterine inertia during labor, length of labor, and the amount of urine in the bladder.

Contraction of the uterus occurs when the mother hears the newborn baby's cry or when she sees or holds the baby. In some hospitals, the baby is put to breast on the delivery table. In all of these instances, oxytocin is released from the mother's hypothalamus, circulates via the bloodstream to the uterus, and causes uterine contraction.

In preparation for this portion of the assessment, the perineal pad is released and the mother's legs are flexed and spread. If spinal or caudal anesthesia was used, it probably will not be possible for the mother to flex her legs. The fundus of the uterus is palpated by placing the side of one hand on top of and slightly cupped under the fundus, while the other hand is placed suprapubically with the exertion of slight pressure as shown in Figure 24-3. Ideally, the fundus

FIGURE 24-3
Hand maneuvers involved in palpation of the fundus of the uterus. (*Courtesy of Abbott-Northwestern Hospital, Minneapolis, Minnesota, Calista Arneson, and A. M. Haukebo.*)

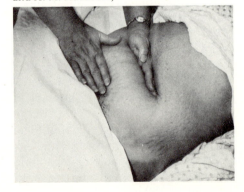

should lie on the midplane of the pelvis, at or below the umbilicus.

If the fundus is boggy, it is *gently* massaged until it contracts and becomes firm. Care must be taken not to overmassage, and hence overstimulate, the fundus. Unnecessary manual stimulation, in the absence of bleeding or increased size of the uterus, may cause overstimulation of the uterine muscles, which will result in undue muscle fatigue, relaxation of the organ, and possible hemorrhage.

The bladder area is observed at this time for signs of distention. If the mother has had intravenous therapy during labor and delivery, the bladder will tend to fill more rapidly because of hydration of body tissues. The palpation maneuver performed by the nurse facilitates observation of the bladder, but in addition to the maneuver outlined above, *limited* pressure is exerted on the fundus by the hand that is cupped above and slightly under the fundus.

If the bladder is filling or full, a bladder bulge will be evident and will feel and appear as a spongy, fluid-filled mass below the uterus and above the symphysis pubis. Figure 24-4 illustrates a full bladder postpartum. The nurse's left hand is shown palpating the fundus of the uterus which is high in the abdomen to the patient's right. The nurse's right hand is shown palpating the full bladder area. The mother may inform the nurse at this time that she has the urge to urinate. However, patients, particularly those who have had a caudal or saddle block, often do not experience the urge to urinate during the first hour postpartum.

A full bladder inhibits contraction of the uterus by elevating the uterus high in the pelvis and displacing it from midline. The mother should be given the opportunity to void, and in the event she cannot, even when nursing measures are employed to stimulate voiding, the nurse should follow the physi-

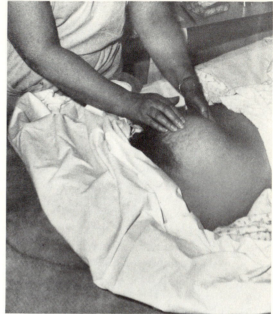

FIGURE 24-4
Palpation of a full bladder on a postpartum patient. The nurse's left hand indicates the fundus of the uterus, which has been displaced to the patient's right by the large, full bladder underlying the nurse's right hand. *(Courtesy of Abbott-Northwestern Hospital, Minneapolis, Minnesota, Calista Arneson, and A. M. Haukebo.)*

cian's orders regarding emptying the bladder.

Expression of the fundus is accomplished by utilizing the same hand maneuvers as those shown in Figure 24-3. In addition, during expression pressure is applied to the fundus with one hand while equal pressure is applied suprapubically with the other hand. Expression is done in sequential 3- to 5-second intervals, with several seconds rest between, until the nurse is sure that clots and free blood held in the uterine cavity have been expressed sufficiently.

After palpation, massage, and expression have been completed, the uterus usually remains firm for a period of time, although the possibility always exists that it may not remain contracted. If there is any doubt regarding the tone of the uterus, or if during the assessment it is believed that bleeding and clotting is heavier than it should be, the nurse must repeat the maneuvers more frequently than the suggested every 15 minutes.

A measurement of the height of the fundus is taken after the fundus is expressed, measuring from the top of the fundus to the umbilicus. Most commonly fingerbreadths are used to measure, as shown in Figure 24-5, but in some institutions a measuring tape is used.

The fundus of the uterus tends to lie closer to the umbilicus in mothers who are multiparous than in those who are primiparous. Multiparas usually have larger uteruses than primiparas, due to repeated stretching of the muscle fibers with subsequent loss of muscle tone. Any condition which has resulted in overdistention of the uterus also predisposes the mother to have a larger uterus.

Perineum

Perineal discomfort is the result of trauma to the area from the episiotomy and is a common complaint of mothers during the first hour postpartum, particularly after the local anesthetic loses its effect. It should be remembered that the episiotomy is a surgical wound in a highly vascular and innervated area of the body, and the nature of its location predisposes the woman who has undergone episiotomy to discomfort.

Women experience various types of episiotomy discomfort. That which is most frequently described is a burning, dull, aching, pulling sensation. Right or left mediolateral episiotomies seem to cause more discomfort than median episiotomies. This is understandable if one takes into account the perineal musculature and skin structure; there is

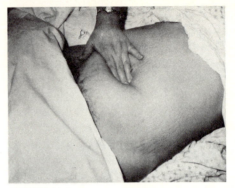

FIGURE 24-5

Measurement of the fundus of the uterus in fingerbreadths, from the top of the fundus to the umbilicus. (*Courtesy of Abbott-Northwestern Hospital, Minneapolis, Minnesota, Calista Arneson, and A. M. Haukebo.*)

more muscle and skin tension on a mediolateral episiotomy than on a median, and hence, more discomfort. This discomfort may become particularly pronounced when the mother changes position in bed, attempts to sit upright, or gets out of bed.

Some physicians order an ice bag applied to the perineum for several hours postpartum. The cold lessens the edema in the area and also has a numbing effect so that the mother's discomfort is not as pronounced.

While inspecting the perineal area during the postpartum assessment, the nurse may observe swelling and/or ecchymosis. This may be indicative of the formation of a perineal or perineal-vaginal hematoma. If a hematoma is present, and if it continues to enlarge, the mother will complain that in addition to severe pain in the perineum, she is experiencing rectal pressure as though she needs to evacuate her bowels.

The nurse can make a positive nursing diagnosis of a hematoma by touching the area *very lightly* with a sterile gauze, or with the patient's perineal pad. If the swelling is more than edema, and is, in fact, the beginning of a hematoma, the mother will complain of extraordinary tenderness when touched. The doctor should be notified immediately. The possible formation of a hematoma is considered when there is any type of perineal swelling postpartum. Once a hematoma begins to form, it may enlarge to an extent that the mother experiences severe perineal pain. Hematomas can become so large that the mother exhibits signs of circulatory shock from extravasation. The importance of inspecting the mother's perineum during the first hour postpartum cannot be overemphasized.

Perineal varicosities are sometimes present, although their occurrence is not frequent. They result from increased uterine pressure on pelvic veins which causes stasis of the blood in the perineal region. Some women are hereditarily predisposed to varicosities both in the perineal area as well as in the lower extremities.

Perineal varicosities may be uncomfortable postpartum. However, in many cases, because intraabdominal pressure has been relieved by birth of the baby, the dull aching and weighty sensations caused by the varicosities is lessened considerably. Then, too, during the fourth stage of labor, any local anesthetic used during delivery may still be effective, decreasing the amount of perineal discomfort experienced.

It is not necessary to carry out complicated procedures for perineal care except those which keep the area as clean and dry as possible. Regular change of perineal pads and linens under the buttocks is required to prevent lochia from becoming dry and adhering to the mother's body. Often it is necessary for the nurse to wash the perineal area and buttocks with mild soap and water to remove lochia not absorbed by the perineal pads. The perineal area approximate to the episiotomy should be washed first with a gentle,

patting motion; care should be taken to wash from the vaginal and episiotomy area toward the rectum.

When checking the perineal pads for amount of lochia, the mother is rolled on her side so that the nurse can accurately determine the amount of bleeding. The lochia is prone to collect under the buttocks and sacral area, and is obscured from sight if the patient is not turned on her side during the assessment.

The lochia during the fourth stage of labor is rubra, neither dark red nor bright red. Normally, it has a fleshy odor, similar to that of fresh blood. Lochia consists of blood from the placental site, shreds of membranes, vernix, lanugo, decidua, and meconium.

During postpartum assessments particular note is taken of the odor, consistency, and color of the lochia. Putrefactive bacteria cause foul-smelling lochia, which is an indication of maternal infection, and therefore possible infant infection. Lochia which contains strings of mucus also indicates infection. Size and consistency of lochial clots are observed and noted in the chart. If the nurse has any doubts as to whether or not the clots contain placental tissue, this should be reported to the doctor and the clots saved for the doctor's inspection.

A constant, *bright red* trickle of lochia from the vagina in the presence of a well-contracted uterus is an indication of fresh bleeding. This is usually the result of cervical or vaginal laceration or both. The doctor is notified immediately so that the laceration can be repaired thereby preventing increased maternal blood loss.

As was discussed previously, nurses may keep a perineal pad count at their own discretion, for purposes of comparison of the amount and character of lochia over a period of time. The pads are kept in a covered container.

Blood Pressure and Pulse

The optimum postpartum blood pressure and pulse recording is that which most closely approximates the mother's antepartum blood pressure and pulse rate, provided these vital signs were within normal limits at that time. If the mother's blood pressure was elevated during pregnancy, it is not uncommon for it to quickly descend to within normal limits (systolic below 140 mmHg, diastolic below 90) during the first hour postpartum.

Excitement after delivery may cause elevated blood pressure and pulse rate in some mothers. Ergonovine may cause some women to experience elevated blood pressure and pulse rate. The combination of general anesthesia, cyclopropane, and oxytocics administered during or after delivery has been cited as a causative agent of elevated blood pressure and pulse in the postpartum patient.

Caudal and saddle block anesthesia have been identified as agents which lower vital signs through their effect on the sympathetic nervous system. Women who have been heavily sedated during labor and delivery exhibit lowered blood pressure recordings and pulse rates.

Blood pressure and pulse recordings as indicators of circulatory shock from hemorrhage are not entirely reliable in that these vital signs initially show only moderate fluctuations even though the mother may be bleeding heavily. After a large amount of blood has been lost, and the circulatory system is no longer able to compensate for the decrease in blood volume, the pulse rate increases rapidly to the extent that it is difficult to count. The blood pressure drops abruptly, although this drop is very often observed *after the pulse rate increases.* For this reason, many physicians, nurse midwives, and experienced maternity nurses believe that pulse rate is a more accurate indicator of the patient's condition than blood pressure.

The mother's vital signs are influenced by her circadian rhythm, or biological clock. Research has shown that the blood pressure is highest between 4 and 6 P.M. and lowest between 1 and 6 A.M. The blood pressure begins to rise, with corresponding rise in pulse rate, early in the morning as the person approaches wakefulness. Considerations of circadian rhythm should be taken into account by the nurse in interpreting the mother's vital signs during the first hour postpartum, as well as through the entire postpartum course.

The pulse rate is usually slower during the postpartum period until the seventh to tenth postpartum day, at which time it returns to the normal rate. This decrease in rate is thought to be associated with the change in the mother's patterns of activity.

Pain

Pain during the fourth stage of labor is most frequently associated with uterine contractions and the episiotomy. Multiparous women are more prone to experience uterine cramping than are primiparous women. The postpartum uterus of a primipara tends to remain in a contracted tonic state unless it has undergone extreme distention, or unless blood clots or placental tissue are retained. A multiparous woman has less uterine tone because of past pregnancies, and consequently her uterus contracts and relaxes rhythmically. These contractions, whether experienced by multiparas or primiparas, are uncomfortable, and their intensity may reach levels which require the nurse to administer a prescribed analgesic to the patient.

Factors other than parity which affect the amount and intensity of postpartum uterine contractions (afterpains) include the amount of urine in the bladder, interaction with the baby including nursing, and the retention of blood or clots within the uterine cavity. As discussed previously, a bladder which is filling or full displaces the uterus and inhibits effective contraction. Interaction with the baby stimulates uterine contractions in that upon seeing, hearing, and nursing the baby, sensory impulses pass to the spinal cord, then through the brainstem, and finally into the hypothalamus, where the production of maternal oxytocin is stimulated.[18] The oxytocin then circulates through the mother's blood to the uterus, where it causes contraction of the uterine muscle. Free blood, clots, and retained placental fragments also affect uterine contractions; their presence stimulates the uterine muscles to contract in an attempt to empty the uterine cavity.

The fact that the newly delivered mother is a primipara should not cause the nurse to view this mother's first hour postpartum complacently. Although this patient has the potential for optimum uterine functioning and tonicity by virtue of her parity, the nurse must care for her as vigilantly as the multiparous patient.

Perineal pain as the result of the episiotomy has been discussed previously, and the reader is referred to this content.

Review of the literature relative to pain reveals that many aspects of pain have been studied by numerous researchers. Laurel Archer Copp, a nurse who has researched and studied pain, made the following interesting observation:

Although doctors and nurses work at the bedside, few have studied . . . the pain experience. The cause and process of pain have been investigated through technology, pharmacology, physiology, and anesthesiology. The religious and the existentialist have described and attempted to account for the place of pain in life. But no one, including the anthropologist, sociologist, and psychologist, has markedly enriched our awareness of the phenomenon of suffering. The course is almost uncharted, though we are indebted to a few patient-authors.[19]

Copp suggests that there are two questions nurses should consider when caring for patients who are experiencing pain.[20] The first focuses on the nurse-patient relationship, and asks: Who are we to that patient? Patients view nurses as people who play out many different roles, some of which include a controller, transporter, communicator, informant, judge, avoider, empathizer, and barterer.[21]

The second question which nurses should ask themselves is: What does pain mean to the patient? In order to answer this question, it is necessary for nurses to put the patient and the pain into context—into a biological, sociological, psychological, anthropological, and cultural context. By doing so the nurse gains a better understanding of how the patient may cope with pain.

It is important for maternity nurses to understand that prolonged pain reduces the mother's ability to cope and reduces her ability to maintain body homeostasis. Pain stimulates the sympathetic nervous system, which in turn stimulates the production and release of adrenalin.[22] The adrenalin stimulates the heart muscle, causing an increase in pulse rate, peripheral vasoconstriction, and possible subsequent rise in blood pressure. These factors in turn affect the body's homeostatic state.

Nurses have little difficulties identifying pain if the postpartum patient is verbal. Presence of the pain is verbalized by the patient and can be validated by an assessment carried out in a physiological and sociocultural context. A plan of action can be formulated in conjunction with the patient, and nursing actions can be implemented that will relieve the pain.

However, the more stoic postpartum patient may not readily verbalize pain; the verbal expression of pain to some people is not socially or culturally acceptable because of tradition or belief systems. The nurse may note with this type of patient that body language reveals a wealth of information. Unusual postures, writhing, frequent position changes, and general restlessness could be clues that the patient is experiencing pain which she is not verbalizing, and which she may need help to verbalize. Blood pressure and pulse may be elevated from pain as the result of increased adrenalin output. The skin may become moist with perspiration; the patient may become nauseated. Behavior reversals may be manifested in that a woman who was cheerful and outgoing may become quietly introverted.

Eileen McLachlan sums up, briefly and appropriately, patient manifestations of pain from which nurses make assessments and upon which nursing actions are based:

People speak of suffering with their cries, their moans, their whimpers. The body also speaks of pain.[23]

The mother's individual, culturally influenced meaning of pain, her unique experience with pain, and her immediate emotional and physiological state influence her reactions to and perception of pain. Anxiety is a reaction closely associated with pain; if the nurse can be with the mother or close by, if truthful explanations for the cause of the pain are offered, and if questions are answered, the patient's anxiety will be lessened.

Analgesics should not be given unjudiciously during the fourth stage of labor, even though maternal-infant attachment may be adversely affected by excessive, unnecessary pain. Nurses must be accountable for the medications they administer, and accountability is contingent upon the conscious utilization of the entire nursing process in identifying and relieving patient pain.

Food and Fluids

The ingestion of food and fluids during the fourth stage of labor is largely dictated by the physician's orders and by the mother's physical condition and needs. Some physicians order fluids and food withheld from the mother until all effects of general anesthesia are completely absent.

Some women experience nausea as a result of the movement of the bed or cart during transfer to the postpartum room; anesthesia; medications during labor and delivery; an empty stomach; or a combination thereof. Tea or a carbonated beverage and dry soda crackers or unbuttered toast are usually tolerated well if the mother shows interest in trying food. Many women want to attempt to eat and drink immediately after delivery, even though nausea may be present. They are quick to attribute their nausea to hunger, and naturally they are thirsty. Often the mother is correct in her assessment, but there are times when she simply cannot tolerate food and fluids. The nurse should anticipate this and place an emesis basin close by, in an inconspicuous but accessible location.

The mother should be encouraged to eat a small amount at first, to eat and drink slowly, and to chew the food well. The degree of hunger and thirst experienced by mothers varies from those who are disinterested in food and fluids to those who are ravenous. The ability of the mother to tolerate food and fluids depends not only on her hunger and thirst but on the *haste* with which she attempts to ingest the nourishment.

Comfort, Reassurance, and Rest

Childbearing is often accompanied by feelings of apprehension on both the mother's and father's part. The environment and personnel are usually strange to them, and they may feel somewhat emotionally insecure during the first hour postpartum even though such insecurity is not a part of their usual emotional character. They may not know quite what to think of the new baby. The father may have heard the mother cry out during labor and delivery, and may be wondering why this happened, and what will happen now. The mother may experience episiotomy discomfort, afterpains, nausea, or leg cramps and may not know why.

The mother and father need reassurance at this time. Ernestine Wiedenbach defines reassurance most appropriately as "the presence of someone who knows what to do."[24] In addition to knowing *what* to do, the maternity nurse should know *how* to do it, *why* it is done, and *when* to do it. This, then, is the essence of reassurance that parents need from the nurse.

Second to reassurance is the need of the mother and father for rest. This is often difficult to accomplish during the fourth stage of labor because of the excitement inherent in the childbearing process. It is difficult for parents to quiet down; there is so much to talk about and share with one another. Other things are also happening which deprive the mother and father of rest. These may be positive, such as visiting with the baby, and they may be necessary, such as the nurse assessing the mother's physical condition.

Although a deep, restorative sleep may not be possible during the first hour postpartum, the nurse must lay the groundwork for deep sleep attainable at a later time. This can be accomplished by expert observation of the patient, watching for signs of uterine atony, deviations in vital signs, perineal hemato-

mas, urinary retention, or other untoward conditions which, unless resolved, will cause the mother sleep loss during a time when necessary deep sleep would otherwise be acquired.

The mother should be encouraged to attempt to rest, if not sleep, during this first hour postpartum. The nurse can facilitate patient rest by careful scheduling of patient care. The mother should not be disturbed unnecessarily, and care should be organized in order that a maximum amount is completed through brief contact during specific intervals.

The mother's legs should be observed and palpated for presence of varicosities, edema, and reddened streaks on the skin. Varicosities may predispose to phlebitis, and edema and reddened streaks on the skin are symptoms of phlebitis.

If the physician is aware of the presence of maternal varicosities, supportive stockings may be ordered to be put on during the fourth stage of labor while the mother is still in bed. Some mothers with varicosities find it helpful and comfortable to have their legs elevated 10 to 15° during the first hour postpartum, and perhaps after that time. This positioning facilitates emptying of stagnant blood from the overdilated vessels.

Proper body alignment is a prerequisite to rest. The nurse can assess if the mother is able to align herself comfortably or whether she needs help. Surely the mother will need help if she has had a saddle block or caudal anesthesia. Sufficient numbers of pillows should be provided to prop her head, arms, legs, and back. The physician's orders must be checked, however, for some physicians do not allow a pillow under the head after a saddle block.

Is the mother warm enough, or is she too warm? Newly delivered mothers often complain of cold feet, a condition that can be easily remedied with warm blankets. Are the bed linens clean, smooth, and secure under and over her? Is her perineal pad clean and in place? Has she had food and fluids, if allowed? The answers to these questions are important for the mother's comfort. The absence or presence, as the case may be, of any one or a combination of conditions outlined above will not be conducive to rest. The nurse has the ultimate responsibility to the patient to help induce rest by promoting her comfort.

Fathers also become tired. They have often spent long hours giving support to the mother through the labor and delivery process. Does the father need a cup of tea or coffee, a sandwich, some milk or juice? What would be quick and nourishing for him from the unit kitchen? Where could he go close by for a quick snack? Perhaps he would rather rest. Is there an easy chair and footstool for him, or an extra pillow? Is the room temperature comfortable for him?

Rest can come only after the mother and father are reassured, only after they feel the nurse knows what to do, how to do it, why it is done, and when to do it. Comfort measures are only a part of reassurance. The mother and father continue to gain reassurance as they assess the competence by which the nurse delivers care duing the postpartum period.

THE CESAREAN SECTION MOTHER AND FATHER

The dynamics associated with the fourth stage of labor differ little between the cesarean section mother and father and those who have been delivered vaginally. One primary difference is that the cesarean section parents often experience a longer time lapse between delivery of the baby and expression of emotions. The opportunity for family interaction is also delayed. These delays can be attributed, in part, to the surgery, the anesthesia, and the subsequent time required to overcome the effects of both. The mother and father need facts and reassurance about the mother's and baby's conditions before they are able to cope with the emotional aspects and role transitions associated with childbearing.

Probably the greatest differences between the cesarean section mother and father and those whose babies were delivered vaginally are observable later in the postpartum period, during which time the parents address themselves to care of a high-risk baby, adjustment of the mother postoperatively, and inherent implications thereof.

The cesarean section mother spends the majority of the first hour postpartum in the postoperative recovery room. The time interval for patient assessments may be more frequent than every 15 minutes and will depend on hospital policy set forth for immediate postoperative care, as well as the immediate condition of the mother. Concentrated attention is given to the mother for signs of abdominal incision bleeding, as well as vaginal bleeding.

The postpartum assessments are conducted with the same maneuvers as those for a vaginally delivered mother. The nurse must be very gentle when palpating the fundus so that unnecessary stress is not placed on the abdominal incision. It is wise to check with the physician before expressing the uterus, for there are different opinions about expression of a cesarean section mother's uterus. Some believe it must be done, with gentleness of course, whereas others believe it should not. Abdominal dressings often prohibit either accurate palpation or effective expression of the uterus. Nursing care of the cesarean section mother during the first hour postpartum is otherwise like that of abdominal surgery patients.

In some hospitals the father is allowed to be with the mother in the postoperative recovery room, if only for a brief time. If possible, the baby should be brought to the parents at this time, but these factors are contingent upon the condition of the mother, the condition of the baby, and hospital policies. When the mother is transferred to the postpartum unit, the nurses responsible for her care will more than likely bear responsibilities not only for care of a postoperative, postpartum patient but also for initiating family relationships. These *in toto* are indeed heavy responsibilities.

CONCLUSION

The first hour postpartum is of critical importance to the well-being of the newly delivered mother. This period is referred to as the fourth stage of labor because the uterus continues to relax and contract just as it did during the first three stages of labor.

Nursing care during this time is focused on the total woman and her family and is founded on an understanding and integration of the physiological, psychological, and sociocultural factors affecting the client. Scientifically based, purposefully organized, judiciously executed nursing care is required during the fourth stage of labor; nothing else is tolerable. Hopefully, this chapter will be informative and beneficial to nurses who care for women during the first hour postpartum, lest they be accused of being

. . . impatient nurses whose one thought is to get the patient off the table and into her room . . . ignorant of the postplacental period (fourth stage of labor) . . . and its proper management . . . a threat to the safety of the mother, especially when the postplacental hour is exclusively entrusted to [them].[25]

REFERENCES

1 Greenberg, Emanuel M.: "The Fourth Stage of Labor," *American Journal of Obstetrics and Gynecology*, 52:746, 1946.

2 Ibid., p. 749.

3 Carlson, Sylvia: "A Practical Approach to the Nursing Process," *American Journal of Nursing*, 72(9):1589–1591, September 1972.

4 Finch, Joyce: "Systems Analysis: A Logical Approach to Professional Nursing Care," *Nursing Forum*, 8(2):177–191, 1969.

5 American Nurses' Association: "Nursing Directors Tackle the Nursing Process, POMR's," *The American Nurse*, vol. 6, November 1974.

6 Hellman, Louis M., and Jack A. Pritchard: *Williams Obstetrics*, 14th ed., Appleton-Century-Crofts, New York, 1971, p. 466.

7 Wiedenbach, Ernestine: *Family-centered Maternity Nursing*, 2d ed., Putnam, New York, 1967, p. 334.

8 Ibid., p. 335.

9 Leininger, Madeleine M.: *Nursing and Anthropology: Two Worlds to Blend*, Wiley, New York, 1970, pp. 20–21.

10 Ibid., p. 21.

11 Caplan, Gerald: *Concepts of Mental Health Consultations, Their Application in Public Health Social Work*, 2d ed., Children's Bureau, Washington, D.C., 1966, pp. 62–63.

12 Fitzpatrick, Elise, Sharon R. Reeder, and Luigi Mastroianni: *Maternity Nursing*, 12th ed., Lippincott, Philadelphia, 1971, p. 302.

13 Hellman and Pritchard: op. cit., p. 471.

14 Jaameri, K. E. U., A. Jahkola, and J. Perttu: "On Shivering in Association with Normal Delivery," *Acta Obstetricia et Gynecologica Scandinavica*, 45(4):383–388, 1966.

15 Goodlin, R. C., L. P. O'Connell, and R. E. Gunther: "Childbirth Chills. Are They an Immunological Reaction?" *Lancet*, 2:79, 1967.

16 Caplan: op. cit., pp. 79–82.

17 *Standards for Obstetric-Gynecologic Hospital Services*, The American College of Obstetricians and Gynecologists, Chicago, 1969, p. 42.

18 Guyton, Arthur C.: *Function of the Human Body*, 2d ed., Saunders, Philadelphia, 1965.

19 Copp, Laurel Archer: "The Spectrum of Suf-

fering," *American Journal of Nursing*, 74(3): 491, March 1974.

20   Ibid., p. 495.

21   Ibid.

22   McLachlan, Eileen: "Recognizing Pain," *American Journal of Nursing*, 74(3):497, March 1974.

23   Ibid.

24   Wiedenbach: op. cit., p. 307.

25   Greenberg: op. cit., p. 749.

BIBLIOGRAPHY

Alland, Alexander: *Adaptation in Cultural Evolution: An Approach to Medical Anthropology*, Columbia University Press, New York, 1970.

Baratz, Stephen S.: "The Unique Culture of the Ghetto," *The Center Magazine*, Center for the Study of Democratic Institutions, Santa Barbara, Calif., July 1969.

Becker, Howard S., et al. (eds.): *Institutions and the Person: Essays Presented to Everett C. Hughes*, Aldine, Chicago, 1968.

Bernstein, Betty: "What Happened to Ghetto Medicine in New York State?" *American Journal of Public Health*, 61:1287, July 1971.

Brasch, R.: *How Did It Begin? Customs and Superstitions and Their Romantic Origins*, McKay, New York, 1967.

Brazelton, T. B., J. S. Robey, and G. A. Collier: "Infant Development in the Zinacanteco Indians of Southern Mexico," *Pediatrics*, 44: 274–290, 1969.

Browne, Ray B.: "Popular Beliefs and Practices from Alabama," *Folklore Studies 9*, University of California Press, Berkeley, 1958.

Caudill, W., and H. Weinstein: "Maternal Care and Infant Behavior in Japan and America," *Psychiatry*, 32:12–43, 1969.

Curtis, Natalie (ed.): *The Indians' Book: An Offering by the American Indians of Indian Lore, Musical and Narrative, to Form a Record of the Songs and Legends of Their Race*, 2d ed., Dover, New York, 1968.

Edwards, J.: "Needed: Patient-oriented Nursing in the Maternity Unit," *Hospital Topics*, 48:83–86, March 1970.

Freedman, D. G., and N. A. Freedman: "Differences in Behavior between Chinese-American and European-American Newborns," *Nature*, 224:1227, 1969.

French, J. G.: "Relationship of Morbidity to the Feeding Patterns of Navajo Children from Birth through Twenty-four Months," *American Journal of Clinical Nutrition*, 20:375–385, 1967.

Gorman, C. N.: "Navajo Vision of Earth and Man," *The Indian Historian*, 6:19–22, 1973.

Hostetler, J. A., and G. E. Huntington: *Children in Amish Society: Socialization and Community Acculturation*, Holt, Rinehart, Winston, New York, 1971.

—— and ——: *The Hutterites in North America*, Holt, Rinehart, Winston, New York, 1967.

Ianni, F. A. J., and E. Story (eds.): *Cultural Relevance and Educational Issues: A Reader in Anthropology and Education*, Little, Brown, Boston, 1973.

Kallen, D. J.: "Nutrition and Society," *Journal of the American Medical Association*, 215:94–100, 1971.

Kiev, Ari (ed.): *Magic, Faith, and Healing*, Free Press, Glencoe, Ill., 1964.

Kluckhohn, C., and D. Leighton: *The Navajo*, Harvard University Press, Cambridge, 1946.

Leacock, Eleanor B. (ed.): *The Culture of Poverty: A Critique*, Simon and Schuster, New York, 1971.

Le Vine, R. A.: "Outsiders' Judgments: An Ethnographic Approach to Group Differences in Personality," *Southwestern Journal of Anthropology*, 22:101–116, 1966.

Lewis, Hylan: "Culture, Class and the Behavior of Low-Income Families," paper presented at the Conference on Lower-Class Culture, June 27–29, 1963, New York; revised August 1965.

——: "Culture, Class and Family Life among

Low-Income Urban Negroes," in Arthur M. Ross and Herbert Hill (eds.), *Employment, Race, and Poverty*, Harcourt, Brace, World, New York, 1967.

Liebow, Elliot: *Talley's Corner: A Study of Negro Streetcorner Men*, Little, Brown, Boston, 1967.

Meltzer, David: *Journal of the Birth*, Oyez, Berkeley, 1967.

————: *Birth*, Ballantine, New York, 1973.

Nader, Laura, and Thomas W. Maretzki (eds.): *Cultural Illness and Health: Essays in Human Adaptation*, American Anthropological Association, Washington, D.C., 1973.

Newman, Lucile F.: "Folklore of Pregnancy: Wives' Tales in Contra Costa County, California," *Western Folklore*, vol. 28, 1969.

Paul, Benjamin D., and Walter B. Miller (eds.): *Health, Culture and Community: Case Studies of Public Reactions to Health Programs*, Russell Sage, New York, 1955.

Randolph, Vance: *Ozark Superstitions*, Columbia University Press, New York, 1947.

Tapia, Jayne A.: "The Nursing Process in Family Health," *Nursing Outlook*, 20:267–270, April 1972.

Ward, M. C.: *Them Children: A Study in Language Learning*, Holt, Rinehart, Winston, New York, 1971.

Werblowsky, R. J. Zwi, and Goeffrey Wigoder (eds.): *The Encyclopedia of the Jewish Religion*, Holt, Rinehart, Winston, New York, 1965.

PART
FOUR

CHILDREARING AND THE NURSING PROCESS

UNIT A

THE NEWBORN

25

The Physiological Basis of Neonatal Nursing*

CYNTHIA LEPLEY

What makes being born so frightful is the intensity, the boundless scope and variety of the experience, its suffocating richness. People say and believe—that a newborn baby feels nothing. He feels everything. Everything—utterly, without choice or filter or discrimination. Birth is a tidal wave of sensation, surpassing anything we can imagine. A sensory experience so vast we can barely conceive of it.

Leboyer, *Birth without Violence*

The effects of the complex interplay of genetic endowment, intrauterine environmental factors, obstetric-pediatric management, and nursing care are manifest in the status of the newborn infant at birth. The major part of the development of the infant

* The author wishes to acknowledge that much of the material in this chapter in the first edition, then prepared by Rose LeRoux and the late Shirley Yee, is included in this edition.

has gone on in utero unperceived by direct clinical observation and largely inaccessible to treatment. Much research has been generated by this perplexing state. Current scientific research focuses on both fetal and neonatal physiology. Although there are many interesting studies available on the subject, there appears to be little absolute agreement among scientists regarding many facets of fetal and neonatal physiology. Some of the facts which have been previously discovered are now interpreted differently. When it was known that babies grew at different rates in utero, the terms *small for gestational age* and *low birth weight* replaced the blanket term *premature*. Because of the changing concepts regarding the fetus and the neonate, nurses who wish to become proficient in their care would do well to consult the most current research studies available on this subject. The basic tenets of infant care persist. They are to provide the newborn infant with protection from harm, adequate food, a stable environment, and bodily contact in which love and security are communicated.

The neonatal period is arbitrarily designated as that time from birth to 28 days of life. It is during this period, especially during the first 24 hours, that the infant is at high mortality and morbidity risk. To provide optimal care to the neonate during this period, the maternity nurse should possess a considerable amount of theoretical knowledge, clinical expertise, and superior judgment. Careful monitoring of the condition of the neonate, manipulation of his or her environment as necessary, and assisting in the infant's transition from intrauterine to a stable extrauterine environment are all part of the nursing role. The nurse must assist the parents in taking on new roles and must recognize potential problems in this area. Early discharge of infants and their mothers from hospitals often precludes the identification of high-risk mother-infant relationships as well as any potential physical problems with the infant. Nurses who work with mothers and their newborn infants would do well to follow them from birth through the first month of life, both in the hospital and in the home setting. It is obvious that it would be in the best interest of the infant to begin care of the potential mother in the preconceptual period.

Most infants are normal when they are born and proceed through the transitional period with a minimum amount of difficulty. Most of the organ systems are prepared to adapt and function in the extrauterine environment. However, many organ systems are not *quite* physiologically mature at birth. Therefore, a neonate does not at birth function physiologically like an adult or even like an older child. The neonatal period is characterized by a considerable amount of instability of many systems; however, each organ system will continue to develop according to its own timetable in an orderly fashion. In order to understand the neonate's behavior the nurse must realize that the observed behavior depends in a large part on an intact and functional physiological mechanism and its relative maturational stages. The term "normal" should not mislead the nurse who cares for newborn infants into assuming that they need any less attention than those infants labeled "high-risk." The nurse should sharpen the ability to examine and observe newborn infants for the accumulation of many and varied insignificant signs which may indicate impending difficulties. Neonatal nursing practice is based on strong theoretical and empirical knowledge derived from direct observation and care of neonates.

The field of neonatal physiology is complex and challenging. This chapter does not purport to cover the subject in depth. Information important to nursing has been extrapolated at the risk of oversimplification. It is strongly recommended that the reader consult current physiology and pediatric texts for more complete information on the subject.

CARE OF THE NEONATE IMMEDIATELY FOLLOWING DELIVERY

The birth of an infant marks the *beginning* of extrauterine existence and the *continuation* of a process of growth and development which began with the fertilization of the ovum by the sperm. At birth, the infant loses the metabolic support of the placenta. Through his or her own breathing, the infant must inhale oxygen, perfuse vital gases through the cardiovascular system, and exhale carbon dioxide. Negotiating successfully from intrauterine to extrauterine life is a major challenge to the neonate. Although most of the neonate's organ systems are prepared to adapt to extrauterine life, they will not reach a state of mature functioning for varying periods of time after birth. This relative immaturity makes it difficult for the newborn infant to adapt to unusually stressful environmental conditions.

A considerable amount of clinical expertise is required of the medical-nursing team in the delivery room. There are times when both mother and infant may be having acute problems, and the delivery-room team must rapidly institute appropriate treatment to each simultaneously. Time is frequently the critical variable affecting a favorable outcome. Therefore, hospitals which assume the responsibility for delivering mothers should provide for expert obstetric and pediatric management. The articulation of obstetrics and pediatrics is nowhere more dramatically illustrated than in the delivery room.

The Establishment of Respirations

The priorities of delivery-room care in regard to the baby are to establish respirations, to monitor the cardiovascular system, and to provide temperature regulation and support. The extent of brain impairment which results from failure to breathe within a few minutes of birth may be greater than is presently documented. Existing evidence supports the proposition that the *prompt onset of breathing should be considered essential* to the neonate's subsequent mental and physical development. Animal studies have indicated that there may be several factors which contribute to the neonate's apparent resistance to the life-threatening effects of anoxia. These factors are the infant's low body temperature, low and variable energy metabolism, low cerebral metabolism, and the amount of blood glucose available. The ability to resist the harmful effects of anoxia are lost shortly after birth. A healthy infant whose mother has not received large amounts of analgesia or anesthesia during labor and delivery should breathe within a few seconds or, at the most, a few minutes after birth. Many infants breathe as soon as the head is delivered.

Physical-sensory and *biochemical* factors appear to stimulate the onset of respiration, but the exact cause remains a subject for research. Among the physical-sensory factors are the rapid expansion of the chest following the compression which has occurred during passage of the infant through the birth canal, the stimulation of the infant's tactile receptors through handling during and immediately following delivery, the abrupt change from a fluid to air environment, and the change from a higher to lower temperature. A powerful effort is required to open alveoli in the lungs, for the surface tension of the alveolar fluid must be overcome. Surfactant which is present in the normal lung assists in overcoming the surface tension. Care should be taken when administering oxygen with prolonged positive pressure by mechanical ventilation, for studies have shown that prolonged ventilation can severely damage the alveolar cells which produce surfactant.[1]

The biochemical changes occur simultaneously with the physical-sensory changes. When the umbilical cord stops pulsating anoxia results from the interruption of the oxygen supplied by the placenta. Carbon dioxide accumulates in the blood, lowering the pH to a point at which the respiratory centers of the medulla are stimulated and breathing should result. Although the initial expiration of the neonate should clear the airway of accumulated amniotic fluid and permit inspiration, it is wise to suction mucus and fluid from the infant's mouth as soon as the head is delivered. This procedure prevents aspiration of this material if the infant gasps with the first breath. A small, soft rubber bulb syringe is usually used for this purpose. A soft catheter attached to a De Lee mucus trap or a mechanical suction machine may also be used. Care must be taken not to traumatize the delicate tissues of the infant's oropharynx. If a large amount of mucus is present, the physician may hold the infant in a head-down position to facilitate drainage from the infant's oropharynx.

Efforts to stimulate crying in the newborn infant are usually limited to gentle rubbing of the infant's back. Slapping the soles of the infant's feet, alternate hot and cold tubbing of the infant, and other such methods are considered dangerous and ineffectual. They only delay the institution of appropriate resuscitation measures.

Every delivery room should be equipped with resuscitation equipment. Personnel who deal with the establishment of respiration in the neonate should be knowledgeable about the procedures proposed by the American Academy of Pediatrics regarding resuscitation of the infant. If a pediatrician is not regularly available in the delivery room, those persons who are available should be trained in resuscitation techniques. Routine procedures should be delayed until respirations are established and maintained in the neonate.

The quality and rate of respirations are extremely variable during the newborn period and are largely diaphragmatic in character. Shallow, slow, and labored breathing is not normal and may require emergency treatment. It is important for the nurse to observe the normal synchronous movements of the infant's thorax and abdomen during respiration to detect early signs of respiratory difficulty. In some newborn infants there may be a few alveoli which do not expand completely for more than a week. Usually these findings are within normal limits.

Changes in the Cardiovascular System

At birth changes occur in the cardiovascular system which result in altered pathways of blood flow and variations in blood volume, pressure, and chemical composition. The clamping of the cord eliminates the supply of oxygenated blood from the placenta. Thereafter the infant must obtain oxygen from the lungs. To accomplish oxygenation of the blood by the lungs several alterations in the anatomic structure of the circulatory system must occur. These changes are brought about by complex biochemical factors in the blood as well as alterations in blood volume and pressure within specific blood vessels. It is beyond the scope of this chapter to discuss the biochemical alterations that precipitate the circulatory changes, but a brief explanation of the structural alterations will be given.

Following delivery the supply of oxygen

from the placenta is removed by the interruption of blood flow through the umbilical cord. The resultant lack of oxygen is one of the factors leading to the first insufflation of the lungs, as has been previously discussed. After the initial inspiration the resistance to blood flow through the lungs is greatly decreased. Blood flowing through the pulmonary arteries increases the pressure in these vessels. The increased pressure is a precipitating factor in the closure of the *ductus arteriosus*. It is probable that the increased oxygen content of the circulating blood in the pulmonary arteries also contributes to the closure. The closure of the ductus arteriosus accompanied by the closure of the *foramen ovale* and the obliteration of the umbilical vessels leads to the establishment of the adult pattern of circulation in which the unoxygenated blood is separated from the oxygenated blood. There is a short interim during which the infant retains some of the fetal

patterns of circulation. Figure 25-1 shows the normal pathways of circulation in the fetus, neonate, and adult.

Table 25-1 illustrates that these circulatory changes are not instantaneous with the first respiration. The ductus arteriosus remains partially patent for 24 to 48 hours, after which it closes functionally. In most infants it remains closed and is obliterated anatomically at about 3 months. However, in cases of neonatal hypoxia the ductus arteriosus may reopen, causing an increased right-to-left shunt. It is probable that some cyanotic episodes in neonates are related to this phenomenon. The flap of the foramen ovale is pushed shut against the atrial septum as soon as the pressure of the blood in the left atrium exceeds that in the right. It is now believed that there is some shunting of blood through the foramen ovale for about the first week following delivery. After this period the foramen ovale remains functionally

TABLE 25-1
Changes in the Circulatory Mechanism at Birth

Structure	Prenatal function	Postnatal function
Umbilical vein	Carries oxygenated blood from placenta to liver and heart	Obliterated to become ligamentum teres (round ligament of liver)
Ductus venosus	Carries oxygenated blood from umbilical vein to inferior vena cava	Obliterated to become ligamentum venosum
Inferior vena cava	Carries oxygenated blood from umbilical vein and ductus venosus and mixed blood from body and liver	Carries only unoxygenated blood from body
Foramen ovale	Connects right and left atria	Functional closure by 3 months, although probe patency without symptoms may be retained by some adults
Pulmonary arteries	Carry some mixed blood to lungs	Carry unoxygenated blood to lungs
Ductus arteriosus	Shunts mixed blood from pulmonary artery to aorta	Generally occluded by 4 months and becomes ligamentum arteriosum
Aorta	Receives mixed blood from heart and pulmonary arteries	Carries oxygenated blood from left ventricle
Umbilical arteries	Carry oxygenated and unoxygenated blood to the placenta	Obliterated to become the vesical ligaments on the anterior abdominal wall

SOURCE: C. Henry Kempe et al., *Current Pediatric Diagnosis and Treatment*, Lange, Los Altos, Calif., 1974, p. 20. Used by permission of the publishers.

closed in the normal person, although it may be anatomically patent to some degree in a few adults.

An important but controversial factor in the hemodynamics of the newborn is the time of clamping of the umbilical cord. The infant receives an additional 50 to 100 ml of blood if clamping is delayed until the cord ceases to pulsate. According to some physicians this extra blood makes available to the

FIGURE 25-1
(a) Fetal circulation; (b) immediate postdelivery circulation; (c) normal circulation.
(*From Ralph C. Benson, Handbook of Obstetrics and Gynecology, 5th ed., Lange, Los Altos, Calif., 1974, pp. 76–77, by permission of the publisher.*)

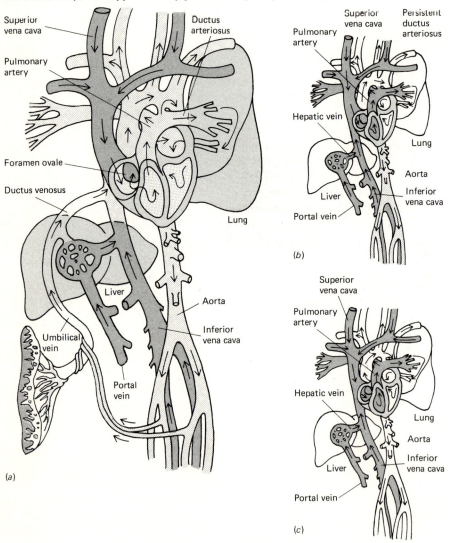

infant an increased amount of iron to be stored and utilized during the first months of life when the infant receives little iron in his or her food. During this time the infant must rely upon the iron which was received during fetal life to satisfy the body's need for this element. Other physicians contend that the advantages of the extra blood have not been clearly proved. In addition, research studies have demonstrated that the increased amount of blood in an infant who is already polycythemic and vulnerable to respiratory distress may produce mild pulmonary edema. Some investigators have noted that the incidence of pulmonary rales and transient cyanosis is more consistently associated with late clamping of the cord.[2] At present the trend seems to be toward early rather than late clamping of the cord. The advantages of the increased iron supply to the infant are considered by many physicians to be less important than the risk of inducing respiratory distress. While there is no undue hurry to clamp the cord, the baby is no longer held below the level of the mother's body to induce more blood flow into the circulation nor is the cord stripped, as was previously done.

Temperature Regulation and Support

Proper temperature regulation of the newborn infant has been shown clearly to increase the infant's chances for survival.[3-5] It is well known that wide variations in temperature can cause death in humans. Adults generally are able to control the temperature of their environment, adjust themselves to it, or remove themselves from it. They can raise their body heat production by shivering, which may increase the metabolic rate of the body by 180 percent over basal levels. They can lower their body temperature by sweating.

By contrast newborn infants have diffi-culty in adapting to even moderate variations in temperature. They have relatively poor resources to resist the effects of both heat and cold. This inadaptability is due in part to the fact that the mechanisms of sweating and shivering are not well developed in the neonate. The sweat and sebaceous glands which are present have little homeothermic function until a month or so following birth. Added to this liability is the newborn's large surface area in relation to body mass and the meager amount of subcutaneous fat which results in poor insulation. The blood vessels therefore lie relatively close to the surface of the skin and are sensitive to environmental temperature. The environmental temperature influences blood temperature, which affects the regulatory centers for temperature control located in the hypothalamus. These factors all contribute to the relative instability of body temperature characteristic of the neonatal period.

Much research is being done regarding the contributions made by various organs and tissues to heat production in the neonate. Brown fat, which has a high mitochondrial content, a rich nerve and blood supply, and a high metabolic rate in vitro, is thought by some researchers to aid in temperature control in the neonate exposed to cold much as it does in the hibernating animal. The in vivo contribution of brown adipose tissue to thermal homeostasis in the newborn infant is not presently known. The largest amounts of this fat are found in the intrascapular region of the neonate's body; some is also found in the thorax and perirenal areas.

Research studies have demonstrated that when neonates are exposed to temperatures lower than their neutral temperature range, they make an effort to increase their metabolism and raise their body temperature by crying, by increased skeletal muscle activity, and by increased respiratory rate. The *neutral temperature range* is defined as that set of environmental conditions in which oxygen consumption is at a minimum.

Increased respiratory rate (leading to increased oxygen intake) as a response to cold is a phenomenon occurring only in the neonate and may be referred to as metabolic or chemical *thermogenesis*. The demand for additional oxygen occurs in response to increased catabolic cell activity during which heat and other forms of energy are released. If the demand for oxygen by the body tissues exceeds the supply over a period of time, the risk of neonatal acidosis increases. In the absence of sufficient oxygen the neonate's cells perform relatively more anaerobic catabolism (e.g., the Embden-Meyerhof pathway of glycolysis) the by-product of which is an increase in blood acids (e.g., lactate). In addition the neonate may become extremely fatigued from breathing rapidly and working hard to obtain additional oxygen. If acidosis develops because of the preceding circumstances, the neonate must be warmed, given oxygen, and treated for acidosis immediately. Judicious monitoring of the neonate's temperature is required to prevent such complications from occurring. Chilling the neonate should be avoided under all circumstances. All procedures, including those of an emergency nature such as resuscitation, should be performed on the neonate in a warm area, such as a heated crib, incubator, or radiant heater.

The prevention of loss of heat from the body is as important as heat production. Infants lose 27 percent of their body heat through evaporation of water from the skin and from the exhalation of water vapor from their lungs. To avoid heat loss through the evaporation of amniotic fluid from the skin the newborn infant should be swaddled in a warm, absorbent blanket and dried. Three percent of body heat is lost by the infant through urine, feces, and warming inspired air. Because 70 percent of body heat is lost through radiation, conduction, and convection, a warmed incubator, heated bed, or radiant heat shield should be provided immediately following birth. To derive maximum benefit from a radiant heat shield the baby should remain uncovered after drying. Such devices should be checked regularly for safety.

To maintain ideal body temperature in the newborn infant, the environmental temperature must be carefully monitored to prevent fluctuations. In addition to controlling the environmental temperature of the neonate, the nurse must observe the infant carefully and frequently. The nurse must discriminate whether crying, restlessness, and increased respirations in the neonate are due to the infant being cold or to other factors.

Essential Care in the Delivery Room

The Apgar Scoring System

The Apgar scoring system provides a systematic and reliable appraisal of the condition of an infant at birth. It is best to use an automatic timer to remind the nurse to take and record the infant's scores promptly at 1 minute and 5 minutes of age. The infant's Apgar score provides valuable information about the infant's condition at birth and has proved to be a reliable predictive instrument. Follow-up studies indicate there is a high positive correlation between infants who have a low Apgar score at 5 minutes of age and subsequent mortality or neurological morbidity in those infants.[6]

The Apgar scoring system is based on the following five signs which are ranked in order of importance. Each sign is evaluated as illustrated in Figure 25-2 and given a score of 0, 1, or 2 according to the degree it is present or absent. The maximum score an infant can receive is 10. Few newborn infants receive scores of 10, as *acrocyanosis* due to vasomotor instability is very common in the

SIGN	0	1	2
Heart Rate	Absent	Slow Below 100	Over 100
Respiratory Effort	Absent	Slow Irregular	Good Crying
Muscle Tone	Flaccid	Some Flexion of Extremities	Active Motion
Reflex Irritability	No Response	Grimace	Cry
Color	Blue Pale	Body Pink Extremities Blue	Completely Pink

FIGURE 25-2
Apgar score chart. (*Photograph from* Apgar on Apgar, *film sponsored by Gerber Products Co., 1967.*)

newborn infant. The *heart rate* is determined by auscultation of the apical pulse. If the heart rate is below 100 the doctor should be notified immediately. *Respiratory effort* and *muscle tone* are evaluated as described in the chart. *Reflex irritability* refers to the infant's response when disturbed by light slapping of the foot, oral suctioning, or insertion of a catheter into the nares. A healthy infant will respond to such irritation by grimacing, crying vigorously, or resisting. In approximately 15 percent of newborn infants the body will be completely pink by 5 minutes of age. In the other 85 percent the hands and feet remain bluish for some period of time. A score of 8 to 10 for a newborn infant is considered good; a score of 5 to 7 is considered moderately depressed; a score of 4 or less indicates a severely depressed infant and resuscitation may be indicated.

The Umbilical Cord

After the umbilical cord has been clamped and cut, it should be examined for the presence of three vessels: two arteries and one vein. A single umbilical artery has been associated with congenital anomalies and is considered a congenital vascular malformation. The nurse should make certain that the clamps are secure and that there is no bleeding from the stump. The stump should remain uncovered to facilitate drying and healing.

Prophylaxis against Ophthalmia Neonatorum

A *1 percent silver nitrate solution* is recommended as prophylaxis against gonorrheal ophthalmia by the National Society for the

Prevention of Blindness. The silver nitrate solution should be instilled so that it will cover all parts of the conjunctival sac. Antibiotic ointments are not recommended as prophylactic agents because there are certain strains of gonococci which are resistant to them and there is concern about infants developing a sensitivity to them.[7]

Infant Identification

When the newborn infant's condition is physiologically stable, the infant should be identified properly. This should be done while the infant is still in the delivery room with the mother. From a legal as well as a moral standpoint, proper identification is an extremely important procedure. Various procedures are used for this purpose. A recommended practice is to secure two identical identification bands to the infant's wrist and ankle. The bands should state the sex of the infant, the mother's full name and hospital admission number, and the date and time of birth. The mother should have a corresponding wristband. The infant's footprints are generally recorded on the baby's hospital record which also contains the mother's right index fingerprint. It is important that prints be recorded carefully, since they are of no value unless they are very clear and legible.[8]

Other Observations

Although a thorough physical examination is usually deferred until the newborn infant has recovered from the birth experience, several important observations are generally made in the delivery room. Color, gross malformations, and unusual body configurations or facies (commonly associated with congenital syndromes) can be readily observed. *Choanal atresia* (obstruction of the posterior nares), which has been associated with many

breathing problems of infants, can be ruled out by holding a hand across the infant's mouth to test if the infant can breathe through the nose. Some physicians recommend passing a soft tube through the mouth into the stomach to rule out esophageal atresia. If aspiration of the gastric contents yields over 20 to 25 ml of fluid, an upper intestinal obstruction may be suspected. This procedure is not without hazard, since accidental irritation of the larynx can cause laryngospasm. Palpating the vertebral column carefully may rule out spina bifida occulta. The amount and color of amniotic fluid associated with delivery, the size of the placenta, and the amount of vernix on the infant should also be recorded.[9]

If the condition of the mother and infant warrants it and the mother so desires, she should be allowed to hold her infant while still in the delivery room. If the father is present, he should be included in these initial family interactions which facilitate taking on new family roles. Some mothers wish to nurse their infants in the delivery room. Nursing is a sound physiological practice which stimulates the pituitary gland to secrete oxytocin, causing the uterus to contract with a resultant decrease in uterine bleeding. Nursing has additional psychological benefits for both mother and infant. Therefore, if the condition of the mother and infant justifies it, the mother's request to nurse her infant in the delivery room should be honored.

CARE OF THE NEONATE IN THE NURSERY

Care of the Neonate in the Transitional or Observation Nursery

The neonate is transferred as soon as possible from the delivery room to a transitional or observation nursery if one is available. Infants who are high-risk or obviously distressed should be transferred directly to an intensive care unit. Priorities for care of the neonate in the transitional nursery should be established. Such priorities are added to those already begun in the delivery room, namely, maintaining respirations and a patent airway, supporting the cardiovascular system, and regulating temperature control. That the first day of life is a critical one for most neonates is reflected in statistics regarding infant mortality rates. Of the total number of infant deaths occurring during the first year, the largest percentage occurs during the first 24 hours after birth; of these deaths, the great majority occur during the first hour after birth.

In light of this, arbitrary priorities for care have been set because neonates are more vulnerable to certain conditions at particular times during their development (e.g., hemorrhagic disease). Prophylactic intervention at these crucial times prevents the development of serious problems. Although certain physiological mechanisms of the neonate have been selected for consideration, this does not imply that all physiological systems are not developing simultaneously (although at different rates). Nor does it imply that the emotional needs of the neonate are any less vital than physiological needs. Underscoring all the care that is given by the nurse to the newborn infant are the infant's basic emotional needs for love, comfort, security, and protection from harm.

The priorities for transitional nursery care are to obtain base-line data regarding vital signs and measurements, to assign the infant a mortality risk rating, to provide an environment which will facilitate transition through the birth recovery period, to provide prophylaxis against neonatal bleeding tendencies, and to observe the neonate carefully for the onset of illness. A method for charting some of this information is shown in Figure 25-3.

Upon admission to the transitional nursery

the infant should be placed in an incubator or warmed bed. Information regarding the antepartum history, the labor and delivery experience, and other relevant information should be recorded on the infant's chart. *Vital signs* should be checked frequently, since they are extremely variable in the neonate. Several consecutive determinations are necessary to establish a base line by which to compare later readings. Preferably the heart rate, respiratory rate, and blood pressure should be taken when the infant is quiet, for they will increase markedly when the infant is crying. In any case, the state of the infant should be noted when the vital signs are recorded. The first temperature should be taken rectally to determine patency of the anus. All subsequent temperatures should be axillary recordings in order to prevent irritation of the rectum and the possibility of frequent stooling. Particular attention should be paid to the fact that *infants with infections often run subnormal or erratic temperatures.* Other signs such as poor feeding, vomiting, diarrhea, or lethargy are much more reliable indications of infection than is temperature.

Accurate measurements of the infant are essential for a number of reasons. They are used to help determine gestational age, as evidence of intrauterine growth retardation, to establish a base line against which to measure later growth of the infant, and to help identify high-risk infants. Measurements of weight, length, and head circumference are usually made in the transitional nursery after the infant has reached a relatively stable condition. These measurements are recorded on forms, as shown in Figure 25-4. Assuming that the infant is over 2 kg, the absolute size of the infant is not as important as the *percentiles* within which each of his or her measurements fall. Weight, height, and head circumference lying in different percentiles increase the probability that the infant has suffered from some intrauterine growth re-

```
                                    Date                              9/1/75

                                    Ward

              Newborn Nurseries     Name

        ADMISSION AND TRANSITIONAL RECORD
                                    Hosp. No.

                                    Mother's Hosp. No.

 Pediatrician Called_____  Mother's Blood Type & RH_____
 Apgar: 1 min____ 5 mins_____      Baby's   Blood Type & RH_____
 Resuscitation, Complications, Comments_____

                        NURSE'S ADMISSION RECORD
 Admit Time to Med-Risk Nurs_____ AM/PM  Calculated Gestational Age_____wks
     Color_____   Clinical  Gestational Age_____wks
     Cry_____   Sole Creases              _____wks
     Respiratory Rate_____            Breast Tissue             _____wks
               Quality_____      Ears                      _____wks
     Heart Rate_____              Vernix                    _____wks
     Blood Pressure: Arm_____      Genitalia                 _____wks
                 Leg_____          Desquamation              _____wks
     Rectal Temp_____                 Resting Position          _____wks
     Activity_____           Recoil                    _____wks
     Birth Wt_____gms                  Ventral Suspension        _____wks
     Lgth    _____cms                  Wrist Angle               _____wks
     HC      _____cms                  Dorsiflexion, foot        _____wks
     Wt/Lgth Ratio_____                NB Class & % Mort
     Anomalies/Remarks_____          Calculated_____
     _____               Clinical  _____
     _____

 Dextrostix_____mg %  Age_____mins
 Periph Hct_____%     Age_____mins
 Central Hct_____%     Age_____hrs

                              _____RN
 ------------------------------------------------------------------------
 Transferred from Medium-Risk Nursery to_____
                                        Date_____Time_____AM/PM
 Lgth of Stay in Medium-Risk Nursery_____hrs/days

                              _____
                                          Signature
 ------------------------------------------------------------------------
                PHYSICIAN'S FINDINGS ON ADMISSION TO NURSERY
                (Use Case Record Form For Complicated Delivery)
 Age_____hrs

                        Signed_____
                               (designate training level)

                        Signed_____
                               (Attending)
```

FIGURE 25-3
Newborn nurseries admission and transitional record. (*By permission from University of Colorado Medical Center, Denver, Colo.*)

tardation. Other reasons for disproportionate measurements include excess edema, abnormalities in the growth of the head, or any number of genetically induced syndromes.

The neonate should be evaluated according to the criteria outlined on a chart similar to that shown in Table 25-2. The estimation of gestational age, vital signs, measurements, and the general condition of the infant are all considered when assigning the infant a mortality risk rating. Figure 25-5 illustrates a mortality risk chart. The mortality risk rating determines whether or not the infant will remain in the transitional nursery or be transferred to an intensive care unit. The birth recovery period is characterized by rapidly changing physiological and behavioral characteristics. The infant's rating may change from low-risk to high-risk at any time during this period. The nurse who cares for neonates must be able to interpret the infant's behavior and symptomatology accurately

FIGURE 25-4
Colorado intrauterine growth charts. Percentiles of intrauterine growth in weight, length, head circumference, and weight/length ratio. (*By permission from Lula O. Lubchenco, et al., "Intrauterine Growth in Length and Head Circumference as Estimated from Live Births at Gestational Ages from 26 to 42 Weeks," Pediatrics, 37:404, 1966.*)

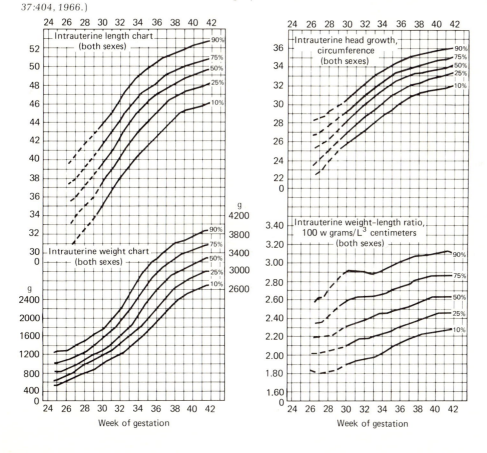

TABLE 25-2
Clinical Estimation of Gestational Age: A Guide

Physical findings		Weeks gestation (Est ga: 24 → 44)
Examination first hours		
Vernix		Appears (24–25); Covers body (30–33); Decrease in amount (39–40); No vernix (42–44)
Breast tissue	Nipples	Barely visible (27–28); Well-defined, raised areola (34–36); Well-defined areola (40–41)
	(breast nodule)	None (29); 1–2 mm (35–36); 4 mm (38); 7 mm or more (41–42)
	Sole creases	None (29–30); 1, Anterior transverse (32); 2, Anterior transverse (35); Anterior ⅔ sole (37–38); Creases involving heel (40–41)
Ear cartilage		Pinna soft, stays folded (27–30); Returns slowly from folding (36); Thin cartilage, springs back (38); Firm, remains erect from head (41–44)
Ear form		Flat, shapeless (29–32); Beginning incurving of periphery (35–36); Partial incurving upper pinna (38–39); Well-defined incurving all of upper pinna (41–43)
Genitalia	Testes and scrotum	Undescended (28–29); Testes high in canal, few rugae (31–33); Testes lower, more rugae (37); Testes descended, pendulous scrotum, rugae complete (41–42)
	Labia and clitoris	Labia majora widely separated, prominent clitoris (28–33); Labia majora nearly cover labia minora (37–38); Labia minora & clitoris covered (41–42)
Hair (appears on head @ 20 weeks)		Eyebrow & lashes (27–28); Fine, woolly hair (33–34); Hair silky, single strands (41–42)
Lanugo (appears @ 20 weeks)		Lanugo over entire body (27); Vanishes from face (28); Slight lanugo over shoulders (34–35); No lanugo (41)
Skin texture		Thin (28–29); Smooth, medium thickness (36–38); Desquamation (42–43)
Skin color and opacity		Translucent, plethoric, numerous venules (abdomen) (28–32); Pink, few large vessels overall (36–37); Pale pink, no vessels seen (42–43)
Skull firmness		Soft to 2½ cm from anterior fontanel (27–31); Springy at edges of fontanel, center firm (35–36); Bones hard, sutures easily displaced (39–40); Bones hard, cannot be displaced (43–44)
Posture	Resting	Lateral decubitus (24–25); Hypotonia (29); Slight increase in tone, lower extremity (31–32); Froglike (34–35); Total flexion (41)
	Recoil	Absent (27); Slight, lower extremities (31–32); None upper extremities / Good lower extremities (34); Slow upper extremities (37–38); Good upper extremities (41–43)

Later examination

		24	25	26	27	28	29	30	31	32	33	34	35	36	37	38	39	40	41	42	43	44
Tone	Heel to ear				No resistance				Slight resistance					Difficult	Almost impossible				Impossible			
	Scarf maneuver					No resistance							Minimal resistance		Fair resistance				Difficulty			
	Neck extensors				Absent				Slight				Fair					Good				
	Neck flexors					Absent						Minimal					Fair				
Reflexes	Moro			Barely apparent			Complete, exhaustible			Good, complete				No adduction				Complete with adduction				
	Pupils to light												React								
	Grasp			Feeble			Fair				Solid, involves arms											
	Rooting			Minimal with reinforcement			Good with reinforcement						Good								
	Crossed extension				Slight withdrawal			Withdrawal				Withdrawal & extension			Withdrawal, extension, adduction						
	Automatic walk					Absent						Minimal		Fair, toes		Good, heels				
	Trunk elevation					Absent						Slight		Good						
	Glabellar tap				Absent					Appears				Present							
	Head turns to light				Absent						Appears				Present					
Clinical estimate, Ga																					
Calculated Ga																					
		24	25	26	27	28	29	30	31	32	33	34	35	36	37	38	39	40	41	42	43	44

Weeks gestation

SOURCE: C. Henry Kempe et al., *Current Pediatric Diagnosis and Therapy*, Lange, Los Altos, Calif., 1974, p. 44, as adapted from Lula O. Lubchenco et al., "Assessment of Gestational Age and Development at Birth," *Pediatric Clinics of North America*, 17:125–145, 1970.

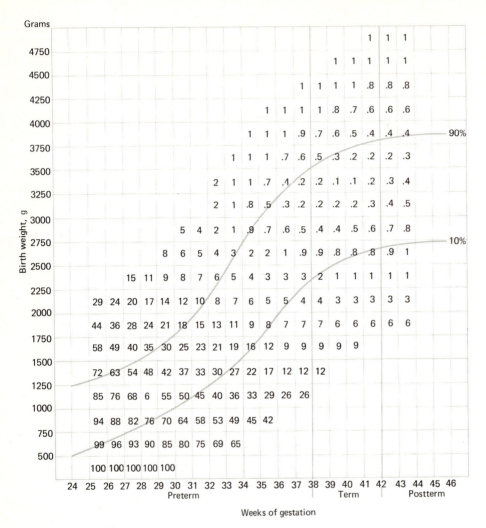

FIGURE 25-5
Neonatal classification and neonatal mortality risk by birth weight and gestational age. (*By permission from Lula O. Lubchenco, "Neonatal Mortality Rate: Its Relationship to Birth Weight and Gestation Age,"* Journal of Pediatrics, 81:814, 1972.)

and refer to a physician for treatment when indicated. The whole nursing process of assessment, plan of action, implementation, and evaulation should continue throughout the neonate's entire hospital stay and is not confined to only one period.

Prophylaxis against Hemorrhagic Disease of the Newborn

All newborn infants demonstrate a moderate deficiency in the vitamin K dependent coagulation factors.[10-12] Most vitamin K absorbed in the body is formed by the action of bacterial flora in the colon. However, this flora is usually absent in the colon at birth. It may take the newborn infant several days to establish a normal flora. Therefore, production by the liver of coagulation factors, such as PTC, prothrombin, proconvertin, and Stuart Prower factor, which depend on vitamin K, is impaired. During this time the infant may develop bleeding problems, such as ecchymosis, bleeding at the site of an injection of medication, bleeding around the umbilical cord, or excessive bleeding at circumcision. This problem, referred to as hemorrhagic disease of the newborn, can be prevented by a single intramuscular injection of water-soluble vitamin K. The usual dose is 1.0 mg, which may be administered to the infant in the delivery room or in the transitional nursery.

Neonatal Behavior during the Birth Recovery Period

Although neonates recover from the birth experience at varying rates, Desmond has identified certain behavioral and physiological patterns which most neonates seem to go through before they reach a stage of relative stability. Desmond describes three overlapping stages characteristic of the birth recovery period. During the *first stage,* which may last for about 30 minutes, the infant may appear alert and active. There is a decrease in body temperature accompanied by an increase in motor activity, respiratory rate, and heart rate. There may be flaring of the *alae nasi,* grunting, and intercostal retractions which may be outward signs of the infant's efforts to accommodate for lowered temperature. Bowel sounds are usually not heard. The infant may have large amounts of mucus which may cause the infant to drool or vomit. During the *second stage,* which may

last from 30 minutes to 2 hours, the infant falls asleep and the respiratory and heart rates slow. During the *third stage,* however, the infant awakens, and the nurse may observe a return of the initial behavior. The heart rate increases; there may be large amounts of mucus, which affect respirations, and there may be periods of apnea. Rapid color changes may be noted which indicate vasomotor instability. Meconium may be passed during this stage. As mentioned previously, vital signs concerning the neonate's heart rate, respirations, and color should be taken and recorded at 15- or 30-minute intervals.[13]

Plethora may occur in the baby at about 6 hours following delivery. At this time the infant's skin appears quite red and may turn to a purplish red when crying. In addition the skin may appear tight and shiny. This phenomenon is a result of the migration of fluid from the blood vessels into the extracellular spaces, resulting in a concentration of red blood cells within the vessels.

A central venous hematocrit over 75 percent can be life-threatening to a newborn and predispose the infant to hemorrhagic and thrombotic tendencies. Small-volume exchange transfusions should be done on infants with symptomatic behaviors. It is controversial whether an asymptomatic neonate with an elevated hematocrit should be exchanged.[14,15]

Within 6 to 8 hours following delivery, the condition of most neonates tends to stabilize; the infant may then be bathed and dressed. A healthy newborn infant may be fed when he or she first appears hungry; this period usually coincides with the completion of the birth recovery period. The first feeding should consist of 5 percent glucose in water. The neonate may take very little of the first feeding or may take several ounces. The nurse should observe and record the infant's ability to suck, the amount of mucus and regurgitation associated with the feeding, and the infant's tolerance for the feeding. When the neonate's vital signs are stable, his or her color is pink, and there are no apparent problems, the infant is transferred into a regular nursery or a rooming-in facility for the remainder of the hospital stay.

Continuing Care of the Neonate

Meticulous attention should be given to the neonate throughout the baby's hospital stay. It is important that the *reasons* for procedures are clearly understood by the personnel who are to carry out these procedures. Even though actual techniques may vary from hospital to hospital, the underlying principles, based on the neonate's physiological and emotional requirements, should be consistent and provide the rationale for the care given. There also should be sufficient staff to carry out the care prescribed. The nurse who carries out the daily activities of feeding, diapering, and keeping the infant clean is in an optimal position for detecting subtle changes in the neonate's condition, appearance, and behavior. Maintaining a patent airway in the neonate is always of primary importance. The nurse should give special attention to proper and firm positioning of the infant on his side after feeding to prevent aspiration of feeding and mucus into the trachea. The nurse should report to the physician promptly any changes which are not in the normal range.

The priorities for care in the regular nursery are to prevent infection, to provide adequate food and fluids, to detect early signs of hyperbilirubinemia, to identify illness, to recognize congenital defects that were not previously noted, and to facilitate positive mother-infant relationships. This may be accomplished by daily systematic observation and examination of the neonate based on knowledge of the baby's physiology and

characteristics. A convenient way to chart these observations is through the use of a checklist similar to that shown in Table 25-3. The nurse can interpret the infant's behavior to the mother and assist her as she endeavors to understand and care for her infant. In the following section the priorities for care in the regular nursery will be discussed in relation to the systems which influence them most obviously. As previously stated all systems work together; a malfunction in one will affect another to some degree. Since the range of normality is fairly wide during the neonatal period, the infant's *normal characteristics* will be presented in chart form along with headings designating their usual manifestations and variations. This will permit the reader to readily note the parameters of normality.

Prevention of Infection

Infants' ability to produce their own immunoglobulins depends on their genetic inheritance.[16] The infant's own immunologic system does not form these immunoglobulins in any significant amount until later in infancy. Therefore, during the first few months of life the infant must depend upon the passive immunity he or she has inherited from his or her mother. The infant's resistance to certain infections depends in large part on the mother's own experience with disease and with active and passive acquired immunity as well as the particular antigens with which the infant comes into contact. Therefore, immunity is a highly individual matter. Some maternal antibodies are transported across the placenta during the last weeks of pregnancy. These antibodies can protect the neonate during the first few months of life from some of the childhood diseases. However, the antibodies inherited against pertussis are inadequate to protect the neonate from this disease, which is very serious during infancy. Immunizations against pertussis as well as diphtheria and tetanus should be started between 1 and 2 months of age. The infant is much more vulnerable to infection than is an adult or even an older child. A wide variety of organisms which may cause minor problems in an older child may cause septicemia in an infant. Septicemia is more common during infancy than at any other time. Viral infections such as herpes simplex, Coxsackie virus, and cytomegalic inclusion disease have grave consequences for the neonate and are associated with a very high mortality and morbidity rate.

Although nursery personnel can do little to alter the neonate's inherited immunity, efforts to prevent infection can be concentrated in four general areas[17]:

1   Infants whose history indicates they have high potential for infection should be *isolated* from other infants. This would include infants born of mothers whose membranes were ruptured for 24 hours or more, infants born outside the delivery room or under unsterile conditions, and infants born of mothers suspected of having infectious disease. It is thought that many cases of neonatal herpes are acquired by infants as they pass through an infected maternal genital tract.

2   Nursery personnel should be required to have regular physical examinations, including a chest x ray. They should be aware of the serious consequences to newborn infants of even a mild infection. Policy should be so established that all illnesses are reported and personnel will refrain from coming to work until they are completely well. No penalty or loss of pay should be feared from this action. Nursery personnel should also be aware of the threat to their own well-being by certain diseases of newborn infants. A pregnant nursery worker exposed to neonatal rubella is a case in point.

3   Meticulous attention to handwashing will reduce the possibility of transmission of common infectious pathogens from infant to infant. All persons should wash their hands for *3 minutes* before handling an infant. This initial scrub should include the hands and the arms up to the area above the elbows. A *1-minute* scrub between babies is required. Hands should be washed scrupulously before and after handling any infant or any object considered contaminated.

4   All formulas and linen should be sterilized. Other nursery equipment should be regularly disinfected.

Provision of Food and Fluid

GLUCOSE REGULATION   As soon as water or glucose feedings are tolerated well and there are no serious problems with regurgitation or with mucus, breast-feeding or full-strength formula feeding is begun. The normal healthy infant should be permitted to regulate the volume and frequency of his or her feedings, provided that calorie, electrolyte, and fluid requirements are met. Milk supplies calcium and phosphorus which the newborn infant needs for the formation of the bony matrix. If the milk is not fortified with vitamin D, the infant should receive a vitamin D supplement to aid calcium absorption. Vitamin D appears to inhibit the destruction of citrate ions which are necessary to form calcium citrate. In this way vitamin D increases the solubility of calcium and aids in calcium ion absorption. Vitamin C, which is required for proper formation of intercellular matrix of connective tis-

TABLE 25-3
Checklist of Significant Observations in Newborn Infants

Healthy findings	Neurological findings
Body temperature	Convulsions
Incubator temperature	Rigid
Weight	Opisthotonos
Respiratory rate	Twitching
Pulse rate	Irritable
Demanding	Hyperactive
Hungry	Tires easily
Sucks well	Less active
Gavages well, but slowly	Lethargic
Resisted gavage	Weak cry
Weight gain	Shrill cry
Good cry	Moro reflex poor or absent
Active	*Cardiovascular findings*
Color stable	
Gastrointestinal findings	Pallor
	Plethora
Gavaged poorly	Cyanosis, circumoral
Sucked poorly	Cyanosis, circumocular
Gagged	Cyanosis, extremities
Drooled	Cyanosis, generalized
Regurgitated	Bleeding (specify area)
Hiccups	*Respiratory findings*
Mucus on gavage tube	
Mucus, other	Oxygen flow (liters/min)
Abdominal distention	Oxygen concentration
Abnormal stool	Shallow respirations

sues—e.g., bone, cartilage, tendons—should also be given daily, as it is poorly supplied by milk and not stored in the body.[18]

The healthy term infant is able to ingest nourishment by sucking and may average 60 to 120 ml of milk per feeding. In general, the healthy neonate is able to digest, absorb, and metabolize milk fairly well. However, as with other factors in the infant's environment, nutritional and fluid intake should be carefully regulated. The infant's early feeding experiences have strong emotional, cultural, and social overtones. Many of the infant's later attitudes toward food and what it symbolizes can be traced back to early experience with feeding. Newborn infants are very sensitive to the feelings of those who feed them—not only toward the infants themselves but toward food in general. The foundations for feeding problems are laid early in infancy.

For infants whose mothers choose not to breast-feed, a 20 cal per 30 ml formula is usually provided on a flexible schedule which ranges from 3- to 5-hour feedings. The minimum fluid and caloric requirement of infants, whose expenditure of energy is within normal limits, is approximately 150 ml and 120 cal per kilogram of body weight per day. Infants usually take from 60 to 120

Sore buttocks	Labored respirations
Weight loss	Deep respirations
Irregular respirations	Umbilical redness
Rest periods, <10 seconds	Umbilical oozing
Rest periods, 10–30 seconds	Alcohol to cord
Apnea, >30 seconds	Pustular rash
Intercostal retractions	Other rash (specify)
Xiphoid retractions	Abscess
Seesaw respirations	Eye discharge
Dilated alae nasi	Skin dry or peeling
Grunting	Skin irritated (specify area)
Cough	*Other*
Sneeze	
Stuffy nose	
Skin findings	
Mottled	
Harlequin syndrome	
Jaundice	
Petechiae (specify area)	
Ecchymosis (specify area)	
Edema	
Dehydration	
Sclerema	

NOTE: The severity of the sign is indicated by +, ++, or +++. If the symptom is present only before or after eating, the abbreviation ac or pc is used. This checklist is used by nurses instead of routine nurses' notes, each column used for one period of observation. The signs observed in the infant are checked, the time and date noted, and the item initialed. If situations other than those listed are present, detailed descriptions are written in the regular nurses' notes. A 24-hour summary of nursing observations is given to the physician at morning rounds. This and the physicians' examinations provide the data on which a decision is made concerning illness.
SOURCE: C. Henry Kempe et al.: *Current Pediatric Diagnosis and Treatment*, Lange, Los Altos, Calif., 1974, p. 54, as adapted from Lula O. Lubchenco, *Pediatric Clinics of North America*, 8:471, 1961.

ml per feeding. To determine if the infant's total intake is adequate, use the following method.

1 Find the amount of formula in milliliters taken per kilogram of body weight, that is, divide the number of milliliters consumed by the infant's weight in kilograms.
2 Determine the daily caloric intake by using the ratio of 20 cal per 30 ml, so if an infant consumed, say, 600 ml, the caloric intake would be 400 cal.
3 Divide the caloric intake by the number

of kilograms of body weight, and check to be sure the result is close to the limit given above.

Food tends to pass rather rapidly through the neonate's stomach. Gastric emptying time varies from infant to infant as well as with the type of feeding given. More undigested protein may pass through an infant's stomach than that of an older child. When the infant's chyme reaches the small intestine, the undigested proteins are handled by protein-digesting enzymes. These enzymes break down the proteins to amino acids which can then be absorbed to provide body protein for the infant. This assumes that the infant's diet provides an adequate supply of protein.

Although neonates readily assimilate disaccharides and monosaccharides, they have little ability to handle long-chain polysaccharides, e.g., cornstarch. This is due to a deficiency of pancreatic amylase in the neonate.

Glucose regulation and a tendency toward hypoglycemia in the neonate depend on a number of interacting factors. Immature liver function in the neonate results in low and unstable glucose concentration in the blood. The factors which may predispose the neonate to hypoglycemia include the infant's high metabolic rate, a relatively long period before the first feedings, and immature liver function. Because the liver cannot perform gluconeogenesis well, glucose stores in the liver are insufficient to keep blood levels of glucose high enough to meet the energy requirements of the infant. If feeding is unduly delayed, the infant becomes hypoglycemic and shows signs of hunger.

Most newborns have a drop in blood glucose levels during the first few hours after delivery. Usually this condition goes unnoticed, but some infants will exhibit signs of hypoglycemia, such as tremors, twitching, limpness, or lethargy. Hypoglycemia is defined as a blood glucose level that is less than or equal to 20 mg per 100 ml of blood in the premature baby and less than 40 mg per 100 ml in the newborn. These infants should have glucose determinations made and, if found to be hypoglycemic, should be given glucose orally or intravenously. The method chosen will depend on the physical condition of the newborn and the degree of hypoglycemia that is present. Prolonged periods of hypoglycemia can cause brain damage in the infant since neurons mainly oxidize glucose as a source of energy.

The neonate absorbs fat slowly from the gastrointestinal tract. The exact cause of this is not known. Because of this slow absorption, it is recommended that infants do not receive formulas with high fat content. Such feedings fail to be absorbed and are merely lost to the body by way of the stools. Currently research is being conducted to discover if there is a possible link between the high incidence of heart disease in the United States and the fact that the great majority of infants in this country are fed cow's milk (which has a higher fat content than breast milk).

FLUID BALANCE Regurgitation during or after a feeding is very common among infants. This is partly due to the labile musculature of the gastrointestinal system which causes reverse peristalsis at times. It is also due to the fact the infant tends to swallow air while sucking. The nurse should be sure that milk fills the entire nipple of the bottle so that the infant will not swallow additional amounts of air while feeding. The nurse should also "bubble" the infant before placing him in the crib. The nurse must discriminate between regurgitation and vomiting in the neonate.

The neonate passes stools frequently; they are softer and more liquid than those of an older child. The nurse must also differentiate between the infant's passing frequent stools and having diarrhea. Since it is often difficult to estimate the amount of fluid and valuable electrolytes lost through vomiting and diarrhea, these conditions present serious problems to the neonate if they develop. The nurse should weigh the baby daily and record the amount and character of each stool passed, the number of voidings, and the number of times and amount the infant vomits. A physician should be notified immediately if the amount of fluid lost seems excessive. Early recognition and treatment of this developing condition is of paramount importance.

The initial stool passed by the baby is a

sticky, greenish black, odorless substance. [See illustration (E) in the color plate.] It consists of the accumulation of secretions in the gastrointestinal tract, called *meconium*. As illustration (F) in the color plate shows, after the baby begins to take milk, the baby's stool goes through a *transitional stage* during which it is yellowish green. When all of the meconium has been expelled the baby's stool is soft and yellow. A normal infant stool is shown in illustration (G) in the color plate. The physician should be notified if the stool deviates from the pattern described. Blood in the stool should be tested to determine whether it is of maternal or fetal origin. Passage of meconium in large amounts indicates the gastrointestinal tract is patent. It is possible for the baby to have a complete or partial obstruction in the upper part of the tract and still pass some meconium. Therefore, it is necessary to record the amount of meconium expelled as well as the fact that it was passed.

In health, neonates are able to regulate a normal fluid load well even though their renal and endocrine systems are immature and their gastrointestinal systems labile. In the face of illness such as infection, vomiting, and diarrhea, however, the infant rapidly gets into difficulty. The neonate has several disadvantages in regard to balancing the volume and composition of body fluids. The infant exchanges fluids 7 times as fast, in relation to body weight, as does an adult and loses more water proportionately. There is a tendency toward acidosis in infants because their metabolic rate is 2 times that of an adult in relation to body mass. Diarrhea can quickly exacerbate this predisposition.

The functional development of the neonate's kidneys is not complete until the end of the first month of life. The neonate concentrates urine to only $1\frac{1}{2}$ times the osmolality of the plasma instead of the normal 3 to 4 times, as in the adult. Because of this renal immaturity the infant does not excrete toxins as efficiently and reabsorb the substances he or she needs as fully as an adult. The influence of the infant's immature endocrine system is also felt. In time of need—e.g., during diarrhea, vomiting, or infection—the neonate is unable to conserve the water the body needs. This is because of the immature functions of both the hypothalamic antidiuretic centers and the distal tubule cells. The neonate is also unable to conserve sodium and other electrolytes when needed because of the immature function of the adrenal cortex and renal distal tubule cells.

The urine of the neonate is scant in amount and pale yellow in color with a low specific gravity and a typical urine odor. One of the signs of some inborn errors of metabolism, however, is a peculiar odor to the urine; it is therefore necessary to note the odor as well as the color of each baby's urine. One of the inborn errors of metabolism, phenylketonuria, can now be detected by a blood test done on the baby after the baby has had 24 hours of a milk diet. This test is being routinely done on all babies before discharge. The infant voids frequently so the nurse usually has an opportunity to observe the force of the urinary stream. If the baby is noted to dribble urine more or less constantly and never exhibits a forceful stream, the possibility exists that there is an obstruction of the urinary tract. Occasionally babies will have a pinkish stain on their diaper which is caused by the presence of uric acid crystals in their urine. This condition will clear spontaneously.

Physiologic Jaundice

Jaundice that occurs on the second or third postdelivery day in a neonate who exhibits no other signs of illness is termed *physiologic jaundice*. This jaundice is a result of the cumulative effects of the hemolysis which is occurring and the immature functioning of the baby's liver. In approximately 50 percent of neonates the liver function is able to keep pace with the breakdown of red cells resulting in no clinical jaundice and little or no increase in serum bilirubin levels. In the remaining infants, most will show a rise in serum bilirubin above the normal level of less than 1 mg per 100 ml of blood. Many of these will demonstrate clinical jaundice.

Two main factors lead to the development of physiologic jaundice: (1) the polycythemia present in the normal newborn and (2) the relative inability of the newborn liver cells to conjugate bilirubin. As hemolysis occurs in the reticuloendothelial system, iron and protein released from the red cells are recirculated in the body for reuse. The toxic substance resulting from hemoglobin destruction is bilirubin which must be conjugated by the liver into a form in which it can be excreted from the body. To be transported to the liver, the bilirubin must be bound to albumin because any free unconjugated bilirubin in the blood is potentially able to bind to brain cells, causing severe brain damage known as *kernicterus*. It is not known why the neonate's brain cells are particularly susceptible to this type of damage. In the liver bilirubin is conjugated (bound to glucuronic acid) and excreted into the bile. From there it passes into the small intestine and out of the body.

Jaundice in the newborn is often difficult to detect but is extremely important to note as soon as it appears. *Any jaundice occurring within 24 hours after delivery must be reported at once.* Infants should be carefully examined in daylight at least once a day to determine the presence of jaundice. Blanching the skin of the chest or forehead is one way of detecting jaundice when it is not readily apparent in the sclerae or nailbeds. Jaundice in the neonate should never be treated lightly even though it is of the so-called "physiological" variety. In the presence of other disease or physiological handi-

caps, the baby may develop kernicterus at blood levels of bilirubin lower than 17 mg per 100 ml. It is necessary to distinguish between true jaundice and the yellow staining of the skin, nails, and vernix due to passage of meconium by the baby during labor and delivery.

Phototherapy is considered useful by some physicians in the treatment of physiological jaundice in selected neonates. The precise reasons for the effectiveness of light in reducing jaundice are not understood at the present time. In addition, the practice has not been in use long enough to be thoroughly evaluated.

Two major problems with this therapy are the possibility of retinal damage and the questionable toxic effect of photochemical products in the body. When phototherapy is ordered the baby is placed unclothed, under cool blue fluorescent lamps.

The suggested footcandles of light to be used is debatable and depends on the type of bulb. To ensure maximum bilirubin breakdown, the light bulbs should be changed at regular intervals. While the baby is under the light, frequent turning is required to promote bilirubin breakdown on all skin surfaces. The eyes must be covered and well protected from the light. Care should be taken, however, to prevent corneal damage from contact with the bandage. The eye patches should be removed at regular intervals to check for any complications. This could be done when the baby is removed from under the lights for feedings.

The infant's temperature and the specific gravity of the urine must be monitored carefully to avoid elevation of temperature and dehydration.

Frequent stimulation by touch and speech is important to develop the infant's trust and to promote awareness of the environment. A careful explanation of the cause of the jaundice and the reason for phototherapy must be given to the parents. They should be encouraged to feed their baby as often as possible while the baby is receiving phototherapy.

Characteristics of the Newborn Infant

Tables 25-4 through 25-9 provide information about the characteristics of the newborn infant and the range of normalcy of those characteristics. The usual manifestation and normal variation of each characteristic is listed, followed by explanatory comments. When indicated, a brief narrative illuminates the information contained in the tables. Table 25-4 shows the range of normal in measurements and vital signs for the neonate. The significance of obtaining accurate data on the size and vital signs of the infant has been discussed in a previous section of this chapter.

General Appearance

Figure 25-6 depicts a typical newborn infant. Note that the head is disproportionately large for the body, comprising one-fourth of the total body length. The center of the baby's body is at the umbilicus rather than at the symphysis pubis as in the adult. The torso appears long and the extremities short. The flexed position in which the baby maintains the extremities contributes to their apparent shortness. The hands are tightly clenched. The neck appears short because the chin rests upon the chest. The baby has a prominent abdomen, sloping shoulders, narrow hips, and a rounded chest. The infant tends to remain in a flexed position resembling that maintained in utero.

Throughout the newborn period, the infant should be carefully observed for *symmetry of body parts* and the *positions* assumed at rest. Asymmetries and unusual positions indicate that the infant should be thoroughly examined for the presence of fractures, paralysis, or other orthopedic defects. Often these asymmetries are within the normal range. They are frequently due to odd positions maintained in utero or unusual presentations during delivery. If the body part can be passively rotated into a normal position with no limitation of motion at the joint, the malposition will usually correct spontaneously as the infant grows. Following a breech delivery, the legs are often flexed on the abdomen for a period of time. It is important for the nurse to be aware of the normalcy of many of the rather odd positions and proportions of the newborn infant so that the appearance can be explained to the mother.

Skin

Table 25-5 describes the major characteristics of the neonate's skin. During the first hours following delivery the infant's skin becomes progressively more plethoric because of the hemoconcentration which occurs at that time. As this decreases the infant becomes more pink but still may become quite red when crying. The ruddy appearance is largely due to the dilation of the superficial blood vessels lying close to the surface of the skin. The residual cyanosis of the hands and feet is more likely caused by sluggish peripheral circulation, as is the mottling which occurs when the infant is chilled. Illustration (*A*) of the color plate demonstrates a moderately plethoric infant with some cyanosis of the hand.

Harlequin color change is an example of vasomotor instability which causes the blood vessels on one side of the newborn's body to dilate while those on the opposite side constrict. This results in a very odd appearance, for there is a sharp line down the center of the infant's body, dividing the reddish half from the blanched half. Harlequin color change appears and disappears sponta-

TABLE 25-4
Normal Range for Measurements and Vital Signs

Characteristic measurements and vital signs	Usual manifestation	Normal variations	Comment
Weight	3,400 g	2,500–4,100 g	Babies above 4,100 g or under 2,500 g are often high-risk. Difficult to measure accurately.
Length	50 cm	44–55 cm	
Head circumference	34–36 cm	32–38 cm	Extremes in size may indicate presence of pathology such as microcephaly, hydrocephaly, or increased intracranial pressure.
Chest circumference	2 cm less than head circumference	7 cm less to 5 cm more than head circumference	Greater variation may indicate head or chest pathology.
Heart rate	120–140 beats/minute	100–160 beats/minute; may be irregular, especially when crying	Rate is influenced by physical activity, crying, state of wakefulness, body temperature, disease, or other defect.
Respiratory rate	30–40/minute	20–60/minute; tends to be irregular	Same things influence respiratory rate which influence heart rate. Some normal babies may have short (10–20 seconds) "resting" periods between respirations.
Temperature	36.5–37°C (axillary)	35.7–37.2°C (axillary)	Axillary temperatures are accurate if properly done. Place bulb of thermometer in axillary region; then hold the arm firmly against body for 1½ minutes. This method avoids irritation of rectum. May run subnormal temperature even with an infection.
Blood pressure	60/20–90/60	60/20–90/60	Blood pressure readings are rarely obtained in neonates.

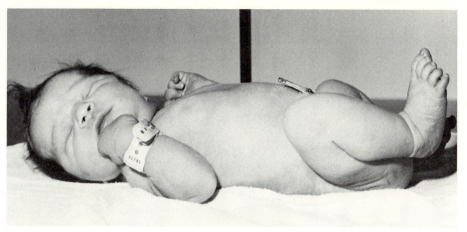

FIGURE 25-6
A normal newborn infant at rest. (*By permission from University of Colorado Medical Center, Denver, Colo.*)

neously and is of no known medical significance. *Pallor* in a newborn is always a grave sign, signifying anemia secondary to internal hemorrhage, erythroblastosis fetalis, or shock due to sepsis or anoxia.

Generalized cyanosis usually indicates an increased need for oxygen. This may be a temporary condition which requires only a few hours of an oxygen-enriched environment, or it may be indicative of serious disease. Nursing responsibilities in dealing with cyanotic infants include careful recordings of when and under what circumstances cyanosis occurred as well as the maintenance of a patent airway and the proper concentration of oxygen in the incubator.

At birth the full-term infant's skin is normally smooth, well hydrated, soft to touch, and covered with varying amounts of lanugo and vernix caseosa. *Desquamation* is common in the first days following delivery. *Rashes* are usually abnormal except for the transient appearance of an urticarial type of rash which has been designated *erythema toxicum neonatorum*. The cause of this rash has not been determined and it disappears

without treatment. Illustration (*B*) of the color plate shows an infant with erythema toxicum neonatorum and lanugo on the back. Lanugo is fine, downy hair found over the back and shoulders of some infants. *Mongolian spots* which appear as bluish black areas over the lower back and buttocks are commonly found in nonwhite newborns. These tend to fade during the first years of life. Telangiectases (capillary hemangiomas) also seem to disappear after infancy, although it is likely that they do not actually become obliterated, but rather the skin becomes thicker, making them less apparent. *Milia*, which are obstructed sebaceous glands appearing as small white papillae over the nose and chin, are illustrated in Figure 25-7. Milia will disappear spontaneously within several weeks.

During early infancy the outer layer of the skin is not an efficient barrier to pathogens. In addition the infant is prone to develop rashes or blisters from trauma that ordinarily would not produce these conditions in an older person. The reasons for the infant's skin sensitivity are not clearly delineated.

TABLE 25-5
Characteristics of Neonate's Skin

Characteristics of skin	Usual manifestation	Normal variations	Comment
Color	Generally pink. Occasional cyanosis around mouth or of hands and feet	Mottling when unclothed. Harlequin color change. May be ruddy for several hours after birth.	Jaundice and pallor are not considered normal. "Physiological" jaundice may occur at 3–5 days of age. *Jaundice occurring within 24 hours of birth is abnormal.*
Consistency and hydration	Soft. Normal turgor. Medium thickness. Subcutaneous fat present	May feel puffy. Amount of subcutaneous fat varies.	Thickness of skin indicates degree of maturity. Poor turgor indicates dehydration.
Condition	Intact and smooth. May be some dryness and peeling	Petechiae over presenting part only. Ecchymosis from forceps. Mongolian spots on back or buttocks. Milia on face particularly on nose. Telangiectases on nape of neck and/or eyelids.	Rashes are abnormal except for erythema toxicum neonatorum. May have pigmented nevi or tufts of hair.
Vernix caseosa	Whitish, greasy material covering body	May be thicker on some babies than on others. Tends to collect in body creases.	Markedly decreased amount or absence of vernix indicates postmaturity. Excessive amount indicates prematurity.
Lanugo	Fine, downy hair on face and shoulders	May be absent.	A large amount of lanugo is indicative of prematurity.
Edema	Present, but not apparent	Often presenting part and eyelids will be obviously edematous.	Obvious, generalized edema is abnormal. Baby will lose 6–10 percent of birth weight within 3–5 days of birth.

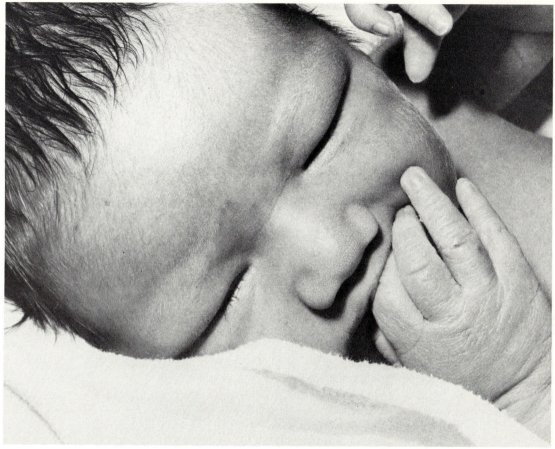

FIGURE 25-7
Milia evident on the nose of a newborn infant. (*By permission from University of Colorado Medical Center, Denver, Colo.*)

However, the fact remains that special care must be taken to prevent skin trauma when cleansing an infant. Some pediatricians recommend that cotton dipped in sterile oil or in a nontoxic bacteriostatic agent be used to clean off the blood and vernix from the infant when the infant is initially bathed. Thereafter cotton balls moistened with warm water may be used for daily cleansing. Gauze is not recommended, since it tends to irritate the skin. Complete baths are not given while the infant is in the nursery, but all the body creases should be cleansed frequently to re-

move collections of material where bacteria may flourish.[19] Care of the umbilical stump is discussed later in the chapter.

Body Segments

The appearance and characteristics of the neonate's body segments are described in Table 25-6.

The common asymmetries of the head are *cephalohematoma* and *caput succedaneum*. Cephalohematoma is caused by trauma to the head during birth which results in subperi-

TABLE 25-6
Characteristics of Neonate's Body Segments

Characteristics of body segments	Usual manifestation	Normal variations	Comment
Head	Usually molded if vaginal delivery, round if cesarean section. Anterior and posterior fontanels and sutures palpable. Fine, silky hair covers scalp.	Less molding occurs if baby is not firstborn or if head has not been engaged long. Size of fontanels and amount of overlapping of sutures varies considerably.	Asymmetries should be noted and evaluated.
Eyes	Dark or slate blue color. Open when awake and not crying. No tears. Equal pupils which react to light. Focuses briefly on face.	Lids may be edematous. Conjunctival hemorrhages may be apparent. Occasional uncoordinated movements normal. Some newborns will produce tears.	Note epicanthal folds, placement of eyes in relation to each other, discharges, persistent uncoordinated movements.
Nose	In midline. Seems flattened. Little nasal bridge. Breathes easily through nose.	May seem deformed due to passage through birth canal. Some mucus present in nares.	Test for patency of nares. Baby should breathe easily with mouth closed. Note nasal discharge.
Mouth	Lips pink. Tongue does not protrude. Sucking initiated when lips touched. Scant saliva.	Epstein's pearls present on gum margins. May have transient circumoral cyanosis. Transient 7th nerve paralysis shown by asymmetrical mouth movements when crying.	Distinguish between Epstein's pearls and thrush. Note abnormalities, i.e., excessive salivation, protruding tongue, high arched palate, lip notches. A short frenulum is considered insignificant. Note cleft lip or palate.
Ears	Well-formed. Cartilage present. Stand out from skull. Placed so that at least part of ear lies above a line drawn from outer canthus of eye to external occipital protuberance.	Preauricular papillomas may be present. Amount of cartilage varies.	Look for branchial clefts, low placement, malformations. Lessened amount of cartilage indicates prematurity.
Neck	Short, straight, head moves freely side to side.		Note webbing, torticollis, masses, restriction of motion, distended veins.
Chest	Almost circular. Symmetrical move-	Milky secretion may be evident from	Observe for retractions, fracture of

Abdomen	ments with respirations. Breast tissue present in both sexes. Rounded and prominent. Respirations are largely diaphragmatic. Umbilical stump dry within several hours of birth. Femoral pulses present, equal.	nipples. Umbilical hernia may be present and is usually insignificant.	clavicle, asymmetry of placement of nipples, and chest expansion. Must make a distinction between a normally prominent abdomen and a distended one. A scaphoid abdomen is abnormal. Diminished abdominal breathing indicates intrathoracic disease. Compare appearance of chest and abdomen. Observe for inguinal hernia. Note signs of bleeding or infection in umbilical stump.
Genitalia	In both sexes, genitalia tend to appear large in relation to rest of baby.	May have increased pigmentation in dark-skinned races. Edema present in breech deliveries.	Examine genitalia carefully for signs of genital ambiguity or other abnormalities.
Female	Labiae appear large, particularly labia minora.	Mucoid or bloody discharge from vagina may be present.	Keep clean by wiping front to back.
Male	Scrotum pendulous. Rugae cover sac. Testes descended. Tight prepuce which is adherent to glans. Meatal opening in center of glans penis.	Size of scrotum and penis varies widely. Testes may be in canal or retract into canal if baby is chilled.	Check for epi- or hypospadius, phimosis, hydrocele. If circumcised, watch for signs of bleeding and infection. If uncircumcised, do not retract foreskin.
Extremities	Generally flexed but can be put through full range of motion passively. Fists clenched. Legs bowed. Plantar fat pad makes feet appear flat.	May retain in utero position when sleeping. Feet may turn in but can be passively turned out.	Observe for gross abnormalities, limitation of movement in any joint, fractures, paralysis. Check for dislocated hip. Count fingers and toes. Note webbing or absence of digits. Note size and shape of hands and feet. Check for simian creases.
Back	Spine straight, easily flexed. When prone, baby can lift head momentarily. Shoulders, scapulae, iliac crests on same plane with each other.	Some asymmetries may be normal if due to unusual fetal position and can be passively corrected.	Check for spina bifida occulta, pilonidal sinus.
Anus	Patent. Proved by passage of meconium or rectal thermometer.	If frequent rectal temperatures have been taken, anus may be irritated.	Note fissures, bleeding. Once patency is determined, take axillary temperatures.

osteal bleeding. It appears several hours after birth and will resorb by two months of age. Usually no treatment is required. Caput succedaneum is edema of the vertex of the head and is caused by pressure on the scalp during labor. It, too, will disappear spontaneously but in a much shorter time than cephalohematoma. The *fontanels* should be palpated frequently during the infant's stay in the nursery to ensure that they are flat. Pulsation of fontanels may be normal. Bulging or tenseness indicates increased intracranial pressure and should be reported immediately. A depressed fontanel may indicate dehydration. The posterior fontanel is much smaller than the anterior fontanel and máy not be palpable during the first hours after birth because of the overriding of the sutures during delivery. It closes any time from birth to two months of age. The anterior fontanel remains open for at least 3 months and may be palpable for as long as 18 months after birth; however, it usually closes between 10 and 14 months.

The eyes, ears, nose, and mouth should be examined for asymmetries, malformations, and placement on the face in relation to each other. In addition to looking at the parts separately, the face as a whole should be carefully observed. Many genetically determined syndromes present with distinctive *facies*. Some of the syndromes are quite obvious, but others can be overlooked unless the proportions of the face are compared to the size of the head and body.

When picked up, the neonate will usually open the eyes; at this time they may be examined for hemorrhages, opacities of the lens, and discharges. If the baby is rotated laterally the baby will develop a *nystagmus* which does not persist after he is replaced in his crib. *Epicanthal folds* can be found in normal Caucasian babies; however, other signs of mongolism should be ruled out before concluding that these are normal.

Keratin cysts commonly known as *Ep-*

stein's pearls appear as white blebs along the gum margins and at the junction of the hard and soft palates. They are a normal manifestation in the newborn infant and can be seen at birth. *Thrush,* which is an infection of the mucous membranes of the mouth usually caused by *Candida albicans,* may appear on the third or fourth day after delivery. The white patches of thrush appear on the tongue and cheeks as well as the gums. This disease should be reported promptly so treatment can be instituted. The production of *saliva is scant* during the first weeks of life. If a baby has a large amount of oral mucus the cause should be determined before the baby is fed. *Tracheoesophageal fistula* is a common cause of this symptom. In addition, a baby with large amounts of mucus needs careful watching to assure that a patent airway is maintained.

The baby's neck should flex, extend, and rotate easily. If limitation of motion is noted, *torticollis,* a shortening of the sternocleidomastoid muscle, may be suspected. The shortening is caused by rupture of the muscle during a difficult delivery or the presence of a tumor in the muscle.

The excessive amount of *breast tissue* found in newborn infants, as well as the occasional secretion of a milklike substance, is produced by the influence of maternal hormones which crossed the placenta. This phenomenon occurs in both sexes and gradually recedes by one month of age.

An abdomen which is unusually flat is called a *scaphoid abdomen.* A common cause of this condition is the presence of a *diaphragmatic hernia* which allows much of the abdominal contents to lie in the thorax. Severe respiratory distress often accompanies this anomaly.

Frequent inspection of the *umbilical stump* is necessary to note bleeding or signs of infection. Seventy percent alcohol is applied daily to prevent the growth of bacteria. In addition, drying of the stump is hastened by leaving it exposed to the air. By the second or third day the stump should be sufficiently dry so that the clamps may be removed. Alcohol applications should be continued until the cord drops off. Since this does not occur until the end of the first week, the mother should be instructed on proper care of the stump.

There is presently some question concerning the advisability of circumcising all male babies. Circumcision is no longer considered a "routine" procedure. Each baby should be evaluated individually and consent from the mother is obtained before the procedure is done. The pros and cons of the procedure should be explained to the mother so that she can make an informed decision. Unless the prepuce is so tight that it obstructs the passage of urine, there is no medical indication for circumcision. However, there are very sound reasons from a physiological standpoint for delaying the procedure until after the first week of life. These reasons include the danger of infection, the bleeding tendencies of the neonate, and the risk of removing too much foreskin if the procedure is not performed carefully.

Neuromuscular Endowment

At birth the normal baby has an intact and fully functioning neuromuscular system. The status of this system is manifested in the muscle tone and strength exhibited by the baby, the spontaneous movements, as well as the responses to various external stimuli, the type and quality of the reflexes, the functioning of the senses, and the overall behavior patterns. The initial physical examination will cover most of these areas; however, continuous evaluation of these items is necessary to assure that the baby is well and stays well.

Early signs of illness appear in the form of relatively small deviations from the normal behavior patterns of the infant. The nurse who handles the baby from day to day is usually the first person to notice these changes. Doctors rely upon the nurse's observations of the baby's behavior during feeding, sleeping, and diaper changes to alert them to the possibility that a given infant is becoming ill or has a previously undetected defect. Changes in behavior point to pathology not only in the central nervous system but in other systems as well.

In evaluating the *muscle tone* of the baby the nurse should check for the *recoil* response in the extremities. If normal recoil is present, the arm or leg will immediately return to the flexed position after being passively extended by the examiner. Another method of determining muscle tone is for the examiner to rapidly move the hand or foot back and forth. The baby will alternately let the part flop and resist flopping during this maneuver. Equal amounts of flopping and resistance to flopping is the normal pattern. When suspended ventrally the baby will not sag into an inverted U position but will exhibit some attempts to lift the head and legs. Likewise in daily handling the infant is not entirely limp as he or she is moved about.

A degree of hyper- or hypotonia may be normal for a given baby just as there are normal variations in the recoil response, joint motility, and resistance to flopping. The difficulty lies in deciding when a given baby's response is normal and when it is not. An obviously flaccid or spastic baby is easily recognized, but it takes familiarity with a number of babies to develop a "feel" for the more subtle manifestations of hyper- or hypotonia. For this reason the baby's general muscle tone should be evaluated every time the baby is handled.

REFLEXES   Table 25-7 lists the common neurological reflexes which are normally present at birth. The normal healthy infant will exhibit all of the reflexes listed in the table and

TABLE 25-7
Common Neurological Reflexes at Birth

Characteristic reflexes	Usual manifestation	Normal variations	Comment
Yawning Stretching Sneezing Burping Hiccoughing	Present in normal newborn.	May be temporarily diminished by central nervous system depression due to maternal medication present in baby's system, anoxia, or infection.	These activities of the baby need to be brought to the mother's attention as mothers are often surprised and frightened if they are not prepared for this behavior.
Rooting	Present. Elicited by softly stroking either cheek, corners of mouth, or upper or lower lip.	Strongest in hungry infant. May disappear after infant has been fed.	If weak or absent, indicative of prematurity, neurological defect.
Sucking	Present. Elicited by placing firm object in baby's mouth.	Normal baby will suck when stimulated in this manner.	Suck should be vigorous with good suction produced. Poor sucking has same causes as poor rooting.
Swallowing	Present. When sucking, infant will swallow any liquid obtained.	May cough, gag, or vomit.	
Moro	Present. Elicited by sudden movement of head and neck causing retroflexion. Response consists of abduction, extension, and adduction of arms with extension of fingers followed by vigorous cry.	If baby is deeply asleep may not respond well. Leg movements may follow arm movement pattern.	Note absence, incompleteness, or asymmetry of Moro reflex. Note changes in Moro from day to day. Note nature of cry (absent, weak, high-pitched, excessive).
Tonic neck	Not always apparent in newborns. Elicited spontaneously when baby is supine if baby turns head to side or can be precipitated by manually turning head to side. Response consists of	Response most prominent between two and four months. Response not sustained in newborn.	Note if response is asymmetrical (stronger on one side than the other). If response is complete, easy to elicit, and sustained in newborn it may indicate central nervous system damage.

	extension of arm toward direction which head is turned and flexion of opposite arm.	
Traction response	Present. Pull baby up by wrists. Head will lag but as reaches upright position head and chest will be in line momentarily, then head will fall forward. Baby will reerect head spontaneously or with slight stimulus.	Head control improves as muscle strength increases.
Incurvature of trunk	Present. Suspend ventrally and stroke sides alternately. Baby should turn pelvis to side stimulated.	Observe general muscle tone as baby is suspended.
Grasping, palmar	Present. Press finger into baby's palm. He should grasp strongly enough to be lifted momentarily from bed.	
Plantar	Present. Prompt flexing of toes upon application of pressure to ball of foot.	
Positive supporting reaction	Present. Lift baby vertically, and baby will usually flex legs. Touch soles to bed and baby will extend legs, then trunk and head.	General muscle tone and condition of baby will affect response.
Placing	Present. Hold baby vertically with one leg out of the way. Move other leg to touch edge of table. Baby will flex knee and try to place foot on table.	
Stepping	Present. Hold vertically. Tilt forward and to one side with feet touching hard surface. Will alternate feet as if walking.	

many others not mentioned. There is some confusion among writers regarding the terminology used in discussing reflexes as well as disagreement concerning the age of appearance and disappearance of a given reflex and the proper manifestation of the reflex. With some reflexes, such as sucking and rooting, the presence or absence is the more important aspect; with others, such as the tonic neck or Moro reflex, the important characteristic is the pattern of the response. In evaluating reflexes the length of time the response is maintained can be important as well as whether or not the response is obligatory.

Research has indicated that the crawling reflex, the automatic walking or stepping reflex, and tendency for babies to push forward with their heads when pressure is applied to the top of their heads facilitate the birth process.[20] While there is no definite proof of this hypothesis, it is easy to conceptualize how these reflexes might work during birth.

After a feeding, nonsocial smiling with the eyes closed may occur. This phenomenon should not be confused with grimacing or facial distortions resulting from flatus. Rather, it should be considered as an early manifestation of the later smiling ability which occurs in babies, as indicated by EEG recordings, in the state which later in life exemplifies the time of maximal dreaming.[21]

Since many factors influence the baby's response to external stimuli, a poor performance at one time is not diagnostic of central nervous system damage. In judging the response, the state of the baby (whether awake, fatigued, sleeping, hungry, or satiated) should be considered as well as the environmental temperature, other stimuli, amount of clothing on the baby, and any disturbing procedures done to the baby prior to the testing. Additional factors to consider are the existence of other congenital defects or birth injuries, the presence of jaundice, other symptoms of illness, and the time and amount of medication given to the mother prior to the infant's birth.

A poor performance at one observation period may increase the nurse's "index of suspicion," but this should be followed by several examinations to determine a pattern of response for this particular baby. The gross abnormalities will be picked up readily, but subtle ones can escape notice for a considerable length of time. Nurses should know what reflexes the baby exhibited at the initial examination so that they can properly evaluate what is seen. If a reflex previously present is lost or diminished, this may be a significant fact to note. The state of the baby at the time the change in response was discovered should be recorded along with the response itself. Figures 25-8 to 25-10 show the sequence of a Moro reaction. Figures 25-11 to 25-15 show typical reflex responses.

SENSES Table 25-8 describes how the neonate functions in regard to basic senses. Although it is difficult to determine what the baby can see and hear, research over the past few years has led investigators to the conclusion that both these senses are better developed in the neonate than was previously thought. The baby does have acute hearing after the middle ear and eustachian tubes have been cleared of amniotic fluid. A baby's response to loud noises consists of a startle, crying, or blinking, or turning of the head toward the sound. When responding to a human voice the infant turns more readily to the voice of the woman than to a man. These responses are the basis for the testing of newborn infants' hearing, which is being done in many nurseries. Although a failure to pass a hearing test in the newborn nursery is not diagnostic of deafness, all babies failing such tests should be referred for later testing.

In regard to vision, it is believed that the

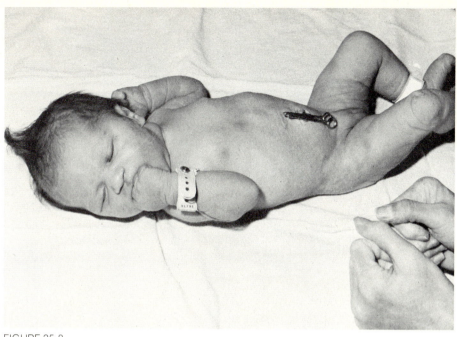

FIGURE 25-8
Baby at rest prior to testing for Moro reflex. (By permission from University of
Colorado Medical Center, Denver, Colo.)

FIGURE 25-9
First stage in Moro response. Note abduction of arms and fanning of fingers. (By
permission from University of Colorado Medical Center, Denver, Colo.)

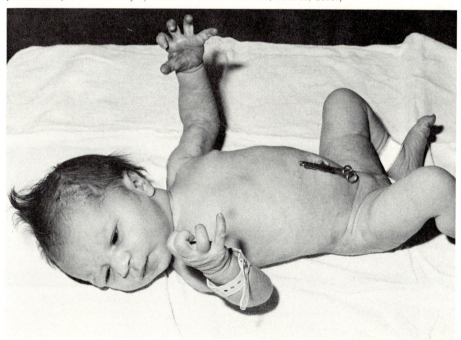

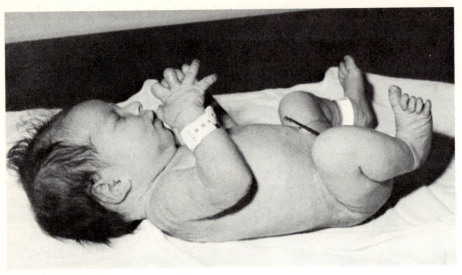

FIGURE 25-10
Second stage in Moro response. Note adduction of arms and flexion of legs.

FIGURE 25-11
Rooting or *reaction des points cardinoux.* [*By
permission from Jerome Hellmuth (ed.),* The Normal
Infant, *vol.* 1, The Exceptional Child, *Special Child
Publications, Seattle, 1967, p. 87.*]

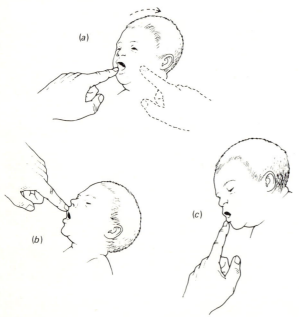

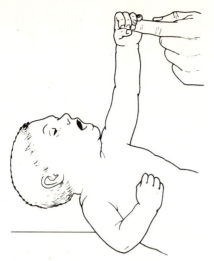
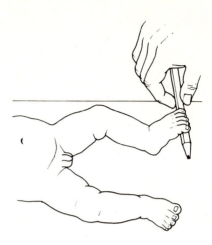

FIGURE 25-12
Grasp reflexes. [*By permission from Jerome Hellmuth (ed.)*, The Normal Infant, *vol. 1*, The Exceptional Child, *Special Child Publications, Seattle, 1967, p. 88.*]

FIGURE 25-13
Tonic neck reflex. [*By permission from Jerome Hellmuth (ed.)*, The Normal Infant, *vol. 1*, The Exceptional Child, *Special Child Publications, Seattle, 1967, p. 100.*]

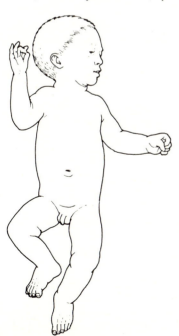
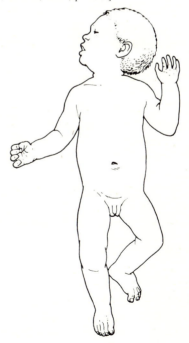

FIGURE 25-14
Reflexes in vertical suspension; positive supporting
reaction. [*By permission from Jerome Hellmuth (ed.),*
The Normal Infant, *vol. 1,* The Exceptional Child,
Special Child Publications, Seattle, 1967, p. 108.]

FIGURE 25-15
Reflexes in vertical suspension; the stepping reaction.
[*By permission from Jerome Hellmuth (ed.),* The
Normal Infant, *vol. 1,* The Exceptional Child, *Special
Child Publications, Seattle, 1967, p. 109.*]

baby can fixate on an object perhaps with both eyes but certainly with one. The peripheral vision is well developed, and the infant has some ability to discriminate colors and patterns. Transient strabismus and nystagmus are normal in the newborn period.

BEHAVIOR As Table 25-9 illustrates, the normal range of behavior for infants is very wide. At one end of the spectrum lie those infants who are placid, rarely cry, respond to stimuli in a muted fashion, and seem relatively indifferent to their environment. At the other end of the scale are those infants who are awake and crying much of the time. They tend to eat rapidly, regurgitate their feeding, and have frequent stools. They seem to be very alert to their environment and are easily disturbed by noises or handling. In between these extremes lie the majority of newborn infants. It is important for the nurse to observe and record the behavior pattern of each infant so changes can be readily identi-

fied. The information obtained can be used by the physician in the diagnosis of disease and by the nurse in helping the mother to become acquainted with her baby. Illustrations (C) and (D) of the color plate depict babies in various states of activity.

A neonatal behavioral assessment has recently been developed by T. Berry Brazelton, M.D. The examination has two main purposes. One of which is to assess the infant's behavior and personality to better help the parents relate to their child, and the other is to use the information to evaluate the neurological development of the child. Dr. Brazelton's examination enables the observer to assess how the infant responds to the environment and to realize what effect this response may have on the caretakers of the infant. Included in this nature-nurture theory are the expectations of the parents for the infant. How, for example, do parents who expected a happy, boisterous infant respond to an infant who is quiet and undemanding?

TABLE 25-8
Characteristic Senses at Birth

Characteristics of senses	Usual manifestation	Comment	Common variations
Vision	Present. Baby blinks to bright light, tap on bridge of nose, or light touch of eyelid. Pupillary light reflex present. Fixates briefly on close objects.	May close lids to bright light or turn toward source of light.	It is normal for baby not to blink to a threatening movement.
Hearing	Present. Blinks to sound.	May respond to sound with eye movements, brief cessation of activity, startle reaction, or crying.	Routine testing of the hearing sense of newborns is performed in many nurseries. If the baby does not pass, baby is usually referred for testing later. However, failure of hearing tests at this age is not diagnostic of deafness.
Touch	Present. Withdraws from painful stimuli including pressure and extremes of temperature.		
Taste	Present. Will have facial grimacing or make sucking motions to the four basic tastes.	May protrude tongue to try to get rid of substance.	Not necessary to test for taste or smell unless infant having trouble sucking.
Smell	Present.	Sense of smell may be stronger in infant than in adult but is hard to test for.	
Kinesthetic	Present.		See responses to change of position listed under reflexes.

TABLE 25-9
Normal Range of Behavior at Birth

Characteristic behavior	Usual manifestation	Common variations	Comment
Activity	Goes through three stages in recovery from shock of birth, then settles into a pattern peculiar to the individual baby.	Ranges from deep sleep to intense activity during crying.	Need to distinguish between normal activity and the extremes of irritability or lethargy. Wide variation in normality.
Awake, not crying	Jerky movements. Symmetrical in arms, alternating in legs.	May be jittery or tremulous. Jaw and ankle clonus common.	Need to distinguish between normal "jitteriness" and convulsive twitching. Watch for symmetry of movements.
Awake, crying	Vigorous movements of all extremities accompanied by loud crying.	May have color changes during crying. Veins on forehead may stand out. May produce tears.	Character (sound quality) and frequency of crying should be noted. Any odd-sounding cries should be reported.
Sleeping	Sleeps quietly and when deeply asleep, is hard to arouse. Spends about 19–22 hours a day sleeping.	May twitch or jerk during sleep. Some babies sleep as little as 16 hours a day.	
Feeding	Sucks vigorously when nipple placed in mouth. Takes 60 to 120 ml at a time.	May regurgitate mucus during early feedings. May vomit mucus, blood, or amniotic fluid.	Some vomiting and regurgitation is normal, but there is a narrow line between normality and pathology.
Voiding	Voids at birth or within 2 to 3 hours.	May not void for 12 hours.	If infant doesn't void by 24 hours, notify doctor. Observe force of urinary stream, color, and odor of urine.
Stooling	Meconium passed during first 24 hours after birth.	May not pass meconium for 48 hours after birth.	Meconium passed before or during birth is suggestive of fetal distress. Note time and amount of meconium expelled.

The Brazelton examination can be done by the nurse in the presence of the parents. They can observe and be taught helpful methods of interacting with their child. Throughout the assessment the parents can observe the infant's use of outside stimuli for self-organization. If the parents are aware that different infants respond in different ways, and that it is possible to deal with such activities, some problems of inadequate parenting may be prevented.

Brazelton, using a small population, has shown that the Brazelton Neonatal Assessment Scale may be a predictor of future abnormalities. More studies should be done in this area to increase data available for possible predictions. For example, if results of the assessment point to possible future abnormalities, preventive measures should be instituted as soon as possible.

REFERENCES

1 Wesenberg, Richard L.: *The Newborn Chest*, Harper & Row, New York, 1973, p. 135.
2 Yao, A. C., et al.: "Expiratory Grunting in the Late Clamped Normal Neonate," *Pediatrics*, 48:865–870, 1971.
3 Hey, E. N., and Bridget O'Connell: "Oxygen Consumption and Heat Balance in the Cot-nursed Baby," *Archives of Disease in Childhood*, 45:335–343, 1970.
4 Hey, E. N., and G. Katz: "The Optimal Thermal Environment for Naked Babies," *Archives of Disease in Childhood*, 45:328–334, 1970.
5 Adamson, Karlis: "The Role of Thermal Factors in Fetal and Neonatal Life," *Pediatric Clinics of North America*, 13:599–619, 1966.
6 Apgar, Virginia: "The Newborn (Apgar) Scoring System: Reflections and Advice," *Pediatric Clinics of North America*, 13:645–650, 1966.
7 *Standards and Recommendations for Hospital Care of Newborn Infants*, 5th ed., Committee on Fetus and Newborn, American Academy of Pediatrics, Evanston, Ill., 1971, pp. 103–104.
8 Ibid., p. 104.
9 Kempe, C. Henry, et al.: *Current Pediatric Diagnosis and Treatment*, Lange, Los Altos, Calif., pp. 42–43, 1974.
10 Hathaway, William E.: "Coagulation Problems in the Newborn Infant," *Pediatric Clinics of North America*, 17:929–942, 1970.
11 Guyton, Arthur C.: *Textbook of Medical Physiology*, 4th ed., Saunders, Philadelphia, p. 998, 1971.
12 Kempe: op. cit., p. 388.
13 Desmond, M. M., et al.: "The Transitional Care Nursery," *Pediatric Clinics of North America*, 13:651–668, 1966.
14 Kempe: op. cit., p. 84.
15 Guyton: op. cit., p. 999.
16 Guyton: op. cit., p. 999.
17 *Standards and Recommendations for Hospital Care of Newborn Infants*, op. cit., pp. 10, 40–42, and 47–54.
18 Guyton: op. cit., pp. 996 and 999.
19 Gellis, Sydney S., and Benjamin M. Kagan: *Current Pediatric Therapy—4*, Saunders, Philadelphia, 1970, p. 655.
20 Freedman, Daniel G.: *Human Infancy: An Evolutionary Perspective*, Lawrence Erlbaum Associates, Hillsdale, N.J., 1974.
21 Ibid.

BIBLIOGRAPHY

Apgar, Virginia, et al.: "Evaluation of the Newborn Infant—Second Report," *Journal of the American Medical Association*, 168:1985–1988, 1958.
Barness, Lewis A.: *Manual of Pediatric Physical Diagnosis*, 4th ed., Year Book, Chicago, 1972.
Barnett, Henry: *Pediatrics*, 14th ed., Appleton-Century-Crofts, New York, 1968.
Benson, Ralph C.: *Handbook of Obstetrics and*

Gynecology, 5th ed., Lange, Los Altos, Calif., 1974.

Brazelton, T. Berry: *Neonatal Behavioral Assessment Scale,* Spastic International Medical Publications, Philadelphia, 1973.

Fink, H. William: "The Newborn at First Glance," *Hospital Topics,* 44:99–101, 1966.

Fitzpatrick, Elise, Sharon Reeder, and Luigi Mastroianni: *Maternity Nursing,* 12th ed., Lippincott, Philadelphia, 1971.

Haynes, Una: *A Developmental Approach to Casefinding,* Children's Bureau, Washington, D.C., 1967.

Hellmuth, Jerome (ed.): *The Normal Infant,* vol. 1, *The Exceptional Infant,* Special Child Publications, Seattle, 1967.

Hymovich, Debra P.: *Nursing of Children: A Guide for Study,* Saunders, Philadelphia, 1969.

Lanzkowsky, Philip, et al.: "Phototherapy—A Note of Caution," *Pediatrics,* 48:969–971, 1971.

Leboyer, Frederick: *Birth without Violence,* Knopf, New York, 1975.

Marlow, Dorothy R.: *Textbook of Pediatric Nursing,* 2d ed., Saunders, Philadelphia, 1973.

McKilligan, Helen R.: *The First Day of Life: Principles of Neonatal Nursing,* Springer, New York; revised by M. Pollock, Heineman, London, 1971.

Nelson, Waldo E., et al.: *Textbook of Pediatrics,* 9th ed., Saunders, Philadelphia, 1969.

Quinn, Norman J.: "Diagnostic Catheter Examinations of the Newborn," *Clinical Pediatrics,* 10:251–256, 1971.

Stuart, Harold C., and Dane G. Prugh (eds.): *The Healthy Child,* Harvard University Press, Cambridge, Mass., 1970.

Watson, Ernest H., and George H. Lowery: *Growth and Development of Children,* 5th ed., Year Book, Chicago, 1967.

Whipple, Dorothy V.: *Dynamics of Development: Euthenic Pediatrics,* McGraw-Hill, New York, 1966.

26

Physical Examination of the Newborn

ANN NOORDENBOS SMITH

Physical examination skills are becoming increasingly important to the nurse as new and extended nursing responsibilities are assumed in the nursery as well as in various community settings. Nurses are being called upon to make initial physical examinations of infants, hospital discharge examinations, and routine follow-up examinations. Community health nurses frequently perform physical examinations of infants in the home setting. In some areas of the country these examinations may follow home delivery. An increasing number of community health nurses are including physical examination as an integral part of a complete infant health evaluation in a well-baby clinic or a child health conference.

This chapter will focus on methods and techniques of examination of the infant. Details of specific findings or normal variations of findings in the newborn and early infancy period are described elsewhere in this text.

GENERAL CONSIDERATIONS

Before beginning the examination the nurse carefully reviews the antepartum history, including the health of the mother during pregnancy, medical supervision, diet, infections or other illnesses, complications of pregnancy, Rh typing and serology, and any drugs taken. Information regarding the birth history includes duration of the pregnancy, birth weight and length, gestational age, kind and duration of labor, type of delivery, sedation and anesthesia, resuscitation required, and Apgar score. The infant's body temperature, weight, respiratory rate, pulse rate, cry, color, and feeding activity are also evaluated. Such information from the infant's and mother's medical histories gives the examiner valuable clues as to where abnormality or pathology may be detected.

A systematic, orderly method is of extreme importance in performing a physical examination. Approaches to the infant may be modified according to varying circumstances; however, even modifications of the nurse's technique of the examination should be done in an orderly sequence so that no part of the examination will be missed.

The basic methods of examination include inspection, palpation, percussion, and auscultation—in that order. The nurse should develop a routine of first looking, then touching, tapping (where appropriate), and then listening.

The system of examination described in this chapter begins with general observation of the infant, proceeds to examination of the skin, feet, lower extremities, genitalia, abdomen, chest, anus, back, neck, upper extremities, head, face, eyes, ears, mouth, and throat and is completed with a basic neurological evaluation. This particular system has the advantage of performing the most uncomfortable parts of the examination (evaluation of the ears, mouth and throat, and elicitation of the startle reflex) last.

The examiner should modify the system of examination according to the situation and the particular infant. For example, in approaching a sleeping infant, it may be best to begin by examining the abdomen and chest. If the infant is crying at the time of examination, one may wish to defer careful examination of the abdomen or the eyes until later. If the examining room is cool, as happens in some well-baby clinics, the nurse may wish to examine the infant's head and extremities first, and then proceed to the parts of the examination which require the infant to be exposed. After becoming familiar and knowledgeable with a systematic method of examination, the nurse then can adapt it to suit the particular circumstances.

The nurse's principal objective while carrying out the examination is to recognize and differentiate normal and abnormal findings, much in the same manner in which any patients are appraised for signs and symptoms pertaining to their condition. Skilled examination requires both broad and specific knowledge of the range of normal physical and behavioral findings of the normal infant. Findings which are dependent upon age or normal physiological processes must be differentiated from those indicating pathology. Abnormalities needing medical attention or correction must be differentiated from those which are self-limited or self-correcting.

Instruments needed for the basic physical examination include:

1 Stethoscope with diaphragm and bell. Of all the nurse's instruments, the stethoscope in particular should become a personal instrument. The earpieces should be large enough and should fit the ears. Familiarity with

one's own stethoscope reduces the possibility of mistaking extraneous sounds for physiological or pathological sounds.

2 Otoscope, preferably with a diagnostic head attachment. Batteries should be replaced frequently. The otoscope light should always be white and bright. Any dimness or suggestion of yellow indicates the batteries or bulb should be changed.

3 Ophthalmoscope. Most ophthalmoscopes are a standard size and fit handles which are interchangeable for otoscopes and ophthalmoscopes.

4 Tongue blade.

5 Measuring tape.

6 Small rattle or other noisemaker.

7 Flashlight or penlight.

Many nurses find it convenient to purchase their own instruments because of the advantage of using a familiar instrument and being able to maintain their instruments in a clean and working condition.

Infants are best examined on a table or in the crib and in an area where good lighting is assured. A pacifier may be used to help quiet the infant during the examination. The examiner's hands should be clean and warm and are washed after examination of areas of the body contaminated by urine and feces before moving to clean areas.

Afterward, a detailed recording is made of the examination, including all pertinent positive and negative findings. This record should be of such quality as to provide valuable base-line data for any other health professionals who may subsequently examine or have responsibility for the infant. A standard checklist for recording the examination is recommended. Adhering to a standardized system of recording the examination, even

though the examination may have been performed in a different order, makes it easier for others to identify specific information more efficiently.

THE EXAMINATION

General Observations

Careful observation of the infant before beginning the actual examination will provide valuable general impressions which can later be confirmed or modified. General size in relation to age is noted; any gross abnormality may be observed. Whether the infant has extra subcutaneous tissue is also noted. The infant's state of consciousness is evaluated—whether awake, irritable, alert, drowsy, lethargic, listless, or asleep. General activity, breathing, movement of extremities, and head and eye movements are observed. The infant's position at rest is studied, including whether the extremities are extended or flexed and any symmetry or asymmetry of position and body parts.

A general impression of skin color is gained. Is the infant ruddy or pale? Is the pigmentation of the skin uniform? Is the infant jaundiced or cyanotic? Does color change in relation to respirations and activity? Respirations are evaluated as to their depth, rate, and degree of regularity. Any change in behavior or activity during the examination is observed. If the infant begins to cry, the quality and pitch of the cry are noted. Crying should be stimulated if it does not occur spontaneously.

While undressing the infant fully in order to perform the examination, evaluation of response to stimulation and of muscle tone is made. Is the infant hypotonic or floppy? Is the infant jittery? Are the arms held in tight flexion? Does the infant startle easily?

NEONATAL PHYSICAL EXAMINATION

Date of Exam_____ Age_____hrs   Wt _____ gms
APPEARANCE AND BEHAVIOR_____ Lgth _____ cms
                                         HC _____ cms
_____   Heart Rate_____
INTEGUMENT_____   Resp Rate_____
                                         Temp _____
_____   BP: Arm_____ Leg_____
HEAD_____
    Fontanelles_____
    Sutures_____

EYES_____
    Conjunctiva_____
    Fundi_____
    Other_____
ENT_____
    Gums_____
    Palate_____
THORAX, LUNGS_____

HEART_____

    Femoral Pulses_____
ABDOMEN_____
UMBILICUS_____
GENITALIA_____
ANUS_____
MUSCULO-SKELETAL_____
    Spine_____
    Hips_____
    Extremities_____

NEUROLOGIC_____

    Developmental (Estimated Gest Age)_____wks
    CNS Pathology_____

    Brazelton_____

IMPRESSIONS_____

_____ Signed_____
                                         (designate training level)
ATTENTING PHYSICIAN'S COMMENTS

                              Signed_____ MD

FIGURE 26-1
A sample of a record of the neonatal physical examination.

Skin

Particular note of the skin is made at the outset of the examination and as each area of the body is examined. Basic morphology of lesions is observed and described whenever possible. Color, consistency, and hydration are noted. Mongolian spots, hemangiomas, presence and amount of vernix caseosa, lanugo, desquamation, macules, or papules are noted. Pallor, beefy red skin, presence of jaundice or cyanosis should be described. The skin is palpated to detect and evaluate any scaling, striae, turgor, edema, or ecchymosis. Skin turgor may be checked over the back of the lower leg or thigh or on the abdomen by grasping the skin between thumb and index finger and allowing the skin to return to its former position and noting whether the skin springs back or a fold persists for several seconds after being released.

Feet and Legs

With the infant in a supine position, color and temperature of the feet are compared, then each foot is examined separately. The toes are counted. Extra digits, webbing, or abnormal spacing between the first and second toe are noted, and length of the toenails and color of the nailbeds are determined.

The Babinski reflex is elicited by stroking the plantar surface of the foot firmly with a sharp object such as the edge of a tongue blade. Grasp reflex of the toes may be elicited by stroking the bottom of the foot at the base of the toes.

Alignment of the foot and leg is noted. The feet at birth are usually held in varus or valgus attitude but can be straightened without forceful manual stretching. Range of motion of the ankle is determined to check for tight heel cords. Flexion and extension of the ankle should have a range of about 130°.

The presence of ankle clonus is checked by stabilizing the leg with the foot held up from the table. With the examiner's thumbs on the distal part of the soles of the feet, the feet are dorsiflexed rapidly 3 to 4 times. One or two continued movements are normal; continued rapid clonic movement is abnormal.

The Achilles deep tendon reflex may be tested by dorsiflexing the foot and tapping the back of the heel with the flat of the finger and noting whether there is an ankle jerk due to plantar flexion of the foot. This reflex is often difficult to obtain in the newborn.

The resting position of the legs is noted. The legs are aligned and examined for bowing or internal or medial torsion of the tibia and knock-knee. A mild degree of bowing or medial rotation is considered normal in the newborn. The muscle mass of the legs is palpated for asymmetry or atrophy. Recoil of the lower extremities is tested by extending and then releasing the legs. Both legs return promptly to the flexed position in the full-term infant.

The patellar deep tendon reflex can be obtained in the newborn by tapping the patella with the flat of the finger. Range of motion of the knee is checked. The legs should fully flex on to the thigh, and the knees should not hyperextend.

Medial skin folds are inspected for symmetry on the anterior and posterior thigh. The presence of extra folds or asymmetry of folds may indicate hip dislocation.

Further investigation for congenital dislocation of the hip is done by flexing the hips and knees, abducting the hips, and applying pressure forward with the examiner's fingers behind the great trochanter. When hip instability exists, a "clunk" is felt and often seen or heard as the femoral head snaps over the posterior acetabular rim into the socket. The hips are then flexed and slightly abducted, and pressure is applied to the upper medial thigh. If a "clunk" is detected, the hip can be dislocated backward.

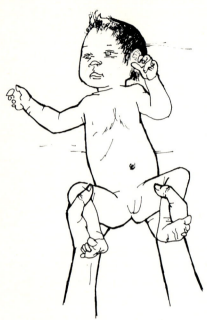

FIGURE 26-2
Investigation for congenital dislocation of the hip is done by flexing the hips and knees, abducting the hips, and applying pressure forward with the examiner's fingers behind the great trochanter. (*Drawing by Dan Manyluk.*)

FIGURE 26-3
The hip is flexed and slightly abducted and pressure is applied to the upper medial thigh. (*Drawing by Dan Manyluk.*)

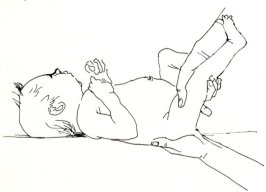

Range of motion of the hip is examined and should be about 160 to 170° in flexion and extension. The thighs flexed at the hip should abduct to an angle of about 160° between the thighs. Limited abduction of one or both hips may indicate the presence of hip dysplasia.

Genitalia

Female genitalia is inspected structurally for the presence of labia majora, labia minora, clitoris, and vaginal orifice. In the newborn the external genitalia are often turgescent, the clitoris and labia minora are prominent, and a hymenal tag may be noted at the vaginal orifice. Any adhesion of the labia minora with occlusion of the vaginal orifice should be detected. Vaginal discharge, if present, is examined. The urethral meatus is difficult to visualize in the newborn; however, voiding should be observed, including the character (gushing or dribbling) of the stream.

In examination of the male genitalia the position of the urethral orifice is noted. The meatal opening should appear as a slit instead of round. In the uncircumcised male during early infancy adhesions may be present between the prepuce and glans of the penis which prevent retraction of the prepuce so that the meatal opening cannot be visualized. This condition is not abnormal unless urinary flow is obstructed or signs of infection are evident.

The scrotum is inspected for symmetry and size. In newborn infants the scrotum may be small and firm or fairly loose, relaxed, and pendulous. Placing the thumb and index finger of one hand over the inguinal canal, the testes are palpated separately between thumb and finger with the other hand. The testes, measuring about 1 cm, and the spermatic cords are the only contents palpable in the scrotum. The presence of any other masses, tenseness, or bulging is abnormal. Stimulation of the cremasteric reflex by stroking the inner aspect of the thigh will cause the testis to rise in the scrotum or into the inguinal canal.

The inguinal area is examined for bulges, which may indicate the presence of hernia, and for lymph nodes. The presence and quality of femoral pulses are checked with the fingertips held firmly along the inguinal ligament.

Abdomen

Inspection of the abdomen precedes palpation, percussion, and auscultation. Abdominal breathing is noted, and respirations are counted. Degree of symmetry or asymmetry of the abdomen is observed. Any fullness, distention, or localized bulging of the abdomen, which may indicate hernia, diastasis recti, or weakness of abdominal musculature, is determined. The condition and turgor of the skin and presence or absence of superficial abdominal veins are determined. The umbilical cord should be carefully inspected for the presence of abnormal redness, wetness of the stump, or odor.

The abdomen is palpated in a systematic manner in order to detect any abnormality in the abdominal musculature or tenderness, organ enlargement, or abdominal mass.

Superficial palpation is performed with the flat surface of the fingers or fingertips, beginning in any one of the quadrants and proceeding in a clockwise manner until the entire abdomen is examined. Any weakness or herniation of the abdominal musculature is recorded as well as whether the abdomen is soft or hard or if tenderness is present. Tenderness is difficult to evaluate in the infant and may be correlated only with irritability or crying during the examination.

The edge or border of the liver may be palpable in the normal newborn. Palpating lightly with the fingertips from right lower to upper quadrant, the liver edge may be detected 1 to 2 cm below the right rib margin. The eleventh and twelfth floating ribs may be mistaken for superficial masses. The tip of the spleen may be felt at times in the normal newborn as a superficial mass in the lateral portion of the left upper quadrant.

After palpating the abdomen lightly, the four quadrants are palpated more deeply with the flat surface of the fingers. The kidneys may be felt immediately after birth. Masses may represent tumors, cysts, or structural abnormalities; all masses should be considered abnormal until adequately explained.

The abdomen is percussed by placing the finger of one hand firmly against the abdominal wall and using the index or middle finger of the other hand as a percussion hammer. All areas of the abdomen are quickly percussed to determine whether increased tympany or resonance is present. Distention of the abdomen and an increase in resonance indicate the presence of gas in the abdomen; distention of the abdomen with little resonance suggests fluid or solid masses in the abdomen.

Auscultation of the abdomen for peristalsis is done by placing the stethoscope firmly

FIGURE 26-4

Palpation is performed with the flat surface of the fingers or fingertips. (*Drawing by Dan Manyluk.*)

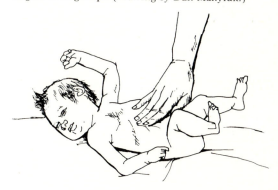

over the abdomen and listening carefully for metallic tinkling sounds. The sounds are of low intensity and occur with an approximate frequency of two to five per minute.

Chest

Inspection of the chest precedes palpation, percussion, and auscultation. Evaluation is made of shape and size; the presence of gross anomalies, tumors, or fractures; a depressed sternum or any asymmetry of the chest; and breathing movements and rate. Particular note is made of intercostal spaces and supra- and substernal areas to detect signs of labored breathing or retractions.

The breasts are inspected for presence of breast tissue, enlargement, signs of infection, development of the nipples and areola, and the presence of any supernumerary nipples, which may appear below the nipple line or in the axillary region.

The chest is examined for bulging or visible heartbeat.

The entire chest is palpated with the flat surface of the fingers or fingertips. The clavicles are examined for tenderness or the presence of crepitance or a bony mass which may indicate fracture. The presence or absence of breast engorgement is confirmed. Location of the apex beat gives information about heart size and location. Any abnormal vibratory thrills are recorded. Examination for lymph nodes in the axillary areas, rarely found in the normal newborn, is performed by gently palpating the chest wall in the axilla with the fingertips.

Percussion of the chest of the newborn infant usually reveals little information because of the difficulty of localizing the vibrations.

The chest is auscultated to determine the rate, rhythm, and quality of heart sounds. Auscultation is best performed with a stethoscope that can be fitted snugly against the chest. A small bell stethoscope is best for localizing specific sounds.

Auscultation of the heart includes listening over the entire precordium, below the left axilla, and posteriorly below the scapula. Special attention is paid to the areas where cardiac valve sounds are best heard—at the apex (mitral), at the second interspace to the left of the sternum (pulmonary), at the second interspace to the right of the sternum (aortic), and at the junction of xiphoid and the sternum (tricuspid). The first heart sound is due to closure of the mitral and tricuspid valves. The second heart sound is due to aortic and pulmonic valve closure.

Attention is given to listening to one thing at a time. First the rate and then the rhythm are determined. Differentiation is made between the first and second heart sounds, and these sounds are compared at the various listening posts; they should be sharp and clear. Extra sounds, sound of poor quality, or murmurs accompanying these heart sounds are considered abnormal.

FIGURE 26-5
In auscultation of the heart, special attention is paid to the areas where cardiac valve sounds are best heard. (*Drawing by Dan Manyluk.*)

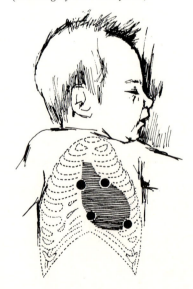

The entire chest is then auscultated for breath sounds in a systematic manner, comparing one side of the thorax to the other. The type of breath sound, the presence of any extraneous sounds, rales, rhonchi, and wheezes are noted. A considerable amount of experience in determining the wide range of breath sounds is necessary before confidence in such evaluation is established. Turning the infant to a prone position, the posterior thorax is examined in a similar manner.

Back and Spine

With the infant in a prone position the entire posterior surface of the infant's body is observed and palpated.

The presence of hair is checked. Hair is sometimes seen over the shoulders and back of the newborn, especially premature infants, but it disappears by three months of age. Tufts of hair anywhere over the spine, especially over the sacrum, may mark the site of a spina bifida occulta or spina bifida. Any masses over the spine or abnormal curvatures of the spine should be noted. The size, shape, and symmetry of the scapulae are determined.

The buttocks and anus are inspected. Presence and character of stool are recorded, and any excoriation or fissure of the anal mucosa should be detected. If a pilonidal dimple is present in the coccygeal area, it should be carefully examined for the presence of infection, which may accompany a pilonidal cyst or sinus.

Neck

Examination of the neck begins while the infant is in a prone position. The neck is inspected for position (torticollis, opisthotonus), swellings, and edema. Webbing of the neck is difficult to determine in the infant and may appear as an extra skin fold on the back of the neck. If the infant lifts the head while in the prone position, this is observed. Motion of the neck is determined by gently rotating the infant's head from side to side and from flexion to extension. The neck is palpated for presence of lymph nodes and masses, and the sternocleidomastoid muscles are also palpated for masses. With the infant in a supine position the trachea is palpated to detect any deviation from the midline.

Arms and Hands

The upper extremities are inspected for congenital anomalies, including absence or defects of parts or all of the extremity. Are the extremities unusually long and thin? Are they broad and short? The position of the arms and hands at rest is observed. Does the infant flex the arms? The full-term newborn will exhibit flexion of the upper extremities with hands held in a grasping or clenched position. The arms are extended by the examiner beside the body; when released, there is prompt flexion at the elbow.

Fingers are checked for the following: clubbing; color and temperature, as well as any difference in color or temperature between the extremities; webbing or the presence of extra digits; length of the fingernails; any unusual shortness or curvature of the little fingers; presence of a simian crease on the palm of the hand. The grasp reflex is elicited by pressing the palmar surface of the hand with the examiner's index finger.

Range of motion of the wrist, elbow, and shoulder is recorded. Flexion of the hand at the wrist is about 110°, and extension is 80°; range of motion at the elbow is about 170°. The shoulder abducts from the trunk about 120°. The entire arm is palpated for any masses or fracture.

The biceps tendon reflex is sometimes difficult to elicit in the newborn. The examiner places the index finger of one hand on the tendon of the biceps muscle in the elbow area. The examiner's ring finger is on the wrist and the middle finger is underneath the arm. Using the index finger of the other hand, the examiner taps the finger which covers the tendon of the biceps. A short contraction can be observed and felt.

Head

The entire occiput is inspected. The shape of the head is examined for asymmetry due to edema, hematoma, molding, presence and character of hair, and condition of the scalp.

The infant's head is next palpated, and particular attention is given to the sutures and fontanels. The sutures are normally felt as ridges immediately after birth and any overriding of the sutures should be noted. Within a day the suture lines may be felt as depressions in the normal infant. The anterior and posterior fontanels are palpated and measured, and the presence of any other fontanel should be noticed. Tension of the anterior fontanel, whether it is depressed or bulging, is determined while the infant is in a sitting position. The normal anterior fontanel can be expected to be slightly depressed when the infant is sitting. Slight pulsations of the anterior fontanel are also normal. Edema of the scalp or cephalohematoma should be detected by palpation.

Measurement of head circumference is done by placing the measuring tape just above the infant's eyebrows and, posteriorly, over the most prominent part of the occiput.

Face

Examination of the face begins with observation for symmetry between the left and right sides and between symmetrical parts. When the infant grimaces or cries it is noticed whether the facial contortions are symmetrical. The skin is inspected for edema, uneven pigmentation, hair, ecchymosis, or lesions. Spacing of the eyes is examined to detect hypotelorism or hypertelorism. Facial expressions of blandness, alertness, fussing, or crying are observed.

Eyes

Examination of the eyes may be difficult in the newborn period because of the tendency for infants to keep their eyes shut or because of periorbital edema. It is usually not helpful to attempt to forcibly hold the eye open. Gentle rocking of the head frequently causes infants to open their eyes.

The structure of the eyelid and eye is inspected for the following abnormalities: bulging or sunken eyes; any drooping, edema, or inflammation of the eyelids; discharge from the eye; conjunctival edema; vascular infection; and scleral hemorrhage. The color of the sclerae should be noted.

The blink reflex may be stimulated by shining a bright light in the eyes. The cornea should be bright and shiny when illuminated by the examiner's light. Any haziness or dullness is abnormal. The color of the iris is noted, as is the shape (round, oval, or irregular) and the size (normal, constricted, or dilated) of the pupil.

The reaction of the pupils to light can be tested by shading one eye with the hand for a moment and checking whether the pupillary response is absent, discernible, or normal.

Whether the eyes are centered or deviated to the left or right and whether nystagmus is present should be recorded.

To use the ophthalmoscope, dim the lights in the room, set the ophthalmoscope at 0 or −1, and direct the ophthalmoscope light at the pupil; a small red-orange circular spot should appear. This is the red reflex, caused by the light shining on the retina, and it indicates that opacities of the lens or other obstructions are not present.

FIGURE 26-6
The ophthalmoscope should be used to check for the
red reflex and make certain there are no opacities
between the lens and the retinas. It is best not to forcibly
hold the lids open. (*Drawing by Dan Manyluk.*)

Nose

The nose is inspected for abnormality of
shape, unusual flattening, flaring of the
nares, patency, or nasal discharge. If sneez-
ing occurs, it should be noted.

Ears

The ears are inspected for size, shape, position, and anomaly. An imaginary line is
drawn between the lateral canthus of the eye
and the most prominent point of the posterior occiput; the top of the ear should fall
above this line.

Hearing is tested by sounding a bell or rattle near the infant's head. Blinking of the
eyes, momentary cessation of activity, or
startle activity indicates a positive response.

Otoscopic examination of the newborn
often yields little information at birth because of the presence of vernix and debris in
the canal, but the eardrum usually is visualized after a few days.

The otoscope is held between thumb and
first finger with the other fingers resting on
the infant's head. With the examiner's other
hand the ear is pulled back and downward to
straighten the canal, and the 3-mm speculum
is introduced gently.

The condition of the canal is first inspected; then the color and landmarks of the
tympanic membrane or eardrum are determined. The color of the normal drum is gray
to bluish white and translucent or opales-
cent. The landmarks of the normal tympanic
membrane are caused by the position of the
membrane in relation to the bones of the
middle ear, particularly the malleus. Infection or other abnormality causes the landmarks to become distorted or absent.

The following landmarks are observed on
the normal eardrum:

1   The umbo or point of maximum con-
    vexity of the drum, which appears as a
    white spot at about the center of the
    eardrum
2   The long process or handle of the mal-
    leus, which appears as a small white
    streak running up and forward from
    the umbo
3   The short process of the malleus,
    which is a small white process at the
    upper end of the malleus
4   The light reflex, which is a sharply de-
    fined cone-shaped reflection from the
    otoscope light, with the apex at the
    umbo and the base in the anterior infe-
    rior portion of the drum

In the infant ear, the tympanic membrane
is normally thicker and more horizontal than
in the older child or adult, and the light reflex may be absent.

Mouth and Throat

An adequate source of light (flashlight or
penlight) and a small tongue blade are required for examination of the mouth and
throat. First the lips are inspected for anoma-

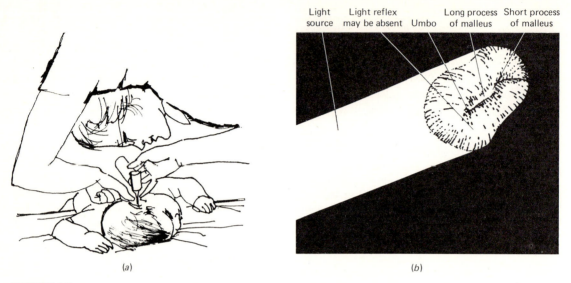

FIGURE 26-7
(a) The otoscope is held between thumb and first finger with other fingers braced
on infant's head or shoulders; the ear is pulled back and downward to straighten the
canal. (*Drawing by Dan Manyluk.*) (b) Schematic illustration of normal
landmarks of the tympanic membrane of the infant ear (right side). (*Drawing
by Dan Manyluk.*)

lies, such as harelip, and for dryness and lesions. The buccal mucosa, gums, and palate are examined, and note is made whether the palate has an unusually high arch and whether a cleft of the hard or soft palate exists.

It may be necessary to palpate the palate with the finger to ascertain whether a submucous cleft palate is present. Bohn's nodules and Epstein's pearls, small retention cysts on the midline of the palate or on the gums, may be detected. The tongue is examined for size and mobility. Generally, if the frenulum can be visualized or if the tip of the tongue is observed extending over the lower gum margin, significant tongue-tie is not present.

While using the tongue blade to hold the tongue on the floor of the mouth, the throat is then examined. The light and tongue blade are employed simultaneously so that when the infant gags the examiner is prepared to view the uvula and pharynx. Presence of the gag reflex and position of the uvula are observed, including bifurcation of the uvula if present.

Neurological Evaluation

The neurological evaluation is usually performed as an integral part of the basic physical examination, although the response of the infant to specific stimuli may be evaluated at the completion of the exam.

During the general observation, certain assessments are made which are most significant in the neurological appraisal. Eye and respiration movement and resting posture and motor activity have been evaluated.

Movement of the arms and legs is observed throughout the exam as to whether the arms and legs are in flexion or extension postures and whether unequal movement of one extremity, jerking, or tremors occur. Facial expression and response to a bell or rattle have been evaluated. The shape and size of the pupils and reaction of pupils to light has been tested. The upper and lower extremities have been moved through their full range of motion and resistance to this movement evaluated. Achilles, knee-jerk, and biceps tendon reflexes as well as palmar and plantar grasp and the Babinski reflex have been tested.

In addition, the rooting reflex is elicited by gently stroking the corners of the mouth and upper and lower lips in the midline. A positive response occurs when the infant opens the mouth or turns the head to the side of the stimulus. The sucking reflex is obtained by placing a finger or pacifier in the baby's mouth and noting the strength of the mouth movements and sucking response.

Grasping the infant's hands and arms, the examiner gently pulls the infant to a sitting position so that the degree of head lag can be observed. It is noted whether the infant's head is in alignment with the body when the infant reaches the vertical position. The degree of head control present with the infant in a sitting position is observed.

Incurvation of the trunk reflex is obtained by holding the infant in a prone position over the examiner's hand. By stroking the infant's back parallel to the spine the examiner detects presence or absence of movement of the pelvis toward the stimulated side.

The automatic walking reflex (stepping reflex) may also be tested. If the infant is held on a forward incline, allowing one foot to touch the table, the infant will right him- or herself with that leg and flex the opposite leg. The opposite action occurs when the other foot touches the table.

The Moro, or startle, reflex is elicited by a loud noise such as clapping near the baby's ear, by striking the table on which the infant is lying, or by lifting the head of the bassinet a few inches and dropping it. The infant's arms, hands, and cry are noted. A complete Moro reflex consists of abduction of the arms at the shoulder, extension of the forearm at the elbow, and extension of the fingers followed by an adduction of the arm at the shoulder. Asymmetrical response, jerkiness or tremor, or slow or weak response are considered abnormal. A vigorous cry should follow the startle.

CONCLUSION

Developing skill in physical examination is becoming increasingly necessary for the nurse, partly because of changing patterns of practice in maternal and child health. Nurses are assuming greater responsibility for evaluating the health status of infants, and the physical examination is one of the basic criteria on which the nurse bases a clinical judgment.

A broad knowledge of normal physical and developmental variations in the newborn infant is required, as well as knowledge of pathological signs and symptoms. When performing the physical examination, the nurse must maintain a high level of suspicion, and all unusual or unexplained findings must be brought to the attention of a physician or other qualified expert and pursued until a satisfactory explanation of the condition is found.

The importance of thoroughness and of developing a methodical system of examination is emphasized. Most signs and symptoms of an abnormal or pathological state are missed, not because of the obscure or esoteric nature of physical findings but because of failure on the part of the examiner to observe and examine the patient carefully and failure to pursue vigorously suspicious or unexplained findings.

Every infant examined by the nurse is unique and must be evaluated in relation to that infant's particular perinatal history. The system of examination should be adapted to the individual infant and to the specific situation.

BIBLIOGRAPHY

Barness, Lewis A.: *Manual of Pediatric Physical Diagnosis,* Year Book, Chicago, 1972.

Brazie, J. V., and Lula O. Lubchenco: "The Newborn Infant," in C. Henry Kempe, Henry K. Silver, and Donough O'Brien (eds.), *Current Pediatric Diagnosis and Treatment,* Lange, Los Altos, Calif., 1974.

Green, Morris, and Julius B. Richmond: *Pediatric Diagnosis,* Saunders, Philadelphia, 1966.

Judge, Richard D., and George D. Zuidema: *Physical Diagnosis: A Physiologic Approach to the Clinical Examination,* Little, Brown, Boston, 1968.

Lloyd-Roberts, G. C.: *Orthopedics in Infancy and Childhood,* Butterworth, London, 1971.

Prechtl, Heinz, and David Beintema: *The Neurological Examination of the Newborn Infant,* The Spastics Society Medical Education and Information Unit, published in association with William Heinemann Medical Books Ltd., London, 1964.

Silver, Henry K., C. Henry Kempe, and Henry B. Bruyn: *Handbook of Pediatrics,* Lange, Los Altos, Calif., 1973.

UNIT B

THE IMPACT OF BIRTH ON THE FAMILY

27

Postpartum Needs of the Family

SHARON SERENA JOSEPH
AND RANA LIMBO PECK

Every family member has a period of readjustment when the new baby arrives; however, the mother's readjustment is perhaps more extensive, since changes occur in her physical state, her habits, and her feelings. During pregnancy and the early puerperium the mother, especially the primipara, finds herself in a tremendous state of emotional flux, and the frontispiece of this book symbolically illustrates many of the emotional struggles occurring within her.

As the frontispiece suggests, the mother senses that the time is near for her to regard the infant as a separate individual; but she hesitates and thinks, "not yet." Hence, her arms enfold the infant more firmly, uniting her body with that of the baby. Later the mother may feel capable of seeing the infant as an individual separate from herself, but then the desire to be one with her child may converge upon her again. "Not yet" may mean that the mother is not ready to give up the baby that was within her body, or it may mean that the mother is hesitant about accepting the overwhelming role of parenthood and the changes that this new role will require the mother and her family to make.

Whether or not a new mother is able to identify feelings similar to those just mentioned, the fact that the woman has recently given birth creates changes in her behavior and emotions. These same emotions, though not quite so extensive, may occur in the husband and siblings as well. This state of flux, which can be referred to as a developmental crisis, provides a unique opportunity for the hospital, clinic, or community health nurse to intervene. Howard J. Parad defines the crisis intervener as one who enters the problem situation and helps those involved to mobilize their strengths in order to move out of the crisis or crisislike state in a manner which is acceptable to those involved.[1] As an intervener, the nurse must possess a thorough understanding of the physical and psychological alterations taking place within the mother as well as an awareness of the dynamics involved in the changing family structure.

IN SEARCH OF SELF

Phases of the Maternal Role

Many deep emotional changes occur within the mother during the puerperium and have been described by Reva Rubin as the phases of taking-in, taking-hold, and letting-go.[2] An understanding of these phases and the variations within them will provide a theoretical base on which to plan nursing care.

Taking-in Phase

This first phase may last from 2 to 3 days, during which time the mother's primary concern is with her own needs—sleep and food.

To some extent, the woman reacts passively and initiates little activity on her own. The mother may find herself ravenously hungry, and the need to satisfy her own hunger may cause her to become apprehensive about her infant's oral intake.

The mother is often quite talkative during this phase and will talk at length about every detail of her labor and delivery experience, as seen in Figure 27-1. It is as if she is attempting to put everything together, to make it more meaningful to her, to absorb the experience and make it part of her inner self. She may repeat and interpret the recent events first to the baby's father and family and then to friends and to anyone who will listen.

This talkativeness is not to be taken lightly by the nurse. As an enthusiastic listener the nurse can help the mother interpret the events so that the whole experience becomes more meaningful to both mother and father.

FIGURE 27-1

A nursing student listens to a mother recount her labor and delivery experience. (*Courtesy of The University of Colorado Medical Center, Denver, Colorado.*)

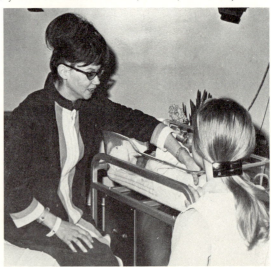

It is also an invaluable opportunity to determine how the mother has perceived the labor and delivery experience and can provide important information for evaluating the future maternal-child relationship. The mother is very perceptive at this time and will sense whether the nurse is interested in her as a person or only in getting her temperature taken and recorded. A few minutes of listening and a few encouraging words can give the mother ego support which is greatly needed as she prepares to enter the second phase.

Taking-hold Phase

About the third postpartum day, the mother begins the taking-hold phase in which the emphasis is placed on the present. She becomes impatient and is driven to organize herself and her life. She has progressed from the passive individual to the one who is in command of the situation. Since the physical changes are so overwhelming to her, she is relieved to know that she can regain control of her body and that everything will return to the prepregnant state. This restoration of self can be divided into five essential needs: nourishment, elimination, comfort, rest, and presence of a supportive figure. When these needs have been met, the mothering tasks become very important, taking priority over all else. If she has difficulty mastering a task, she becomes intolerant of herself, feeling that she is a failure, that she is inadequate, and that the baby is rejecting her.

The new mother is trying hard to be perfect, although she is often quite unsure of herself. A task that appears simple to the nurse may seem monumental to the mother; for as Rubin points out, the mother looks but does not see. Common sense becomes most uncommon, and what looks simple becomes difficult. The following situation illustrates this point. The nurse sees that a mother is having difficulty diapering the baby and relieves the mother of her frustration by diapering the baby neatly, quickly, and efficiently. In reality what has happened is that the well-meaning nurse has made the mother feel inadequate. The mother wonders if she will ever handle the baby as well as the nurse, and because her security is threatened, she becomes frightened at the prospect of caring for her infant.

The nurse should recognize the mother's fears and desires which are so evident during this phase. The greatest contribution to the mother at this time is staying with her while she diapers the baby, and complimenting her on a job well done. The nurse must determine what has priority for the mother at the time—teaching or ego support.

A similar situation might occur during feeding. If the mother has difficulty getting the baby to nurse or to take the bottle, she is likely to interpret this as rejection of her by the infant; hence, she again feels inadequate in her mothering tasks. Successes at this time are important events in the development of a warm and healthy mother-child relationship.

The taking-hold phase lasts about 10 days. Once the mother has taken control of her own physical being and taken hold of the mothering tasks, she is able to extend her energies to her mate and other children. The nurse should recognize this course of events and help the father understand what is happening to his mate who was once so loving and caring. He may feel left out and needs to understand that this is a temporary situation during which he will probably have to give more than he will receive. A few timely words to a father can do much toward maintaining a satisfying union.

Since this is a time when the mother is taking hold of many things and is striving to master new tasks, teaching is an important and significant aspect of nursing care. Another point to remember is that the mother is curious about many things concerning herself and the baby and is willing to learn and to try new ways. It is perhaps unfortunate that many mothers are discharged from the hospital on the third postpartum day. This means that the hospital nurse never sees the mother during the taking-hold phase; hence, the best opportunities for teaching are missed. Many hospitals have organized teaching programs hoping that the new mothers will absorb some of the material presented. Such programs are of value and should be developed, but ideally the nurse would use physiological and psychosocial knowledge of the postpartum woman and teach to meet the individual needs. It would also warrant a nurse skilled in observation who can use creativity in presenting information to the patient without appearing perfect and omniscient. The mother seeks assistance in self-actualization, not competition in the art of mothering.[3]

Letting-go Phase

The third phase of Reva Rubin's description of the restorative process is the letting-go phase. As the frontispiece of this book illustrates, the woman often has difficulty letting go of the infant as part of her body. The cutting of the umbilical cord is the first step in the infant's journey to independence, for once the cord is cut the infant depends on his or her own body to perform the life tasks of eating, breathing, and eliminating waste products.

The mother often feels a deep loss because what was once part of her body and her imagination is now reality and separate from her. The woman may quietly grieve over this loss. Many changes have taken place within her, and a new life awaits her; however, she must first accept the baby as a person, with a distinct personality, and second, she must establish new norms for herself, her baby, and her family.

Conflicts of the Maternal Role

The arrival of the baby creates many conflicts within the mother even though she may have planned for this child for several months. Whether the pregnancy was planned or not, the presence of a helpless infant brings about changes in the mother's life-style. The new mother may find herself in a double-bind situation. The traditional values of the self-sacrificing, forebearing mother are often in conflict with the more liberated, self-fulfilling goals the woman has for her own life.[4] The following five conflicts were described by Ross Laboratories in a study on maternal attitudes.[5]

Dependency and Independency

The mother's need to be dependent is very real during the early puerperium. It is as if she is at first overwhelmed with what she has done—delivered a baby. The new mother finds that a dependent role is safe and secure, but her situation demands that decisions be made. The attainment of maturity and independence is what she has strived for since childhood, and her new role reinforces the achievement of this goal. She is caught in conflict between doing what she knows is expected of her—making independent decisions for her baby—and doing what she feels more secure in doing—letting others make decisions for her and her baby. Ultimately, of course, she is forced to make such decisions, but she often feels she has inadequate experience on which to base them. The teenage mother needs special consideration regarding this conflict, since she is also experiencing a dependent-independent conflict between adolescence and adulthood. Most adolescents feel that they have functioned as an adult by delivering a baby, but they are not necessarily ready to assume the responsibility of motherhood. They may use role play a great deal as they attempt to "try on" being called mother.

Idealized and Realistic Role

During pregnancy the mother may have daydreamed about what it would be like after the baby was born, seeing herself rocking and cuddling the infant, very content and satisfied with life. During the weeks following delivery, she comes to see her mothering role more realistically, and it includes getting up at night to feed the baby and changing and laundering the diapers as well as rocking the baby and cooing fondly over the infant. The reality of caring for a helpless infant is forced upon the mother who may feel guilty because she considers the baby a lot of work.

Love and Resentment of Infant

Infants have many needs for which they are dependent on the mother to fulfill, and since they do not know patience, they will vocally make their wants known. The mother retains many of the needs she had prior to the arrival of the baby, and conflict may arise as she tries to fulfill both her needs and her infant's. She sometimes finds her needs incompatible with the infant's, and although she loves her baby, she may resent the intrusion on her privacy. Many times the woman was treated as someone special while she was pregnant, and now that the baby has come, everyone's attention is on the infant. She may resent this fact and at the same time feel remorse because she has such feelings.

Self-Fulfillment and Motherhood

When a baby comes into the family, the woman finds that she is no longer just a woman and mate. She has become woman, mate, and mother, which requires a change in her self-concept. Previous to the birth she may have seen herself as a schoolgirl, a companion, a career girl. Some of these roles may now seem incompatible with her new role as mother; hence, conflict may arise. She may find it difficult to give up her career, and although many women continue to work following delivery, adequate arrangements must be made for the infant's care.

Love for Father and Infant

Previous to the baby's birth, the woman may have devoted much of her time to her mate, and now she finds her time must be divided between the baby and the baby's father. Both she and her mate may find this difficult to accept. The mother feels conflict within her because she wants to continue to give the same attention to her mate, but she finds that the baby often interrupts and demands her attention.

Often the woman settles the conflict within by becoming so involved with the infant that she forgets that the father still needs much of the attention she gave him prior to the baby's arrival. The woman should be reminded that she remains first a companion and then a mother. A woman who has a happy relationship will find that she is a happier mother.

Postpartum Blues

With all the physiological and psychological changes taking place within the mother, she is prone to postpartum depression, or "blues." Rubin defines postpartum depression as the gap between the ideal and reality.

The new mother's self-expectations may exceed her capabilities, resulting in *cyclical* feelings of depression.[6] Some predisposing factors affecting the development of postpartum blues include a first pregnancy, a pregnancy in later childbearing years, ambivalence toward the woman's own mother, social isolation, long and/or hard labor, anxiety regarding finances, marital disharmony, and crisis in the extended family.[7]

The new mother may be unsure of herself in her new role; hence, too many well-meaning suggestions and words of advice may cause her to become tense and upset. She worries about obtaining the approval of her neighbor or her mother yet resents all their knowledgeable advice. She needs encouragement and acceptance from these people, and an occasional helpful hint may be welcomed. In anticipation of such frustration the nurse might suggest that the new mother listen and take what advice fits into her lifestyle and politely ignore the rest. The mother should be encouraged to relax with her infant and do things as she wishes. The baby will survive in spite of inexperienced mothering.

If the mother finds that she is easily upset during the early puerperium, she should be reminded that this is normal and is due to the many changes occurring within her. The nurse should let her know that it is all right for her to cry if she feels like it. Many women feel that they are "going crazy" and are losing control of their emotions, since one minute they are happy and the next they are sad. The nurse should encourage her to talk about her feelings and above all let her know that these reactions are normal. Some women have a delayed postpartum depression which may occur as late as 3 to 4 weeks after delivery. A father who is made aware of these emotional changes in the new mother can provide understanding and support for her during this unsettled time.

The Multiparous Mother

The mother having her second child may say that she feels so much more confident with this baby than she did with her first, as she is more secure in the mothering tasks. She may jokingly say that she will enjoy this baby because she learned from her first child. It is important for the nurse to remember that the woman who has other children will still pass through Rubin's three phases and still feels emotional conflicts following the delivery.

It is also appropriate for the maternal-child nurse to discuss with the mother how she plans to manage sibling rivalry that may arise when the new baby is brought home. A mother may say that there will be no problems; however, the nurse might remind her that the first child has received the parents' entire attention and, like most human beings, will find it difficult to share the limelight. The nurse should learn the ages of the other children and incorporate knowledge about the various age groups in conversations with the mother as the nurse helps to prepare her for eventual discharge. The task of discussing sibling rivalry with the postpartum mother is frequently overlooked; however, it can be of prime importance in attempting to maintain an intact, content family. These mothers often miss their older children very much while they are in the hospital, and it is frequently the first lengthy separation for both mother and child.

One woman was quite anxious to see her two-year old child and could not wait to be discharged. On the day of discharge she was prepared to receive a warm welcome from her toddler. Instead of hugs and kisses she found the child wanted nothing to do with her. The mother was crushed and quite depressed. The child was upset with the mother because she had left him, and 2 days seemed an eternity to a child who had no concept of time. Since the child was hurt by his mother's absence, he was unsure whether he would accept her back so readily. The mother needed to be aware of how the child felt and to act appropriately. A woman in this situation can be encouraged to spend time with the older child each day—time which is that child's alone. A gift for the older child from the mother when she arrives home from the hospital often serves to remind the child of his or her importance. This is just one of the many experiences that a woman may face when she returns to her other children. The arrival of a new baby causes change for every member of the family and is a time of developmental crisis for all involved.

Development of the Maternal-Child Relationship

Because the mother is the primary source of socialization for the infant during the first year of life, it is advisable to have an understanding of how she initially establishes a relationship with her new baby; for it is she who conveys warmth, affection, distance, and rejection as she conducts her caretaking tasks, becoming the chief influence in the infant's life. Much has been written about the importance of a good mother-child relationship, a product of her adjustment to the new infant. It is of great importance for the maternal-child nurse to recognize the characteristics of a healthy and normal mother-infant relationship in contrast to one which deviates from the norm. The nurse's knowledgeable intervention at this time could be crucial in the lives of the new mother and growing child.

The pregnant woman's attitude toward the fetus, though not so much her attitude toward the pregnancy itself, has been found to correlate closely with her initial contribution to the mother-infant relationship.[8] The

mother who has been very emotionally attached to the baby within her is more likely to remain that way after the birth. On the other hand, it is usual for someone who has viewed the fetus in an intellectual, detached way to be much less demonstrative and affectionate toward her newborn.

Definition and Description

One cannot adequately define a mother-child relationship solely by viewing the mother, for the system of interrelating is a circular one in which the mother responds to the baby on the basis of how she perceives the infant's needs. Concurrently, through activity, appearance, size, and actions the infant communicates to the mother, generating a response from her. In a healthy relationship this response is an effort by the mother to satisfy the infant's needs primarily on the basis of the baby as an individual, and not according to the mother's own need for self-fulfillment.[9]

The first interaction between mother and baby is one of exploration and examination. When a mother is able to see her infant for the first time and the infant is nude, she will rapidly progress from poking her fingertips at the baby's extremities to encompassing the trunk with her palm.[10] The time required for the new mother's initial investigation varied from 4 to 8 minutes in one group studied, but a longer time is needed if separation after delivery has been prolonged. The description of maternal exploration is a species-specific behavior and important for a nurse to understand because the nurse is able to provide the mother with the opportunity, time, and privacy to fulfill this needed release of initial maternal behavior.

Interest in the baby's eyes is demonstrated repeatedly by new mothers when they see or hold the baby for the first time. A statement such as, "Come on now, open your eyes," often heard from new mothers, reflects this intense interest in having eye-to-eye contact with the infant. Desire for the *en face* position was demonstrated in all the mothers in the study mentioned above as they explored the infants,[11] as shown in Figure 27-2.

In order to execute nursing care which is of optimum benefit to the new mother, it is helpful to assess how she and the baby interact. A new mother may appear very frightened and disturbed when her baby is brought to her. She may become much less fearful if the baby's father enters the room, but may still be obviously upset by having relatives or friends view this initial encounter with her offspring. The mother often does not feel an immediate warm attachment to her baby, and the baby's father may warm up to the infant faster than she does. During pregnancy she may have viewed the fetus intellectually,

FIGURE 27-2

A new mother shows intense interest in her baby's eyes. (*Courtesy of The University of Colorado Medical Center, Denver, Colorado.*)

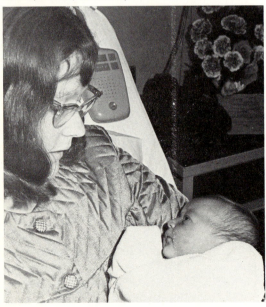

without a strong emotional tie. Now that she is face to face with her "little stranger," she is unsure of herself and seems awkward when she finally handles the baby. She may at first feel more comfortable looking at the baby, rather than holding the baby.

Gerald Caplan, in his description of initial maternal behavior, has coined the term "maternal time lag"[12] to identify the span of time required for a new mother to feel that the baby really belongs to her. The importance of understanding and assisting the mother becomes more obvious as ongoing care is given, for mothers experiencing this time lag may carry out tasks with less affection and fondling than they will when the infant has become less of a stranger to them and have a difficult time with diapering, feeding, bathing, etc. The baby's needs are seen objectively rather than felt subjectively because the infant is not perceived as an extension of the mother, and, therefore, she cannot respond to the baby's needs as quickly and assuredly as she will later. Breast-feeding may be more difficult, especially in finding a suitable position, since she cannot sense the baby's discomfort as she can her own. The nurse needs to be a role model, demonstrating a maternal figure. The mother handles intellectual information well, such as what toys to buy, how to dress the baby, or what temperature to keep the bedroom; however, the primary goal of nursing care for this mother involves being a strong mother figure, meeting first the mother's own needs as always, and then going on to being very affectionate toward the baby. That includes cooing, fondling, cuddling, talking—all demonstrating maternal warmth. These mothers may never have been exposed to what "mother love" entails; therefore, a well-prepared nurse can interpret the verbal and nonverbal communication the mother gives and show her this type of caring. The mother may be confused because she did not respond to her infant with instant love. The nurse can relieve the mother's concern by assuring her that the lag in maternal feelings is normal, whether she is a primipara or multipara.

One views in contrast Caplan's description of the mother who during her entire pregnancy has displayed a strong emotional attachment to the fetus. She talks to the unborn child, calling him or her by a pet name. These mothers usually name their babies early, talk incessantly about the joys of pregnancy, and have a very close relationship with the baby soon after birth.

The frontispiece of this book illustrates the emotions of this mother as she gazes fondly down at her child and the two figures become one. After delivery the mother shows a great deal of warmth and affection toward her baby, and as one views the mother and child, the feeling of oneness pervades. She is able to endow the new baby with a personality but does not yet see the infant as an individual apart from herself. Normal behavior of the newborn such as regurgitating, soiling diapers, and crying are all perceived subjectively, as though they were happening to the mother herself. The maternal time lag is much shorter and may in some mothers appear to be absent. It is difficult for this mother to "let go," but the acquisition of the maternal role up to that point seems relatively easy, even natural. These mothers cuddle their babies a great deal, deriving pleasure from the sharing of warmth. Breast-feeding appears easy and natural, usually continues successfully, and the nurse notices a certain look of contentment on the mother's face as she nurses.

The mother who maintains a very close relationship with her baby needs guidance in seeing the child as an individual. The nurse who says, "Look how he raises his head," or "Did you see how startled she was by the loud noise?" is pointing out individual characteristics. During the hospital stay, this mother may respond very poorly to intellectual information; however, she will seem receptive to instruction involving motor activities with the baby, such as feeding, bubbling, diapering, bathing, etc.

Assessment of the Relationship

In evaluating the mother's relationship with her infant it is helpful if the nurse has more to depend upon than observational skills. Dr. Dane Prugh uses a series of questions when he interviews new mothers which can be employed, as well as Caplan's theory, as predictive tools in assessment of the mother-infant relationship.[13] The nurse may wish to use all or some of these questions to obtain a more realistic picture of the new mother's feelings now and prior to the birth of her baby. They may be used in any order after the first question.

1   How are you feeling? Do you have any concerns about the baby or about how the baby looks to you? This is a warm-up question, but it may produce some interesting information. It is a good idea to first ask the mother how *she* is feeling because practically everyone who enters the room will go to the baby first. Once she has given information about herself, then the question can be asked about the baby. Some of her concerns about the baby are small ones, such as milia or erythema toxicum, but she may also bring to the interviewer's attention the fact that the baby's eyes are draining or that the baby's jaundice has increased a great deal since the evening before. This time can be used for explanations and reassurance.

2   What is the baby's name? When did

you choose the name? After the mother tells the interviewer what the baby's name is, it is well to explore with her how she chose the name. One mother admitted very freely that her baby's first and middle names were chosen after people she disliked intensely. Or a mother may name a boy after his father, who is abusive to her. In these cases, negative feelings may be projected toward the new infant because of the child's name, thereby creating a high-risk situation which should be carefully followed by the community health nurse. The parents who cannot agree on a name may be signaling that they cannot agree on other issues either, and marital problems can be inferred. The time the infant's name was chosen is useful in determining the feelings the mother had toward the fetus. The emotionally attached mother as described by Caplan usually names her baby early, while the unemotional, intellectual mother may still be trying to decide on a name the day she is discharged from the hospital.

3   How did you feel when you felt the baby move for the first time? Mothers who have established a strong relationship with the fetus and who will predictably relate well with the new infant say that they were excited, elated, and could not wait to have the father feel the baby move in utero. A mother who is having a more difficult time relating to the baby may describe the baby's movements as painful or generally a nuisance, and many times she will go into detail about how the baby kept her awake at night and made it difficult for her to breathe.

4   Did you have a mental picture of the baby around the time when the baby moved or later in the pregnancy? Many mothers who have very positive responses to the other questions cannot remember having any mental image of the fetus. Others say they pictured the fetus as a tiny infant. Concern about the response to this question is elicited when the mother says she saw the fetus as, for example, a one-year old. This mother may be fearful of her ability to care for the baby during the first year if for some reason she could not picture the baby as an infant. It is normal to have occasional frightening dreams about the baby; however, recurring unpleasant dreams or none at all reveal anxiety or ambivalence relating to the baby.

5   When asking this next question, the interviewer should preface it with a statement similar to, "Most women having a baby for the first time think they will feel immediate maternal warmth, but it is completely normal not to feel this way for a while." Then the question can be asked, "How is it with you?" or "How has it been for you?" Phrasing the question in this way elicits a truer response than asking the woman if she feels like a mother, since everyone answers affirmatively to that question. By prefacing the suggested question with such a statement, the mother feels much more comfortable in admitting her real feelings. By asking this question, the nurse is able to see if the mother is experiencing a maternal time lag, and it gives the nurse an opportunity to put the mother at ease regarding her feelings about the baby. It is surprising to watch the look of relief pass over many mothers' faces when they are told it is normal to have a lag in their maternal feelings. Clues may

have been given prior to asking this question such as, "I just can't believe this baby is really mine," or "It seems impossible that I'm a mother." Dr. Prugh feels that the time lag averages somewhere between 12 to 15 hours and 3 to 4 days; however, he and Caplan both acknowledge that it may last a period of months and still be normal.

Basic maternal behavior is best understood if the preceding types of new mothers are placed at opposite ends of a continuum. It is essential for the nurse to comprehend maternal behavior as constantly changing, with each mother a little different from the next. Viewing behavior on a continuum exemplifies this state of flux and demonstrates the variety of "normal." Most new mothers cannot be placed at one end of the continuum or the other, but rather fall somewhere in between, exhibiting behaviors from each end. The usefulness of the theory appears clearer as one plans and executes nursing care for a patient during the postpartum period. Even though either end of the continuum describes a healthy mother, the nurse is able to hasten the mother's progress to the goal of either "letting-go" or attainment of maternal feelings by realizing her approximate position on the continuum at the time.

The usefulness of the community health nurse cannot be overemphasized, since it is this nurse who will have contact with the mother long after her hospital stay. Besides being a resource person, role model, and health counselor, the community health nurse is in the best position to evaluate the new mother's progress in relation to role taking and attainment of maternal feelings. Since the maternal lag may normally last up to a month or 6 weeks, intervention can be planned if the lag is prolonged. And con-

sidering that the emotional separation between mother and infant may not occur until 7 months, ongoing care seems of utmost importance.

Nursing Intervention

Maternal behavior is learned; it is acquired through years of observation, personal experience, play acting, and development of a self-concept. Because maternal behavior is learned, it should be the goal of every maternal-child nurse to help a mother attain a feeling of comfort with her baby in performing mothering tasks. In some instances this process takes longer than others, but it should always be uppermost in the nurse's mind. This feeling of comfort cannot be achieved without letting the mother try things for herself, but with anticipatory guidance from the nurse. Seeing that she can perform as a mother is a great reward for both patient and nurse and, finally, is a tremendous ego strengthener. There is a certain amount of safety and security associated with the hospital environment because of the presence of doctors, nursing personnel, technical equipment, and even the hospital routine. The mother who has not been helped during her hospital stay to gain a feeling of comfort and confidence with her new infant has not been given optimal care. The process does not end in the hospital, but it must have its beginnings there if there is to be stability in the family environment following hospitalization.

The maternal-child nurse has other unique responsibilities to the family, including involvement with them during hospitalization of the mother and infant. Parents at times can feel overwhelmed by all the medical people around them whom they feel are so knowledgeable. This is especially true when either mother or baby is ill. A medical problem during this period of developmental crisis in the family is easily misinterpreted by the individuals involved. The parents at times view the situation as worse than it is, or they do not have an understanding of the facts and the probable outcome. At this point the nurse should be available to the parents as a source of strength and a resource person. A doctor's explanation is often filled with medical terminology that should be clarified. The nurse is in the position to realize that parents seldom grasp the meaning the first time they are informed of their baby's illness, however minor the illness is. They hear only that something is wrong, and immediately fear and anxiety block out whatever follows. It is not unusual to approach parents to whom the pediatrician has just given a careful description of their infant's heart murmur and hear one of them ask, "I think he said our baby has a heart murmur. What is a heart murmur anyway?"

If the baby's illness requires that the infant be transferred to an intensive care area or forbids the infant to be brought to the mother's room, the involvement continues as the nurse accompanies the parents to visit the baby. The nurse's presence and continued support at this time help alleviate some of the parents' anxiety and is an act of nursing care which is greatly appreciated.

The nurse should communicate an attitude of caring, characterized by a free and easy environment with as few rules as possible. New mothers are especially sensitive to criticism, and guidance by a nurse who has communicated this sense of caring to the mother will be accepted without hurt feelings and tears. The maternity unit is no place for a stern and rigid nurse. Harshness and criticism are confusing and upsetting when the mother knows she is doing her best. When teaching is done with love and understanding, an entirely different attitude is conveyed to the mother; therefore, when ego

strength is weak, as it often is during this time of passivity and dependency, it is important to emphasize the positive in what the mother is capable of doing.

THE CHANGING BODY

Anatomic Alterations

Physiological changes occur throughout the pregnancy, labor, delivery, and the puerperium. The nurse should assume the responsibility of keeping the mother informed of the processes which are taking place within her body and of helping her learn of their physiological importance.

The Uterus

Following the delivery of the placenta, the uterus, which now weighs almost 900 g, normally contracts into a hard mass about the size of a grapefruit and should be palpated in the midline halfway between the umbilicus and the symphysis pubis. Within the next 12 hours the uterus rises to the level of the umbilicus or slightly below, after which time it rapidly begins to decrease in size. On the fifth postpartum day, it should be approximately 4 to 5 fingerbreadths below the umbilicus and should weigh about 450 g.

By the tenth postpartum day, the uterus has descended into the true pelvis and is no longer palpable abdominally. By 6 weeks the uterus has fully involuted and weighs about 60 g, which is slightly more than its nulliparous weight. The muscle cells decrease in size, but the exact mechanism of this process is unknown.[14] Involution may be less rapid when the uterus has been markedly overdistended as in the cases of polyhydramnios, multiple gestation, a large baby, or in the grand multipara.

During the early postpartum days, the endometrium is also undergoing rapid change.

The lining, exclusive of the placental site, resembles a large desquamating wound which is restored by the end of the third week. The placental site heals less rapidly, requiring up to 6 weeks and leaving no permanent scar tissue at the site.

The Cervix

Following the third stage of labor, the over-distended cervix appears soft and flabby; unlike the endometrium, the cervix begins a simultaneous process of healing and regeneration. During the first 2 days postpartum, two fingers can be readily inserted into the cervix, but by the end of the first week it scarcely accommodates one finger. Anatomically, the internal cervical os returns to its tightly closed state and the external os remains slightly open, but because of the delivery process itself, the cervix never regains its nulliparous appearance.

The Vagina

The vagina, which is greatly distended during the birth process, becomes relaxed and edematous following delivery. It slowly diminishes in size but never regains its pregravid state, with rugae beginning to reappear around the third week. Most women are unaware of any change in size or tonicity of the vagina following labor and delivery; however, occasionally a mother will complain of dyspareunia (painful intercourse) which is usually the result of a tender perineal scar secondary to the episiotomy repair.

The Abdominal Wall

After delivery, the muscles of the abdominal wall are soft and flabby, but if tone has been maintained during pregnancy, the abdominal muscles usually return to their normal state by the end of 6 weeks. Unfortunately,

poor muscle control antepartally requires additional time for regaining muscle tone, and a slight protuberance of the abdomen may be evident for as long as 3 to 12 months; in fact, the muscles may never return to their prepregnant state.

Stretch marks, or striae gravidarum, are caused by a rupture of the elastic fibers in the skin, as shown in Figure 27-3. These marks appear as brownish or pinkish streaks on the abdomen and breasts and less frequently on the hips and thighs. Gradually the striae become silvery white but never completely fade, a fact which often causes the mother some distress since she may not feel comfortable in a two-piece bathing suit.

The rectus muscles, which are divided by a narrow muscular sheath, may show a marked separation, or diastasis. This condition prevents adequate support of the abdominal organs but is lessened by attention

FIGURE 27-3
Striae gravidarum as seen in the postpartum patient. (*Courtesy of The University of Colorado Medical Center, Denver, Colorado.*)

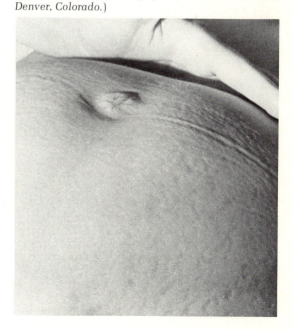

to proper exercise, diet, rest, and posture during pregnancy. Diastasis of the rectus muscles can be felt quite easily during a postpartum fundus check, as the rectus muscles are prominent and displaced laterally, and the fundus can be palpated just through the abdominal wall.

The Breasts and Lactation

The breast is composed of 15 to 24 lobes separated from one another by fatty tissue. These lobes are divided into lobules, each lobule containing a certain number of acini, or alveoli, as illustrated in Figure 27-4. To understand milk production, it is necessary to be aware of the structure of an alveolar cell. The constituents of breast milk are manufactured in the lining of the alveolar

cell, the epithelial layer. After this process, the myoepithelial cells in the walls of the alveoli contract, forcing the milk from the alveoli into small ducts. These ducts connect with larger ones called lactiferous ducts, which have orifices on the surface of the nipple.

The mechanism of milk production and ejection (called letdown) is determined hormonally. During pregnancy, the circulating estrogen, progesterone, and chorionic somatomammotropin (CST) have been preparing the breast for lactation. The estrogen primarily affects the ducts; the progesterone affects the alveoli.[15] The exact role of CST is still unknown at this time. Immediately after the delivery of the placenta, those hormone levels diminish, thereby activating the anterior lobe of the pituitary to release pro-

FIGURE 27-4
A cross section of the lactating breast. (*Reproduced from Richard M. Applebaum, "The Modern Management of Successful Breast Feeding,"* Pediatric Clinics of North America, 17:205, 1970. By permission of the publisher.)

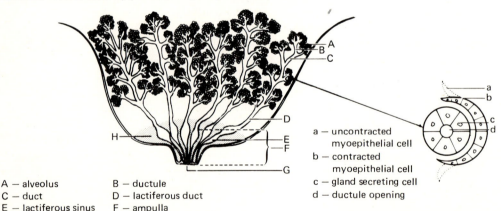

A — alveolus   B — ductule
C — duct   D — lactiferous duct
E — lactiferous sinus F — ampulla
G — nipple pore   H — areolar margin

a — uncontracted myoepithelial cell
b — contracted myoepithelial cell
c — gland secreting cell
d — ductule opening

With full development of the ovarian-uterine menstrual cycle, groups of gland secreting cells (alveoli) bud from the small ducts (ductules). The alveoli, under the influence of prolactin from the pituitary gland, secrete milk.

MICROSCOPIC SECTION OF ALVEOLUS
Gland secreting cells layer in a circle about the ductule opening. About the alveolus is a contractile cell called a myoepithelial cell. With commencement of sucking, this cell under the influence of oxytocin from the pituitary gland contracts and squeezes the milk into the duct system. This reflex is called *the letdown.*

lactin, which acts on the epithelial cells of the alveoli, stimulating them to produce milk. This process, which takes from 2 to 4 days, is enhanced by the sucking stimulus of the baby.

Sucking also triggers the release of oxytocin by the posterior lobe of the pituitary, thereby initiating the letdown reflex. The oxytocin causes contraction of the myoepithelial cells as well as the uterine myometrial cells. The truly amazing part of this reflex is once a woman is conditioned to nursing, the cry or thought of a baby is sufficient to activate letdown of the milk.

Breast milk is bluish white in color and appears to be very watery. It is high in both lactose and fat, low in protein and phosphate.[16] The composition is reversed in its precursor, colostrum, which is normally found in the alveoli during the latter phase of pregnancy. Colostrum, a yellowish fluid, which is high in antibodies, is an excellent food for the baby during the 2 to 3 days before the milk comes in. Breast milk is quite often mixed with colostrum for a week or longer. (See Table 27-1.)

Drugs such as antibiotics, sulfonamides, bromides, iodides, certain cathartics, large doses of salicylates, certain anticoagulants, and alcohol are absorbed into breast milk. Milk of magnesia and mineral oil are safe laxatives, heparin may be used as an anticoagulant, but tetracycline and oral anticoagulants are definitely contraindicated for a nursing mother.

The Lochia

During the early weeks of the puerperium there is a vaginal discharge varying in amount and color called lochia. Lochia rubra occurs during the first 2 to 4 days of the puerperium and consists of blood from the placental site, shreds of membranes and decidua, vernix, lanugo, and meconium. By the fourth day, the lochia has turned a brownish or dark red color, has a fleshy odor, and may last from 4 to 10 days. Lochia serosa, as it is called, is composed of blood, wound exudate, leukocytes and erythrocytes, shreds of decidua, cervical mucus, and many microorganisms. After the tenth day, the lochia is whitish yellow due to the increased number of leukocytes and is called lochia alba. Lochia may last anywhere from 3 to 6 weeks. If lochia rubra occurs following the appearance of lochia alba, it is usually a warning sign of possible postpartum complication. Rest and oxytocics are indicated in an attempt to avoid a late postpartum hemorrhage.

Many mothers worry about clots, and the nurse should inform the mother that small clots are not unusual, but large clots or any tissue in the discharge are considered abnormal and should be reported. At times it is difficult to differentiate between clots and tissue. Tissue is stringy, has a whitish cast to it, and may look like hamburger meat; a clot is red, dissolves on crumbling, and on gross examination has the appearance of liver. If there is any question, the specimen should be saved for observation by the physician. If the lochia remains red beyond 4 days, it indicates slow involution of the uterus which could be caused by retained placental fragments. Early ambulation causes the uterus to involute more quickly, and the duration of lochia rubra is therefore shortened. A strong, offensive odor is an indication of infection and should be reported to the physician and noted on the patient's chart.

The nurse is responsible for checking the color, amount, and odor of the lochia. This is usually done about every 4 hours during the first day following delivery and at least once a day throughout the remainder of the mother's hospital stay. It is helpful to the mother if she understands the color changes of the vaginal discharge and how long she

TABLE 27-1
Natural Milks and Prepared Milks Used in Infant Feeding*

Milk or formula	Milk:water ratio†	cal/ml	Approximate percentage composition, g/100 ml				Approximate electrolyte composition					mg/liter
							meq/liter					
			Protein	Carbohydrate	Fat	Minerals	Na	K	Cl	Ca	P‡	Fe
Human milk, mature, average	Undiluted	0.70	1.2	7.0	3.8	0.21	7	14	12	17	9	1.5
Cow's milk, market, average	Undiluted	0.70	3.3	4.8	3.7	0.72	25	35	29	62	53	1.0
Cow's milk, evaporated, many brands	1:1	0.75	3.8	5.4	4.0	0.8	28	39	32	65	59	1.0
Cow's milk, powdered:												
Klim, Borden	1:7	0.70	3.3	4.7	3.5	0.7	22	35	28	58	48	1.0
Commercial premodified milks:												
Infant Formula, Baker§	1:1	0.70	2.2	7.0	3.3	0.6	17	23	19	42	37	7.9
Bremil with Iron, Borden	1:1	0.70	1.5	7.0	3.5	0.5	11	16	13	35	18	8.5
Bremil, Powder, Borden	1:8	0.70	1.5	7.1	3.5	0.4	16	36	13	35	18	8.5
Modilac, Gerber	1:1	0.70	2.2	7.8	2.7	0.4	17	27	19	42	37	10.6
Enfamil, Mead§	1:1	0.70	1.5	7.0	3.7	0.3	11	19	12	32	32	8.5
Olac, Mead§	1:1	0.70	3.4	7.5	2.7	0.7	22	41	29	60	58	trace
Nan Powder, Nestlé	1:7	0.70	1.6	7.3	3.4	0.3	11	20	11	17	22	
Lactogen Powder, Nestlé	1:6	0.70	2.5	8.0	3.6	0.5	11	22	14	34	27	
Lactogen Powder, Full Protein, Nestlé	1:5.5	0.70	3.5	8.2	3.0	0.8	16	30	17	47	38	
Prodieton Powder, Nestlé	1:5	0.70	3.3	11.0	3.4	0.7	16	32	21	55	37	
Similac with Iron, Ross¶	1:1	0.70	1.8	6.6	3.4	0.4	12	26	18	34	30	12
Similac Powder with Iron, Ross¶	1:8	0.70	1.8	6.6	3.4	0.5	17	31	17	41	30	12
Similac PM 60/40 Powder, Ross	1:8	0.70	1.5	7.2	3.4	0.2	7	14	12	17	10	
SMA S-26, Wyeth§	1:1	0.70	1.5	7.2	3.6	0.25	7	14	12	21	21	8

Data supplied by processors or assembled from other sources.
* Figures given are for normal dilution.
† Number of milliliters of milk to number of milliliters of water. (Most powdered milks may also be prepared by adding 1 level tablespoonful or special measuring spoonful of powder to each 60 ml of water.)
‡ Calculated for valence of 1.8.
§ Also available in powdered form with similar composition.
¶ Also available without iron supplementation.

SOURCE: Reproduced from Waldo E. Nelson, et al. (eds.), Textbook of Pediatrics, 9th ed., Saunders, Philadelphia, 1969, p. 154. By permission of the publisher.

can expect it to last. It is also wise to caution her about the odor of the lochia so that she may report any abnormalities to her physician should they arise during the weeks following her discharge from the hospital.

Lochia contains large amounts of bacteria which may not cause problems for one mother but may be highly infectious to another; therefore, clean technique is of utmost importance when caring for these patients.

Clinical Manifestations

Body Temperature

Definitions of what constitutes a temperature elevation vary. A postpartum patient is described as febrile if her temperature exceeds 38°C in any two consecutive 24-hour periods excluding the first 24 hours;[17] however, temperatures between 37.5 and 38°C may be indicative of a beginning infection. A temperature that is defined as an elevation by a particular physician or hospital should be rechecked at least every 4 hours until it has remained in the normal range for two successive 4-hour periods.

Slight temperature elevation in the postpartum patient is common, and it is important for the nurse to understand this in order to assess and report changes in body temperature knowledgeably. The most common reason for a temperature rise during the first 24 hours is dehydration. Since labor is such hard work, a laboring patient may perspire profusely; the loss of fluid, along with the fact that oral fluids are often restricted and intravenous fluids sometimes omitted, may lead to dehydration and a slight increase in temperature. This elevation responds to an increase in fluids, sometimes as much as 4,000 ml in a 24-hour period. A patient is usually unaware of her temperature elevation and may need constant encouragement to take sufficient oral fluids. She may prefer

juices or coffee to water, and these preferences should be honored by the nurse in the plan of care. One must be careful, however, of water intoxication due to the overzealous administration of fluids.

In rare instances, a temperature elevation in the first 24 hours is not due to dehydration but to a previously existing infection. This viral or bacterial infection can usually be distinguished from dehydration. The patient with an infection experiences chills, temperature spikes, and a feeling of general malaise; the dehydrated patient commonly exhibits a flushed face, dry skin or mucous membranes, and is unaware of any temperature elevation. The two most common causes of a sudden increase in temperature after the first day are endometritis (puerperal fever) and urinary tract infection.

An elevation in temperature on the third or fourth day postpartum was once considered to be due to breast engorgement. This concept of "milk fever" has been shown to be a fallacy, for most of these temperature elevations are secondary to an infectious process. In rare instances, however, extreme engorgement may lead to a sudden, short-lived temperature spike not lasting more than 12 hours. Special attention should be paid to the comfort of a patient with a fever. As the fever decreases, the patient may experience diaphoresis. A blanket or sponge bath is comforting, and she may appreciate a cool cloth for her face during the elevation.

The Pulse

Bradycardia is common in the early puerperium. The heart rate usually averages between 60 and 70 but may drop to 50 or even lower on the first or second day. In a woman who is nervous or who has lost a large amount of blood, this drop in pulse may not be as dramatic. The bradycardia is not as evident if there is early ambulation, except in the early morning before arising. By the seventh to the tenth day, the pulse has returned to normal. A sudden spike in pulse taken while the woman is resting may be indicative of an early infection.

Uterine Afterpains

The uterus of a primipara generally maintains a state of tonic contraction unless blood clots or placental fragments remain in the uterine cavity. When these conditions exist, the uterus actively contracts in an effort to remove them. The uterus loses some of its tonicity if it has been unduly stretched. Rather than maintaining a state of sustained contraction, the muscles relax and contract at intervals in an attempt to return to normal. This cycle is interpreted as waves of pain, commonly referred to as afterpains. Mothers who breast-feed feel these pains more strongly, since the oxytocin released as the baby nurses also stimulates contraction of the uterus.

These afterpains may last as long as 7 days but usually diminish in intensity after the third day. The nurse must remember that many women require an analgesic for this pain. Having the mother lie on her abdomen often eases the discomfort, and the nurse should encourage the mother to empty her bladder. A full bladder elevates the uterus high in the pelvis which necessitates stronger uterine contractions in order for the uterus to return to its normal position and size. It is important for the nurse to be sympathetic as the mother may be quite uncomfortable while the pains persist.

The Bowels

Early ambulation has helped the problem of constipation during the puerperium but has not eliminated it. Several contributing factors to the new mother's difficulties with elimination are the relaxed abdominal and intestinal muscles, the cleansing enema before delivery, and lack of solid food during labor.

The fluid imbalance which may occur as the lactating breasts demand more fluids and the body eliminates much fluid is another cause of constipation, and therefore the postpartum mother should be encouraged to have an adequate fluid intake. If proper muscle tone has been maintained during pregnancy, the possibility of developing postpartum constipation is lessened.

A painful episiotomy and/or sore hemorrhoids hinder evacuation by preventing a woman from bearing down to aid in elimination. A topical anesthetic spray, sitz baths, ice packs, analgesics, or ointments may help to relieve some of the perineal discomfort. A laxative may be ordered routinely or as needed; however, a mild laxative should be given by the evening of the second day if the patient has not yet had a bowel movement. Some doctors order small enemas or suppositories if there has been no bowel movement by the morning of the third day.

The Urine

There is an increased amount of body fluids during pregnancy, and when the delivery is over, diuresis ensues in the body's effort to return to its nonpregnant metabolic state. This diuresis usually occurs during the second to fifth postpartum days, and there may be as much as 3,000 ml of urine excreted in a 24-hour period. It is not unusual to find sugar in the urine caused by the lactose being produced by the mammary glands as they are preparing for milk letdown. This is most noticeable during establishment of lactation and when the mother is weaning. Proteinuria is often present due to breakdown of the cells of the uterus during the process of involution. The proteinuria usually disappears by the third day, but may continue in trace amounts until involution is complete.

It is sometimes difficult for the mother to urinate following delivery, but she should void within 4 to 8 hours after the birth. There are certain factors contributing to the mother's difficulty with voiding during the first 12 hours:

1 Trauma to the bladder due to the pressure in labor of the fetal head against it
2 Edema of the urethra and vulva due to the birth process
3 The decrease in intraabdominal pressure immediately postpartum secondary to the distention of the pregnant abdominal wall
4 Possible decrease in the sensitivity of the bladder for several hours, depending on the kind of anesthesia the mother has received

What effect does a distended bladder have on the mother? It can prevent the uterus from contracting properly, thus increasing the chances of a postpartum hemorrhage. If the nurse notices that the bleeding is heavier than normal, the mother should be encouraged to void in an effort to decrease the amount of bleeding. A distended bladder may cause the mother to void small amounts, often less than 100 ml, which indicates that she is not emptying her bladder, and residual urine can cause infection.

Bladder distention can be detected in several ways. The mother may complain of feeling full, or she may be distended and be totally unaware of the problem. If the uterus is displaced above the umbilicus and deviated to the right or left, this is usually indicative of a full bladder. A soft puffiness just above the symphysis is also a sign of a full bladder. It is the nurse's responsibility to make pertinent observations and report the findings to the physician.

There are several techniques of preventing overdistention of the bladder. Once again early ambulation is encouraged, since it is easier for the mother to void if she is able to get up to the bathroom. Many women find it difficult or impossible to void on a bedpan or in a reclining position (in the case of a woman who has had spinal anesthesia). If she is unable to void, the nurse should encourage fluids. A warm sitz bath and/or shower, pouring warm water over the symphysis and labia, having the mother concentrate on voiding, or encouraging her to blow bubbles through a straw in a glass of water may serve as stimulants which aid in emptying the bladder.

If these measures are unsuccessful, the physician may order the mother to be catheterized. The catheter will rarely remain in the bladder longer than it is necessary to empty it of urine. If the mother has been voiding small amounts, less than 100 ml, the physician may order the nurse to catheterize the patient for residual urine immediately after voiding. If there is more than 150 ml of residual urine, he may request that the catheter remain in place for 24 hours. Usually after 24 hours, the edema of the urethra and vulva decrease enough so that the mother does not have difficulty voiding. When the catheter is removed, culture and sensitivity should be obtained, and the nurse should encourage the mother to drink fluids and to void within 6 to 8 hours following the removal of the catheter. The amount voided should be recorded on the patient's hospital record, as well as the position of the uterus following the voiding.

The Circulation

An increase in blood fibrinogen has been noticed during the first postpartum week which may be a contributing factor in the development of thrombophlebitis. Early ambulation helps to decrease the possibility of thrombophlebitis by preventing venous stasis.

There is an increase in the number of leukocytes, especially if the labor has been long. The white blood cell count may be as high as 30,000 at the end of the first week, but this does not necessarily indicate an infection.[18] The leukocytosis demonstrates that the body has mobilized its defense system against possible infection and aids in the many repairs taking place within the body.

The hemoglobin or hematocrit is checked on the third postpartum day and should not differ significantly from the value during early labor. If the difference is marked, it usually indicates a considerable blood loss. The mother who is anemic may require additional time during the day for rest and sleep, and she may be given iron either orally or parenterally prior to discharge from the hospital.

During pregnancy, the body carries approximately 2 additional liters of blood which are eliminated by the renal system and by diaphoresis within the first 2 weeks postpartum. The diaphoresis occurs frequently during the night and categorically has been called "night sweats." Heavy sweating may continue for as long as 3 weeks; therefore, daily bathing, frequent clothing changes, and protection from chilling are essential.

Circulation to the lower extremities is often sluggish during pregnancy because of the pressure of the uterus, preventing adequate drainage of the pelvic vessels. Following delivery it is important to promote good circulation which can be done partially through proper positioning. The mother who is supine or in an extreme Fowler's position decreases the flow of blood to the legs. The best position to enhance circulation to all areas of the body is to elevate the head of the bed to about a 45° angle and to

elevate the knees slightly, thus allowing a free flow of blood to and from the lower extremities.[19] When the mother is sitting on the side of the bed, her feet should not be dangling, since this constricts the popliteal arteries and veins. She should have her feet resting flatly on a chair, preventing constriction of any of the major vessels, and crossing of the legs should be discouraged. These suggestions are especially beneficial to the mother who has difficulty with varicosities. The physician in such cases may recommend that the patient wrap her legs in elastic bandages or wear elastic hose. The legs should be rewrapped at least twice a day and whenever necessary. Usually the superficial varicosities will improve noticeably within the first few days postpartum as a result of the marked decrease in total blood volume, but the larger veins may never return to their normal size.

The Perineum

Sutures used in repair of the episiotomy dissolve in about 3 weeks, and care of the perineum during this time centers mainly on cleanliness. Mothers should be taught to dry their perineal area from front to back, blotting rather than wiping, since improper cleansing may cause contamination of the urinary meatus and a resulting urinary tract infection. Taking frequent sitz baths in the hospital and using a bathtub at home are good practices to keep the area clean and to promote healing; however, a separate washcloth should be used for the perineum. Doctors will sometimes prescribe ice packs to be applied to the perineum during the first 12 to 24 hours to prevent or decrease edema, which is the primary cause of initial discomfort. After this time, a patient finds the warm or hot sitz bath more soothing and comforting than the ice packs. A perineal heat lamp may be ordered, but dry heat may cause a pulling or drawing of the sutures. Therefore, moist heat is preferable.

Lacerations of the perineum extending back to or including the rectal sphincter cause added discomfort. The same suggestions that were described above for general episiotomy care are employed. Topical anesthetics, ointment, and analgesics also aid in reducing the pain of a laceration or troublesome episiotomy.

Ovulation and Menstruation

If the mother is not nursing, menstruation will usually return within 6 to 12 weeks following delivery. The menses may not recur for as long as 18 months in the nursing mother but usually return in approximately 4 months. Ovulation occurs in 6 to 8 weeks in the nonlactating mother and in approximately 11 weeks in the lactating mother. The nursing mother should be made aware that breast-feeding is not to be considered a form of contraception, since she may ovulate without first menstruating.

The first menstrual period following delivery may be heavy and last longer than a normal menses, and it is not unusual for small clots to be passed. Some women have irregular periods for a few months as the body continues to attempt to regain its nonpregnant normal state. It is the responsibility of the nurse to inform the mother of these facts so that she will not become alarmed when any of the above mentioned events occur.

Special Needs

A mother's need for sleep during the early puerperium has been described as sleep hunger. Immediately after delivery she may be elated and wide awake, but soon she becomes extremely tired and needs rest. This overwhelming need to rest may descend upon the postpartum patient at any time. A wise nurse senses this need and allows time for morning and/or afternoon naps. It may be necessary for the nurse to alter somewhat hospital routines, such as temperature taking or a sitz bath, if a mother is in the midst of this deep sleep.

The appetites of new mothers vary tremendously. Some crave food almost immediately after delivery and continue to eat large meals while others prefer small portions. Snacks between meals are usually welcomed, especially by nursing mothers. The nurse should keep in mind individual differences and varying nutritional requirements in caring for the postpartum patient.

The need for increased fluids has been discussed previously. A mother may not feel thirsty; therefore, an explanation of why fluids are important will usually motivate her to drink adequate amounts.

THE ART OF FEEDING

Whether a mother chooses to breast- or bottle-feed, she will undoubtedly find herself eager for the feeding instruction and guidance given to her by the nurse. Many women believe that babies naturally know how to eat and that regardless of how a mother elects to feed her infant, the infant will accept the food with only a minimal amount of effort on her part. Experience has shown this to be a fallacy, for certain learned skills are required for feeding to be successful. Feeding is a primary caretaking responsibility executed by the mother in the care of her newborn infant, and for this reason it is an area that should not be taken lightly by the nurse. Success in feeding brings delight and a feeling of accomplishment to the new mother, while failure at getting the baby to eat may bring about depression or a feeling of rejection, thus upsetting the desired pattern of events during the postpartum period.

The mother should select the method of feeding that seems best for her, giving special consideration to her husband's feelings; however, the nurse's responsibility to the mother includes antepartum and postpartum education on certain facts about both breast- and bottle-feeding. It is the purpose of this section to help the nurse become aware of the hows and whys of feeding so that, in turn, the nurse can serve as a resource person to the new mother, giving her needed guidance in whatever method of feeding she has selected for herself and her new infant.

Breast-feeding

A study conducted at the University of Colorado Medical Center[20] showed that of the clinic population which the center serves, 34 percent of new mothers chose to nurse their babies in the immediate postpartum period. Follow-up at 1 month indicated that only one-half of those women were still nursing, and of that group, slightly over half of them had nursed babies before. It is worthwhile to note that of the mothers who had stopped nursing, one-third had done so at the ill-considered advice of a physician. Antepartum instruction and rooming-in were not found to influence whether a mother continued nursing or not, although 69 percent of the breast-feeding mothers chose rooming-in.

In contrast, 43 consecutive patients seen in a private practice had a success rate which was much higher than that found in the clinic population. Of the 80 percent who chose to nurse, 94 percent were still nursing at 1 month. The patients who had stopped did so at the advice of a pediatrician. From this study, one concludes that a higher socioeconomic level and more education seem to correlate positively with successful nursing;

however, an understanding of breast-feeding and its problems by both physician and nurse is certain to raise the success rate of poorer or less educated women.

Some mothers are hesitant to breast-feed because they feel they will be constantly tied down to the baby with little free time for themselves and their husbands. Others have been told that breast-feeding is superior because it brings the mother and baby closer emotionally and makes the infant feel more secure. The facts are that when a nursing mother is ready, she can go out and leave the baby at home; and the chief benefits of breast-feeding in most instances are physiological, rather than psychological, for a mother who bottle-feeds can certainly feel as close to her infant as one who breast-feeds.

Although a large number of the babies born in the United States are bottle-fed, there seems to be a trend toward breast-feeding by younger mothers. They select the more natural way of feeding but are sometimes disillusioned to find that this natural way takes a great deal of patience and skill.

Many breast-feeding mothers throughout the country have received needed help from a group of women who belong to an organization called La Leche League. The term *la leche* is taken from the Spanish language and simply means "the milk." This organization was established in Illinois in 1956 by a group of women who nursed their babies successfully and wanted other women to have equally rewarding experiences.[21] La Leche League is found in most areas, and breast-feeding mothers should be made aware of the group. The league provides a list of telephone numbers of women who have nursed their infants and are willing to help others with common problems arising during the nursing experience. They also have meetings for expectant mothers where they discuss breast-feeding and teach the women how to prepare for nursing.

Benefits to the Mother

There are well-known and documented physiological benefits to the breast-feeding mother. In studies conducted on women of various cultures throughout the world it has been shown that mothers who nurse have a markedly decreased chance of developing breast cancer. In Western culture breast-feeding has been on the decline in the last few generations while during the same time mammary cancer is on the rise. In a study done in Boston on 473 women with breast cancer, it was concluded that there is an increased incidence of developing cancer in women who nursed less than 3 months.[22] This study does not establish cause and effect, but it does point out an association between breast cancer and nursing. The reason may be a function of suppression of ovarian hormones. This is substantiated by the fact that both pregnancy and lactation suppress ovarian function and the incidence of breast cancer is decreased in multiparous women and mothers who have breast-fed. New mothers who do not wish to nurse may be given estrogenic or estrogenic/androgenic drugs to suppress lactation. Due to increased blood coagulability, the incidence of thrombophlebitis, although quite low, is 4 to 10 times higher in these women than in their nursing counterparts.[23] For this reason, some physicians will not administer such drugs. Occasionally women who have taken lactation inhibitors find that on the third postpartum day or later the breasts become engorged. It is necessary to make these mothers aware of this possibility and give instructions regarding comfort measures such as application of ice bags to the breasts, use of mild analgesics, and use of a tight brassiere.

Postpartum uterine involution is more rapid in mothers who breast-feed. Therefore, delayed postpartum hemorrhage is also less common, and there is less chance of uterine perforations with the insertion of an intrauterine device for contraception at the routine 6-week postpartum examination.

Though breast-feeding should never be depended upon as a means of contraception, lactation has been shown to suppress ovulation for 75 days postpartum in almost 100 percent of mothers who do not supplement their infants with bottle or solid food. Thus, breast-feeding, for a short time, is probably preferred to contraceptive hormones which produce hypercoagulability if given soon after delivery. These oral hormones also lessen the milk supply, at times causing the entire supply to dry up.

Benefits to the Baby

Dr. J. David Baum suggests several benefits to the breast-fed baby,[24] some of which are listed below. The colostrum and breast milk provide antibody protection against several types of viruses, including all three varieties of polio, and the Coxsackie Type B which causes newborn myocarditis and aseptic meningitis. The oral polio vaccine exhibits a high failure rate when given to infants who are being breast-fed.

Breast-fed babies show a marked decrease in respiratory infections and gastroenteritis. Lysozyme, an enzyme with antiseptic qualities that destroys foreign protein, is thought to play a significant part in the destruction of invasive organisms in the gastrointestinal tract. Especially important here is its attack on *Escherichia coli* organisms, the chief cause of gram negative sepsis of the newborn. Breast milk, with its high lactose content and poor buffering quality, keeps the pH of the stomach lower. Since *E. coli* may grow at a pH of 7.1, the increased acidity caused by breast milk inhibits its growth and possible resulting infection.[25] Along with lysozyme, secretory IgA, an immunoglobulin, is resistant to enzyme breakdown and gives the gastrointestinal tract additional resistance to invading microorganisms.

Allergic disorders such as infantile eczema, asthma, and hay fever are much less common in breast-fed babies. The mechanics by which the body uses breast milk to protect against these allergies is not fully understood; however, it is known that cow's milk is highly allergenic, and antibodies to cow's milk are found in high concentrations in formula-fed infants soon after birth.

Neonatal tetany is not seen in exclusively breast-fed babies.[26] This condition is caused by the high phosphorus level in prepared formulas. There is an inverse relationship between serum phosphate and serum calcium; therefore, as the infant ingests more and more phosphorus, the calcium level drops, causing symptoms of tetany. Artificial feeding also provides the infant with a high concentration of fatty acids, which may contribute to the condition by binding calcium in the gastrointestinal tract.

The sodium and solute concentration in formulas is much higher than in breast milk. In some cases, the solute load is too great, and overloading of the kidneys occurs.

It is observed that quite often obese infants become obese adults or at least have a problem maintaining a desired weight. Since the weight gain of a breast-fed infant is less than that of a bottle-fed one, obesity becomes an important consideration when evaluating the two types of infant feeding. It is sometimes difficult for parents to see the thinner baby as healthier than the chubby cherub because for many years it was maintained that a fat baby was a healthy one. Only recently has this statement been challenged, bringing with it the need for explanation and encouragement by the nurse to the mother whose baby is breast-fed and not gaining weight as rapidly as bottle-fed counterparts.

Malocclusion is an improper placement of the teeth and may involve teeth, bone, and muscle tissues. Because of the forward tongue thrust used by the bottle-fed baby to control the flow of milk into the mouth, the likelihood of malocclusion is greater than in breast-fed infants.[27] (See Figure 27-5.)

Helping the Mother Begin

During the first 2 to 3 days postpartum, the mother's breasts secrete colostrum. The nurse should remind the mother that the yellowish secretion provides nourishment and maternal immunities for the infant, and that sucking during the immediate postpartum period helps to bring in the milk more quickly.

Help and encouragement are essential during these early days if the mother is to have a successful breast-feeding experience. The nurse should be available to help the mother during all feedings, especially the first few. In a rooming-in situation, it is not difficult for the nurse to arrange to be nearby when the baby begins to feed. A demand schedule means that not all babies will be feeding at the same time; hence, the nurse can give individualized help to the mother.

Before the mother begins to breast-feed, she should make sure her hands are clean. It is not necessary for the mother to wash her nipples before each feeding because, as was previously stated, breast milk contains an antiseptic. If the infant is crying hard when brought to the mother, she should first calm the infant by holding the baby firmly and closely and by talking gently. An upset baby who is put to breast does not realize the nipple is in the mouth and will continue to cry loudly which tends to upset the mother and frustrate the infant. Once the baby is calm, the baby will be able to grasp the nipple and begin sucking.

There are several positions which the

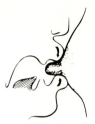

Notice how lips clamp "C" shape in nipple areolar concave junction fitting "like a glove". Cheek muscles contract.

Tongue thrusts forward to grasp nipple and areola.

BREAST

Nipple moves against hard palate as tongue whips <u>backward</u> bringing areola into mouth. NEGATIVE pressure is created by tongue and cheeks against nipple. <u>Suction effect</u> is created.

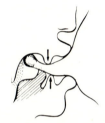

Gums compress areola squeezing milk into back of throat where <u>suction</u> occurs against nipple. Milk flows against hard palate from high pressure system to negative pressure at back throat.

BOTTLE

<u>Large rubber nipple strikes soft palate</u> (with gagging) and displaces proper tongue action. Tongue moves <u>forward</u> with "anterior tongue thrust" against gums to control milk overflow into esophagus. Lips flange "O" shape. Compression does not occur. Cheek muscles relax.

FIGURE 27-5

Sucking mechanism at the breast and bottle. (*Reproduced from Richard M. Applebaum, "The Modern Management of Successful Breast Feeding," Pediatric Clinics of North America,* 17:203, *1970. By permission of the publisher.*)

mother may assume while breast-feeding. She should be familiar with the different positions so that she may decide upon those most suitable for her and the baby. The one used most frequently is the sitting position shown in Figure 27-6. The mother sits in the bed or a chair, and holding the infant securely, she places the infant's arm underneath her arm, thereby aligning the baby's mouth with her nipple. To get the baby to turn toward the breast, the mother strokes the cheek close to her, causing the infant to root for the nipple.

Many mothers find that a side-lying position is especially convenient during the night feedings or when a period of rest and relaxation is needed. Figure 27-7 illustrates two variations of this position. She may lie on her side with head and back supported by

FIGURE 27-6
Proper positioning is important for successful nursing. (*Courtesy of The University of Colorado Medical Center, Denver, Colorado.*)

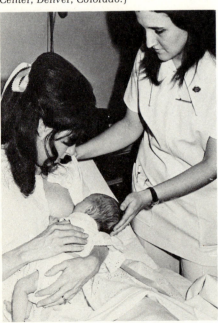

pillows. The baby is placed close enough to her so that the nipple touches the baby's lips and the baby is able to grasp it easily. At other times the mother may want to rest her weight on her elbow as she gets the baby into position.

While the mother is learning the art of nursing, she may find it necessary to grasp the breast with index and middle fingers and guide the nipple into the baby's mouth, as shown in Figure 27-8. If the baby is slow to take hold, the nurse might suggest that the mother express a few drops of colostrum or milk onto the baby's lips which often entices the infant to grasp the nipple.

The proper placement of the nipple is on top of the baby's tongue with as much of the areolar area as possible in the mouth. A common misconception is that all of the areola must be in the baby's mouth in order for the baby to nurse or suck properly. The nurse can tell if the baby is sucking correctly through careful observation of the sucking process. A clicking sound is noted as the infant swallows, but other sucking noises are probably indicative of an improper grasp on the nipple. Also, the nurse can observe the areola being drawn in as the baby sucks, indicating proper mouth positioning.

During the early days of nursing, the mother should be cautioned not to feed too long at any one feeding as her nipples will become sore. It is recommended that she nurse from 3 to 5 minutes at frequent intervals during the first day, from 5 to 7 minutes during the second day, and from 7 to 10 minutes during the third day. In a week she should be able to nurse 10 minutes on the first side and 20 minutes on the second side.

The mother should encourage the baby to nurse from both breasts at each feeding, alternating the side on which she begins. A suggestion to help the mother remember which side to start on at the next feeding is to have her put a safety pin in the bra strap

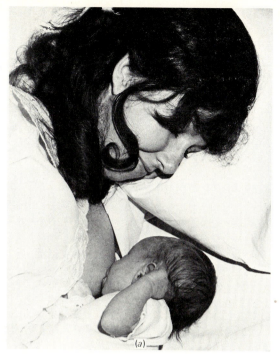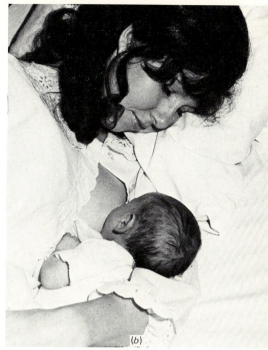

FIGURE 27-7
This mother demonstrates two side-lying positions for nursing. Her left arm in
picture (a) is under the pillow and in picture (b), it encompasses the baby. (*Courtesy
of The University of Colorado Medical Center, Denver, Colorado.*)

on the side on which she will begin to nurse
the next time. The baby should nurse on both
breasts because babies suck hardest on the
first side and get about 90 percent of the milk
in that breast during the first 5 to 10 minutes
of nursing. Using both breasts provides the
necessary stimulus to keep up a sufficient
amount of milk production in the breasts.
This is especially important during the early
weeks of nursing.

Not all babies want to nurse for 20 minutes
on the second side, and the mother should be
reassured that the baby takes as much as
needed. Some infants begin suckling quite
easily at the first feeding, and others require
more help in getting started. The mother may
feel that it is so easy when the nurse gets the
baby started but quite difficult when she is

trying to get the baby to suck by herself. The
nurse can remind the mother that both she
and the baby are learning to nurse and that
once they begin working as a team, she will
have no problems getting the baby to suck.

The newborn is very sleepy and often
drifts off to sleep soon after starting to nurse.
Once the infant gets a little food in the stomach, he or she feels warm and comfortable
next to the mother and promptly goes to
sleep. In a short while the baby will awaken
and demand to eat again. Such situations can
be avoided if the mother is taught how to
keep the baby awake during the feeding.
When the mother is ready to nurse, she can
loosen the blankets around the baby so that
the infant is not quite so warm and drowsy
during the feeding. If this does not work, she

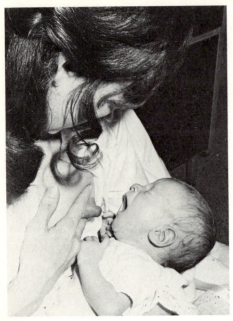

FIGURE 27-8
Compression of the areolar area facilitates the baby's initial grasp on the nipple. (*Courtesy of The University of Colorado Medical Center, Denver, Colorado.*)

may try any of the following: rub the soles of the baby's feet, stroke the abdomen, loosen or remove the shirt, change the baby's position, or place a cool cloth on the baby's forehead. If the mother has difficulty keeping the baby awake, a nurse should be available to help her with the baby, and ease the mother's frustration.

The procedure of *alternate massage*[28] is suggested for use in the early nursing experience when the baby is sleepy in order to empty the breasts as completely as possible. Very often, a new baby begins sucking with vigor, and then it is noticed that after a minute or so the infant starts taking long, slow, rhythmic sucks. When these long, slow sucks become short and fast, or if the infant takes rest periods too frequently, alternating massage of the breast with the sucking will stimulate more milk to be released from the ducts. The shorter, more rapid sucking of the infant indicates the milk is flowing less freely, creating negative pressure, which contributes to nipple soreness.

The massage should begin only after the character of the sucking changes, otherwise the milk will flow too quickly and cause choking. The breast is massaged from the back and middle portion near the axillary area toward the nipple. After several massages the infant will begin taking long, slow sucks again as the milk flows freely. The position of the fingers can be rotated to stimulate as much of the breast tissue as possible.

When the baby is finished nursing, the mother should not pull the infant off the breast but should learn to release the suction on the nipple by using any of the following suggestions: gently squeezing the infant's cheeks; putting her finger into the side of the baby's mouth and releasing the suction, as shown in Figure 27-9; pressing inward on the areola near the nipple; or gently but firmly pulling downward on the baby's chin with the pad of her finger or thumb. If she tries to remove the baby without first breaking the suction, the infant will continue to suck while being pulled away, causing the mother discomfort and quite possibly sore nipples.

Common Problems of Breast-feeding

ENGORGEMENT   About the third day, when the milk begins to come in, engorgement may cause some problems for the mother. Hopefully she will be in the hospital when this occurs so that she may receive guidance from the nurse. Engorgement is a process of swelling and hardening of the breast tissue brought about by milk being released into the ducts with an increase in blood and lymph supply to the breast. It usually reaches a peak between the third and fifth postpartum days and lasts about 48 hours. The condition is usually more marked in a primipara or in the multipara who has not nursed previously.

The degree of discomfort from this non-inflammatory process varies with each individual; however, most women experience at least mild swelling and tenderness. Though it is impossible to empty a breast completely, the severity of engorgement is lessened by frequent nursing. This decreases the fullness of the breasts and clears the ducts for passage of the milk. Engorgement usually begins at the top or outer aspect of the breast and extends into the axillary area where a small nodule may be palpated. This stage is often referred to as the milk "coming in." An ex-

FIGURE 27-9
The mother releases the baby's suction on the nipple by inserting her finger into the corner of the baby's mouth. (*Courtesy of The University of Colorado Medical Center, Denver, Colorado.*)

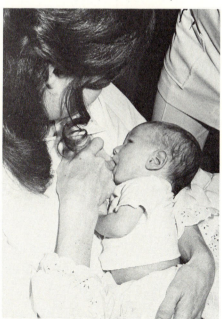

tremely engorged breast shows induration extending into the areolar and nipple areas, a condition which needs immediate attention to facilitate the baby's nursing. The breast may show red striations and appear shiny as a result of the overstretching of the skin. If engorgement is allowed to progress to this point, decreasing the fullness of the breast (the primary treatment) becomes quite difficult.

Other treatment includes a good supportive bra, heat or ice packs, and perhaps a mild analgesic. If it is difficult for the baby to grasp the nipple and areola because of extensive engorgement, hot packs, manual expression (Figure 27-10), or a hand breast pump may be utilized to obtain a small amount of milk from the breast prior to nursing, thereby softening the tissue. Occasionally a nipple shield is used for a short time at the beginning of the feeding which will draw out the nipple so that when the shield is removed, the infant will be able to suck directly from the breast. If ice packs are used between feedings to decrease swelling and relieve the pain, then hot packs will usually be needed to stimulate letdown at feeding time. A mother who is in pain may be tense and irritable. The nurse can help her relax by administering an analgesic about $\frac{1}{2}$ hour prior to the feeding which enables her to be more comfortable when the baby is ready to nurse. The mother needs to be reminded that this is a temporary condition.

Once the milk is in, some mothers complain that it comes out too quickly, causing the baby to choke. If this occurs, the nurse can suggest that the mother express the fast flowing milk into a cup until the stream slows down. Once some of the tension is relieved, the mother should have no problem getting the baby to nurse with ease.

The mother is often concerned with how frequently she should nurse her baby. It is wise to keep in mind that some infants have

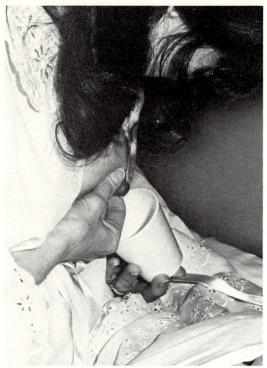

FIGURE 27-10
Milk can be manually expressed from the breast by compression of thumb and index finger behind the areola. Pressure is exerted backward rather than forward on the breast. (*Courtesy of The University of Colorado Medical Center, Denver, Colorado.*)

a greater need to suck than others and may want to nurse more often not because of hunger but to satisfy an inborn need to suckle. These same infants may not be content with a pacifier. Such things should be taken into consideration when discussing frequency of nursing the infant.

WORRIES OF THE NURSING MOTHER "Will the baby smother while I am nursing?" The woman who has large breasts will find it necessary to push down on some of the breast tissue with her finger to facilitate the baby's breathing. She should be reminded that the baby will instinctively stop sucking if he is unable to breathe.

"Is the baby getting enough milk?" Mothers may often be overly concerned with how many milliliters the baby takes at a feeding. Often the hospital nurse will weigh the baby prior to the feeding and then following the feeding. The nurse announces to the mother that the baby took 60 ml and is doing well or that only 30 ml were taken and this is not enough. Such procedures only make the mother more apprehensive about how much the baby gets. The nurse can be helpful by telling the mother that if the baby is voiding 6 or more times a day and if the urine is pale in color, then he is getting enough fluid. Another way of telling if the baby is getting a sufficient amount of milk is if he or she does not demand to feed for 2 to 3 hours between nursings. The nursing mother needs to be encouraged to relax and not to worry so much about time and amount.

"My milk is too watery." This is another common concern of nursing mothers. Breast milk is bluish white and appears watery like skim milk; the mother should be reassured that this is the proper appearance of the milk.

"My baby has a bowel movement every time I nurse her, and she has diarrhea." Breast-fed babies often have an explosive bowel movement with each feeding and others will go as long as 5 days or even longer without a bowel movement. Breast milk is high in water content, which helps prevent constipation. The stool from a nursing baby is loose and varies from a bright yellow-gold to a brownish green; unlike stools from the bottle-fed baby, it has no strong odor.

"Can I eat spices or chocolate when I am nursing?" This is another frequent misconception about breast-feeding. Occasionally some babies will react to such foods by having loose stools and gastric distress. In general, the baby will have no problems if the mother eats spices and chocolate in moderation. If she notices that a particular food seems to be causing the baby some distress, she should eat the food again and observe the infant's reaction to it. If it causes the baby gastrointestinal distress, it would be wise for her to avoid that particular food while she is nursing.

"Can I diet while I am nursing a baby?" Crash diets are not recommended for anyone and especially not for a nursing mother; however, there is no reason why a woman cannot lose weight and nurse at the same time, though weight loss may be slower. La Leche League recommends a 3,000-ml fluid intake for the lactating mother, and the American Dietetic Association states that only 500 extra calories per day is necessary to maintain an adequate milk supply.[29] An increase in protein intake is also important for the breast-feeding mother, especially the teenage nursing mother. Many physicians suggest that those who nurse continue to take vitamins while lactating, and, as with nonnursing mothers, good food habits are stressed.

"How can I breast-feed if my baby is sick or premature?" When a mother wishes to obtain breast milk for a premature or ill infant who is not able to nurse, an electric breast pump provides a rapid and complete emptying of the breasts. The milk can be saved and brought to the hospital for the baby. The nurse should be familiar with the availability and workings of an electric pump, which can be bought or rented from a hospital supply house. Another type of pump, called the Ora-Lac, utilizes suction from the woman's mouth in place of the electric motor. The Ora-Lac may be more comfortable and less expensive for the mother than the electric pump. An alternative method is to manually express the breast milk.

SORE AND CRACKED NIPPLES Some soreness of the nipple area is a frequent occurrence in a nursing mother; the degree of tenderness, however, is dependent on many things, most of which the knowledgeable maternity nurse

can alleviate. A conscientious woman who has prepared her breasts antepartally is less likely to experience soreness after delivery, but the preparation is not a guarantee that she will be able to nurse without discomfort. Since the skin of blondes and redheads is more sensitive than that of dark-skinned women, they usually experience more soreness of nipples. A sore nipple carefully examined may appear to have small fissures or cracks on the surface of the skin. Proper steps to promote healing should be taken so that breast-feeding may continue. Some helpful hints the nurse should give to the mother as soon after delivery as possible, if the instruction has not been done antepartally, are discussed below. The preferential treatment of sore or cracked nipples involves healing them *before* they inhibit or temporarily stop the breast-feeding experience.

Nursing mothers should be instructed to clean the nipple area with plain water only, omitting soap and astringents such as alcohol, tincture of benzoin, or witch hazel. The cleansing need only be done once a day and is not necessary before each feeding. If mothers are concerned that the breast will be unclean for the baby, they can be reassured by the knowledge that the lysozyme in breast milk is an antiseptic. For an especially sensitive nipple, the nurse may suggest the use of a cotton ball instead of a cloth for cleaning the area.

An excellent method of preventing or reducing nipple soreness and cracking is air-drying of the nipples for 10 to 15 minutes after each feeding. The mother might leave the flaps of her nursing bra open, or insert small tea strainers, with the handles removed, inside the cups of her bra to promote free circulation of air with the flaps closed. Plastic-covered pads or plastic-lined bra cups are to be avoided, for moisture that is retained inside the bra next to the nipple increases the chances of skin breakdown and slows healing and toughening of the skin.

Most doctors recommend that a vitamin or pure lanolin ointment be applied to the nipples after they have been air-dried to promote healing and toughening of the skin. If an ointment is used after nursing, it should be gently but completely rubbed in so that air is allowed to reach the nipples. The ointment used should be one which is harmless to the baby so that unnecessary cleansing of the breast can be avoided.

To minimize soreness it is usually recommended that nursing time be increased gradually, as mentioned in the previous section. Mothers who overdo by letting the baby nurse as long as the baby wishes right from the beginning usually become quite uncomfortable by the second day. Since it is the frequency of the feedings, not the length of time of sucking at each feeding, that determines milk supply and the time of the first letdown, one is justified in suggesting to the mother that she limit the length of the initial feedings.

Some mothers change positions for each feeding, thereby putting the greatest pressure of the baby's suck on different areas of the nipple. She might lie down, sit on the edge of her bed, sit in a rocking chair, place the baby on a pillow in her lap, or hold the baby's head with her hand rather than cradling it in her arm. These are all variances which the mother may wish to try before leaving the hospital while the nurse can help and give suggestions.

Engorgement frequently leads to sore nipples; therefore, prevention of severe engorgement should be a prime concern of the nurse caring for a nursing mother. An extremely swollen breast causes the baby to grasp the nipple area improperly because the baby is not able to draw a large amount of the areolar area into the mouth. So instead of compressing and sucking, the baby merely chews on that part of the breast which is available—the nipple.

Treatments with a sunlamp or gooseneck lamp with a 20-watt bulb are both recommended for sore or cracked nipples. An ultraviolet bulb may be purchased and used in any ordinary lamp socket or stand, thereby giving the healing warmth of a sunlamp without purchasing the expensive equipment. Mothers who use an ultraviolet light must shield their eyes, and expose their skin no longer than $\frac{1}{2}$ minute the first day, 1 minute the next 2 days, and 2 minutes the fourth and fifth days. If there is any sign of reddening of the skin, the mother should be instructed to go back to $\frac{1}{2}$ to 1 minute and begin working up again. She should be positioned about 4 feet from the lamp, and the treatment should only be done once a day. Using an ordinary light bulb, the mother may sit closer to it (about 46 cm) and she does not need to shield her eyes. The exposure time can be lengthened to 5 to 10 minutes at a time which can be repeated several times a day. Treatment with dry heat as mentioned above can be initiated when nipple soreness is noticed; but if the skin has broken down and is bleeding from the fissures, treatment is essential.

If the soreness is quite uncomfortable for the mother, nursing less frequently will not decrease her discomfort because then the baby will be nursing from an overfull breast. It is better to limit nursing time to 10 minutes on each side rather than to nurse less often. The baby should start on the side that is less sore to stimulate milk ejection; once letdown has occurred the baby can be changed to the other side. If breasts are equally tender, application of a hot cloth or towel to the breasts just prior to nursing will trigger milk ejection, after which the baby can be put to breast. If the soreness or cracking is so severe that feeding must be discontinued on one side, the milk from that breast can be manually expressed for 24 to 48 hours, and the baby can nurse from the other side. The hand expression should be used along with air-drying, light, and ointment.

Sore or cracked nipples can be a major problem for a mother who is intolerant of pain or one who has been led to believe that nursing a baby is a simple procedure. It is, therefore, the responsibility of the nurse to constantly remind the mother that this soreness is temporary and that her discomfort will subside. So often a mother will say, "If I have to go through this every time I nurse, I'm not going to be able to do it." All the suggestions presented previously must be combined with sympathy, understanding, and encouragement from the nurse to help the mother through this particular time in her nursing experience.

BLISTERED NIPPLES   A nipple which is blistered is usually indicative of improper sucking by the baby. It most often is caused by the infant grasping only the nipple, and not the areolar area. The nipple remains at the front of the baby's mouth, where the action of tongue and gums causes blistering. These blisters may bleed when they are broken, which is not harmful to the baby but may frighten the mother. Prevention here is certainly preferable to cure. A mother may not realize the baby is not sucking properly unless the nurse observes the feeding and points this out to her. Ultraviolet light and resting the nipple for 24 to 48 hours are the preferred methods of treatment.

ANXIETY OR OVEREXERTION   Anxiety, upset, or emotional trauma influence milk ejection; therefore, a mother who is not able to relax prior to nursing may find that her milk will not let down. If at all possible, she should be encouraged to lie down while nursing and concentrate on relaxation of her entire body. If lying down is not possible, perhaps she could put her feet up and read a magazine. Because of the close relationship between thoughts of the mind and actions of the body,

her main goal must be gearing her thoughts toward something other than the cause of her upset. If the emotional upset is continual over a period of time, the doctor may prescribe an oxytocic nasal spray to aid in letdown. The nasal spray is also useful when overexertion or lack of rest inhibits milk ejection.

MASTITIS   Mastitis frequently presents itself as soreness in a particular area of the breast, usually accompanied by induration and erythema. A nursing mother with these symptoms should consult her doctor. Often she will be able to continue nursing as long as treatment of the infection has begun. A breast abscess which requires incision and drainage will not interfere with nursing once it is healed. The mother can continue nursing on the unaffected breast and hand express the milk from the abscessed one.

THE BABY WHO WILL NOT SUCK   An infant who refuses to suck at the breast or who thrusts the tongue toward the roof of the mouth presents a special problem. These babies will almost always suck beautifully from a bottle nipple; therefore, it is imperative not to supplement them with an artificial nipple. Besides causing the baby to become accustomed to it, the mother loses all confidence when she sees her baby refuse her breast and gulp down milk from a bottle. Supplements may be given with a spoon, cup, or an eyedropper. The eyedropper is preferred in this situation because milk can be dribbled down over the breast into the baby's mouth, hopefully helping the baby to begin sucking from the breast. Another suggestion is to express some colostrum from the breast.

INADEQUATE MILK SUPPLY   The mother who says she does not have enough milk for her baby probably is not nursing often enough. This complaint is frequently heard at about 6 weeks and then again at 3 months, both times that babies have growth spurts. The nurse should inform the mother of this and also remind her that the oftener the baby nurses, the more milk she will have. If she would feed the baby frequently (every 2 hours or even more often) during her waking hours, she will find that her supply will increase. *The milk supply is directly related to the frequency of nursing—the more often the baby nurses and empties the alveoli, the more milk is produced.* The supply and demand concept is sometimes hard to remember when a baby is awakening every hour to 2 hours to be fed; therefore, the community health nurse can give encouragement to the mother during these frustrating times.

Special Considerations

WEANING   It is not unusual for a new mother to ask the nurse how long she should continue to nurse the baby. Some women nurse for as short a time as 6 weeks and others will nurse for over a year. A mother may decide to stop breast-feeding because she wishes to, while at other times it is the baby who gradually weans himself or herself.

When the baby is to be weaned, the easiest and most comfortable way to do so is gradually. The nurse might suggest that the mother eliminate one breast-feeding a day and cup or bottle-feed at that time. In a few days, the mother may again eliminate another nursing and feed the baby twice by cup or bottle. She should continue in this manner until her milk has dried up. La Leche League suggests that the mother wean the baby when the infant seems to be less interested in the breast.[30] They also suggest that the mother not offer the child the breast unless the child wants it; this allows the child to initiate the weaning. If the baby is recovering from an illness or teething, or if there has been an emotional upset in the family, wean-

ing should be delayed. The baby's life should be calm and happy when the weaning is begun so that the infant has only one new situation with which to contend.

SUPPLEMENTAL FEEDING   Supplementary or complementary feedings are defined here as formula, water, or glucose water given after breast-feeding, or in place of a breast-feeding once the mother's milk is well established. Many hospitals use the supplementary bottle following a breast-feeding until the mother's breasts fill with milk. The idea of the supplementary feeding is to keep the baby hydrated and satisfied; however, if the mother's colostrum supply is adequate and the baby appears satisfied after breast-feeding, the bottle should not be forced. It may be that the greatest harm done by feeding a baby supplements with a bottle is teaching the mother a psychological dependence on the bottle, undermining confidence in her ability to breast-feed. Varying opinions exist as to the appropriateness of *ever* supplementing through a bottle nipple, since the milk flows easier from such a nipple and the infant's suck is weakened. In an infant whose suck is weak and who is not nursing well, it is preferable to supplement using a spoon, cup, or eyedropper so that the suck will be stronger when the infant does nurse. In discussing supplementary feedings, the nurse should encourage the parents to consider spending some evenings out together and leave a bottle at home for the baby. She may wish to manually express the milk from her breasts into a bottle or to mix an artificial feeding. After lactation is well established, her milk supply will not be noticeably lessened by giving the baby an occasional bottle. Some mothers feel tied to their babies, thinking that they either cannot go out or must take the baby along. A word of encouragement from the nurse to take an evening off can go a long way in easing the mother's anxiety.

NURSING TWINS A mother who wishes to breast-feed twins should be given some hints from the nurse before time for discharge. After she gets home she will be doubly busy and will appreciate having the art of nursing well under way. A modified demand schedule might be suggested to her so that her entire day is not spent feeding; that is, when one twin is awake and ready to eat, she awakens the other and feeds him at the same time. The milk supply will be adequate because of the supply-and-demand principle of breast milk. When she nurses both of them at once, the new mother will need to sit up, holding the twins in her lap, as shown in Figure 27-11, or at her sides with their bodies on pillows. She can experiment with them in her lap with them facing the same direction, or with both of them facing toward her. The mother may choose to breast-feed twin A and

FIGURE 27-11
This mother demonstrates one way of positioning twins while nursing. (*Courtesy of The University of Colorado Medical Center, Denver, Colorado.*)

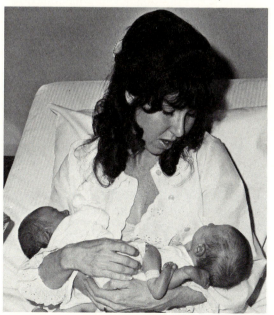

bottle-feed twin B at one feeding, and at the next feeding breast-feed twin B and bottle-feed twin A. La Leche League is a helpful resource for the mother who is nursing multiple infants.

THE WORKING MOTHER It is very possible to have a full-time job and still breast-feed. Often mothers will mention to the nurse while they are in the hospital that they plan to stop nursing and go back to work in 6 weeks. If they do wish to continue to nurse longer than that and must go back to work, they can come home to feed the baby once during the day; if that is not possible, they can hand express the milk at work and save it for the baby-sitter to give to the baby during the next day. Hand-expressed milk can be stored in a freezer for as long as 1 month and in a deep freeze for 3 months. Recent findings on frozen breast milk indicate that some nutrients are lost in the freezing process; however, occasional supplemental feeding of breast milk which has been frozen is felt to be adequate for the healthy infant.

LEAKING BREASTS It is common for the second breast to leak as the baby nurses on the first side because of the milk letting down in both breasts at the same time. In order to keep the mother's clothes dry a washcloth may be inserted into her bra on the second side. Most new mothers who breast-feed will have some leaking of the breasts between feedings for at least the first few weeks until lactation is well established. Nursing pads are available which can be inserted into the bra to absorb the leakage; however, they are not recommended because they prevent air from circulating freely due to the plastic coating. For this reason cotton handkerchiefs or other lightweight fabric is preferable. Perineal pads should not be used because they contain deodorants which might irritate the nipple and breast. If letdown occurs unexpectedly while out in public, the new mother should be instructed to very unobtrusively press her forearms against her breasts for a few seconds until the tingling sensation stops.

Bottle-feeding

If the mother chooses to bottle-feed her baby, the nurse should support this decision and help her learn the art of formula feeding. One of the first things a bottle-feeding mother asks about is sterilization. Many pediatricians still believe that sterilizing is necessary; however, the current trend is toward a clean technique rather than a sterile one. The mother should be instructed to wash the bottles and nipples, and they can be washed with the rest of the dishes. A bottle brush should be used for cleaning whether the bottles are washed in a dishwasher or by hand, as milk which is dried in the bottom of the bottle or in the nipple provides an excellent medium for growth of bacteria.

The kind of formula used will vary, and most pediatricians have a preference. Some mothers will use the prepared formulas and others the evaporated milk formula which is cheaper. If the woman has been instructed to use a prepared formula, she will find it comes in three forms: powdered milk, concentrated liquid, and ready-to-use. The powdered milk is the least expensive, but most difficult to prepare as many women have difficulty getting the powder to dissolve in the water. The nurse might suggest that she use hot water in preparing the bottle, and some mothers find that they need a beater to remove the lumps from the milk. If she chooses the concentrated liquid form, this is prepared by adding equal amounts of milk and water. She should be advised to buy this by the carton as it is cheaper than buying one can at a time. The ready-to-use formula is the most expensive and needs no preparation.

Once a can of milk has been opened, it should be stored in the refrigerator and used within 24 hours. New mothers should be reminded of the high sodium content of soft water and instructed to use nonsoftened water in formula preparation.

In the past, mothers made enough formula to last 24 hours; however, the current trend is to prepare one bottle at a time to decrease the incidence of bacterial growth in the milk. Warm water can be used to mix with the milk to bring it to room temperature so that heating the bottle will be unnecessary.

Some pediatricians are beginning to recommend that the mother start feeding her baby milk with 2 percent butterfat after the first month. This milk has less animal fat and is high in protein. They have suggested that the high carbohydrate content in the prepared formulas causes the baby to become hungry more frequently; hence, the baby eats more and gains weight rapidly, thus generating new fat cells.[31]

How much the baby takes varies from feeding to feeding and from infant to infant. If the baby is fed on demand, the baby will be hungry at the time of the feeding and will take what is necessary. As with the breast-feeding mother, the woman who is bottle-feeding should try to keep the baby awake so that the baby does not take just enough for brief satisfaction and then fall asleep. The infant is getting enough if the infant can go from 3 to 4 hours between feedings.

When the mother is ready to feed the baby, she should assume a comfortable position and try to be as relaxed as possible. Since this is the time when the baby gets to know the mother, and has the opportunity for warmth and security, propping the bottle should be discouraged. Propping is also dangerous to the infant, because the infant may choke on the milk if the mother is not near enough to help in case of difficulty. The bottle should be held so that no air is in the nipple when the baby is sucking, and the nipple should be completely filled with milk. A baby may take about 20 minutes to eat, and the mother should plan for this time as she arranges her daily schedule.

Bubbling the Infant

Both breast- and bottle-fed babies will need to be bubbled during, following, and sometimes prior to the feeding. The baby who has been quite fussy before the feeding may need to be bubbled first, since crying causes an infant to swallow a lot of air. Air in the stomach often causes the baby to feel full before taking much milk. The air displaces the milk, thereby filling the stomach and sometimes causing the baby to regurgitate.

A mother may bubble the baby quite frequently during the feeding; however, she should be aware that each time the baby takes hold of the nipple, a mouthful of air is swallowed before the seal is complete. It is sufficient to bubble the newborn infant about every 30 ml and the older baby about every 60 ml. The breast-fed baby can be bubbled when changing breasts. The mother should learn to know her baby, and if the infant seems to need bubbling more frequently, she should do so. The baby is bubbled at the end of the feeding to rid the stomach of air which could cause gas pains or regurgitation.

The baby may be bubbled by having the mother put the baby over her shoulder and gently rub the back, as pictured in Figure 27-12. It is not necessary to pat the baby vigorously, since this often causes the infant to spit up whatever has just been eaten. Another position which is good for bubbling is for the mother to set the infant on her lap, placing her hand under the baby's jaw to support the head, and lean the baby forward as she gently rubs the back. The nurse can suggest that the mother try both methods so

that she can provide some variety for the infant. Some infants will burp quickly, and others require a longer period of time and greater patience on the part of the mother.

Pacifiers

All babies have a strong sucking need, and it seems appropriate to discuss pacifiers briefly. Many women antepartally object to them; however, they find that when the baby is taken home and is fussy for no explainable reason, a pacifier settles the baby by fulfilling the need for sucking. This urge to suck, which is felt by the infant as an uncomfortable sensation in the mouth,[32] usually disappears by four to five months of age; therefore, a mother should be encouraged to allow the infant to wean himself from the pacifier at that age if the baby has lost interest in it. The nurse should reassure a mother who feels guilty about using a pacifier that her infant's need to suck is normal and natural and that a pacifier is preferable to the child's thumb.

The Nuk Sauger pacifier is ideal, since it is shaped like the nipple on the mother's breast as the baby sucks (Figure 27-13), and orthodontists feel it lessens the chance of malocclusion later in life. Occasionally a baby will refuse this kind of pacifier, and the mother should not hesitate to try one of the other varieties readily available in most drugstores and supermarkets.

ENVIRONMENT

Establishment of a suitable environment plays an essential part in fostering the beginning of healthy family interrelationships. (See Figure 27-14.) In order for this environment to be favorable for the family, it must be planned according to a philosophy of maternity care geared to the needs of the family

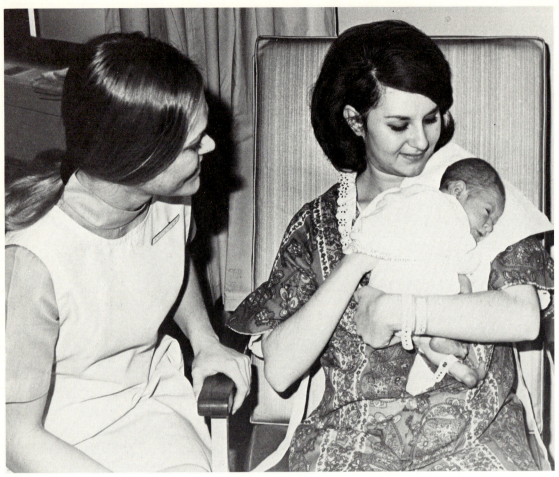

FIGURE 27-12
The most common position for bubbling an infant. (*Courtesy of The University of Colorado Medical Center, Denver, Colorado.*)

and the individual mother and infant. This basic philosophy must be one of freedom and direction with a minimum of strictness and regimentation. The success or failure of the environment as a positive phase during this developmental crisis is dependent on each nurse's own commitment to family-centered maternity care. The nurse must assimilate the philosophy and in some cases pass it on to other personnel in order to maintain the tone of the entire unit. To de-

velop such a philosophy, the nurse must have a sound understanding of the physical and psychological changes occurring within the mother and the family at the time of the baby's arrival.

Availability of the Baby

In order for the family concept to be continuous, it is obvious that the baby must be available to the mother whenever she

FIGURE 27-13
The Nuk Sauger primary exerciser. Two views of the
Nuk Sauger bottle nipple. (*Courtesy of Rocky Mountain
Dental Products Co.*)

wishes. This means that the maternity unit
should be set up in one of two ways: (1) a
central nursery regarded by the staff as a
place where the baby is kept when the
mother does not wish the baby at her bedside, or (2) rooming-in.

A rooming-in unit is designed with the
baby's crib always at the mother's bedside or
with a nursery adjacent to the mother's room
available. In some units the baby is with the
mother 24 hours a day, and she is the primary caretaker at all times. In other instances, rooming-in is modified so that the
baby is kept in the adjacent nursery during
the night. In either setup, if the mother is in
need of rest or is unable to care for the baby
for a period of time, ideally she should be
able to return the baby to a nursery.

With the central nursery, the baby is taken
to and from the nursery as the mother desires. As the term implies, there is one nursery for all the babies which is centrally located in relation to the mothers' rooms.

A pilot study[33] done at the University of
Colorado Medical Center brought the idea of
rooming-in back to its initially defined function—to provide an atmosphere for the
family to remain together from the time of
delivery. Because of studies done by Klaus
and Kennell[34] and Kennell et al.[35] showing
the harmful short- and long-term effects of
maternal-infant separation, it was decided to
manipulate the environment and prevent
separation completely. Newly delivered
mothers and their infants were admitted directly to the rooming-in unit from the delivery room, thus avoiding the traditional
separation of parents and baby immediately
after delivery. The nurse was able to observe
and be a part of the initial interaction between parents and infant, an experience
which was found to be most satisfying to the
nurses involved in the study. Time-honored
routines such as immediate application of
silver nitrate to the infant's eyes, delayed
first feeding, emptying of the stomach with a
mucous trap, total body bathing, and observation of the infant while in an incubator
were dispensed with in order to duplicate
the naturalness and flexibility of a home delivery. The positive response of the parents
and the excellent condition of the infants
may lead the nurse to reevaluate the hospital-imposed separation of the family following delivery.

Availability of the Nurse

Besides the availability of the baby, the success of a family-centered program is also dependent on the availability of the nurse.
Ideally the nurse responsible for the mother's
care should also be responsible for the baby's
care, for the two should be regarded as one
unit. This negates the traditional titles of
"postpartum nurse" and "nursery nurse"
and develops the term "maternal-child
nurse." This expands the nurse's role far beyond the one of custodial caretaker; it initiates creativity and purposefulness in planning and executing care. Separation of the

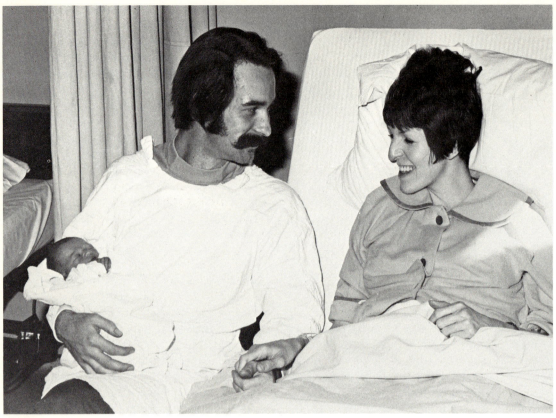

FIGURE 27-14
The father is welcome in a family-centered maternity unit. (*Courtesy of The
University of Colorado Medical Center, Denver, Colorado.*)

two nursing roles leads to anxiety and frustration within the parents because the questions concerning their baby must often be referred to someone else. The separation of the
two roles also leads to conflicts between the
postpartum and nursery nurses, as each feels
his or her role to be more important. The lack
of communication between the two areas is
also a source of difficulty in providing optimal patient care; however, when division of
the two roles in unavoidable, it is each individual nurse's responsibility to be aware of

both mother and baby, keeping a direct line
of communication open to the nurse in the
other area.

When the family-centered concept is practiced, the nurse has the opportunity to observe early mother-child and family interactions, intervene when appropriate, and be
involved in teaching. This expands the
nurse's role far beyond the one of custodial
caretaker and enables the nurse to be creative
and purposeful in planning and executing
care.

Visiting Policies

Visiting policies are an important part of postpartum care, and even though it is a controversial issue, it is one which needs to be considered carefully. First there is concern about infection being passed from visitors to the baby. Current theory reveals that clean technique by all those coming in contact with the baby is adequate for protection of the infant. This involves washing hands thoroughly, and placing a cover gown over street clothes; it does not include wearing a mask. Most hospitals limit the number of visitors coming into the mother's room at any one time, and usually a restriction is placed on who can be in the room when the baby is with the mother. These restrictions need to be periodically and realistically evaluated so that unnecessary restrictions are not placed on the family for the benefit of the hospital routine and nursing personnel.

The mother's rest must be considered when establishing visiting policies. It has been mentioned that she requires a great deal of sleep during the early puerperium; therefore, it may be wise at times to be aware of the mother's fatigue and intervene by suggesting that visitors leave. The nurse should realize that it may be difficult for the mother to make that suggestion herself when she is being visited by close relatives or friends.

The more progressive institutions now allow grandparents and great-grandparents to hold and feed the baby during the hospital stay; however, in the mobile society of today in which married children are often far away from parents, the mother may wish to have as visitors a best friend, sister, or other close relative. One wonders why these people are kept from the mother at a time when it is important for her to share such a great event in her life with others to whom she is close. Another logical question may be why a grandparent is regarded as cleaner than a friend.

Siblings are not to be forgotten in establishing visiting policies. A flexible unit should provide opportunity for the mother to visit her other children either by having a lounge area next to the maternity unit for that purpose or by letting the child or children visit the mother in her hospital room. Included in this same idea is the importance of allowing siblings to see the new baby, as in Figure 27-15. Some family-centered hospitals are now permitting siblings to touch and hold the new baby, as in Figure 27-16. These hospitals have not noted any increase in infections among the newborns since more lenient visiting policies have been in effect.

Demand Feeding

Adherence to a strict feeding schedule promotes the idea to mothers and nurses that babies are fed by the clock rather than according to their own hunger needs. As discussed above, however, hunger needs vary according to body size, activity, output, and the type of feeding (whether by breast or bottle). The mother who tries to feed an infant who is not hungry, but who is due to eat by the clock, finds herself frustrated and anxious as she perceives the baby's disinterest as rejection of her. This is a prime example of a baby's negative contribution to the mother-infant relationship, which could be a positive contribution if the baby were ready to eat. When a mother feels rejected, confidence in her mothering tasks is weakened, and depression is often the outcome. This feeling of rejection is heightened if the baby is being breast-fed. Demand feeding, therefore, is regarded as essential to provide an environment that gives the mother the best possible

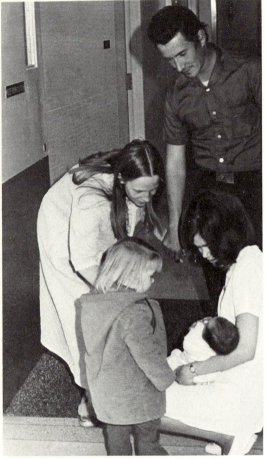

FIGURE 27-15
Proud parents share in three-year old Tina's first
encounter with her new sister. (*Courtesy of The
University of Colorado Medical Center, Denver,
Colorado.*)

chance to have a successful feeding experience.

Demand feeding allows the nurse to spend
more time with each mother, since most of
the babies will be eating at different times. It
also portrays an idea of flexibility and individual needs which were previously mentioned as important concepts in family-
centered care.

Routines and Willingness to Change

Hospital routines interfere with administration of individualized nursing care. The day
begins with checking temperature at 6 A.M.,
doctors' rounds at 7 A.M., and breakfast at
8 A.M. By this time the groggy mother is encouraged by the nurse to take her bath in
order to be ready for the infant's morning
feeding, which is usually about 10 A.M. It
would seem that these regimented schedules
meet the needs of nurses and doctors, but not
the mother. Many mothers complain about
the lack of sleep while they are in the hospital. During the day when a mother is beginning her restorative process, which requires
added sleep, hospital routine consistently
interrupts and interferes with this restoration. It is indeed a challenge for the maternal-child nurse to provide individualized
care in spite of the hospital-imposed routines.

FIGURE 27-16
Kristianne gets a close-up view of her brother while
visiting her mother in the hospital. (*Courtesy of Pete
Stofflet, Director of Public Relations, Allied Jewish
Federation of Denver, Denver, Colorado.*)

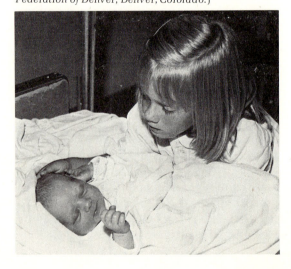

GUIDANCE AND
EVALUATION DURING
THE PUERPERIUM

Teaching of the parents during the post-partum period is a task that should not be overlooked by the nurse. Instruction given during the antepartum period needs rein-forcement, and many times the actual birth of the baby precipitates questions and prob-lems that were not foreseen. The situations for learning are easily found on the post-partum unit; however, how and when to do the teaching has long been a problem. The mother is in the hospital for such a short time that the nurse must be skillful and creative in teaching without overloading the mother with too much information.

There are several considerations to be made before any teaching is done. The woman should be physically comfortable, have some motivation to learn, and the place selected for the teaching situation should be calm and quiet. The teacher should not pre-sent a threat to the mother and should also be relaxed and comfortable in that role. The at-mosphere should be one in which the mother feels free to ask questions and discuss her feelings.

Individualized Teaching

Because pregnancy and birth are normal events and the postpartum mother has few physical needs, the nurse has more time to spend doing individualized teaching. (See Figure 27-17.) The nurse needs to assess where the mother and/or the family are in the developmental crisis of pregnancy and deliv-ery. For instance, a woman who has had four babies may need counseling in how to man-age that many children at home; whereas the greatest need of the primipara who has never held a small baby is learning to feel com-fortable with her infant. Likewise, the new

father who expresses anxiety that the baby might break may need a nurse nearby when he first holds his infant. Parents who have not had a baby for several years will probably require the same support and assistance that the first-time parents need.

The emphasis in many hospitals is on the techniques of bathing, formula preparation,

FIGURE 27-17
The health practitioner performs the discharge physical examination and teaching at the mother's bedside. (*Courtesy of The University of Colorado Medical Center, Denver, Colorado.*)

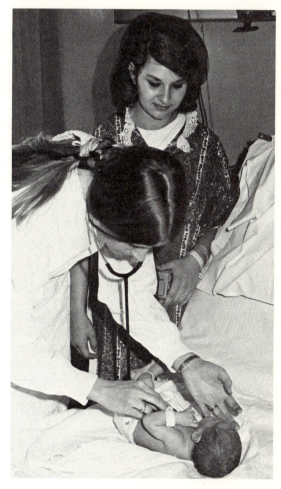

bubbling, etc. Techniques are an important part of teaching, but until the parents feel comfortable in holding the baby, they probably will not comprehend much of what is taught to them about tub bathing the infant. That is why the main focal point of teaching with these parents should be in helping them rely on their own observational abilities and their common sense. A mother who continues to use soap daily on her baby's dry, flaky skin needs teaching which stresses observation of the baby over routine. If a mother is assisted in thinking through the symptoms of illness in a new baby, she will probably remember them better than if a nurse were to present them to her in a lecture.

In contrast to the first-time mother is the multiparous woman who has recently had an infant and seems very comfortable in caring for the new baby. She may not be interested in attending a bath class but is deeply concerned about how the other children in the family will accept the new baby. This may require a nurse to sit down and discuss possible and realistic ways to introduce the infant to the other family members.

Group Teaching

Teaching may be done through a lecture during which a nurse gives information to mothers in a group situation in which there is a give-and-take between the mothers, as pictured in Figure 27-18. Ideally the group sessions are conducted by a nurse who is able to guide the discussion and present information where appropriate. This is not an easy task, since the group will probably meet just once and for a short time. The mothers will probably have sore perineums and will not want to sit for any length of time. It takes a skilled nurse to create an exciting group discussion and to realize that the postpartum mother is undergoing a great deal of stress.

The teaching plan should be flexible so that the nurse is able to work with the mother when she is receptive to learning. Though there are many problems involved with group teaching, it is recommended that the nurse experiment with the method. A group situation along with individualized teaching can do much in preparing the mother to return to her home environment with confidence in herself and her mothering tasks.

Postpartum Exercises

During the early puerperium the mother should learn the value of exercising and getting her weight back to her prepregnant state. It frequently happens that a woman never quite loses the weight gained in pregnancy or gets her abdominal muscles back in shape; hence, with each succeeding pregnancy she finds herself adding a few extra pounds and her muscles becoming more and more relaxed. For this reason it is advisable to have the mother begin selected exercises while she is still in the hospital, and she should be encouraged to continue them at home. Now is the time for her to tone and tighten her stretched muscles and to lose whatever weight she has gained during pregnancy.

Our society has become somewhat obsessed with weight, and the current trend favors slender women. Obesity is a common occurrence, and this is an excellent time to work on preventing such a problem. To encourage the overall health of the woman, it is advisable to take this opportunity to show her how to get her weight and muscle tone back to normal. A woman's figure influences her self-image and feeling of general well-being.

The mother will have many demands on her time after she goes home, so it is not wise to give her too many exercises. It is better to select a more realistic regimen for the mother

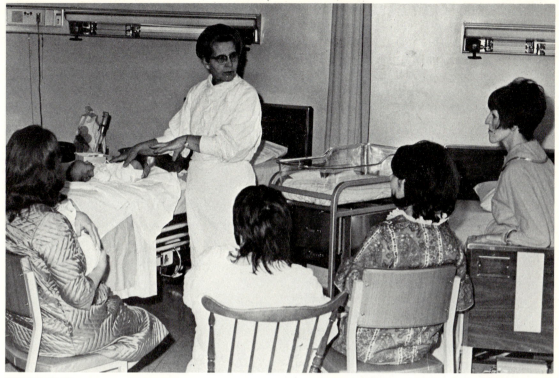

FIGURE 27-18
The nurse guides a group of mothers in a discussion on infant care. (*Courtesy of The University of Colorado Medical Center, Denver, Colorado.*)

to achieve and maintain. Several drug companies publish pamphlets on postpartum exercises, and the nurse might review them and select one for use on the postpartum unit. Many hospitals have prepared mimeographed sheets on postpartum exercises which are handed out to the mothers, and sometimes the physical therapist gives the instruction. It is helpful to give the mother written material so that she will have something to refresh her memory when at home. It is the nurse's responsibility to be knowledgeable about the exercises and to teach them as appropriate.

The following exercises are very basic and can be easily taught. There are many others, but these have been found to be beneficial to

the postpartum mother during the early days after delivery. They require regular daily practice if success is to be the outcome. It is wise to remind the woman that exercising will not decrease her weight, but it will tone the muscles. A sensible diet plus exercise should be recommended to the mother who wants to regain her figure.

1   Deep abdominal breathing used to strengthen the diaphragm (Figure 27-19a). Begin on the first postpartum day. Take a deep breath, raising abdominal wall, and exhale slowly. To ensure that exercise is being done correctly, place one hand on the chest and

one on the abdomen. When inhaling, the hand on the abdomen should be raised and the hand on the chest should remain stationary. Repeat exercise 5 times.

2   Head and shoulder raising. On the second postpartum day lie flat without a pillow and raise head until the chin is touching the chest. On the third postpartum day raise both head and shoulders off the bed and lower them slowly (Figure 27-19b). Increase gradually until able to do 10. This is a less strenuous exercise which helps to tone the abdominal muscles.

3   Leg raising (Figure 27-19c). This exercise may be begun on the seventh postpartum day. Lying down on the floor with no pillow under the head, point toes and slowly raise one leg keeping the knee straight. Lower the leg slowly. Gradually increase to 10 times each leg. On the ninth postpartum day, slowly raise both legs together. This is an excellent exercise for strengthening abdominal muscles.

4   Pelvic tilt (Figure 27-19d). Lie flat on the floor with knees bent, inhale, and while exhaling flatten the back hard against the floor so that there is no space between the back and the floor. While doing this, tighten abdominal muscles and the muscles of the buttocks.

5   Kegal exercise. This exercise is used to strengthen and tone the muscles of the pelvic floor. The mother should be instructed to do this daily for the rest of her life. Exercise can be done lying on the floor with ankles crossed or sitting in a chair with knees apart and feet flat on the floor. Tighten the muscles around the anus as if to control a bowel movement and then tighten the muscles around the vagina and urethra

as if to stop urine in midstream. Now hold these muscles tightly to the count of 6 and then relax. This exercise can be done on the first postpartum day; it also increases the circulation to the perineal region, hence promoting faster healing of the episiotomy.

6   Sit-ups (Figure 27-19e). In 2 weeks, the mother may begin sit-ups, slowly increasing the number until she is able to do at least 10. Lie flat on back with hands on hips. Slowly raise head, shoulder, and trunk until attaining a

(a)

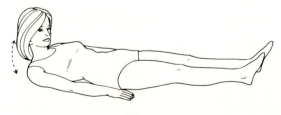

(b)

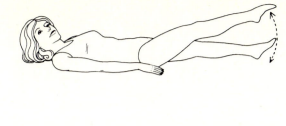

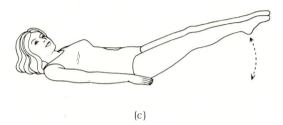

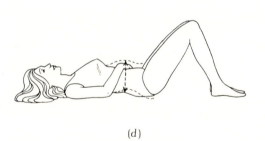

(c)

(d)

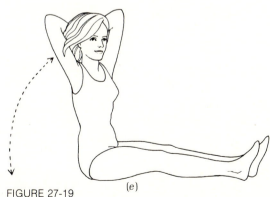

(e)

FIGURE 27-19
Postpartum exercises. (*Courtesy of Elizabeth Riska Townsley.*)

sitting position. This is another good exercise for toning and strengthening abdominal muscles.

After 2 weeks the mother may do almost any exercise she chooses. It is wise to remind her that if she notices that the lochia turns bright red after she has been exercising, she should stop for a few days until the bleeding is no longer bright red. If the mother does these six exercises faithfully and follows a careful diet, she should be able to regain her figure quickly.

Evaluation of Learning

In an effort to evaluate the learning that has taken place in the hospital, the nurse can arrange time to sit down and talk with the mother about how she feels regarding herself, the baby, and the events that have just taken place. If a bath demonstration has been given, the nurse may suggest to the mother to bathe the infant again when the nurse is available to check on the learning and answer any additional questions. It is extremely important that the mother be made to feel comfortable while doing this. In some hospitals, the nurse may have a mother who has had other children give the bath demonstration while the nurse guides the group discussion. Some mothers would enjoy doing this, and others would feel very threatened by talking before a group. The nurse should be flexible enough to try a variety of teaching methods.

Information should be obtained as to the kind of help the mother will have at home. This help might be a mother, mother-in-law, sister or other close relative, next-door neighbor, or a hired person. Those mothers who will be left alone at home should be given a telephone number to call, either that of the postpartum unit or the community health nurse. The establishment of a warm, friendly relationship with the mother in the hospital becomes even more important as discharge day nears. The mother who has become close to a nurse or nurses will be much more likely to call if she experiences any difficulty than will the mother who felt alone and without aid in the hospital.

Follow-up on the teaching that has been done is also a necessary function of the community health nurse. This nurse is the person most able to evaluate the learning that has taken place since the visiting nurse is able to see the mother in her home. The hospital nurse can begin a teaching program, and the community health nurse can add to and follow up on it. Such a system requires good communication between staff and agency. It is the hospital nurse's responsibility to initiate the community health referral if none has been made and to communicate exactly what the mother has been taught, how the woman reacted to it, and the nurse's evaluation of what has occurred during the hospital stay. In a family-centered maternity program, no one nurse can do all things for the patient, but via effective communication, excellent nursing care can be carried out.

In summary, teaching is the focal point of nursing on the postpartum unit, whether it is done formally or informally. It provides a continuous challenge for the nurse and offers an opportunity to be creative.

The Mother with a Cesarean Section

The mother with a cesarean section provides the nurse with an excellent opportunity for teaching, since she is hospitalized longer and has more time to develop a relationship with the nurse. During the early days following surgery, the mother's main concern will be with her physical well-being. She will need medication to ease her discomfort and

more physical care than the routine postpartum mother. This woman tends to recover quickly and by the end of the first or second day she is beginning to take an interest in the infant.

If the mother had general anesthesia for her surgery, there may be a greater lag in maternal feelings than in the mother who had the cesarean section under a regional block. The mother who is awake and able to see the baby immediately after birth usually feels that she has been an active participant in the delivery and is able to take hold of the maternal role more quickly; whereas the mother who has been put to sleep for the surgery may find that emotionally she is not as involved with the infant during the early puerperium. The mother whose cesarean section is planned and without a long labor may demonstrate a shorter maternal lag than the one who has an emergency section and no chance to prepare psychologically for the delivery. All these things must be taken into consideration as the nurse plans the patient's care and teaching.

Sexual Adjustment in the Puerperium

The usual minimal recommended time for resuming sexual intercourse is 2 weeks postpartum, though time limits will vary. The nurse may alleviate potential problems by discussing the reasoning for any limitations and sexual readjustment during the puerperium; however, each couple will ultimately make their own decision in this area.

Studies reveal that tension and fatigue may prevent the woman from relaxing and enjoying sexual intercourse.[36] Other women fear that the episiotomy will not be completely healed, and yet others respond with increased sensitivity to sexual stimulation following the birth of a baby.

Many nursing mothers find that the vaginal tissue is dry and sexual intercourse is uncomfortable. This is due to a lack of hormone stimulation to the area and is easily remedied by having her physician prescribe a vaginal cream. Some mothers find breastfeeding sexually stimulating, which may lead to feelings of embarrassment and eventual discontinuation of nursing.

In preparing the patient for returning to her normal life-style, it is important for the nurse to include some guidance and/or information regarding sexual relations following pregnancy and delivery.

The 6-Week Check

The new mother should return to be examined by her doctor about 6 weeks postpartum. The purpose of this visit is to ensure that the puerperium has progressed normally, and it is important because it may be the last medical contact with the mother unless she has a problem or until she becomes pregnant again. This check consists of a thorough pelvic and breast examination, measurement of blood pressure and weight, a urinalysis, and sometimes a hematocrit and rubella immunization. The visit provides the doctor with information needed to assess the mother's progress through the puerperium and also enables the woman to ask questions and bring to the doctor's attention any special concern. The 6-week examination is an excellent time to instruct the woman in breast self-examination if she is not already familiar with the procedure, and she should also be reminded of the importance of annual or semiannual Papanicolaou smears, the test for cervical cancer.

REFERENCES

1   Parad, Howard J. (ed.): *Crisis Intervention: Selected Readings,* Family Service Association of America, New York, 1965, p. 2.

2   Rubin, Reva: "Puerperal Change," *Nursing Outlook,* 9(12):753–755, December 1961.

3   Bergersen, Betty S., et al. (eds.): *Current Concepts in Clinical Nursing,* vol. I, Mosby, St. Louis, 1967, p. 391.

4   Duffey, Margery, et al. (ed.): *Current Concepts in Clinical Nursing,* vol. III, Mosby, St. Louis, 1971, p. 220.

5   Ross Laboratories: *A Study in Maternal Attitudes,* Medical Department, Ross Laboratories, Columbus, Ohio, 1959.

6   Bergersen: op. cit., p. 389.

7   Heitler, Susan M.: *Postpartum Depression: A Multi-dimensional Study,* unpublished dissertation, New York University, New York, February 1975, p. 38.

8   Caplan, Gerald: *An Approach to Community Mental Health,* Grune & Stratton, New York, 1961, p. 90.

9   Ibid., p. 103.

10 Klaus, Marshall, John Kennell, et al.: "Human Maternal Behavior at the First Contact with Her Young," *Pediatrics,* 46:188, August 1970.

11 Ibid., p. 190.

12 Caplan: op. cit., p. 90.

13 Prugh, Dane: personal communication, Nov. 21, 1974.

14 Hellman, Louis M., and Jack A. Pritchard: *Williams Obstetrics,* 14th ed., Appleton-Century-Crofts, New York, 1970, p. 465.

15 Ibid., p. 470.

16 Kagan, B. M., et al.: "Feeding Premature Infants—Comparison of Various Milks," *Pediatrics,* 15:376, January–June 1955.

17 Hellman and Pritchard: op. cit., p. 471.

18 Hellman and Pritchard: op. cit., p. 473.

19 Smith, Christine: *Maternal-Child Nursing,* Saunders, Philadelphia, 1963, p. 174.

20 Bowes, Watson A., Jr., Sharon Joseph, and Rana Peck: unpublished data, 1971.

21 La Leche League International: *The Womanly Art of Breastfeeding,* 13th ed., Interstate, Danville, Ill., 1971, p. 151.

22 Moore, Francis D., et al.: "Carcinoma of the

Breast," *New England Journal of Medicine*, 277:294, 1967.

23 Daniel, D. G., H. Campbell, and A. C. Turnbull: "Puerperal Thromboembolism and Suppression of Lactation," *Lancet*, 2:288–289, 1967.

24 Baum, J. David: "Nutritional Value of Human Milk," *Obstetrics and Gynecology*, 37(1):126–129, January 1971.

25 Bullen, Catherine, and A. T. Willis: "Resistance of the Breast-fed Infant to Gastroenteritis," *British Medical Journal*, Aug. 7, 1971, p. 342.

26 Baum, J. David, et al.: "Hypocalcaemic Fits in Neonates," *Lancet*, 1:598, Mar. 16, 1968.

27 Graber, T. M.: *Orthodontics, Principles and Practice*, 3d ed., Saunders, Philadelphia, 1972, pp. 323–324.

28 Iffrig, Sister M. C.: "Nursing Care and Success in Breast Feeding," *The Nursing Clinics of North America*, 3:347–349, June 1968.

29 Mitchell, Helen S.: "A Symposium: Recommended Dietary Allowances Up to Date," *Journal of the American Dietetic Association*, 64:149–150, February 1974.

30 La Leche League International: op. cit., p. 131.

31 Lubchenco, Lula O.: personal communication, Jan. 6, 1975.

32 Fraiberg, Selma H.: *The Magic Years*, Scribner, New York, 1959, p. 70.

33 Andresen, Mary, Lula O. Lubchenco, and Rana Peck: unpublished data, August 1971.

34 Klaus, Marshall, and John Kennell: "Mothers Separated from Their Newborn Infants," *Pediatric Clinics of North America*, 17(4): 1035, November 1970.

35 Kennell, John H., et al.: "Maternal Behavior One Year after Early and Extended Postpartum Contact," *Developmental Medicine and Child Neurology*, 16:172–179, 1974.

36 Falicov, Celia J.: "Sexual Adjustment during the First Pregnancy and Post Partum," *American Journal of Obstetrics and Gynecology*, 117(7):996–1000, Dec. 1, 1973.

BIBLIOGRAPHY

Anderson, Edith H., et al. (eds.): *Current Concepts in Clinical Nursing*, vol. 4, Mosby, St. Louis, 1973.

Applebaum, Richard M.: *Abreast of the Times*, copyright, Richard M. Applebaum, 1969.

———: "The Modern Management of Successful Breast Feeding," *Pediatric Clinics of North America*, 17(1):203–225, February 1970.

———: "The Physician and a Common Sense Approach to Breast Feeding," *Southern Medical Journal*, 63(7):793–799, July 1970.

Bergersen, Betty, et al. (eds.): *Current Concepts in Clinical Nursing*, vol. 2, Mosby, St. Louis, 1969.

Brazelton, T. Berry: *Infants and Mothers*, Dell, New York, 1969.

Brown, Marie Scott: "Drug Contaminants and Nutrients in Human Milk," *Keeping Abreast Journal*, 1(1), January–March 1976.

Countryman, Betty A.: "Hospital Care of the Breast-fed Newborn," *American Journal of Nursing*, 71(12):2365–2367, December 1971.

Davis, M. Edward, and Reva Rubin: *Obstetrics for Nurses*, 17th ed., Saunders, Philadelphia, 1962.

Derthick, Nancy: "Sexuality in Pregnancy and the Puerperium," *Birth and the Family Journal*, 1(4):5–9, Fall 1974.

Egli, G. E., N. S. Egli, and Michael Newton: "The Influence of Number of Breast Feedings on Milk Production," *Pediatrics*, 27(2):314–317, February 1961.

Fitzpatrick, Elise, Sharon Reeder, and Luigi Mastroianni, Jr.: *Maternity Nursing*, 12th ed., Lippincott, Philadelphia, 1971.

Haire, Doris, and John Haire: *Implementing Family-centered Maternity Care with a Central Nursery*, Childbirth Education Association of New Jersey, Hillside, N.J., 1968.

Ingalls, A. Joy, and M. Constance Salerno: *Maternal and Child Health Nursing*, 2d ed., Mosby, St. Louis, 1971.

Lesser, Marion, and Vera Keane: *Nurse-Patient*

Relationships in a Hospital Maternity Service, Mosby, St. Louis, 1956.

McLennan, Charles E.: *Synopsis of Obstetrics,* 9th ed., Mosby, St. Louis, 1974.

Nelson, Waldo E., Victor C. Vaughn, and R. James McKay (eds.): *Textbook of Pediatrics,* 9th ed., Saunders, Philadelphia, 1969.

Newton, Michael, and Niles Newton: "Postpartum Engorgement of the Breast," *American Journal of Obstetrics and Gynecology,* 61(3): 644–667, March 1951.

Newton, Niles: *Maternal Emotions,* Hoeber-Harper, New York, 1955.

——— and Michael Newton: "Mothers' Reactions to Their Newborn Babies," *Journal of the American Medical Association,* 181(1):206–210, July 21, 1962.

Peplau, Hildegard: "Anxiety in the Mother-Infant Relationship," *Nursing World,* 134:11, 33–34, May 1960.

Reed, Constance: *Rapid Post Natal Figure Recovery,* Ortho Pharmaceutical Corp., Rantan, N.J., 1968.

Rubin, Reva: "Attainment of the Maternal Role, 1, Processes," *Nursing Research,* 16(3):237–245, Summer 1967.

———: "Attainment of the Maternal Role, 2, Models and Referrants," *Nursing Research,* 16(4):342–346, Fall 1967.

———: "Basic Maternal Behavior," *Nursing Outlook,* 9(11):683–686, November 1961.

———: "Maternal Touch," *Nursing Outlook,* (11):828–831, November 1963.

Sawin, Clark T.: *The Hormones: Endocrine Physiology,* Little, Brown, Boston, 1969.

Stuart, Harold C., and Dane G. Prugh (eds.): *The Healthy Child,* Harvard University Press, Cambridge, Mass., 1960.

Taylor, E. Stewart: *Beck's Obstetrical Practice,* 9th ed., Williams & Wilkins, Baltimore, 1971.

28

Significant Others in Childrearing

ELIZABETH J. WORTHY

In previous chapters the impact of the birth of an infant on the family and the tasks and relationships of the primary family unit have been studied. The focus has now shifted to those infants for whom the primary family cannot provide full care or whose parents (or parent) elect to place them with other members of their family, other family units, or in group care. The societal context within which alternate care for infants and young children has developed, the needs and the resources available to the primary family, factors which enter into the choice of a placement for a child, and the nursing function in alternate care situations will be explored in this chapter.

There are two major thrusts to family life: (1) the basic biological nature and needs of its members and (2) the requirements of the society in which it exists and which it subserves by preparing its offspring to live within it.[1] The dependency of the young child and the time which must elapse before he or she can take care of his or her own needs make it imperative that the child be raised in a favorable environment and by people to whom the child's welfare is as important as their own. "His dependency and his prolonged attachment to them (family and extra-family members) provide major motivation and directions for his development into a member of society."[2] All that an individual experiences later is perceived and understood according to foundations established during these early years.

Many pressures are exerted on the family in present-day society. Margaret Mead summed them up over two decades ago when she stated, "We now expect a family to achieve, alone, what no society has ever expected an individual family to achieve unaided. In effect, we call upon an individual family to do what a whole clan used to do."[3] The developing family as seen by Mead is founded on a somewhat narrow base. Economic pressures, job security, emotional immaturity, and mobility are only a few of the threats which can seriously undermine family stability.

In reviewing trends in the development and restructuring of the American family, Talcott Parsons has pointed out that the family has now become a more differentiated unit and that its functions in relationship to other units have become more specialized.[4] The loss of functions to some other units has already occurred. These include the school and peer group, the mass media, business units, and many other social institutions. Parsons has also described the comparative "isolation" of the nuclear family, emotionally, economically, and geographically. He did not see the restructuring of the family as a general tendency toward dissolution. Rather, he believed that, as the role and function of the primary family unit became more highly differentiated from other units in society, its main functions would emerge,

thus resulting in greater stability. In his opinion the role differentiation of both parents and children becomes a focal point. The "shift in balance of the sex roles," as viewed by Parsons, leads to the mother taking over more of the managerial functions within the family, including that of the management of childrearing. The father then assumes more of the "chairman of the board" functions and maintains, through his occupational role, the field of extrafamily relations, rather than being the supreme authority in his own home. The mother, having longer and more intimate contact with their child, increases the emotional intensity and dependency of the parent-child unit and reduces the amount of conformance to a final authority expected from him. The child is regarded more as an individual who has some part in decision making and who is led rather than forced to higher levels of growth.[5] The high degree of emotional intensity, the relative isolation of the primary unit, and the comparative lack of extrafamily contacts can provide difficulty for the child when he is first exposed to extrafamily groups, whether in preschool or grade school situations.

Typically a family develops through predictable sequences of growth stages. "Before one family unit has completed its cycle, its grown children have been launched to start out on theirs. Most twentieth-century families have the privilege of seeing a second, third, or even fourth life cycle spin off as children rear their children who grow up and have children, who in turn repeat the family life cycle pattern while older members of the family are still living."[6] Family life cycles have altered considerably during this century. Because of improved health care, and social and economic conditions, Albrecht[7] has predicted that five, or even six, contemporaneous generations of families may be likely in the future.

Reuben Hill's study of three-generation families has confirmed ongoing interaction in a continual flow from one generation to the next.[8] He found sharing of activities, visiting, and help exchanges among the three generations; the most frequent interaction was between adjacent generations. Each generation turned to the kinship network for help in solving problems, the middle generation being the "lineage bridge" between older and younger generations. The elderly might have problems with illness or household management; the parent generation may need emotional gratification; and the childbearing generation may require help with finances or child care. This degree of interdependence was advanced by "heavy involvement" of the middle generation, who give more assistance up and down the generation ladder than they receive. The three-generation family received less help from health, religious, social, or welfare agencies, compared with that which they received from their own family members. In 1 year alone, over 3,780 instances of different kinds of help (in illness, with finances, in child care, and in household and emotional crises) were reported. In each generation, members consistently reported receiving more help than they gave to others. Thus, the popular picture of the modern family as a small susceptible nucleus which is not sustained by other thoughtful relatives is not reflected in this research. Observation and experience evidences a modified extended family within a sound network of generational involvement.

The evidence alluded to above, while not taking all possible points of view into consideration, permits us to review some aspects of the societal context in which alternate care for infants and growing children has become necessary. Families have become smaller and their functions more specialized; although more family members are living longer, and a rich network of relationships between generations is possible, there are many threats to family development and stability. Some of these are discussed below.

THREATS TO FAMILY STABILITY AND THE MAINTENANCE OF AN INTER-RELATIONAL NETWORK

The Single-Parent Family

There are a growing number of single-parent families in which the parent, usually the mother, seeks to raise young children alone. In 1974 it was reported that 62 percent of women heads of families in the labor force had children under five years of age.[9] Figures for one metropolitan area in the state of Washington indicated that 9,446 women in the labor force had 14,000 children under six years of age.[10] Of these, 2,212 women heads of families had 3,300 children under six years of age. The figures are consistent with the national trend, which indicates that one-third of children under six years of age have mothers in the labor force and that many of these are women heads of households who are divorced, widowed, or separated.[11]

In 1974, according to Urie Bronfenbrenner, one out of every six children under eighteen years of age in the United States lived with one parent, and one out of every eight infants under three had a single parent: widowed, divorced, separated, or unwed. There is an increase in both the divorce and illegitimacy rate.[12]

Of necessity many of the women who are single parents will join the labor force if they do not wish or are ineligible for public assistance. The personal and family problems of the single parent are multiple. According to Goode, contemporary American society has failed to define a role for her; what she may or may not do within the family setting is not prescribed. Lacking such prescriptions, Goode concludes that many participants in marital dissolution could be expected to undergo considerable personal disorganization.[13] The above factors could also affect the young child's ability to cope with this crisis situation and the child's adaptation to a new way of life. At this point both parents might be unavailable to give support to the child—the father geographically, the mother emotionally. The position of either or both parents in the extended family is also altered. The supportive network of relationships may no longer be available to them. One or both may move to another area or withdraw from relatives, friends, and neighbors, alienating themselves from a society in which there is no formal position for them.

There has been progressive fragmentation and isolation of the family within the United States during the past few years. The middle-class families of the seventies are becoming more like the low-income families of the sixties. The need to develop a support system for both parents and children within the United States is great.[14]

The Impact of Poverty, Mobility, and Family Discord

The impact of these three factors on the family unit has been well documented. Working women in the poverty group, white or nonwhite, single or wed, carry many burdens, such as discrimination (racial, economic, sex), inadequate preparation for work or for family life, lower wages, and a higher probability of family disruption. They may be able to cope with many of these burdens but may be overwhelmed by the cumulative effects of chronic economic dependency: periodic or continuous unemployment, debts, inadequate housing, poor standards of housekeeping, resultant malnutrition, apathy, and inability to profit from experience. The low-income families are often repeaters in the poverty cycle and may be considered, by their more affluent neighbors, to be the troublemakers in their communities.

The *mobility*, either forced or habitual, of many families in cities or rural areas weakens the interacting network of the extended family and again leaves the family or single parent alienated from society and from the supports which, inadequate as they may be, could be available to them. Much time and energy needs to be expended by individuals and groups in order to learn how to work with or within a system of care, be it social, economic, or health. Families who are on the move soon give up as each system presents its complexities, time after time. The causes of family discord have been described by many authors. Moses sums them up as stemming from the facts that (1) the original choice of a partner may have been largely a compromise for one or both partners; (2) the needs of both, which may act as motivator of behavior, are constantly changing; (3) the demands of one partner or another may be inconsistent, contradictory, incompatible, or out of touch with reality; and (4) communication is frequently inadequate between partners who may have had little opportunity to learn how the other partner thinks or perceives.[15]

Infants born into such families may fail to thrive physically, emotionally, and intellectually if the interacting climate is unstable. They may be unplanned, unwanted, neglected, or even abused. One should hasten to say that higher-income groups, especially those who have limited psychosocial resources, are not exempt from such problems.

The Working Mother

In March 1973, 4.8 million mothers in the national labor force had 5.9 million children under six years of age and at that time women comprised 44 percent of the national labor force.[16]

Women supposedly achieve their goals in

family life by being competent partners and mothers. Economic, sociocultural, and personal pressures can make this goal difficult to achieve. Some women become disillusioned with the tasks of motherhood and housekeeping for which they may have little aptitude, and they may need to get away from what they consider to be a "humdrum" existence. Some wish to compete with men in occupations hitherto considered reserved for men only, while others seek to work in occupations or professions for which they are already highly skilled. It is obvious that not all women who work are in the lower-income groups. In many instances a desire for a higher standard of living is supported by two wage earners in a family. All married women, ill- or well-prepared, are at a serious work disadvantage when compared with men and single women. They may not have access to the basic support systems for child care, housekeeping, illness care, or preventive health and social services. Such services are often inconveniently located and run impersonally, and many women are reluctant to use them, even if available. The extended family network may be absent or fragile in texture—mothers tend to work too hard and for too long in order that they might "break even" financially.

It appears that many family units can and do provide for at least some of the intra- and extrafamily needs of their young children through utilization of some available resources. It is also evident that the so-called multiproblem family, within which factors such as poverty, mobility, and marital discord threaten the stability of the family unit, may not be able to make such provision. To whom shall they turn? How can and does the community attempt to supplement or, in some instances, replace the extended family? What specific measures can be adopted in order to protect vulnerable infants and young children from the damaging effects of early inadequate environments, whether these be in their natural homes, the homes of relatives or sitters, or in a group setting? How can we preserve the positive features of a warm and challenging home setting in which there is a working mother and supplement her care?

ALTERNATE CARE FOR YOUNG CHILDREN

Problems and Resources

Until very recently no official planning or allocation of resources has been offered, at any level, to assist with the development of alternate care programs for infants and children under three years of age. In fact, such programs were discouraged, although the need for "suitable" placement for infants has been present for many years. Parents could not, and have not, waited for official sanction.

Findings from a national study revealed that over 45 percent of the mothers surveyed who worked full time had found placements for their children under three years old at home with father, with siblings over sixteen years of age (27.5 percent), or with nonrelatives in the home (17.8 percent). Placement in the home of a relative was also high (22 percent). The corresponding figures for those mothers who worked part time were: care in the home with relatives, 36.4 percent (almost 4 percent of these relatives were under sixteen years of age); care in the home by nonrelatives, 8.8 percent; and placement in the home of a relative, 9.4 percent. The 4.1 million mothers who were working or looking for work in 1968 (the number increased to approximately 4.8 million in 1973) had over 2 million children under three years of age. Mothers without husbands were more likely to be working than those with husbands; 27 percent of the mothers in the labor force with husbands had children under six years old, but 51 percent of the mothers in the labor force without husbands had children under six years old. Thirty-two percent of nonwhite (as opposed to 17 percent of white) working mothers provided the main source of income for their families. Many mothers of children under three years old chose part-time rather than full-time work. Mothers in all socioeconomic groups have felt and expressed guilt feelings about leaving their young children at a time when they are considered to be highly vulnerable to adverse factors in their environment.[17] Conversely, to quote Robinson, "Many mothers can function more happily as mothers and as individuals when they are away from home part of the day; many children, too, can profit from the brief time in the care of others."[18]

The depth of satisfaction which mothers experience when they obtain care for children outside the home varies greatly. Mothers of young children and those who lead a busy and overburdened life caring for older children seem more likely to be dissatisfied. When the children are cared for in their own homes by relatives or baby-sitters, mothers have been found to be more satisfied. They also appear to be more satisfied if they expect relatively little of an unpaid neighbor or a grandparent. In the national study the relatively small number of mothers working full time who placed their young children in the homes of nonrelatives or in group day care arrangements or who looked after them themselves at work were more satisfied with group day care, even though their expectations of this service were higher.

In one small unpublished study of 41 mothers whose infants were born in a university hospital setting in a metropolitan area, the investigator studied the types of substitute care which mothers used in the early weeks and months of life.[19] His findings included the fact that 37 percent of full-time working mothers were leaving their infants with others for a large part of the week. Over half the infants had been left overnight in the care of others, 15 percent before the age of two months. The mothers all experienced difficulties in making such arrangements and also in arranging temporary baby-sitting services. They were more satisfied with care in the home. When the infants were out of the home for 6 to 8 hours in the care of others, 30 percent of the mothers expressed dissatisfaction with such provisions. Poor quality of care and higher cost were the main reasons for their dissatisfaction. Dissatisfaction increased to 50 percent if only low-income mothers were considered. The investigator also found that 35 percent of the mothers who were most affected by this lack of "good" alternate care placements would have returned to work if satisfactory arrangements could have been made. In this study, low-income mothers were the most dissatisfied, presumably because they were even less able to pay for "good" care, if it existed. This dissatisfaction may also have kept them from entering training programs through which they could increase their incomes and thus be able to afford "better" care, if it existed.

A survey of 516 urban families was carried out in North Carolina in 1965.[20] Approximately half these families were nonwhite. Highly pertinent questions were asked. How many infants experienced supplemental mothering during part of the day, in or out of their homes? Who supplied the care? What age was the infant when this care was provided? How satisfied was the mother? What was the potential demand for such services? What were the other preferences? The answers were equally pertinent to our discussion.

More than half of the white children and

almost half of the nonwhite children were under six months of age when someone other than the mother had begun to care for them regularly. Two-thirds of these white infants were placed in settings away from their homes. For nonwhite infants, 32 percent were experiencing supplementary care—18 percent in their own homes and 14 percent away from home. Sixteen percent of the total sample were in daytime care outside their own homes. Two-thirds of these white infants were in day-care homes, while half the nonwhite infants were in the homes of relatives.

Most of the mothers were satisfied with the arrangements they had made. There were more dissatisfactions among nonwhite mothers and among mothers whose infants were in care away from home. The sample included mothers from low-, middle-, and high-income groups, and the study indicated that 90 percent of the low-income infants and 83 percent of the middle-income infants were being cared for by relatives or sitters in their own homes, while only 50 percent of the high-income group had their children cared for in their own homes, and 26 percent had arranged for care outside the home.

Also, most of the mothers in this sample indicated that they would be working regularly if dependable sources of care were available. Most expressed a preference for care of children in their own homes. There was a marked preference for a nursery center for group care among both white and nonwhite families, but only one-third of the white mothers and fewer of the nonwhite mothers gave this as their first choice.

Many federal training programs, such as the Manpower Development and Training Act, the Job Corps for Women, the Work Incentive Program, and the training programs under the Economic Opportunity Act, provide opportunities for unskilled women to obtain training so that they may work to support their families. Some of these programs also supplied group care programs for the children of their trainees who were under contract. The Report of the President's Commission on the Status of Women has emphasized that more women would be joining the labor force and would be remaining in it.[21] Women's liberation movements all over the United States have stressed the need for supplemental care for children so that women could be free to seek work if they should wish to do so and that they be placed in a position of equality with men in relation to access to the basic support systems for child care mentioned previously. Employers are increasingly turning to the provision of day-care programs as a means of attracting and keeping women employees.

Young infants who require more permanent placement outside the home because of total parental inability to provide care and protection for them include the infants of unwed teenagers without resources, of abusive or emotionally disturbed parents, and of rejective parents of unplanned or handicapped infants. Parents such as these provide society with the responsibility for many infants, whose numbers are gradually decreasing, but for whom the initial placement from the hospital nursery is still a serious consideration.

According to Marion Howard, 1 out of every 10 young women in the United States has a baby before she is eighteen years old, and some have more than one. For those who conceive prior to sixteen years of age, the incidence of repeated pregnancy increases. Sixty percent of these young women are married at the time of birth, but over half of them will be divorced within 5 years. Eighty-five percent of these young mothers keep their babies and many of them have to work.

If the grandmother cares for the infant while the teenage daughter is working, she tends to take the infant away from the mother emotionally, and a continuous struggle around the baby and the baby's care develops.

Many young singles decide to relinquish their child at about age three. While adolescents are not primarily child abusers, they do tend to neglect their children.[22]

Adoption or foster homes are still considered to be the arrangement of choice for most infants, but homes for nonwhite infants are not readily available because of sociocultural pressures, and the reluctance to accept interracial adoption persists.

In many communities, agencies exist to identify all such infants, preferably before birth, to provide parental counseling for the natural parents and their families, and to actively recruit adoptive and foster parents. Social and economic support similar to that which natural parents require will prevent many of these infants from being placed in institutional care. But there are still a proportion, the "hard to place" or "unadoptable," among them, for whom group care in institutions is inevitable, either on a temporary or more permanent basis. This group has been estimated at several hundred thousand and includes those over two years of age, the nonwhite, and the handicapped, who may require special care.

For the unwed teenager who wishes to keep her infant, special programs have been developed to aid her in remaining within an educational setting during pregnancy and following the birth of her infant. This has created a new demand for infant care during school hours. More than 200 such educational programs have received federal support, and according to Caldwell, of 67 infant care programs recently surveyed, one-third were concerned with the needs of school age parents.[23]

There has been much concern over the past 10 to 15 years about the needs of teenage parents. They were and are considered "at risk" medically, socially, and educationally. Many of the girls dropped out of school, and became ashamed, depressed, and unhappy; as unskilled workers they were unable to obtain or hold down a job when the baby, whom they or their families invariably put up for adoption, was dispatched to a waiting family. Intervention programs were focused on antepartum care and medical supervision of the pregnancy, often in a maternity home setting or a private household away from the girl's own community. The young fathers received little or no attention.

Many teenage parents have expressed strong desires to raise their infants, either in the parental home or in a separate living situation. The mother is most likely to be involved, on a long-term basis, in such a plan for childrearing.[24] Among the community services which might now be available to her, and to the father, should he remain in the picture, are:

1   Support for the development and improvement of her own parenting skills, while she is still able to continue with her general education. Even though she may be living with her parents out of economic necessity, she could be looking to a future in which she might be independent financially and able to assume more responsibility for the care of her infant.
2   The provision of role models in child care situations such as group infant day-care centers or family day-care homes, or in her own home where a mother or grandmother has undertaken to help raise the infant. With role-model supervision, the teenage parent can increase her competence in caring for the infant.
3   The provision of special classes, often evening classes, relating to child

growth and development, infant nutrition, child care, health care, and other related topics, which are available to both young parents.

4 The development of supportive health care services and teaching programs related to health care for parent and child, so that health supervision can be ensured throughout the antepartum and postpartum periods, infancy, and childhood. This includes hospitals, child health clinics, and school health services involving preventive programs, and requires special efforts to "reach out" to these young families. Case-finding and care programs must be available to teenagers at a time and in a place where they are likely to be able to receive and benefit from such programs. It is important that assistance be both positive and constructive so that future childrearing activities are founded on a solid base.

5 The development of infant care programs in or close to the schools in which parent or parents are receiving their education, for example, at a YWCA, a high school, or a community center. This enables teenage parent and child to be together for at least part of the day, and can facilitate learning about child care to a marked degree.

6 The provision of supportive relationships from agency personnel in the community, so that these young people who are indeed parents, but who have had limited opportunities to make informed decisions, can learn to make their own decisions, gain the respect of their families, increase their independence, and accept the responsibilities of family life.

The need for acceptable facilities for child care in a variety of situations has been illustrated. Communities all over the country are often unable or unwilling to help the mothers of young children to make arrangements for care which will be in the best interests of children and families. However, an increasing number of communities are being forced to become aware of the situation as parents and professionals become increasingly vocal about needs and problems.

Informal Sources

It is evident that many informal sources of care for children exist. Grandparents, aunts and uncles, siblings, high school students, unemployed adults of both sexes, some with interest in or aptitude for child care, are available to parents. Communes provide care for the children of their members—a "multiple parenting" situation. Neighborhood groups in some areas cooperate to provide care for individual infants and children or for groups. That parents use these sources is clear, but reported dissatisfactions indicate that informal sources are considered insufficient to meet the needs for quality care of young children in a community.

Members of the modified extended family continue to operate within an interrelational network despite threats to existence of the family. However, because informal sources are too few in number and threats to family stability high, there has been, for many years, a need for communities to help supply alternate sources of supplemental care through formal channels.

Formal Sources

Formal resources are many and varied, and considerable confusion has existed among parents and professionals alike because of the wide range of programs offered, the wide age span of the children requiring care, the overlaps and gaps in the services provided, the terminology used to describe the resource, the quality of the services provided, the number available within a given community at a given moment, and the costs to the community. State or federal standards regulating the operation of such resources, "recommended" standards, and statements of principles of care also vary considerably. They may require only that zoning, fire safety, and sanitation requirements be met, or they may include highly complex educational, social, or health regulations, many of which cannot be measured quantitatively.

The formal sources of alternate care for infants and young children usually include:

1 *Institutional care*, either in large (up to 300 infants) or small (10 to 15) institutions.
2 *Foster family care*, typically of four to six children, under six years of age (and including one or two infants) in a private home.
3 *Family day-care home*, also including up to six children and one or two infants in a private home. The infants include the foster mother's own children.
4 *Group day-care home*, including up to 12 children, in a private home and requiring additional employees. Infants are not usually placed in these settings.
5 *Group day care* of over 12 children in a hall, school, church, or other building planned and used for this specific purpose.
6 *Adoptive care* in a private family, arranged preferably through a social agency in order to protect both groups of parents and children alike and to provide the adoptive parents with all the responsibilities and joys of the primary family unit.
7 *The expansion and use of homemaker services* to provide help for families

with infants and young children, in their own homes.
8 *Parent-Child Centers*, a component of Head Start, began in 1967 in a number of cities throughout the United States and aimed at preserving links between mother and child. Several of these centers offer infant care programs.

Making the Choice for Infant Care

The choice of a program for infant care is determined by many factors. In most instances parents want to do what they think is best for their child, but they may lack the personal knowledge and skill, as well as social, economic, and extrafamily resources, to fulfill their role as parents and to meet their child's needs. Many young parents have had little or no preparation in parenting, probably the most important function of their lives, and according to Marion Howard, their desire for parenthood waxes and wanes.[25]

Professionals' sensitivity should help them identify family (adult and child) strengths and weaknesses. The strengths should be emphasized and built upon, while support is being provided where weaknesses exist. Information can be shared with teenage parents while they and their baby grow, and they can be helped to structure their time and energy more effectively as they progress through adolescence.

Since many parents have not progressed through adolescence, they themselves are still dependent and have not had many of their needs met, which in turn inhibits them from meeting the needs of another. Parents should be provided information, support, and counseling service to help them understand their difficulties, and they should definitely be included in decision making.

If the parents are experiencing a crisis situation and seem to be unable to cope with their anger, frustration, and depression, assistance from a child protection agency may be indicated. For the child's safety, removal from the home either temporarily or permanently may be necessary.

The Availability and Acceptability of a Source of Care to the Parents

Geographically, economically, culturally, or emotionally, either on a long- or short-term basis, the proximity to, knowledge of, and involvement of parents in the program have proved to be essential to its success in many instances. The mother, especially, needs to have close ties with the director and the facility in order to have input into the program on behalf of her infant and to receive reports of progress or specific activities—educational, social, or health—in which the infant is involved. In those instances in which the community, through one of its social agencies, takes over total responsibility for care, even temporarily, the professional has the same responsibility for close contact and involvement.

The Type and Scope of Services Offered by the Resource Selected by the Family

Parents and professionals alike need to have information about the goals and scope of the programs offered, especially if they will include infant stimulation programs which are liable to enrich the infant's daily life and which could be transferable into his or her own home, when possible. Powell describes these programs as "arranging circumstances in the environment that reinforce a child's strengths and skills . . . and capitalize on readiness to learn new tasks and skills."[26] Health and developmental screening programs and nutritional and social services, as well as basic care, may also be available to the infant and parents.

AGE AND DEVELOPMENTAL LEVEL OF THE INFANT AT THE TIME OF PLACEMENT

The infant's ability to make such a transfer will depend on the support and information provided for the parent or primary caretaker and the gentle easing of the infant into the care situation during the transition period. In discussing group care of infants, Provence reassures all concerned about the ability of the normal infant to make this transition and to continue to develop normally if the caretaker can provide for the infant in a manner in which development is supported rather than interfered with.[27]

The Stability of the Arrangements for Care

The importance of consistency of care has been alluded to. The haphazard nature of many informal child care situations has also been reported. It should be possible to plan group care for an infant so that changes in caretaking and learning environment are kept to a minimum.

The Ability of the Primary Family to Adjust to Placement of the Child

Long-term goals for the placement of the child in the home again (or in a setting approximating a home, should he or she be in an institution and should it be deemed necessary and desirable by parent and professional) must be kept constantly in sight.

The Changes in Professional Attitudes toward Placement of Infants and Young Children

Concern has long been expressed about childrearing in group situations in the United States. This concern was early associated with studies of institutionalized infants who demonstrated severe distortion of physical, emotional, and cognitive development.[28–32] Concern has also been expressed by Ribble about the rights of infants—the infant's need and right for personalized mothering care in the early weeks and months of life.[33] However, it is evident that the preservation of the nuclear family unit is not always possible. Alternate resources may have to be found for infants without families, sometimes on a permanent basis. In other situations in which only temporary help is needed, or when day care can be provided, a support system which will assist family members to retain as much parental responsibility as they can tolerate at a given point may be all that is required. The conclusion has persisted, however, that care for infants and young children within the family is always superior to that in any institution or care situation outside the home, however well organized this may be.[34] Professional attitudes are beginning to change. Mavans et al., writing about care in *Early Child Care: The New Perspective*, reminds professionals that:

1 Many mothers make "casual" and "shifting" arrangements for the care of their young children for a variety of reasons. (This, it must be said, is often necessary as so few resources exist in some communities.)
2 The number of foster homes often lags behind the demand. Infants may be shifted from one to another, with little long-term planning and often as a matter of dire necessity. It is very hard to supervise such arrangements.
3 The patterns of childrearing observed in some segments of the country tend to perpetuate some physical, emotional, and intellectual handicaps from one generation to another; opportunities can and do exist to break into this cycle of events and help infants to grow and develop into sturdy children and adults, freed from some of these deficits.
4 A number of other countries continue to use and to be enthusiastic about group care for infants.[35]

Robinson, in discussing the changing attitudes of professionals, sums up his thinking in relation to day care as, "what was at issue was 'deprivation of stimulation' and 'deprivation of (generalized) mothering' and that separation from the mother for a portion of the day would not lead to the dire results formerly predicted."[36]

In a discussion on group care in the United States, Whittaker says that recent governmental statements seem to indicate that the federal government may be shifting its policy, as expounded at the First White House Conference on Children in 1909 and reiterated at every such conference since, that "the home is the highest and finest product of civilization and that children should not be separated from their parents by reasons of poverty alone," to the present (1971) proposed welfare regulations that "the home is the highest and finest product of civilization for some children and that children may be separated from their parents (at least for day care) for reasons of poverty, alone."[37] He points out that it is essential that we separate the question of effectiveness of group care for young children, as an alternative to the nuclear family, and the separation of certain groups of young children from their families solely because they are poor. Evidence has certainly been growing that poverty homes are often poorly suited to the needs of young children and that the relationship of some young children to their own mother does not necessarily enhance their intellectual and social growth.

Caldwell has reminded us that there has been much wariness about planning definitive programs for young infants within what she terms a "developmental milieu." There has been an implicit assumption in many communities that any setting which preserves life through its ability to meet basic needs for shelter, food, and protection from hazards was adequate for the care of young infants. Caldwell has examined some of the basic assumptions relative to the provision of short-term care for infants and concludes that from the scientific and lay literature and from the practices in health and welfare agencies one could infer that the optimal learning environment of the young child was (1) in the child's own home, (2) within the context of a warm and loving relationship, (3) with the child's mother or a close mother figure, and (4) under conditions which provide for a wide variety of input, both social and cognitive. However, she questions whether one should support the first factor so enthusiastically if (2), (3), and (4) could reasonably be obtained outside the home.[38] Many professionals are trying to keep an open mind about infant care programs and are attempting to evaluate the quality of the mothering experiences which the infant receives rather than the amount of time he spends outside the home.

A report prepared for the Child Development/Day Care Workshop in Warrenton, Virginia, in July 1970 states:

Much of the movement in rethinking child care services for infants and toddlers came from three sources: research showing the crucial importance of the experiences in the first three years of life for later development; research on the effects of an enriched environment during those early years; and a long and serious look at the effects of Headstart and similar programs, where two con-

clusions were drawn: (a) programs must begin before children are three years old, and (b) most important of all, parents must be involved in the programs. *Only when the entire family unit is strengthened will there be important and lasting changes in the child.* Parents want and need good child care programs. Parents care about the welfare of their children. They must be helped to achieve this [italics supplied].[39]

GROUP CARE FOR CHILDREN
Economics

The willingness of this nation to pay for the quality child care programs which have been and will be devised by parents and professionals has been questioned many times. These programs, if they be of the quality required, will demand long-term commitment to the goals of care, to the recruitment and training of personnel to staff such activities, and to funds to support them so that they can be of major benefit to those who need them most. Costs of group care programs vary tremendously according to the type and level of program, the quality of care offered, and the area of the country in which they are located. Family day-care costs have been estimated at about $2,000 per child per year without considering capital investment in home and equipment. Day care now being offered is likely to be in the range of $1,000 to $2,000 per year per child. This is dangerously low—acceptable costs are more likely to be in the range of $2,400 per year per child under three years old; again, this is without including capital investments and without the addition of research activities, which have pushed the cost of some programs up to $8,000 per year per child. Public assistance programs offer $5.00 per day per child on an average, i.e., approximately $1,200 per year per child. If the infant is to receive a program which will enhance growth and development rather than provide for custodial care, the high cost is inevitable. All parents are not able to contribute toward the costs of care. Capital expenditure for space, equipment, program materials, staff salaries and inservice training, and health and social work service (often donated) will all add to the costs. It is small wonder that housing in church basements, poorly prepared personnel, restricted programs, low salaries, donated services, and low prestige are the rule rather than the exception in child care services. Infant care centers, mostly experimental in nature, have fared better because of strict licensing arrangements but have faced the same financial problems and the transient nature of the services provided, as money runs out.

One of the many aspects of group child care is depicted in Figure 28-1, which shows a daily assessment of a child in a day-care center.

Licensing Standards

Standards for group care services are published by each state, and mandatory licensing is the rule rather than the exception, although in some areas the regulations are not rigorously enforced. National professional organizations have also published recommended standards, for example, the American Public Health Association (1967),[40] the Child Welfare League for America (1969),[41] the American Academy of Pediatrics (1971) (the latter relating specifically to the health care of infants under three years old),[42] and the Office of Child Development (formerly the Children's Bureau).[43]

The Day Care and Child Development Council of America, Inc., has prepared a statement of principles relating to the development of a locally controlled, publicly supported, and universally available child care system (1971).[44] Community-coordinated

FIGURE 28-1
A daily assessment of a child in a day-care center.

child care (4C) programs have been developed in approximately 150 communities in an effort to coordinate child care programs and provide maximum use of available funds, staffing, and facilities. This program emphasizes local efforts and citizen participation in child care.

The Needs of Infants

The needs of infants in group care have been variously described; Huntington and Provence summed them up succinctly in 1970:[45]

The infant must have his health and nutritional needs met in addition to clothing and shelter. He needs an adult's assistance in providing for his physical comfort, in managing his bodily activity, in protecting him from hazards to health and safety, and in caring for him when he is sick or injured.

The infant needs to be able to form an attachment to one major caretaker; someone who cares for him and he for her. This should not compete with maternal care when this is available, but be supplementary to it. In the fulfillment of his basic physical needs, both mother and caretaker can deepen their attachment to this specific infant. Other persons may well care for him and will of necessity do so, but mother or principal caretaker are around to assist him to form attachments to these other persons in his life.

Infants need lots of company, people who will interact with them in a loving, caring manner and who will respond to their behavior by talking to them, playing with them, caressing them, feeding them, bathing them, or dressing them. To quote Huntington and Provence, "Language is one of the least expensive and most accessible tools we have for interacting with children and supporting their increasingly complex understanding of the world."[46]

Infants need new and challenging activities and experiences within their physical and social environment so that they remain active and interested in it and revel in its variety.

Infants need to be able to learn through constant personal exploration of their life spaces. The more they learn, the more they are stimulated, and the more they continue to learn.

Infants need some order and predictability in their physical and social world. Routine periods for sleep, rest, feeding, and quiet periods are a balancing force for a rich and stimulating learning environment.

Infants need adults to set limits for them, to know what is acceptable social and physical behavior and what is not and to deal with resulting frustrations in such a manner that learning continues to take place.

Infants need to be able to develop happy, confident self-images through the quality of people and of experiences to which they are exposed. The sturdy personality of the toddler and preschool child who has successfully handled early developmental tasks reflects the attainment of trust and personal autonomy as he or she relates to others.

Infants and young children need to feel that others love and respect them for what they are. Their ability to model the behavior of others allows them to pick up many of the attitudes and values of these significant others. These become a part of the child; some of this can be taught but most of it is caught in these early years.

Characteristics of the Environment

With these needs of infants in mind, what are the salient features of the environment in which the infant in group care can grow and develop?

A group care environment should be a stimulating, learning environment in settings both indoor and outdoor. Warmth, comfort, bright colors, and soft and rough textures should be available, and the environment should be free from physical hazards and contain the necessary services (care, protection, food) and equipment, all of which will ensure the continuing growth and development of the young child.

A group care environment should offer a "relatively high frequency of adult contact, utilizing a relatively small number of adults."[47] These adults are carefully screened for personal and health characteristics, preferably prepared in early childhood education, education, basic nurturing, and health care (including dental care) and are provided with stimulating inservice training programs.

A group care environment should offer a carefully planned daily program which will meet the needs of infants at various levels of development. The program should include activities, rest, a balanced nutritional intake provided at appropriate intervals, sleep periods, quiet periods, listening or singing to music, opportunities for indoor and outdoor play, and for practice of newly acquired physical, intellectual, and social skills.

A group care environment should maintain close contacts with the community through parent (or mother) meetings or classes in order to facilitate ideas about infant development, behavior, or problems; informal personal discussion with parents; the use of volunteer caretaking or social or health services; excursions into the community; an active public relations program to allow the community access to the center through the use of articles, pictures, and other media; and home visiting by staff.

The Health Program

The main thrust of a health program would be directed toward the control of infection; the prevention of accidents and other environmental hazards; the promotion of health through screening, immunization programs, developmental testing, nutritional assessment, and parent and staff education; and the recognition and referral of developmental deviance or disease in infants to appropriate sources. The following questions might well be asked of an adequate health care program for infants:

1   Has the infant had a pre-entry medical examination? Was the mother or principal caretaker present? Are health records complete? Is the immunization schedule up to date? Does he or she have a private physician, attend a public clinic, or does the child need to be referred for medical or nursing supervision? Have other disciplines been involved in the child's care at any time?
2   Has an assessment of the infant's health and developmental status been carried out since the infant was placed in group care? By whom? When? How

often has it been repeated? What tools and techniques were employed? What were the major problems identified? What priorities were set? Where are the records filed?
3   What long-term and short-term goals of health care were established for this young infant in group care? Was a plan of care devised? To whom was this plan communicated? When and how was the plan implemented? What family and community resources were explored and utilized?
4   What was the outcome of this plan of care? What criteria for evaluation were established? How was the promotion of health and the treatment of illness related to other activities and programs in the group care setting?

Nursing Function

The nursing function in group care settings is closely related to the answers to the preceding questions. Nursing can and does play a prominent role in the prevention, identification, treatment and care, and referral to other resources of many young children in group care.

Although the infant care center is required by state regulation in many states to be under general medical supervision, this is often limited to advisement regarding standards of medical care to be observed, preadmission medical examination of specific children, and incenter clinics set up for the prevention and early identification of disease.

Each infant should be under the health supervision of a physician or public clinic, and parents are encouraged to obtain such supervision.

The infant care center is also required to obtain the services of a registered nurse, or in some instances, a licensed practical nurse who undertakes the major responsibility for the development and maintenance of a health program, an outline of which follows:

1 Consultation to the director and staff on matters relating to the health of the children is provided by health professionals, such as the nurse (and social worker, dental staff, and nutritionist, when available). The health program should be the outcome of discussions between these groups and the parents, and all parents must be made aware of the program in order for it to be effective.

2 Written policies and procedures regarding standing orders for minor acute illnesses, first aid, major medical emergencies, and the inability of most agencies to administer medication must be available to director and staff. These are developed by the nurse and center staff in consultation with a physician.

3 All persons in contact with the children must be in good health and free from communicable disease. Regular checks are necessary in order to ensure that this is accomplished.

4 Regular monitoring of the physical, social, and emotional environment in which the child is receiving care must be considered.

5 General health supervision, including evidence of the pre-entry medical examination to exclude previous illness or disability; an assessment of the child's present health; the status of the immunization program and its regular updating for each infant; the screening of developmental progress; and conferences with the parents and agency staff to provide for their ongoing input are all regular features of the health program. Identification of the specific health needs of each infant or group of infants and the development of plans to meet these needs would follow. Evaluating the effects of these plans and their implementation is a major responsibility of the nurse, director, and parent together. The nurse plays a prominent role in teaching the agency staff to:

a Recognize acceptable standards of health in an infant

b Carry out a simple health examination on a regular basis

c Identify a child who is sick or in need of care (physical, emotional, nutritional, dental, social, etc.); recognize developmental deviance

d Provide for sickness care where this is required

e Maintain safety standards and carry out first aid measures efficiently

f Perform hand-washing and cleansing and placement procedures related to the direct care of a young infant and his or her environment, based on accurate knowledge and understanding of existing needs

g Report and record all information clearly

h Ensure that the nutritional status of each child is adequate and that nutritional intake in the center is sufficient for the child's growth and development

i Provide for childrearing activities such as toilet training, bathing, feeding, intellectual and social stimulation, and mothering activities so that close links with the child's regimen at home are preserved

Setting up group training sessions for both staff and parents, which cover any or all of the points raised above has been found to be most effective. Focusing on a health or social problem identified by the staff and then moving on to other pertinent areas provides the nurse with an entrance point into the system at a time when interest is high.

The nurse, as a citizen, also plays an important part in the identification of the need for child care programs in a community, in working actively with citizen groups toward the development of a variety of such programs, in order to meet the wide variety of needs. Contacts with agencies and planning groups should also enable the nurse to help monitor quality of care as well as quantity.

CONCLUSION

While the needs and resources described above are still far from reaching a meeting point, group care for infants at all income levels is growing. The low status and poor quality of some present services are improving. The financial support is beginning to emerge. In an article written for *Saturday Review* in February 1971, Bettye M. Caldwell provides strong direction for the future:[48]

At this moment in history, when we are on the threshold of embarking on a nationwide program of social intervention offered through comprehensive child care, we let ourselves prattle about such things as cost per child, physical facilities, or even community control. And when we begin to think big about what kinds of children we want to have in the next generation, about which human characteristics will stand them in good stead in a world changing too rapidly, we fall back on generalities such as care and protection. Yet any social institution that can shape behavior and help instill values and competencies and life-styles should also shape policy. Early child care is a powerful instrument for influencing patterns of development and the quality of life for

children and adults. Because of its power, those who give it direction must not think or act with timidity.

REFERENCES

1   Lidz, Theodore: "The Family as the Developmental Setting," in Anthony E. James and Cyrille Koupernik (eds.), *The Child in His Family*, Wiley, New York, 1970, pp. 19–39.
2   Ibid., p. 24.
3   Mead, Margaret: "What Is Happening to the American Family?" in *New Emphasis on Cultural Factors*, Family Service Association of America, New York, 1947.
4   Parsons, Talcott: *Family Socialization and Interaction Process*, The Free Press, Glencoe, Ill., 1955, pp. 3–33.
5   Ibid., p. 215.
6   Duvall, Evelyn: *Family Development*, 4th ed., Lippincott, Philadelphia, 1970, pp. 106–132.
7   Albrecht, Ruth: "Intergeneration Parent Patterns," *Journal of Home Economics*, 46:31, January 1954.
8   Hill, Reuben: *Family Development in Three Generations*, Schenkman, Cambridge, Mass., 1970, chap. 4.
9   Hoffman, L. W., and F. Ivan Nye: *Working Mothers*, Jossey Bass, San Francisco, 1974.
10 League of Women Voters of Seattle: *Child Care: Pieces in the Puzzle*, U.S. Department of Labor, Employment Standards, Administration Women's Bureau, April 1974.
11 ———: *Child Care: We Care*, U.S. Department of Labor, Employment Standards, Administration Women's Bureau, 1971.
12 Bronfenbrenner, Urie: "Who Cares for America's Children?," in Victor C. Vaughn, III, and T. Berry Brazelton (eds.), *The Family, Can It be Saved?*, Year Book Medical Publications, Inc., Chicago, 1976, p. 6.
13 Goode, William J.: *After Divorce*, Free Press, Glencoe, Ill., 1956, p. 186.
14 Bronfenbrenner: op. cit., pp. 10–11.

15　Moses, Harold: "A Note on Marital Discord," *Child and Family*, 5(3):54–56, Summer 1966.

16　*Voice for Children*, Day Care and Child Development Council of America, Inc., December 1974, p. 3.

17　Low, Seth, and G. Spindler: *Child Care Arrangements of Working Mothers in the United States*, Children's Bureau Publication no. 461, Washington, D.C., 1968.

18　Robinson, Halbert B.: unpublished paper, 1971.

19　Rowles, Roger: "A Study of Caretakers of Young Babies Born at University Hospital," unpublished research project, University of Washington, 1969.

20　Keister, Mary Elizabeth: *Patterns of Daytime Care of Infants under Three Years of Age*, summary report, Guilford County, N.C., 1965.

21　*American Women*, Report of the President's Commission on the Status of Women, Washington, D.C., 1963.

22　Howard, Marion: "The Young Parent Family," in Victor C. Vaughn, III, and T. Berry Brazelton (eds.), *The Family, Can It Be Saved?*, Year Book Medical Publications, Inc., Chicago, 1976, pp. 240–241.

23　Caldwell, Bettye: "What Does Research Teach Us about Children under Three?" *Children Today*, 1(1):6–11, January 1972.

24　*Sharing*, Consortium of Early Childbearing and Childrearing, National Child Health Service, U.S. Department of Health, Education, and Welfare, Winter 1975.

25　Howard: op. cit., pp. 242–248.

26　Barnard, Kathryn, and M. L. Powell: *Teaching the Mentally Retarded Child: A Family Care Approach*, Mosby, New York, 1972.

27　Provence, Sally: *Guide for the Care of Infants in Groups*, Child Welfare League of America, New York, 1967.

28　Bakwin, H.: "Emotional Deprivation in Infants," *Journal of Pediatrics*, 35:512–521, 1949.

29　Bowlby, John: *Maternal Care and Mental Health*, World Health Organization, Geneva, 1952.

30　———: "The Nature of the Child's Tie to His Mother," *International Journal of Psycho-Analysis*, 38:350–373, 1958.

31　Provence, Sally, and Rose C. Lipton: *Infants in Institutions*, International Universities Press, New York, 1960, pp. 9–52.

32　Spitz, Rene A.: "Hospitalism: An Enquiry into the Genesis of Psychiatric Conditions in Early Childhood," in Ruth S. Eissler, et al., *The Psychoanalytic Study of the Child*, vol. I, International Universities Press, New York, 1945, pp. 53–74.

33　Ribble, Margaret A.: *The Rights of Infants*, Columbia, New York, 1943.

34　Wolins, Martin: "Some Theory and Practice in Child Care: A Cross Cultural View," *Child Welfare*, 42:369–377, 1963.

35　Mavans, Allen E., et al.: "The Children's Hospital in Washington, D.C.," in Laura L. Dittman (ed.), *Early Child Care: The New Perspectives*, Atherton, New York, 1968.

36　Robinson: op. cit.

37　Whittaker, James: *Group Care in America: Review and Preview*, unpublished paper, 1971.

38　Caldwell, Bettye M.: "What Is the Optimal Learning Environment for the Young Child?" *American Journal of Orthopsychiatry*, January 1967, pp. 8–21.

39　Huntington, Dorothy, and Sally Provence (cochairpersons): *Child Development/Day Care Workshop*, Airlie House, Warrenton, Virginia, July 23–30, 1970. (Guiding Principles of Early Child Care, years 1–12.)

40　American Public Health Association Committee on Child Health: *Health Supervision of Young Children*, 3d ed., American Public Health Association, New York, 1960.

41　*Standards for Day Care Services*, Child Welfare League of America, New York, 1964.

42　*Standards for Day Care Centers for Infants and Children under Three Years*, American Academy of Pediatrics, Evanston, Ill., 1971.

43 Huntington, D. S., S. Provence, and Ronald K. Parker (eds.): *Day Care, 2, Serving Infants*, U.S. Department of Health, Education, and Welfare, Office of Child Development, Report no. 72-8, 1972.
44 Day Care and Child Development Council of America: *Statement of Principles*, 1971.
45 Huntington and Provence: op. cit.
46 Ibid.
47 Caldwell, Bettye M., and Julius B. Richmond: "The Children's Center in Syracuse, New York," in Laura L. Dittman (ed.), *Early Child Care: New Perspectives*, Atherton, New York, 1968, p. 342.
48 Caldwell, Bettye: "A Timid Giant Grows Bolder," *Saturday Review*, Feb. 20, 1971, pp. 47–53 and 65–66.

BIBLIOGRAPHY

Brazelton, T. Berry: *Infants and Mothers*, Dell, New York, 1969.

———: *Toddlers and Parents*, Delacorte, New York, 1974.

Care of Children in Day Care Centers, World Health Organization, Geneva, 1964.

Care of Well Children in Day Care Centers and Institutions, Technical Report Series no. 256, World Health Organization, Geneva, 1963.

Class, Morris E.: "Licensing for Child Care—A Preventive Welfare Service," *Children*, September–October 1968.

Deprivation of Maternal Care: A Reassessment of Its Effects, World Health Organization, Geneva, 1962.

Dittman, Laura: *Children in Day Care with Focus on Health*, U.S. Department of Health, Education and Welfare, Children's Bureau, 1967.

——— (ed.): *Early Child Care: The New Perspectives*, Atherton, New York, 1968.

Elardo, Richard, and Betty Pogan: *Perspectives on Infant Day Care*, Southern Association on Children under Six, 1972.

Evans, E. B., and George Saia: *Day Care for Infants*, Beacon, Boston, 1972.

Hazelkorn, Florence (ed.): *Mothers at Risk*, Adelphi University School of Social Work Publications, Garden City, N.Y., 1966.

Hille, Helen M.: *Food for Groups of Young Children Cared for during the Day*, U.S. Department of Health, Education and Welfare, Children's Bureau, 1969.

Howell, Mary C.: "Employed Mothers and Their Families I and II," *Pediatrics*, 52(2), August 1973; 52(3), September 1973.

Keyserling, Mary Dublin: *Windows on Day Care*, National Council of Jewish Women, New York, 1972.

Murphy, Lois B.: "Children under Three: Finding Ways to Stimulate Development," *Children*, March–April 1969, pp. 46–52.

———: *Nutrition and Feeding: Infants and Children under Three in Group Day Care*, U.S. Department of Health, Education and Welfare, 1971.

Provence, Sally: "Children under Three: Finding Ways to Stimulate Development, II," *Children*, March–April 1969, pp. 53–62.

———: "Guide for the Care of Infants in Groups," Child Welfare League of America, New York, 1967.

Recommendations for Day Care Centers for Infants and Children, American Academy of Pediatrics, Evanston, Ill., 1973.

Standards of Child Health Care, American Academy of Pediatrics, Evanston, Ill., 1967.

U.S. Department of Health, Education, and Welfare: *Children Today*, vol. I, January–February 1972. (Formerly entitled *Children*; entire issue devoted to day care for children.)

Walters, James, and Nick Stinnet: "Parent and Child Relationships, A Decade of Research," *Journal of Marriage and the Family*, 33(1), February 1971.

Yarrow, Leon J.: "Maternal Deprivation: Toward an Empirical and Conceptual Reevaluation," *Psychological Bulletin*, 58:459–490, 1961.

PART

FIVE

COMPLICATIONS OF CHILDBEARING AND CHILDREARING

UNIT A

COMPLICATIONS OF CHILDBEARING

29

Psychological and Socioeconomic Implications*

BARBARA CABELA

Complications which occur in or result from any phase of the maternity cycle, whether they affect the pregnant woman, new mother, or the infant, have an impact on everyone closely involved with the family unit. In the home, in the clinic, and in the hospital the nurse is in a strategic position to care and to help; therefore, it is essential to be knowledgeable about the various complications; to be aware of the usual physical, psychological, and socioeconomic sequelae; and to be able to employ skills of assessment, development of a plan of action, implementation, and evaluation. In many instances no other member of the health team has as much knowledge of the total situation or as great

* This chapter was written by the author in her private capacity. No official support or endorsement by the Department of Health, Education and Welfare, Public Health Service, is intended or should be inferred. The author wishes to acknowledge the impact of Florence G. Blake's guidance and support in helping this nurse expand and practice her philosophy of nursing care.

an opportunity to provide care as does the nurse.

Before considering the effects of complications of childbearing upon the infant and family, it is necessary to briefly review the effects of an uncomplicated pregnancy and a healthy, intact baby. Even though these more usual and desirable conditions prevail, the couple may very quickly be aware that all things did not happen exactly as planned nor do the feelings anticipated prior to the pregnancy always arise. The pregnant woman may resent the change in her body. The attractive, valued figure disappears. The new mother who eagerly anticipated motherhood may not feel motherly after delivery. Although she chose to terminate her career, at least temporarily, she may long for the stimulation and satisfaction experienced as a member of the working world. The expectant father may resent his partner's wish to decrease the number of social activities which he formerly enjoyed. The new father may feel responsible for the pain experienced by his partner during labor and delivery. Both parents are often concerned over increasing expenses. The infant may only faintly resemble the idealized baby pictured in the parents' minds prior to delivery. Usually these are minor or temporary problems or disappointments coped with readily by most parents. If their relationship is healthy, they are able to express their feelings and they are able to resolve differences. Consideration of the above, however, should make one begin to think about the potential for the disturbing impact which the complicated pregnancy or the infant who deviates from normality has on the family unit.

COPING WITH STRESS AND CRISIS

The Concept of Coping

Regardless of the nature of the problem and whether it affects the parents, the infant, or both, one major goal of the nurse as well as other members of the health team is to help the family unit cope with the stress or crisis in the most constructive way possible. The concept of coping is sometimes used to describe all adjustment behavior, whether it be maladaptive, maintains equilibrium, or is growth-producing. The use of defense mechanisms such as repression, denial, reaction formation, and rationalization represents an attempt to diminish the recognition or impact of experiences which may be distressing to the individual. They allow the person to avoid dealing fully with unpleasant situations or unacceptable ideas. Although in some instances these mechanisms may be essential for the person to continue functioning, they are, objectively, less healthy ways of handling stress or crisis situations than the positive coping behavior described by some authors. This indicates that the term "coping" is not compatible with maladaptive behavior.

Coping as used in this chapter is defined as adaptive behavior which is reality-oriented, purposeful, and under the control of the individual. It is an active and thoughtful approach used by the person to deal with stress of crisis.[1] Coping behavior is a positive process by which the person maintains equilibrium or grows under disturbing conditions and masters new problem situations. It does not include the mechanisms of defense nor does it have a negative adjustment connotation. The ability to cope is related to past experiences and present resources.

The Nature of Stress and Crisis

Much research has been done on the physical and psychological aspects of stress and crisis. Although a variety of approaches have been used to study stress and crisis and some scientists have emphasized the physical while others concentrated on the psychological, there are some helpful similarities in the research which may be used to provide a framework for understanding what takes place and how to help those affected by the complications of childbearing.

There is difficulty differentiating between stress and crisis in the literature, as the two tend to overlap. Lazarus states that "stress conveys the idea that the person or animal is beset by powerful pressures which greatly tax the adaptive resources of the biological or psychological system."[2] According to Parad and Caplan, "a crisis is a period of disequilibrium overpowering the individual's homeostatic mechanisms."[3] In general, crisis seems to describe an event which is sudden in onset, requires rapid action, tends to establish a demarcation line, and is limited in time. A stress situation, on the other hand, usually develops gradually, demands less in terms of action, is difficult to isolate, and often continues for a prolonged period. Consequently, a crisis situation may be more easily identified and dealt with more readily by those in crisis as well as members of the health team. This places an added burden on members to remain alert for stress-producing situations because stress, when unrelieved, seems to have a greater potential for the development of neurotic behavior patterns.

Hill describes the course of adjustment to crisis graphically as the "truncated form of a roller-coaster."[4] The crisis, which may be dulling initially, is followed by a drop in organization as the individual or group realizes the implications of the event, the lowest point of disorganization. With the initiation of adjustment responses the recovery period begins, and a new level of reorganization is sought. The level of reorganization attained depends on the adequacy of the adjustment made for those involved.[5]

Both stress and crisis situations necessitate changes in behavior if the person is to resume the equivalent level of functioning which was achieved prior to the disturbing event. Adaptation may include altering present behavior patterns, learning and using new behavior, or drastic reorganization of one's goals and life-style. Although certain events tend to produce stress or be viewed as a crisis almost universally, there is wide variation in response to situations both individually and culturally. An event which is stressful for one person or family unit may represent a crisis to a second and create only minor discomfort in a third. These situations represent the extremes; however, it is critical that the nurse and other members of the health team remain open intellectually and emotionally to the patient's and family's subjective views of potentially disturbing occurrences regardless of objective expectations.

GENERAL ASPECTS OF NURSING CARE

Through the nursing care provided, the nurse helps the patient and family unit cope with stress and crisis. Nursing care is composed of four major aspects, or elements. These are assessment, development of a plan of action, implementation, and evaluation.

Assessment

Assessment includes two primary components, observation and interpretation, which result in a nursing diagnosis. Observation includes listening attentively, looking perceptively, and eliciting responses purposefully. Information about both the physical and psychological status of the patient is collected. What is the patient saying and with what inflection? How does the patient or family member appear? What is the degree of muscle tone? Is there much or little facial expression? Which questions are answered and ignored? What is the response to encouragement of verbalization?

As the nurse gathers data, the process of interpretation is also begun. Comparison of the different kinds of information obtained is made for consistency. Does the patient's appearance correlate with verbal expression? The nurse analyzes behaviors singly and as part of the whole picture. Lethargy may indicate depression or result from physical exhaustion. Cultural patterns and socioeconomic factors are reflected in the patient's behavior and responses. The Mexican-American woman who smiles cheerfully and agrees readily with all suggestions may be responding to what she believes are the dominant culture's expectations.

Based on knowledge and analysis of observations, the nurse formulates one or more tentative hypotheses (nursing diagnoses) about the situation. These take into account both the nurse's and the patient's perception of the situation, and the patient's problems, needs, strengths, and limitations in dealing with it.

Included as an integral part of nursing assessment is validation of the nursing diagnosis. Validation is accomplished in a number of ways. The nurse encourages the patient or family members to expand a statement they have made by saying something like, "Tell me more about that." The nurse verbalizes an interpretation to the patient for confirmation or denial. It can be suggested that other people often feel a certain way under similar circumstances. The nurse compares the findings with those of other caretakers and begins planning nursing intervention with the patient and family.

Development of a Plan of Action

Assessment of the status and behavior of those for whom the nurse is providing care forms the foundations upon which plans for nursing intervention are made. Nursing care plans are written descriptions of nursing diagnoses, needs, and goals; patient and family strengths and limitations; and care components. The nursing diagnosis encompasses or is expanded by a set of nursing care problems to be addressed through nursing intervention. Patient needs based on nursing assessment and discussion with patient and family are described. Nursing intervention is planned to help the patient and family meet these needs. Mutual goals of patient, family, and nurse give direction and provide a means for determining the correctness of assessment and effectiveness of intervention. Listing strengths and limitations of the patient and family in coping with the stress or crisis enhances the nurse's ability to select care components (nursing interventions) which utilize strengths as fully as possible and diminish the effect of patient and family limitations. Finally, specific nursing care measures or interventions are outlined. These are nursing actions designed to enable the patient and family to cope with the situation as effectively as possible. They may include doing things for the patient at least temporarily, but the desired outcome is for the patient and family to gain or regain the highest level of independent functioning possible.

Implementation

Nursing intervention is the implementation of the nursing care plan. However, the nursing care plan undergoes continuous development; and observation, interpretation, and validation are never completed. Living, whether it occurs in the hospital or outside of it, is dynamic. Therefore assessment and evaluation are ongoing processes which are used to determine when a plan of nursing care requires modification. Only then can nursing care promote growth for the patient and family and provide maximum opportunities for the nurse to learn.

What is nursing intervention or implementation of the nursing care plan and what does it entail? It is the purposeful use of self—of one's knowledge, past experiences, and skills—and of prescribed medications and treatments to help the patient regain the previous level of physical health if this is possible, and to enhance the patient's and family's ability to cope with stress-producing or crisis-inducing experiences. Implementation is action, the physical laying on of hands or the application of principles of psychology, sociology, and anthropology to the process of interaction with the patient. In most instances it is a blending of the three. Nursing action is a stimulus which brings about a response or reaction which requires the use of another element of the nursing process—evaluation.

Evaluation

Evaluation is the process of deciding if and to what extent nursing care has been effective. Are the patient's needs being met? Is progress being made toward the achievement of the goals? Are the patient and the family unit coping with the stress or crisis? Evaluation often results in a recycling of all or part of the process of nursing care. Continued observation usually yields new information. Behavioral response to nursing care may indicate a need for different interpretation and intervention. Failure of the patient to make satisfactory progress may require alterations in nursing diagnosis, care plan, and action, and in the evaluation which follows. This process of nursing care continues for whatever period of time the nurse-patient relationship continues and regardless of whether there is frequent, prolonged contact, as in the hospital setting, or intermittent contact, as occurs frequently in the community.

THE NURSE AND THE NURSING PROCESS

During the process of nursing care there is, in addition to the direct effect of planned intervention, a secondary and vitally important indirect effect. This effect is related to the person of the nurse. Culturally, socially, experientially, who the nurse is colors how the care is provided. Attitudes, values, and beliefs influence the nurse's behavior toward patients, often without awareness of either patient or nurse. Much is written about why it is necessary for the nurse to understand and accept the patient. It is also important that the nurse gain increasingly more understanding of self. Nurses need to know who they are and where they are. Achieving self-awareness and recognizing the impact of self in the patient-nurse interaction is difficult because it forces one to look honestly at oneself, and this may be painful. However, nurses cannot hope to understand and accept the recipient of nursing care until they are able to do it first for themselves, and respect how it modifies personal nursing ability as well as patient response.

Another essential consideration in regard to the nursing process is the fact that it is not only the patient and family unit who are acted upon and affected. Nursing care involves interaction among people, and through the experience the nurse can also grow, learn, and change. If the nurse takes this opportunity to recognize how the provision of nursing care affects self, the reward of sharing the experience will enhance the person of the nurse, and the patient will receive a higher level of care. Nursing care, then, involves interaction between a minimum of two people, and failure to recognize the implications this has for the outcome is very much like operating in a vacuum.

COMPLICATIONS OF CHILDBEARING

Complications of the childbearing process are a potential source of stress or crisis for the pregnant woman or new mother and her family unit. The nurse attempts to help those involved cope with and emerge from the experience at the highest health level possible.

The term family unit as used in this chapter refers to the people who are closely tied to the patient emotionally whether or not they are related by blood or marriage. The definition of family and the individual's attachment to its different members will vary culturally. Currently in our society, the meaning of family is changing and is inconsistent across groups. The important consideration for the nurse is recognition and inclusion of significant others in the nursing process.

Complications of the childbearing process may occur in any phase of the cycle from conception until mother and infant have been assessed as healthy or normal. The particular kinds of stress or crisis and how the individual and the family unit cope with these complications as well as the therapeutic nursing intervention will vary and are influenced by several factors: the nature and severity of the complication, the phase of the cycle during which it occurs, the person(s) affected, the sociocultural background of the patient and family unit, the strengths and limitations of those involved, and their previous coping ability.

Complications of Early Pregnancy

Spontaneous abortion is one of the potential problems of the first trimester. During this early stage of pregnancy the woman has probably not yet experienced the feeling of movement and life within her body. Consequently she has not developed the same feeling of attachment to the embryo or fetus and the sense of the full reality of pregnancy which will evolve during the second trimester. Even though pregnancy has been confirmed and the woman has noted the early signs of pregnancy such as amenorrhea, fullness and tingling in her breasts, and unexpected episodes of nausea and vomiting, she usually does not have the feeling that "this is really happening to me."

Loss of the embryo or fetus through spontaneous abortion during the first trimester, therefore, involves different responses than does a stillbirth or newborn death. Particularly if this is a first pregnancy, the woman is likely to question her womanhood. Despite the current diminishing of the tendency to equate womanhood and fulfillment with motherhood, many women are still emotionally and culturally tied to the older concept. Even if spontaneous abortion does not threaten her status as a woman, she may undergo a loss of self-esteem or a weakening of self-concept. She may well feel something is wrong with her. Why is her body incapable of completing this pregnancy? If the pregnancy was desired, the woman who aborts experiences frustration at not reaching her goal of motherhood. She will be concerned and more apprehensive about the outcome of future pregnancies. She may wonder whether or not she will become pregnant again. There may be guilt feelings related to real or imagined failure to comply with restrictions and/or taboos imposed by pregnancy and the wish that she were not pregnant which every woman has at some time during her pregnancy. Guilt feelings are further increased if the pregnancy is unwanted. In this instance, the feeling of relief at its termination may provide another source of recrimination. Spontaneous abortion may also cause the pregnant woman anxiety or fear for her own health or life. In the event of massive hemorrhage which may accompany incomplete abortion, there is sufficient evidence to support her fears.

The woman's partner also has feelings of his own to handle. His primary concern is likely to be for his partner's welfare and safety. "Is she going to be all right?" is his question, whether verbalized or not. Should death result from or be related to any phase of the pregnancy, he may experience remorse as the person responsible for the pregnancy.

If he was unhappy about the pregnancy, he may, like his partner, feel responsible for the loss of the embryo or fetus. The male's sense of manhood is less vulnerable to the threat occasioned by spontaneous abortion than is his partner's sense of womanhood. Manhood is apparently related to sexual function and the ability to impregnate. However, production of an infant with defects may have similar implications for both partners. Another factor which may influence the attitude or response of the male whose partner aborts spontaneously is his disappointment over the loss and a need to blame someone. If this need exists, he may hold the physician responsible or he may blame his partner even though there is no reason to blame either. It is essential when dealing with psychological aspects of distressing situations to remember that feelings and emotions may be illogical.

Guilt Feelings

Feelings of guilt are frequently associated with complications of the childbearing process. When people are faced with unexpected, distressing events such as spontaneous abortion or the birth of an infant with a congenital anomaly, the frustration experienced often seeks release through determination of cause. Responses and feelings dating back to their childhood years are likely to be aroused. During the socialization process the child learns cause and effect relationships very early. A great number of behaviors take on a "right" or "good" versus "wrong" or "bad" connotation. If the child is "right" or "good," rewards are forthcoming. If the child is "wrong," or "bad," punishment follows. As the superego develops the child becomes the regulator of self. Even when the "wrong" or "bad" is not discovered by parents, the child feels guilty and blameworthy. Adults to a greater or lesser degree are subject to remnants of the early training process. At a time when anxiety is high and emotion affects intellectual processes, adults are particularly vulnerable to guilt feelings.

Guilt is often expressed or alluded to verbally. "What did I do wrong?" or "I wonder if I took some medicine I shouldn't have," indicate feelings of responsibility for the abortion of the fetus or for the occurrence of a congenital defect in an infant. Sometimes these statements are related to a specific incident. In other instances they reflect a more general feeling that "there must be a reason for this to have happened." In order to help the person express these feelings and work through them the nurse can encourage the person to verbalize more about the concern. Appropriate responses to these kinds of questions or statements might include: "I wonder why you feel you did something wrong," or, "You've asked why this happened several times. Is there something specific that concerns you?" Nursing intervention is designed to help the parents talk about and deal with their own feelings. It is rarely helpful for the nurse to speculate about possible causes.

There are instances when the nurse should not attempt to handle the problems that are uncovered. Help from other professionals with more background in psychological and psychiatric counseling should be obtained when defensive behavior such as withdrawal and hyperactivity are severe or prolonged. Additional help is also indicated when there is evidence that guilt is caused by attempted abortion or drug use during the pregnancy or when the abortion or infant with defects is perceived as deserved punishment for infractions unrelated to the pregnancy.

Guilt may be particularly upsetting and difficult to handle when the complication occurs in an unwed pregnancy. Although pregnancy outside legal marriage is accepted more readily than in previous years, it remains a moral issue for many people. These attitudes tend to heighten the woman's and sometimes the man's guilt feelings. It, too, is a situation for potential perception of the complication as punishment by both the couple and others.

Economic Factors

At times complications of early pregnancy create economic problems for the couple. Added stress can be anticipated if they do not have health insurance, either private or through governmental agencies, to cover expenses, or if the female partner's employment is a major source of income and she is unable to work for a period of time. Included among the former are a group of people in our society who have marginal incomes. They tend to manage as long as there are no major (for them) unexpected expenses. Unless they are employed by an organization which provides or requires health insurance, this item tends to be left out of the budget. Whether the problem is spontaneous abortion or total breakdown of the car needed for travel to work, the expense is too great for them to handle and is a source of stress. Many are faced with prolonged periods of payments to hospitals or loan companies which constantly threaten their frail financial balance. Others are unable to deal with this added stress and feel hopeless and helpless in their struggle for self-maintenance. The male's self-esteem is particularly vulnerable under these conditions, and his partner, as well as others, can further decrease his feelings of self-worth by their reaction and because of their own anxiety.

This kind of situation is especially difficult for a young couple early in family life. It imposes an additional stress factor at a time when there are already many adjustments to be made and when their resources for dealing with stress and crisis as a couple are limited. The nurse cannot ignore this aspect of the lives of the people for whom care is given. The nurse will often have to involve other professionals and agencies in helping the family find and use resources, but the recognition of potential economic stress and the effect it has on the patient and family unit are well within the province of nursing care.

Nursing Care

What then are the implications for nursing care in spontaneous abortion and other complications of early pregnancy which result in loss of the embryo or fetus and which may cause some concern for the pregnant woman's health or life? The nurse's initial contact with the woman is often in an emergency setting or an unplanned hospital admission. The primary responsibility of the health care team is to ensure the survival of the pregnant woman. However, during the period of emergency care, the nurse has an opportunity to observe the reactions of the patient and her partner or family. Appropriate reassurance of both is essential. The nurse who *makes* time to listen to the expressed fears of the patient and family can help them sort out the realistic fears from those which are not. This allows the nurse to increase people's ability to cope by explaining what is being done and will be done to care for the patient. It also provides specific help which can be related to the source of fear and anxiety rather than stating such platitudes as, "Everything will be fine," which is generally not helpful. If verbal expression of fear is absent, the nurse can make use of behavioral cues such as facial expression or increased motor activity. The nurse might say, "You look worried. Tell me about it," or, "You look upset. Let's talk about your concerns." If the father of the child or the family is separated from the patient for a period of time, it is important that they be given information about the condition of the patient at intervals. This gives those waiting accurate information with which to deal and lets them know that the health team cares about and understands what they are experiencing.

Following the initial emergency care for spontaneous abortion (discussed in Chapter 30), the potential problems discussed earlier need to be considered to determine how the woman and family unit are coping with the event and its ramifications. In order to plan and carry out appropriate nursing care, the nurse needs to observe and make interpretations about the following: the relationship and communication of the couple or of the patient and significant other, patient and family source and use of support, expression of feelings by the couple related to self-concept, patient reaction to future pregnancy, patient and family response to loss, expression of guilt feelings by the couple, and socioeconomic and cultural data.

A nursing diagnosis based on the information obtained through observation and interpretation can then be made and appropriate nursing intervention planned. If the woman appears depressed and has talked little about what she has experienced, the plan might include provision for one nurse to give most of the patient's care, allowing this nurse to spend extra time with the patient and discuss with the patient feelings common to others in her situation. If the patient is able to disclose feelings of unworthiness, is grieving, or perceives a second pregnancy as too risky, the nurse has an opportunity to help the patient deal constructively with her thoughts and feelings. Then she can begin to direct her energies toward resumption of previous activities and development of new goals. However, if the patient does not show signs of coping, the nurse needs to involve other members of the health team, help initiate appropriate referrals, and aid the family in planning for continuing care. It is important that hospital personnel consider the patient's possible need for care in other than the hospital setting. Hospitalization is usually an extremely brief experience, and discharge rarely coincides with resolution of the patient's problems. The nurse, regardless of the employment setting, has a responsibility to help families plan for, and in some instances arrange for, continuing care.

Complications during the Second and Third Trimesters

Complications which arise during and after the 4th or 5th month of pregnancy pose different kinds of problems for the pregnant woman and family unit. Consequently, although the theoretical basis of nursing care is unchanged, the nurse will be dealing with stress and crisis initiated by other types of problems. It is usually near the end of the 4th month that the pregnant woman experiences the first sensation of fetal movement. This is probably the single most significant and confirming sign of pregnancy for the woman. Other signs of pregnancy become more apparent than they were during the first trimester. These factors increase the sense of the reality of approaching motherhood and strengthen feelings of attachment for the fetus. Early feelings of disappointment or denial of pregnancy, unless deep-seated, have to an extent usually been resolved, and the pregnant couple begin to prepare physically and psychologically for the birth of the baby.

There is a second aspect of the later stages of pregnancy which also influences the consideration of complications. Potential threats to the woman's health and life increase as she nears term. Depending on one's viewpoint, the pregnancy itself may complicate a pre-existing condition, such as cardiac disease. Complications during the third trimester of pregnancy also have potential for causing ambivalent feelings in the pregnant woman and her family unit. Fear and anxiety about the health and life of the pregnant woman and her unborn child may arouse conflicting emotions. At times the family or some members of it are faced with making a choice which will provide a relative advantage for either the woman or fetus in terms of health and life. This is a difficult situation for everyone.

As with spontaneous abortion, guilt is commonly generated in the pregnant couple by any threat to the fetus. Because of the increased danger for his partner, the male is more likely to feel deep concern especially if the procreation of a child was of greater importance to him than to his partner. Failure to obtain early antepartum care and a negative response of health professionals to this omission also heighten the feelings of guilt.

Feelings of resentment toward the father may be engendered by complications of pregnancy. Again, the need to blame someone may be apparent. "You did this to me," or, "If it weren't for the pregnancy, I would be okay" are often nonverbalized but behaviorally expressed feelings of the pregnant woman whose health or life is threatened even temporarily by complications of pregnancy. These feelings pose a serious problem to communication and mutual support. If delivery is accomplished successfully for mother and baby, remnants of these feelings, if not coped with adequately, may negatively influence the development of a healthy mother-child relationship. They also may carry over to future pregnancies.

The woman's self-esteem may decrease as a result of her inability to carry out successfully a "normal" function of women. Both partners are likely to see themselves as less worthy if the potential danger to the fetus is great. There is often a feeling of "There must be something wrong with me" on the part of both. This phenomenon is particularly evident among individuals who have experienced limited or little success in life.

Economic factors are more often of greater concern with complications which occur in the later stages of pregnancy. Problems such as toxemia and cardiac disease usually require termination of employment. Increased medical care often associated with periods of hospitalization adds to the financial burden. The couple may have planned carefully with usual expenses in mind and the benefit of the woman's salary until very near term. This kind of budget may be destroyed by complications of the second and third trimesters. Insurance benefits may not cover the complications of pregnancy which affect either the mother or infant.

Fear for the survival or normality of the fetus is a very realistic concern when complications such as placenta previa or premature labor occur. The nurse and other members of the health team must be able to give the woman and family unit accurate information. Honest appraisal of the situation and communication with the woman and family, and respect for their intelligence and ability to cope, help to establish a feeling of trust. Allowing or encouraging the patient to talk about her fears for the unborn child often enables her to gain perspective, work through feelings, utilize support, and cope with the stress or crisis. If survival of the fetus is highly unlikely, as with early premature labor or signs of severe fetal distress, anticipatory grief work may be initiated by the woman and/or her partner. Whether or not this improves coping ultimately depends on the extent to which it is accomplished and the eventual outcome of the pregnancy. Anticipatory grief work will be discussed in more detail later in this chapter.

Birth of an Infant Who Deviates from Normality

The birth of an ill or premature infant or a baby with a defect confronts the family unit with a situation they may have feared throughout the pregnancy. If the pregnancy was desired and the infant's arrival eagerly anticipated, the parents are faced with concern for the infant's survival or reduced potential for normal development at a time when they expected to feel pleasure and fulfillment. If the pregnancy was unwanted, the crisis for the mother and father may be even greater because of guilt feelings and/or interpretation of the outcome as punishment.

Parents of infants who are seriously ill or who have a major defect that is apparent at or shortly after birth invariably ask themselves one or more of the following questions: "Will the infant survive?" "What residual effects will there be?" "Will we be able to take care of the child?" "How will this complication change our plans and goals?" "Will we be able to afford the care this child needs, now and later?" "Why did this happen to me (us)?" "Did I (we) do something to cause the problem?" Other questions and concerns will also be formulated in the minds of the parents, but in general the above are the most common.

Although these concerns are generally felt by parents, they may not be expressed verbally. The failure of mothers and/or fathers to verbalize these questions and feelings is a warning signal to the nurse which indicates the need for further investigation.

Denial

Denial is one of the defense mechanisms employed by parents when told their infant has a congenital defect, particularly one in which most of the signs and symptoms are internal. Denial is an inability to acknowledge the reality situation because it is extremely painful or distressing. Instead, the opposite of the real facts is accepted as true. Denial serves a protective function initially. It allows parents time to gather their resources and find more constructive ways of dealing with an unpleasant reality. However, its continued use in the presence of evidence to the contrary is an unhealthy sign. Denial

is often difficult for nurses and other members of the health team to handle. It may result in hostile challenges of professional knowledge and ability. In addition, it is easy to reinforce the parents' denial by agreeing with them in regard to negative signs of defect. Generally, nursing intervention encourages parents to deal with the reality of the situation following the initial impact of the stress or crisis. Grief work over the loss of the expected normal child must be done, and feelings of frustration, guilt, and disappointment expressed. When parents have begun to deal honestly with their feelings, information regarding corrective measures provides them with knowledge which they can use in coping with the problem. When coping mechanisms are absent or seriously diminished, attempts to break down the defense mechanism of denial may leave the person unable to function. In this instance additional help is needed.

Nursing Responsibilities

The nurse caring for the family of the infant with a problem such as respiratory distress syndrome or congenital heart disease must remain aware of and plan to meet the needs common to most new families as well as aid other team members in meeting these needs. All mothers need to talk about their labor and delivery experience to clear up any misconceptions they may have and to express their feelings about the experience. In this way the mother is able to finish the psychological work of labor and delivery and move away from the experience with a realistic picture of what took place. Hopefully she can also feel that she is a worthwhile person.

The mother who has delivered a baby who deviates from normality has all the usual needs as well as other needs for care resulting from her anxiety about the infant's fate and the possibility of feelings of decreased self-esteem related to the production of an infant with defects. If concerns of members of the health team as well as family and friends are focused mainly on the infant, the mother may be reluctant to discuss those experiences and feelings which center directly on her. The nurse must include the psychological work of normal labor and delivery in the patient care plan and demonstrate a genuine interest in and concern for the mother's well-being.

In addition, the nurse needs to observe the father's behavior and his interaction with his partner carefully to determine whether or not he is able to provide the love and support he would normally give to her. He, too, may be overwhelmed with concern for the infant and the uncertain future and thus may be blind to his partner's needs or be unable to meet those of which he is aware. If this is happening, the nurse and other members of the team must support the father until he becomes ready and able to provide the love and support his partner requires.

There are, of course, many instances when a crisis of this nature brings marriage partners closer together and strengthens their ability to cope. However, this is far from universal and seems to be a function of the strength of the relationship and the success of the couple in coping with previous crises. It is imperative that the nurse make careful observations and interpretations of the behavior of the father and mother in relation to themselves and each other. In this way there is a basis for making a nursing diagnosis and planning appropriate nursing intervention.

The birth of an infant who deviates from normality often precipitates an economic crisis for the mother and father. Medical care of the seriously affected infant is extremely costly and may be prolonged for weeks, months, or even a lifetime. Not all health insurance policies cover unusual care for the newborn, and it is possible for families to incur debts under these circumstances which they are never able to pay. At times sufficient outside resources to help the family do not exist. However, there are many resources for financial aid such as handicapped children's programs and tax-supported hospitals. Referral or making arrangements for help is one aspect of nursing responsibility. Depending on the setting, this may require nothing more of the nurse than referral to the social service department, or it may entail locating an appropriate resource and helping the family learn to use it. Nurses and physicians need knowledge of available resources and awareness of the extent of financial liability incurred by the family as a result of care provided.

Relationship Formation with Parents and Siblings

The birth of an infant who deviates from normality is usually a crisis situation for the family unit, particularly if there is little hope of the child approaching normal appearance, intellectual ability, or physical functioning. The response to the infant usually includes elements of rejection and overprotection. Either response may be dominant, and both have serious implications for the satisfactory adjustment of the parents, child, siblings, and other family members. Inability to accept the infant who deviates from normality distorts the development of mother-child and father-child relationships. Parents may overtly neglect the infant or covertly punish the infant for the distress and problems precipitated by the birth. Necessary rearrangement of financial priorities and disruption of major goals may be blamed on the child. Guilt feelings caused by the birth of the infant who deviates from normality as well as the parents' reaction to this child may result in parents unnecessarily giving up important goals and providing less in time and material goods for other children in order to do every-thing possible for the child with a defect. When this happens siblings feel loss and resentment; this distorts the sibling relationship with the new baby and may negatively affect their own growth and development.

Some families are unable to cope with a crisis of this nature and break up under the strain. Other families remain intact physically but at a tremendous emotional cost to all. Families faced with this kind of crisis need help and support from many sources. Health professionals, clergymen, extended family members, friends, and employers contribute to successful resolution. Nursing care which increases the family's coping ability utilizes individual and family strengths, allows for expression of feelings, supports and guides appropriately, and helps the family deal with reality. Teaching the family specific techniques for providing the special care needed by their child increases their confidence and ability to cope. Care for these families is initiated with the birth of the infant and continues after discharge from the hospital. In varying ways and degrees it will be necessary for an indefinite period of time. The quality of early care, however, is extremely important and has tremendous implications for healthy adjustment and later care.

DEVELOPMENT OF PARENTING BEHAVIOR AND SKILLS

Maternal Attachment and Motherliness

Motherliness or mothering behavior in the human being is the result of a complex interweaving of physiological processes, including hormonal regulation, and psychological factors influenced by the mother's own mothering, environment, and culture.[6] Additionally, reciprocal interaction with each child alters the expression of motherliness. Intense maternal feelings are seldom experienced at the time of delivery or on initial contact with the infant. Maternal feelings appear to develop gradually and partially as a result of early contacts between mother and infant.

Affectional bonding between mother and infant begins during the antepartum period and continues after the birth of the baby. Identified significant events are confirmation of pregnancy, awareness of fetal movement, birth of the baby, seeing the baby, eye-to-eye contact between mother and infant, and touching the baby.[7] Events occurring in the immediate postpartum period may critically affect maternal attachment. Mothers seek eye-to-eye contact with their infants, and newborn babies have a remarkable ability to attend and follow during the first hours of life.[8] Klaus et al.[9] studied normal newborns and their mothers during their initial contact $\frac{1}{2}$ to $13\frac{1}{2}$ hours after delivery. They found a rapid progression from maternal fingertip touching of the infant's extremities to maternal palming of the infant's trunk and encompassing contact over a 10-minute period. Within 5 minutes there was marked increase in eye-to-eye contact. In the first hours and days after birth mothers become more relaxed and secure in handling their infants. Cuddling behavior increases and the mother talks to her infant. In many ways the new mother begins to identify this baby as a member of the family and as a distinct person. Progressive maternal attachment is reflected in the mother's interest in learning to care for her infant and to plan for the infant's care at home.

Increasing understanding of the process of maternal attachment suggests that early and/or prolonged separation as well as infant behavior in response to initial maternal overtures may have serious implications for the establishment of maternal attachment.

Fatherhood and Fatherliness

Fatherhood, too, has biologic as well as emotional roots. The instinctual drive for survival is the biologic basis of fatherhood.[10] Interwoven with this instinctual drive are the father's developmental experiences, his identification with his own father, the father's identification with this child, and his ability to accept the role of protector and provider.[11] Fatherliness develops in part as a result of each father's initial dependency on his mother. The quality of mothering he received as an infant and child as well as how he accomplished the developmental tasks of overcoming maternal dependence and identifying with the father and his roles affect the development of fatherliness. Fatherliness is expanded in interaction with the child. It develops as the father touches, holds, and becomes confident in caring for the child. Positive responses from the infant cement the bond even further, and as the father plays with and teaches his own child, the feelings of fatherliness grow.

INADEQUATE PARENTING

Inadequate parenting may result from the failure of maternal attachment or the failure to develop fatherliness. Inadequate parenting is the frequent inability of one or both parents to meet the basic needs of the child for food, physical care, protection, and healthy emotional development; it may also involve inflicting physical injury on the child.

Potential Outcomes for the Child

Children whose parents do not meet their needs adequately may be affected in one or more of the following ways. The child may be physically injured, suffering bruises, burns, or fractures. Severe undernourishment or failure to thrive may occur. The child may be sexually abused or exploited. Medical care may not be obtained for a child with an obvious illness. Adequate shelter or sleeping facilities may not be provided. The child may be emotionally neglected, and miss out on experiences which usually result in the child feeling secure, loved, wanted, and a worthwhile person. Emotional disturbance may occur in the child as a result of frequent stress and crisis and high levels of tension and frustration in the home. Educational programs or schooling may be neglected.

Characteristics of Abusing and Neglecting Parents

Investigators studying child abuse and neglect have identified behavioral and situational characteristics of abusing and neglecting parents.[12–14] Those who abuse and neglect children tend to be "normal" people unable to handle stress and crisis appropriately in a critical period. Abusive acts are rarely willful, deliberate, or intentional. In most instances abusive and neglecting parents are not mentally ill.

Many times parents are emotionally immature and inexperienced and are unable to cope adequately even with everyday tensions and anxieties. Some parents have limited intellectual capacity and are unable to provide the complex environment children need for healthy growth and development. Marital conflict may result if siblings use one parent against the other parent, or may be caused by other stress-inducing conditions in the home. Abusing and neglecting parents may be repeating a family pattern in which they were abused or neglected as children. Inadequate parenting may occur in families who become trapped in a continuous state of crisis. Use of alcohol or other drugs to cope with stress and crisis may be underlying factors. Inability to seek and use help and support from others is often found. Abusing and neglecting parents frequently have difficulty dealing with any criticism of their parenting capabilities and often make unrealistic performance and behavior demands on the child. In some instances one observes the child "caring" for the parent.

Early Identification and Prevention

Indications of potential parenting problems are often discernible in the antepartum and perinatal periods. An unwanted pregnancy or one in which an unsuccessful abortion attempt was made is a potential problem situation. Couples who experience multiple problems which they are unable to handle adequately or resolve during the antepartum period, including significant family discord, may need help. Failure to make specific plans for the baby and infant care, or unrealistic anxiety about the outcome of pregnancy and the mother's or parent's ability to care for the infant, are also significant indicators.

During the labor, delivery, and postpartum period the potential for inadequate parenting may be recognized. Negative attitudes or feelings in the mother or father about the unborn child should be further explored. Labor and delivery which are experienced as extremely difficult and in which the pregnant woman is unable to utilize support and/or is inadequately supported by her partner may leave the new mother with many negative feelings which color her developing relationship with her infant. In the postpartum period, failure to progress toward maternal attachment as described earlier is another warning signal to the health care team. Most mothers become more relaxed and comfortable in handling their infants. They begin to identify the infant as a member of the family, discovering characteristics in the infant

which resemble their own, the father's, or those of other relatives. They are interested in learning to care for their infant and plan for the baby's care at home. Disturbance in this pattern or identification of primarily negative characteristics in the infant suggest that maternal attachment is not progressing well.

No single indicator is predictive of later child abuse or neglect. However, the health care team needs to be alert for early signs of difficulty and has a responsibility to gather additional data and follow up or arrange for further care when they have evidence of potential inadequate parenting.

Intervention Techniques

Early intervention and help when signs of inadequate parenting are present may prevent later child abuse and neglect. Counseling of one or both parents by understanding, helpful professionals often results in growth of self-confidence and parenting skills. Counseling should be oriented toward strengthening the parents' positive abilities for child care and protection. Ongoing instruction in child care and childrearing techniques and provision of models for healthy parenting often enable parents to become increasingly skillful in caring for their infant. Helping the parents to identify supporting people or arranging for a warm, caring person to visit the home and become a friend to a mother who is isolated helps to meet the parent(s) need for care. Provision of day care, baby-sitting, or other alternate child care services allow the parent to get out from under when the pressures are great and/or provide time to pursue their other interests. Help in solving socioeconomic difficulties from established agencies or through advocacy can remove or decrease sources of stress and crisis.

In most communities there are a variety of agencies which provide one or more of the above services. Community health nursing, child welfare programs, mental health centers, and homemaker services, as well as clinic and private medical care, are available in many smaller communities and provide a nucleus for ongoing care for parents in need of assistance. Identification and referral of those who show signs of inadequate parenting and coordination of care and services in the community are critical factors in the prevention of child abuse and neglect and the provision of needed services. Agencies need to work together, often designating that person who seems most successful in reaching the family as the primary care person.

In larger communities there are often specialized services for problems of child abuse and neglect. Interdisciplinary child abuse teams, hot lines, crisis nurseries or centers, and family day care or live-in care may be available. Personnel providing these services are knowledgeable about child abuse, neglect, and treatment and may be able to provide needed services or help select appropriate services for particular families. When actual child abuse or neglect is suspected or known, law enforcement and judicial authorities are also involved. Ideally they are included in the community core group of people concerned with inadequate parenting and child abuse and neglect. Almost any community could have a team of people from the public and private sector involved in planning, education, coordination, and policy making directed toward the prevention, identification, and early treatment of child abuse and neglect.

COMPLICATIONS RESULTING IN DEATH OF THE INFANT

Death of a newborn is difficult for parents and professional health workers alike to accept. If the infant has serious defects or is in danger of death at an early age, feelings are ambivalent and people try to rationalize the death. However, it is still a tragic event because of the sharp contrast between the occurrence and the expectation.

Material which has been covered earlier is applicable to this situation. Guilt feelings, loss of self-esteem, depression, withdrawal, inability to communicate effectively are common following the death of a newborn. Nursing care consists of the same basic elements. Support and appropriate intervention are essential. Although grief has been mentioned previously in this chapter, the grief reaction and grieving process have not yet been dealt with in depth.

Grief and the Grieving Process

Grief is a normal physical and psychological reaction to loss. The loss may be of a loved person or an object for which the individual has developed strong attachments; it may be loss of a body part or function or a subjective loss of love or self-esteem. The loss itself, regardless of the object, apparently triggers a grief reaction. Although much research has been done on grief and grieving, Lindemann's classic study still forms the basis for identifying the characteristic symptoms and course of acute grief.[15] He lists the symptoms of the normal grief reaction as "(1) somatic distress, (2) preoccupation with the image of the deceased, (3) guilt, (4) hostile reactions, and (5) loss of patterns of conduct."[16] Recovery from an acute grief reaction and the amount of time required depend on the person's ability to do the grief work. Successful grief work requires that the person allow himself to feel the distress caused by the loss and to express these feelings. It involves "emancipation from the bondage to the deceased, readjustment to the environment in which the deceased is missing, and the formation of new relationships."[17] If the person is able to do the necessary grief work and the grief reaction is uncomplicated, the usual duration is 4 to 6 weeks.[18]

Even though Lindemann's work deals primarily with grief occasioned by the death of a loved person, his concepts and observations are applicable to grief resulting from other kinds of loss. The grieving process and grief work have many implications for those concerned with the psychological aspects of complications of the childbearing process. Grief reactions may follow death of the embryo, fetus, or infant; death of the mother; loss of self-esteem due to inability to carry the fetus to term or due to production of an infant with defects; surgical removal of one or more of the female reproductive organs; and loss of the anticipated healthy infant with the birth of an infant who deviates from normality. In these instances a grief reaction in the woman and her partner should be anticipated by the nurse and other members of the health team. Nursing intervention should be geared to helping the family unit through the grieving process. Because the period of hospitalization is often brief, appropriate referral and follow-up in the community is essential. Initial emotional distress and expression of feelings should be present shortly after the stress or crisis situation. Absence of appropriate reaction should alert the hospital caretakers to the need for additional care.

If the woman and the family unit are experiencing and expressing the emotion associated with loss and grief, their potential for carrying out the necessary grief work is good. The person or persons deeply affected by the loss face the three major tasks outlined by Lindemann: (1) They must break the ties to the lost object or person. The parents of the newborn who dies must return home empty-handed and put away the clothing and furniture prepared for the baby. They have to deal with the fact that the pregnancy is over and the outcome was unsuccessful. (2) They must adapt to the altered environment. The parents of an infant born with an abnormality must grieve for the anticipated normal infant. In his place they must learn to accept and love an infant whose care may be complex and time-consuming, who may be in danger of death now or at some later time, and whose condition may require expensive care and equipment. (3) Finally they must develop new attachments. The woman who aborts spontaneously and feels her self-concept and her womanhood threatened by this event must recognize her other talents and abilities as a person and as a woman. She may plan to resume a successful career which previously brought many satisfactions or look forward to another pregnancy at a later time.

In addition to the grief reaction precipitated by actual loss there is another type of grief, anticipatory grief, which occurs with potential loss such as when a soldier leaves for war or during a critical illness in a loved person.[19] Anticipatory grief is a protective mechanism which allows the person to prepare for the crisis or loss in advance and plan for his adjustment to the loss. All of the symptoms of the acute grief reaction may be present. When the actual loss does occur, the normal grief reaction is diminished, and the loss is often accepted as inevitable and probably for the best. Statements such as, "At least he isn't suffering anymore," or, "She wouldn't have been normal," verbally indicate anticipatory grief work has been done. However, if the expected loss does not happen and anticipatory grief work has taken place, the person is faced with another stress or crisis. The emotional ties which have been broken must be rebuilt. Changed plans and altered goals must be rearranged to again include the surviving person.

Anticipatory grief can occur with some complications of the childbearing process. If the pregnancy has been difficult and there has been concern for the survival of the fetus, particularly in the later stages of pregnancy, anticipatory grief work may have been accomplished. To protect themselves from the impact of a fetal death near term or a stillbirth, the pregnant woman and her partner may have prepared for such an event and even started to plan individually or together for a future pregnancy or possible adoption. When this happens, the birth of a live infant will evoke a response which may be difficult to understand unless the nurse is aware of the phenomena of anticipatory grief. At a time when hospital personnel expect the new parents to be extremely delighted and happy, the nurse may encounter disbelief and a flat reaction instead. A mothering attitude may be slow to develop, and interest in and concern for the infant may be diminished. Guilt related to the parents' feelings of detachment from the infant may increase their distress.

Another occasion for anticipatory grief work is the birth of a baby whose condition is or becomes critical, such as in the case of a small premature infant or a baby with a serious cardiac defect. Parents are and should be aware of the fact that this infant may not live. They do not give up hope for their baby's survival, but they usually try to prepare themselves for the possible death of their infant. The amount and degree of anticipatory grief work done will vary with the duration of the critical period and their interpretation of the infant's chances for survival. Decreasing queries about the baby's condition and fewer visits to the nursery may indicate that anticipatory grief work is in progress. If the infant dies, the grief reaction will be less acute, but if the baby survives they will have to establish an attachment to the infant.

Nursing care must be planned to allow for gradual adjustment of the parents to the new circumstances. They may be baffled at their own reaction. Understanding acceptance of their feelings, provision of an environment in which they can discuss them freely, and information which will help them gain insight about what has taken place enable the parents to cope more effectively with this additional stress or crisis.

THE INFLUENCE OF CULTURAL FACTORS

The significance of cultural factors on the person's perception of stress or crisis, on the manner of dealing with complications, and on the effect on nurse-patient interaction has been alluded to previously. However, because the impact of culture is frequently ignored or responded to in terms of stereotyped expectations, it is important to emphasize culture specifically. "Since culture defines *a way of life for a designated group of people,* the nurse must understand the particular way of life for a defined patient, family, or social group. . . ."[20]

The culture in which a person grows up substantially influences attitudes, values, beliefs, and habit patterns. Often this influence is unrecognized, and even when the person demonstrates intellectual awareness of these factors, emotional response may not be altered. The person's cultural background provides a basis for decisions regarding behavior under ordinary circumstances and when faced with new situations. Culture also influences the consumer's expectations of providers of care in terms of roles and functions and perception of health and health practices. When a person enters a health care system or hospital dominated by people of another cultural group, misunderstanding and conflict may result.

The institution or agency itself is, in a way, a subculture with an ingroup of employees and an outgroup of patients. In addition, the behavior, beliefs, and attitudes of individual members of the health care team are influenced by the particular cultural group to which each member belongs. In order to meet the needs of patients from different cultural settings, the nurse must develop cultural awareness as well as self-awareness.[21] Cultural awareness is gained by studying other cultural groups, contacting and interacting with people of differing cultural backgrounds, and by caring for patient members of diverse cultures.[22]

Aspects of life about which knowledge of cultural background is particularly relevant to the nurse include medical practices, religious beliefs, family composition and relationships, and economic status. Some would not include economic status under cultural factors, but when poverty or wealth are of long duration, there is rationale for identifying the members of those groups as part of a particular culture or subculture. The cultural definition of pregnancy, belief or nonbelief in an afterlife, the role of grandparents, and whether the usual diet is high in starch with little protein or gourmet foods should influence nursing care. Listening to the patient, demonstrating behaviorally that the patient is a worthwhile person, and involving the patient in the care plan enable the nurse to care for the patient culturally and individually.

CONCLUSION

Much of the material in this chapter has dealt with negative responses and distressing situations. This is done purposefully because of the nature of the subject and the importance of recognizing and caring for the various problems described. However, if application is made unthinkingly and without consideration of the people involved—nurse and patient—the goal of this chapter—to help people care for people—will be unmet. The nurse can not and should not expect to have the capacity to meet every need presented by patients. The nurse will meet many of these needs well, and even under the distressing circumstances described there is satisfaction in providing care and observing growth.

REFERENCES

1 Blake, Florence G., F. Howell Wright, and Eugenia H. Waechter: *Nursing Care of Children*, 8th ed., Lippincott, Philadelphia, 1970, pp. 17–18.

2 Lazarus, Richard S.: *Psychological Stress and the Coping Process*, McGraw-Hill, New York, 1966, p. 10.

3 Parad, Howard J., and Gerald Caplan: "A Framework for Studying Families in Crisis," in H. J. Parad (ed.), *Crisis Intervention: Selected Readings*, Family Service Association of America, New York, 1965, p. 56.

4 Hill, Reuben: "General Features of Families under Stress," in H. J. Parad (ed.), *Crisis Intervention: Selected Readings*, Family Service Association of America, New York, 1965, p. 45.

5 Ibid., pp. 45–48.

6 Benedek, Therese: "Motherhood and Nurturing," in E. James Anthony and Therese Benedek (eds.), *Parenthood: Its Psychology and Psychopathology*, Little, Brown, Edinburgh and London, 1970, pp. 153–155.

7 Klaus, Marshall H., and John Kennell: "Mothers Separated from Their Newborn Infants," in Richard E. Behrman (ed.), *The Pediatric Clinics of North America*, 17(4): 1020–1021, November 1970.

8 Klaus, Marshall, et al.: "Human Maternal Behavior at First Contact," *Pediatrics*, 46(2): 190–191, August 1970.

9 Ibid., p. 187.

10 Benedek, Therese: "Fatherhood and Providing," in E. James Anthony and Therese Benedek (eds.), *Parenthood: Its Psychology and Psychopathology*, Little, Brown, Edinburgh and London, 1970, p. 171.

11 Ibid., pp. 171–174.

12 Kempe, C. Henry, and Ray E. Helfer (eds.): *Helping the Battered Child and His Family*, Lippincott, Philadelphia, 1972.

13 Helfer, Ray E., and C. Henry Kempe (eds.): *The Battered Child*, University of Chicago Press, Chicago, 1968.

14 Steele, Brandt F.: "Parental Abuse of Infants and Small Children," in E. James Anthony and Therese Benedek (eds.), *Parenthood: Its Psychology and Psychopathology*, Little, Brown, Edinburgh and London, 1970, pp. 449–477.

15 Lindemann, Erich: "Symptomatology and Management of Acute Grief," *American Journal of Psychiatry*, 101:141–148, 1944.

16 Ibid., p. 142.

17 Ibid., p. 143.

18 Ibid., p. 144.

19 Knight, James A., and Frederic Herter: "Anticipatory Grief," in Austin Kutscher (ed.), *Death and Bereavement*, Charles C Thomas, Springfield, Ill., 1969, pp. 196–201.

20 Leininger, Madeleine M.: *Nursing and Anthropology: Two Worlds to Blend*, Wiley, New York, 1970, p. 99.

21 Ibid., p. 98.

22 Ibid., pp. 97–99.

BIBLIOGRAPHY

Baldwin, Alfred L.: *Theories of Child Development*, Wiley, New York, 1967.

Blake, Florence G.: *The Child, His Parents, and the Nurse*, Lippincott, Philadelphia, 1954.

Brazelton, T. Berry: *Infants and Mothers*, Delacorte, New York, 1969.

Callahan, Sidney Cornelia: *Parenting: Principles and Politics of Parenthood*, Doubleday, Garden City, N.J., 1973.

Erickson, Erik H.: *Childhood and Society*, 2d ed., Norton, New York, 1963.

———: *Identity: Youth and Crisis*, Norton, New York, 1968.

Gessell, Arnold, Frances Ilg, and Louise Bates Ames, in collaboration with Janet Learned Rodell: *Infant and Child in the Culture of Today*, rev. ed., Harper and Row, New York, 1974.

Harris, Cheryl Hall: "Social Problems Surrounding the High-Risk Infant," in Edith H. Anderson et al. (eds.), *Current Concepts in Clinical Nursing*, vol. 4, Mosby, St. Louis, 1973, pp. 100–109.

Hinshaw, Ada Sue: "Early Planning for Long-Term Care of Children with Congenital Anomalies," in Betty Bergerson et al. (eds.), *Current Concepts in Clinical Nursing*, Mosby, St. Louis, 1967, pp. 284–291.

Kübler-Ross, Elisabeth: *On Death and Dying*, Macmillan, New York, 1969.

LeMasters, E. E.: *Parents in Modern America*, Dorsey, Homewood, Ill., 1970.

Leslie, Gerald R.: *The Family in Social Context*, Oxford, New York, 1967.

Lipkin, Gladys B.: *Psychosocial Aspects of Maternal-Child Nursing*, Mosby, St. Louis, 1974.

Moore, Mary Lou: *The Newborn and the Nurse*, Saunders, Philadelphia, 1972.

Murphy, Lois: *Personality in Young Children*, Basic Books, New York, 1956.

Redmann, Ruth E.: "Black Child—White Nurse: A Nursing Challenge and Privilege," in Margery Duffey (ed.), *Current Concepts in Clinical Nursing*, vol. 3, Mosby, St. Louis, 1971, pp. 106–114.

Rubin, Reva: "Cognitive Style in Pregnancy," *American Journal of Nursing*, 70:502–508, 1970.

Schaffer, H. R. (ed.): *The Origins of Human Social Relations*, Academic Press, London, 1971.

Schoenberg, Bernard, et al. (eds.): *Loss and Grief: Psychological Management in Medical Practice*, Columbia, New York, 1970.

Scott, Diane: "Crisis Intervention," in Betty Bergerson et al. (eds.), *Current Concepts in Clinical Nursing*, Mosby, St. Louis, 1967, pp. 392–399.

Selye, Hans: *The Stress of Life*, McGraw-Hill, New York, 1956.

Wiedenbach, Ernestine: *Clinical Nursing: A Helping Art*, Springer, New York, 1964.

———: *Family-centered Maternity Nursing*, Putnam, New York, 1967.

30

High-Risk Complications of Pregnancy*

BARBARA O'NEIL LOWE

The philosophy of maternity family-centered nursing has significant implications for the nurse:

Nurses are functioning as primary care agents in the delivery of health care for normal pregnant women.

Changing roles in the delivery of health care warrants consideration for aspects of prevention and management of the high-risk maternity patient.

Health professionals are developing collaborative teams and delineating role functions, which involve professional sharing.

* In preparation of this chapter, the author wishes to acknowledge the assistance provided through consultation service by Paul Wexler, M.D., FACOG Assistant Clinical Professor, Department of Obstetrics-Gynecology, University of Colorado Medical Center and Chairman, Department of Obstetrics-Gynecology, General Rose Memorial Hospital, Denver, Colorado.

These interdependent and intradependent responsibilities of the health care team are an endeavor to reduce complications of pregnancy.

Knowledge of placental physiology and its significant relationship to fetal growth and development have been disclosed within the past decade and have helped reduce maternal and fetal mortality. The antepartum screening process adds another qualitative dimension for the maternity nurse. The maternity nurse is committed to continue to reduce mortality and morbidity rates, which implies a responsibility and accountability for the nurse to function in the preventative role in the delivery of health care to all pregnant women.

For purposes of this chapter, high-risk pregnancy is defined as one in which the pregnant woman may evidence a myriad of factors, antecedent to and coincidental with pregnancy, that may increase the risk for maternal and fetal outcome. Recognition of these factors and their interrelationships by the nurse provides a basis for identifying the high-risk pregnant woman. Early recognition of these factors helps lessen the dangers to both the potential high-risk maternity client and her fetus.

Table 30-1 represents an overview of significant maternal factors that constitute criteria for a high-risk pregnancy. This table is *not* all-inclusive; no one single factor constitutes a high-risk category. It is the combination of factors presented by the pregnant woman that sets up a base line of symptomatology which then allows the nurse to recognize, assess, and plan for the delivery of optimal health care to the pregnant woman.

TABLE 30-1
Maternal Factors Contributing to High-Risk Pregnancy

Biological factor	Variable	Significance
Age	a Very young, 11–17 years old	1 Immature reproductive system 2 Increase in prematurity 3 Increase in toxemia 4 Psychologically immature and irresponsible
	b Primigravida over 35 years old and the over-40-year old pregnant woman	1 Increase in obstetrical complications 2 Increase in genetic complications
Race	Oriental and black women giving birth to low-birth-weight babies (small for gestational age)	1 Reasons for low-birth-weight black babies not known but probably due to economic deprivation 2 More cesarean sections in Oriental women due to smaller body structures
Parity	a Multiparity—2 or more pregnancies b Grandmultiparity—6 or more pregnancies	1 Increase in maternal complications, e.g., hemorrhage 2 Increase in multiple gestation
Nutrition	a Deprivation—less than 4 kg weight gain by 30 weeks gestation b Obesity—80 kg weight gain or more	1 Increased chance for disturbances in maternal and fetal development 2 Increased risk for toxemia, gestational diabetes
Pharmacologic hazards	a Iatrogenic and/or self-medication b Drug abusers including alcohol	1 May initiate alterations in embryologic development

		2 Increase in fetal neurologic complications 3 Alterations in psyche
Reproductive factors	a Placenta previa/abruptio placenta b Incompetent cervix c Infertility d Pelvic disorders, skeletal and/or soft tissue masses	1 Significant increase with subsequent pregnancies 2 Increased risk for spontaneous abortions 3 Increased psychological stress/anxiety
Genetic dysfunction and paternal influence	Hereditary diseases, diabetes, ABO-Rh isoimmunization	1 Increased risk of congenital pathology for fetus 2 High-risk outcome for fetus

Psychological factor	Variable	Significance
Irresponsible pregnancy	Unwanted pregnancy and baby	Increased stress altering intrauterine environment
Treatment for a psychotic or neurotic condition	a Previous postpartum depression b Suicide threats c Personality disorders	May increase risk *after* pregnancy in psychotic or neurotic problem
Stress factors	Inappropriate coping mechanisms	Alters perception of pregnancy, inability to adapt to mothering role

Socioeconomic factor	Variable	Significance
Economic deprivation	Prevents adequate nutrition and decreases availability of health care facility	Increased risk for prematurity and all other maternal complications
Education	a Incomplete or deprived of education b Limits understanding for health care c Inability to recognize problem areas of pregnancy	1 Increased risk due to lack of awareness in seeking health care 2 Increased prematurity and embryological defects of fetus
Frequent pregnancies without spacing	a Lack of family planning information b Nonuse of family planning techniques available	Increased maternal and fetal complications
Teenage pregnancy	a Change in moral codes b Lack of responsibility for sexual activities	1 Increased risk of prematurity 2 Increase in complications of pregnancy 3 Increase in psychological problems 4 Neglectful in overall health care

Cultural factor	Variables	Significance
Ethnic group	a Wide diversity in cultural tradition throughout the world b Cultural heritage ingrained and responds slowly to change in society c Cultural influences on attitudes and beliefs toward pregnancy	1 May decrease seeking early antepartum care 2 Alteration of cultural components causing increased maternal conflicts increasing anxiety and stress

Pregnancy history	Variables	Significance
Antecedent and/or coincidental factors	a Preterm deliveries (before 38 weeks) b Preterm infants c Length of hospitalization (for mother and infant) d Dystocia problems e Pregnancy beyond 42 weeks	1 Multiple gestations 2 Reproductive anomalies 3 Increased perinatal (maternal-fetal) mortality 4 Postpartum complications; neonatal problems

f Bleeding complications		5 Breech, cesarean section
g Polyhydramnios		6 Uterine inertia, atony, fetal anomalies
		7 Hormonal and reproductive disorders, e.g., hydatidiform mole
		8 Gestational diabetes, fetal anomalies

Medical history	Variables	Significance
Antepartum disease	*a* Cardiovascular	1 Major factor for increased maternal demise
	b Renal	2 Increased chances for toxemia
	c Diabetes	3 Increased chances for large-for-gestational-age baby (over 4,200 g)
	d Anemia	
	e Intercurrent and infections	4 Decreased placental perfusion
	f Environmental: decrease in O_2, e.g., high altitude, pollution, chemicals, smoking	5 Rubella, chronic urinary tract infections, and thrombophlebitis
		6 Increased risk for premature deliveries, premature and small-for-gestational-age infants

BLEEDING COMPLICATIONS OF PREGNANCY

The major contributing factors to maternal morbidity and mortality are the bleeding complications of pregnancy. The most common hemorrhagic conditions and their predisposing factors will be discussed in this chapter.

Abortions

Abortion is defined as the premature termination of pregnancy before the time of fetal viability. This is a variable concept that usually depends on individual state laws. The term abortion may have a negative connotation with some lay people who use miscarriage interchangeably and often as a substitute for abortion.

Simplistically, abortions are classified as (1) spontaneous or (2) elective or induced. This chapter will focus on spontaneous abortions. Elective and induced abortions are reviewed in Chapter 11.

Most early trimester bleeding occurs between the 8th and 12th weeks of pregnancy. Embryonic and fetal causes account for 50 to 60 percent of early abortions, whereas maternal factors account for 15 percent. The remaining percentage, 20 to 25 percent, are primarily due to an interrelationship of fetal-maternal forces.

Spontaneous abortions are classified as follows:

1 Threatened: previable conceptus jeopardized but pregnancy may continue
2 Incomplete inevitable: expulsion of partial products of conception but abortion is imminent
3 Complete: expulsion of entire conceptus and membranes
4 Habitual: expulsion of the products of conception in three or more sequential pregnancies
5 Missed: fetal death in utero with retention of products of conception for 4 to 5 weeks

Commonalities of signs and symptoms for spontaneous abortions exist, but specific symptoms which differentiate the types are discussed under the subheadings below.

Threatened Abortion

A threatened abortion is one in which the previable conceptus is jeopardized but the pregnancy may continue. The patient presents to the physician, maternity nurse practitioner, or midwife about 3 weeks after conception with bright red vaginal bleeding, mild cramping similar to menstrual discomfort, and a slight backache. Examination by the physician reveals objective signs of pregnancy with no cervical dilatation. Hypotheses which attempt to account for the etiology of bleeding at this time vary. One hypothesis is related to hormonal insufficiency in that a decrease in progesterone may lead to an increase in myometrial activity; labor may ensue, creating a threatened spontaneous abortion.

The medical regimen for threatened abortions is symptomatic and may include bed rest, sedation, uterine relaxants, and hormonal therapy, none of which have proved scientifically valid due to the lack of precise knowledge of etiologic factors.

Nursing management includes obtaining a complete obstetric history, and the nurse should instruct the patient to report immediately to the physician whenever vaginal bleeding occurs. If bleeding persists, hospitalization may be necessary. Frequent monitoring of vital signs is imperative, as well as evaluating the amount of bleeding on perineal pads. The nurse alerts the patient to the need for adhering to the therapeutic regimen for the maintenance of pregnancy.

After bleeding has subsided, the patient may be allowed to resume her usual activities. Restoration of psychological homeostasis is a primary nursing intervention because the potential loss of pregnancy is a very stressful event for the pregnant woman and her family. The nurse is a major support system at this time of heightened anxiety.

The initial history procured provides clues about the client's perception of pregnancy. Some questions a nurse might ask are: "Was this a planned or unexpected pregnancy?" or "How do you think this pregnancy will affect your life?" Further information about socioeconomic, cultural, and emotional factors allows the nurse to assess interrelationships which concern the client.

When confronted with the possibility of loss, the grief and grieving process differs among individuals and depends upon the coping mechanisms of the client. Refer to Chapter 29 for information about the grieving process.

Incomplete Abortion

An incomplete abortion is the partial expulsion of the products of conception usually prior to the 10th week of gestation. The placenta frequently remains adherent to the uterus. Profuse bright red vaginal bleeding begins that may produce hemorrhagic shock. The decreased circulating blood volume leads to decreased venous return to the heart which is evidenced by falling arterial blood pressure and tachycardia. The physical examination reveals dilatation of the cervical os, signaling that abortion is inevitable.

The medical regimen is to hospitalize the patient and surgically intervene by dilatation and curettage (D&C) without further delay. The nursing management includes ordering "stat" blood type and cross-match in preparation for a possible transfusion. Vital signs are constantly monitored until the patient's condition is stabilized. Intravenous fluid replacement is instituted to prevent further hypovolemia. Preoperative preparation of the patient is necessary. The administration of intravenous oxytocin is controversial due to the inherent pressor-antidiuretic properties. Therapeutic results are achieved with the physician and nurse interacting as a team. The nurse supports the patient psychologically by intervening to reduce the high anxiety and stress that may accompany this crisis situation.

Complete Abortion

A complete abortion is the expulsion of the entire products of conception—fetus, placenta, and membranes. The patient presents with vaginal bleeding and may experience suprasymphysial discomfort. Physical examination reveals cervical dilatation with evidence of protruding conceptual products. The major physiologic cause is unknown but includes a multiplicity of fetal-maternal factors identified in Table 30-2.

The treatment is bed rest, which may or may not require hospitalization. Constant observation for bleeding pre- and postabortion is imperative. The major role for nursing intervention is the maintenance of physiological and psychological homeostasis for the patient.

Habitual or Recurrent Abortion

A habitual or recurrent abortion is one that occurs in three or more sequential pregnancies. The primary pathologic factor is thought to be due to faulty intrauterine environment. Genetic and chromosomal abnormalities are the probable causes for this type of abortion in early pregnancy. Physiological and psychological maternal factors account for late gestational recurrent abortions.

The client usually presents a complex obstetric history. The interview includes the outcome of all previous pregnancies. Specific data with reference to the completed gestational age is significant for evaluation of the client's high-risk potential. After the subjective data are obtained, a complete physical examination and diagnostic work-up is done. This includes serum studies for estriol levels, hematologic and chemistry status, urine estriols, and a chest x ray. The medical treatment is dependent upon the results of the physical examination and results of the diagnostic survey.

A major nursing intervention is to interrupt the cyclical feedback created by the repetition of pregnancy, loss, pregnancy, loss, etc. The desire for pregnancy complicated by repeated loss increases stress for the woman and her family. The nurse explores the woman's feelings regarding pregnancy and determines in conjunction with other health team members if genetic counseling

TABLE 30-2
Major Pathophysiologic Causes for Complete Spontaneous Abortions

Embryonic-Fetal 50–60%	Maternal 15–20%	Unknown 20–25%
1 Disorganization of germ plasm	1 Faulty maternal environment, e.g., systemic infections	Fetal-maternal interrelationship
2 Ovular defects, i.e., blighted ovum	2 Severe nutritional deprivation	
3 Chromosomal aberrations	3 Abnormal pathologic conditions of reproductive tract	
4 Faulty placental development, i.e., molar degeneration	4 Endocrine dysfunctions	
	5 Coincidental disease pathologies, e.g., ABO-Rh incompatibility	
	6 Accidental trauma, radiation	
	7 Psychogenic factors	

is appropriate. Refer to Chapter 20, which discusses the emotional components of pregnancy.

Table 30-3 gives the general nursing goals which should be included in the care of the patient with spontaneous abortion.

Missed Abortion

A missed abortion is frequently a midtrimester occurrence of fetal death with retention of the products of conception in the uterus for 4 to 5 weeks. It is assumed that fetal demise occurs first followed by decreasing placental function, but there is no clear etiologic explanation for the prolonged retention of the products of conception. Medical research indicates that estrogen decreases more rapidly than progesterone, and estrogen deprivation will reduce myometrial contractibility which prevents expulsion of the products of conception.[1]

The patient usually has an uneventful first trimester of pregnancy: amenorrhea, nausea, and uterine growth are within normal limits. There is a gradual decrease in the signs of pregnancy as evidenced by weight loss and common subjective complaints such as "I don't feel pregnant anymore" and "I'm losing weight." There is usually no frank vaginal bleeding or pain associated with missed abortion.

Upon physical examination, palpation of the uterus reveals limited or no growth, and the uterus is smaller in size than expected for gestational age. This results from amniotic fluid absorption and maceration of the fetus. A comparative evaluation of menstrual dates and expected fetal and uterine growth is necessary. A discrepancy may be predictive for early detection of missed abortion.

The retention of the degenerating products of conception can become problematic since this can inhibit coagulation and platelet function which aggravates the hemor-

TABLE 30-3
Nursing Goals with Spontaneous Abortion

Assessment	Management/intervention
1 Obtain complete history, specifically obstetric and gynecologic.	1 Establish rapport, using therapeutic communication skills for interviewing and data collection.
2 Determine gestation; note onset and type of bleeding, with/without cramping or discomfort, expulsion of tissue or clots.	2 Arrange for patient to see physician immediately; instruct patient to save all perineal pads and specimens of tissue or clots for inspection by the physician and the attending nurses.
3 If hospitalized, request laboratory tests as ordered by physician: blood type and cross-match, complete hematologic studies, serum and urine estriols, hormonal assay.	3 Complete bed rest with legs elevated about 20°; no enemas or laxatives; decrease environmental stimuli; monitor vital signs until stable; promote and maintain physiologic homeostasis; use therapeutic approach to reduce anxiety and stress; administer medications as ordered by physician.
4 Observe for symptoms of hemorrhagic shock, decreased blood pressure, increased pulse, weak and thready pulse, cold, clammy skin, apprehension, cyanosis.	4 Control hemorrhage; record vital signs every 15 minutes; monitor intake and output; administer O_2 as indicated; start intravenous with Y setup to prevent severe hypovolemia and allow for blood transfusion.
5 If surgery is indicated, prepare patient by teaching pre- and postoperative expectations.	5 Discuss with patient and family emergency measures the physician may initiate: surgical permit, surgery, anesthesia, transfusions.

rhagic process. This condition is known as disseminated intravascular coagulation (DIC). The disseminated intravascular coagulation mechanism may occur when thromboplastinlike substances enter maternal circulation from contaminated amniotic fluid due to fetal autolysis as in missed abortion. Simultaneous activation of the clotting and fibrinolytic systems result in hypocoagulability of the blood with concurrent diminution of clotting factors.[2] Circulatory disequilibrium exists and requires immediate evaluation, diagnosis, and treatment to prevent further maternal complication.

Medical treatment is not definitive, but recent literature states that once the diagnosis is confirmed, expulsion of uterine contents is mandatory to prevent the possibility of serious complications.[3] Intravenous infusion of oxytocin has been used effectively; this stimulates the uterus to contract, thereby expelling its contents.

Missed abortion creates a psychological dilemma for the patient, her family, and the nurse. The nurse should be alert to the signs of impending complications and coagulation defects which include subjective statements like the following: "Perhaps I am not really pregnant," "My gums bleed when I brush my teeth," or "I have frequent nosebleeds lately." The nurse should assume a directive role and keep the woman informed regarding her condition. Simple explanatory comments which invite client inquiry will help the woman to ask questions and express her feelings about the situation. This approach allows the woman and her family to gain an understanding and explore their coping process in dealing with this high-risk maternal complication of pregnancy. Focusing on the woman's concerns and feelings and giving knowledgeable reassurance, with factual information, can prove to be a therapeutic role for the nurse.

Molar Pregnancy

Although uncommon, the obstetrical phenomenon called molar pregnancy merits some discussion. In the United States, the incidence is 1 out of every 1,500 pregnancies in women under twenty and over forty years of age. The etiological factor is nonspecific, but it is thought to be primarily of placental origin. Epidemiology studies of pregnant women reveal protein deprivation and viral disease as predisposing factors to molar pregnancies.

The most common molar pregnancy seen is the hydatidiform mole. (See Figure 30-1.) Hydatidiform mole is defined as the hydropic degeneration of the chorionic villi with proliferation of the trophoblastic cells. Pregnancy progresses with the normal signs and symptoms. Between the 16th and 20th week of gestation, intermittent vaginal bleeding occurs. It is dark brown in color

FIGURE 30-1
Uterus containing a hydatidiform mole. (*By permission from Louis Hellman and J. Pritchard,* Williams Obstetrics, *Appleton-Century-Crofts, New York, 1971. With permission of publisher.*)

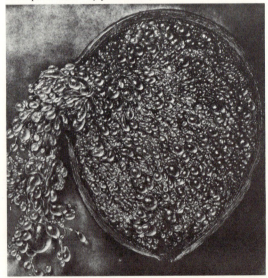

with vesicular, bubblelike discharge. The uterus is measurably larger than that expected for the duration of pregnancy identified. The patient complains of excessive nausea and vomiting. Physiologically, the changes are thought to result from an increase in human chorionic gonadotrophin (HCG) stimulation.[4] Early eclamptogenic-like symptoms, such as hypertension, may appear.

Diagnosis of molar pregnancy can be confirmed by ultrasound. Once diagnosed, uterine evaluation is necessary and is usually accomplished by an intravenous infusion of oxytocin which produces uterine contractions, and hence spontaneous delivery. Hemorrhage and infection are frequent complications of molar pregnancies; such pregnancies are therefore designated high-risk.

In the majority of molar pregnancies, the degenerative process is benign. The patient who has had a molar pregnancy must be carefully followed, at least every 3 months, with serum hormonal assays of HCG. Elevation of these levels is indicative of a malignant, metastatic invasion process called choriocarcinoma. If the patient has evidence of widespread metastases, chemotherapy and radiation show promising results followed eventually by a total hysterectomy. Nursing management is focused upon crisis intervention techniques and anticipatory guidance to help the patient and her family to cope with the nature of the crisis.

Ectopic Pregnancy

An ectopic pregnancy is one in which implantation develops outside the uterine cavity. Implantation may occur in the sites identified in Figure 30-2. The physiologic mechanisms involved in gamete transporta-

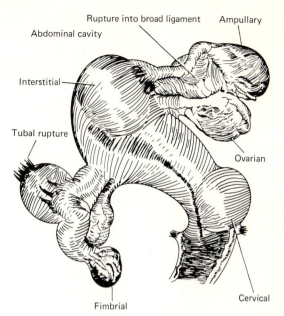

FIGURE 30-2
Sites of ectopic pregnancies. (*By permission from Ralph C. Benson,* Handbook of Obstetrics and Gynecology, *5th ed., Lange, Los Altos, Calif., 1974. With permission of publisher.*)

tion after fertilization, hence implantation, are:

1   The direction of flow with tubal fluid
2   Tubal ciliary activity
3   Tubal contractility
4   Sperm motility

Alteration of these factors can result in an ectopic pregnancy. Ninety percent of ectopic pregnancies occur in some portion of the fallopian tubes. The primary theory of etiology is endosalpingitis, a tubular inflammatory disease which occludes the lumen and prevents the passage of the fertilized ovum into the uterus.

The frequency of ectopic pregnancy is 1 in every 250 conceptions.[5] The high-risk factors for consideration are:

1 History of infertility
2 History and frequency of pelvic inflammatory disease (PID)
3 History and frequency of venereal disease—particularly gonorrhea
4 History of previous ectopic pregnancy[6]

Age is a significant factor in that 40 percent of the cases occur between the ages of twenty and twenty-nine. Pregnant women from the lower socioeconomic strata show a significantly higher number of ectopic pregnancies.[7] This is primarily due to a higher incidence of pelvic inflammatory disease. The alternative life-style patterns of today may change the sociologically defined populus who develop ectopic pregnancies.

Clinical manifestations for tubal pregnancy are those of normal pregnancy. The onset of vaginal bleeding occurs at approximately the 6th to 8th week of pregnancy. The patient reports to the physician, maternity nurse practitioner, or midwife with subjective complaints of amenorrhea, "spotting," and lower abdominal pain of moderate to severe quality. A common subjective complaint is pain radiating to the shoulders and/or side of the neck. This referred pain is the result of bleeding into the peritoneal cavity and overstimulation of the vagus nerve. Cullen's sign, a bluish discoloration in the periumbilical area, indicates intraperitoneal hemorrhage.

Upon physical examination, the classical objective signs of pregnancy are seen. Vaginal examination reveals severe tenderness with cervical manipulation. Vascular collapse and hypovolemic shock may follow. Differential diagnosis is of primary importance to prevent rupture of the ectopic gestation. Surgical intervention is the usual treatment of choice.

The patient with an ectopic pregnancy is a high-risk obstetrical patient. The nurse should be aware of the signs of ectopic pregnancy. Constant monitoring of vital signs will identify alterations in the cardiovascular system. The nurse should refrain from administering enemas and vaginal examination to prevent excitation of internal organs and introduction of infection. An elevated temperature is clinically significant as an indication of infection. The major nursing management is to prevent hemorrhagic shock. Intravenous fluid should be started while awaiting the blood crossmatch.

The nurse intervenes during this situational crisis which is an actual threat to the patient's life. The patient and her family may express anxiety and feelings of helplessness. The priority nursing goal is to assist the patient and her family in coping with this crisis. Therapeutic techniques of crisis intervention should be incorporated into the total family care.

Third-Trimester Bleeding

There is an increased risk of antepartum hemorrhage during the third trimester of pregnancy. Bleeding is never considered normal during pregnancy, and the most critical type of bleeding is that of placental origin. Placental bleeding is a life-threatening crisis for the mother and her baby. Two important clinical entities that result in placental bleeding are placenta previa and abruptio placenta.

Placenta Previa

Placenta previa is the abnormal implantation of the placenta near the lower uterine segment as opposed to the fundal portion of the uterus. There are three major types of previa. (See Figures 30-3 to 30-6.)

The incidence of placenta previa is 1 in every 150 pregnancies, but the specific etio-

FIGURE 30-3
Partial placenta previa. (*By permission from Ralph C. Benson,* Handbook of Obstetrics and Gynecology, *5th ed., Lange, Los Altos, Calif., 1974. With permission of publisher.*)

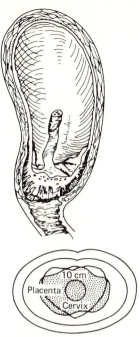

FIGURE 30-4
Complete placenta previa. (*By permission from Ralph C. Benson,* Handbook of Obstetrics and Gynecology, *5th ed., Lange, Los Altos, Calif., 1974. With permission of publisher.*)

logic factors are obscure. Medical researchers state that endometrial deficiencies and decreased muscularity in the fundus of the uterus seem to play a significant role in this abnormality.[8]

Candidates who are more susceptible to placenta previa include (1) older parous women, (2) multiparous women, (3) women who have had previous cesarean sections or uterine surgery, and (4) women with uterine anomalies. These high-risk variables lend support to etiologic theories.

The classical presenting symptom is *painless vaginal bleeding.* The progressive dilatation of the lower uterine segment during the third trimester of pregnancy leads to disruption of the placental tissues. Thus a significant amount of placental bleeding oc-

curs which may result in hemorrhage, and the risk of perinatal mortality increases proportionately. The major maternal hazards are shock and infection, and prematurity and fetal hypoxia are complications for the baby.

If placenta previa is suspected, the therapeutic regimen is best accomplished by conservative treatment. Hospitalization with complete bed rest is recommended. Bleeding usually subsides within 24 hours, and after bleeding ceases, the abdomen will be relaxed when palpated.

Close observation of the patient is a major nursing responsibility. In addition the nurse can obtain an accurate history pertaining to the onset and character of bleeding. The physician will want to know if the bleeding is associated with any pain. All perineal

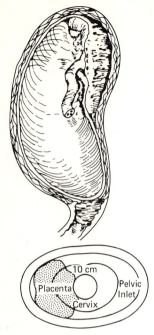

FIGURE 30-5
Normal placenta. (*By permission from Ralph C. Benson, Handbook of Obstetrics and Gynecology, 5th ed., Lange, Los Altos, Calif., 1974. With permission of publisher.*)

FIGURE 30-6
Low implantation. (*By permission from Ralph C. Benson, Handbook of Obstetrics and Gynecology, 5th ed., Lange, Los Altos, Calif., 1974. With permission of publisher.*)

pads should be saved for evaluation of the amount and type of blood loss. This data will help the physician to make a differential diagnosis. The nurse monitors the fetal heart tones because abnormal presentations are frequent with placenta previa and location of fetal heart tones will aid in the diagnosis. Maternal vital signs are taken and recorded every 5 to 15 minutes if there is active bleeding. Sedation is usually ordered to reduce the patient's overt fear and anxiety. A clear liquid diet is ordered due to the prospects of impending surgery.

X rays have been used to diagnose placenta previa, and ultrasound shows promise as a diagnostic tool in earlier detection. A positive diagnosis of placenta previa is made by a sterile vaginal examination. The deliv-

ery room must be ready for a spontaneous vaginal delivery and/or for cesarean section. In institutions where the delivery room cannot fill these two needs, the surgical suite is notified of a possible cesarean section. To prevent hypovolemia, an intravenous infusion is started and whole blood that has been typed and cross-matched should be available.

Once the clinical diagnosis and type of placenta previa (see Figures 30-3 to 30-6) is confirmed, the physician elects the safest and most expedient manner for delivery. If vaginal delivery is selected, an amniotomy with oxytocic augmentation may be initiated and effective. The nurse places the patient in semi-Fowler's position, which reduces the risk of a prolapsed cord by compressing the fetal presenting part against the cervix. Fetal heart tones are monitored immediately after the amniotomy and at least every 15 minutes thereafter until delivery. A patient with complete placenta previa is delivered by cesarean section.

The overall nursing goal is to promote physiological and psychological homeostasis which is accomplished by astute assessment and management of physiologic problems. By providing support and reassurance to the patient during the crisis, the nurse will help her maintain her psychologic homeostasis.

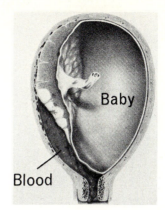

FIGURE 30-7
Partial separation (apparent hemorrhage). (*Adapted from Ross Aid Charts, by permission.*)

Abruptio Placenta

Abruptio placenta is defined as the premature separation of a normally implanted placenta—usually after the 24th week of gestation. It occurs in 1 out of every 150 pregnancies,[9] and a great deal of controversy is presented in the medical literature relative to the etiology of abruptio placenta. There is data, however, to support the increase in frequency of abruption occurring with eclamptogenesis, folic acid deficiency, and vascular changes resulting in hypertension.

There are two types of abruptio placenta: apparent or external hemorrhage and concealed or internal hemorrhage. The severity of the symptoms depends on the degree of placental separation. (See Figures 30-7 to 30-9 and Table 30-4.) Apparent abruptio placenta is a partial separation of the placenta associated with obvious external bleeding, whereas concealed abruptio placenta may be a partial and/or a complete separation of the placenta characterized by a rigid, boardlike uterus. There is retroplacental bleeding that may extrude into the endometrial and myometrial layers of the uterus; thus the patient complains of severe abdominal pain.

Conditions which predispose the pregnant woman to abruptio placenta are sudden alteration in the vascular dynamics, supine hypotensive syndrome, overdistention of the uterus as with twinning, precipitous labor, and shortened umbilical cord. The pathogenesis of abruptio placenta is thought to be a retroplacental hemorrhage of the decidua which causes placental separation.[10] Bleeding infiltrates the uterine wall behind the placenta reducing myometrial contractibil-

FIGURE 30-8
Partial separation (concealed hemorrhage). (*Adapted from Ross Aid Charts, by permission.*)

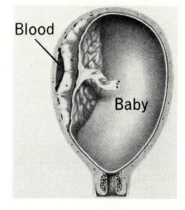

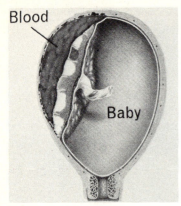

FIGURE 30-9
Complete separation (concealed hemorrhage). (*Adapted from Ross Aid Charts, by permission.*)

ity and producing uterine apoplexy. This is termed *Couvelaire uterus*, a dramatic consequence of abruptio placenta.

Generally the patient with abruptio presents with or without vaginal bleeding a firm contracted uterus and moderate to severe uterine tenderness. Fetal heart sounds may or may not be present.

The maternal complications from abruptio placenta are hypovolemic shock with resultant vascular collapse and disseminated intravascular coagulation. Normally, a retroplacental clot forms when the placenta detaches. In abruptio placenta, tissue necrosis occurs, and it is believed that tissue thromboplastin from the placental site enters maternal circulation initiating disseminated intravascular coagulation.[11]

Abruptio placenta, a life-threatening situation for both the pregnant woman and her baby, necessitates early accurate diagnosis and immediate action. The woman is admitted to the intrapartum unit where maintenance of adequate circulating blood volume is the primary therapeutic aspect of nursing and medical management.

It is essential that the nurse be able to recognize the classical signs and symptoms exhibited by the patient with placenta

abruptio. These include assessment and monitoring of the maternal vital signs and fetal heart tones; palpation of the uterus for contractions and relaxation; and evaluation of subjective complaints regarding the severity of pain disassociated with uterine contractions. It is not uncommon for a normal laboring patient to complain of sudden sharp discomfort in the lower quadrant of the abdomen, which may be a warning sign of grade 0 placental separation. (See Table 30-4.) The physician should be notified immediately.

A diagnostic survey of major blood coagulation tests is ordered and includes the fibrin split products, prothrombin time, bleeding and clotting time, hematocrit, and fibrinogen levels. The results of these tests aid in accurate diagnosis and will expedite the course of action. There is a significant decrease in the hematocrit, hemoglobin, and fibrinogen levels and increase in bleeding and clotting times. Prothrombin and pro-

TABLE 30-4
Scale for Delineating Severity of Abruptions

Grade	Symptoms
0	No evidence of clinical symptoms; usually not recognized until placental inspection after delivery; occurs in 30 percent of abruptions.
1	External bleeding present; one-third of the placenta may be separated; no signs of fetal distress present; occurs in 45 percent of abruptions.
2	External or internal hemorrhage; tetanic uterine contractions; mild to severe pain; evidence of fetal distress; fetal heart tones may be absent; occurs in 15 percent of abruptions.
3	External or internal hemorrhage; maternal shock; uterine tetany; intrauterine fetal demise; occurs in 10 percent of abruptions.

SOURCE: Table adapted from Helmuth Vorheer, "Disorders of Uterine Functions during Pregnancy, Labor and Puerperium," in Nicholas S. Assali (ed.), *Pathophysiology of Gestation,* vol. I, Academic, New York, 1972.

thrombin consumption levels are impaired and/or prolonged.[12,13]

Nursing management requires initiation of an intravenous infusion with a Y setup to prevent further hypovolemic shock. Administration of whole blood, blood substitutes such as plasma, and plasma expanders is frequently done. A decrease in circulating blood volume causes maternal and fetal hypoxia, and to help augment this deficit, oxygen is administered.

Oral and intravenous intake is recorded accurately. An indwelling catheter is inserted to monitor hourly urinary output. The minimal output should be between 30 to 60 ml per hour. Oliguria, or decreased urinary output, indicates renal and/or tubular necrosis.

Controversy abounds in the literature regarding the administration of vasopressors for the hemorrhaging patient. The stated therapeutic value is that vasopressors increase myocardial contraction and sustain blood pressure until blood is available. The use of corticosteroids has a desirable hemodynamic effect and potentiates the action of the vasopressor agents.

Delivery must be accomplished as soon as possible for the safety of the mother and fetus. It is theorized that activating the myometrium diminishes the intravascular coagulation process. When fetal distress is apparent, a cesarean section is done. If the concealed hemorrhage has infiltrated the uterine wall, a *Porro cesarean section* immediately followed by a hysterectomy may be necessary.

HYPERTENSIVE SYNDROMES OF PREGNANCY

A great deal of controversy exists relative to the classification of toxemias of pregnancy. The American College of Obstetricians and Gynecologists have delegated this task to an ad hoc group, the committee on terminology. This group is charged with the responsibility of delineating criteria by which specific pathologic patterns associated with the hypertensive disorders are influenced by pregnancy. The ad hoc committee has arbitrarily suggested the following categories:[14]

1 Acute hypertensive disorders of pregnancy: preeclampsia and eclampsia (toxemia)
2 Chronic essential hypertensive disorders antecedent to or coincidental with pregnancy

The above categories serve as a model for the presentation of the pathogenesis, therapeutic medical regimen, nursing assessment, intervention, and management of this high-risk maternity patient.

Acute Hypertensive Disorders

Toxemia of pregnancy, a disease process found uniquely in the human species, ranks third among the chief causes of maternal mortality. The reproductive wastage resulting from toxemia is reported to be approximately 25,000 fetal and neonatal deaths in the United States per year.[15]

The incidence of toxemia reflects the amount of medical care received. It is well to point out that until recently, approximately 25 percent of all pregnant women received *no* antepartum care. Lack of precision in interpreting the criteria defined as toxemia cases by hospitals, clinics, and private physicians adds another dimension for skepticism. However, the reported incidence reveals that toxemia occurs in 1 out of every 15 pregnancies. Toxemia is seen more frequently in the young primigravidas, ages fourteen to nineteen years; in primigravidas over thirty years old; and in patients with pre-existing metabolic disorders. Socially, educationally, and economically deprived women also have a higher incidence of toxemia. Attributable factors are the lack of recognition of the adverse symptomatology related to pregnancy, nutritional deprivation, and more specifically the inability to obtain quality maternity care.

The primary role for the maternity nurse is early recognition of the myriad of factors contributing to the toxemias of pregnancy. Once identified, the nurse can intervene specifically with the clientele served to help eradicate the high-risk potential. Astute antepartum screening by the health team may be the key to the prevention of toxemia.

Toxemia is a condition universally recognized and one which is unique usually to the last half of pregnancy. It may begin during the last trimester as well as in the early puerperium. Toxemia of pregnancy has no etiologic implication to a circulating toxin in the blood, and it is characterized by a cardinal triad of symptoms. This triad is called *EPH gestosis:* E = edema, P = proteinuria, and H = hypertension. The chronological order for appearance of these symptoms is hypertension, edema, and proteinuria.

Preeclampsia is characterized by the development after the 24th week of gestation of one or more of the cardinal symptoms. If, however, the patient presents with two or more of the cardinal symptoms, this is a warning sign of increasing severity.

The most severe form of toxemia is eclampsia. The severe preeclamptic patient can progress to the eclamptogenic state. Classically, eclampsia is characterized by the cardinal triad and the occurrence of one or more convulsions; coma may follow.

Pathogenesis

Toxemias of pregnancy have been called diseases of multiple theories, and to date, no one definitive etiology is known. It is known, however, that toxemia occurs only in the pregnant state without respect to the presence or absence of a fetus (i.e., with hydatidiform mole). This suggests the placenta and/or the uterus as probable causative agents. Termination of pregnancy, either artificially or by natural means, alleviates the cardinal symptoms that activate the eclamptogenic state in a pregnant woman.

The normal homeostatic mechanisms are dramatically intensified during pregnancy. In a pathologic state of pregnancy such as toxemia, major alterations in the renal and circulatory systems are demonstrated. Many clinical researchers support the theory of generalized arteriole vasoconstriction as the primary entity for the symptoms presented in toxemia.

The physiological mechanisms of the renal system are dependent on the circulatory system. Alterations in renal function, however, are commonly seen in the preeclamptic woman. A reversal of the factors which influence the excretion of sodium has been observed; thus sodium retention occurs. There is also conclusive evidence to indicate altered glomerular functions. In the eclamptic woman the glomerular filtration rate decreases while the renal vascular resistance increases.[16]

Of considerable interest is the regulation and biosynthesis of the renin-angiotensin-aldosterone system.[17] Renin, an enzyme, is produced and stored in the juxtaglomerular cells. It then converts circulating renin to angiotensin I. A converting enzyme that is of pulmonary origin splits off two amino acids leaving angiotensin II. Angiotensin II is said to be the most potent vasopressor known present in humans. An immediate effect of angiotensin II is vasoconstriction of the peripheral arterioles and increased systemic blood pressure. It also stimulates the secretion of aldosterone from the adrenal cortex. Aldosterone secretions result in sodium retention, expansion of the intravascular volume, and increased blood pressure. The exact mechanism of how angiotensin II exerts its effect on the glomerular cells is unknown, but this negative-feedback regulatory system defends the basis for the classical triad of symptoms displayed in the toxemias of pregnancy.

Psychopathogenesis

The interplay of the psyche with organic factors deserves recognition. Much has been written about the important role of emotions and personality in the development of toxemia. Some authors have stated that toxemia may be a disease of adaptation, concluding that prolonged physiological and psychological stress can result in hyperactivity of the hypothalamic-pituitary system.[18] Other sources state that there is frequently a preexisting concealed personality aberration; this has been suggested by the results of some retrospective and prospective research studies.[19] Psychodynamically, the patient is unable to cope with stress effectively, and personality decompensation results.

The psychotherapeutic regimen involves bolstering the patient's self-confidence by displaying a concerned attitude and listening attentively to the patient's problems.

Clinical Criteria for Toxemia

EDEMA Edema is the accumulation of extracellular fluid in the tissues which initially may be localized, but sudden excessive weight gain and generalized edema may be the first sign of impending preeclampsia. A weight gain of 0.8 kg per week or 2.4 kg per month has been identified as the criterion for suspecting preeclampsia. There is a direct correlation between sudden weight gain and abnormal retention of sodium. Hypoproteinemia may be another factor resulting in edema formation.

Edema is first noticeable on the feet (pedal) and the lower end of the tibia (pretibia). As it becomes more generalized, it is found in the eyelids, hands, and face, particularly upon arising. With the external evidence of edema present, the working diagnosis is made that a similar internal condition exists. Intracranial edema gives rise to subjective complaints including nausea and vomiting, frontal headache, and visual disturbances.

PROTEINURIA Proteinuria (albuminuria) is the presence of increased amounts of protein in the urine. Normally, only traces of protein are excreted in the urine, less than 80 to 100 mg (8 to 10 g) in a 24-hour period.[20] Since glomeruli influences or urinary protein absorption, impairment of these structures may lead to proteinuria. Progressive renal ischemia contributes to hypertension.

HYPERTENSION The criterion for defining hypertension is variable. Hypertension in pregnancy is defined as a rise of 30 mmHg or more in systolic blood pressure and a rise of 15 mmHg or more in the diastolic reading.[21] The adult blood pressure recommended by the American Heart Association is 140/90 absolute. To evaluate the clinical meaning of the blood pressure reading, the woman must be at rest. Blood pressure must be taken on two separate occasions at least 6 hours apart. Accuracy is necessary to make a differential diagnosis in view of the classification index. The combination of the triad—edema, proteinuria, and hypertension—with other deviations from normal provides for a diagnosis of toxemia.

General Management and Therapeutic Regimen

Because of the insidious onset of toxemia, knowledgeable antepartum screening is needed. The initial screening includes a complete physical examination and history.

The height, weight, and blood pressure are recorded and a urine specimen is obtained. It is significant to note any family history of hypertension, renal or cardiovascular disease, diabetes, and toxemia of pregnancy. Some scholars believe there is a familial tendency related to the occurrence of toxemia.[22]

Some obstetricians impose dietary salt intake restrictions and the use of diuretics during late pregnancy. The assumption was formerly that restriction of salt prevents or controls the symptoms of toxemia. This management is controversial and some believe potentially hazardous to maternal and fetal well-being.[23]

Caloric restrictions during pregnancy also need reassessment. There seems to be a direct correlation between the nutritional status of the pregnant woman and the wellness of the newborn. The widespread singular or joint practice of weight control and sodium restriction during pregnancy is believed to be a contributory factor to low-birth-weight infants.

The major objectives for management of toxemia are control of preeclampsia and prevention of eclampsia. Management of the woman with mild toxemia is usually on an outpatient basis. Frequent antepartum examinations are essential, particularly if the history indicates the possibility of toxemia.

A high protein diet with vitamin supplements is recommended. Foods high in sodium content, such as potato chips, ham, bacon, and smoked pork, should be avoided. A nutritionally balanced diet of 1,800 to 2,200 calories is adequate to provide for the necessary fetal growth and development.

The woman is confined to her home, and is placed on bed rest with limited activity. Mild sedation is recommended to decrease the physiological components of fear, stress, and anxiety. Some researchers believe that antihypertensives reduce placental perfu-

sion.[24] Therefore, adequate circulation to the fetus is diminished, perhaps producing fetal hypoxia and malnutrition.

If mild preeclampsia progresses, hospitalization is required and a therapeutic regimen continues with a more vigorous plan of care. The patient should be placed in a private room on complete bed rest; the blood pressure is monitored every 3 hours when awake; intake and output is recorded; and the patient is weighed daily, preferably in the morning. Diagnostic plasma volume and urinary clearance tests are ordered. Tests to determine fetal well-being and placental function are needed to determine plan of care.

Daily examination of the retina with the ophthalmoscope is recommended to detect early vascular changes, because retinal changes occur as toxemia progresses. The use of sedatives and anticonvulsant medications may be indicated if the blood pressure reaches maximum limits.

Again, the criteria varies from physician to physician, but a blood pressure of 160/110 mmHg demands vigorous treatment to prevent convulsions and cerebral vascular accidents. Phenobarbital and magnesium sulfate are chemotherapeutic drugs that can be used after the therapeutic drugs of choice.

Magnesium sulfate may be administered initially intravenously as a slow drip in a 10 percent solution for immediate action; however, it is usually administered intramuscularly with a 7-cm needle. It is common practice to inject 0.5 ml of a local anesthetic in combination with 5 ml of the prescribed dosage of magnesium sulfate into the gluteus maximus. No more than 5 ml should be given into any one site. This procedure is recommended to minimize the discomfort associated with magnesium sulfate administration and absorption. Magnesium sulfate causes burning and sloughing of the tissues at the site of injection. If frequent administration of the drug is necessary, rotation of sites is imperative. Magnesium sulfate carries considerable hazards, including decreased urinary output (below 100 ml per hour), decreased respiratory efforts (below 16 per minute), and decreased neurological responses (absence of the knee-jerk reflex). When any one of these symptoms occurs, magnesium sulfate is discontinued. In cases of overdose, the antidote is calcium gluconate solution administered intravenously very slowly. This definitive management plan should prevent increased cerebral vasoconstriction which leads to convulsions and coma.

Nursing Management

The first member of the health team usually encountered by the pregnant woman is the maternity nurse, who takes the complete initial history. The data gathered include a complete family history with recognition of cultural variations and socioeconomic status and a review of each physiological system. The woman's reproductive history is of prime importance, and the nurse should obtain pertinent information about previous pregnancy outcomes. The woman's subjective assessment of her current general health status and that prior to pregnancy is relevant.

These data become a base line for the delivery of optimum quality maternity care for the pregnant woman and her family. An overall nursing goal priority is achieved through knowledgeable assessment, planning, and management of the potentially high-risk pregnant woman.

Prevention and control begin with the initial antepartum visit at which time the nurse assesses physical findings in light of high-risk factors. Weight, height, and blood pressure are recorded, and a urine specimen is obtained. The nurse, depending on knowledge, education, and expertise may perform an abdominopelvic examination.

Laboratory tests may include a Venereal Disease Research Laboratory test, rubella and antibody screening, Rh determination, blood type, and hematocrit. Hemoconcentration is commonly present in toxemia.

A major responsibility of the nurse is that of communicating effectively with the pregnant woman. Open communication between the maternity nurse and the client promotes the client's understanding of the pregnancy as well as of the continuous changes that are occurring. The nurse explains the rationale for the care prescribed.

The value of frequent antepartum visits is to assess the course of the toxemic condition. These visits also provide an opportunity for the nurse to teach the woman about a well-balanced diet and good hygiene, and to look for and recognize early warning signs of impending crisis. With each subsequent visit, the nurse will reassess and change the nursing care plan in view of the present problem. Subjective complaints that reveal an increase in symptoms such as vertigo, headaches, and visual disturbances should be reported to the physician. One of the last warning signs preceding a convulsion is the subjective complaint of epigastric pain. This is due to engorgement and stretching of the liver capsule.

If preeclampsia progresses to eclampsia, magnification in subjective complaints and the clinical picture necessitate hospitalization. Eclampsia precautions are instituted when the woman is admitted to the hospital. An emergency tray is placed at the patient's bedside. This tray includes a mechanical airway; an assortment of emergency medications such as sedatives, antihypertensives, diuretics, cardiotonics, and antidepressants; and an adequate supply of syringes, tourniquets, needles, and alcohol swabs. Suction and oxygen must be readily available, and an intravenous infusion is started.

The eclamptic patient requires intensive

nursing care, and the nurse must constantly observe and monitor the patient carefully. As with all high-risk crisis situations, the nurse is responsible for communicating the procedures to the patient and her family, and an opportunity is provided for the patient and her family to ventilate their feelings. The psychological stages of adaptation to a crisis, real or potential, vary with individuals, and how the patient and her support system members perceive the pregnancy is vital.

The situational crisis of a high-risk pregnancy and the potential of a high-risk infant is a real psychological threat. Much depends on the coping mechanisms and the alternative patterns the patient and family use in the adaptive process.

Physical disequilibrium tends to create additional patient stress and thereby heightens anxiety and fear. Feelings of anger, guilt, and helplessness are common, and the patient becomes more dependent on health team members for decision making.

The adaptative process is somewhat sequential; the coping mechanisms usually associated with this crisis are rationalization, denial, depression, disorganization, and acceptance. The use of denial, the disallowing of reality, is the initial attempt on the part of the patient to resolve the emotional conflict. This process closely resembles that of the grieving process discussed in Chapter 29.

The nurse provides anticipatory guidance to support the patient and her family through the toxemia crisis. A calm and responsive milieu created by the nurse will help the patient and her family with the acceptance of the temporary crisis situation. One of the most effective tools a nurse can implement is sensitivity to and understanding of the patient and her concerns. Nursing management must be governed by the patient's behavior. This requires the develop-

ment of a therapeutic interpersonal relationship between the nurse, patient, and the family support system.

The advancement of the physical crisis occurs with the onset of a convulsion. Twitching begins with the facial muscles and moves in a downward direction encompassing spasm of all the muscles. Tonic-clonic-type convulsions are seen in the eclamptic state. These attacks vary in intensity, severity, and duration. Constant monitoring of the vital signs to detect increasing hypertension and respiratory embarrassment is necessary. The nurse maintains a patent airway, and observes the patient for impending convulsions. Hourly measurement of intake and output is required to detect renal damage. This will be evidenced by oliguria (less than 100 ml per hour). The patient is protected from injuries that may result from uncontrolled thrashing during a convulsion; padded side rails decrease this hazard. The use of restraints is not recommended since they may increase fear and anxiety and contribute to self-injury. The well-being of the fetus is jeopardized by this tumultuous situation, and the physician usually elects to deliver the patient, particularly if gestation is 36 weeks and beyond.

The prognosis for the mother with advanced toxemia and her high-risk infant can be favorable with astute and vigorous management. The physician and maternity nurse, working as a team, are determining factors in preventing mortality and morbidity resulting from toxemia.

Essential Hypertension and Pregnancy

A question remains as to when a pregnant woman is diagnosed as essential hypertensive antecedent to pregnancy. It can be argued that women who start pregnancy with a blood pressure of 140/90 are latent cases of hypertension; by most criteria, hypertension developing prior to the 20th week of gestation is termed essential hypertension, a condition uncommon before thirty years of age.[25] It is not uncommon for essential hypertension to be revealed on early routine antepartum examination. The blood pressure determination is 160/100 or more.

There is a strong familial tendency toward this type of hypertension. When taking the initial history, the nurse must ask about the family history in specific terms, in the form of the medical history of parents, grandparents, and siblings. If deceased, the age and cause of death is significant.

Further evaluation with respect to renal symptoms (edema, proteinuria, hematuria, and retinal examination) should be pursued. If there is a rise in blood pressure prior to the onset of proteinuria, essential hypertension is suspected. Differential laboratory tests may distinguish essential hypertension.

Preeclampsia can develop in the patient with essential hypertension, in which case the onset of preeclampsia is earlier and more severe. There is great concern for the welfare of the fetus due to the dramatic reduction in placental functioning. This is particularly true if proteinuria is present.

The management consists of frequent monitoring of the blood pressure and urine. Depending on the progress of the clinical symptoms, hospitalization may be indicated. The use of antihypertensives has proved to be questionable and unrewarding, for these drugs further reduce placental sufficiency, thereby increasing the risk for the fetus.[26] Laboratory tests to determine fetal well-being and placental function are repeated frequently.

The nurse assesses the clinical status of the patient, bearing in mind the symptoms and differences between acute (toxemia) and chronic hypertensive disease in pregnancy. The nursing management includes all that has been identified for the toxemic patient, and the prognosis for the woman who develops acute hypertension of pregnancy is favorable when the treatment is prompt and rigorous. The fetal outcome is less favorable. An increase in perinatal mortality occurs when the blood pressure rises. The causes of fetal morbidity and mortality are intrauterine death, prematurity, and respiratory distress syndrome. Fetal outcome is thought to be related to the duration of the disease process and the general vascular degeneration involving all the arteries, but particularly the uterine arteries.

The pregnant woman with essential hypertension is a prime candidate to develop preeclampsia concomitantly. Maternal mortality may occur following a sudden increase in blood pressure accompanied by preeclampsia-eclampsia. Death results from cerebral hemorrhage, left ventricular failure, or pulmonary complications.

There are other disease processes that alter the hypertensive mechanisms, such as chronic renal disease, coarctation of the aorta, pyelonephritis, and urinary calculi. The physician and the maternity nurse must be alert for these medical disorders. Early antepartum screening promotes optimal management and decreases mortality and morbidity.

INFECTIONS DURING PREGNANCY

When a pregnant woman develops a systemic infection, alterations in the intrauterine environment can occur. The incidence of pregnancy complicated by an infectious process is variable, but it is thought to be approximately 5 percent of all pregnancies.[27] The more virulent organisms, virus and bacteria, can be transmitted via the placenta and have deleterious effects upon the fetus. There is a higher incidence of intrauterine viral and bacterial infections among the lower socioeconomic groups. Early recognition and detection of infections by the nurse enhances the quality of maternal and fetal outcome. The maternity nurse operates preventively with early client immunoglobin screening determinations.

Some medical literature states that there is seldom an absolute correlation between maternal viremia and embryopathy.[28] The inability to resolve this statement with specific rationale is a medical dilemma. It is thought that fetal immunologic responsiveness occurs at approximately the 20th week of gestation.

The classical teratogens in early gestation are rubella and *cytomegalovirus* (CMV). The concept of time relative to cell replication and cell differentiation is a major factor in the teratogenicity of these viruses.

Rubella

Rubella, commonly known as German measles, is basically a mild disease. When contracted in the first 90 days of pregnancy, however, it has teratogenic effects on embryonic growth and development. The fetal defects include congenital heart disease, cataracts, hearing loss, and mental retardation.

Rubella virus has an incubation period of 11 to 17 days from the acquisition of the infection to the onset of the rash. The rash is that of a fine maculopapular eruption. The mode of transmission is aerosol dissemination, and portals of infection are the nasopharynx.

The clinical picture of rubella is difficult to distinguish from many other infectious processes. The symptoms include mild fever, malaise, coryza, and polyarthritis. In the past, tenderness of the suboccipital nodes has been used as the symptom for definitive diagnosis, but this may prove faulty since exact diagnosis can only be made on serologic determinations. Posterior cervical and postauricular lymphadenopathy is very common. The presence of a fine maculopapular rash appears first on the face and moves to the trunk and extremities within 3 days. The rash fades rather quickly. The rubella virus circulates in the maternal blood during the incubation period which is antecedent to the onset of the rash. The degree of insult to the conceptus depends largely upon the stage of gestation and the stage of organogenesis. Confirmation of diagnosis depends on the epidemiologic evidence of the disease in the community and positive serologic data.

If a woman who suspects pregnancy or in whom pregnancy has been confirmed develops a febrile illness and rash suspicious of rubella, an immediate hemagglutination-inhibition antibody (HAI) screening should be obtained. The rubella virus appears in the maternal blood within 24 to 48 hours after the appearance of the rash. If the HAI titer is less than 1:8 the woman has not had rubella but is now a prime suspect. When the HAI titer is 1:16 or more, this indicates the woman has had the disease, developed antibodies, and is no longer susceptible to rubella.[29]

Congenital rubella, acquired in utero, is demonstrated by an elevation of the immunoglobin IgM, and isolation of the rubella virus confirms the diagnosis. The manifestation of congenital heart defects, cataracts, deafness, and other anomalies will evidence support for the intrauterine infection.

The presence of pre-existing antibodies in a pregnant woman can be reassuring because the fetus is not in jeopardy. Immunization of all females prior to menarche with live attenuated rubella virus has been recommended by the United States Public Health Service.[30] Pregnancy must be prevented for 2 months after immunization. Administration of the vaccine in the early postpartum period is suggested for those women never having had rubella.

To decrease the effect of rubella embryopathy, antepartum screening is necessary. All pregnant women should be required to have a HAI antibody screening test on the first antepartum visit. In most instances, careful history taking and serologic screening will provide for a working diagnosis.

Professional people exposed to the risk of rubella infection should be screened for HAI titer. These include physicians, nurses, midwives, paramedical personnel, and school teachers. This pragmatic approach would identify persons who serve as vectors in the dissemination of the rubella infection among the childbearing population. Of major importance is the HAI titer screening of all personnel responsible for direct maternal and infant care in the obstetric unit.

It is judicious for the nurse to realize the consequences of rubella, namely fetal wastage, severe congenital anomalies, and mental retardation. Community screening of all females for susceptibility to rubella may reduce the risk of maternal infection and fetal complications.

Cytomegalovirus

Cytomegalovirus (CMV) is transmitted from intimate contact with body fluids that contain the infectious material, such as endocervical mucus, colostrum, urine, and transfused blood. If a primary infection occurs during gestation, fetal infection may develop. Following primary infection in the pregnant woman, there is prolonged viuria which is characteristic of CMV disease.

The clinical manifestations of CMV are similar to those presented by infectious mononucleosis. The symptoms are usually general malaise, lethargy, hepatomegaly, and sudden onset of high fever lasting for as long as 3 weeks. The distinguishing absence of pharyngitis and cervical lymphadenopathy reinforce the diagnosis.

Chronic infections of the female genital tract play an important role in the epidemiology of CMV. Research demonstrates a higher neonatal infection rate in infants whose mothers have persistent vaginal infections.[31] There is also a higher incidence in the firstborn of very young primigravidas perhaps due to the lack of exposure to CMV. Overt congenital CMV is always the result of hematogenous dissemination and is capable of infecting the fetus regardless of gestational time.

Conditions associated with the infant at risk who has been infected by CMV are prematurity, low birth weight, microcephaly, and disseminated intravascular coagulation. The complications advance with each trimester. Unlike other viruses, CMV can occur with subsequent pregnancies.

The diagnosis is confirmed by maternal serologic tests which detect antibodies to this virus. The complement fixation titer is contingent on the presence of specific IgG antibodies in the serus. The complement fixation titer has a fourfold rise when the maternal infection is present.

The neutralization titer is more specific in detecting susceptibility to CMV disease. The neutralization titer is a reflection of both IgG and IgM antibodies. A more expedient and definitive method to detect the presence of CMV is to culture the maternal and fetal urine. There is no specific treatment for the disease although antiviral chemotherapy has been considered, but with reservation.

This virus has the ability to disseminate throughout the immediate environment. Therefore, isolation of the infant from the mother and other infants in the nursery is recommended until the maternal urine culture and antibody status can be determined.

Adequate history taking and routine antibody screening may reduce the risks to the fetus. The threat of carrying an infected infant who is at risk is anxiety provoking, and separation of the high-risk infant from the mother may delay the development of positive mother-infant relationships.

The nurse must provide physical and emotional support to the pregnant woman and her family during such a crisis. See Chapter 20, "Emotional Considerations for the Pregnant Family," in which the nursing management and intervention tools are well delineated.

Venereal Disease

Venereal diseases are communicable, infectious diseases that are contracted almost exclusively through sexual contact. The most common is gonorrhea; the most serious is syphilis. In recent years, gonorrhea has reached epidemic proportions in the United States. The highest incidence is among young adults twenty to twenty-four years old, followed next by teenagers fifteen to nineteen years old. Changing social, moral, and sexual standards, and easier access to contraception, have been implicated as factors in the venereal disease epidemic. Over 1 million new cases are reported annually in the United States.[32] Syphilis can be transmitted to the fetus through the transplacental barrier and gonorrhea during parturition.

Neisseria Gonorrhea

Gonorrhea, a gram-negative diplococcus which was discovered in 1879, is transmitted during sexual intercourse almost without exception. Epidemiologists state that from 3 to 5 percent of a given segment of the population harbor the infection.[33] In 1973, gonorrhea was the most prevalent reportable communicable disease. These findings support the use of Credé's method, the application of ophthalmic prophylaxis into

each eye of the newborn infant after delivery to prevent gonococcal ophthalmic neonatorum.

The symptoms appear within 2 to 5 days after sexual contact with an infected person, but many women are asymptomatic; therefore, delay in seeking medical attention is common. Generally, when the woman begins to have dysuria, urinary frequency, and increased leukorrhea of greenish yellow color she becomes suspicious and reports to the clinic for diagnosis. During this period, systemic infections can occur, namely salpingitis, cervicitis, and arthritis. If gonorrhea is untreated, the symptoms last from 10 days to 2 weeks. The woman may still harbor the organism and thus become a source of reinfection. An attack of gonorrhea confers no immunity to subsequent infections.

Frequently, women seek treatment from local VD clinics or neighborhood health clinics, and nurses are probably the first people with whom these women interact. To be effective in the treatment, control, and management of this epidemic disease, the nurse must be nonjudgmental in approach and attitudes. Establishing a therapeutic rapport with the client is of primary importance because the pregnant woman who contracts gonorrhea is anxious and concerned about the welfare of her baby. The nurse will need to counsel the woman regarding gonorrhea, providing information about its transmission and the symptoms of the disease. Prevention and treatment are the major focuses for the nurse. The sharing of this knowledge with an individual or a group of women is within the realm of nursing, and as a professional member of the health team the nurse can utilize communication media for informing the public and disease control agencies.

The maternity nurse encounters many women with a major subjective complaint of leukorrhea. Skill is required in the collection of specimens for differential diagnosis. A vaginal exam is done using a bivalve speculum which facilitates visualization. Smears are obtained separately from the vagina, urethra, cervical os, and rectal areas.

To obtain a specimen for culture, sterile swabs are used, and the specimen is inoculated on separate Thayer-Martin (TM) media plates. The swab should be rolled on the TM media in a Z fashion.

When it is necessary to send the specimen to a central laboratory for culture, such as with cases involving nurses who practice in a rural health area, Transgrow bottles containing medium are used.

The therapeutic approach is to obtain a high blood level of an effective antibiotic for a short duration. For the irresponsible client, parenteral administration may be necessary. The use of probenecid with penicillin has been recommended by the Communicable Disease Control Center. With large doses of penicillin, the gonococci die within 2 to 9 hours after therapy begins. The use of probenecid in combination with penicillin is reported to increase the efficacy of the action of penicillin.[34] The nurse assesses the patient's previous history in view of allergic response to penicillin. Tetracyclines are avoided in the pregnant woman due to the teratogenic effects on the fetus.

Syphilis

Syphilis is a complex infectious disease caused by the spirochete *treponema pallidum*. It is a systemic disease transmitted almost exclusively by sexual contact. It can be transmitted to the infant transplacentally via the bloodstream after the 20th week of gestation, resulting in congenital syphilis.

Syphilis is divided into two major stages, primary and secondary. Primary syphilis is characterized by a chancre at the site of infection, and has an incubation period of 10 to 90 days after contact. Upon examination a hard, indurated, painless ulcer type of lesion is frequently seen at or near the clitoris, accompanied by regional lymphadenopathy. Secondary syphilis is characterized by a generalized, papular (or grouped follicular), symmetrical, pruritic rash, which may occur up to 6 months following the development of the chancre. The skin eruptions, which may be accompanied by a low-grade fever, heal within 2 to 8 weeks.

After the unmedicated client is noninfectious, the disease is termed latent or tertiary syphilis. Since syphilis is a systemic disease, invasion of the central nervous, cardiovascular, and respiratory systems may develop from 10 to 20 years after the latent period.

Diagnostic laboratory data are essential for definitive diagnosis. In primary syphilis, a dark-field microscopic examination is made, which is the direct examination of a moist lesion. To avoid confusion with other spirochetal organisms, the dark-field exam is done by an experienced microbiologist.

The Venereal Disease Research Laboratory (VDRL) and the fluorescent treponemal antibody absorption tests (FTA-ABS) tests are the serologic diagnostic tests specific for syphilis. The VDRL shows a positive reading in 1 to 3 weeks after a primary lesion. The results are interpreted as nonreactive 1+ to 4+, and the VDRL titer tends to be high in secondary syphilis. The FTA-ABS readings are expressed in positive or negative results depending on the nontreponemal antigen response. Administration of large doses of penicillin is the specific treatment for all forms of syphilis. The dose is regulated daily until a total of 4.8 million units has been given. An alternative dose plan is the administration of procaine penicillin intramuscularly for 10 consecutive days.

The presence of a chancre and a positive

serology in a pregnant woman necessitates treatment. Analysis of cerebrospinal fluid is also necessary to develop a therapeutic plan of care for the pregnant woman and the fetus. The usual chemotherapy is limited with the pregnant woman because of the teratogenicity of tetracyclines. Penicillin G is preferred, but if the woman is hypersensitive, erythromycin can be used in the second and third trimester. The damage to the fetus is minimal if the disease is acquired and the woman is treated in early gestation.

Treponema pallidum affects all organs including the placenta. There is morphological evidence, however, suggesting that prior to the 5th month of gestation there is no placental involvement.

Serological surveillance of the high-risk population for venereal disease should be a primary focus for the maternity nurse. Venereal disease control should begin in antepartum and postpartum clinics, family planning clinics, and private physicians' offices. The nurse, functioning in a primary care role, frequently initiates the plan of care.

The areas for nursing management and intervention are:

1 Complete history taking including a comprehensive sexual history
2 Screening of all females—particularly the high-risk candidates
3 Educating and teaching clients to increase their awareness of venereal disease
4 Maintaining personal confidentiality
5 Reporting all cases to community health system

There is still a great deal of stigma associated with contracting a venereal disease. The nurse must reassure the client regarding the outcome for herself and the fetus. Early detection and prompt treatment will provide an uneventful outcome in a large majority of cases.

Herpes Simplex II

The organism herpes virus is of DNA origin. Herpes simplex type II is considered to be a venereal infection of the lower genital tract, and in review of the literature, there is evidence to support an alarming increase of herpes II. Some reports indicate that it is approaching the epidemic proportions of gonorrhea. The highest incidence occurs in women who are in the second and third decades of life. Herpes II is seen more frequently in sexually active women with multiple sex partners. It is also prevalent in lower socioeconomic populations.

The predisposition to herpes II seems to be associated with clients who have abnormal systemic diseases and inadequate antibody antigen responses. This group includes the women who have allergies, diabetes, and hypogammaglobulinemia.

The clinical manifestations of primary herpes II are multiple lesions on the vulva, vagina, and/or cervix occurring 2 to 7 days after contact with the virus, with communicability of 7 to 10 days. Subjective complaints of leukorrhea, local genital discomfort, dysuria, scant bleeding, and dyspareunia along with general malaise and fever are common. Regional lymphadenopathy is found on physical examination.

Secondary or recurrent herpes, in contrast to primary herpes, is more confined with less involvement. Local symptoms rather than systemic symptoms predominate. Vaginal discharge and discomfort are the subjective complaints.

There seems to be a threefold increase in spontaneous abortions when the maternal infection is of primary origin.[35] Prematurity is noticeably increased in women who develop herpes II vulvovaginitis after the 20th week of gestation. Herpes II is devastating to the fetus in the immediate neonatal period (24 to 48 hours). Mortality is over 60 percent, and if the infant survives, 50 percent will have neurological and ocular sequelae.

The medical management depends upon clinical evidence of the number, size, and distribution of the lesions. If systemic symptoms occur, an amniocentesis may be done 3 to 4 weeks after the onset of the primary infection. This procedure can provide data for documentation of fetal involvement.

A pap smear should be obtained, since herpes II may have an oncogenic effect on the cervix.[36] The woman should also have an antibody serological screening evaluation. Cytologic analysis of a cell from the lesion can often lead to a positive diagnosis. A biopsy of a lesion will also confirm the diagnosis.

Local anesthetic agents are used to decrease the discomfort, and the use of tannic acid is beneficial in reducing the edema, tingling, and burning sensations. Controversy exists regarding the treatment of herpes II with steroids since they cause viral replication.

The role of the nurse, in a nonjudgmental approach, is to obtain a complete sexual history with emphasis on the woman's sexual behavior patterns. Seeking information about the sexual contacts is primary for control of herpes II due to the communicability.

Current research states that there is a relationship between herpes genitalis and cervical cancer.[37] It has been found that 80 percent of women with cancer of the cervix have antibodies to herpes simplex II. Cancer of the cervix is more prevalent in the lower socioeconomic group and in those that engage in heterosexual activities early in life. Other interrelated and correlated theories proposed are related to the incidence of venereal disease as it relates to the incidence of cervical cancer. Further scientific research is necessary to document these hypotheses.

With active primary lesions, delivery by cesarean section is preferred if membranes are intact or have been ruptured less than 4 hours. If time permits, a culture of amniotic fluid is recommended to detect presence of the virus and determine the route for delivery.

Group B Hemolytic Streptococci

Hemolytic streptococcus is a gram-positive organism that grows in chains. It has been isolated in the female genital tract, and a large percentage of women of childbearing age harbor this organism. The prevalence of group B hemolytic streptococci in the vaginal flora has not seemed to increase the pathogenic response in the pregnant woman. Researchers believe that the probability of group B hemolytic streptococci is underestimated.[38] However, there is a wide spectrum of associated pathologic conditions that are demonstrated during pregnancy resulting from hemolytic streptococcus B, which include pyelonephritis, sepsis from induced abortion, puerperal sepsis, pneumonitis, and neonatal sepsis.

By and large, penicillin is the drug of choice for hemolytic streptococcus B. If the patient is hypersensitive to penicillin, Cephalathin is recommended. The therapeutic regimen is an initial loading dose followed by 10 to 14 days of therapy.

Trichomonas Vaginalis and Candida Albicans

Trichomonas is a flagellated motile protozoan, and the viability and growth of the organism is dependent on its environment.

When the pH of the vagina is 4.9 to 7.5, the protozoan can survive and grow. The organism commonly infects the vagina, cervix, and urethra but may also infect the Bartholin and Skene's glands. Trichomonas is transmitted through sexual intercourse exclusively, and it is estimated that 15 to 20 percent of the female population worldwide are infected.[39]

During pregnancy, the symptoms are exacerbated by the increased levels of progesterone which elevate the pH of the vaginal flora and enhance growth of the protozoa. Acute emotional crisis is also thought to aggravate the symptoms of trichomoniasis. There seems to be a higher than normal association of trichomoniasis and cancer of the cervix. Diagnosis is confirmed by wet smear identification culture and cytological smears.

Candida albicans is a fungus commonly harbored in the vagina of pregnant women. Higher levels of estrogen in pregnancy favor the abundance of glycogen in the vaginal mucosa, supporting fungal growth. *Candidiasis* (moniliasis) is more common in women using oral contraceptives as well as those using antibiotics indiscriminately.[40] Diabetic women and potential pregnant diabetics have an increased incidence of candidiasis.

It is reported that 50 percent of infants born to mothers who harbor *C. albicans* subsequently develop the clinical manifestations of a disease referred to as *thrush*. Local antifungal therapy is prescribed. Painting the vulva and vagina with 1 percent gentian violet before the initiation of antifungal therapy relieves the pruritis.

Nursing Management

The overall nursing management for trichomonas vaginitis and candidiasis is to obtain a vaginal smear for a wet prep test. The microscopic results will aid in differential diagnosis and thereby provide a specific chemotherapeutic plan. The nurse assesses the client's personal hygiene to determine if clarification and education is indicated. The woman should be instructed to wipe her vulva from front to back to prevent reinfection. Sitz baths may alleviate pruritis and reduce edema. The woman should be instructed to avoid bubble baths and perfumed feminine deodorants, so frequently advertised, since these alter the vaginal flora. If vaginal suppositories or ointments are prescribed, instruction of how to use them is a primary nursing role. Avoidance of sexual intercourse is recommended, but if this is unacceptable, the use of condoms is suggested.

Helping the woman deal with vaginal infections requires an empathetic approach from the nurse because vaginal infections, regardless of etiology, carry a stigma, which may alter the woman's self-esteem and increase her anxiety. Reassurance from the nurse that this condition is not uncommon in the female population may reduce the level of anxiety.

MEDICAL COMPLICATIONS DURING PREGNANCY

Heart Disease

Recent statistics show a marked decline in maternal mortality for pregnant women with pre-existing heart disease, but cardiac disease still ranks as the fourth cause of maternal mortality.[41] Contributing factors for this decline are the advancement in the knowledge of cardiovascular physiology as well as colleague sharing and management of the cardiac pregnant woman by the obstetrician, internist, and the maternity nurse practitioner. There is still need to provide the pregnant cardiac woman the astute assessment and management received by the general cardiac population.

The hyperdynamic circulatory changes that occur during pregnancy are well documented in the medical literature. It is stated that these circulatory alterations are considered the most important of all system changes due to the effect on maternal and fetal homeostasis.[42]

Cardiovascular research substantiates that the circulating blood volume and maximum cardiac output increase approximately 40 percent by the end of the first trimester, and there is a continued expansion during the second trimester followed by a gradual leveling throughout the remainder of pregnancy and in the early puerperium.[43] The circulatory parameters that increase during pregnancy are the total blood volume, plasma volume, cardiac output, and red cell mass. Peak levels of these parameters are reached between the 28th and 35th weeks of gestation. This depicts cardiovascular activity occurring in the normal uncomplicated pregnant state.

The maternity nurse must be cognizant of the cardiovascular alterations that occur during pregnancy because when pregnancy is superimposed upon a woman with organic heart disease, the physiologic changes are magnified.

Rheumatic heart disease and its sequelae, mitral stenosis, constitute the majority of heart disease cases encountered by the obstetrician and maternity nurse. In the past 20 years, there has been a significant decline in rheumatic heart disease due to early detection and improved therapeutic management.

Pregnant women with a congenital heart lesion comprise a significant number of the maternity populus. With the advent of corrective cardiac surgery and restorative medical management, young girls with a congenital cardiac anomaly survive to become reproductive. Although less common, organic heart disease, namely heart block, COR pulmonale, thyrotoxic heart disease, myo-cardical infarction, and Marfan's syndrome may become evident during pregnancy.

The New York Heart Association has developed a four-category classification index for heart disease (shown below) based on the patient's history and presenting disability.[44] To date, this is an operational tool for evaluating cardiac function of a pregnant woman. The cardiovascular status dictates the management and therapeutic regimen.

Class I: Cardiac disease present; can do routine physical activity without limitations

Class II: Cardiac disease present; normal physical activity causes palpitations, dyspnea, or anginal discomfort

Class III: Cardiac disease present; decrease in ability to perform normal physical activity; marked discomfort and excessive fatigue

Class IV: Cardiac disease present; inability to perform any physical activity without discomfort; a decompensated state

When a pregnant woman presents with subjective symptoms of cough after minimal exertion, palpitation, dyspnea, or edema, the nurse suspects coexisting heart disease. A careful history is taken, with emphasis on familial, congenital and/or acquired organic heart disease. If the history reveals significant predisposing factors to cardiac disease, further investigation is necessary, which may include serum laboratory study, chest x ray, urinalysis, electrocardiogram, arterial and venous blood pressure readings, and apical and radial pulse evaluations. Variations from the normal clinical picture add support to the diagnosis of heart disease. The prevention of pulmonary edema and congestive heart failure are primary considerations for the physician and the nurse.

The role of the nurse is to assess the physical status as well as cultural and psychosocial aspects of the woman's condition at frequent intervals. Antepartum visits every 2 weeks are recommended; with close supervision, the nurse will be able to detect early warning signs of impending cardiac failure. The onset of cardiac failure is usually gradual. The woman often expresses subjective complaints of a cough without evidence of a respiratory infection. Upon auscultation, however, the examiner hears persistent rales which remain audible after two or three deep inspiratory efforts. The presence of increasing edema and tachycardia are also critical warning signs of decreasing cardiac function. Subjective complaints from the woman include statements like "My whole leg is swollen," "My heart is pounding like a trip-hammer," and, "I couldn't sleep last night because my heart was pounding like a drum." The therapeutic regimen varies according to the degree of cardiac involvement.

The nurse must articulate the medical management into the plan of care for the woman. The priority nursing goals should include:

1. *a* Limitation of physical activity by encouraging frequent rest periods daily; recommend at least 10 hours of sleep at night (classes I and II).
   b Complete bed rest to hospitalization (classes III and IV).
2. Frequent communications with the woman and her family to relay significant data necessary to minimize further complications.
3. Discussion of alternatives available with the woman for decreasing anxiety and stress in the environment: e.g., utilize homemaker services for house-work and child care; decrease stimulus overload.
4. Utilization of available community resources.
5. Instruction for alterations in diet planning. Sodium restriction may be required. Minimal weight gain (7.5 to 9 kg) is encouraged to prevent further cardiac overload. Encourage foods rich in iron to decrease anemia complications.
6. Implementation of the medical regimen that usually consists of providing sedation, digitalis preparations, diuretic therapy, and oxygen as indicated.

Depending on the severity and advancement of the cardiac problem, the physician may elect to terminate the pregnancy. It should be reemphasized that peak levels of the cardiac parameters previously stated occur during the 7th and 8th months of pregnancy. Once this crisis has passed, successful vaginal delivery can be accomplished under local or regional anesthesia.

The most critical maternal crisis occurs within the first 24 hours after delivery. Resurgence of the expanded circulating blood volume may initiate cardiac failure. The maternal physiological readjustments return to the prepregnant status in approximately 2 to 4 weeks postpartum.

Diabetes

Diabetes mellitus, a major endocrine disorder, is the inability of the beta cells of the pancreas to metabolize glucose properly. Current research in molecular biology reveals that glucagon is equally important in diabetes as insulin. Whereas insulin is deficient in diabetes, glucagon is present in excess and difficult to decrease. A major research breakthrough was the discovery of a newly isolated hormone, somatostatin, that can suppress the release of both insulin and glucagon.[45] It then became apparent that glucagon plays a critical role in the pathology of diabetes.

It has been found that: (1) hyperglucagonemia is present with every type of hyperglycemia; (2) when the secretion of glucagon and insulin are suppressed, hyperglycemia is absent; and (3) with the somatostatin-induced suppression of glucagon there is restoration of normal blood sugar levels and certain other symptoms of diabetes are eliminated.[46] There seems to be a delicate balance that exists between glucagon and insulin. An in-depth review of diabetes mellitus is recommended to recall the complexity of carbohydrate metabolism.

Diabetes mellitus is a coincidental endocrine disease process that may coexist with pregnancy. Some researchers consider pregnancy a diabetrogenic state; dramatic hormonal alterations effect changes in carbohydrate metabolism even in the normally healthy pregnant woman. Insulin is circulating as early as the 8th week of gestation, and this increases significantly by the third trimester of pregnancy.

Two mechanisms have been described for maintaining normoglycemia during pregnancy:[47]

1 A check-and-balance system involving the destruction of increased insulin production by placental lactogen
2 An increase in the glomerular filtration rate with a decrease in the tubular reabsorption of glucose

Placental lactogen seems to be the main antagonist that keeps the circulating insulin in check to prevent hypoglycemia.

There is a delicate balance between glucose production and glucose metabolism during pregnancy. Increased demands for fetal growth and development may overtax the maternal production of insulin, which affects glucose metabolism. The fetus derives its glucose exclusively from maternal sources.

The effect of diabetes on pregnancy is awesome. It is a major cause of perinatal morbidity and mortality, and the incidence is 1 in every 200 to 300 pregnancies in the United States.[48]

According to the classification of diabetes established by the American Diabetic Association, diabetes during pregnancy is a moderately inconsequential entity that can be managed without too much difficulty. Overt and latent diabetics, who superimpose pregnancy upon already severe disorders, are much higher-risk patients. Priscilla White, in her classic article published in 1949, devised the following classification index for diabetes and pregnancy.[49]

Class A: Pregnant women whose glucose tolerance test is only slightly abnormal. Fetal survival is high; dietary regulation is minimal, and no insulin is required.
Class B: Pregnant women whose diabetes is of less than 10 years' duration, whose disease began at age twenty or older, and who have no vascular involvement.
Class C: Pregnant women whose diabetes began between age ten and nineteen, whose disease has lasted from 10 to 19 years, and who have minimal vascular involvement.
Class D: Pregnant women whose diabetes has lasted 20 years or more, whose disease began before age ten, and who have greater vascular involvement.
Class E: Pregnant women in whom calci-

fication of the pelvic arteries has been demonstrated on x ray.

Class F: Pregnant women whose diabetes has caused nephropathy.

This is perhaps the most cogent frame of reference for developing nursing assessment, for action planning and for intervention in caring for the pregnant diabetic woman.

There is a high-risk group who are predisposed to diabetes and its complications in pregnancy. They include the following:

1 Clients who are known diabetics
2 Clients with a family history of diabetes mellitus
3 Clients who are obese, due to alteration of carbohydrate metabolism
4 Women who have delivered a baby weighing 4,500 g and over
5 Women with a past obstetrical history of unexplained stillbirths and/or neonatal deaths
6 Women whose pregnancy was associated with polyhydramnios and/or preeclampsia
7 Women with infertility problems

The clinical assessment and management begin with the collaborative efforts between the pregnant woman, internist, obstetrician, and maternity nurse. The overall goal of management is to maintain the balance between insulin and glucose with emphasis on optimum maternal and fetal outcome.

Early detection and diagnosis of diabetes is primary, and a complete health history and physical examination provide a base line of data for the identification of the risk factors. The client's weight (evidence of gains or losses) may be significant in detecting alterations in metabolism. A routine blood pressure evaluation is obtained to help identify circulatory problems, hypertension, and/or preeclampsia.

The type of infection, the healing time, and therapeutic treatment is specific information that must be assessed by the nurse. The nurse should focus particularly on genitourinary, vaginal, and recurrent upper respiratory infections. Frequent urinary tract infections can be a clue to the possibility of kidney damage. Candidiasis increases during pregnancy, but more so in the diabetic pregnant woman. The healing process is delayed in the pregnant woman with diabetes as a result of decreasing vascularization.

Of utmost importance for the nurse is the client's dietary patterns and activity routine. A complete dietary history is obtained with the number of calories, protein, fat, and carbohydrates spelled out clearly. Assessment of the activities of daily living for the client will describe how she copes physically with the disease process.

The key to the clinical management for the pregnant diabetic is to maintain the fasting blood glucose levels between 90 and 110 mg per 100 ml and the 2-hour postprandial blood sugar below 170 mg per 100 ml. Insulin is adjusted according to fasting blood sugar levels, and the 2-hour postprandial blood sugar levels. The usual prescription is a combination of intermediate or long-acting insulin with regular insulin in the morning and an additional dose of regular insulin after the evening meal. The nurse must thoroughly discuss with and explain this rigid regimen to the client. A demonstration in the use of the syringe, aseptic technique, types of insulin, and sites of injections is the focus of the teaching plan for the nurse. Oral hypoglycemia agents are contraindicated during pregnancy due to potential fetal teratogenicity.

Diet for each individual is based upon normal nutritional needs expressed in terms of total caloric requirements. The diabetic woman prior to pregnancy is probably familiar with the dietary regimen, but modifications may be needed. The usually prescribed diet for pregnant diabetics is from 1,800 to 2,200 calories, with 90 g of protein.[50] This is divided into three equal meals and an evening snack. The diabetic food exchange list, published by the American Diabetic Association, provides a guideline for measurement and variety of foods to be included. The 1,800 to 2,200 calorie 90-g protein diet will maintain a stable blood glucose level as well as meet the demands of the growing fetus.

Estimation of fetal well-being and placental function must be determined, and laboratory tests used are noted on the chart in Table 30-5. The results of these tests are decisive factors in initiating labor or delivery of the baby. Placental researchers have indicated that during the last 3 to 4 weeks of gestation, the placenta has periods of insufficiency. To reduce macrosomia (a large baby) and deliver a live fe'us, a cesarean section is performed.

The role of the nurse is extensive; teaching is the focus, and the nurse should know how to develop a teaching/learning tool with behavioral objectives for the individual client. *The Process of Patient Teaching* by Dr. Barbara Redman is an excellent resource.

TABLE 30-5
Evaluation of the Fetal-Placental Unit (Laboratory Tests to Determine Fetal Status and Placental Function)

Fetal	Maternal
Ultrasound cephalometry. Done from 32d week of gestation to term. Determines growth of biparietal diameters—failure of growth on three consecutive occasions is a warning sign of retarded fetal growth and chronic fetal distress.	Measure twenty-four hour urinary estriol levels from mother starting the 32d week of gestation to term. Figures are charted against a standard normal range. May be done weekly and then daily. Normal is 10–40 mg/day in late pregnancy. If 4–12 mg, indicates fetal growth retardation; 1–4 mg in danger of dying; 1 mg indicates intrauterine death. Urinary estriol levels are low in mothers with toxemia, diabetes, and pyelitis. This test determines the status of both the fetal and placental unit.
Lecithin/sphingomyelin /L/S) ratio shake test. Withdraw amniotic fluid by amniocentesis, place in tube, add ethanol, and shake. If stable bubbles appear, adequate pulmonary maturity is present. The higher the ratio, the more mature the fetal lungs. A ratio of less than 2:1 is indicative of hyaline membrane disease.	Maternal serum evaluation of HPL. HPL, human placental lactogen, reflects the integrity of the placenta and mirrors the curve of fetal growth. Serum evaluation can be done from 8–36 weeks of gestation. A persistent value of 4.0 mg/ml on three occasions from the 36th week on is a warning of placental insufficiency and fetal distress.
Amniography. Introduction of radiopaque contrast media into amniotic sac. As the fetus ingests amniotic fluid, the contrast media is swallowed. Anomalies can be detected. The fetus who is too moribund to swallow the media is at risk for delivery.	Oxytocin challenge test (OCT). OCT is the administration of 5 to 10 units of oxytocin per 1,000 ml IV solution to promote uterine contractions at 3–5 minute intervals, lasting 60 seconds. The contractions and fetus are monitored. The OCT may last from 1–3 hours and be repeated. The absence of any later decelerations constitutes a negative test which means the fetus is well and the placental function is sufficient. A positive OCT means the fetus is compromised and cannot withstand labor.
Amnioscopy. Insertion of a conical speculum through the cervical os—inspection of the amniotic fluid through an intact fetal membrane—can detect fetal distress.	

The nurse assesses the client's ability to understand the disease, and communicates the following to her:

1   Scientific terminology in lay phraseology
2   The necessity for dietary control
3   Early identification of abnormal symptoms
4   Recognition of accurate measurement of the dose and type of insulin, as well as the rotation of sites for administration
5   Reason for meticulous skin care
6   Methods to prevent injury and infection

The nurse, a key person on the health team, interacts with the client frequently, and recognizes that the client's anxiety level may be markedly increased when pregnancy is complicated by diabetes or vice versa. The educational background of the nurse provides the necessary physiologic, psychosocial, and cultural support for the pregnant diabetic woman.

Thyrosis

One of the major physiologic changes which occurs during pregnancy is the increased hormone secretion by the thyroid gland which alters the delicate balance maintained through thyroid function. The most abundant thyroid hormones are thyroxine (T_4) and triiodothyronine (T_3). In the pregnant state, a mild hyperplasia of the thyroid gland exists. As the thyroid enlarges, there is a proportionate increase in the production of T_4. T_3 also becomes more active during pregnancy and is capable of transplacental crossing. There is a specific physi-

ologic feedback mechanism that operates between the hypothalamus and the adenohypophysis or anterior pituitary gland. This system exerts a stimulating effect on the thyroid gland to maintain the necessary amounts of T_3 and T_4.

Pregnancy rarely occurs with severe hypothyroidism or hyperthyroidism. There is a relatively high incidence of infertility in clients with either condition. If pregnancy does occur, it is possible to consider that a marginal hypo- or hyperthyroidism condition exists. Spontaneous abortions, prematurity, and toxemia are common untoward complications for the woman, and the fetus is endangered in either condition with the possibility of mental retardation.

The thyroid status of all pregnant women should be determined on the initial antepartum visit by use of the *free thyroxine index* (FTI). The range for the FTI is 2.6 to 7.2 mg per 100 ml of serum.[51] In hyperthyroidism, the FTI is increased. Other significant laboratory data include the protein–bound iodine serum test (PBI, the T_3 uptake, and the basal metabolic rate (BMR) test. The therapeutic regimen depends upon the clinical symptoms and diagnostic laboratory results.

In hyperthyroidism, the client complains of increased appetite despite weight loss, peripheral vasodilatation in the extremities, and tachycardia or palpitations. The management is individualized to the client's gestational age of pregnancy. Mild sedation with phenobarbital is usually prescribed to reduce the tachycardia. Antithyroid drugs, such as propylthiouracil, may be administered with caution, however.

The clinical picture of hypothyroidism is one of a gradual onset of lethargy, cutaneous thickening, mental confusion, and insensitivity to cold with confirmation of the diagnosis made through evaluation of the laboratory data. The therapeutic regimen is usually oral administration of crude thyroid extract. Careful monitoring via laboratory tests allows for regulation of the dosage.

The overall therapeutic management of the pregnant woman with thyroid dysfunction includes a well-balanced nutritional diet, a quiet, relaxing atmosphere, and judicious implementation of the medical therapeutic regimen.

Jaundice

Viral Hepatitis

Viral hepatitis, a major health problem unrelated to pregnancy, is the most common cause of jaundice during pregnancy. The effect of viral hepatitis on pregnancy depends upon the virulence as well as the term of gestation when acquired. The onset of the disease in the last trimester is more ominous for both the woman and the fetus than if it were acquired earlier in pregnancy.

The clinical symptoms of viral hepatitis may be present during the first or second trimester but since the symptoms of nausea, vomiting, and fatigue are attributed to pregnancy rather than a disease process, the condition may go undiagnosed until later in pregnancy. Differential diagnosis, a necessary measure, is done through laboratory screening.

The client complains of increased epigastric pain, vomiting, and general malaise followed shortly by jaundice. Confusion in diagnosis exists since the symptoms correlate with those of advanced toxemia.

The etiology is unknown, but there are hypotheses that relate the causative factor to protein malnutrition.[52] Pregnant women who suffer from nutritional deprivation and others who have taken large doses of tetracyclines for infections during preg-

nancy are the high-risk candidates. Maternal and fetal complications advance as the disease progresses.

Cholelithiasis

The biochemical adjustments of pregnancy may promote the formation of gallstones. There is an increase in circulating cholesterol with higher concentrations present in the bile. The effect of certain hormones is to cause atony and stasis of the gallbladder, but rarely does a biliary obstruction occur during pregnancy as a result of this mechanism.

This condition is seen more frequently with the multigravida in late pregnancy or the early puerperium. When the client becomes jaundiced, clinical evaluation of the urine and stools is necessary. Radiography will lend credence for a differential diagnosis, and surgery may become necessary.

Anemia

Anemia refers to a reduction in the oxygen-carrying capacity of the blood below normal values. A pregnant woman is diagnosed as anemic if the hemoglobin is less than 10.6 g per 100 ml of whole blood. Acute or chronic blood loss and iron deficiency anemia are the major causes for anemia in pregnancy.

There is an increase in the iron requirement during pregnancy. See Chapter 17 for the specific requirement. In the third trimester, the fetal and placental demands increase abundantly, resulting in depletion of the maternal iron stores. The maternal iron stores are seldom ample to meet the parasitical requirements of the fetoplacental unit, which can result in iron deficiency anemia.

Oxygen deprivation and tissue hypoxia is first evident in the vital organ system.

This accounts for some of the presenting symptoms, namely headache, fatigue, pallor, and dyspnea.

The therapeutic regimen for controlling iron deficiency anemia includes an iron-rich diet composed of such foods as lean organ meats, eggs, green leafy vegetables, and fruit; administration of oral iron supplements to augment the total hemoglobin mass; and frequent laboratory evaluations.

Anemia due to blood loss can be acute or chronic. The acute phase may be associated with bleeding complications of pregnancy and postpartum hemorrhage. Hypovolemia, a major complication, requires blood volume replacement immediately to correct a potential maternal crisis. Intravenous infusions of lactate Ringer's solution and whole blood is a treatment of choice to provide for adequate tissue perfusion. Chronic blood loss may go unrecognized until such a time as hypovolemic shock occurs. Abruptio placenta is an obstetrical complication that exemplifies undetected blood loss.

Sickle-cell anemia, a dominant genetic disorder seen predominantly in the black population, is intensified during pregnancy. A sickle-cell crisis may be precipitated after a physiologically stressful pregnancy due to the increase of circulating sickle-shaped red cells. Maternal and fetal mortality is greater than that of the general obstetrical population.

Early identification is imperative to prevent a sickle-cell crisis situation. Some researchers suggest that administration of iron and folic acid supplements abate further hemoglobinopathy. A therapeutic plan of treatment includes symptomatic and palliative alleviation of pain and genetic counseling.

The maternity nurse should gather a base line of signs and symptoms to enable early recognition of medical disease processes that coexist in pregnancy. Skillful observa-

tion and astute listening by the nurse will enhance the early control of the hemoglobinopathies seen in pregnancy.

MULTIPLE GESTATIONS

The phenomenon of multiple pregnancy occurs in two specific ways: the simultaneous fertilization of two ova by two spermatozoa resulting in fraternal/dizygotic twins, who may be of the same or different sexes; or twinning, which results from the abnormal development of a single ovum fertilized by a single sperm. The latter are termed identical/monozygotic twins, and are always of the same sex. (See Figure 30-10.)

The incidence of twinning, prior to and excluding the fertility-drug-induced twins, was reported to be 1 in every 90 to 95 deliveries.[53] The black population has a higher incidence of multiple-ova multiple pregnancies than the white population. Twinning is rare among orientals.

In a multiple pregnancy, the uterus is overdistended for accommodation of the two fetuses. Placental and membrane development are altered. With identical twins, there is usually one placenta, one chorion, and two amnions, which creates a

FIGURE 30-10

Placental variations in twinning. (*By permission from Ralph C. Benson, Handbook of Obstetrics and Gynecology, 5th ed., Lange, Los Altos, Calif., 1974. With permission of publisher.*)

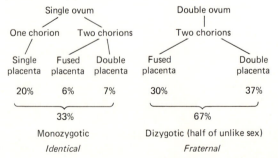

high-risk situation for one fetus who may suffer oxygen and nutritional deprivation. Fraternal twins have two placentas and two membranes. (See Figure 30-11.) The type of twinning is determined at delivery with the inspection of the placenta(s) and membrane(s). Microscopic examination provides definitive confirmation. The perinatal

FIGURE 30-11
Amniotic membranes of twins. (By permission from Ralph C. Benson, Handbook of Obstetrics and Gynecology, *5th ed., Lange, Los Altos, Calif., 1974. With permission of publisher.)*

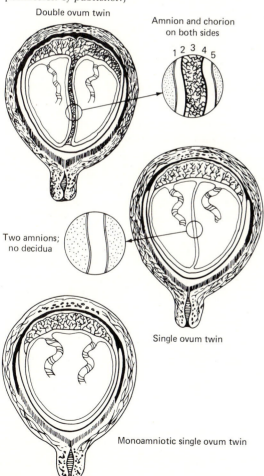

mortality rate is higher with identical twins since they are frequently more preterm and immature. The mother is also a high-risk patient. The physiologic demands of a twin pregnancy are magnified to a far greater degree than a single gestation. There is marked overdistention of the uterus, and the myometrial stretching causes irritability that leads to premature labor, hence premature infants.

The high-risk complications of toxemia, anemia, and circulatory overload are more common in multiple pregnancies. An abnormal amount of amniotic fluid (polyhydramnios) is produced, and although the etiology is unknown, it may be a compensatory survival mechanism. The increasing size of the uterus and its weight produce subjective complaints of backache, edema of the lower extremities, and varicosities of the vulva. As the pregnancy progresses, complaints of dyspnea are common.

A bimanual examination usually confirms the suspicion of multiple pregnancy. Auscultation of fetal heart tones in opposite quadrants is also suggestive of twins. Definite diagnosis can be made by radiography after the 20th week of gestation. (See Figure 30-12.)

To avoid fetal and maternal complications, delivery should be spontaneous, but frequently labor is dysfunctional. With judicious care and constant monitoring, however, an oxytocin infusion may be beneficial.

The nurse provides measures to alleviate the minor discomforts associated with multiple gestation. Bed rest is recommended at frequent intervals during the day. Dietary assessment and planning with the patient is imperative to reduce the risk of anemia.

When the client and her family are informed of a multiple pregnancy, the nurse needs to provide appropriate psychological support. Anticipatory guidance and prepara-

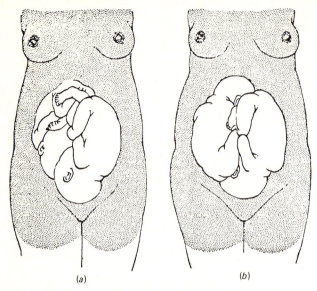

(a)   (b)

FIGURE 30-12
(a) Both twins presenting vertex. (b) One vertex and one breech presentation. (By permission from Ralph C. Benson, Handbook of Obstetrics and Gynecology, 5th ed., Lange, Los Altos, Calif., 1974. With permission of publisher.)

tion are essential. The nurse assists the woman and her family through the stages of shock, disbelief, and acceptance. Knowledge of the woman's adaptation and coping mechanisms are fundamental.

PSYCHOPATHOLOGICAL PROBLEMS

Hyperemesis Gravidarum

Hyperemesis gravidarum, defined as excessive vomiting in pregnancy, usually beyond the first trimester, frequently ceases after the 16th week of gestation. It is unknown in certain cultural groups, for example, most Asian peoples, but there is evidence to support the notion that hyperemesis develops even within these groups as they become acculturated into Western society.

No one specific etiologic factor is known. There are physiological alterations during pregnancy that can be specifically identi-

fied as presumptive causes, while on the other hand, psychological research studies reveal it may be an expression of neurotic behavior. There is evidence to support both schools of thought. New perspectives have been opened by the fact that hyperemesis is not caused by a single pathognomonic or psychogenic factor.[54] The phenomenon of the psyche interacting with the soma is greatly magnified in the hyperemesis gravidarum woman. In considering the organic hypothesis, undoubtedly there is a basic disturbance in carbohydrate metabolism in early pregnancy, which is primarily the result of increased metabolic demands for glucose.

Intractable vomiting, such as seen in severe hyperemesis, is accompanied by significant weight loss, alterations in the acid-base balance, and development of hepatic disorders such as fatty infiltration of the liver and mild jaundice. Clinical tests for liver function, however, demonstrate normal values in the hyperemesis woman.

Literature reviews state that hyperemesis gravidarum and anorexia nervosa bear certain resemblances. Certainly both are manifestations of a psychodynamic conflict. Some researchers say that anorexia nervosa occurs because the mother does not want to relinquish her daughter to adulthood, and the psychogenic problem for the hyperemesis patient is reported to be one of morbid fear in assuming adult sexuality.[55] More specifically, it is the fear of the role delineation and expectations of the adult sex role—womanhood and motherhood.

A London study of 100 primigravidas revealed that hyperemesis or intractable vomiting was found in women who were rejecting the maternal role.[56] These women demonstrated ambivalence in the development of the mother-child relationship. The nausea and vomiting are transient somatic evidence of rejection and denial of the pregnancy.

The symbolic meaning of food has been investigated. As an infant the need for food requires dependency from another, namely the mother. The maternal desire to "be a good mother," as imposed by society and the grandmother, is intensified in the client who may be basically insecure. The inability to respond from a mature emotional framework is threatened. Psychodynamically, overeating symbolizes the gratification response to impregnation. The absence of food, or starvation, has symbolic meanings related to fear and guilt.

The elevation of HCG during pregnancy is well validated. HCG is greatly increased in the woman with multiple gestation and hydatidiform mole. The pregnant woman who presents with hyperemesis should be evaluated for the existence of these high-risk conditions rather than categorized as a neurotic woman.

All theories must take multiple factors into account. Therapeutic management is a combination of treating symptoms from an organic base and using psychotherapeutic techniques, which results in treating the whole person.

A family-centered maternity care approach by the nurse is a functional strategy for prevention of hyperemesis. A complete history and physical examination is done with emphasis placed on the psychological history of the client and members of her support system. The physician and/or maternity nurse must be alert for underlying emotional conflict relative to the pregnancy. A diagnostic work-up may be necessary to rule out underlying pathology including systemic infections, cerebral irritation, and diabetes of pregnancy. A complete neurological and mental status examination is also recommended. Antiemetic suppositories have been used with efficacy.

The nurse continuously assesses and reassesses the client's behavior, verbal and nonverbal. Positive suggestion therapy is a valuable communication tool for the nurse to implement.

Hospitalization may become necessary to monitor electrolyte imbalance and improve nutritional status. A quiet, secure, and relaxing environment enhances recovery. Psychotherapy and hypnosis have proved to be beneficial for the hyperemesis patient.

Pseudocyesis

Pseudocyesis, defined as a false pregnancy, was described as early as 300 B.C. According to the medical literature, it is not an uncommon occurrence; it is seen more frequently in infertile women and postmenopausal women, and it even occurs sometimes in men.[57] The woman's intense desire for pregnancy is converted into physiological manifestations. This wish fulfillment is on an unconscious level, and may be a symptom of conversion hysteria. Another theory is that the woman had a strong unconscious oedipal attachment to her father, resulting in rivalry with and resentment toward her mother, which is expressed in the woman's desire to have a baby of her own.

Pseudocyesis is often misdiagnosed and sometimes confused with the woman who has a missed abortion. The physical signs and symptoms presented by the client are frequently magnified, and include menstrual alterations, specifically amenorrhea, usually lasting for 9 months. Amenorrhea, often mentioned as a symptom of depression, supports the contention that the single most important etiologic factor for pseudocyesis is the depression mechanism.

It is not uncommon for the woman to report feeling fetal movement. Roentgenography, used for definitive diagnosis of pregnancy, is always negative. After psychotherapy, there is a reversal of the physical symptoms which support the theory that pseudocyesis is of psychogenic origin.

The primary management of pseudocyesis is psychotherapy, and phenothiazines and antidepressants have also proved beneficial. The nursing management is to articulate the therapeutic plan of care established by the psychiatrist.

REFERENCES

1 Vorheer, Helmuth: "Gestational and Puerperal Uterine Disorders," in Nicholas S. Assali (ed.), *Pathophysiology of Gestation*, Academic, New York, 1972, p. 205.
2 Hasson, H. M.: "The Role of Enzymes in Disseminated Intravascular Coagulation," *Journal of Obstetric, Gynecologic and Neonatal Nursing*, 3(3):27–28, 1974.
3 Vorheer: op. cit., p. 205.
4 Vorheer: op. cit., p. 211.
5 Benson, Ralph C.: *Handbook of Obstetrics and Gynecology*, 4th ed., Lange, Los Altos, Calif., 1971, pp. 225–226.
6 Ibid., pp. 226–227.
7 Ibid., pp. 227–232.
8 Vorheer: op. cit., p. 226.
9 Hellman, Louis, and Jack Pritchard: *Williams Obstetrics*, 14th ed., Appleton-Century-Crofts, New York, 1971, p. 624.
10 Ibid., p. 627.
11 Hasson: op. cit., p. 28.
12 Benson: op. cit., p. 238.
13 Vorheer: op. cit., p. 224.
14 Hellman and Pritchard: op. cit., p. 686.
15 Russell, P. T., and Allen Shade: "Prostaglandins in the Toxemia of Pregnancy," *Journal of Obstetric, Gynecologic and Neonatal Nursing*, 3(5):52, 1974.
16 Chesley, Leon: "Kidneys, Fluids and Electrolytes," in Nicholas S. Assali (ed.), *Pathophysiology of Gestation*, Academic, New York, 1972, p. 397.
17 Ibid., pp. 418–432.
18 Ringrose, C. A.: "Psychopathology of Toxaemia of Pregnancy," in John G. Howells (ed.), *Modern Perspectives in Psycho-Obstetrics*, Brunner/Mazel, New York, 1971, pp. 283–289.
19 Ibid., p. 284.
20 Hellman and Pritchard: op. cit., p. 691.
21 Ibid., p. 686.
22 Ibid., p. 701.
23 *Maternal Nutrition and the Course of Pregnancy*, National Academy of Sciences, Washington, D.C., 1971, pp. 183–185.
24 Ibid., pp. 184–186.
25 Hellman and Pritchard: op. cit., p. 687.
26 Assali, N. S., and C. R. Brinkman: "Circulatory and Respiratory Adjustments," in Nicholas S. Assali (ed.), *Pathophysiology of Gestation*, Academic, New York, 1972, pp. 333–340.
27 Montif, Gilles R.: *Infectious Diseases in Obstetrics and Gynecology*, Harper & Row, New York, 1974, p. 42.
28 Ibid., p. 32.
29 Ibid., p. 73.

30 Ibid., p. 72.
31 Ibid., p. 43.
32 Millar, J. D.: "The National Venereal Disease Problem," in *Epidemic Venereal Disease*, Mosby, St. Louis, 1972, pp. 10–13.
33 Ibid., pp. 11–12.
34 Montif: op. cit., p. 109.
35 Kaufman, Raymond, and William E. Rawls: "Herpes Genitalis and Its Relationship to Cervical Cancer," *Cancer*, 24(6):258–264, September–October 1974.
36 Ibid., pp. 258–260.
37 Ibid., pp. 258–262.
38 Montif: op. cit., pp. 113–118.
39 Montif: op. cit., p. 207.
40 Montif: op. cit., p. 245.
41 Benson: op. cit., p. 301.
42 Assali and Brinkman: op. cit., pp. 270–297.
43 Assali and Brinkman: op. cit., pp. 270–297.
44 Hellman and Pritchard: op. cit., p. 779.
45 Maugh, Thomas: "Diabetes (III): New Hormones Promise More Effective Therapy," *Science*, 188:920–923, 1975.
46 Ibid., pp. 920–923.
47 Cranley, Mecca S., and Sue A. Frazier: "Preventive Intensive Care of the Diabetic Mother and Her Fetus," *Nursing Clinics of North America*, 8(3):489–499, 1973.
48 Benson: op. cit., p. 337.
49 White, P.: "Pregnancy Complicating Diabetes," *American Journal of Medicine*, 7:609, 1949.
50 Lerch, Constance: *Maternity Nursing*, Mosby, St. Louis, 1974, pp. 130–133.
51 Barnes, Cyril G.: *Medical Disorders in Obstetrics Practice*, 4th ed., Blackwell, London, 1974, chap. 15, pp. 307–318.
52 Montif: op. cit., pp. 77–82.
53 Benson: op. cit., p. 215.
54 Chertok, Leon: "The Psychopathology of Vomiting of Pregnancy," in John G. Howells (ed.), *Modern Perspectives in Psycho-Obstetrics*, Brunner/Mazel, New York, 1972, pp. 269–281.
55 Ibid., p. 280.
56 Ibid., pp. 269–281.
57 Barglow, Peter, and Edward Brown: "Pseudocyesis," in John G. Howells (ed.), *Modern Perspectives in Psycho-Obstetrics*, Brunner/Mazel, New York, 1972, pp. 52–65.

BIBLIOGRAPHY

Aladjem, Silvio: *Risks in the Practice of Modern Obstetrics*, Mosby, St. Louis, 1972.
Baird, James T.: *Parity and Hypertension*, U.S. Department of Health, Education, and Welfare, March 1972.
Barber, Hugh R. K., and Edward A. Graber: *Surgical Disease in Pregnancy*, Saunders, Philadelphia, 1974.
Bennett, A. David, et al.: *Immunization during Pregnancy*, American College of Obstetricians and Gynecologists Technical Bulletin, March 1973.
Brunner, Lillian, and Doris Suddarth: *Textbook of Medical-Surgical Nursing*, 3d ed., Lippincott, Philadelphia, 1975.
Burchell, R. Clay: "Professional Perspectives on Abortions," *Journal of Obstetric, Gynecologic and Neonatal Nursing*, November 1974, p. 25.
Conklin, Mary M.: "DIC in the Pregnant Patient," *Journal of Obstetric, Gynecologic and Neonatal Nursing*, June 1974, p. 29.
De Alvarez, Russell R.: "Hypertensive Disorders in Pregnancy," *Clinical Obstetrics and Gynecology*, March 1973, pp. 47–71.
Finnerty, Frank A.: "Management of Hypertension in Toxemia of Pregnancy," *Hospital Medicine*, January 1975, pp. 52–65.
Frohlich, Edward D. (ed.): *Pathophysiology-altered Regulatory Mechanism in Disease*, Lippincott, Philadelphia, 1972.
Guyton, Arthur C.: *Textbook of Medical Physiology*, 4th ed., Saunders, Philadelphia, 1971.
Hall, Joanne, and Barbara Weaver: *Nursing of Families in Crisis*, Lippincott, Philadelphia, 1974.
Halstead, Lois: "The Use of Crisis Intervention in Obstetrical Nursing," *Nursing Clinics of North America*, March 1974.

Hawkins, D. F. (ed.): *Obstetric Therapeutics*, Bailliere Tindall, London, 1974.

Hobel, Calvin J., et al.: "Prenatal and Intrapartum High-Risk Screening," *American Journal of Obstetrics and Gynecology*, 117(1): 1–9, September 1973.

Keller, C., et al.: "Counseling the Abortion Patient Is More Than Talk," *American Journal of Nursing*, 72(1):102, January 1972.

Krupp, M., and M. Chalton: *Current Medical Diagnosis and Treatment*, Lange, Los Altos, Calif., 1974.

Mayer, Gloria: "Disseminated Intravascular Coagulation," *American Journal of Nursing*, 73(12):2067–2069, December 1973.

McCartney, Charles P.: "Hypertension in Pregnancy," *Obstetrics and Gynecology Annual*, 1973, pp. 85–101.

McLennan, C., and E. C. Sandberg: *Synopsis of Obstetrics*, Mosby, St. Louis, 1974.

Messer, Joseph V.: "Heart Disease in Pregnancy," *The Journal of Reproductive Medicine*, 10(3): 102–106, March 1973.

Methany, Norma, and W. D. Snively: *Nurses Handbook of Fluid Balance*, 2d ed., Lippincott, Philadelphia, 1974.

Naismith, W. C., et al.: "Simultaneous Intravenous Infusion of Prostaglandin E_2 (PGE_2) and Oxytocin in the Management of Intrauterine Death of the Fetus, Missed Abortion and Hydatidiform Mole," *The Journal of Obstetrics and Gynecology of the British Commonwealth*, 81:146–149, February 1974.

National Academy of Sciences: *Maternal Nutrition and the Course of Pregnancy*, Washington, D.C., 1974.

Pfizer Laboratories: *Epidemic—Venereal Disease*, 2d International Venereal Disease Symposium, New York, 1973.

Pour-Reza, Maryam, et al.: "Serum Creatinine, Urea and Protein Level Changes in Hydatidiform Mole," *Journal of the American Medical Association*, 230(4):580–582, October 1974.

Redman, Barbara Klug: *The Process of Patient Teaching in Nursing*, Mosby, St. Louis, 1968.

Ryan, George F.: "Improving Pregnancy Outcome via Regionalization of Prenatal Care," *Journal of Obstetric, Gynecologic and Neonatal Nursing*, 3(4):38–40, July–August 1974.

Sarvis, B., and H. Rodman: *The Abortion Controversy*, 2d ed., Columbia University Press, New York, 1974.

Schoenberg, Bernard, et al.: *Loss and Grief—Psychological Management in Medical Practice*, Columbia University Press, New York, 1971.

Schwartz, L., and J. L. Schwartz: *The Psychodynamics of Patient Care*, Prentice-Hall, Englewood Cliffs, N.J., 1972.

Sharp, Elizabeth S.: "Symposium on Restructuring Maternity Care," *Nursing Clinics of North America*, June 1974.

Sheehan, H. L., and J. B. Lynch: *Pathology of Toxemia of Pregnancy*, Churchill Livingstone, London, 1973.

Shontz, Franklin C.: *The Psychologic Aspects of Physical Illness and Disability*, Macmillan, New York, 1975.

Speroff, Leon: "Toxemia and Pregnancy—Mechanism and Therapeutic Management," *American Journal of Cardiology*, 32:582–590, September 1973.

Sullivan, Jay M.: "Blood Pressure in Pregnancy," *Progress in Cardiovascular Diseases*, 16(4):375–392, February 1974.

Tsai, Albert, et al.: "Diabetes and Pregnancy," *Journal of Reproductive Medicine*, 11(1):23–28, July 1973.

Van Dersall, William R.: "How to be a Good Communicator—and a Better Nurse," *Nursing '74*, 4(12):57–64, December 1974.

Wahl, Charles W.: "The Art of Taking the Sexual History," *Ortho Panel*, Raritan, N.J., 1974.

Walbert, D., and J. Butler (eds.): *Abortion, Society and the Law*, Case Western, Cleveland, 1974.

White, P.: "Pregnancy Complicating Diabetes," *American Journal of Medicine*, 7:609, 1949.

Wynn, Ralph M.: *Obstetrics and Gynecology: The Clinical Care*, Lea & Febiger, Philadelphia, 1974.

31

Complications during Labor and Delivery

KARYN S. KAUFMAN

Labor and delivery is the process whereby the mature products of conception are expelled by the action of rhythmic uterine contractions. When studying this process, it is often helpful to examine its three primary components:

1 The powers—uterine contractions
2 The passengers—fetus, cord, placenta, membranes, and amniotic fluid
3 The passage—maternal pelvis and reproductive organs

In order for a normal labor and delivery to occur each of these components must be within the range of normalcy. When abnormalities are present in one or more of them, a complicated labor and delivery exists to some degree.

The primary abnormalities of these three components will be discussed in this chapter. It is necessary, however, to emphasize the interrelatedness of the powers, the passengers, and the passage. An abnormality in one of them will frequently occasion abnormalities in the other two. However, by assessing each component individually, cause and effect relationships may be established.

POWERS

Premature Labor

When the rhythmic contractions of labor begin before the 37th week of gestation, premature labor exists. The incidence of this complication is 7 to 13 percent of all births. Because of the immediate care needed at delivery, this is considered a complication of the intrapartum period, even though the actual labor and delivery may be uncomplicated. The cause of most premature labors is unknown. Less than half of them are associated with maternal disease conditions such as toxemia or chronic hypertension.[1]

Treatment of premature labor is directed to stopping the labor if this is possible. The pregnant woman is confined to bed and may receive medication to inhibit uterine contractions. Ethanol which inhibits oxytocin and vasodilators which inhibit uterine contractility are being used with some success. These medications are usually administered according to protocols which provide large initial doses and then subsequent doses based on uterine contractions and vital signs. These women need frequent monitoring of their vital signs, hydration status, possible side effects, and close observation of the fetal condition.[2]

If labor is too far advanced at admission, it may be impossible to stop contractions. In other cases the labor proceeds in spite of the medications. The nursing care of the patient is then influenced by the knowledge that premature infants have a lower margin of reserve for tolerating the stress of labor and can become hypoxic more quickly than the full-term infant. During labor, therefore, the pregnant woman will receive little or no systemic analgesia in order to prevent central nervous depression of the fetus. Careful monitoring of the fetal heart rate for patterns of distress is very important in view of the lowered tolerance of stress. The greater incidence of malpresentations may contribute to additional problems which will be considered later in this chapter.

The actual gestational age of the fetus is also taken into consideration in the nursing care of this patient. Preparation for delivery begins early in the labor and varies for the 28-week fetus as compared with the 37-week fetus. If multiple gestation is the precipitating factor in the premature labor, preparations for more than one infant have to be made. The following is suggested as a guide which can be adapted to individual situations.

1 Warming equipment in the delivery room turned on ahead of time. A servo-thermal-controlled unit is preferable for smaller prematures.
2 Resuscitation equipment in the delivery room with appropriate size masks, endotracheal tubes, and laryngoscope blade.
3 Equipment to monitor infant temperature, pulse, and respirations.
4 Personnel in attendance who are skilled in immediate newborn care.
5 Equipment available that provides warmth and oxygen for transporting the infant to a premature facility.
6 Informing nursery staff of expected premature infant, gestational age, significant maternal conditions, evidence of fetal distress in labor.

7 Discussing with parents the potential problems and preparations being made for their infant.

Uncertain estimated delivery date (or estimated date of confinement, EDC), or disease conditions of the mother or placenta that alter normal growth patterns of the fetus, sometimes make it difficult to know what size infant to anticipate at delivery. Tests to establish fetal age and maturity are available and can be a useful adjunct in making specific preparations for delivery.[3]

When a premature infant is delivered, it is important that trauma to the soft premature skull is minimal. Frequently an episiotomy is performed to reduce perineal resistance when the head is delivering. A spontaneous delivery is generally preferred. The nurse can assist the mother to push at appropriate times and to avoid long, forceful pushing.

The cord is clamped and cut quickly, and the baby placed in a heated crib for care. The nurse participates in the immediate newborn care, keeps the parents informed about the infant's condition, and alerts the premature facility to the infant's birth and condition.

Dysfunctional Labor

Uterine contractions normally increase in frequency, duration, and intensity as labor progresses, but with full relaxation of the muscle between contractions. During this resting stage there is the minimum of intrauterine tension. This minimum tension, called tonus, is in the 8 to 12 mmHg range.[4] Normal labor contractions may reach an intrauterine pressure of 50 to 60 mmHg at the acme of the contraction. The contractions effect dilatation of the cervix and descent of the fetus over a period of time.

Graphically, labor progress is seen to be an S-shaped curve.[5] (See Figure 31-1.) These curves are based on mean values for duration of labor in primigravidas and multiparas. Limits of normal variation have been statistically derived, but clinically, when values outside those time limits are seen, the labor process is abnormal.[6]

Precipitous Labor

Graphically, precipitous labor is an abnormally accelerated curve in which the total time for the labor and delivery process has been defined by some to be under 3 hours.[7,8] The uterine contractions are increased in frequency, duration, and intensity. Intrauterine pressures are often above 50 mmHg with each contraction. The high level of uterine activity allows little rest time between contractions. Uterine blood flow may be sufficiently reduced to impair oxygen transfer across the placenta, culminating in fetal distress. The forceful contractions, particularly combined with minimally resistant maternal tissue, may propel the fetus rapidly through the maternal passage. The dangers of this are damage to the fetal head from rapid expulsion and/or an unattended delivery.

Whenever high levels of uterine activity are observed the nursing care must include close observation of fetal heart rate patterns and insurance that the patient is not left alone. If delivery is rapid and uncontrolled, the fetus should be carefully evaluated for injury. The circumstances of delivery should always be reported to the nursery staff to ensure ongoing assessment.

Prolonged Labor

The upper limits of normal duration of the various phases of labor (latent phase, active phase, deceleration phase, and second stage)

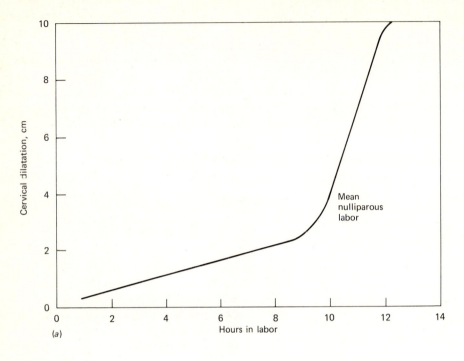

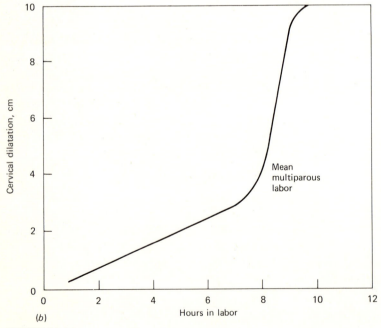

FIGURE 31-1
Labor progress curves (mean values). (*From Emanuel Friedman, "Synthetic Oxytocin," American Journal of Obstetrics and Gynecology, 74:1118–1124, 1957.*)

have been defined.[9] Total length of labor is not as valuable an index of prolonged labor as assessment of progress of each phase of labor. Prolonged labor would therefore be an appropriate label for several different labor patterns, e.g., labor which begins slowly and progresses minimally for 12 to 15 hours, labor which progresses normally for a time and then fails to progress for several hours, or labor which progresses normally to near the end of the first stage and then is protracted beyond 1 to 2 hours.[10] (See Figure 31-2.)

These dysfunctional labor progress curves are associated with dysfunctional uterine contractions. One type of contraction pattern is characterized by a decline in the frequency, duration, and intensity of the contractions. This pattern may occur in response to maternal exhaustion. When energy stores are depleted, the uterus cannot contract efficiently. If maternal exhaustion is causing the decline in uterine activity with resultant loss of labor progress, the accompanying symptoms are dry mucous membranes, acetonuria, elevated pulse, and often an elevated temperature.

Another cause of diminished uterine activity is the influence of medication. Either systemic analgesics or continuous local anesthetics given too early in the labor process have an adverse effect on uterine activity.

A second type of dysfunctional contraction pattern develops when mechanical obstruction is responsible for lack of labor progress. Soft tissue rigidity, inadequate emptying of the bladder or bowel, relative cephalopelvic disproportion, and/or malpresentation of the fetus occur in these instances. The uterine contractions may increase in frequency, duration, and intensity and be accompanied by greater pain. Secondarily the contractions may slow in response to maternal exhaustion if the labor is prolonged because of the obstructive phenomenon.

Treatment of prolonged labor is directed to the underlying problem. Adequate hydration and energy replacement with oral or

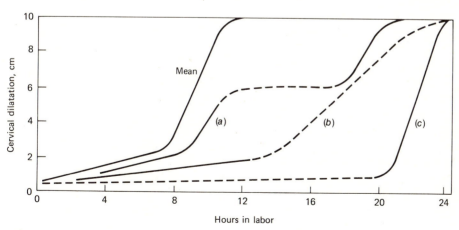

FIGURE 31-2
Major labor aberrations compared with the mean labor curve of nulliparas.
(a) A prolonged latent phase; (b) protracted active phase dilatation; (c) secondary arrest of dilatation. (*Adapted by Emanuel Friedman from J. P. Greenhill, Obstetrics, 13th ed., Saunders, Philadelphia, 1965.*)

intravenous fluids may be enough stimulus to increase uterine activity. Oxytocic augmentation of labor can also be utilized to increase the activity level. The maternal pelvic soft tissue as well as the presentation, position, and size of the fetus are evaluated if it appears there is a mechanical obstruction present.

Nursing care includes keeping the patient well hydrated in conjunction with comfort measures to help prevent maternal exhaustion. Providing for elimination needs keeps the bladder and bowel from impeding labor progress. When prolonged labor occurs, close attendance is essential to encourage the patient who often feels fatigued and discouraged because of slow labor progress. The fetus must also be evaluated for any symptoms of distress. Prolonged labor may tax the ability of the fetus to cope with the repetitive stress of contractions.

Induced Labor

A decision may be made to induce labor rather than await the spontaneous onset of labor (uterine) contractions. The decision can be *elective*, i.e., without medical indication, or *indicated* because of an unfavorable prognosis in awaiting spontaneous labor.

The method of induction may be rupturing the membranes artificially and then waiting for the onset of contractions. When the cervix is soft and partially dilated, contractions will often begin within a short time. Once labor begins, the progress is like that of a normal labor of spontaneous onset.

Administering oxytocics is a frequently used method of inducing labor contractions. These drugs may be given by buccal or parenteral routes. An intravenous drip of a diluted oxytocic is a common method. Amniotomy sometimes accompanies oxytocic administration. The resulting labor is

accelerated when compared to the graph of normal labor.[11] (See Figure 31-3.) When the cervix is favorable, contractions usually begin within a short time after initiating the oxytocic. The frequency, duration, and intensity of contractions are monitored carefully, and increments in dose are based on the contraction pattern. The uterine tonus is often elevated when oxytocics are used.

Nursing observations include timing the contractions and noting whether relaxation of the uterine muscle occurs between contractions. Prolonged contractions and/or inadequate uterine muscle relaxation may impair uterine blood flow and result in fetal hypoxia. The patient often needs assistance to cope with the contractions of an induced labor because she may experience frequent, strong contractions from the onset, as opposed to spontaneous labor where the frequency, duration, and intensity of contractions increases gradually.

Third- and Fourth-Stage Complications

When delivery of the fetus is completed, the uterus must continue to contract to expel the placenta and membranes. Faulty contractions in the third stage may fail to accomplish placental separation, and the placenta will be manually removed.

In the fourth stage the uterus must contract around the exposed blood sinuses to prevent postpartum hemorrhage. When the uterus has contracted inefficiently during labor, it can be anticipated that there will be greater difficulty with uterine contraction in the fourth stage. If contractions were stimulated during labor with oxytocin, then this stimulation will usually be necessary after delivery. In practice most patients receive some amount of oxytocin during the third and fourth stages for prophylactic reasons.

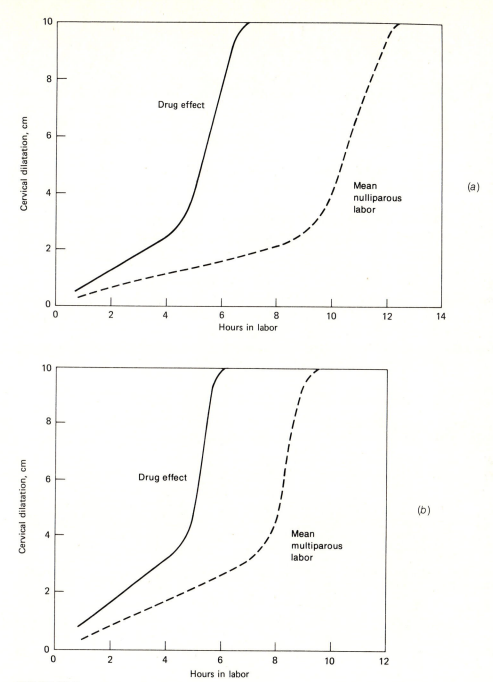

FIGURE 31-3
Comparison of labor curves when oxytocin is used. (*From Emanuel Friedman,*
*"Synthetic Oxytocin,"*American Journal of Obstetrics and Gynecology, *74:1118–*
1124, 1957.)

PASSENGERS

Fetus

Physiological Response to Labor

In spite of current knowledge we cannot accurately predict which fetus will become distressed during labor. Rather, a designation of *high risk* is applied to those situations in which the likelihood of fetal problems is high. For example, the fetus of the diabetic, toxemic, Rh-sensitized, hypertensive, or hypotensive mother is at risk. More elaborate lists and scoring systems have been devised and are useful adjuncts in assessing which fetus needs to be most closely observed and evaluated.[12]

Disturbances in fetal physiologic functioning can be detected by evaluating the fetal heart rate pattern in relation to uterine contractions. Fetal monitoring equipment provides the most useful data about fetal heart rate patterns because it obtains and visually records continuous data. This equipment is usually not available for monitoring all labors; therefore the high-risk fetus receives first priority for its use. Three primary heart rate patterns are identified and described by Hon.[13] (See Figures 31-4 to 31-6.)

The early deceleration pattern apparently develops during a uterine contraction in response to fetal head compression which induces a vagal reflex that briefly slows the fetal heart rate. The pattern is most commonly seen late in labor when the fetal head is well down in the maternal pelvis and/or after rupture of membranes when the uterine wall is in direct contact with the fetal head. The early deceleration pattern is usually benign, but it may precede a late deceleration pattern or become a pronounced pattern of repetitive and large drops (50 beats per minute or more) in fetal heart rate. Either of these patterns is associated with fetal distress.[14]

The late deceleration pattern is an ominous pattern, particularly when persistent. Fetal hypoxia and acidosis result from this pattern which reflects placental insufficiency. Fetal-maternal gas exchange is markedly reduced.

Variable deceleration patterns result from varying degrees of compression of the umbilical cord during uterine contractions. This pattern is seen in 85 to 90 percent of the clinically diagnosed cases of fetal distress. The pattern may be transient or may gradually become more severe. Metabolic acidosis less frequently accompanies this type of fetal distress.

FIGURE 31-4

Early deceleration pattern. Head compression. (*From Edward H. Hon,* An Introduction to Fetal Monitoring, *Harty, New Haven, Conn., 1969.*)

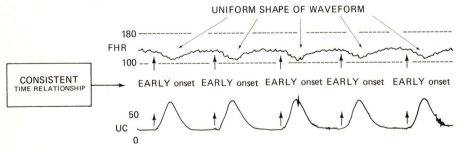

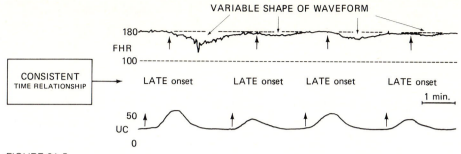

FIGURE 31-5

Late deceleration pattern. Uteroplacental insufficiency. (*From Edward H. Hon,* An Introduction to Fetal Monitoring, *Harty, New Haven, Conn., 1969.*)

The traditional criterion for defining fetal distress (heart rate below 120 or above 160 beats per minute between contractions) has limited application to these three primary patterns. The late deceleration pattern may fall entirely within the acceptable range, yet the pattern can be associated with marked fetal distress. Listening only to the fetal heart rate between contractions with a conventional fetoscope makes identification of these patterns difficult, if not impossible. The most useful way of using the conventional fetoscope is to begin listening during the decrement phase of the contraction (as soon as comfortable for the patient) and count the heart rate for consecutive 15-second intervals. The counting is continued well into the rest period between contractions. This method allows the nurse to determine whether a deceleration took place as the contraction was ending and the length of the recovery period to the normal base-line rate. This detects a persistent late deceleration pattern, the most ominous for the fetus, and may help detect a variable deceleration pattern.

The base-line fetal heart rate is simply the rate seen most of the time. A base-line tachycardia (above 150 to 160 beats per minute) may accompany a late or variable deceleration pattern and is further suggestive of fetal distress. A base-line tachycardia without these deceleration patterns may be a symptom of early distress, but it is also

FIGURE 31-6

Variable deceleration pattern. Cord compression. (*From Edward H. Hon,* An Introduction to Fetal Monitoring, *Harty, New Haven, Conn., 1969.*)

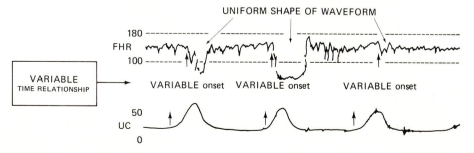

associated with maternal fever and fetal immaturity. A base-line bradycardia is significant when it gradually and progressively worsens and/or when it becomes sustained at somewhere below 90 to 100 beats per minute. The normal base-line heart rate is reactive; i.e., it constantly oscillates 5 to 10 or more beats per minute. This reactivity is produced by the constant interaction of the sympathetic and parasympathetic cardiac responses. A smooth, straight base line often indicates compromise of the central nervous system, and its appearance should be noted and reported, and the fetus evaluated.[15]

It is possible to assess fetal acid-base status by sampling small amounts of scalp blood. Correlation of blood pH values with heart rate patterns provides additional information about the type and degree of fetal distress.

The passage of meconium by the fetus in a cephalic presentation is assumed to be evidence of hypoxia. The presence of meconium is not a consistent finding with the heart rate patterns associated with fetal distress.[16]

Medications administered to the patient may also affect the fetus. For example, local anesthetic agents injected into the paracervical region for labor analgesia may produce a fetal bradycardia persisting for several minutes. Medications which depress the central nervous system such as narcotics, barbiturates, magnesium sulfate, and tranquilizers may smooth the base-line fluctuation. Systemic narcotic analgesics given to the patient in labor cross the placenta and can depress the fetal respiratory center. If delivery occurs while the drug is exerting its peak effect, the fetus may have difficulty initiating spontaneous respirations. The timing of administration of medications to the patient is as important as the dosage.

Whenever symptoms of fetal distress are observed, the initial actions are to place the patient in the lateral position, give oxygen by mask, discontinue oxytocics, and bring the symptoms to medical attention. If the distress does not respond to treatment and becomes progressively more profound, operative delivery may be necessary if vaginal delivery is not imminent. Regardless of the mode of delivery, preparations for immediate infant resuscitation should be made in advance.[17] Equipment and personnel such as described earlier in this chapter will be necessary.

Fetal Presentation, Position, and Size

Abnormal presentation, position, and size of the fetus increase the incidence of complications because of the following:

1 If the presenting part is smaller than the vertex, which is normally the presenting part, the potential for a prolapsed cord increases. *Example:* A foot presenting in a breech presentation predisposes to a prolapsed cord. (See Figure 31-7.) Five percent of breech presentations are complicated by a prolapsed cord.[18]

2 A smaller presenting part descending in the maternal pelvis is not as efficient a dilator of maternal tissue as the larger bony head in a normal presentation. Therefore, larger aftercoming fetal parts may not descend easily, resulting in a difficult delivery. *Example:* In a breech presentation the feet and legs may deliver easily, but the shoulders and head may deliver with difficulty. Special forceps may need to be used. (See Figure 31-8.)

3 A larger than normal diameter may cause a relative disproportion between the fetus and the maternal pelvis. *Example:* A very large baby in normal position, a face or brow presentation

FIGURE 31-7
Footling breech. (*From Harry Oxorn and William Foote, Human Labor and Birth, Appleton-Century-Crofts, New York, 1964. By permission of the publisher.*)

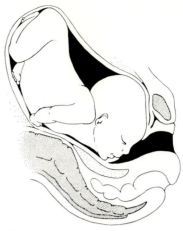

FIGURE 31-9
Lateral view of a face presentation. (*From Harry Oxorn and William Foote, Human Labor and Birth, Appleton-Century-Crofts, New York, 1964. By permission of the publisher.*)

with a larger presenting diameter of the head, or an anomalous head or abdomen may not be able to deliver through an average pelvis. (See Figure 31-9.)

4　An abnormal fetal position will affect the mechanisms of labor necessary for delivery. *Example:* A posterior position of the vertex may rotate to a direct occiput posterior position for delivery. Delivery of the head will then be accomplished primarily by flexion rather than by extension, as in occiput anterior positions. (See Figures 31-10 and 31-11.)

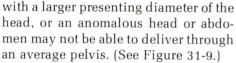

FIGURE 31-8
Forceps to the aftercoming head. (*From Harry Oxorn and William Foote, Human Labor and Birth, Appleton-Century-Crofts, New York, 1964. By permission of the publisher.*)

FIGURE 31-10
Flexion beginning in the occiput posterior position. (*From Harry Oxorn and William Foote, Human Labor and Birth, Appleton-Century-Crofts, New York, 1964. By permission of the publisher.*)

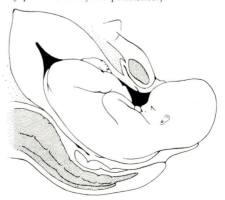

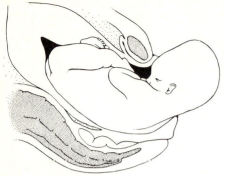

FIGURE 31-11
Flexion completed in the occiput posterior position.
(*From Harry Oxorn and William Foote,* Human Labor and Birth, *Appleton-Century-Crofts, New York, 1964. By permission of the publisher.*)

The most common malpresentation is a breech presentation. It accounts for 3 to 4 percent of the 5 percent of all deliveries in other than the vertex presentation.[19]

There are some specific nursing care measures pertinent to the care of a patient with the fetus in a breech presentation. Knowing that the possibility of a prolapsed cord is increased, the nurse should carefully observe the fetal heart rate pattern for symptoms of cord circulation interference. (See Figure 31-6.) Because of poor fetal-pelvic fit, the membranes tend to rupture early, further predisposing to a prolapsed cord. When membranes rupture, the perineum should be promptly observed for any obvious cord prolapse, and the fetal heart rate evaluated. The presence of meconium in a breech presentation is *not* a good indicator of fetal distress but is related to pressure on the fetal abdomen as descent occurs.

A frequent problem with breech presentations is that the small lower extremities and/or buttocks can reach the pelvic floor before the cervix has completely dilated. The patient develops an urge to push because of this pressure, but she must be coached in breathing techniques to prevent pushing until the cervix is completely dilated. Successful delivery of the head in a flexed position necessitates full dilatation of the cervix unless the fetus is small.

If the lower extremities deliver through the vaginal introitus before the rest of the fetus can be delivered, it is helpful to keep a warm cloth around them while awaiting completion of the delivery to help prevent cooling of the fetal body.

The mechanisms of a frank breech delivery are illustrated in Figures 31-12 to 31-20.

Other malpresentations occur less commonly than the breech presentation. If the malpresentation or large fetal size predisposes to a cephalopelvic disproportion, the dysfunctional labor curves of prolonged labor often appear. Certain face presentations and brow presentations that spontaneously correct themselves with good flexion of the fetal head may prolong labor until the flexion occurs, but labor progress and delivery subsequent to flexion should be normal. Large infants in normal position may cause difficulty at delivery because of increased head and shoulder size. Whenever the labor is prolonged and/or the delivery is

FIGURE 31-12
Breech crowning. (*From Harry Oxorn and William Foote,* Human Labor and Birth, *Appleton-Century-Crofts, New York, 1964. By permission of the publisher.*)

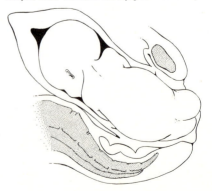

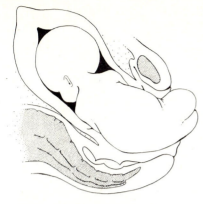

FIGURE 31-13
Birth of posterior buttock. (*From Harry Oxorn and William Foote, Human Labor and Birth, Appleton-Century-Crofts, New York, 1964. By permission of the publisher.*)

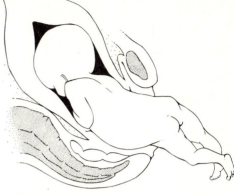

FIGURE 31-15
Feet born, shoulders engaging. (*From Harry Oxorn and William Foote, Human Labor and Birth, Appleton-Century-Crofts, New York, 1964. By permission of the publisher.*)

difficult, the infant may be depressed at delivery. In addition to adequate resuscitation, the baby should be examined for possible birth injury. Cephalohematomas, brachial or facial nerve injury from pressure on the face and axilla during delivery, and even broken bones (most often the clavicle) can result from a traumatic delivery.

Malpresentations such as a shoulder presentation with a transverse lie (Figure 31-21) or a cord prolapse with any presentation will necessitate cesarean section. If labor is not progressing well with a face or brow presentation, or a breech presentation, then cesarean-section delivery is also indicated.

FIGURE 31-14
Birth of anterior buttock. (*From Harry Oxorn and William Foote, Human Labor and Birth, Appleton-Century-Crofts, New York, 1964. By permission of the publisher.*)

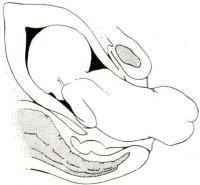

FIGURE 31-16
Descent and internal rotation of shoulders. (*From Harry Oxorn and William Foote, Human Labor and Birth, Appleton-Century-Crofts, New York, 1964. By permission of the publisher.*)

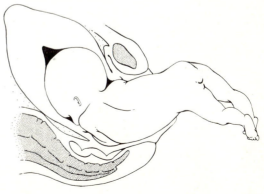

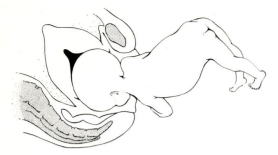

FIGURE 31-17
Posterior shoulder born, head has entered pelvis. (*From Harry Oxorn and William Foote*, Human Labor and Birth, *Appleton-Century-Crofts, New York, 1964. By permission of the publisher.*)

FIGURE 31-19
Internal rotation and beginning flexion of head. (*From Harry Oxorn and William Foote*, Human Labor and Birth, *Appleton-Century-Crofts, New York, 1964. By permission of the publisher.*)

Placenta

Placental Function

During labor the placenta must continue to provide the maternal-fetal gas exchange. Placental function is dependent on blood flow through the intervillous space where diffusion of gases takes place. Strong uterine contractions can effectively reduce uterine blood flow and therefore affect the gas exchange. Maternal toxemia or chronic hypertension can interfere with normal blood flow to the intervillous space because of vessel

constriction. Maternal hypotension will also reduce the uterine blood supply.

Maternal-fetal gas exchange is also influenced by the amount of placental surface area available. A small placenta, an infarcted placenta, or a partially prematurely separated placenta will reduce the available exchange surface.

An edematous placenta (seen with diabetic mothers and with erythroblastosis) may compromise gas diffusion across the intervillous space.

Placental aging is also known to occur.

FIGURE 31-18
Anterior shoulder born, descent of head. (*From Harry Oxorn and William Foote*, Human Labor and Birth, *Appleton-Century-Crofts, New York, 1964. By permission of the publisher.*)

FIGURE 31-20
Flexion of the head is complete. (*From Harry Oxorn and William Foote*, Human Labor and Birth, *Appleton-Century-Crofts, New York, 1964. By permission of the publisher.*)

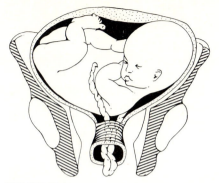

FIGURE 31-21

Transverse lie with a prolapsed cord. (*From Harry Oxorn and William Foote*, Human Labor and Birth, *Appleton-Century-Crofts, New York, 1964. By permission of the publisher.*)

Placental function may peak any time in the last weeks of pregnancy and then follow a downhill course. If the onset of labor occurs when placental functioning is less than optimal, gas exchange with the added stress of labor contractions may be compromised. This phenomenon is witnessed with postmature infants who often have a malnourished appearance. Placental aging is responsible for diminished transfer of nutrients to the fetus. This more complicated function is likely to be compromised first, and then later the gas exchange function.

The primary test of placental function is assay of maternal urine for 24-hour levels of estriol. Serial urine collections (daily, every other day, etc.) are obtained from the pregnant woman to evaluate placental output of estriol. In normal pregnancies, the output increases progressively to term. The mean value at 28 weeks is about 12 mg per 24 hours and rises to 25 mg per 24 hours at 40 weeks.[20] Persistent low values or a significant drop from one reading to the next may signal placental dysfunction. Close observation and monitoring of the fetus is indicated.

When estriol levels are known to be at critical levels, or when any of the previously described conditions that interfere with maternal-fetal gas exchange are present in labor, the fetal heart rate pattern is carefully evaluated for distress patterns, particularly late deceleration curves. (See Figure 31-5.) This characteristic deceleration of heart rate 30 seconds or more after the peak of the contraction with slow return to the base-line rate is symptomatic of diminished gas exchange. In response to the low oxygen levels the fetus develops a relative bradycardia. Administering 6 to 7 liters of oxygen by mask to the woman to raise the maternal blood concentration of oxygen and increase the gradient at the placental exchange site may assist in correcting the pattern. If the contraction pattern is one of high activity, the uterus may need to be rested to increase the uterine blood flow and promote better gas exchange. Placing the patient in the lateral position may help reduce uterine activity. If oxytocin is being administered the infusion rate may have to be reduced to lower uterine activity. Because the placental insufficiency pattern is an ominous sign, corrective steps should be taken as soon as it is detected.

Placenta Previa and Abruptio Placentae

The placenta is normally implanted on the upper wall of the uterus. When abnormal implantation of the placenta occurs, complications result when the placenta encroaches on the cervical opening. Blood vessels are exposed near the cervix, and vaginal bleeding is the first symptom of *placenta previa*. This bleeding is classically described as painless, bright red, and rarely of sufficient amount with the initial episode to produce maternal fatality. The incidence of this complication is about 1 in every 150 deliveries. The cause of the abnormal implantation is unknown.[21]

The initial bleeding episode may occur in the latter part of pregnancy without the presence of labor. When the fetus is quite immature and the initial amount of blood is not great, the pregnant woman may be treated with bed rest and close observation for any recurrence of bleeding. Continuing hemorrhage, the presence of labor contractions, or a distressed fetus necessitate prompt delivery. As the cervix dilates in labor, a small or large portion of placenta may be exposed, depending on its actual location. The cervical dilatation is apt to tear through more blood vessels, resulting in further bleeding. Unless there is only a margin of placenta near the dilating cervix and labor is progressing quite rapidly, delivery is most often accomplished by cesarean section.

A normally implanted placenta that separates from the uterine wall before the fetus has delivered is called *abruptio placentae*. Varying degrees of abruption are apparently possible. Only a small marginal area may separate, or the entire placenta may detach from the uterine wall.

The symptoms of severe abruptio placentae are vaginal bleeding, a rigid tender uterus, pain, and fetal distress or death. In perhaps 20 percent of cases there is no apparent vaginal bleeding. These cases are described as concealed hemorrhage, i.e., blood from the exposed vessels remains retroplacental and is trapped between the placenta and the uterine wall. Uterine tenderness is very evident, and maternal vital signs may reflect the blood loss even though no external bleeding is evident.[22] The patient may experience shoulder-strap pain.

The greater number of cases involve a separation of only one or two cotyledons. This may produce some vaginal bleeding, but maternal vital signs are stable and fetal

distress is not evident. In milder forms the most characteristic symptom may be failure of the uterus to relax between contractions. Again, the amount of maternal blood loss, status of labor, and/or the presence of fetal distress will influence the mode of delivery.

A secondary complication of abruptio placentae is hypofibrinogenemia. Whenever abruptio placentae is suspected, clotting times are checked to detect this problem.

The nurse must recognize that any vaginal bleeding developing during labor (as distinguished from normal bloody show) or present at labor onset is abnormal. The immediate cause of the bleeding may not be apparent, but placental bleeding is always suspected. It is important to estimate the amount of blood being lost. Pads, linen, etc., can be weighed and their amounts compared to comparable dry articles. Vital signs must be monitored every 10 to 15 minutes. Pulse rates generally change before blood pressure readings. The presence of other symptoms are also evaluated: pain, uterine tenderness, and uterine rigidity between contractions. Whenever placenta previa is suspected, the cardinal rule is *no* vaginal or rectal examination unless it is done under circumstances where an immediate cesarean section can be performed because massive hemorrhage can result if placental tissue is torn when an examination is attempted.

The fetus must be closely evaluated since placental bleeding obviously compromises placental function. Profound distress or death can occur swiftly in severe cases. In milder cases in which labor is progressing, the nurse should watch for late deceleration patterns or other fetal distress symptoms.

Blood is drawn for clotting time and is typed and cross matched in the event blood replacement is needed. An intravenous infusion should be in place. Preparations for emergency delivery and infant resuscitation should be made when indicated.

Umbilical Cord

The vessels of the umbilical cord are responsible for transporting nutrients, oxygen, and waste products between the fetus and placenta. Interference of cord circulation predisposes the fetus to distress.

Mechanical interference occurs if the cord becomes compressed between the fetal presenting part and the maternal pelvis. When an overt prolapse occurs, this is treated as an emergency situation and immediate delivery is accomplished. When the cord is visible at the vaginal introitus, it is observed for pulsation. If pulsation is slowing, it is sometimes possible to place gloved fingers against the presenting part firmly enough to take pressure off the cord while preparations are made for delivery. Placing the pregnant woman in the Trendelenburg position may also aid in reducing pressure on the cord. The nurse can protect the protruding cord by packing it with wet, sterile normal saline packs. If this is done, precautions must be taken *not* to compress the cord. Emergency intervention is not indicated if cord pulsation is absent, since this is evidence of fetal death.

If the cord is positioned so that each contraction produces cord compression, a variable deceleration pattern will be seen on a fetal monitor tracing. (See Figure 31-6.) The immediate treatment is to change the pregnant woman's position, since this may also change the position of the cord, and administer oxygen. If the pattern continues, the woman's position is changed again (side to side, to Trendelenburg, to sitting, etc.) until the pattern is corrected. In most instances the pattern improves with this measure. If no response is evident and the pattern becomes progressively worse (longer, lower decelerations), operative delivery may be necessary. Prolonged cord compression can produce considerable fetal distress.

Loops of cord around the fetal neck or abdomen, a knot in the cord, or an abnormally short cord represent other potential interferences with cord circulation. The observations and treatment of fetal distress are those described above.

Membranes and Amniotic Fluid

Rupture of membranes normally occurs at any time during the labor process. When membranes have been ruptured 24 hours prior to the onset of labor, this is termed premature rupture of membranes. Such a premature rupture predisposes the woman and fetus to infection. The pregnant woman may develop amnionitis, an intrauterine infection, and the fetus may develop pneumonia or septicemia. The classic signs of such infection will be maternal symptoms of increased pulse rate, elevated temperature, and presence of a foul-smelling vaginal discharge. During labor the fetal heart rate may show sustained tachycardia in response to maternal fever. At delivery the infant will often possess the same characteristic odor of the infected uterine contents. Respiratory distress may be evident. Both mother and infant will need close observation following delivery.

Rupture of membranes is also related to prolapse of the umbilical cord. Whenever there is a poor fetal-pelvic fit, the sudden release of fluid from the uterus when membranes rupture may "wash" the cord down along or past the presenting part. It is always important to evaluate fetal heart rate when membranes rupture, and particularly so when a malpresentation or a high presenting part occurs.

There is normally about a liter of amniotic fluid present by the end of gestation. The fluid is normally clear, although suspended particles such as vernix, lanugo, and epithelial cells are usually seen. Discolored fluid is not normal and reveals fetal difficulties. Green-tinged amniotic fluid is stained from meconium and is evidence of an episode of fetal hypoxia. Yellow fluid is seen with erythroblastotic infants; bilirubin in the amniotic fluid causes this discoloration. Bloody amniotic fluid is usually symptomatic of fetal blood loss into the amniotic sac.

Abnormally large amounts (polyhydramnios) or small amounts (oligohydramnios) of amniotic fluid have been associated with fetal anomalies. Fetal swallowing and urination play a role in amniotic fluid formation. Esophageal and central nervous system anomalies have been found with polyhydramnios, and urinary system anomalies have been found with oligohydramnios.

The close association between amniotic fluid status and fetal status led to widespread testing of the amniotic fluid as a means of determining fetal condition. Amniocentesis is a relatively low-risk method of obtaining samples of fluid for study. Many laboratory determinations can be performed which reflect fetal biochemical function and maturity. A selected list of these determinations include creatinine, sodium, protein, and the lecithin-sphingomyelin (L/S) ratio. The L/S determination is the one test most useful for establishing the relative maturity of fetal lungs and, therefore, the likelihood of encountering respiratory distress syndrome during the postpartum period.[23,24]

PASSAGE

Pelvis

The obstetric or true pelvis is a complete bony ring bounded laterally by the ischial bones, posteriorly by the sacrum, and anteriorly by the pubic bones. The various dimensions of the pelvis are the ultimate limits of the birth passageway. The fetal head must be able to negotiate these dimensions, or vaginal delivery will be impossible.

The primary planes of the obstetric pelvis are the inlet, the midplane (the plane of least dimension), and the outlet. (See Figure 31-22.) With reference to an average size, full-term fetus, there are identified average and minimum measurements for each of these planes.

The pelvic inlet is formed by the sacral promontory, the iliopectineal lines on the iliac bones, and the superior border of the symphysis pubis. The narrowest diameter of the inlet is usually the anteroposterior diameter. When this measurement is normal, then the inlet is assumed to be of adequate size. The minimum normal measurement for this anteroposterior diameter is 10 cm. This measurement would theoretically still allow

FIGURE 31-22
Planes of the pelvis. (*From Harry Oxorn and William Foote,* Human Labor and Birth, *Appleton-Century-Crofts, New York, 1964. By permission of the publisher.*)

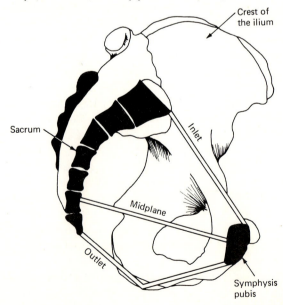

the average term fetus with a biparietal head diameter of 9.5 cm to pass through the inlet.

The pelvic midplane passes through the ischial spines. The distance between the ischial spines forms the transverse diameter of the pelvic midplane and represents the smallest diameter of that plane. The minimum normal measurement of that diameter is 9.5 to 10 cm. A transverse diameter measuring less than that will not permit internal rotation of a normal size fetal head to the occiput anterior position.

The pelvic outlet is formed by the inferior border of the symphysis pubis, the ischial tuberosities, and the last sacral vertebra. The distance between the ischial tuberosities is the transverse diameter of the outlet. This distance and the angle of the subpubic arch influence the amount of space available at the outlet.

Architecturally the pelvis varies in shape and dimension. Four pelvic types have been described: the gynecoid, the android, the anthropoid, and the platypelloid. The characteristics of the ideal gynecoid pelvis make it most suitable to childbearing. Probably 40 percent or more of the female population have pelvises with characteristics of the gynecoid pelvis.[25] A detailed discussion of the differences among the four types can be found in medical obstetric texts. The important points to realize are that classic pelvises are rare, that any individual woman may have a mixture of characteristics, and that the actual diameters are relevant only in relation to fetal size.

During labor, therefore, the pelvis with "borderline" measurements may be no problem for a small fetus. A normal pelvis may be inadequate when contractions are insufficient to mold the fetal head and expel it from the passage or when a malpresentation occurs. The different pelvic shapes can contribute to fetal malpositions and presentations; e.g., the fetal vertex may rotate to the occiput posterior position for delivery rather than the occiput anterior if there is more room in the posterior portion of the lower pelvis, or the small breech may present when the pelvis is small and narrow.

When a relative cephalopelvic disproportion does occur in labor, symptoms of prolonged labor with cessation of progress appear. X-ray pelvimetry can be performed during labor to obtain measurements of pelvic dimensions and fetal head size. However, clinical labor progress is the most important factor in the management of a relative disproportion no matter what the actual dimensions.

Soft Tissue

The soft tissue of the maternal generative tract lies between the pelvic bones and the fetus. Abnormalities of the soft tissue can also reduce the size of the birth passage.

Tissue resistance can influence labor progress. A rigid cervix will dilate slowly and lead to prolonged labor. Stretched tissue and poor muscle tone can contribute to rapid precipitous labors. Tissue resistance is primarily responsible for the longer primigravid labor as compared to subsequent labors.

Space-occupying tumors, such as uterine fibroids, may contribute to malpresentations. Small fibroids located high in the fundus are compatible with normal labor and delivery, but fibroids in the lower segment or cervical area may prevent descent of the fetus.

Congenital anomalies of the uterus, cervix, or vagina may influence whether normal labor and delivery is possible. Severe anomalies that play a role in infertility or repeated spontaneous abortion obviously prevent normal labor and delivery. Slight anomalies may not even be discovered until the time of labor and delivery. A partial septum in the uterus may reduce the available space for fetal growth and predispose to premature delivery. A septum in the cervix will prevent normal cervical dilatation in labor. An incompetent cervix which dilates without the presence of labor contractions is associated with premature delivery.

Trauma to maternal tissues is a complication of vaginal delivery. The cervix or the vaginal mucosa may sustain lacerations in the delivery process. The perineum may also be torn. Perineal tears are classified according to the tissue involved in the laceration. First-degree tears involve the vaginal mucosa at the vaginal outlet and/or the perineal skin and fourchette. Second-degree tears involve torn muscle in the perineal body. Third-degree tears involve the perineal body and the rectal sphincter. Fourth-degree tears extend through the rectal sphincter and involve the rectal mucosa. Third- and fourth-degree lacerations can result from extensions of an episiotomy. Lacerations along the labia minora and around the urethra can also occur. It is important that lacerations are identified and repaired to effect hemostasis and to promote proper healing and perineal muscle support.

In the fourth stage of labor it is important for the nurse to detect any vaginal bleeding that is unrelated to uterine atony. A laceration of the cervix or vagina that may have been overlooked can produce a constant trickle of bright red blood in the immediate postpartum stage. Reexamination of the patient and suturing of the laceration may be necessary to prevent undue blood loss.

Hematomas can also form under the perineal skin. If they are small, they will be noticeable only by the skin discoloration and tenderness they cause. Large hematomas can form under the vaginal mucosa and may cause extreme pain and symptoms of shock if the blood loss is great. The nurse should be particularly concerned about complaints of rectal pressure during the fourth stage, since this may well be symptomatic of a hematoma.

DELIVERY

Throughout this chapter it has been noted that forceps delivery and cesarean section are often the treatment for a complication of labor. These methods of delivery prevent the pregnant woman and fetus from becoming compromised by a prolonged and/or difficult labor.

Forceps Delivery

Forceps delivery is a means of assisting the pregnant woman to deliver the fetus through the vaginal passage. Forceps are applied by a skilled physician to the fetal head. During a uterine contraction, pull is exerted on the forceps while the woman pushes, if possible. The pull on the forceps always coincides with a contraction since this obtains maximum force. The sum of the pushing force plus the pulling force is needed for effective use of forceps.

Outlet (low) forceps are used when the fetal head has reached the perineal floor and the position of the head is occiput anterior. The outlet (low) forceps delivery assists the woman in the final expulsion of the fetus through the vaginal outlet.

In a midforceps delivery the forceps are applied after engagement of the fetal head in the pelvis. The station is at least 0 and it may be +1 or +2, and the cervix is completely dilated. It is possible for a midforceps delivery to be done safely by a highly skilled operator, but it is a complex procedure, and one which is seldom used. The infrequency of its use decreases the operator's skill and increases the infant's vulnerability. A difficult delivery may be anticipated through careful monitoring and assessment which alerts the operator to the safest method of delivery.

Many different kinds of obstetric forceps are available. Some forceps have special uses; e.g., Piper forceps are applied to the after-coming head in a breech presentation. (See Figure 31-8.) Forceps are curved to fit the fetal head (cephalic curve) and also to fit the maternal pelvis (pelvic curve). A forceps application is illustrated in Figure 31-23. The choice of particular forceps for delivery rests with the physician.

Cesarean Section

Cesarean section is an operative procedure for delivery of the fetus. An incision is made into the abdominal wall and into the uterus itself. The infant, as well as the placenta and membranes, is delivered through the incision. The uterus and abdominal wall are then sutured. Generally the uterine incision is made in the thinner lower segment in a transverse direction. This incision is associated with less blood loss, and less tendency to rupture at the incision site in successive pregnancies. The alternative incision is the "classic," longitudinal midline uterine inci-

sion. This incision is now used less frequently than the low transverse incision. It may, however, be the choice when cesarean section is performed because of a low-lying placenta.

Cesarean section is now associated with low maternal mortality and morbidity figures. The availability of good anesthetics, skilled nurse anesthetists, anesthesiologists, and obstetric surgeons, blood banks, and antibiotics have reduced the risks to a minimum level. Care of the patient after cesarean section is similar to that of a patient undergoing abdominal surgery.

Fetal mortality and morbidity figures are higher for emergency cesarean-section deliveries than for vaginal deliveries. Many cesarean sections are performed because of a jeopardized fetus, so these higher rates are expected. The incidence of respiratory distress is also higher in infants delivered by cesarean section, particularly in premature infants; this could be the result of a combination of factors. When the fetus passes through the *birth canal*, pressure on the chest helps rid the fetus of amniotic fluid accumulated in the lungs and bronchi. This, of course, is not the case with cesarean-

FIGURE 31-23
Correct forceps application. (*From Harry Oxorn and William Foote,* Human Labor and Birth, *Appleton-Century-Crofts, New York, 1964. By permission of the publisher.*)

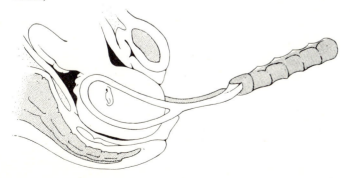

section delivery. An emergency cesarean section is not done unless the fetus and/or the mother is in difficulty.

IMPLICATIONS FOR THE NURSING PROCESS

Nursing the patient in labor demands continual assessment of the dynamic nature of the labor process. Complications may occur at any point in the labor or may be present at its onset.

An initial assessment takes into consideration significant past and present history related to labor and delivery. The presence of maternal disease conditions that influence placental function is very important information. Obtaining information about the pattern of contractions prior to hospital admission, status of fetal membranes, history of any vaginal bleeding, length and description of past labors, and the gestational age of the current pregnancy helps the nurse plan the patient's care.

In addition to this history the current status is assessed. Observing hydration status, level of fatigue, and the amount and type of discomfort provides more information for the nursing care plan. Measuring the vital signs, the frequency, duration, and intensity of contractions, and the fetal heart rate contributes data about maternal and fetal response to this labor. By palpating the abdomen the nurse can obtain information about fetal position, presentation, and size. A nurse properly trained in vaginal or rectal examination procedure can obtain information about fetal position and station and status of membranes as well as cervical dilatation and effacement.

As labor continues, the nurse is particularly alert for signs of fetal distress, dysfunctional labor progress, and symptoms of altered maternal homeostasis, such as altered vital signs, dehydration, or abnormal bleeding.

Patients who experience a complication of the labor and delivery process need expert nursing care to meet their needs. Nursing care measures for specific problems have been mentioned throughout this chapter.

The nurse must also be able to assess the impact of the complication on the cultural, emotional, and psychosocial needs of the pregnant woman and her family. The childbearing experience is a developmental crisis in family life. When there is a complication of the childbearing process, the developmental crisis is compounded by a situational crisis. The behavior of the pregnant woman and her family may become disorganized. Denial is often an initial reaction to the appearance of symptoms such as premature labor contractions or leaking amniotic fluid. The pregnant woman may try to reassure herself that she is experiencing a stomachache or is losing some urine. Anxiety and fear are normal feelings when complications develop. These feelings interfere with the ability to listen and take in information. The woman and her family may ask the same questions repeatedly.

Studies in crisis intervention have shown that the only way to successfully survive a crisis is to be aware that it exists.[26,27] Explanations, to be effective, must be appropriate for the family's coping mechanisms. If they are experiencing denial, they may need help acknowledging that a crisis exists and that it is usual to feel frightened and anxious. Explanations should be appropriate and repeated as often as necessary. Whenever possible, explanations should be made jointly to parents; in this way both receive the same message, and their communication is kept clear. Positive communication to the parents—e.g., "It's good that you came right in," "Yes, you did the right thing," or, "You're telling me just what I need to know"—can help alleviate anxiety and improve coping abilities. Ascertaining the parents' goals for participation in the labor and delivery and helping them achieve these goals if possible will enhance their feelings of adequacy. Providing false reassurance or statements like "Just leave everything to us" places the parents in a childlike position and may increase anxiety.

The parents should have opportunity for contact with their newborn as soon after delivery as possible. The value of early contact is well described in the literature.[28,29] If the newborn is small and/or distressed, it is usually possible to provide time for the mother (parents) to see and touch the baby as soon as the baby's condition is stabilized, even if the baby is being transferred to an intensive care facility. If the mother experiences complications and/or has a general anesthetic, the baby can often be brought to her as soon as her condition stabilizes. By giving clear descriptions and explanations of events, acknowledging realistic concerns, and staying with the parents, the nurse can provide effective supportive care.

The nurse must also relate to a variety of health care professionals who are involved in managing complications of labor and delivery. Communicating pertinent information, taking initial corrective steps, and anticipating and preparing for interventions are specific actions that enable the nurse to function as a productive member of a multiprofessional team; a team which greatly increases the chance of successfully resolving a complication of the labor and delivery process.

REFERENCES

1 Hellman, Louis M., and Jack A. Pritchard: *Williams Obstetrics*, 14th ed., Appleton-Century-Crofts, New York, 1971, pp. 526–528.

2 Cibils, Luis A., and Frederick P. Zuspan: "Pharmacologic Control of Premature Labor," *Clinical Obstetrics and Gynecology*, 16:199–210, 1973.

3 Hasselmeyer, Eileen G.: "Indices of Fetal Welfare," in B. Bergerson, et al. (eds.), *Current Concepts in Clinical Nursing*, vol. 2, Mosby, St. Louis, 1969, pp. 298–318.

4 Oxorn, Harry, and William R. Foote: *Human Labor and Birth*, 2d ed., Appleton-Century-Crofts, New York, 1968, p. 361.

5 Friedman, Emanuel A.: *Labor, Clinical Evaluation and Management*, Appleton-Century-Crofts, New York, 1967, pp. 27–31.

6 Ibid., pp. 36–37.

7 Hellman and Pritchard: op. cit., p. 849.

8 Oxorn and Foote: op. cit., p. 366.

9 Friedman: op. cit., pp. 36–39.

10 Ibid., pp. 45–50.

11 Ibid., pp. 314–315.

12 Effer, S. B.: "Biochemical and Biophysical Indices of Fetal Risk," *Clinics in Perinatology*, 1:161–163, 1974.

13 Hon, Edward H.: *An Introduction to Fetal Monitoring*, Harty, New Haven, 1969, pp. 21–60.

14 Russin, Ann, et al.: "Electronic Monitoring of the Fetus," *American Journal of Nursing*, 74:1294–1299, 1974.

15 Ibid., p. 1297.

16 Hon: op. cit., p. 46.

17 Auld, Peter A. M.: "Resuscitation of the Newborn," *American Journal of Nursing*, 74:68–70, 1974.

18 Oxorn and Foote: op. cit., p. 195.

19 Oxorn and Foote: op. cit., p. 195.

20 Beischer, N. A., et al.: "The Incidence and Significance of Low Estriol Excretion in an Obstetric Population," *The Journal of Obstetrics and Gynaecology of the British Commonwealth*, 75:1024–1033, 1968.

21 Hellman and Pritchard: op. cit., pp. 610–611.

22 Hellman and Pritchard: op. cit., pp. 623–631.

23 Gluck, Louis, et al.: "Diagnosis of the Respira-

tory Distress Syndrome by Amniocentesis,'' *American Journal of Obstetrics and Gynecology*, 190:440–445, 1971.

24 Effer, S. B.: ''Amniocentesis—Methodology, Complications and Interpretation,'' *Recent Progress in Obstetrics and Gynaecology, Proceedings of the VII World Congress of Obstetrics and Gynaecology*, Moscow, Aug. 12–18, 1973, published by Excerpta Medica, Amsterdam, 1974.

25 Hellman and Pritchard: op. cit., pp. 313–316.

26 Caplan, Gerald: *Principles of Preventive Psychiatry*, Basic Books, New York, 1964, pp. 288–296.

27 Parad, Howard J. (ed.): *Crisis Intervention: Selected Readings*, Family Service Association of America, New York, 1965.

28 Klaus, Marshall H., et al.: ''Maternal Attachment, Importance of the First Post-partum Days,'' *The New England Journal of Medicine*, 286:460–463, 1972.

29 Kennell, John H., and Marshall H. Klaus: ''Care of the Mother of the High-Risk Infant,'' *Clinical Obstetrics and Gynecology*, 14:926–954, 1971.

UNIT B

COMPLICATIONS OF CHILDREARING

32

Postpartum Care of the High-Risk Mother

VIRGINIA GRAMZOW KINNICK

A great deal of literature about the high-risk mother and her infant is oriented toward the mother's pregnancy, the hazards for her fetus, and the condition and care of the baby following delivery. Although much has been written about the role of the nurse in working with parents who have produced a still-born or a high-risk baby, little has been written about this care in relation to the mother when her condition continues as high-risk into the puerperium.

During the first 48 hours after delivery the high-risk mother may have many more physical problems than one whose maternity cycle has been uncomplicated, whether a "perfect" baby has been produced or not. The chances of an abnormal baby, however, whether premature or one with birth defects, are much greater for this mother. She will be concerned about the welfare of the baby, but because of her physical condition, will have less energy to cope with what she may perceive. Her concern about her ability to care for this child may be magnified and distorted during this time.

The purpose of this chapter is to present some implications of what a continued high-risk condition to the mother during the puerperium means to her, to her family, and to her mothering role, when accompanied by either a normal or a high-risk baby. Certain basic nursing considerations will then be discussed in relation to the needs presented by the mother's condition and the condition of her baby. Specific high-risk conditions that can continue into the puerperium will be presented, and implications for the nursing care required for these specific complications will be discussed.

CONCERNS CREATED BY THE MOTHER'S CONDITION

The Mother's Experience

For the woman who has complications during the early puerperium, Rubin's "taking-in phase" may be more obvious and will probably last for a longer period than if no complications were present. The early puerperium involves extensive physiological changes which may cause a crisis in many existing medical complications or overlapping complications of pregnancy. Until the mother's physical imbalance has been restored, she may not fully become a part of the taking-in phase as described for the mother with a normal puerperium. If she has not delivered a healthy or normal baby, this phase will be extremely difficult. She will probably be more concerned about her baby during this phase than will the mother of a healthy baby. She will also be besieged with a mixture of feelings of grief, anxiety, and guilt about her role in not producing the "perfect" baby.

It is important for the high-risk mother to have an opportunity to relive her labor and delivery experience and resolve some of the fantasies she may have about them. The nurse should encourage the mother in her efforts to do this and should help her realistically appraise a difficult labor and delivery experience and/or her role and her partner's role in producing an abnormal baby if this has occurred. It is important to this couple that they have been "good parents" throughout the woman's maternity cycle. If the mother confronts her anxieties and resolves her fantasies of guilt, she will be more ready to enter the taking-hold phase of the puerperium and to develop a healthy self-concept of her maternal role.

As the woman who has been ill in the early puerperium enters the taking-hold phase, she experiences a greater sense of body loss than other women. Her worries about her lack of control over her body will increase her anxieties about herself and her baby, whom she may not have yet seen. She may be anxious about her ability to function as a mother in the presence of her physical incapacities, about how this experience will permanently affect her body function, and about the effect of these multiple stresses on the family unit. She may feel overwhelmed by the problems that confront her.

Since the mother's illness may have prevented contact with her baby, it is important that contact be promoted as soon as her condition allows. Maternal feelings do not come automatically, and the mother needs to be aware that early and continuous contact with her baby will encourage the growth of her feelings for the baby.[1] Also of importance in helping this woman develop maternal feelings is support and encouragement of her ability to fulfill the mothering role in spite of medical problems or other physical problems that affected her in the early puerperium. Even healthy women usually have concerns about their ability as mothers, and the concerns of the high-risk mother during the puerperium must be even greater.

As the high-risk mother becomes acquainted with her baby, she is also involved in the restoration of her body function. Rubin stresses the importance that intolerance of inadequacies plays as a motivating factor.[2] The woman who is intolerant of the inadequacies of her body must be taught how to cope with these inadequacies appropriately as well as to stabilize them so that she can regain control. For the patient with hyperthyroidism, it may be a rapid process involving the basic body functions of a normal puerperium plus taking medications for her condition. For the patient with cardiac disease, it may be a very slow and frustrating process which involves a great amount of bed rest that seems incompatible with the mothering role during the weeks to follow. She may find it difficult to accept the help that she will need.

The Father's Concerns

Initially, many demands are made upon the father. Depending upon the extent of maternal complications, his greatest concerns will be for his partner. However, he will probably have innumerable anxieties. Other predominant concerns could involve anxiety about the baby's condition if a healthy baby was not produced, feelings of guilt about his role in the problems connected with his partner's condition, economic considerations, and concerns about other children. He needs the opportunity to express some of his feelings and resolve his anxieties so that he can be more supportive to his partner and family. He also needs to know what is being done for his partner, which frequently involves clarification of information presented to him by the doctor and other health care personnel.

The parents' ability to cope with the problems that confront them depends on multiple factors which include their own existing personalities, previous encounters with the maternity cycle, their relationship with each other, and the number of stressful situational factors occurring at the time of this crisis. Situational factors include the kind of nursing and medical attention they receive during the mother's hospitalization.

Nursing Implications

Nursing personnel may find it difficult at times to handle their own feelings and concerns for this family, especially if the mother during the first 48 hours experiences superimposed complications. The nurses working with the couple should have the opportunity to express their feelings to someone available to them outside the immediate nursing situation. Conferences should be held daily by the health team to discuss some of the problems involved and to develop an ongoing care plan. The concerns of this couple also involve the baby they have produced. These concerns and further implications for nursing care in relation to them will be discussed in the section Concerns Created by the Infant's Condition.

The intervention of nursing and medical personnel during the early puerperium can have strong influence in how this couple copes with the problems that confront them. Fear of criticism or disapproval of the feelings they express creates increased and unresolved anxieties within the parents, and, in turn, they begin to project blame on others or themselves. Other children or the spouse may become the scapegoat for these unexpressed anxieties.[3]

To help the couple ventilate some of their concerns, the nurse should help them to develop trust in the health team. It is important then that this couple be assigned the same nurse each day so that this person becomes a familiar figure to both parents. The concern and respect the health team shows for them, the truthfulness and objectivity of answers to the parents' questions, and the skill and thoughtfulness with which the nurse carries out physical care of the mother will all be factors in developing this trust. If the mother is not fully conscious during the first 48 hours after delivery, when a medical crisis may occur, the nurse will be directing intensive physical care to the mother and intensive emotional support toward the father.

During periods of stress, people do not accurately hear what is being said to them. The nurse must recognize that the father may need an opportunity to ventilate certain anxieties before he can understand some of the explanations the health team has for him about the mother's condition. During these times, the father may become quite sensitive to nonverbal communication. When nursing personnel retreat or seem to avoid communication with him, they may be reinforcing his fears that he is not being told everything. The patient, depending on her awareness, may react in the same way. She is especially sensitive to nonverbal or verbal communication in relation to the condition of her baby. The anxieties of both parents are increased if their questions are avoided, ignored, or not answered to their satisfaction.

The nurse needs to be aware of what the couple has been told about the mother's condition. Facts may need to be repeated and reinterpreted, and the feelings expressed by both should be accepted. The nurse should be available almost constantly until the physiological equilibrium has been restored; this way the nurse becomes a familiar and important person to both parents.

The nurse plays an important role in coordinating the rehabilitation activities of the new mother with her care of her newborn. The nurse who has become a symbol of trust to the parents is of utmost assistance to the couple throughout this phase. This relationship is of extreme importance in helping the mother to gain confidence in her mothering role. The patient must be taken at the pace compatible with her emotional and physical health and the health of her baby. It is also important for the nurse to support the father and increase his awareness of the support his partner needs from him. Both parents must be involved in plans made for the care of the baby and mother in the home. The family unit can be strengthened through sensitive nursing care.

The couple must become fully aware of how the mother's health will be permanently affected by the complications in her pregnancy and puerperium as soon as the medical team knows. If the physiological equilibrium has been reestablished during the first 48 hours following delivery, there is probably minimum change from her nonpregnant physical condition. The prognosis of specific conditions, however, does vary and will be discussed in a later section.

Communication between the couple can be encouraged by the health team by involving both parents in all reports and discussion of the mother's and baby's condition. The father needs the support of the health team but also needs to be made aware of what to expect of his partner's behavior and how he can be of help to her.

Implications of Family Planning

The need for family planning is an important area for these couples. Not only is it important in respect to the mother's health and the health of future babies, but it is important in the relationship between the mother and her partner.

The couple should be encouraged to discuss the subject of birth control together. The most effective family planning method is probably that method freely chosen by the couple after careful education in what is available and what is most appropriate for the mother's condition. With some medical conditions, the need for specific measures may be essential for the mother's health so that few, if any, alternatives are available. However, if the couple is not encouraged to privately discuss the subject and what it means to each of them after the crisis they have encountered with this pregnancy, their sexual relationship may suffer profoundly as a result of their mixed feeling and fears of a future pregnancy. They should be encouraged to seek early assistance from the physician.

When the primipara has a high-risk pregnancy and she produces a stillborn or a baby with anomalies, the couple may have many mixed emotions about family planning. They need the opportunity to ventilate some of these mixed feelings in an accepting atmosphere. Genetic counseling services may be of help in contributing to their knowledge of their risk in future childbearing.

In some situations, the physician may strongly advocate sterilization of the woman. Sterilization may be very difficult for any female to accept, depending on multiple factors which include number of living children, religious orientation, and marital relationship.

CONCERNS CREATED BY THE INFANT'S CONDITION

Women whose pregnancies are classified as high-risk have an increased chance of not being able to produce a normal, healthy baby. A high-risk mother may give birth to a stillborn baby, a premature baby, or a baby with a congenital defect. Parental response to the baby's condition and the nurse's role in the situation are significant aspects of postpartum care.

A discussion of the grieving process and parents' response to the death of a newborn infant is discussed in Chapter 29. Understanding of the concept of grieving is also basic to care of parents who do not give birth to a "normal" newborn, for example, a couple who give birth to a premature or a baby born with congenital defects. The awareness and appropriate use of this knowledge by the nurse caring for these parents is essential in giving effective postpartum care.

If the babies born to high-risk mothers need intensive nursing care, it is common practice to separate them from their mothers in the postpartum period. In some situations, the baby may even be transferred to a hospital in another city. The effect of separation on maternal attachment to the baby needs further study. Nursing personnel, however, need to be aware of implications created by this separation and the importance of the nurse's role in facilitating maternal attachment.

Effects of Early Separation on Maternal Behavior

When babies are born with high-risk conditions, they are immediately taken to a special nursery where they receive intensive nursing care. Separating babies and mothers during the early postpartum days when high-risk babies are born is a practice almost unique to the Western world. In this situation, medical and nursing personnel play an important role in helping the mother to develop a positive maternal attachment toward her baby. Recent research indicates that lack of early contact between mother and baby does delay maternal attachment. Some researchers believe the separation may even be a factor in some disturbed mother-child relationships. Figure 32-1 indicates other major aspects that contribute to maternal behavior and also

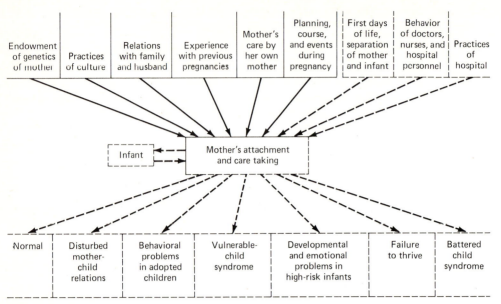

FIGURE 32-1

Disorders of mothering: A hypothesis of their etiology. Solid lines indicate determinants which are ingrained; dashed lines indicate factors which may be altered or changed. (*From M. Klaus and J. Kennell, "Mothers Separated from Their Newborn Infants,"* Pediatric Clinics of North America, *17:1015, 1970, by permission.*)

the possible results of that behavior. It is important to note that Klaus's hypothesis includes only three factors* that can be altered to change maternal behavior. These three factors can be altered by medical and nursing personnel who are responsible for isolating mother and baby for the purpose of saving the baby's life. Now that we have the knowledge and methods to help many babies survive physically, we need to focus on facilitating a healthy emotional environment for them. That environment begins with the mother, and Klaus has presented health personnel with great responsibility in this area.

Klaus and his coworkers are involved in

----

* The three factors are "en face" eye to eye contact, fingertip touching of extremities initially and quickly, and finally massaging, encompassing palm contact of infant's trunk.

research that provides direction as to how maternal attachment can be facilitated by good hospital practice, and supportive medical and nursing care. One of their studies involved parents of premature babies. One group of parents entered the high-risk nursery soon after their babies were born, were able to touch their babies, and gradually became involved with simple care as each baby's condition allowed. The researchers did not detect any increase in occurrence of infection, a concern of many nursery personnel.[4] Another group of parents of premature babies were not allowed into the high-risk nursery to touch their babies until their babies were 20 days old. Results indicated differences in maternal behavior between the two groups as late as 6 months after delivery.[5]

Another study, conducted by Kennell,

Jerauld, and associates, assessed the effect of
the amount of contact time on maternal attachment of mothers. Their study utilized
mothers who had given birth to healthy
babies. Only mothers who planned to bottle-
feed their babies were included in the study.
One group of mothers were involved in routine postpartum practice; they were separated from their babies shortly after birth,
with an opportunity to look at their babies 6
to 12 hours later; actual contact occurred
with the first feeding and every 4 hours
thereafter. The second group was given increased time with their babies soon after
birth and an extended amount of time each
day for 3 days. There was a total of 16 hours
difference in contact time. As a result, measurable differences in maternal behavior were
found between the two groups, both at 1
month and at 1 year, with the greatest maternal attachment occurring with the group
having extended contact.[6]

Parental Response to Prematurity

If the mother has complications throughout her pregnancy, premature labor is an additional shock. Neither parent has had the
opportunity to prepare psychologically for
the baby, and frequently the parents have not
completed physical preparations for a new
baby in the home. If the couple has other
children, these children are not prepared for
the disequilibrium that occurs in the family,
such as the sudden departure of their
mother, the anxiety they see in their father,
and the new baby, who is responsible for the
changes.

Many couples are also unprepared for the
labor and delivery experience. They may
have feelings of guilt that they did something to initiate labor. Many women who
have experienced a premature delivery will
describe it as having unreal qualities. Following delivery, these parents tend to have
increased anxieties about whether their baby
is alive or if it will live. Anticipatory grieving, as discussed in Chapter 29, will usually
occur if the parents have any concerns about
whether the baby will live or not. There is
also great concern about the presence of deformities and mental retardation.[7]

Another kind of grief frequently felt by
parents of a premature baby is expressed as a
sense of failure to produce the perfect baby
they expected. The one exception, however,
is the mother who has lost babies previously.
She will probably experience a sense of
achievement if her baby lives regardless of
the baby's limitations.[8]

Nursing Implications

It is important that the mother sees her baby
as soon as she is able in order to help her
minimize some of the fantasies that she may
have created as well as to begin establishing
a mother-infant relationship. If the mother's
condition prevents her from seeing the baby
early, the father can be encouraged to assist
her by reporting his observations. A nurse
should be with the parents to help them express the concerns about what they see and
support them as necessary. The early visits
may be upsetting to the parents when they
see the small size and general appearance of
their baby, with accompanying intravenous
tubings, incubator, or other awesome equipment.

One of the most difficult problems the
nurse encounters with the parents is that of
being objective and truthful in answering
questions related to their infant's condition.
Members of the health team frequently
underestimate parents' ability to cope with
stress and they have a tendency to reassure
parents when reassurance is not indicated. If
the baby dies, the shock and grief are far
greater for them if they have not been kept
currently informed of their infant's critical

condition, but have been led to believe that the baby's condition is stable and satisfactory.

Trust is established through giving correct information and being open and honest. Parents can accept the loss of a child, painful as it may be, far better than they can accept misinformation, evasiveness, and dishonesty.

Frequently, the intensive care nursery is not on the maternity floor where the mother is hospitalized. Open lines of communication between the nursery and parents are important to help minimize their anxiety about their baby. Effective methods of communication need to be established and coordinated by the nurse caring for the parents and the nurse caring for the baby. Coordination is necessary, since opening these lines of communication should later include opportunities for the mother to touch and/or hold her baby as soon as it is physically possible for both.

Minimizing separation between the newborn baby and mother is always important in the development of a healthy maternal role and infant security. This process involves reports which include the baby's behavioral characteristics and feeding pattern. When the mother is able, she should be wheeled to the nursery to see her baby and supported as necessary with her first glimpse and physical contact with the baby, as discussed previously. It is extremely difficult for the mother if the personnel do not help her to feel that this baby is hers, and if she does not have an opportunity to touch, hold, or feed her baby before she leaves the hospital.

Personnel must be patient and supportive with the mother in her mothering role. In particular, she needs much reassurance and guidance in the feeding experience, which is largely the basis of her attitude in the total care. Feeding is her first maternal task and thus, a very important one in which to be successful. The goal of the personnel at this time is to help her gain confidence in her capabilities to care for her baby. She also needs to be aware that the development of maternal feelings is a gradual process, even with mothers of full-term babies, and it is common for a greater emotional lag to occur with mothers of premature babies because of their separation and lack of contact.

It may be difficult for this mother to return home without a baby. She and her husband must be made aware of the importance of the mother being able to return to the nursery for feeding experiences. The nurse should also encourage the mother to call at any time about her baby.

Both parents should be prepared for the baby's arrival in the home; they should understand how their baby's needs will vary from a normal baby in special areas such as feeding patterns and growth and development, and also how this baby is "potentially normal."[9] Upon return of both mother and baby to the home, appropriate community referrals should be made.

Parental Response to an Infant with Defects

The reactions of parents to the birth of a child who has a deformity are based on several factors, the primary factors being the severity and location of the deformity. Other factors include when they are informed, their amount of energy at the time, and their past experience with the condition.[10]

It is important that parents be told about the presence of a deformity in their baby soon after delivery. A perfect baby is expected, and the longer they assume this perfect baby has arrived, the more they suffer when eventually informed otherwise. This delay also causes distrust of personnel and bitterness which could be directed toward the child as well as those working with the couple.

Initially, the parents feel shock and shame. It is especially difficult for the woman who has had a high-risk puerperium and, thus, already a sense of inadequacy about her own body. Since the baby is still considered an extension of herself, her sense of inadequacy and failure as a woman is heightened.[11]

Neither parent, especially the mother, is ready to accept their baby until they have had an opportunity to express their grief and release some of their feelings of disappointment and failure.[12,13] If these feelings are not expressed to someone, the formation of the relationship between this mother and her child can be detrimentally affected. Sometimes personnel accuse these mothers of rejecting their babies during this period, since they are not yet ready to accept them. However, this process is important in the mother's formation of her relationship with her baby and should be understood rather than censured. Both parents need to be aware of the normality of this behavior.[14]

Nursing Implications

A nurse should be available to parents when they are informed of the baby's abnormality. It is important that all personnel be aware that anger or hostility could be directed at them and understand its basis. The nurse must be able to accept this expression of their feeling and understand it as an initial phase of the grieving process, and support them in their mourning.

The parents' perception of the attitudes and behavior of personnel toward them immediately after the birth of their baby has great influence on the family's attitude toward their baby and how they cope with the problems created. The nurse demonstrates caring and respect for the parents even though they have produced an imperfect baby. Our society places great emphasis on the physical and intellectual "wholeness" of

its people. The health team is the first contact these parents have with attitudes toward them and their baby. This contact is at a particularly sensitive time for them, and they are intensely aware of all nonverbal communication and behavior of the health team.

As the mother begins to cope with her feelings, early contact with her baby is essential. When it is time for her to begin the basic mothering task of feeding her infant, the nurse must continue to support and reassure her in her abilities and in the nurse's acceptance of her and her baby. The health team must begin to teach the parents about the defect and what it will mean to the child as well as discuss realistic plans for rehabilitation. Appropriate referrals are essential for this family.

The parents must also be helped to prepare for the handling of reactions from other children. They must be aware that sibling rejection is normal with a healthy child and does not arise because they have not presented a perfect baby.[15]

Another great concern of parents who give birth to a defective child is their probability of producing another child with the same problems. This subject is discussed in Chapter 12 in the section on genetic counseling.

Concerns of the Nurse

Nursing care of parents and babies in the presence of a defect can be very difficult because of multiple feelings within the nurse. Feelings of shock, distaste, or pity toward the baby may be prominent negative feelings. If these feelings are present, it becomes difficult for the nurse to either develop or maintain a meaningful relationship with the parents in helping them through the process of developing their own healthy acceptance of their baby. It is again essential that nursing personnel be aware of their own feelings and can discuss and ventilate them with others so that these feelings are not resolved at the expense of the parents and their child.

The nurse must be aware of feelings aroused by the parents' reactions toward the baby, too. More discussion of how the individual nurse is personally affected when caring for these babies and their families can be found in Chapter 33.

Family Reorganization

It should be obvious that the support given to parents through the early puerperium has important implications for the reorganization of the family. If they have been effectively assisted through the early puerperium, they will be ready to accept help in becoming aware of the needs of each other and other family members.

Initially, the mother may feel overwhelmed by the demands made upon her. She must face possible limited physical capacities and must care for her new baby, as well as any other children in the home. The father, too, may feel frustrated by the new demands that are made on him. Each parent can be helped to become aware of what these demands mean to each other and to the children in the family, and how to handle them.

Caplan believes that family equilibrium is determined by whether individual needs are "perceived, respected, and gratified."[16] He does not believe that the individual family member suffers greatly if his or her needs are perceived and respected even if the family cannot meet all of them. For example, parents can be prepared to expect periods of regression from the toddler as being the norm; and, just as importantly, they learn to perceive and respect the needs for attention in the toddler in order to reestablish family equilibrium and to promote healthy emotional development in their child.

It is also important that one family member, such as the father, does not assume all family responsibilities such as household chores, care of the children, and the like, for an extended period of time. When this occurs, that individual's emotional and physical reserves may be eventually depleted, resulting in further disequilibrium of the family system. All family members need to plan how they can share responsibilities and be aware of resources to assist them if necessary.

Basically, the nurse should encourage the couple to discuss needs of other children in the home and guide them in making plans for how the mother can divide her time among her family members, including the father, and still get the rest she needs. Home planning should be discussed with the mother and father as a team, helping them to freely discuss their concerns and anxieties. Both parents should be informed of community agencies which can be of assistance to them in their adjustment into the home.

SPECIFIC HIGH-RISK CONDITIONS

There are many conditions in a high-risk pregnancy that are not abruptly terminated with delivery of the baby. Obvious examples include women who have a coincidental medical complication such as diabetes or cardiovascular disease. Since many nursing textbooks are oriented to the normal maternity cycle, nurses are often at a loss in knowing how these conditions are affected during the puerperium. Furthermore, they are probably not accustomed to caring for maternity patients with medical complications unless they work in high-risk centers, where high-risk mothers are often referred. The majority of maternity nurses in general hospitals may suddenly be called upon to use knowledge and skills not commonly needed. It is extremely important for the patient involved to have confidence in those who are caring for her.

The nurse needs to be aware of how the puerperium affects the coincidental conditions and how, in turn, these conditions may affect the puerperium. The first 48 hours after delivery involve significant changes in the body which produce a crucial period for many complications. The nursing care in this period is of utmost importance for these patients.

The following sections will discuss how continuing complications of pregnancy are affected by the physiological adaptation of the puerperium and, in turn, how they affect the puerperium. Nursing implications of integrating physical care of the two conditions will be discussed. However, specific nursing care of a medical condition will not be covered, since this is done thoroughly in any medical nursing textbook which should be found on maternity units. It should be the responsibility of the nursing staff to hold conferences for purposes of refreshing the knowledge of nurses who care for these patients and helping auxiliary personnel in observing and understanding symptoms that are presented by the patient's condition.

Coordination and continuity of nursing care is of utmost importance in the care of these patients with the multiple problems presented with both their condition and that of their babies. These patients have a greater need for rest than others, but many more demands for tests and treatments are made upon them. Rather than one doctor, they may be seeing the obstetrician, pediatrician, internist, and even interns or residents in the hospitals where they are present. Dietitians, social workers, and laboratory personnel may also have contact with the patient. It is the nurse who has prime responsibility for coordinating the activities of all these people so that the needs of the patient will be best fulfilled.

Discussion of emotional support is found in the previous sections. The following sections will include basically the physical care of each complication discussed.

CARDIOVASCULAR CONDITIONS

Cardiac Disease

After delivery occurs, there is a 20 to 40 percent increase in blood volume.[17] The blood that previously supplied the uterus is emptied into the general circulation, increasing cardiac output. For the person who has cardiac disease, the danger of congestive heart failure is again present in the first 48 hours following delivery—the first hour is the most crucial.

A moderate amount of blood loss following delivery reduces the total blood volume and aids the heart in its work. However, too much blood loss is a problem because of the anemia that results. If the cardiac patient requires blood during the postpartum period, packed cells would probably be given rather than overloading the circulatory system with whole blood.

The physiological diuresis of the body during the second to fifth days postpartum helps to establish physiological equilibrium. However, the nonpregnant cardiac output level is not usually reached until almost 2 weeks postpartum.[18]

Psychic stimuli following delivery play a less important role in increasing cardiac output than during labor. Much anxiety is relieved by the termination of pain during delivery process.[19]

The patient who develops puerperal infections and mastitis is also in danger of developing bacterial endocarditis. Most cardiac patients are put on prophylactic antibiotics following delivery and are often discouraged from breast-feeding by some doctors for this reason. Slight infections can also trigger congestive heart failure in cardiac patients. It is important that the patient be protected from upper respiratory infections as well as puerperal infections and mastitis.

The New York Heart Association[20] has used the following criteria to group cardiac patients into four functional classes:

Class I patients have no limitation of physical activity. Ordinary physical activity causes no discomfort; they do not have symptoms of cardiac insufficiency and do not have anginal pain.

Class II patients have slight limitation of physical activity. Ordinary physical activity causes excessive fatigue, palpitation, and dyspnea or anginal pain.

Class III patients have a moderate to marked limitation of physical activity. During less than ordinary activity they experience excessive fatigue, palpitation, dyspnea, or anginal pain.

Class IV patients are unable to carry on any physical activity without experiencing discomfort. Even at rest they will experience symptoms of cardiac insufficiency or anginal pain.

Most cardiac patients usually deliver vaginally at term and produce healthy babies which may be smaller than average size. However, those patients in class IV who have had severe hypoxia late in pregnancy may have intrauterine deaths or premature deliveries.[21] Some doctors discourage the mother from breast-feeding because they want to reduce any potential hazards of infection. However, most believe that mothers who are in classes I and II may be allowed to breast-feed if they so desire. Mothers in classes III and IV are usually discouraged from breast-feeding because of the increased demands on the fluid and metabolic status.[22]

When the woman has cardiac disease, especially if she has had congestive heart failure at any time, family planning is important. Most doctors believe these patients should be prepared for a method of contraception before they return home. However, postpartal sterilization is usually not indicated for the patient whose condition is well compensated, and patients who have recently suffered congestive heart failure are poor surgical risks.[23]

Nursing Implications

Regardless of etiology, the greatest danger to these patients during the first 48 hours following delivery is congestive heart failure. Factors in the postpartum period which increase this possibility include the increased cardiac output at this time, slight puerperal infections, anemia from excess blood loss, and undue physical strain. Nursing care of cardiac patients during the postpartum is directed at prevention of the above mentioned factors and intensive observation for early symptoms of congestive heart failure.

Two early symptoms of congestive heart failure are edema and shortness of breath; thus, the mother should be observed closely for the presence of edema and changes in the apical pulse as well as the rate of respirations. If she is bedridden, the edema is found first in the posterior regions of the thighs and sacrum. If she is not on bed rest, the edema will probably be located in the area of the ankles. The mother's weight is not usually a reliable indicator of edema during the early puerperium.[24] The apical pulse should be checked closely for any arrhythmias or changes. The care of patients with congestive heart failure is thoroughly discussed in medical nursing textbooks.

The normal physiology of increased cardiac output cannot be changed. However, prevention of increased circulatory overload is important. If an intravenous infusion accompanies the patient from the delivery room, the rate of flow should be determined by the doctor and regulated with great care by the nurse. As the patient begins to eat, low-sodium diets are important in prevention of fluid retention. The patient will probably be on diuretics at this time for the same purpose. The total fluid intake and output should be carefully recorded.

It is important for the nurse to closely observe the patient's blood loss and condition of the fundus in the early hours postpartum so that anemia from blood loss is checked as closely as possible. Oxytocics will probably be given, although Ergotrate is usually avoided because of its effect on the circulatory system.[25] Frequent manual determination of the condition of the fundus is essential, since an increased flow from a boggy fundus could be detrimental. The amount of blood loss that could cause anemia will vary with each patient, depending on such factors as previous hemoglobin and blood loss at delivery.

Although the patient may decide not to breast-feed, especially patients in classes III and IV, estrogen is not usually given to these patients for suppression of lactation because of the fluid retention that results. They will need to be assisted in the relief of breast engorgement when it occurs and in accompanying comfort measures.

Prevention of infection is always important in the puerperium. However, it becomes even more essential with the cardiac patient, since any infection will add increased stress and/or the increased risk of endocarditis. As mentioned previously, the patient may be on prophylactic antibiotics, but this factor should not cause a relaxation in good perineal and breast care.

Undue physical stress is also a factor in causing congestive heart failure. The amount of physical activity tolerated by each patient will vary. However, during this period of increased cardiac output, it is important that activity be limited for all cardiac patients.

It is important for these patients not to strain when passing a stool. As the patient strains she tenses the thorax and holds her breath, causing changes in cardiac output and pressure. These changes may cause tachycardia and lead to cardiac arrest. This activity not only occurs when straining with a stool, but can also occur when getting onto a bedpan or moving around in bed. The patient should be taught to exhale during these activities rather than hold her breath.[26] Appropriate stool softeners, ordered by the doctor, should be started early in the puerperium to alleviate straining during defecation. The sluggish peristalsis of the bowel that occurs during labor and delivery and lack of early ambulation in the puerperium add to the problem of bowel elimination for the cardiac patient.

If the pulse is taken after exertion, it can be a good measure of impending congestive heart failure. Only a few minutes should be needed for the mother's pulse to return to normal after an activity has ceased, such as getting out of bed. A great length of time for the pulse to return to normal may indicate congestive heart failure.

The prevention of thromboembolic complications is important for the cardiac patient. The patient who is on bed rest should be encouraged to move her legs frequently and may be required to wear elastic stockings. Ambulation, as soon as it is considered safe, is advisable. Other methods of prevention are discussed in the section on thrombophlebitis.

Long-Term Plans

Patients with cardiac disease must continue on the regimen necessary in the nonpregnant state. If congestive heart failure has occurred at any time throughout the pregnancy, a stricter regimen may be needed. It is essential for all of these mothers to have a strict pattern of rest in the following weeks to again prevent the possibility of congestive heart failure from overactivity and lack of rest. Long-term planning will be essential in the nursing care of these patients. Many community agencies may be of value to this family, such as those involved in household services, since help in the home is essential for these mothers. The American Heart Association also has pamphlets available to help mothers find easier ways of accomplishing household responsibilities. Family members need to be aware of this need for help so as not to place undue expectations on the new mother.

Phlebothrombosis

During pregnancy and in the puerperium, the circulatory system undergoes some specific changes which can increase the tendency for venous thrombosis if preventive measures are not taken. Chances of venous thrombosis are greatly increased during the puerperium when stasis of blood in the legs occurs and with the increased clotting ability of the blood at this time. The tendency is even greater with patients who have had cesarean sections and those who have been on bed rest in the last week or more of pregnancy, as in some high-risk pregnancies.

Phlebothrombosis is a venous thrombosis without the presence of an infectious process. The symptoms are usually masked. It is rarely encountered in the average, healthy, postpartum patient; it occurs more frequently in women over forty years old or in younger women if obesity is present. There is a greater risk with emboli in this form of venous thrombosis than with thrombophlebitis.

Thrombophlebitis

The presence of a slight puerperal infection and direct injuries to a vein predispose to thrombophlebitis, which is a clot formed as a result of an inflammation of the walls of the vein. Thrombophlebitis can be present in the ovarian and uterine veins, and veins of the broad ligament, which would be referred to as pelvic thrombophlebitis; or it can be present in the veins of the leg, which is referred to as femoral thrombophlebitis.

Pelvic Thrombophlebitis

Symptoms indicating the presence of this condition begin with chills and a high fever. The causative organism is usually anaerobic streptococcus which can be cultured from the bloodstream only during a chill. Otherwise, its presence is difficult to detect. This condition does not usually appear until the second week postpartum. During the time of the chill and peak in her fever, the mother seems extremely ill. At other times she may appear and feel well.

The inflammation can rise higher and higher, or the thrombosis may limit it. As the inflammation extends, the thrombus can also be broken into a mass of pus with small emboli eventually breaking away. The result can be lung abscesses or even pleurisy or pneumonia. The metastatic infection can also occur in the kidneys.

The use of anticoagulants is important to prevent more clots from being formed and to decrease the possibility of pulmonary embolism. An antibiotic specific for anaerobic streptococcus is used to combat the organism present in the bloodstream.

Femoral Thrombophlebitis

Symptoms indicating the presence of this condition usually do not occur in the immediate postpartum period. They begin with pain in the affected leg accompanied by a temperature elevation. As in most cases of phlebitis, the temperature fluctuates between high elevations and normal, often confusing the clinical picture with temperature fluctuations caused by low-grade uterine inflammation, which are characteristic of the second and third postpartum days. However, the pulse remains elevated and ordinarily is elevated out of proportion to the temperature. The affected area will be hotter to touch than the rest of the leg or the other leg. Edema will be present; the degree of edema depends on the amount of obstruction in the vein and the location of the vein in which there is an embolus. Upon passive dorsiflexion of the foot of the leg suspected of having thrombophlebitis, the patient may experience pain in the calf and popliteal areas, indicating the presence of deep venous thrombosis. The presence of pain during this maneuver is known as a positive Homan's sign. However, a negative Homan's sign (the dorsiflexion maneuver *without* pain) is an unreliable indicator that thrombophlebitis is *not* present, due to the fact that some patients with thrombophlebitis present a negative Homan's sign.

Thrombophlebitis is often referred to as *phlegmasia alba dolens,* and also as "milk leg," especially when extensive edema is present. The latter term was coined when it was believed that the edema was actually milk present in the leg. Perhaps this was because the skin over the area of swelling becomes tense and white, and lactation may cease when an acute febrile process is present.[27] It may take several weeks for the inflammatory process to heal, and recurring edema may continue to be a problem for years.

Nursing Implications

The most important aspect of care is prevention. During the postpartum period, this includes early ambulation to prevent stasis of blood in the leg and the prevention of puerperal infection. Changing the position of patients who have had cesarean sections should be done frequently, and they should be encouraged to move their legs while in bed. If there is no contraindication for other conditions, elevation of the foot of the bed can be beneficial in assisting venous drainage for those requiring bed rest. The knee gatch should not be elevated, and the patient should not lie in bed with legs or ankles crossed, since this puts added resistance on venous return.

When the patient is initially ambulated after delivery, she should be assisted in walking periodically rather than allowed to sit. Sitting on the edge of the bed or sitting in a chair increases pressure on the veins in the legs, which predisposes to clot formation. Elastic stockings may be ordered by the physician for patients whose condition predisposes to the formation of clots, such as cardiac patients who may be on bed rest, or women with existing varicosities. With thrombophlebitis, a cradle is used to keep the bedclothes off the affected leg. The affected leg should never be rubbed or massaged.

There are basically two types of treatment for thrombophlebitis depending upon whether the superficial or deep leg veins are affected. With superficial thrombophlebitis topical heat is applied locally to the area. The patient is not on bed rest, she wears support stockings when ambulating, and anticoagulants are usually not administered. Patients with deep thrombophlebitis are kept on strict bed rest until the anticoagulant regimen is stabilized, after which time ambulation is allowed. These patients also wear support stockings when out of bed. Only if the femoral thrombophlebitis is secondary to septic pelvic thrombophlebitis is the patient given antibiotics.

Pulmonary Embolism

Pulmonary embolism usually results from the development of phlebothrombosis rather than thrombophlebitis, making it difficult to detect warning signs before the actual damage occurs. However, knowledge of the conditions which predispose to phlebothrombosis helps preventive measures to be implemented. Predisposing conditions include congestive heart failure and hypothyroidism as well as the combining factors discussed in the section on venous thrombosis.

The seriousness of a pulmonary embolism depends on the size of the embolus. A large embolus causes sudden death within a few minutes or hours in a patient who previously appeared healthy. A smaller embolus is not usually fatal, but there is a great possibility that other emboli, and larger ones, will be released into the bloodstream and that repeated episodes will occur which could be fatal.

Symptoms of pulmonary embolism include sudden and intense chest pain, severe shortness of breath, and cyanosis. The pulse is feeble and irregular. If the patient does not die soon after the attack, a high concentration of oxygen is given and anticoagulant therapy is started. The anticoagulant therapy does not affect clots that are already formed but does prevent formation of more. Medication is given to help relieve apprehension.

Nursing Implications

The most important aspect of care is prevention of any form of venous thrombosis. In the postpartum period this includes early ambulation and other measures to prevent stasis of blood in the legs and prevention of puerperal infection.

When the patient survives the first pulmonary embolism, she must be on strict bed rest and virtually physically inactive. Emboli may be dislodged during movement, resulting in death. Oxygen is started immediately, and since anticoagulant therapy will also be ordered by the physician, the patients must be observed closely for unusual bleeding. Any apprehension should be relieved if

possible. Most patients who are still alive after 6 hours will probably recover completely.[28]

ENDOCRINE DYSFUNCTIONS

Diabetes

Insulin needs of patients during the third trimester of pregnancy usually increase. During the immediate postpartum period there is an abrupt drop in the need for insulin, and if the dosage is not reduced prior to delivery or immediately following, insulin shock could occur. Other metabolic changes that normally occur as the body rapidly returns to its nonpregnant state sometimes make diabetes difficult to control in the immediate puerperium. The mother's diabetic condition should be fully stabilized within 72 hours postpartum.[29]

In the last weeks of pregnancy and during lactation, lactose is produced in the breast. If lactation is inhibited, lactose spills over into the bloodstream and is excreted into the urine. Lactosuria is sometimes misleading at this time, so blood sugar determinations are frequently done for a more accurate regulation of the insulin requirement. Lactosuria will still be found during lactation but is usually clinically insignificant. The patient should check her urine during lactation following the early puerperium. Lactose demonstrates a negative test for glucose with the Clinistix, although Benedict's solution tests positive for sugar.[30]

Diabetic women are more likely to develop toxemia and polyhydramnios during their pregnancy than other women. If eclampsia develops, the nurse is also involved in the care of this condition as described in the section on postpartum eclampsia. Polyhydramnios increases the mother's tendency to hemorrhage in the postpartum period due to overdistention of the uterine muscle fibers with resultant loss of tonicity. Thus, a diabetic patient presents multiple conditions which require intensive nursing care. However, with a well-controlled diabetic condition throughout pregnancy and close supervision of the pregnancy, toxemia may be prevented and the diabetic condition may remain unchanged from the nonpregnant condition.

In women with diabetes, labor is sometimes induced 2 weeks prior to term because fetal death tends to occur more frequently during this period of time. As a result, even though the infant may be large for gestational age, the infant could be preterm if a discrepancy in dates exists.

Since diabetics have less resistance to infection, those mothers with a longer duration of the disease are sometimes discouraged from breast-feeding their babies. Cracked nipples may be extremely difficult to heal and even develop into serious infections. Breast-feeding may also decrease the stability of their diabetic condition, especially when weaning the baby, since their intake and lactation needs will vary. The decision to breast-feed depends on the seriousness of the patient's diabetic condition, her baby's condition, and her doctor.

If the diabetes is well controlled throughout pregnancy, the mother's diabetic condition during the postpartum period should gradually return to her nonpregnant status. In women who have had long-lasting diabetes, however, the maternal vascular system may show greater changes than caused by aging alone.[31] Women with gestational diabetes may find that their condition will return to latent diabetes, but with each pregnancy and with age, clinical diabetes will eventually become permanent.[32]

Women who produce large babies, especially if the baby is a stillborn at term, frequently are suspected of latent diabetes. Sometimes 2-hour postprandial blood sugars are done on these women in the early puerperium. If high blood sugar is determined, a glucose tolerance test is done. If latent diabetes is detected, these patients are counseled regarding the effect of weight gain and the significance of pregnancy and age in manifestation of the clinical condition. Their future pregnancies are closely supervised to prevent intrauterine death at term.

Nursing Implications

Nursing care in the early puerperium of diabetic mothers is directed at factors which help to stabilize their diabetic condition and result in a healthy obstetric outcome. The mode of delivery, preferably vaginal, influences the nursing care. Cesarean sections are not done unless indicated by the obstetric condition. For example, a woman with a severe diabetic condition whose cervix is "not ripe" for induction will probably have a cesarean section; cesareans may also be done in cases of cephalopelvic disproportion due to a large but immature baby.

Fluctuation of the diabetic condition in the early puerperium requires blood sugar determinations as well as the usual urine checks as ordered by the doctor. In a mild form of diabetes, only frequent urine checks might be done, and insulin dosage will be regulated accordingly. A short-acting insulin may be used until stabilization occurs. The nurse must observe the patient for signs of hypoglycemia and impending insulin shock, which is most common during this period, and also must be alert for signs of diabetic coma.

The patient's diabetic condition begins to fluctuate in the presence of an infectious process; therefore good perineal care and breast care is again emphasized. The patient must understand the importance of good hygiene in relation to her postpartum care while she is in the hospital and in the home setting. Slight puerperal infections can make the management of the diabetic condition difficult, so infections should be reported immediately.

If polyhydramnios was present during pregnancy, the tendency toward hemorrhage is increased during the postpartum period. These patients must be checked closely in the early puerperium for bleeding complications.

Thyroid Dysfunctions

Hyperthyroidism

Physiology of the puerperium seems to have minimum effect on hyperthyroidism. The basal metabolic rate is increased during the last trimester of pregnancy but returns to normal within a week after delivery.

These patients have usually been on antithyroid activity medications during pregnancy to help produce a euthyroid state. The dosage of the antithyroid medication will probably be reduced in the first week of the puerperium. Since these drugs are excreted into the breast milk, these mothers are not allowed to breast-feed.[33]

If these patients are overtreated with antithyroid medications, their pregnancies frequently result in abortions, fetal anomalies, and an overly suppressed fetal thyroid. Toxemia and postpartum hemorrhage could also occur with poor management of the hyperthyroid condition superimposed on pregnancy.[34]

Nursing Implications

Much of the nursing care in the puerperium of the patient depends on the medical control of her thyroid condition. The nurse should be alert for increasing apprehension and tachycardia, suggesting an impending thyroid storm or crisis. Laboratory tests to determine thyroid status will probably be done until the thyroid condition is again stabilized to determine medication dosages.

Prevention of postpartum hemorrhage may be an important factor, depending on the status of thyroid activity at the time of delivery. Toxemia may also be present. Otherwise, nursing care will basically involve a normal puerperium.

Hypothyroidism

There is little discussion in the literature on the postpartum care of the patient with hypothyroidism. The severe form of this condition is associated with sterility. When milder forms of the condition are present and untreated, the problems that occur are usually related to the ability to become pregnant and the maintenance of the pregnancy. If untreated, premature delivery and congenital anomalies are frequently present when the pregnancy is maintained.[35] Women who are being treated for their hypothyroidism and in whom a euthyroid state is present usually have a normal childbearing course.

COMPLICATIONS SPECIFIC TO PREGNANCY

Postpartum Eclampsia

Postpartum eclampsia is a complication of toxemia of pregnancy characterized by convulsions. Approximately one-fourth of all toxemia cases have their first convulsion in the postpartum period and are, thus, designated as postpartum eclampsia.[36] Patients who have experienced convulsions before the puerperium can also continue to have them within the first 48 hours after delivery. Close observation of these patients is as essential during this time as it is prior to delivery. Obviously, the dangers are the same, with the potential threat of convulsions occurring during sleep. The blood pressure tends to be somewhat labile but usually high.

Nursing personnel should not relax observations and care of these patients because delivery has occurred. Spontaneous recovery usually does not occur for 48 hours after delivery, so continued vigilance is important during this time.

Owing to sedation during this time, the mother may be unable to breast-feed until as late as the fourth or fifth day postpartum. Haynes reports that with a group of posteclamptic patients approximately half developed postpartum psychosis.[37] These patients should be observed for signs of this condition.

Nursing Implications

Principles of nursing care of the eclamptic patient in the postpartum period are essentially the same as in the antepartum period. Basic differences, obviously, relate to the empty uterus. The nurse must use great care and gentleness in determining blood loss and checking the fundus so that convulsions are not triggered. Judgment as to fluctuations in blood pressure must be accurate in relation to blood loss and the eclamptic condition.

Since the level of hypertension may not return to normal for several weeks, these mothers should be put on low-sodium diets and maintained on these until there is a decrease in their blood pressure. It is difficult to determine immediately if permanent hypertension will result following postpartum eclampsia. However, it is more likely to persist in older women. Essential hypertension seems more likely to result when the patient is already predisposed to it.

Multiple Pregnancy

A woman with a multiple pregnancy is susceptible to multiple complications in the puerperium. Her chances of having toxemia, including eclamptogenic toxemia, are greatly increased compared to the woman with a single fetus. The danger of postpartum hemorrhage is also heightened as a result of the overdistention of the uterus, which results in uterine atony after delivery. These patients should not only be checked closely for prevention of excessive blood loss, but preparations should be made to replace blood loss if necessary.

Premature labor is quite common with a woman who has a multiple pregnancy. Thus, prematurity, fetal death, and fetal trauma at birth are more common problems with the multiple pregnancy than with a single fetus.

Nursing Implications

Immediate physical care of a woman with a multiple birth in the puerperium is basically directed at prevention of postpartum hemorrhage and appropriate nursing care in the presence of toxemia.

A combination of difficult emotional situations could be present, depending on the condition of the babies and whether a multiple pregnancy was expected or not. The nurse must be aware of a mother's need to grieve for a stillborn baby even though she has a second baby who is healthy and normal. If a second baby was not expected, it may not be as difficult for the mother because she would not have been prepared psychologically or made preparations in the home.

REFERENCES

1 Caplan, Gerald: *Concepts of Mental Health and Consultation, Their Application in Public Health Social Work,* 2d ed., Children's Bureau, Washington, D.C., 1966, pp. 62–63.
2 Rubin, Reva: "Body Image and Self-esteem," *Nursing Outlook,* 68:20–21, June 1968.
3 Owens, Charlotte: "Parents' Response to Premature Birth," *American Journal of Nursing,* 60:1118, August 1960.
4 Klaus, M., and J. Kennell: "Care of the

Mother," in Marshall Klaus and Avroy Fanaroff (eds.), *Care of the High Risk Neonate*, Saunders, Philadelphia, 1973, p. 102.

5   Ibid., p. 102.

6   Kennell, John, Richard Jerauld, et al.: "Maternal Behavior One Year after Early and Extended Post Partum Contact," *Developmental Medicine and Child Neurology*, 16:173–178, April 1974.

7   Kaplan, D. M., and E. A. Mason: "Maternal Reactions to Premature Births Viewed as an Acute Emotional Disorder," *American Journal of Orthopsychiatry*, 30:541, July 1960.

8   Ibid., p. 542.

9   Ibid., pp. 544–545.

10   Kaullas, J.: "The Child with Cleft Lip and Palate—The Mother in the Maternity Unit," *American Journal of Nursing*, 65:121, April 1965.

11   Waechter, Eugenia: "The Birth of an Exceptional Child," *Nursing Forum*, 9:204, 1970.

12   Ibid., pp. 204–212.

13   Kaullas: op. cit., p. 122.

14   Waechter: op. cit., p. 209.

15   Waechter: op. cit., p. 215.

16   Caplan: op. cit., pp. 42–43.

17   Lerch, Constance: *Maternity Nursing*, Mosby, St. Louis, 1970, p. 109.

18   Haynes, D. M.: *Medical Complications during Pregnancy*, McGraw-Hill, New York, 1969, p. 69.

19   Ibid., p. 72.

20   Criteria Committee of the New York Heart Association, Inc.: *Nomenclature and Criteria for Diagnosis of Diseases of the Heart and Blood Vessels*, 5th ed., The New York Heart Association, New York, 1955.

21   Hellman, Louis M., and J. Pritchard: *Williams Obstetrics*, Appleton-Century-Crofts, New York, 1971, p. 781.

22   Haynes: op. cit., p. 99.

23   Haynes: op. cit., p. 99.

24   Shafer, K., J. Sawyer, A. McCluskey, E. Beck, and W. Phipps: *Medical-Surgical Nursing*, 5th ed., Mosby, St. Louis, 1971, pp. 314–315.

25   Mendelson, C. L.: *Cardiac Disease in Pregnancy*, Davis, Philadelphia, 1960, p. 77.

26   Johnson, B. J.: "Effects on Cardiovascular Function," *American Journal of Nursing*, 67:782, April 1967.

27   Fitzpatrick, E., S. Reeder, and L. Mastroianni: *Maternity Nursing*, 12th ed., Lippincott, Philadelphia, 1971, p. 498.

28   Barnes, Cyril: *Medical Disorders in Obstetric Practice*, 4th ed., Blackwell, Oxford, 1974, p. 249.

29   Babson, S. G., and R. C. Benson: *Management of High-Risk Pregnancy and Intensive Care of the Neonate*, 2d ed., Mosby, St. Louis, 1971, pp. 74–78.

30   Barnes: op. cit., p. 287.

31   Cavanaugh, Denis, and M. R. Talisman: *Prematurity and the Obstetrician*, Appleton-Century-Crofts, New York, 1969, p. 75.

32   Barnes: op. cit., p. 291.

33   Gerbie, Albert: "Endocrine Diseases Complicated by Pregnancy," in D. M. Haynes, *Medical Complications during Pregnancy*, McGraw-Hill, New York, 1969, p. 354.

34   Babson and Benson: op. cit., pp. 51–52.

35   Babson and Benson: op. cit., p. 52.

36   Hellman and Pritchard: op. cit., p. 701.

37   Haynes: op. cit., p. 54.

BIBLIOGRAPHY

Anderson, Betty, et al.: *Interruptions in Family Health during Pregnancy*, vol. II, *Childbearing Family*, McGraw-Hill, New York, 1975.

Caplan, Gerald: *Concepts of Mental Health and Consultation, Their Application in Public Health Social Work*, 2d ed., Children's Bureau, Washington, D.C., 1966.

———: "The Mental Hygiene Role of the Nurse in Maternal and Child Care," *Nursing Outlook*, 2:14–19, January 1954.

Hall, Joanne, and Barbara Weaver: *Nursing of Families in Crisis*, Lippincott, Philadelphia, 1974.

Johnson, B. J.: "Effects on Cardiovascular Function," *American Journal of Nursing*, 67:781–782, April 1967.

Klaus, Marshall, R. Jerauld, N. Kreger, et al.: "Maternal Attachment: Importance of the First Post Partum Days," *New England Journal of Medicine*, 286:460–463, 1972.

Klaus, Marshall, and John Kennell: "Mothers Separated from Their Newborn Infants," *Pediatric Clinics of North America*, 17:1015–1037, November 1970.

Klaus, Marshall, J. Kennell, N. Plumb, et al.: "Human Maternal Behavior at the First Contact with Her Young," *Pediatrics*, 46:187–192, 1970.

Leifer, A., P. Leiderman, et al.: "Effects of Mother-Infant Separation on Maternal Attachment Behavior," *Child Development*, 43:1204–1217, 1972.

Lytle, Nancy: *Maternal Health Nursing*, Brown, Dubuque, Iowa, 1967.

Makinson, D. H.: "Medical Disorders of Pregnancy," *Nursing Mirror*, 128:15–17, January 10, 1969.

———: "Medical Disorders of Pregnancy, Part II," *Nursing Mirror*, 128:42–45, January 17, 1969.

Owens, C.: "Parents' Reactions to Defective Babies," *American Journal of Nursing*, 64:83–86, November 1964.

———: "Parents' Response to Premature Birth," *American Journal of Nursing*, 60:1113–1118, August 1960.

Prugh, Dane G.: "Emotional Problems of the Premature Infant's Parents," *Nursing Outlook*, 1:461–464, August 1953.

Rose, Patricia Ann: "The High Risk Mother-Infant Dyad—A Challenge for Nursing?" *Nursing Forum*, 6:94–102, 1967.

Rubin, Reva: "Puerperal Change," *Nursing Outlook*, 9:753–755, December 1961.

Stevens, Bette A.: "Postpartum Eclampsia," *Nursing Mirror*, 123:331–332, Jan. 13, 1967.

Wiedenbach, Ernestine: *Family-centered Maternity Nursing*, Putnam, New York, 1967.

33

Care of High-Risk Infants and Their Families

JANE M. BRIGHTMAN AND
STEPHANIE CLATWORTHY

The process of labor and delivery and the need for immediate adjustment to the external world create stress and crisis for all newborns. The majority of infants adapt well with little or no difficulty. Some, however—infants at risk—cannot or do not adapt with the same degree of ease. Predisposing the infant to difficulties during the adjustment phase of life are certain maternal and environmental conditions. Also implicated are conditions which exist within the infant at birth or which appear soon thereafter. Table 33-1 lists the factors which commonly contribute to the vulnerability of the neonate. With or without any of the other factors noted in this table the majority of high-risk infants are premature or of low birth weight.

In an attempt to improve care and to decrease neonatal morbidity and mortality, those infants who are at risk during the first few days and weeks of life have been singled out for special attention. According to Nelson, the term "high-risk" infant has been

TABLE 33-1
Criteria for High-Risk Pregnancy

Previous pregnancy history
  Grand multiparity, six previous pregnancies (beyond 16 weeks gestation)
  Cesarean section
  Premature infants—by weight and gestational age
  Neonatal deaths—perinatal
  Infant or child with mental retardation or cerebral palsy or prolonged neonatal hospitalization
  Midtrimester loss
  Isoimmunization
  Other pregnancy complications requiring hospitalization or unusual care, e.g., third trimester bleeding
  Difficult vaginal deliveries
  Large baby—over 4,200 g
  Infertility
  Previous major congenital anomalies
  Postpartum hemorrhage

Medical history
  Hypertension
  Renal disease
  Diabetes
  Thyroid disease (bona fide)
  Cardiovascular disease
  Collagen disease—lupus erythematosus, etc.
  Neurological disease
  Chronic pulmonary disease

Current pregnancy complications
  Age—under 16, over 40 (primipara 35 or over)
  Weight—80 kg or over
  Excessive weight gain—14 kg
  Inadequate weight gain—4 kg by 30 weeks gestation
  Preeclampsia
  Significant uterine bleeding after 12 weeks gestation
  Anemia—hematocrit 30%—not responding to treatment
  Multiple pregnancy
  Failure of uterus to enlarge (McDonald measurement—more than 3 weeks behind gestational dates on two occasions)
  Polyhydramnios
  Intercurrent disease, e.g., rubella, persistent urinary tract infections, thrombophlebitis, etc.
  Pregnancy beyond 42 weeks from last menstrual period
  Breech
  Incompetent cervical os
  Premature rupture of membranes
  Rh-negative, nonsensitive

SOURCE: Courtesy of the University of Colorado Medical Center, Denver, Colorado.

coined to designate infants who should be under close observation by the most interested and experienced nurses available and visited frequently by a physician until complications arising from the circumstances leading to the increased risk may no longer reasonably be expected.[1] Table 33-2 indicates risk percentages calculated at one health care institution.

The aim of special care for high-risk infants is not only to save lives but also to afford this child the potential to attain maximum fulfillment. Inherent in this is the need to support family development in the crisis created by the birth of a high-risk infant.

Discussion in this chapter will cover the most common problems associated with infants at risk, except intrauterine growth defects, which are discussed in Chapter 34.

Depending upon the situation, certain needs have been identified as being common to all infants and families in a risk situation. The relative importance of specific needs may vary in each instance. For example, measures aimed at maintenance of respirations are of high priority for infants with respiratory distress syndrome.

THE NEEDS OF THE FAMILY

The birth of a child is considered to be a normal maturational crisis within any family unit. The response of the parents to their new child is individual and will be influenced by what the birth of a new baby means to them. Does the mother see this child as her gift to her partner—or perhaps to her mother? Does the family view this birth as an achievement in keeping with social status? What is their perception of their ability and desire to be parents of this child? At any rate, the parents' expectations invariably include that their child will surpass or at least attain their level of sociocultural accomplishment.

TABLE 33-2
Neonatal Morbidity Risk

Condition	Risk based on antepartum information only, %	Risk based on antepartum, intrapartum, and immediate condition of newborn, %
Previous neonatal death	8.1	
Previous low-birth-weight infant	5.1	
Mother's age less than 17 years	6.0	
Incompetent cervix	32.5	
Placenta previa, abruptio, antepartum hemorrhage	31.0	
Attempted abortion, suicide, drug intoxication	13.8	
Prolapsed cord	17.1	
Breech position	13.5	
Other labor complications*	27.2	23.8
Abnormal presentation at delivery	24.6	10.7
Maternal diabetes	40.7	33.3
Rh and other isoimmunization	39.4	34.5
Antepartum abdominal/major surgery, accident	30.5	14.0
Premature rupture membranes	27.6	12.3
Toxemia	22.4	14.0
Amniocentesis	7.8	6.6
Multiple gestation	7.2	− 8.5
Prenatal care: none	9.4	4.2
1–3 visits	7.6	3.8
4–7 visits	4.4	3.0
8+ visits	1.3	2.2
Fetal distress	11.5	5.2
Cesarean section	10.5	5.5
Other delivery complications		10.4
Mother's age over 30 years		2.7
Male infant		1.8
Active resuscitation, delivery room		8.3
		Birth weight–gestational age morbidity score (from chart) × 0.78 ———
	Total ———	Total ———

* Induction, pitocin stimulation, uterine inertia, contracted pelvis.
SOURCE: Based on University of Colorado Medical Center live-born data, July 1, 1966, to June 30, 1968. Courtesy of the University of Colorado Medical Center, Denver, Colorado.

In most instances, the birth of a baby is a time of much joy accompanied by congratulations and wishes of well-being from family and friends. This is not the case when the infant is in a vulnerable situation. The atmosphere becomes one of watchful waiting, and responses are guarded. When a family first learns their baby is considered to be in a life-threatening situation, their initial response, a manifestation of their grief, is that of disbelief and denial: "No, it can't be, not my baby!" The parents begin to mourn the loss of the perfect baby of their fantasies. As they begin to accept the reality of this situation, their greatest fear is that their baby will die.

Nursing Intervention

This is a very painful time for the parents. It is the responsibility of the nurse to help them to tolerate what they see, hear, and feel. Often at this time, the parents, and especially the mother, are separated from their child in an attempt to "spare them the pain." The baby is whisked off to a special nursery or even to another hospital; the mother is placed in a private room, usually at the end of the hall, and all maternal care activities are supposedly geared to letting her rest. This careful neglect will not change the situation but will simply postpone dealing with reality. Rather than being helped by caring professionals to deal with the pain, the parents may be left to suffer alone. A nurse with insight will not be the instrument of such neglect. Fortunately, there is a growing awareness on the part of the health team of the needs of these families. Each of us needs help with a difficult situation at some time, and it is not particularly easy to help parents express and deal with their sorrow. The nurse who is helping the family in crisis may also be in need of support.

Separation of parents and infants should be avoided when possible. The early postpartum period is important in the development of effective parenting and family patterns. Studies have shown not only the immediate effects upon parents and infants, but also the enduring effects which separation has upon childrearing practices.[2] It is important to help parents to understand the responsibilities of their roles. This includes the "normal" postpartum maternal needs for rest, proper diet, and support. Siblings at home will need additional support from parents because they too are experiencing a crisis situation. Where local regulations permit, children should be permitted to visit their siblings. Figure 33-1 demonstrates family inclusion. A view through the nursery window is helping these brothers and sisters

cope with the crisis surrounding the birth of their new family member. In addition, mothers, fathers, and significant others demonstrate that they have only delegated and not relinquished their responsibilities by active involvement with the child. This may include caring for the infant, or, as in the case of a very sick infant, watching and asking questions when they do not understand a particular treatment.

Development of Support

The nurse is a vital member of the health team to the family with a high-risk infant. Through the unique position of the nurse, support and guidance can be provided to the family during times of stress. Assisting the family in coping with their grief as well as assuming the parenting roles is essential. Figure 33-2a, b, and c, depicting "progression of touch," shows healthy parental response which can be encouraged, guided, and supported by members of the health team, who realize the need for and importance of parental involvement. The literature puts much emphasis on mothering patterns, but helping the father assume his role is equally important. It is our belief that the man involved must be helped to assume his role and not be pushed into the role of "co-conspirator with the medical team" in an attempt to "spare the mother." The couple who are helped to deal openly with their feelings are in a better position to support each other.

Cognizance and insight into the nurse's own feelings, values, and knowledge are needed before support can be given. For example, if the nurse does not believe the family should grieve, or is unaware of the family's attempts to handle their grief, the family's coping mechanisms may be hindered or obstructed.

Being supportive may mean different

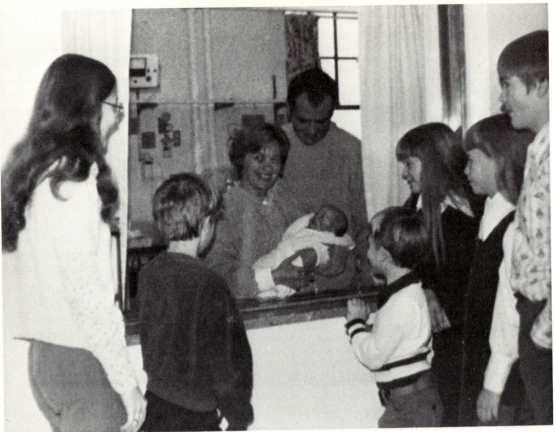

FIGURE 33-1
When local regulations permit, children should be permitted to visit their sibling.
A view through the nursery window is helping these brothers and sisters cope with
the crisis surrounding the birth of their new family member. (*By permission from
Sioux Valley Hospital, Sioux Falls, South Dakota.*)

things to each of us. Generally, we believe that it involves conveying a feeling of caring to the family. It means letting them know that we will be with them as they experience the pain of their crisis. It also means providing an environment in which the couple feels they can safely express feelings as they experience them. Initially the nurse must identify the strengths within a family and help sustain these strengths. This process may involve modifying established routines.

For example, a couple may be adapting to the situation when they are together, but when forced to separate they are no longer able to cope. This is the family that needs extended visiting privileges with privacy provided as appropriate. Any routine not essential to the well-being of mother or infant should be questioned.

To be supportive, the nurse must deal with the situation openly and honestly. This is a time when the nurse and physician must

(a)

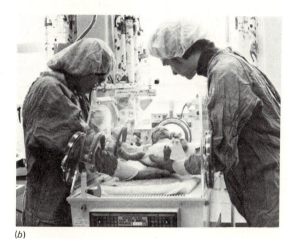

(b)

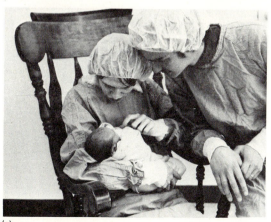

(c)

confer in planning for this family and should discuss how questions will be answered. The parents at this time are searching for information and tend to ask similar questions of different people. Our answers need to reinforce each other if we are to help parents understand what is happening and to foster a trusting relationship. Understanding of the situation and ability to adjust are further strengthened when the mother is allowed to remain on the maternity unit and is not forced into isolation within the unit.

With many newborns, it is the father who is more likely to be excluded or separated from his child because of hospital policies and practice. However, when a child is transferred to a pediatric setting for more intensive care, the father is more likely to have closer contact with his child. The father may then become a major person to help the mother understand and deal with the reality of their problem. The father may be of similar help when the mother is unable to visit the nursery to see her child because of maternal complications such as hemorrhage, or cesarean section.

Providing families with photographs of the infant is a useful nursing intervention. Pictures of infants assist mothers to deal with the reality of the birth, even if they have limited contact with their infant. Photographs are useful in explaining to siblings that they have a new brother or sister. In addition, photographs assist parents in dealing with the reality of grief and loss should the infant die. At this time, the only reality of their experience may be the picture of the lost child.

The nurse is the key person to help the

◄
FIGURE 33-2
Parents should be guided in their developing relationship with their at-risk infant according to their level of readiness and the condition of the baby. (*By permission from St. Luke's Hospital, New Bedford, Mass.*)

family become involved with their infant. The ability of the nurse to recognize the readiness of the family to proceed to develop their involvement with their infant will be of prime importance. As in any guidance situation, the nurse must proceed at the family's own pace.

Development of Trust

In dealing with the parents, the nurse may begin to identify clues that relate to the parents' feelings of guilt. Some degree of searching to place blame—on self, others, events, or fate—is not unusual. The mother may begin to recall events in the pregnancy which to her seem related. For example, she may say to herself: "I shouldn't have gone on vacation"; "I fell during the fifth month"; "I took aspirin before I knew I was pregnant." Inherent in this are feelings of failure at not being able to produce a healthy child. The nurse should listen very carefully to notice whether guilt feeling persists or whether the mother's ideas begin to focus on the care of her child. Because guilt will be compounded when the parents cannot care for their child as they expected, the nurse should encourage the involvement of the parents with their child as soon as possible. When the mother's condition or the child's condition limits the contact, parents may vicariously share in the experiences through a trusted nurse. The nurse's approach to parents and the baby must convey respect for the responsibility with which the nurse is entrusted. It must never be forgotten to whom this baby belongs; otherwise the nurse may be viewed by the mother as a competitor. This will further any feelings of failure the mother may have.

Trust becomes even more important when the mother is discharged, but the child must stay for further care. Plans for discharge become of greater import for this family.

Parents must return home, and the mother must become reacquainted with her other children and they with her. The children will need support for they have expected mother to return with a new baby. Plans will be needed to foster the continuance of the parents' involvement with their infant. (See Figure 33-3.) An infant who requires special care or extended hospitalization may present a financial burden to the family. The nurse must be cognizant of these factors and make appropriate referrals. During the period of hospitalization, the nurse has the opportunity to evaluate the family needs. Many families with high-risk infants will require additional nursing care over a period of time. When this is indicated the nurse should initiate plans for continuance of nursing care. The aid of a maternal–child health clinical specialist found within the community or the hospital may be enlisted. Referral to the pediatrician's nurse or the community nurse may be appropriate. The nurse must be aware of the resources available within the community to facilitate appropriate aid for each individual family.

FIGURE 33-3
This mother (right), discharged home without her baby, visits the nursery daily to participate in her baby's care and to discuss the baby's progress with the nurses. (*By permission from St. Luke's Hospital, New Bedford, Mass.*)

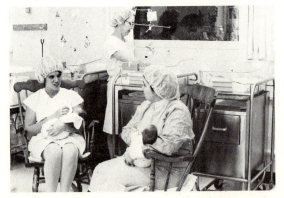

THE NEEDS OF A HIGH-RISK INFANT

Conservation of Energy

All newborn infants may have difficulty conserving their energy at birth, and with the high-risk infant this becomes imperative if life is to be preserved. Conservation of energy can be studied from a variety of approaches. In this discussion, it will be mentioned as it relates to preservation and support of body temperature, support and maintenance of respirations, provision of adequate food and fluid intake, and prevention of infection.

Control of Body Temperature

The infant must be maintained in an environment that is neither too warm nor too cold. Either condition will stress the metabolic process as the infant attempts to adjust to this environment, thereby increasing the oxygen and calorie requirement. Immaturity of the central nervous system, lack of subcutaneous fat, and a high proportion of body surface to weight will contribute to loss of body heat. This process is accentuated to an even greater extent in the premature infant. Chilling may lead to acidosis making it even more difficult for the infant to cope with the environment.

The axillary area is the preferred site for measuring the infant's body temperature. Illness is reflected in changes of skin temperature before that of core or rectal temperature. Taking rectal temperatures may create additional stimuli and increase stooling, which may cause loss of body fluids and electrolytes. Perforation of the rectum by the thermometer has been reported. The infant's temperature should be maintained at 36.5°C. The infant's temperature will respond directly to the temperature of the environment; therefore, incubators or infant warmers are utilized to provide a more reliable means of stabilization of the environmental temperature. (See Figure 33-4.) Both the infant's body temperature and the temperature of the environment should be recorded frequently.

While raising the infant's body temperature, the incubator should be 2 degrees higher than the body temperature. When the infant's temperature reaches 36.5°C, the nurse should adjust the incubator temperature in accordance with the infant's needs. If the temperature of the incubator is 1.2 to 3.1°C lower than the infant's body temperature, it is likely that the infant is utilizing a great amount of energy reserve to maintain body temperature level. The temperature of the incubator may be influenced by direct sunlight, proximity to air-conditioners, outside temperature, or opening of portholes; thus infant temperature and incubator temperature should be checked and recorded at frequent intervals. The frequency is determined by the size and condition of the infant, and may range from 1 to 3 hours.

Portholes on all incubators should be closed at all times, for a small active premature infant could fall through a porthole if the mattress is level with the openings. Air ventilation is provided by a motor which pulls in room air through a filter that removes very minute dust particles. There are a variety of mechanical devices available to assist the nurse in monitoring the infant's and incubator temperature which help reduce unnecessary handling of the infant; however, these devices must be checked for accuracy by the nurse when the infant's temperature is taken, as well as in between times. For immediate awareness of temperature change, the infant and the incubator should be independently monitored as long as the infant has difficulty in stabilizing his temperature.

Infants placed in incubators for temperature control must be left undressed and uncovered so the flow of warm air will have

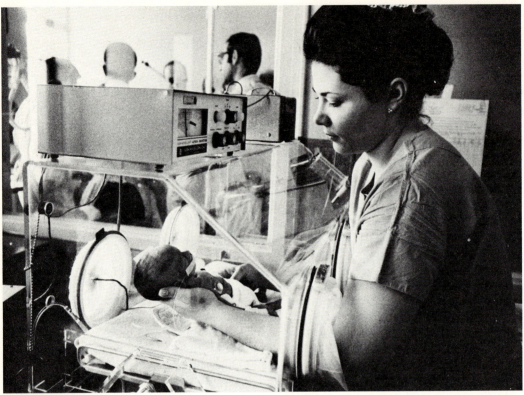

FIGURE 33-4
This infant's body temperature is being maintained through the use of an incubator.
Note the apnea monitor and oxygen analyzer on top of the incubator. The tape on
the infant's face is securing the feeding tube. (*By permission from the Isolette Division
of Air Shields, Inc.*)

contact with the body surface. In addition, the infant who is uncovered is more easily observed by the nurse. When it is necessary to care for or handle the infant in an incubator, body temperature should be recorded before and after to determine the degree of heat loss and the infant's ability to maintain body temperature. When the infant is taken out of the incubator, the infant should be wrapped in warmed blankets.

Infant Warmer and Humidity

When an infant warmer is utilized to maintain body temperature, the instructions accompanying the equipment should be fol-

lowed closely. There are a variety of models available. Some make use of a skin thermistor while others are regulated according to room temperature.

Humidity in the environment must be maintained to prevent additional fluid loss and dehydration. Humidity will also assist in the dilution of infant secretions, enabling the infant to eliminate these with greater ease. If humidity is not controlled by the central ventilating unit, then distilled water should be added to the reservoir of the incubator.

If the incubator or warmer is no longer necessary for the care of the infant and the infant's temperature has been stabilized, the weaning process may be started. This is done by gradually decreasing the temperature of the incubator or warmer and frequently monitoring the infant's body temperature. As the temperature is lowered in the incubator or warmer, the infant may be dressed in a shirt, diaper, and receiving blanket. Once the incubator or warmer is at room temperature and the infant's temperature is maintained at 36.5°C, the infant can be placed in a bassinet.

Maintenance of Respirations

Any infant having respiratory difficulties will be considered at risk. The degree of potential danger is directly related to the infant's gestational age and cause of distress. The nursing care of such an infant is based upon the infant's needs as well as the severity of distress.

Signs of Respiratory Difficulties

The appearance of an infant in respiratory difficulty follows a sequential pattern as the severity increases and is dependent to some degree upon the cause. The initial sign may only be increase in respirations which tend to be more rhythmic in nature. The apical pulse becomes more rapid. Retractions begin; usually the first to appear are subcostal, spreading to the substernal, intracostal, suprasternal, and clavicular areas. (See Figure 33-5.)

Initially the infant's color is pink, but as the compensatory mechanisms become less effective, the infant develops circumnasal-oral pallor and then cyanosis. At this time, nasal flaring on inspiration occurs. Depending upon etiology and energy stores, inspiratory stridor or expiratory grunt appear. The infant's respirations become abdominal,

FIGURE 33-5

Pictorial representation of retractions. This chart is used as an index of respiratory distress by grading each of five arbitrary criteria from 0 to 2: 0 indicates no difficulty; grade 1, moderate difficulty; and grade 2, maximum difficulty. The "retraction score" is the sum of these values; a total score of 0 indicates no dyspnea, and a score of 10 denotes maximum respiratory distress. (*By permission from Mead Johnson & Company, Evansville, Ind.*)

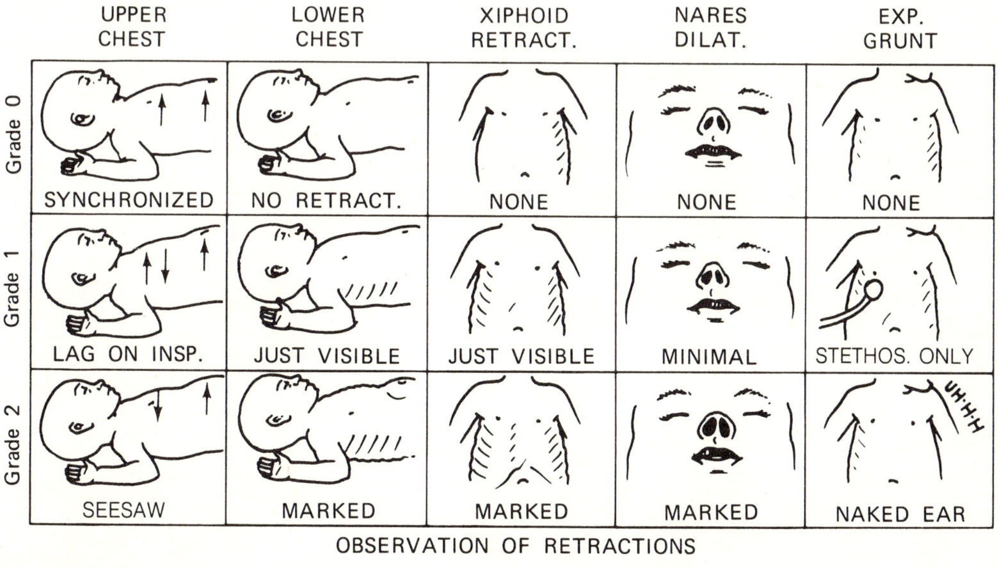

OBSERVATION OF RETRACTIONS

and seesaw breathing patterns are evident. Since the infant is now utilizing a great deal of energy to breathe, the infant's temperature may begin to drop, and close surveillance is required. Too rapid cooling or warming tends to increase apnea. The cardiac system, in its attempts to compensate, may begin to evidence signs of failure, such as palpable liver and spleen and increased edema. Failure and death impend when the heart rate begins to fall, and respirations, although rapid, are frequented with increasing apneic spells. This resembles the Cheyne-Stokes breathing pattern.

Use of Positioning to Support Respirations

Positioning becomes of prime importance for the infant who is having respiratory difficulties and should be individualized. In some cases, elevation of the head of the mattress will allow less pressure on the diaphragm from the abdominal contents. Care should be taken to prevent the infant's arms from lying on the chest. This will only serve to increase the energy needed to lift the chest for inspirations. Flexion and abduction of the infant's arms will permit greater expansion of the thoracic area. An infant in respiratory difficulty will utilize abdominal muscles to a greater extent; therefore, diapers, if used, should be applied loosely around the abdomen.

To further enhance the infant's respirations, it may be necessary to extend the neck slightly to prevent or lessen tracheal obstruction. This is easily done by placing a diaper roll under the infant's shoulders. Caution must be taken not to extend the neck too greatly, making it difficult for the infant to swallow secretions. In addition, the nurse must watch that the diaper roll does not become displaced. An active infant can cause the roll to slide under the head, causing flexion of the neck with narrowing of the

trachea, thus increasing the infant's respiratory distress.

To facilitate drainage of fluids within the chest, the infant should be turned from side to back to side every 1 to 2 hours. This infant should not be placed in a prone position, for the infant will then be supporting the total body weight on chest and abdomen.

Chest physical therapy may be added to the regimen if pooling of secretions becomes a problem.

Feeding Problems Associated with Respiratory Difficulties

Feeding the infant with respiratory difficulties may create medical and nursing problems. The infant who cannot breathe with ease will have difficulty in sucking and swallowing. The infant who is having mild respiratory distress and has no other contraindications may, in rare instances, be able to bottle- or breast-feed. Special attention should be given to clearing the airway prior to feeding. The clearer the airway, the easier the infant can nurse. Milk products tend to increase the amounts of mucus; in addition, milk that is aspirated will create more problems than clear fluids. For these reasons, the infant may be placed on clear fluids for a period of time. Sucking is a basic need of all newborns; therefore, whenever possible, bottle- or breast-feeding is preferable, providing it does not overtax the infant's energy stores. If the infant cannot tolerate the stress of sucking, then tube feeding will be necessary. Some infants do very well alternating bottle- or breast-feeding and tube feeding.

Evaluation of which schedule is best for the individual infant can be done as the nurse cares for the child. Many physicians allow the nurse to make this decision and will write appropriate orders providing the nurse some latitude of decision making based on observations and knowledge of the infant. When the physician does not share decision making with the nurse, it then becomes necessary to bring the needs and desires of the infant to the physician's attention.

Regardless of the method of feeding, there are two main considerations in feeding the infant in respiratory difficulty: (1) the stomach must not be distended. Overdistention restricts the thoracic area and increases the chance of regurgitation, vomiting, and aspiration. (2) Energy reserves must be maintained. The infant may be able to feed well for 10 to 15 minutes for a total of 30 to 60 ml and then be too fatigued to finish the feeding. For these two prime reasons, infants with respiratory difficulties do better with more frequent feedings of smaller amounts. For the infant who cannot tolerate oral or tube feedings, the parenteral route will be the only source of fluids and calories.

Oxygen and Humidity Needs

The infant who has lowered blood PO_2 and increased blood PCO_2 levels or the infant who demonstrates clinical cyanosis or duskiness will require additional oxygen. Oxygen may be administered to an infant through an incubator, mask, or plastic hood. The infant's chest should be exposed since accurate observation of respirations is imperative.

Humidity may need to be increased according to the severity and cause of the respiratory distress. There are a variety of humidifiers available: ultrasonic sound, fine misters, moist air, and warmed or cooled mist. One type is shown in Figure 33-6. The nurse must be knowledgeable as to the type of humidifier used on a specific infant. Nursing care of the infant receiving additional humidity will create several additions to the nursing plan of care. When warmed or cooled mist is utilized, the temperature

of the incubator must be adjusted accordingly. The concentration of humidity should never interfere with observation of the infant.

Oxygen delivered through a hood should be warmed and humidified. The sensors of the face are especially sensitive, and constant exposure to cold oxygen may result in cold stress even though the rest of the body is in a thermoneutral environment.

For the past 30 years, optimal oxygen concentration and therapy for high-risk newborns have received and are receiving intensive study. Too little or too much oxygen may produce serious complications. Oxygen must be given at the direction of the physician; however, the nurse is the primary person available to provide constant observation of the infant and is usually the first one to recognize the need for oxygen. Through the nurse's constant attendance and knowledge, recognition of subtle changes in behavior and color can be made. The physician who visits once or twice daily may be less able to detect change. The nurse must be aware of the conditions of lighting (day, night, natural, or artificial light), since this may influence the infant's color. Changes in activity must be considered in relation to such things as feeding times and treatments.

The nurse can observe for signs of hypoxia, but there is no clinical picture for oxygen toxicity; arterial blood–PO_2 levels are the only accurate guide.

COMPLICATIONS OF OXYGEN THERAPY Increased concentration of oxygen may have to be breathed by the infant to maintain a circulating PO_2 level sufficient to meet the cellular demands of the body. However, when increased oxygen is supplied, the risk of pulmonary oxygen toxicity is present. Increased amounts of oxygen create an increased inability of the lungs to assimilate the gas,

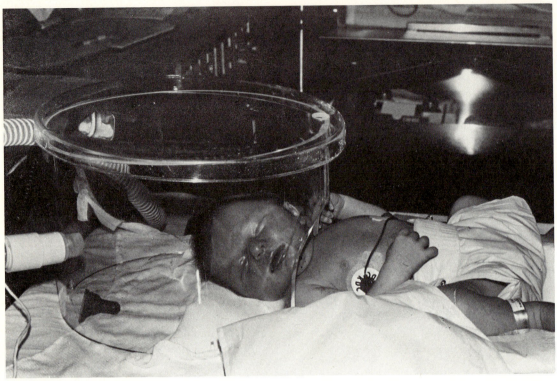

FIGURE 33-6
This infant is receiving humidified oxygen via a hood. The hood allows for regulated
concentration while the infant is maintained in a normal environment. (*Courtesy
of Mr. and Mrs. C. R. Alexander.*)

thus increasing the need for more oxygen.
High concentrations of oxygen (70 to 80
percent) given for even short intervals or
slightly increased oxygen levels for a long
period of time result in a loss of pliancy and
a thickening of the alveolar and vascular
structures, interfering with the gas exchange.
This will lead to atelectasis and increased
cellularity of the lung. The cilia become
paralyzed, thus making the removal of secretions more difficult. Therefore, the infant
may become dependent on the oxygen.

Hyperoxemia must exist before damage of
tissue other than the lung develops. A main
concern is retrolental fibroplasia. Hemorrhage and scar formation are identified with

an ophthalmoscope. If scarring is found in
the macular area, blindness will occur. The
incidence of this condition is directly related
to the maturity of the infant. Some believe
that the infant less than 27 to 28 weeks of
gestation is so susceptible that retrolental
fibroplasia will occur if oxygen is supplied
in the amount necessary to prevent brain
damage. The only way of identifying toxic
levels of oxygen is through measurement of
oxygen tension of blood. It cannot be evaluated through observation nor through predictable regulated concentration. Frequent
samplings of arterial blood for oxygen tension are vital.

The maintenance of a prescribed amount

of oxygen is dependent on the equipment utilized for administration. The concentration will depend on the flow of oxygen (liters per minute) and the loss of oxygen through the use of portholes, or around hoods or masks. It was formerly believed that the concentration of 40 percent oxygen was a safe maximum level in preventing retrolental fibroplasia. It is now realized this figure is not an absolute, as the primary concern is the maintenance of adequate arterial oxygen tension. Each time the amount of oxygen is increased, the flow rate and oxygen concentration levels should be recorded to assist in the evaluation of the infant. If PO_2 levels are too high, oxygen should be decreased slowly in decrements of 5 to 10 percent with careful monitoring of vital signs, oxygen concentration, and blood PO_2.

The use of intravenous therapy to control acidosis may cause an abrupt rise in arterial PO_2. Arterial oxygen tension should be determined before and after any changes in oxygen or parenteral therapy, and the infant should be closely observed.

The nurse working with infants requiring oxygen therapy should be aware that oxygen supports combustion. The hazards of oxygen are markedly increased with the use of electrical equipment; therefore, all electrical equipment should be grounded.

Suctioning

The infant with respiratory difficulties or any newborn during the first 24 hours of life may have difficulties handling secretions. It is imperative that suction equipment be close at hand and that the nurse be skilled in its use.

Depending upon the size of the infant, a number 8 or 10 French catheter is sufficient. A small container of water with a suction machine is the only other equipment necessary. For the infant who is not apneic, it may be helpful to restrain the arms before beginning. The catheter may be lubricated with water. The infant's head should be held securely and the machine turned on. Gently insert the tube through the nostril. When obstruction is met, lift the tube straight up to make the natural turn of the nasal passage. The tube should then be passed until the infant gags (esophagus) or begins to cough (trachea). Once the tube is properly placed in the trachea, suction should be applied as the tube is slowly rotated and withdrawn. Care should be taken so that suctioning is brief because air as well as secretions are being aspirated from the lung. This procedure should be repeated in the opposite nostril. Each time the suction catheter is inserted, irritation of the mucosa occurs, creating an increase in the production of mucus. In addition, passage of a suction catheter or feeding tube may stimulate the vagus nerve, creating bradycardia. For these reasons, suctioning should be done only as necessary. Because of the strong potential of triggering the gag reflex, suctioning should be done prior to feedings.

Once the procedure is completed, all equipment should be discarded, and a new suction catheter and container of water placed with the machine at the side of the incubator. Because of the potential traumatic effect of electrical suction, the de Lee mucus trap is preferred by many clinicians. Suctioning can be accomplished through the nose or mouth.

Resuscitation

Every nurse working with infants should be highly skilled in infant resuscitation. Infants demonstrating apnea may only require gentle stimulation to resume respiration on their own. A piece of gauze placed under the infant's axillary area or foot and tied to the

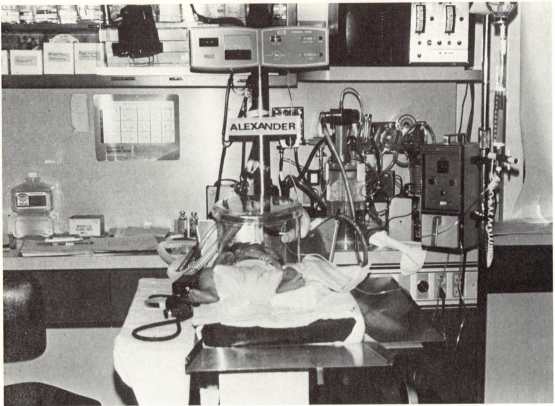

FIGURE 33-7
Much equipment is utilized to monitor the progress of high-risk infants. Parents
should be prepared to see their child attached to all of this equipment. Understanding
its purpose and function will reduce some of the anxiety for the parents. (*Courtesy
of Mr. and Mrs. C. R. Alexander.*)

top of the incubator for gentle tugging without having to open portholes will provide
adequate stimulation for most infants. If this
fails, rubbing the feet and legs or *gentle*
squeezing of the chest will produce respirations. If these measures fail to produce respiration within 20 seconds, more vigorous
resuscitation will be necessary.

Before resuscitation is begun, the airway
must be cleared and the infant's neck slightly
extended. This can be done easily with a
diaper roll. Effective resuscitation of the
infant, like the adult, is only done when the

infant is lying on a hard surface. The newer
models of incubators have a firm enough
mattress so that resuscitation can be instituted there; however, if the infant is in a
bassinet or on a soft mattress, the infant
should be placed immediately on a table or
some other firm surface.

Once positioned, the first two fingertips
(one finger on a premature infant) should be
placed on the midsternum. Gentle, but firm,
pressure should be applied to depress the
sternum not more than 2.5 cm at 100 to 120
beats per minute; a quick respiration should

follow every 3 beats. Excessive pressure could result in laceration of the liver. Simultaneous ventilation and cardiac massage could result in pneumothorax or pneumomediastinum. The respirations may be mouth to mouth, but most institutions now have a bag ventilator with a mask that fits snugly over the infant's nose and mouth. Insufflation should be strong enough to raise the chest but not so strong that a lung is ruptured. A bag ventilator should have an escape valve which prevents excessive air pressure. Sometimes air is pumped into the stomach as well as the lungs. When abdominal distention occurs, a gastric tube should be passed to relieve the air pressure and thus increase the chest capacity.

Resuscitations of this nature must be started immediately to prevent brain damage and death. The physician should be notified immediately, but the nurse should not wait for the physician's arrival to begin resuscitation.

When maintenance of respirations becomes a critical problem the infant may be intubated, and continuous respiratory assistance is provided with positive pressure. (See Figure 33-8.) Great nursing skill is now required, and the infant should not be left alone. If additional equipment or supplies are needed, the nurse caring for the infant must ask for someone else to bring them.

Food and Fluid Requirements

The required water, calorie, and electrolyte intake of the newborn baby is dependent upon the infant's rate of expenditure and body stores of these substances. When caring for an infant at risk, the need for additional calories, fluids, or electrolytes must be evaluated frequently in accordance with the needs of the individual infant. The nurse must be knowledgeable in fluid and electrolyte balance and skillful when collaborating

with the physician in planning for the nutritional needs of a high-risk infant. It is not the purpose of this chapter to discuss in depth the physiological responses inherent in nutritional needs with pathological disorders but to center on nursing knowledge and skills necessary to help the infant maintain calorie, fluid, and electrolyte balance.

Oral Feeding

The infant has strong oral needs at birth. Through the mouth, the infant will gain pleasure and satisfaction of hunger. By having oral and hunger needs met promptly with a nipple to suck on and warm arms to snuggle in, the infant learns trust.[3]

The infant is born with a sucking ability and a swallow reflex. However, the infant must learn to coordinate sucking with swallowing before bottle- or breast-feeding can bring pleasure and nutrition. Infants who cannot suck, swallow, or coordinate these activities are at risk. The inability to suck may be secondary to mouth or palate deformities, central nervous system depression, immaturity, or limited energy stores.

FIGURE 33-8
This infant's respirations are being assisted by means of a positive pressure respirator which has been connected to a nasally inserted endotracheal tube. (*By permission from Massachusetts General Hospital, Boston, Mass.*)

An infant who is considered at risk should be bottle- or breast-fed whenever possible to meet oral needs and develop the infant's trust in a caring person. However, when the infant cannot be fed by bottle or breast, modifications of feeding must be instituted.

For the infant who has a weakened suck or who needs to conserve energy while sucking, a variety of nipple and feeding tools are available. Most of these nipples are made of soft rubber. Some are longer or broader in length and diameter to assist the infant.

Breast-feeding

If the high-risk infant can tolerate it, the infant should be allowed the comfort and satisfaction of being breast-fed, when this is the method chosen by the parents. Although the basic principles of breast-feeding are applicable, some adaptation of the procedure may be necessary. The infant who should conserve energy may need to be fed every 2 hours. Although it is generally considered unwise to give a breast-feeding infant a bottle, as this may interfere with adaptation to the breast, the infant who needs to maintain energy reserves while meeting nutritional needs may require supplemental bottle feedings. Nursing judgment is required to determine which pattern is most appropriate for a given infant and mother. Some infants and mothers do very well if breast-feeding is supplemented by bottle-feeding. Other infants, with less energy, may have to alternate breast- with bottle-feeding. When the infant cannot tolerate all breast-feeding, or in some instances any breast-feeding, the mother must be strongly supported. Mother and nurse should plan together for the best means of maintaining a milk supply. This may be through manual expression and/or the use of breast pumps. The mother who wishes to breast-feed but cannot will need much encouragement. This is best done by praising her for those things she can do and by keeping her well informed of her infant's condition. This will assist in the reinforcement of reality. In addition, the mother who must continue pumping her breasts must be given reason and encouragement. This direct guidance can be very therapeutic to the mother in a crisis situation. It may also help her to accept her mothering role, for she can then feel that she is doing something for her baby and can see the results of her actions.

Feeding the Infant Who Is Unable to Suck

For a baby who cannot tolerate sucking, such as those with cardiac conditions, other devices have been developed to assist the feeding. The eyedropper has been used successfully for many years, but it is a tedious method at best. Of greater assistance is the use of a 5- to 10-ml syringe with a rubber tube about 3.7 to 5 cm in length attached. The rubber tubing allows the formula to be placed further back in the infant's mouth. Neither of these methods of dripping formula into the infant's mouth provides the infant with the pleasurable feel of a nipple. The feel of a nipple is very important, and becomes of even greater importance to the infant who will not be able to feed with a bottle for a prolonged period. At times calorie requirement takes precedence over sucking needs, and the infant may be fed from a small cup.

Extreme caution must be taken whenever the drip method of feeding is utilized with the eyedropper or syringe, for the danger of aspiration is increased greatly. The infant should be held and an area provided for the infant to lie down, if necessary. Suction equipment should be available. This type of feeding can be very fatiguing for the infant; thus, about 30 to 45 minutes should be allowed to provide for rest periods. Frequent bubbling will be necessary since the infant is more likely to swallow air. Again, the feeding should be as pleasurable as possible; both nurse and baby will enjoy the rest periods spent holding and cuddling. Once the stability of the infant is ascertained, the mother can be taught to use these devices when she demonstrates readiness.

Tube Feeding

The immature infant, the one in respiratory distress, or the one with central nervous system disorders may not be able to coordinate sucking and swallowing. For these infants the primary method of feeding is by gavage. Disposable gavage sets are available with a variety of sizes and length of tubes. The tube should be selected in accordance with the size of the infant. The infant's head is elevated and the abdomen and chest exposed. The infant's arms are restrained to prevent accidental displacement of the tube. The tube is measured from the bridge of the nose to the xiphoid cartilage.

The tube may be inserted into a nostril or the mouth. The nostril is the choice selection if the tube is to be left in place. Some believe the nose is contraindicated, as it causes irritation to the mucosa and creates an increase in mucus secretions. The newborn breathes only through the nose and the foreign body markedly decreases breathing capacity. Some believe a tube should not be left in place as this creates a constant production of mucus. The newborn's eustachian tubes are broad and short; therefore, a nasogastric tube left in place provides a source for developing otitis media. Others believe that leaving the tube in place is less traumatizing and less stressful, since it does not have to be passed every 2 to 3 hours. It is usually the practice to pass the tube through the mouth when it is not to be left in place. This eliminates irritation to the nasal mucosa, and the tube provides some oral

stimulation simultaneously with the filling of the stomach, which is more normal and causes very little expenditure of energy for the infant when skillfully done.

After the infant is elevated, chest and abdomen exposed, and hands are secured, the nurse should hold the infant's head in one hand, lubricate the tube with water, and insert the tube to the back of the throat. This may stimulate swallowing, which opens the glottis, allowing the tube to be passed with greater ease. Each time the infant swallows, the tube should be inserted another 2.5 to 5 cm. There is no reason to rush this procedure, as speed is not required. The tube should be inserted until the mark is reached which should place the tip of the tube within the stomach. If obstruction is met, *stop*. The procedure should be started over again, but the tube must not be forced.

There are three ways to ascertain whether the tube is in place:

1 Place the end of the tube in water; if bubbles appear and correspond to the infant's respirations, the tube is in the trachea. The infant will probably cough and choke. Some bubbles may appear if there was air trapped in the stomach, but these will cease and are not related to respirations.
2 Aspirate gently. The appearance of gastric contents will be proof that the tube is in the stomach.
3 Gently insert a small amount of air with a syringe into the stomach and listen with a stethoscope over the stomach for a bubbling sound. If any of these tests leave any doubt that the tube is placed in the stomach, withdraw the tube and begin again.

Once the tube is in place, it is taped to the infant's cheek. With some infants it is necessary to aspirate the gastric contents to measure the amount of absorption of the previous feeding. The contents must be replaced in the stomach or the infant may lose vital electrolytes and enzymes necessary to absorb and utilize the next feeding. The amount returned is considered when planning the amount to be administered at the current feeding.

The barrel of a syringe or a special cylinder is then attached to the feeding tube. Generally these are small to prevent the pressure of the flowing fluid from becoming too great. A 5- to 10-ml syringe can be used quite efficiently. It is wise to begin the feeding with 1 ml of clear fluid. Should the tube be misplaced, the infant would demonstrate immediate respiratory changes, indicating the tube to be in the trachea. Should this occur, clear water will create far less hazards than formula.

OBSERVING THE INFANT DURING TUBE FEEDING
While the feeding is in process, the infant's response should be carefully observed. The amount of solution may be ordered by the physician, but many times it is determined by the observations of the infant's tolerance to the feeding. The rate of flow should be slow; approximately 20 minutes will be needed for the average feeding.

To determine the infant's tolerance to the feeding, several factors should be considered. Distention of the abdomen will occur; however, caution should be taken to avoid overdistention, as this could lead to vomiting and aspiration and/or further embarrassment of respirations. The flow rate should be steady; however, if the infant shows distress, do not hesitate to stop the feeding and allow the infant to rest prior to completion. When the fluid will no longer flow with gravity, maximum capacity has usually been attained. At *no* time should formula be pushed into the infant. If the infant does not tolerate the amount of feed-

ing ordered, merely discontinue the feeding and report the results to the physician.

When discontinuing the feeding, clamp the tube securely and gently remove it. The infant should then be positioned comfortably and in a manner that will prevent aspiration if vomiting should occur. Emptying time of the stomach may be somewhat enhanced and the possibility of regurgitation and aspiration reduced by placing the infant on the right side and elevating the bed or mattress for 20 minutes following the feeding.

The infant who can tolerate it should be held and cuddled following tube feeding, as this aspect of feeding is denied when tube feeding is being used. Some infants prefer to be held and cuddled prior to the feeding. The nurse who communicates with the infant will learn which the infant prefers.

As the infant's needs for tube feeding decrease, the infant will begin to develop sucking motions while being fed. This should be supported with the use of pacifiers initially, and as tolerance increases, the infant may be bottle-fed for one or two feedings each day. As the infant progresses, the number of bottle-feedings will gradually increase. Some infants, usually those who are immature, may develop "lazy" tendencies and prefer the tube feeding to bottle, since hunger is relieved with little effort on the infant's part. This phenomenon may also be increased with the infant who has not been taught that pleasure can be found in a nipple and that there is further benefit in being held. By introducing nipple feedings very gradually, this behavior can often be avoided.

Intravenous Therapy

The infant whose fluid and calorie needs cannot be met orally will need parenteral therapy. It is recognized that parenteral therapy may be necessary for other reasons, such as administration of medication; however, regardless of the purpose, an intravenous administration of fluid and calories will influence the infant's feeding needs. The preferable site for an intravenous infusion is believed to be in a peripheral vein. In some situations, the umbilical artery is utilized. An umbilical catheter with radiopaque markings is used, and its position after insertion is checked by x ray. The infant receiving parenteral fluids needs careful and astute observations. Such an infant's fluid needs are greater than an adult's in proportion to body surface and weight, and the infant can easily be placed in an unbalanced situation.

An intravenous feeding is best administered with the use of an infusion pump which provides a more accurate and constant flow rate. This does not excuse the nurse from the responsibility of closely observing the infant. Some pumps will continue functioning after the drip chamber has emptied, exposing the infant to the danger of air embolism. A new model automatically sounds an alarm and stops pumping when the chamber is empty. Any of these pumps, however, will continue operating when fluid is going into the tissues, so that the infant must be watched closely for signs of infiltration. (See Figure 33-9.)

Several means can be utilized to assist the physician in the evaluation of the infant's needs for intravenous fluids. Infants receiving parenteral fluids should have their urine output measured so that an accurate record of total intake and output is obtained. Each time the infant voids, specific gravity should be measured as an indicator of the urine concentration. The urine should also be checked for glucose.

The weight of the infant is an indication of adaptation to parenteral fluids. Some infants receiving parenteral fluids may be weighed as often as every 12 hours; others may be weighed every 24 hours. Initial baseline weights should include all equipment in use so that monitors do not have to be disconnected to weigh the infant. Generally, a weight gain or loss of 100 g over a 24-hour period is considered to be sufficiently significant to alter the rate of flow.

Calorie Needs

The fluid and calorie needs of the high-risk infant are basically the same as for the full-term or "normal" infant. The difference must be based on the specific needs demonstrated by the individual infant. The infant who is not tolerating oral fluids well will obviously require additional fluids. The infant who is depleting energy stores rapidly, such as in the case of an infant with respiratory distress syndrome, will require additional calories. The more immature the infant, the greater the needs for carbohydrates, as the infant will be expending a great deal of energy to adapt to the extrauterine environment. This is further complicated by the infant's inability to store carbohydrates because of the immaturity of the body systems. For this reason the premature infant is sometimes given formula containing 24 calories per 30 ml. Carbohydrates should be maintained in proper amount. Too little carbohydrate can lead to hypoglycemia, a condition that attributes to central nervous system disturbances and mental retardation. This condition is found very frequently in the premature infant, infants of diabetic or prediabetic mothers, and the small-for-gestational-age infant. Hypoglycemia also becomes of great concern for the infant in stress situations, such as during cooling, respiratory distress syndrome, sepsis, or cardiac difficulties. It appears that whenever an infant is placed in a crisis situation, whether metabolic or environmental, the infant is likely to deplete carbohydrate levels rapidly.

Hypoglycemia has also been found with

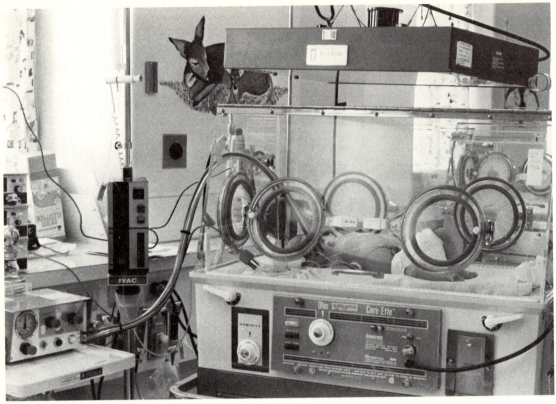

FIGURE 33-9
This infant's infusion is being monitored by pump. Should the burette of fluid
become empty, this pump will automatically stop the flow of solution and signal an
alert. Also visible is a positive-pressure respirator. (*By permission from St. Luke's
Hospital, New Bedford, Mass.*)

the infant who suddenly has parenteral
fluids discontinued. This is due to the fact
that with the increase of circulating glucose
from the fluids, the infant produces additional insulin. When the glucose is suddenly
discontinued, the overproduction of insulin
rapidly depletes the available glucose levels;
thus, hypoglycemia develops. If not severe,
the infant will be able to automatically compensate. Some hypoglycemic infants exhibit
no sign of the condition; others may appear
hyperirritable, jittery, restless, or lethargic.
These symptoms can occur with electrolyte
imbalance, particularly when calcium or

potassium imbalances are present, and it is
essential that blood be drawn immediately so
that a laboratory diagnosis can be made.

Hyperalimentation

When an infant must be maintained on
parenteral fluids to the exclusion of oral
feedings or cannot utilize nutrients taken
orally, hyperalimentation has proved to be
an effective method of maintaining a required
nutritional state. The infant's nutritional
needs are calculated, and a nutrient solution
composed basically of carbohydrates, pro-

tein hydrolysate, vitamins, calcium, sodium, potassium, and magnesium is prepared by the pharmacist. This is usually infused through a catheter inserted surgically into the vena cava via the external or sometimes the internal jugular vein. An infusion pump set at a constant rate is used.

Nursing interventions must be directed toward use of aseptic technique in care of catheter, and positioning of infant to prevent kinking of tubing. Continued assessment of the infant receiving hyperalimentation includes awareness of the signs of the following complications: infection—general or local phlebitis, thrombosis of the vessels, pneumothorax, embolism, hypoglycemia, electrolyte imbalance, and amino acid imbalance.

Prevention of Sepsis

Prevention of infection is of prime importance in any newborn nursery. The import of these precautions becomes magnified when caring for the infant at risk. The infant at risk will have a decreased resistance to infection and thus will be more susceptible and vulnerable. The additional stress of an infection may be all that is necessary for a complete collapse of the infant.

In addition to increased susceptibility, the infant at risk is subjected to many procedures and treatments which may compromise the infant's first line of defense, i.e., injections, suctioning, intravenous infusion, additional personnel, and prolonged hospitalization. It becomes obvious, then, that scrupulous adherence to aseptic technique be observed.

People are the primary source of infection in a hospital setting. For this reason, the number of people admitted to a nursery caring for high-risk infants should be limited to only those necessary to the care of these infants. Whenever possible, nursing staff should be permanently assigned to the special care nursery and should not be asked to "float" to other areas. Delivery of supplies should be made outside the nursery. Personnel coming from other departments should be limited so that whenever possible the same person comes from the x-ray area or from a particular laboratory.

It must be stressed, however, that parents are necessary to provide care for the infant and must be allowed to participate in the care of their child whenever possible. If one takes time to explain precautions necessary to safeguard their child, parents are usually quite willing and able to adhere to them. In fact, some become quite observant and may raise questions concerning others' observance of techniques.

Should an infant develop any symptoms indicative of an infectious process, the infant should be removed from the nursery at once. There is no way to effectively isolate an infant other than by room isolation. It is true that while an infant is in an incubator, the infant is isolated from other infants. However, whenever portholes are opened, transmission of airborne organisms becomes possible.

EFFECT OF DRUGS
Narcosis

An infant may require special attention if the infant is demonstrating the effect of analgesics or anesthetic drugs which the mother received during labor or delivery. The infant may be sleepy, have sluggish respirations, and be reluctant to take feedings. This baby needs to be observed closely so that supportive measures may be instituted, if necessary. This narcosis is usually transitory, and these babies tend to do well subsequently.

Effects of Drug Addiction

Infants born to mothers addicted to habituating drugs such as heroin are being recognized and treated in increasing numbers. About 80 to 90 percent of infants born to actively addicted mothers will manifest withdrawal symptoms, and most of these infants will begin to show evidence of withdrawal within the first 24 hours of life. Supportive measures are generally used to control discomfort, irritability, and purposeless movements. The signs and symptoms which have generally been observed include tremors, irritability, hyperactivity, vomiting, poor food intake, high-pitched, shrill cry, diarrhea, and fever. Dehydration and malnutrition occur secondary to the vomiting, diarrhea, constant activity, and wakefulness manifested by these infants. Among the first signs to appear and the last to disappear are hyperactivity and flushing.

Phenobarbital, diazepam (Valium), methadone, chlorpromazine (Thorazine), and paregoric are some of the drugs used in treating infants suffering from narcotic withdrawal syndrome.

Rather than dealing with affected infants, a better approach would be to treat women early in pregnancy. They prove, however, to be unreliable informants concerning their drug habits. There is evidence that later in pregnancy the fetus responds to the mother's withdrawal with hyperactivity so that it may be necessary to wait until after delivery and support mother and infant separately during the withdrawal process.

NECROTIZING ENTEROCOLITIS

Necrotizing enterocolitis, a serious condition affecting high-risk infants, is being recognized both earlier and in more infants than in the past. This condition, which is especially prevalent among premature infants, has appeared at anywhere from six hours to twenty-one days of age. It is characterized by abnormal distention, bilious vomiting, and roentgenographic signs of ileus. Further manifestations include pneumatosis intestinalis, intestinal perforation without antecedent illness, bloody diarrhea, metabolic acidosis, and sudden cardiovascular collapse.

The cause of this condition remains elusive, although a number of factors have been implicated as possibilities. Some of the most popular theories include congenital deficiency of the bowel wall, trauma from umbilical catheters either directly or through irritating solutions, dissection of air along the root of the mesentary from the stomach, and damage to intestinal mucosa from early feedings of hypertonic solutions such as high-calorie glucose and formula stronger than 20 calories per 30 ml.

Infectious causes have also been considered, although research seems to indicate that microorganisms play a secondary role.

Conservative medical therapy is being used to a much greater extent than it was formerly; surgical resection of the damaged bowel is being resorted to far less frequently than it was in the past. Convalescence following surgical intervention is a long tedious process and not without complication.

NEONATAL JAUNDICE

During the first few days of a baby's life, nurses make frequent, systematic observations of the skin to note the appearance of jaundice. The rise in serum bilirubin responsible for the yellow hue may have several causes. One of these, the phenomenon of physiological jaundice, was discussed in an earlier chapter. Other predisposing factors include high doses of vitamin K, drugs such as sulfisoxazole given to the mother during pregnancy, infections such as rubella, and maternal diabetes. The most common cause, however, is hemolytic disease of the newborn due to blood group incompatibility. Bilirubinemia beyond physiological bounds, or hyperbilirubinemia, exists when serum bilirubin levels approach 18 to 20 mg per 100 ml. The term hyperbilirubinemia of the newborn is usually reserved for infants whose primary problem is a deficiency or inactivity of bilirubin transference rather than an excessive load of bilirubin for excretion.

The liver of the newborn produces little or no glucuronyl transferase, the enzyme necessary for the excretion of bilirubin. In each of the aforementioned instances, the concern with rising bilirubin levels rests with the possibility of its being deposited in the basal nuclei of the brain. This results in a condition known as kernicterus, which leads to cerebral damage or death. The critical level of serum bilirubin is approximately 20 mg per 100 ml, although lower levels may be significant in the premature infant. The bilirubin unconjugated by the liver is also referred to as indirect bilirubin after the laboratory procedure used in its determination. This circulating bilirubin is bound to albumin and, hence, is unavailable for deposition in tissues. The amount of free bilirubin in the tissues cannot be measured; however, it is felt that determining the degree of saturation of serum albumin can provide a clue to this.

Phototherapy

In order to help the body to excrete excess bilirubin, a therapeutic intervention whereby the infant is exposed to an artificial light source has been developed. Phototherapy breaks down tissue bilirubin into products which thus far seem to be nontoxic and easily excreted. The infant should be completely undressed when placed under the lights, and the position of the infant should be changed about every 2 hours. The baby's body temperature should also be monitored closely because it will be affected by such factors as (1) light source, whether cool blue light or a heat-producing source; (2) use of an incubator or an open crib; and (3) temperature of the room. The light source needs to be checked regularly, since the energy output of any bulb decreases markedly after 200 hours of use, resulting in a decrease in the rate of decline of serum bilirubin. Some record of the number of hours a bulb has been in use should be kept attached to the equipment. (See Figure 33-10.)

The full effects of exposure to light on the infant's biological rhythms is not yet known, which leads one to believe it should be used with caution. Careful observation of the infant's eating and sleeping patterns is important, since changes may indicate a need to reevaluate the therapy. Studies with experimental animals have demonstrated retinal damage. For this reason, it is imperative that the baby's eyes be protected. When applying eye patches, the nurse must be certain that the baby's eyes are closed to prevent corneal abrasion. A common side effect of phototherapy is loose stools which may appear greenish because of the increased excretion of bilirubin. The infant will need additional water to compensate for this fluid loss. The nurse caring for this infant must remember that the infant must not be left suspended in this "limbo" indefinitely. Feeding time provides a good opportunity to take the infant away from the lights, remove the eye covering, and hold the infant. The infant still has need for visual and tactile stimulation as well as comfort.

HEMOLYTIC DISEASE OF THE NEWBORN

The main characteristics of hemolytic disease of the newborn are hyperbilirubinemia and anemia. Although this condition can result from the blood-group incompatibility, the difficulties usually arise when an Rh-negative woman is carrying an Rh-positive fetus. The Rh factor, a dominant trait, is an antigen present on the red blood cells of 85 percent of the white and 93 percent of the black population. Unlike the ABO system, there are no naturally occurring anti-Rh antibodies. An Rh-negative person will produce anti-Rh antibodies upon exposure to Rh-positive red blood cells, such as during a blood transfusion or an Rh-incompatible pregnancy.

Fetal and maternal circulations are separate entities and there is no mixing of blood. Late in pregnancy, and especially during the intrapartum period, there is appreciable placental transfer of fetal red blood cells to the pregnant woman. She responds by producing antibodies against the Rh factor which, on first exposure, begin to show up in her serum a few days after delivery. Since

FIGURE 33-10
This infant is receiving phototherapy. Note the mask covering the infant's eyes.
(*By permission from St. Luke's Hospital, New Bedford, Mass.*)

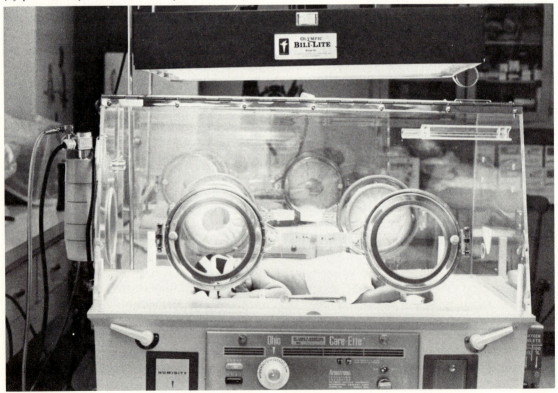

the production of antibodies takes time, the first Rh-incompatible baby usually escapes disease unless the mother has been sensitized by an Rh-incompatible blood transfusion or previous abortion of an incompatible fetus.

In subsequent Rh-incompatible pregnancies, the woman will produce Rh antibodies earlier and in increasing numbers. These antibodies then cross the placenta and begin destroying the fetal Rh-positive red blood cells. The fetus compensates by increasing red blood cell production, and hence, increased numbers of erythroblasts appear in the fetus's circulation. In fact, the presence of these immature cells was the source of the older name for this disease—erythroblastosis fetalis. The problem usually increases in severity with each successive Rh-incompatible pregnancy.

The affected infant will appear pale as a result of the anemia and will become jaundiced, usually within the first day of life. The immature liver is unable to conjugate for excretion the increased amount of bilirubin resulting from the destruction of erythrocytes. Thus, this infant may be in danger of developing kernicterus.

Treatment of Hemolytic Disease

The goal of any treatment is to reduce bilirubin levels and to correct the anemia. There are still circulating antibodies within the infant's system, causing hemolysis.

In severe cases, such as when the indirect bilirubin is approaching 20 mg per 100 ml (or cord bilirubin is greater than 5 mg per 100 ml) or the degree of anemia is severe, an exchange transfusion is performed. In this procedure, Rh-negative blood is transfused usually via the umbilical vein. Using a three-way stopcock attached to a catheter, a small amount of the infant's blood is withdrawn (usually about 10 ml), and then a similar amount of the Rh-negative blood is injected. This continues until the transfusion is complete. Using 500 ml of whole blood, it has been estimated that 85 to 90 percent of the infant's blood will be replaced. The amount of blood used depends upon the size and condition of the infant. The aims of an exchange transfusion are (1) to increase the hemoglobin level sufficiently to suppress production of Rh-positive cells, (2) to keep serum bilirubin below dangerous levels, and (3) to remove both free antibodies and antibody-coated cells. Rh-negative blood is used to prevent further hemolysis by remaining antibodies.

This is a stressful procedure for the infant. The infant's body heat must be maintained and vital signs must be frequently and carefully noted. Some nurseries have equipment which permits constant monitoring. The infant's extremities are restrained. Restraints must be applied so that they are effective but not constricting. Resuscitative equipment must be at hand. The nurse usually has the added responsibility of recording the amounts of blood withdrawn and transfused along with the baby's reaction to the procedure.

Phototherapy is used by some physicians in conjunction with exchange transfusions to help reduce the number of transfusions necessary for any one infant. Phototherapy alone, except in mild cases, is not a treatment for hemolytic disease of the newborn, since it does not correct anemia, nor does it remove circulating antibodies.

In very severe cases, the anemia is accompanied by edema, fluid in serous cavities (hydrops fetalis), and heart failure. In an attempt to save those infants who previously died in utero, intrauterine transfusions have met with some success. Intrauterine deaths were usually the result of severe anemia.

Rh-negative cells are injected into the peritoneal cavity of the fetus where they are absorbed into the circulation. The need for this procedure can be determined by amniocentesis. This is performed when indicated by the pregnant woman's rising antibody titer. Spectrophotometric analysis of amniotic fluid bilirubin provides a guide in assessing the severity of the hemolytic process in the fetus.

Prevention of Hemolytic Disease Due to Rh Incompatibility

Since maternal antibodies are usually not present until a few days after the first delivery, and it is usually succeeding infants who are affected, prevention is aimed at suppression of maternal antibody production. A form of passive immunization has been used successfully for this. RhoGAM (Rho [D] immunoglobulin [human]) can be administered to the mother within 72 hours after delivery or abortion if she shows no evidence of antibody production. The mechanism of action is demonstrated in Figure 33-11. RhoGAM must be administered after every abortion and every Rh-incompatible birth to prevent Rh sensitization.

ABO Incompatibility

Incompatibility of the ABO groups occurs more frequently than that caused by the Rh factor. It usually occurs when the woman is type O and the fetus is A or B. Hemolytic disease due to ABO incompatibility is usually less severe than that due to Rh incompatibility, although it can produce every gradation of disease seen with Rh incompatibility and demands similar treatment. The main difference is that prior sensitization is not required, since A and B antibodies are already present in the mother's blood and thus the firstborn can be affected.

RESPIRATORY DISTRESS SYNDROME

Respiratory distress syndrome, formerly called hyaline membrane disease, is the chief reason for high perinatal death rates. It has been responsible for 25,000 to 30,000 deaths of newborns each year in the United States. The etiology of respiratory distress syndrome is still uncertain. The incidence, however, appears to be limited primarily to the premature infant usually less than 38 weeks of gestation who is apparently grown for gestational age. The disease has been found in about 60 percent of infants less than 28 weeks of gestation but in practically no full-term infants. Hyaline membrane disease has a tendency to be familial. It was previously thought that infants of diabetic mothers were more susceptible to the disease; however, recent studies indicate that diabetes is a predisposing factor only in that prematurity may be increased. Until recently, it was believed that cesarean-section infants were more prone to develop the disease; however, it is now thought that only the reason for the cesarean section may influence its development. Racial factors do not seem to apply. Although asphyxia in the perinatal period is common, it is not a prerequisite. Hyaline membrane disease is found primarily in the immature infant, following a period of air breathing, usually in the first few hours of life.

Low surfactant levels have been demonstrated in infants with respiratory distress syndrome. Surfactant acts by reducing surface tension in the alveoli, thereby maintaining their patency at the end of the respiratory cycle. When surfactant levels are low, alveoli tend to collapse following expiration, and each breath the infant takes is nearly as strenuous as the initial one. Two surface-active phospholipids which can be identified and measured are lecithin and sphingomyelin. Concentrations of these two

How Rh disease develops...

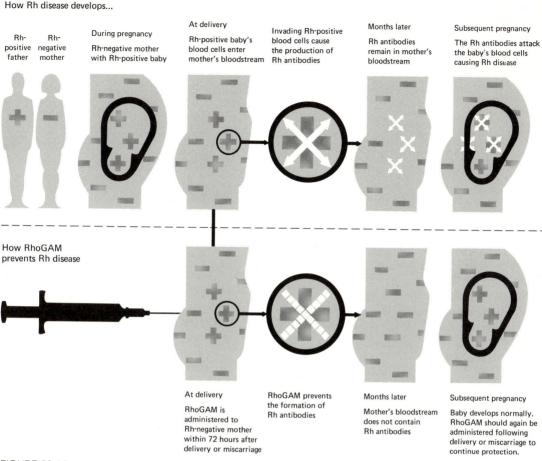

FIGURE 33-11

Mechanism of Rh disease production and the utilization of RhoGAM as a preventive measure. (*By permission from Ortho Diagnostics.*)

substances in the amniotic fluid bear an unusual relationship to each other during pregnancy and are referred to as the L/S ratio. The lecithin concentration rises sharply at about 35 weeks gestation. The L/S ratio is valuable in predicting maturity of the fetal lung. Hyaline membrane disease seldom occurs when L/S ratios are in excess of 2.0. Investigators are studying the use of steroids administered to the mother when premature labor is a threat in an attempt to accelerate fetal lung maturation.

Clinical Manifestations

Clinical manifestations of the disease usually begin shortly after birth. Initially, the infant develops increased respirations and slight subcostal retractions. As the disease progresses, the respirations become more rapid and labored. Retractions on inspiration spread to include supra- and substernal and clavicular areas. Abdominal or seesaw respirations may develop.

An expiratory grunt develops in an attempt to prolong expiration, increasing alveolar pressure and facilitating diffusion of inspired oxygen.

The laboratory findings indicate a decrease in oxygen–PO_2 levels and an increase in carbon dioxide–PCO_2 levels. The acidity of the blood is increased, and there is a decrease in buffer substances, creating a metabolic and respiratory acidosis. The degree of the acidosis will depend on the severity of the disease and the amount of medical support provided.

If the disease is not controlled at this point, the infant will develop severe retractions and greatly labored breathing. The infant will remain cyanotic even with increased amounts of oxygen. The pulse rate will begin to drop, and the infant will appear to be flaccid and exhausted. Apneic spells will become more frequent, and resuscitation with mechanical assistance will become necessary.

Several methods which augment or substitute for the expiratory grunt have been employed in an attempt to stabilize the alveoli and prevent their collapse. Continuous positive airway pressure (CPAP) maintains pressures above zero at the end of expiration. This provides ventilatory assistance without the use of a mechanical respirator. A variety of means have been used to provide continuous positive airway pressure, including an endotracheal tube, a tightly fitting face mask, and, more recently, a device which is attached nasally.

If it becomes necessary to insert an endotracheal tube and use a positive-pressure mechanical respirator, the same end can be achieved by setting the respirator controls so that the pressure is above zero at the end of the respiratory cycle, usually around +4. This technique is called positive-end expiratory pressure (PEEP).

The attempt to prevent alveolar collapse when a negative-pressure respirator is used is referred to as continuous negative pressure (CNP). These are all complex procedures which require the presence of a highly skilled team.

Nursing Intervention

The prognosis for the infant with respiratory distress is greatly dependent upon the quality and quantity of nursing care provided. The infant who is in acute crises requires the full attention of one nurse who possesses the knowledge and skill to identify, diagnose, and intervene, and evaluate action taken on a minute-to-minute basis.

Minimal stress on the infant is maintained through providing a thermoneutral environment, administering humidified oxygen in amount and method prescribed, and meeting fluid and caloric requirements parenterally.

Assessment of action taken is accomplished through careful monitoring of blood gases, monitoring urine for glucose and specific gravity, and maintaining constant control of body temperature.

Complications

The infant with respiratory distress syndrome is a candidate for several complications. The development of these complications is greatly dependent upon the maturity of the infant and severity of the disorder. In addition to the apnea that has been previously mentioned, pneumothorax, pneumomediastinum, cardiac failure, sepsis, intravascular coagulation, intercranial hemorrhage, and hyperbilirubinemia may appear. These will need appropriate treatment if they occur.

The nurse caring for these infants will become very much involved and should be cautioned that there is an equally great need for communicating with and supporting the family. Because of the closeness of the nurse to the infant, giving the parents information and support becomes vital. If the parents cannot visit the nursery, the nurse should plan to spend some time each day with them. Whenever the parents are willing and able to enter the nursery, they should be encouraged to come in for a close look at their child and to touch the infant, even through the incubator.

When the infant begins to recover, the nurse should gradually transfer as much of the caretaking as possible to the mother. This may mean teaching the mother how to hold her baby while an intravenous infusion is in place or how to instill a gavage feeding. Mothers can be taught to do these things if there is someone who is willing to share the information.

THE PREMATURE INFANT

Premature infants have the same needs for adjustment to their environments as full-term infants. The difference is that the premature infant is more dependent on assistance from the health team, as the infant has been early deprived of the warmth and security of the mother's womb. The closer the premature infant's gestational age is to term, the more the infant will resemble the full-term infant in appearance and behavior. The degree of immaturity is relative to gestational age. The younger, more immature infant has more difficulty adjusting to the external environment. (See Figure 33-12.)

An infant born prior to 37 weeks gestation is considered to be premature. Traditionally, emphasis has been placed on weight, and a premature was described as an infant weighing 2,500 g or less at birth. Weight as a sole criterion is believed to be inadequate, since it fails to take into account the following: (1) infants who are premature by weight but have a gestational age of 37 weeks or greater (true of one-half of infants premature by weight), (2) the infant whose low birth weight is due to genetic or racial factors and who exhibits no other sign of immaturity, and (3) those infants whose birth weight is greater than 2,500 g but who have a gestational age less than 37 weeks. The mortality rate of the third group of infants is 3 to 4 times greater than the term infant of equal weight.

Because of these factors, the premature or immature infant should be identified by evaluation of weight and gestational age. When the nurse evaluates the gestational age of an infant, the history of the mother's last menstrual period is of great importance; however, this information is not always known or accurate. Therefore, there are other guidelines for determining the maturity of the infant. Tables 25-2 and 33-3 list some of the differing appearances of newborns with various gestational ages, and Table 33-4 depicts weight-gestation classification.

Incidence

In 1961 the expert committee on maternal-child health of the World Health Organization recommended that the term "premature" be replaced by the more appropriate term "low birth weight" and that the term premature be used only for infants born less than 37 weeks after the beginning of the mother's last menstrual period. Since the majority of statistical data available in the last 30 years included both premature and low-birth-weight infants, some concepts related to the premature infant may need alteration when new data, specific for the premature, have been acquired. Since the statistical emphasis on gestational age, as well as birth weight, is relatively recent, the real incidence of prematurity has not been adequately determined. In the United States, the incidence of live infants born weighing

TABLE 33-3
Estimation of Gestational Age by Various Parameters

Feature	28	29	30	31	32	33	34	35	36	37–40
Clinical										
Chest	Narrow in anteroposterior diameter —————————————————————————→									More cylindrical
Skin	Tense, shiny, watery in appearance, more "fitted" ——————————→									Less "edematous" in appearance
Hair	Lanugo present over body; scalp hair fine, "matted," feathery ——→									Coarser, separated strands
Nipple masses	Under 2 mm in diameter ———————————→								4 + mm ——→	7 + mm
Ear cartilages	Soft, pliable, underdeveloped cartilages ———————————————→								Creases in anterior 2/3 ——→	Many creases over sole
Genitalia	Male—scrotum poorly developed, testes undescended or in canals ——→									Male—scrotum pendulous, rugated testes in scrotum
	Female—large clitoris, gaping labia majora ——————————————→									Female—labia majora developed
Neurologic										
Activity	More generalized and athetoid; global, quiet sleep, cry feeble ——→						More localized movements, brief in duration; active sleep— eye movement, grimaces, etc; cry strong			
Muscle tone	Hypotonic, all limbs flaccid and touching mattress ——————————→							All extremities flexed ——→		

Weeks of gestation

Posture	Beginning of thigh flexion at hip	Froglike position	
Heel-to-ear maneuver	Heel-to-ear, no resistance	Beginning of resistance	
Scarf sign	No resistance, elbow passes midline of trunk		More resistance, elbow may not cross midline of trunk
Owl sign	Head turned over shoulder, no resistance, chin over shoulders		Chin reaches to shoulder resistance
Reflexes			
Moro	Complete but exhaustible	Complete	
Grasp	Feeble	Solid	
Suck	Present but weak	Stronger and synchronous with swallowing	
Pupillary response	Absent	Present	
Automatic walk	Absent	Present	
Radiologic			
Distal femoral epiphysis		Calcification	Calcification
Proximal tibial			Calcification
Hematologic			
Nucleated RBCs/100 WBCs		Greater than 10/100 WBCs	Less than 10/100 WBCs
Hemoglobin F concentration		90–95%	50–85%
Amniotic fluid studies			
Creatinine	Less than 2 mg/100 ml	2 mg/100 ml	
Sebaceous cells	Less than 1%	1–10%	10–50%

SOURCE: Sophie H. Pierog and Angelo Ferrara. *Approach to the Medical Care of the Sick Newborn,* Mosby, St. Louis, 1971.

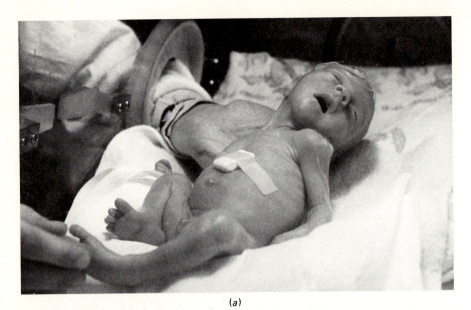

(a)

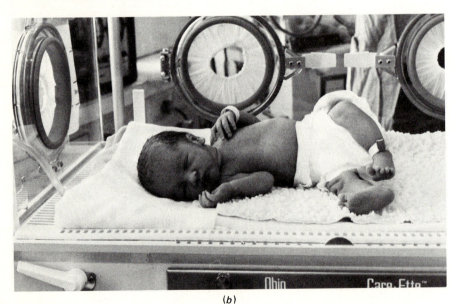

(b)

FIGURE 33-12

(a) A premature infant who is young and in a risk situation. Note the lack of subcutaneous fat and lack of muscle tone. The infant's abdomen is distended following
her tube feeding. The device taped to her abdomen is a sensor for an apnea monitor.
(By permission from New England Medical Center—Boston Floating Division. Photo-
graphed by Boston University School of Nursing, Media Services Department.)
(b) A premature infant who is more mature. Note subcutaneous fat, flexion of
extremities. The sheepskin under the baby is used to protect the pressure areas from
breakdown. (By permission from St. Luke's Hospital, New Bedford, Mass.)

TABLE 33-4
Weight-Gestation Classification (Modified after Yerushalmy)

	Gestation, weeks	Weight, g	Percent of total deliveries	Mortality rate, %	Group characteristics	Special problems
Group I Immature Premature	all*	< 1,501	1.0 ± 0.2	60–75	Thin, fragile, red skin Eyes closed Edematous	Temperature control Enzymatic deficiencies (hyper-bilirubinemia, hyaline membrane disease)
Group II Premature Preterm	< 37	1,501–2,500	2.0 ± 0.3	10–15	Relatively hypotonic Weight loss 10–20%	Susceptibility to infection Apnea and cyanosis, capillary hemorrhage Retrolental fibroplasia
Group III "Small-for-dates" Undergrown Fetal malnutrition Dysmature	> 36	1,501–2,500	3.0 ± 0.5	3–5	Often malnourished with dry and peeling skin Anxious, open-eyed Increased tone and activity Minimal weight loss	Increase in congenital anomalies, intrauterine infection Perineal asphyxia Pulmonary hemorrhage Hypoglycemia
Group IV "Large-for-dates"	< 37	> 2,500	3.0 ± 1.0	2–4	Often inactive Characteristics of groups I and II	Problems of groups I and II
Group V "Normal"	> 36	> 2,500	90.0 ± 3.0	0.5	Normal Occasionally undernourished and dysmature	Generally healthy

* Less than 1% more than 36 weeks.

SOURCE: S. Gorham Babson and Ralph C. Benson, *Management of High-Risk Pregnancy and Intensive Care of the Neonate*, 2d ed., Mosby, 1971; modified after J. Yerushalmy, "The Classification of Newborn Infants by Birth Weight and Gestational Age," *Journal of Pediatrics*, 71:164, 1967.

2,500 g or less is 7.2 percent for white infants and approximately 14 percent for non-whites.[4]

Related Factors

Using the definitions of premature and low birth weight for gestational age, it is difficult to separate the causal factors associated with each. Thus far, certain factors have been identified as being associated with premature or low weight for gestational age infants. Nelson and Babson and Benson have attributed some of the maternal factors to include obstetric problems such as toxemia, premature separation of the placenta, placental insufficiency, intercurrent maternal disease, and incidental surgery. Also having some relationship to premature and low birth weight, although not necessarily causal, are the age and parity of the mother (primipara under sixteen or over forty years old), marital status, height, fatigue level, cigarette smoking history, history of previous difficult pregnancy, fertility difficulties, race, socio-economic level, and poor nutritional status. Although largely theoretical, the paternal role is being investigated. The factors thus far implicated include older age of father, chronic alcoholism, diabetes mellitus, and the presence of Rh-positive genes when the mother is Rh-negative. Fetal factors associated with prematurity include multiple births, hydramnios, and abnormalities of the cord. The incidence of prematurity drops to a relative low of 5 to 6 percent in areas where there is a higher socioeconomic status.[5] There are a number of reasons attributed to this discrepancy, although it is unclear which predominate. These include maternal education, nutrition, housing conditions, hygiene, interest in pregnancy, and antepartum care.

Prognosis

The mortality and morbidity rates of premature infants and low-birth-weight infants are considerably higher than those of the full-term infant. Following discharge from the hospital, the mortality rate of low-birth-weight infants is 3 times that of full-term infants during the first 2 years of life.[6] Since many of these deaths are attributable to infection, they seem at least theoretically preventable. Premature infants, barring any other physical difficulties, generally lag behind in growth and development, as compared to the full-term infant for the first 2 years of life. The larger the premature at birth, the more closely the infant will resemble the full-term infant in achievement of developmental tasks. The smaller the infant at birth, the greater the incidence of mental retardation, cerebral palsy, and neurological defects. This fact could be attributed to the higher incidence of cerebral anoxia and hemorrhage in the premature infant.

Nursing Care

The nursery admission of a premature infant is often an emergency situation, as with any infant at risk. An initial evaluation is done to rapidly ascertain the need for immediate lifesaving measures. Because of the immaturity of the premature's central nervous system and lack of subcutaneous fat, the infant needs support of body temperature. Depending on color and respirations, oxygen may need to be administered. Parenteral therapy may be started immediately on infants who appear to be in respiratory difficulty or whose electrolytes are unbalanced. In most instances, these infants will have blood drawn to determine the status of electrolytes and blood gases. If sepsis is of concern, parenteral fluids may be started to facilitate antibiotic therapy. The maintenance of body temperature is imperative and must not be overlooked during the emergency admission procedure; therefore, the use of an infant warmer is of great benefit.

Once the emergency treatments have been completed, the infant is placed in the incubator or warmer. Nursing care now becomes of primary importance for the survival of the infant. Frequent recordings of the infant's vital signs are required. The temperature may be more labile in the premature than in the full-term infant. The premature's axillary temperature should be maintained at 36.5°C. Apical pulse rate will be weak, irregular, and rapid. Respirations are irregular. It is hard to establish norms for respiratory rates in the premature. According to Fitzpatrick et al., two patterns have been associated with a low mortality rate and have thus been described as "normal." In the first pattern, about 40 respirations per minute occur from birth onward without any significant fluctuations; in the second pattern, rates over 60 respirations per minute occur in the first hour with no significant increase and a subsequent decline. A significant increase would be a rise of 15 or more above that recorded for the first hour of life. The earlier the gestational age, the more prone the infant is to periods of apnea. Gentle stimulation by rubbing the chest or gently compressing the thorax is usually adequate to start respirations. It appears the infant sometimes just forgets to breathe. Because pulse and respiration rates are irregular, they must be counted for a full minute. In addition to this, the nurse must observe for expiratory grunt and retractions which are indicative of respiratory distress. With the variety of electrical equipment available to assist the nurse in monitoring the vital signs of infants, it is imperative that the nurse be familiar with the

equipment in use and cognizant of the potential electrical hazards. These may be compounded with the use of compressed gases and oxygen. The leads for these monitors are usually attached with adhesives or jellies, which can irritate the skin. It is therefore necessary, to maintain the integrity of the skin, that these leads be removed and then reapplied after the skin has been cleaned.

After the initial lifesaving measures have been instituted and the condition of the infant evaluated, the team must decide if the infant can be maintained in their nursery or if transfer to a regional neonatal referral center is necessary. This decision must be based not only on the condition of the infant, but on the availability of skilled nurses and physicians on a 24-hour basis. If transfer is determined necessary, a portable incubator with oxygen equipment attached should be used, and a registered nurse who is skilled in infant resuscitation should accompany the infant. Whenever possible, provision should be made for the mother to see her infant prior to transfer. The mother will need to be prepared by the nurse for the experience of seeing her infant in an incubator and perhaps surrounded by strange equipment. She may even be helped to hold or to touch her baby. This is a difficult period for the parents and for the nurse, since the possibility exists that this is the last time they will see the infant. The mother who has seen her infant is more ready to deal with the reality of the birth and the tasks of grieving.

There are many components to the care of the premature infant. One of the concerns is conservation of the infant's energy and support of the immature systems. Maintenance of body temperature through use of the incubator is common practice. Because of the immaturity of the infant's nervous system, sucking ability may be too weak to permit nursing a bottle, and tube feedings may be necessary. Vomiting is common because of an immature cardiac sphincter; therefore, small frequent feedings will be necessary. Prevention of aspiration and vomiting can be assisted by slightly elevating the head of the mattress. The elevated head may also assist the respirations.

Positioning

Positioning of the premature is of prime importance. The premature's muscles are very weak and underdeveloped. The immaturity of the skeletal system permits molding of bones in relation to positioning. This is readily visible in the premature's skull bones. There is little or no subcutaneous fat, allowing for pressure areas to be prevalent. The skin is thin and easily broken down. Therefore, sheepskin and bubble pads can be used to prevent breakdown of skin over bony prominences.

The position of the premature infant should be changed every 2 hours. This will enhance ventilation and expansion of the lungs and stimulate circulation. Care must be taken, however, not to position the infant so there is constriction to the thoracic or abdominal area, as this may interfere with the infant's respirations.

Care must also be taken when applying diapers to a premature infant. If the diaper is too large, the hips may be hyperextended and externally rotated. If the hips are immobilized in this position for a period of time, deformities to the hips may occur. Therefore, if small diapers are not available, regular disposable diapers can be cut in half.

Complications

The premature infant has a tendency to bleed secondary to the fragility of the capillaries and low plasma prothrombin levels. This

may be manifested as petechial or ecchymotic areas. Careful observation of the infant is required with special attention to the cord as it may be prone to secondary bleeding. Intercranial capillaries are particularly susceptible; therefore, observation should include watching for signs of increased intercranial pressure or bleeding.

Both the full-term and premature infant have a high hemoglobin concentration at birth. The cord blood hemoglobin on both a full-term and premature baby of 1,200 g is approximately 17 g per 100 ml. In a premature infant below 1,200 g the hemoglobin is approximately 15.6 g per 100 ml. In both the premature and full-term infant there is a normal decline in hemoglobin concentration due to the interaction of several factors. The first is a relative decrease in the bone marrow erythropoietic activity. There is also a relative increase in the rate of hemolysis as well as a hemodilution due to the rapid expansion of the blood volume. The above factors are more extreme in the low-birth-weight infant and result in a more severe anemia at an earlier age. In the premature, the hemoglobin may drop to a level of 6 to 7 g per 100 ml at the third to seventh week. This guideline is helpful in evaluating whether or not an existing anemia is the result of a pathological process. In addition, a number of pathological processes and/or indiscriminate drawing of blood specimens may be superimposed upon this "physiological" anemia, creating a more severe anemia.

The majority of premature infants tend to become jaundiced on the second to fourth day of life. The level of serum bilirubin tends to be related to the gestational age of the infant. The immature liver is unable to conjugate the bilirubin created by the breakdown of red blood cells.

The premature infant has an increased susceptibility to infection and is less able to handle infection than the full-term infant.

Also, the skin and mucous membranes of the premature are less protective. Treatments such as intravenous infusions may further break down this first line of defense and create new portals of entry. The premature has a lowered white blood cell count which does not respond with the expected elevation to infection. Prematures have poor antibody-forming ability, and they are lacking in immune bodies transmitted via the placenta.

Particular care must be taken to assure that proper aseptic technique is carried out at all times. This may require repeated instructions to parents and hospital staff who visit and care for the premature infant. Parents learn the necessary precautions quite readily and are usually quite eager to do what is best for their baby.

Nutritional Needs

Feeding practices for premature and low-birth-weight infants have undergone evaluation and change over the years and still vary. In general, it is believed that early feeding will contribute to a lower morbidity and mortality by preventing depletion of nutrients and maintaining biochemical homeostasis. Hypoglycemia and hyperbilirubinemia will be lessened. The premature infant in good condition with active peristalsis should be given 5 to 10 percent glucose water orally by six to twelve hours of age. Infants in poor condition, such as respiratory distress, should not receive oral feedings, but should receive parenteral fluids. According to the infant's tolerance, the water feedings will gradually be replaced by milk feedings until fluid and calorie needs are being met.

The premature infant will have to be fed more frequently than the full-term infant. Generally speaking, infants weighing less than 1,350 g will have to be fed every 2 to 3 hours. As the infant approaches 1,600 g,

the feeding schedule will approach 3 to 4 hours. The premature who is being bottle-fed initially needs to learn to coordinate sucking and swallowing. The nurse must remember the importance of conservation of energy and not allow the baby to become chilled or fatigued during feeding. Any feeding which takes longer than 20 minutes will probably be tiring to the premature. The smaller the premature infant, the less likely the infant is to demonstrate hunger; therefore, the baby may have to be awakened for feeding. The premature weighing less than 1,350 g may not have an adequate suck, swallow, or gag reflex and therefore may require tube feeding with a nasogastric tube or, in the case of an infant in severe respiratory distress, a gastrostomy tube. However, the insertion of a gastrostomy tube requires a surgical procedure and usually is not the first choice. An example of a feeding guide is demonstrated in Table 33-5.

DEVELOPMENTAL NEEDS OF HIGH-RISK INFANTS

It is difficult to distinguish specific emotional needs of the premature infant because similar needs have been demonstrated by other infants who have required prolonged care in incubators and separation from family. In general, the primary concern is the absence of opportunity for the infant to meet developmental tasks at the same time or in the same manner as does the "normal" infant.

First, let us consider a few of the basic tasks that all infants must complete. If one considers Erikson's first stage of man, trust versus mistrust, or Freud's pleasure produces learning, and applies this to the premature or high-risk infant, one can immediately see inherent danger. The premature can have little trust when the infant has literally been pushed into supporting his or

TABLE 33-5
Feeding Guide for Premature Infants under 2,000 g

		Volume ranges daily			
		ml/kg		ml/lb	
Formula	Age, days	Immature*	Undergrown*	Immature	Undergrown
10% glucose	0	20	30	9	14
Half 10% glucose	1	30	45	14	20
and half full-strength	2	40	60	18	26
	3	50	75	22	32
	4	60	90	26	40
	5	70	105	30	48
Full-strength formula	6	80	120	35	55
(24 cal/30 ml)	7	90	135	40	60
	8	100	150	45	70
	9				
	10	110	160	50	75
	12	120	160	55	75
	15	130	160	60	75
	20	140	160	65	75

* *Immature* refers to the very small, weak, and hypotonic premature infant. *Undergrown* infants are those who are small for their gestational age and who have a greater need for calories.

1   The volume ranges allow a choice of feeding amounts. Most premature infants are more safely fed in the lower ranges. *Supplemental parenteral fluids will be necessary if dehydration, lethargy, or excessive weight loss occurs.*
2   Multiply infant's weight (kilograms or pounds) by volume to be given for that day and divide by 12 (number of feedings) for amount to be fed at 2-hour intervals.
3   Infants on reaching 1.5 kg (3 lb 5 oz) should be placed gradually on a 3-hour feeding schedule (total volume given, divided by eight feedings).
4   Infants on the bottle and on reaching 1.8 to 2 kg (4 to 4½ lb) may be fed on a modified demand basis and at increased feeding intervals. Volume taken may range *above* 200 ml per kg (90 ml per lb).

Exceptions:
1   Infants in poor condition *for any reason* require a delay in oral feedings and the institution of parenteral fluids *from the first few hours of life.*
2   Any baby with distention, cyanotic or apneic attacks, or vomiting should have feedings stopped and condition evaluated.
3   A stomach residual (at the time of the next gavage feeding) of over 1 ml indicates a delay in emptying time. Feedings should be reduced and the event reported to physician for evaluation.
4   Malnourished infants require glucose and water soon after birth to support brain metabolism, due to deficient glycogen stores in liver.

SOURCE: S. Gorham Babson and Ralph C. Benson, *Primer on Prematurity and High-Risk Pregnancy*, Mosby, St. Louis, 1966, p. 107.

her own life far in advance of the full-term infant. The premature or any high-risk infant will have little development of pleasure if the infant is being stuck and poked, and is frequently in pain or discomfort. The infant can hardly learn trust or pleasure if the infant's primary contact with other people usually creates additional discomforts because of necessary treatments and procedures. In addition, high-risk and definitely premature infants are frequently denied satisfaction of basic needs. The infant who is denied oral intake cannot suck unless a pacifier has been provided.[7] The vision of an infant in an incubator is blurred and distorted when the infant looks through the plastic sides; should the infant require phototherapy, the infant is completely without vision. Also, the infant in an incubator has distorted hearing. Within the incubator, there is the constant noise of the motor, and it is possible that other noise may enter the incubator when people bang the incubator or talk in the near vicinity. It is also possible that such sound that enters the incubator may reverberate on all six surface areas, creating unpleasant sounds and perhaps painful stimuli. In an attempt to provide a less distorted environment, some health care teams are maintaining high-risk infants in warming units or bassinets where feasible.

Nursing Approach

It becomes apparent that nursing care must be geared to assist the infant in meeting primary developmental tasks as well as physiological needs.

The first nursing approach might well be the assignment of one nurse to be the infant's caretaker for the entire stay in the nursery. This would provide the infant the opportunity to become familiar with the nurse's touch, smell, and sound of voice. Is this not what "normal" infants experience with their mothers? The nurse would also become more cognizant of the infant's communication patterns and means of satisfying the infant's needs. Whenever care is to be provided, the nurse should talk to and fondle the infant, even if this must be done through portholes. Holding the baby's arm or stroking the head will provide contact with another person and will not endanger the infant in any way. As soon as possible, the infant should be held and cuddled.

Visual stimulation should also be pro-

vided. According to studies and observations of Dr. T. Berry Brazelton, infants respond more readily to animate, spherical visual stimuli than to inanimate objects,[8] and while small brightly colored mobiles suspended in an incubator may provide some visual stimuli, they are a weak substitute for a human face.

Auditory stimulation is also more effectively accomplished through the human voice than through other means that might be instituted. Research has shown that the newborn infant responds more readily to the high-pitched voice of a female than to that of the male.[9]

FAMILY ADJUSTMENT TO THE HIGH-RISK INFANT

It should be obvious to the reader that the nurse caring for a high-risk infant must be acutely observant as well as informed. An infant in a risk situation poses a special threat to the parents. Their greatest fear—death of their child—is close to being realized. Parents seek to protect themselves from the pain of this threat by withdrawing from their association with the baby. They begin to grieve in anticipation of the baby's death. Although this anticipatory grief begins as a protective mechanism, if the parents do not receive assistance in dealing with their feelings, it is possible that they will grieve the baby out of their lives. This has tremendous implications for childrearing practices should the baby survive. If the parents have emotionally separated from this child, they will find it difficult to establish effective parenting patterns. They may tend to continue to consider this child vulnerable to serious illness or accident and even destined to die during childhood. To them, the child is only on tenuous loan and not really theirs.

The children involved in this process have been known to demonstrate a variety of problems. They may have difficulty with separation. These parents will rarely use babysitters but may leave the child with grandparents on occasion. Sleep problems may be manifest, and when the time comes these children may develop a school phobia. These parents may become overprotective and overindulgent, but since they tend not to set limits, the child may be overly dependent, disobedient, and uncooperative. Although the mother cannot seem to control this behavior, she may be quite restrictive of the child's activity, keeping the child in the playpen excessively or forbidding such activities as tricycling. The mother, and later her child, may become overly concerned with body function, leading to hypochondriasis.

This is just an overview of some of the disordered childrearing practices that may result from a grief reaction which did not cease when the threat to the infant's life was over. Kaplan and Mason have identified four tasks which must be completed by the mother of a premature infant in order to prevent the parenting problems described. The first task, that of *anticipatory grief*, involves a withdrawal from the relationship already established with the child so that she still hopes the baby will survive but simultaneously prepares for death. Second, she must *face and acknowledge her maternal failure to deliver a normal full-term baby*. The grief and depression are signs that she is struggling with these tasks. These are healthy responses and usually last until the baby's chances for survival seem secure. The remaining tasks need to be performed while baby is recovering. The third task involves *resumption of the previously interrupted process of relating to the baby*. In the case of the premature infant, the mother has not had the same length of time to prepare for the mothering role which is afforded the mother of the full-term infant.

The mother has been preparing herself for a loss, but as the baby begins to improve, she must respond with hope and anticipation of recovery. There is usually a point at which the mother really believes her baby will survive. This turning point may be related to a change in baby's weight, change in feeding pattern or activity, or even a change in the nurse's manner.

In the fourth task, the mother must *understand how this baby differs in relation to special needs and growth patterns*. It is also important that she sees these special needs as being temporary and that they will yield in time to more normal patterns.

It is believed that each of these tasks must be accomplished in the order in which they are listed. A successful outcome is considered to be one in which the mother regards the baby as potentially normal, gives the baby realistic care, and takes pride and satisfaction in that care.[10]

Although these tasks have been specifically identified for the mother of the premature infant, we feel that there is some applicability to both parents and that the situation could relate to any infant in a vulnerable condition. It is the nurse's role to help parents accomplish these tasks.

Often, in the case of the high-risk infant, the mother is discharged from the hospital some time before the baby is ready to go. What is the effect upon siblings when mother returns home without the promised baby? Our response to this question is based largely upon experiences. In those instances in which parents have not been able to cope successfully with the threat to their child's life, their overattentiveness to this baby may limit the time and energies available for other children. This can then set the stage for jealousy and rivalry. On the other hand, parents who are able to accomplish Kaplan and Mason's four tasks seem to be able to use the time alone with their children to prepare them for baby's homecoming.

TRENDS IN INTENSIVE CARE NURSERIES

Nurseries across the country have demonstrated that care can be truly family-centered without sacrificing the safety of the infants. Families are encouraged to have contact with the infant and parents are encouraged to become involved in the infant's care. In place of rigid visiting hours, many intensive care nurseries encourage flexibility, and visits by parents may be at any time mutually agreed upon by themselves and the nurse. In addition, phone calls are accepted day or night. Parents are told that a call to the nursery may help in coping with a sleepless night. Some intensive care centers provide a sleeping room for families or make contractual arrangements with nearby hotels or motels.

A unique, close relationship often develops between families and the members of the health team caring for their babies. In these situations, one is truly able to sense the warmth and hope surrounding an otherwise stressful setting.

FAMILY ADJUSTMENT TO LOSS OF THE INFANT

Despite all of the efforts of the health team, some infants at risk do not survive. There is no easy way to tell parents that their child has died; a direct approach seems to be best. Families of high-risk infants usually have experienced some anticipatory grief; however, once their greatest fear has become reality, they find themselves in an acute crisis situation. At this time, families need specific directions regarding their immediate tasks of funeral and burial procedures. Parents should be encouraged to participate in these plans, since participation enforces reality of loss and allows the parents to work through the grieving process. Siblings can be helped

to deal with their loss by being allowed to participate in funeral activities.

In the immediate weeks following loss, parents will need continued support from the health team to foster interactive grieving by the family instead of isolated grieving by each member. Parents need to know that children are handling grief in a healthy manner when they engage in acting out events surrounding the death and in open discussion of same. Anger, acting out, regression, and disturbed sleep patterns are all normal behaviors for the child who has experienced a crisis.

One sign of the parents' acceptance of the loss is their dismantling of the nursery. Friends and relatives who wish to be helpful should support them in this task rather than relieve them of it.

Fathers seem to find it particularly difficult to talk about their sad feelings with their mates. A sign that the father is not dealing with his grief in a healthy manner is when he does not seem to have time to share his feelings about the loss of his child. He takes on additional responsibilities, such as an extra job, to keep himself very busy.

Pregnancy should not be contemplated until resolution of this grief work is complete so that the next child will be accepted as a separate individual and will not be seen as a replacement or duplicate of the dead child. At such times the focus of the health team, which had been providing support to the family as well as directly caring for the infant, is to assist with the grieving process. One neonatal center recognizes its unique relationship with the family and believes that a particular family should not be "discharged" until all of its members can be pronounced healthy. Guidance is provided for the family by regular contact which starts immediately after the infant's death. The next contact occurs in 3 days and then again after 4 to 6 months. Further guidance is provided if needed during the interim. Hope-fully, more people involved in the care of high-risk infants will recognize that their re-sponsibility to the family does not end with the death of the infant.

REFERENCES

1 Nelson, Waldo E., Victor C. Vaughn, and R. James McKay: *Textbook of Pediatrics,* 9th ed., Saunders, Philadelphia, 1969, p. 360.

2 Klaus, Marshall H., and John Kennell: "Mothers Separated from Their Newborn In-fants," *Pediatric Clinics of North America,* 17:1015–1035, November 1970.

3 Erikson, Erik H: *Childhood and Society,* 2d ed., Norton, New York, 1963, p. 72.

4 Nelson: op. cit., p. 365.

5 Nelson: op. cit., p. 366.

6 Nelson: op. cit., p. 370.

7 Erikson: op. cit., pp. 251–254.

8 Brazelton, T. Berry: *Neonatal Behavioral Assessment Scale,* Lippincott, Philadelphia, 1973, p. 21.

9 Ibid., p. 23.

10 Kaplan, David M., and Edward Mason: "Maternal Reactions to Premature Birth Viewed as an Acute Emotional Disorder," *American Journal of Orthopsychiatry,* 30: 118–128, July 1960.

BIBLIOGRAPHY

Abramson, Harold (ed.): *Resuscitation of the Newborn Infant,* Mosby, St. Louis, 1973.

Babson, S. Gorham, and Ralph C. Benson: *Man-agement of High Risk Pregnancy and Inten-sive Care of the Neonate,* Mosby, St. Louis, 1971.

Barnett, C. R., Herbert P. Leiderman, Rose Grob-stein, and Marshall Klaus: "Neonatal Separa-tion: The Maternal Side of Interactional De-privation," *Pediatrics,* 45:197, February 1970.

Behrman, Richard E.: *Neonatology-Diseases of the Fetus and Infant,* Mosby, St. Louis, 1973.

Brann, Alfred W., Jr., and Jose M. Montalvo: "Bar-biturates and Asphyxia," *Pediatric Clinics of North America,* 17:851, November 1970.

Chernick, V.: "Continuous Negative Chest Wall Pressure Therapy for Hyaline Membrane Dis-ease," *Pediatric Clinics of North America,* 2:407, 1973.

Cohen, Sanford N., and William A. Olson: "Drugs That Depress the Newborn Infant," *Pediatric Clinics of North America,* 17:835, November 1970.

Finnegan, Loretta P., and Bonnie A. MacNeu: "Care of the Addicted Infant," *Ameri-can Journal of Nursing,* 74:685–963, April 1974.

Fitzpatrick, Elise, Sharon Reeder, and Luigi Mas-troianni: *Maternity Nursing,* 12th ed., Lippin-cott, Philadelphia, 1971.

Fogerty, Sarah: "The Nurse and the High Risk In-fant," *The Nursing Clinics of North America,* 8:533, 1973.

Gluck, Louis, and Maria Kulovich: "Fetal Lung Development: Current Concepts," *Pediatric Clinics of North America,* 20:367, 1973.

——— et al.: "Perinatal Prediction of Respiratory Distress Syndrome," *Program and Abstracts,* American Academy of Pediatrics Society, Inc., 81st Annual Meeting, Atlantic City, May 1971.

Green, Morris, and Albert J. Solnit: "Reactions to the Threatened Loss of a Child: A Vulnerable Child Syndrome," *Pediatrics,* 34:58, 1964.

Greenbaum, Edward I., et al.: "Rectal Thermom-eter Induced Pneumoperitoneum in the New-born," *Pediatrics,* October 1969, pp. 539–542.

Hall, Calvin, and Gardner Lindzey (eds.): *Theories of Personality,* Wiley, New York, 1957.

Hathaway, William: "Coagulation Problems in the Newborn," *Pediatric Clinics of North America,* 17:929, November 1970.

Hill, Reba M., and Murdina Desmond: "Manage-ment of the Narcotic Withdrawal Syndrome in the Neonate," *Pediatric Clinics of North America,* 10:67–85, 1963.

Hosack, Alice Marie: "A Comparison of Crises: Mothers' Early Experiences with Normal and

Abnormal First Born Infants," unpublished doctoral thesis, Harvard University, 1968.

Kahn, Erick, Lois Neuman, and Gene-Ann Polk: "The Course of the Heroin Withdrawal Syndrome in Newborn Infants Treated with Phenobarbital or Chlorpromazine," *Journal of Pediatrics,* 75:495–500, September 1969.

Kennedy, Janet: "The High Risk Maternal Infant Acquaintance Process," *The Nursing Clinics of North America,* 8:549, 1973.

Kitterman, Joseph A., Roderic H. Phibbs, and William H. Tooley: "Catheterization of Umbilical Vessels in Newborn Infants," *Pediatric Clinics of North America,* 17:4, November 1970.

Korones, Shilaton B.: *High Risk Newborn Infants,* Mosby, St. Louis, 1972.

Kumpe, Mary, and Leonard Kleinman: "Care of the Infant with Respiratory Distress Syndrome," *The Nursing Clinics of North America,* 6:25–37, March 1971.

Lindemann, Erich: "Symptomatology and Management of Acute Grief," *American Journal of Psychiatry,* 101:141–148, 1944.

Lubchenco, Lula O.: "Assessment of Gestational Age and Development at Birth," *Pediatric Clinics of North America,* 17:125, February 1970.

Lutz, Linda, and Paul H. Perlstein: "Temperature Control in Newborn Babies," *The Nursing Clinics of North America,* 6:15–23, March 1971.

Marlow, Dorothy: *Textbook of Pediatric Nursing,* Saunders, Philadelphia, 1969.

Nelson, Nicholas M.: "On the Etiology of Hyaline Membrane Disease," *Pediatric Clinics of North America,* 17:943, November 1970.

O'Brien, Richard, and Howard Pearson: "Physiologic Anemia of the Newborn Infant," *Journal of Pediatrics,* 79:132–138, July 1971.

Ortho Diagnostics: *Blood Group Antigens and Antibodies as Applied to Hemolytic Disease of the Newborn,* Ortho Diagnostics, Raritan, N.J., 1968.

Owens, Charlotte: "Parents' Reactions to Defective Babies," in Nancy A. Lytle (ed.), *Maternal Health Nursing,* Brown, Dubuque, Iowa, 1967.

Parad, Howard J. (ed.): *Crisis Intervention: Selected Readings,* Family Service Association of America, New York, 1965.

Perlmutter, J. F.: "Drug Addiction in Pregnant Women," *American Journal of Obstetrics and Gynecology,* 99:569, 1969.

Pierog, Sophie, and Angelo Ferrara: *Approach to the Medical Care of the Sick Newborn,* Mosby, St. Louis, 1971.

Segal, Sydney: "Oxygen: Too Much, Too Little," *The Nursing Clinics of North America,* 6:39–53, March 1971.

Sinclair, John C., John M. Driscoll, William C. Heird, and Robert W. Winters: "Supportive Management of the Sick Neonate: Parenteral Calories, Water, and Electrolytes," *Pediatric Clinics of North America,* 17:4, November 1970.

Torma, M. J., et al.: "Necrotizing Enterocolitis in Infants," *American Journal of Surgery,* 126:761, 1973.

Virney, Norman, and John Reynolds: "Epidemiological Aspects of Neonatal Necrotizing Enterocolitis," *American Journal of Diseases of Children,* 128:186, 1974.

34

Intrauterine Growth Deviations

KATHARINE A. McCARTY AND
GLADYS MARY SCIPIEN

REACTIONS TO THE BIRTH OF A DEFECTIVE INFANT

In a society in which physical and intellectual attainment is an ideal, the birth of a defective infant is a tragic event for the individual, the family, and society. A pregnant woman and her mate plan for the arrival of their infant both physically and psychologically. Physically the woman is concerned about the changes within her own body. Her doctor's visits are generally centered around her blood pressure, her weight, her urine, and the fetal heartbeat. She may or may not begin to purchase articles for her infant early in pregnancy. Psychologically many changes are also occurring. She is concerned about her changing body image and whether she will regain her normal figure. Will changes need to be made in her family living situation? Will there be alterations in relationships between her and her partner and among the other children?

The fear of having a defective infant is a periodic concern of many pregnant women. She may express her concern and question openly when she states, "My niece is having corrective surgery for a harelip. What are the chances of this happening to my baby?" Or her fears may not be overtly expressed. Frequently clues to her fears are expressed in the form of, "I don't care what I have as long as the baby is healthy and normal." At the time of delivery one of the first questions a mother asks is, "Is my baby normal?" Regardless of what the doctor or nurse says to her, she will want to examine her infant and see for herself that her infant is normal.

The birth of a defective infant is a crisis for the mother and the family. A crisis manifests itself when the normal course of living is upset. In a state of crisis, the usual patterns of solving problems are not adequate, and nursing intervention can be meaningful. Each mother reacts differently to a defective infant. This reaction may be demonstrated by her refusal to talk about the infant, her silences, her outbursts of tears, or casualness about the infant. Her reaction will be influenced by her own past experiences with her parents and siblings as well as by other significant events in her life.[1]

Nurses' reactions to the birth of a defective infant will *also* be influenced by the degree and extent of the abnormality as well as their own past experiences with their family and community. A female nurse will often have thoughts and concerns about what kind of a mother she will be and whether she will rear her child differently from her own experiences. Through mass media, nurses are constantly reminded of the rights and place of the physically and mentally handicapped in society.

Predictions of genetic engineering and the ethical questions that arise are subjects of many newspaper and magazine articles. Nurses, too, think about their own reproductive ability and the possibility of bearing a defective infant. Facing the crisis of the birth of a defective infant is upsetting. Negative feelings of disgust and physical withdrawal from the infant are normal reactions. Many questions arise: Did the mother or father do or take something that predetermined the defect? Is an extensive, costly rehabilitation period worthwhile? In the case of some defects, the repulsion of seeing the infant is so overwhelming to the entire personnel involved in the care of the baby that the baby is left isolated from all but minimal care. A cognitive approach to the understanding of intrauterine defects is an essential basis for a nursing care plan. An understanding of the feelings that arise within nurses, the family, and ward personnel is essential before nursing intervention can be considered. Feelings about defective infants are a part of everyone and need to be expressed and discussed. The feelings of the nurse need to be overtly expressed to health care colleagues in order for the parents and family to receive the help which they need.

Interdisciplinary Team Approach

An interdisciplinary team approach to the care of the infant and the infant's family is primary. Frequently intensive, supportive medical and/or surgical care may be needed over a period of years. The availability of nutritional, physical therapy, social, and nursing care services must be provided for infant and family in the hospital and the community. Each member of the team can contribute toward total care when there is mutual respect among the team members. The family in its initial shock and grief may reach out to or withdraw from the individual team members. Sensitivity to what is happening to the mother and family is of prime importance in assessing the needs of the family at this time.

Individual team members also can derive support from each other in order to help the family.

The Nurse as a Member of the Interdisciplinary Team

The nurse is often in an enviable position in relation to patient care and may be the only member of the team who gives direct nursing care to infant, mother, and father. Observation, formulation, implementation, and evaluation of a nursing care plan for the mother and infant are essential. Elements of the nursing care plan for the infant can be demonstrated and discussed with the mother. Initially, the mother may be timid about the care of her infant. Her concerns about the physical appearance and care of her baby may intensify her feelings about producing a defective infant. She will need patience and understanding from the nurse and repeated demonstrations of care. As a team member, the nurse will have knowledge of the condition of the infant and the mother may need help in cognitively grasping what is wrong with her infant. An initial explanation about the infant's condition may not have been heard or understood by the mother and family. Repeated explanations are often necessary. The mother must be allowed the opportunity to express her fears and concerns about the infant. Misinformation can be clarified and added information can be given. As a helping person, the nurse must be prepared for the negative responses and irrational attitudes of the mother and family. These expressions need to be placed in a rational context by understanding and clarifying the issues.

In times of crisis, people reach out to others for comfort and support. The ways in which mothers reach out at this time may differ from mother to mother. She may, in turn, accept and reject those who are helping her. Understanding what the mother is experiencing at the time will enable the nurse to provide the supportive nursing care needed. As a member of the team, the nurse's caring role will be an essential ingredient in providing humanistic care to the mother, the infant, and the family.

CAUSES OF INTRAUTERINE GROWTH DEVIATIONS WHICH AFFECT STRUCTURE OR FUNCTION

The birth of a child is never an isolated, solitary event. As the umbilical cord is cut, it is replaced by other ties that bind each infant to the infant's parents, the community, and society. This is particularly true in the case of a child born with a birth defect or anomaly.

There are about 200,000 infants born each year with significant intrauterine growth deviations which affect structure as well as function, and these defects are second only to accidents as a cause of death in childhood. It is a significant community health problem when one considers the rehabilitation, education, and the sequential surgical procedures these infants and children undergo in the process of survival. They spend approximately 6 million days in hospitals each year, at costs exceeding millions of dollars.

Indeed, our society faces a tremendous dilemma. As sophisticated diagnostic tools identify severe defects more readily, surgical interventions improve technically, and antibiotic therapy expands, the survival rate has increased. Although medical and surgical complications may occur at intervals, these infants and children can now live useful, productive lives. The demands made and the challenges presented to nurses and other members of a health team are overwhelming, but the rewards and satisfactions experienced in working with these children and their parents are most gratifying.

It is important to remember that the prognosis of these infants and children has changed drastically. For verification one need only review the mortality figures of 10 or 15 years ago. A contributing factor in reducing the death rate has been the mobilization of an interdisciplinary team approach. Another issue which has been identified is the interaction of the financial, social, and psychological problems of handicapping. They are no longer ignored or dismissed, for they affect each member of the family in some way. The interdisciplinary team can greatly enhance resolution through realistic guidance, support, and understanding. The nurse who works so closely with these infants and their families is a logical coordinator of team-related activities.

Unfortunately these particular intrauterine growth deviations occur frequently and contribute substantially to infant morbidity and mortality. Prevention, detection, and management appear to be of paramount importance. Better health care, a more effective, co-ordinated team approach, and more realistic operational long-term planning are imperative in meeting the needs of these children, their parents, and society.

For the purposes of clarity the authors define a congenital anomaly as a defect of body structure or function present at birth and noted upon the routine inspection of an infant in the delivery room or newborn nursery. In utilizing this definition particular abnormalities such as the inborn errors of metabolism, mental retardation, or those anomalies which manifest themselves later in life have been purposefully excluded. However, in view of current practice in new-

born nurseries, it is essential that phenylketonuria be discussed.

Birth defects or congenital anomalies may be divided into two categories. A major anomaly is one serious enough to cause death or result in severe handicapping of the infant, and examples are meningomyeloceles or a severe form of cyanotic congenital heart disease such as transposition of the great vessels. On the other hand, a minor anomaly such as a club foot or syndactyly will not prove to be a serious impediment to a normal life or the realization of a full life expectancy.

Most human malformations are believed to be due to an interaction of both genetic and environmental influences—a combination of all internal factors present in the fertilized egg, and all external factors which may affect its growth in utero. About 20 percent of the causes of these abnormalities can be attributed to environmental causes (viruses, radiation, and drugs), with another 20 percent resulting from hereditary factors (phenylketonuria, cystic fibrosis, or sickle-cell anemia). The remaining 60 percent are probably due to an interaction of heredity and environment.[2]

Developmentally the fetus is most susceptible to teratogenesis at three crucial stages. The first is during oogenesis. The second is during the period of late blastula and early gastrula formation when the initial differentiation of presumptive organ regions is made and the three germ layers (endodermal, mesodermal, and ectodermal) are established. The last critical stage is whenever a major organ or system is being developed.

There is intense intracellular metabolic activity during these phases. Any harmful agents introduced which do not destroy the entire embryo exert some effect upon the anatomic or physiological processes being developed.

Viral Infections

Rubella

The role of viruses as possible teratogenic agents first became evident in 1941 during an epidemic in Australia when Gregg reported large numbers of children born with certain abnormalities to mothers who had had rubella early in their pregnancies. According to the National Foundation/March of Dimes, the rubella epidemic which swept across the United States in 1964 caused some 50,000 abnormal pregnancies, resulting in some 20,000 live-born babies with birth defects and about 30,000 fetal deaths.

These pregnant women who had rubella during their first trimester gave birth to infants with congenital heart disease, cataracts, deafness, and developmental brain anomalies as well as mental retardation. With the isolation of the rubella virus from human fetal tissue in 1963, subsequent research has indicated the persistence of the virus in a chronic state in the newborn infant. It has continued to be isolated from urine and conjunctival smears from 18 months to 2 years after an infant's birth. Such information has grave implications for pregnant women with whom these infants may come in contact as well as for pediatric areas and personnel caring for them during hospitalization.

The effect of the rubella virus upon the embryo has been confirmed and conclusively demonstrates its lethal character. Yet to be proved or disproved is the theory proposed by some investigators that infants conceived 1 year or more after their mothers had been infected by rubella were born malformed.[3] Is there a rubella carrier state mothers assume which is hazardous to subsequent pregnancies? Some physicians advise women not to become pregnant until 18 months after exposure.

Cytomegalovirus

Another virus which is associated with chronic infection in humans is the cytomegalovirus, which crosses the placental barrier and initiates a chronic infection in the developing fetus. There is no definitive evidence to indicate the period in pregnancy when the embryo is most susceptible.

Cytomegalovirus has been known to cause hydrocephalus, microcephalus, focal cerebral dysfunctions, mental retardation, deafness, and optic atrophy in addition to visceral and skeletal malformation. Very little is known of transmission. Cytomegalic inclusion disease is more common than rubella but is probably not as devastating to the fetus.

Coxsackie Virus

A longitudinal study in Michigan has recently pointed to the hazards of Coxsackie virus infections during the first trimester of a pregnancy. Mothers who demonstrated Coxsackie virus, Type B, in serological studies delivered offspring with various cardiovascular anomalies.[4] At this time it appears that the cardiovascular system is the only one affected.

The rubella virus and cytomegalovirus have been repeatedly documented as influencing forces upon the developing embryo. The results of the Michigan study implicating the Coxsackie virus are being accepted as valid and reliable. Although other viruses such as mumps and influenza have also been linked with deformities, this has not been absolutely proved.

Knowledge regarding malformations due to viral infections is meager. There are many questions still to be answered. Why do certain viruses cross placental barriers to produce these intrauterine growth deviations?

How can a virus as innocuous as rubella be responsible for such devastating handicaps? How arc thcy able to produce chronic infections in the presence of antibodies in the fetus and newborn?

Congenital Syphilis

Syphilis continues to be a major concern for those interested in and responsible for community health. Congenital syphilis is passed from the pregnant woman to the fetus through the placenta. Transplacental infection by *Treponema pallidum* before the 16th week has not been documented; therefore, it is believed that this fetal infection occurs after the midgestational period. Although there is a greater incidence of abortions in infected pregnant women, it is also important to note that these women have 8 times the normal number of stillborns.[5] Penicillin is the most frequently used drug for treatment of syphilis. Treatment of the pregnant woman through the second trimester effects the cure of the fetus, and results in the third trimester are almost always excellent. Most states require serologic examinations of all pregnant women. An important step in eradication is to check pregnant women not only in early pregnancy but in the last trimester.

There are two clinical forms of congenital syphilis—*early*, in children under two years, and *late*, beyond the age of two. Early congenital syphilis is often characterized by cutaneous or mucous membrane lesions, often vesicular or bullous, particularly involving the palms of the hands and the soles of the feet. Hepatosplenomegaly, pseudoparalysis or painful limbs, anemia, jaundice, and rhinitis are some of the most common symptoms presented by a newborn with congenital syphilis.

It is apparent that early treatment of the pregnant woman with syphilis can eradicate the problem of congenital syphilis.

Drugs

In 1961–1962, thousands of German infants were born with gross abnormalities involving all extremities, as extensive as total absence of limbs, complete phocomelia, or any variation thereof. Subsequent investigations revealed that practically all the mothers who delivered these children had taken the sedative Thalidomide during the early part of their pregnancies. In this instance the relationship between the medication and the deformities was conclusive. As a result of this tragedy the United States Food and Drug Administration tightened regulations pertaining to drug approval. The most important lesson learned was that no pregnant woman should take any drugs without the approval of her physician.

There are investigations regarding the use of hallucinogenic substances in pregnancy and the delivery of a deformed infant; however, the published reports are conflicting in the conclusions reached. Zellweger et al. have reported chromatid breaks in peripheral white cells of LSD (lysergic acid diethylamide) users and the delivery of babies with malformed legs.[6] On the other hand, Gardner et al. have collected data which reveal no damage to chromosomes of mothers who admitted using LSD and who also delivered infants with abnormalities.[7] It appears that the collection and careful analysis of data on lysergic acid intake in relation to the condition of the infant at birth are needed before the question of whether LSD has teratogenic properties in humans can be answered. At this time, the information, the observations, the data are too scanty to be considered reliable.

Most of the studies related to the use of methamphetamines and the incidence of anomalies have been confined to animal research in which a causal relationship has been demonstrated. One group of investigators revealed a 38 percent frequency of anomalies, including defects of the heart, central nervous system, skeletal system, and face. Nora et al. in 1967 clearly stated there was no causal relationship between maternal dexamphetamine ingestion and congenital heart disease, but in continuing their study at Baylor they have reconsidered their statement and now urge a large-scale investigation of the drug and its effects. They appear to have doubt regarding the nonexistence of a relationship.[8]

It should be obvious that the investigation of teratogenic agents is extraordinarily difficult. An additional explanation for the lack of clear-cut evidence regarding the influence of a drug upon the developing embryo and fetus is that the possible teratogen may also produce an abnormality only in an individual with a hereditary predisposition. Evidence must support a causal relationship between the drug taken in pregnancy and its adverse effect upon the infant delivered.

Radiation

There is absolutely no doubt that radiation causes somatic damage to the embryo and fetus. There is an extreme susceptibility to the effects of radiation, particularly in the earliest phases of neural development, for this is the period of major organogenesis. The period from 2 to 6 weeks is probably the most damaging, but unfortunately this is also the period during which the pregnancy may be unsuspected. A classic study frequently referred to in the literature found that 11 of 11 fetuses irradiated in the first 2 months of a pregnancy showed extensive damage; 7 of 11 irradiated between 3 and 5 months demon-

strated defects; and 3 out of 13 fetuses exposed between the 6th and 9th months were abnormal at delivery. It should be apparent that exposure at later stages of gestation may cause less obvious deviations.

Among the most common kinds of growth deviations noted in infants irradiated in utero are microcephaly, anencephaly, microphthalmia, cataracts, mental retardation, midline defects of the central nervous system such as meningoceles, and other diverse skull malformations.

These grave consequences should be considered when radiation procedures arc carried out upon a pregnant woman. For example, radioisotope studies should not be done during the second half of a menstrual cycle because of the possibility of an unsuspected early pregnancy. The male partner may also experience chromosomal damage. If a physician is conscious of severe fetal damage which might have occurred, patients should be advised of their right to a therapeutic abortion.[9]

Environmental irradiation or radiocontamination also contributes to concern regarding the causes of deformities. This is a frustrating area, for there is little human control over atmospheric contamination which occurs after testing nuclear weapons or nuclear accidents. The anomalous effects of environmental radiocontamination have been most dramatically documented since the Nagasaki and Hiroshima, Japan, nuclear blasts.

IDENTIFIABLE INTRAUTERINE GROWTH DEVIATIONS IN THE NEWBORN

The Nervous System

When one considers the various internal and external forces which influence the embryo, in addition to the complexities associated with the differentiation of tissue, it is no wonder that intrauterine growth deviations occur. Midline anomalies of the central nervous system are usually identified as major birth defects. The most commonly seen are spina bifida occulta, meningocele, myelomeningocele (meningomyelocele), and myelocele.

The etiology of these developmental defects is unknown. Since the closure of the neural tube is completed in the embryo by the fourth week of gestation, these midline neurological conditions must occur at that time.

Spina Bifida

Spina bifida occulta results from the incomplete fusion of the spines and laminae which constitute the neural arch of the vertebrae, without an external protrusion of the intraspinal contents. They are most commonly found in the lower segment of the back, although they may occur anywhere along the vertebral column.

A protrusion through the spina bifida which forms a soft, saclike appearance along the spinal axis is a meningocele which contains cerebrospinal fluid and meninges within the sac. An even more severe defect is a myelomeningocele (meningomyelocele) which is also an external protrusion including fluid and meninges in addition to the spinal cord and/or nerve roots. (See Figure 34-1.)

Meningoceles and myelomeningoceles are covered by a thin, transparent membrane and a thicker, irregular epithelium or normal skin. The neurological manifestations accompanying a meningocele are generally slight, but the symptoms associated with a meningomyelocele vary, depending upon the extent of the defect as well as the site of the mass. Observing an infant with a menin-

FIGURE 34-1
Sacral meningocele. (*By permission from the University of Colorado Medical Center, Denver, Colorado.*)

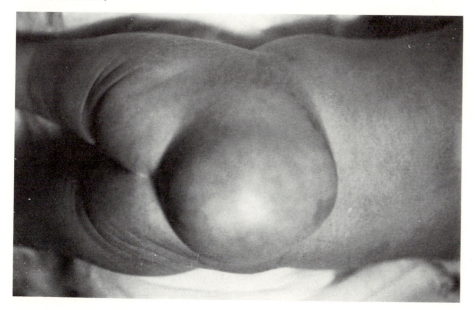

gomyelocele a nurse notices the constant dribbling of urine, the absence of sphincter control, and deformities of the feet, indicative of extensive damage.

The location of the deviation determines the extent of neuromuscular involvement, particularly of the lower extremities. There may be paralysis, flaccidity, spasticity, or no involvement whatsoever. Differentiating a meningocele from a meningomyelocele may be dependent upon the nurse's astute observation of symptoms being presented by the newborn. (See Figure 34-2.)

A myelocele, the most severe of defects associated with spina bifida occulta, is a mass of nervous tissue representative of underdeveloped embryonic tissue, which appears as a disorganized, protuberant ulceration along the back. Although it is surgically correctable, it may be incompatible with life.

NURSING RESPONSIBILITIES These neurological conditions, if amenable to surgery, are corrected in the early days of life. In the period before correction, the infant must be handled most cautiously. Rupture, infection, irritation or leakage from the sac are all possible, and as such, they are life-threatening to the newborn. Careful handling and avoiding any pressure over the mass as well as positioning become extremely important measures for nursery personnel to perform conscientiously.

Head circumference is taken and recorded daily. The anterior fontanel should be checked frequently for symptoms of increasing tension, indicative of developing hydrocephalus. Neurological evaluation of sphincter control can be realized through observation and by recording the character and number of voidings and stools. These infants' nutritional needs must also be met, but whether the baby may be held for feedings will depend upon the physician's preference and the nurse's confidence in handling ability.

Skin care is important, too, particularly around the sac and surrounding skin. The specific care associated with the deformity and the use of a dressing or a topical ointment will again depend upon the neurosurgeon's orders.

Hydrocephalus

Another neurological abnormality noted at delivery is hydrocephalus, which is characterized by an abnormal increase in cerebrospinal fluid volume within the intracranial cavity. (See Figure 34-3.) Unless otherwise stipulated, hydrocephalus refers to internal hydrocephalus in which the fluid accumulates under pressure within the ventricles.

There are two differentiations which must be made for clinical clarity. Noncommunicating, or obstructive, internal hydrocephalus is an obstruction within the ventricles which prevents the fluid from entering the subarachnoid space. Communicating internal hydrocephalus occurs when the obstruction is located in the subarachnoid cisterns at the base of the brain and/or within the subarachnoid space.

The head of an infant with this growth deviation may be normal or just slightly enlarged at birth. The suture lines are wide, and the anterior fontanel, which may be bulging, is also broader and wider than usually felt in the newborn. The bridge of the nose may also be flat and broad in addition to the forehead having a bulging appearance. As the fluid increases there may be a downward displacement of the eyes, which is frequently referred to as the "setting sun" sign. In severe form, the head size increases rapidly, the infant's cry is shrill and high-pitched, and the baby is irritable and restless. In many instances, increase in head circumference can be arrested through a successful ventricular shunt.

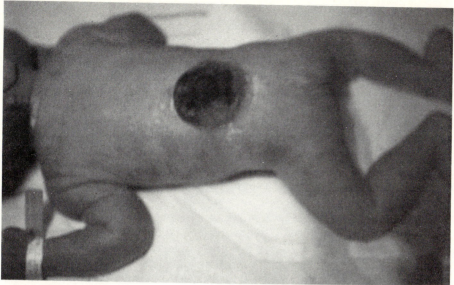

FIGURE 34-2
Lumbar myelomeningocele. (*By permission from the University of Colorado Medical Center, Denver, Colorado.*)

FIGURE 34-3
Hydrocephalus. (*By permission from the University of Colorado Medical Center, Denver, Colorado.*)

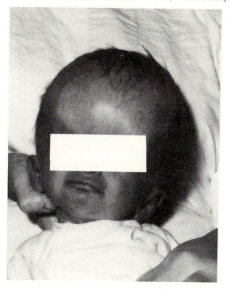

NURSING RESPONSIBILITIES As in the case of infants with other neurological problems, careful observation is imperative. Head circumference measurements and size and fullness of the anterior fontanel should be recorded, and any changes in behavior should be reported.

An adequate nutritional intake is essential, but when an infant is irritable or vomiting, feedings may become a problem. In such instances techniques should vary and be flexible in meeting the needs of the individual baby. Small, frequent feedings are sometimes much more effective than adhering to rigid nursery routines.

Positioning may be a potential problem, particularly when the head is growing rapidly, and the infant is prone to developing pressure areas. Frequent position changes, a meticulously dry and clean bassinet, and the use of lamb's wool will deter skin breakdown. It is also important that the infant be turned cautiously, for the increase in head size can place an additional strain on the baby's neck.

All of these infants have very specific needs, and in meeting them nurses occasionally become involved in the management of care. These newborns have very definite emotional needs which are sometimes overlooked, particularly if the defect is large, and the nurse is hesitant in handling the baby. Dexterity comes through experience, and the physical contact the infant may enjoy when being held in one's lap or in being cuddled is very important. Such an endeavor may support and encourage others to do likewise.

The Gastrointestinal System

Cleft Lip and Palate

Cleft lip or a cleft palate is one of the more frequently seen anomalies which involves the upper lip or palate. The fusion of maxillary or premaxillary processes normally occurs between the 5th and 8th weeks of embryonic development. The palatal processes fuse about 1 month later. Incomplete fusion results in a cleft lip, a cleft palate, or both. (See Figures 34-4 and 34-5.)

The incidence of this impaired fusion is about 1 in 800 births. As with other growth deviations, the specific cause is unknown; however, some studies indicate a strong genetic influence.

A cleft lip (harelip) is seen more frequently in males, varying in severity from a small notch to a total separation extending into the floor of the nose. Whether unilateral or bilateral, these clefts usually involve the dental ridges, hence additional anomalies of deformed, supernumerary, or absent teeth present themselves later in a child's development.

A cleft palate occurring alone or in asso-

ciation with a cleft lip is seen more frequently in females. This malformation may involve only the uvula or may extend into or through the soft and hard palates. When seen with a cleft lip the defect may involve the midline of the soft palate and extend into the hard palate, exposing one or both sides of the nasal cavities, depending on whether it is a unilateral or bilateral cleft palate.

NURSING RESPONSIBILITIES The role of the nursery nurse in caring for an infant with these problems is defined by the plastic surgeon who will be repairing the lip or palate. Maintenance of an adequate nutritional state is the most immediate problem. If only the lip is involved, surgical repair may be done soon after birth. Should the anomaly be extensive, however, surgery may be delayed and the lip repaired at 6 to 8 weeks of age, while the palate may not be repaired for 12 to 15 months or longer. The operative schedule depends upon the infant's physical status and the surgeon's preference. (See Figure 34-6.)

An important aspect of newborn care then will be teaching the parents how to feed their baby. It is best to feed these infants in a sitting position with any one of the several varieties of nipples or syringes available. These include a soft, cross-cut rubber nipple, a cleft palate nipple, or a "duck bill" nipple. Some plastic surgeons prefer to use a rubber-tipped syringe or medicine cup at least until the lip is repaired. Should a syringe or medicine cup be used, it is important to remember to direct the flow of formula toward the side of the mouth, thereby decreasing the possibility of aspiration. Since these babies cannot create suction, they tend to become irritable and frustrated in their attempts to feed. Regardless of the feeding method used, the rate of flow of the formula must be adjusted to each individual baby.

Since these infants characteristically swal-

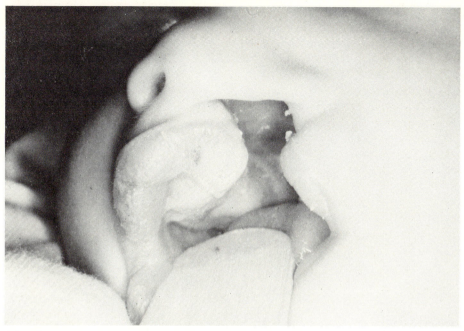

FIGURE 34-4
Unilateral cleft lip and palate. (*Courtesy of Richard Waldon, M.D., Mineola, New York.*)

FIGURE 34-5
Bilateral cleft lip and palate. (*By permission from the University of Colorado Medical Center, Denver,*

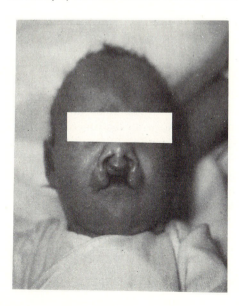

low large amounts of air, frequent burping is essential. Rest periods should be provided in order to avoid tiring the infant. When a mother begins to feed her baby, reassurance, patience, and the understanding of nursery personnel are important components of this learning situation. A mother frequently finds herself "all thumbs"—frightened at the prospect of feeding her baby—and yet she must learn, for feeding will be her responsibility upon discharge. The initial clumsiness will be overcome once the infant's sucking attempts are coordinated with the formula being given, and the mother will become more comfortable and more confident in her ability to care for the baby. Praise and encouragement from the nurse will help reduce the parents' anxiety.

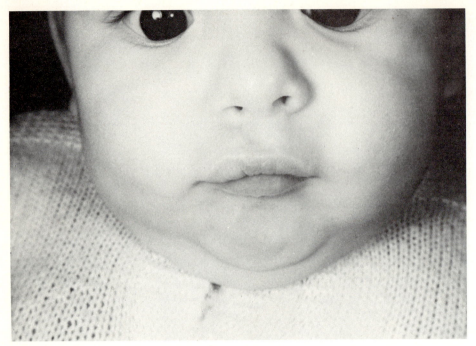

FIGURE 34-6
Successful repair of right unilateral cleft lip. (*Courtesy of Richard Waldon, M.D.,*
Mineola, New York.)

Tracheoesophageal Fistula

A problem detected before or at the time an
infant is given the first fluids by mouth is a
tracheoesophageal fistula, possibly accompanied by an esophageal atresia. In the embryo, by the 4th week the laryngotracheal
groove develops into the larynx, trachea, and
primordial lung tissue, while the esophagus
is elongated as the heart and lungs push the
stomach caudally. By the 8th week the
esophageal lumen is formed. Various anomalies occur as a result of the failure of these
processes to be completed correctly.

The most common form of esophageal
atresia and tracheoesophageal fistula seen in
about 90 percent of the cases is the upper
portion of the esophagus ending in a blind
pouch at or just above the bifurcation of the
trachea, while the lower portion from the

stomach is connected to the trachea by a
short, fistular tract.

Tracheoesophageal fistula is sometimes associated with polyhydramnios which alerts
personnel to observe these infants more
closely.

NURSING RESPONSIBILITIES   One of the nurse's
primary responsibilities in caring for newborn infants is accurate astute observation
and being able to differentiate normal from
pathological conditions.

Some of the symptoms indicative of a
tracheoesophageal fistula which the nurse
can observe are excessive mucus or constant
drooling from the corner of the mouth. When
the infant is fed for the first time, the nurse
notes that the first swallow or two is normal,
but suddenly the fluid returns through the
nose and mouth, the baby is coughing, gag-

ging, cyanotic, and struggling for breath. The infant may even stop breathing. A second attempt to feed results in the same sequence of events.

Since early diagnosis is imperative and surgical intervention is the only definitive treatment, early nursing assessment of the infant's status is essential. Even though immediate surgery is desirable, complications such as pneumonia, dehydration, or electrolyte imbalance may delay action until the surgical risk is reduced.

The baby is kept in an upright position to avoid leaking of gastric juices into the trachea and lungs. Gentle suctioning is used to remove mucus from the mouth and esophagus. These infants are usually placed in incubators and receive humidified oxygen. The episodes of respiratory difficulty can be relieved, and the viscosity of the secretions decreased. Antibiotics and intravenous therapy are initiated during the preoperative period.

The uneventful recovery of these infants depends upon cooperative planning and skill of the health team.

Imperforate Anus

Abdominal distention or the absence of meconium may be indicative of an obstruction of the intestinal tract. Embryologically the differentiation of tissue and the separation into two closed systems, dorsally the rectum and ventrally the bladder and urethra, occur by the 8th week. Interference with development of the anal-rectal structures gives rise to a variety of anomalies. Although the true incidence of imperforate anus is unknown, it is estimated that about 1 in 1,000 infants needs some major surgical correction. (See Figure 34-7.)

The diagnosis is made when no anal opening is found, there is no passage of meco-

nium, the nurse cannot insert a small gloved finger into the rectal canal, or the "blind pouch" of the cavity is palpable. Later abdominal distention develops. It is not uncommon for a tracheoesophageal fistula to be accompanied by an imperforate anus.

NURSING RESPONSIBILITIES The diagnosis can be made by observation, insertion of a catheter, or by digital examination. Observation of the newborn permits the detection of the anomaly, unless it is the simple type having a thin membrane covering the anal orifice, which can be diagnosed on delivery.

Occasionally a nurse does not suspect an obstruction for a day or two after delivery. This gross oversight can be prevented by a thorough digital examination at birth. The absence of meconium coupled with some abdominal distention may be the first clues given by the infant to indicate some intestinal obstruction. X rays reveal the extent of the malformation and permit the surgeon to plan the most appropriate intervention.

Gastroschisis and/or Omphalocele

At birth, a neonate may be delivered with viscera protruding through and lying out of the abdominal cavity because of a malformation of the abdominal wall. (See Figure 34-8.) Such a defect may be gastroschisis or omphalocele. Gastroschisis is located below and separate from the umbilicus without a sac or covering, whereas an omphalocele is centrally located, includes the umbilicus, and may have a sac or covering (the sac may disintegrate in utero).

The failure of the embryonic tissue of the abdominal layers to develop and mature properly is the cause of gastroschisis. An omphalocele is present as a result of an impaired fusion of the abdominal lateral folds by the 10th week of uterine life.

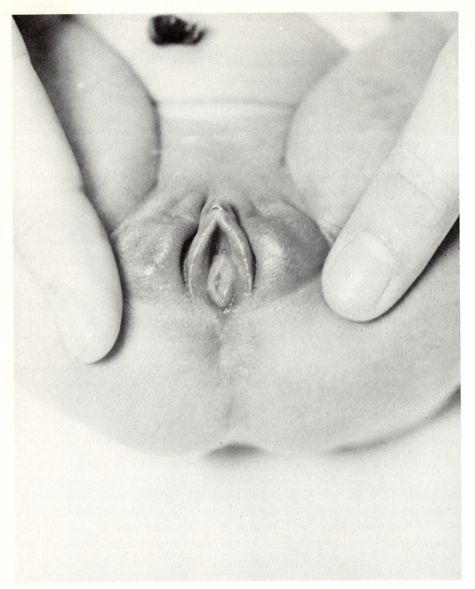

FIGURE 34-7
Imperforate anus. (*Courtesy of Lawrence Pickett, M.D., Yale University, New Haven, Conn.*)

NURSING RESPONSIBILITIES Careful handling of the malformation is one of nursing's most important functions. For survival it is essential that infection, rupture, or drying of the peritoneal sac does not occur.

These infants are usually repaired soon after delivery. Pediatric surgeons frequently pass a nasogastric tube which is attached to low intermittent suction to prevent abdominal distention. There is usually an order to keep the defect covered with sterile towels or sterile sponges (without cotton fill), keeping either one moist with sterile saline solution until the infant is transferred to the operating room. Monitoring vital signs, keeping the involved area covered and moist, and checking the suction apparatus are important nursing procedures.

The Genitourinary Tract

Malformations of the genitourinary system are common; however, many of them do not produce any symptoms or disturbances in function during the neonatal period. These are usually demonstrated as the infant grows and develops.

Exstrophy of the Bladder

One deviation in intrauterine growth involving the genitourinary tract which is readily identified at birth is exstrophy of the bladder. (See Figure 34-9.) Characterized by an absent anterior wall over the bladder area, there may be a complete or partial exposure of bladder mucosa. The exposed mucosa is bright red, has numerous folds, and is most

FIGURE 34-8
Omphalocele. (*Courtesy of Lawrence Pickett, M.D., Yale University, New Haven, Conn.*)

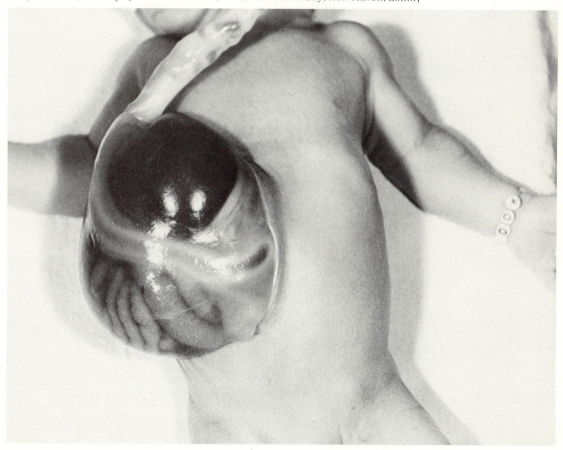

sensitive to touch. In the male, anomalies such as an undescended testes, a short penis, epispadias, and inguinal hernias may also be present. These conditions compound parental concern.

NURSING RESPONSIBILITIES The anomaly is obvious at birth. There is urine seepage onto the abdominal wall from the involved structures. Excoriation of the surrounding skin may occur, and there is also the constant odor of urine. Ulceration of the exposed bladder mucosa may occur. Meticulous hygiene and skin care are necessary to prevent any infections from developing, for such an occurrence may involve the kidneys.

Each infant is different, and depending upon the extent of the deformity as well as

the surgical timetable, parents are sometimes taught to care for their infants before the operative procedure is done. Seeing the exstrophy initially, mothers usually become frightened and distressed. Cleansing the skin around the defect may be particularly difficult for them to do. The parents' dexterity in handling the baby as well as their ability to retain their composure whenever viewing the exstrophy comes with experience and time.

For the nurse the emphasis should be on prevention of infections or the formation of ulcerations on the mucosa. This can be accomplished by placing sterile petrolatum gauze dressings over the exposed areas. Stool contamination and urine odor retention can be avoided by frequent diaper changes.

FIGURE 34-9
Exstrophy of the bladder.

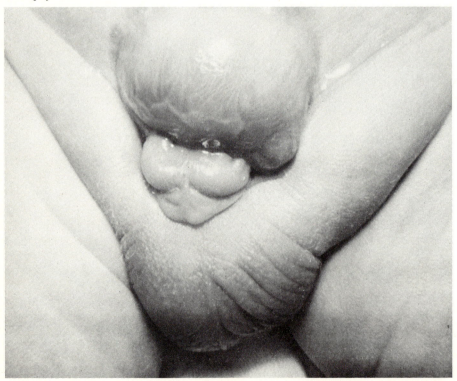

Diapers should be loosely applied to avoid any pressure over the exposed bladder.

Care given in the nursery and clearly demonstrated to a mother, coupled with a relaxed atmosphere which is conducive to questions, frequently reduces the stress and anxiety experienced by the mother. With the acceptance, encouragement, and understanding of the nurse, a mother begins to feel comfortable in caring for her baby.

Hypospadias

One of the most common malformations of the male genitourinary system is hypospadias, in which the urethral orifice is ventral and posterior to its normal opening. While the meatus usually occurs near the glans, it may occur anywhere along the shaft of the penis. If the infant should void while he is in the delivery room, the defect could be identified then, otherwise it may go undetected until a voiding is actually observed.

NURSING RESPONSIBILITIES   The care associated with this intrauterine deviation does not differ from that given to other babies in the nursery. Physical complications may be minimal; however, the social, financial, and psychological implications may be many. The nurse should be prepared to answer parents' questions honestly and realistically so that they can plan for the future welfare of the child.

The Circulatory System

The circulatory system does not escape anomalous formation in utero; however, these defects are not usually noted at birth or within a few days following delivery. Cyanosis may not be manifested until the ductus arteriosus begins to close. Infants at three to six weeks of age may be admitted to pediatric units with rapid respirations, no weight gain, tachycardia, and signs of congestive heart failure.

Transposition of the Great Vessels

A condition which usually occurs in infants large for gestational age and diagnosed during the first few days of life is transposition of the great vessels. The primary symptom which manifests itself soon after delivery is cyanosis. In transposition of the great vessels the aorta arises from the right ventricle, and the pulmonary arteries from the left ventricle. With the systemic veins returning to the right atrium and the pulmonary veins emptying into the left atrium, two independent circuits are present. This condition is incompatible with life unless the foramen ovale or ductus arteriosus remains open or there is an intraventricular or intraatrial septal defect.

A large number of these newborns are salvaged with the use of the *ballon atrial septostomy*. This palliative measure is important for the intraatrial baffle technique which realizes total correction at a later age. The Mustard procedure, an innovative surgical intervention, necessitates removal of the atrial septum and the creation of an intracardiac baffle (with Dacron or tissue), forming a tunnellike structure which runs across the receiving chamber, diverting pulmonary venous return to the tricuspid valve and systemic venous return to the mitral valve. It can result in acyanotic infants and toddlers who gradually resume full activity and lead reasonably normal lives.[10]

NURSING RESPONSIBILITIES   Cyanosis may not be present at delivery; therefore, observation of the infant in the nursery is important. Rapid respirations, dyspnea, and cyanosis are the initial symptoms presented. When the infant is fed for the first time the nurse notes that the sucking reflex is poor and that the respirations are rapid and may be in excess of 80 or 100 per minute. The baby's color is dusky and not the pink that is characteristic of newborns. The baby appears to be too busy breathing to eat.

The diagnosis is made early and a septostomy or surgical intervention occurs soon after confirmation. The time spent in the nursery before any procedure is done is most important to that baby's survival. Astute observations are essential, for this condition changes rapidly.

Congestive heart failure may occur, and the nurse should be aware of the manifestations. Poor sucking, rapid respirations, and increasing cyanosis together with sudden weight gain, edema, and retractions and nasal flaring are indicative of the infant's deteriorating condition.

The problem of feeding becomes a major issue for the nurse. The infant tires easily and is utterly exhausted when attempting to suck. More frequent feedings, a high-calorie formula, and frequent rest periods will permit a more sufficient intake. It is not unusual for the nurse to take as long as 45 minutes to feed the infant, and it is imperative that enough time be taken to ensure adequate nutrition.

If diuretics are being given, weight should be checked accurately at 8-hour intervals and the urinary output carefully noted, for both will indicate the success of the therapy to the cardiologist. In administering a digitalis preparation in the digitalization process, vital signs should be monitored hourly. These nursing measures are applicable when adjusted and individualized to meet the needs of the infant with other forms of congenital heart disease.

Tetralogy of Fallot

Another cardiac condition which may be present, but which may not necessarily manifest itself in the delivery room or in the newborn nursery, is tetralogy of Fallot. The presence of pulmonary stenosis, a ventricular septal defect, dextroposition of the aorta, and a right ventricular hypertrophy constitute this congenital heart disease.

Hemodynamically, as the right ventricle contracts, resistance at the pulmonary stenosis shunts unoxygenated blood across the ventricular septal defect into the aorta. The persistent arterial unsaturated state results in cyanosis. It is the most common condition accompanied by persistent cyanosis and accounts for three-fourths of the cyanotic congenital heart diseases in children over the age of one year. The nurse should remember, however, that the cyanosis which is characteristic of this disease may not be present at birth, for as long as the ductus arteriosus remains open sufficient blood flows through the lungs to prevent this manifestation.

The great strides made in cardiac surgery, both palliative and total corrective procedures, have resulted in lowering the mortality rate and improving the prognosis.

Pulmonary Atresia

In this anomalous condition, cyanosis generally appears soon after birth, and as the heart progressively enlarges, congestive heart failure may occur. The presence of a small right ventricle and tricuspid valve results in blood entering the left atrium via the foramen ovale or an atrial septal defect. Generally the prognosis is poor.

Pulmonary Stenosis

It is important for the nurse to remember that pulmonary stenosis may exist as a separate entity or with associated defects of the atrial or ventricular septum. In the most common type of isolated pulmonic stenosis the valve cusps are dome-shaped, with a small central or eccentric opening. The obstruction of the blood flow from the right ventricle to the pulmonary artery results in an increased systolic pressure as well as hypertrophy of the right ventricle. The symptoms vary according to the degree of stenosis from mild to severe. In the latter, peripheral cyanosis may be present. Prognosis is correlated with the severity of the condition.

The Musculoskeletal System

There are two anomalies of the musculoskeletal system which are commonly seen in the newborn nursery, and they are easily diagnosed. In both instances early recognition and treatment is essential for successful correction. The longer a condition goes unidentified, the more severe the deformity becomes, the more difficult the repair, and the less favorable the prognosis.

Congenital Dislocation of the Hip

In the newborn, congenital dislocation of the hip usually exists as a potential dislocation rather than an actual dislocation. The hip joint which develops from mesoderm emerges at about the 7th embryonic week, but at birth the fetal, cartilaginous state persists. The delay in ossification seems to be due to insufficient pressure of the femoral head into the acetabulum during fetal life, thereby delaying ossification of the ball-and-socket joint.

It is found in females 6 times more frequently than in males, and unilateral dislocations are about twice as common as bilateral dislocations. In the United States congenital dislocation of the hip is disproportionately high among the Navaho Indians.

On examination of the infant there is an asymmetry of the gluteal and inguinal folds on the affected side. They appear to be higher than the folds on the unaffected side. A shortening of the involved leg is also evident. When the baby moves both legs the ob-

servant nurse notes there is less motion in the affected leg because of a limitation of abduction of the affected hip.

Congenital Club Foot

About 95 percent of the infants born with a club foot are of the *equinovarus* type. The entire foot is inverted, the heel is drawn up, and the forefoot is abducted. There is a deep transverse crease that is also seen on the sole of the foot. If able to walk, the baby would be walking on the ankle rather than the sole of the foot. (See Figure 34-10.)

Occurring in 1 in 800 births, it is found twice as frequently in males as in females. This deformity of the foot is identified at birth; however, it must be differentiated from a positional deformity of the foot which can be attributed to an infant's position in utero.

NURSING RESPONSIBILITIES A nurse is in a unique position to detect these particular problems in the nursery. As the newborn is cared for, the nurse can note the height of the gluteal and inguinal folds, and can also contribute the information necessary to distinguish a positional deformity from a club foot. The parents will need information regarding the anomaly, but the nurse's emphasis should be upon the need for long-term

FIGURE 34-10
Club feet (bilateral) in a neonate. (*By permission from the University of Colorado Medical Center, Denver, Colorado.*)

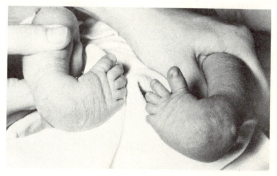

follow-up. Their questions should be answered honestly and in terms readily understandable.

THE ROLE OF THE NURSE IN INTERHOSPITAL TRANSPORTATION

The special nursing care of a neonate requiring surgery begins when the diagnosis is made and ends when the infant is returned to the parents. Early diagnosis increases the chance for survival, and the nurse's contributions to early detection of an anomaly cannot be overemphasized.

Occasionally once the diagnosis is made these infants are transferred to larger, specialized pediatric areas where the surgery may be performed. In these instances, pertinent information should accompany the infant. The nurse who accompanies the baby is expected to share this information with the nursing personnel who will be assuming the responsibility of caring for the baby. Of particular value are the symptoms presented by the baby, the condition at the time of delivery, and the behavior of the baby in the nursery. Fathers who accompany their infants are usually so distraught they cannot be expected to relate information which medical personnel consider essential data.

Should it be impossible for a nurse to accompany the infant, then a detailed, written set of nursery notes sent with the baby will be helpful to the receiving nursing personnel. Still another alternative could be a phone call to the head nurse of the ward to which the child will be admitted. A nursing assessment and evaluation of an infant's condition is gratefully appreciated by those who will be directly involved in caring for the baby. It helps them understand the infant's status before arrival and permits the assembly of all necessary equipment essential to the baby's care.

Frequently overlooked in the hurried arrangements for transfer is the operative permit, and the result is that surgery is sometimes delayed until legal permission is obtained. This is true when the father does not accompany the baby. Arrangements for telegram consents or other legal forms acceptable to the receiving hospital will facilitate the interhospital transfer.

Under ideal conditions a nurse accompanying the infant should find a vehicle properly equipped for such transportation. Oxygen and suction should be available and ready for use. The infant should be kept warm, properly positioned, and appropriate measures taken to maintain fluid balance. The infant's birth, the tests essential for diagnosis, and now the transferral to another hospital are all extremely traumatizing and contribute to the baby's deteriorating physical status. We should never forget what this tiny individual is experiencing in the struggle for survival.

IDENTIFIABLE METABOLIC AND CHROMOSOMAL DEVIATIONS IN THE NEWBORN

Phenylketonuria

The disease known as phenylketonuria (PKU) is an inborn error of metabolism which, without treatment, results in mental retardation. Phenylalanine is an essential amino acid present in all protein foods. The primary biochemical defect in PKU is the absence of the liver enzyme phenylalanine hydroxylase which transforms phenylalanine to tyrosine, permitting further metabolism. In a child with PKU, the excessive phenylalanine is unable to be converted to tyrosine, and it builds up in the tissues, including the brain, and spills into the urine as phenylpyruvic acid, phenylacetic acid, orthohydroxyphenylacetic acid, and the excessive phenylalanine.

If this metabolic disorder is present, as a newborn takes in food there should be an accumulation of phenylalanine. The Guthrie test, a simple blood test which involves a heel puncture, permits an early diagnosis. There are also some health care facilities which utilize urine analyses for the detection. Regardless of the method, testing is usually done about the third day, and it is mandatory in most states. This is the example of an instance in which mental retardation can be prevented by preventing phenylalanine intake from infancy. Substitute diets should be implemented immediately after confirmation so that the brain will be permitted to develop normally.

Nursing Responsibilities

The nurse's prime responsibility is to ensure that the appropriate blood or urine test is done before the baby is discharged from the nursery. Different hospitals have different procedures for collecting the appropriate sample. It is important that the test be done before the infant is discharged from the nursery, and that the infant has had 120 ml of formula, 20 calories per 30 ml, prior to the blood work. Since this metabolic error is easily detected, it is imperative that nursery nurses assume the responsibility of verifying the fact that appropriate tests have been done. Dietary management and the prevention of mental retardation can occur only through early detection.

INTRAUTERINE GROWTH DEVIATIONS AFFECTING BIRTH WEIGHT

The developing fetus is part of a delicately balanced biological unit which also includes the mother's environment, the mother, and the placenta. Any external and internal factors which affect any component of this inte-gral unit are reflected in the neonate at delivery. Unfortunately, only a few of these adverse conditions are understood and can be associated with growth deviations in utero. These infants, whether small or large for their gestational age, contribute to the morbidity and mortality of the so-called high-risk infants.

Infants Small for Gestational Age

About one-third of all newborns weighing less than 2,500 g are considered small for their gestational age and therefore represent another type of intrauterine growth deviation.[11] These are the infants identified in the literature as small for date, demonstrating fetal malnutrition, fetal undergrowth, or intrauterine growth retardation. Some authors term these infants *dysmature* in an effort to unify the various terms. Although the terminology may be confusing, it is important to remember that most of these infants weigh less than 2,500 g. They have failed to achieve expected size for the duration of their gestational period, which may be 38 weeks or longer. The small-for-date infant differs greatly from the premature, who has developed normally but has failed to remain in utero long enough to achieve full-term size.

On visual examination these babies are long and thin, with dry skin and diminished skin turgor. They are much more active and alert than their premature counterparts. They have creases on their soles, and their hair is coarse, straight, and silky compared to the fine, fuzzy hair found in premature infants. The ear cartilage is also very well developed, with sharp ridges, and these small-for-date infants also have firm skull bones. When palpating the area around the anterior fontanel, it is hard and thick right up to the edge of the fontanel, not at all like the soft, cartilaginous feeling of a premature's skull bones. Lanugo is not found in infants demonstrating growth retardation.

Causes of Poor Fetal Growth

The weight of an infant at birth in relation to gestational age portrays, to some extent, the intrauterine environment and the effects of maternal influences. Factors which affect growth may originate in the fetus, the mother, the placenta, or the mother's environment.

Congenital anomalies, such as congenital heart disease; chromosomal aberrations, such as Down's syndrome; and teratogenic, genetic, and metabolic diseases are frequently associated with reduced growth potentials. A causal relationship has been established between rubella and cytomegalovirus and small-for-date infants.

The pregnant woman's nutritional status has a primary influence upon the developing embryo, although it probably has little effect prior to the third trimester when requirements are relatively low. Some of the most vulnerable women entering pregnancy are adolescents with poor eating habits. Such habits contribute substantially to the increase in severe preeclampsia as well as the increased incidence of small-for-gestational-age infants.[12]

The fetus usually receives adequate nutrients from maternal sources during gestation, enabling the fetus to build up stores of glycogen and fat late in pregnancy which will tide the infant over the period from birth to when feeding begins. Should these stores be inadequate, an infant's glucose level falls as the available energy sources are mobilized, and hypoglycemia may occur.

Maternal infections which involve the fetus can occur through the placenta (transplacentally) or via the amniotic fluid. The former relates to the presence of the offending organism in the mother's bloodstream, while the latter refers to an ascending type of infection. Bacteria and fungi commonly infect the fetus via the amniotic cavity; viruses, protozoa, and spirochetes usually infect the fetus transplacentally.

Women with hypertensive cardiovascular and/or renal disease also may deliver infants who are small for their gestational age. Pregnant women at either end of the age spectrum tend to deliver smaller babies, as do women who have children at intervals of less than 2 years. Likewise, women who give birth at intervals of 6 years or more tend to deliver infants demonstrating fetal malnutrition.

In utero single infants and twins develop at the same rate until 29 to 32 weeks of gestation when the growth rate of twins slows down.[13] When fetal malnutrition occurs in a twin pregnancy, it usually does so in only one fetus. Such twin sets are of markedly different weights. (See Figure 34-11.)

A third factor which affects growth is the

FIGURE 34-11
Male twins. The infant on the left is appropriate for gestational age (AGA) while his sibling on the right demonstrates fetal malnutrition (SGA). (*Courtesy of Joseph Kennedy, Jr., M.D., Boston, Mass.*)

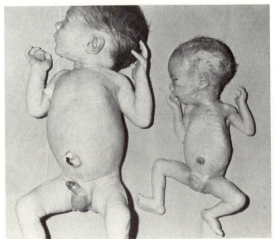

placenta. Site of the implantation and its development, composition, and metabolism play an important role in fetal development. Some etiologic placental causes which interfere with the main nutritional supply line of the fetus include (1) limitation of uterine blood flow, (2) reduced maternal concentration of essential nutrients, (3) reduced effective area for placental exchange, and (4) impaired diffusion or active transport across placental membrane. All contribute to fetal malnutrition.[13]

There are some placental lesions which are potentially harmful to the developing fetus and result in small-for-date babies. The most common include an abnormal insertion of the cord, an abnormal placental outline, insufficient vascular patterns, and multiple infarctions. However, the ability to identify these causes of impaired placental transfer is most difficult—until the baby is born.

The pregnant woman's environment also exerts its influence upon the developing fetus. Women in low socioeconomic circumstances with little education and little or no antepartum care tend to deliver malnourished infants. Women who smoke as well as women who live at high elevation also tend to deliver infants with growth retardation.

Nursing Responsibilities

An initial nursing problem identified at birth is the limited ability of these infants to conserve heat. They are of small size and have a scanty amount of subcutaneous fat. However, they have a large surface area compared to their weight, they are wet, and the cool air-conditioned surroundings result in heat loss by evaporation, convection, and radiation. These environmental stresses can lead to a slower recovery from birth and an exhaustion of fat and glycogen stores, and increase the risk of hypoglycemia. All efforts must be taken to prevent heat loss.

The nurse should observe these infants very carefully, and feedings are usually started early. Although active, vigorous babies free of tremors may develop hypoglycemia, generally these infants are jittery, listless, depressed, and occasionally they may have apneic episodes. A knowledge of the consequences of hypoglycemia, the degree of cerebral impairment, and its contribution to infant mortality and morbidity emphasizes the need for close nursing observation.

Hypoglycemia

With a blood sugar level below 30 mg per 100 ml, hypoglycemia may occur within 24 hours of delivery. Its signs and symptoms include jitteriness, tremors, and/or seizures. It is important for a nurse to know that four types of newborns are at great risk of developing hypoglycemia: (1) progeny of diabetic mothers; (2) infants of low birth weight who may have experienced intrauterine malnutrition; (3) neonates with metabolic or genetic problems such as glycogen storage disease or maple syrup disease; (4) critically ill newborns with increased metabolic needs. As a precautionary measure, a heel stick is incorporated into the admission procedure from which a Dextristix and hematocrit can be done to help identify correctable problems immediately. Those infants whose Dextristix is 40 mg per 100 ml or below and who are able to take oral feedings are usually given glucose in water or formula immediately, which normally corrects the situation. Infants with severe hypoglycemia (less than 20 mg per 100 ml), however, are given 10 percent glucose in water intravenously at a rate of 100 ml per kg per day.

If the fetal malnutrition has been of long duration, heart failure may present itself after delivery. It is also important to note the number of voidings per day, for there may also be renal failure. Sometimes pediatricians order weights to be done on each nursing shift. It is essential to remember that the general condition of a small-for-gestational-age infant is such that physical deterioration has long preceded birth, and there are many systems involved. Careful examination is imperative.

Since these infants are usually difficult to feed, they are frequently on 3-hour feeding schedules. It is interesting to note that there is an immediate weight gain which characteristically differentiates the malnourished infant from the premature counterpart. It suggests rehydration of a dehydrated state rather than actual tissue growth.

Sometimes these infants are placed on high-calorie formulas. Occasionally, diarrhea may develop because the ability of the intestinal tract to absorb is quite limited during the early days of life.

Polycythemia

An easily recognized problem in the neonate is polycythemia. The normal hemoglobin range at birth is 14.7 to 21 g per 100 ml, with a hematocrit of 45 to 65 g per 100 ml. A neonate whose blood values are greater than normal is plethoric in appearance. Neonatal polycythemia is being reported with increasing frequency, particularly in those infants small for gestational age. Nurses working with newborns who demonstrate intrauterine growth retardation should watch for signs of plethora and complications such as seizures, respiratory distress, tachycardia, congestive heart failure, or hyperbilirubinemia.

The central nervous system signs may be seen very early after birth, and they include excessive jitteriness and convulsions, as well as a poor suck, lethargy, and hypotonia. The polycythemia and associated hyperviscosity apparently result in decreased cerebral circulation, producing brain ischemia.

In most instances no cause can be identified. Usually phlebotomies are done, and the blood is replaced with equal volumes of plasma reducing the cell mass and hyperviscosity. These modified exchange transfusions improve the newborn's status and there are no recurrences.

On the admission of a newborn, the nurse evaluates the baby's color and uses blood from the heel stick to evaluate the hematocrit which provides additional data in identifying polycythemia.

The nurse has a significant role in preventing complications. Protecting the infant from an initial, devastating heat loss, noting tremors, ensuring an adequate oral intake, and observing any changes in behavior assist the small-for-gestational-age infant in adjusting more satisfactorily to the new environment.

Infants Large for Gestational Age

Infants delivered of diabetic mothers tend to be large for gestational age, and demonstrate still another growth deviation—the large-for-date baby. Fetal hyperinsulinism in response to maternal hyperglycemia is postulated as the cause of the large size of these infants. However, it does not explain the large size of babies delivered to prediabetic women. Longitudinal studies have indicated that women who delivered infants weighing 4,550 g or more developed diabetes later in life, and therefore the diabetic and prediabetic states pose a hazard to the developing fetus. Maternal corticotrophin has also been suggested as contributing to the largeness and cushingoid features of these infants.

These babies frequently weigh more than 4,550 g; have round "cherub's" cheeks; and are large, plump, and puffy looking with buried eyes, short necks, and red skin. Their

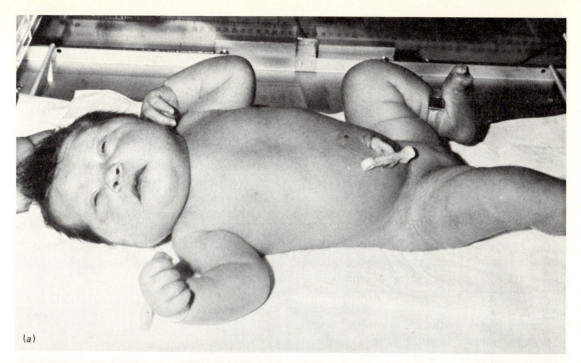

(a)

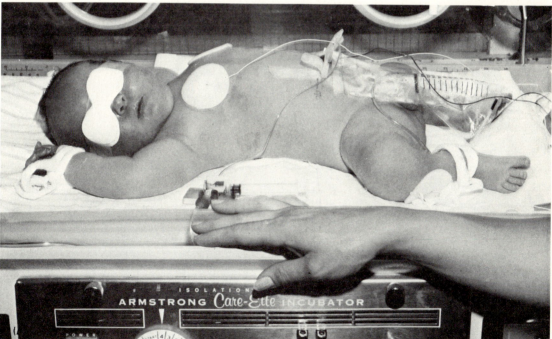

FIGURE 34-12

(a) A large-for-gestational-age (LGA) newborn, the product of a diabetic mother. (*Courtesy of Joseph Kennedy, Jr.,* *M.D., Boston, Mass.*) (b) A large-for-gestational-age (LGA) newborn, the product of a diabetic mother. The figure illustrates intensive care required in some instances. (*By permission from the University of Colorado Medical Center,* *Denver, Colorado.*)

overweight appearance is deceiving, for the maturity of these babies does not correspond to their actual weight, but to a lower weight.[14] (See Figure 34-12.)

Mortality rates are quite high, as is the incidence of intrauterine death after 36 weeks. Some studies have indicated that the incidence of congenital anomalies is 2 to 4 times the expected rate. Anomalies of the lumbosacral region, such as meningomyelocele, occur most frequently. Interestingly enough, despite their large size, these infants seem to have an increased vulnerability to disease.

These large-for-date neonates appear also to have a higher incidence of congenital heart disease than the offspring of nondiabetic mothers. The incidence is 5 times the number expected in the general population, with transposition, ventricular septal defect, and coarctation of the aorta seen in more than half of the cases. It is difficult to relate gestational influence of maternal diabetes with the incidence of congenital heart disease. However, some investigators have implicated the importance of the age of the mother at the onset of diabetes. The newborn of a diabetic mother may mimic the signs and symptoms of heart disease, with cardiomegaly, dyspnea, or the presence of a murmur, but cyanosis and the lack of a response to oxygen serves as an indicator of serious congenital heart disease. An electrocardiogram appears to be the most consistent, reliable tool in a diagnostic evaluation.[15]

Nursing Responsibilities

Sometimes the babies of diabetic mothers are admitted directly to special care nurseries because of the high incidence of respiratory distress syndrome in these infants. In addition to the usual newborn appraisal, the nurse may assist the pediatrician in aspirating gastric contents, a procedure routinely performed on these infants.

Vital signs are monitored at least every hour, and strict attention is given to the physical status of the infant. Tremors, hyperirritability, cyanosis, and restlessness are detected and reported immediately.

Feedings of glucose and water are started 2 to 3 hours after delivery. If seizure activity is noted, intravenous glucose may be started after blood sugar levels are drawn. In these instances intravenous therapy may continue until the baby is taking fluids well by mouth.

These infants are a challenge to the nurse working in a nursery, for the baby's physical status may change rapidly; the happiness enjoyed by a diabetic mother, however, in taking her infant home is the result of the nurses' conscientious efforts.

CONCLUSION

Advancements in technology, diagnostic procedures, and the field of genetics have necessitated an exploration of the role of the nurse in antepartum genetics. In view of the legal, moral, and ethical implications of current research and practice, nurses must become conscientiously and actively involved in these considerations.

Utilization of an interdisciplinary team approach is essential. The advantages of such an approach cannot be overemphasized. If the infant is to survive, to grow and develop, and to be accepted as a productive member of society, then both infant and family must be provided with the skills, knowledge, and understandings of every discipline striving together to achieve individualized, humanistic care.

REFERENCES

1 Solnik, Albert J., and Mary H. Stark: "Mourning and the Birth of a Defective Child," *Psychoanalytic Study of the Child*, 16:525, 1961.

2 The National Foundation/March of Dimes: *Facts: 1975*, White Plains, New York, 1975, pp. 7–8.

3 Plotkin, S. A., and W. J. Mellman: "Rubella in the Distant Past as a Possible Cause of Congenital Malformations," *American Journal of Obstetrics and Gynecology*, 108(3):387, Oct. 1, 1971.

4 Brown, Gordon: "Maternal Virus Infections and Congenital Anomalies," *Archives of Environmental Health*, 21(3):362–365, September 1970.

5 Caldwell, Joseph G.: "Congenital Syphilis: A Nonvenereal Disease," *American Journal of Nursing*, 71(9):1768, September 1971.

6 Zellweger, Hans, et al.: "Is Lysergic Acid Diethylamide (L.S.D.) a Teratogen?" *Lancet*, 7525:1066, Nov. 18, 1967.

7 Gardner, L. I., Salma Regina Assemany, and Richard L. Nev: "Deformities in a Child Whose Mother Took L.S.D.," *Lancet*, 7659:1290, June 13, 1970.

8 Nora, James T., et al.: "Dexamphetamine: A Possible Trigger in Cardiovascular Malformations," *Lancet*, 7659:1290, June 13, 1970.

9 Cooper, George, Jr., and Byron Cooper: "Radiation Hazards to Fetus and Mother," *Clinical Obstetrics and Gynecology*, 9(1):11–21, March 1966.

10 Rowe, R. D., et al.: "Long Term Management of Heart Defects," *Pediatric Clinics of North America*, 21(4):854–855, November 1974.

11 Hunscher, Helen A., and Winslow T. Tompkins: "Influence of Maternal Nutrition on the Immediate and Long-Term Outcome of Pregnancy," *Clinical Obstetrics and Gynecology*, 13(1):138, March 1970.

12 Cassady, George: "Body Composition in Intrauterine Growth Retardation," *Pediatric Clinics of North America*, 17(1):79, February 1970.

13 Page, Ernest W.: "Pathogenesis and Prophylaxis of Low Birth Weights," *Clinical Obstetrics and Gynecology*, 13(1):82, March 1970.

14 Pederson, Jorgen: *The Pregnant Diabetic and Her Newborn*, Scandinavian University Books, Munksgaard, Copenhagen, 1967, p. 61.

15 Rowland, Thomas W., et al.: "Congenital Heart Disease in Infants of Diabetic Mothers," *The Journal of Pediatrics*, 83(5):815–820, November 1973.

BIBLIOGRAPHY

Abramson, Harold: *Symposium on the Functional Physiopathology of the Fetus and Neonate*, Mosby, St. Louis, 1971.

Adamson, Karlis: *Diagnosis and Treatment of Fetal Disorders*, Springer-Verlag, New York, 1968.

Apgar, Virginia, and Gabriel Stickle: "Birth Defects—Their Significance as a Public Health Problem," *Journal of the American Medical Association*, 204(5):371–374, April 29, 1968.

———: "Assessment of Gestational Age and Development at Birth," *Pediatric Clinics of North America*, 17(1):125–130, February 1970.

Austin, R. Lee: "Congenital Malformations," *Postgraduate Medicine*, 46(5):193–195, November 1969.

Bernfeld, Merton R.: "Progress in Birth Defects Research," *California Medicine*, 112(2):26–42, February 1970.

Cooke, Cynthia W., et al.: "Fetal and Maternal Outcome in Asymptomatic Bacilluria of Pregnancy," *Obstetrics and Gynecology*, 36(6):840–844, December 1970.

Davies, Pamela A.: "Bacterial Infection in the Fetus and Newborn," *Archives of Diseases in Childhood*, 46(245):1–27, February 1971.

Drillien, C. M.: "The Small for Date Infant; Etiology and Prognosis," *Pediatric Clinics of North America*, 17(1):9–24, February 1970.

Elizan, Teresita, and Okingele Fabije: "Congenital and Neonatal Anomalies Linked with Viral Infections in Experimental Animals," *American Journal of Obstetrics and Gynecology*, 106(1):147–165, January 1, 1970.

Ferreira, Antonio J.: *Prenatal Environment*, Charles C Thomas, Springfield, Ill., 1969.

Fishbein, Morris: *Birth Defects*, Lippincott, Philadelphia, 1963.

Franciosi, Ralph A.: "Fetal Infection via Amniotic Fluid," *Rocky Mountain Medical Journal*, 67(10):32–34, October 1970.

Fuchs, Fritz, and Lars L. Cedarquist: "Recent Advances in Antenatal Diagnosis by Amniotic Fluid Analysis," *Clinical Obstetrics and Gynecology*, 13(1):178–201, March 1970.

Greene, John W., Jr., and John L. Dukring: "Diabetes and Pregnancy," *Journal of Tennessee Medical Association*, 64(2):113–118, February 1971.

Hecht, Frederick, and Everett W. Lovrien: "Genetic Diagnosis in the Newborn," *Pediatric Clinics of North America*, 17(4):1039–1053, November 1970.

Hendricks, Charles H., and William Brenner: "Toxemia of Pregnancy: Relationships between Fetal Weight, Fetal Survival, and the Maternal State," *American Journal of Obstetrics and Gynecology*, 109(2):225–233, Jan. 15, 1971.

Hughes, Walter T.: "Infection and Intrauterine Growth Retardation," *Pediatric Clinics of North America*, 17(1):119–124, February 1970.

Important Facts about the Diagnosis of Birth Defects in Early Pregnancy, The Genetics Unit, The Walter E. Fernald State School, Waltham, Mass.

Kasirsky, Gilbert, and Martin F. Tansy: "Teratogenic Effects of Methamphetamine in Mice and Rats," *Teratology*, 4(2):131–134, May 1971.

Klein, Jerome, and S. Michael Marcy: "Infection in the Newborn," *Clinical Obstetrics and Gynecology*, 13(2):321–347, June 1970.

Lenz, W.: "How Can the Teratogenic Action of a Factor Be Established in Man?" *Southern Medical Journal*, 64:41–47, February 1971.

————: "Malformations Caused by Drugs in Pregnancy," *American Journal of Diseases of Children*, 112(2):99–106, August 1966.

Lubchenco, Lula, and Harry Bard: "Incidence of Hypoglycemia in Newborn Infants Classified by Birth Weight and Gestational Age," *Pediatrics*, 47(5):831–838, May 1971.

Lugo, G., and George Cassady: "Intrauterine Growth Retardation," *American Journal of Obstetrics and Gynecology*, 109(4):615–622, Feb. 15, 1971.

MacVicar, John: "Chorioamnionitis," *Clinical Obstetrics and Gynecology*, 13(2):272–290, June 1970.

Milunsky, Aubrey, et al.: "Prenatal Genetic Diagnosis, Part I," *New England Journal of Medicine*, 283(25):1370–1381, Dec. 17, 1970.

————: "Prenatal Genetic Diagnosis, Part II," *New England Journal of Medicine*, 283(26):1441–1446, Dec. 24, 1970.

————: "Prenatal Genetic Diagnosis, Part III," *New England Journal of Medicine*, 283(27):1498–1503, Dec. 31, 1970.

Navarrette, V. N., et al.: "Subsequent Diabetes in Mothers Delivered of a Malformed Child," *Lancet*, 2(7681):993–994, 1970.

Nelson, Waldo E., Victor C. Vaughan, III, and R. James McKay: *Textbook of Pediatrics*, 9th ed., Saunders, Philadelphia, 1969.

North, A. Frederick: "Small for Date Neonates," *Pediatrics*, 38(6):1013–1018, December 1966.

O'Brien, John S., et al.: "Tay-Sachs Disease: Prenatal Diagnosis," *Science*, 172(3978):61–64, April 2, 1971.

Parad, Howard J. (ed.): *Crisis Intervention: Selected Readings*, Family Service Association of America, New York, 1970.

Patrick, Marguerite J.: "Influence of Maternal Renal Infection on the Fetus and Infant," *Archives of Diseases of Childhood*, 42(222):208–213, April 1967.

Richards, J. D.: "Congenital Malformations and Environmental Influences in Pregnancy," *British Journal of Preventative and Social Medicine*, 23(4):218–225, November 1969.

Rubin, Alan (ed.): *Handbook of Congenital Malformations*, Saunders, Philadelphia, 1967.

Rubin, Reva: "Cognitive Style in Pregnancy," *American Journal of Nursing*, 70(3), 1970.

Schneck, L., et al.: "Prenatal Diagnosis of Tay-Sachs Disease," *Lancet,* 2(7647):582–584, Mar. 21, 1970.

Scipien, Gladys Mary, et al.: *Comprehensive Pediatric Nursing,* McGraw-Hill, New York, 1975.

Sever, John L.: "Viral Infections and Malformations," *Federation Proceedings,* 30(1):114–117, January–February 1971.

Shanklin, D. R.: "Influence of Placental Lesions on the Newborn Infant," *Pediatric Clinics of North America,* 17(1):25–42, February 1970.

Siegel, Morris, Harold T. Fuerst, and Vincent F. Guinee: "Rubella Epidemicity and Embryopathy," *American Journal of Diseases of Children,* 121(6):469–473, June 1971.

Sternberg, Joseph: "Irradiation and Radiocontamination during Pregnancy," *American Journal of Obstetrics and Gynecology,* 108(3): 490–511, Oct. 1, 1970.

Terris, Milton, and Edwin Gold: "An Epidemiological Study of Prematurity," *American Journal of Obstetrics and Gynecology,* 103(3): 358–379, Feb. 1, 1969.

Toledo, T. M., et al.: "Fetal Effects during Cyclophosphomide and Irradiation Therapy,"
Annals of Internal Medicine, 74(1):87–91, January 1971.

Tompkins, Winslow T.: "National Efforts to Reduce Perinatal Mortality and Morbidity," *Clinical Obstetrics and Gynecology,* 13(1): 44–56, March 1970.

Usher, Robert H.: "Clinical and Therapeutic Aspects of Fetal Malnutrition," *Pediatric Clinics of North America,* 17(1):169–183, February 1970.

Von Schilling, Karin C.: "The Birth of a Defective Child," *Nursing Forum,* 7:424–439, April 1968.

Wallace, Helen: "Factors Associated with Perinatal Mortality and Morbidity," *Clinical Obstetrics and Gynecology,* 13(1):13–43, March 1970.

Yamazaki, James N.: "A Review of the Literature on the Radiation Dosage Required to Cause Manifest Central Nervous System Disturbances from in Utero and Postnatal Exposure," *Pediatrics,* 37(5):877–897, May 1966.

Yeung, C. Y.: "Hypoglycemia in Neonate Sepsis," *Journal of Pediatrics,* 77(5):812–817, November 1970.

GLOSSARY

abortion Termination of pregnancy prior to viability of the fetus, i.e., less than 20 to 24 weeks gestational age.

abortorium An institution in which only abortions are performed.

acrocyanosis Cyanosis of fingertips and other extremities.

affinal bonds Relationships developed through marriage.

anaerobic catabolism The breakdown, in the absence of free oxygen, of organized substances into simpler compounds with the resultant release of energy.

anoxia Absence or deficiency of oxygen, as reduction of oxygen in body tissues below physiologic levels.

autosomes The chromosomes in the body other than the sex (X and Y) chromosomes.

azoospermic A condition in which sperm is absent in the semen.

bicornuate uterus A double uterus.

bilirubin The orange- or yellow-colored pig-ment in bile produced by the breakdown of hemoglobin and excreted by the liver cells.

caput succedaneum Swelling produced on the presenting part of the fetal head during labor.

cephalohematoma A localized effusion of blood beneath the periosteum of the skull of a newborn infant caused by disruption of the vessels during birth.

choanal atresia Congenital obstruction of the posterior nares.

chromosome The microscopic, rod-shaped bodies (46 in humans) which develop from cell nucleus material and contain the genes.

colostrum The "first milk" secreted from the lactiferous glands.

consanguinity Blood relationship to another person.

deoxyribonucleic acid A complex protein which is the carrier of genetic information and consists of adenine and guanine, which are purines, and two pyrimidines, thymine and cystosine.

desquamation   Shedding of cells from the skin or mucous membrane.

dilatation of cervix   The enlargement of the external os from an orifice a few millimeters in size to an opening large enough to allow the passage of the infant. A cervical opening approximately 10 cm in diameter is usually considered complete dilatation.

ductus arteriosus   A communicating channel between the aorta and the pulmonary artery of the fetus.

ductus venosus   A fetal blood vessel that connects the umbilical vein and the inferior vena cava.

dyspareunia   Painful sexual intercourse experienced by females.

ecchymosis   Skin discoloration resulting from extravasation of blood into the skin or mucous membrane.

eclampsia   Acute toxemia of pregnancy characterized by convulsions and coma occurring during pregnancy, labor, or the puerperium.

effacement   A thinning and shortening of the cervix which occurs during late pregnancy and/or labor.

effleurage   A stroke used in massage.

epicanthus   A fold of skin extending from the root of the nose to the median end of the eyebrow and covering the inner canthus and caruncle. It is a characteristic of the Mongolian race and may occur as a congenital anomaly in Caucasians.

Epstein's pearls   Small, white epithelial cysts along both sides of the median raphe of the hard palate. Commonly found in newborn infants.

erythema toxicum neonatorum   An urticarial condition affecting newborns in the first few days of life. The lesions consist of dead white papules grainy to the touch, with or without surrounding areas of redness.

erythroblastosis fetalis   A blood dyscrasia of the newborn characterized by agglutination and hemolysis of erythrocytes; usually caused by incompatibility between the infant's blood and the mother's.

esophageal atresia   A condition in which the esophagus ends in a blind pouch or narrows into a thin cord; usually occurs between the upper and mid third of the esophagus.

facies   The expression or appearance of the face; certain congenital syndromes present with a specific facial appearance.

fontanel   An unossified space or "soft spot" lying between the cranial bones of the skull of a fetus.

foramen ovale   The septal opening in the fetal heart that provides a communication between the atria.

gene   A factor responsible for the transmission of hereditary characteristics to offspring.

generative   Capable of reproducing.

genotype   The hereditary combination of genes in human beings.

gestation period   The number of completed weeks of pregnancy calculated from the first day of the last menstrual period.

gravida   The number of times a woman has been pregnant.

hemoconcentration   An increase in the number of red blood cells resulting from a decrease in the volume of plasma.

hirsutism   The excessive growth of hair, or growth of hair in unusual areas of the body.

homeothermic   Referring to an animal which maintains its internal temperature at a specified level regardless of its environmental temperature.

hydatidiform mole   Cystic proliferation of chorionic villi resembling a cluster of grapes.

hydrocephalus   An excess of cerebrospinal fluid within the ventricular system.

hydrocephalus, communicating   Cerebral fluid that circulates into the lumbar thecal space.

hydrocephalus, noncirculating   Ventricular fluid that does not empty into the lumbar thecal space.

hyperbilirubinemia   An excessive amount of unconjugated bilirubin in the blood.

hyperemesis gravidarum   Excessive vomiting during pregnancy.

hypersomnia   Excessive need for sleep.

hypofibrinogenemia   A deficiency of fibrinogen in the blood.

hypospadias   A condition in which the urethral orifice is at some point between the scrotal raphe and the base of the glans penis.

hypoxia   A broad term meaning diminished availability of oxygen to the body tissues.

idiopathic respiratory distress syndrome (hyaline membrane disease)   A severe respiratory condition found almost exclusively in preterm infants.

inborn error of metabolism   A hereditary disease caused by a deficiency of a specific enzyme.

jaundice   A condition characterized by a yellow color of the skin, the whites of the eyes, the mucous membranes, and body fluids that is due to deposition of bile pigment resulting from excess bilirubin in the blood.

kernicterus   A clinical syndrome in newborn infants manifested by pathological changes in the central nervous system resulting from deposition of unconjugated bilirubin in certain nuclei of the brain.

lanugo   Fine, downy hair growing over the body of the fetus.

large for gestational age   An infant above the 90th percentile.

lightening   The descent of the fetal head into the pelvic inlet.

lochia   The vaginal discharge during the puerperium, consisting of blood, mucus, and tissue.

lochia alba   The thin, colorless discharge which follows lochia serosa on about the 10th postpartum day and may last from the end of the third to the sixth postpartum week.

lochia rubra   The color description of the red, sanguinous vaginal flow which follows delivery and which lasts two to four days postpartum.

lochia serosa   The serous, pinkish-brown watery discharge which follows lochia rubra and lasts until about the 10th postpartum day.

lysozyme   An enzyme with antiseptic qualities which destroys foreign protein.

meconium   Dark green mucus material in the intestine of the full-term fetus. It constitutes the first stools passed by the newborn infant.

meiosis   The process by which germ cells divide.

milia   Distended sebaceous glands which produce tiny pinpoint papules on the skin of newborn infants. Commonly found over the bridge of the nose, chin, and cheeks.

mitochondrion   A filamentous or granular component (organelle) of cytoplasm, the principal site of oxidative reaction by which the energy in foodstuff is made available for endergonic processes in the cell.

mitosis   The process of somatic cell division by which multicellular organisms multiply.

Mongolian spots   Benign bluish pigmentation over the lower back, buttocks, or occasionally over the extensor surfaces. May be present at birth, particularly in dark-skinned races.

mucus-trap suction apparatus   A type of suction apparatus used in aspirating the nasopharynx and trachea of a newborn infant. It consists of a catheter with a mucus trap which prevents mucus from the baby from being drawn into the operator's mouth.

neonatal period   From birth to 28 days.

nursing process   The basis of systematic, conscious, organized nursing care, the steps of which are assessment, development of a plan of action, implementation of the plan, and evaluation. These steps are nondiscrete at times, and are used concurrently and recurrently.

nystagmus   Involuntary rhythmic oscillation of the eyeball—horizontal, vertical, or rotary.

omphalocele   A defect resulting from failure of closure of the abdominal wall or muscles whereby abdominal viscera is covered by a thin membrane only.

ophthalmia neonatorum purulent   Infection of the eye of the newborn, usually caused by gonococcus.

parity   The number of viable infants live or dead that a woman has delivered.

perinatal   A period of time beginning at 20 weeks gestation extending through the 28th day postpartum.

perinatalogist A physician with expertise in fetal and neonatal care.

phenotype The physical appearance of a person.

phenylketonuria A congenital disease caused by a defect in the metabolism of the amino acid phenylalanine. The condition is hereditary and results from lack of an enzyme, phenylalanine hydroxylase, necessary for the conversion of the amino acid phenylalanine into tyrosine.

phototherapy The therapeutic measure used in the treatment of hyperbilirubinemia.

placenta A disclike vascular structure in the impregnated uterus which nourishes and removes waste products from the fetus.

placenta abruptio A premature separation of a normally implanted placenta.

placenta dysfunction A placenta that is failing to meet fetal requirements.

placenta marginal A condition that exists when the placental edges are not firmly attached to the wall of the uterus.

placenta previa A placenta which is implanted in the lower uterine segment so that it partially or completely covers the internal os of the cervix.

plethora A condition marked by vascular turgescence, excess of blood, and fullness of pulse.

pluralistic society Multiple cultures living side by side.

premature infant A liveborn infant of less than 38 weeks gestation.

pseudocyesis False pregnancy.

psychological miscarriage Lack of love for the infant.

resuscitation Restoration of life or consciousness of one apparently dead or whose respiration has ceased.

retrolental fibroplasia A condition resulting from high oxygen tension in the arterial blood which may cause retinal vasospasm leading to ischemic injury to the retina.

scaphoid abdomen An abdomen with a hollowed interior wall.

shirodkar Operative procedure for correcting an incompetent cervix.

skin turgor Normal fullness of the tissue.

small for gestational age An infant who falls below the 10th percentile.

spermatogenesis The process by which mature spermatozoa are formed and during which the diploid chromosome number is reduced to the haploid.

spina bifida occulta A congenital defect of the walls of the spinal canal caused by the lack of union between the laminae of the vertebrae.

stillborn Born without life.

striae gravidarum Reddish streaks on the abdomen, thighs, and breasts during pregnancy from overstretching; the streaks turn silvertone in time.

surfactant A substance formed in the lungs that helps to keep the small air sacs extended by virtue of its ability to reduce the surface tension.

telangiectasis The presence of small, red focal lesions, usually in the skin or mucous membrane, caused by dilation of capillaries, arterioles, or venules.

teratogenic agent Virus, irradiation, or drugs, the exposure to which can damage the fetus in a pregnant woman.

term infant A liveborn infant of between 38 and 42 weeks completed gestation.

tetralogy of Fallot A common cardiac malformation consisting of pulmonary stenosis, ventricular septal defect, dextroposed aorta, and hypertrophy of the right ventricle.

thermogenesis The production of heat, especially in the body.

thrombocytopenic purpura A hematological disorder in the newborn in which the bleeding time is prolonged, platelets are greatly decreased, and there is cell fragility.

thromboembolus A blood clot in a vein.

thrombophlebitis Inflammation of a vein developing before the formation of a thrombus.

thrush Infection of the oral membrane by a fungus, usually *Candida albicans*. It is characterized by white patches on a red, moist, inflamed surface and may occur anywhere in the mouth.

torticollis Wryneck; stiff neck caused by spasmodic contraction of neck muscles drawing the head to one side with the chin pointing to the other side. Congenital or acquired.

toxemia Disorders occurring during pregnancy or early puerperium which are characterized by one or all of the following: hypertension, edema, albuminuria, and, in severe cases, convulsions and coma.

tracheoesophageal fistula A congenital anomaly in which there is an abnormal tubelike passage between the trachea and the esophagus.

vernix caseosa A cheeselike substance which covers the skin of the fetus.

APPENDIX

Standards of Maternal and Child Health Nursing Practice*

INTRODUCTION

Nursing practice is a direct service, goal directed and adaptable to the needs of the individual, family, and community during health and illness. Professional practitioners of nursing bear primary responsibility and accountability for the nursing care clients/ patients receive. The purpose of standards of nursing practice is to fulfill the profession's obligation to provide and improve this practice.

The standards focus on practice. They provide a means for determining the quality of nursing which a client/patient receives regardless of whether such services are provided solely by a professional nurse or by a professional nurse and nonprofessional assistants.

The standards are stated according to a

* Reprinted with permission of the American Nurses' Association.

systematic approach to nursing practice: assessment of the client's/patient's status, planning nursing actions, implementation of the plan, and evaluation. These specific divisions are not intended to imply that practice consists of a series of discrete steps, taken in strict sequence, beginning with assessment and ending with evaluation. The processes described are used concurrently and recurrently. Assessment, for example, frequently continues during implementation; similarly evaluation dictates reassessment and replanning.

These standards for nursing practice apply to nursing practice in any setting. Nursing practice in all settings must possess the characteristics identified by these standards if patients are to receive high-quality nursing care. Each standard is followed by a rationale and examples of assessment factors. Assessment factors are to be used in determining achievement of the standard.

Implementation of the standards will be facilitated by use of the standards as a basis for evaluating nursing practice by:

a The individual nurse (self-evaluation)
b Nurses (peer view)
c Nurses with superior clinical expertise
d Nurse administrators

In addition to evaluation of nursing practice by nurses, nurses will solicit and be responsive to an evaluation by:

a Interdisciplinary colleagues
b Clients/patients
c Official and voluntary accrediting agencies
d Community representatives

DEFINITION

Maternal and child nursing practice is a direct service to individuals, their families, and the community during childbearing and childrearing phases of the life cycle. It is a dynamic process involving specific activities which are goal directed and adapted to the needs of individuals and families during health and illness. The primary responsibility and accountability for nursing care clients/patients receive is that of the maternal child nurse. It is given independently and in collaboration with nursing colleagues and/or with members of other health disciplines.

PHILOSOPHY

Maternal and child nursing practice is based on nursing knowledge, principles, and concepts drawn from the biological, physical, and social sciences and from the humanities. These principles and concepts are selected and synthesized into the theoretical basis for maternal and child nursing practice. Regardless of the setting in which nursing is practiced (hospital, home, school, community, etc.), basic concepts and principles are used to describe, explain, and predict human development and behavior potential. A thorough understanding of the interrelatedness of the cultural, psychosocial, spiritual, and physiological influence on the individual and the family is essential to effective practice.

Maternal and child nursing practice includes independent, dependent, and interdependent functions. Independent functions are those activities performed by the nurse which are not prescribed nor subject to the control of nonnurse personnel. Dependent functions are those delegated by another member of the health team. Interdependent functions are derived from collaboration with members of the interdisciplinary team.

The health plan for care and cure evolves from the assessment and evaluation made by each member of the health team. Responsibility for the development of total health services for the entire community is shared with all health-related disciplines. Such comprehensive care should be geared to economic efficiency and intelligent use of personnel.

SKILLS

The skills needed in maternal and child nursing practice are multiple: intellectual, communication, observation, and manual (technical). Intellectual skills are essential in making judgments, assessing success and failure, developing new concepts, developing goals and plans for the future, seeking new knowledge, and scientifically investigating clinical problems. Communication skills are important in interviewing, teaching, guidance, and counseling. They are also necessary for effective collaboration with health team members and with the family. Observational skills are important to the assessment and evaluation of the health status. Manual skills are an essential part of the total nursing process and must be used in conjunction with other skills. All of these skills are essential to planning, implementing, and evaluating nursing care during the preconceptual, conceptual, childbearing, childrearing, and childhood phases of the life cycle.

The way in which the nurse utilizes knowledge and skills is contingent upon her awareness and understanding of self as a therapeutic agent, as well as upon her ability to weld these knowledges and skills into effective practice.

A systematic approach to assessment, interpretation, planning, implementation, evaluation, and reassessment of care is inherent in this process.

Effective practice is planned and evaluated independently and in collaboration with nurse colleagues, others on the interdisciplinary health team, and with representatives of the community.

PREMISES

Maternal and child nursing practice is based on the following premises:

1 Survival and the level of health of a society is inextricably bound to maternal and child health.
2 Maternal and child nursing practice respects the human dignity and rights of individuals.
3 Maternal and child nursing practice is family-centered.
4 Maternal and child nursing practice focuses on the childbearing/childrearing phases of the life cycle which include the development of sexuality, family planning, interconceptual care, and child health from conception through adolescence.
5 Maternal and child nursing makes a significant difference to society in achieving its health goals.
6 Man is a total human being: his psychosocial and biophysical self are interrelated.
7 Human behavior shapes and is shaped by environmental forces and as such sets into motion a multitude of reciprocal responses.
8 Through his own process of self-regulation the human being attempts to maintain equilibrium amidst constant change.
9 All behavior has meaning and is influenced by past experiences, the individual(s) perception of those experiences, and forces impinging upon the present.
10 Growth and development is ordered and evolves in sequential stages.
11 Substantive knowledge of the principles of human growth and development, including normative data, is

essential to effective maternal and child nursing practice.

12 Periods of developmental and traumatic crises during the life cycle pose internal and external stresses and may have a positive or negative effect.

13 Maternal and child nursing provides for continuity of care and is not bound by artificial barriers and exclusive categories which tend to restrict and delimit practice.

14 *All* people have a right to receive the benefit of the delivery of optimal health services.

GOALS

Maternal and child nursing practice is aimed at:

1 Promoting and maintaining optimal health of each individual and the family unit

2 Improving and/or supporting family solidarity

3 Early identification and treatment of vulnerable families

4 Preventing environmental conditions which block attainment of optimal health

5 Prevention and early detection of deviations from health

6 Reducing stresses which interfere with optimal functioning

7 Assisting the family to understand and/or cope with the developmental and traumatic situations which occur during childbearing and childrearing

8 Facilitating survival, recovery, and growth when the individual is ill or needs health care

9 Reducing reproductive wastage occurring at any point on the continuum

10 Continuously improving the quality of care in maternal and child nursing

11 Reducing inequalities in the delivery of health care services

REASONS FOR STANDARDS

Standards prepared for the profession exceed the minimum requirements for licensure.

1 To assist the profession in evaluating the quality of practice in any setting

2 To serve as a tool for self-evaluation

3 To provide a common base for practitioners to coordinate and unify their efforts in the improvement of practice

4 To provide a common base for practitioners and others concerned to coordinate their efforts in the improvement of health care

5 To identify the elements of independent, dependent, and interdependent functions of practice

6 To provide one of the bases for planning and evaluating educational programs preparing practitioners

7 To help employers understand what to expect of the practitioner

8 To inform society of our concern for the improvement of practice

9 To assist the public in understanding what to expect from practice

10 To provide one measure by which eligibility for certification of individual practitioners can be determined by the Division on Maternal and Child Health Nursing Practice

11 To encourage a philosophy of comprehensive rather than compartmentalized maternal and child care

12 To develop a measure by which the achievement of maternal and child nursing goals can be evaluated

Standards of Maternal and Child Health Nursing Practice

I Maternal and child nursing practice is characterized by the continual questioning of the assumptions upon which practice is based, retaining those which are valid and searching for and using new knowledge.

II Maternal and child nursing practice is based upon knowledge of the biophysical and psychosocial development of individuals from conception through the childrearing phase of development and upon knowledge of the basic needs for optimum development.

III The collection of data about the health status of the client/patient is systematic and continuous; the data are accessible, communicated, and recorded.

IV Nursing diagnoses are derived from data about the health status of the client/patient.

V Maternal and child nursing practice recognizes deviations from expected patterns of physiologic activity and anatomic and psychosocial development.

VI The plan of nursing care includes goals derived from the nursing diagnoses.

VII The plan of nursing care includes priorities and the prescribed nursing approaches or measures to achieve the goals.

VIII Nursing actions provide for client/ patient participation in health promotion, maintenance, and restoration.

IX Maternal and child nursing practice provides for the use and coordination of all services that assist individuals to prepare for responsible sexual roles.

X Nursing actions assist the client/ patient to maximize his health capabilities.

XI The client's/patient's progress or lack of progress toward goal achievement is determined by the patient/client and the nurse.

XII The client's/patient's progress or lack of progress toward goal achievement directs reassessment, reordering of priorities, new goal setting, and revision of the plan of nursing care.

XIII Maternal and child nursing practice evidences active participation with others in evaluating the availability, accessibility, and acceptability of services for parents and children and cooperating and/or taking leadership in extending and developing needed services in the community.

STANDARD I

Maternal and child nursing practice is characterized by the continual questioning of the assumptions upon which practice is based, retaining those which are valid and searching for and using new knowledge.

Rationale:

Since knowledge is not static, all assumptions are subject to change. Assumptions are derived from knowledge or findings of research which are subject to additional testing and revision. They are carefully selected and tested and reflect utilization of present and new knowledge. Effective utilization of these knowledges stimulates more astute observations and provides new insights into the effects of nursing upon the individual and family. To question assumptions implies that nursing practice is not based on stereotyped or ritualistic procedures or methods of intervention; rather practice exemplifies an objective, systematic, and logical investigation of a phenomenon or problem.

Assessment factors:
Therefore in practice, the MCN:

1   Critically examines and questions accepted modes of practice rather than relying on ritualistic or routinized modes of practice
2   Utilizes current and new knowledge in identifying and questioning the validity of the assumptions which form the bases of nursing practice
3   Continuously expands and improves nursing practice by utilizing theories and research findings in search for alternative solutions
4   Actively shares new knowledge and approaches with colleagues and others in the community

STANDARD II

Maternal and child nursing practice is based upon knowledge of the biophysical and psychosocial development of individuals from conception through the childrearing phase of development and upon knowledge of the basic needs for optimum development.

Rationale:

A knowledge and understanding of the principles and normal ranges in human growth, development, and behavior are essential to MCN practice. Concomitant with this knowledge is the recognition and consideration of the psychosocial, environmental, nutritional, spiritual, and cognitive factors that enhance or deter the biophysical and psychological maturation of the individual and family.

Assessment factors:
Therefore in practice, the MCN:

1   Observes, assesses, and describes the developmental level and/or needs of the individual within the family before performing any actions
2   Involves the individual and family in the assessment and planning of care
3   Works with individuals and groups utilizing knowledge of the psychosocial, environmental, nutritional, spiritual, and cognitive factors inherent in the family or group environment

STANDARD III

The collection of data about the health status of the client/patient is systematic and continuous; the data are accessible, communicated, and recorded.

Rationale:

Comprehensive care requires complete and ongoing collection of data about client/patient to determine the nursing care needs and other health care needs of the client/

patient; all health status data about the client/patient must be available for all members of the health care team.

Assessment factors:

1 Health status data includes:
 a Growth and development
 b Biophysical status
 c Emotional status
 d Cultural, religious, socioeconomic background
 e Performance of activities of daily living
 f Patterns of coping
 g Interaction patterns
 h Clients'/patients' perception and satisfaction with their health status
 i Client/patient health goals
 j Environment (physical, social, emotional, ecological)
 k Available and accessible human and material resources
2 Data are collected from:
 a Client/patient, family, significant others
 b Health care personnel
 c Individuals within the immediate environment and/or the community
3 Data are obtained by:
 a Interview
 b Examination
 c Observation
 d Reading records, reports, etc.
4 Format for the collection of data:
 a Provides for a systematic collection of data
 b Facilitates the completeness of data collection
5 Continuous collection of data is evident by:
 a Frequent updating

 b Recording of changes in health status
6 The data are:
 a Accessible on the client/patient records
 b Retrievable
 c Confidential

STANDARD IV

Nursing diagnoses are derived from data about the health status of the client/patient.

Rationale:

The health status of the client/patient is the basis for determining the nursing care needs. The data are analyzed and compared to norms.

Assessment factors:

1 The client's/patient's health status is compared to the norm to determine if there is a deviation, the degree and direction of deviation.
2 The client's/patient's capabilities and limitations are identified.
3 The nursing diagnoses are related to and comparable with the totality of the client's/patient's health care.

STANDARD V

Maternal and child nursing practice recognizes deviations from expected patterns of physiologic activity and anatomic and psychosocial development.

Rationale:

Early detection of deviations and therapeutic intervention are essential to the prevention of illness, to facilitating growth and developmental potential, and to the promotion of optimal health for the individual and the family.

Early detection requires that minute deviations be recognized, often before the individual or his family is aware that such deviations exist. The nurse has a unique opportunity to observe and assess the patient and his family, particularly in the community setting.

Assessment factors: Therefore in practice, the MCN:

1 Demonstrates a thorough understanding of the range of normal body structure and function by detecting signs and symptoms which are not within normal limits
2 Identifies the variety of coping mechanisms which may serve an adaptive function or represent maladaptive patterns of response
3 Searches for improved means of detecting impairment of physical and emotional function
4 Searches for improved means of detecting physical, psychological, or environmental situations which may lead to impaired function
5 Instructs the individual and family in recognizing and understanding deviations

STANDARD VI

The plan of nursing care includes goals derived from the nursing diagnoses.

Rationale:

The determination of the desired results from nursing actions is an essential part of planning care.

Assessment factors:

1 Goals are mutually set with the client/patient and significant others:
   a They are congruent with other planned therapies.
   b They are stated in realistic and measurable terms.
   c They are assigned a time schedule for achievement.
2 Goals are established to maximize functional capabilities and are congruent with:
   a Growth and development
   b Biophysical status
   c Behavioral patterns
   d Human and material resources

STANDARD VII

The plan of nursing care includes priorities and the prescribed nursing approaches or measures to achieve the goals.

Rationale:

Nursing actions are planned to promote, maintain, and restore the client's/patient's well-being.

Assessment factors:

1 Physical measures are planned to manage (prevent or control) specific client/patient problems and clearly relate

to the nursing diagnosis and goals of care, e.g., ADL, use of self-help devices, etc.

2 Psychosocial measures are specific to the client's/patient's nursing care needs and to the nursing care goals, e.g., techniques to control aggression.

3 Teaching-learning principles are incorporated into the plan of care and objectives for learning stated in behavioral terms, e.g., specification of content for learner's level, reinforcement, readiness, etc.

4 Approaches are planned to provide for a therapeutic environment:
   a Physical environmental factors, e.g., control of noise, control of temperature, etc.
   b Psychosocial measures are used to structure the environment for therapeutic ends, e.g., paternal participation in all phases of the maternity experience.
   c Group behaviors are used to structure interaction and influence the therapeutic environment, e.g., conformity, territorial rights, locomotion, etc.

5 Approaches are specified for orientation of client/patient to:
   a New roles and relationships
   b Relevant health (human and material) resources
   c Modifications in plan of nursing care
   d Relationship of modifications in nursing care plan to the total care plan

6 The plan includes the utilization of available and appropriate resources:
   a Human resources—other health professionals
   b Material resources
   c Community

7 The plan is an ordered sequence of proposed nursing actions.

8 Nursing approaches are planned on the basis of current knowledge.

STANDARD VIII

Nursing actions provide for client/patient participation in health promotion maintenance and restoration.

Rationale:

The client/patient and family is provided the opportunity to participate in the nursing care. Such provision is made based upon theoretical and experiential evidence that participation of client/patient and family may foster growth.

Assessment factors:

1 The client/patient and family are kept informed about:
   a Current health status
   b Changes in health status
   c The total health care plan
   d The nursing care plan
   e Roles of health care personnel
   f Health care resources

2 The client/patient and family is provided with the information needed to make decisions and choices about:
   a Promoting, maintaining, and restoring health
   b Seeking appropriate health care personnel
   c Maintaining and using health care resources

STANDARD IX

Maternal and child nursing practice provides for the use and coordination of all services that assist individuals to prepare for responsible sexual roles.

Rationale:

People are prepared for sexual roles through a process of socialization that takes place from birth to adulthood. This process of socialization, to a large extent, is carried out within the family structure. Social control over child care increases in importance as humans become increasingly dependent on the culture rather than upon the family unit. The culture of any society is maintained by the transmission of its specific values, attitudes, and behaviors from generation to generation. Attitudes and values concerning male and female roles develop as part of the socialization process. Attitudes toward self, the opposite sex, and toward parents will influence the roles each individual assumes in adulthood and the responsibilities accepted.

Assessment factors: Therefore in practice, the MCN:

1. Utilizes resources available in the social and behavioral sciences to help her understand the attitudes and values of individuals and families with whom she is working
2. Utilizes opportunities available to her to promote those attitudes and values conducive to emotional and physical health and family solidarity, without imposing her own value system
3. Encourages society to provide the resources needed to help people prepare for responsible sexual roles

4. Interprets to other health personnel the needs of individuals and families as she sees them and attempts to understand the needs as seen by other health personnel
5. Works with other health personnel to develop services which promote optimal health and family solidarity

STANDARD X

Nursing actions assist the client/patient to maximize his health capabilities.

Rationale:

Nursing actions are designed to promote, maintain, and restore health. A knowledge and understanding of the principles and normal ranges in human growth, development, and behavior are essential to MCN practice.

Assessment factors:

1. Nursing actions:
   a. Are consistent with the plan of care
   b. Are based on scientific principles
   c. Are individualized to the specific situation
   d. Are used to provide a safe and therapeutic environment
   e. Employ teaching-learning opportunities for client/patient
   f. Include utilization of appropriate resources
2. Nursing actions are directed to the physical, psychological, and social behavior associated with:
   a. Ingestion of food, fluid, and nutrients
   b. Elimination of body wastes

  c Locomotion, exercise
  d Temperature and other regulatory mechanisms
  e Relating with others
  f Self-fulfillment

STANDARD XI

The client's/patient's progress or lack of progress toward goal achievement is determined by the patient/client and the nurse.

Rationale:

The quality of nursing care depends upon comprehensive and intelligent determination of the impact of nursing upon the health status of the client. The client is an essential part of this determination.

Assessment factors:

1 Current data about the client are used to measure his progress toward goal achievement.
2 Nursing actions are analyzed for their effectiveness in goal achievement of the client.
3 The client/patient evaluates nursing actions and goal achievement.
4 Provision is made for nursing follow-up of particular patients to determine the long-term effects of nursing care.

STANDARD XII

The client's/patient's progress or lack of progress toward goal achievement directs reassessment, reordering of priorities, new goal setting, and revision of the plan of nursing care.

Rationale:

The nursing process remains the same but the input of new information may dictate new or revised approaches.

Assessment factors:

1 Reassessment is directed by goal achievement or lack of goal achievement.
2 New priorities and goals are determined and additional nursing approaches are prescribed appropriately.
3 New nursing actions are accurately and appropriately initiated.

STANDARD XIII

Maternal and child nursing practice evidences active participation with others in evaluating the availability, accessibility, and acceptability of services for parents and children and cooperating and/or taking leadership in extending and developing needed services in the community.

Rationale:

Knowledge of services presently offered to parents and children is the first step in determining the effectiveness of health care to all in the community. When it is recognized that needed services are not available, accessible, or acceptable, the nurse takes leadership in working with consumers, other health disciplines, the community, and governmental agencies in extending and/or developing these services. Services must be continually evaluated, expanded, and changed if they are to improve the health and well-being of all parents and children within our society.

Assessment factors: Therefore in practice, the MCN:

1 Applies and shares the cultural and socioeconomic concepts which help her understand the differences in the unique needs of individuals and families

2 Recognizes the need for available health services for all parents and children in the community

3 Utilizes the services and resources presently available

4 Works with consumers, nurse colleagues, other health disciplines, the community, and governmental agencies in evaluating the availability, accessibility, and acceptability of services to all parents and children in the community

5 Participates actively with significant others in initiating changes in the delivery of health services and/or developing new services to enable each individual in the family to function at his optimum capacity and to enhance family unity

INDEX

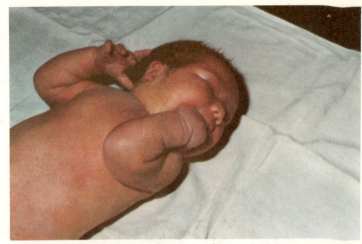

(A) Moderately plethoric infant with acrocyanosis.

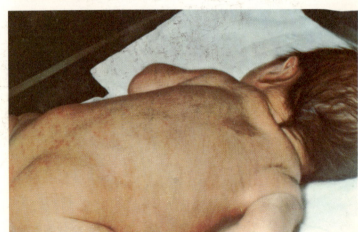

(B) Newborn with erythema toxicum neonatorum and lanugo.

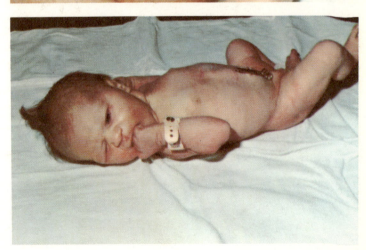

(C) Infant awake and alert.